The Cambridge Handbook of Romance Linguistics

The Romance languages and dialects constitute a treasure trove of linguistic data of profound interest and significance. Data from the Romance languages have contributed extensively to our current empirical and theoretical understanding of phonetics, phonology, morphology, syntax, semantics, pragmatics, sociolinguistics and historical linguistics. Written by a team of world-renowned scholars, this Handbook explores what we can learn about linguistics from the study of Romance languages, and how the body of comparative and historical data taken from them can be applied to linguistic study. It also offers insights into the diatopic and diachronic variation exhibited by the Romance family of languages of a kind unparalleled for any other Western languages. Asking what Romance languages can do for linguistics, this Handbook is essential reading for all linguists interested in what a knowledge of the Romance evidence can contribute to linguistic theory.

ADAM LEDGEWAY is Professor of Italian and Romance Languages at the University of Cambridge. Recent publications include *The Cambridge History of the Romance Languages. Vols 1–2* (2011–13), *The Cambridge Handbook of Historical Syntax* (2017) and *The Oxford Guide to the Romance Languages* (co-edited with Maiden, 2016).

MARTIN MAIDEN is Professor of the Romance Languages at the University of Oxford. Recent publications include *The Cambridge History of the Romance Languages, Vols 1–2* (2011–13) and *The Oxford Guide to the Romance Languages* (co-edited with Ledgeway, 2016).

CAMBRIDGE HANDBOOKS IN LANGUAGE AND LINGUISTICS

Genuinely broad in scope, each handbook in this series provides a complete state-of-the-field overview of a major sub-discipline within language study and research. Grouped into broad thematic areas, the chapters in each volume encompass the most important issues and topics within each subject, offering a coherent picture of the latest theories and findings. Together, the volumes will build into an integrated overview of the discipline in its entirety.

Published titles

The Cambridge Handbook of Phonology, edited by Paul de Lacy
The Cambridge Handbook of Linguistic Code-switching, edited by Barbara E. Bullock and Almeida Jacqueline Toribio
The Cambridge Handbook of Child Language, Second Edition, edited by Edith L. Bavin and Letitia Naigles
The Cambridge Handbook of Endangered Languages, edited by Peter K. Austin and Julia Sallabank
The Cambridge Handbook of Sociolinguistics, edited by Rajend Mesthrie
The Cambridge Handbook of Pragmatics, edited by Keith Allan and Kasia M. Jaszczolt
The Cambridge Handbook of Language Policy, edited by Bernard Spolsky
The Cambridge Handbook of Second Language Acquisition, edited by Julia Herschensohn and Martha Young-Scholten
The Cambridge Handbook of Biolinguistics, edited by Cedric Boeckx and Kleanthes K. Grohmann
The Cambridge Handbook of Generative Syntax, edited by Marcel den Dikken
The Cambridge Handbook of Communication Disorders, edited by Louise Cummings
The Cambridge Handbook of Stylistics, edited by Peter Stockwell and Sara Whiteley
The Cambridge Handbook of Linguistic Anthropology, edited by N.J. Enfield, Paul Kockelman and Jack Sidnell
The Cambridge Handbook of English Corpus Linguistics, edited by Douglas Biber and Randi Reppen
The Cambridge Handbook of Bilingual Processing, edited by John W. Schwieter
The Cambridge Handbook of Learner Corpus Research, edited by Sylviane Granger, Gaëtanelle Gilquin and Fanny Meunier
The Cambridge Handbook of Linguistic Multicompetence, edited by Li Wei and Vivian Cook
The Cambridge Handbook of English Historical Linguistics, edited by Merja Kytö and Päivi Pahta
The Cambridge Handbook of Formal Semantics, edited by Maria Aloni and Paul Dekker
The Cambridge Handbook of Morphology, edited by Andrew Hippisley and Greg Stump
The Cambridge Handbook of Historical Syntax, edited by Adam Ledgeway and Ian Roberts
The Cambridge Handbook of Linguistic Typology, edited by Alexandra Y. Aikhenvald and R. M. W. Dixon
The Cambridge Handbook of Areal Linguistics, edited by Raymond Hickey
The Cambridge Handbook of Cognitive Linguistics, edited by Barbara Dancygier
The Cambridge Handbook of Japanese Linguistics, edited by Yoko Hasegawa
The Cambridge Handbook of Spanish Linguistics, edited by Kimberly L. Geeslin

The Cambridge Handbook of Bilingualism, edited by Annick De Houwer and Lourdes Ortega

The Cambridge Handbook of Systemic Functional Linguistics, edited by Geoff Thompson, Wendy L. Bowcher, Lise Fontaine and David Schönthal

The Cambridge Handbook of African Linguistics, edited by H. Ekkehard Wolff

The Cambridge Handbook of Language Learning, edited by John W. Schwieter and Alessandro Benati

The Cambridge Handbook of World Englishes, edited by Daniel Schreier, Marianne Hundt and Edgar W. Schneider

The Cambridge Handbook of Intercultural Communication, edited by Guido Rings and Sebastian Rasinger

The Cambridge Handbook of Germanic Linguistics, edited by Michael T. Putnam and B. Richard Page

The Cambridge Handbook of Discourse Studies, edited by Anna De Fina and Alexandra Georgakopoulou

The Cambridge Handbook of Language Standardization, edited by Wendy Ayres-Bennett and John Bellamy

The Cambridge Handbook of Korean Linguistics, edited by Sungdai Cho and John Whitman

The Cambridge Handbook of Phonetics, edited by Rachael-Anne Knight and Jane Setter

The Cambridge Handbook of Corrective Feedback in Second Language Learning and Teaching, edited by Hossein Nassaji and Eva Kartchava

The Cambridge Handbook of Experimental Syntax, edited by Grant Goodall

The Cambridge Handbook of Heritage Languages and Linguistics, edited by Silvina Montrul and Maria Polinsky

The Cambridge Handbook of Arabic Linguistics, edited by Karin Ryding and David Wilmsen

The Cambridge Handbook of the Philosophy of Language, edited by Piotr Stalmaszczyk

The Cambridge Handbook of Sociopragmatics, edited by Michael Haugh, Dániel Z. Kádár and Marina Terkourafi

The Cambridge Handbook of Task-Based Language Teaching, edited by Mohammed Ahmadian and Michael Long

The Cambridge Handbook of Language Contact: Population Movement and Language Change, Volume 1, edited by Salikoko Mufwene and Anna Maria Escobar

The Cambridge Handbook of Language Contact: Multilingualism in Population Structure, Volume 2, edited by Salikoko Mufwene and Anna Maria Escobar

The Cambridge Handbook of Romance Linguistics

Edited by
Adam Ledgeway
University of Cambridge

Martin Maiden
University of Oxford

CAMBRIDGE
UNIVERSITY PRESS

University Printing House, Cambridge CB2 8BS, United Kingdom

One Liberty Plaza, 20th Floor, New York, NY 10006, USA

477 Williamstown Road, Port Melbourne, VIC 3207, Australia

314–321, 3rd Floor, Plot 3, Splendor Forum, Jasola District Centre, New Delhi – 110025, India

103 Penang Road, #05–06/07, Visioncrest Commercial, Singapore 238467

Cambridge University Press is part of the University of Cambridge.

It furthers the University's mission by disseminating knowledge in the pursuit of education, learning, and research at the highest international levels of excellence.

www.cambridge.org
Information on this title: www.cambridge.org/9781108485791
DOI: 10.1017/9781108580410

© Cambridge University Press 2022

This publication is in copyright. Subject to statutory exception and to the provisions of relevant collective licensing agreements, no reproduction of any part may take place without the written permission of Cambridge University Press.

First published 2022

A catalogue record for this publication is available from the British Library.

ISBN 978-1-108-48579-1 Hardback

Cambridge University Press has no responsibility for the persistence or accuracy of URLs for external or third-party internet websites referred to in this publication and does not guarantee that any content on such websites is, or will remain, accurate or appropriate.

În amintirea lui Marius Sala
1932–2018

Contents

List of Figures	page xxiv
List of Tables	xxv
List of Contributors	xxx
List of Abbreviations	xxxii

1 Data, Theory, and Explanation: The View from
   Romance   *Adam Ledgeway and Martin Maiden*   1
  1.1 Introduction   1
  1.2 The View from Morphosyntax and the Case of
       Functional Categories   3
    1.2.1 From Latin to Romance: The Rise of Functional
           Categories   3
    1.2.2 Linguistic Variation   6
      1.2.2.1 Parameters   6
      1.2.2.2 Language Universals   12
      1.2.2.3 Typological Variation   15
      1.2.2.4 The Interfaces   18
      1.2.2.5 Interim Conclusions   21
    1.2.3 What Romance Can Do for Syntactic Theory   21
      1.2.3.1 Pro-drop Parameter   21
      1.2.3.2 Verb Positions   25
      1.2.3.3 Mapping the Left Periphery of the Clause   27
      1.2.3.4 Interim Conclusions   33
    1.2.4 What Linguistic Theory Can Do for Romance   34
      1.2.4.1 Word Order   34
      1.2.4.2 Pro-drop Parameter Revisited   37
      1.2.4.3 The *Placiti cassinesi*   40
      1.2.4.4 Dual Complementizer Systems   45
      1.2.4.5 Nominal Functional Structure   47

    1.3 The View from Romance Palatalization   54
        1.3.1 Sketch of the Two Major Romance 'Waves' of Palatalization and Their Consequences   54
        1.3.2 The Palatalization of the Velars and the Emergence of a Sound Change   58
        1.3.3 When Does Phonological Conditioning of Morphological Alternation 'Stop'? Comparative Romance Evidence   65
        1.3.4 When Does the Morphologization of a Sound Change 'Start'? Comparative Romance Evidence   71
        1.3.5 'Standard Language Bias' in Historical Linguistic Analysis   79
        1.3.6 What Is a Romance Language? Could There Be an Answer in Morphology?   86
    1.4 Conclusion   93

Part One   What Is a Language?

2 Origins of Romance   *Nigel Vincent*   97
    2.1 Introduction   97
    2.2 Attestation vs Reconstruction: The *DÉRom* Controversy   99
    2.3 Texts and Times: The Chronology of Latin   105
    2.4 The Issue of 'Submerged' Latin   109
    2.5 The Role of Language Contact   110
    2.6 Reconstruction and Levels of Language: Three Case Studies   114
        2.6.1 The Verb GO   114
        2.6.2 Control and WANT VERBS   115
        2.6.3 Recomplementation   118
    2.7 Conclusion and General Lessons   120
3 Documentation and Sources   *Alvise Andreose and Laura Minervini*   123
    3.1 Introduction   123
    3.2 Sources for the Study of Late Latin and Early Romance   126
        3.2.1 Sources of 'Vulgar Latin' or 'Late Latin'   126
        3.2.2 The Problem of Transition   127
        3.2.3 The Earliest Testimonies of Romance Languages   128
    3.3 Medieval Romance *Scriptae*   130
        3.3.1 Introduction   130
        3.3.2 Literary Texts   131
        3.3.3 Documentary and Practical Texts   134
    3.4 The Codification of Romance Languages in the Modern Age   135
        3.4.1 Printed Sources   135
        3.4.2 National Languages, Regional Languages, and Dialects   137
        3.4.3 Grammar and Dictionaries   138

3.5 Dialectological Enquiries, Linguistic Atlases, and
      Dialectometry   140
      3.5.1 The Beginnings of Dialectological Enquiries and
            Linguistic Cartography   140
      3.5.2 After the *ALF*: Traditional and New Linguistic Atlases 142
      3.5.3 Historical Atlases and Dialectometry   144
  3.6 Corpus Linguistics   146
      3.6.1 The Beginnings of Corpus Linguistics   146
      3.6.2 Oral Corpora and Historical Corpora   146
4 Variation in Romance   *Diego Pescarini and Michele Loporcaro*   150
  4.1 Introduction   150
  4.2 Systematic Variation: The Case of Subject Clitics   150
      4.2.1 Subject Clitics and the Null Subject Parameter   151
      4.2.2 Expletive Subject Clitics and Agreement   153
      4.2.3 Subject Clitics vs Verbal Agreement   155
      4.2.4 Gaps   158
      4.2.5 Syncretism   160
      4.2.6 Pantiscu, an Outlier   161
  4.3 Auxiliary Selection and Auxiliary Splits   162
      4.3.1 Lexical and Semantic Factors   163
      4.3.2 The Syntactic Gradient   164
      4.3.3 Person-Driven Variation and Splits   166
      4.3.4 Variation in Mixed Auxiliation: Give to Morphology
            What Belongs to Morphology   172
      4.3.5 An Outlier: *Do*-Support in the Dialect of Monno   176
  4.4 Modelling Linguistic Diversity   177

Part Two Phonetics and Phonology
5 Structure of the Syllable   *Giovanna Marotta*   183
  5.1 Preliminary Remarks   183
  5.2 Syllable Structure and Quantity in Latin   184
  5.3 The Fate of Quantity in Romance Languages   186
      5.3.1 Vowel Length   186
      5.3.2 Open Syllable Lengthening   187
  5.4 Syllable Constituents   189
      5.4.1 Romance Nuclei   189
      5.4.2 Unstressed Nuclei   190
      5.4.3 Romance Onsets   191
      5.4.4 Romance Codas   194
  5.5 Phonological Processes   196
      5.5.1 Diphthongization   196
      5.5.2 Palatalization   198
      5.5.3 Lenition   200

5.6 Lexical Stress	200
5.7 Parametric Variation in Metrical Patterns	203
5.8 Syllable and Rhythm	204
5.9 'Western' versus 'Eastern' Romance	206
6 Sandhi Phenomena *Max W. Wheeler and Paul O'Neill*	209
6.1 Introduction	209
6.2 Vowel Sandhi	212
6.2.1 Elision of [ə] in Eastern Continental Catalan	212
6.2.1.1 Stressed Vowel Followed by an Unstressed Non-high Vowel [ə]	212
6.2.1.2 Unstressed Non-high Vowel [ə] Followed by a Stressed Vowel	214
6.2.1.3 Contact between Unstressed Vowels	214
6.2.2 Elision in French	215
6.3 Inter-word Vowel–Consonant Contact: V.#C	216
6.4 Inter-word Consonant–Consonant Contact: C.#C	217
6.4.1 Consonant Contacts in Majorcan Catalan	218
6.4.2 Consonantal Contact in Occitan	222
6.4.3 Lexicalization in C.#C Contacts	223
6.4.3.1 French *Liaison*	223
6.4.3.2 Initial Geminates from Coda Assimilation: *Rafforzamento Fonosintattico*	227
6.4.3.3 Aspiration of /s/ in Andalusian Spanish	231
7 Effects of Stress *Judith Meinschaefer*	234
7.1 Introduction	234
7.2 Metrical Structure, Stress Assignment, and the Prosodic Hierarchy	236
7.2.1 Introduction	236
7.2.2 Prosodic Structure	236
7.2.3 Word Stress	237
7.3 Phonological Effects	240
7.3.1 Introduction	240
7.3.2 Effects of Prominence	240
7.3.2.1 Vowel Lengthening	240
7.3.2.2 Diphthongization	242
7.3.3 Effects of Non-prominence	243
7.3.3.1 Introduction	243
7.3.3.2 Vowel Deletion	243
7.3.4 Vowel Reduction	247
7.4 Effects of Metrical Constituency	248
7.4.1 Introduction	248
7.4.2 Consonant Gemination	248
7.4.3 Vowel Insertion	250
7.4.4 Compensatory Lengthening	250
7.4.5 Clash Resolution	252

	7.5	Morpholexical Effects	253
		7.5.1 Alternations in Verb Roots	253
		7.5.2 Alternations in Function Words	257
		7.5.3 Minimality Requirements on Lexical Words	257
8	The Notion of the Phoneme *Benedetta Baldi and Leonardo M. Savoia*		261
	8.1	Introduction	261
	8.2	The Phoneme	262
	8.3	Conditions for Phonemes: Linearity, Invariance, and Biuniqueness	263
	8.4	Phonemes and Historical Changes	273
	8.5	Features Theory and Generative Phonology	276
	8.6	Approaches to Complex Phenomena: Phonology as Externalization	282
	8.7	Concluding Remarks	290
9	Typologically Exceptional Phenomena in Romance Phonology *Eulàlia Bonet and Francesc Torres-Tamarit*		292
	9.1	Introduction	292
	9.2	Phoneme Inventories	293
		9.2.1 Front Rounded Vowels	293
		9.2.2 Galician *Geada*	294
		9.2.3 The Voiced Velar Stop in Asturian	295
		9.2.4 Spanish *Ceceo*	296
		9.2.5 Retroflex Consonants in Sardinian and Italo-Romance Varieties	297
		9.2.6 Palatal Stops in Raeto-Romance	298
		9.2.7 Glottal Stops in Campidanian Sardinian	299
	9.3	Syllabic Structure	300
		9.3.1 Word-Initial and Word-Medial Consonant Clusters	300
		9.3.2 Final Consonantal Clusters with Rising Sonority in Insular Catalan	302
	9.4	Segmental Processes	302
		9.4.1 Vowel Devoicing	302
		9.4.2 Diphthongization of Long Vowels in Canadian French	303
		9.4.3 Gliding of High Vowels and Palatalization in Romanian	304
		9.4.4 Glide Strengthening in Romansh	306
		9.4.5 Velar Nasals in Northern Italian Dialects and Galician	307
		9.4.6 Nasal Place Neutralization towards [m] in Spanish	308
		9.4.7 Word-Final Deletion of /r/ and /n/ in Catalan	309
		9.4.8 Campidanian Sardinian Lenition	309
		9.4.9 Intervocalic Fortition in Salentino	310
		9.4.10 Final Affrication of /ʒ/ in Catalan	311
		9.4.11 Campidanian Sardinian Rhotic Metathesis	311
		9.4.12 Palatalization of /s/ in Coda Position in Portuguese	313
		9.4.13 Onset Clusters in Ribagorçan Catalan	314

9.5 Suprasegmentals — 314
    9.5.1 Plural Morphemes and Low Tone in Occitan — 314
    9.5.2 Moraic Verbal Morphemes in Friulian — 315
    9.5.3 Truncated Vocatives — 316

Part Three   Morphology

10 Phonological and Morphological Conditioning   *Franck Floricic and Lucia Molinu* — 321
    10.1 Introduction — 321
    10.2 Allomorphy of the Definite Article — 322
    10.3 Subject Clitic Allomorphy — 324
    10.4 Possessive Allomorphy — 326
    10.5 Stem Allomorphy — 329
        10.5.1 Verb Allomorphy — 329
        10.5.2 Nominal Allomorphy — 335
        10.5.3 Adjectival Allomorphy — 338
    10.6 Affix Allomorphy — 340
    10.7 Conclusion — 343

11 The Autonomy of Morphology   *Louise Esher and Paul O'Neill* — 346
    11.1 Introduction — 346
    11.2 Origins of the Autonomy of Morphology — 347
    11.3 Autonomy of Morphology from Phonology and Semantics and the Notion of the Morpheme — 350
    11.4 A Typology of Morphomic Structures in Romance — 351
        11.4.1 Metamorphomes — 352
            11.4.1.1 The Concept at Issue — 352
            11.4.1.2 Source of Four Common Romance Metamorphomes — 354
            11.4.1.3 Behaviour of Metamorphomes — 358
        11.4.2 Rhizomorphomes (Inflexional Classes) — 361
            11.4.2.1 The Concept — 361
            11.4.2.2 Exponents of Rhizomorphomes — 362
    11.5 Theoretical Reflections and Considerations — 365

12 Suppletion   *Martin Maiden and Anna M. Thornton* — 371
    12.1 Definitions of Suppletion — 371
    12.2 Typology and Distribution of Romance Suppletions — 375
        12.2.1 Introduction — 375
        12.2.2 Ordinal vs Cardinal Numerals — 375
        12.2.3 Comparatives and Superlatives — 377
        12.2.4 Inflexional Morphology of Personal Pronouns — 379
        12.2.5 Inflexional Morphology of Verbs, Nouns, and Adjectives — 380
    12.3 General Determinants and Conditions of Suppletion as Reflected in the Romance Data — 386
        12.3.1 Sound Change as Determinant of Suppletion — 386
        12.3.2 Incursive Suppletion and Its Causes — 387

12.3.3 The Paradigmatic Distribution of Suppletion	396
12.3.4 The Role of Phonological Resemblance in Determining Incursive Suppletion	397
12.4 Conclusion	398

13 Inflexion, Derivation, Compounding *Chiara Cappellaro and Judith Meinschaefer* 400
   13.1 Introduction 400
   13.2 Basic Characteristics of Inflexion, Derivation, and Compounding in Romance 402
      13.2.1 Introduction 402
      13.2.2 Inflexion 402
      13.2.3 Derivation 404
      13.2.4 Compounding 405
   13.3 Distinctions in Form and Constituency 406
      13.3.1 Introduction 406
      13.3.2 Morphophonological Alternations 408
      13.3.3 Prosodic Constituency 410
      13.3.4 Morphological Ellipsis in Coordination 413
   13.4 Issues and Challenges: Inflexion and Derivation 417
      13.4.1 Introduction 417
      13.4.2 Typical Properties Illustrated with Romance Data 418
      13.4.3 Two Case Studies 421
         13.4.3.1 Introduction 421
         13.4.3.2 Synchrony: Italian Ambigeneric Nouns with -a Plural 421
         13.4.3.3 Diachrony: Latin -sc- 423
   13.5 The Interaction of Inflexion, Derivation, and Compounding in 'Conversion' 426
      13.5.1 Introduction 426
      13.5.2 Derivation without Affix 426
      13.5.3 Word-Level Conversion as Derivation 427
      13.5.4 Syntactic Conversion 429
      13.5.5 Formations without a Base 430

14 Evaluative Suffixes *Antonio Fortin and Franz Rainer* 434
   14.1 Introduction 434
   14.2 Zwicky and Pullum's Criteria for Expressive Morphology 435
      14.2.1 Introduction 435
      14.2.2 Pragmatic Effects 436
      14.2.3 Promiscuity with Regard to Input Category 437
      14.2.4 Promiscuity with Regard to Input Basehood 438
      14.2.5 Imperfect Control 438
      14.2.6 Alternative Outputs 439
      14.2.7 Interspeaker Variation 440
      14.2.8 Special Syntax 440
   14.3 Evaluative Affixes in Semantic and Pragmatic Theory 442
      14.3.1 Introduction 442

	14.3.2 Heterogeneous Meanings and Uses of the Diminutive	442
	14.3.3 Semantic versus Pragmatic Accounts	444
	14.3.4 Romance Evaluative Affixes in Formal Semantics	446
14.4	Diminutives outside Verb Inflexions in Romance	448
	14.4.1 Positional Mobility of Evaluative Suffixes in Latin and Romance	448
	14.4.2 Diminutive Suffixes outside Verbal Inflexion	449
	14.4.2.1 Romanian	449
	14.4.2.2 Italian (Dialect of Lucca, Tuscany)	450
	14.4.2.3 Occitan (Gévaudan Dialect)	450
	14.4.2.4 Spanish	451
	14.4.2.5 Brazilian Portuguese	452
	14.4.3 Lessons for General Linguistics	454
14.5	Conclusion	457
15	Counting Systems *Brigitte L. M. Bauer*	459
15.1	Introduction	459
15.2	Early Systems of Quantification	460
15.3	Numerical Counting	461
	15.3.1 Bases and Arithmetical Operations	462
	15.3.2 Bases and Arithmetical Operations in Romance/Latin	463
	15.3.3 Order of Meaningful Elements	466
15.4	Types of Numeral	469
	15.4.1 Latin vs Romance Numerals	469
	15.4.2 A Systemic Difference	471
	15.4.3 Grammatical Marking on Numerals	472
15.5	Potential Effects of Language Contact: Romanian Teens and Decads	473
	15.5.1 Romanian Teens	474
	15.5.2 Romanian Decads	475
15.6	Vigesimals: Language Contact or Internal Development?	476
	15.6.1 Vigesimals in Romance	478
	15.6.2 Formal Characteristics of Vigesimal Forms in Romance	480
	15.6.3 Vigesimals in Other Languages	481
	15.6.4 Origins of Vigesimal Forms in Romance	483
15.7	Decimal System in Romance	484

Part Four   Syntax

16	Argument Structure and Argument Realization *Víctor Acedo-Matellán, Jaume Mateu, and Anna Pineda*	491
16.1	Introduction	491
16.2	Unaccusativity and Unergativity	493

	16.3 The Clitic SE	501
	16.4 Datives	507
	16.5 Lexicalization Patterns	512
	16.6 Concluding Remarks	517
17	Agreement *Roberta D'Alessandro*	519
	17.1 Introduction	519
	17.2 Phrase Structure Rules for Agreement	520
	17.3 Spec-Head Agreement	523
	17.3.1 Agreement in a Spec-Head Configuration	525
	17.4 Agreement in the Minimalist Program	528
	17.4.1 Participial Agreement Revisited	528
	17.4.2 Unaccusatives	533
	17.5 Morphological Agreement	534
	17.5.1 Rich Agreement and Null Subjects	535
	17.5.1.1 Agreement and Subject Clitics	539
18	Alignment *Sonia Cyrino and Michelle Sheehan*	544
	18.1 Introduction	544
	18.2 On the Diachrony of Alignment in Romance	547
	18.3 Auxiliary Selection	555
	18.3.1 Frequent Patterns	556
	18.3.2 Rarer Patterns	559
	18.4 Past Participle Agreement	561
	18.4.1 Frequent Patterns	561
	18.4.2 Rarer Patterns	563
	18.5 SE-Passives	564
	18.6 Word Order	566
	18.7 Other Phenomena	567
	18.7.1 INDE-Cliticization	567
	18.7.2 Absolute Participles and Participial Adjectives	568
	18.8 Conclusion	569
19	Complex Predicates *Adina Dragomirescu, Alexandru Nicolae, and Gabriela Pană Dindelegan*	571
	19.1 Outline and Scope	571
	19.2 Delimitations and Diagnostics	572
	19.2.1 What Is a Complex Predicate?	572
	19.2.2 Diagnosing Monoclausality	573
	19.3 Auxiliaries	576
	19.3.1 Introduction	576
	19.3.2 Auxiliary-Verb Constructions Based on HABERE 'Have'	576
	19.3.3 Auxiliary-Verb Constructions Based on ESSE 'Be'	579
	19.3.4 Auxiliary-Verb Constructions Based on Other Verbs	580
	19.3.5 TAM Make-up of Auxiliaries	581

	19.4 The Periphrastic Passive	582
	19.4.1 Synthetic vs Analytic	582
	19.4.2 Frequency and Distribution	582
	19.4.3 Participle Agreement	583
	19.4.4 The Reflexive Passive	583
	19.4.5 Inventory of Passive (Semi-)Auxiliary Verbs	584
	19.4.6 The Double Passive	587
	19.4.7 The Position of Constituents in the Passive Periphrasis	588
	19.4.8 Monoclausal Properties	589
	19.5 Aspectual Periphrases	591
	19.6 Modal Complex Predicates	594
	19.7 Causative Complex Predicates	596
	19.7.1 Introduction	596
	19.7.2 FACERE Causatives	597
	19.7.2.1 The *Faire-infinitif* Construction	598
	19.7.2.2 The *Faire-par* Construction	599
	19.7.3 LAXARE Causatives	599
	19.7.4 MANDARE Causatives	600
	19.8 Complex Predicates with Perception Verbs	600
	19.9 Conclusions: What Romance Languages Tell Us about Complex Predicates	601
20	Dependency, Licensing, and the Nature of Grammatical Relations *Anna Cardinaletti and Giuliana Giusti*	604
	20.1 Introduction	604
	20.2 Parallels between Nominal Expressions and Clauses	605
	20.2.1 Split IP, Split CP, and Verb Movement	605
	20.2.2 The Adjectival Hierarchy and the Position of N	608
	20.3 Encoding and Licensing of Grammatical Relations	614
	20.3.1 Encoding the Subject	616
	20.3.2 Encoding Objects	618
	20.3.3 Possessives	622
	20.4 Long-Distance Dependencies	624
	20.4.1 A-Movements	624
	20.4.2 Clitic Movement	626
	20.4.3 A′-Movements	630
	20.5 Pronominal Dependencies	632
	20.5.1 Binding	632
	20.5.2 Control Constructions	634
	20.6 Conclusions	635
21	Parametric Variation *Adam Ledgeway and Norma Schifano*	637
	21.1 Introduction	637
	21.2 Sentential Core	642
	21.2.1 Subject Clitics	642

	21.2.2 Auxiliary Selection	646
	21.2.2.1 Tense and Mood	647
	21.2.2.2 Person and Argument Structure	648
	21.2.2.3 Diachronic Considerations	650
	21.2.2.4 Summary	651
	21.2.3 Verb-Movement	652
	21.2.4 Negation	656
	21.2.4.1 Correlation between Verb-Movement and Jespersen's Stages	659
21.3	Left Periphery	663
	21.3.1 Grammaticalization of (In)definiteness on C	663
	21.3.2 Weak/Strong C	666

Part Five Semantics and Pragmatics

22 Word Meanings and Concepts *Steven N. Dworkin* 673
  22.1 Traditional Approaches to Lexical Change 673
  22.2 Grammaticalization and Pragmatic-Semantic Change 675
  22.3 Prepositions and Prepositional Phrases 682
  22.4 Degrammaticalization (or Lexicalization?) 684
  22.5 Discourse Markers and Semantic-Pragmatic Change 686
  22.6 Subjectification and Evidentiality 690
  22.7 A Concluding Observation 692

23 Key Topics in Semantics: Presupposition, Anaphora, (In)definite Nominal Phrases, Deixis, Tense and Aspect, Negation
Chiara Gianollo and Giuseppina Silvestri 695
  23.1 Introduction 695
  23.2 Presupposition 695
    23.2.1 Introduction 695
    23.2.2 Presupposition and (In)definiteness 696
    23.2.3 Presupposition Autonomy and Triggers 697
    23.2.4 Presuppositionality and Case Marking 698
        23.2.4.1 Presuppositionality and Differential Object Marking 698
        23.2.4.2 Presuppositionality and Greek-Style Dative 699
  23.3 Anaphora 700
    23.3.1 Introduction 700
    23.3.2 Pronominal Anaphora 700
        23.3.2.1 Intrasentential Anaphora 700
        23.3.2.2 Discourse Anaphora 702
    23.3.3 Temporal Anaphora 704
  23.4 (In)definite Nominal Phrases 705
    23.4.1 Introduction 705
    23.4.2 Articles: Distribution, Functional Load, Diachronic Emergence 705
    23.4.3 Indefinites 708

23.5 Deixis ... 709
   23.5.1 Introduction ... 709
   23.5.2 Spatial Deixis ... 710
   23.5.3 Temporal Deixis ... 713
   23.5.4 Person Deixis ... 714
23.6 Tense and Aspect ... 715
   23.6.1 Introduction ... 715
   23.6.2 Imperfectivity and Perfectivity in Present and Past ... 716
   23.6.3 Tense, Aspect, and Modality: Imperfect and Future ... 720
23.7 Negation ... 721
   23.7.1 Introduction ... 721
   23.7.2 Negative Concord ... 722
   23.7.3 Diachronic Developments ... 723
   23.7.4 Pragmatically Marked Negation ... 725

24 Speech Acts, Discourse, and Clause Type   *Alice Corr and Nicola Munaro* ... 728
24.1 Introduction ... 728
24.2 Clause Type ... 728
   24.2.1 Declaratives ... 729
   24.2.2 Interrogatives ... 730
   24.2.3 Exclamatives ... 737
   24.2.4 Imperatives ... 741
   24.2.5 Optatives ... 745
   24.2.6 Concluding Remarks ... 747
24.3 Speech Acts and Illocutionary Force ... 747
   24.3.1 Theoretical Approaches to Speech Acts ... 749
      24.3.1.1 The View from Speech Act Theory ... 749
      24.3.1.2 The Role of Syntax ... 750
      24.3.1.3 The Role of Prosody ... 751
   24.3.2 Mapping Form to Function: Insights from Romance ... 752
      24.3.2.1 The Role of Polarity ... 754
      24.3.2.2 Word Order, Complementizers, and Verb Movement ... 755
      24.3.2.3 Disambiguating Discourse ... 758
   24.3.3 Syntactic Encoding of 'Speech Act' Information ... 759
24.4 Conclusion ... 761

25 Address Systems and Social Markers   *Federica Da Milano and Konstanze Jungbluth* ... 763
25.1 Introduction ... 763
25.2 From Latin to Romance: Expressing Politeness by Pronouns ... 765
25.3 Forms of Address between Lexicon and Grammar in Use Today ... 767
   25.3.1 Noun Phrase: Nominal Forms of Address ... 767
   25.3.2 Pronominal Forms: Address Systems ... 769

	25.3.3 Vocatives	772
	25.3.4 Paradigms and Their Variation: Losses and Gains	773
	25.3.5 Typological Patterns of Address Systems	774
25.4	Changing Address Systems across Time	775
25.5	Conclusion	781

26 Information Structure *Silvio Cruschina, Ion Giurgea, and Eva-Maria Remberger* 784

26.1	Introduction	784
26.2	Focus, Focalization, and Focus Types	785
	26.2.1 Introduction	785
	26.2.2 Focus and New Information	786
	26.2.3 Focus Types and Focus Fronting	788
	26.2.4 Focus Types and Clefts	793
26.3	Topicalization Constructions and Types of Topics	793
	26.3.1 Introduction	793
	26.3.2 Topic-Marking and Givenness-Marking	795
	26.3.3 Different Types of Topics in the Left Periphery	797
	26.3.4 Different Syntactic Constructions and Their Derivation	800
26.4	Subject Placement	805
	26.4.1 Introduction	805
	26.4.2 Status of Preverbal Subjects	805
	26.4.3 Subject Inversion: Narrow Focus and Thetic Sentences	808

Part Six Language, Society, and the Individual

27 Register, Genre, and Style in the Romance Languages *Christopher Pountain and Rodica Zafiu* 817

27.1	Definitions	817
	27.1.1 Register	817
	27.1.2 Genre	819
	27.1.3 Style	819
	27.1.4 Some Dimensions of Register, Genre, and Style	820
27.2	Register	821
	27.2.1 'Spoken' and 'Written' Language	821
	27.2.1.1 The Identification of *français populaire*	823
	27.2.1.2 The Boundaries of Spoken and Written Register	824
	27.2.1.3 Subregisters	825
	27.2.1.4 Jargons and Slangs	826
	27.2.2 Variation According to Register	827
	27.2.3 Some Particular Phenomena	828
	27.2.3.1 Affective Suffixes	829
	27.2.3.2 Dislocation	829

27.2.3.3 Passive	831
27.2.3.4 Relativizers	832
27.2.3.5 Future Tense Functions	834
27.2.3.6 Morphological Variation	835
27.2.3.7 Discourse Phenomena	835
27.3 Genre	836
27.4 Style	838
27.4.1 'Good' Style	838
27.4.2 Literary Style	839
27.5 The Importance of Diaphasic Variation in the History of the Romance Languages	841
27.5.1 'Learnèd' Influence	842
27.5.2 The Relative Distance between Registers	842
27.5.3 Attitudinal Factors	843
27.6 Conclusion	843
28 Contact and Borrowing *Francesco Gardani*	845
28.1 Introduction	845
28.2 Effects of Language Contact	847
28.3 Borrowing	850
28.3.1 Phonological Borrowing	852
28.3.2 Prosodic Borrowing	854
28.3.3 Morphological Borrowing	856
28.3.4 Syntactic Borrowing	858
28.4 The Upper Limits of Borrowing	861
28.5 Linguistic Factors Favouring Grammatical Borrowing	864
28.6 Borrowability Hierarchies	866
28.7 Conclusion	868
29 Diamesic Variation *Maria Selig*	870
29.1 Defining Diamesic Variation	870
29.1.1 'Spoken' and 'Written' Language	870
29.1.2 Diamesic Variation, the Architecture of Varieties, and Register Theory	871
29.1.3 Three Dimensions of Diamesic Variation: Medial, Sociolinguistic, and Functional Aspects	872
29.1.4 Synchronic Variation and Processes of Standardization	874
29.2 Effects and Consequences of Diamesic Variation	876
29.2.1 Written and Spoken Latin: The Sociophilological Approach	876
29.2.2 The Dynamics of Late Latin: Diglossia, Restandardization, and Polynormativity	879
29.2.3 Spoken Varieties and Linguistic Change	883
29.2.4 Inscripturation: Romance Vernacular Varieties and the Transition to Written Use	887

		29.2.5 *Scriptae*: 'Invisible Hands' and Linguistic Centralizations	890
		29.2.6 Codifications: 'Grammatization' and 'Standard Ideologies'	893
		29.2.7 Mass Literacy, Restandardization, and New Media	894

30 Social Factors in Language Change and Variation
John Charles Smith   898
  30.1 Introduction   898
  30.2 Variation and Change   899
  30.3 Social Variables   900
   30.3.1 Time   900
   30.3.2 Place   901
   30.3.3 Age   902
   30.3.4 Class   903
   30.3.5 Gender   904
   30.3.6 Ethnicity   905
   30.3.7 Style and Register   905
   30.3.8 Medium   907
   30.3.9 Attitude and Lifestyle   907
   30.3.10 Concluding Remarks   908
  30.4 Transmission and Diffusion   908
  30.5 Simplification and Complexification   911
  30.6 Diglossia and Linguistic Repertoire   915
  30.7 Code-Switching and Contact Vernaculars   917
  30.8 Language Death   918
  30.9 Societal Typology and Language Change   919
  30.10 Standardization   922
  30.11 *Ausbau* Languages and *Abstand* Languages   925
  30.12 Conclusion   928

Index   930

Each chapter has selected references. The full references can be found online at the following page: www.cambridge.org/Romancelinguistics

Figures

4.1	Distribution of languages according to the number of contrastive exponents in the paradigms of verbs (y-axis) and subject clitics (x-axis)	page 157
4.2	Distribution of patterns per number of gaps: diffusion of dialects in the sample vs probability	158
4.3	Presence of 1SG and 2SG clitics in the *ASIt* dataset	159
4.4	Presence of 1SG and 2SG clitics in four linguistic areas (northern Italo-Romance)	159
4.5	Number of clitic systems with gaps and/or syncretic items in Manzini and Savoia's (2005) dataset	160
4.6	Number of non-syncretic and non-null exponents per person	160
4.7	Auxiliary forms by person with unergative verbs in our sample (76 dialects, 36 auxiliation patterns)	170
4.8	Auxiliary forms by person with unaccusative verbs (76 dialects, 40 auxiliation patterns)	171
4.9	Diffusion of E forms (by percentage): unergatives vs unaccusatives. Sample: 76 dialects	171
4.10	Diffusion of the free alternation between E and H forms (by percentage): unergatives vs unaccusatives. Sample: 76 dialects	171
11.1	Conceptualization of the *Lexical Hypothesis*	349
28.1	Thomason and Kaufman's (1988) borrowing scale	867
30.1	The family tree model of Romance (Version 1)	909
30.2	The family tree model of Romance (Version 2)	909

Tables

1.1	Synthetic vs analytic marking of core grammatical categories in Latin and Romance	page 4
1.2	Ripano nominal and present indicative paradigms	16
1.3	Typology of null subjects	22
1.4	(Old) Romanian	57
1.5	Old Italian	57
1.6	Portuguese	58
1.7	Effects of palatalization of velars in some Romance languages	59
1.8	Differential treatment of reflexes of [kw] in Italian and Romanian	62
1.9	Differential palatalizing effect of proto-Romance plural *-e in Italian and Romanian	62
1.10	Failure of expected palatalization of velar consonants in 'western' Romance first conjugation present subjunctives vs expected palatalization in Romanian	64
1.11	The distribution of velar alternants in the Romanian verb	66
1.12	The Romanian velar~palatal alternation unique to *a fugi* 'flee'	66
1.13	Recurrent alternation pattern in old Italian verbs	69
1.14	Sporadic analogical extension of L-pattern alternants into the gerund in old Italian	69
1.15	Absence of extension of L-pattern velar alternants into the old Italian gerund	70
1.16	Root-final -s in verbs which also have velar~palatal alternations	71
1.17	Root-final -s in verbs which also have roots ending in dentals	71

1.18	Introduction of root-final velars into verbs in root-final [d] (here [de] > [ɟe]) in Oltenian	72
1.19	Exceptional effects of metaphony on mid vowels in the present tense of the verb in La Cervara	75
1.20	Ordinary metaphony of low mid vowels vs hypermetaphony: examples from the *AIS*	76
1.21	Metaphony of [a] in Agnone	76
1.22	Metaphony of [a] in the verb in Agnone	77
1.23	Presence in old Italian vs absence in old Romanian of expected palatalization in the third person plural present indicative	80
1.24	Non-palatalized reflexes of Latin 3PL UENIUNT 'come' vs reflexes of (original) palatalization in 1SG UENIO 'come' in some central and southern Italian dialects (*AIS*)	82
1.25	Reflexes of Latin FIERI 'happen, become, be made' continued in the Romanian verb BE	83
1.26	Reflexes of Latin FIERI (> hʲi-) in the Aromanian verb BE	83
1.27	'L-pattern' effects of sound change in Portuguese and old Italian	90
1.28	'Coherent' levelling and innovatory adjustments of the Italian variant of the L-pattern in modern Italian	91
1.29	Innovatory L-pattern alternation in Portuguese *perder* 'lose'	91
1.30	Creation of L-pattern suppletion in Galician dialects	91
4.1	Expletive clitics in impersonal environments	155
4.2	Patterns of gaps and syncretism in the paradigms of subject clitics (left) and verbal forms (right)	157
4.3	Gaps in subject clitic paradigms in dialects of northern Italy and Romansh	158
4.4	Implicational scale for auxiliary selection	165
4.5	Patterns of split auxiliation with unergative verbs in our sample (76 dialects)	167
4.6	Patterns of split auxiliation with unaccusative verbs in our sample (76 dialects)	169
4.7	Perfective auxiliation in the dialect of Aliano (province of Matera)	173
4.8	Perfective auxiliation in the dialect of Viguzzolo (province of Alessandria)	173
6.1	French numeral allomorphy	224
10.1	The article in Aranese (Canejan-Bausen)	322
10.2	Plural *-s* in Allez-et-Cazeneuve	323
10.3	Paradigms of Fr. *baisser* 'lower', *tourner* 'turn', *refuser* 'refuse'	325
10.4	Paradigms of French vowel-initial *écouter* 'listen', *aimer* 'love', *oser* 'dare'	327
10.5	French possessives	328
10.6	Masculine possessives in Cabranes	328

10.7	Feminine possessives in Cabranes	328
10.8	Differentiation of the root according to whether it is stressed or unstressed in Asturian (Somiedo)	329
10.9	Old Occitan present indicative and present subjunctive paradigms	330
10.10	Gemination triggered by labiovelar glides	331
10.11	Stress shift due to the existence of a heavy (disyllabic) ending	331
10.12	Second person singular allomorphy in Romanian	333
10.13	Non-palatalization of the velar in Italian *-are* verbs	333
10.14	Italian *fuggire* 'flee', *leggere* 'read'	334
10.15	*correr* 'run' or *pendre* 'take' in Azanuy	335
10.16	Brazilian Portuguese plural formation	336
10.17	Adjectival allomorphy before nouns in French	339
10.18	Feminine and plural adjective formation in La Litera	340
10.19	Place assimilation in Italian	340
10.20	Castilian *-dad*, etc.	341
10.21	Diminutive formation in Campidanian Sardinian	342
10.22	Diminutive formation in Logudorese Sardinian	342
10.23	French suffix *-esque* / *-este*	343
10.24	Italian imperfect indicative	343
11.1	Paradigmatic distribution of four Romance metamorphomes affecting finite forms: the N-pattern, the L/U-pattern, PYTA, and Fuèc	353
11.2	Paradigm of Pt. *saber* 'know'	356
11.3	Reflexes of Latin *infectum* forms for It. *portare* 'carry' and Cat. *veure* 'see'	356
11.4	Cat. *moure* 'move'	358
11.5	Present-tense forms of Pt. *dever* 'owe', *mover* 'move', *beber* 'drink' and the *-ir* verbs *servir* 'serve', *dormir* 'sleep', *vestir* 'dress'	360
12.1	Degrees of suppletion between Italian placenames and ethnonyms	374
12.2	Suppletion in Romanian ordinal numerals	375
12.3	Suppletion in Romance ordinal numerals	376
12.4	Suppletion in Romance ordinal numerals	376
12.5	Suppletive comparatives in Latin and some Romance languages	377
12.6	First person tonic pronouns	379
12.7	Second person tonic pronouns	380
12.8	BE (etyma: ESSE, FUISSE (suppletive perfective of ESSE) 'be'; FIERI 'become'; STARE 'stand'; SEDERE 'sit')	381
12.9	GO (etyma: IRE 'go'; UADERE '"go" making an "impressive … showy advance"'; AMBULARE (or possibly *ambiˈtare) 'walk'; FUISSE 'have been')	382

12.10	MUST (etyma: DEBERE 'must, owe'; *estoˈpere 'must, be necessary') Surmiran Romansh (Savognin)	383
12.11	GIVE (etyma: DARE 'give'; DONARE 'give, grant, bestow')	383
12.12	FIND (etyma: AD+FLARE 'sniff out'; *troˈpare 'find') South-eastern Sicily	383
12.13	TAKE (etymon: LEUARE 'raise') in Romanian	383
12.14	FIT (etyma: CAPERE 'take'; COLLIGERE 'gather in') in Larouco, Province of Ourense, Galicia	383
12.15	PULL (etyma: TRAHERE 'pull'; *tiˈrare 'pull') in Romansh (Prez)	384
12.16	WANT ((a) etymon: *voˈlere 'want'; (b) etyma: *voˈlere, Sl. *voliti* 'want')	384
12.17	SAY (etymon: DICERE 'say') in Surselvan Romansh	384
12.18	DRINK (etymon: BIBERE 'drink') in Lugo (Romagna, Italy)	384
12.19	FALL (etyma: CADERE 'fall'; *kasiˈkare 'fall') in Casacalenda (Molise, Italy)	384
12.20	HEAR (etyma: SENTIRE 'feel'; INTENDERE 'understand') in Modica, Sicily	385
12.21	EXIT (etyma: EXIRE 'go out'; It. *uscio* 'doorway' < OSTIUM) in Italian	385
12.22	Istro-Romanian suppletive aspectual distinctions	385
12.23	Suppletion in imperative of COME (etyma: UENIRE; Gk. ἔλα [ˈela]; AMBULARE 'walk')	385
12.24	EYE (etymon: OCULUM 'eye') in French	386
12.25	SMALL and BIG (etyma: *ˈmiku 'small' + MINUTUS 'chopped small, fine-grained' and MAIOR 'larger, major' + *matjuˈkatu 'knobby') in Megleno-Romanian	386
12.26	Derivationally related lexemes containing diminutive suffixes of different origin (etyma of the suffixes: *-ˈinu; *-ˈettu (plural *-ˈitti))	386
12.27	Derivationally related lexemes containing diminutive suffixes of different origin (etyma of the suffixes: -ELLA; Sl. *-ˈika) in Romanian	386
12.28	Preterite of HAVE in S. Michele di Ganzaria (Sicily, AIS map 1700, point 875)	397
13.1	Italian noun *divano* 'sofa.(M)SG'	403
13.2	Italian adjective *buono* 'good.MSG'	403
13.3	Romanian noun *fată* 'girl.(F)SG'	403
13.4	Nominal output examples	404
13.5	Adjectival output examples	404
13.6	Verbal output examples	404
13.7	Subordinate, coordinate, and attributive compounds	405
13.8	Romance compounds	406
13.9	Derivational diminutive affix	406

13.10	Italian diphthongization and palatalization	408
13.11	Palatalization in the Italian verb *vincere* 'win'	409
13.12	Italian palatalization in inflexion, derivation, and compounding	409
13.13	Italian inflexion and word-formation	410
13.14	Suffixed words: no prosodic boundary between stem and suffix	411
13.15	Prefixed words	411
13.16	Italian compounds	412
13.17	European Portuguese	413
13.18	Portuguese inflexional wordforms	418
13.19	Standard Portuguese 'the new pupil(s)'	419
13.20	Non-standard Brazilian Portuguese 'the new pupil(s)'	419
13.21	It. *parlare* 'speak' and *chattare* 'chat (online)' vs *andare* 'go'	419
13.22	Defectiveness. Sp. *partir* 'part' vs *blandir* 'brandish'	420
13.23	Syncretism: It. BUONO 'good' vs VERDE 'green'	420
13.24	Standard Italian inflexion class system	422
13.25	Italian *uov-o* 'egg'	422
13.26	Italian *uov-o* 'egg' vs *uov-a* 'eggs'	423
13.27	Italian *mur-o/-i* 'wall/-s' and *mur-a* 'walled perimeter'	423
13.28	Italian *finire* 'finish'	425
13.29	Romanian *a păți* 'suffer'	426
13.30	Derivation of deverbal nouns without affixation	426
15.1	Formation of cardinals in some standard Romance languages	465
15.2	Formation of Latin numerals	470
17.1	Verb agreement paradigm in (colloquial) Brazilian Portuguese, present indicative of *cantar* 'sing'	535
17.2	Null (vs overt) subjects in transcribed interviews according to structural context	536
18.1	The Auxiliary Selection Hierarchy	557
18.2	Reflexive auxiliary hierarchy	558
18.3	Person-based auxiliary selection in Abruzzo	560
18.4	Variable auxiliary selection (Loporcaro 2011a)	561
19.1	Auxiliary-verb constructions vs other monoclausal constructions	575
21.1	Typologies of Romance verb-movement	652
21.2	Correlation between PI and (un)interpretability	655
21.3	Verb-movement and negation typologies	659
24.1	Possible intonational contours and corresponding communicative functions for Sp. *bebe la limonada* 's/he drinks the lemonade'	751
30.1	The interpretation of variation according to age	903
30.2	Wikipedias in Romance varieties	927

Contributors

Víctor ACEDO-MATELLÁN, University of Oxford
Alvise ANDREOSE, Università di Udine
Benedetta BALDI, Università degli Studi di Firenze
Brigitte L. M. BAUER, The University of Texas at Austin and Max Planck Institute for Psycholinguistics, Nijmegen
Eulàlia BONET, Centre de Lingüística Teòrica, Universitat Autònoma de Barcelona
Chiara CAPPELLARO, University of Oxford
Anna CARDINALETTI, Università Ca' Foscari Venezia
Alice CORR, University of Birmingham
Silvio CRUSCHINA, University of Helsinki
Sonia CYRINO, University of Campinas
Roberta D'ALESSANDRO, Utrecht University
Federica DA MILANO, Università di Milano-Bicocca
Adina DRAGOMIRESCU, 'Iorgu Iordan – Alexandru Rosetti' Institute of Linguistics of the Romanian Academy and University of Bucharest
Steven N. DWORKIN, University of Michigan
Louise ESHER, CNRS – LLACAN (UMR 8135)
Franck FLORICIC, Université de Paris 3, Sorbonne Nouvelle and LPP (CNRS)
Antonio FORTIN, University of Oxford
Francesco GARDANI, University of Zurich
Chiara GIANOLLO, Alma Mater Studiorum, Università di Bologna
Ion GIURGEA, 'Iorgu Iordan – Alexandru Rosetti' Institute of Linguistics of the Romanian Academy
Giuliana GIUSTI, Università Ca' Foscari Venezia
Konstanze JUNGBLUTH, European University Viadrina Frankfurt
Adam LEDGEWAY, University of Cambridge
Michele LOPORCARO, University of Zurich
Martin MAIDEN, University of Oxford

Giovanna MAROTTA, University of Pisa
Jaume MATEU, Centre de Lingüística Teòrica, Universitat Autònoma de Barcelona
Judith MEINSCHAEFER, Freie Universität Berlin
Laura MINERVINI, Università degli Studi di Napoli Federico II
Lucia MOLINU, Université de Toulouse 2, Jean Jaurès and BCL (CNRS)
Nicola MUNARO, Università Ca' Foscari Venezia
Alexandru NICOLAE, 'Iorgu Iordan – Alexandru Rosetti' Institute of Linguistics of the Romanian Academy and University of Bucharest
Paul O'NEILL, University of Sheffield
Gabriela PANĂ DINDELEGAN, 'Iorgu Iordan – Alexandru Rosetti' Institute of Linguistics of the Romanian Academy and University of Bucharest
Diego PESCARINI, CNRS, Université Côte d'Azur
Anna PINEDA, University of Cologne
Christopher POUNTAIN, Queen Mary University of London
Franz RAINER, WU Vienna
Eva-Maria REMBERGER, University of Vienna
Leonardo M. SAVOIA, Università degli Studi di Firenze
Norma SCHIFANO, University of Birmingham
Maria SELIG, University of Regensburg
Michelle SHEEHAN, Newcastle University
Giuseppina SILVESTRI, University of California, Los Angeles
John Charles SMITH, University of Oxford
Anna M. THORNTON, Università dell'Aquila
Francesc TORRES-TAMARIT, SFL, CNRS, Université Paris 8
Nigel VINCENT, The University of Manchester
Max W. WHEELER, University of Sussex
Rodica ZAFIU, 'Iorgu Iordan – Alexandru Rosetti' Institute of Linguistics of the Romanian Academy and University of Bucharest

Abbreviations

*	unattested or reconstructed form or usage
**	ungrammatical form or usage
(?)?	(very) dubious form or usage
?	substandard/non-standard form or usage
#	(i) pragmatically infelicitous
	(ii) word boundary
Ø	zero (null), covert form
>	becomes, yields
<	comes from, derives from
ˈ	(primary) word stress
ˌ	(secondary) word stress
=	cliticized to
ː	long/lengthened
.	syllable boundary
||	utterance boundary
ι	intonational phrase
φ	phonological phrase
ω	prosodic word
π	foot
σ	syllable
μ	mora
√	root
1 / 2 / 3	first/second/third person
A	subject of a transitive clause
A-position/movement	argument position/movement
A'-position/movement	adjunct position/movement
ABL	ablative
Abr.	Abruzzese (dialect group of Abruzzo, upper south-eastern Italy)

ABS	absolutive
ACC	accusative
AcI	accusative and infinitive construction
ACT	active voice (morphology)
addr	addressee
ADDU	*Atlas lingüístico Diatópico y Diastrático del Uruguay*
ADJ	adjectival
A(dj)(P)	adjective (phrase)
ADN	adnominal case form
ADV	(i) adverbal case form
	(ii) adverbial
Adv(P)	adverb(ial) (phrase)
Agn.	Agnonese (northern Molisan dialect of Agnone, upper southern Italy)
Agnell.	Andreas Agnellus of Ravenna
AGR	agreement (morphology)
Agr(P)	agreement (phrase)
AgrO(P)	object agreement (phrase)
AgrS(P)	subject agreement (phrase)
AIS	*Atlante Italo-Svizzero* or *Sprach- und Sachatlas Italiens und der Südschweiz*
Alb.	Albanian
ALF	*Atlas Linguistique de la France*
ALG	*Atlas Linguistique de la Gascogne*
Alg.	Alguerès (Catalan dialect of city of Alghero, north-western Sardinia)
Alt.	Altamurano (central Pugliese dialect of Altamura, upper south-eastern Italy)
AN(A)	adjective-noun(-adjective) order
Anc.	Anconitano (central eastern Marchigiano dialect of city of Ancona, eastern central Italy)
And.	Andalusian (variety of Spanish spoken in region of Andalusia, southern Spain)
AOR	aorist
Ara.	Aragonese (Pyrenean Ibero-Romance language spoken in Aragon, north-eastern Spain)
Arl.	Ariellese (eastern Abruzzese dialect of Arielli, upper south-eastern Italy)
Arm.	Armenian
Arn.	Aranese (Pyrenean Gascon dialect of Occitan spoken in the Val d'Aran, north-western Catalonia, Spain)
ARo.	Aromanian (Daco-Romance dialects spoken in Greece, Albania, Bulgaria, Serbia, and the Republic of Macedonia)

ASH	Auxiliary Selection Hierarchy
ASIt	*Atlante Sintattico d'Italia*
ASP	aspect(ual) marker
Asp(P)	aspect(ual) (phrase)
ASRT	assertive
Ast.	Asturian (dialect group of north-western Spain)
A-topic	aboutness topic
ATR	advanced tongue root
Aug.	Augustine
AUX	auxiliary
(1-/2-/3-)aux	(1-/2-/3-)auxiliary system
b.	born
Bad.	Badiot (Ladin dialect spoken in Val Badia, Dolomites of Alto Adige/southern Tyrol, north-eastern Italy)
Bal.	Balearic (Catalan)
BCE	before the Common Era
Bcl.	Barceloní (Catalan of city of Barcelona)
Bel.	Bellunese (northern Venetan dialect of city of Belluno, north-eastern Italy)
BEN	benefactive (case)
Bol.	Bolognese (eastern Emilian dialect of city of Bologna, north-eastern Italy)
BrBgm.	Brazilian Bergamasch (variety of the dialect of the city of Bergamo now spoken in Botuverá, Santa Catarina, Brazil, following migrations from eastern Lombardy in nineteenth and twentieth centuries)
Brg.	Borgomanerese (north-eastern Piedmontese dialect of Borgomanero, north-western Italy)
BrPt.	Brazilian Portuguese
Bsq.	Basque
C	(i) central
	(ii) consonant
c.	circa
C-drop	complementizer drop
Caes.	Caesar
B.G.	*de Bello Gallico*
Cal.	Calabrian (dialect group of Calabria, extreme south-west of Italy)
Car.	Carrarese (northern Tuscan dialect of Lunigiana, central Italy)
Cat.	Catalan
CCR	Central Coincidence Relation

CE	Common Era
ch.	chapter
Ch.	Chinese
Cic.	Cicero
Agr.	*De Lege agraria*
Att.	*Epistulae ad Atticum*
Cael.	*Oratio pro Caelio*
Clu.	*Pro Cluentio*
Fam.	*Epistulae ad familiares*
Leg. Man.	*Pro Lege Manilia*
Off.	*De officiis*
Phil.	*Orationes Philippicae*
CIL	*Corpus Inscriptionum Latinarum*
Cl	clitic
CLat.	Classical Latin
ClLD	clitic left-dislocation
ClRD	clitic right-dislocation
CM	comparative method
CMPR	comparative
COLL	collective
coll.	colloquial
COMP	complementizer (position)
COND	conditional
Cos.	Cosentino (northern Calabrian dialect of city of Cosenza, extreme south-west of Italy)
C(P)	complementizer (phrase)
Cpd.	Campidanese (dialect group of Campidania, southern Sardinian)
Crs.	Corsican
Cst.	Castilian
C-topic	contrastive topic
Ctz.	Catanzarese (central southern Calabrian dialect of city of Catanzaro, extreme south-west of Italy)
Cvl.	Castrovillarese (northern Calabrian dialect of Castrovillari, extreme south-west of Italy)
d.	died
Dan.	Danish
DAT	dative
Dch.	Dutch
DEF	definite(ness)
Deg(P)	degree modifier (phrase)
DEM	demonstrative
DÉR	*Dictionnaire Étymologique Romane*
DET	determiner (category)

DIM	diminutive
dir. trans.	direct transitive clause
DO	direct object
DOM	differential object marking (or marker)
D(P)	determiner (phrase)
DRo.	Daco-Romance
e	empty category
E	(i) Romance outcome of ESSE 'be' (ii) event time
ECM	exceptional case marking
Egd.	Engadine (Romansh dialect of Engadine Valley, south-east Switzerland)
Eng.	English
Eon.	Eonavian
EPP	extended projection principle (a syntactic requirement that every clause shall have a subject)
ERG	ergative
ESID(s)	extreme southern Italian dialect(s)
EuPt.	European Portuguese
EuSp.	European Spanish
Ext.	Extremaduran (dialect group of Extremadura, central western Spain)
F	feminine
F	feature
f.	and following page
FAM	familiar
Fas.	Fassano (Ladin dialect spoken in the Val di Fassa, north-eastern Trentino, north-eastern Italy)
Fin(P)	finiteness (phrase)
Flo.	Florentine
FLMS	feminine-like masculine singular form
Foc(P)	focus (phrase)
FP	functional projection
fr.	fragment
Fr.	French
Frl.	Friulian (dialect group of Friuli, north-eastern Italy)
Frp.	Francoprovençal (Gallo-Romance dialects spoken in central eastern France, western Switzerland, and north-western Italy)
FUT	future
fv	final vowel
G-topic	given topic
GaR.	Gallo-Romance

GB	Government-Binding Theory
GEN	(i) gender feature
	(ii) genitive
Gen.	Genoese
GER	gerund
Ger.	German
Glc.	Galician (Ibero-Romance language of north-western Spain)
Grk.	Greek
Gsc.	Gascon
Gvd.	Gévaudanais (Occitan variety spoken in central southern France in the Départment of Lozère)
H	(i) Romance outcome of HABERE 'have'
	(ii) heavy syllable
	(iii) high functions and contexts (of language use)
H–	high phrasal accent
H*	high pitch accent
H*+L / H+*L	falling complex pitch accent (stressed syllable aligned with high/low pitch accent)
H%	high boundary tone
HAS	higher adverb space
HON	honorific
HOR	hortative
HT	hanging topic
Hygin.	Hyginius
Fab.	*Fabulae*
i	interpretability
IbR.	Ibero-Romance
Ils.	Illasian (south-western Venetan dialect of Illasi, north-eastern Italy)
IMP	imperative
IMPS	impersonal
IND	indicative
indir. trans.	indirect reflexive transitive clause
indir. unerg.	indirect reflexive unergative clause
INF	infinitive
I(nfl)(P)	inflexion(al phrase)
IntP	interrogative phrase
INTJ	interjection
IPFV	imperfective (aspect)
IRo.	Istro-Romanian (Daco-Romance variety spoken in Istria, Croatia)
Isc.	Ischitano (Campanian dialect spoken on island of Ischia in the Bay of Naples, upper south-west of Italy)

It.	Italian
ItR.	Italo-Romance
K(P)	Case (phrase)
L	(i) (any given) language
	(ii) light syllable
	(iii) low functions and contexts (of language use)
L–	low phrasal accent
L*	low pitch accent
L*+H / L+*H	falling complex pitch accent (stressed syllable aligned with low/high pitch accent)
L%	low boundary tone
L1/2	first/second language
Lad.	(Dolomitic) Ladin
LAmSp.	Latin American Spanish
LAS	lower adverb space
Lat.	Latin
Lec.	Leccese (southern Salentino dialect of Lecce, extreme south-east of Italy)
Leo.	Leonese (dialect group of north-western Spain)
lex	lexical
LF	Logical Form
Lf1	low-frequency formant
Lgd.	Lengadocien (Occitan dialects of Languedoc, southern France)
Lig.	Ligurian (dialect group of Liguria, north-western Italy)
lit.	literally
Liv.	Livy (*Ab urbe condita*)
Lmb.	Lombard (dialect group of Lombardy, central northern Italy)
Lnc.	Lancianese (south-eastern Abruzzese dialect of Lanciano, upper south-eastern Italy)
LOC	locative
Log.	Logudorese (dialect group of Logudoro, north-western Sardinia)
LP	left periphery
Luc.	Lucanian (dialect group of upper southern Italy)
M	masculine
Mac.	Maceratese (central Marchigiano dialect of Macerata, central Italy)
Maj.	Majorcan (Catalan)
Mar.	Marchigiano (dialect group of Le Marche, central eastern Italy)

med	medieval
Mes.	Messinese
Mil.	Milanese
Mod	modern
MR	Metaphony Rule
MRK	marker
MSLF	masculine singular liaison form
Mus.	Mussomelese (central Sicilian dialect of Mussomeli, extreme south of Italy)
mvt	movement
n.	(foot)note
N	(i) nasal consonant
	(ii) north(ern)
NA	noun–adjective order
Nap.	Neapolitan
NCL	noun class
NEG	negator
Neg(P)	negation (phrase)
NID(s)	northern Italian dialect(s)
NOM	nominative
N(P)	noun (phrase)
NPD	non-prototypical derivation
NPI	(i) negative polarity item
	(ii) non-prototypical inflexion
NR	Neutralization Rule
Nuo.	Nuorese (Sardinian dialects of Nuoro and province, north-eastern Sardinia)
O	(i) object
	(ii) old
OBL	oblique case (form)
OBV	obviative
Occ.	Occitan
OCSl.	Old Church Slavonic
OSL	open syllable lengthening
OT	Optimality Theory
OV	object–verb order
p	grammatical property or behaviour
p.	page
Pad.	Paduan (southern Venetan dialect of city of Padua, north-eastern Italy)
Pal.	Palmero Spanish (Island of La Palma, Canary Islands)
PART	partitive

PASS	passive
PD	prototypical derivation
PEJ	pejorative
PER	person
Petr.	Petronius
Sat.	*Satyricon*
PF	Phonological Form
PFV	perfective (aspect)
PI	(i) paradigmatic instantiation
	(ii) prototypical inflexion
Pie.	Piedmontese (dialect group of Piedmont, north-western Italy)
PIE	proto-Indo-European
PL	plural
Pl.	Plautus
Capt.	*Captiui*
Cas.	*Casina*
Cur.	*Curculio*
Epid.	*Epidicus*
Most.	*Mostellaria*
Plin.	Pliny (the Younger)
Ep.	*Epistulae*
Plm.	Palermitano (north-western Sicilian dialect of city of Palermo, extreme south of Italy)
PLPF	pluperfect
p-movement	prosodically conditioned movement
POSS	possessive (form)
Poss(P)	possessive (phrase)
P(P)	preposition(al phrase)
PRED	predicator
PREP	preposition(al)
pro($_{GEN}$)	null pronominal argument (with generic, arbitrary reference)
PRO	phonetically null pronoun
PROG	progressive
PRS	present tense
PRT	preterite
Prv.	Provençal Occitan (Occitan dialects spoken in Provence, south-eastern France)
PSR	Phrase Structure Rules
PST	past
Pt.	Portuguese
PTC	particle
PTCP	participle

Ptl.	Putoleano (Campanian dialect of Pozzuoli in north-eastern outskirts of Naples, upper south-western Italy)
Pgl.	Pugliese (dialects of upper south-eastern Italy)
PVFV	palatalization of velars before front vowels
PYTA	perfecto/pretérito y tiempos afines (= Romance continuants of Latin perfective forms)
QT	question tag
R	reference time
RaeR.	Raeto-Romance
REC	recursive
REFL	reflexive
reg.	regional
REL	relative/relativizer
restr	restructuring
retr.	retroherent clause
RF	*raddoppiamento* (or *rafforzamento*) *fonosintattico* 'phonosyntactic doubling (or strengthening)'
Rip.	Ripano (southern Marchigiano dialect of Ripatransone, central Italy)
RL	recipient language
Rmc.	Romanesco (now defunct dialect of Rome)
Rmg.	Romagnol (dialect group of Romagna region, north-eastern Italy)
Rms.	Romansh (dialects spoken in south-eastern Swiss Canton of Graubünden/Grisons/Grigioni/Grischun)
Ro.	Romanian
Ros.	Rossellonès (Catalan dialect of Roussillon, Pyrénées-Orientales, south-eastern France)
Ru.	Russian
Rv(P)	resultative light verb (phrase)
S	(i) south(ern) (ii) speech time (iii) subject
S_A	intransitive (ACTOR/AGENT) subject of an unergative clause
SA	speech act
Sal.	Salentino (dialect group of Salento, southern Puglia, extreme south-east of Italy)
Sall.	Sallust
BI.	*Bellum Iugurthinum*
Sav.	Savoyard (Francoprovençal variety spoken in the historical territory of the Duchy of Savoy in present-day France (Savoie and Haute-Savoie) and Switzerland (Canton of Geneva))

SBJV	subjunctive
SC	small cause
SCL	subject clitic
Sen.	(i) Seneca (the Younger)
	(ii) Senese (dialect of Siena, central northern Tuscany)
Sey.	Seychellois (Seychelles) creole
SG	singular
Sic.	Sicilian
SID(s)	southern Italian dialect(s)
SL	source language
Sl.	Slavonic
Slc.	Sanleuciano (north-eastern Campanian dialect of San Leucio del Sannio, upper south-western Italy)
S_O	intransitive (THEME/UNDERGOER) subject of an unaccusative clause
SOV	subject–object–verb order
Sp.	Spanish
Spec	specifier position
Spkr	speaker
Srd.	Sardinian
Srs.	Surselvan (Romansh dialect, south-eastern Switzerland)
Subj(P)	subject of predication (phrase)
SVi.	Sanvitese (northern Venetan dialect of San Vito di Cadore, north-eastern Italy)
SVO	subject–verb–object order
TAM	tense, aspect, and mood
Ter.	Terence
Andr.	*Andria*
Hec	*Hecyra*
Top(P)	topic (phrase)
T(P)	tense (phrase)
trans.	transitive clause
Trn.	Trentino (dialect group of Trento, north-eastern Italy)
Trp.	Trapanese (north-western Sicilian dialect of city of Trapani, extreme south of Italy)
Tsc.	Tuscan
Tur.	Turinese (central Piedmontese dialect of city of Turin, north-western Italy)
TV	thematic vowel
u	uninterpretable
UG	Universal Grammar

unacc.	unaccusative clause
unerg.	unergative clause
USID(s)	upper southern Italian dialect(s)
V	vowel
Ṽ	nasalized vowel
V1	verb-initial clause / word order
V2	verb-second syntax / word order
V3	verb-third clause / word order
Vals.	Valsuganotto (Trentino dialect of Valsugana, north-eastern Italy)
Vâo.	Valdôtain (Francoprovençal variety spoken in Aosta Valley, north-western Italy)
Vbc.	Verbicarese (dialect of Verbicaro spoken in Lausberg Zone of northern Calabria, southern Italy)
Ven.	Venetan
Ver.	Veronese (Venetan dialect of city of Verona, north-eastern Italy)
Vgl.	Vegliote (defunct Dalmatian dialect formerly spoken on island of Veglia (Krk))
Vlc.	Valencian (Catalan)
Vnt.	Venetian
VO	verb–object order
voc	vocative
v(P)	light verb (phrase)
V(P)	verb (phrase)
VS	verb–subject order
VSO	verb–subject–object order
W	west(ern)
Wal.	Wallon (French dialect of Wallonia, southern Belgium)
WALS	*World Atlas of Language Structures*
Wel.	Welsh
WhP	embedded wh-phrase projection

1

Data, Theory, and Explanation: The View from Romance

Adam Ledgeway and Martin Maiden

1.1 Introduction

This is a book about doing linguistics by using data, comparative and historical, from the Romance languages. It explores what we can learn about linguistics from the study of Romance, rather than taking the more traditional approach of asking what we can learn about the structure and history of the Romance languages through the application of general linguistic principles and assumptions. In short, it asks not what linguistics can do for Romance, but, rather, what Romance can do for linguistics.

The Romance languages are among the most widely studied and researched language families in modern linguistics. Data from Romance have always been prominent in the linguistic literature and have contributed extensively to our current empirical and theoretical understanding of phonetics, phonology, morphology, syntax, semantics, pragmatics, sociolinguistics, and historical linguistics. Their prominence reflects the richly documented diachronic variation exhibited by the Romance family, which, coupled with our extensive knowledge and abundant textual documentation of the ancestral language, Latin, offers insights into a range of variation through time and space certainly unparalleled for any other Western languages. In short, the Romance languages and dialects constitute a treasure house of linguistic data of profound interest and importance not merely for Romance linguists, but for linguists generally. Indeed, this perennially fertile and still underutilized linguistic testing ground has a central role to play in challenging linguistic orthodoxies and shaping and informing new ideas and perspectives about language change, structure, and variation. This book takes seriously the idea that our knowledge and understanding of the many fields of linguistics have been and continue to be considerably enhanced – but in many cases shaped – by investigations of the Romance data. It is therefore meant not for the exclusive use and interest of Romance linguists,[1] but for general linguists interested in the insights that a knowledge of the Romance evidence can provide for general issues in linguistic theory.

By exploring a range of comparative Romance data, this book contributes to a series of core questions and issues in linguistics, namely I. *What Is a Language?*; II. *Phonetics and Phonology*; III. *Morphology*; IV. *Syntax*; V. *Semantics and Pragmatics*; VI. *Language, Society, and the Individual*. The 30 chapters have been written, often collaboratively, by 50 internationally recognized Romance linguists, who were invited to contribute in these areas both on the basis of their expertise in specific fields of linguistics and for their expert knowledge of the relevant comparative Romance data. They have been encouraged to take a personal view of the principles and areas that have been influential in a particular subarea, bringing to bear the results of their own recent research wherever appropriate.

What follows in this introductory chapter is also a 'personal view' of Romance linguistics, but one that adopts a slightly different perspective from that taken in the rest of the book. At first sight, what we do in the remainder of this chapter may appear quirky, incoherent, perhaps even self-indulgent. Rather than addressing a particular topic in linguistic theory from a Romance perspective, we have chosen to explore our own, personal, experiences of doing Romance linguistics, and of how working with data from the Romance languages has made us reflect on wider issues in general linguistics. Recurrent themes in our work have been, respectively, morphosyntactic change (Ledgeway) and sound change and its morphological consequences (Maiden). Within those areas, however, we have each concentrated here on a particular aspect, Ledgeway on the grammatical expression of functional categories and Maiden on Romance palatalization and its consequences. Now these two topics may seem to be the most curious of bedfellows, and indeed there is probably no significant overlap between them whatever. Moreover, each of these topics has led us along a number of different, and perhaps unexpected, sidetracks and byways but not, we think, dead ends! The result may seem eclectic and diffuse, but that is not

---

[1] There are numerous valuable manuals and handbooks, including classic comparative-historical and massively-detailed encyclopaedic treatments such as Meyer-Lübke (1890–1902), Lausberg (1965–66), Holtus, Metzeltin, and Schmitt (1988–2005), and Ernst, Gleßgen, Schmitt, and Schweickard (2003–08), and the three volumes co-edited by the current editors (viz. Maiden, Smith, and Ledgeway 2011; 2013; Ledgeway and Maiden 2016), as well as a new De Gruyter series *Manuals in Romance Linguistics* (general editors: Günter Holtus and Fernando Sánchez-Miret) with a projected 30 or so volumes dedicated to individual Romance varieties, sub-branches of Romance, and specific Romance phenomena and themes. Then there are the many very useful smaller-scale works on comparative Romance such as Hall (1974), Elcock (1960; 1975), Harris (1978), Harris and Vincent (1988), Posner (1996), Alkire and Rosen (2010), Ledgeway (2012a), as well as detailed structural treatments of some of the better-known individual Romance languages (e.g. Maiden 1995; Penny 2000, 2002; Azevedo 2005; Fagyal, Kibbee, and Jenkins 2006; Pană Dindelegan 2013, 2016; Maiden et al. 2021).

the point. These topics are simply two representative fragments of the vast intellectual enterprise of Romance linguistics, and we believe that they have led us to the kind of conclusions that would also emerge if Romance linguists working in any other subdomains were invited to reflect on their personal experience of doing Romance linguistics. And what are those conclusions? That the comparative-historical study of the Romance languages can most effectively illuminate our understanding of human language, and particularly of language change, if it seeks to explain, rather than merely to describe, linguistic facts; that such explanation should be informed by, and can in turn illuminate and refine, general linguistic theory; but above all, and most fundamentally, that Romance linguistics can make its most powerful contributions to general linguistics when Romance linguists exploit to the maximum the extraordinary wealth of historical and comparative *data* which the Romance languages offer them.

1.2 The View from Morphosyntax and the Case of Functional Categories

1.2.1 From Latin to Romance: The Rise of Functional Categories

One of the most striking morphosyntactic differences between Latin and Romance has traditionally been taken to involve a distinction between morphology and syntax:[2] whereas Latin predominantly makes recourse to synthetic structures, Romance makes greater use of analytic structures, a development often interpreted as the surface reflex of a change in the basic ordering of head and dependency according to a well-known typological distinction from which many other basic properties are said to follow (Greenberg 1966; Lehmann 1974; Harris 1978: 4–6; Bauer 1995: 13).[3] By way of illustration, consider Table 1.1, where we see that, in contrast to Romance, Latin lacks functional categories, in that none of the core grammatical categories such as subordination, tense, aspect, mood, transitivity, or definiteness is expressed analytically (cf. Ledgeway 2012a: ch. 4). At the same time, there is significant synchronic variation across Romance as to which of the functional categories are lexicalized and the distinctions they overtly mark. For instance, only French lexicalizes all the available heads of the functional projections in Table 1.1, including an overt transitive/causative light v(erb) *fait* 'made', whereas Italian only optionally encodes the partitive distinction through an overt DET(erminer) *del* 'of.the (= some)' (cf. Stark 2008). By contrast, Romanian fails to overtly lexicalize either of

---

[2] See, among others, von Schlegel (1818), Bourciez (1956: 23), Harris (1978: 15f.), Schwegler (1990), Posner (1996: 156f.), Vincent (1997a), Ledgeway (2011b: 383–87; 2012a: ch. 2; 2017a).

[3] Harris (1978: 16), Vincent (1988: 55f., 62f.; 1997b: 166), Bauer (1995), Oniga (2004: 52), Ledgeway (2011b: §5; 2012a: ch. 5; 2014b; 2018a).

Table 1.1. *Synthetic vs analytic marking of core grammatical categories in Latin and Romance*

		COMP		Infl		v		DET	
Lat.	Dico/Uolo	Ø		eum	Ø	Ø	coxisse	Ø	panem.
Fr.	Je dis/veux	qu'		il	a/ait	fait	cuire	du	pain.
It.	Dico/Voglio	che			ha/abbia	Ø	cotto	(del)	pane.
Ro.	Spun/Vreau	că/să			a/fi	Ø	copt	Ø	pâine.
	I.say/want	that$_{(REALIS/IRREALIS)}$		him/he	has$_{IND}$/(be)$_{SBJV}$	made	bake(d)	some	bread
	'I say that he has/I want him to have baked some bread.'								

these functional categories, but uniquely displays robust marking on the COMP(lementizer) *că/să* 'that' for the realis/irrealis opposition (Gheorghe 2013b: 468–70), otherwise paralleled in the indicative/subjunctive distinction realized through the clausal INFL(exion) on the perfective auxiliary *a/ait* and *ha/abbia*, in turn further distinguished by way of a HAVE/BE split (viz. *a/fi*) in Romanian (Ledgeway 2014a). In short, we observe minimal differences among otherwise highly homogenous systems which can be read both vertically (Latin ⇒ Romance) and horizontally (French ⇒ Italian ⇒ Romanian) as cases of diachronic and synchronic/diatopic microvariation, respectively.

We thus conclude that marking of clausal boundaries, various verb-related grammatical categories, and definiteness and quantification in Romance is lexicalized by functional markers belonging to the categories of COMP(lementizer), AUX(iliary), light v(erb), and DET(erminer). In current theory, grammatical elements of this type are generally considered to head their own functional projections CP, I(nfl)P, vP, and DP which provide the locus of grammatical information for the clausal, sentential, verbal, and nominal groups, respectively. On this view, one of the most significant generalizations of the traditional synthesis-analysis approach can now be recast in terms of the emergence of these functional categories (Vincent 1997a: 105; 1997b: 149; Lyons 1999: 322f.) which, at least according to one view (though cf. Horrocks 2011; Ledgeway 2012a: ch. 5), were either entirely absent from Latin or only present in incipient form.

Although a consideration of the lexicalization or otherwise of the head positions made available by a universal structure of functional projections provides an elegant way of drawing a morphosyntactic typological distinction between Latin and Romance, it does not offer any further insight into the thorny question of how Romance can be distinctively and exhaustively defined purely on linguistic grounds (Section 1.3.6). Clearly, there are many other language families and areal groupings that equally show extensive evidence for the use of functional categories in similar ways to the Romance languages. Nonetheless, detailed study of Romance functional categories constitutes a fruitful and insightful area of investigation which can both throw light on the comparative history of Romance and offer us important lessons in general linguistic theory. Indeed, differences in functional categories are best studied comparatively within a single family of languages where dimensions of variation between otherwise highly homogeneous linguistic systems of the family are often minimal, thereby allowing us to pinpoint what precisely may vary and the linguistic mechanisms underpinning such variation. In this respect, the richly documented diachronic and synchronic variation exhibited by the Romance family (cf. Section 22.2) offers privileged access to a range of variation through time and space unparalleled for other Western languages.

The Romance languages therefore offer us a valuable experimental testbed to investigate the ways in which current theories claim that it is possible for the morphosyntax of languages to vary. Building on the insights of the Borer–Chomsky Conjecture (cf. Baker 2008: 353), the relevant dimensions of Romance microvariation can be taken to lie in the functional lexicon and, in particular, in the overt lexicalization of specific formal feature values of individual functional heads and the functional categories that realize them (Borer 1984; Chomsky 1995). These feature values are not set in isolation, inasmuch as dimensions of variation ostensibly form an interrelated network of implicational relationships whereby the given value of a particular functional category may, in turn, entail the concomitant activation of associated lower-order grammatical choices, whose potential surface effects may consequently become entirely predictable, or indeed rule out other morphosyntactic properties. In what follows, we therefore consider a selection of representative case studies of comparative morphosyntactic variation which highlight a number of significant differences in the featural make-up of the functional heads C-T-v-D and their associated domains – the left periphery, the inflexional core of the sentence, the verb phrase, and the nominal group – and the parametric options they instantiate. By marrying, on the one hand, traditional Romance philological and dialectological scholarship through the study of syntactic microvariation across time and space with, on the other, the insights of recent syntactic theory, we show how a detailed, expert knowledge of the full extent of the Romance evidence can both test and challenge our theories of morphosyntax and expand the empirical linguistic data on which they are based. Unfortunately, non-standard Romance varieties are too often overlooked in this respect, even though they offer fertile, and frequently uncharted, territory in which to study microvariation. Such microvariation frequently reveals significant differences of real theoretical significance which would not otherwise be visible by simply comparing the grammars of the standard Romance languages (cf. the discussion of gender and number in Section 2.2).

Following a brief introduction in Section 1.2.2 to morphosyntactic variation across Romance in relation to parameters (Section 1.2.2.1), universals

(Section 1.2.2.2), language typology (Section 1.2.2.3), and the interfaces (Section 1.2.2.4), in Section 1.2.3 some case studies of microvariation across Romance are explored which highlight what Romance can do for syntactic theory by way of testing, challenging, and expanding our theory of language and the empirical base. By the same token, the tools and insights of current theories of syntax can also be profitably used to throw light on many of the otherwise apparently inexplicable facts of Romance microvariation, the topic of Section 1.2.4 where the role of syntactic theory for Romance is explored through the exploration of a number of Romance case studies which have traditionally proven, at the very least, extremely difficult to interpret in a unitary and satisfactory fashion.

1.2.2 Linguistic Variation

1.2.2.1 Parameters

One area where research into Romance functional categories has proven particularly influential is the investigation of linguistic parameters, those dimensions of linguistic variation along which natural languages are said to vary (for in-depth discussion, see Chapters 4 and 21, this volume, and Roberts 2019: §1.2; Ledgeway 2020b).[4] Linguistic variation is not free or wild, but is subject to specific structural conditions which restrict the possible limits of variation of all natural languages. To cite just one simple example, it is well known (cf. Cheng 1997; Roberts 2019: ch. 7) that languages vary according to whether *wh*-interrogatives must be fronted to the C-domain, as in most Romance varieties (1a–b), or whether they must remain *in situ* as in Chinese (1c). Yet, in other languages *wh*-fronting is not so systematic, but shows a mixed distribution. This is the case in Brazilian Portuguese, colloquial French, and many dialects of north(-eastern) Italy, where the fronting or otherwise of *wh*-interrogatives variously depends on their phonosyntactic and discourse-pragmatic status (cf. also Section 20.4.3; Section 24.2.2). For instance, in the north-eastern Italian dialect of Lamon clitic and tonic variants of the *wh*-interrogative WHAT occur in fronted (2a) and *in situ* (2b) positions, respectively, and can even co-occur (2c), whereas discourse-pragmatically marked interrogatives such as D(iscourse)-linked complex *wh*-phrases (2d) invariably undergo fronting (De Cia 2018: 22f., 118).[5]

---

[4] For examples and discussion of a phonological parameter, see Section 5.7.

[5] See Munaro (1998), Ambar et al. (2001), Munaro, Poletto, and Pollock (2001), Munaro and Poletto (2002), Benincà and Poletto (2005), Kato and Mioto (2005), Manzini and Savoia (2011), Kato (2013), Bonan (2019), De Cia (2019). Note, however, that many of these analyses maintain that insituness is only apparent, with the *wh*-interrogative raising to the lower or higher left periphery, variously accompanied by remnant movement. If correct, then the relevant fronting parameter displays a uniform behaviour across Romance.

(1) a. **Cine** crede John că ~~cine~~ a cumpărat cărțile? (Ro.)
    b. **¿Quién** cree John que ~~quién~~ ha comprado los libros? (Sp.)
       who believe.PRS.3SG John that have.PRS.3SG bought.PTCP the books(.DEF)
    c. John xiangzin **shei** mai-le shu? (Ch.)
       John believe who buy-ASP book
       'Who does John believe has bought the books?'

(2) a. Sa- g- a -li dat a Simon? (Lamon)
    b.   G- a -li dat che a Simon? (Lamon)
    c. Sa- g- a -li dat che a Simon ? (Lamon)
       what= DAT.3= have.PRS.3 =SCL.3MPL give.PTCP what to Simon
       'What did they give Simon?'
    d. **Che casa** a -lo fat su Toni? (Lamon)
       what house have.PRS.3 =SCL.MSG do.PTCP up Toni
       'Which house did Toni build?'

Among those varieties which display overt fronting of *wh*-interrogatives it is possible to further distinguish between those which allow multiple fronting and those that do not (Bošković 2002): at first blush Slavonic (3a) belongs to the former group, whereas Romance (3b) appears to belong to the latter group (cf. Giurgea and Remberger 2016: 870). However, a more extensive examination of the Romance facts reveals a more nuanced picture in that, unlike other Romance varieties, Romanian (3c) requires multiple fronting (Rudin 1988).

(3) a. **Kto čto** ~~kto~~ kupil **čto**? (Ru.)
    b. **¿Quién** (**qué) ~~quién~~ ha comprado **qué**? (Sp.)
    c. **Cine ce** ~~cine~~ a cumpărat ~~ce~~? (Ro.)
       who what bought what
       'Who has bought what?'

In this respect the behaviour of Romanian appears to parallel that of Slavonic, hardly a surprising result given the widespread borrowing, not just of lexical, but also of functional features across languages of the so-called Balkan Sprachbund. Nonetheless, a closer look at the Romanian facts reveals that the features of the C-head which license multiple *wh*-fronting also impose ordering restrictions absent in Slavonic (Gheorghe 2013a). More specifically, in contrast to most Slavonic varieties where the order of multiple fronted *wh*-constituents is generally unconstrained (cf. 3a, 4a), in Romanian their order shows a sensitivity to superiority effects such that, for example, the subject must precede the object (cf. 3c vs 4b) and arguments must precede, in turn, all adjuncts (4c).

(4) a. **Čto kto** ~~kto~~ kupil ~~čto~~? (Ru.)
    b. **Ce cine** ~~cine~~ a cumpărat ~~ce~~? (Ro.)
       what who bought
       'Who bought what?'

c. (**Când) **Cine când** ~~cine~~ a cumpărat-o ~~când~~? (Ro.)
   when   who when   have.PRS.3SG buy.PTCP=it
   'Who bought it when?'

Consequently, the evidence of Romanian – today still too often overlooked in so-called comparative overviews of Romance – is fundamental for the study of the parameters and sub-parameters involved in the licensing of *wh*-fronting, since it exceptionally presents a mixture of both typical Romance and non-Romance options yielding apparently hybrid grammatical choices. By comparing in this way Romanian not only with other Romance languages, but also with the neighbouring Slavonic varieties it has come into contact with over time (cf. also Chapter 28, this volume), it is possible to isolate the properties of individual functional heads of the C-domain responsible for the fronting of *wh*-interrogatives and model the internal hierarchical organization of the options they instantiate. For example, keeping technical details to a minimum, the formal structural characterization of the variation observed so far in the licensing of the *wh*-interrogatives can be captured by way of (5).

(5)

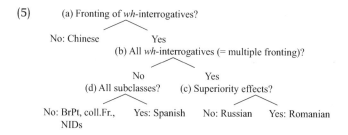

Conceived along the lines of (5), parametric variation can be interpreted in a scalar fashion and modelled in terms of a series of hierarchical and implicational relationships (for further discussion, see Section 21.1). The simplest and least marked options that uniformly apply to all functional heads, are placed at the very top of the hierarchy, but, as one moves downwards, variation becomes progressively more restricted with choices becoming progressively more limited to smaller and smaller proper subsets of features and contexts. This gradual cascading effect produced by the options presented in (5) highlights how variation in relation to the ability of the C-domain to attract *wh*-interrogatives is not uniform but, rather, licenses differing degrees of surface variation in accordance with the growing markedness conditions that accompany the available parametric options as one moves down the hierarchy.

The simplest and least constrained option (viz. 5a) is exemplified by Chinese where all *wh*-interrogatives simply remain in their base positions in all cases, since the C-head is inert and hence unable to license *wh*-fronting to the clausal left periphery. In all other varieties, by contrast, the relevant parameter shows a more marked setting, in that the C-head requires some degree of *wh*-fronting. The least marked option (viz. 5b) among these varieties is instantiated by languages where C indiscriminately attracts all *wh*-interrogatives giving rise to multiple fronting, inasmuch as the effects of the parameter are uniform since the 'rule' affects all *wh*-interrogatives without exception. In this respect, languages such as Chinese, on the one hand, and multiple-fronting languages, on the other, represent simpler and comparatively unmarked options, in that the C-head in these varieties either indiscriminately fails to attract any *wh*-interrogative or, on the contrary, systematically attracts all *wh*-interrogatives. However, as we have seen, within the subclass of languages specified positively for the option of multiple *wh*-fronting there is an additional split which introduces a further restriction in relation to the linear order of fronted *wh*-interrogatives (viz. 5c). While in Slavonic languages such as Russian the order of fronted constituents is largely unconstrained, in Romanian their order falls under specific structural conditions constrained by superiority effects. Finally, option (5d) identifies those varieties where the C-head licenses a more restricted type of fronting limited to a maximum of just one *wh*-interrogative. Such varieties do not, however, form a homogeneous grouping but can be further divided into at least two further subclasses according to whether *wh*-fronting displays a uniform or mixed behaviour. In languages such as Spanish and most other Romance varieties all *wh*-interrogatives may be fronted without exception, whereas in varieties such as Brazilian Portuguese, colloquial French, and many north(eastern) Italian dialects fronting only applies to specific subclasses of *wh*-interrogative.

Over recent years the significance of Romance dialects for the study of parametric variation has also been increasingly recognized. These prove particularly insightful since, although neighbouring dialects tend to be closely related to each other displaying in most cases a high degree of structural homogeneity, they often diverge minimally in significant ways which allow the linguist to identify and observe what lies behind surface differences in particular parametric settings across a range of otherwise highly homogenized grammars. By drawing on such microvariation, it is possible to determine which phenomena are correlated with particular parametric options and how such relationships are mapped onto the syntax. By way of example, consider the so-called dative shift construction, a phenomenon attested in a number of Germanic languages whereby an underlying indirect object such as the RECIPIENT *to Mary* in (6a) can be reanalysed and promoted to direct object. Consequently, in the double object variant in (6b) *Mary* now occurs without the dative marker *to* and precedes the THEME *a book*. Furthermore, it has been claimed that the possibility of dative shift is linked to another structural property, that of stranding prepositions in *wh*-questions and relative clauses, as demonstrated in (6c).

(6) a. John gave a book [to **Mary**].
b. John gave [**Mary**] a book.
c. [**Who**] did John give a book [PP to [DP who]]?

Romance, by contrast, has been claimed to display neither dative shift nor preposition stranding (Kayne 1984; Larson 1988: 378; Holmberg and Platzack 1995), as the sharp ungrammaticality of the Portuguese examples in (7b–c) demonstrates:[6]

(7) a. O João deu um livro [à **Maria**]. (Pt.)
the João give.PST.PFV.3SG a book to.the Maria
b. **O João deu [a **Maria**] um livro. (Pt.)
the João give.PST.PFV.3SG the Maria a book
c. **[**Quem**] deu o João um livro [PP a [DP quem]]? (Pt.)
who give.PST.PFV.3SG the João a book to

However, this apparent Germanic-Romance parametric contrast, ultimately related to properties of the light *v* head and its extended projection, is contradicted by a number of Romance dialects where something very similar, if not identical, to dative shift, is found (Demonte 1995; Sornicola 1997: 35f.; Ledgeway 2009a: 844–47; cf. also Section 16.4), witness the representative Neapolitan examples in (8).

(8) a. Giuanne nce rette nu libbro [a **Maria**]. (Nap.)
Gianni DAT.3= give.PST.PFV.3SG a book to Maria
'Gianni gave a book to Maria.'
b. Giuanne a rette [a **Maria**] nu libbro. (Nap.)
Gianni ACC.3FSG= give.PST.PFV.3SG DOM Maria a book
'Gianni gave Maria a book.'
c. **[**Chi**] rette nu libbro [PP a [DP chi]]? (Nap.)
who give.PST.PFV.3SG a book to
'Who did he give a book to?'

The RECIPIENT argument *a Maria* 'to Maria', the underlying indirect object in (8a), has been promoted to direct object in (8b) where *a* is no longer the indirect object marker but, rather, the differential object marker

---

[6] Note the orthographic and phonetic distinction in (7a–b) between the articulated preposition *à* [a] 'to the' (< *a* 'to' + *a* [ɐ] 'the.FSG') and the feminine singular definite article *a* [ɐ] 'the.FSG'.

of specific animate objects, as shown by: (i) the position of *a Maria* in front of the THEME *nu libbro*; and (ii) by the fact that *a Maria* is now referenced by an accusative clitic pronoun *a* 'her' on the verb, and not the third person dative pronoun *nce* in (8a). Other neighbouring southern dialects, by contrast, such as Cosentino (cf. Ledgeway 2000: 46–52) exhibit a more constrained type of dative shift, inasmuch as RECIPIENT arguments (cf. *cci* 'to her' in 9a) may only surface as direct objects (cf. *a* 'her' in 9b) in monotransitive clauses. A similar dative–accusative alternation is also found in a number of non-standard Ibero-Romance varieties (Pineda 2016; 2020), including (central) Catalan (10a), various Spanish varieties (10b), and Asturian (10c).

(9) a. Gianni **cci** scriva (na littera). (Cos.)
 Gianni DAT.3=write.PRS.3SG a letter
 b. Gianni **a** scriva (**na littera). (Cos.)
 Gianni ACC.3FSG=write.PRS.3SG a letter
 'Gianni will write her (a letter).'

(10) a. En Joan (**li**/) **la** telefona. (non-standard Cat.)
 the Joan DAT.3= ACC.3FSG= phone.PRS.3SG
 'Joan rings her.'
 b. Al día siguiente **la** telefoneó para invitar**la** al
 at.the day following ACC.3FSG= phone.PST.PFV.3SG for invite.INF=ACC.3FSG to.the
 cine. (non-standard Sp.)
 cinema
 'The following day he phoned her to invite her to the cinema.'
 c. Telefoneé**lu** (/?-**y**). (Ast.)
 phone.PST.PFV.1SG=ACC.3MSG (/=DAT.3)
 'I rang him.'

These dialectal varieties reveal therefore three important things. First, dative shift is not a simple Germanic vs Romance parametric option (see also Pineda and Mateu 2020: iv–vii). Second, the supposed link between dative shift and preposition stranding, argued to be derivable from a single parametric option (cf. 6c vs 7c), does not hold. Rather, the presence of both phenomena in languages like English simply represents a fortuitous combination rather than the principled outcome of a particular parametric setting, since preposition stranding is not found in those same Romance varieties which license dative shift (cf. 8c). This conclusion is further confirmed by Romanian which, in contrast to other standard Romance languages but in line with neighbouring Slavonic patterns, also displays a number of lexicalized double object constructions (Pană Dindelegan 1968; 2010; 2013: 65–72) in which the RECIPIENT is marked accusative even in the presence of a THEME argument (11a–c), but which once again fails to license preposition stranding (11d).

(11) a. Imprudența   aceasta l-   a   costat   viața. (Ro.)
       imprudence.DEF this ACC.3MSG=have.PRS.3SG cost.PTCP life.DEF
       'This act of folly cost him his life.'
    b. Am   întrebat-o   ceva. (Ro.)
       have.PRS.1SG ask.PTCP=ACC.3FSG   something
       'I asked her something.'
    c. Îi   învățau   limba   engleză. (Ro.)
       ACC.3PL= teach.PST.IPFV.3PL language.DEF English
       'They were teaching them English.'
    d. **Cine vorbeau   [PP **despre** [DP ~~cine~~]]? (Ro.)
       who   speak.PST.IPFV.3PL   about
       'Who were they speaking about?'

Third, it is incorrect to subsume all instances of accusative marking of RECIPIENT arguments under the generic heading of dative shift, since some Romance dialects prove sensitive to the mono- vs ditransitive distinction. It follows therefore that what might otherwise be taken to represent the surface reflexes of a single parametric setting in dialects like Neapolitan, namely the accusative marking of all RECIPIENT arguments irrespective of whether they occur in mono- or ditransitive clauses, turns out in fact to conceal two distinct structural operations in the light of evidence gleaned from Cosentino, non-standard (central) Catalan and Spanish varieties, and Asturian.

1.2.2.2 Language Universals

Romance also has much to contribute in the area of so-called universal principles of language, essentially a system of rules forming part of the genetic endowment known as Universal Grammar which is believed to hold of all human languages (cf. also Section 21.1). A good illustration of the valuable role that Romance can play in testing linguistic universals concerns the licensing of nominative Case. Within current theory, it is assumed that Infl, the locus of verbal inflexion, may be specified as [±Agr], featural specifications which in turn are argued to correlate with the verb's ability or otherwise to license a nominative Case-marked subject. This [±Agr] distinction is supported by the evidence of many of the world's languages, including French, where finite verbs license nominative subjects (12a), but non-finite verbs such as infinitives and gerunds, which lack overt morphological agreement, only allow null (Caseless) PRO subjects (12b):

(12) a. Vous   rentrez   à   la   maison. (Fr.)
        you   return.PRS.IND.2PL   to   the house
        'You return home.'
     b. Avant de $\emptyset_i$/**Jean rentrer,   vous$_i$ avez   téléphoné. (Fr.)
        before of Ø   Jean return.INF   you   have.PRS.2PL phone.PTCP
        'Before going home, you rang.'

Yet, the evidence of Romance dialects reveals that the supposed universal correlation between the specification of Infl and the availability of nominative Case is entirely spurious (Ledgeway 1998; 2000: ch. 4; Mensching 2000). In particular, dialects from the length and breadth of the Romance-speaking world demonstrate an abundant use of overt nominative subjects in conjunction with infinitival verbs:

(13) a. L' üsu l' è d' acatâ tütu u **padrùn**. (Lig.)
the usage SCL be.PRS.IND.3SG of buy.INF all the boss
'It is customary for the boss to buy everything.'

b. Nun sgarrava mai l' uri soi, senza dàricci corda **nuddu**. (Sic.)
NEG err.PST.IPFV.3SG never the hours its without give.INF=DAT.3 wind nobody
'It always kept time without anyone ever having to wind it up.'

c. E' di prima à mettasi **idda** in vinochju, altari ùn si ni fighjulaia più (Crs.)
and of before to put.INF=self she in knee altar NEG self= of.it= look.PST.IPFV.3SG more
'Until she knelt down, you couldn't look at the altar.'

d. Su postinu est colatu prima de arrivare **jeo**. (Srd.)
the postman be.PRS.IND.3SG pass.PTCP before of arrive.INF I
'The postman passed by before I arrived.'

e. Eu trabalha per **elo** s' amusa. (Occ., Gvd.)
I work.PST.IPFV.1SG for she self= enjoy.INF
'I would work so that she could enjoy herself.'

f. ¿Qué tú me recomiendas para **yo** entender la lingüística? (Cuban Sp.)
what you me=recommend.PRS.IND.2SG for I understand.INF the linguistic
'What do you recommend for me so that I can get an understanding of linguistics?'

Examples such as (13a–f) which illustrate the so-called 'personal' infinitive (cf. Ledgeway 1998; 2000: ch. 4; Bentley 2014) highlight how traditional interpretations of finiteness in terms of a binary distinction are untenable, inasmuch as apparently non-finite forms function to all intents and purposes on a par with finite forms (cf. also Section 2.6.2). Indeed, we are led to conclude that finiteness cannot be understood in terms of superficial morphological marking alone, but, rather, must be interpreted as a scalar notion also including reference to semantico-syntactic criteria. Framing these observations in terms of the features T(ense) and Agr(eement) of the functional category Infl, the traditional binary opposition can be recast in accordance with the typological options in (14a–d) illustrated here by Romanian examples.

(14) a. [+T, +Agr] ⇒ indicative
Ion se trezeşte / trezea / trezi / trezise. (Ro.)
Ion self= wake.PRS.IND.3SG wake.PST.IPFV.3SG wake.PST.PFV.3SG wake.PLPFV.3SG
'Ion wakes/was waking/woke/had woken up.'

b. [+T, −Agr] ⇒ personal infinitive
Am plecat / Plec / Voi pleca înainte de a
have.PRS.1SG leave.PTCP leave.PRS.1SG AUX.FUT.1SG leave.INF before of to

```
            se      trezi           Ion. (Ro.)
            self=   wake.INF        Ion
            'I (have) left/leave/will leave before Ion wakes up.'
         c. [−T, +Agr] ⇒ subjunctive
            Vreau       / Voiam             să          se      trezească       Ion. (Ro.)
            want.PRS.1SG  want.PST.IPFV.1SG  PRT_IRREALIS  self=wake.SBJV.3  Ion
            'I want/wanted Ion to wake up.'
         d. [−T, −Agr] ⇒ canonical (control) infinitive
            Ion_i   doreşte          a      Ø_i  se     trezi. (Ro.)
            Ion     wish.PRS.IND.3SG  to          self=  wake.INF
            'Ion wishes to wake up.'
```

Appealing to ideas developed in Ledgeway (1998; 2007), to which the reader is referred for a detailed treatment, the featural specification in (14a) represents canonical finite indicative verb forms which, from a semantico-syntactic perspective, show the greatest degree of temporal and referential autonomy, in turn, reflected morphologically by explicit marking for person, number, and tense. At the other extreme, the specification in (14d) identifies canonical control infinitives which lack any semantico-syntactic autonomy, as reflected by the complete absence of any morphological marking (cf. Sections 2.6.2, 20.5.2). Consequently, in contrast to indicative forms, such infinitival forms are limited to embedded contexts, where they depend on their associated matrix verb to supply their personal and temporal reference. In particular, the identity of the null infinitival subject is 'controlled' by a matrix argument (cf. Williams 1980; Hornstein 1999; Landau 2013), whereas the temporal frame of the infinitival clause is invariably interpreted as posterior to the matrix reference time, thereby giving rising to the obligatory irrealis unrealized future reading of the infinitival tense (Stowell 1982).

Specifications (14b–c), by contrast, represent intermediate points between (14a,d) on a scale of finiteness. The former identifies the personal infinitive which, despite lacking morphological marking for person, is nonetheless specified positively for the feature tense (cf. Ledgeway 2000: §4.4.2). Unlike control infinitives, the personal infinitive does not receive an obligatory irrealis interpretation but, rather, is referentially free in that its temporal frame can be located as simultaneous (13a–b), anterior (13c–d), or posterior (13e–f) to the matrix reference time. As a consequence, the personal infinitive can be taken to express a non-specific tense relative to the matrix predicate, thereby capturing the fact that the tense of the personal infinitive is always free though interpretatively bound by that of the matrix. Finally, the specification in (14c) provides an accurate description of the formal properties that distinguish subjunctive verb forms. Although endowed with overt marking for person and number (hence the featural specification +Agr), subjunctive verb forms lack the referential temporal freedom of the personal infinitive (cf. Maiden 2016a: 111) but, rather, typically yield an irrealis interpretation (Stowell 1982; Ledgeway 2000: §4.4.2) similar to that observed with the canonical control infinitive (hence the featural specification −T).[7]

1.2.2.3 Typological Variation

Data like those exemplified in (13a–f) also illustrate how investigations of Romance and especially its dialects frequently reveal that the extent of typological variation within Romance, and indeed even within and beyond Indo-European, can prove to be considerably greater than is traditionally assumed and often of a typologically 'exotic' nature (for some phonological examples, see Chapter 9, this volume). In this respect, one only has to think of such examples as the Romance inflected infinitives (15a), gerunds (15b), and participles (15c),[8] which, as hybrid categories, present further problems for the traditional binary interpretations of finiteness reviewed in Section 1.2.2.2 (cf. Ledgeway 2007c):

(15) a. É doado supoñer-**en** as cousas. (Glc.)
    be.PRS.IND.3SG easy suppose.INF-AGR.3PL the things
    'It is easy for them to assume things.'
  b. Não saíndo-**mos** de casa, morrâmos à fome. (EuPt., Ervedosa do Douro)
    not leave.GER-AGR.1PL of home die.PRS.1PL at.the hunger
    'If we don't leave the house, we'll starve to death.'
  c. dato-**no**-sse insembla salute como convenne (ONap.)
    give.PTCP-AGR.3PL=self together greeting as require.PST.PFV.3SG
    'after having greeted one another as was customary'

Another acute example comes from the unique 'infectious' development of inflexion across all functional categories in the Marchigiano dialect of Ripatransone.[9] Simplifying somewhat, in addition to some expected person/number agreement, the Ripano finite verb simultaneously displays masculine/feminine gender agreement with the subject, not to mention the possibility of agreement with third person so-called neuter subjects, by means of final inflexional vowel contrasts which appear quite remarkably to have

---

[7] From the perspective of Romanian and the dialects of the extreme south of Italy this conclusion is not at all surprising, inasmuch as the distribution of subjunctive clauses in these varieties largely coincides with the use of the canonical control infinitive in other Romance varieties. Note finally that, alongside the subjunctive, the specification in (14c) also picks out the so-called inflected infinitive discussed in Section 1.2.2.3, underlining the intuition that the subjunctive is little more than an infinitive endowed with overt marking for person.

[8] See, among others, Maurer (1968), Carballo Calero (1981), Loporcaro (1986), Jones (1993: 78–82), Longa (1994), Vincent (1996; 1998), Ledgeway (1998: 41–46; 2000: 109–14; 2009a: 585–90; 2012a: 293–95), Mensching (2000), Lobo (2001).

[9] See Parrino (1967), Lüdtke (1974; 1976), Mancini (1993), Harder (1998), Ledgeway (2012a: §6.3.4), Paciaroni and Loporcaro (2018), D'Alessandro (2020).

Table 1.2. *Ripano nominal and present indicative paradigms*

	Nominal			Verbal			
	Masculine	Feminine	Neuter	Person	Masculine	Feminine	Neuter
Singular	fijj**u**	fijj**e**	prəʃutt**ə**	1			
				2	magn**u**	magn**e**	
				3			piov**ə**
Plural	fijj**i**	fijj**a**		1	magnem**i**	magnem**a**	
				2	magnet**i**	magnet**a**	
				3	magn**i**	magn**a**	

been grafted onto the verbal paradigm from the nominal paradigm. This is shown in Table 1.2 by a comparison of the nominal and verbal paradigms of *fijj-* 'son, daughter' and *prəʃuttə* 'ham', on the one hand, and *magnà* 'eat' and *piovərə* 'rain' on the other.

Far from being limited to finite verbs, such a rich and complex system of agreement has come to permeate all instantiations of Infl, including so-called non-finite verb forms such as perfective participles (16a), gerunds (16b), and (rhizotonic) infinitives (16c).

(16) a. Lu frəki / le frəkine è **ddərmitu** / **ddərmite**. (Rip.)
        the boy   the girl   be.PRS.3SG sleep.PTPC.MSG sleep.PTCP.FSG
        'The boy / the girl has been sleeping.'
    b. Mamme stieve   cucənenne (Rip.)
        mum   stand.PST.IPFV.FSG cook.GER.FSG
        'Mum was cooking.'
    c. Sai   **skrivu**   / **skrive** ? (Rip.)
        know.PRS.2SG write.INF.MSG   write.INF.FSG
        'Do you know how to write?'

However, these agreement features are not limited to Infl in Ripano, but are extended to all functional heads and the categories they host (Ledgeway 2012a: 308–10).[10] As such, overt agreement with the clausal subject is found on parts of speech including in the C-domain *wh*-interrogatives (17a), in the *v*-domain predicative nominal complements (17b), and quite exceptionally within the nominal domain prepositions (17c), a behaviour which aligns Ripano with languages such as Welsh.

(17) a. C'aveti   **peuri**   / C'aveta   **peura**. (Rip.)
        have.PRS.2MPL fright.MPL   have.PRS.2FPL fright.FPL
        'You are afraid.'

---

[10] For a full discussion of the phonological, morphological, and syntactic conditions operating on the distribution of Ripano agreement, see Paciaroni and Loporcaro (2018).

b. **quannu** passu / **quanne** passe lloka (Rip.)
when.MSG pass.MSG when.FSG pass.FSG there
'whenever I/you/(s)he pass(es) by there'

c. **vəcinu** lu mara / **vəcine** le case (Rip.)
near.MSG the.MSG sea.MSG near.FSG the.FSG house.FSG
'near the sea/house'

We turn finally to a brief examination of the Romanian imperative. In contrast to other Romance and Indo-European languages,[11] the Romanian second person singular positive imperative frequently (though not systematically) marks, outside of the first conjugation, a transitivity distinction through an inflexional alternation between the desinences *-i* and *-e* which respectively encode the intransitive and transitive nature of the verb (Pîrvulescu and Roberge 2000; Zafiu 2013: 36f.; Maiden 2016a: 108; Maiden et al. 2021: 304f.).

(18) a. Fierbi! (Ro.)
boil.IMP.2SG
'Boil!'

a'. Fierbe macaroanele! (Ro.)
boil.IMP.2SG macaroni.DEF
'Boil the macaroni!'

b. Arzi! (Ro.)
burn.IMP.2SG
'Burn!'

b'. Arde toate documentele! (Ro.)
burn.IMP.2SG all.FPL documents.DEF
'Burn all the documents!'

c. Adormi! (Ro.)
fall.asleep.IMP.2SG
'Go to sleep!'

c'. Adoarme-l! (Ro.)
put.to.sleep.IMP.2SG=ACC.3MSG
'Put him to sleep!'

Data like these, which reflect a transitivity feature encoded in the verb (presumably a formal feature of the light *v* functional head), prove truly remarkable. In Romance finite verbs display inflexional marking for the

---

[11] Even outside the imperative, formal marking of transitivity proves extremely rare cross-linguistically, as highlighted by Trudgill's (2011: 73f., 105f.) remarks about the exceptional formal distinction between transitive and intransitive infinitives (the latter marked by final *-y*) in some English dialects of the south-west of England, e.g., Dorset *he can't hit it* vs *he can't swimmy*.

subject, not the object.¹² Inflexional marking on the verb referencing the object, by contrast, is restricted in Romance to non-finite verb forms such as the perfective participle in accordance with well-documented diachronic and diatopic variation (Loporcaro 1998; 2016). The Romanian examples in (18) highlight therefore two important typological considerations. First, the Romanian positive imperative shows an inflexional distinction for transitivity which is otherwise unparalleled in most languages of the world (cf. n. 11). Second, it is a frequent traditional observation that one of the most notable characteristics of the imperative is its lack of any inflexional marking or, at the very least, very minimal inflexional marking in accordance with a widespread cross-linguistic tendency (Pott 1859: 613; Bybee 1985: 173; Maiden 2006; 2007; Floricic 2008: 10; Ledgeway 2014c). Yet, the Romanian facts do not readily fit with this picture in that Romanian not only presents an inflexional alternation in contrast to the otherwise robust cross-linguistic tendency towards inflexional invariance, but also a minimal inflexion which encodes a typologically unusual distinction concerning the object.

1.2.2.4 The Interfaces

Functional categories also have an important role to play in understanding those linguistic phenomena whose surface form and formal licensing represent the convergence of two or more areas of the grammar. Indeed, investigation of the interfaces has figured prominently in much recent generative research thanks to developments such as phase theory (cf. Chomsky 2001; 2008), which postulate through the cyclical Spell-Out operation a direct mapping between narrow syntax and the conceptual-intentional and sensorimotor interfaces, and the cartographic enterprise (cf. Rizzi 1997; 2004; Cinque 1999; 2002; 2006; 2010; Belletti 2004; Benincà and Munaro 2010), which attempts to build semantic and pragmatic representations into the formal morphosyntactic architecture of the clause.¹³ In both cases functional categories and their associated projections prove fundamental: phases represent autonomous phonological and semantico-syntactic derivational domains defined in terms of the functional heads C, v, and D and their extended projections, whereas cartographic analyses assume richly articulated functional structures composed of a universally

---

¹² A notable exception is the dialect of Ripatransone where, under specific conditions, the finite verb may also encode the features of the object in conjunction with those of the subject (cf. Ledgeway 2012a: §6.3.4).

¹³ See, among others, Burkhardt (2005), Späth (2007), Grohmann (2009), Ramchand and Reiss (2012), Rothman and Slabakova (2011). Studies of the interfaces in relation to Romance data include Rizzi and Savoia (1993), Zubizarreta (1998), Elordieta et al. (2003), D'Imperio et al. (2005), Rao (2008), Silvestri (2009), Folli and Ulbrich (2010), Scheer (2011), Cruschina (2012), D'Alessandro and Scheer (2015), Fischer and Gabriel (2016), Manzini and Savoia (2016), Ledgeway (2018b; 2021a), Cruschina, Ledgeway, and Remberger (2019).

fixed order of projections which transparently encode and license various grammatical distinctions.

In this respect, Romance functional categories present the linguist with many valuable opportunities to study the linguistic interfaces, offering numerous insights into how different components of the linguistic system – syntactic, phonological, morphological, semantic, and pragmatic – do not necessarily operate in isolation but, rather, interact to license phenomena whose nature and distribution can only be fully understood in terms of the formal mapping between the interfaces. Consider, for instance, *rafforzamento fonosintattico* or *raddoppiamento fonosintattico* (RF) 'phonosyntactic reinforcement/doubling', a phonological process of sandhi assimilation in the dialects of southern Italy whereby a class of words that historically ended in a final consonant (e.g., PLUS > Cos. *cchiù* 'more') cause the lengthening or strengthening of the initial consonant of the following word in word$_1$ + word$_2$ sequences (e.g., Cos. *cchiù* [m:]*ele* 'more honey').[14] It is not, however, a simple phonological rule whose application is based on pure linear adjacency, but shows sensitivity to structural configuration (Ledgeway 2009a: 46f.; 2018b). By way of illustration, consider the possible effects of the third person singular finite verb *vena* 'comes' (cf. < Lat. UENIT) on the form of the feminine singular definite article (< (I)LLAM) in the Cosentino near-minimal pairs in (19a–b), where under RF the vibrant represents the restoration of an underlying word-initial Latin long lateral (viz., [ll]- > [dd]- > [ḍḍ]- (> [ɭɭ]-) > [r/ɾ]-).

(19) a. Quannu vena (**r)a primavera, mi sientu ggià miegliu. (Cos.)
    when come.PRS.3SG the spring me= feel.PRS.1SG already better
    'When(ever) spring comes, I already start to feel better.'
  b. Quannu vena **(r)a primavera, m' affittu na casa a ru mare. (Cos.)
    when come.PRS.3SG the spring me=rent.PRS.1SG a house at the sea
    'When the (= this) spring comes, I'll rent a house by the sea.'

In (19a), but not in (19b), the definite article cannot occur in its 'reinforced' variant with the initial vibrant despite immediately following the third person singular finite verb, but assumes its simple vocalic realization. As a result, the semantico-pragmatic reading of the two immediately postverbal subjects is not the same in (19a–b). In the former, the subject, although definite, is not referential but, rather, receives a generic interpretation, hence the unbounded reading of *quannu* 'whenever'. In (19b), by contrast, *quannu* has its bounded interpretation and the postverbal definite subject, now marked by RF, is concomitantly fully referential, identifying a specific and known referent salient in the discourse or the extra-linguistic

---

[14] Cf. Rohlfs (1966: 235–38), Loporcaro (1988; 1997b), Maiden (1995: 72–76), Fanciullo (1997), Sampson (2016: 675f.). For further discussion in this volume, see also Sections 6.4.3.2 and 7.4.2.

context which we can characterize as topical (hence the reading 'the/this spring').

The distribution of RF observed in these examples therefore highlights how Cosentino formally distinguishes between postverbal non-referential definite subjects and their referential variants. Given the assumption that for RF to take place Word$_1$ and Word$_2$ must surface in the same phasal domain (cf. Ledgeway 2018b; 2021a), there emerges a principled explanation for the facts in (19a–b). In particular, adopting Belletti's (2004; 2005) seminal idea that the edge of the *v*-domain makes available a lower left periphery with dedicated Topic and Focus positions (cf. also Section 26.2.3), we can assume a direct mapping between syntax and pragmatico-semantic interpretation such that all referential constituents, when not raised to the higher left periphery within the C-domain, target a Topic or Focus position within the lower left periphery, whereas all non-referential constituents remain *in situ* within the lexical VP (cf. also Diesing's 1992 Mapping Hypothesis). Consequently, we can associate the minimal pair in (19a–b) with the structural representations in (20a–b), where the presence of RF on the postverbal definite subject in (20b) signals a referential reading of the subject raised to SpecTop, namely, 'When the (= this) spring comes', whereas its absence in (20a) correlates with a non-referential interpretation of the definite subject *in situ*, namely, 'Whenever spring comes'.

(20) a. Quannu vena [$_\text{TopP}$ ——— [$_\text{vP}$ ~~vena~~ [$_\text{VP}$ ~~vena~~ a primavera]]], ...
 b. Quannu vena [$_\text{TopP}$ [$_\text{Spec}$ ra primavera] [$_\text{vP}$ ~~vena~~ [$_\text{VP}$ ~~vena a primavera~~]]], ...

Following Ledgeway and Lombardi (2005), the finite verb in Cosentino targets a low functional head situated above the *v*-VP complex. It therefore follows that RF is licensed with referential postverbal subjects such as (20b) where the finite verb (viz. Word$_1$) and the immediately postverbal constituent (viz. Word$_2$) are transferred to the phonological component of the grammar in the same higher phasal cycle, since the postverbal subject surfaces in the left edge of the lower *v*P phase from where, in accordance with the Phase Impenetrability Condition, it remains accessible to phonosyntactic processes of the higher CP phase. In (20a), by contrast, the postverbal subject from its *in situ* position remains inaccessible to the potential RF effects of the third person singular finite verb, since it is contained within the lower *v*P phase from where it is sent to the phonological component in the lower cycle before the spell-out of the RF trigger in the higher phasal cycle.

We therefore see that the distribution of Cosentino RF involves an isomorphic mapping of syntax and phonology at the interfaces, with phonological domains aligning with syntactic domains to externalize in the phonological component syntactic information which, in turn, may spell out key semantico-pragmatic distinctions such as referentiality and topicality. In particular, the licensing of RF is constrained by specific locality conditions which can be exhaustively computed and modelled in terms of a phase-theoretic cartographic approach, providing new and interesting data to further test the nature and computation of phasal domains ultimately defined in terms of specific functional projections. At the same time, we have seen that these same structural representations explicitly encode semantico-pragmatic information through the activation or otherwise of (lower) left-peripheral positions which, though not necessarily linearly distinguished on the surface, witness the immediately postverbal position of both subjects in (19a–b), nonetheless leave their mark in the phonological component which reads and externalizes these postverbal positions in distinct phasal cycles. We thus witness in these examples the output of an interaction of the syntactic, phonological, semantic, and pragmatic components of the grammar which contrive to derive strings which can be read at each of the interfaces.

1.2.2.5 Interim Conclusions

From the preceding introductory discussion, it is clear that the wealth of Romance standard and especially dialectal data, although frequently overlooked, have a great deal to contribute to research into such areas as parametric variation, linguistic universals, typological variation, and the interfaces. Nonetheless, the syntax of the dialects still represents a relatively poorly understood area of Romance linguistics, to the extent that there still remains a considerable amount of fieldwork to be done in recording and cataloguing the linguistic diversity within the Romània, as well as in bringing such facts to the attention of the wider linguistic community. With this in mind and keeping the technical detail to a minimum, in what follows a number of issues relating to the syntax of Romance will be discussed under the two broad headings of what Romance can do for syntactic theory and what syntactic theory can do for Romance. Under the former heading a number of assumptions will be reviewed about language structure and variation that have been proposed in the literature, demonstrating how in the specific cases examined the Romance data contradict such principles and parameters, rendering them either invalid or in need of further elaboration. Under the latter heading, by contrast, some of the less familiar and more problematic aspects of Romance syntax will be brought to light which can be shown to find an enlightening interpretation in light of current theoretical assumptions.

1.2.3 What Romance Can Do for Syntactic Theory
1.2.3.1 Pro-drop Parameter

One of the best known and most widely studied parameters is the so-called pro-drop (or null subject) parameter (for recent overviews, see Biberauer,

Holmberg, Roberts, and Sheehan 2009; Koeneman and Zeijlstra 2021; and Roberts 2019: ch. 3). Limiting our attention to Romance and Germanic, it is traditionally claimed that, with the exception of modern French, morphological Agr(eement) for person and number on the Romance verb is sufficiently rich to license a null subject (21a), whereas in such languages as English Agr is so impoverished that that it is unable to recover the identity of a null pronominal subject which must instead be phonologically expressed (22a; cf. also Section 17.5.1). By the same token, it is also assumed (cf. Chomsky 1981: 28; Rizzi 1986: 410; Haider 2001: 285; Koeneman and Zeijlstra 2021: §2.2.3) that expletive (or non-referential) pronouns are null in the former (21b) but overt in the latter (22b).

(21) a. Ø   (/Él)   llora. (Sp.)
        Ø   he   cry.PRS.IND.3SG
     b. Ø / **Él / **Ello llueve. (Sp.)
        Ø   he   it   rain.PRS.IND.3SG

(22) a. He/ **Ø cries.
     b. It Ø rains.

On a par with others, Rizzi (1982: 143) derives this supposed universal distinction from the pro-drop parameter, which he argues yields the four language types illustrated in Table 1.3.

Table 1.3. *Typology of null subjects*

Subject pronoun	Type 1 English	Type 2 Spanish	Type 3 German	Type 4 ?
null referential	−	+	−	+
null expletive	−	+	+	−
	non-pro-drop language	consistent pro-drop language	partial pro-drop language	

Language types 1 and 2 are exemplified by English and Spanish, respectively. In Spanish both null expletives and null referential pronouns are licensed, an example of a so-called consistent pro-drop language (Holmberg and Roberts 2010), whereas in English both types of null pronoun are excluded. Type 3 is argued to characterize German, an example of a so-called partial pro-drop language where, in contrast to referential pronouns which are invariably overt (23a), (certain classes of) overt expletive pronouns are only licensed when they occur in clause-initial position to satisfy the surface V2 requirement (23b–c):

(23) a. Er   / **Ø   weint. (Ger.)
        He   Ø   cry.PRS.IND.3SG
     b. Es   wird   heute   getanzt. (Ger.)
        it   become.PRS.IND.3SG today   dance.PTCP
     c. Heute wird   Ø / **es getanzt. (Ger.)
        today become.PRS.IND.3SG Ø   it   dance.PTCP
        'There is dancing going on today.'

On the other hand, Rizzi (1982: 143) explicitly argues that type 4 languages with overt expletive subjects but null referential subjects are 'excluded for intrinsic reasons'. However, the evidence of a number of non-standard Romance varieties demonstrates that type 4 languages do indeed exist. For example, although Neapolitan is a pro-drop language (24a), it also displays structures such as those in (24b) where the subject position is filled by the overt expletive *chello* 'that' (Sornicola 1996; Ledgeway 2009a: 290–94; 2010a), a pattern replicated by a number of other non-standard Romance varieties (25a–g).

(24) a. Ø / **Isso**   chiagne. (Nap.)
        Ø   he   cry.PRS.3SG
     b. Ø / **Chello** chiove. (Nap.)
        Ø   that   rain.PRS.3SG

(25) a. El   sera   verdade   que   o   centro   fala   e   a   periferia non
        it   be.FUT.3SG   truth   that the   centre   speak.PRS.3SG and the periphery NEG
        responde? (Glc.)
        reply.PRS.IND.3SG
        'Is it true that the centre speaks while the periphery fails to reply?'
     b. **Ele** era   umas   dores   de   cólica   enorme! (EuPt., Unhais da Serra)
        it   be.PST.IPFV.3SG some   pains   of   colic   enormous
        'It was a horrible case of stomach cramps!'
     c. ¡**Ello** hay   un   búho   en   el   techo! (Dominican Sp.)
        it   have.PRS.IND.3SG   an   owl   in   the rood
        'There's an owl on the roof!'
     d. **Ell**   és   veritat! (Bal.Cat.)
        It   be.PRS.IND.3SG   true
        'It is true!'
     e. **Iddu** cchi   mm'   importa? (Ctz.)
        it   what   me=   matter.PRS.3SG
        'What does it matter to me?!'
     f. Ma   **iddu** chi   cc'   è   cosa? (Plm.)
        but it   what   there=   be.PRS.3SG   what
        'What is it?!'
     g. **kɔ**   pløj. (Corrèze, Nocc.)
        that   rain.PRS.IND.3SG
        'It is raining.'

With the exception of the northern Occitan example in (25g), for which see Oliviéri (2009) and Kaiser, Oliviéri, and Palasis (2013), in most cases the use of the overt expletive in such examples is associated with specific pragmatic functions (Sornicola 1996: 325f.; Ledgeway 2003; 2009a: 290f.; Hinzelin 2009; Corr 2015; 2016), typically marking the illocutionary force of the clause as exclamative (cf. 25b,c,d) or interrogative, often with rhetorical overtones (cf. 25a,e,f), a usage which still requires much more detailed investigation. Summing up, the data considered here lead us to conclude, with Kaiser, Oliviéri, and Palasis (2013), that the ability to drop referential pronouns and the licensing of overt expletives are not necessarily mutually exclusive or, for that matter, two interrelated properties of a single pro-drop parameter (cf. also Roberts 2019: ch. 3). At the same time, however, as argued in Ledgeway (2010a), the overt expletives of most of these Romance dialects cannot be equated *tout court* with those of languages like English and French in view of the marked pragmatic functions of the former and the purely syntactic nature of the latter.

The wealth and extent of the Romance evidence is such that our typology of null subjects does not, however, stop here. Turning our attention to medieval Romance, it has long been noted that null subjects in these varieties display an asymmetric distribution,[15] a pattern more robustly represented in Gallo-Romance (French, Occitan, and northern Italian dialects) than either in Ibero-Romance or central-southern Italo-Romance (Wolfe 2018). In particular, whereas in root clauses null subjects are freely licensed (26a–c), in subordinate clauses pronominal subjects must usually be phonologically expressed (27a–c), although not interpreted as emphatic or contrastively focused. Illustrative in this respect are the old French and old Umbro-Tuscan examples in (27a,c), where, despite the coreference of main and embedded clause subjects, the latter is overtly realized yielding a structure which would be judged ungrammatical, for example, in modern Spanish or Italian where the presence of an overt pronoun in the same context would typically signal switch reference.

(26) a. Et lors vint Ø en sa chambre (OFr., *Histoire ancienne* 604.16)
and then come.PST.PFV.3SG Ø in her room
'And then she came into her room'
b. Del cor Ø sospir e dels olhs Ø plor (OPrv., *Era·m cossehlatz, senhor* 19)
of.the heart Ø sigh.PRS.IND.1SG and of.the eyes Ø cry.PRS.IND.1SG
'I sigh from the heart and cry from the eyes'
c. manifestamente Ø l' hoe veduto nelle cose [...] (OTsc., *Novellino* 3)
manifestly Ø it=have seen in.the things
'I have seen this clearly in those things [...]'

---

[15] Adams (1987), Hirschbühler and Junker (1988), Dupuis (1989), Roberts (1993: §3.2), Benincà (1994; 2006; 2010: §3.2.1), Salvi (2004: 16f., 26–31), Dufter (2010), Ledgeway (2012a: 74f.; 2021b: §§2.2.3–4).

(27) a. Por ce qu' ele_i estoit tostans en doute qu' ele_i ne perdist ce
for this that she_i be.PST.IPFV.3SG always in doubt that she NEG=lose.PST.SBJV.3SG this
qu' ele_i trop amoit (OFr., *Histoire ancienne* 604.7)
that she too love.PST.IPFV.3SG
'Because she was always in doubt that she would lose what she so dearly loved'
b. Non es meravelha s' **eu** chan / Melhs de nul autre
not be.PRS.IND.3SG wonder if I sing.PRS.IND.1SG better of no other
chantador (OPrv., *Era·m cossehlatz, senhor* 1–2)
singer
'It is no wonder if I am a better singer than all others'
c. Elli_i conosce certamente ch' **elli**_i avea ucciso lo migliore
he know.PRS.IND.3SG certainly that he have.PST.IPFV.3SG kill.PTCP the best
cavaliere del mondo (OUmb.-Tsc., *Tristano Riccardiano* 238.6–7)
knight of.the world
'He certainly knows that he had killed the best knight in the land'

This asymmetrical distribution leads us to conclude that null subjects in medieval Romance were not licensed exclusively, if at all, by rich verb agreement for person and number, insofar as the featural specification of Infl is equally rich in both root and subordinated clauses, but by a structural property (to be discussed in Section 1.2.4.2) which aligns the verb with distinct functional positions in both clause types. Indeed, the unreliability of verb morphology as a diagnostic for correctly predicting the distribution of null subjects is further evidenced by Ripano, a pro-drop variety, where we have seen that finite verbs (cf. Table 1.2) privilege the marking of gender over that of person, witness the three singular persons of the paradigm *magnu* (MSG) vs *magne* (FSG), despite traditional claims that the licensing of null subjects is directly linked to (the overt marking of) the person feature.[16] In summary, the null pronominal types seen in medieval Romance and Ripano cannot be readily accommodated in terms of current theories of a binary null subject parameter (cf. also Oliviéri 2009; Kaiser, Oliviéri, and Palasis 2013) and, in particular, the typology of null subjects predicted by such models as that observed in Table 1.3 which ultimately reduce the distribution of null pronominals to the availability of rich morphological Agr for person on the functional head Infl lexicalized by the finite verb.

1.2.3.2 Verb Positions

Exploiting the fixed positions of VP-adverbs like ALWAYS as a diagnostic indicator of the left edge of the *v*-VP complex, it is possible to distinguish between overt verb-raising languages like French (28a), where the finite

---

[16] Cf. Koeneman and Zeijlstra (2021: §2.1), who claim that in consistent pro-drop languages the minimal requirement for the licensing of null subjects is that the verb morphology express at the very least person and number.

verb raises to the Infl position to the left of VP-adverbs, and languages like English (28b), where the verb remains *in situ* to the right of such VP-adverbs and the Infl position is not overtly lexicalized in the syntax, a difference traditionally retraced to the respective richness of verbal inflection in the two languages (Emonds 1978; Pollock 1989; Belletti 1990).

(28) a. Jean [Infl skie [v-VP souvent ~~skie~~]] (Fr.)
     b. John [Infl Ø [v-VP often skis]] (Eng.)

Nonetheless, recent research has revealed a much more nuanced interpretation of Romance verb movement than these familiar broad-brush treatments which classify Romance *tout court* as having overt verb movement (for in-depth discussion, see Sections 17.3, 20.2.1, 21.2.3; and Schifano 2018). Following the seminal work of Cinque (1999), Infl is now commonly interpreted as a general label for the rich inflexional area of the clause (the I-domain) made up of a series of distinct functional projections dedicated to marking various temporal, aspectual, modal, and voice distinctions ranging over the lexical verb, its arguments, and possible adjuncts which can also be identified by the semantically corresponding adverbial modifiers they host (cf. also Cinque 2002; 2006; Belletti 2004; Rizzi 2004). Armed with these assumptions about a universal fixed hierarchy of adverb positions and corresponding functional projections, it is now possible to construct a fine-grained typology of Romance varieties along the lines of (29):

(29) a.   [IP...   [v-VP...   ]]
                              normalmente   todavía veo   todo   ~~veo~~ (Sp.)
     b.   di solito   vedo   ancora   ~~vedo~~   tutto ~~vedo~~ (It.)
     c. je **vois**   d'habitude   ~~vois~~   encore   ~~vois~~   tout   ~~vois~~ (Fr.)
         I see.PRS.IND.1SG   usually   see.PRS.IND.1SG still   see.PRS.IND.1SG all
         'I can usually still see everything.'

Although in all three varieties exemplified in (29) the finite lexical verb invariably leaves its base position to vacate the verb phrase, witness its position to the left of the completive adverb ALL/EVERYTHING immediately adjacent to the *v*-VP, it raises to different functional projections within the I-domain as illustrated by its differential position with respect to different adverb classes. For example, in Spanish (29a) the finite verb raises to the head position of the continuative aspectual projection immediately below the adverb STILL, whereas in Italian (29b) it raises slightly higher to the head position of the habitual aspectual projection below the adverb USUALLY, and in French (29c) it raises to the highest available position above all adverb classes.

On the basis of evidence like this, a number of surface differences across Romance can be interpreted in terms of the varying extent of verb movement around different adverb classes. Traditionally there have been many attempts to relate the extent of movement to the richness or otherwise of the verb's inflexional features (Roberts 1985; Lightfoot and Hornstein 1994; DeGraff 1997; Rohrbacher 1997; Vikner 1997; Biberauer and Roberts 2010; Zwart 2020). In essence, approaches of this type attempt to derive syntactic operations from cross-linguistic morphological differences in individual languages (cf. also the discussion of the *Mirror Principle* in Section 17.3). Admittedly, this view finds some initial support in the Romance vs Germanic contrast in (28a–b) where the Romance verb form, undoubtedly the inflexionally richest of the two, raises the highest. However, a brief comparison of the results reported in (29a–c) above suffices to dispel such an approach, inasmuch as all the Romance varieties exemplified are what may be termed inflexionally rich languages, yet they display some quite marked differences in the extent of finite lexical verb movement. This conclusion is further substantiated by the observation that much of the rich inflexion of the modern French verb, unlike that of Spanish or Italian, is predominantly orthographic, yet it shows higher verb movement of finite lexical verbs than the other two varieties.

Thus, to conclude, the rich comparative evidence of multiple verb positions observed across Romance forces us to postulate a richer functional structure for the clause than has traditionally been assumed. More generally, it has been established that from an empirical and a theoretical perspective broad-brush characterizations of Romance as invariably involving overt V-raising prove neither descriptively nor explanatorily adequate, inasmuch as a more nuanced picture has to be recognized. At the same time, this same evidence has highlighted the danger of assuming a direct correlation between the richness of inflexion and the extent of verb movement.

1.2.3.3 Mapping the Left Periphery of the Clause

As seen in the previous section, one area of considerable interest in much recent syntactic research has been the role of of functional categories in throwing light on the fine structure of the clause (for an overview, see Cruschina and Ledgeway 2016). Standardly, the structure of the clause in a typical SVO language, of which all the modern Romance varieties are arguably examples, has been taken to present (at least) the positions indicated in the linear template in (30a), exemplified from Italian in (30b):

(30) a. Subject Aux   Adverb   Verb   Object   Adjunct(s)
     b. Ugo   ha   sempre   preparato   la   pasta a cena. (It.)
        Ugo   have.PRS.IND.3SG always prepare.PTCP the   pasta at dinner
        'Ugo has always made pasta for dinner.'

The linear arrangement in (30a–b) highlights how the confines of the sentential core can be identified with the preverbal subject position situated at the left edge of IP and the complement or adjunct position situated at the right edge of v-VP (31a). However, following the seminal work of Rizzi (1997), in recent years research within generative syntax has increasingly focused on the investigation of the C-related functional categories and the positions they lexicalize within the left periphery (cf. also Benincà and Munaro 2010), the syntactic space immediately to the left of the sentential core (31b).

(31) a. $[_{IP}$ S Aux $[_{v\text{-}VP}$ V O (X)]]
      b. [Periphery ... $[_{IP}$ S Aux $[_{v\text{-}VP}$ V O (X)]]]

Unsurprisingly, a considerable amount of work on the split C-domain has been conducted on the basis of the rich (dialectal) microvariation offered by Romance varieties (for an overview and relevant bibliography, see Ledgeway 2012a: 154–71, and Section 20.2.1), which in many cases provide invaluable overt evidence with which to map the fine structural organization of the left periphery. In particular, the left periphery, traditionally defined in terms of CP and its associated Spec(ifier) and head positions hosting *wh*-operators and complementizers (Chomsky 1986: §1; cf. also Section 1.2.2.1), respectively, is now conceived as a split domain, hierarchically articulated into several fields and associated projections (for an in-depth overview, see Chapter 26, this volume). Revealing in this respect are Italian topicalization examples such as (32a–c), where one of the constituents of the sentential core in (30b) conveying old/given information has been fronted to the left periphery and picked up, where available, by a resumptive clitic pronoun on the verb in the sentential core, a case of (clitic) left-dislocation.[17] Yet, this does not exhaust all available structural possibilities, as demonstrated by the examples in (33a–d) where as many as two constituents have been fronted under (clitic) left-dislocation, illustrating the fact that topic is a recursive category capable of multiple realizations within the same utterance.

(32) [Topic$_{OLD}$ [S V Adv O (X)]]
   a. [La pasta$_i$, [Ugo la$_i$ prepara   sempre a   cena.]] (It.)
       the pasta   Ugo it= prepare.PRS.IND.3SG always at dinner
   b. [Ugo$_i$,   [lui$_i$ prepara   sempre la pasta a cena.]] (It.)
       Ugo   he   prepare.PRS.IND.3SG always the pasta at dinner
   c. [A cena,   [Ugo prepara   sempre la pasta.]] (It.)
       at dinner   Ugo prepare.PRS.IND.3SG   always the pasta

---

[17] In these and following examples we indicate topicalized constituents by underlining, contrastively focalized constituents by small caps, and informationally focalized constituents with bold.

(33) [Topic_OLD   [S V Adv O (X)]]
   a. [Ugo_i, la pasta_j, [lui_i la_j pepara   sempre a cena.]] (It.)
      Ugo the pasta   he it= prepare.PRS.IND.3SG always at dinner
   b. [La pasta_j, Ugo_i   [lui_i la_j prepara   sempre a cena.]] (It.)
      the pasta Ugo_i   he it= prepare.PRS.IND.3SG always at dinner
   c. [Ugo_i, a cena   [lui_i prepara   sempre la pasta.]] (It.)
      Ugo at dinner   he prepare.PRS.IND.3SG always the pasta
   d. [A cena, la pasta_i [Ugo la_i prepara   sempre.]] (It.)
      at dinner the pasta Ugo it= prepare.PRS.IND.3SG always

Further support for the richly articulated structure of the left periphery comes from a consideration of focus structures such as the Italian examples in (34), where a constituent of the sentential core in (30b) is fronted under corrective focus to correct a previous assertion (cf. 34a–c). Significantly, however, fronted focused constituents are not in complementary distribution with fronted topicalized constituents, as the traditional simplex CP structure with its single left-peripheral position presupposes, but can co-occur with left-dislocated topics in the strict order Topic + Focus, as shown in (35a–d).

(34) [Focus_NEW   [S V O (X)]]
   a. [SEMPRE   [Ugo prepara   la pasta a cena.]] (It.)
      always   Ugo prepare.PRS.IND.3SG the pasta at dinner
   b. [A CENA   [Ugo prepara   sempre la pasta.]] (It.)
      at dinner   Ugo prepare.PRS.IND.3SG always the pasta
   c. [LA PASTA   [Ugo prepara   sempre a cena.]]
      the pasta   Ugo prepare.PRS.IND.3SG always at dinner

(35) [Topic + Focus   [S V O (X)]]
   a. [Ugo_i, SEMPRE   [lui_i prepara   la pasta a cena.]] (It.
      Ugo always   he prepare.PRS.IND.3SG the pasta at dinner
   b. [Ugo_i, A CENA   [lui_i prepara   sempre la pasta.]] (It.)
      Ugo at dinner   he prepare.PRS.IND.3SG always the pasta
   c. [La pasta_j, SEMPRE [Ugo la_i prepara   a cena.]] (It.)
      the pasta always   Ugo it= prepare.PRS.IND.3SG at dinner
   d.** [SEMPRE la pasta_i [Ugo la_i prepara   a cena.]] (It.)
      always the Pasta   Ugo it= prepare.PRS.IND.3SG at dinner

Evidence like this from Italian and other Romance varieties highlights that the existence of a single left-peripheral position is empirically inadequate. Rather, the relevant left-peripheral positions must be reconceived as distinct pragmatico-syntactic spaces along the lines of Benincà and Poletto (2004), according to which we can identify from left to right at least two fields termed Topic and Focus, respectively (see also Cruschina 2012; Cruschina and Ledgeway 2016: §31.3.4). Not only is this demarcation between both fields justified at a pragmatico-semantic level, in that elements appearing in the Topic field are generally interpreted as 'old' or 'given' information whereas the Focus field is typically associated with informationally 'new' elements, but it also finds confirmation at the syntactic level. For instance, in contrast to elements appearing within the Topic field, which often call for a resumptive pronominal (clitic) where available (cf. 32a–b, 33a–d), those appearing within Focus (cf. 34c) prove incompatible with a pronominal copy. Moreover, it has already been observed that topic is a recursive syntactic category allowing several reiterations within a given utterance, whereas focus is restricted to just one occurrence per utterance.

Robust evidence like this demonstrates that topicalized and focused constituents target distinct spaces within the left periphery, forcing us to recognize a representation of the C-domain along the lines of (36).

(36)   [CP Comp [TopP Topic^{REC} [FocP FOCUS [IP …]]]]

1.2.3.3.1 Complementizer Positions

In addition to the Topic and Focus fields highlighted above, the left periphery of the clause also hosts subordinators or complementizers. Alongside finite complementizers derived from QUOD/QUID 'that' and QU(I)A '(because >) that' which introduce tensed clauses (cf. (a) examples below), Romance varieties also present a series of non-finite complementizers derived from the prepositions AD 'to' and DE 'of, from' to introduce infinitival clauses (cf. (b) examples below), which to all intents and purposes parallel the use of their finite counterparts.

(37) a. Et gouyat$_i$ qu' aymeré que [IP Ø$_{i/j}$ dansèsses dap ére.] (Gsc.)
the young.man that like.COND.3SG that Ø dance.PST.SBJV.2SG with her
'The young man would like you to dance with her.'

b. Et gouyat$_i$ qu' aymeré a [IP Ø$_{i/*j}$ dansa dap ére.] (Gsc.)
the young.man that like.COND.3SG to Ø dance.INF with her
'The young man would like to dance with her.'

(38) a. Digues-li$_i$ que [IP Ø$_{i/*j}$ vingui!] (Cat.)
tell.PRS.SBJV.2SG=DAT.3 that Ø come.PRS.SBJV.3SG

b. Digues-li$_i$ de [IP Ø$_{i/*j}$ venir!] (Cat.)
tell.PRS.SBJV.2SG=DAT.3 of Ø come.INF
'Tell him to come!'

Despite appearances, the presumed parallelism between finite and non-finite complementizers is not, however, perfect, as revealed by their respective positions in relation to topics and foci: whereas finite complementizers precede topics and foci (39a), non-finite complementizers invariably follow both types of fronted constituent (39b).

(39) a. So   che, la data, [IP l'   ho   sbagliata]. (It.)
       know.PRS.IND.1SG that the date   it= have.PRS.IND.1SG mistake.PTCP
    b. So,   la data, di [IP averla   sbagliata]. (It.)
       know.PRS.IND.1SG the date of   have.INF=it mistake.PTCP
       'I know (that), the date, I got (it) wrong.'

Romance evidence like this forces us to assume that the Topic and Focus fields outlined above are, in turn, closed off upwards by a higher complementizer position (termed Force) marking the illocutionary force of the clause and hosting such items as the Romance finite declarative complementizer *que*/*che* 'that', and downwards by a complementizer position (termed Fin(iteness)) specifying the modality and/or finiteness of the clause and hosting such items as the Romance infinitival complementizers *de*/*di* 'of', as schematicized in (40).

(40)   [Periphery *que*/*che*$_{Force}$ + Topic^{REC} + FOCUS + *de*/*di*$_{Fin}$ [IP...]]

In fact, some Romance varieties present dual finite complementizer systems which appear to exploit both the higher and lower complementizer positions within the left periphery (cf. also Sections 2.6.2, 21.3.1). This is the case in Romanian and many southern Italian dialects,[18] which contrast an indicative/realis complementizer (QU(I)A 'because' > *că*/*ca*) which lexicalizes the higher complementizer position, and therefore precedes topics and foci (41a), and a subjunctive/irrealis complementizer (SI 'if' > Ro. *să*, QUOD/QUID 'that' > USID *co*/*che*, QUO(MODO), (QUO)MODO 'how' > Sal. *cu*, Cal./NESic. *mu*/*mi*/*ma*) that lexicalizes the lower complementizer position, and therefore follows topics and foci (41b):

(41) a. Cred   [CP că   MÂINE   [IP merg   la teatru.]] (Ro.)
       believe.PRS.IND.1SG that$_{REALIS}$ tomorrow   go.PRS.1SG to theatre
       'I believe that I'm going to the theatre TOMORROW.'
    b. Vreau   [CP MÂINE   să   [IP merg   la teatru.]] (Ro.)
       want.PRS.1SG   tomorrow that$_{IRREALIS}$ go.PRS.1SG to theatre
       'I want to go to the theatre TOMORROW.'

Additional compelling evidence for these two complementizer positions comes from those varieties which allow the simultaneous lexicalization of both positions around a fronted topic or focus constituent. These so-called 'recomplementation' structures are found across a wide range of Romance varieties (Ledgeway 2012a: §4.4.2.2; cf. also Section 2.6.3), including many early Romance texts (42a–b; Wanner 1998; Paoli 2003a; Ledgeway 2004:

---

[18] For Romanian see, among others, Dobrovie-Sorin (1994: 93–111), Alboiu and Motapanyane (2000: §4.2), and for southern Italy Calabrese (1993), Lombardi (1997; 1998), Ledgeway (1998; 2004; 2005; 2006; 2007c; 2009b; 2012b; 2016: §63.3), Manzini and Savoia (2005, I: 455–501, 650–76), Ledgeway and Lombardi (2014), Colasanti (2018), Groothuis (2019), Andriani, Groothuis, and Silvestri (2020: §3).

§4.3.2.2; 2005: 380–89; Vincent 2006; Munaro 2016), and a number of modern Italo-Romance dialects (42c; Paoli 2002; 2003a; 2003b; 2005; D'Alessandro and Ledgeway 2010) and modern Ibero-Romance varieties (42d; Demonte and Fernández-Soriano 2009; Gupton 2010: 227–34; Villa-García 2010; 2015; Martínez Vera 2020).

(42) a. Onde dize Josepho *que* en casa de so padre *que* le
where say.PRS.IND.3SG Josepho that in house of his father that him=
llamaron primiera mientre Ciro (OSp.)
call.PST.PFV.3PL first -ly Ciro
'Where upon Josepho said that in his father's house he was originally called Ciro'

b. èy manifesta cosa *che* homo che se ave a defendere
be.PRS.IND.3SG obvious thing that man that self= have.PRS.IND.3SG to defend.INF
a la patria soa intre li amici e li canussienti suoy *cha*
to the fatherland his among the friends and the acquaintances his that
ave a chesta parte gran prerogativa e gran avantayo (ONap.)
have.PRS.IND.3SG at this part big prerogative and big advantage
'it is abundantly clear that, a man who has to defend himself in his own country among his friends and acquaintances, has in this respect considerable privilege and advantage'

c. A Teeja a credda *che* a Maria ch' a parta
the Teresa SCL believe.PRS.IND.3SG that the Mary that SCL leave.PRS.SBJV.3SG
duman. (Lig.)
tomorrow
'Teresa believes that Mary will leave tomorrow'

d. Dixéronme *que* a esse rapaz *que* o coñecemos na
say.PST.PFV.3PL=me that DOM that boy that him= know.PST.PFV.1PL in.the
festa. (Glc.)
party
'They told me that we met that guy at the party.'

Finally, unique within Romance is the situation found in Béarnais Gascon since around the sixteenth century, where the [+finite] feature of affirmative root clauses is exceptionally spelt out in the systematic lexicalization of the lower complementizer position C_{Fin} through the complementizer *que* 'that' (see also Section 21.3.2).[19] Cross-linguistically, explicit typing of declarative force in this way represents an extremely rare option (cf. Lyons 1968: 307; Bybee 1985: 147; Cinque 1999: 130; Franco 2013; see also Section 24.2.1), yet Gascon highlights how models of language need to accommodate it. Firm proof that root-clause *que* spells out the lower complementizer head is provided by the observation that, apart from object clitics, nothing can intervene between *que* and the finite verb so that all preverbal lexical subjects must occur to the left of *que*. This latter observation highlights the fact that, unlike in other Romance varieties, there is

[19] For extensive discussion and analysis, see Ledgeway (2020a) and sources cited therein.

apparently no preverbal subject position within the sentential core in Gascon, such that all subjects have to be syntactically fronted to a topicalized (typically if old and definite; 43a) or focalized (typically if new and indefinite; 43b) position within the left periphery. These facts find an immediate explanation if we assume that *que* lexicalizes the C$_{Fin}$ position, since finiteness is standardly assumed to license nominative Case, hence Gascon would appear to have grammaticalized the locus of finiteness and, by implication, the licensing of nominative subjects within the left periphery, as happens in Verb Second (V2) varieties, rather than in the sentential core. Indeed, Ledgeway (2020a) shows how this exceptional typological development is externally motivated, being ultimately the result of contact with a non-Romance language, Basque, and can be formally integrated into the V2 Parameter if the latter can be satisfied by direct insertion ('external merge') of *que* in in the C$_{Fin}$ head rather than V-movement to the same (cf. also Ledgeway 2008).

(43) a. [$_{TopP}$ La   Maria [$_{FinP}$ qu'   [$_{IP}$ apara   las pomas.]]] (Gsc.)
              the   Maria   that   collect.PRS.IND.3SG   the apples
          'Maria gathers up the apples.'
      b. [$_{FocP}$ **Quauque trufandèr** [$_{FinP}$ que [$_{IP}$ vos   dirà...]]] (Gsc.)
              whatever   joker   that   you=   say.FUT.3SG
          'Any joker will tell you ...'

This analysis is further supported by the behaviour of embedded declarative clauses such as (44) where both complementizer positions are simultaneously realized: whereas *que* continues to lexicalize C$_{Fin}$ on a par with root declaratives, from where it follows fronted topics and foci, subordination is marked in the higher C-position Force, also lexicalized by *que* 'that' but which precedes fronted topics and foci.

(44) Que   sémble   [$_{ForceP}$ que [$_{FocP}$ TOUTS [$_{FinP}$ que [$_{IP}$ pouderém   sénse
      that   seem.PRS.IND.3SG   that   all   that   can.COND.1PL without
      pénes   debisa   parié.]]]] (Gsc.)
      difficulties speak.INF   equally
      'It seems that we can all speak equally without problems.'

On the basis of the Romance evidence reviewed in the preceding sections, the fine structure of the left periphery can be summarized as in (45):

(45) [$_{ForceP}$ *que/che* [$_{TopP}$ Topic^{REC} [$_{FocP}$ FOCUS [$_{FinP}$ *de/di/che/sā/cu/mu* [$_{IP}$...]]]]]

1.2.3.4 Interim Conclusions

The discussion so far has highlighted the importance of Romance data, and especially those from the still underutilized non-standard varieties and dialects, in making us rethink some of our most basic assumptions about language structure and variation in relation to individual functional heads and the functional categories that lexicalize them. In particular, we have seen that standard interpretations of the null subject parameter prove insufficient in terms of the limited range of null and overt pronominal subject types they predict, the limited predictive power of rich inflexion in the distribution of null subjects, and the non-universality of inflexion for person in licensing null subjects. Within the verbal domain we have established that the now classical typological distinction between verb-raising and non-verb-raising languages, which places Romance among the former, proves empirically inadequate. By contrast, we have observed that the extent of verb movement across Romance varies enormously, revealing a whole host of different positions which can, in turn, be taken to spell out the vast range of functional projections that make up the rich architecture of the sentential core. In a similar vein, this rich functional design of the clause has been shown to extend to the left periphery, where the Romance evidence forces us to recognize a richly articulated functional space composed, at the very least, of Topic and Focus fields sandwiched, in turn, between two complementizer positions.

1.2.4 What Linguistic Theory Can Do for Romance
1.2.4.1 Word Order

Undoubtedly one of the most striking differences between medieval and modern Romance varieties is manifested in the often radically differing word order patterns they permit in root clauses. By way of illustration, consider the old Neapolitan sentences in (46a–b) and their modern Italian translations in (47a–b):

(46) a. e **viechy** reduceva   ad etate iuvenile (ONap.)
           and old reduce.PST.IPFV.3SG to age juvenile
           'and she could make the old young again'
      b. <u>de poy queste parole</u> ademandao   lo messayo licencia (ONap.)
           after these words ask.PST.PFV.3SG the messenger leave
           'And following these words the messenger asked permission to leave'

(47) a. e riportava   i vecchi a età giovanile (It.)
           and bring.back.PST.IPFV.3SG the old to age juvenile
      b. <u>dopo queste parole</u> il messaggiere domandò   licenza (It.)
           after these words the messenger ask.PST.PFV.3SG leave

(46a–b) illustrate a frequent early Romance structure in which the preverbal position is occupied by some constituent other than the subject, namely the direct object (*viechy*) and a non-subcategorized adverbial phrase (*de poy queste parole*), respectively. In the former case, the fronted rhematic direct object, which conveys new information, constitutes an example of informational focus (Lambrecht 1994: ch. 5; Cruschina 2012), and contrasts sharply with many modern Romance varieties such as Italian (cf. 34–35), where preposing of rhematic constituents is only found under quite restrictive pragmatic conditions to license corrective focus, insofar as rhematic objects conveying informational focus canonically occur in postverbal position (cf. 47a). Similarly, example (46b) demonstrates how when the preverbal position is occupied by a constituent distinct from the subject, the latter, whenever overtly realized, is generally required to follow the verb, giving rise to an apparent case of verb-subject inversion. Significantly, in this and similar examples of inversion the subject does not simply follow the verb but also precedes any other sentential constituents (subcategorized or otherwise), witness the order subject (*lo messayo*) + direct object (*licencia*) in (46b). In modern Italian, by contrast, postverbal subjects generally follow their associated objects and other sentential constituents, and in such cases are typically associated with rhematic interpretations, whereas the postverbal subject in (46b) is clearly thematic. Consequently, in the modern Italian translation in (47b) the thematic subject obligatorily occurs in preverbal position.

Word order patterns like these, which can be readily replicated for other early Romance varieties, have led a number of linguists to argue that medieval Romance word order is characterized by a V2 constraint, the origins of which can be retraced to late Latin (Ledgeway 2017b).[20] During this V2 stage sentences consist therefore of two principal parts (48a), a sentential core (IP) with fixed S V O Adv order on a par with what we have already witnessed in Section 1.2.3.3 for modern Romance, and a richly articulated left periphery (CP) along the lines of (45) to whose lowest C position (Fin) the finite verb raises in root clauses, where it is preceded by one or more elements fronted from the sentential core to the Topic and Focus fields to be assigned a pragmatically salient reading. In embedded clauses, by contrast, the left periphery generally hosts an overt Comp(lementizer) and the finite verb is consequently forced to remain within the sentential core, yielding the order S+V+O+Adv (48b). Thus, as the following representative early Romance examples demonstrate, alongside S+V+X (48c) we also frequently find in main clauses O+V(S) (48d), IO+V(S) (48e), O_{PP}+V(S) (48f), and Adv+V(S) (48g), whereas embedded clauses invariably display rigid S+V+O+Adv (48h):

---

[20] See, among others, Skårup (1975), Vanelli, Renzi, and Benincà (1985), Vanelli (1986; 1999), Adams (1987), Fontana (1993; 1997), Roberts (1993), Benincà (1994; 1995; 2006; 2013), Lemieux and Dupuis (1995), Ribeiro (1995), Vance (1995; 1997), Lombardi and Middleton (2004), Salvi (2004; 2012; 2016: 1005–09), Labelle (2007), Ledgeway (2007b; 2008; 2017b; 2021b), Lombardi (2007), Radwan (2011), Salvesen (2013; 2014), Bech and Salvesen (2014), Poletto (2014), Steiner (2014), Wolfe (2015a; 2015b; 2015c; 2015d; 2018a), Cruschina and Ledgeway (2016: 571f.). For an analysis of V2 in old Romanian, see Nicolae (2015: 155–98), Nicolae and Niculescu (2015), and Dragomirescu and Nicolae (2015).

(48) a. [LeftPeriphery Top / Foc V [SententialCore S V̶ O Adv]]
b. ... [LeftPeriphery Comp [SententialCore S V O Adv]]
c. [CP Lo cavaliere *prese* [IP l̶o̶ ̶c̶a̶v̶a̶l̶i̶e̶r̶e̶ ̶p̶r̶e̶s̶e̶ i marchi]] (OTsc., *Novellino* 4)
   the knight take.PST.PFV.3SG   the marks
   'The knight took the marks'
d. [CP **Grande duelo** *avien* [IP las yentes
   great   sorrow have.PST.IPFV.3PL the peoples
   cristianas a̶v̶i̶e̶n̶ ̶g̶r̶a̶n̶d̶e̶ ̶d̶u̶e̶l̶o̶]] (OSp., *Mío Cid* 29–30)
   Christian
   'The Christian peoples felt great sorrow'
e. [CP A ceste paroles *respont* [IP la reine r̶e̶s̶p̶o̶n̶t̶ ̶a̶ ̶c̶e̶s̶t̶e̶ ̶p̶a̶r̶o̶l̶e̶s̶]] (OFr., *M.Artu* 59, 84)
   to these words reply.PRS.IND.3SG the queen
   'The queen replied to these words'
f. [CP D'ALGUÑAS COUSAS me *calarei* [IP m̶e̶ ̶c̶a̶l̶a̶r̶e̶i̶ ̶d̶'̶a̶l̶g̶u̶ñ̶a̶s̶ ̶c̶o̶u̶s̶a̶s̶]]
   of some things myself=fall.silent.FUT.1SG
   (OPt., *Diálogos de S. Gregório* 1.5.25)
   'I shall remain silent about certain matters'
g. [CP **Luenh** *es* [IP lo castelhs e la
   far   be.PRS.IND.3SG the castle and the
   tors e̶s̶ ̶l̶u̶e̶n̶h̶]] (OOcc., Rudel, *Pro ai del chan essenhadors* 3.1)
   tower
   'Far is the castle, far is the tower'
h. la *honret* [CP q' [IP **ella fetz** so q' el
   her=honour.PST.PFV.3SG that she do.PST.PFV.3SG that that he
   volc]] (OPrv., *Era·m cossehlatz, senhor* 30,1)
   want.PST.PFV.3SG
   'And he honoured her such that she did what he wanted'

In conclusion, it has been seen that the fine structure of the sentential core (Section 1.2.3.3) and the left periphery (Section 1.2.3.3.1) independently established above on the basis of modern Romance data provide us with the necessary pragmatico-syntactic tools to interpret the facts of medieval Romance word order. However, above it was simply assumed that the finite verb in root clauses raises to the lowest C-head Fin, although the fine structure of the C-domain in (45) makes available two C-head positions. This has led some to argue that under V2 syntax the finite verb may also target the highest position C_{Force}. Following Roberts (2012; 2015), Wolfe (2015d; 2018), and Dadan (2019: ch. 3), it is thus possible to recognize a typology, according to which V2 grammars differ in terms of whether the finite verb targets a low position C_{Fin} (49a) or a high position C_{Force} (49b) within the C-domain.

(49) a. [FrameP [Spec] [ForceP [Spec] [TopP^{REC} [Spec] [FocP [Spec] [FinP V_{Fin} [TP V̶$_{F̶i̶n̶}$...]]]]]]
b. [FrameP [Spec] [ForceP [Spec] V_{Fin} [TopP [FocP [FinP [TP V̶$_{F̶i̶n̶}$...]]]]]]

The representations in (49) make some precise and testable predictions about the types of structures that can be generated in both types of V2 grammars. In a V-in-Fin V2 grammar (cf. 49a) the verb sits in the lowest head position C_{Fin} from which it can be preceded, potentially simultaneously, by a focus (SpecFocP), one or more topics (SpecTopP[REC]), and a frame element (SpecFrameP).[21] In a V-in-Force grammar (cf. 49b), by contrast, the possibilities are greatly reduced since the verb targets the higher C$_{Force}$ head, from where it can only be preceded by a fronted focalized or topicalized constituent in SpecForce (> V2) and additionally by a frame element in SpecFrameP (> V3). Grammars of the former type have been argued to characterize, among others, medieval southern Italo-Romance varieties (cf. Ledgeway 2007b; 2008) as well as late Latin (Ledgeway 2017b), where we witness V-to-Fin raising with optional fronting of one or more constituents to the left periphery (> SpecFocP, SpecTopP[REC], SpecFrameP). Consequently, it is correctly predicted that in these V2 varieties, alongside frequent linear V2 orders, V1 and V3* orders are not only possible but also not insignificant. On the other hand, V2 grammars of the latter V-in-Force type have been argued to characterize medieval Gallo-Romance (cf. Wolfe 2018; Ledgeway 2021b), where V-to-Force movement is accompanied by obligatory fronting to SpecForceP, be that of a focus or a topic. This correctly predicts a much stricter surface V2 linearization where V1 and V4 orders are extremely rare, if not entirely absent/impossible, and where V3 orders are attested, but are qualitatively constrained since the only position above SpecForceP is SpecFrameP such that V3 orders necessarily instantiate Frame+Topic/Focus sequences.

1.2.4.2 Pro-drop Parameter Revisited

Returning to our observation regarding the distribution of null subjects in medieval Romance (cf. examples 26–27 in Section 1.2.3.1), this same generalized raising of the finite verb to C(omp) under V2 also provides us with an elegant and highly natural explanation for the asymmetric distribution of null subjects in early Romance. In particular, when the verb raises to the vacant C position, null subjects are freely licensed (50a), whereas in subordinate clauses, where the finite verb is forced to remain *in situ* within the sentential core, pronominal subjects must be phonologically expressed (50b), although not interpreted as emphatic or contrastively focused.

(50) a. Et lors vint Ø en sa chambre (OFr.)
and then come.PST.PFV.3SG Ø in her room
'And then she came into her room'
b. Por ce qu' ele$_i$ estoit tostans en doute qu' ele$_i$ ne perdist ce
for this that she be.PST.IPFV.3SG always in doubt that she NEG= lose.PST.SBJV.3SG this
qu' ele$_i$ trop amoit (OFr.)
that she too love.PST.IPFV.3SG
'Because she was always in doubt that she would lose what she so dearly loved'

---

[21] As documented in the literature (cf. Benincà and Poletto 2004; Ledgeway 2010b), frame elements sit outside the clause proper above ForceP and introduce a dislocated topical constituent, typically represented either by a (hanging) topic or by a scene-setting/circumstantial adverb(ial) that spells out the spatial-temporal coordinates of the utterance (cf. also Section 26.3.3).

This asymmetrical distribution leads us to conclude that null subjects in medieval Romance were not licensed exclusively, if at all, by rich verb inflexion for person and number, but, by a property which the finite verb uniquely acquires by raising to the vacant C position, presumably the locus of finiteness in medieval Romance (cf. Ledgeway 2012a: §3.4.1). Now we have just seen in Section 1.2.4.1 how medieval Romance V2 can be classified according to a V-in-Fin and V-in-Force typology, the latter type characterizing medieval Gallo-Romance varieties where the root-embedded asymmetry in the distribution of overt and null pronominal subjects is strongest, if not systematic. Superficially, this asymmetrical distribution might lead us to hypothesize that the functional head responsible for the licensing of pro-drop in medieval Gallo-Romance is C_{Force}, since null subjects occur in root V2 contexts where the finite verb targets C_{Force}, but not in embedded contexts where the verb only raises to Infl and its associated subject can only be realized by an overt pronominal. Less frequently, however, we also find in medieval Gallo-Romance examples of embedded V2 (cf. Salvi 2004: ch. 1; Benincà 2006: 24), in which the finite verb exceptionally raises to C_{Fin} with concomitant fronting of one or more constituents to the left periphery, since the C_{Force} position is already lexicalized by the subordinating complementizer (51a). Such cases can be unambiguously identified in that they deviate from the otherwise predominant embedded SVO pattern (viz. V-in-Infl; cf. 48b), displaying an immediately preverbal constituent other than the subject (cf. Salvesen and Walkden 2017), and the subject, if pronominal, can be null (51b) as in canonical root V2 contexts.

(51) a. ...[$_{ForceP}$ que [$_{Top/FocP}$ Topic/Focus [$_{FinP}$ V [$_{IP}$ pro V]]]]
b. Tantost com ele sot [...] que ·vii· nés i avoit Ø
soon as she know.PST.PFV.3SG that 7 ships there= have.PST.IPFV.3SG Ø
chargees (OFr., *Histoire ancienne* 598.8)
load.PTCP
'As soon as she found out [...] that he had 7 ships fully laden there'

Significantly, this observation that null subjects are also possible in cases of embedded V2 involving V-in-Fin forces us to identify the licensing of pro-drop with C_{Fin}, through which the finite verb passes *en route* to C_{Force} in root V2 contexts, since if the relevant head were C_{Force}, then this would incorrectly predict the ungrammaticality of null subjects in embedded V2. This is a natural conclusion given the traditional strong association of Fin(iteness) with inflexional reflexes of number and person which presumably license and spell out the relevant phi-feature specification of the null subject.

Finally, it is interesting to note how this archaic pattern in the asymmetrical distribution of null subjects has been exceptionally retained in modern Corsican (Marchetti 1974: 25, 51, 85, 94, 119). In particular, Corsican behaves as a canonical Romance null subject variety in root clauses (52a–b), but in embedded contexts requires referential (52a–c) and non-referential (52d) pronominal subjects to be overtly realized, albeit in reduced clitic form (cf. tonic/clitic *eio/e, o* (1SG), *tù/tu* (2SG), *ellu/ella / (e)llu/(e)lla* (3M/FSG), *noi/no* (1PL), *voi/vo* (2PL), *elli/elle / (e)lli/(e)lle* (3M/FPL)).

(52) a. Ø avemu da fà e divuzioni à tutti i santi chè **no**
      (we) have.PRS.IND.1PL from do.INF the devotions to all the saints that we=
      truvemu. (Crs.)
      find.PRS.IND.1PL
      'We'll pray to all the saints we meet.'
   b. Ø e cumprerete à u scagnu quand'è **vo** falate. (Crs.)
      (you) them= buy.FUT.2PL a the office when you= descend.PRS.IND.2PL
      'You buy them at the office when you go down.'
   c. **Eo** ogni volta ch' o tornu in Cervioni, è ch' o u sentu
      I each time that I=return.PRS.IND.1SG in Cervione and that I= it= hear.PRS.IND.1SG
      u nostru chjoccu mi mette sottusopra. (Crs.)
      the our chiming me= put.PRS.IND.3SG under.over
      'Each time I go back to Cervione and hear our chiming bell I get overcome.'
   d. Ch' **ellu** un ci sia troppu rumore! (Crs.)
      that it= not there= be.PRS.SBJV.3SG too.much noise
      'Make sure that there isn't too much noise!'

This distribution of null and overt pronouns is however only superficially similar to medieval Romance, in that modern Corsican is not a V2 variety with the finite verb occurring in the sentential core in all cases, irrespective of the realization of the pronominal subject. However, when the finite verb does raise to the C-domain, as happens in partial interrogatives (53), realization of the clitic subject pronoun is blocked in a similar fashion to what was seen for medieval Romance (cf. 50a).

(53) [CP QUANDU falate [IP Ø ~~falate quandu~~?]] (Crs.)
     when descend.PRS.IND.2PL Ø
     'When are you coming down?'

In conclusion, these modern Corsican data highlight the force of reanalysis in syntactic change, whereby the original asymmetrical distribution of null and overt pronominal subjects, the surface output of an underlying V2 grammar, has been subject to reanalysis and realigned with a non-V2 grammar in which their distribution is no longer licensed by specific functional heads targeted by the finite verb (viz. C_{Fin} ⇒ null/overt vs Infl ⇒ overt), but, presumably, by a [±root] distinction borne by the finite verb raised to a position within the I-domain. This example shows, in turn, how the cluster of properties associated with a given parameter, V2 of the V-in-Force type in this particular case, are not intrinsically bound together but, rather, represent separate microparameters which can also be licensed individually under other scenarios. For example, formal registers of modern French and many dialects of north(eastern) Italy continue to license raising of the finite verb to the C-domain in specific marked non-veridical contexts (cf. Ledgeway 2015a; Section 21.3.2), but have lost focus-fronting to the left periphery (54a). This contrasts with most dialects of southern Italy which, despite having lost non-veridical V-to-C movement, have retained focus-fronting to the C-domain (54b; cf. Ledgeway 2020b).

(54) a. Ven-lo staseìra teu pari? (Rueglio)
      come.PRS.IND.3SG=SCL.3MSG this.evening your father
      'Is your father coming this evening?'
   b. 'O pate songh' io! (Nap.)
      the father be.PRS.IND.1SG I
      'I'm the daddy!'

Together with the modern Corsican facts in (52a–d), we thus see how three individual reflexes of the medieval Romance V2 parameter, namely, V-to-C movement, focus-fronting, and the asymmetrical root-embedded distribution of null and overt pronominal subjects, are today distributed as independent residues across different modern Romance varieties, although none of the varieties involved displays a V2 grammar today.

1.2.4.3 The *Placiti cassinesi*

We now turn to the area of Romance philology and, in particular, the *Placiti cassinesi*.[22] Leaving aside the *Indovinello veronese* (Tuchel 1964; De Angelis 2003; Pescarini in press), which presents many Latin features (cf. n. 11 in Section 3.2.3), these four brief, formulaic, sworn declarations composed in Capua, Sessa Aurunca, and Teano (all situated in the modern-day southern Italian region of Campania) and dating between 960 and 963 are generally taken to represent the first documented attestations of the vernacular within the Italian Peninsula. Below we reproduce the first of these, the *Placito capuano* from March 960, which relates to a land dispute between the abbot of Montecassino and a certain Rodelgrimo who claimed, through inheritance, ownership of the lands which the abbot maintained had been the property of the monastery of St Benedict of Montecassino for 30 years. In the absence of any official documentation of ownership, the judge ordered the abbot to produce three witnesses to authenticate his claim, each of which was reported to have sworn the oath in (55):

(55) Sao ko kelle terre, per kelle fini que ki contene,
     know.PRS.IND.1SG that those lands for those confines that here contain.PRS.IND.3SG
     trenta anni le possette parte sancti Benedicti.
     thirty years them= possess.PST.PFV.3SG party saint.OBL Benedict.OBL
     'I know that, those lands, within those borders which are contained here [in the document/map before me], have belonged for thirty years to the part [= monastery] of St. Benedict [of Montecassino].'

---

[22] Bartoli (1944–45), Folena (1960), Castellani (1973: 59–76), Bianchi, De Blasi, and Librandi (1993: 211f.), Michel (1996), Ledgeway (2011a; 2012c).

Although a very short text, the *Placito capuano* is not without its problems, raising a number of qualitative and interpretive issues for the philologist (cf. Section 3.2.3). In particular, given the extremely brief and formulaic nature of the text, it is legitimate to question what is the value, if any, of the linguistic evidence that such a short piece can genuinely offer the historian of the language. Indeed, this is a problem which arises with many of the earliest attestations of the Romance vernacular including, for example, the earliest Romance text, the *Strasbourg Oaths* of 842, another short sworn oath produced in an early French dialect of disputed origin.[23]

Another unresolved issue thrown up by the *Placito capuano* concerns the correct reconstruction of the pragmatico-semantic interpretation of the fronted constituents stacked up at the beginning of the embedded clause (namely, *kelle terre, per kelle fini ..., trenta anni*), our reading of which is without doubt greatly hindered by the limited nature of our textual evidence. Again this is a frequent problem faced by philologists reading early texts, which in many cases only offer a rather brief glimpse of the language, especially when they only exist in fragmentary form, and whose linguistic physiognomy is often deliberately limited by the specific style and register of the text type.

A final observation concerns the appearance of the complementizer *ko* 'that' in (55). Contrary to expectations in light of the discussion of dual complementizer systems above (cf. Section 1.2.3.3.1), the epistemic main clause predicate *sao* 'I know' selects for an indicative clausal complement headed, not by the expected indicative/realis complementizer *ca*, but by what appears to be the subjunctive/irrealis complementizer *ko* (< QUOD), a variant of *che* (< QUID). How are we then to interpret the appearance of *ko* in this instance? Is it an example of a scribal error, or should it be taken at face value? As we shall see below, a consideration of this question in light of our preceding discussion of the fine structure of the left periphery provides an illuminating solution.

Putting together the results of the discussions of the previous sections regarding the fine structure of the left periphery of the clause (Section 1.2.3.3) and the philological evidence of the *Placito capuano*, it becomes clear that a knowledge of the relevant linguistic and philological facts can profitably complement one another. We begin by observing how, despite only providing a glimpse of the early vernacular, the *Placito capuano* is of immense interest both to the historian of the language and the historical linguist since, although a very short text, it is nonetheless astonishingly rich in linguistic evidence. More specifically, it is quite remarkable that such a short text, and the first one from the Italian Peninsula no less,

---

[23] See Tabachovitz (1932), Ewert (1935), Lüdtke (1963; 1966), Castellani (1969; 1978), López (1994), Ayres-Bennett (1996: 16–30), Balibar (1997: 61–68), Beck (2014).

should provide such extensive early evidence of the fine structure of the left periphery and, above all, incontrovertible proof for the existence of the two left-peripheral fields postulated in Section 1.2.3.3, which, in turn, hold the key to a proper pragmatico-semantic interpretation of the fronted constituents stacked up at the beginning of the embedded clause. In particular, the rigid ordering of the Topic + Focus fields postulated in Section 1.2.3.3, together with the observations regarding the potential recursion of topics but not foci, which is limited to a single occurrence, allows us to infer that the left periphery of the embedded clause hosts two thematicizations within the Topic field, namely, *kelle terre* 'those lands' (picked up by the resumptive clitic pronoun *le* 'them') and *per kelle fini que ki contene* 'with those borders which are contained here', and a contrastive focus *trenta anni* '(for) thirty years' within the Focus field, as represented in (56).

(56) Sao [ForceP ko [TopP kelle terre, per kelle fini que ki contene,
know.PRS.IND.1SG that those lands for those confines that here contain.PRS.IND.3SG
[FocP TRENTA ANNI [IP le possette parte sancti Benedicti.]]]]
thirty years them= possess.PST.PFV.3SG party saint.OBL Benedict.OBL
'I know that, those lands, within those borders which are contained here [in the document/map before me], have belonged for thirty years to the part [= monastery] of St. Benedict [of Montecassino].'

Turning now to the unexpected use of the complementizer *ko* (< QUOD) rather than *ca*, this too finds a principled explanation in terms of the structural organization of the complement clause. As demonstrated in Ledgeway (2004; 2005), in the early dialects of southern Italy, including those of Campania, the distribution of the two complementizers *co*/*che* (< QUOD/QUID) and *ca* (< QU(I)A) is not quite as neat as the traditional descriptions reviewed in Section 1.2.3.3.1 would lead us to expect. Whereas all types of subjunctive/irrealis clause are introduced by *che*, indicative/realis complement clauses are headed either by *ca* or *che*. Simplifying the facts somewhat (for detailed discussion, see Ledgeway 2005: §3), it will suffice to note here that either *ca* (57a) or *che* (57b) are employed when the left periphery of an embedded indicative/realis clause does not contain any topics or foci, whereas *che* alone is found in the presence of fronted topics/foci (57c), as witnessed by the following old Neapolitan examples:

(57) a. Homero [...] dice a li suoy libri ca [IP foro nave
Homer say.PRS.IND.3SG to the his books that be.PST.PFV.3PL ships
MCLXXXVI] (ONap.)
1186
'Homer [...] says in his books that there were 1186 ships'
b. Purriase ben dicere che [IP fo causa multo legiere] (ONap.)
can.COND.3SG=self well say.INF that be.PST.PFV.3SG cause very light
'it could indeed be said that there was very little reason for it'

c. Considerava che [TopP a quista insula de Colcosa [...], [IP non se nce
consider.PST.IPFV.3SG that to this island of Colchis NEG self= there=
poteva gire se non per mare]] (ONap.)
can.PST.IPFV.3SG go.INF if not by sea
'He thought that, this island of Colchis [...], was only accessible by sea'

Given these distributional facts, it is possible to argue that old Neapolitan had just one indicative complementizer generated in the lowest complementizer position (C_{Fin}) as *ca*: whenever raised to the higher complementizer position (C_{Force}), as proves obligatory whenever topics or foci are present, it surfaces in the form *che* (namely, *ca*$_{C-Fin}$ vs *che*$_{C-Force}$). In short, the overt form assumed by indicative uses of *co/che* is interpreted as nothing more than the surface morphological reflex of raising *ca* from its base position to the higher complementizer position within the left periphery. Indeed, this analysis is directly supported by old Neapolitan recomplementation examples such as (42b) above where, crucially, the higher complementizer invariably surfaces in the morphological form *co/che* but the lower position is always spelt out as *c(h)a*, and never *vice versa*.

In this light, we can now return to the initially mysterious selection of *ko* in the *Placito* in (55). It turns out after all that the use of *ko* here is not a scribal error, but reflects the availability and use of two different complementizer positions determined by the informational structure of the embedded clause (cf. 58a) which, as noted in (56), contains a contrastively focused constituent preceded by two topicalized constituents. It is the activation of these Topic-Focus fields in the embedded left periphery which is directly responsible for the presence of *ko*, inasmuch as the complementizer is forced to surface in the higher complementizer position in the presence of fronted topics or foci where it is spelt out as *ko* (58b). It now comes as no surprise therefore that the complementizer *ca* (or its graphic variants *cha*, *ka*) should not be employed in (55).

(58) a. ... [CP ko/che Topic + FOCUS ka/c(h)a [IP...]]
b. Sao [CP ko$_i$ kelle terre, per kelle... TRENTA ANNI ka$_i$ [IP...]]

This example also highlights the dangers of dismissing too hastily the linguistic attestations offered to us by even the most meagre of philological evidence. In this particular case, the *Placito capuano* provides an invaluable early example of the *ca* vs *co/che* alternation, which is not attested again in the textual record for the Campania region for at least another 350 years. Thanks however to this early attestation, it is possible to conclude with confidence that the relevant complementizer alternation and associated positions licensed by the absence/presence of fronted topics and foci, otherwise richly attested in texts from the fourteenth century onwards

(Ledgeway 2004; 2005; Vincent 2006), must date back to at least the tenth century. Of course, it might be objected that the linguistic evidence of the texts is so formulaic that its value for the linguist is questionable on a number of counts. Indeed, a comparison of the *Placito capuano* with the other three *Placiti cassinesi* produced three years later in the nearby localities of Sessa Aurunca (59a) and Teano (59b–c) reveals such an extraordinarily high level of structural, discourse, and lexical uniformity across all four texts that it would seem naïve to imagine that all four sworn oaths faithfully reproduce authentic, spontaneous tokens of the spoken vernacular of the time.

(59) a. Sao cco kelle terre, per kelle fini que tebe mostrai
know.PRS.IND.1SG that those lands for those confines that you.DAT show.PST.PFV.1SG
Pergoaldi foro, que ki contene, et trenta anni
Pergoaldi.OBL be.PST.PFV.3PL that here contain.PRS.IND.3SG and thirty years
le possette.
them= possess.PST.PFV.3SG
'I know that, those lands, within those borders which I have shown you, and which are contained here [in the document/map before me], belonged to Pergoaldo [the abbot of the monastery of San Salvatore] and that he owned them for thirty years.'

b. Kella terra, per kelle fini que bobe mostrai, sancte Marie
that land for those confines that you.DAT show.PST.PFV.1SG saint.OBL Maria.OBL
è, et trenta anni la possette parte sancte Marie.
be.PRS.IND.3SG and thirty years it= possess.PST.PFV.3SG part saint.OBL Maria.OBL
'That land, within those borders which I have shown you [in the document/map before me], belong to [the monastery of] Santa Maria [di Cengla], and were possessed by the part [= monastery] of Santa Maria [di Cengla] for thirty years.'

c. Sao cco kelle terre, per kelle fini que tebe mostrai,
know.PRS.IND.1SG that those lands for those confines that you.OBL show.PST.PFV.1SG
trenta anni le possette parte sancte Marie.
thirty years them= possess.PST.PFV.3SG part saint.OBL Maria.OBL
'I know that those lands, within those borders which I have shown you [in the document/map before me], have belonged for thirty years to the part [= monastery] of Santa Maria [of Cengla].'

On the contrary, given the nature of the four oaths, which all had the specific purpose of persuading the court that a set of disputed lands had been in the possession of a given monastery for thirty years and consequently a legitimate part of the latter's estate, it is more than likely that the individuals enlisted by the Church to serve as 'independent' witnesses, presumably under the promise of personal financial reward, were given very precise instructions regarding what they were required to swear under oath. Nonetheless, it would be rash to disregard the evidence of these four short, highly formulaic written testimonies on these grounds alone; rather, given the Church's deliberate efforts to place presumably authentic-sounding words and structures of the vernacular in the mouths of their witnesses, it is still possible to see in the language of these four texts a deliberate hypercharacterization of some of the most salient traits of the spoken language of the time such as the fronting of topicalized and focused constituents, which still constitutes to this day a characteristic feature of the spoken, rather than written, registers of Romance (cf. Duranti and Ochs 1979; Schweickard 1986; Rossi 1999; Cruschina 2012). In short, the *Placiti* presumably reflect competence rather than performance.

To sum up, the discussion in this section has demonstrated that, when theory and philological evidence are considered together, the results of traditional philological and linguistic scholarship can be considerably enhanced (cf. Section 2.7). In particular, current theoretical assumptions about the design and architecture of the left periphery of the clause provide us with some novel and powerful tools to shed light on the interpretation and linguistic choices of one of the earliest Romance texts. At the same time, the *Placiti cassinesi* provide independent and robust evidence for these same syntactic assumptions. In short, and as abundantly demonstrated in this case study, linguistics and philology should complement each other to produce enlightening results, rather than be seen as alternatives to be pursued in isolation from each other.

1.2.4.4 Dual Complementizer Systems

In Section 1.2.3.3.1 it was observed how Romanian and a number of southern Italian dialects employ a dual complementizer system which distinguishes between a realis complementizer derived from QUIA 'because' (> Ro. că, SItR. ca) and an irrealis complementizer derived from QUID/QUOD 'that, which' (> USID che, chi/co), QUO(MODO)/(QUO)MODO 'how' (> Sal. cu / SCal. mu, ma, mi) or SI 'if' (> Ro. să): while the former heads clauses selected by declarative and epistemic predicates typically marked by the indicative (60a), the latter is employed after predicates such as volitionals that characterize the state or events of their complements as unrealized at the time of speaking typically marked by the subjunctive when available (60b).

(60) a. Su'   ssicuru c'   a ttie nu tte   tice   none. (Lec.)
        be.PRS.IND.1SG sure that$_{REALIS}$ to you NEG you= say.PRS.IND.3SG no
        'I'm sure that he won't tell you no.'
    b. Spettamu   lu miètecu nesciu cu   nni   fazza   la lizzetta. (Lec.)
        wait.PRS.1PL the doctor our   that$_{IRREALIS}$ DAT.3= do.PRS.SBJV.3SG the prescription
        'We're waiting for our doctor to give him the prescription.'

Furthermore, it was noted above how both complementizers differ with respect to their relative positions in conjunction with fronted topicalized and focused constituents. For instance, as the preceding Leccese examples demonstrate, while *ca* precedes all such fronted elements (cf. 60a), *cu* must follow (cf. 60b). Facts like these led us to propose in terms of Rizzi's (1997) split CP perspective that the realis complementizer (e.g., *ca*) lexicalizes the higher C_Force head and the irrealis complementizer (e.g., *cu*) the lower C_Fin head, as sketched in (61):

(61)　[ForceP *ca*_REALIS [TopP Top [FocP Foc [FinP *cu*_IRREALIS [IP …]]]]]

A further distinction between the two complementizers which, at first sight, does not seem to immediately follow from (61) concerns their phonological realization (Calabrese 1993; Terzi 1994; 1996; Ledgeway 2013; 2015b). For example, while in Salentino *ca* must always be pronounced (62a), *cu* may optionally remain unpronounced (62b), a case of C-drop.

(62)　a.　Te　　prumettu　　**(*ca*)　　tornu. (Sal.)
　　　　　you= promise.PRS.1SG　that_REALIS return.PRS.1SG
　　　　　'I promise you that I will return.'
　　　b.　Ogghiu　　　(*cu*)　　llu faci　　　　stare　　cittu. (Sal.)
　　　　　want.PRS.1SG that_IRREALIS it= make.PRS.2SG stand.INF quiet
　　　　　'I want you to shut him up.'

Strikingly, even in those Romance varieties which do not display a dual complementizer system it is not infrequent for the finite complementizer *que/che* to remain phonologically unpronounced, on condition that it introduces an irrealis complement (63b), but not, crucially, when it introduces a realis complement (63a).[24]

(63)　a.　Sabem　　　　　**(*que*) esperes. (Cat.)
　　　　　know.PRS.IND.1PL　that　wait.PRS.IND.2SG
　　　b.　Preguem　　　　(*que*) esperis. (Cat.)
　　　　　pray.PRS.IND.1PL　that　wait.PRS.SBJV.2SG
　　　　　'We know/ask that you wait.'

In view of the superficial similarity in the conditions regulating the distribution of C-drop in varieties with dual complementizer systems and languages such as Catalan with apparently only one complementizer, it is tempting to extend the analysis of dual complementizer systems to languages of the latter type. In particular, we have established on the basis of dual complementizer systems that C-drop is a property uniquely licensed by the lowest C-related position, presumably involving a residual V2 effect (cf. Section 1.2.4.2) with raising of the modally-marked finite verb to C_Fin in the absence of the irrealis complementizer (Poletto 2001), but not by the realis complementizer which lexicalizes the highest C-related position C_Force and hence unavailable to finite verb-raising under V2. By the same token, in its irrealis uses standard Romance *que/che* must also lexicalize C_Fin, thereby explaining its complementary distribution with finite verb-raising under

---

[24] See further the discussion in Section 21.3.2, as well as Ledgeway (2016: 1021f.) and references cited therein.

C-drop, in contrast to its realis uses where it lexicalizes the highest position C_{Force}.

In short, we are led to conclude that the dual complementizer system explicitly attested for such varieties as Romanian and the dialects of southern Italy must also be assumed to hold more generally for Romance where, despite the two complementizers not being lexically distinguished (cf. also Ledgeway 2009b; Ledgeway and Lombardi 2014), the relevant distinction between the two homophonous complementizers *que/che* is marked indirectly by their differential positions within the left periphery and their compatibility with C-drop (64a–c).

(64) a. [ForceP Ø   [Top/FocP [Fin *que/che*$_{IRREALIS}$ [IP V$_{SBJV}$]]]]
     b. [ForceP Ø   [Top/FocP [Fin V$_{SBJV}$ [IP ~~V$_{SBJV}$~~]]]]
     c. [ForceP *que/che*$_{REALIS}$ [Top/FocP [Fin Ø   [IP V$_{IND}$]]]]

1.2.4.5 Nominal Functional Structure
1.2.4.5.1 Articles

An area of spectacular diachronic and synchronic microvariation in Romance regards the numerous dimensions of variation characterizing the Romance nominal group,[25] many of which can be captured in terms of the functional categories and associated functional structure that make up the DP. An obvious place to start is Quintilian's oft-quoted remark 'noster sermo articulos non desiderat' ('our language has no need of articles'), highlighting a salient typological difference between Latin and Greek in nominal functional structure of a parametric nature. Effectively, Quintilian's observation distinguishes between languages that lack articles such as Latin, which fail to grammaticalize definiteness overtly in the syntax through the lexicalization of the D(eterminer) position with a definite article (cf. Bošković 2005a; 2005b; 2008; Ledgeway 2012a: §4.2.2.1), and varieties like Romance, which from around the eighth century (Ledgeway 2012a: 96) grammaticalized the marking of definiteness on D through a weakened form of the Latin distal demonstrative ILLE 'that' or, less frequently, the Latin intensifier IPSE '-self, same' (> Bal./Costa Brava Cat. *es/sa*, Srd. *su/sa*). In accordance with the cross-linguistic generalization that marking of indefiniteness is dependent on the prior availability of marking for definiteness (Longobardi and Guradiano 2009; Keenan 2011; Longobardi

---

[25] See also Longobardi (1994; 2012), Guardiano and Longobardi (2005; 2017a; 2017b), Longobardi and Guardiano (2009), Longobardi, Guardiano, Silvestri, Boattini, and Ceolin (2013), Ledgeway (2007a; 2015a), Longobardi, Ghirotto, Guardiano, Tassi, Benazzo, Ceolin, and Barbujani (2015), Longobardi, Ceolin, Ecay, Ghirotto, Guardiano, Irimia, Michelioudakis, Radkevic, Luiselli, Pettener, and Barbujani (2016), and Giusti (2016).

2012: 308–15), it is possible to further derive the fact that, despite presenting a definite article, the earliest Romance varieties often still fail to grammaticalize the [±count] distinction on D and hence lack an indefinite article in their earliest attestations. Indeed, systematic usage of the indefinite article, which continues a weakened form of the Latin numeral for 'one' (< UNUM/-AM), does not become established until around the fourteenth century (Pozas Loyo 2010: ch. 5; Maiden 1995: 121; Ledgeway 2012a: §4.2.1). Before then bare DPs are employed for non-particularized referents (65a), whereas the indefinite article is reserved for particularized new referents (65b), presumably a residue of its numeral origin (Parry and Lombardi 2007: 91f.). In the modern languages, by contrast, indefinite DPs, whether particularized or not, require the article (65c):

(65) a. **Enfant** nos done   qui seit   a ton talent (OFr., *Vie de Saint Alexis* 5.5)
child us= give.IMP.2SG who be.PRS.SBJV.3SG to your wish
'Give us a child of your pleasing'

b. **Un fi** lor   donet (OFr., *Vie de Saint Alexis* 6.3.)
a son to.them= give.PRS.IND.3SG
'He gave them a son'

c. Busco   **una minyona** que em neteja/netegi   la casa. (Cat.)
search.PRS.IND.1SG a maid that me= clean.PRS.IND/SBJV.3SG the house
'I'm looking for a maid who is cleaning/to clean my house.'

Although in later stages of Romance that grammaticalize both the definite and indefinite articles the definite article displays considerable attenuation of its original deictic force, increasingly coming to mark shared cognition between speaker(s) and addressee(s), it still retained considerable identifying force, witness its exclusion in early texts with unique, abstract, and generic referents (66a; cf. Parry and Lombardi 2007: 83f.; Renzi 2010: 318f., 329f., 332–37), a usage often fossilized in modern proverbs and set expressions (66b–c). In the modern languages, by contrast, shared cognition between speaker(s) and addressee(s) assumes increasing importance, such that the article is now generally required with unique, abstract, and generic referents (66d).

(66) a. leichatz estar **ypocresie** (OGsc., *Disciplina clericalis* 1v.32–33)
let.IMP.2PL be.INF hypocrisy
'let hypocrisy be'

b. Parar/desparar **taula** (Cat.)
lay.INF/clear.INF table
'To lay/clear the table'

c. **Noblesse** oblige (Fr.)
nobility oblige.PRS.IND.3SG

d. **Dreptatea** este lumina vieții. (Ro.)
justice.DEF be.PRS.IND.3SG light.DEF life.GEN.DEF.SG
'Justice is the light of life.'

This difference between earlier and later stages of Romance can be captured through a microparametric opposition between weak and strong D languages (Guardiano and Longobardi 2005). Languages of the former group include early Romance varieties which do not require overt association in the syntax between N and D, hence kind-reference is not explicitly lexicalized on D, witness the absence of the article in old Galician examples such as *e les quede* **libertad** *de poder cobrar de lor herederos* (*Historia de la Santa A. M. Iglesia de Santiago de Compostela* 73) 'and may they retain (the) **freedom** to be able to inherit'. In strong D languages such as modern Romance varieties, by contrast, kind-reference is licensed through explicit association of N and D in the syntax, witness the obligatory use of an expletive article in such modern Galician examples as ***(a) escravitude é todo o contrario da liberdade* '(the) slavery is the complete opposite of (the) freedom'. In this respect, many Balearic Catalan varieties and, to a lesser extent Catalan dialects spoken along the Costa Brava, prove particularly revealing in that they show a further dimension of synchronic microvariation on 'strong' D which explicitly marks a lexical distinction between the deictic and expletive functions of the article through the opposition between IPSE-derived (67a) and ILLE-derived (67b) articles, respectively (Ledgeway 2012a: 100–03).

(67) a. **Sa** mort d' en Joan (MajCat.)
 the death of the Joan
 'Joan's death'
 b. Pensam en **la** mort. (MajCat.)
 think.PRS.IND.1PL in the death
 'We think about death.'

1.2.4.5.2 Noun Positions

Among the strong Romance D varieties we can further observe a parametric distinction between those that exhibit N(-to-D)-raising and those that do not. Particularly instructive in this respect are adjective-noun orders (for an overview and relevant bibliography, see Ledgeway 2012a: 50–57). Simplifying somewhat, prenominal and postnominal adjective positions typically correlate with the following respective interpretations in the modern standard varieties of Romance:[26] (i) inherent/non-inherent (68a); (ii) descriptive/distinguishing (68b); (iii) subjective/objective (68c); and (iv) figurative/literal (68d).

---

[26] See further Arnholdt (1916), Sandfeld and Olsen (1960: 98–114), Alisova (1967), Reiner (1968), Lapesa (1975), Vincent (1986; 2007: 57–61), Bernstein (1993), Giorgi and Longobardi (1991), Bosque (1996), Berruto (1998), Pountain (1998), Demonte (1999), Abeillé and Godard (1999), Radatz (2001), Cinque (2010), Gonzaga (2004), Ledgeway (2007a; 2012a: §3.2.2.1), Andriani (2015; 2018), Giusti (2016: 545–49).

(68) a. un **àrid** desert vs una regió **àrida** (Cat.)
        a   arid   desert   a   region   arid
        'an arid desert' vs 'an arid region'
b. unas **interesantes** películas vs unas películas **interesantes** (Sp.)
        some interesting films   some films interesting
        'some interesting films' vs 'some films which are interesting'
c. une (**splendide**) maison (**splendide**) (Fr.)
        a   splendid   house   splendid
        'a splendid house'
d. nu **vècchiə** chəmbagnə vs nu chəmbagnə **vècchiə** (Bar.)
        a   old   companion   a   companion   old
        'an old (= of long standing) friend' vs 'an old (= in years) friend'

In early Romance, by contrast, the distribution of adjectives was quite different, insofar as contrastive readings were not necessarily associated with the postnominal position as in modern Romance, but could equally be licensed in the prenominal position (Ledgeway 2007a; 2009a: 214f; Vincent 2007; Thiella 2008; Giusti 2010: 599–609; Brăescu and Dragomirescu 2014). This is illustrated in the following near-minimal pairs, where the adjective in each case invariably gives rise to a contrastive reading irrespective of its pre- or postnominal position.

(69) a. pro **christian** poblo vs lo nom **christiien** (OFr., *Strasbour Oaths / Sequence of S. Eulalia*)
        for Christian people   the name Christian
        'for the Christian people' vs 'the Christian name'
b. La **carnal** amor del spiritu et el desseo **carnal** (OSp., *Libro de actoridades*)
        the carnal love of.the spirit and the desire carnal
        'Carnal love of the spirit and carnal desire'
c. li **spagnoli** soldati vs le compangnie **spagnole** (ONap., *Cronaca dei tumulti* 34–35 / 65)
        the Spanish soldiers   the companies Spanish
        'the Spanish soldiers' vs 'the Spanish troops'

Strikingly similar is the situation found in modern Wallon (Bernstein 1991; 1993: ch. 4; Bouchard 2002), where all adjectival classes, apart from those expressing nationality (70d), occur in prenominal position (70a–c), perhaps representing a conservative feature, although we cannot exclude the (reinforcing) influence of neighbouring Flemish varieties. Language contact with Croatian presumably also explains the preferred preposing of adjectives in Istro-Romanian (Zegrean 2012: 91–96), as illustrated in (71a–c). Once again, the exception is represented by nationality adjectives, at least the class in *-an*, witness the contrast in (71d).

(70) a. on **neûr** tchapê (Wal.)
        'a black hat'
b. du l' **corante** êwe (Wal.)
        of the running water
        'some running water'

c. lès **cûts** pans (Wal.)
    'the cooked loaves'
d. le peûpe **italyin** (Wal.)
    the people Italian
    'the Italian people'

(71) a. (**negre**) pâre (**negre**) (IRo.)
         black bread black
         'brown bread'
     b. doi (**otrovni**) šarpel'i (**otrovni**) (IRo.)
         two poisonous snakes poisonous
         'two poisonous snakes'
     c. (**uscăte**) lemne (**uscăte**)
         dried wood dried
         'dried wood'
     d. ur (**taljanksi**/**taljan) fečor (**taljan/taljanksi**) (IRo.)
         a Italian boy Italian
         'an Italian boy'

By contrast, in a number of, especially non-standard, Romance varieties including Occitan (72a; cf. Wheeler 1988: 268), Sardinian (72b; cf. Jones 1993: 42), and central-southern Italian dialects (72c; cf. Rohlfs 1969: 330; Ledgeway 2007a; Andriani 2015; 2018), the prenominal adjectival position is extremely restricted and generally replaced by the postnominal position, which is neutral to the contrastive vs non-contrastive distinction:[27]

(72) a. lo (****vièlh**) pònt **vièlh** d' Avinhon (Lgd.)
         the old bridge old of Avignon
         'the old Avignon bridge'
     b. na (****piccerella**) maruzza **piccerella** (Nap.)
         a small snail small
         'a small snail'
     c. una (****nova**) mákkina **nova** (Srd.)
         a new car new
         'a new car'

Exploiting the analysis in Section 1.2.3.2 of variable verb positions around different adverbial classes distributed across the clause, it is possible to make sense of the variation witnessed in (69)–(72) along parallel lines in terms of the varying extent of N(oun)-movement in relation to different adjectival classes (cf. also Section 20.2.2). In particular, different adjectival positions can be reinterpreted as the surface reflex of the head noun

---

[27] Cf. the postnominal position of the adjectives in (69a–c) with the corresponding prenominal position in their French (le **vieux** pont d'Avignon) and Italian (una **piccola** lumaca; una **nuova** macchina) translations.

variously moving across a universally fixed series of at least seven different adjectival classes situated immediately above the NP within the functional structure of the DP (cf. Cinque 1994; 2010; Giusti 2016: 545), as summarized in (73):

(73)   [DP (N) [AP1 Adj_Quantity (N) [AP2 Adj_Quality (N) [AP3 Adj_Size (N) [AP4 Adj_Age (N) [AP5 Adj_Form (N) [AP6 Adj_Colour (N) [AP7 Adj_Origin [NP N]]]]]]]]]

Assuming the much-simplified structure in (74a) in which AP_1 and AP_2 can be broadly understood as the functional 'areas' in which the various subclasses of non-contrastive and contrastive adjectives, respectively, are generated, we can formally capture in a highly simple manner the differences between the non-standard varieties in (72a–c) on the one hand and standard Romance varieties (68a–d) on the other: in the former the nominal head typically raises to the highest available position above the highest adjectival projection (AP_1), which hosts non-contrastive adjectives from where it precedes both non-contrastive and contrastive adjectives (74b), whereas in the latter the noun only targets the higher adjectival field (viz. AP_1), from where it precedes contrastive adjectives but follows those with a non-contrastive reading (74c):

(74)   a.   ...   (N)   [AP1 Adj_Contr.   (N)   [AP2 Adj_Non-contr.   [NP N̶]]]
       b.   ...lo   pònt   [AP1 [vièlh]   p̶ò̶n̶t̶   [AP2   [NP p̶ò̶n̶t̶]]] (Lgd.)
       c.   ...le   [AP1 [vieux]   pont   [AP2   [NP p̶o̶n̶t̶]]] (Fr.)

By the same line of reasoning, we can explain the frequent prenominal position of contrastive adjectives in early Romance (cf. 69a–c) by assuming that N-raising is only optional in the early varieties (75a–b), since, as noted in Section 1.2.4.5.1, these were originally weak D languages which initially did not require overt association in the syntax between N and D, namely, N(-to-D)-raising, independently yielding the observed adjective-noun order. As observed above, this archaic pattern is still preserved to the present-day in Wallon and Istro-Romanian, where the nominal head only moves at most to the left of the subclass of contrastive adjectives encoding nationality/origin (76a–b). Nonetheless, these are both strong D languages since they require the use of the article with, for example, generic reference (77a–b), highlighting how low N-raising is compatible with both weak (e.g., early Romance) and strong (e.g., Wallon, Istro-Romanian) D grammars, although in the latter case the relevant cluster of properties appears to be the output of adstratal contact with Flemish and Croatian.

(75)   a.   li   [AP1   [AP2 [spangnoli]   [NP soldati]]] (ONap.)
             the   Spanish   soldiers
       b.   le   [AP1 compangnie   [AP2 [spangnole]   [NP c̶o̶m̶p̶a̶n̶g̶n̶i̶e̶]]] (ONap.)
             the   companies   Spanish

(76) a. lès [AP1 ... [AP2 [cuts] pans... [NP pans]]] (Wal.)
       the   cooked loaves
    b. le [AP1 ... [AP2 ... peûpe [AP2-Origin italyin] [NP peûpe]]] (Wal.)
       the   people   Italian

(77) a. **Les** omes sont pus sovint bilingues ki **les** femreyes. (Wal.)
       the men be.PRS.IND.3PL more often bilingual that the women
       'Men are more often bilingual than women.'
    b. **Căprele** mârâncu iărba. (IRo)
       goats.DEF.FPL eat.PRS.IND.3PL grass.DEF.FSG
       'Goats eat grass.'

In conclusion, there are truly striking parallels between the nominal and verbal domains and the functional structures associated with these, as revealed by the fixed positions of distinct classes of adjectival and adverbial modifiers, respectively. In particular, we have seen how different diachronic and diatopic varieties of Romance provide clear evidence for some considerable microvariation in terms of the extent of N-movement and its effects on semantico-pragmatic interpretation at the interfaces. Among the various patterns observed, we have also identified a strong diachronic tendency for Romance nouns to climb progressively higher within the available nominal functional structure, the end result of which has given rise in a number of non-standard varieties to a syntactic neutralization of the erstwhile interpretive difference between contrastive and non-contrastive adjectival readings.

1.2.4.5.3 Expletive Articles

Although the preceding discussion forces us to conclude that, with the exception of Wallon and Istro-Romanian, D and the functional field above NP uniformly attracts N in modern Romance to yield the typical noun-adjective$_{Contrastive}$ order, further fine-grained differentiation of this particular microparameter is required to understand the observed split among Romance varieties in relation to the licensing of proper names through the use or otherwise of an expletive article (Longobardi 1994). The relevant difference is to be interpreted in terms of which types of N can be attracted by D in individual Romance varieties. The least marked option is that which characterizes varieties such as standard Spanish, where D indiscriminately attracts all types of N, including proper names which overtly raise to D and therefore prove incompatible with the definite article, e.g., (**el*) *Juan*/(**la*) *Juana* '(the) John/(the) Jane'. The more marked and restrictive option is exemplified by varieties such as European Portuguese where D fails to attract proper names, a small and lexically definable subclass of nominals, which, by virtue of the strong D setting, can only be rescued through merger of an expletive article in D, e.g., *o João*/*a Joana* 'the John/the Jane'. Catalan varieties have moved the furthest in this direction (Wheeler, Yates, and Dols 1999: 67f.), developing a specialized paradigm for proper names based on clitic reflexes of DOMINUS/-A 'master/mistress' > en/na in Balearic Catalan (e.g., *en Joan/na Joana*) and on a blend of DOMINUS- and ILLE-derived forms in the standard language (e.g., *en Joan/la Joana*).

Once again this is a simplification of the relevant Romance facts, in that there are further microparametric distinctions involved which, for space limitations, we cannot discuss in detail here. For example, while standard Italian appears to pattern with Spanish in all relevant respects with personal proper names, e.g., (**il) *Gianni*/(**la) *Gianna*, the two languages differ with respect to proper names denoting large geographical expanses, e.g., It./Sp. **(*la*)/(**la) *Francia* '(the) France'. However, even in Spanish there are certain lexical exceptions where the article proves obligatory, e.g., **(*la*) *India* '(the) India', **(*El*) *Reino Unido* '**the** United Kingdom' (but cf. (**la) *Gran Bretaña* '(**the**) Great Britain'), or optional, e.g., (*la*) *Argentina* '(**the**) Argentina', (*el*) *Canadá* '(**the**) Canada'. A similar distribution, though often with different class membership (cf. Sp./Pt. (**la) *España*/**(*a*) *Espanha* '(the) Spain', (*el*) *Brasil*/**(*o*) *Brasil* '(**the**) Brazil'), also obtains in Portuguese where the article is generally excluded, e.g., (**a) *França* '(the) France', (**o) *Portugal* '(the) Portugal', but in some cases is obligatory, e.g., **(*a*) *Índia* '(**the**) India', **(*o*) *Japão* '(**the**) Japan', and in others is optional, e.g., (*a*) *Uganda* '(**the**) Uganda', (*o*) *Timor Leste* '(**the**) East Timor'. Such unpredictable lexically-based variation, which is often subject at the same time to considerable diatopic and idiolectal variation, is indicative of nanoparametric variation. In a similar fashion, in Romanian and northern-central regional varieties of Italian, D attracts only masculine proper names, e.g., Ro. *Ion(**ul)* 'John(=**DEF**)', It. (**il) *Gianni* '(the) John', but not feminine proper names which must occur with an expletive article, namely, Ro. *Ioana* 'Jane=**DEF**' < *Ioană* + -*a* 'Jane + =DEF', NCIt. *la Gianna* (cf. Cornilescu and Nicolae 2015; Ledgeway 2017c). To our knowledge, the reverse situation, namely, obligatory N-to-D raising with feminine proper names coupled with the obligatory use of expletive articles in conjunction with masculine proper names, is not found in any Romance variety in line with general assumptions regarding the relative markedness of gender categories (viz. masculine > feminine). In sum, data like these highlight once again the role of functional categories such as those associated with the D-domain in licensing extensive Romance microvariation.

1.3 The View from Romance Palatalization

1.3.1 Sketch of the Two Major Romance 'Waves' of Palatalization and Their Consequences

The history of the major Romance palatalizations can be thought-provoking in several quite different respects. Before we see what these are, we need a preliminary sketch of the palatalizations in question. The phonological process of palatalization has occurred in various ways over the history of the Romance languages. It is a cross-linguistically common phenomenon which has a fairly simple articulatory explanation as an assimilation: see, e.g., Anderson (1973: 106–08); Trask (1996a: 60f.; 1996b: 254f.; 2000: 243). Many manifestations of the phenomenon in Romance are locally restricted and of relatively late date (see, e.g., Loporcaro 2011: 143–50; Repetti 2016), but the two palatalizations discussed in what follows are 'Romance' in the sense that their effects are part of the shared inheritance of all Romance languages, and this is because they operated at an early date. The first palatalization (see, e.g., Loporcaro 2011: 144; Repetti 2016: 658–62) is attested (from inscriptional evidence) in the second century, and involves the emergence of a novel series of palatal consonants (Latin had no palatals apart from the glide [j]). These arose by assimilation of certain consonants to an immediately following 'yod' (i.e., the glide [j]), often resulting in the 'absorption' of the yod into the preceding consonant.[28] As well as producing palatalization, [j] often caused affrication of preceding consonants, so that the first palatalization is also a major source of novel affricate consonants. The second palatalization (see, e.g., Loporcaro 2011: 147f.; Repetti 2016: 662–64) appears, on the basis of inscriptional evidence, to have occurred in or by the fifth century, and involves a change such that velar consonants [k] and [g] are palatalized (principally yielding the affricates [tʃ] and [dʒ], but with various subsequent developments according both to geographical area and to phonological environment). As we see later, the effects of this second palatalization are to be observed over a more restricted geographical area than those of the first palatalization.

Both palatalizations can be usefully illustrated from their effects on inflexional morphology. Indeed, these morphological consequences of the palatalizations will crop up repeatedly in what follows. In some Romance varieties (occasionally in Italo-Romance and very systematically in Romanian)[29] the second palatalization produced alternation between singular and plural in nouns and adjectives (e.g., SG PORCUS 'pig' ~ PL PORCI > It. por[k]o ~ por[tʃ]i, Ro. por[k] ~ por[tʃ]i; Ro. SG SICCUS 'dry' ~ PL SICCI > Ro. se[k] ~ se[tʃ]i),[30] but the most dramatic effects of both palatalizations, across the Romance languages, are to be seen in the verb. An important point in what follows is that, in many Romance languages, both the first and the second palatalization produced allomorphy in the final consonant of lexical

---

[28] There was a proliferation of new yods in late Latin because the Latin unstressed vowels /e/ and /i/, when immediately followed by a vowel, became [j].

[29] For discussions of why the phenomenon is rare in Italo-Romance, and why the (masculine) plural forms originate specifically in Latin nominative (rather than accusative) case-forms, see Maiden (1996; 2000).

[30] The morphology of nouns and adjectives was such that there happened to be no potential for the creation of *alternations* by the first palatalization.

roots of non-first conjugation verbs such that the first person singular present indicative,[31] and some or all forms of the present subjunctive, come to share a distinctive root allomorph.[32] That both types of palatalization create the same paradigmatic *pattern* of alternation is actually coincidental. The phonological environment for palatalization by yod was met just in the first person singular present and in throughout the present subjunctive; in contrast, the phonological environment for palatalization of velars was extensively met throughout the paradigm of the relevant verbs, *except* in first person singular present indicative, and throughout the present subjunctive. The two palatalizations effectively operated on complementary sets of paradigm cells.

A fine-grained account of how the effects of the palatalizations (and affrications) have played out in the historical morphology of the Romance languages is beyond our scope here (see also Section 10.5.1). There are many details and apparent or real exceptions that require special and lengthy explanations: for discussions, see Maiden (2010; 2011b; 2018: 122–48); Maiden et al. (2021: 350–56). Among these complications are the fact that in Romanian the first and second person subjunctive forms have been replaced by indicative forms, and that in Italian the expected alternant is now often absent in some verbs in the first and second persons plural of the present subjunctive. Nonetheless, the broad effects of the palatalizations can be illustrated by the verb forms in Tables 1.4–1.5. Subsequent sound changes in some Romance varieties have meant that the original palatal (or affricate) nature of the alternants may no longer be directly apparent as such, although Italian (Table 1.5) stays fairly close to what are likely to have been the origin products of the palatalizations. Yet the alternations illustrated in Tables 1.4–1.6 are all, in origin, the direct results of palatalization. The choice of 'old' Italian and 'old' Romanian in these examples is motivated by the fact that by the twentieth-century analogical levelling had rather obscured these original effects.

The most important point to note here is that the Romance languages, generally, have acquired, as a result of the palatalizations, a recurrent pattern of alternation such that forms of the present subjunctive share a distinctive root allomorph with the first person singular present indicative (and in some cases also with the third person plural present indicative). This is an observation to whose significance we will return in Sections 1.3.5 and 1.3.6 where, perhaps surprisingly, we will see that these facts have a

---

[31] First conjugation verbs never presented the appropriate environment for creation of alternation caused by yod. These verbs were in principle exposed to the 'second palatalization' in their present subjunctive, but what actually happened here is discussed in Section 1.3.2.

[32] In Italian and some other central Italo-Romance dialects these effects include the third person plural present indicative. In Romanian the effects of the second, but not the first, palatalization extend slightly further, in that they include the third person plural present indicative.

Table 1.4. (Old) Romanian

(a) Effect of palatalization by yod

	1SG	2SG	3SG	1PL	2PL	3PL
PRS	vă[dz]u 'see'	vedzi[33]	vede	vedem	vedeți	vădu
SBJV	----	----	va[dz]ă	----	----	va[dz]ă
PRS	au[dz]u 'hear'	audzi	aude	audzim	audziți	audu
SBJV	----	----	au[dz]ă	----	----	au[dz]ă
PRS	sa[j]u 'jump'	sari	sare	sărim	săriți	saru
SBJV	----	----	sa[j]e	----	----	sa[j]e

(b) Effect of palatalization of velars

	1SG	2SG	3SG	1PL	2PL	3PL
PRS	zicu 'say'	zi[tʃ]i	zi[tʃ]e	zi[tʃ]em	zi[tʃ]eți	zicu
SBJV	----	----	zică	----	----	zică
PRS	împingu 'push'	împin[dʒ]i	împin[dʒ]e	împin[dʒ]em	împin[dʒ]eți	împingu
SBJV	----	----	împingă	----	----	împingă

Table 1.5. Old Italian

(a) Effect of palatalization by yod

	1SG	2SG	3SG	1PL	2PL	3PL
PRS.IND	va[ʎʎ]o 'am worth'	vali	vale	valemo	valete	va[ʎʎ]ono
PRS.SBJV	va[ʎʎ]a	va[ʎʎ]i	va[ʎʎ]a	va[ʎʎ]amo	va[ʎʎ]ate	va[ʎʎ]ano
PRS.IND	te[ɲɲ]o 'hold'	tieni	tiene	tenemo	tenete	te[ɲɲ]ono
PRS.SBJV	te[ɲɲ]a	te[ɲɲ]i	te[ɲɲ]a	te[ɲɲ]amo	te[ɲɲ]ate	te[ɲɲ]ano
PRS.IND	ve[ddʒ]o 'see'	vedi	vede	vedemo	vedete	ve[ddʒ]ono
PRS.SBJV	ve[ddʒ]a	ve[ddʒ]i	ve[ddʒ]a	ve[ddʒ]amo	ve[ddʒ]ate	ve[ddʒ]ano

(b) Effect of palatalization of velars

	1SG	2SG	3SG	1PL	2PL	3PL
PRS	di[k]o 'say'	di[tʃ]i	di[tʃ]e	di[tʃ]emo	(dite)	di[k]ono
SBJV	di[k]a	di[k]i	di[k]a	di[tʃ]amo	di[tʃ]ate	di[k]ano
PRS	le[gg]o 'say'	le[ddʒ]i	le[ddʒ]e	le[ddʒ]emo	le[ddʒ]ete	le[gg]ono
SBJV	le[gg]a	le[gg]i	le[gg]a	le[ddʒ]amo	le[ddʒ]ate	le[gg]ano

bearing on such issues as the tendency for linguists inappropriately to take the perspective of standard languages in their analysis of historical

---

[33] The [dz] found in the second person singular (ve[dz]i) and also in the first and second persons plural of some verbs (au[dz]im, au[dz]iți) is of different origin from and probably of later date than that found in first person singular and the subjunctive. See Maiden (2011b: 64).

Table 1.6. Portuguese

(a) Effect of palatalization by yod

	1SG	2SG	3SG	1PL	2PL	3PL
PRS.IND	te[ɲ]o 'have'	tens	tem	temos	tendes	têm
PRS.SBJV	te[ɲ]a	te[ɲ]as	te[ɲ]a	te[ɲ]amos	te[ɲ]ais	te[ɲ]am
PRS.IND	ve[ʒ]o 'see'	vês	vê	vemos	vedes	vêem
PRS.SBJV	ve[ʒ]a	ve[ʒ]as	ve[ʒ]a	ve[ʒ]amos	ve[ʒ]ais	ve[ʒ]am
PRS.IND	fa[s]o 'do'	fazes	faz	fazemos	fazeis	fazem
PRS.SBJV	fa[s]a	fa[s]as	fa[s]a	fa[s]amos	fa[s]ais	fa[s]am

(b) Effect of palatalization of velars

	1SG	2SG	3SG	1PL	2PL	3PL
PRS.IND	digo 'say'	dizes	diz	dizemos	dizeis	dizem
PRS.SBJV	diga	digas	diga	digamos	digais	digam

analyses, and on the fundamental question of how Romance languages are to be defined. We begin, however, by looking at how the palatalizations can make us reflect on the nature of sound change, and the relation between sound change and morphologization.

1.3.2 The Palatalization of the Velars and the Emergence of a Sound Change

The Romance palatalization of velars before front vowels (PVFV), illustrated from alternation in verbs (and some nouns and adjectives) in Section 1.3.1, operates across the board, wherever the relevant phonological environment is met. Some further examples, this time from non-alternating environments, are given in Table 1.7.[34]

Romance PVFV seems to offer a classic scenario in which sound change occurs regularly and apparently without exception. Where PVFV does not occur, the reason is apparently geographical (the sound change simply failed historically to occur in a particular area, again across the board), or chronological (apparent counterexamples to PVFV simply postdate the historical period at which the sound change operated), or 'analogical' (morphological alternations originally triggered by the sound change have subsequently been removed by so-called analogical levelling, often attributed to a preference for a one-to-one correspondence between form and meaning).

---

[34] The Spanish forms given in Table 1.7 are in standard European Spanish. The consonant [θ] (elsewhere [s]) can be shown to go back to an affricated outcome of the velar before a front vowel.

Table 1.7. *Effects of palatalization of velars in some Romance languages*

Latin	Italian	Romanian	Spanish
CIUITATEM 'town'	[tʃ]ittà	[tʃ]etate	[θ]iudad
GELU 'frost, ice'	[dʒ]elo	[dʒ]er	[j]elo
GENERUM 'son-in-law'	[dʒ]enero	[dʒ]inere	[j]erno
CENAM 'dinner'	[tʃ]ena	[tʃ]ină	[θ]ena
PACEM 'peace'	pa[tʃ]e	pa[tʃ]e	pa[θ]
LEGES 'laws'	le[ddʒ]i	le[dʒ]i	le[j]es
PISCEM 'fish'	pe[ʃʃ]e	pe[ʃt]e	pre[θ]

The best example of the 'geographical' exception comes from Sardinian (or at least central Sardinian dialects), which systematically lacks PVFV (cf. Lausberg 1966: 315f., 322f.). The physical and cultural isolation of Sardinia probably explains why the island was unaffected by PVFV – a phenomenon which is not attested in inscriptions until the fifth century and may not have reached all parts of a fracturing late Roman Empire. That geographically isolated areas within some linguistic domain may fail to participate in innovations that originate outside those areas is unremarkable.[35] Apparently all we would need to do, then, for Sardinian is to adjust the statement that the Romance languages underwent palatalization of velars before front vowels so as to exclude at least one, isolated, place, Sardinia. And this is what manuals of Romance linguistic regularly and understandably do. An example of the 'chronological' type of exception is Ro. *gem* 'I moan' [dʒem] < Lat. GEMO, Ro. *înțelege* 's/he understands' [intseˈledʒe] < Lat. INTELLEGIT, with the expected palatalization, but *ghem* [gem] 'ball of wool',[36] or *inteligenție* [inteliˈgentsije] 'intelligentsia', without it. These words fail to undergo PVFV because the former comes from late Latin *ˈglemu, and developed as [gem] only in relatively recent linguistic history, while the latter is a twentieth-century loanword from Russian. Both forms simply postdate the period at which PVFV operated. All that is needed here is to state a chronological limit after which the sound change ceased to operate and after which these words must have entered the language or developed velar + palatal sequences. Analogical levelling could be illustrated from Italian (see also Section 10.5.2). This language does have the

---

[35] This does not mean that isolated or peripheral areas are inherently linguistically archaic. There is simply no reason in principle why they should be, and it is perfectly possible for innovations to occur in them which do not occur elsewhere. But the language of isolated areas is liable to be *different* from the cognate languages from which they are separated. Nor should we ever assume that areas that seem 'isolated' today were necessarily so in the past; for a valuable object lesson on this point, see Varvaro (1984).

[36] More accurately, [gʲem], since velars in modern Romanian automatically display a small degree of phonetic palatalization (but not affrication) in modern Romanian. For more discussion of types of palatalization at work in modern Romanian, see Section 9.4.3.

expected velar ~ palatal alternation between singular and plural in SG *porco* ['pɔrko] 'pig' ~ PL *porci* ['pɔrtʃi], or SG *amico* [a'miko] 'friend' ~ PL *amici* [a'mitʃi], but not in SG *secco* ['sekko] 'dry' ~ PL *secchi* ['sekki], or SG *fungo* ['fuŋgo] 'mushroom' ~ PL *funghi* ['fuŋgi]. The latter non-palatalized cases can surely be assigned to analogical levelling: we may assume that the alternation was originally present (e.g., ['fuŋgo] ~ PL ['fundʒi]) as a result of regular sound change operating before the front vowel of the plural ending, but that it was then eliminated, quite plausibly on the model of countless other nouns and adjectives whose roots do not alternate for number, a development perhaps additionally motivated by a desire to unify form with meaning.[37] So far, so good. Most manuals of Romance historical linguistics indeed create a fairly tidy view in which this sound change occurred across the board, and if there are exceptions they can be neatly assigned to these well understood categories. Most of the time, this procedure is perfectly justified. But if we pay proper attention to *all* the historical-comparative information available to us, the picture becomes much more nuanced, fragmentary, and blurred.

Linguists should always ask themselves how plausible the changes they postulate are, in the light of what we know about the history of the people who speak the relevant languages. For many families of related languages we may have little or no knowledge of the broader historical context in which changes occur, but for Romance linguistics the possibilities are often different and Romance linguists should avoid too abruptly extirpating purely linguistic facts from the wider historical context in which they occurred. This is a point on which the Italian Romanist Alberto Varvaro repeatedly insisted, and it is one that he happens to have illustrated with reference to the Romance palatalization of velars. For example, Varvaro (2004a: 88) is critical of Wartburg (1967) for the 'summary and uninterested way' in which the latter treats some 'cases of regional conservatism in the development of Latin', including palatalization of velars. Varvaro observes that the modern extension of the phenomenon over almost the whole Romance domain (and its presence in all those Romance languages which have attained the status of a national or literary language, apart from some geographically marginal or apparently isolated areas), should not blind us to the fact that this sound change (like any other) was an innovation whose current geographical spread could not have been achieved overnight, and indeed that it was a late innovation which appears to postdate the fall of the western Roman Empire. In fact, failure to participate in PVFV is crucially not limited to Sardinian and this, in Varvaro's view, is significant. Varvaro (2004a: 88–90) observes that the (voiceless) velar is preserved intact in

---

[37] The apparent levelling is the overwhelming majority case in modern Italian. For a more nuanced account of the historical mechanisms involved, and the possible additional role of semantic factors, see Maiden (2000).

palatalizing contexts in loans from Latin into Germanic, Greek, Slavonic, and Berber (and, albeit partially, Maghreb Arabic): e.g., German *Keller* < CELLARIUS 'cellar', *Kiste* < CISTA 'chest', Berber *akîker* < CICER 'chickpea', *iger* < AGER 'field' (see, e.g., Tagliavini 1969: 173, 177). Varvaro also notes evidence that in the Romance of the Moselle area PVFV did not take place before the sixth century. All this must mean, Varvaro contends, that the current geographic spread of PVFV can date from no earlier than the end of the western Empire and that the phenomenon spread over almost the entire Latin area when political unity had already disintegrated, at a period of maximum fragmentation when new, smaller, political units were emerging. In short, just because a phenomenon is geographically widespread does not mean that it is ancient nor (we may add) that it emerged abruptly and spread easily and uniformly over the Empire. This perspective should make us wonder whether PVFV was as straightforward a process as simple 'before and after' comparisons between Latin and the Romance languages might suggest.

The sense that PVFV first spread in a tentative, non-uniform, way is augmented by a closer look at the comparative details. First, absence of PVFV turns out to involve not only isolated areas of the Romània (Sardinian) but also the far less isolated Vegliote Dalmatian – which is in a geographically intermediate position between Italo-Romance and Daco-Romance. There is indeed palatalization of velars before front vowels in Vegliote, but the phenomenon seems recent and in fact independent of the more widespread Romance examples of PVFV. In Vegliote, inherited velar consonants do not show palatalization before inherited mid front vowels (e.g., 'kaina 'dinner' < CENAM, ge'lut 'cold' < GELATUM). There is PVFV before high front vowels (Bartoli 1906: §425; Lausberg 1966: 316; Solta 1980: 148f.), but this development appears to be an independent, modern phenomenon, since some of the high front vowels in question have emerged in the recent history of the language (e.g., tʃol 'arse' < *kyl < CULUM; tʃil 'sky' < *kjelu < C(A)ELUM). In short, there is no good evidence that 'Romance' PVFV ever occurred in Vegliote either.

At first glance, PVFV in Romanian looks to be exactly the same historical phenomenon as PVFV in Italian, and many manuals of Romance linguistics (e.g., Lausberg 1966: 316, 323) assume or imply that they are indeed historically the 'same' phenomenon.[38] Closer scrutiny reveals some thought-provoking differences, however. In other Romance languages, Latin [kwi] or [kwe] become [ki] or [ke] but this change 'counterfeeds' PVFV, and is therefore clearly later than it, since the resulting [ki], [ke] do not undergo

---

[38] See also Varvaro's remarks (Varvaro 2004a: 88f. n. 46) on similar assumptions made by Mihăescu (1983).

Table 1.8. *Differential treatment of reflexes of [kw] in Italian and Romanian*

Latin [kw]	Italian [k]	Romanian [tʃ]	
QUAERERE	[k]*iedere*	[tʃ]*ere*	'ask for'
QUI	[k]*i*	[tʃ]*ine*	'who(?)'
AQUILAM	(a[g]*ila*)	a[tʃ]*eră*	'eagle'

Table 1.9. *Differential palatalizing effect of proto-Romance plural *-e in Italian and Romanian*

*ˈvakke 'cows'	> It. ˈvakke (*vacche*)	Ro. *ˈvatʃe > vatʃ (*vaci*)
*ˈlarge 'broad.$_{FPL}$'	> It. ˈlarge (*larghe*)	Ro. *ˈlarge > lardʒ (*largi*)

palatalization. In Romanian, in contrast, these same outcomes *do* undergo palatalization (Table 1.8).[39,40]

Another respect in which Romanian differs from Italo-Romance in the range of 'input' to PVFV involves the desinence -[e] of feminine plural nouns and adjectives.[41] In Italian this ending *never* triggers palatalization of preceding velars. Maiden (1996) argues that this is probably because the ending developed via a process -[as] > *-[ai] whose final stage, -[e], emerges only after PVFV has ceased to be productive in Italo-Romance. Yet the same ending, with the same origin, *always* triggers PVFV in Romanian (Table 1.9). Note that in Romanian feminine plural -[e] often subsequently became -[i] (then frequently losing its syllabic value altogether):

Finally, nearly all Romance languages systematically fail to present the expected palatalization of velars in the present subjunctive of first conjugation verbs, historically characterized by the desinence -[e]. For example It. [ˈkariki] *carichi* 'load$_{PRS.SBJV.SG}$' not **[ˈkaritʃi] *carici*, Sp. [ˈkarʝe] *cargue* not **[ˈkarχe] *carge*, the non-occurring forms being the expected output if palatalization had originally happened. This is a fact to whose significance we return later, but we should note that, in contrast, Romanian systematically does present the expected palatalization in the first conjugation present subjunctive (e.g., third person [iŋˈkartʃe] *încarce* not **[iŋˈkarke] *încarche*).

A possible interpretation of the foregoing facts is that PVFV applied in Romanian at a later historical stage than it did in Italo-Romance. This interpretation is supported by a series of observations, made a century ago, which the major manuals of historical Romance linguistics have

---

[39] For the *-ne* at the end of the Romanian form of 'who' in Table 1.8, see Maiden et al. (2021: 177).

[40] The modern standard Italian form *aquila* 'eagle' in Table 1.8, retaining the pronunciation [kw], may be a learnèd borrowing from Latin. The old Tuscan form *aghila*, given here, happens to show voicing of the velar as well as loss of the labial glide.

[41] In Romanian the feminine plural inflexional ending is also the ending of the feminine singular genitive-dative case-form.

frankly overlooked. In the 1920s Petar Skok (1926: 408) argued that a proper understanding of Balkan Romance palatalizations and their relation to PVFV elsewhere in the Romance world could only be gained by taking into account not only the purely linguistic details but also the historical circumstances in which the eastern Romance languages evolved, and the evidence of non-Romance languages with which they were in contact. Skok carefully documents Romance loans in south Slavonic, which took place during the period of Slav settlement along the Adriatic coast, and demonstrates the complete absence of palatalization in those loans. Skok's conclusion (as also suggested by the evidence of Dalmatian, discussed above) is that PVFV was absent on the Romance-speaking Adriatic littoral. After the arrival of the Slavs, according to Skok, the remaining nomadic Romance speakers of the interior were cut off from the urban linguistic models of the coast. Skok reaches the radical conclusion that Romanian palatalization is actually a post-sixth-century innovation *independent* of the PVFV that we see in 'western' Romance languages (Skok 1926: 409).

So was there one general Romance PVFV, or were there at least two independent PVFVs? Our purpose here is not to provide a 'right answer', but merely to show how our understanding of linguistic change (in this case, of a particular phonological change) may become far more nuanced if we carefully scrutinize not only the 'internal' linguistic details but also the 'external' historical facts. We do not have to accept either of the extreme positions (straightforward, monogenetic, almost pan-Romance, palatalization of velars vs fragmented, independent, polygenetic palatalizations occurring separately in the 'west' and the 'east'). One could perfectly well imagine a situation in which PVFV was, so to speak, 'in the air', with possibly more educated, and therefore perhaps linguistically more conservative, urban, speakers who tended not palatalize velars before front vowels, and less educated and more rustic ones who tended to do so. In fact, a scenario in which palatalization of velars was originally 'latent', with some parts of the population tending to produce it more than others, would perhaps help us better understand how it was ever possible for palatalization to fail to occur in medieval or modern 'western' Romance present subjunctives, mentioned earlier. Some examples are given in Table 1.10.[42]

In this case in 'western' Romance it is conventionally assumed (e.g., Penny 2002: 177 for Spanish) that regular PVFV at first took place, but that the resultant alternation was then removed from the present subjunctive as an effect of analogical levelling in favour of the velar alternant, the latter being by far predominant in the inflexional paradigm of the relevant verbs. Of course analogical levelling of the effects of palatal~velar alternations

---

[42] The only exceptions of which we are aware in any Romance language outside Romanian occur in old French (see Fouché 1967: 202).

Table 1.10. *Failure of expected palatalization of velar consonants in 'western' Romance first conjugation present subjunctives vs expected palatalization in Romanian*

	1SG	2SG	3SG	1PL	2PL	3PL
Portuguese *ro*[g]*e* 'ask'		*ro*[g]*es*	*ro*[g]*e*	*ro*[g]*emos*	*ro*[g]*eis*	*ro*[g]*em*
Spanish *to*[k]*e* 'touch'		*to*[k]*es*	*to*[k]*e*	*to*[k]*emos*	*to*[k]*éis*	*to*[k]*en*
Catalan *pa*[g]*i* 'pay'		*pa*[g]*is*	*pa*[g]*i*	*pa*[g]*em*	*pa*[g]*eu*	*pa*[g]*in*
Languedocien *to*[k]*e* 'touch'		*to*[k]*es*	*to*[k]*e*	*to*[k]*em*	*to*[k]*etz*	*to*[k]*en*
Italian *to*[kk]*i* 'touch'		*to*[kk]*i*	*to*[kk]*i*	*to*[kk]*iamo*	*to*[kk]*iate*	*to*[kk]*ino*
Romanian *ro*[g] 'ask'		*ro*[dʒ]*i*	*roa*[dʒ]*e*	*ru*[g]*ăm*	*ru*[g]*aţi*	*roa*[dʒ]*e*
to[k] 'chop'		*to*[tʃ]*i*	*toa*[tʃ]*e*	*to*[k]*ăm*	*to*[k]*aţi*	*toa*[tʃ]*e*

(and of many other kinds of alternation) are commonplace in the history of the Romance verb, but such levellings simply do not show anything like the sheer, absolute, exceptionlessness we see in the first conjugation. So complete is the lack of evidence for any original palatalization of velars in Romance first conjugation present subjunctives that Maiden (1992: 305 n. 21) actually implies that PVFV simply *never happened* in the first conjugation. It is undoubtedly plausible that analogical pressure played some role: after all, the relevant first conjugation verbs show the velar alternant in all forty-odd cells of their inflexional paradigm with the exception of just the six cells of the present subjunctive. But the utterly exceptionless rejection of the expected palatalization would make much more sense if we assumed that they took place in a linguistic world where palatalization of velars was still latent, a *tendency* in the linguistic system, and where the 'balance of power' between phonological pressure for the assimilation to take place and morphological pressure to maintain a one-to-one relationship between lexical meaning and the forms of the lexical root was very far from settled. In a memorable metaphor, Varvaro (2004c: 41) once likened the widespread yet still curiously 'patchy' and geographically sporadic emergence of another sound change (so-called *yeísmo*, whereby original [ʎ] > [j], in different varieties of Spanish), to an 'epidemic' in which a 'virus' is present throughout a community but only develops full-blown symptoms in some individuals (i.e., here and there, but not everywhere). Perhaps the initial situation with PVFV was the same. Let us put together all the comparative evidence from the history of PVFV: localized exceptions in areas that were by no means obviously isolated, evidence from loans that PVFV had not taken place in the early history of Balkan Romance; curious discrepancies between the input to PVFV in Romanian and other Romance languages; the remarkable wholesale failure of the expected PVFV to occur in one morphologically defined category. In this light, perhaps we should be thinking not of a discrete across-the-board sound change, but of a scenario much more similar to that postulated by Varvaro for Spanish *yeísmo*, such that in the early Romance world the sound change was possible, but nowhere firmly established and where norms lacking the palatalization still existed. The 'fuller picture', obtained by considering as many of the available facts as possible, certainly makes any notion of an abrupt and general transition from velars to their palatalized forms look simplistic.

We are hardly being original here in proposing what is, in effect, a 'variationist' approach to phonological change (or to language change more generally). The importance of such an approach in Romance linguistics is explored in far more detail in Section 30.2, to which readers are referred. The point here, rather, is that our minds should be open to the possibility that apparently very simple changes may have emerged in a situation of linguistic variation, and that careful scrutiny of the comparative-historical facts, even at a distance of centuries, may point us in just that direction.

1.3.3 When Does Phonological Conditioning of Morphological Alternation 'Stop'? Comparative Romance Evidence

It is usually easy to demonstrate that some alternation originally triggered by sound change has become 'morphologized': for example, once the relevant pattern of alternation is analogically extended outside the original phonological conditioning environment, so that its occurrence cannot be analysed as a phonological effect of that environment, or where there is abundant other evidence that the original triggering sound change is long defunct in the language.[43] But even indisputably morphologized alternations can still display a surprising sensitivity to phonological environment. Comparative scrutiny of dialectal variation in Romanian verb morphology brings to light a surprising situation, in which a change which is indisputable evidence for the morphologization of an alternation type reveals a residual sensitivity to phonological environment. In the inflexional paradigm of Romanian verbs, the velar~palatal alternation in second and third conjugation verbs is distributed in such a way that the velar alternant

---

[43] For further discussion and references, see for example Bybee (2001: 55, 96–98).

Table 1.11. *The distribution of velar alternants in the Romanian verb*

infinitive	gerund		present	subjunctive
lin[dʒ]e	lin[g]ând	1SG	lin[g]	lin[g]
		2SG	lin[dʒ]i	lin[dʒ]i
		3SG	lin[dʒ]e	lin[g]ă
		1PL	lin[dʒ]em	lin[dʒ]em
		2PL	lin[dʒ]eți	lin[dʒ]eți
		3PL	lin[g]	lin[g]ă

Table 1.12. *The Romanian velar~palatal alternation unique to* a fugi *'flee'*

infinitive	gerund		present	subjunctive
fu[dʒ]i	fu[dʒ]ind	1SG	fu[g]	fu[g]
		2SG	fu[dʒ]i	fu[dʒ]i
		3SG	fu[dʒ]e	fu[g]ă
		1PL	fu[dʒ]im	fu[dʒ]im
		2PL	fu[dʒ]iți	fu[dʒ]iți
		3PL	fu[g]	fu[g]ă

occurs just in the first person singular and third person plural present tense, in the third person of the subjunctive, and in the gerund. The distributional pattern of the velar is exactly correlated with historically non-palatalizing environments (i.e., with an original following non-front vowel). We may take the example of the verb *a linge* 'lick' (Table 1.11). Note that the vowel spelled *â* in standard Romanian is the high central [ɨ]; crucially, it is not a front vowel.

Dozens of Romanian second and third conjugation verbs follow this pattern. However, there happens to be only one *fourth* conjugation verb,[44] namely *a fugi* 'flee, run', which also displays the velar~palatal alternation. This verb shows exactly the same inflexional distributional pattern as in second and third conjugation verbs, but deviates from it specifically in respect of the gerund. Here, in the standard language, we find not the velar alternant as in second and third conjugation verbs, but instead the palatal alternant. This fact has an entirely straightforward historical phonological explanation: the fourth conjugation gerund ending is *-ind*, and therefore contains the environment for PVFV (Table 1.12).

What is the wider dialectal picture for the same verb? The data offered by the Romanian linguistic atlases offer a kind of 'chequer board' image in which one may find in one place the gerund type [fu'dʒind] with the

---

[44] That there is only one such fourth conjugation verb in modern Romanian is basically a historical accident.

expected palatal as in standard Romanian,[45] but in the next place the type [fuˈɟind] with the velar. That the velar alternant should appear in many dialects also in the gerund of *a fugi* is not surprising, given that, as we have seen, in all other Romanian verbs that have the velar~palatal alternation the velar also occurs in the gerund. But one thing is remarkably conspicuous by its absence: we find [fuˈdʒind] and we find [fuˈɟind] but we absolutely *never* find a perfectly conceivable – indeed expected – third alternative, namely [fuˈɟind], in which the velar would have been analogically extended on the analogical model of second and third conjugation verbs, but the characteristic gerund ending of the fourth conjugation *-ind* were nonetheless preserved. So the analogical introduction of [ɟ] always entails the parallel appearance of the ending -[ind]. There is absolutely no phonological impediment in Romanian – nor has there been for many centuries – to the existence of a potential **[fuˈɟind], in which the velar is followed by a front vowel: compare, for example, ModRo. *ghimp* [ɟimp] 'thorn', *ghete* [ˈɟete] 'boots', [kin] 'torture'. Nor, it may be added, is there any constraint against the reverse situation, where such a palatal is not followed by a front vowel: e.g., *geam* [dʒam] 'window', *magiun* [maˈdʒun] 'plum jam', *ciori* [tʃorʲ] 'crows', *deci* [detʃ] 'so' (the orthographic front vowels following the velars in these examples have a merely diacritic value). Yet, despite the lack of phonological obstacles to the contrary situation, the analogical generalization of [ɟ] is always and unfailingly accompanied by the selection of a non-fourth-conjugation gerund ending containing a non-front vowel, -[ɨnd] -*ând*.

The absolutely crucial point here is that the analogical change in the root allomorph *must* have chronologically preceded (or at least been simultaneous with) the replacement of the inflexional ending -[ind] by -[ɨnd]. One's first assumption may be that first the ending -[ind] was somehow replaced by -[ɨnd] and that only then was the velar alternant selected. This is essentially to say that the selection of the velar alternant is phonologically motivated, and it suggests that the alternation between the palatal affricate and the velar is actually conditioned by the phonological environment. But this analysis cannot be correct, since it would make *a fugi* the only fourth conjugation verb in which such a replacement of the gerund ending has ever taken place; no other fourth conjugation verb has a gerund ending -[ɨnd] (spelled -*ând*), and postulating such a change just to account for *fu*[ɟ] *ând* would be utterly ad hoc. In contrast, the analogical replacement of [dʒ] by [ɟ] is very clearly motivated morphologically: it is beyond doubt that the gerund type *fu*[ɟ]*ând* involves the analogical extension of a pattern of alternation whose current distribution is fundamentally *morphological, not phonological*, in nature. The extension is motivated by the fact that in all other

---

[45] The dialectal data may be directly observed in *ALRII* map 2153; *NALROltenia* map 924; *ALRRMunteniaDobrogea* map 543.

verbs with the relevant alternation, the velar alternant also occurs in the gerund. The change cannot be phonologically motivated because, *a priori*, fourth conjugation verbs have the ending *-ind*, and *a fugi* was, and firmly remains in all other respects, a fourth conjugation verb. Nonetheless, when the morphological change occurs, it actually brings with it the selection of a gerund ending containing the non-front vowel characteristic of non-fourth conjugation gerunds. Why? These facts suggests a residual sensitivity on the part of speakers to what is, in universal terms, clearly a more 'natural' environment for a velar alternant to occur in, given the availability of a choice between the alternants [dʒ] by [g]. The implication is that speakers prefer *fu*[g]*ând* over a potential and phonologically perfectly possible **fu[g]*ind* simply because the language provides two types of gerund ending and the former is simply the phonologically more natural possibility of the two. If this inference correct, then an indisputably morphological phenomenon, while not phonologically triggered, has not entirely broken free from phonological conditions on the distribution of the alternation.

In fact, Romanian is not the only Romance variety in which the diachronic behaviour of velar~palatal alternations in the gerund shows sensitivity of a clearly morphologized alternation to phonological environment – this time of a negative kind. The Italian [g]~[dʒ] alternation is clearly no longer triggered by a following front vowel. This can easily be demonstrated by medieval and modern examples such as *lun*[g]*i* ~ *lun*[g]*e* ('long' M/F.PL), [g]*iro* 'dormouse', [k]*iedere* 'ask', *par*[k]*i* 'parks', *pes*[k]*e* 'peaches', and significantly by old Italian present subjunctive forms such as *le*[gg]*i* 'read', *cres*[k]*i* 'grow'. The [g]~[dʒ] and [k]~[tʃ] alternations in old (and modern) Italian have a paradigmatic distribution such that the velar alternant occurs in the first person singular and third person plural present indicative and in most forms of the present subjunctive (see also Section 1.3.6). However, this distributional pattern is not limited to velar~palatal alternations, because other sets of alternants, of various origins, show the same alternation pattern. For example, in old Italian, the verbs *leggere* 'read', *morire* 'die', and *tenere* 'hold' (Table 1.13).

A much fuller account of the linguistic facts presented here will be found in Maiden (2018: 84–166). Note that the gerunds for the relevant class of verbs end in *-endo* and therefore contain a front vowel immediately following the root. The point of interest here is that in old Italian the three gerunds *faccendo* 'doing', *sappiendo* 'knowing', and *vegnendo* 'coming'[46] happen to show the same root allomorph as the present subjunctive and (according to verb), the first person singular present indicative and third person plural present indicative: 1SG.PRS.IND *faccio*, 3SG.PRS.SBJV *faccia*, GER *faccendo*; [1SG.PRS.IND *so*], 3SG.PRS.SBJV *sappia*, GER *sappiendo*;

---

[46] The modern forms (which already existed as well in old Italian) are *facendo, sapendo, venendo*.

Table 1.13. *Recurrent alternation pattern in old Italian verbs*

infinitive	gerund			present	subjunctive
le[dʤ]ere	le[dʤ]endo	1SG		le[gg]o	le[gg]a
		2SG		le[dʤ]i	le[gg]i
		3SG		le[dʤ]e	le[gg]a
		3PL		le[gg]ono	le[gg]ano
infinitive	gerund			present	subjunctive
mo[r]ire	mo[r]endo	1SG		muo[j]o	muo[j]a
		2SG		muo[r]i	muo[j]i
		3SG		muo[r]e	muo[j]a
		3PL		muo[j]ono	muo[j]ano
infinitive	gerund			present	subjunctive
te[n]ere	te[n]endo	1SG		te[ɲɲ]o	te[ɲɲ]a
		2SG		tie[n]i	te[ɲɲ]i
		3SG		tie[n]e	te[ɲɲ]a
		3PL		te[ɲɲ]ono	te[ɲɲ]ano

Table 1.14. *Sporadic analogical extension of L-pattern alternants into the gerund in old Italian*

INF	1SG.PRS.IND	3SG.PRS.SBJV	GERUND	
potere 'be able'	posso	possa	possendo	or *potendo*
vedere 'see'	veggio	veggia	veggendo	or *vedendo*
tenere 'hold'	tegno	tegna	tegnendo	or *tenendo*
piacere 'please'	piaccio	piaccia	piaccendo	or *piacendo*
avere 'have'	ho	abbia	abbiendo	or *avendo*
volere 'want'	voglio	voglia	vogliendo	or *volendo*

1SG.PRS.IND *vegno*, 3SG.PRS.SBJV *vegna*, GER *vegnendo*. This paradigmatic distribution is exceptional from a synchronic morphological point of view, but it is attributable to a regular historical phonological change operating specifically in these verbs. These gerunds then served as an analogical model whereby many other verbs, albeit only occasionally and variably, extended their present subjunctive alternant into the gerund (Table 1.14).

Yet there is one class of verbs that never participates in this analogy,[47] namely those with velar~palatal alternants (Table 1.15). The lack of velar alternants in the gerund seems impossible to explain in purely morphological terms: other verbs with similarly distributed alternants readily

---

[47] We base the claim that such forms *never* occur on the observation that the *Opera del Vocabolario Italiano* (*OVI*) online database of thirteenth- and fourteenth-century Italo-Romance texts does not yield any such gerunds for verbs with root-final velars, whereas gerunds of the other kinds are amply attested there. See also Vanelli (2010: 1467f.).

Table 1.15. *Absence of extension of L-pattern velar alternants into the old Italian gerund*

INF	1SG.PRS.IND	3SG.PRS.SBJV	GERUND
pian[dʒ]*ere* 'weep'	*pian*[g]*o*	*pian*[g]*a*	*pian*[dʒ]*endo* never **pian[g]*endo*
dire 'say'	*di*[k]*o*	*di*[k]*a*	*di*[tʃ]*endo* never **di[k]*endo*
cre[ʃ]*ere* 'grow'	*cre*[sk]*o*	*cre*[sk]*a*	*cre*[ʃ]*endo* never **cre[sk]*endo*

participate in the analogy. Nor can a purely phonological explanation hold water, since, as we have seen, there is no constraint against velars before front vowels in Italian. Rather, we seem to be in the presence of something more nuanced and complex: a tentative, and ultimately ephemeral, morphological innovation seems to have been effectively 'deterred' by the fact that the result would have been the replacement of a palatal alternant by a velar alternant in a phonological environment in which the palatal seems more 'natural' (as witness the very fact that in Romance, and cross-linguistically, velars tend to palatalize before front vowels). And there are perhaps echoes here of an observation that we made earlier concerning the notable failure of otherwise general PVFV to occur in Romance present subjunctives, except that in that case it is almost as if a tentative incipient sound change was deflected by morphological pressure within the inflexional system of the first conjugation.

There have been periods in the history of linguistic theory when morphology has effectively been evicted from it altogether. A great deal of structure in morphology, and especially the type of paradigmatic alternation discussed above, originates in sound change, and the analysis of such phenomena has often been gravely distorted by what may be termed a 'phonologizing bias', the belief that they should be treated as phonologically conditioned even in synchrony, especially where the original conditioning environment survived at least vestigially. Many linguists, in reaction to this tendency,[48] have devoted much energy to asserting the truly morphological nature of allegedly phonological phenomena, and one example of this might be Maiden (2009b). Maiden there argues against attempts by Burzio (2004) to force a synchronic phonological analysis of the modern Italian facts including velar~palatal alternations, sometimes by what was, as Maiden avers, the illegitimate resurrection of long dead phonological conditioning environments. However, data of the kind cited above from old Italian gerunds suggests that a properly comparative and historical perspective of the facts from the velar~palatal alternations make the case for a more nuanced and less polarized theoretical stance, in which some role can

---

[48] For a discussion of many of the issues see, e.g., Bybee (2001).

be accorded to phonological conditioning while also recognizing that alternations may be fundamentally morphologized. For a further review of these issues, see Maiden (2013: 31–38).

1.3.4 When Does the Morphologization of a Sound Change 'Start'? Comparative Romance Evidence

The 'overlapping' nature of the transition from phonological causation to morphologization of alternation is apparent from other comparative Romance data. These suggest that speakers begin to associate the alternations created by sound change with the marking of morphosyntactic distinctions at a surprisingly early stage. Clear illustrations of this claim from the history of the Romance languages are provided by two phenomena which, while not directly a matter of palatalization, are in different ways related to it. We saw in Table 1.4 the typical pattern of allomorphy produced by PVFV, such that a velar alternant survives in the first person singular and third person plural of the present, alternating with a palatalized root-final consonant in the remainder of the paradigm. However, many of the relevant verbs, such as *a linge* 'lick', have past participles, supines, preterites, and pluperfects in root-final -s (Table 1.16).

The past participle, supine, preterite, and plurperfect in -s is a characteristic of a great many second and third conjugation verbs, not merely those with velar-palatal alternations. Thus standard Romanian *a tunde* 'shear' (Table 1.17).

Table 1.16. *Root-final -s in verbs which also have velar~palatal alternations*

infinitive		present	subjunctive	
lin[dʒ]e	1SG	lin[g]	lin[g]	
	2SG	lin[dʒ]i	lin[dʒ]i	
	3SG	lin[dʒ]e	lin[g]ă	
	3PL	lin[g]	lin[g]ă	
past participle/supine			preterite	pluperfect
lin[s]		3SG	lin[s]e	lin[s]ese

Table 1.17. *Root-final -s in verbs which also have roots ending in dentals*

infinitive		present	subjunctive	
tunde	1SG	tund	tund	
	2SG	tunzi	tunzi	
	3SG	tunde	tundă	
	3PL	tund	tundă	
past participle/supine			preterite	pluperfect
tun[s]		3SG	tun[s]e	tun[s]ese

Table 1.18. *Introduction of root-final velars into verbs in root-final [d] (here [de] > [ɟe]) in Oltenian*

	present	subjunctive
1SG	tũŋg	tũŋg
2SG	tũnz	tũnz
3SG	'tũɲe	'tũŋgə
3PL	tũŋg	'tũŋgə
past participle (etc.)		tũns

In some dialects, however, the verb *tunde* (among others) has been subject to an analogical change such that the root-final [d] has been analogically replaced by [g] in certain parts of the paradigm. The reasons for this kind of replacement are considered in detail in Maiden (2011b) but, very briefly, the fact that both verbs like *a tunde* and those like *a linge* share past participles, preterites, and pluperfects in [s] seems to have facilitated an analogical change such that *a tunde* follows *a linge* in acquiring root-final [g] in in the gerund, in the first person singular and third person plural present, and in the third person subjunctive. An example from the Oltenian dialect of Godineşti (*NALROltenia* point 942) is in Table 1.18.

What is of particular theoretical interest here, however, is the fact that the original nasal [n] has been replaced by velar [ŋ] wherever [g] has replaced root-final [d] in *a tunde*. At first glance this looks utterly uninteresting, indeed trivial. It is, after all, a wholly natural phonetic process of assimilation of a nasal to the position of articulation of an immediately following consonant; it is a banal phonetic phenomenon and one repeatedly observed across the world's languages. Yet a comparative perspective on the data provided by the Oltenian linguistic atlas for this verb holds a major surprise. As described in more detail in Maiden (2009a; 2011b), where the analogical [g] was introduced there has, in many localities, subsequently been a counter-reaction such that the etymologically 'correct' dental has been restored and has ousted the analogically introduced [g]. Yet the Oltenian linguistic atlas shows that there are localities in north-eastern Oltenia (e.g., point 935 Dobriţa) in which, in the third person subjunctive of *a tunde*, the replacement of [g] by [d] has not entrained the replacement of the allophone [ŋ] by the allophone [n], so that what we find is not expected **'tũndə, but actually 'tũŋdə, with a highly marked sequence of a velar nasal followed by dental consonant. This development is so unlikely, given our normal assumptions about the phonetic behaviour of preconsonantal nasals, that one might suspect a mishearing on the part of the investigator, or even a banal misprint in the linguistic atlas where the data appear. It is important to emphasize, therefore, that this is not observed just once, in one locality: the atlas presents the morphology of this verb for multiple localities in Oltenia, and in no less than *nine separate places*, from different informants, the exact same unexpected result was obtained. The fact that the evidence is repeated independently gives us confidence in saying that we are in the presence of something that, however unusual, is real.

The explanation of what we observe is in one respect quite obvious: the continued presence of the velar nasal clearly reflects the earlier presence of [g]. The distribution of that velar was clearly morphologized, in that it was associated with a morphosyntactically specified set of paradigm cells. Yet the purely allophonic velar nasal survives in the relevant paradigm cells even after its phonological conditioner (the velar [g]) has been replaced. That this 'allophone' [ŋ] survives in the phonologically quite unnatural environment of a following dental is clear proof that it, too, had become 'morphologized', and had been associated directly with the feature specification 'third person subjunctive'. Morphology has, so to speak, been 'snatched from the jaws of phonology', and a distribution which seemed exquisitely and naturally dependent on phonological environment turns out to be quite 'unnatural' and arbitrary, having become associated with a morphosyntactic context. The relevant dialects contain many other cases where the [n]~[ŋ] alternation remains correlated, in the verb and elsewhere, with the difference between non-velar and velar environments, e.g., Dobriţa third person subjunctive [ˈplıŋɡə] 'weep' vs present [ˈplındʒe] 'he weeps'. On the evidence of the [ˈtũŋdə] type in the same dialect, we are bound to suspect that the [ŋ] of subjunctive [ˈplıŋɡə] is already a morphologized marker of subjunctive there too. In short, the detailed comparative-historical perspective provided by, for example, a linguistic atlas can offer clear evidence that even 'low level', allophonic and apparently purely phonetically-conditioned alternations may become morphologized.

The case of the Oltenian morphologization of nasal assimilation before velars is not the only one in which comparative Romance dialectology has offered insights into the relation between phonological conditioning of alternation and the morphologization of alternants. 'Metaphony' is a phenomenon attested in the history of many Romance languages, and extensively attested in Italo-Romance, whereby an unstressed (and usually word-final) high vowel ([i] or [u]) triggers assimilatory raising of a preceding stressed vowel. In Italo-Romance varieties the potential input to metaphony typically includes stressed high mid vowels ([e] and [o]), stressed low mid vowels ([ɛ] and [ɔ]), and stressed [a]. The input to metaphony is regionally variable: whereas in most dialects the high and low mid vowels undergo the assimilation, metaphony of stressed [a] is much rarer. The output of metaphony is also variable. The 'teleology' of a phonological assimilation is naturally the minimization of the phonological distance between input and conditioning environment, so there is a sense in which the most 'natural' outcome of metaphony would be the raising of *all* stressed vowels to the height position of the conditioning vowels unstressed [i] and [u]. This never happens: stressed [e] and [u] are indeed raised, respectively, to [i] and [u]. But the low mid vowels [ɛ] and [ɔ] show two kinds of metaphonic outcome, either as the diphthongs [je] and [wo] or as raising to [e] and [o],[49] while metaphony of [a], when it occurs, usually yields raising (and fronting) to [ɛ] or [e]. In short, metaphony of non-high vowels yields only a *partial* adjustment towards the height position of the conditioning vowels.

The foregoing facts are amply illustrated in manuals of Italo-Romance historical linguistics (e.g., Rohlfs 1966). Yet there is an intriguing type of exception to them found, principally,[50] in central and southern Italian dialects of Lazio, Marche, Abruzzo, Molise, and Puglia. This is a phenomenon which, until recently, had gone all but unnoticed, and whose significance only becomes apparent through a properly comparative survey of the linguistic atlases and by systematic scrutiny of descriptive studies of individual dialects. These exceptions are constituted by the fact that, sporadically but over a wide range of dialects, *in the verb and only in the verb, the degree of raising produced by metaphonic raising, and the range of input to metaphonic raising, is greater than in any other part of the grammar*. Before we address the structural details, it is worth pointing out how scattered and elusive the relevant data are. So much so that, for example, they escape mention even by Rohlfs in his magisterial surveys of Italo-Romance phonology and morphology (Rohlfs 1966; 1968). The first allusion to them of which we are aware occurs however in Merlo (1909: 77f.), presented again in Merlo (1922: 13, 15, 19, 20), who mentions what he regards as a 'minor disturbance due to analogy' in some Lazio dialects such as that of La Cervara where we find that in the verb, and only in the verb, the metaphonic output of low mid vowels is not the otherwise regular [e] and [o] (e.g., SG [ˈpɛde] 'foot' – PL [ˈpedi], SG [ˈɛnte] 'tooth' – PL [ˈenti], FSG [ˈbbɔna] 'good' – MPL [ˈbboni], FSG [ˈmɔrta] 'dead' – MPL [ˈmorti]), but the output expected for higher input vowels (i.e., for the inputs [e] and [o]), namely [i] and [u]). Thus the present indicative forms of some verbs in stressed low mid vowels (Table 1.19).

Merlo (1909: 77f.) believes that such forms have been created on the analogy of verbs that contain high vowels and therefore have regular metaphonic alternants [i] and [u], such as 1SG [ˈmeno] 'beat' ~ 2SG [ˈmini], or 1SG [ˈsposo] 'marry' ~ 2SG [ˈspusi]. Such an analysis is much more problematic than Merlo appears to think, but to understand why appeal purely to morphological analogy is inadequate, a much broader comparative perspective is instructive. That perspective is difficult to achieve, because there is no dialect in which *hypermetaphony* (the label which Maiden 1991 applied to this phenomenon) applies without exceptions, so

---

[49] The historical relation between these two outcomes is controversial (see, e.g., Maiden 2016b), but not immediately relevant here.

[50] As Maiden (1991: 180) points out, there are similar developments in some northern Italo-Romance dialects, but we will concentrate here on central-southern Italo-Romance varieties. We will focus on the phenomenon as it is manifest in lexical roots of verbs but, as Maiden (1991) shows, the thematic vowel [a] can also be affected and, where it is affected, this is often in the absence of any other metaphony of [a].

Table 1.19. *Exceptional effects of metaphony on mid vowels in the present tense of the verb in La Cervara*

1SG	ˈlɛo 'lift'	ˈpɛrdo 'lose'	ˈsɛnto 'feel'	ˈtrɔo 'find'	ˈkɔtʃo 'cook'	ˈmɔro 'die'
2SG	**ˈlii** *not* **ˈlei	**ˈpirdi** *not* **ˈperdi	**ˈsinti** *not* **ˈsenti	**ˈtrui** *not* **ˈtroi	**ˈkutʃi** *not* **ˈkotʃi	**ˈmuri** *not* **ˈmori
3SG	ˈlɛa	ˈpɛrde	ˈsɛnte	ˈtrɔa	ˈkɔtʃe	ˈmɔre
3PL	ˈlɛanu	**ˈpirdu** *not* **ˈperdu	**ˈsintu** *not* **ˈsentu	ˈtrɔanu	**ˈkutʃu** *not* **ˈkotʃu	**ˈmuru** *not* **ˈmoru

the evidence is mainly scattered and fragmentary. This means that careful sifting through the available sources is needed in order to obtain historical insights. For an overview of the relevant descriptive sources (including the two major linguistic atlases, the *AIS* and the *ALI*, and some 20 independent descriptions of different dialects of central Italy), and exemplification of how they can be assembled in order to gain a deeper historical insight into the emergence of hypermetaphony, see for example Maiden (1991: 181–84). The linguistic atlases are the obvious first port of call in trying to establish the extent and nature of hypermetaphony, but even then the evidence is hard to spot. For example, and limiting ourselves here (for reasons of space) just to cases of metaphony of the low mid back vowel [ɔ], we may compare examples of regular metaphony of this vowel in non-verb forms (e.g., *AIS* maps 76 MPL *morti* 'dead'; 184 FSG *grossa*, MPL *grossi* 'large'; 710 FSG *buona*, MPL *buoni* 'good'),[51] with verb forms that have the potential to display hypermetaphony: thus, *AIS* map 649/51 2SG.IMP vs 2SG.PRS.IND of *dormire* 'sleep'), 1683 (3SG.PRS.IND vs 2SG.PRS.IND of *trovare* 'find'), 1694 (3SG.PRS.IND vs 2SG.PRS.IND of *potere* 'be able'), 1696 (3SG.PRS.IND vs 2SG.PRS.IND of *morire* 'die'). The masculine plural forms in Table 1.20(a),[52] and the second person singular forms in Table 1.20(b), ended historically -i, and their vowels were therefore subject to metaphony.

The most important thing that the various dialectological sources, *taken together*, bring to light is that in the verb we can have not only a different kind of metaphonic output from that otherwise expected, but even the presence of metaphony where none would be expected at all. At issue here is principally metaphony of stressed [a]. In Agnone (Ziccardi 1910) metaphony of [a] is historically triggered only by reflexes of historically underlying unstressed [i], never by historically underlying unstressed [u]. Moreover, the

---

[51] In many Romance varieties, such as Italian, the adjective meaning 'dead' is also the past participle of the verb 'die'. Hypermetaphony is never observed, however, in past participles, whose morphological behaviour is generally like that of adjectives.
[52] The same pattern of alternation illustrated in Table 1.20(a) for adjectives is found in nouns.

Table 1.20. *Ordinary metaphony of low mid vowels vs hypermetaphony: examples from the AIS*

(a) Regular metaphony ([ɔ] > [o]) in adjectives

	FSG MPL	FSG MPL	MPL
Capestrano	'bɔna 'boni	'grɔssa gross	
Trasacco		'rɔssa 'rossa	'mortə
Sonnino		'rɔssa 'rosso	'morte
S.Giovanni Rotondo	'bɔnə 'bonə	'grɔssə 'grossə	'mortə

(b) Hypermetaphony ([ɔ] > [u]) in some verbs

	3SG 2SG	3SG 2SG	3SG 2SG	3SG 2SG
Capestrano		pɔ pu		'dɔrmə durmə
Trasacco				'dɔrmə durmə
Sonnino	'trɔva 'trove	pɔ po	'mɔre mure	'dɔrme durmə
S.Giovanni Rotondo	'trɔva truvə	pɔ pu	'mɔrə murə	'dɔrmə durmə

Table 1.21. *Metaphony of [a] in Agnone*

SG	PL
'a.sənə (< *'a.se.nu) 'donkey'	'ɛ.sə.nə (< *'a.se.ni)
'kwan.də (< *'kwan.tu) 'how much'	'bɛf.fə (< *'baf.fi) 'moustache'
ju.'kẹa.tə (< *'jo.'ka.tu) 'played'	sul.'dje.tə (< *'sol.'dat.i) 'soldiers'

regular output of metaphony of [a] is differentiated according to phonological environment: in closed syllables and in proparoxytones it yields [ɛ] while in open syllables it yields the diphthong [je] (Table 1.21).

However, in the verb, and only in the verb, we find that the output of metaphony of [a] in closed syllables is systematically that expected in open, rather than closed, syllables, namely [je]. It should be added that [je] is also the regular output of metaphony of the low mid vowel [ɛ] (e.g., 2SG.PRS 'sjendə < *'sɛnti 'feel; hear'). The fact that in this dialect metaphony of [a] is never triggered by unstressed [u] would also lead us to expect that metaphony of [a] would never occur in verbs whose third person plural present ended historically in *-u(no); but in Agnone metaphony does occur in just such verb forms (Table 1.22).[53]

The situation in the dialect of Arpino (Lazio; Parodi 1892: 300) is even more dramatic. There is no metaphony of [a] at all here, *except in the verb*: e.g., 1SG.PRS.IND 'mannə 'send' (< *'mando) ~ 2SG.PRS.IND 'mjennə

---

[53] Given the broadly expository nature of this presentation, we cannot here enter into finer details of analysis. Suffice it to say that there are grounds for scepticism about Ziccardi's suggestion (1910: 431) that such forms in the third person plural are purely analogical (and therefore independent of phonological conditioning). Rather, there is comparative evidence to suggest that third person plural metaphony of [a] occurs only where there was an original final unstressed [u].

Table 1.22. *Metaphony of [a] in the verb in Agnone*

1SG	ˈpartə 'leave'	< *ˈparto	ˈkandə 'sing'	< *ˈkanto
2SG	ˈpjertə (not **ˈpɛrtə)	< *ˈparti	ˈkjendə	< *ˈkanti
3SG	ˈpartə	< *ˈparte	ˈkandə	< *ˈkanta
3PL	ˈpjertənə (not **ˈpartənə)	< *ˈpartuno	ˈkandənə	< *ˈkantano

(< *ˈmandi) vs SG ˈannə 'year' (< *ˈannu) ~ PL ˈannə (< *ˈanni).[54] The same situation, with metaphony of stressed [a] found only in the verb, is repeated in the dialect of Martinsicuro (Mastrangelo Latini 1976) on the Abruzzo/Marche border. In some dialects (e.g., of the Gargano peninsula, or Veroli in Lazio) a similar situation is found for stressed [ɔ]: this vowel is either not subject to metaphony at all, or not subject to metaphony by *-u in closed syllables, but in the verb, and only there, this vowel undergoes hypermetaphony in metaphonizing environments (see Maiden 1991: 185).

The implication of these facts is remarkable. What would we say about hypermetaphony if, instead of being rigidly confined to the verb, it occurred more or less sporadically across the lexicon, without morphologically defined restrictions? Surely we would say that it is an unsurprising and wholly *natural* phonetic phenomenon?[55] And that is exactly what it is. It is natural that an assimilatory process should *assimilate*, that it should yield outputs maximally close, phonologically, to the conditioning environment. It is equally natural that the assimilation should apply to the maximum possible range of phonological inputs, that it should bring all more open vowels closer to the assimilating vowels. Hypermetaphony is a paradox: a phonetically natural phenomenon somehow confined to a purely morphological environment.

Some linguists, for example already Merlo (1909: 77f.), might react to hypermetaphony by trying to argue that it is, in fact, essentially a matter of morphological analogy. Merlo thinks that the hypermetaphonic type 1SG [ˈpɛrdo] 'lose' ~ 2SG [ˈpirdi], 1SG [ˈmɔro] 'die' ~ 2SG [ˈmuri], is analogically modelled on regular metaphonic alternation in verbs with high mid vowels, such as 1SG [ˈmeno] 'beat' ~ 2SG [ˈmini], 1SG [ˈsposo] 'marry' ~ 2SG [ˈspusi]. But such an analysis is problematic because [ˈmeno] ~ [ˈmini], [ˈsposo] ~ [ˈspusi] involve a *different alternation* from [ɛ] ~ [i], [ɔ] ~ [u], and there is simply no precedent in the language for the novel alternation [ɛ] ~ [i], [ɔ] ~ [u]. One might respond that there *is* a precedent insofar as [i] or [u] alternate in the inflexional paradigm with other stressed vowels. But in this case one would predict that either of these two metaphonic vowels could come to alternate

---

[54] Parodi (1892) and Mastrangelo Latini (1976) view this situation as a *remnant* of once more widespread metaphony of [a]. But there is no good reason to take this view: see Maiden (1991: 184) and, more generally, Maiden (1987).

[55] Perhaps one that was diffusing gradually through the lexicon.

with *any* other vowel: why not [ˈparto] 'leave' ~ **[ˈpurti] or [ˈdɔrmo] 'sleep' ~ **[ˈdirmi]? And why should only the metaphonic alternants [i] and [u], and not also [e] and [o], alternate in this way? Why not [ˈparto] 'leave' ~ **[ˈporti] or [ˈdɔrmo] 'sleep' ~ **[ˈdermi]? If Merlo's hypothesis does not seem at first glance implausible, it is because of an assumption that he does not explicitly state, namely that the supposed analogy applies to the two input vowels, [ɛ] and [ɔ], which are those *phonetically most similar* to [e] and [o] and for which [i] and [u] would actually be quite 'natural' phonological outputs of metaphony.[56] Merlo's analysis tacitly acknowledges the 'phoneticity' of the phenomenon. If we then take all the comparative evidence for hypermetaphony into account, and particularly the propensity of stressed [a] to undergo metaphony in the verb but not outside the verb, appeals to morphological analogy seem wholly inadequate. Rather, the maximal comparative-historical perspective suggests, quite simply, that the phonetic process of metaphony has a particular propensity to occur within the inflexional paradigm of the verb. Hypermetaphony is simply a manifestation of the phonetic process of metaphony which is also exquisitely sensitive to a morphologically specified context, that of the verb. How this is to be explained remains moot: the point is that the facts taken together show us that something needs explaining. For example, Maiden (1991: 232–45) surmises that the inflexional paradigm of finite verb forms is generally 'vulnerable' to incipient sound change in the Romance languages,[57] precisely because the inflexional paradigms of Romance verbs comprise multiple word forms which may be differentiated from each other by patterns of sometimes extreme allomorphy which may involve considerable phonological distance between alternants, whereas nouns and adjectives characteristically show rather little root allomorphy (usually only for number and/or gender). Maiden speculates that this characteristic 'looseness' of the verb in some way licensed speakers to 'unleash' latent phonological tendencies that were liable to produce more extreme forms of allomorphy.[58] Maiden's

---

[56] An alternative analysis of the data presented in Table 1.20 might say that hypermetaphony is purely phonological and that the local output of metaphony of low mid vowels [ɛ] and [ɔ], namely [e] and [o], simply 'feeds' metaphony of high mid vowels, in that it undergoes further raising to [i] and [u]. Such an analysis could not escape that hard morphological fact that hypermetaphony is restricted to the verb and therefore irreducibly morphological. Nor would it be able to explain those cases where vowels that do not otherwise undergo metaphony actually do so just in the verb, or the existence of hypermetaphony in dialects where the output of metaphony of low mid vowels is not [e] and [o] but rather a diphthong (on metaphonic diphthongs see Maiden 2016b).

[57] Past participles, although part of the inflexional paradigm of the Romance verb, have inflexional properties of adjectives and, like other adjectives, never show hypermetaphony. Other non-finite forms of the verb (gerund, infinitive) do not show generally the conditioning environment for metaphony.

[58] Contrast, for example, modern Italian, where the inflexional paradigms of nouns and adjectives contain at most four different word forms and where allomorphy in the root is rare (e.g., MSG *alto* 'high', FSG *alta*, MPL *alti*, FPL *alte*), and verbs —which may display around 40 different word-forms, sometimes with idiosyncratic kinds of root-alternation (for example, 3SG.PRS.IND *vale* 'is worth', 3SG.PRS.SBJV *valga*, 3SG.FUT *varrà*, 3SG.PST.PFV *valse* or 3SG.PRS.IND *ha* 'has', 3SG.PRS.SBJV *abbia*, 3SG.FUT *avrà*, 3SG.PST.PFV *ebbe*). It is also noticeable that suppletion (see Chapter 12, this

idea is a surmise whose plausibility could probably only be tested by typological comparison: the question one would need to ask is whether it is the case cross-linguistically, in language whose word-classes show very different degrees of morphological variation, whether the more morphologically varied classes also show systematic susceptibility to phonological innovation.[59] The crucial point here is that careful scrutiny of geolinguistic variation in the Italo-Romance data suggest that morphologization and the processes of phonological change are not mutually exclusive but may overlap and interact from the very inception of a sound change.[60] And this in turn should lead us to ask why.

1.3.5 'Standard Language Bias' in Historical Linguistic Analysis

Another kind of deviation from the historically predicted morphological effects of palatalization occurs in old Romanian. In some respects it may seem quite minor, indeed it is rarely commented on at all, but a recent attempt to account for it happens to exemplify a distorting perspective on the analysis of language change which, in fact, can be observed in a number of other respects in Romance linguists (and no doubt beyond). There are times when Romance linguistics can provide models of what *not* to do in historical linguistics!

Latin verbs of the fourth conjugation (with a few other verbs of the third conjugation) had third person plural present indicative forms that ended in -IUNT. The -I- of such forms would have become [j] in early Romance and this [j] should, in turn, automatically have triggered palatalization of a preceding consonant. A similar development would have been expected to occur in the first person singular present indicative and throughout the present subjunctive (the relevant changes are discussed and illustrated in Section 1.3.1). Yet comparison of Romanian with Italian yields a surprise: both languages historically duly display the expected effects of palatalization in the first person singular present indicative and in the present subjunctive, but Romanian systematically deviates from Italian in

---

volume) in Romance languages is found almost exclusively in verbs, and scarcely ever in nouns and adjectives. See also Maiden (2018: 296–300) for the radically different morphological nature of Romance nouns and adjectives as opposed to verbs.

[59] Readers may sense an apparent contradiction with another claim by Maiden, mentioned in Section 1.3.2, that the verb may have been *resistant* to an incipient sound change, namely the palatalization of velars. In fact, the two claims are mutually reinforcing, although we do not have space here to go into details (for which see Maiden 2018: 277–83). Briefly, the verb forms at issue are first conjugation present subjunctives, and Maiden argues that first conjugation verbs are distinguished from other conjugation classes precisely by their relative lack of root allomorphy (and especially consonantal allomorphy), rather as nouns and adjectives are distinguished overall from verbs by lack of root allomorphy. So the fundamental claim is that sound changes may be sensitive to contrasting degrees of characteristic allomorphy.

[60] The issue continues to preoccupy synchronic linguists working from an experimental perspective, as well. See, for example, Strycharczuk and Scobbie (2016).

Table 1.23. *Presence in old Italian vs absence in old Romanian of expected palatalization in the third person plural present indicative*

	Latin	old Italian	palatalized?	old Romanian	palatalized?
1SG.PRS.IND	UENIO	*vegno* 'come'	yes	*viu* 'come'	yes
3SG.PRS.IND	UENIT	*viene*	no	*vine*	no
3PL.PRS.IND	UENIUNT	*vegnono*	yes	*vin*	no
3SG.PRS.SBJV	UENIAT	*vegna*	yes	*vie*	yes
	Latin	old Italian	palatalized?	old Romanian	palatalized?
1SG.PRS.IND	SALIO	*saglio* 'go up'	yes	*saiu* 'jump'	yes
3SG.PRS.IND	SALIT	*sale*	no	*sare*	no
3PL.PRS.IND	SALIUNT	*sagliono*	yes	*sar*	no
3SG.PRS.SBJV	SALIAT	*saglia*	yes	*saie*	yes

the third person plural present indicative by not showing the expected effect of palatalization. As Table 1.23 shows, unlike old Italian,[61] old Romanian third person plural present indicatives pattern with (for example) the unpalatalized third person singular:

Our concern here is not to identify the particular reason for the unexpected behaviour observed in Romanian,[62] but to underscore the perils for reliable linguistic reconstruction of a perspective which ignores the full range of comparative-historical data. So long as we limit ourselves to comparing these two standard Romance languages (Italian and Romanian), Italian seems 'well-behaved', taking into account etymology and the expected regularity of sound change, while Romanian appears to be a deviant requiring an explanation specific to it. It seems evident, then, that this explanation should be sought in some circumstance peculiar to Romanian, and an obvious candidate is language contact. Indeed, in the Slavonic variety with which Romanian is known to have been in contact during the Middle Ages ('middle Bulgarian') a similar pattern of alternation can be shown to have existed,[63] with an alternant (caused by a historically underlying yod) present in the first person singular present but absent for regular historical phonological reasons in the third person plural of the present tense. Details of the relevant middle Bulgarian patterns and their history will be found in Elson (2017: 879). Since Italian, in contrast, has never had any significant contact with Slavonic, the apparently deviant behaviour of Romanian seems plausibly explicable by a particular historical fact, contact with Slavonic, which is absent from the history of Italian and distinctive of Romanian alone.

---

[61] The relevant effects are best illustrated from older forms of these standard languages. As mentioned in Section 1.3.1, they have been complicated or effaced by analogical changes in the more recent history.
[62] For an attempt to do this, at least in part, see Maiden (2020).
[63] But not, overall, an identical one given that, for example, Slavonic has no present subjunctive.

Such an explanation has indeed been proposed,[64] and at first sight it may appear an attractively elegant one. There is, after all, abundant evidence of Slavonic influence on Romanian morphology – although, it must be said, in the realm of derivational, not inflexional, morphology (see Maiden 2021). But it is an explanation which begins to deflate just as soon as one begins to consider the facts from an adequately comparative perspective. The first question any historical linguist should ask of any proposed explanation for a particular language, is 'How do the same historically underlying structures play out in all the other, cognate, varieties to which we have access?' The plausibility of any proposed historical explanation stands or falls on the comparative evidence. In the case at hand a wealth of relevant dialectal data from non-standard varieties is available, and we are bound to ask what they tell us. The information regarding the fate of the expected palatalization in third person plurals from the dialects of Romania and from Romanian's sister Daco-Romance varieties does indeed support (or at least does not contradict) what we see in (old) Romanian. The problem is comparison of Romanian, or more broadly Daco-Romance, with just 'Italian'. 'Italian' may today be the national standard language of Italy, but it is essentially the continuant of the medieval dialect of Florence – it is merely one of thousands of different 'Italo-Romance' dialects, and we cannot legitimately take it as a proxy for the vastly varied Italo-Romance domain. We need to ask how the other Italo-Romance dialects behave with respect to the third person plural morphology at issue, if we are to make any valid comparison with Romanian.

Even a glance at the Italian linguistic atlases begins to make us see both 'Italian' and Romanian in a different light. The *Sprach- und Sachatlas Italiens und der Südschweiz* (*AIS*) has several maps or plates providing information on the relevant third person plural forms (e.g., AIS 1661, 1691, 1695, 1696, 1699), and they contain a surprise. In most parts of Italy for which an answer is discernible,[65] notably the centre and south, the relevant third person plural present indicatives turn out to behave *exactly as they do in Romanian*: there is no palatalization, even though the effects of the expected palatalization (or allomorphs reflecting the presence of original palatal allomorphs, see, e.g., Maiden 2011a: 236–40) are firmly present in the first person singular present indicative. Table 1.24 gives the example of the verb COME from localities in central and southern Italy, and compares it with Romanian.

This picture, showing (original) palatalization in the first person singular but not in the third person plural, is faithfully confirmed by other linguistic

---

[64] See Elson (2017: 889f.).
[65] In some areas, especially the north, phonological or morphological changes have simply obscured the historically underlying developments.

Table 1.24. *Non-palatalized reflexes of Latin 3PL UENIUNT 'come' vs reflexes of (original) palatalization in 1SG UENIO 'come' in some central and southern Italian dialects* (AIS)

	1SG.PRS	3PL.PRS
Scanno, Abruzzo	ˈvjeŋgə	ˈvjeːnənə
Trevico, Campania	vɛŋk	ˈvjennə
Vernole, Puglia	ˈɛɲu	ˈɛːnune
San Chirico Raparo, Basilicata	ˈvɛɲgu	ˈvjɛːninu
Mistretta, Sicily	viˈeɲu	viˈeːnu
old Romanian	*viu*	*vinu*

atlases (e.g., ALI map 1695) and by an abundance of monographic and journal studies of individual Italo-Romance dialects (see Maiden 2020; 2021 for more details). In fact, with the exception of Italian and some other dialects of central Italy, in the overwhelming majority not just of Italo-Romance, but of Romance languages for which it is possible to have an answer, the position turns out to be that found in Romanian: the expected palatalization does not occur in the third person plural present indicative. This means that while the lack of palatalization in the third person plural is indeed anomalous from a historical phonological point of view, from a comparative and morphological point of view it turns out to be Italian that is 'anomalous' while Romanian is simply a 'normal Romance language'. This fact is invisible just so long as one focuses too closely on the standard language, or treats it as a proxy for a dialect area of which it is a mere member, but once it becomes visible it simply nullifies appeal to Slavonic influence as the historical explanation of the Romanian facts.

What matters for our present purposes is not the specific explanation of the facts, but the need to utilize to the maximum the perspective of dialectal variation when setting about any kind of historical reconstruction. The case of the Romanian third person plural is not isolated. There is a sense, indeed, in which 'familiarity' (the fact of being characteristic of some well-known standard language) sometimes seem to breed, if not exactly 'contempt', at least a misleading disregard for historical reality in Romance linguistics. As another example, in which, this time, it is a rather too narrow focus on standard Romanian which is to blame, we may look at the suppletive morphology of the Romanian verb BE. Most parts of the paradigm of this verb continue forms of Latin ESSE 'be', but the subjunctive (together with the infinitive and gerund) is derived from a different Latin verb FIERI 'happen, become, be made' (Table 1.25).

Analysis of the historical morphology of this verb has been distorted by viewing it through the 'lens' of modern standard Romanian. Because in the modern language the reflexes of FIERI are (among the finite verb forms) uniquely associated with the subjunctive, many historical linguists

Table 1.25. *Reflexes of Latin* FIERI *'happen, become, be made' continued in the Romanian verb* BE

	PRS	SBJV
1SG	sunt	fiu
2SG	ești	fii
3SG	este	fie
1PL	suntem	fim
2PL	sunteți	fiți
3PL	sunt	fie

Table 1.26. *Reflexes of Latin* FIERI (> hʲi-) *in the Aromanian verb* BE

	PRS.IND	SBJV
1SG	'esku/hʲiu̯	hʲiu̯
2SG	'eʃtʲ / hʲii̯	hʲii̯
3SG	'e̯aste	'hʲie/'hʲibə
1PL	hʲim	hʲim
2PL	hʲitsʲ	hʲitsʲ
3PL	sən/sun	'hʲie/'hʲibə

(Philippide 2011: 479; Capidan 1925: 174; Bourciez 1956: 541; Rothe 1957: 114; Rosetti 1986: 148) have simply assumed that these forms are derived directly from the Latin present subjunctive of FIERI, namely 1SG FIAM, 2SG FIAS, 3SG FIAT, 1PL FIAMUS, 2PL FIATIS, 3PL FIANT. While it is very likely that the third person singular and plural form *fie* derives from subjunctive FIAT and FIANT, derivation of the other forms from the subjunctive of FIERI is surprisingly insouciant of historical phonology: the present subjunctives FIAM, FIAMUS, FIATIS, at least,[66] simply *cannot* yield *fiu, fim, fiți*; the only phonologically possible outcomes would be **fie, *fiem or **fiam, **fiați. Rather, *fiu, fii, fim, fiți* are, instead, all perfectly regular outcomes of the Latin present *indicatives* FIO, FIS, FIMUS, FITIS, a set of forms which happen not to be continued as present indicatives in Romanian. The moment the wider dialectal picture is explored, it becomes even more surprising that the Romanian forms should ever be analysed as original subjunctives. For in at least two (Aromanian and Megleno-Romanian) of the other three major branches of Daco-Romance,[67] reflexes of indicative FIMUS, FITIS provide the sole first and second person present indicative forms of the verb BE, while in some varieties of these two branches FIO, FIS provide the first and second person singular forms as well (Table 1.26).

---

[66] The status of 2SG *fii* is more ambiguous, but it is not a direct phonological reflex of FIAS.

[67] There is also some, more problematic, evidence for the presence of reflexes of FIERI in the present indicative of the verb BE in the fourth branch, Istro-Romanian (see Maiden and Uță Bărbulescu in progress).

Now the usual reaction of linguists to these facts has arguably been ill-judged: for example, Streller (1904: 5, 11), Capidan (1925: 173; 1932: 488), and Rosetti (1986: 148) have all asserted that these present indicative forms in Aromanian or Megleno-Romanian are analogically imported *from the subjunctive*, despite the very obvious fact that not only formally, but also functionally, they correspond perfectly to the Latin present indicatives. The only conceivable motivation (as overtly acknowledged by Streller 1904: 11) for their making this assumption is the fact that such forms are only found in the subjunctive but not in the indicative *in standard Romanian*. We have here what might be termed 'standard language bias'. Rather than allowing the comparative dialectal facts to guide the analysis of the standard language itself, linguists have allowed the modern standard language to guide the analysis of the dialects and thereby the entire morphological history of the verb BE, even in the standard language. The approach taken even ignores the 'internal' comparative evidence of each of Aromanian, Megleno-Romanian, and Daco-Romanian, for in each the first and second person subjunctive forms of *all* verbs are demonstrably derived, historically, from the present indicative. Neglect of comparative data has led to a serious methodological failure, by obfuscating the obvious implication that proto-Daco-Romance must have had reflexes of FIERI in the present indicative. This conclusion is, by the way, again supported by comparative Romance data: medieval northern Italian dialects (Rohlfs 1968: 272;1969: 129f.; Michaelis 1998; Cennamo 2003) shows present-tense reflexes of FIERI, where this verb was used both as the passive auxiliary BE, and also survived in its original meaning of 'become, happen'. For example, from the early fourteenth century Milanese *Volgarizzamento in antico milanese dell'Elucidario* (78):

(78) Doncha nuy **fimo** crucificadi con Criste al mondo [...] per la vivanda del So corpo nuy **fimo** una medexima cossa con Criste

'So we **are** crucified with Christ in the world [...] by the food of His body we **become** one with Christ.'

Sardinian also preserves reflexes of what were originally present indicative forms of FIERI (see Wolf 2014).

This is by no means the only example in Romance linguistics in which the historical analysis of an aspect of a standard language has been compromised by too narrow a focus with the standard language itself, lacking a more balanced comparative perspective. Loporcaro (1997a) points out the distorting effects of taking analyses devised to explain the structure of *modern Italian* and projecting them backwards into diachrony to explain phonological history. At issue is Italian *raddoppiamento fonosintattico* (see Sections 1.2.2.4 and 6.4.3.2), that phenomenon whereby the initial consonant of a word is lengthened principally if it is immediately preceded by a word-final stressed vowel. For modern standard Italian, the phenomenon lends itself to explanation as an effect of prosodic constraints on syllable structure. However, Loporcaro (1997a: 40) writes 'any hypothesis on the origin of R[addoppiamento] F[onosintattico] in Italian, formulated on the basis of internal data, must on the one hand be evaluated by sifting through the available direct documentation, following forward through time the diachronic path that led from Latin to Tuscan-based standard Italian, in its written attestations. And, on the other hand, that hypothesis will need to be confirmed by the reconstructive arguments which can be developed on the strength of evidence provided by other Romance varieties'. This is exactly what Loporcaro does, and the path of evolution that he reconstructs via careful comparison with 'other Romance varieties' (especially other Italo-Romance varieties) offers a different and far more plausible account of the development of the phenomenon than could be achieved by projection backwards in time from modern Italian, showing on comparative grounds that *raddoppiamento* orginates in Italian, as elsewhere in Italo-Romance, as an effect of consonant assimilation at word boundaries, which later undergoes locally differentiated types of extension and reanalysis over time.

A further possible example of the benefits of a comparative as opposed to a 'standard-language-oriented' perspective involves the controversial question of the origins of diphthongization of proto-Romance low mid vowels in open syllables in Italian,[68] e.g., *'tɛ.ne > *tiene* 's/he holds', *'kɔ.re > *cuore* 'heart'.[69] Maiden (2016b: 32) detects a historic tendency, particularly among Italian scholars, and perhaps most of all in the work of Arrigo Castellani,[70] to treat Italian (and the Tuscan dialect from which it emerged) as a 'special case' which has somehow developed in an independent way from other (Italo-)Romance varieties.[71] But is Italian so special? Taking a comparative-historical perspective, however, Maiden emphasizes how the diphthongization found in Tuscan resembles diphthongization in other (particularly central and southern) Italian dialects where it is the product of the assimilatory process of metaphony (see Section 1.3.4). Maiden (2016b: 19–23), pointing out that an alleged significant difference between metaphonic diphthongization of low mid vowels and Tuscan diphthongization of low mid vowels, namely that in Tuscan the phenomenon is limited to open syllables, is actually compatible with what we also know about medieval forms of metaphony in central Italy, where there is evidence that metaphony, too, was restricted to open syllables. He also shows that the exceptions to diphthongization in Italian and modern Tuscan dialects nearly always involve words that would not historically have met the phonological environment for metaphony, or would not have alternated

---

[68] See also Section 7.3.2.2.
[69] For a description of the history of the issues, see Sánchez Miret (1998).
[70] E.g., Castellani (1980a–1980e).
[71] See also Section 5.5.1.

morphologically with forms historically in inflexional -[u] or -[i] subject to metaphony, such as the invariant b[ɛ]ne 'well', n[ɔ]ve 'nine', or also, for example, dialectal m[ɛ]le 'honey', effectively a *singulare tantum*, lacking a plural (and therefore not alternating with a form in -[i]). Those interested may judge for themselves which account they find more convincing, but there is no doubt that the issues cannot be adequately assessed without viewing Italian in a properly comparative respective, and this is valid for the Romance languages more generally. Standard Romance languages are obviously 'special' in that, for different reasons, they have risen to prominence as prestigious varieties. But from a strictly linguistic perspective, it can be a serious mistake to consider them as any more 'special' than their sister varieties.

1.3.6 What Is a Romance Language? Could There Be an Answer in Morphology?

Perhaps surprisingly, it will be suggested here that the morphological repercussions of Romance palatalization might even provide one kind of answer to the fundamental question 'what is a Romance language?'. This is a question to which there is, perhaps equally surprisingly, no obviously 'right' answer. The standard response, as given for example by the *Encyclopaedia Britannica*,[72] is that Romance languages are those historically 'descended' or 'derived' from Latin. This is a purely historical definition, which carries the implication of continuous intergenerational transmission. It does not explain where the *difference* with Latin lies, although the Romance languages are conventionally labelled in a way that distinguishes them from their ancestor.[73] There is a lively controversy about the historical and cultural circumstances that might have induced Romance speakers to perceive themselves as speaking something other than Latin, which we will not address here (see, e.g., Wright 1982; 2016; Varvaro 2013). The question we want to explore, rather, is whether there is any possible, purely linguistic, definition of what a Romance language is. What, if anything, do all Romance languages have linguistically in common that would distinguish them from other languages, including Latin?

One might seek some unique, and shared, trait in phonology or in morphosyntax, but it is not clear that any characteristic exists that strictly

---

[72] See www.britannica.com/EBchecked/topic/508379/Romance-languages (consulted 10 March 2021). The *Encyclopaedia* actually says that the Romance languages are 'derived' from 'Vulgar Latin', defined as a 'spoken form of non-Classical Latin'.

[73] However, see the term 'neo-Latin' in the title of Tagliavini (1969), *Le lingue neolatine*. Note also that some Romance varieties, *Ladino* (a name for Judaeo-Spanish), or *Ladin* (the Romance variety spoken in the region of the Dolomites) preserve popular forms of the word 'Latin' (see Müller 1963). Terms such as *rumantsch/romansh* or the Romanian term *român* 'Romanian' also show continuity with Latin ROMANICUS or ROMANUS 'Roman'. For more discussion of the naming of Romance languages see, e.g., Wright (2013; 2016).

meets these criteria. A great deal of what the Romance languages have in common in those domains recurs repeatedly across the world's languages. For example, probably all Romance languages have the five 'cardinal' vowels [i, e, a, o, u], or distinguish singular from plural, or have at least two grammatical genders, or have a basic subject-verb-object word order,[74] but these are properties observable across numerous languages of the world. Chapter 9 of this volume explores a number of typologically unusual features in Romance phonology, for example, but none of these seems to meet the criterion of being unique to, yet shared across, the Romance languages.

Clearly a uniquely defining linguistic characteristic of Romance languages will need to be maximally *idiosyncratic*, and thereby maximally unlikely to be shared by other languages. Could we perhaps find it in the *lexicon*, where the principle (cf. Saussure 1968: 100f.) of arbitrariness in the relation between form and meaning is at its most prominent? There are several reasons why this, too, would be unsatisfactory. It is certainly true that there is a common core lexicon inherited by all Romance languages (see for example Dworkin 2016: 580), comprising semantically basic items such as DIE, BE BORN, SKY, TOOTH, HAND, FINGER, SON, DAUGHTER, as well as a range of function words such as personal pronouns or prepositions, but this etymologically shared lexicon still fails to unite the Romance languages. This is because of the disruptive effects of sound change: all Romance languages, for example, retain reflexes of Lat. DIGITUS for 'finger', but Sp. *dedo*, Cat. *dit*, Fr. *doigt* ([dwa]), Srs. *det*, Ro. *deget* have little more than the initial voiced dental in common, and even that is not true for all Romance varieties. There are southern Italo-Romance varieties where, by regular sound change, this word begins with some other consonant or with none: e.g., Nap. [ˈritə], Isc. [lit], Sora (province of Frosinone) [ˈitə] (see Rohlfs 1966: 204f.).[75]

Another problem is that lexical criteria could lead us to count as 'Romance' some languages which are generally regarded as deserving a different classification. Thus, some 'creole' languages have predominantly Romance lexicons, but that does not automatically make them Romance languages. The 'Romance' creoles (see Bollée and Maurer 2016: 447–67) are widely considered not to be 'Romance languages' precisely because, although they have a largely Romance-derived lexicon, they have not inherited the distinctive phonological, morphological, or syntactic systems

---

[74] The first two criteria do not in fact distinguish Romance from Latin, either. For further discussion of word order see, e.g., Salvi (2016).

[75] It needs to be said, also, that lexical items can be borrowed from one language into another, and far more easily than grammatical or phonological structures. For example, on one estimate (Finkenstaedt and Wolff 1973), Latin- or Romance-based vocabulary constitutes nearly 60 per cent of the lexicon of modern English, but that does not make English a 60 per cent Romance language.

of the relevant Romance languages.⁷⁶ The final difficulty is that probably all of the 'shared' vocabulary is shared because it is inherited from Latin, so that the lexical criterion would not differentiate Romance from Latin.

'Arbitrariness' is of course also encountered in morphology. Could morphology be the domain in which linguistic 'Romanceness' could be located? The answer is probably yes, but in a very specific respect. Derivational affixes or inflexional desinences often present similar arbitrariness in the relationship between form and meaning as we find in the lexicon, but we run into exactly the same problems as we have seen for the lexicon. What is common to all Romance languages in their derivational or inflexional inventory is likely also to be shared with Latin yet to have become phonologically differentiated beyond recognition across Romance. For example, virtually all Romance languages share a second person plural marker derived from Latin -TIS,⁷⁷ but -TIS is not uniquely Romance precisely because it is shared with Latin.⁷⁸ It cannot constitute a modern pan-Romance second person plural desinence because of the multiplicity of its modern phonological reflexes: e.g., CANTATIS 'you sing' > Pt. *cantais*, Cat. *canteu*, Fr. *chantez* [ʃõte], Log. [kanˈtaːðes], Srs. *canteis*, It. *cantate*, Ro. *cântaţi* [kɨnˈtatsʲ]. However, it is suggested in what follows that it is in another aspect of inflexional morphology that we might encounter phenomena that meet our definitional criteria. They are 'arbitrary' to a very high degree yet, if the following analysis is correct, they could be part of all Romance speakers' abstract and active knowledge of the organization of their morphological system, in such a way, indeed, as to guide and condition diachronic change.

Our example is the pattern of allomorphy historically caused by the palatalizations. As we saw in Section 1.3.1, an effect of the palatalizations in early Romance was to confer on all Romance varieties a pattern of alternation such that presence of a root allomorph in the present subjunctive cells, or in the first person singular present indicative cell, implies the presence of that same alternant in all the other cells. In central

---

[76] The view that Romance-based creoles are not strictly Romance languages does not, of course, mean that they are one bit less worthy of study by linguists, but it does mean that they may be more effectively understood from a 'creole' rather than a 'Romance' perspective. See, for example, the rich literature on the theoretical significance of the emergence of creoles (e.g., Holm 1988; Manessy 1995; Hazaël-Massieux 1996; Mufwene 2002). However, for an intriguing example of a characteristic and idiosyncratic feature of Romance verb morphology, namely conjugation-marking vowels, being continued in a creole language see Luís (2011).

[77] The reservation is prompted by the possibility that the Italian second person plural endings originate in the Latin *imperative* ending -TE (see Maiden 2007: 159–61). Even then, the formative [t] would be underlyingly common (in the historical sense) to all Romance languages.

[78] It is also non-distinctive by being part of the common Indo-European inheritance: compare, for example, Lat. UIDETIS 'you.2PL see', It. *vedete*, but also Croatian (Slavonic) *videte*. On this basis an unwary observer might conclude that these three languages belong to the same family, while French (*voyez* [vwaje]) was unrelated to any of them!

Italo-Romance and for a subset of verbs in Romanian (the reasons are ultimately a matter of regular historical phonology: see, e.g., Maiden 2020). Maiden (e.g., 2018: 84) labels this paradigmatic distributional pattern the 'L-pattern'; the variant that includes the third person plural present indicative is labelled the 'U-pattern'. These two labels are strictly arbitrary; indeed, they are necessarily arbitrary since the relevant patterns are not describable in terms of any phonological or functional labels. However, for ease of reference here we will use the label 'L-pattern' to cover both of them (after all, the U-pattern subsumes the L-pattern). Two assumptions are crucial: that the original phonological conditioning of the L-pattern is defunct, and that the set of paradigm cells defined by the effects of the original sound changes is fundamentally 'incoherent', in that it is not plausibly reducible to any semantic or functional common denominator. What, after all, does the class of present subjunctive and first person singular present indicative cells have significantly and uniquely in common? Now these assumptions are far from uncontroversial, but our purpose here is expository: see especially Maiden (2018: 161–66) for references to, and discussion of, the relevant debate. Maiden's view is that the L-pattern belongs to that class of entities which Aronoff (1994) describes as 'morphomes', autonomously morphological entities conceived as functions lacking any inherent connexion with a specific form or a specific meaning yet serving systematically to relate form and meaning in the morphological system (see further Sections 11.3–4). In our case, and put informally,[79] the palatalizations gave rise to a pattern of allomorphy which has persisted long after the original phonological motivation has become defunct. Its paradigmatic distribution becomes synchronically arbitrary, lacking any common set of distinguishing morphosyntactic or phonological features. Yet, crucially, the L-pattern, historically found across the Romance languages, commonly displays diachronic 'coherence', in that real or potential exceptions to it tend to be removed or resisted, and changes affecting any of the specified cells in the L-pattern equally affect all the others 'in lockstep'. Moreover, the L-pattern often acts as a 'template' for the distribution of innovatory kinds of alternation which have no connexion whatever with the sound changes which originally created the L-pattern.

It is not possible here to describe anything like the full range of coherence and innovations respecting the L-pattern over the history of the Romance languages (for detailed exemplification see Maiden 2018: 93–122), and all we can do here is to give some brief indicative examples. Table 1.27 illustrates L-pattern effects produced by phonetically regular palatalizations in Galician-Portuguese and in Italian. Galician-Portuguese is represented here

---

[79] For more detailed theoretical discussions of the issues, see Maiden (2018: 236–41).

Table 1.27. 'L-pattern' effects of sound change in Portuguese and old Italian

(a) Portuguese

	1SG	2SG	3SG	1PL	2PL	3PL
PRS.IND	tenho 'have'	tens	tem	temos	tendes	têm
PRS.SBJV	tenha	tenhas	tenha	tenhamos	tenhais	tenham
PRS.IND	vejo 'see'	vês	vê	vemos	vedes	vêem
PRS.SBJV	veja	vejas	veja	vejamos	vejais	vejam
PRS.IND	faço 'do'	fazes	faz	fazemos	fazeis	fazem
PRS.SBJV	faça	faças	faça	façamos	façais	façam
PRS.IND	venho 'come'	vens	vem	vimos	vindes	vêm
PRS.SBJV	venha	venhas	venha	venhamos	venhais	venham
PRS.IND	digo 'say'	dizes	diz	dizemos	dizeis	dizem
PRS.SBJV	diga	digas	diga	digamos	digais	digam

(b) Old Italian

	1SG	2SG	3SG	1PL	2PL	3PL
PRS.IND	soglio 'am wont'	suoli	suole	solemo	solete	sogliono
PRS.SBJV	soglia	sogli	soglia	sogliamo	sogliate	sogliano
PRS.IND	veggio 'see'	vedi	vede	vedemo	vedete	veggiono
PRS.SBJV	veggia	veggi	veggia	veggiamo	veggiate	veggiano
PRS.IND	vegno 'come'	vieni	viene	venimo	venite	vegnono
PRS.SBJV	vegna	vegni	vegna	vegnamo	vegnate	vegnano
PRS.IND	dico 'say'	dici	dice	dicemo	dite	dicono
PRS.SBJV	dica	dichi	dica	dicamo	dicate	dicano

by modern Portuguese, and Italian by the medieval form of the language (which better exemplifies the effects of regular palatalization than the modern language).

The diachronic 'coherence' of these alternation patterns lies in the fact that they either survive intact, or are lost completely. The alternations are often subject to analogical levelling, but when that happens it affects all the relevant cells of the paradigm at once. That is to say that there are no 'halfway houses', with the alternant removed in some cells of the paradigm but not in others, and therefore the L-pattern is never violated. Sometimes, the alternants may undergo novel adjustments in their form, but these adjustments operate in all cells in which those alternants occur, apparently at once. Thus, in modern Italian, the historical alternation between *veggi*-[veddʒ]- and *ved*- has been removed in favour of *ved*-, but it has been removed *completely* (not, say, just in the subjunctive, or just in the first person singular and third person plural present indicative). The alternant *vegn*-[vɛɲɲ]-, has been analogically replaced in the modern language by

Table 1.28. *'Coherent' levelling and innovatory adjustments of the Italian variant of the L-pattern in modern Italian*

	1SG	2SG	3SG	1PL	2PL	3PL
PRS.IND	vedo 'see'	vedi	vede	vediamo	vedete	vedono
PRS.SBJV	veda	veda	veda	vediamo	vediate	vedano
PRS.IND	vengo 'come'	vieni	viene	veniamo	venite	vengono
PRS.SBJV	venga	venga	venga	veniamo	veniate	vengano

Table 1.29. *Innovatory L-pattern alternation in Portuguese* perder *'lose'*

	1SG	2SG	3SG	1PL	2PL	3PL
PRS.IND	perco 'lose'	perdes	perde	perdemos	perdeis	perdem
PRS.SBJV	perca	percas	perca	percamos	percais	percam

Table 1.30. *Creation of L-pattern suppletion in Galician dialects*

	1SG	2SG	3SG	1PL	2PL	3PL
PRS.IND	ˈkoʎo 'fit'	ˈkaβes	ˈkaβe	kaˈβemos	kaˈβeðes	ˈkaβeŋ
PRS.SBJV	ˈkoʎa	ˈkoʎas	ˈkoʎa	koˈʎamos	koˈʎaðes	ˈkoʎaŋ

veng- [vɛŋg]-,[80] but this replacement, again, has happened equally in the present subjunctive[81] and in the two cells of the present indicative (Table 1.28).

Portuguese, like Italian, shows 'coherent' levellings and adjustments, but it also acquires at least one completely novel and unprecedented alternation, whose origins are frankly mysterious. The old Galician-Portuguese verb *perder* 'lose' would not have been expected to show any kind of L-pattern consonantal alternation. Yet at some point, and for some reason (Maiden 2018: 115), *perd-* began to acquire consonantal alternants including *perc-* (where *c* = [k]). This novel alternation, wherever it comes from, takes as its distributional template the L-pattern (Table 1.29).

In some Galician dialects (which show the same kind of inherited L-patern alternation in the verb as their sister variety Portuguese), two etymologically distinct verbs meaning 'fit, be containable in', namely *coller* and *caber*, have coalesced suppletively (see also Section 12.2.5) into a single inflexional paradigm. The distributional pattern they adopt is again the L-pattern (Table 1.30).

---

[80] For a discussion of the motivation, see Maiden (2011a: 238f.)

[81] The first and second persons plural of the present subjunctive are exceptions and develop in a different way. This is a widespread phenomenon in Italian, whose nature is explored in Maiden (2010).

These are just a few illustrative examples from two far-separated Romance languages. The broader claim, made for example by Maiden (2018) is that this (and some other) patterns, unprecedented in Latin, exist across the Romance languages and generally show the same historical characteristics of 'coherence' in the face of morphological innovations. This would mean that we have a genuine candidate for a defining structural characteristic of a Romance language. This characteristic is arbitrary in that it is morphomic, and the kind of diachronic evidence that we have seen suggests that this pattern is 'psychologically real' for all native Romance speakers. Coherence, and the fact that the L-pattern is repeatedly seen to act as a template for morphological innovation, are only explicable if Romance speakers generally have an abstract sense that the allomorph of any one of relevant set of cells must be identical to all of the others. Our claim that the pattern is a defining characteristic of Romance would of course be compromised if it turned out that an identical pattern existed outside Romance, but precisely because the Romance 'L-pattern' is the complex consequence of series of disparate historical sound changes acting on a disparate and idiosyncratic set of paradigm cells in the early Romance verb it is inherently unlikely that exactly this pattern could ever recur in another language family.[82]

This claim is certainly a bold one, but it has the virtue of being empirically testable on modern speakers as well as in diachrony. Very little experimental testing of the psychological reality of such structures in modern speakers has actually been done, however. The results of the tests that have been done to date (Nevins et al. 2015) have been interpreted as showing that our claim is not in fact true for modern adult speakers of Portuguese, Spanish, and Italian, but the methods and conclusions of that research are problematic (see, e.g., Maiden 2018: 165f.; 2021: 90) and it is certain that further experimental research is needed to test speakers' reactions to artificially engendered violations of the L-pattern, or to tasks in which speakers are asked to produce the set of present indicative and present subjunctive forms for made-up verbs with novel, invented, forms of root allomorphy. The prediction is, of course, that such violations would tend to be rejected, and that the experimentally made-up allomorphs will tend to be distributed according to the L-pattern. Such work remains to be done, but the diachronic evidence nonetheless indicates that there must at least

---

[82] This observation does not imply, as has recently been claimed (Herce 2019; but Maiden 2021a), that typological comparisons of morphomic structures across language families are impossible. Rather, it is inherently unlikely (although not logically impossible) that the particular details of a morphomic structure such as the L-pattern could ever occur outside the Romance languages. Claims that allegedly unique morphomic patterns are in reality not morphomic because they are more widely attested cross-linguistically tend to rest on a failure to grasp the precise details of such patterns (cf. Andersen 2010; Nielsen 2019). It is just possible, also, that morphomic patterns might be *borrowed* from one language into another, although the evidence for this is elusive (see Maiden in progress).

have been a point in the past where the L-pattern was a defining characteristic of Romance languages. It may be added that even those who are doubtful about the validity of morphomic claims of this kind for the *modern* synchrony of Romance languages (see, e.g., Embick 2016: 304; cf. Maiden 2020: 90), tend to concede that the relevant diachronic developments attest to the existence in the past of the kind of abstract morphological knowledge which is postulated.

Whether the 'L-pattern' can be regarded as a defining characteristic of Romance languages will continue to be debated. It can at least stand as an example of how one might go about seeking to establish such a definition. That approach consists of looking for diachronic and comparative evidence for speakers' knowledge of, and ability to replicate, truly arbitrary patterns of mapping between form and grammatical meaning unique to a particular language family. In fact, it recasts the question 'what is a Romance language?' as 'what kind of linguistic knowledge is specifically shared by all and only native speakers of Romance languages?'

1.4 Conclusion

Although modern linguistics as a discipline developed in large part out of the philological study of individual languages and language families such as Romance, it is a striking characteristic of contemporary research in both linguistics and in Romance studies that the traditional link between the two disciplines is often not as strong as it might be. To be sure, analyses within Romance linguistics which fail to take account of enlightening ideas and principles from linguistic theory risk overlooking and/or misconstruing the relevance of all or part of the available empirical evidence they are so at pains to correctly reconstruct, evaluate, and interpret. By the same token, linguistic analyses which are blindly driven by theory-internal considerations with insufficient regard for actual data as offered by textual corpora and the numerous dialectal varieties of Romance run the risk of presenting a largely idealized and unhelpfully selective representation of the available linguistic evidence. The result may be a partial theory which is only capable of accounting for a subset of the available data and that largely ignores the imperfections and irregularities characteristic of real linguistic productions.

The discussions of the preceding sections may seem eclectic and heterogeneous, but their common theme has been that when theory and Romance evidence are considered together, the results are mutually enhancing. The discussion has also shown how careful and detailed consideration of the Romance linguistic data can open our eyes to problems, possibilities, and approaches sometimes overlooked by mainstream linguistic theory.

Selected References

Below you can find selected references for this chapter. The full references can be found online at the following page: www.cambridge.org/Romancelinguistics

Ledgeway A. (2007a). 'La posizione dell'aggettivo nella storia del napoletano'. In Bentley, D. and Ledgeway, A. (eds), *Sui dialetti italoromanzi. Saggi in onore di Nigel B. Vincent* (*The Italianist* 27, Special supplement 1). Norfolk: Biddles, 104–25.

Ledgeway A. (2010b). 'The clausal domain: CP structure and the left periphery'. In D'Alessandro, R., Ledgeway, A., and Roberts, I (eds), *Syntactic Variation. The Dialects of Italy*. Cambridge: Cambridge University Press, 38–51.

Ledgeway A. (2012a). *From Latin to Romance: Morphosyntactic Typology and Change*. Oxford: Oxford University Press.

Ledgeway A. (2015a). 'Parallels in Romance nominal and clausal microvariation', *Revue roumaine de linguistique* 60: 105–27.

Ledgeway A. (2017a). 'Syntheticity and analyticity'. In Dufter, A. and Stark, E. (eds), *Manual of Romance Morphosyntax and Syntax (Manuals of Romance Linguistics)*. Berlin: De Gruyter, 837–84.

Ledgeway A. (2020b). 'The north–south divide: parameters of variation in the clausal domain', *L'Italia Dialettale* 81: 29–77.

Maiden, M. (1991). *Interactive Morphonology. Metaphony in Italy*. London: Routledge.

Maiden, M. (1992). 'Irregularity as a determinant of morphological change', *Journal of Linguistics* 28: 285–312.

Maiden, M. (2013). 'Semi-autonomous morphology: a problem in the history of the Italian (and Romanian) verb'. In Cruschina, S., Maiden, M., and Smith, J. C. (eds), *The Boundaries of Pure Morphology*. Oxford: Oxford University Press, 24–44.

Maiden, M. (2016a). 'Romanian, Istro-Romanian, Megleno-Romanian, and Aromanian'. In Bentley, D. and Ledgeway, A. (eds), *Sui dialetti italoromanzi. Saggi in onore di Nigel B. Vincent* (*The Italianist* 27, Special supplement 1). Norfolk: Biddles, 91–125.

Maiden, M. (2016b). 'Italo-Romance metaphony and the Tuscan diphthongs'. *Transactions of the Philological Society* 114: 198–232.

Maiden, M. (2018). *The Romance Verb. Morphomic Structure and Diachrony*. Oxford: Oxford University Press.

Maiden, M. (2021a). 'The morphome'. *Annual Review of Linguistics* 7: 89–108.

Maiden, M. (2021b). 'Establishing contact: Slavonic influence on Romanian morphology?' *Journal of Language Contact* 14: 24–52.

Part One

What Is a Language?

2
Origins of Romance

Nigel Vincent

2.1 Introduction

It is no accident that in his introduction to the comparative method (CM), Michael Weiss begins by examining sets of vowel and consonant correspondences in a selection of Romance languages before going on to show how the inventories reconstructed in this way compare very favourably with what we know about Latin from the written record.* In his words: '[a] test case like the Latin-Romance one ... gives us confidence that the method should work within its built-in limits for cognate languages without a recorded quasi-ancestor' (Weiss 2017: 132). By the same token, precisely because there is such a rich body of textual evidence for Latin, the Romanist W. D. Elcock (1960: 33) could state with confidence that '[i]t is the special privilege of Romance philologists that they are not compelled to rely entirely upon reconstruction'. In their different ways, remarks like these imply a priority for 'real', that is to say attested, data over the hypothetical patterns that result by applying the CM and similar techniques based on our understanding of the general principles of linguistic structure and organization. For this reason, while the idea of a proto-language that can be reconstructed by comparing material from the surviving members of a family or sub-family is central to historical research into families such as Germanic, Indo-European, Algonquian, and Oceanic, the concept of proto-Romance has played only a marginal role in the majority of comparative Romance studies (see Dworkin 2016: 2f. for some discussion and background) and figures hardly at all, for example, in a major reference work such as Ledgeway and Maiden (2016). Things may change, however, in the

---

* Thanks for their comments and suggestions to: Jim Adams, Éva Buchi, James Clackson, Eleanor Dickey, Roger Lass, Adam Ledgeway, Martin Maiden, George Walkden, and Michael Weiss.

wake of the project initiated – not uncontroversially, it must be said – in 2008 under the name *Dictionnaire Étymologique Roman* (*DÉRom*). We will examine the debate around this project in Section 2.2, but first let us consider a particular case as a way of appreciating the complexity of factors and circumstances at play.

The set of cognate items Pt./Srd. *tia*, Sp. *tía*, It. *zia*, OOcc. *sia* all meaning 'aunt' leads via the CM to a reconstructed form */ˈtia/, given that the sound change sequence [t] > [ts] > [s] is the most natural way of connecting the different initial consonants. The companion male terms Pt. *tio*, Sp. *tío*, Srd. *tiu*, It. *zio* 'uncle' reinforce this conclusion and yield a corresponding masculine */ˈtiu/. The problem is that these reconstructions cannot plausibly be mapped onto any of the Latin words in this semantic domain: AMITA 'paternal aunt', MATERTERA 'maternal aunt', PATRUUS 'paternal uncle', AUUNCULUS 'maternal uncle'. The answer here is provided by Greek where the relevant items are *thia* (θεία), *thios* (θεῖος), which must have been borrowed into part of the Latin-speaking territory. It is worth noting, however, that the reconstructions would have to stand even if we did not have the Greek evidence to justify them. Note further that the Greek terms do not distinguish between maternal and paternal lineage. They thus not only provide a source for the abovementioned Romance forms but also align with, and maybe even help to explain, the fact that in other Romance languages which do have direct derivatives of the Latin items such as Fr. *oncle*, Ro. *unchi* < (AU)UNCULUS and Ven. *amia*, OFr. *ante*, ModFr. *tante*, Ro. *mătușă* < AMITA, the etymological maternal terms have been generalized in meaning. To this mix we can now add a third set of items: Lad./Ven./IRo. *barba*, Frl. *barbe*, Vgl. *buarba* all meaning 'uncle'. Here the required reconstruction is semantic: an entirely plausible but unattested metonymic shift from the Latin feminine noun BARBA 'beard', in the light of which it comes as no surprise that the languages which have adopted this term have had to look elsewhere for their 'aunt' word, either with reflexes of Lat. AMITA (Lad. *meda*) or by borrowing (Vgl. *tsi*) or by new coinages such as Pie. *magna* < (AMITA) MAGNA 'great (aunt)'.

This example serves to highlight the different factors which have to be considered when we investigate the origins of the Romance languages. In addition to reconstruction – phonological, morphosyntactic, and semantic – and textual attestation, we must take into account borrowing both from non-Romance languages and between sister languages, as with the Istro-Romanian form *barba*, which is generally taken to be a loan from Venetian. There are also regional patterns which call for explanation. Thus, reflexes of *thios/-a* occur across the whole of Iberia and in those languages spoken around the shore of the Mediterranean, while the epicentre of *barba* appears to be directly north and south of the Alps, and the reflexes of AUUNCULUS are found as far apart as France and Romania but not in between. In the following sections, therefore we look in more detail at the role of reconstruction across all linguistic levels, at the range and variety of the textual attestation, and at the social, regional, and chronological variation of Latin within the Roman world.

2.2 Attestation vs Reconstruction: The *DÉRom* Controversy

For Romanists the question of the relation between attested material and reconstructed forms and meanings has been brought into renewed focus in recent years through the launching – by the French scholar Éva Buchi and her German colleague Wolfgang Schweickard supported by a team of younger researchers – of their project to develop a new Romance etymological dictionary, the *Dictionnaire Étymologique Roman* (*DÉRom*). We begin by reviewing the motives behind this initiative and the principles on which it is based before considering some of the criticisms that have been levelled at it.[1]

The key here is to be found in the expression 'quasi-ancestor' in the above quotation from Weiss. The written language that we call Latin cannot by definition be the source of the modern Romance languages, since linguistic change typically proceeds via the spoken language, even if in literate societies there may over time be more or less significant interactions between spoken and written norms. There is a danger therefore that we will miss things or make the wrong generalizations if we do not have some independent check on how we use the written evidence, valuable though that undoubtedly is. The *DÉRom* therefore represents an attempt to move away from what its originators label 'graphocentrism' by deploying the set of generally agreed and phonetically grounded principles implicit in the CM as a control on the interpretation of written Latin. In that sense, it is in effect the reverse of the situation in Weiss's example: the CM is being used to check conclusions derived from the written language rather than the written evidence being used to validate the accuracy of the CM.

To this end, Buchi and Schweickard started by identifying a corpus of some 500 lexical items with a (more or less) pan-Romance distribution and then applied the techniques of CM – supplemented where appropriate by internal reconstruction based on patterns of morphophonemic alternation – to yield a series of etyma that are recorded in the dictionary in phonemic

---

[1] In addition to challenges on grounds of principle there has been some criticism of the way the *DÉRom* entries are formatted, both with respect to the online version – available at www.atilf.fr/DERom/ and last consulted for present purposes on 19 November 2018 – and the printed version (Buchi and Schweickard 2014; 2016). However we will not go into this aspect of the matter here; for some discussion and references see Dworkin (2016) and Weiss (2017). For a very positive assessment of the methodology of the *DÉRom* project by an expert historical specialist from a different language family, see Lass (2018).

notation, prefixed with an asterisk and labelled 'proto-Romance'. The inspiration here is very much that of Robert A. Hall's project for a comparative grammar and in particular Hall (1974). As input to this process the project uses data derived from a core set of Romance languages called 'obligatory' and which figure in all the entries. These languages are: Daco-Romanian, Istro-Romanian, Megleno-Romanian, Aromanian, Vegliote, Istriot, Italian, Sardinian, Friulian, Ladin, Romansh, French, Francoprovençal, Occitan, Gascon, Catalan, Aragonese, Spanish, Asturian, Galician, and Portuguese, chosen for the most part because of their well-attested historical record. In this context, the presence of different varieties of Romanian is justified by the relatively short period of historical attestation in that part of the Romance-speaking territory coupled with the need to ensure appropriate representation of eastern Romance. In addition, where there are gaps in the record, other so-called 'optional' Romance varieties have been called upon. For example, the fact that the Lombard word for bridge *pont* is feminine merits its inclusion as evidence of this gender for this item within Italian territory even though the standard Italian word *ponte* is masculine (Andronache 2013).

Key properties of the phonological system that emerges following this procedure include a nine-vowel inventory /i ɪ e ɛ a ɔ o ʊ u/ plus the diphthong /au/ but with no role for contrastive vowel length, a consonant inventory consisting of /p b t d k g kʷ ɸ β s m n r l/, and stress which is phonemic rather than being predictable from segmental structure. Perhaps not surprisingly, this system corresponds very closely to that argued for in Loporcaro (2011a), where the focus is prospective, seeking to understand the patterns of phonetic and phonological change that have generated the modern Romance systems, rather than retrospective or reconstructive.

In addition to phonological reconstruction, the *DÉRom* also seeks to recover some morphological properties such as inflexion classes and gender. The latter is particularly interesting since it provides an instance where the reconstructed system is richer and more diverse than what might be arrived at on the basis of textual evidence alone. The bounds are set on the one hand by groups of Romance cognates all of which are masculine, that is to say, they have an ending in -*o*/-*u* < Lat. -UM in those languages which have a clear marker of this kind:[2] */ˈɸiliu/ > It. *figlio*, Sp. *hijo*, Ro. *fiu* 'son'; */kaˈβallu/ > It. *cavallo*, Pt. *cavalo*, Srd. *cuaddu* 'horse'; */ˈannu/ > It. *anno*, Sp. *año*, Ast. *añu*, to which we can add */ˈtiu/ for the *tio*/*zio*/*tiu* words for 'uncle' cited above. These are balanced by a set of cognate feminines: */ˈɸilia/ > It. *figlia*, Sp. *hija*, Frl. *fie*, Ro. *fiică* 'daughter'; */ˈrɔta/ > It. *ruota*, Fr. *roue*, Srd. *roda* 'wheel'; */ˈɛrba/ > Fr. *herbe*, ARo. *iarbă*, Cat. *herba*

---

[2] Here and elsewhere, in the interests of space, I give only partial sets of cognates. For the full sets the reader is referred to the relevant entries of *DÉRom*.

'grass', plus */ˈtia/ for the 'aunt' words. Sometimes, the semantics is the decider, as when a reconstructed masculine */ˈbarba/ 'uncle' sits beside a feminine */ˈbarba/ 'beard, chin'. In contrast to these is a set of forms where the Romance reflexes vary in gender but where the attested Latin forms are all masculine. Thus, for example, in comparison with the Latin masculine DENS 'tooth' we have both masculine It. *dente*, IRo. *dinte*, Frl. *dint*, Sp. *diente* and feminine Srd. *dente*, Cat. *dent*, Frp. *din*. A similar diversity of reflexes is attested for PONS 'bridge', MONS 'mountain', PANIS 'bread', SAL 'salt' among others. Comparative evidence shows a regional split in the genders of these items and leads to the conclusion that an original masculine was first replaced by a feminine and then in some parts of the Romance territory reverted to masculine (Dardel 1965; 1976).

A somewhat different scenario concerns items which in Latin were neuter such as LAC 'milk' but where once again the Romance reflexes have different genders: masculine Srd. *latte*, Vgl. *l̮uat*, Fr. *lait* beside feminine Sp. *leche*, Cat. *llet*, Gsc. *leit*, Ven. *late*. A complicating factor here is that the form *lapte* in all varieties of Romanian that are input to the *DÉRom* are, following traditional usage, also labelled 'neuter', something which seems to imply continuity from Latin. However, the term 'neuter' in Romanian grammars refers not, as it does in Latin, to a distinct class of items with their own inflexions (albeit involving many syncretisms with other genders) but to a set of words that consistently have the morphology of the masculine in the singular and the feminine in the plural: thus *caiet(e)* 'notebook(s)' has a zero singular like *băiat* 'boy' but the plural *-e* like *fete* 'girls'. This has led to debates over the years as to whether the neuter is indeed a separate gender in modern Romanian, as argued most recently by Loporcaro (2018: §4.4), or whether there are simply two genders and a set of heteroclitic items (Maiden 2016a). And here the *DÉRom* has altered its stance over the years, as described in Buchi and Greub (2016), first simply accepting the Latin neuter as given but then, recognizing the methodological inconsistency of this procedure, opting for a reconstructed masculine */ˈlakte/ before finally accepting Loporcaro's arguments and reverting to neuter. The difference is that now the choice of neuter is motivated by attested modern Romance data, providing us with a case in which the diversity of forms and systems in the modern languages allows for the reconstruction of a much more complex history than emerges from attested Latin alone.

The term 'neuter' has yet another sense when it is applied to the distinction observable in pairs such as Nap. *o pane* 'the loaf of bread' vs *o ppane* '(the) bread', where the meaning of the form without doubling of the initial consonant is 'count' and with doubling is 'mass'. Although many of the items where the doubling applies are originally Latin neuters referring to substances such as MEL 'honey' and UINUM 'wine', the pattern has been extended, as here, to an original masculine like PANIS 'bread' and, as

Ledgeway (2012: 105f.) shows, to nominalized adjectives like *o ttriste* 'sadness' and borrowings like *o bblues* 'blues music'. In Asturian, by contrast, we find the mass/count distinction realized on postnominal and predicative adjectives so that, for example, the feminine count *la casa* 'the house' is accompanied by the adjective *fría* 'cold' while *la tsiche* 'milk' is followed by the mass form of the adjective *frío*. The latter also goes with the masculine noun *el café* 'coffee' in contrast to *fríu* with the masculine *el pie* 'the foot' (Loporcaro 2018: 160). Once again patterns like these suggest, as indeed Loporcaro (2018: 282f.) concludes, that the development of gender and number from Latin to Romance is considerably more complex than the textual evidence of Latin and the Romance standard languages would allow and that the comparative analysis of non-standard and dialectal data is essential if we are to reconstruct that history in all its proper detail (for other cases, see the extensive discussions in Chapter 1, this volume). In particular, the traditional observation that the transition from Latin to Romance involves the loss of the neuter gender cannot be maintained. It is interesting, too, in the context of this debate that the position of the *DÉRom* is closer to that argued for by Loporcaro and farther removed from the view of proto-Romance nominal morphology advocated by Hall (1974).

The *DÉRom* breaks into even more contentious territory with the insistence on coupling reconstructed forms with reconstructed meanings since, when it comes to the latter, a core set of robust and well-tested techniques is not available (see the review in Urban 2011). And yet this move is necessary if consistency is to be achieved, since meanings as well as sounds may have changed with respect to the Latin ancestor even when one is to be found. Thus, the proto-form */kaˈβallu/ needs to be glossed simply as 'horse' and not further specified as a packhorse or horse for riding as with the Latin lexeme CABALLUS. Of course, in simple cases there will be no discrepancy; the 'son/daughter' meanings reconstructible for the proto-forms */ˈɸiliu/ and */ˈɸilia/ map straightforwardly onto the Latin terms FILIUS and FILIA. What unites both the CABALLUS and the FILIUS/-A type items is that they can be reconstructed to a single meaning and are accordingly labelled by Buchi (2012) 'monosemic' as opposed to the more complex polysemic items where different semantic threads have to be disentangled. One of her examples is our already discussed item */ˈbarba/, which in various parts of the Romance territory has come to mean not just 'beard' but also 'chin', a meaning not attested in Latin texts.[3] More complex is the case of */ˈkuɛre-/, which has two principal semantic reflexes: 'ask for' in DRo. *cere*, OIt. *cherere*, ModIt. *chiedere*, Occ. *querre*, and 'want' as in Log. *kèrrere*, Sp./Pt. *querer*. To these the *DÉRom* entry adds a third, namely 'seek', with the cited examples

---

[3] In the special case of old Neapolitan the two meanings are associated with distinct forms, the local reflex *vàrv(e)ra* 'chin' and the Tuscan import *bbarba* 'beard' (Ledgeway 2009: 94 n. 8).

including again DRo. *cere* and OIt. *cherere*, which raises the thorny question that faces all lexicographers, diachronic and synchronic, of when meanings are to be treated as distinct. Here comparison with written Latin confirms that the 'seek' and 'ask for' meanings belong together as part of an older semantic stratum. Conversely, the development of the sense 'love' builds on and comes later than the 'want' sense: compare It. *volere bene* and Pt. *querer bem*. Thus, by allowing – in the online version at least – the possibility of consulting entries via the 'sememes', the *DÉRom* eases the path of enquiry for the modern researcher. We come back to this item in the examples in Section 2.6.2.

What all the dimensions discussed above – phonological, morphological, and semantic – demonstrate is a clear commitment on the part of the compilers of the *DÉRom* to a realist interpretation of the outcome of the reconstructive enterprise. Reconstruction is not simply a means of summing up the differences of form across a related set of languages; it is rather an attempt to shed light on and analyse stages of a language that have been lost from direct historical view, but nonetheless are to be conceived of as real entities subject to the general principles that govern linguistic structure (see Lass 2018 for recent discussion).

It is perhaps inevitable, but unfortunate nonetheless, that the *DÉRom* is usually compared with one of the field's classic reference works, Meyer-Lübke's *Romanisches etymologisches Wörterbuch* (*REW*) (third fully revised edition, 1935). The two enterprises are by no means incompatible and there is ample room for both in the current research landscape. That said, it is instructive to note some of the principal differences between the two. First, as we have said, all the entries in *DÉRom* are prefixed with an asterisk to indicate their reconstructed status, whereas in *REW* only unattested items are so marked, something which arguably implies an unmerited distinction in status between the two types of entry. Second, *DÉRom*, at least in the online version, can be consulted both by form (*signifiants*) and by meaning (*signifiés* or 'proto-sememes'), where the latter are glossed in French as the chosen metalanguage of the whole project.[4] The nearest analogue in *REW* is the index of German–Romance equivalents, though this is by no means as systematic and extensive. Third, the focus of *REW* is much wider. There are close to 10,000 entries, since the aim is to provide coverage of the whole family even where items are only attested in particular subsets of languages. By contrast, the entries in *DÉRom* are considerably more detailed, often constituting mini-essays on the phonology, morphology, syntax, and

---

[4] This in turn reflects the fact that it can no longer be assumed that all Romanists are familiar with German. Indeed, Weiss (2017: 129f.) expresses his own reservation about this decision to use French in this role in the light of the prevalence of English in the world of international science. Regardless of the merits of this debate, in the present chapter our glosses will be in English.

semantics of the items in question: the online entry for */ˈβad-e-/ 'go' in *DÉRom*, for example, is some 5,000 words in length. This, as we will see in Section 2.6.1, opens it up as a valuable resource for reconstructing a wider range of morphosyntactic patterns.

The pros and cons of the *DÉRom* have been debated over the years since the project's inception (see Dworkin 2016 and Weiss 2017 for discussion and references). However, there can be little doubt that its most trenchant critic has been Alberto Varvaro (see Varvaro 2011a; 2011b and the responses from Buchi and Schweickard 2011a; 2011b), for whom the *DÉRom* is simply redundant, first because we already have the excellent etymological enterprise which is the *REW* plus for many individual languages independent and very extensive projects such as the *Lessico etimologico italiano* (Pfister and Schweickard 1979–) and the *Diccionario crítico etimológico castellano e hispánico* (Corominas and Pascual 1991–97), and second because we have the rich documentation of Latin. To go into detail on the various Romance etymological projects would take us too far off course, but the second point is central to the current debate. Varvaro writes (2011a: 300): '[t]o apply in the case of Latin and the Romance languages the methodology which is imposed on us (because of circumstances and not of our own choosing) in the case of Indo-European and the prehistoric Indo-European languages would be like studying the history of Napoleonic France with the methods that are normal in the domain of prehistory'.[5] However, such an analogy implies a parallelism between linguistic and socio-political history which is only in part justified. Languages have structures and systems which can be studied and analysed independently of their social context, as a vast body of general linguistic research has demonstrated. While one must surely agree with Varvaro in many of his other writings (see Maiden 2019 for discussion and references) about the undesirability of too rigid a split between 'internal' and 'external' linguistic history, the fact remains that there is no inconsistency in analysing for example the vowel inventory or the gender classes of an attested and a reconstructed language in the same terms. Indeed it would be hard to do otherwise given the basic assumptions of uniformitarianism (Lass 2018: 160f.). The problem would only present itself if the reconstructed system were taken to replace the attested one, but as Buchi and Schweickard make clear in their replies to Varvaro the intention is to bring the two together not to separate them. In that sense the reconstructed proto-Romance is not an autonomous system but simply provides part of the picture of a complex state of affairs in which spoken and written norms were co-present, as indeed they are in many modern societies.

---

[5] I translate here from the original Italian.

It is true, as Varvaro (2011a: 301) notes, that proto-systems tend to be reductive and to eliminate the sociolinguistic variation that is characteristic of any complex community, but no textual record, even one as rich and varied as we have for Latin, is ever complete. Moreover, as we have seen with the example of the neuter, there will be occasions when the reconstructed pattern transcends and enriches what the texts alone can tell us. More than anything else, therefore, what the debate about *DÉRom* brings into question is the relation between the written and the spoken language and hence the reliability of textual evidence. In the next section therefore we move on to a brief overview of the historical profile and textual variety of Latin.

2.3 Texts and Times: The Chronology of Latin

Languages do not have natural breaks or stages except those that are artificially imposed by the availability of written evidence or by the communities where they are spoken or by those who study them. For some languages, the scholarly tradition has established a chronological sequence of periods such as Old French, Middle French, and Modern French or Old High German, Middle High German. The grounds for making the distinction and the timing differ from language to language even within the same family, so one cannot for example generalize across the 'Old' or 'Middle' stages of different languages (Lass 2000; Smith 2020). It is for this reason that the term 'Old Romance', although sometimes found in the literature, makes no sense. Rather these labels work within individual linguistic traditions (see for example Smith 2002 on the issues around the concept of Middle French). At least, however, such usages are consistent in the chronological sense that modern follows middle and middle follows old. When we come to Latin, things are rather more complex, in part because the tradition of language naming predates modern scholarship and has been driven more by cultural and literary concerns than changes in linguistic structure. A key concept here was *latinitas*, an overtly prescriptive notion defined by writers such as Varro (116–27 BCE) as 'pure' Latin avoiding 'barbarisms' and 'solecisms' (Chahoud 2007: 43), and thus allied to the idea of *sermo urbanus* 'city speech' and contrasted with *sermo rusticus* 'country speech' and *sermo uulgaris* 'popular speech'. These definitions in terms of register and residence were balanced by a chronological but still literary notion of *prisca latinitas* 'old Latinity' which recognized particular words and turns of phrase to be found in early poets and playwrights as no longer in everyday use. Such usages came back into favour amongst writers such Aulus Gellius (second century CE) with the rise of the cult of archaism.

The upshot is that in modern discussions two sets of terms are found: chronological labels such as early and late Latin beside socio-cultural ones like vulgar and classical Latin. In and of itself, this dichotomy is not problematic, since any language will exhibit variation along a number of dimensions: diatopic, diamesic, diastratic, and diachronic. There is a risk, however, when the two are collapsed so that classical is defined both in terms of register and style and chronologically as occupying what we may call the 'long first century BCE' ending with the death of Augustus in 14 CE, a definition accepted for example in Pinkster (2015). This in turn opens the door to thinking of vulgar Latin as a separate language and one which can be treated as a successor to Classical Latin as in the recent proposal by Adamik (2015), so that changes are formulated as a mapping from one to the other. It is preferable to think of Latin as a multi-dimensional historical continuum, albeit one which can be broken down into stages as and when the available data allows or requires it. To this end, we briefly summarize the divisions that have been proposed (for more discussion and references see Vincent 2016a).

The earliest Latin texts go back to the seventh century BCE and are in the main very brief inscriptions and religious dedications, important for our understanding of the relations between Latin and other Italic languages but of less immediate relevance to the Romanist. However, from the third century BCE there is a substantial body of material – in the literature variously labelled as 'early', 'old', or 'archaic' Latin – in which it is possible to find words and structures which seem to prefigure Romance developments. For example, the words for 'ear' in Romance Sp. *oreja*, Cat. *orella*, Fr. *oreille*, It. *orecchia*, Ro. *ureche* imply as etymon not the base form AURIS 'ear' but the diminutive AURICULA found in the sense of '(outer) ear' as early as Plautus and still with that sense in modern Spanish. Similarly, the source of Fr. *menace*, Srd. *minatta*, Pt. *ameaça* 'threat' must be the Plautine MINACIA rather than the classical equivalent MINAE 'threats', while *coquinare* 'to cook', whence It. *cucinare*, Cat. *cuinar*, Frl. *kuziná*, is only ever attested in Plautus (254–184 BCE). Apparent diachronic discontinuities of this kind in turn have led to the hypothesis of 'submerged' Latin to which we return in the next section.

Conventionally, early or old Latin is taken to go down to the end of the first century BCE, though with different endpoints proposed by different scholars. More important, though, than the precise date are two developments that begin to take shape around that time and which have opposing consequences for those who seek to trace the origins of the Romance languages. On the one hand, there is the consolidation of the move to define a pure and correct language – what Rosén (1999) calls the 'crystallization' of classical language – which has the effect of building a prescriptivist wall behind which anyone seeking to reconstruct the spoken language will not always find it easy to penetrate. At the same time, there is an increasing diversity of text types, especially private letters and various kinds of treatise and technical writings devoted to architecture, farming, military matters, and so forth. These not only increase the range of vocabulary but are less subject to, though not entirely free from, the stylistic norms of the classical language. Particularly valuable are texts where the original has survived and can be precisely dated. Thus, Clackson and Horrocks (2007: 238–43) examine in detail the contents of a wax tablet which begins by stating its date of composition as seventeen days before the kalends of October (in modern notation, 15 September 39 CE). The name 'Caesar' occurs here three times in the genitive and is always spelt *Cessaris*, indicating both that the inherited diphthong *ae* had already monophthongized and uncertainty in the use of geminates, the latter further evidenced by *scripssi*, *suma*, and *mile* beside classical SCRIPSI 'I wrote', SUMMA 'total', and MILLE 'thousand'. Such texts thus allow us to complement the relative chronology achieved through the CM.

Like early Latin, the label 'late Latin' has various boundaries, but from the Romanist's perspective the most helpful distinction is that drawn by Herman (1998; cf. also Section 3.2). His first phase covers the period from the first to the sixth century CE and is marked by a set of changes – loss of contrastive vowel length, deletion of final consonants, loss of some case distinctions – that are pan-Romance. In the second phase, running from the sixth to the end of the eighth century, the languages begin to distinguish themselves in terms of patterns of case marking, development of verbal periphrases and so forth. Within the first of these phases, some scholars have also sought to identify a particular variety called Christian Latin, associated with writers such as Tertullian (ca. 155–ca. 240 CE) and Augustine (354–430 CE) but perhaps most obviously with the translation of the Bible known as the Vulgate, by Jerome (347–420 CE). As Burton (2011) notes, the main interest here has been lexical but some syntactic patterns have also figured. Galdi (2016) discusses one such, namely COEPI/INCIPIO 'begin' + infinitive as an emergent future periphrasis. His study demonstrates that while COEPI retains its lexical value throughout, INCIPIO does indeed develop a future meaning, in his words 'probably as a loan shift of Greek μέλλω', but this usage does not move beyond Christian writing. Drinka (2017: 132–38) likewise concludes that Christian Latin exhibits numerous Greek influences but that for the most part these do not generalize beyond the writings of that religious community.

Finally, we must mention Medieval Latin. The label is chronological, but what is referred to is not a stage in the historical evolution of the language but rather a diverse set of codified grammatical norms and stylistic practices taught in monasteries and universities rather than constituting anyone's mother tongue. These are too rich and various to be summarized here, but we will briefly consider one such body of texts and the general lessons that we can derive from them. Sornicola et al. (2017) is a detailed study of the grammar, lexis, and scribal practices of an archive of legal documents from the ninth century CE preserved at the abbey of Cava de' Tirreni in Campania. As with many such collections of medieval texts, the vocabulary is limited by the topic but there are still lessons to be learnt. For instance, many of the documents relate to inheritance and so we find a range of family terms including for 'uncle' only *barba*, although southern Italy falls within the area where reflexes of *thios* are the norm. This discrepancy is to be explained by the fact that the documents reflect the importation from the north of Langobardic legal practices, hence the fact that the term BARBANUS in these documents has been glossed with PATRUUS. Similarly, the word for 'brother' is *germanus*, source of the usual word for that relation in Ibero-Romance (Sp. *hermano*, Cat. *germà*, etc.), but here used in the more technical sense of 'son of father' as contrasted with *germanus uterinus* 'son of mother', and in contrast to the modern regional forms derived from Lat. FRATER.

In the domain of morphosyntax, we find a mix of innovative and conservative traits. Thus, attested here is an early use of the preposition *da* (< DE AB) to mark both source and the agent in a passive construction just as in modern Italian and modern Campanian varieties, and noun plurals such as *emptori* 'buyers' – compare It. *rettori* 'rectors' and *pittori* 'painters' – beside the classically correct *emptores*. The system of verbal inflexion likewise combines classical forms with new analogical formations such as *poteo* 'I can' (built to the stem *pote-* as in It. *potere* 'to be able') beside *posso* (< POSSUM 'I can').[6] Noteworthy too in the context of our discussion in Sections 2.4–5 of the emergence of the Romance perfect periphrasis is the fact that the recurrent transactional expression *habeo traditum* means 'I possess (something) which has been handed down to me' and not 'I have handed something down'. When it comes to clause combining, particularly striking is the frequent attestation of QUOMODO both in the comparative meaning 'as, like' seen in Fr. *comme*, Sp. *como*, etc. and in something nearer to the function that leads to its reflexes in the southern Italian complementizers *cu* and *mu* (De Angelis 2013; Ledgeway 2016: 269).

More generally, these texts – and many other instances across the whole of the Romance-speaking territory – provide a valuable part of the story, but for the full picture to emerge we need to work back from the modern forms as well as forward from the written material.

---

[6] Michael Weiss points out that formations like this are already attested in the Italic language Oscan spoken in this region, such as third person singular present subjunctive *pútíad* 's/he may' for classical POSSIT.

2.4 The Issue of 'Submerged' Latin

As we have noted, the traditional labels for identifying types of Latin are not exclusively chronological. In particular, since Classical Latin is defined principally in terms of register and style, words and structures may be attested in poetry and prose produced before the establishment of such norms, only to disappear or occur less frequently in classical texts and then re-emerge at a later stage (cf. also Section 29.2.1). Herein lies the essence of the hypothesis of 'submerged' Latin first advanced in Marx (1909). On this view, for example the Plautine passage *uir me habet despicatam* (Pl., *Cas.* 186) lit. 'husband.NOM me.ACC have.PRS.3SG despise.PST.PTCP.ACC.FSG' has been seen as an early precursor to the Romance periphrastic perfect (cf. Sections 4.3, 18.3, and 21.2.2) and has been translated as 'my husband has despised me.' A careful reading in context, however, indicates that a more accurate rendering would be 'my husband holds me in contempt' with *habet* acting as a main verb with its widely attested sense 'hold, consider' and *despicatam* as a secondary predicate. As Haverling (2016) shows in detail, this kind of usage continues through the classical era and into later texts. Augustine (Aug. *In psalmos enarrationes* 76.4, fourth century CE), for example, writes *sic habes scriptum in libro Job* meaning 'you find it written thus in the book of Job' and not 'you have written ...'. Similarly, the oft-cited passage from Gregory of Tours (*Vitae patrum* 3.1, sixth century CE) *episcopum cum duce et civibus invitatum habes* means 'you have the bishop together with the duke and citizens as an invited guest' and not 'you have invited ...'. Haverling (2016: 200) concludes: 'There is ... no particular connection between early and late Latin in this case, since the development seems to be a steady, gradual and rather slow one.'

What this example shows is the need for attentive construal in context, something that is of course only possible when there is a body of texts available for consultation and analysis. Another instance of the same kind is the claim that early evidence of suppletion with 'go' verbs is to be found in a usage such as Plautus (Pl. *Cur.* 621) *ambula in ius* lit. 'walk.IMP.2SG in court.ACC (= walk to court!)' with the reply *non eo* 'NEG go.PRS.1SG (= I'm not going)'. Rosén (1999) argues that this is to be explained on the basis of the phonetic weakness of the monosyllabic imperative *i* of the verb IRE 'go', and hence a preference for the corresponding form of the verb AMBULARE 'walk', the etymological source of ModFr. *aller* 'go'. However, as Adams (2013: 792–820) shows in detail, this passage must be understood as 'walk to court (as opposed to being forcibly transported)' and he further notes that there are in the region of 120 instances of the imperative *i* in Plautus so we have no reason to believe that the playwright was averse to its use when appropriate. That said, there is no doubt that the attestation of monosyllabic forms of IRE declines with the passage of time, but the process is gradual and consistent with their displacement by forms of UADERE in the paradigm of 'go' verbs in various Romance languages.

A third case which has received considerable attention in the literature is the relation between the dative and the sequence AD 'to(wards)' + NP as the complement of verbs of saying, giving, and the like. The classical norm requires the dative in such cases, whereas all the Romance languages show the prepositional pattern. Against this background the use by Cato (234–149 BCE) of AD in the sentence *ad praetores et consules uinum honorarium dabant* (*Orationes* fr. 132) lit. 'to praetor.ACC.PL and consul.ACC.PL wine.ACC honorary.ACC they.gave (= they gave wine to the praetors and consuls as a token of esteem)' seems to anticipate Romance usage (cf. also Section 29.2.1). Adams and De Melo (2016: 96) argue, however, that in contexts such as this where the gift is sent rather than handed over directly in person, it is the movement involved which determines the choice of the prepositional alternative. Similarly, Baños Baños (2000) shows that while Cicero uses AD more frequently than the dative with the verb SCRIBERE 'write', the reverse is true with Seneca despite the fact that Seneca is writing almost a century later. Once again the explanation is that in Cicero's case the letters were actually sent by courier to the recipient, whereas Seneca's letters are a literary device with a virtual rather than real addressee. It is only in the late Latin period that we start to find precursors of Romance usage and the preference for AD over the dative even when no movement is involved.

What all the examples reviewed in this section show is that before conclusions can be drawn about morphosyntactic change, a range of factors need to be taken into account; in particular genre, register, meaning, and construction type (cf. also Chapter 27, this volume). Considerations of this kind obviously depend on access to a substantial body of texts and would therefore seem in part to justify Varvaro's scepticism concerning the *DÉRom* project discussed above. Paradoxically, however, they also confirm that the directionality and chronology of the changes which have been studied are in the main linear and sequential. New constructions emerge and over time embed themselves in the language, either creating new oppositions and contrasts or provoking the loss of an older construction, something which is very much in line with the assumptions of the CM.

2.5 The Role of Language Contact

So far the discussion has centred, not unreasonably, on forms and meanings in Latin, but it must be remembered that the Roman empire was linguistically very diverse with many languages being spoken over the full extent of the imperial territory (for details see Adams et al. 2002; Adams

2003). What is perhaps less typical of large empires is that there was also a degree of bilingualism at its very centre, with a special role for Greek both as a language that formed part of the core curriculum for the educated elite and as the language of immigrant communities in the centre and south of the Italian peninsula. In consequence there are many Greek loanwords in Latin and also, as recently emphasized by Dickey (2018), many Latin loanwords in Greek. When examining the textual sources, it is important to distinguish loans from codeswitching (Adams 2003: 18–29), but from the perspective of reconstruction this is less of a problem since by definition anything that has survived across some or all the Romance languages must have been integrated into the earlier linguistic system. We have already seen an example of this with the Greek words *thios, thia* 'uncle, aunt'. Another such case is the source of the word for 'leg' in a range of Romance languages: Cat. *camba*, Fr. *jambe*, Srd. *kamba*, It. *gamba*. These items license a proto-form */ˈkamba/ or */ˈgamba/, but it is the knowledge of the Greek word *kampé* which tells us that the historically underlying initial consonant was voiceless. At the same time, it is only the textual evidence that tells us that the context of the borrowing is veterinary language and that the term originally referred to the lower part of a horse's leg before generalizing its meaning in Romance (Adams 1982: 9).

When it comes to syntax, the question of borrowings from Greek is much less certain. Simple similarity of patterns is not sufficient. Thus, ancient Greek already had a well-developed system of definite articles and, as Adams (2003: 763) observes, 'the earliest uses of Latin demonstratives with article function directly imitate Greek usages, as for example in Plautus ... But it was centuries after Plautus that the article function was established in non-Grecising Latin, and it has to be assumed that there were influences additional to mere imitation of Greek.' Similarly, Vincent (2016b) notes the parallels between early uses of Lat. FACERE and Grk. ποιέω 'make, do' in combination with an infinitive in a way that seems to anticipate the Romance causative construction as in Fr. *il fera lire le roman à ses étudiants* 'he will make his students read the novel'. There is, however, a significant difference in that the Romance constructions tend to have agentive subjects, whereas both the early Latin and the Greek examples are restricted to natural forces such as the sun and the wind as in *uentus fecit spissescere nubem* (Lucretius *De rerum natura* 6.176, first century BCE) 'the wind has made the cloud thicken'. Examples with agent subjects akin to Romance only appear with any frequency some five centuries later. More generally and having surveyed a range of possible syntactic Grecisms, Einar Löfstedt (1959: 99) observes: '[i]t is impossible not to conclude that, interesting and noteworthy as they may be, [these Grecisms] nevertheless exercised no decisive or lasting influence upon the structure of Latin as a whole', a view endorsed more recently by both Coleman (1975: 147) and Adams (2003: 763).

The question of the relation between the two languages has recently been reopened by Drinka (2017), who has made the most detailed and persuasive case to date for Greek influence on Latin syntax in her account of the rise and spread of the periphrastic perfect construction. The variant of this construction with alternating BE and HAVE auxiliaries according to the argument structure of the lexical verb is attested both in Romance (French, Italian) and Germanic (Danish, German), and even where it is not attested in the modern languages (English, Swedish, Spanish, Sicilian) there is diachronic evidence of the earlier existence of the alternation (cf. Section 21.2.2). Thus, the Italian distinction between *Giorgio è corso alla stazione* lit. 'George is run to the station', i.e., 'George has run to the station' with the BE auxiliary expressing motion, and *Giorgio ha corso per due ore* 'Giorgio has run for two hours' with the HAVE auxiliary expressing activity is paralleled by Danish *hun er gået* 'she has gone (away)' with BE versus *hun har gået* 'she has walked' with HAVE when the verb *gå* 'go, walk' is used in the activity sense. And just as old Spanish had *son venidos* 'they are come' where the modern language has *han venido* 'they have come', so in Old English we find *hie sind gecumene* lit. 'they are come' in contrast to modern English *they have come*. At the same time, a periphrasis of this kind is not widespread among the languages of the world and therefore it is hard to believe that its co-occurrence in two families as geographically close as Romance and Germanic is attributable to independent developments. In consequence, many have argued that the Germanic patterns are the result of contact with Latin (though see Heine and Kuteva 2006 for a dissenting voice). Drinka (2017: ch. 9) adopts a similar position, albeit with a continuing role for Greek especially in relation to Gothic, and interprets the Romance developments in the context of what, following van der Auwera (1998), she calls the 'Charlemagne Sprachbund'.

The question then is: how did Latin acquire the construction? The standard answer is that it developed internally through the grammaticalization of HABERE 'have' plus the past participle of transitive and unergative verbs beside and as a complement to the use of ESSE 'be' to express the perfect of passives, deponents, and in due course unaccusative verbs (Ledgeway 2012: 317–19; cf. also Sections 19.3.2–3). It is this integrated system which is then, so to speak, exported to Germanic.[7] Drinka raises the question of what triggers this chain of developments, and argues that the answer lies in a parallel HAVE construction in Greek which served as the model for various writers, among whom she singles out in particular Vitruvius (first century BCE), author of the technical treatise *De architectura*. The problem here lies

---

[7] Here is not the place to go into the further question whether the Germanic HAVE/BE alternation is to be reconstructed to the proto-language or whether, as Drinka (2017: ch. 9) argues, Latin influenced each language independently at different periods and in different ways.

in the fact that, as she notes, in the classical and immediately post-classical era there are very few attested examples of HABERE with a past participle, and for those that are found the intended meaning appears to be possessive rather than perfective. These facts in turn suggest an alternative explanation akin to Adams' argument cited above in the case of the definite article: early examples of a more or less slavish adoption of Greek models in particular writers and a later independent grammaticalization process. Such a conclusion would also appear to chime better with the data discussed by Haverling (2016). However, there is not space here to debate the matter fully. The important point in the present context is that countervailing hypotheses such as these could not even be formulated, let alone resolved, were it not for the availability of a rich body of texts, which can be explored in both quantitative and qualitative terms.

We have concentrated here on Greek and the nature of syntactic contact. For other languages such as Celtic and Germanic, and at earlier stages various languages of the Italian peninsula, whether cognate with Latin (Oscan, Umbrian) or not (Etruscan), the inheritance in Romance is by and large lexical: see Adams (2003) and Weiss (2020: ch. 42) for discussion and references. An exception is Latin! Not only is Latin in one form or another the source of the Romance languages, it is also in its formal, written, and prescribed version a factor which helps to shape the individual languages, especially those which come to act as national or regional standard languages. One hallmark of this is what have come to be called 'learnèd' sound patterns. For example, while the stressed vowel in It. *pésce* 'fish' is [e], as would be expected by regular sound change from PISCEM, the Italian technical adjective *piscatorio* 'of, related to fishing' retains the original Latin vowel. Similarly, It. *ghiaccio* 'ice' exemplifies the regular development of Lat. [Cl] > [Cj], but the associated Italian adjective *glaciale* 'glacial' does not. At the same time, there is no general rule that adjectives do not undergo sound changes – contrast It. *biondo* from the Germanic loan *blund* beside Fr. *blond* – and hence anyone seeking to apply the CM to forms like this would have to be on their guard about which forms to choose as input to the comparison.

A different kind of learnèd influence is that which derives from translation. Consider forms such as Sp. *habiendo hablado* 'having spoken' or Fr. *étant venu* 'having (lit. 'being') come'. Given the evidence we have seen above for the perfect periphrasis with HAVE and BE as part of the emergent Romance verbal systems already in the sixth or seventh centuries BCE, it would be natural to fill out the reconstructed paradigm with these periphrastic or compound participles. In fact, however, we know from the textual tradition that such forms only come into use from the thirteenth century onwards when they were coined in vernacular translations of Latin classics, as when Virgil's *sic ore effata* (Aeneid 2.524) is rendered in Italian as *ed avendo così parlato* 'and having thus spoken' in Ciampolo de Meo's fourteenth-century translation (Vincent 2016a: 13). Examples such as this are yet another demonstration of the way the CM can yield relative chronology, but for absolute dating we need textual evidence of one kind or another.

2.6 Reconstruction and Levels of Language: Three Case Studies

Having reviewed the textual tradition, we return in this final section to the CM and in particular to the contested domain of syntactic reconstruction. Here too we will see that the *DÉRom* is an invaluable resource even if the project itself is more centrally concerned with form and meaning at the lexical level.

2.6.1 The Verb GO

If we consult the *DÉRom* via the sememe 'aller' ('go') we access an entry divided into two sub-parts, the first */ˈβad-e-/ labelled 'original' and the second */ˈβ-a-/ described as 'evolved' (*évolué*). Each is then broken down into three sub-categories: full verb of movement; inchoative-ingressive semi-auxiliary which may subsequently combine with an infinitive to yield a future periphrasis; co-extensive semi-auxiliary which may subsequently combine with the *gerundio/gérondif* to produce a progressive periphrasis. So far so good and already much more detailed and precise than the entry 9117 *vadĕre* in the *REW*. By dividing things in this way the entry also implicitly makes the point that the formal development of the GO verbs in Romance is independent of their lexical and grammatical content. There are various patterns of suppletion (cf. also Chapter 12, this volume): for example, Spanish has *ir* for the infinitive, a present tense that uses *va-* throughout, and a preterite *fui, fuiste*, etc. derived from the BE verb, while in Galician reflexes of Lat. IRE provide the first and second person plurals of the present as well as the infinitive, forms which in French, by contrast, derive from Lat. AMBULARE. However, whatever the pattern, in most varieties the same forms are used both in the full lexical meaning GO and in the various periphrases: exceptions here are Catalan, some Aragonese dialects, and Occitan (Jacobs and Kunert 2014). By contrast the periphrases vary across the languages so that modern French does not have the GO progressive pattern and only Italian has GO plus past participle in the modal passive sense: *va fatto* 'go.PRS.IND.3SG do.PTCP (= it must be done)'. And while GO plus the infinitive has a future meaning in French it has a preterite meaning in Catalan and Occitan but only the full lexical meaning in Italian. This diversity is consistent with the constructions arising in Herman's second phase mentioned above. At the same time the Latin textual evidence for these patterns is scanty at best.

The only way, therefore, that we can come to a complete picture of the changing forms and functions of GO in Romance is via detailed cross-linguistic and cross-dialectal comparison.

2.6.2 Control and WANT Verbs

Our second case study concerns the form and interpretation of the complement of verbs meaning WANT (cf. also Section 20.5.2). Cross-linguistically, we find languages such as English in which an infinitival structure is used with both co-referential and disjoint arguments as in (1), languages such as Modern Greek in which a finite clause is used in both circumstances (2) and languages such as French in which the co-referential pattern has an infinitive while the disjoint pattern requires a finite clause (3) (Haspelmath 2013).

(1) a. Bill wants to come.
    b. Bill wants Fred to come.

(2) **Greek**
    a. O   Kostas   theli   na   erthi.
       DEF   Kostas   want.PRS.3SG   COMP   come.PRS.3SG
       'Kostas wants to come.'
    b. O   Kostas   theli   na   erthi   o   Yanis.
       DEF   Kostas   want.PRS.3SG   COMP   come.PRS.3SG   DEF   Yanis
       'Kostas wants Yanis to come.'

(3) **French**
    a. Pierre   veut   venir.
       Pierre   want.PRS.IND.3SG   come.INF
       'Pierre wants to come.'
    b. Pierre   veut   que   Paul   vienne.
       Pierre   want.PRS.IND.3SG   COMP   Paul   come.PRS.SBJV.3SG
       'Pierre wants Paul to come.'

The French pattern is also found across the whole family with the exception of extreme southern Italian dialects and the varieties of Daco-Romance, where we find instead a pattern very similar to Greek (cf. Section 1.2.3.3.1). Thus, compare Spanish and Vegliote Dalmatian in (4) and (5) with Salentino and Romanian in (6) and (7):

(4) **Spanish**
    a. Quiero   venir.
       want.PRS.IND.1SG   come.INF
       'I want to come.'
    b. Quiero   que   Juan   venga.
       want.PRS.IND.1SG   COMP   Juan   come.PRS.SBJV.3SG
       'I want Juan to come.'

(5) **Vegliote (Maiden 2016b, ex. 112)**
    jal 'bule   ven'dur toʧ   per'ko
    he   want.PRS.IND.3SG   sell.INF everything   because
    la   'tsua niena blaja   ke   la ven'dua.
    DEF his mother want.IPFV.3SG COMP it=sell.PRS.SBJV.3SG
    'he wants to sell everything because his mother wants him to sell it'

(6) **Salentino (Calabrese 1993)**
    a. Lu   Karlu ole   ku   bbene   krai.
       the Carlo want.PRS.IND.3SG   COMP come.PRS.IND.3SG   tomorrow
       'Carlo wants to come tomorrow.'
    b. Lu   Karlu ole   ku   bbene   lu   Maryu.
       the Carlo want.PRS.IND.3SG   COMP come.PRS.IND.3SG   the Mario
       'Carlo wants Mario to come.'

(7) **Romanian**
    a. Vreau   să   vin.
       want.PRS.1SG   SA   come.SBJV.1SG
       'I want to come.'
    b. Vreau   ca   Ion să   vină.
       want.PRS.1SG   COMP   Ion SA   come.SBJV.3SG
       'I want Ion to come.'

Sardinian by contrast allows an infinitival construction even with non-co-referential subjects (Jones 1993: 268):

(8) **Sardinian**
    a. Non keljo   vennere.
       NEG want.PRS.IND.1SG   come.INF
       'I don't want to come'
    b. Non keljo   a   vénnere   tue.
       NEG want.PRS.IND.1SG   to   come.INF you.NOM
       'I don't want you to come.'

Given this range of modern data, there are (at least!) four diachronic questions which arise. How are we to explain:

(a) the pattern of alternation between finite and non-finite? Here the textual tradition is rich and helpful and allows us to document the emergence of a system of finite complementation introduced by reflexes of QUID, QUOD, QUIA, and QUOMODO in lieu of the Latin accusative and infinitive construction. Examples were already noted for early Latin by Bennett (1910: 130), who commented that in some contexts 'the causal notion is usually very slight, *quia* having the force rather of "that"'. The construction becomes more widespread and frequent with the passage of time (Cuzzolin 1994; 2013). However, even without such textual evidence we would be forced to reconstruct a set of finite complementizers on the basis of forms such as Pt./Sp./Cat./Fr. *que*, It. *che*, Srd. *chi*, Sal. *cu*, and Ro. *că* accompanied in different contexts by finite verbs, either indicative or subjunctive (Ledgeway 2012: §4.4). This development goes hand in hand with the recession of the classical accusative and infinitive construction, so that the infinitive is now only possible with co-reference, or what is traditionally known as the prolative infinitive.

(b) the generalization of the finite? This is best seen as an extension of the Balkan *Sprachbund* (Joseph 1983; Friedman and Joseph 2021), and is undoubtedly to be attributed to Greek influence but at a much later historical stage than the Greek borrowings discussed above. In other words this is a contact effect rather than an internally motivated development.

(c) the generalization of the infinitive? This is part of a wider phenomenon whereby some Romance languages develop infinitival constructions with a nominative subject (cf. Bentley 2014 on Sicilian, and Section 1.2.2.2 for the wider Romance picture) while others have so-called inflected infinitives which agree with their subjects in a fashion usually associated with finite verbs (Campidanese, old Neapolitan, Portuguese; cf. Section 1.2.2.3).

(d) the shift from UELLE to QUAERERE? The Latin verb meaning 'want' is UELLE, built on a root that can be reconstructed back to proto-Indo-European and the source of the corresponding item in numerous Romance languages (Fr. *vouloir*, It. *volere*, Frl. *volê*, Ro. *vrea*). It is paradoxical, therefore, that when one consults the *DÉRom* via the sememe 'vouloir' the only form given is */ˈkuɛre-/, which corresponds to Lat. QUAERERE 'seek'. As we noted in Section 2.2, this etymon is listed with three meanings: 'seek', 'ask for', 'want', of which 'seek' is undoubtedly the oldest. In fact, Marx (1909) in his pursuit of submerged Latin had already adduced Terence *quid sibi hic uestitus quaerit* (*Eunuchus* 558) 'what does this garment mean?' as having an implicit sense of 'want'. However, it is only later as with Tacitus *qui mutare sedes quaerebant* (*Germania* 2) 'who want to change places' and especially with Christian writers such as Tertullian that we find uses that anticipate the Romance development (Maggiore 2014). It is striking too that the Romance reflexes of both Latin items display properties of so-called restructuring. Thus, compare It. *lo vuole fare*, Sp. *lo quiere hacer*, and Srd. *lu keret fákere* 'it= want.PRS.IND.3SG do.INF (= he wants to do it)', where the clitic object of the infinitive is attached to the finite WANT verb. This effect is a systematic property of control structures in a range of languages (Grano 2015).

In this example, then, we have seen two further dimensions that constitute an essential part of modern historical work in the syntactic domain. In addition to reconstruction and attestation, we have the insights emerging from the general linguistic theory of complementation, and more precisely the theory of control, supplemented and interacting with the establishment of cross-linguistic patterns of typological diversity.

2.6.3 Recomplementation

In addition to the single occurrences of complementizers discussed in the previous section, some modern varieties attest to the occurrence of double or iterated complementizers (cf. also Section 1.2.3.3.1),[8] the first occurring before the whole embedded clause and the second after the initial focalized or topicalized item. Thus, in colloquial Spanish (9) and Portuguese (10) we find examples (complementizers in bold) such as:

(9) Susi   dice   **que** a   los   alumnos,   (**que**) les
     Susi   say.PRS.IND.3SG   that   to   the   pupils   that   to.them=
     van   a   dar   regalos. (Sp.)
     go.PRS.IND.3PL   to   give.INF   gifts
     'Susi says that they are going to give presents to the students.'

(10) Duvido   **que** a   Ana **que** goste   de ópera. (Pt.)
     doubt.PRS.IND1SG   that   the Ana   that   like.PRS.SBJV.3SG of opera
     'I doubt that Ana likes opera.'

And Paoli (2007: 1058) cites the following from a conservative variety of Turinese:

(11) Gioanin   a   spera   **che** Ghitin   **ch'** as
     Giovanni   SCL=   hope.PRS.IND.3SG   that   Margherita   that   SCL.self=
     në   vada   tòst. (Tur.)
     thence=   go.PRS.SBJV.3SG   soon
     'Giovanni hopes that Margherita leaves soon.'

This phenomenon has been called 'recomplementation' (Villa-García 2012) and might be dismissed simply as a modern development – which in these varieties it may well be – were it not for the fact that it is also widely attested in medieval Romance (for a richer selection of examples, see Wanner 1998; Vincent 2006; and Ribeiro and Torres Morais 2012):

(12) je te adjure ...   **que** ta   fille   Tarsienne **que** tu   ne   la
     I you=beseech.PRS.1SG   that   your daughter   Tarsienne that you not her=
     donnes   a   marriage a   autre que   a   moy (Apoll. f48b, fourteenth-c. Fr.)
     give.PRS.SBJV.2SG to   marriage to   other that to   me
     'I beg you not to give your daughter Tarsienne in marriage to anyone but me'

---

[8] The term 'dual complementizer' is also found (for example Ledgeway 2012: 170) with reference to those varieties which have different complementizers in different modal contexts. This is a distinct phenomenon from the one we address here, though it too is something whose early history we can reconstruct (as indeed Ledgeway does) and for which the textual evidence from Latin provides only partial support.

(13) le   aveva   ditto   **che** se sua maistà voleva   lo
     him= have.PST.IPFV.3SG say.PTCP that if his majesty want.PST.IPFV.3SG the
     stato suo **che** se   llo venesse   a ppigliare co   la spata in
     state his that self= it= come.PST.SBJV.3SG to take.INF with the sword in
     mano (*Ferraiolo* 148v.1–2, fifteenth-c.-Nap.)
     hand
     'he had said to him that if his majesty wanted his territory he should come to take it with his sword in his hand'

(14) Non credati   vuy **che** cascuna creatura **che** nasce
     not believe.PRS.SBJV.2PL you that each   creature that be.born.PRS.IND.3SG
     che Deo IN   QUILLO PUNTO comandi   lu suo
     that   god in   that   point command.PRS.SBJV.3SG the his
     nascimento (*Libro di Sidrac* 9v.16–17, mid fifteenth-c. Sal.)
     birth
     'Do not believe that for each creature who is born God at that point commanded his birth'

Given that this construction is to be found in a range of text types and across a spread of medieval varieties from Castile through to southern Italy, it is not unreasonable to reconstruct it to the period in which the complementizer system is taking shape, but as to when within that period exactly it is hard to say. As already noted, the CM yields only a relative chronology and not an absolute one. And on this occasion Latin texts are of little help since recomplementation is virtually unattested there. An exception from the texts from Cava de' Tirreni referenced in Section 2.3 is (15) (cited and discussed by Greco 2017: 295–98):

(15) scriptum   est   ut femina   qui   parentes   non
     write.PTCP be.PRS.IND.3SG that woman.NOM who.NOM relative.ACC.PL not
     habuerit   ut in mundium   palatjii   subiacerent[9]
     have.SBJV.PFV.3SG that in protection.ACC palace.GEN come.under.SBJV.IPFV.3PL
     'it is written that a woman who does not have relatives should come under the protection of the palace'

In principle, too, we need to exclude independent innovation. Although the structural parallels both as regards the position of the iterated complementizers and the intervening categories might seem to render this alternative less likely, occasional examples of a similar pattern in Old English (Salvesen and Walkden 2017: 180 n. 15) show that the Romance developments discussed here are not unique.

While we find doubling of the finite complementizers, we do not for the most part find a parallel iteration of pre-infinitival particles such as Fr. *de* 'of', *à* 'to' and It. *di* 'of', *a* 'to', a fact which would follow naturally if,

---

[9] The plural verb *subiacerent* after the singular subject *femina* is best construed as agreement *ad sensum*; the principle of protection applies to all such women and not just one.

following Rizzi (1997), it is assumed that the finite and non-finite items occupy different structural positions, *Force* and *Fin* respectively. But in this instance one body of texts provides a significant challenge. The Sardinian legal documents from the thirteenth century known as the *Condaghe Silki* contain numerous examples like the following, in which the purposive expression *in fine* 'in order to' contains two occurrences of *de* surrounding the protasis of the embedded hypothetical:

(16) in fine de si lu perdea   custu de torraremi   saltu (OSrd.)
      in end of if it= lose.PST.IPFV.3SG this of return.INF=me woodland
      'so that if I were to lose this, he would give me the woody terrain in return'

However, here the most natural conclusion would seem to be that this is a local idiosyncrasy, arguably connected to the different role of the infinitive in Sardinian noted above, and not a case where the textual evidence leads us to overturn what has been reconstructed across the wider family on general linguistic grounds.

2.7 Conclusion and General Lessons

A recurrent theme in this chapter has been the contrast between data derived from texts and data which depend on reconstruction and the application of general linguistic principles. This in turn raises the question of what the relation is between these two and between the disciplines – philology and general linguistics – that they in turn depend on. Sornicola (2011: 48f.) is in no doubt when she writes:

> At the close of the nineteenth century, Schuchardt held that a Romanist should be a general linguist before addressing problems of historical linguistics ... In the twentieth, in different ways, Coseriu and Malkiel attempted the difficult task of reconciling general linguistics and historical linguistics, but their work shows the importance of being a Romanist before being a general linguist.

In a different vein, Fleischman (2000: 51f.) also expresses concerns about the way general linguistics has interacted over the years with textual philology:

> What linguistics held out to philology at the end of the nineteenth century was a methodology for systematizing, reifying, and in the process, one must acknowledge, denaturing its object of study in the name of linguistic description.

On this view, both writers of grammars of older languages – in her case old French, but the lesson is a more general one – and editors of older texts have been induced by ideas derived from general linguistics about the centrality of structure to overemphasize the uniformity of the language or text under investigation. Fleischman's plea to introduce into the study of language change some of the ideas of variationist sociolinguistics is well taken and is reminiscent of the concerns expressed by Varvaro about the role of the CM within the *DÉRom* project. At the same time, as we have seen with Latin-Romance gender patterns, GO verbs and (re)complementation, there are instances where reconstruction can lead to a richer and more nuanced system than that derivable from the textual record alone. The lesson to be learned, I would suggest, from the evidence surveyed in this chapter is not to set linguistics and philology, the CM and texts, the *DÉRom* and the *REW*, against each other but to deploy each as and when appropriate. They are compatible not contradictory, and the picture will be clearest when the light from both is shone on the target (cf. also Section 1.2.4.3).

Selected References

Below you can find selected references for this chapter. The full references can be found online at the following page: www.cambridge.org/Romancelinguistics

Adams, J. (2013). *Social Variation and the Latin Language*. Cambridge: Cambridge University Press.
Buchi, E. and Schweickard, W. (2011). 'Ce qui oppose vraiment deux conceptions de l'étymologie romane. Réponse à Alberto Vàrvaro et contribution à un débat méthodologique en cours', *Revue de Linguistique Romane* 75: 628–35.
Corominas, J. and Pascual, J. A. (1991–97). *Diccionario crítico etimológico castellano e hispánico*. Madrid: Gredos.
Dardel, R. (1965). *Recherches sur le genre roman des substantifs de la troisième déclinaison*. Geneva: Librairie Droz.
Drinka, B. (2017). *Language Contact in Europe. The Periphrastic Perfect through History*. Cambridge: Cambridge University Press.
Dworkin, S. N. (2016). 'Do Romanists need to reconstruct Proto-Romance? The case of the *Dictionnaire Étymologique Roman (DÉRom)* project', *Zeitschrift für romanische Philologie* 132: 1–19.
Elcock, W. D. (1960). *The Romance Languages*. London: Faber & Faber.
Hall, R. A. (1974). *Proto-Romance Phonology*. New York: Elsevier.
Haverling, G. (2016). 'On the use of *habeo* and the perfect participle in earlier and later Latin'. In Adams, J. and Vincent, N. (eds), *Early and Late Latin: Continuity or Change?* Cambridge: Cambridge University Press, 180–201.
Lass, R. (2018). [Review of Buchi and Schweickard (eds) (2014) and (2016)], *Zeitschrift für romanische Philologie* 134: 580–87.

Ledgeway A. (2012). *From Latin to Romance: Morphosyntactic Typology and Change*. Oxford: Oxford University Press.

Ledgeway, A. and Maiden, M. (eds) (2016). *The Oxford Guide to the Romance Languages*. Oxford: Oxford University Press.

Loporcaro, M. (2011a). 'Syllable, segment and prosody'. In Maiden, M., Smith, J. C., and Ledgeway, A. (eds), *The Cambridge History of the Romance Languages. Vol I: Structures*. Cambridge: Cambridge University Press, 50–108.

Loporcaro, M. (2018) *Gender from Latin to Romance: History, Geography, Typology*. Oxford: Oxford University Press.

Maiden, M. (2016a). 'Romanian, Istro-Romanian, Megleno-Romanian, and Aromanian'. In Ledgeway, A. and Maiden, M. (eds), *The Oxford Guide to the Romance Languages*. Oxford: Oxford University Press, 91–125.

Meyer-Lübke, W. (1935). *Romanisches etymologisches Wörterbuch*, 3rd ed. Heidelberg: Carl Winter.

Pfister, M. and Schweickard, W. (1979–). *Lessico etimologico italiano*. Mainz: Akademie der Wissenschaften und der Literatur.

Rosén, H. (1999). *Latine Loqui: Trends and Directions in the Crystallization of Classical Latin*. Munich: Wilhelm Fink.

Sornicola, R. (2011). 'Romance linguistics and historical linguistics: reflections on synchrony and diachrony'. In Maiden, M., Smith, J. C., and Ledgeway, A. (eds), *The Cambridge History of the Romance Languages. Vol I: Structures*. Cambridge: Cambridge University Press, 1–49.

Varvaro, A. (2011). 'La 'rupture étymologique' del *DÉRom*. Ancora sul metodo dell'etimologia romanza', *Revue de linguistique romane* 75: 623–27.

Weiss, M. (2017). [Review of Buchi and Schweickard (2014)], *Kratylos* 62: 127–53.

3

Documentation and Sources

Alvise Andreose and Laura Minervini

3.1 Introduction

The study of Romance languages is characterized by a richness and depth of documentation that makes it possible to follow their development seamlessly from the late Latin stage to the present – a perhaps unique case in linguistics.*

Until relatively recently, knowledge of the history of Romance languages was based only on written sources. By the nineteenth century – within the movement, broadly inspired by Romanticism, for recovery of popular traditions – dialect texts began to be transcribed directly from the voices of speakers. How much this material was consciously or unconsciously manipulated by researchers is another matter. The first field-based dialectal enquiry on Romance was published in the last years of the century, leading to the creation of the *Atlas Linguistique de la France* by Jules Gilliéron (see Section 3.5): the results of interviews carried out in different places in France were projected in cartographic form, forming the basis of the atlas.

It was only from the early twentieth century that direct access to oral documentation of Romance languages became possible, thanks to voice-recording techniques. Among the oldest was the *Phonogrammarchiv* of the *Kaiserliche Akademie der Wissenschaften* of Vienna, established in 1899 with the aim of collecting and preserving a wide range of 'voices of the world'. In this ambitious project there are many field-based works on Romance languages: e.g., Istro-Romanian, Balkan Judaeo-Spanish, Romansh, Romagnol

---

* This chapter is the result of close collaboration between the authors. Sections 3.1 and 3.5–6 are particularly the work of Minervini, Sections 3.2–4 the work of Andreose. All consultations of online sites took place in November 2018.

dialects, Friulian, Dolomitic Ladin, all accompanied by recordings and transcriptions of significant historical value that can still be consulted.[1]

During the twentieth century, research into living Romance languages and dialects based on interviews with speakers became common practice, with increasingly accurate techniques. The linguistic atlases and the corpora of spoken varieties created during the last 30 years are a precious asset for present and future studies (see Sections 3.5–6). For the (remote) past, Romance linguistics is based on a corpus of written documents of variable size and content according to historical stage and geographical area: it covers 12 centuries (from the ninth), with texts mainly dating back to the modern and contemporary age, topographically distributed in a far from homogeneous way – for instance, there is no direct documentation of the Balkan-Romance varieties of the Middle Ages. It includes texts of various kinds, in manuscripts or printed books, written on parchment, paper, or etched in stone or on metal. This is an undoubted advantage if compared with the tradition of studies (e.g., of sub-Saharan African or of Semitic languages) devoid of temporal depth due to a total or partial lack of written sources or to the absence of documentation from the 'prehistoric' phase.

Despite such a privileged situation, the use of written sources for the reconstruction of past phases of living languages, observable today in all their complexity, presents problematic aspects that must be addressed with a clear awareness of its limitations. Writing traditions are usually conservative: linguistic changes can be recorded in the written code even centuries after their appearance in the spoken form; dating can be supported by relative chronology, but only from the first attestations of specific forms in written texts. Moreover, writing traditions rarely reflect more informal and sociolinguistically lower registers, and therefore tend to conceal stigmatized and/or sub-standard traits of a language: this is even truer in periods of limited access to writing, when literacy was the monopoly of a narrow sociocultural élite.

For example, contemporary French uses a graphic system dating from the Middle Ages, which does not reflect the fundamental phonetic and phonological changes that had already occurred in the late Middle Ages and about which we know only indirectly (errors in rhymes, copyists' mistakes, explicit statements in manuals for foreign speakers)[2]; the recurrent spelling reform attempts promoted by French institutions have had very limited outcomes in this sense. However, contemporary spoken French also shows a series of morphosyntactic phenomena (disappearance of the synthetic preterite, substitution of the synthetic future tense with the periphrasis

---

[1] See Liebl (2007; 2014). The history of the *Phonogrammarchiv* and the set of recordings are available at www.oeaw.ac.at/phonogrammarchiv/.

[2] For example, the case of *oi* for [wa] studied by Chauveau (2012).

using the verb *aller* 'go', use of cleft sentences with *c'est* 'it is', tendency to use the impersonal *on* 'one' instead of *nous* 'we', etc.), which are not all necessarily recent, but for which it is difficult to find documentation in the texts of the past.[3]

The idea that the problems associated with the conservatism and normativism of Romance writing traditions can be overcome, at least in terms of graphic and phonetic correspondences, by observing those languages as they appear in different writing systems is often illusory. Romance texts in Arabic, Hebrew, Greek, and Cyrillic characters, free of the influence of the Latin graphic model, may illuminate individual points of historical phonetics, but generally once a norm has been stabilized, these texts reveal a degree of conventionality no lesser than that of contemporary texts in Latin characters. Then there are also the problems deriving from interference with locally used graphic systems – such as the Romance texts written in Greek characters from Sardinia (eleventh to thirteenth centuries) and southern Italy (thirteenth to sixteenth centuries) (see De Angelis 2016; Maggiore 2017; Strinna 2017) – and the interpretative uncertainties of writing systems which had emerged for use with other linguistic types, such as Hispanic texts written in Arabic and Hebrew script (*aljamiados*), which offer a partial and imprecise representation of vowels.[4]

Equally unsatisfactory are attempts to access colloquial varieties through written texts that, intentionally or not, allow glimpses of features belonging specifically to spoken language (agreements *ad sensum*, dislocations, hanging topics, deictics, etc.). These include early texts written before there was clear syntactic codification, literary and legal texts aiming to mimic speech, or practical texts produced by poorly educated writers (see, for example, Dardano 2007; Guillot et al. 2015; Trifone 2017: 167–83). Such texts are of great interest as they can give glimpses of a very varied linguistic phenomenology that normally escapes diachronic analysis, but it must be recognized that the medium of writing is never neutral in its effects. Regardless of the degree of control exercised by the writers, it inevitably compresses and suppresses the variation, fluidity, and indeterminacy characteristic of spontaneous speech. No written text is able to reproduce the strategies and enunciative processes typical of oral communication. Furthermore, since orality is a dimension in which languages naturally live and evolve, this is obviously a major obstacle for the study of how linguistic systems work, from a diachronic as well as synchronic point of view.

---

[3] For a general overview see Koch and Oesterreicher (2011: 154–83); Ernst (2015: 88–98); Rossi-Gensane (2016); for the specific case of *c'est*, cf. Dufter (2006).

[4] For these and other problems concerning the interpretation of *aljamiado* texts, see Galmés de Fuentes (1984: 47–60) in relation to the so-called *mozarabic* texts; Varvaro and Minervini (2008: 162–66) for the Judaeo-Spanish ones; and for the issues related to Romanian texts in Cyrillic characters, see Mareș (2015).

Nonetheless one must acknowledge the important function of written documentation in the understanding of a complex, multifaceted, but partly inaccessible linguistic reality. The answer to those who see written texts as purely artificial, almost as an unnecessary veneer that cloaks and misrepresents another, 'truer', reality,[5] is careful and circumspect use of written sources; this remains the main path for a critical interpretation of the language facts of the past, together with historical-comparative reconstructions.

3.2 Sources for the Study of Late Latin and Early Romance

3.2.1 Sources of 'Vulgar Latin' or 'Late Latin'

Numerous indications suggest that, as early as the first century BCE, there was a diaphasic differentiation in the Latin-speaking part of the Empire between a formal register – so-called 'Classical' Latin – and an informal register, referred to in ancient sources as *sermo familiaris, cotidianus*, or *uulgaris* (see Dickey and Chahoud 2010: ch. 3; cf. also Sections 2.3 and 29.2.1). It is probable that from the imperial age, the low variety began to distance itself grammatically and lexically from the high register, to the point of giving rise to diglossia, i.e., the coexistence of two linguistic systems in a hierarchical and complementary relationship within the same social community. Only the high register was endowed with social prestige and used for written texts. The use of the low register – traditionally called 'vulgar Latin' starting from Schuchardt (1866–68) – was limited to everyday oral communication.[6] Nevertheless, some categories of text can provide partial information on this variety, because they contain incorrect forms deviating from Classical norms, foreshadowing Romance developments (so-called Romanisms or vulgarisms). The main sources of 'vulgar Latin' (also known as 'popular Latin', 'informal Latin', or 'late or imperial Latin') are: the grammatical treatises that stigmatized the phenomena of contemporary language use considered to deviate from standard forms; works whose language was shaped, more or less consciously, on forms of speech (theatrical works, letters, Petronius' *Satyricon*, Christian texts); and texts composed by writers of modest culture or semiliterate scribes (technical literature, inscriptions, etc.).[7] Linguists who try to reconstruct the characteristics of vulgar Latin and its diachronic development seek out deviations from the norms of Classical Latin (errors, hypercorrections, innovations) contained in these sources which can be framed as part of the

---

[5] Such as Wright's proposal (1982; 2013) to consider early medieval Latin texts as instances of logographic writing, concealing a much more evolved language. Against this see, among others, Torreblanca (2010) and Varvaro (2013).

[6] For the issue of whether labels such as 'vulgar' are better written in English with upper- or lower-case initial letters, and the associated implications, see Maiden, Smith, and Ledgeway (2011: xxif.).

[7] See the classification by Renzi and Salvi (1994). Also see the wide anthological choices accompanied by linguistic commentary in Iliescu and Slusanski (1991) and Adams (2016).

development from Latin to Romances languages, but can often be observed from ancient times in less controlled registers of the language.[8]

3.2.2 The Problem of Transition

In the early centuries of the Middle Ages, Latin became the exclusive domain of a very small class of literates and semi-literates (ecclesiastics, judges, notaries). Overall, the general lowering of the cultural level of the literate classes between the sixth and eighth centuries resulted in a deterioration in the quality of written language. Alongside a high tradition, which made use of an elegant, albeit conventional, Latin, there was an increase in mistakes in the manuscripts, often due to interference. The language of these texts often reflects the presence of underlying forms of speech. For that reason, they are an important source for knowledge of Romance languages in these centuries lacking documentation.

Thanks to the growing availability of reliable editions and the refinement of techniques of enquiry, it is now possible thoroughly to investigate those deviations from the Classical norm that, at all levels of language, expose the linguistic structures of Romance languages in their initial phase. Attention has focused above all on some historiographical sources from Merovingian Gaul, written in a vigorous but linguistically modest and often incorrect Latin. These texts are particularly rich in Romance characteristics: the *Historia Francorum* by Gregory of Tours (b. ca. 538–d. 594) and the so-called *Fredegarius* (seventh century). Legal-administrative texts (cartularies, documents relating to sales and donations, collections of laws, etc.), glosses and glossaries written in Gaul, the Iberian Peninsula, and Italy between the early Middle Ages and the beginning of the late Middle Ages, have been of great use.[9]

During these centuries, the orientation of Latin towards spoken language cannot always be attributed to writers' poor skills. The marked Latin–Romance hybridism of some texts is a conscious attempt to diminish the distance between the two codes. The clear separation between the Romance used by the mass of illiterates and the written language, the domain of a few, pushed the latter to seek an intermediate code, which had to be at least partly similar to the spoken language, especially in fields of communication where contact between the two languages was inevitable. According to Lüdtke's controversial hypothesis (Lüdtke 1964), communication between literates and illiterates was possible through two indirect channels: from the speaker to the writer to the reader, or from the writer to the listener, through the mediation of a reader. In the first case, the writer tried to

---

[8] See, for instance, Väänänen (1963), Herman (2000), Kiesler (2006), Adams (2013).
[9] Excellent examples of philological and linguistic analysis of this type of text are the recent studies by Sornicola et al. (2017) and Carles (2011).

reproduce a text originally pronounced or conceived in Romance according to the graphic-morphological system of Latin; in the second case, the writer tried to facilitate communication with an illiterate or poorly literate recipient through a modest and simplified Latin, adhering syntactically and lexically to the spoken language. It is actually in this written tradition, sometimes designated *latinum circa romançum* 'Latin approximating to Romance' (Avalle 1965) or *scripta latina rustica* 'rustic Latin writing' (Sabatini 1996), that the first hints of a progressive awareness of the difference between Romance and Latin must be sought; and it is possible to see here the ground being laid for the formation of the first Romance *scriptae* (see Section 3.3) that emerged from the ninth and tenth centuries and established themselves during subsequent centuries.

Such documents are a fundamental source of information about the 'submerged' phase of Romance languages. However, they often present considerable interpretative problems. It must be remembered that, at root, one must always postulate an interference between two separate codes, not only from the phonological and morpho-syntactic point of view, but also from the diamesic, diaphasic, and diastratic point of view: Romance, the language of oral interaction and the only means of communication among the illiterate, passed through the filter of Latin, the written language of the literate and semi-literate. In some cases, the radical difference between the two codes allows scholars to ascertain confidently what traits belong to one language or the other. However, it often happens that the boundary is not so clear-cut. In particular, it is difficult to determine whether the presence of Latin spellings, forms, or constructions can be ascribed to the persistence of scriptural conventions used for centuries (and, in parallel, to the absence of models for the rendering into writing the nascent vernacular languages), or whether they actually reflect a stage of Romance in which the 'new' structures had not yet been established. Difficulties are encountered in the dating of texts which lack information on the context of their drafting. The same is true for diatopic classification: where there are no lexical elements clearly identifiable as dialectal, the analysis of phono-morphological data generally seems insufficient to determine a precise location.

3.2.3 The Earliest Testimonies of Romance Languages

The oldest attestations of Romance languages date back to the ninth and tenth centuries.[10] These texts show a marked difference from the series of

---

[10] The so-called *Indovinello veronese* (late eighth to early ninth century), which many scholars consider the oldest vernacular testimony in Italian – and more generally, in Romance (Tagliavini 1964: 457–60; Castellani 1973: 13–30) – should instead be more appropriately classified as part of the Latin-Romance hybrid text typology mentioned above (Renzi and Andreose 2015: 207f.; cf. also Section 1.2.4.3).

intermediate writings mentioned above: here, there is a clear awareness of the difference between Latin and Romance. In what is considered the earliest document in a Romance language, the Strasbourg Oaths (see Villa and Lo Monaco 2009), the parts in vernacular are linguistically distinct from those in Latin. However, this does not mean that the document is totally exempt from the hybridism that characterizes texts from previous centuries. As with other archaic testimonies, the language of the Oaths raises many interpretative problems (cf. also Section 1.2.4.3), above all from a diatopic perspective, as can be seen from the numerous and often contrasting hypotheses that have been formulated to date (see Avalle 1966: 97–144; Becker 1972: 47–55; Castellani 1980a; 1980b). According to some scholars, the coexistence of northern and southern features in the text locates it in a transition zone between the French and Occitan domains (Poitou, Francoprovençal area, etc.). According to other scholars, the document is written in an artificial language, a koiné, understandable by all members of Charles' heterogeneous army. It must be emphasized that the language of the Oaths is very different from that of other Gallo-Romance texts from the ninth to tenth centuries. Its apparently archaic aspect probably does not reflect embryonic French. It seems to depend on the use of spellings and forms of the Merovingian *scripta* used in the chancery which wrote the text (Keller 1969).

In the other two Romance documents certainly datable to the ninth century, the *Graffito della Catacomba di Commodilla* (first half of the century) and the *Sequence of Saint Eulalia* (878/882), the vernacular writing is more developed. Although the influence of the contemporary Latin *scripta* is perceptible, especially in the representation of vowels, the two texts have clear diatopic characteristics. The *Graffito* bears phenomena typical of the ancient vernacular of its place of production, Rome (Sabatini 1966; 1987); the *Sequence* – contained in the final sections of a Latin manuscript transcribed at the abbey of Saint-Amand – is characterized by several linguistic features of north-eastern varieties of France: Wallon, Picard, and Champenois (Opfermann 1953).[11]

From the tenth century, the number of Romance texts progressively increased,[12] especially in the Oïl and Occitan areas of France. In Italy, the written use of vernacular is rare in the eleventh to twelfth centuries, becoming established in some areas only from the thirteenth. A similar delay occurs in the Iberian Peninsula, where testimonies in Romance prior to the eleventh century are utterly sporadic. A tradition of writing in the vernacular began slowly to emerge only in the twelfth century (in the first

---

[11] Further information in Hartmann and Frank (1997: II, 9, 214).
[12] For an updated list of chrestomathies and anthologies of early Romance texts of the origins, see Iliescu and Roegiest (2015).

half in Catalonia, in the second in Castile; see Hartmann and Frank 1997: I, 28–42).

The situation of the Romanian domain, geographically and historically isolated from the rest of the Romània, is very different. The prestige of Slavonic, long the official language both in the religious and in the administrative field, confined this language to exclusively oral communication for centuries. The earliest surviving texts in Romanian, written in Cyrillic characters, date from the sixteenth century (Gheție 1974).

The oldest Romance documents are often heterogeneous both in form and content, and therefore not easily classifiable. This is reflected in the fact that the classifications proposed so far have been based on different taxonomic criteria. Renzi and Salvi's classification (Renzi and Salvi 1994: 239–49) is fundamentally based on the distinction between religious and lay texts. Koch's (1993) categorization takes two variables into account: the 'medial' realization of the utterance (phonic vs graphic), and the way of conceiving the text in relation to the communicative situation (immediacy vs communicative distance). In Frank and Hartmann (1997), the documents are divided into nine main categories, with several subclasses, essentially on the basis of their genre and their pragmatic function. In order to assess the sociocultural prestige acquired by several traditions of writing, it is important also to consider the methods of text preservation, distinguishing between scripts intended to be transmitted for their legal, religious, or literary value, and scripts not intended to be deposited in archives or libraries (Petrucci 1994: 48–52; see also Renzi and Andreose 2015: 212–15).

3.3 Medieval Romance *Scriptae*

3.3.1 Introduction

By the end of the early Middle Ages, the Romance domain was fragmented into myriad varieties. It formed a dialectal continuum from the Atlantic to the Adriatic. Only some of these varieties were written, usually the varieties of the places that played a major political, economic, or cultural role in the territory: major abbeys, royal and aristocratic courts, and – from a certain date – cities. Some areas began to codify certain *scriptae*, i.e., more or less coherent systems of writing conventions, characterized by the use of specific signs to indicate phonemes that were not part of Latin and circumscribed to specific areas of use: literary, documentary, chancery, etc. (Kabatek 2013: 151–55; cf. also Section 29.2.5). These *scriptae* are a fundamental resource for the study of the Romance languages in their most ancient phase. However, for reasons to be explained, they offer only a faint and partial image of the multifaceted linguistic reality of Medieval Romance Europe.

3.3.2 Literary Texts

In order to legitimize once and for all the use of writing in Romance, it was necessary to establish a prestigious literary tradition, above all in the poetic field. Throughout the Romània, the most ancient literary testimonies have religious content. From the second half of the eleventh century in the French and Occitan area, there are testimonies of religious poems of considerable length, which were probably intended to be recited or sung outside liturgies, perhaps during processions, votive festivals, or pilgrimages: e.g., *Sancta Fides*, *Boeci*, *Vie de Saint Alexis*. The appearance of the first lay literary documents (epic poetry, courtly lyric) – initially in the French and Occitan domains (end of the eleventh century), later in Iberia (twelfth to thirteenth centuries) and in Italy (late twelfth to early thirteenth century) –[13] marked a point of no return in the establishment of a written tradition of Romance languages. Towards the end of the Middle Ages, there was a continuous increase in the number of literary testimonies in the vernacular and, at the same time, a progressive multiplication of production centres. These testimonies, despite their importance, present several linguistic problems.

Firstly, until the advent of printing, the only way to disseminate a text was to copy it by hand. This transmission system involved all types of text: literary, but also legal, religious, and scientific texts. The tradition of a text, that is, the set of testimonies that have transmitted it, is simply the series of transcriptions to which it has been subjected. With the multiplication of copies, transcription mistakes increased and more or less voluntary innovations were introduced into the original texts. Copyists tended to adapt the language of the text to their own habits, above all their phonetic ones, eliminating forms of the source text that were felt as archaic or foreign to their own speech. All medieval works whose originals have not been preserved are 'mixed', or 'stratified' texts, in which elements dating back to the original version are mixed, often in a disorderly way, with new elements attributable to the subsequent series of transcriptions by copyists who have left traces of their language in the texts. Thus, several 'diachronies', or several synchronic strata, coexist in the 'synchrony' of the surviving text, each of which is generally characterized by particular diatopic traits.

Segre (1979: 14, 56–64) usefully describes each manuscript as a 'diasystem': the result of the overlapping of successive systems, the original system being contaminated by the copyists' or redactors' systems. Many

---

[13] An interesting case is Sardinia, where documentary texts began to be written entirely in Romance as early as the second half of the eleventh century and became more frequent over the twelfth and thirteenth centuries. The first attestations of Sardinian are documents written in the chanceries of the sovereigns who governed the island. Valuable testimonies of ancient Sardinian are also the *condaghi*, registers in which legal acts relating to religious communities were transcribed.

works from the earliest period have been transmitted via a unique, non-original transcription. In this case, the primary aim of a linguistic analysis is to recognize the most recent linguistic elements of the text, i.e., those attributable to the copying phase, in order to isolate the original linguistic characteristics of the work. Cases in point are the *Vie Sant Lethgier* and *Passion* (tenth century), two poems in octosyllables, contained in the final sheets of a Latin manuscript from Clermont-Ferrand. Both are characterized by a composite language with numerous southern features. For the former, a Wallon-Picard origin has been hypothesized, with a later transcription in the Occitan area. The latter was probably done by a writer from Poitou who was exposed to southern linguistic influences (Linskill 1937; Avalle 1962; 1967).

For the literature of the subsequent centuries, works are more frequently transmitted by two or more exemplars, none of which is the original. In this case, to restore the original features of the text there is not only the problem of a stratigraphic analysis of the manuscript, but also the critical comparison between the surviving exemplars (Contini 2007). It is useful to note that the philological discipline that deals specifically with the edition of texts, 'textual criticism' or 'ecdotics', uses very different methodological orientations to tackle the problem of restoring the linguistic and graphic features of the original. The textual criticism of 'Lachmannian' orientation based on the method described by Karl Lachmann (b. 1793–d. 1851; cf. Timpanaro 2005) is grounded in the *recensio*, i.e., the classification of exemplars based on shared mistakes, and in the correction of texts through objective criteria. This procedure allows one to choose the substantial variations to be accepted in a text. However, it rarely provides useful tools for the choice of formal variants.

In general, the practice provides for the adoption of the language and graphic style of the testimony in the upper levels of the *stemma codicum* (the family tree that represents the relationship between manuscripts) which more faithfully reflects the author's linguistic habits. However, in some traditions (for example, the works of Dante), this method is not practicable and the recreation of the original linguistic character of the texts is achieved through a screening and comparison of the manuscripts that are diachronically and diatopically closer to the original (Stussi 1991: 14–17; Trovato 2014: 229–41). Thus, the critical text does not replicate the appearance of an existing copy from a graphic and linguistic point of view; it is the product of a reconstructive hypothesis, with the risks of arbitrariness that this entails. The textual criticism of 'Bédierian' orientation – inspired by the ideas of the French philologist Joseph Bédier (b. 1864–d. 1938) – emphasizes how every medieval exemplar has its own graphic, linguistic, and textual physiognomy. To prevent the assemblage of readings of various manuscripts from leading to the invention of a historically non-existent text, the usual practice is to replicate faithfully the substance and form of the document that emerges as closest to the original, correcting the text only where it is manifestly erroneous (Trovato 2014: 77–108). The risks associated with this method are very high, because the editor simply abstains from distinguishing what should be attributed to the author and what depends on the graphic and linguistic habits of the copyists (Stussi 1987: 1121–23; 1991: 15f.).

Another aspect that should be considered in the linguistic analysis of literary texts is the strong tendency to codify medieval literary language and, consequently, its relative stability in time and space. Literary, and above all poetic, texts, usually belong to an existing tradition of language, so that their language only partially reflects that used by their author. They incorporate typical phonological, morphological, and lexical traits that can be classified into diachronic and diatopic contexts sometimes very distant from those in which they were produced. Moreover, there is the tendency, especially in 'high' poetry of courtly inspiration, to eliminate the more locally marked features and terms perceived as typical of 'low' varieties and registers. At every historical stage, the elaboration of a literary language usually involves stylization of the spoken language and consequent impoverishment of its diatopic, diaphasic, and diastratic diversity.

A special category of literary texts is represented by translations. The establishment of a Romance literary tradition and the progressive expansion of its audience favoured the translation of texts that until then were accessible only by the classes that knew Latin (clergy, lawyers, etc.). This phenomenon involved works belonging to the most varied fields, from classical epic to history, from treatises (rhetoric, philosophical-moral, scientific) to narratives, from religious to didactic literature.[14] In Italy, Portugal, Castile, and to a lesser extent, Catalonia, translations from Latin were soon flanked by those from French. The Castilian domain also translated abundantly from Arabic (Bossong 1979; Wright 2007: 1266f.). The greater or lesser adherence of the language of these texts to that of their models depends essentially on the affinity between source and target language, and on the translator's competence and culture. In translations from Latin or other Romance languages, the sectors that were more exposed to the pressure of the original linguistic model, were syntax and lexicon. In particular, it should be noted that, thanks to translations from Latin, the Romance lexicon provided itself with new words relating above all to abstract concepts and specialized terminology. Latin also influenced the word-formation sector (prefixation, suffixation, and composition), favouring the introduction of structures that Romance languages had not originally inherited.

---

[14] On translations during the Middle Ages see Kittel et al. (2004–11, II: 1263–374). On translations in the French and Italian domains see *GRLMA*, VIII/1, 219–65 (by F. Bérier); X/2, 201–54 (by B. Guthmüller).

3.3.3 Documentary and Practical Texts

When Romance secular poetry began to be written, Romance languages also appeared in non-literary texts for special purposes which, until then, had been written in Latin: legal, legislative, administrative documents, etc. In these areas, when a Romance variety began to be written, it was at the expense of Latin, the language of writing par excellence throughout the Middle Ages and sometimes even in the modern age. In Castile, Catalonia, and Portugal, a central role was played by royal courts, which elaborated and disseminated chancery *scriptae* – and, in some cases, literary *scriptae* – of great prestige. In France and central and northern Italy, the rise of the new bourgeois class proved decisive for the establishment of a documentary tradition in Romance. This new class, mostly unused to Latin, needed a written language for its activities that was neither time-consuming nor difficult to learn. The participation of increasingly large sections of the population in the political and economic life of cities gave a strong impulse to the use of Romance languages in private legal documents and then in public documents (e.g., statutes, regulations, laws).

In Latin juridical texts of the tenth to eleventh centuries, one finds attestations of vocabulary or short sentences in Romance, inserted into the 'free' parts of some documents. The practice of drafting documents entirely in vernacular (especially in the private domain) increased progressively in the twelfth to fourteenth centuries, with different methods and times from region to region (Frank and Hartmann 1997: IV–V). Documentary writings constitute a fundamental resource for the study of Romance languages in their medieval phase, not only for their early emergence and relative abundance, but also for their specific textual features (Stussi 1987: 110–12). Texts that fall into this type of production have the great advantage of being datable and locatable with a good degree of certainty, because they generally bear the date and the place where they were written and the writer's name. Moreover, compared with literary works, they are less subject to linguistic stratification phenomena due to text transmission, because they have come down to us in their original version or in a contemporary or slightly later copy. For these reasons, the increasingly numerous editions of documentary texts produced in several regions of the Romance domain are a fundamental tool for the knowledge of the linguistic conditions of medieval Europe, particularly for investigating a specific synchronic section of a Romance language.

Documentary texts offer little variety in their vocabulary and morphology, with strongly repetitive phrasal structures. Moreover, from a syntactic point of view, their language is often modelled on the formulae of legal Latin, above all in the initial and final parts of the documents. The influence of Latin is also reflected in the graphic-phonetic structures of these texts. It should be remembered that *scriptae* are systems of compromise between the phonological reality of a language and the pre-existing Latin graphic tradition. This explains, for instance, the significant presence of etymological spellings. Within some spheres of script (documentary, chancery, etc.) there is a strong conservativeness, which can cause long-term preservation of spellings and archaic forms. Finally, when a documentary tradition in various Romance languages became consolidated, this type of writing tended to lose the most markedly local linguistic features and orient itself towards forms of regional or supra-regional koinés, generally modelled on the *scriptae* of the most important localities.[15]

Practical texts (minutes, notes, letters) lie outside the limits of the documentary sources, being written for the needs of daily life and not for official use, and are permeable to typical traits of spoken language. The great usefulness of these testimonies from a linguistic point of view is counterbalanced by their scarcity in the earliest centuries (e.g., the *Conto navale pisano* in Italy, the *Nodicia de kesos* in Spain). Unlike legal texts, they were not intended to be kept in archives or libraries; for this reason, they have been lost more easily. Interesting testimonies of the popular varieties of language are the practical writings of the 'semi-literate', which become increasingly common from the fifteenth and sixteenth centuries (D'Achille 1994). Among the most ancient attestations in the Italian domain, are the fifteenth-century *Ricordi* by the Neapolitan Loise De Rosa and the *Libretto di Conti di Maddalena pizzicarola in Trastevere*, dating from the beginning of the sixteenth century (Formentin 1998; Petrucci 1978).

3.4 The Codification of Romance Languages in the Modern Age

3.4.1 Printed Sources

The invention of printing, which revolutionized the world of culture and books from the second half of the fifteenth century, accelerated the standardization of Romance and non-Romance languages, spreading authoritative models of writing and imposing normalized spelling systems. It is no coincidence that the first major works of Romance grammatography and lexicography (see Section 3.4.3) are contemporary with or a few years older than the advent of printing. In the passage from the manuscript format to printed books there is progressive levelling of the oscillations

---

[15] It is instructive to consider Occitan, whose use in the documentary field is very early. By the end of the tenth century, Occitan expressions were being inserted into Latin documents in the form of quotes. This practice became more frequent (especially in feudal oaths) during the next century. The first document entirely in vernacular is Ademar Ot's will of 1102, chronologically contemporary with the poetic activity of the 'first' troubadour William IX of Aquitaine. Thereafter, the number of documents in Occitan gradually increased, until the establishment of an actual documentary *scripta* with strong graphic-linguistic homogeneity (Brunel 1926; 1952; Frank and Hartmann 1997, I: 42).

linked to the different local and personal habits, characteristic of the medieval *scriptae*. Spelling is generally simplified, with a reduction in abbreviations and graphemes that bear no phonetic value.[16] Consistent criteria are gradually imposed in the use of diacritic signs (accents, apostrophes, etc.), punctuation, and the separation of words. The editorial revision process often undergone by printed works also entailed the adaptation of the language of the texts to that of the literary models in vogue, above all from a phonetic and morphological point of view, with consequent levelling of diatopic differences.

In general, printing favoured the spread of the hegemonic languages, greatly reducing the space for written expression of those varieties that, for historical reasons, had remained confined to the urban, provincial, or regional contexts. The new technique may have had the effect of increasing the availability and circulation of written texts, but it determined a progressive reduction of the range of languages used in writing, compared with the Middle Ages.

Printing played a key role in the creation of a written tradition of Romanian, in a part of Eastern Europe under the sway of the Turks and dominated by Slavonic culture. The Slavonic tradition of the Orthodox Church meant that Romanian was written in Cyrillic characters until the mid nineteenth century. The earliest surviving document in Romanian is *Psaltirea Hurmuzaki*, a copy, datable to the first decade of the sixteenth century, of a translation of the Psalms made in the previous century (Mareş 2000). The earliest surviving document spontaneously written in Romanian is a letter of 1521 from the boyar Neacşu of Câmpulung to Hans Benkner, mayor of Braşov. These documents clearly continue an existing written tradition. There are other liturgical manuscripts in the sixteenth century: the Voroneţ Codex, containing the translation of part of the Acts of the Apostles; the Voroneţ Psalter, the Scheian Psalter, containing translations of the psalms (Gheție and Mareş 1985; 2001). The turning point came with the translation of the Four Gospels (*Tetraevanghelul*), printed in 1560–61 by a printer of Greek origin, the deacon Coresi, in Braşov (Gheție and Mareş 1994). With this work, Coresi printed at least another ten texts, and others were printed at the same time elsewhere. This flowering of texts was essentially due to the initiative of exponents of the reformed churches (Lutheran and Calvinist) among the German and Hungarian populations of Transylvania. They had the effect of gradually legitimizing the written use of Romanian in the Orthodox faith as well: among others, the verse translation of the Psalter by the Metropolitan of

---

[16] This tendency did not apply to French, which underwent a systematic Latinization (and sometimes, Hellenization) due to scholarly and literary influence during the Renaissance. This led to the introduction of etymologizing and conservative spellings into French (Beaulieux 1927).

Moldavia, Dosoftei (1673), and the monumental Bucharest Bible (1688). At the same time, the writing of Romanian extended to other domains: notarial, legal (Lucaci, *Pravila*, 1581), historiographical (Mihail Moxa, *Cronograf*, 1620; Grigore Ureche, *Letopisețul Țării Moldovei*, 1642–47; Miron Costin, *Letopisețul Țării Moldovei de la Aron Vodă încoace*, 1675), and literary (*Cărțile Populare* 'popular books'), etc. (Gheție 1997).

3.4.2 National Languages, Regional Languages, and Dialects

The Romance languages that emerged as major literary languages at the beginning of the modern era were Italian, French, Spanish, and Portuguese, while Occitan, Catalan, Galician, and other locally used varieties that had had a written use in the Middle Ages experienced temporary or permanent eclipse. In the same period, Romanian timidly made its first steps.

Most of the Romance varieties that had been written in the Middle Ages for legal, administrative, practical, religious, and often artistic purposes, gradually gave way to the nascent 'national' languages. Initially, even the varieties then prevailing in various states for literary reasons or political prestige were typical merely of a sometimes very limited area. The influence of these languages on the myriad local varieties began to be felt very early in some areas of the Romània (thirteenth century in France, in Castile and in Portugal, fourteenth century in Italy). A real hegemony was established during the sixteenth century, when Spanish, Portuguese, French, and Italian occupied a large part of the space filled by local varieties in the written language, territory by territory, also replacing Latin over the centuries.

It is also during the sixteenth century that the Greco-Latin term 'dialect' was introduced first in Italy and then in the rest of Europe, to designate a local variety different from the national one. Henceforth, this term started to indicate the varieties spoken locally and sociolinguistically or culturally subordinated to the hegemonic language. This involved only written language at an early stage. The oral use of local varieties continued in many regions with great vitality, lasting until the late twentieth century and, in some cases, until today. Although the written use of regional varieties has regressed considerably since the sixteenth and seventeenth centuries, in some traditions it has remained alive. The case of Italy is significant, where dialects have had a literary use in what is generally called 'dialect literature'. This has given rise to genuine masterpieces, especially in theatre and poetry. These texts constitute a fundamental source of knowledge of many dialectal varieties in the historical stages that precede nineteenth-century scientific dialectology. The use of this documentation for linguistic purposes requires caution: in some cases, the parodic, caricatural, or expressionistic intent might have led the author to hypercharacterize dialectal features, distorting the reality of the spoken language.

A specific case are those varieties that, characterized by a strong historical and cultural identity from the beginning, played a very important role in the Middle Ages in the literary and administrative domain, subsequently losing their importance because of the expansion of national languages: Occitan (Kirsch 1991; Kreminitz 1991), Galician (Brea 1994), Catalan (Casanova 1991; Lüdtke 1991). In these domains, there was a phase of strong reduction of written sources that began roughly in the sixteenth century, continuing until the nineteenth, when various movements of cultural revival promoted the recovery of indigenous linguistic heritage, especially in the lexicographical and grammatical field. They encouraged the written use of the language in literature. In Catalonia and Galicia, the ideas of the nineteenth-century cultural movements found fulfilment in the policies of normalization and officialization of the language, implemented by local authorities since the end of the 1970s. Occitan too was recognized by the French Republic as a regional language (1951), but the dialectal fragmentation and the progressive loss of competence among the population strongly limited its social use, both in written and oral form.

3.4.3 Grammar and Dictionaries

The sixteenth century was the 'century of the norm'. The increasing conviction that the varieties imposing themselves as languages of culture and, in many cases, as languages of the nascent modern states, had importance and dignity, paved the way for the idea that they were worthy of detailed grammatical analysis (Renzi and Salvi 1994: 40f.; Metzeltin 2007: 151–54). In the first half of the sixteenth century (and in some cases even as early as the fifteenth) the first valuable linguistic works devoted to Romance varieties began to be produced.[17] With respect to similar traditions in other European countries, the early lexicography and grammaticography of the 'national' Romance languages, with the exception of Romanian, were distinguished both by their precociousness, and by the quality of their outcomes. This activity was often connected to the debate concerning the linguistic and orthographic 'norm' to be adopted in the nascent nation-states. The first Romance grammars and dictionaries not only provide fundamental sources for information about the vocabulary and the phonological, morphological, and syntactic structures of Italian, Spanish, Portuguese, and French over the fifteenth–seventeenth centuries, and, in some cases, over the fourteenth–seventeenth centuries, but also offer a particularly favourable vantage point from which to better understand the processes of language standardization that began with the dawn of the modern era.

---

[17] Livet (1859), Kukenheim (1932), Trabalza (1908). See also Metzeltin (2004; 2007: 155–78) and Sanson (2013).

In Italy, grammatical reflection started in the fifteenth century. Leon Battista Alberti (b. 1404–d. 1472) wrote an (unpublished) *Grammatichetta* of Florentine around 1435. The first Italian printed grammar was published by Giovanni Francesco Fortunio in 1516, under the title of *Regole grammaticali della volgar lingua*. In 1525 the *Prosa della volgar lingua* by Pietro Bembo was published, the third book of which is actually a grammatical treatise. In Spain the *Gramática de la lengua castellana* by Antonio de Nebrija was published in 1492, and can fairly be considered the first major grammar of a Romance language. In Portugal, Fernão de Oliveira wrote and published the first grammar of Portuguese (1536). Another important grammar is by João de Barros (1540), also the author of a *Diálogo em louvor da nossa linguagem* (1540). In France, the excellence of the national language with respect to Latin and Greek was supported for the first time by Joachim du Bellay in his *Deffence et illustration de la langue francoyse* (1549). The first grammars are slightly earlier: *L'esclarcissement de la langue francoyse* by John Palsgrave (1530), written in English, and the treatise *In linguam gallicam isagωge* by Jacques Dubois (1531), written in Latin. The first description of French written in French is *Le tretté de la grammère françoèze* by Louis Meigret (1550).

In the same years, the first dictionaries of Romance languages were published. This kind of linguistic work, unknown to classical antiquity and the Middle Ages, made its appearance at the beginning of the modern age and, through successive adjustments, achieved its final form in the seventeenth century. The diffusion of dictionaries contributed considerably to the regulation of national languages and the achievement of their normative balance. In Spain, lexicographic activity was very early and intense: suffice it to mention the bilingual vocabularies *Universal vocabulario en latín y romance* by Alfonso Fernández de Palencia (1490), the *Lexicon hoc est Dictionarium ex sermone latino in hispaniensem* (1492) and the *Dictionarium ex hispaniensi in latinum sermonem* (1495?) by Nebrija, and the monolingual *Tesoro de la lengua castellana o española* by Sebastián de Covarrubias y Horozco (1611). In France, the great scholar and typographer Robert Estienne published a *Dictionarium Latinogallicum* in 1538 and a *Dictionnaire Francoislatin* in 1539. Italian lexicography was born with *Le tre fontane* by Niccolò Liburnio (1526) and *La fabrica del mondo* by Francesco Alunno (1546–48). However, the first great European dictionary is that by the Academicians of the Crusca, published in 1612, after a project created by Lionardo Salviati. Following the Crusca model, in France, the *Dictionnaire de l'Académie françoise* (1694) was published, and in Spain the *Diccionario de la lengua castellana* of the Royal Academia Española was published between 1726 and 1739. For Portuguese, there is the *Dictionarium ex lusitanico in latinum sermonem* by Jerónimo Cardoso (1562), although the most important lexicographical works date from the eighteenth century: among others, the *Vocabulario portuguez e latino* (bilingual) by Rafael Bluteau (1712–28), from which António de Morais Silva drew the *Diccionario da lingua portugueza* (1789).

3.5 Dialectological Enquiries, Linguistic Atlases, and Dialectometry

3.5.1 The Beginnings of Dialectological Enquiries and Linguistic Cartography

In the second half of the nineteenth century, dialectological studies acquired an important role and received academic recognition due to the rise of historical-comparative linguistics. This led to an exceptional increase in data on dialects, the scientific study of which began in the Romance area thanks to Graziadio Isaia Ascoli, one of the founders of modern dialectology. His researches, based mainly on written texts, identified within the Romance dialectal *continuum* the Raeto-Romance and the Francoprovençal dialectal groups. In 1873 Ascoli developed the concept of 'isofone' ('isophones'), that may be considered the forerunner of the more successful 'isogloss', i.e., an imaginary line defining the areas sharing the same linguistic feature, thus representing its geographic boundary.[18]

The existence of dialectal boundaries was, in that period and also afterwards, a highly debated topic: distinguished linguists and philologists contemporaneous with Ascoli, such as Hugo Schuchardt and Paul Meyer, denied the possibility of establishing borders between dialects, stating that only the geographical extent of single features might be ascertained. Against their criticism, Ascoli maintained the legitimacy of his methods and the value of its results, the discovery and description of linguistic discontinuities in space. Though criticized by linguists for different shortcomings, isoglosses are still used as effective instruments for classifying languages and dialects and documenting the areal distribution of linguistic features; since an isogloss is meaningful only in relation to other isoglosses, different configurations of isoglosses have been observed and described by linguists.[19]

Fostered by dialectological enquiries, linguistic cartography first developed in the Germanic world during the last quarter of the nineteenth century. Before detailing this development, destined for great things in the field of Romance linguistics, it is important to remember that dialectological enquiries were and still are not necessarily intended for drawing

---

[18] The word 'isogloss' is first documented in August Bielenstein's work on Latvian dialects (Bielenstein 1892). Ascoli's terminology (*isofona, isomorfa, isolessi, isosema*) is scarcely used even in the Italian tradition of dialectological studies.

[19] For an appraisal of the concept of isogloss and for various configurations of isoglosses see Chambers and Trudgill (1997: 89–103), Grassi et al. (1997: 57–60), Loporcaro (2009: 10–25), Girnth (2010: 112–16).

linguistic atlases. As a matter of fact, the distribution of linguistic features in space is not the focus of all dialectological research: thus, linguists working within the structuralist or the generative paradigm have often exploited the extraordinary dialectal diversity of the Romance-speaking world, without paying particular attention to its geographical dimension. For instance, more or less recent studies in Italian dialectology (Belletti 1993; Repetti 2000; Manzini and Savoia 2005; Benincà, Ledgeway, and Vincent 2014) use dialects as a rich and powerful reservoir of linguistic data, that may provide important contributions to phonological and (morpho)syntactic theory. On the contrary, scholars of language and dialect geography have not been much involved in linguistic theorizing: the integration of geolinguistic data into general linguistic theory is a relatively recent accomplishment (Chambers and Trudgill 1997: 15).

Leaving aside early attempts such as Johann Andreas Schmeller's map in his work on the Bavarian dialects (1821) or Bernardino Biondelli's *Atlante linguistico d'Europa* (1841), rigorous linguistic geography may be said to begin with Georg Wenker. His exploration of German dialects was based on a questionnaire of 40 standardized sentences, distributed by post to schoolmasters all over the country (1887–88); the (mainly phonological) information collected from about 45,000 locations was successively plotted over 1600 maps. The result was the *Sprachatlas des deutschen Reichs* (1889–1923), whose material represents one of the world's largest databases in dialectology and geolinguistics.[20] Wenker did not mean to explicitly challenge the Neogrammarian claim about the exceptionlessness of sound changes, but the result of his research revealed a previously unknown and apparently random heterogeneity: without rejecting the existence of sound laws, Wenker documented the spatial distribution of linguistic features, that might vary word for word.

A student of Paul Meyer's, the Swiss scholar Jules Gilliéron was aware of Wenker's works when he projected and directed his *Atlas Linguistique de la France (ALF)*.[21] Aiming at recording the geographical diversity of dialects in France, Gilliéron established a network of 639 survey points in the French linguistic area and entrusted a single collaborator, Edmond Edmont, with the task of collecting data in the specific areas. For each location, a speaker was selected to answer the same questionnaire, using a phonetic transcription for the answers. The results of the enquiry, which took place between

---

[20] Wenker's *Sprachatlas des deutschen Reichs* was actually preceded by three undertakings on a smaller scale: *Das rheinische Platt* (1877), *Sprachatlas der Rheinprovinz nördlich der Mosel* (1878), and *Sprach-Atlas von Nord- und Mitteldeutschland* (1881), with partially different approaches. For Wenker's works and methods see Lameli (2010: 574–76), Scheuringer (2010: 159–62).

[21] Like Wenker's, Gilliéron's research activity also started by documenting a relatively small area, the Canton of Valais, in his *Petit atlas phonétique du Valais roman (sud du Rhône)* (1880). For the *ALF* enterprise, see Chauveau (2002: 72–83), Lameli (2010: 574–78), Swiggers (2010: 274f.).

1897 and 1901, led to the creation of 1920 linguistic maps, in the 20 volumes of the atlas published between 1902 and 1910 (Gilliéron and Edmont 1902–10). With respect to his German harbinger, Gilliéron's methodological innovations – direct data collection, narrow phonetic transcription, detailed extralinguistic information, inclusion of different linguistic sublevels (phonology, morphology, lexicon, syntax), orientation to the daily life of the informants – were extremely influential in the field of geolinguistics. Moreover, in the *ALF* 'display maps' – that is, maps transferring the tabulated responses for each item onto a map – were first used, while Wenker, who was interested in the areal structuring and boundaries of German dialects, used 'interpretive maps', showing the distribution of variants prevailing in each region (Chambers and Trudgill 1997: 25; Girnth 2010: 101). Display maps have a primarily documentational function, since they give direct access to the original data, and remain the kind of mapping commonly used in Romance atlases, whereas interpretive maps are favoured in the German and English tradition (Goebl 2018: 11). Finally, it worth noting that Gilliéron originally intended to map dialectal synchronic variation, but soon realized that the areal distribution of linguistic forms (especially lexical items) might provide insights into the diachronic dimension; linguistic geography was thus shifting towards 'linguistic geology' (Swiggers 2010: 275).

3.5.2 After the *ALF*: Traditional and New Linguistic Atlases

Gilliéron's masterpiece did not receive unanimous approval at that time. Its data were incorporated into the *Französisches Etymologisches Wörterbuch* (*FEW*) by Walter von Wartburg (1922–2002) and thereby indirectly contributed to subsequent developments in French linguistics and dialectology. The *ALF* also constituted a model for the linguistic cartography of the 1920s and 1930s: among others, the *Atlas Lingüistic de Catalunya* (*ALC*) by Antoni Griera (1923–29, then 1962–64); the *Sprach- und Sachatlas Italiens und der Südschweiz* or *Atlante Italo-Svizzero* (*AIS*) by Karl Jaberg and Jakob Jud (1928–40); *Atlasul lingvistic român* (*ALR*) by Sextil Puşcariu, Sever Pop, and Emil Petrovici (Pop 1938–42, Petrovici and Pătruţ 1956–72); and the *Atlas Lingüístico de la Península Ibérica* by Tomás Navarro Tomás, whose history was troubled by the Spanish Civil War (the only volume published so far dates from 1962, but its surveys date from the 1930s).[22]

The *AIS* is probably the most successful result of this generation of Romance linguistic atlases. Gilliéron's disciples, Jaberg and Jud, were inspired by his approach; yet they differ from him in some fundamental

---

[22] For a general overview of Romance language cartography see Chauveau (2002), Cugno and Massobrio (2010), Swiggers (2010).

points. They entrusted their field-based enquiry to academic collaborators (Paul Scheuermeier, Gerhard Rohlfs, and Max Leopold Wagner), rather than to a self-taught man like Edmond Edmont, whose linguistic inexperience had seemed to Gilliéron a guarantee of objectivity in the processing of the data. They accepted multiple informants for the same locality and thus a diversification of the answers to the questionnaire, whereas Gilliéron always considered the testimony of a single informant to be sufficient. They also included in the network of localities some medium to large cities (Turin, Milan, Venice, Bologna, and Florence), recognizing their role as points of attraction for (macro)linguistic communities, and turning away from the 'ruralist' bent of the *ALF*. This attitude was due to the peculiar situation of the Italian dialects, whose use was not restricted to rural environments, and it paved the way for the development of urban dialectology in the second half of the twentieth century. What is more, the *AIS* paid careful attention to the historical and sociological interpretation of the linguistic maps, to which a great amount of information was added by the fieldworkers: even the reactions of the informants were recorded, as well as their uncertainties and self-corrections, their feelings about their own dialect and those of their neighbours, etc. Such information helped understanding the dynamic of the clash between different linguistic systems in contact, what Jaberg named 'linguistic biology'. Finally, the German title of the *AIS*, that is *Sprach- und Sachatlas*, is an explicit reference to the research method *Wörter und Sachen*, based on the idea that the history of words goes hand in hand with that of the objects they designate. Thus, the *AIS* is also an impressive collection of ethnographic materials, thousands of sketches, drawings, and pictures complementing the linguistic maps. Accordingly, Jaberg and Jud's work may be said to have transformed the linguistic atlas into an outstanding scientific tool for ethnographic and sociolinguistic research.[23] The *AIS* was a model for many atlases in Romance-speaking world and also beyond it; in 1931 Jakob Jud and Paul Scheuermeier went to the US in order to train the fieldworkers for the *Linguistic Atlas of the United States and Canada*, a project coordinated by Hans Kurath.

The atlases published afterwards developed along two main lines, involving the choice of smaller areas, with a denser network of localities and more structured questionnaires than those used for national atlases, and the deepening of the ethnographic and sociolinguistic dimension, already present to some extent in the *ALF* and above all in the *AIS*. These two directions could also intersect, giving rise to enquiries and then to linguistic atlases on a regional or sub-regional scale with a sociolinguistic and/or

---

[23] For the *AIS* see Cugno and Massobrio (2010: 50–58), Swiggers (2010: 281, 291).

ethnographic orientation. The development of voice-recording technologies eliminated or at least reduced one of the most complicated issues for dialectologists and authors of atlases of the beginning of the century, namely data distortion unconsciously introduced by those transcribing the informants' answers. The availability of portable recording instruments in fact made it normal practice to record and document more or less spontaneous interviews with the local speakers. Advances in information technology allowed the creation of large databases and the development of more advanced types of atlases.

Without listing the major accomplishments in this field, suffice it here to mention the names of Albert Dauzat, director of the project of the *Nouvel atlas linguistique de la France par régions* (NALF, various volumes published from the 1940s), and Manuel Alvar, who directed several Spanish regional atlases, including Andalusia, Canary Islands, Aragon (published from the 1960s).[24] As representative of the latest generation of linguistic atlases, it is worth mentioning Hans Thun's *Atlas lingüístico diatópico y diastrático del Uruguay* (ADDU, Thun and Elizaincín 2000), which aims to solve the problem of monodimensionality of linguistic atlases. Rejecting the traditional representation of linguistic space as an 'instant snapshot' (Thun 2010: 511), this pluridimensional atlas takes into account all possible variables of the informants, age, sex, sociocultural class, etc., and projects them onto maps. The result is a dynamic picture where innovations and archaisms coexist at the phonetic, lexical, and grammatical levels. The ADDU is part of an ambitious project of research on the anthropo-geographic zone of the River Plate (Río de la Plata): the analysis of the linguistic situation in this macro-region is developed in various atlases, that present an integrated view of the contacts between Spanish, Portuguese, and Guaraní standard and sub-standard varieties, and the languages and dialects of the late-arriving minorities. This research relies on an expanded model of linguistic space and fosters a methodological discussion about aims and techniques of contemporary geolinguistics and its conceptual framework.[25]

3.5.3 Historical Atlases and Dialectometry

The structure of the atlas, understood as a set of linguistic maps, can also be used in historical linguistics. This is the case with the *Atlas des Formes et des Constructions des Chartes Françaises du 13e siècle* by Anthonij Dees (1980), in which a series of graphic, phonetic, morphological, and syntactic features extracted from 3,400 French documents, dated and located on the basis of

---

[24] For Dauzat, Alvar, and their atlases, see Swiggers (2001; 2010: 284–90), García Mouton (1996: 70–74; 2006: 167f.).

[25] For the *ADDU* and related projects see Dietrich (2010: 309–12) and Thun (2010).

extralinguistic criteria, are projected onto a map of medieval France with 87 geographical points. The results thus obtained were then used by Dees to create the *Atlas des Formes Linguistiques des Textes Littéraires de l'Ancien Français* (1987), which offers a systematic comparison of 200 literary texts with those of the documents already analysed, obtaining 517 maps and a series of proposals for a localization of variable reliability.[26] Apart from minor corrections, Dees charters' atlas is generally considered a useful and effective tool in historical dialectology, while his literary texts' atlas is undoubtedly weaker, given the linguistic stratification of medieval manuscripts (Section 3.3.1).[27] Dees' seminal work evolved along two main directions: the scriptological analysis of his corpus of literary texts, the so-called *Nouveau Corpus d'Amsterdam* (Section 3.6.2), and dialectometrical interpretations of his maps (see below).

Geolinguistic data have often been the subject of quantitative work, and Dees himself was keenly interested in this line of research; his original 'localization counts' (*calculs de localisation*) for old French literary texts has been recently discovered and re-used (Goebl and Smečka 2016). Results of great importance in this field have been achieved by dialectometry, from the 1970s. This discipline deals with establishing relations of dialectal similarity and difference by synthesizing the materials supplied by linguistic atlases through statistical and taxometric procedures. The term *dialectométrie* was coined in 1973 by Jean Séguy, author of the *Atlas Linguistique de la Gascogne* (ALG), which aimed to condense the information offered by the *ALG* maps through a (then new) methodology for measuring the structural distance between dialects. Among the Romanists who have worked on the project, after Séguy, is Hans Goebl, who has subjected the materials of both the ALF and the AIS to an integral dialectological analysis, with interesting results; for Goebl and his 'Salzburg School', the dialectometric method, submitting data to numerical synthesis and a systematic cartographic elaboration, is the main way to discover the deep geolinguistic structures and laws that regulate their development.[28] One hundred years after Wenker, the problem of diverging isoglosses could be solved, according to dialectometricists, thanks to cumulative areal classifications and global interpretation of linguistic atlas data: with the paradox that the branch of linguistics that first drew attention to the problems related with sound laws, ended up establishing its own, genuine spatial laws. Dialectometry, in fact, positions itself within the tradition of qualitative geolinguistics, which it intends to improve via quantitative means.

---

[26] For the methodology and results of the work, see Dees (1988); for other research following Dees' methodology see van Reenen and van Reenen Stein (1988) and Merisalo (1988).

[27] Dees was aware of this weakness, which he tried to compensate for in various forms (Dees 1987: xvi–xviii).

[28] For an introduction to dialectometric methodology, see Séguy (1973) and Goebl (1981; 2010).

3.6 Corpus Linguistics

3.6.1 The Beginnings of Corpus Linguistics

The elaboration of textual corpora for linguistic studies has developed since the 1950s, and thanks to advances in computer science since the 1980s it has acquired its typical traits: the corpus is normally large, computer-readable, and designed for linguistic analysis. Born in the Anglo-American environment and faced with the Chomskyan distrust of performance data, corpus linguistics found extensive application in Romance studies, with excellent results.[29] We now have a great variety of corpora of the main Romance languages, with various methodologies and objectives: written or spoken, monolingual, bilingual, or multilingual, reference or special, sample or monitor, raw or annotated, etc.[30] *Stricto sensu* corpora should be distinguished from databases and text archives, even if the difference is more nuanced than it may seem. We will examine some particularly significant experiences in Romance linguistic studies.[31]

Some pioneers of corpus linguistics prior to the spread of computers were Aurélien Sauvageot and Georges Gougenheim, who coordinated the first research on *Français fondamental* (1951–54); Sauvageot, Gougenheim, and their team's work was born in the field of language didactics and aimed at developing lexical frequency lists based on spontaneous speech recordings. The results were surprising and have led to the questioning of many of the *idées reçues* about phonetics, syntax, and vocabulary of spoken French, as well as practices of field surveys and data transcription. This caused such a violent reaction in the academic world that Gougenheim decided to destroy all the recordings, for fear that their poor quality could fuel further controversy.[32]

3.6.2 Oral Corpora and Historical Corpora

Following the model of the enquiry used for *Français fondamental*, Spain (*Español fundamental*, 1963–70) and Portugal (*Português fundamental*, 1970–84) organized similar works. Among the later spoken corpora is that on the literate norm of the major South American cities, promoted by Juan Manuel Lope Blanch since the 1960s and subsequently extended to Madrid and Seville (*Macro-Corpus de la Norma Culta*, MC-NC); that assembled by Claire Blanche Benveniste and the *Groupe Aixois de Recherches en Syntaxe* at the

---

[29] We do not distinguish between *corpus-based* and *corpus-driven linguistics*; for the distinction cf. Tognini Bonelli (2010: 18f.), as well as the discussion in McEnery and Hardie (2012: 5f., 147–52).

[30] For the characteristics of the several types of corpora (which of course can overlap) see Stubbs (2004), Hundt (2008).

[31] For an overview of the corpora of the main Romance languages see Iliescu and Roegiest (2015); for oral corpora, also Pusch (2002).

[32] The history of research on *Français fondamental* was reconstructed by Rivenc (2006).

Université de Provence since 1975 and based on interviews conducted mostly in south-eastern France; and that developed by Tullio De Mauro and his team for the production of a large frequency-lexicon of spoken Italian (*Lessico dell'italiano parlato*) consisting of some 60 hours of interviews conducted between 1990 and 1992 in Milan, Florence, Rome, and Naples.[33]

Research based on such corpora contributed to the description of the phonology, grammar, and lexicon of spoken Spanish, French, and Italian; only written language had traditionally been the object of linguistic analysis, together with the native speaker's intuition in generative studies. Scholars were first enabled to study these languages quantitatively, that is in probabilistic terms, observing what is central and typical in each language and what is not: even departing from the norm (so-called 'mistakes') was attentively evaluated, when its quantity was noticeable, since it revealed features of grammar restructuring (Blanche Benveniste 1996). Finally, some distinctive features of languages used in natural, spontaneous interactions have emerged, that confirm the findings of scholars such as Michael Halliday (1985) and Douglas Biber (1988; 2006) working on English language corpora.

An area where Romance corpus linguistics was more fruitful is that of multilingual speech corpora: this development was spurred by the peculiar situation of the Romance languages, which share so much of their grammar, still differing from each other, and French overall, in many significant features. In this perspective it is worth mentioning the C-ORAL project (2001–04), funded by the European Union, which produced a collection of spontaneous Italian, French, Spanish, and Portuguese speech corpora of the total size of about 123 hours, allowing the first contrastive study of speech in the Romance field.[34]

Romance corpus linguistics relies now on several megacorpora of written and oral language, such as the *Corpus de Referência do Português Contemporâneo*, a corpus of (European) Portuguese with some 311 million words, based on texts of different genres, collected mostly after 1970; the *Corpus de Referencia del Español Actual*, which contains texts collected between 1975 and 2004, divided in half between Spanish of Spain and America, for some 160 million word, with its recent offspring, the *Corpus del Español del Siglo XXI*; and *Frantext*, amounting to some 270 million words, mostly from literary texts (and to a lesser extent scientific and technical texts) of the nineteenth and twentieth centuries.[35] But also medium- to small-size

---

[33] The Spanish macro-corpus is available on CD-ROM (Samper Padilla et al. 1998); transcriptions of interviews and studies are available in a series of monographs, the first by Lope Blanch (1971); the French corpus was partially published in print by Blanche Benveniste et al. (2002); the *Lessico dell'italiano parlato* was published by De Mauro et al. (1993), while the audio files are accessible online (www.parlaritaliano.it/index.php/it/volip).

[34] The corpus is published on DVD and accompanied by a printed volume (Cresti and Moneglia 2005).

[35] See Bacelar do Nascimento (2000), Mendes (2016), Rojo (2016), Cappeau and Gadet (2015). The corpora are (partially or completely) accessible online: http://alfclul.clul.ul.pt/CQPweb/, www.rae.es/recursos/banco-de-datos/crea, www.rae.es/recursos/banco-de-datos/corpes-xxi, www.frantext.fr.

corpora have been fruitful in the domain of Romance linguistics:[36] again, we may note the important role played by dialectological enquiries, prompted by the great dialectal fragmentation of the Romance-speaking world. An excellent model of data collection and interpretation is offered by the *Corpus Oral y Sonoro del Español Rural* directed by Inés Fernández Ordóñez, where key grammatical topics of Spanish linguistics – such as the clitic system or the *neutro de materia* ('mass neuter') – are investigated through the data recorded in fieldwork in rural Castile, transcribed and stored online.[37]

As for the historical perspective, once we acknowledge the primacy of the English language corpora, that were worked out early and have acquired huge dimensions (Cantos 2014), we may find some original developments in Romance corpus linguistics. Relying on the notion of *scripta* (Section 3.3), a new branch of Romance historical dialectology has arisen since the 1970s termed *scriptologie* (Goebl 1975; 1979; Glessgen 2012): it aims at describing from a quantitative viewpoint the linguistic variation observed in medieval handwritten texts, mainly at the grapho-phonetic and morphological levels. Dated and localized texts are preferred, since they allow precise diatopic and diachronic identifications; in this framework the importance of great chanceries as writing centres (*lieux d'écriture*) is highlighted which promoted their own *scripta*, with regional or sub-regional diffusion (Glessgen 2008).

When *scriptologie* employs cartographic devices, connecting the medieval situation with the modern one, it approaches or even coincides with the dialectometrical methodology (Section 3.5.3); not by chance, Hans Goebl and his Salzburg School are active in both subdisciplines. One of its most notable accomplishments is Paul Videsott's work on the *scriptae* of medieval northern Italian texts (Videsott 2009): the aim is that of measuring the distance between those *scriptae* and contemporary standard Italian, via the statistical analysis of 320 linguistic features found in 2,064 texts. The results, as is often the case in scriptological works, show a remarkable similarity between the medieval and the modern dialectal landscapes, the basic assumption being that of linguistic continuity across a long chronological span.

The problem of literary *scriptae*, normally more mixed than documentary *scriptae*, is directly addressed by the project of the *Nouveau Corpus d'Amsterdam*, based on the annotated digital edition of Dees corpus of literary texts (Section 3.5.3), re-edited, updated, and improved (Kunstmann and Stein 2007; Glessgen and Vachon 2013).[38]

---

[36] For the advantages of small, carefully balanced corpora see Hundt and Leech (2012).
[37] See Fernández Ordóñez (2011); the corpus is available online: www.corpusrural.es/.
[38] The *Nouveau Corpus d'Amsterdam* is available online for registered users: https://sites.google.com/site/achimstein/research/resources/nca.

Finally, we observe that scriptological research is not common in the Ibero-Romance domain, where the same notion of *scripta* did not take root (Sánchez-Prieto Borja 2012). That is not to say that Ibero-Romance historical linguistics and dialectology lack important textual corpora: on the contrary, the great quantity of historical corpora has prompted a serious discussion about their goals and functions, and the possibility of better exploiting their data (Kabatek 2016).

Selected References

Below you can find selected references for this chapter. The full references can be found online at the following page: www.cambridge.org/Romancelinguistics

Adams, J. (2013). *Social Variation and the Latin language*. Cambridge: Cambridge University Press.

Auer, P. and Schmidt, J. E. (eds) (2010). *Language and Space. Vol. 1: Theories and Methods*. Berlin: de Gruyter.

Cugno, F. and Massobrio, L. (2010). *Gli atlanti linguistici della Romània. Corso di geografia linguistica*. Alessandria: Edizioni dell'Orso.

Dees, A. (1980). *Atlas des formes et des constructions des chartes françaises du 13e siècle*. Tübingen: Niemeyer.

Frank, B. and Hartmann, J. (1997). *Inventaire systématique des premiers documents des langues romanes*. Tübingen: Narr.

Gheţie, I. (ed.) (1997). *Istoria limbii române literare. Epoca veche (1532–1780)*. Bucharest: Editura Academiei Române.

Iliescu, M. and Roegiest, E. (eds) (2015). *Manuel des anthologies, corpus et textes romans*. Berlin: de Gruyter.

Kabatek, J. and Benito Moreno, C. (eds) (2016). *Lingüística de corpus y lingüística histórica iberorrománica*. Berlin: de Gruyter.

Kittel, H., House, J., and Schultze, B. (eds) (2004–11). *Übersetzung. Translation. Traduction: ein internationales Handbuch zur Übersetzungsforschung*. Berlin: de Gruyter.

Lameli, A., Kehrein, R. and, Rabanus, S. (eds) (2010). *Language and Space. An International Handbook of Linguistic Variation. Vol. 2: Language Mapping, Part I*. Berlin: de Gruyter

Metzeltin, M. (2004). *Las lenguas románicas estándar. Historia de su formación y de su uso*. Oviedo: Academia de la Llingua Asturiana.

Trovato, P. (2014). *Everything You Always Wanted to Know about Lachmann's Method: A Non-Standard Handbook of Genealogical Textual Criticism in the Age of Post-Structuralism, Cladistic, and Copy-text*. Padua: Libreriauniversitaria.it.

4

Variation in Romance

Diego Pescarini and Michele Loporcaro

4.1 Introduction

This chapter sets out to show how the study of linguistic variation across closely related languages can fuel research questions and provide a fertile testbed for linguistic theory.* We will present two case studies in structural variation – subject clitics and (perfective) auxiliation – and show how a comparative view of these phenomena is best suited to providing a satisfactory account for them, and how such a comparative account bears on a number of theoretical issues ranging from (rather trivially) the modelling of variation to the definition of wordhood, the inventory of parts of speech, and the division of labour between syntax and morphology.

4.2 Systematic Variation: The Case of Subject Clitics

French, northern Italian Dialects, Ladin, and Romansh are characterized by the presence, with variable degrees of obligatoriness, of clitic elements stemming from Latin nominative personal pronouns.

Subject clitics are not a minor peculiarity scattered across several varieties, but a macro-phenomenon, which has been studied extensively in the past decades (see Poletto and Tortora 2016 for a recent overview). On the theoretical side, subject clitics raise several questions regarding the nature of null subject languages and the relation between pro-drop and agreement (cf. also Sections 10.3, 17.5.1.1, and 21.2.1).

---

* This article was conceived and written jointly; nevertheless, for academic purposes Diego Pescarini is responsible for Sections 4.2–4.2.5, 4.3.5, and 4.4, Michele Loporcaro for Sections 4.1, 4.2.6, and 4.3–4.3.4.

4.2.1 Subject Clitics and the Null Subject Parameter

It is worth recalling that the null subject parameter cuts across the area of subject clitics: northern Italian dialects exhibit subject clitics (cf. 1a), but, unlike French, they exhibit the canonical properties of null subject languages, i.e., they are not subject to the so-called *that*-trace effect (cf. 2) and allow free inversion (cf. 3). For these reasons, clitics in northern Italian dialects have often been analysed as agreement markers, rather than fully-fledged pronouns (Rizzi 1986; Brandi and Cordin 1989).[1]

(1) a. Parla   italiano. (It.)
       speak.3SG   Italian
    b. **(Il)   parle   italien. (Fr)
       3SG.NOM=   speak.3SG   Italian
    c. **(El)   parla   italian. (Ver.)
       3SG=   speak.3SG   Italian
       'He speaks Italian.'

(2) a. Chi   hai   detto   che _   ha   scritto
       who   have.2SG   say.PST.PTCP   that   have.3SG   write.PST.PTCP
       questo   libro? (It.)
       this   book
    b. **Qui   as-tu   dit   qu' _   a   écrit
       who   have.2SG=2SG.NOM   say.PST.PTCP   that   have.3SG   write.PST.PTCP
       ce   livre? (Fr.)
       this   book
    c. Ci   ghe-to   dito   che _   ga   scrito
       who   have.2SG=2SG   say.PST.PTCP   that   have.3SG   write.PST.PTCP
       sto   libro? (Ver.)
       this   book

(3) a. È   arrivato   Gianni. (It.)
       be.3SG   arrive.PST.PTCP   Gianni
    b. **Est   arrivé   Jean. (Fr.)
       be.3SG   arrive.PST.PTCP   Jean
    c. L'   è   rivà   Giani. (Ver.)
       3SG= be.3SG   arrive.PST.PTCP   Gianni.
       'John has arrived.'

Given this state of affairs, it is tempting to treat subject clitics as affixes. In this respect, the notion 'clitic' has fuelled a huge debate, which is understandable since it is an 'umbrella term', as Zwicky (1994: xiii) puts it, and '[u]mbrella terms are names for problems, for phenomena that present "mixed" properties of some kind, not names of theoretical

---

[1] In the following examples, the gloss NOM is used only for pronominal clitic subjects.

constructs'. As examples of the ongoing debate, consider, for instance, Bermúdez-Otero and Payne (2011), who question the legitimacy of Zwicky's (1977: 4) category of 'special clitics', to which Romance pronominal clitics are usually ascribed. These, on the other hand, 'are better regarded as elements which are neither canonical affixes nor canonical clitics' according to Spencer and Luís (2013: 147). And there is indeed plenty of evidence that they cannot be reduced to (word-level) affixes.[2] For instance, in some modern Romance varieties, pronominal clitics can be separated from their hosts by an intervening adverbial, which never happens with affixes (see Ledgeway and Lombardi 2005: 80–82) and subject clitics, unlike inflexional affixes, often undergo subject-clitic inversion in interrogative clauses. At the same time, however, Romance pronominal clitics differ from corresponding full pronouns in several respects (cf., e.g., Kayne 1975; van Riemsdijk 1999: 2–4; Russi 2008: 4–7). This means that, even if subject clitics were considered agreement markers, they would differ in nature from agreement affixes, a possibility excluded in some typological accounts of the word vs affix divide (Bickel and Nichols 2007).

With this in mind, let us entertain the hypothesis that subject clitics in a non-null-subject language like French are fully fledged pronouns, whereas clitics in null-subject languages are (non-affixal) agreement markers. Loporcaro (2012: 176) argues for a principled distinction between *clitic subjects* (i.e., fully-fledged pronouns that, from a morpho-phonological point of view, are clitics) and *subject clitics* (i.e., non-argumental clitic markers expressing agreement features). Further evidence seems to support the hypothesis: in northern Italian and Tuscan dialects, but not in French, subject clitics can double a non-dislocated subject, follow negation, and cannot be dropped under coordination:

(4) a. Nessuno gli ha detto nulla. (Flo.)
 no.one 3SG= have.3SG say.PST.PTCP nothing
 b. **Personne il n' a rien dit. (Fr.)
 no.one 3SG.NOM= NEG= have.3SG nothing say.PST.PTCP
 'Nobody has said anything.'

(5) a. Un tu compri mai mele. (Flo.)
 NEG 2SG= buy.2SG never apples
 b. Tu n' achètes jamais de pommes. (Fr.)
 2SG.NOM= NEG buy.2SG never of apples
 'You never buy apples.'

(6) a. La canta e la balla. (Flo.)
 3FSG= sing.3SG and 3SG= dance.3SG

---

[2] A conceivable alternative consists in analysing Romance clitics as phrase-level affixes: cf., for example, Bermúdez-Otero and Payne (2011) for discussion and criticism.

b.   Elle   chante   et   danse. (Fr.)
     3FSG.NOM=   sing.3SG   and   dance.3SG
     'She sings and dances.'

However, Poletto (2000) shows that northern Italian dialects, although behaving like null-subject languages, do not always allow doubling, do not always display the order negation > clitics, and, under certain circumstances, allow the omission of certain clitic forms in coordinated structures. At the same time, corpus studies have shown that in French varieties such as colloquial metropolitan French as well as Quebec, Ontario, and Swiss varieties of French (see Palasis 2015 and references therein), subject clitics and NP/DP subjects (including strong pronouns) co-occur even if the latter are not dislocated, which has led some scholars to conclude that French clitic subjects, at least in certain varieties, are also in fact agreement markers (subject clitics, in Loporcaro's 2012 terms).

To conclude, clitic elements with nominative etymology are attested in both null and non-null subject languages, but their syntactic behaviour differs in the two types of language in several respects (above all, doubling of a clause subject). This suggests that clitic subjects in non-null subject languages may have a pronominal status, whereas subject clitics in null-subject languages cannot, although the correlation between the syntactic properties of subject clitics (and clitic subjects) and the divide between null/non-null subject languages is more complicated than previously thought (Poletto 2000; Roberts 2014; Palasis 2015).

4.2.2 Expletive Subject Clitics and Agreement

In this section, we discuss the conclusion of the previous section in the light of evidence from dialects exhibiting expletive subject clitics.

Some northern Italian dialects – null subject languages, according to the traditional subdivision – exhibit expletive subject clitics in impersonal clauses. For instance, in the dialect of Monno the non-agreeing/expletive clitic *el* in (7b–c) co-occurs with postverbal subjects and weather verbs.[3]

(7) **Monno, Lombardy**
    a. Le   matele   le   lavarè   zo   i   piacc.
        the   girls   3FPL=   wash.FUT.3   down   the   dishes
        'The girls will wash the dishes.'
    b. El   salta   zo   le   foe.
        3MSG=   drop.3   down   the.FPL   leaf.PL
        'Leaves are falling.'

---

[3] The patterns in (7) and (8) are broadly reminiscent of the distinction between *canonical* and *expletive* null subject languages (see D'Alessandro 2015 for a recent overview).

    c.   El   plof.
         3MSG= rain.3
         'It is raining.'

In other dialects, such as Triestino, subject clitics are optional if the subject is preverbal,[4] whereas the clitic never occurs with a postverbal subject (cf. 8b), or in impersonal contexts (cf. 8c; more on impersonals below).

(8) **Trieste (*Syntactic Atlas of Italy*, http://asit.maldura.unipd.it/)**
    a.   Le   mule   (**le**)   laverà   i   piati.
        the girl.PL 3FPL= wash.FUT.3 the.PL plate.PL
        'The girls will wash the dishes.'
    b.   Casca   le   foie.
        drop.3 the.FPL leaf.PL
        'Leaves are falling.'
    c.   Piovi.
        rain.3
        'It is raining.'

The idea that agreement markers act as expletives needs further discussion. First, subject expletives are normally regarded as placeholders, i.e., dummy elements having the same status as phrasal subjects. This definition, however, is at odds with the behaviour of subject clitics in dialects that allow doubling (cf. 8a): since clitics and phrasal subjects co-occur, it is unlikely that subject clitics, namely agreement markers, can satisfy any syntactic requirement related to the subject position.

Second, if subject clitics were agreement markers, they would occur across-the-board, i.e., in all impersonal constructions such as (8b–c) or in prototypical subject-less contexts such as imperatives, contrary to fact. It is worth noting that Romance imperatives normally exhibit agreement endings, therefore the absence of subject clitics cannot result from a generalized impoverishment of agreement morphology in imperative contexts. Rather, central Romance varieties exclude subject clitics precisely in those contexts where phrasal subjects are ruled out, which amounts to saying that the distribution of subject clitics mirrors that of strong subject pronouns.

As for impersonal contexts, Renzi and Vanelli (1983) observed that expletive clitics are more readily found with weather verbs and,[5] to a lesser

---

[4] Benincà and Poletto (2004a) argue that in Paduan subject clitics are mandatory when the subject is dislocated. Additionally, in some varieties subject clitics must be dropped in certain environments such as restrictive (vs appositive) relative clauses or subject-wh interrogatives, whereas similar omissions never target fully fledged agreement markers.

[5] This is reminiscent of partial pro-drop languages (cf. Section 1.2.3.1), but recall that here we are dealing with dialects which are pro-drop, although they have subject (expletive) clitics.

Table 4.1. *Expletive clitics in impersonal environments*

Variety	Weather verb	Existential construction	Raising construction	Arbitrary construction	Impersonal necessity
Carcare	U ciov	U j-è	U smija …	U s diz	U bsogna
Cesena	E piov	U j-è	E per …	U s dis	Ø bsogna
Monno	El plof	El g'e	El par	Ø s dis	Ø gna
Rocca P.	El piof	L'è	Ø somea	Ø se dis	Ø moza
Aldeno	El piove	Ø gh'e	Ø par	Ø se dis	Ø bisogna
	'it rains'	'there is …'	'it seems that …'	'one says'	'it is needed …'

extent, with existentials and impersonal *si* constructions. Some dialects require an expletive clitic to occur with the modal verb expressing impersonal necessity ('it is necessary to'), but – to the best of our knowledge – this happens if and only if the expletive clitic occurs in the remaining impersonal contexts. Hence, the distribution of expletive clitics in impersonal environments also follows an implicational scale, illustrated in Table 4.1 (from Pescarini 2014 with modifications).

4.2.3 Subject Clitics vs Verbal Agreement

Even if they were agreement markers, it is not clear why subject clitics should 'double' the information conveyed by verbal endings. The naïve hypothesis is that subject clitics emerged to disambiguate person agreement (or license null subjects, in the terms of Roberts 2014) after verb endings had merged via sound change.[6] In fact, however, many dialects with subject clitics have very transparent verb morphology and, among dialects with a complete set of subject clitics, these are often syncretic or optional (cf. the formative *i* in 9a–f). Consequently, if clitics were meant to 'counterbalance' the loss of verb endings, why is the inventory of clitics more syncretic than that of endings?

(9) Gruyère, Switzerland (De Crousaz and Shlonsky 2003)
    a. Me (i) medzo dou fre.
          I   1SG= eat.1SG of.the cheese
          'I am eating cheese.'
    b. Tè te medzè dou pan.
          you 2SG= eat.2SG of.the bread
          'You are eating bread.'
    c. Li (i) medzè chin ti lé dzoa.
          he 3MSG= eat.3SG that all the days
          'He eats that every day.'

---

[6] This issue parallels the discussion on the relationship between richness of verb agreement and pro-drop (e.g., Taraldsen 1980; Matasović 2018: 45–48).

d. No no medzin rintyé la demindze.
   we 1PL= eat.1PL only the Sunday
   'We eat only on Sundays.'
e. Vo vo medzidè avu no.
   you.PL 2PL= eat.2PL with us
   'You are eating with us.'
f. Là (i) medzon to cholè.
   they 3PL= eat.3PL all alone
   'They are eating all alone.

Roberts (2014: 196f.) elaborates on the following typology of morphological systems on the basis of the lack/presence of overt agreement markers on subject clitics and finite verbs:

(10) SCL [+agr] V [+agr] 'fully redundant', null-subject system
      SCL [+agr] V [−agr] non-null-subject system
      SCL [−agr] V [+agr] a non-redundant null-subject system
      SCL [−agr] V [−agr] (usually) a complementary system

However, no system is 'pure' as, for instance, a dialect can be fully redundant in the singular and non-redundant or complementary in the plural. On average, all systems are redundant. Table 4.2 reports data from a sample of ten varieties regarding the co-occurrence of subject clitics and verbal forms of the present indicative (regular verbs). Even factoring out morphophonological aspects (sandhi phenomena, e.g., liaison, irregular verbs, suppletion, gaps), the taxonomy in (10) looks somewhat idealized.

Once the data in Table 4.2 are plotted into a Cartesian diagram (Figure 4.1) representing the number of contrastive exponents in the paradigms of verbs (y-axis) and subject clitics (x-axis), we may notice that all dialects occur in the upper-right part of the plan, which means that the total possible number of distinctive combinations always exceeds the six persons of the paradigm. The tendency (dotted) line suggests that the morphological richness of the verbal and clitic systems correlate inversely, but the hypothesis needs to be tested on the basis of a larger set of data.

From a qualitative point of view, the hypothesis of an inverse relation between the verbal and proclitic domain is particularly promising in the case of the first person plural and second person plural, which normally display idiosyncratic exponents in the verbal paradigm (e.g., suppletive or non-rhizotonic forms), whereas the corresponding clitics are missing or syncretic (more on this below). If the whole paradigm is examined, however, the impoverishment of verb inflexion may be considered a possible factor in shaping clitic paradigms, but verbal morphology per se cannot be regarded as a necessary condition for the emergence of clitic systems.

Table 4.2. *Patterns of gaps and syncretism in the paradigms of subject clitics (left) and verbal forms (right)*

Pigna (Lig.)		Cortemilia (Pie.)		Donceto (Lmb.)		Casola (Tsc.)		Chioggia (Ven.)	
1SG$_a$	1SG$_a$	1SG$_a$	1SG$_a$	1SG$_a$	1SG$_a$	1SG$_a$	1SG$_a$	0	1SG
2SG	2SG$_b$	2SG	2SG$_b$	2SG	2SG$_a$	2SG	2SG$_a$	2SG	2SG
3SG	3SG$_a$	3SG	3SG$_a$	3SG$_a$	3SG	3SG$_b$	3SG$_a$	3SG$_a$	3SG$_a$
1PL	1PL$_c$	1PL$_a$	1PL	1PL$_a$	1PL	1PL$_a$	1PL	0	1PL
2PL$_a$	2PL$_c$	2PL$_b$	2PL$_b$	2PL$_a$	2PL	2PL	2PL	0	2PL
3PL	3PL$_b$	3PL$_b$	3PL	3PL	3PL	3PL$_b$	3PL	3PL	3PL$_a$
4	3	4	4	4	5	4	4	4	5

French		Gruyère (Frp.)		Breil (Occ.)		Vallader (RaeR.)		Badiot (Lad.)	
1SG	1SG$_a$	1SG$_a$	1SG	0	1SG$_a$	1SG	1SG	1SG$_a$	1SG
2SG	2SG$_a$	2SG	2SG$_a$	2SG	2SG	0	2SG	2SG	2SG
3SG	3SG$_a$	3SG$_a$	3SG$_a$	3SG	3SG	0	3SG	3SG	3SG$_a$
1PL	1PL	1PL	3SG	0	1PL	0	1PL	1PL$_a$	1PL
2PL	2PL	2PL	1PL	0	2PL$_a$	0	2PL	2PL$_a$	2PL
3PL	3PL$_a$	3PL$_a$	2PL	0	3PL	3PL	3PL	3PL	3PL$_a$
6	4	4	5	3	5	3	6	4	5

Key: 0 = gaps; subscripts (a, b, c) mark syncretism. The number of contrastive exponents is given in the shaded row.

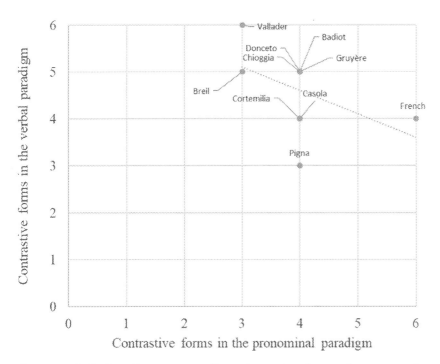

Figure 4.1 Distribution of languages according to the number of contrastive exponents in the paradigms of verbs (y-axis) and subject clitics (x-axis)

4.2.4 Gaps

Calabrese (2011) quantifies Manzini and Savoia's (2005) data (from 183 varieties) on the distribution of gaps. What follows elaborates on Calabrese's in-depth examination, combined with quantitative observations on other datasets, e.g., the *Atlante Sintattico d'Italia* (ASIt) covering 182 more dialects.

Among Manzini and Savoia's (2005) 183 paradigms (from northern Italian and Romansh dialects), 72 are defective, as seen in Table 4.3, which lists the patterns attested in at least two or more varieties, with a diffusion > 0.005.

By combinatorics (see also Heap 2000; 2002), a 6-cell paradigm allowing gaps is supposed to generate 64 possible patterns. Hence, the probability of developing a non-defective paradigm is lower (1/64) than the probability of developing a system with gaps. Probability and actual diffusion are compared in the graph in Figure 4.2.

Leaving full paradigms aside, the distribution of defective patterns looks rather regular as it follows the curve of probability. However, it is worth noting that among the 20 possible patterns with three gaps, only one

Table 4.3. *Gaps in subject clitic paradigms in dialects of northern Italy and Romansh*

number of gaps	5	4	4	3	2	2	0
number of dialects	3	4	6	39	3	4	111
diffusion[a]	0.02	0.02	0.03	0.21	0.02	0.04	0.60
1SG	0	0	0	0	1	0	1
2SG	1	1	0	1	1	1	1
3SG	0	1	1	1	1	1	1
1PL	0	0	0	0	0	0	1
2PL	0	0	0	0	0	1	1
3PL	0	0	1	1	1	1	1

[a] = number of dialects / 183.

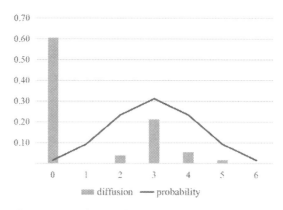

Figure 4.2 Distribution of patterns per number of gaps: diffusion of dialects in the sample vs probability

system is broadly attested, viz. that featuring only second person singular, third person singular, and third person plural clitics (this system has a diffusion of 0.21, one system in five).

The diffusion of the above pattern is confirmed by further data from the ASIt database. We have plotted the presence of first person singular and second person singular clitics in the 182 varieties surveyed there. Four possible patterns are expected:

- Ø, Ø: both first person singular and second person singular are missing;
- Ø, 2: the first person singular is missing;
- 1, Ø: the second person singular is missing;
- 1, 2: both clitics are attested.

As shown in the bar chart in Figure 4.3, the patterns in which the second person singular clitic is missing are unattested or very marginal.

The diagram in Figure 4.4 shows the diffusion of the same four patterns in four linguistic areas of northern Italy. We can observe that the pattern [Ø, 2] is strongly predominant in Venetan dialects. Hence, in this case areal factors might play a role, although areal explanations per se cannot capture the overall asymmetry in the make-up of clitic paradigms.

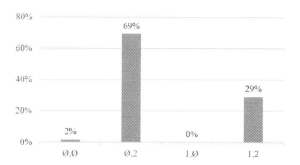

Figure 4.3 Presence of 1sg and 2sg clitics in the *ASIt* dataset

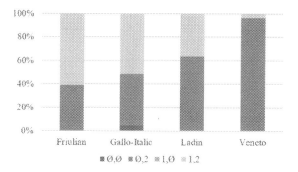

Figure 4.4 Presence of 1sg and 2sg clitics in four linguistic areas (northern Italo-Romance)

Building on similar data, previous studies revealed some robust trends in the form of implicational statements (see further the discussion in Section 23.2.1):

(11) a. 2 > 3 > 6 > 5 > 4 > 1   (Renzi and Vanelli 1983)
     b. 2 > 3 > 6 > 1 > 4/5   (Cabredo Hofherr 2004; Calabrese 2011)
     c. 2 > 6 > 3 > 4 > 1 > 5   (Heap 2000)

Heap (2002), Oliviéri (2011), and Calabrese (2011) among others tried to formulate higher-grade generalizations, although all accounts based on feature geometries are eventually challenged by counterexamples.

4.2.5 Syncretism

Subject clitics exhibit systematic syncretism, i.e., identity of exponence across paradigm cells. The graph in Figure 4.5 illustrates the distribution of syncretisms and gaps in the 183 paradigms reported in Manzini and Savoia (2005).

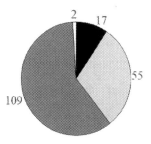

■ +syncretism +gaps ▢ −syncretism +gaps
▨ +syncretism −gaps ▯ −syncretism −gaps

Figure 4.5 Number of clitic systems with gaps and/or syncretic items in Manzini and Savoia's (2005) dataset

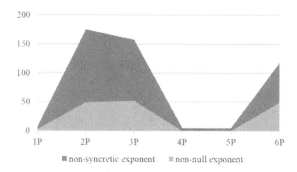

Figure 4.6 Number of non-syncretic and non-null exponents per person

Almost all dialects exhibit either syncretism or gaps. Moreover, gaps and syncretism seem tightly linked. As Calabrese (2011: 311) points out, '[w]e find zeros in all of the cases where we have syncretic exponents'. The correlation between the two phenomena is illustrated in Fig. 4.6 diagram, which represents the number of overt (light grey) and idiosyncratic exponents (dark grey) for each person. Despite the different dimensions – which are due to the larger amounts of systems with syncretism (Figure 4.6) – the two areas have the same shape.

4.2.6 Pantiscu, an Outlier

For all central Romance dialects addressed so far, despite huge variation, the following holds true: (a) distributionally, the (non-)occurrence of subject clitics obeys morphological (see Sections 4.2.4–5) and syntactic constraints; and (b) functionally, subject clitics encode exclusively the inflexional categories of person, number, and (for the third person) gender, marking subject agreement on a par with the verb's contextual inflexion (in Booij's 1994; 1996 terms). There is, however, just one Romance variety for which (a)–(b) do not hold. This is also an outlier geographically, as it is spoken far from the central Romance area stretching from Bordeaux to the Alps to Florence, from which we have drawn examples so far. Pantiscu, the Sicilian dialect spoken on the island of Pantelleria, was shown (by Loporcaro et al. 2010; Loporcaro 2012) to possess subject clitics whose occurrence is not dictated by syntax and whose function consists in marking the progressive value of the aspect category, in addition to person, number, and (for the third person) gender.

(12) **Pantelleria**
    a.   ɖɖʐa   pɪtˈtʃɔtta   (ˈɪ)ɖɖʐa pasˈsɪa.
        that.FSG girl.SG   3FSG=   stroll.3SG
        'That girl is taking a walk.'
    b.   ˈɪɖɖʐʊ e   maˈrɪːa ʊn   ɖʐɪ   ˈfannʊ ˈnɛnte.
        3MSG   and Maria   NEG 3PL= do.3PL nothing
        'He and Maria are not doing anything.'
    c.   ˈjɛ   ʊɲɲɛ   ˈmantʃʊ (**mai).
        1SG NEG.1SG= eat.1SG   never
        'I am not eating.'
    d.   ɖɖʐʊ   pɪtˈtʃɔtto ˈsempe ke (**ɖɖʐʊ) ˈkʊrre
        that.MSG boy.SG   always that   3MSG= run.3SG
        'That boy always runs.'

Examples (12a–d) contain present tense forms that could be replaced by the imperfect, the only other imperfective tense in the indicative mood. Note that in (12a–c) there occurs a pronominal element (3FSG, 3PL, and 1SG, respectively), which could be omitted, but this is not what happens in reality because without the pronominal element the clauses would be aspectually unmarked, compatible with both perfective (*praesens pro futuro*) and imperfective non-progressive readings. Compare (12d), where ˈsempe 'always' forces a habitual reading and causes 3MSG ɖɖʐʊ to be ungrammatical, while with ɖɖʐʊ and without ˈsempe (12d) would mean 'that boy is running'. Progressive, in other words, is expressed by pronominal elements, which (a) agree with the clausal subject, (b) co-occur with a subject NP, and (c) test positively for clitichood diagnostics: to mention just one, in (12b–c) the clitics follow, rather than precede, preverbal negation (ʊnn),[7] thus occupying a position from which all subject NPs are barred (see Loporcaro 2012: 757f. for other tests). Thus, Pantiscu has subject clitics, like northern Italian dialects, but unlike the latter these subject clitics are not syntactically obligatory nor semantically void, expressing – in addition to number, gender, and person – an aspectual value which is usually encoded in the verb's inherent inflexion. In line with this, pronominal progressives are barred in contexts where progressives are cross-linguistically excluded (e.g., with state-denoting verbs). A final remarkable point is that Pantiscu subject clitics are all syntactic clitics but, again contrary to central Romance dialects, they are not uniformly phonological clitics. As exemplified in (12a), third person clitics have a full form, bisyllabic and homophonous with the stressed personal pronoun, occurring in free variation with a reduced unstressed monosyllabic form (both seen in 12b), but first and second persons lack reduced forms, so that subject clitics are fully homophonous with subject pronouns (e.g., ˈtʊ ʊn tʊ ˈmantʃi 'you are not eating').

4.3 Auxiliary Selection and Auxiliary Splits

Romance languages and dialects all feature auxiliary verbs, defined as 'a lexically designated closed class of verbs whose defining property is that they inherit their subject' (Rosen 1997: 112). While, under many definitions, modal verbs are also labelled 'auxiliaries', modals differ from auxiliaries proper in that they reinitialize (i.e., bestow a thematic role on) their subject argument. By contrast, perfective auxiliaries (cf. 13–14), whose sole function is to form (perfective) periphrastic verb forms, do not.

(13) a. María ha   comido (el   arroz). (Sp.)
         María has   eaten   the rice

---

[7] (12b–c) are from Khamma, a rural outlying part of Pantelleria, whose dialect allows progressive subject clitics to co-occur with negation, while most speakers from central Pantelleria resort to the alternative pan-Romance progressive construction whenever negation is involved.

b. Marie a mangé (le riz). (Fr.)
   Marie has eaten the rice
   'Mary has eaten (the rice).'

(14) a. María ha entrado. (Sp.)
       María has entered
    b. Marie est entrée. (Fr.)
       Marie is entered
       'Mary has come in.'

As the examples show, Spanish and French display diverging distributions: while French preserves an auxiliation contrast, which arose in proto-Romance (cf. La Fauci 1988), with auxiliary E selected in unaccusative (14b) and H in unergative/transitive clauses (13b), Spanish has generalized auxiliary H.[8] There is a huge literature on this twofold binary contrast, i.e., the syntactic contrast (13b) vs (14b) within languages such as French – or Italian and Sardinian – and the contrast between French-type 2-aux Romance varieties and languages such as Spanish – or Portuguese, Catalan, and Romanian. However, this is just the tip of the iceberg, since variation in auxiliation readily reveals itself as much more pervasive, as soon as one widens the scope of inquiry beyond the standard languages. As it happens, less known non-standard dialects display a kaleidoscope of auxiliation options, whose rationalization poses fascinating analytical challenges and yields insights into basic issues of linguistic theory, such as those mentioned in Section 4.1.

4.3.1 Lexical and Semantic Factors

Semantic and lexical factors, relevant to this variation, can only be briefly sketched here (see also discussion in Section 23.2.2). TAM-driven splits occur in several varieties: Romanian has auxiliary H in the indicative present perfect and auxiliary E in other tenses/moods (Ledgeway 2014), and comparable splits occur in Italian and Catalan dialects (Loporcaro 2016: 813f.). *Aktionsart* (in particular (a)telicity) and agentivity correlate with auxiliary selection in intransitives: Sorace (2000) put forward an Auxiliary Selection Hierarchy (ASH) which has telic change of location verbs like (14) at the top, selecting auxiliary E categorically, and verbs designating non-motional process at the bottom, with categorical auxiliary H, and five more semantic classes in between, selecting E with decreasing

---

[8] As shown by La Fauci (1988), split auxiliation, like other unaccusativity-related phenomena, was established in proto-Romance as one of the manifestations of active/inactive alignment, while generalization of just one auxiliary is part of a later drift towards the reestablishment of a more consistent accusative/nominative alignment (cf. also Section 18.3).

likelihood and showing variation (cf. Legendre and Sorace 2003: 196; cf. also Section 16.2). Along these lines, some studies (e.g., Cennamo 1999; 2002; 2008; Aranovich 2003; Bentley 2006) contend that unaccusativity can be reduced to semantics and that a syntactic representation of unaccusativity can be entirely dispensed with. However, Loporcaro (2011; 2015; 2016) has shown that, alongside semantic gradience (ASH), an orthogonal syntactic gradient is to be recognized, as first proposed in Loporcaro (1999: 213) within Relational Grammar and adapted to other frameworks in Bentley (2010) and Ledgeway (2012: 321). While the ASH may (see Aranovich 2003 for old Spanish) or may not (see Loporcaro 2015: 67–71 for old Sicilian and old Neapolitan) play a role in shaping variation and change, this is unquestionably a subordinate role, since this variation is observed within the limits of syntactically defined classes of predicates.

Lexical factors play a role in the Romance drift 2-aux > 1-aux, involving gradual depletion of the set of E-selecting unaccusatives, as observed when comparing Italo-Romance (with about 300–400 such verbs) with modern French, where this set shrinks to around 30, and northern and American Oïl dialects in which just one or two verbs still select aux E (examples and references in Loporcaro 2016: 812).

Reference to the lexicon is found in approaches to auxiliation which capitalize on the alleged (change in) the 'lexical' specification of, say, auxiliary *haber* 'have' in (the diachrony of) Spanish. This view, criticized in Loporcaro (2007b: 175f.), will not be further considered here.

4.3.2 The Syntactic Gradient

An advance in research on variation in Romance auxiliation was the recognition that, as more dialects are considered, the (seemingly) binary contrasts in (13)–(14) become part of an implicational scale: French and Spanish occupy the two extremes on one dimension, while on the other axis unaccusatives and unergatives/transitives are the endpoints.[9]

In between, the steps of the scale are shaped by auxiliary choice with different types of reflexive construction. For instance, type (b) is exemplified by the Apulian dialect of Lesina (M. Carosella, p. c.; Loporcaro 2007b: 192):

(15) Lesina (Foggia) Clause type:
 a. 'jɛss 'ɛ 'mmɔrt. unaccusative
  she is died.FSG
  'She has died.'

---

[9] E and H in Table 4.4 represent the majority case, but what is crucial is the auxiliation contrast or lack thereof. Thus, while for option (f) in Table 4.4 generalization of H is most widespread, Portuguese – with generalized *ter* 'hold; have' – and the dialects of central-southern Italy (Tuttle 1986: 267 on Terracinese) and of Catalonia (cf. Alcover 1903: 470f.; Fabra 1912: 136 on Rossellonès) which generalized aux E are instances of the same type.

b. 'jɛssə tʃ 'ɛ lla'vatə. direct transitive
    she REFL.3 is washed
    'She has washed herself.'

c. 'jɛssə tʃ 'ɛ rrəspʊn'nʊtə 'sola. (monadic)
    she REFL.3 is answered alone indirect unergative
    'She has answered to herself.' E

d. 'jɛssə tʃ 'a lla'vat i 'manə. H
    she REFL.3 has washed the hands indirect transitive (dyadic)
    'She has washed her hands.'

e. 'iss 'a 'rrɔtt a bbut'tɪɟɟə/ 'a kkammə'nat as'sa.
    he has broken the bottle has walked a.lot transitive/unergative
    'He has broken the bottle / has walked a lot.'

As seen in (15), this dialect like Logudorese Sardinian (option b in Table 4.4; cf. data in Loporcaro 2016: 809) selects auxiliary H not only with ergatives/transitives but also with dyadic reflexives, the only reflexive predicates to feature a distinct initial subject and direct object, while all the other reflexive constructions pattern with unaccusatives in selecting auxiliary E. The auxiliary E/H divide can occur at other points on the scale (cf. Loporcaro 2016: 814f. for details): most options are attested in modern dialects, except for option (d), which is illustrated with old Florentine and (variably) old Castilian in Loporcaro (2015: 63–65). Crucially, discontinuous options (say, auxiliary E in unaccusatives and indirect unergative reflexives vs auxiliary H elsewhere) are unattested. This can hardly be coincidental and calls for a formal explanation, which has been provided under the form of a parametric rule in Loporcaro (2007b: 193; 2011: 82). However, structural variation in auxiliary selection by no means reduces to the six options in Table 4.4.

Table 4.4. *Implicational scale for auxiliary selection*

	INACTIVE					ACTIVE
			Reflexive			
	unacc.	retr.	dir. trans.	indir. unerg.	indir. trans.	trans./unerg.
a. French	E					H
b. Logudorese Srd.	E					H
c. Picernese	E					H
d. old Florentine	E					H
e. Leccese	E					H
f. Spanish						H

4.3.3 Person-Driven Variation and Splits

In the examples in (13)–(14) and (15), third persons are representative of homogeneous paradigms, displaying auxiliary E or H throughout. Several Italo-Romance dialects depart from such uniformity in that they show free variation and/or complementary distribution of E/H depending on verb person. The dialect of Ruvo di Puglia (province of Bari; Manzini and Savoia 2005, II: 724f.) illustrates both cases:

(16)　　Ruvo di Puglia
　　　　1SG　'sɔ / 'aɟɟə　　drəm'meutə/və'neutə.
　　　　　　　am　have.1SG　slept/come
　　　　2SG　'si　　　　　 drəm'meutə/və'neutə.
　　　　　　　are.2SG　　　slept/come
　　　　1PL　'ɔmmə　　　 drəm'meutə/və'neutə.
　　　　　　　have.1PL　　slept/come
　　　　'I/you.SG/.PL have slept/come.'

In the dialect of Ruvo di Puglia, all classes of verbs select auxiliary E/H in free variation in the first person singular, while in the second person singular only auxiliary E is grammatical and in all plural persons (exemplified with first person plural in 16) only auxiliary H is grammatical. However, the person split in (16) is just one among a host of different options displayed by Italian dialects. While there is an extensive literature on such mixed systems (e.g., Giammarco 1973; Tuttle 1986; Bentley and Eythórsson 2001; Ledgeway 2003; 2009: 618–20; 2019; Vecchio 2006), Manzini and Savoia (2005, II: 682–727, 784–91; III: 2–34) provide by far the largest first-hand dataset available, with 50 dialects showing person splits and possibly free variation in some persons in addition.[10] To these (unreferenced in Tables 4.5–6), we will add the dialects mentioned in further sources providing full paradigms: Giammarco (1973) (eight dialects), Tuttle (1986) (5 dialects), Loporcaro (1999; 2001; 2007b) (2, 1, and 4 respectively), Ledgeway (2003; 2009: 618–20) (1) (these sources are abbreviated M&S, G, T. L1, L2, L3, and Le respectively in Tables 4.5–6), adding up to a convenience sample of 76 dialects with person splits, which we will use to draw some generalizations on auxiliary distribution. The dialects are scattered over Italy: Abruzzo 20, Basilicata 4, Calabria 5, Campania 6, Lazio 13, Marche 4 (all from the southernmost province of Ascoli Piceno), Molise 6, Piedmont 5 (all Lombard dialects are from the eastern fringes of the region), Puglia 12. The skewing depends on the sources available and, more importantly, on the fact that such split systems occur in the mentioned areas, not

---

[10] Ledgeway (2019) presents an analysis of perfective auxiliation which covers not only person splits but also all the factors disregarded here (mentioned in Section 4.3.1), whose discussion would exceed the scope of the present chapter (though, for discussion, see also Section 23.2.2).

Table 4.5. *Patterns of split auxiliation with unergative verbs in our sample (76 dialects)*

		#	1SG	2SG	3SG	1PL	2PL	3PL
a.	Poggio Imperiale	1	E	E	E	H/E	E	E
b.	Pàstena-Castelpetroso	1	E	E	E	E	E	H/E
c.	Roccasicura	1	H/E	E	E	E	E	E
d.	Cori (T),[a] Miglionico	2	E	E	E	E	E	H
e.	Pescocostanzo	1	E	E	H	E	E	E
f.	Gallo Matese	1	H/E	E	E	E	E	H/E
g.	Monteroduni	1	H/E	E	E	E	E	H
h.	Vastogirardi	1	H	E	H	E	E	E
i.	Amandola, Bellante, ecc.[b]	21	E	E	H	E	E	H
j.	Veroli (T)	1	H/E	E	H/E	E	E	H/E
k.	Capracotta	1	H	E	E	H/E	H/E	E
l.	Amaseno (T)[c], S. Vittore, Viticuso	3	H/E	E	H	E	E	H
m.	Guardiaregia	1	H/E	E	H	H/E	H/E	H/E
n.	Sassinoro	1	H/E	E	H/E	H/E	H/E	H/E
o.	Secinaro	1	H/E	E	H	H/E	H/E	H
p.	Agnone	1	H/E	E	H	H	H	H/E
q.	Lanciano (G)	1	E	E	H	H/E	H/E	H
r.	Bisceglie2,[d] Giovinazzo, Pietransieri (L3)	3	E	E	H	H	H	H
s.	Ruvo di Puglia	1	H/E	E	H=E	H	H	H
t.	Bitetto	1	H	H	H=E	H/E	E	H
u.	Montenerodomo, Popoli	2	E	E	H	H	H	H
v.	Castelvecchio Subequo, Molfetta	2	H/E	E	H	H	H	H
w.	Minervino Murge	1	H/E	H/E	H	H/E	H/E	H
x.	Vasto (G)	1	H	E	H/E	H	H	H
y.	Altamura (L3)	1	H/E	H/E	H/E	H/E	H/E	H
z.	Trecate	1	H/E	E=H	E	E	E=H	E
aa.	Cerano	1	H/E	E=H	E	H/E	H/E	E
bb.	Morcone, Frigento[e]	8	H	H	E	H	H	H
cc.	Bisceglie1; Introdacqua, Scanno (G)	3	H	E	H	H	H	H
dd.	Notaresco (G)	1	E	H	H	H	H	H
ee.	Padula, Monteparano	2	H	H	H/E	H	H	H
ff.	Canosa di Puglia	1	H/E	H	H	H	H	H
gg.	Gravina di Puglia	1	H/E	H	H=E	H	H	H
hh.	Briga Novarese, Masserano	2	H	E=H	H	H	H	H
ii.	S. Giorgio d. Sannio	1	H	H	E=H	H	H	H
jj.	Naples (Le), Aliano, Viguzzolo	3	H	H	H	H	H	H

[a] Tuttle (1986: 270), checked in Chiominto (1984: 178).
[b] Amandola, Bellante, Borgorose-Spedino, Campii, Canosa Sannita, Colledimacine, Ortezzano, Pontecorvo, San Benedetto del Tronto, Sonnino, Torricella Peligna, Tufillo (M&S); Avezzano, L'Aquila, Pescara (G), Roiate, Subiaco (T), Colonna, Zagarolo (L1), Servigliano (L2), Acquafondata (L3).

^c Amaseno (Tuttle 1986: 233, checked in Vignoli 1920: 71).
^d This is Manzini and Savoia's (2005) description of the dialect of Bisceglie (Bari), diverging from that given by De Gregorio (1939) indicated as Bisceglie 1 below.
^e In addition to Morcone and Frigento (Manzini and Savoia 2005, III: 22f., 26f.), six more dialects belong here (those of Albidona, Alessandria del Carretto, Nocara, Oriolo, Rocca Imperiale, Rotondella; see Manzini and Savoia 2005, II: 784–91) which the authors (2005, II: 779) claim to select auxiliary H uniformly. Consider, for example, the following data from Albidonese (II: 784f.):

i. 'ɛ ddɔrˈmutə/bbəˈnutə.   's/he has (lit. is) slept/come'
ii. 'jɛ kkwənˈtɛntə.   's/he is happy'
iii. 'ya 'famə.   's/he is hungry' (lit. 'has hunger')

The authors argue that the third person singular auxiliary form in (i) must belong to 'have', like those in other persons, because it is not homophonous with the copula (ii). However, they neglect the fact that the corresponding form of 'have' (which they provide, (iii)) is clearly distinct, both segmentally and because it does not cause word-initial consonantal fortition (*raddoppiamento fonosintattico*), while the form of 'be' does, both as a copula and as an auxiliary. That the forms of 'be' in those two functions may diverge, with a more reduced one occurring as an auxiliary, is an independently well-known phenomenon.

in others: thus, in southern Italy, no split system occurs in Sicily, while in northern Italy the only area featuring relevant phenomena, as noted as early as Salvioni (1902: 208), straddles Lombardy and Piedmont.

By way of a preliminary observation, let us recall that, as shown in Loporcaro (2001; 2007b), split systems can be mapped onto the scale in Table 4.4, provided that one focuses not on the individual auxiliary morpheme selected but rather on the contrast patterns between the classes of predicates selecting different combinations. Thus, some split systems select the same person-sensitive combination for all classes of predicates, and are hence instances of 1-aux systems (option (f) in Table 4.4), while others display two or even three contrasting options, whereby unaccusatives and unergatives/transitives represent the opposite poles and the different classes of reflexives pattern in different ways.[11]

Among dialects showing person-split auxiliation, 21 exhibit the scheme EEHEEH with unergatives/transitives, 10 of them also with unaccusatives, while the other 11 display EEEEEE with unaccusatives. The remaining 53 varieties exhibit alternative person-split auxiliation patterns.[12]

Consider first unergatives. As shown in Figure 4.7, with unergatives E is favoured in the 2sg, H in the 3pl, whereas free variation of H/E is rather frequent in the 1sg.[13]

Comparing the paradigms in Table 4.5, we note that no dialect has only E with unergatives, whereas a few have only H (jj) (these are listed here because they present a person split with unaccusatives; see options y, z, and jj in Table 4.6). Focusing on the similarities and differences across persons, we

---
[11] This has been shown for selected dialects in Loporcaro (2001; 2007b) but would be impossible given the present sample, because of the crucial gaps in the data usually provided by sources, as discussed in Loporcaro (2015: 65).
[12] For simplicity, we limit our discussion to the compound perfect, since several of the dialects in the sample also show TAM-related splits of the kind mentioned in Section 4.3.1 (for further discussion, Section 23.2.2).
[13] Key (also valid for Figure 4.9 and Tables 4.5–6): E = 'be', H/E = 'have/ be' in free variation, H = 'have', E=H = syncretic form of both auxiliaries, H-E = 'have' and 'be' according to phonological context (shape condition).

Table 4.6. *Patterns of split auxiliation with unaccusative verbs in our sample (76 dialects)*

		#	1SG	2SG	3SG	1PL	2PL	3PL
a.	Amandola, Borgorose-Spedino, etc.[a]	11	E	E	E	E	E	E
b.	Roccasicura, Vastogirardi	2	H/E	E	E	E	E	E
c.	Pàstena-Castelpetroso	1	E	E	E	E	E	H/E
d.	Briga Novarese	1	E	E=H	E	E	E	E
e.	Cori (T), Miglionico	2	E	E	E	E	E	H
f.	Pescocostanzo	1	E	E	H	E	E	E
g.	Gallo Matese	1	H/E	E	E	E	E	H/E
h.	Monteroduni	1	H/E	E	E	E	E	H
i.	Capracotta	1	H	E	E	H/E	H/E	E
j.	Bellante, Campli, Canosa Sannita, etc.[b]	11	E	E	H	E	E	H
k.	Trecate	1	H/E	E=H	E	E	E=H	E
l.	Cerano	1	E	E=H	E	H/E	H/E	E
m.	Pietransieri	1	E	E	E	H/E	H/E	H/E
n.	Amaseno (T), S. Vittore, Viticuso	3	H/E	E	H	E	E	H
o.	Veroli (T)	1	H/E	E	H/E	E	E	H/E
p.	Montenerodomo, Popoli	2	E	E	E	H	H	H
q.	Secinaro	1	H/E	E	E	H/E	H/E	H
r.	Guardiaregia	1	H/E	E	E	H/E	H/E	H/E
s.	Agnone	1	H/E	E	E	H	H	H/E
t.	Scanno	1	H	E	E	H	H/E	H/E
u.	Bitetto	1	H	E	H-E	H/E	E	H
v.	Masserano	1	H	E=H	H/E	H	H/E	E
w.	Altamura	1	H/E	H/E	E	H/E	H/E	H/E
x.	Sassinoro	1	H/E	E	H/E	H/E	H/E	H/E
y.	Naples (Le), Minervino Murge	2	H/E	H/E	H/E	H/E	H/E	H/E
z.	Viguzzolo	1	H/E	H/E	H/E	H/E	H/E	H
aa.	Ruvo di Puglia	1	H/E	E	H-E	H	H	H
bb.	Padula	1	H/E	E	H/E	H	H	H
cc.	Castelvecchio Subequo	1	H/E	E	E	H	H	H
dd.	Bisceglie2, Giovinazzo	2	E	E	H	H	H	H
ee.	Molfetta	1	H/E	E	H	H	H	H
ff.	Vasto (G)	1	H	E	H/E	H	H	H
gg.	Lanciano (G)	1	H	E	H	H	E	H
hh.	Gravina di Puglia	1	H/E	H	H-E	H	H	H
ii.	Bisceglie1, Introdacqua (G)	2	H	E	H	H	H	H
jj.	Albidona, Aliano, Morcone, ecc.[c]	8	H	H	E	H	H	H
kk.	Notaresco (G)	1	E	H	H	H	H	H
ll.	Canosa di Puglia	1	H/E	H	H	H	H	H

Table 4.6. (cont.)

		#	1SG	2SG	3SG	1PL	2PL	3PL
mm.	Monteparano, Frigento	2	H	H	H/E	H	H	H
nn.	S. Giorgio d. Sannio	1	H	H	E=H	H	H	H

[a] Amandola, Borgorose-Spedino, Colledimacine, Ortezzano, Poggio Imperiale, Torricella Peligna, Tufillo (M&S); Colonna, Zagarolo (L1), Servigliano (L2), Roiate (T, checked with Orlandi 2000: 124).
[b] Bellante, Campli, Canosa Sannita, Pontecorvo, San Benedetto del Tronto, Sonnino (M&S); Avezzano, L'Aquila, Pescara (G), Subiaco (T), Acquafondata (L3).
[c] To Albidona, Aliano and Morcone (data in Manzini and Savoia 2005, III: 30, 22) must be added the following five dialects, for the reasons explained above in note d to Table 4.5.: Alessandria del Carretto, Nocara, Oriolo, Rocca Imperiale, Rotondella.

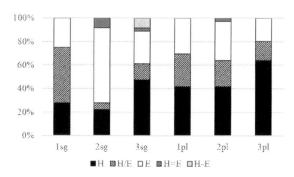

Figure 4.7 Auxiliary forms by person with unergative verbs in our sample (76 dialects, 36 auxiliation patterns)

observe that first person plural and second person plural nearly always have the same auxiliary choice (three exceptions: a, t, z in Table 4.5), whereas in the first person singular E mostly occurs if it occurs in the second person singular as well (one exception, dd in Table 4.5), and the same goes without exception for plural persons (note that in z in Table 4.5 the 2pl form is syncretic).[14]

With unaccusatives (Figure 4.8), the 2sg remains the person in which auxiliary E is most widespread, though increased usage of E in the 3sg is observed.

If we now focus on distribution across paradigm cells within each system, we see that some dialects (option a in Table 4.6) have only E (as previously mentioned, they appear here because they exhibit a person split with unergatives). No dialect exhibits only H with unaccusatives.

Implications among persons parallel those seen for unergatives, first person plural and second person plural very often share the same pattern and in the first person singular and the plural persons, E tends to occur if it

[14] In Tables 4.5–6, auxiliation patterns are ordered so that prevailing selection of E and H cluster at the top and bottom, respectively. Occurrence of the third option (free variation) precludes a strictly monotonic display. The column labelled # indicates the number of distinct dialects in the sample representing each distribution.

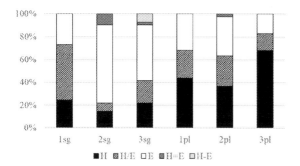

Figure 4.8 Auxiliary forms by person with unaccusative verbs (76 dialects, 40 auxiliation patterns)

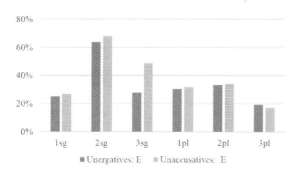

Figure 4.9 Diffusion of E forms (by percentage): unergatives vs unaccusatives. Sample: 76 dialects

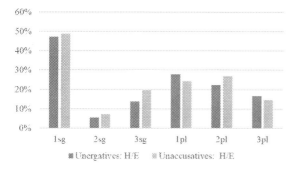

Figure 4.10 Diffusion of the free alternation between E and H forms (by percentage): unergatives vs unaccusatives. Sample: 76 dialects

occurs also in the second person singular. The graphs in Figures 4.9–4.10 illustrate the comparison between unergatives and unaccusatives. Figure 4.9, which represents the frequency of E forms, shows that unaccusativity correlates with an increase of E in the third person singular and, to a lesser extent, in the remaining persons but the third person plural.

Free variation of H/E, plotted in Figure 4.10, increases most, with unaccusatives (vs unergatives), in the third person singular and second person plural, less markedly so in the first person singular and second person singular, while the reverse tendency is observed elsewhere.

To sum up, the following generalizations emerge from Tables 4.5 to 6, and Figures 4.7 to 10:

(17) Generalizations
 a. All-H and all-E paradigms are attested only with unergatives and unaccusatives, respectively;
 b. We observed a correlation with unaccusativity in some persons: auxiliary E is much more frequent in the third person singular and less markedly in the second person singular, and the same holds (with lesser skewing) for E/H free variation, where the second person plural also shows a similar imbalance;
 c. E is the most frequent option in the second person singular;
 d. First person singular and plural persons tend to have E if and only if second person singular also has E.

A complementary perspective on split systems thereby emerges, compared with that in Loporcaro (2007b: 185f.) which stressed the theoretical consequences of the freedom of combination in auxiliary choice within person-split systems. Since each paradigm cell represents an independent variable, which can host one of three values (E, H, or E/H), this yields in principle $3^6 = 729$ possible combinations for 1-aux mixed systems, $729^2 = 531,441$ for 2-aux mixed systems, and $729^3 = 387,420,489$ for 3-aux mixed systems. What we have now seen, even on the basis of this very limited random sample, is that not all conceivable options and combinations occur with the same frequency. In the following sections, we will try to make sense of the distributional generalizations in (17) and address the significance of these results for the modelling of variation and the other theoretical issues raised in Section 4.1.

4.3.4 Variation in Mixed Auxiliation: Give to Morphology What Belongs to Morphology

The generalizations in (17a–b) mention unaccusativity, an eminently syntactic concept, and are indeed often treated as though they were syntactic in nature. We will argue, however, that they are best accounted for within inflexional morphology in terms of verb paradigm structure. This view was first proposed in Loporcaro (1999: 213) and further elaborated on in Bentley and Eythórsson (2001: 70f.) and Loporcaro (2001: 462, 470; 2007b: 186); we will provide new and cogent arguments in support of it.

Considered in itself, (17a) would appear a bona fide syntactic generalization: if only auxiliary E is selected with unaccusatives and only H with unergatives, at first sight this seems liable to be stated in terms of a syntactic rule in the same way as (the first clause of) the French/Italian (non-mixed) auxiliation rule: i.e., 'select auxiliary E if and only if the final

Table 4.7. *Perfective auxiliation in the dialect of Aliano (province of Matera)*

	1SG	2SG	3SG	1PL	2PL	3PL
a. unergatives	H	H	H	H	H	H
b. unaccusatives	H	H	E	H	H	H

Manzini and Savoia (2005, III: 30–32).

Table 4.8. *Perfective auxiliation in the dialect of Viguzzolo (province of Alessandria)*

	1SG	2SG	3SG	1PL	2PL	3PL
a. unergatives	H	H	H	H	H	H
b. unaccusatives	H/E	H/E	H/E	H/E	H/E	H

Manzini and Savoia (2005, II: 20–22).

subject is an initial direct object; select auxiliary H elsewhere'. To see that this move would be wrong, one needs to consider auxiliation in its entirety, within split systems such as, for instance, Alianese or Viguzzolese (jj in Table 4.5, and z, and jj in Table 4.6).

In both systems, the 'elsewhere condition' could be as in standard Italian or French, but the positive specification cannot be stated as 'select aux E', given that the latter occurs only in the third person singular in (b) in Table 4.7 while in (b) in Table 4.8 it is in free variation with H except in the third person plural. Thus, the rule must refer to the auxiliation patterns b (positive specification) vs a (elsewhere case) rather than to the individual auxiliary morphemes.[15] The same holds for selection of auxiliary E in type (a) in Table 4.6.

Of course, it is not by chance that in these dialects, as well as in the others in type (jj) in Table 4.5, auxiliary H is homogeneously selected in the elsewhere case. Likewise, it is hardly by chance that auxiliary E is selected uniformly with unaccusatives in the dialects of type (a) in Table 4.6. Rather, these are remnants of the proto-Romance auxiliation rule, in which the two auxiliation patterns could be labelled 'auxiliary E' vs 'auxiliary H' for short. However, as soon as the systems became mixed, such a descriptive shortcut becomes illegitimate. In other words, (17a) has a syntactic reason, which however pertains to a past stage, like the light from a distant star: synchronically, it has nothing to do with syntax.

---

[15] In addition, since reflexives pattern with unaccusatives, not unergatives, the rule must include the same restriction (the final 1, namely the surface subject, is a non-multiattached [= non-reflexive] initial 2, namely object) as in the non-mixed systems of type (e) in Table 4.4.

The same goes for the quantitative skewing of auxiliaries E and H across classes and persons in (17b). Here, the strongest correlation with unaccusativity is observed in the third person singular, which is hardly surprising in view of the fact that this is cross-linguistically the grammatical person that hosts more contrasts, whenever these are distributed unevenly across paradigms (cf. Greenberg 1975: 41–43).

Generalizations (17c–e) are also purely morphological: in a nutshell, there is no longer a (syntactic) reason for the second person singular to host auxiliary E most frequently (17d) than there is for, say, the first person plural of the present indicative in Italian to be copied from the corresponding person of the present subjunctive via a rule of referral (Thornton 2005: 132). An alternative view claims that occurrence of auxiliary E in the first person singular and second person singular is derived syntactically and depends on a person-split of the kind observed in languages with ergative alignment in which only first and second person pronouns align accusatively (Manzini and Savoia 1998: 130f.; 2005, II: 729–31). Objections to this use of Silverstein's (1976) hierarchy have been raised in Bentley and Eythórsson (2001: 73), Loporcaro (2007b: 195–97). Figures 4.8–10 show that the dialects for which this has been argued were cherry-picked from among a host of different options which are not amenable to such a syntactic explanation.

A further clear indication that the occurrence of E/H in different persons is a matter of inflexional morphology, not syntax, comes from syncretisms (cf. Cennamo 2010; Loporcaro 2016: 814), which usually result from blends of the forms of auxiliaries E/H, as seen, for example, in a'ʃi 'fættə 'you.SG have done' in the dialect of Ortona a Mare (province of Chieti, see Giammarco 1973: 165) which has 1-aux H except in the second person singular, where it blends forms of 'have' and 'be' ('a and 'ʃi in neighbouring dialects). Unlike subject clitics (Sections 4.2.4–5), gaps do not occur, since the auxiliary is the carrier of finite verb morphology in these verbal periphrases and thus cannot be missing.

Crucial evidence regarding the status of person-driven alternations is provided by three dialects of central Apulia, those of Ruvo, Gravina, and Bitetto (data from Manzini and Savoia 2005, II: 724–26; III: 29f.). All three dialects present person-splits (see the patterns in types s, t, gg of Table 4.5, and types u, aa, kk of Table 4.6). In all persons but the third singular – as exemplified for Ruvo in (16) – either E or H or free variation of H/E occur, while only Bitettese contrasts unergatives with unaccusatives, whose auxiliary differs just in the second person singular. In the third person singular, however, a phonologically-conditioned complementary distribution is observed:

(18) Ruvo di Puglia
    a.   'ɛ   drəm'meutə / və'neutə // s   'ɛ   la'vɔtə.
        be.3SG slept   come   REFL.3 be.3SG washed

b.   'ɔv   aʃpətˈtɔtə / arrəˈvɔtə // s   ɔv   asˈsɛisə.
        have.3SG   waited   arrived   REFL.3   have.3SG sat
        'S/he has slept/come/washed him-/herself/arrived/waited.'

(19) Gravina di Puglia
   a.   'je   ddərˈmoutə / vvəˈnoutə / mˈmurtə // s   'e   laˈvətə.
        be.3SG   slept   come   died   REFL be.3SG   washed
   b.   'av   aˈpirtə la 'portə // s   'av   asˈsisə.
        have.3SG   opened the door   REFL.3 have.3SG sat
        'S/he has slept/come/died/washed himself/opened the door/sat down.'

(20) Bitetto
   a.   'ɛ   drəmˈmeutə / vəˈneutə // s   'ɛ   llaˈvitə.
        be.3SG   slept   come   REFL be.3SG   washed
   b.   'av   arrəˈvitə / aˈpirtə // s   'av   aˈpirtə.
        have.3SG   arrived   opened   REFL.3 have.3SG opened
        'S/he has slept/come/washed him-/herself/arrived/opened/it opened.'

As seen in (18)–(20), auxiliary E is selected with verbs of all classes whose participle begins in a consonant, while auxiliary H occurs before vowel-initial participles. Now, if the two third person singular forms were selected by a syntactic rule, this would violate the principle of phonology-free-syntax:

> syntax can be sensitive to abstract properties realized in the distribution of phonological features, but not to the specific phonological features. ... no language has a syntactic rule stipulating that some constituent begin with an obstruent, or have no more than two syllables, or contain only unrounded vowels, or have stress on its penultimate syllable. (Zwicky 1996: 4477)

There is indeed a more economical solution. Once one admits that person-driven auxiliation is specified morphologically, one can derive (18)–(20) via a shape condition of the kind accounting for the distribution of *a/an* in the English indefinite article, which 'specifies aspects of the phonological shape of i[nflectional]-forms, but "postlexically" – by reference to triggers at least some of which lie outside the syntactic word.' (Zwicky 1986: 310). This specification:

> is not part of the lexical entry for the word, because it refers to the following syntactic context. It is not a phonological rule of English, for it applies only to the indefinite article and has no general applicability to phonological domains. It is a condition on shape that overrides the lexical entry for the indefinite article and stipulates that another shape is called for. (Pullum and Zwicky 1988: 262)

In our case, too, replacement of 'ɛ by 'ɔv/'av prevocalically does not follow from a phonological rule but is sensitive to the postlexical phonological context, in a way syntactic rules never are. This description would be out of reach for theories which derive the specific forms of auxiliaries from syntactic factors, such as Kayne's (1993) approach to person-mixed auxiliation systems. According to Kayne (1993: 3), '"Have" is identical to "be" but for the incorporation of an abstract preposition.' In our case, the movement leading to incorporation of the abstract preposition P° would be triggered by a following initial vowel, which would constitute an unprecedented exception to phonology-free syntax. Conversely, if selection of ˈɔv/ˈav prevocalically is effected by a shape condition, the problem evaporates and we gain cogent evidence that auxiliaries E/H in mixed systems are not selected by a syntactic rule. The syntax goes so far as to decide that perfective auxiliation obeys one of the distribution options (a)–(e) in Table 4.4 attested for 2-aux systems (or one of the three patterns contrasting in 3-aux systems). Then, however, exactly which auxiliary is selected in which person, is specified by the morphology, that may allow, albeit rarely, for phrasal allomorphy as in (18)–(20), comparable with that observed for the English indefinite article.

4.3.5 An Outlier: *Do*-Support in the Dialect of Monno

In the previous sections we focused on perfective auxiliation and, so far, we have taken for granted that the sole role of Romance auxiliaries is that of carrying TAM and agreement features. However, the Italo-Romance dialect of Monno (Benincà and Poletto 2004b) exhibits a peculiar system of auxiliation in which perfective auxiliaries of the H/E type are in complementary distribution with the auxiliary *fa* ('do'),[16] which occurs only in interrogative main clauses. As illustrated in (21), Monnese exhibits subject clitic inversion in main clause interrogatives, like many other northern Italo-Romance dialects, but, unlike the surrounding dialects, Monnese does not allow the inversion of lexical verbs (21a). To form an interrogative clause in simple tenses, auxiliary *fa* is inserted, while the lexical verb occurs in the infinitive form, see (21b). Conversely, in compound tenses, it is the perfective auxiliary that undergoes inversion and therefore, the insertion of the *fa* auxiliary is ruled out, see (21c).

(21) a. **maja-l?
        eat.PRS.3SG=3SG
    b. fa-l   majà?
        do.PRS.3SG=3SG eat.INF?
        'Does he eat?'
    c. **fa/à-l   majà?
        do/has.PRS.3SG=3SG eaten
        'Has he eaten?'

---

[16] A comparable phenomenon is attested in old and middle French (Miller 1997).

The same holds for wh-questions in (22), except for questions on the subject. Also, as in English, *fa*-support is excluded from embedded clauses. Unlike English, the Monnese *fa* auxiliary does not occur in negative declaratives and cannot carry emphasis.

(22) a. **ke maja-l?
       what eat.PRS.3SG=3SG
    b. ke fa-l majà?
       what do.PRS.3SG=3SG eat.INF?
       'What does he eat?'
    c. ke **fa/à-l majà
       what do/has.PRS.3SG=3SG eaten
       'What has he eaten?'

Lastly, unlike English, lexical subjects and strong pronouns are not subject to (auxiliary) inversion. Hence, Monnese differs from all other Romance dialects in showing a specific auxiliation system in main interrogative clauses.

4.4 Modelling Linguistic Diversity

The data illustrated so far raise several questions regarding the modelling of linguistic diversity: do the above phenomena result from a finite set of (universal) discrete parameters or emerge from a *continuum* of language-specific options? The notion *parameter* has been subject to extensive debate and criticism for decades (more on this below). Conceptually, parameters differ from concrete properties as the former are inferred from the latter and, in the end, are speculative in nature.

In origin (for an overview, see Chomsky and Lasnik 1993), parameters were mainly conceived as (binary) choices between alternative instantiations of the same invariable and universal property (called *Principle*).[17] For instance, given the Principle that all syntactic structures are binary branching (Kayne 1984), a parameter is needed to establish which branch precedes the other (i.e., head-complement vs complement-head), giving rise to opposite word orders e.g., VO vs OV, P-N vs N-P.

Being linked to principles, parameters have been argued to be universal: our I(nternal)-Language is therefore endowed with a finite and invariable set of parameters, while languages differ with respect to the value (positive or negative) of each parameter. In this sense, parameters are not only abstract generalizations, but 'real' mental objects, hard-wired in our brain, and possibly, innate. In fact, acquisition is conceived as a process of parameter setting, in which the value of each parameter is fixed on the basis of

---

[17] On binarity, see Clark and Roberts (1993).

the external experience. The parametric hypothesis has led to strong predictions regarding the way in which grammatical systems vary, are acquired, and eventually lost in the case of pathologies.

The above 'strong' claims, typical of the early Principles and Parameters framework, have been questioned by several scholars, claiming that (certain) parameters are in fact *epiphenomenal*. On the one hand, the parametric hypothesis has been completely discarded by scholars such as Newmeyer (2004), Haspelmath (2008), who claim that parameters are idiosyncratic clusters of language-specific properties. Other scholars, on the other hand, have reformulated the theory of parameters by claiming that (macro-) parameters of the early Principles and Parameters framework may be better conceived as clusters (or hierarchies) of micro-parameters (Baker 2001; see also Roberts and Holmberg 2005 and Longobardi and Roberts 2010, who reply to Newmeyer 2004 and Evans and Levinson 2009, respectively).

A clue to the hierarchical organization of parameters comes from cases in which grammatical properties isolate concentric subsets of languages, e.g., Language 1 exhibits a subset of the phenomena that characterize Language 2, etc. Entailment/subset relations hold also within languages belonging to the same family/group and, in this respect, implications of the kind overviewed in the above sections may help scholars in modelling parametric hierarchies (see Ledgeway 2019 on auxiliation systems, as well as the extensive discussion in Section 21.2.2).

Furthermore, under a hierarchical model of parametric variation one might explain why certain empirical domains, e.g., subject clitics or perfective auxiliaries, are subject to a higher degree of cross-linguistic variation than others, e.g., object clitics or modal auxiliaries. Assuming that parameters are organized into sub-hierarchies, higher-level parameters are expected to affect entire sub-hierarchies, thus resulting in a higher degree of crosslinguistic variation in certain empirical domains.

However, regular, systematic variation – the kind that can be easily captured by hierarchies – is always amenable to external explanations, i.e., a subset of the speakers of language L1 has developed a subvariant L2, which in turn has been subject to further differentiation giving rise to the subvariant L3, and so on. In this way, languages gradually shift from one to another giving rise, in synchrony, to hierarchies of the type L1 > L2 > L3. Hence, hierarchies do not provide conclusive evidence in favour of parameters because, in Haspelmath's words, one 'runs the risk that he will discover shared innovations that have purely historical explanations, rather than properties that are shared because of the same parameter setting.' (2008: n. 8).

Pleading for the notion 'micro-parameter', Manzini and Savoia (2005, I: 120) claim that gaps in the distribution of subject clitics (Section 4.2.4) result from the micro-parametrization of the Null Subject Parameter (Section 4.2.1), which 'cannot be defined for the entire language, but must be applied to the individual forms of the paradigm' (translation in Roberts 2014: 178). Roberts (2014: 179), however, argues against such a radically microparametric approach, which would 'mak[e] the number of possible grammatical systems hyperastronomical' and which fails to make it clear that many of the instances so treated are not parametric 'but rather represent unpredictable taxonomic variants'. This critique resonates with the view of auxiliary selection defended in Section 4.3, and the whole issue has far-reaching implications for the modelling of free variation occurring both in subject clitics and auxiliation systems. A widely held view, prominently defended by Kroch (1994), has it that morphosyntactic variation is best formalized in terms of coexisting and competing grammars.[18] This is the position endorsed in Manzini and Savoia's (2005, II: 740) account of mixed auxiliation: '[i]n terms of theory, the seeming optionality in auxiliary choice is to be traced back to the co-presence of different grammars'. In this view, 'optionality must be treated as an instance of (micro-)bilingualism' (Manzini and Savoia 2007: 76). Loporcaro (2007a: 333) argues that this is hardly plausible since, as said in concluding Section 4.3.3, just for auxiliary selection, combination options grow exponentially, so that one should be prepared to cope with millions of different 'grammars', whose number should in turn multiply by any single variation point in other fragments of grammar. This computational argument parallels the aforementioned objections levelled by Roberts (2014: 178f.), discussing subject clitics, against the 'strictly local' view of microparameters advocated by Manzini and Savoia (2005, I: 357). For auxiliation, the otherwise 'hyperastronomical' number of possible grammars is aptly constrained as soon as the division of labour between syntax and morphology proposed in Section 4.3.3 is adopted: what is really syntactic is the choices along the scale in Table 4.4, while the specific auxiliary (or combination of auxiliaries) selected, in each dialect with person splits, is a matter of morphology, to be treated on a par with other aspects of the shape of verb inflexional paradigms, which are not for the syntax to predict.

On a similar note, radically microparametric approaches are at odds with relatively rare systems such as the subject clitic system of Pantiscu or the *do*-support system of the dialect of Monno. The functional elements of Monnese, for instance, derive from the same late Latin/proto-Romance inventory characterizing nearby dialects, which, unlike Monnese, have never developed *do*-support. Again, if structural differences hinged only on properties of the functional lexicon, how did the singularity of Monnese emerge? What kind of internal factors triggered such a peculiar innovation if the functional 'ingredients' of the grammar were the same as in neighbouring vernaculars?

---

[18] Objections to Koch, addressing, like the original proposal, variation across English dialects, have been raised, for instance, by Pietsch (2005) and Haser and Kortmann (2009).

Without resorting to high-level parameters, we think that a principled answer to this kind of questions cannot be advanced.

Selected References

Below you can find selected references for this chapter. The full references can be found online at the following page: www.cambridge.org/Romancelinguistics

Calabrese, A. (2011). 'Investigations on markedness, syncretism and zero exponence in morphology', *Morphology* 21: 283–325.

Cennamo, M. (2008). 'The rise and development of analytic perfects in Italo-Romance'. In Eythórsson, T. (ed.), *Grammatical Change and Linguistic Theory: The Rosendal Papers*. Amsterdam: Benjamins, 115–42.

Clark, R. and Roberts, I. (1993). 'A computational approach to language learnability and language change', *Linguistic Inquiry* 24(2): 299–345.

Kayne, R. (1993). 'Toward a modular theory of auxiliary selection', *Studia Linguistica* 47: 3–31.

La Fauci, N. (1988). *Oggetti e soggetti nella formazione della morfosintassi romanza*. Pisa: Giardini (English translation: La Fauci, N. (1994). *Objects and Subjects in the Formation of Romance Morphosyntax*. Bloomington, IN: IULC).

Ledgeway, A. (2019). 'Parameters in the development of Romance perfective auxiliary selection', in Cennamo, M. and Fabrizio, C. (eds), *Historical Linguistics 2015. Selected Papers from the 22nd International Conference on Historical Linguistics*. Amsterdam: Benjamins, 343–84.

Loporcaro, M. (2007b). 'On triple auxiliation in Romance', *Linguistics* 45: 173–222.

Loporcaro, M. (2012). 'A new strategy for progressive marking and its implications for grammaticalization theory: the subject clitic construction of Pantiscu', *Studies in Language* 36(4): 747–84.

Manzini, M. R. and Savoia, L. M. (2005). *I dialetti italiani e romanci. Morfosintassi generativa*. Alessandria: Edizioni dell'Orso.

Poletto, C. and Tortora, C. (2016). 'Subject clitics: syntax'. In Ledgeway, A. and Maiden, M. (eds), *The Oxford Guide to the Romance Languages*. Oxford: Oxford University Press, 772–85.

Roberts, I. (2014). 'Subject clitics and macroparameters'. In Benincà, P, Ledgeway, A., and Vincent, N. (eds), *Diachrony and Dialects: Grammatical change in the Dialects of Italy*. Oxford: Oxford University Press, 177–201.

Rosen, C. (1997). 'Auxiliation and serialization: on discerning the difference'. In Alsina, A., Bresnan, J., and Sells, P. (eds), *Complex Predicates*. Stanford: CSLI, 175–202.

Zwicky, A. (1996). 'Syntax and phonology'. In Brown, K. and Miller, J. (eds), *Concise Encyclopedia of Syntactic Theories*. Oxford: Elsevier, 300–05.

Part Two

Phonetics and Phonology

5

Structure of the Syllable

Giovanna Marotta

5.1 Preliminary Remarks

The syllable is a representational primitive of phonological structure, with an autonomous cognitive status.* It organizes segments into constituents (onset, rhyme, nucleus, and coda) and provides the context for phonotactic constraints and the grounding for explanation for regularities of segment organization, as well as for language change. Language acquisition and pathology confirm the cognitive relevance of the syllable both for the speaker and the listener (Guasti 2002). Therefore, we believe that linguistic theory still cannot dispense with it, despite efforts to claim that it is only an epiphenomenon.[1] In particular, our understanding of phonological change can benefit strongly from the notion of the syllable, since it makes it simpler to find commonalities and mutual relations in the distribution of different processes, thus offering a more grounded interpretation even in cases of great variation such as that occurring in the Romance domain.

The last quarter of the twentieth century was the golden age of the syllable. When non-linear generative models began to be developed in the United States, the syllable became a crucial topic of phonological representation (Goldsmith 1990; Kenstowicz 1994). After fifty years, most phonologists still use the same syllable constituents and adopt the same hierarchical formal pattern. Following the mainstream of generative phonology, the syllable structure adopted in this chapter recognizes the *Rhyme* as a high-order constituent (on a par with *Onset*), which dominates the *Nucleus*

---

* I am grateful to Edoardo Cavirani and Francesco Rovai, who read this chapter in a preliminary version and made compelling comments.

[1] The notion of syllable is criticized by models that refer to natural phonology (cf. Donegan and Stampe 1979; Dziubalska-Kołaczyk 2002) as well as in exemplar and emergent frameworks, which are more phonetically-driven (cf. Bybee 2002; Johnson 2006). See van Oostendorp (2013) for discussion.

and the *Coda*. The fundamental reason for such an internal hierarchical structure is the relevance of the *Rhyme* to syllable weight. For instance, many natural languages are sensitive to *Rhyme* structure in stress rules. The Latin stress algorithm is a typical case: a (heavy) rhyme comprising a long vowel or a diphthong has the same weight as a syllable with a short vowel and a consonant in coda: the prosodic weight is determined by *Rhyme* structure.

Romance languages testify to the sensitivity of phonological developments to syllable structure. Some processes selectively target nuclei in open syllables, whereas onsets and codas trigger other kinds of change.

5.2 Syllable Structure and Quantity in Latin

The syllable structure of Latin is typologically unmarked (Marotta 1999b; Maddieson 2011; Schmid 2012: 45–57): the vowel inventory is quite small; consonant clusters are relatively limited in type and number; inflexional morphology prevents the formation of sequences of consonantal morphemes.

The major markedness trait is segmental length: both vowels and consonants contrast in Latin with regard to duration, in open as well as in closed syllables, regardless of stress position; e.g., ROSĂ 'rose' (NOM) vs ROSĀ (ABL); UĔNIT '(he/she) comes' vs UĒNIT '(he/she) came'; ŎS 'bone' vs ŌS 'mouth'; COLIS '(you) cultivate' vs COLLIS 'hill'; ANUS 'old woman' vs ANNUS 'year'(Giannini and Marotta 1989). Quantity markedness is supported by typological studies: only a small number of languages which have a large inventory of vowels also exhibit the contrast V vs V: (Maddieson 1984: 129; 2001: 544). Recent phonetic studies proving the effects of lexical stress on segmental duration have confirmed that vowel quantity is often a recessive property of phonological systems (Lehnert-Lehoullier 2013), since diachronic changes favour loss of vowel length contrast.[2] On the other hand, the development of vowel openness contrasts from an original length opposition is well attested, shortness generally becoming associated with more open segments and length with more closed segments (Lahiri 2015). This scenario is perfectly compatible with the evolution of a large number of Romance languages, in particular those exhibiting the contrast between mid-open and mid-closed vowels (cf. Section 5.4.1).

Preservation of vowel quantity had probably been confined to the high registers of Latin (Pulgram 1975; Vineis 1984; Marotta 2015). Along the historical path of the language, a number of phonological processes testify

---

[2] This does not mean that vowel quantity is always destined to be lost. For instance, a new contrast in vowel length has emerged in some Romance dialects after the quantity collapse (cf. Section 5.4.1).

to a general drift towards loss of vowel quantity, especially in unstressed syllables. The main phenomena concern general shortening of final vowels in closed syllables except those ending in -s; e.g., ANIMĂL 'animal' (NOM) vs ANIMĀLIS (GEN); LECTŎR 'reader' (NOM) vs LECTŌREM (ACC) (Weiss 2009: 128), vowel shortening in hiatus (e.g., PLĒRE 'to fill' vs PLĔŌ 'I fill'), and the *correptio iambica* 'iambic shortening' (e.g., MODŌ > MODŎ 'only; presently'; MALĒ > MALĔ 'badly': cf. Leumann 1977: 111, §123; Weiss 2009: 126).

In agreement with such evolutionary drift, long vowels tend to become decreasingly frequent in the history of Latin, especially in unstressed syllables, whereas the length of the nuclei tends to be determined by stress and syllable structure, according to the general principle of isochronism: long vowel in stressed open syllable; short vowel elsewhere (Loporcaro 2015; Marotta 2016).

Classical Latin shows a low degree of complexity in syllable structure. Its template comprises heavy and light nuclei, i.e., long and short vowels (e.g., RO.TA 'wheel', MŪ.RU(M) 'wall'); diphthongs count as heavy (e.g., CAE.LUM 'sky'). The onset could be associated with zero, one, or two consonants; e.g., A.MOR 'love', FA.CE.RE 'to do', PRE.ME.RE 'to press'.³ The coda could be empty or filled by one or two consonants; e.g., A.NUS 'old woman', FAC.TUS 'done', SANC.TUS 'holy'. In principle, syllables could be light, heavy, and superheavy, according to the number of skeletal slots associated with the rhyme constituent. Superheavy syllables were normally stressed, less frequent, and subject to segmental constraints (Marotta 1999b; Lehmann 2005; 2010). In particular, they could have the following formats only:

(a) complex nucleus + simple coda; e.g., STĒL.LA 'star', ŌR.DO 'order', SCRĪP.TUS 'written', ĀC.TUS 'driven' (by Lachmann's Law; cf. Leumann 1977; Weiss 2009);
(b) simple nucleus + complex coda; e.g., SANC.TUS 'holy', CARP.TUS 'picked'; DICUNT '(they) say';
(c) simple nucleus + complex coda + -s in word-final position; e.g., ARX 'castle', STIRPS 'stem', FALX 'sickle'.

In a complex coda, the two consonants obey the sonority sequencing constraint (Sievers 1881; Clements 1990; Blevins 1995): the first is a sonorant, unspecified for [place], whereas the second is an obstruent with variable place of articulation. A morpheme boundary obligatorily occurs after the coda. The Latin coda is anyway the richest constituent of the syllable since it can be filled by zero, one, two, or even three segments, at least in word-final position. This enlargement of the coda is motivated by the morphosyntactic function of the endings in Latin.

---

³ On the tri-consonantal clusters with initial s-, see Section 5.4.3.

5.3 The Fate of Quantity in Romance Languages

5.3.1 Vowel Length

Latin vowel quantity did not survive as such in any Romance variety (Weinrich 1958; Lausberg 1969; Loporcaro 2015). From the first centuries of the Christian era the shortening of vowels in unstressed syllables and in closed stressed syllables favoured the emergence of the isochronic principle governing the distribution of vowel quantity: long vowels in stressed open syllable; short vowels elsewhere.

Allophonic vowel lengthening depending on syllable structure and stress still occurs in Italian, Sardinian, central and southern Italian dialects (cf. also Section 7.3.2.1), according to the so-called *Strong Rhyme Constraint*, which requires a heavy rhyme in a stressed syllable (Marotta 1999a); e.g., RŎTAM 'wheel' > It. [ˈrwɔːta], Srd. [ˈrɔːða], Cal., Sic. [ˈrɔːta] in open stressed syllables; SACCUM 'sack' > It. [ˈsakːo], Srd. [ˈsakːu], Cal., Sic. [ˈsakːu] in stressed closed syllables.

In Spanish and Catalan, too, vowels are lengthened to some degree in stressed open syllables (Borzone de Manrique and Signorini 1983; Recasens 1996; Roca 1999), although to a lesser degree than in Italo-Romance. In French no vowel length has survived today; the sporadic contrast between [ɛ] and [ɛː] (e.g., *faite* 'do.PTCP.FSG' with [ɛ], and *fête* 'party' with [ɛː]; Walter 1997; Durand, Laks, and Lyche 2002; Durand and Lyche 2003; 2008) originates from the compensatory lengthening due to the loss of a sibilant in the coda (< FESTA).

Further historical developments give rise to a new phonological contrast of vowel quantity in some Romance varieties, for instance, in Gallo-Romance and Gallo-Italian dialects, in Ladin and Friulian (Salvi 1997: 287f.; Vanelli 1997; Baroni and Vanelli 1999). The occurrence of the new vowel quantity is connected with the loss of the original geminate consonants (cf. Haudricourt and Juilland 1949; Lüdtke 1956; Loporcaro 2007; 2015; Filipponio 2012; see also Chapter 8, this volume). In these varieties, the widespread processes of syncope and apocope have substantially altered the structure of the word. Varieties where no vowel quantity occurs (such as Piedmontese and Lunigiana dialects) coexist alongside other systems showing a /V ~ Vː/ contrast (e.g,. Emilian and western Lombard dialects). At the same time, new contrasts emerge in the quality of vocalic segments, in particular for mid vowels (Section 5.4.2).

The combined action of various phonological developments (i.e., degemination, loss of long vowels in unstressed syllables and in stressed closed syllables, vowel lengthening in stressed open syllables, apocope, syncope) has resulted in more or less heavy structural modifications of the prosodic structure of the word. Due to the variable applicability of the processes listed above, after the loss of the original Latin vowel quantity, the Romance domain is characterized by the following generalizations:

(a) open syllable lengthening rule (Italian and central and southern Italo-Romance dialects);
(b) emergence of a new vowel length contrast (some Gallo-Romance and Gallo-Italian dialects);
(c) partial lengthening in open syllables (Ibero-Romance).

5.3.2 Open Syllable Lengthening

Weinrich (1958: 17) had already noticed the strict relation between syllable structure and quantity collapse, although he did not explicitly refer to the notion of syllable. In considering the distribution of both long vowels and consonants, he underlined the lexical frequency of trochees, with variable (i.e., long or short) stressed vowel. In his opinion, the incoming and increasingly widespread isochronism readily favoured the lengthening of short vowels in open syllables as well as the shortening of the long vowels in closed syllables. Recent studies on the distribution of short and long nuclei in the Latin lexicon have pointed out that the percentage of long vowels was particularly low in closed unstressed syllable, whereas long vowels occurred especially in open stressed syllables (Marotta and De Felice 2019).

Despite the analogies concerning their distribution and prosodic function, vowels and consonants showed different sociophonetic values with regard to length. In Latin spoken at a low social level, vowel quantity could be ignored or even changed into tenseness since the first centuries of the Christian era (Vineis 1984; Marotta 2015; 2016), whereas consonant gemination had been a sociolinguistic marker, being associated with features of familiarity and rusticity (Giannini and Marotta 1989).

Although consonant gemination, too, is typologically marked (Laver 1994: 436), the collapse of vowel quantity preceded the loss of consonant gemination. Whereas vowel quantity did not survive as an inherited trait in any Romance language or dialect (Section 5.3.1), consonant gemination is still present in a part of the Romance domain, although with variable distribution and functional load. In particular, Italy and the dialects of southern Italy still show a systematic contrast between short and long consonants, regardless of manner and place of articulation; e.g., It. *cane* 'dog' - *canne* 'reeds'; Nap. 'e [f]iglie 'the sons' vs 'e [f:]iglie 'the daughers' (Ledgeway 2009: 49). The assimilation processes often triggered by syncope common in the spoken Latin of the Republican age progressively increased the number of geminates in late Latin and then in proto-Romance; e.g., OCTO > It. *otto* 'eight', AURICULA > It. *orecchia* 'ear'.

In sum, in the sociolinguistic repertoire of Latin, the feature of length had opposite values in vowels and consonants: the production of long vowels was a sociophonetic positive marker, typical of a high register, whereas gemination had a negative value, as it was associated with low registers. In variants such as BĀCA / BĂCCA 'berry', CŪPA / CŬPPA 'cup', MŪCUS / MŬCCUS 'mucus' the first form belonged to the high register, the second to the low register (Benedetti and Marotta 2014). Since these prosodic alternations involved a stressed syllable, the phenomenon became a clear clue of the isochronism spreading through the Romance domain (Weinrich 1958) which gave rise to *open syllable lengthening* (OSL) in the stressed syllable.

In this scenario, the rule of OSL is often attributed to so-called proto-Romance, although we might wonder whether a proto-Romance variety ever existed as a language spoken in all the territories where Latin varieties were spoken after the collapse of the Roman empire. More probably, OSL was already a rule of late Latin (with reference to language register and speakers' education) in the first centuries of the Christian era. The strong correlation between vowel length, stress, and syllable structure has been active in the language for a long time, as quantitative lexical data clearly show (Marotta and De Felice 2019). At the outset it was probably a variable rule, subject to conditionings of various kinds (e.g., literacy of the speakers, communicative context), and it later became increasingly frequent, spreading even into more educated milieux and marking the definitive loss of vowel quantity.

A final remark concerns the trigger of OSL. Loporcaro (2011a: 77) claimed that the collapse of vowel quantity began in utterance-final position, due to prepausal lengthening. Note that prepausal lengthening is a prosodic universal, taking place in all phonological systems without any considerable impact on the prosodic arrangement of languages. It is a phonetic phenomenon due to the inertia of the articulatory organs. At the end of a phrase, it has the function of signalling the syntactic boundary. Note also that this lengthening affects not only the last segment of the word but extends over a time interval that includes the last syllable and sometimes also the penultimate. From these two observations, we would expect an apparently universal process such as prepausal lengthening to move from the utterance and phrase levels to the word level in all the varieties, provided that it undergoes phonologization and that no other process intervenes. So if we have varieties in which vowels (both stressed and unstressed) get lengthened phrase-finally, we would expect this lengthening process to gradually climb up, e.g., to the word level. However, the phonologization of prepausal lengthening into phrase-level and word-level phonology is not automatic. Finally, and more importantly, prepausal lengthening occurs regardless of the structure of the final syllable, whereas OSL specifically targets open stressed syllables.

In my opinion, internal structural reasons better explain the evolution of the vowel system, since the Latin lexicon already contained a considerable number of trochaic words with a long vowel (Marotta and De Felice 2019). This prosodic template could easily have become a prototype and spread throughout the lexicon, regardless of the original vocalic quantity of stressed syllable. Therefore, the first context for the emergence of OSL was the short vowel in a penultimate stressed syllable.

5.4 Syllable Constituents

5.4.1 Romance Nuclei

A set of typologically unmarked features is shared by every Romance variety. First, the Romance languages confirm the so-called 'size principle' stating that larger inventories of phonemes are more likely to contain cross-linguistically uncommon segments (Maddieson 2001; 2011: 544). Second, the inventory of unstressed vowels is normally smaller than that of stressed ones, in agreement with a general typological trend. The difference between stressed and unstressed vowels is significant not only with reference to the segment inventories but also with respect to the phonological processes involved (cf. Section 5.5). For instance, in Italian seven segments occur in stressed syllables (/i e ɛ a ɔ o u/) but only five in unstressed syllables (/i e a o u/). In many Romance varieties, unstressed nuclei undergo centralization processes and even deletion with consequent reduction of potential phonetic outcomes (*infra*).

In stressed syllables the number of vocalic phonemes is variable, going from the five vowels of Spanish to the 16 contrastive nuclei of French, with nasalization and the development of front rounded vowels. Many Gallo-Italian dialects have more than ten vowels, due to the emergence of a new quantitative contrast.

Synchronically, vowel systems show wide restorations that have modified the alleged proto-Romance picture. Traditional notions like archaic or innovative systems, 'western' or 'eastern' vowel systems may be useful more for understanding language evolution than for the description of contemporary empirical data. Due to the intrinsic and variable dynamic force of phonological systems, single vowel systems not only have often undergone further developments, but also continue to show phonological alternations and changes.

The strongest innovation in vowel inventories is found in French and in other Gallo-Romance varieties and Gallo-Italian dialects. Indeed, the occurrence of front rounded vowels is a typical feature of 'northern Romance'; e.g., Fr. *peu* 'little', with [ø], *peur* 'fear', with [œ], *lune* 'moon' with [y]; Occ. *madur* [maˈdy] 'ripe' (Wheeler 1988: 247); Lmb. *lüna* [ˈlyːna] 'moon', [ˈtøt] 'all', [ˈbrøt] 'ugly.ᴍ', brüta [ˈbryta] 'ugly.ꜰsɢ' (Loporcaro 2007); Tur. füma [ˈfyma] '(s/he) smokes'; Gen. rêusa [ˈrøːza] 'rose' and lûxe [ˈlyːʒe] 'light' (noun) (Schmid 2015; cf. Section 9.2.1).

Quite marked is also the occurrence of stressed central vowels in Romanian (Vasiliu 1989: 1; Chițoran 2002: 7). The phoneme inventory of this language contains the vowels /ɨ ə/, e.g., var [var] 'whitewash' ~ văr [vər] 'cousin' or sun [sun] 'I ring' ~ sân [sɨn] 'breast'. These two centralized vowels are relatively uncommon in association with stressed nuclei among the languages of the world (cf. Maddieson and Precoda 1990), whereas they are much more frequent in unstressed syllables, as also in Romanian.

Another feature that characterizes northern Romance and that makes it more different from Latin and from the other Romance varieties is the emergence of vowel quantity. Although Latin vowel quantity has disappeared everywhere (Sections 5.2, 5.3.1), a new contrast of vowel length reappeared in northern Romance as a consequence of phonological changes involving the rhyme structure of the syllable (degemination) and the nucleus (open syllable lengthening, diphthongization, apocope). For instance, long vowels contrast with short vowels in the Francoprovençal varieties of Savoy, in Ladin varieties of the Dolomites, in Friulian (Vanelli 1997; Baroni and Vanelli 1999) and Lombard dialects (Sanga 1997: 254f.).[4]

Phrasal prominence plays a role too: stressed syllables at the lexical level may lose their prominence within a wider domain, with consequent changes in phonetic production.

Many dialects of southern Italy show an alternation between vowels or onglide diphthongs in internal position of the word and offgliding diphthongs in the phrase final domain, where the highest degree of prominence, associated with the final foot, is realized. Rohlfs (1966: §12) had already noted alternations occurring in the phrasal domain such as [ˌbːɔːnu ˈmiediku] 'good doctor' vs [ˌmɛdiku ˈbuonu] 'good doctor' (Adrano, Sicily), [u ˈproimə] 'the first' vs [u ˌprimə ˈmiːsə] 'the first month' (Vico del Gargano, Foggia). Offgliding diphthongs, typical of dialects of southern Italy, occur in association with the last stressed syllable, i.e., with the phrasal accent in prepausal position. More recently, alternations sensitive to sentence phonetics have been reported for Altamura (northern Apulia), Verbicaro (northern Calabria), and Agnone (Molise) (Loporcaro 1988: 42; Silvestri 2009; Loporcaro 2011b: 132f.).

5.4.2 Unstressed Nuclei

Unstressed vowels have been affected by different kinds of reduction according to their position in the word. Two fundamental processes are

---

[4] See Loporcaro (2015) for a detailed discussion.

observed: deletion or centralization, though only the first has significant consequences at the level of syllable structure as well as of word length.

In general, post-tonic position is the primary target of vowel deletion. Syncope is indeed very frequent in Romance languages; e.g., AURICULA 'ear' > Fr. *oreille*, It. *orecchia*, Sp. *oreja*; OCULUS 'eye' > Fr. *oeil*, It. *occhio*, Sp. *ojo*; CALIDU(M) 'warm' > Fr. *chaud*, It. *caldo*. However, it is more pervasive in some areas than in others; e.g., PECTINE(M) 'comb' > Fr. *peigne*, Sp. *peine*, but It. *pettine*, Ro. *pieptăn*; FRAXINU(M) 'ash tree' > Fr. *frêne*, Sp. *fresno*, but It. *frassino*, Ro. *frasin*; POLLICE(M) 'thumb'> Fr. *pouce*, but It. *pollice* (Lausberg 1969: §284). Syncope is still productive in some varieties of Portuguese, even in pre-tonic syllables (cf. Section 7.3.3.2.2).

Apocope also occurs, especially in French and Gallo-Italian dialects; e.g., NASU(M) 'nose' > Fr. *nez*, Mil. [naːz]; late Lat. LACTE(M) 'milk' > Fr. *lait*, Frl. [lat]; CRUDU(M) 'raw' > Fr. *cru*, Bol. [kruːd], but It. *crudo*; PERDERE 'to lose' > Fr. *perdre*, Rms. [ˈpjarder], but It. *perdere*. In Spanish, apocope is essentially restricted to final *-e* preceded by a single coronal consonant; e.g., *canal* 'canal', *valor* 'value'. In Italian, verb inflexional forms are the primary target of final vowel deletion (*troncamento*), in internal position of the phrase and utterance; e.g., *fare* 'to do' > *far*; *hanno* '(they) have > *han*. Note that in disyllabic words, apocope overlaps with syncope. In case of aphaeresis, the first vowel drops, with the emergence of complex and aberrant consonant clusters; e.g., HOSPITALEM > Bol. [zbdɛːl] 'hospital' (Section 5.4.3).

Centralization occurs in many Romance varieties (for instance, Catalan, Portuguese) and is typical of the dialects of southern Italy, where final vowels are lost apart (optionally) from *-a*; e.g., Nap. [maˈriːtə] 'husband', [ˈbɔːnə] 'good' (F).

New unstressed nuclei also emerge in the diachronic developments from Latin. Prosthesis is generalized in French, Spanish in words beginning with original *s+C* clusters; e.g., SCHOLA 'school' > Fr. *école*, Sp. *escuela*; SPONSU(M) 'husband' > Fr. *époux*, Sp. *esposo*. Epithesis is attested too. For instance, Tuscan varieties add a final [e] in words ending in a consonant, with concomitant gemination of the final segment; e.g., *bar* 'bar' [ˈbarːe], *COOP* (the name of a supermarket) [ˈkopːe]. The process works even in loanwords; e.g., *ticket* [ˈtihetːe]. The same happens in Campanian dialects, where the new nucleus is a centralized vowel, according to the general phonological rule of centralization in final syllables: e.g., *pulman* 'coach' > [pulˈmanːə], *valzer* 'waltz' > [valˈtsɛrːə] (Ledgeway 2009: 34).

5.4.3 Romance Onsets

In general, the onset shows more stability than the coda. All the consonants that were allowed in this structural position in Latin also occur in the Romance varieties; i.e., stops and fricatives (both voiceless and voiced), with the canonical places of articulation bilabial, labiodental, dental, and velar (i.e., [p b f v t d s k g]); nasals and liquids (i.e., [m n ŋ l r ɾ]), plus the glottal fricative [h] in Romanian. The main innovation concerning the onset is the introduction of two new series of consonants, palatals and affricates. The phonological change thus involves both place and manner of articulation. Palatal consonants occur in almost Romance languages, their number and type varying language-specifically; e.g., in French, two fricatives [ʃ ʒ] and the nasal [ɲ]; in Spanish, the voiceless affricate [tʃ] and the (quite rare in use) lateral [ʎ], in Italian, the voiceless fricative [ʃ], two affricates [tʃ dʒ], the liquid [ʎ] and the nasal [ɲ]. The type and number of dental affricates may also vary along the Romance continuum (e.g., Italian and southern Italo-Romance dialects [ts dz]; Romanian [ts]), although in this case there are varieties lacking this class of consonants; e.g., French and many Gallo-Italic dialects.

Palatal segments originate from the development of the configuration C+j +V, where the yod (if not original) is the product of an earlier loss of syllabicity in the hiatus configuration i/e+V; e.g., IACEO '(I) lie > *'jakjo > It. *giaccio* ['dʒatʃːo]; IUNIUM 'June' > *'junju > It. *giugno* ['dʒuɲːo]. Affricates have the same origin; e.g., PUTEUM 'shaft' > *'potju > It. *pozzo* ['potːso]; Ro. *puz* [puts]; MEDIUM 'half' > *'mɛdju > It. *mezzo* ['mɛdːzo] (cf. Lausberg 1969: §453–55; Repetti 2016: 659).

In languages with geminates, dental affricates are intrinsically long in intervocalic position. For instance, It. *mazzo* 'bundle' ['matːso], *razzo* 'rocket, missile' ['radːzo]; words with [ts dz] in initial position select the allomorph of the masculine definite article ending in a vowel, confirming their status as long segments at the underlying level; e.g., *lo zucchero* 'the sugar', *lo zio* 'the uncle'.

Some phonotactic constraints apply to palatal and affricates, suggesting their special status with regard to the other consonants inherited from Latin; for instance, dental affricates are not found word-initially in Catalan; palatal [ɲ] and [ʎ] are quite rare in the Italian lexicon word-initially. In general, affricates do not enter into tautosyllabic clusters, that is they fill the onset position alone; e.g., sequences such as **[tsr], **[dzm] or **[tʃr], **[dʒm] are not admitted, although they do agree with the strength hierarchy. However, many exceptions are found in Gallo-Italian dialects (in particular, Emilian and Lunigianese; e.g., ['tʃreˑʒa] 'cherry') as well as in Campidanese Sardinian (e.g., ['tʃreːβu] 'deer'; see below).[5]

In agreement with typological trends, the most common cluster occurring in complex onset is *muta cum liquida*, inherited from Latin and surviving in Romance languages with the format [obstruent + liquid], since the stop underwent lenition in some systems (cf. Section 5.5.3); e.g., LIBRU(M)

---

[5] The syllabification of these complex clusters as onsets is however questionable and depends on the theoretical model assumed. Here it is sufficient to note their occurrence at the beginning of the word.

'book' > It. [ˈliːbro], *libro*, Pt. *livro* [ˈliːvɾu], Cst. *libro* [ˈliːβɾo]; CAPRA(M) 'goat' > It. *capra*, Ro. *capră* vs Sp. *cabra* with [β]; MAGRU(M) 'thin' > It. *magro* [ˈmaːgro]. In some varieties, clusters with the lateral in second position are less frequent, due to the palatalization of l; e.g., CLAUE(M) 'key' > It. *chiave* [ˈkjaːve]; PLATEA(M) 'square' > It. *piazza* [ˈpjatːsa] (but Fr. *clé*, *place*). In particular, the so-called coronal syndrome (Kenstowicz 1994) applies, since the clusters /tl/ and /dl/, already absent in Latin (Marotta 1999b), occur only in loanwords from Classical Greek; e.g., It. *atlante*, Cat. *atlas* 'atlas'.

The syllable boundary in the clusters *muta cum liquida* has long been debated. The stress shift from the original antepenultimate syllable (testifying to the syllable boundary before the cluster) to the penult in some words seems to testify a change in the syllabification; e.g., INTEGRU(M) 'whole' > Sp. *entero*, Fr. *entier*, It. *intero*, TENEBRAS 'darkness' > Sp. *tinieblas*, Fr. *ténèbres* (but It. *tènebre*, with persistent stress on the first syllable). Data from Apulian dialects are especially interesting for this respect (see Loporcaro 2011a: 91f.).

In many languages other consonant clusters not obeying the sonority sequencing are avoided via repair strategies. For instance, in loanwords from Greek showing C+N or C+s, vowel epenthesis or deletion of the first consonant occurs in Spanish, Portuguese, Catalan, Italian; e.g., Pt. *psicologia* [pisikoloˈʒiːɐ] 'psychology'; (substandard) It. *psicologia* > *sicologia* or *pissicologia*; Sp. *pneumático* [neuˈmatiko] 'tyre', *psicología* [sikoloˈxia] 'psychology'. The process of segmental reduction is more frequent in low registers of the language.

Besides stop + liquid clusters (e.g., *prinde* 'catch', *clei* 'glue'), Romanian also admits /h/ + /l/, /r/ as complex onsets; e.g., *hlizi* 'to giggle', *hrană* 'food', whereas the cluster /m/ + liquid, occurring only in words of Slavonic origin (e.g., *mlădios* [mləˈdi joˈs] 'slender'; *mreană* [ˈmrɛ̯anə] 'barbel'; Chițoran 2002: 14) should be considered heterosyllabic, by not obeying the *Sonority Principle* (Clements 1990; Kenstowicz 1994).

Even looser constraints apply in the case of Gallo-Italian dialects and varieties of French, where vowel deletion (in the multiple facets of aphæresis, apocope, and syncope) has led to shorter words with long sequences of consonants. Emilian dialects clearly show this enrichment of consonant clusters: Bol. [ˈstmɛːna] 'week', [tʃtiˈmɔːni] 'witness', [pkæŋ] 'mouthful'; Lunigiana [ˈʃtmaːna] 'week' (Filipponio 2012; Cavirani 2015; 2018). Depending on speech rate, in these clusters a short central vowel (schwa) may be produced by the speaker, because of a complex interconsonantal contact. However, note that the appearance of this non-etymological vocoid should be rather considered a case of an intrusive vowel, determined by purely articulatory reasons (Cavirani 2015). Campidanese Sardinian also shows aberrant clusters in initial position of the word via metathesis (Cossu 2019); e.g., /sirˈbɔnɛ/ > [sriˈβɔːni] 'wild boar'; /mɛrˈkunis/ > [mreˈkuːnizi]

'Wednesday'; /ˈtsurfuru/ > [ˈtsruːfuru] 'sulphur', [tʃr], /ˈtʃerbu/ > [ˈtʃreːβu] 'deer'.

A special case is the cluster /s/+C, inherited from Latin. Its heterosyllabification abides by the *Sonority Principle*, if a stop is in second position. In many Romance languages (e.g., Spanish, Portuguese, Sardinian, Catalan, French), vowel epenthesis (with /e/ or schwa) occurs before word-initial clusters beginning with /s/; e.g., SCHOLA(M) 'school' > Sp. *escuela* [esˈkwela], Pt. *escola* [əsˈkɔlɐ], Cat. *escola* [əsˈkɔlə], Fr. *école* [eˈkɔl], Srd. [isˈkɔla]. Deletion of preconsonantal [s] in the history of French provides additional evidence for its association with the coda position and for the heterosyllabic status of sC clusters: cf. It. *festa*, Fr. *fête* 'party'. The three-consonant clusters of the form sC1C2, already allowed in Latin, remain broadly stable and obey the same syllabic constraints: STRATA(M) > It. *strada* 'street', SCRIPTUM > Sic. [ˈskritːu] 'written', SCRIBERE 'to write' > Sp. *escribir* [eskriˈβir], Cat. *escriure* [əsˈkriwrə].

5.4.4 Romance Codas

The coda is the syllable constituent most affected by phonological change. In most Romance varieties the coda is constrained by restrictions concerning types and number of segments, with the exception of French and Gallo-Italic dialects, in which phonotactic constraints are much more relaxed (see Section 5.4.3). Since Kiss (1972), it is usual to speak of coda weakening, which is usually exemplified by the loss of gemination and the reduction of consonant clusters occurring in a vast part of the Romance domain.

However, the empirical data only partially confirm this claim. If some languages have lost the final consonants of Latin (e.g., Italian, many southern Italo-Romance dialects, Romanian), final *-s* has been retained in a quite high number of other languages (e.g., Sardinian, Spanish, Portuguese, French, Catalan). While internal clusters comprising two obstruents have been reduced in a part of the original lexicon in some varieties (e.g., OCTO 'eight' > Sp. *ocho* [ˈotʃo], Fr. *huit* [ɥi(t)]; RUPTUM 'broken' > Sp. *roto* [ˈroto]), in others gemination occurs, with preservation of the original closed syllable (e.g., It. *otto* [ˈɔtːo]; Nap. [ˈɔtːə]).[6] The preservation of a voiceless obstruent in the onset (cf. the Spanish examples above) suggests that the consonant remained in coda for a long time before being deleted; otherwise, that is, if the original stop had been in a post-vocalic position, the lenition would have taken place.

The palatalization and affrication processes occurring in Romance languages are an instance of fortition rather than lenition, because, in systems

---

[6] Though the geminate output testifies a sort of 'weakening', since the segment in the coda loses its place of articulation, more significant is the preservation of the syllable structure in terms of weight units (Marotta 1995).

allowing gemination, the new segments often surface as long; e.g., MEDIUM 'half' > It. *mezzo* (Section 5.5.3). The same *rafforzamento fonosintattico* (Italian and central-southern Italo-Romance dialects; see Section 6.4.3.2) can be considered another case of preservation of the original structure, since the loss of the final consonant of the first word is compensated by the gemination of the initial consonant of the second word, thus ensuring the maintenance of the mora associated to the coda; e.g., Lat. CANTAUIT BENE > *kan'taw b'bɛne > It. *cantò bene* [kanˈtɔ ˈbːɛːne] 'sing.PST.PFV.3SG well (= s/he sang well)'.

Apart from the developments of consonant clusters, new complex codas appear in Romance varieties (especially in northern Romance) via apocope and syncope; for instance, in Carrarese (Lunigiana) consonant clusters respecting the *Sonority Sequencing Generalization* (Blevins 1995) occur in word-final position, together with others that violate the scale; e.g., HERBA(M) > Car. [ɛrb] 'herb', TRISTE(M) > [trist] 'sad', TEPIDU(M) > [tepd] 'lukewarm', LIBRU(M) > [libr] 'book' (Cavirani 2015). Likewise, sequences not obeying the *Sonority Sequencing Generalization* occur in French, e.g., *arbre* [aʁbʁ] 'tree'.

Coda weakening is well grounded in the case of Latin superheavy syllables, which do not survive as such in any Romance language. The repair strategies include simplification of the consonant cluster (e.g., SANC.TUS 'holy' > It., Sp. *santo*; Fr. *saint*, with a nasalized vowel) as well as vowel shortening (e.g., STĒL.LA 'star' > It. *stella*) and degemination (Fr. *étoile*, with diphthongization; SCRĪP.TUS 'written' > Fr. *écrit* also with apocope).

The vocalization of laterals via velarization can also be considered an instance of coda weakening; e.g., FALCE(M) > Sic. [ˈfawtʃə] 'sickle', Fr. *faucher* 'to scythe' [foˈʃe] (with further monophthongization of aw); MALU(M) > EuPt. [ˈmaɫ] 'evil', but BrPt. [maw]; CALIDU(M) > Pontremolese [kau̯d], COLAPHU(M) > [kurp] 'blow' (Cavirani 2015).

Regressive assimilation processes are also positive evidence for coda depletion; for instance, voice assimilation affects the sibilant in preconsonantal position; e.g., Sp. *esto* 'this' with [s], *mismo* 'same' with [z]; It. *pasto* 'meal' with [s], *risma* 'ream' with [z]. On the other hand, progressive assimilations can be fortition processes. The voicing of unvoiced stops occurring in southern Italy after a nasal consonant could therefore be considered counterevidence, e.g., Nap. '*n campagna* [ŋ gamˈbaɲːə] 'in the countryside' (Ledgeway 2009: 87).

In conclusion, to speak of a generalized coda weakening in the transition from Latin to Romance is far from reality. Rather, a sort of balance between opposing trends might be proposed: on the one hand, reduction of syllable complexity (deletion and weakening of consonants in coda) favouring open syllables and at the same time giving rise to new geminate consonants; on the other, word shortening (via syncope, apocope) producing new closed syllables and new formats of coda. Both trends occur in Romance languages to different degrees, as reduction of syllable complexity is stronger and more frequent in some varieties (such as Italian and Spanish), whereas syllable deletion prevails in others (e.g., French, Catalan, Romanian). Note that, even in this case the traditional dichotomy between western and eastern Romania does not hold (Section 5.9).

5.5 Phonological Processes

5.5.1 Diphthongization

The development of onglide (i.e., rising) diphthongs is certainly one of the most innovative aspects of the evolution of the Romance languages (cf. also Section 7.3.2.2). Classical Latin only had the falling diphthongs AE, OE, AU. The diphthong AU apparently is universally present in the early stages of Romance and surviving nowadays in some dialects of southern Italy as well as in Romanian and Occitan. Rising diphthongs were basically absent in Latin, since the sequences where a vowel is preceded by a semivowel (e.g., IACIO '(I) throw', UOLO '(I) want', with [j]-, [w]-, respectively) should be considered sequences of onset plus nucleus.

In the Romance developments (and probably already in the spoken Latin of the Christian era), the palatal glide gives rise to many palatalization processes. The same holds for high front vowels in hiatus preceded by a consonant; e.g., IACEO '(I) lie > It. *giaccio*; IAM 'already' > It. *già* [dʒa], Fr. *déjà* [de'ʒa]; MEDIUM 'half' > *'mɛdju > It. *mezzo*, Ro. *miez* (cf. Lausberg 1969: §§453–55). In fact, the context of /i/ in hiatus determined a change in the syllable structure: i > j, i.e., from vowel to glide, triggering and feeding the palatalization processes in late Latin, and then in the Romance languages (Section 5.5.2).

The rounded semivowel exhibits a relatively free distribution in Latin, since it may occur in initial position (e.g., UOLO '(I) want'; UULPES 'fox'), between vowels (LAUO '(I) wash'), after a consonant and before a vowel (ARUA 'arable field', NOM-ACC.PL; SILUA 'forest'). The combinability of Latin semivowels with all vowel timbres confirms their nature as consonants.

The Romance evolution indicates that both [j] and [w] originally acquired consonantal value: [j] develops into an affricate or fricative; e.g., IANUARIUS 'January' > *jenuarju > It. *gennaio*, Fr. *janvier*, Cat. *gener*, Pt. *janeiro*; [w] becomes a fricative; e.g., UELUM 'veil', with [w] > It. *velo*, Fr. *voile* (see Lausberg 1969: §§329–30).

The new rising diphthongs in Romance languages arise from an original mid vowel; e.g., It. *uomo* 'man' < HOMO; It. *piede* 'foot', Fr. *pied* < PEDE(M) (cf. below). Some dialects suggest that the phonological development from a vowel into a diphthong could be understood as the development of a new complex configuration with two skeletal slots linked to the syllable nucleus. In Italian there is strong evidence for the association of the onglides with the onset position because of their free distribution; e.g., It. *piede* 'foot', *miele* 'honey', *pioggia* 'rain', *uomo* 'man', *fuoco* 'fire', *quindi* 'thus'. Moreover, in varieties showing OSL, such as Italian, the stressed vowel of a rising diphthong is lengthened, suggesting that the mere diphthongization does not comply with the *Strong Rhyme Constraint*; e.g., It. [ˈpjɛːde], [ˈfwɔːko]), and therefore that the onset is not part of the rhyme.

Evidence from the dialects of southern Italy, however, might suggest that onglides may be associated with the syllable nucleus rather than the onset, since the application of *rafforzamento fonosintattico* (RF; see Section 6.4.3.2) is blocked in case of initial [j]- in the metaphonetic diphthong *-ie-*, suggesting its association with the nucleus, with consequent protection from RF; e.g., Cal. *ieri* 'yesterday' but *oja, nu ieri* 'today, not yesterday', and not ***oja, nu* [ggʲ]*eri*' versus NON IOCAT > *nu* [ggʲ]*oca* 'he doesn't play', from Latin initial *i-*, like *d(i)-/d(-e)*, which systematically undergo RF (e.g., Cal. *iurnata* 'day' > *chi* [ggʲ]*urnata!* 'what (a) day!').

Romance varieties also show falling diphthongs as developments from stressed vowels in open syllable; e.g., Pgl. [ˈteila] 'canvas' < TELA (Stehl 1980; 1988); Isc. [ˈfaitekə] 'liver' < FICATUM (Russo 2010); similar outputs in the Basilicata dialect of Venosa (Fanciullo 1988).

According to the traditional approach, there is a strong correlation between stressed open syllable and vowel lengthening (cf. Section 5.2). The emergence of falling diphthongs is therefore considered 'spontaneous' as it is crucially due to the lengthening of the stressed vowel via breaking of the nucleus: the maintenance of the same articulatory configuration for a certain period of time almost automatically leads to a change in the gestures with the consequent production of new phonetic segments. However, in a number of Romance varieties diphthongs also occur in closed syllables; e.g., FORTE(M) > Cst. *fuerte* (but It. *forte*) 'strong'; OSSU(M) 'bone' > southern Vnt. *wosso* (It. *osso*); also in some Apuan areas (Carpitelli 1997: 119–23), in northern Calabria (Rohlfs 1966: §10) as well in the Campanian area of Pozzuoli and Ischia (e.g., [ˈtraɪtːsə] 'braid'; Russo 2010). Note that the occurrence of offgliding diphthongs in closed syllables gives rise to super-heavy rhymes, a marked structure in typological terms and a quite infrequent configuration within the Romance domain (Barry and Russo 2002).

On the origin of Romance diphthongs two main hypotheses have been proposed: diphthongization has been related to vowel lengthening (Wartburg 1950: 122f.; Lüdtke 1956: 82f.; Loporcaro 2011a: 120–22) or to metaphony (Schürr 1956; 1965; 1970; 1972; Lausberg 1969; Maiden 1995: 54; 2016a; 2016b).

It is possible to object to both hypotheses. If diphthongization is a result of vowel lengthening (and if this is in turn related, as has been suggested, with prepausal lengthening), we should expect many more instances of falling diphthongs (than the rising ones occurring in most Romance languages), and this is not the case (cf. above). Moreover, it becomes difficult to explain why vowel nuclei of rising diphthongs are subject to OSL in those varieties still exhibiting it; e.g., Lat. PEDE(M) 'foot' > It. [ˈpjɛːde], HOMO 'man' > It. *uomo* [ˈwɔːmo], like MANU(M) > 'hand', It. [ˈmaːno] (Marotta 1988). On the other hand, if diphthongs arise from the process of metaphony, the earlier and more frequent metaphonic outcome should be a diphthong instead of a raised vowel, whereas philological data consistently indicate just the opposite throughout the Romance domain. And even in this case, falling diphthongs instead of rising should be expected more frequently. Furthermore, metaphony may occur without diphthongization (e.g., in Portuguese or Sardinian) and in parallel diphthongization does not imply metaphony. For instance, Italian seems to be insensitive to metaphony; yet it does have diphthongization in stressed syllables.[7]

Furthermore, in Tuscan dialects the simple vowel [ɔ] occurs instead of the diphthong [wɔ]; e.g., Tsc. *bòno* 'good', *òvo* 'egg', *mòvo* '(I) move', instead of standard It. *buòno*, *uòvo*, *muòvo*. We might wonder if [ɔ] is the direct continuation of the original Tuscan picture, where diphthongization (in stressed syllable of prominent words) was in alternation with simple middle vowel (in words deprived of primary stress); e.g., Tsc. *bon amico* 'good friend', also attested as a surname in the region, i.e., *Bonamico*. Indirect evidence in favour of the metaphonetic origin of the diphthongization could be the lack of diphthong in forms as It. *bene* 'well', *nove* 'nine', which could be related to the absence of the trigger (i.e., final high vowel), since these words lack metaphonizing inflexions. On the other hand, toponyms like *Siena*, *Fiesole* do not support the metaphonetic origin of diphthongization in Tuscany.

As a final remark on the topic of diphthongization, let us recall a parallel phonological process giving rise to onglide diphthongs in some languages, i.e., the developments of cluster -Cl- into Cj-; for instance, e.g., PLATEA(M) 'square' > It. [ˈpjatːsa], CLAUE(M) 'key' > It. *chiave* [ˈkjaːve] (Lausberg 1969). This process ended up conspiring with the emergence of diphthongization, although the relative chronology of the two processes is far from being definite.

5.5.2 Palatalization

The label 'palatalization' covers a set of processes with variable output sharing the same feature, i.e., the fronting of a consonant gesture due to a front high vowel or glide, i.e., [i j].

The target of palatalization is the syllable onset, with major repercussions on the preceding rhyme (Marotta 1995). Due to the process of palatalization

---

[7] On the special position of ancient Aretino, see Castellani (1970), Loporcaro (2011b: 120), Maiden (2016b).

not only the number but also the types of onset increase with respect to Latin, since palatal and affricates emerge in the consonant inventories of the Romance languages (cf. Section 5.4.4).

The first context giving rise to palatal segments is C[-labial]iV: the vowel in hiatus easily changes into a palatal glide, a segment with a strong dynamic force; e.g., FACIE(M) 'face' > It. *faccia* with [tʃ:], Fr. *face* (with [s], but with [ts] until the sixteenth century; cf. Loporcaro 2011b: 144), RATIONE(M) > It. *ragione* 'reason' with [dʒ], Sp. *razón*, Occ. *razò*, Fr. *raison* (all with [dz] in the Middle Ages); BRACHIUM 'arm' > It. *braccio* with [tʃ:], Ro. [brats]; MEDIUM > It. *mezzo* 'half' with [d:z]; DIURNUM > It. *giorno* with [dʒ]; Fr. *jour*, 'day' with [ʒ]. The same happened to the sequence C[- labial]eV, since *e* in hiatus became *i*, and then *j*; e.g., PLATEA(M) > It. *piazza* 'square' with [t:s], Sp. *plaza*, Fr. *place*; PUTEUM > Ro. [puts], Mil. [pos] 'well, shaft' (Repetti 2016: 659).

In the sequence jV, the normal output is a palatal fricative or affricate; e.g., IUGUM 'yoke' > It. *giogo* with [dʒ], Fr. *joug* with [ʒ]; *iocu(m)* 'play' > It. *gioco* with [dʒ], Fr. *jeu* with [ʒ], Cat. [ʒɔg], Pt. [ˈʒogu].

Another typical context for palatalization is represented by the sequence C[+velar]i/e; e.g., CIUITATEM 'city' > It. *città*; AMICI 'friends' > It. *amici*; PACE(M) 'peace' > It. *pace*, CAELUM 'sky' (AE > [ɛ]) > It. *cielo*, all with [tʃ]; Sp. *cinco, cielo*, both with [θ], Fr. *cinq, ciel*, with [s], Pt. *cinco, ceu*, with [s]. The fronting has been more recent in this context, probably because the yod was not involved. Note that Logudorese Sardinian has maintained the original velar consonant; e.g., CIMICE(M) 'bed bug', CENTUM 'one hundred', CENA(M) 'dinner' > Srd. *kimige, kentu, kena*.

Palatalization is also involved in the clusters C[+ sonorant]jV. With the coronal nasal, in some Romance languages the complex segment [ɲ] is produced; e.g., UINEA(M) 'vineyard' > It. *vigna*, Sp. *viña*, both with [ɲ]. The development of the sequence lj shows a remarkable variety of outputs; it palatalizes in Italian; e.g., FAMILIA 'family' > It. *famiglia*; PALEA(M) 'straw' > It. *paglia*, both with [ʎ]; in other languages fricatives occur as a secondary reflex of the palatalization; e.g., Sp. *paja* [ˈpaxa] 'straw'; in many dialects of southern Italy palatal obstruents occur (e.g., FILIU(M) 'son' > Sic. *figghiu*); in Rome a long glide [j:] is produced (*fijjo*); similarly in French (*paille* [paj]; in southern Tuscany the sequence remained unchanged (*filio, familia*).

In varieties exhibiting consonant gemination, the output of j-clusters is often a long segment; for instance, in Italian, the new segments /ts dz ʃ ʎ ɲ/ emerging from the processes of palatalization are intrinsically geminate (apart from the palato-alveolar affricates). In the development of the sequences iV, eV, the first segment switches from front vowel to glide j. However, the structure does not change in terms of syllable weight since the mora lost by the vowel is retrieved via gemination of the new palatal segment; e.g., FILIU(M) = three moras corresponding to the three nuclei; It. [ˈfiʎ:o] with still three moras. Despite the apparent change the structure is therefore preserved (whereas in other cases a syllable is lost; e.g., RATIONE (M) > It. *ragione* [ra'dʒoːne] 'reason': from four to three syllables).

For the morphological aspects of palatalization, see Sections 10.5.1–2.

5.5.3 Lenition

Among the processes involving consonant segments, lenition is one of the most pervasive in Romance languages (Brandão de Carvalho et al. 2008; Loporcaro 2011b: 150–54). The term 'lenition' is here used as a cover term referring to the weakening of obstruents associated with an onset position occurring in post-vocalic context. In fact, depending on whether the previous syllable is closed or open, the next onset will be stronger or weaker, respectively (Coda-Mirror effect, Ségéral and Scheer 2011). Romance varieties exhibit a wide set of weakening phenomena targeting an onset not preceded by coda or pause (weak position).

The different development of voiceless stops /p t k/ traditionally provides a criterion for the traditional division between the eastern and western Romània (Wartburg 1936); for instance, CAPRA(M) 'goat' > It. *capra*, Ro. *capră* vs Sp. *cabra* with [β], Fr, *chèvre*; ROTA(M) 'wheel' > It. *ruota*, Ro. *roată* vs Sp. *rueda* with [ð], Fr. *roue*; FORMICA(M) 'ant' > It. *formica*, Ro. *furnică* vs Sp. *hormiga*, with [ɣ], Fr. *fourmi* (Schmid 2016). However, sonorization may occur in some lexemes also in Italian, as in *strada* < STRATA(M) 'street', *lago* 'lake' < LACU(M). Moreover, a typical process of Tuscan Italian is so-called *gorgia toscana* (lit. 'Tuscan throat'), which is precisely a spirantization process that changes a stop into the corresponding fricative; e.g., *amico* 'friend' [a'miːxo] or [a'miːho], *dito* 'finger' ['diːθo]; the process occurs in sandhi too; e.g., *la Coca Cola* 'the Coke' [la 'hɔha 'hɔːla] (Marotta 2008; cf. also Section 6.4.3.2). Sardinian data are even more problematic, since voiceless stops are maintained in Nuorese, whereas lenition occurs systematically in Campidanese and Logudorese, e.g., *sa terra* [sa 'ðɛrːa] 'the earth', and *su cane* [su 'ɣaːnɛ] 'the dog', challenging the traditional dichotomy between western and eastern Romance once more.

The end point of the lenition chain, i.e., segment deletion, can be found in some lexical sets of many Romance varieties; e.g., Fr. *vie* [vi] 'life' < UITA(M). In western Tuscan (Pisa and Livorno), [x h] may even be deleted: e.g., [a'miːo] 'friend' < AMICU(M); ['mɛːdio], ['mɛːdjo] 'doctor' < MEDICU(M), ['baːo] 'worm' < BACU(M) (Rohlfs 1949: 322).

5.6 Lexical Stress

Lexical stress has not normally changed position. In general, the syllable which was prominent in Classical Latin remains stressed, although the word length may change; e.g., MATÚRU(M) 'ripe' > It. *matúro*, Sp./Pt. *madúro*; MATRE(M) 'mother' > It./Sp. *mádre*, Fr. *mère*. Stress preserves the original position even in French and other Gallo-Romance varieties, where widespread processes of apocope and syncope have considerably reduced the syllable nuclei, increasing the number of monosyllabic or oxytonic words; e.g., SÁLICE(M) 'willow' > It. *sálice*, Nap. [ˈsalətʃə], Sp. *sauce* [ˈsawθe], Fr. *saux* [so].

The exceptions to this general rule probably do not represent real Romance innovations but the emergence of pronunciations already occurring in low sociolinguistic varieties of Latin. In particular, in trisyllabic words with *muta cum liquida*, the stress occurred on the antepenultimate syllable in Classical Latin. In Romance languages, these forms often become trochaic, suggesting a shift in the syllable boundary; e.g., ÍNTEGRU(M) 'whole' > It. *intéro*, Sp. *entéro*, Fr. *entier*. Sequences -io-, -ie-, -eo- which were disyllabic in Classical Latin and stressed on the first vowel undergo stress shift due to the loss of the first nucleus with concomitant palatalization of the previous consonant (Section 5.5.3); e.g., FILÍOLUS 'son' > It. *figliolo* [fiˈʎɔːlo], Fr. *filleul* [fiˈjœl] 'godson'; LINTÉOLU(M) 'bed sheet' > It. *lenzuolo* [lenˈtswɔːlo], Sp. *lenzuélo*, Fr. *linceul* [lɛ̃ˈsœl] 'shroud' (Lausberg 1969: §149). In compound verbs, stress often moves from the prefix to the verb root, for analogical reasons; e.g., RÉCIPIT '(he/she) receives' > It. *riceve* [riˈtʃeːve], Fr. *reçoit* [ʁəˈswa] such as RECIPIO '(I) receive' > It. *ricevo* [riˈtʃeːvo]. It is worth noting that these all stress shifts point towards the same rhythmic pattern, namely the trochaic one (see below and also Section 7.2.3).

The nature of stress in Latin has been long debated. At present, the prevailing opinion does not confer a melodic accent to Latin, despite recognizing the relevance of length in the phonological system. Lexical stress in the Romance languages has a dynamic and expiratory nature, although the degree of the intensity is variable along the Romance space. In particular, stress is more intense in Gallo-Romance, due to the interference with other languages (see Section 5.8), whereas in Italian and southern Italian dialects segment duration still plays a relevant role, as vowels are long in stressed open syllables (Section 5.3). The relation between lexical stress and rhythmical structure has also to be considered, since different timings can affect stress production and perception.

Although the position of lexical stress does not normally change in the evolution from Latin to Romance varieties, there is clear evidence that the role of stress has drastically changed. In particular, starting from the lower registers and spreading through the sociolinguistic repertoire of Latin, the phonological importance of stress progressively increases in strict correlation with the loss of vowel length contrast. Therefore, the phonological balance between the two prosodic factors shifts from vowel quantity to stress, that is, from the segmental to the prosodic structure: in Latin the position of lexical stress was governed by the weight of the penultimate syllable, due to intrinsic vowel quantity as well as to the structure of the rhyme; in the Romance domain, after the collapse of vowel quantity, stress strongly influences the length of syllable nuclei (Section 5.3.2).

The relevance of stress is proved by the different fate of the vowels depending on their prosodic status. As a general trend, stress preserves the nuclei and their main articulatory features, whereas the lack of prominence makes the syllables weaker and favours a series of changes connected with articulatory weakening (see Sections 5.4.1–2).

In many Romance languages, stress is free and distinctive. Italian, Friulian, Romanian, and Ibero-Romance show minimal pairs: Sp. *sábana* 'sheet' vs *sabána* 'savannah'; It. *cápito* 'I turn up' vs *capíto* 'understood' vs *capitò* 'it happened'; Ro. *ácele* 'the needles' vs *acéle* 'those.FPL'. Stress is also free and distinctive in dialects of northern Italy: Ven. [faˈdiga] 'labour' vs [fadiˈga] 'to labour' (Zamboni 1974: 15). However, in Spanish, Catalan, Occitan, Italian, Portuguese, Romanian, Sardinian, and Ladin, the lexical prominence is more frequently associated with the penultimate syllable than with the others; for instance, in Italian, stress is located in the penultimate syllable in 93 per cent of disyllabic words and in 81 per cent of trisyllabic words (Mancini and Voghera 1994). The same trend towards a trochaic pattern is found in some dialects of southern Italy, where in phrases comprising sequence of verb plus clitics, the consonant of the first clitic geminates and primary stress shifts from the verb root to the penultimate syllable, e.g., Nap. [ˈpɔrta] 'bring!', [ˈpɔrtalə] 'bring it!', but [pɔrtaˈmiːlə] 'bring it to me!'; Nap. [ˈfravəkə] 'build!', but [fravəˈkalːə] 'build it!' (Bafile 2008; 2012; Ledgeway 2009: 33–35). Likewise, Occitan tends to avoid dactylic feet and to fix stress on the penultimate syllable, e.g., *lagréma* 'tear', *perségue* 'peach', *silába* 'syllable', *classíca* 'classical', *credúla* 'credulous', regardless of the etymon (Wheeler 1988).

A completely different pattern emerges in French and Gallo-Romance varieties (northern Italian dialects included), due to the spread of apocope and syncope which have deleted post-tonic nuclei (Section 5.4.3), increasing the number of words stressed on the final syllable.

Though stress is considered free in the lexicon of many Romance languages, there is wide evidence that the penultimate syllable of the word is the preferred stress position cross-categorically. In other terms, the trend already occurring in the Latin lexicon (Marotta and De Felice 2019) becomes even stronger in Romance systems. On the other hand, the morphological structure often makes the position of the prominence predictable, since inflexional and derivational morphemes may be attractors or repellers of stress; for instance, in verb inflexion, It. *mangiámo*, Sp./Pt. *comémos* '(we) eat'; It. *vedéva* '(he/she) was seeing', Sp. *vió* '(he/she) saw', It. *vedeváte* '(you.PL) were seeing', Sp. *víste* '(you.SG) saw'; in derivational processes, It. *távolo*, Sp.

mésa 'table' vs It. *tavolíno*, Sp. *mesíta* 'small table'. Many morphemes preserve the same attractive or repulsive power that they had in the ancestor language; for instance, *-icus* for adjectives was a stress-repeller, while *-atus* for past participles was a stress-attractor; the same happens for their Romance descendants; e.g., Sp./It. *fantástico* 'fantastic'; Sp./It. *amádo/ amáto* 'loved'.

5.7 Parametric Variation in Metrical Patterns

Considering the parameters of metrical phonology, the lack of a general rule for the assignment of lexical stress makes the use of traditional parameters of metrical phonology less advantageous in Romance languages than in Latin. If the head of the foot is set leftwards for the majority of the Romance languages, in French and Gallo-Romance varieties the fall of the post-tonic syllables has often changed the metrical shape of the word, favouring an iambic pattern.

Even in languages where trochaic foot is the unmarked structure, it is impossible to claim a strict setting of left-headedness, because words with final stress do occur in the lexicon, with a not negligible frequency; e.g., It. *città* 'town'; Sp. *jamón* 'ham'. It is also worth observing that the oxytonic pattern is the only new one in the Romance varieties with respect to their ancestor, since in Latin no word could be stressed on the final syllable of a polysyllable (apart from some words arising from apocope, like ILLÁC, ILLÚC).

Boundedness is also a critical notion. Leaving aside French (and its varieties) and Gallo-Italian dialects, in the other Romance languages the trochaic foot, even if extremely frequent, it is not the only left-headed metrical pattern, since dactylic feet also occur, e.g., It. *távolo* 'table', *célibe* 'celibate'; Sp. *pícaro* 'sly', *pálido* 'pale' (Marotta 1999a; Piñeros 2016).

The parameter of quantity-sensitivity (Hayes 1995) has changed its format: in Latin, lexical stress was assigned on the basis of vowel quantity as well as of syllable structure, whereas Romance languages show quantity-sensitivity regarding syllable structure only, thus reducing its scope and importance (see also Chapter 7, this volume). In summary, Romance stress is a lexical property, thus it is unpredictable (except for French and Gallo-Italian dialects) and cannot be accounted for in a mere parametric framework.

Despite the general trend towards the preservation of the original locus of lexical stress, some new trends may be observed. For instance, in contemporary Italian young people (especially in the northern regions) tend to produce dactylic feet instead of the original trochaic ones, probably because of the interference with English, e.g., *édile* 'building.ADJ', *móllica* 'crumb; soft part of loaf', *persuádere* 'to persuade', *sálubre* 'healthy' (Marotta 1999a).

5.8 Syllable and Rhythm

Syllable structure also plays a role in the rhythmic organization of the utterance, with crucial reference to the so-called 'timing' (Pike 1945). Living languages are usually classified into rhythmic classes placed on a typological continuum with the two opposite poles of stress timing and syllable timing (Bertinetto 1989; Schmid 2012). A very broad line of research has focused on measuring vowels and consonants and their intervals (Ramus, Nespor, and Mehler 1999; Grabe and Low 2002; Dellwo and Wagner 2003; Bertinetto and Bertini 2008). However, quantitative metrics only reflect physical segmental durations, which may be influenced by many variables in the performance of the speaker, e.g., speech rate, accuracy in the production, sociolinguistic context, and so on. The perception of rhythm seems to be related more to structural properties of the language (like the complexity of syllable structure or the fate of unstressed vowels) than to simple differences in the acoustic length of segments (Dauer 1983; Gill 1986; Nespor, Shukla, and Mehler 2011). Therefore, the competence of speakers is couched on formal schemata that reflect more general and abstract rhythmical patterns, produced by the speakers in other human dynamic behaviours (e.g., music, poetry, movement; Marotta 2012).

A great number of Romance varieties are traditionally considered syllable-timed, e.g., Spanish, Italian, Romanian, Friulian, many Italian dialects (Marotta 1985; Dascălu 1998; Ramus, Nespor, and Mehler 1999; Dellwo and Wagner 2003; Wheeler 2005). On the other hand, Gallo-Romance varieties can be considered closer to the stress-timed pole, due to the frequent vowel centralization or deletion and the consequent higher complexity in syllable structure. The same is true for European Portuguese, which has experienced a striking reduction of word length, whereas the phonologically more archaic variety of Brazilian Portuguese has maintained a simpler syllable structure. Some southern Italian dialects could also be placed in the middle of the rhythmic continuum between the two ideal poles of syllable timing and stress timing (Trumper, Romito, and Maddalon 1991; Schmid 2000).

Timing has only recently received the attention of Romance linguists. Special attention is given to the historical development of unstressed vowels. The tendency to centralize or delete unstressed nuclei has been considered the strongest cue for stress timing whereas the maintenance of unstressed vowels is associated with syllable timing. In particular, Loporcaro (2011a: 107f.) claimed that proto-Romance might have shifted from syllable timing (typical of Classical Latin) towards the stress-timed pole. Since reduction of unstressed segments and syncope are classic symptoms of stress timing, their massive occurrence in the history of French becomes the main evidence in favour of his hypothesis. The trend towards the heterosyllabication of -Cr/l/j- clusters documented in the Latin–Romance transition as well as in some central-southern Italian dialects may be another argument for the shift towards stress timing (Loporcaro 2011a; Section 5.4.3).

However, a large area of the Romance domain has neither encountered major processes of segmental reduction nor shows clear signs of heterosyllabic scan of *muta cum liquida* clusters. Therefore, the alleged stress timing of proto-Romance appears to be essentially restricted to the area of French and its varieties, including the Gallo-Italian dialects (Varvaro 2014). As discussed, proto-Romance is certainly a useful notion for historical philology. However, it does not correspond to a uniform linguistic reality inasmuch it combines data historically recorded with elements taken from the Romance outcomes, not to mention the vast geographical area involved and the wide temporal extension.

In historical linguistics, there seems to be no great evidence in favour of a sudden shift from one timing to another in a temporal span of a few centuries, save in cases of language contact. The Romance area where prosodic processes strictly related with the alleged stress timing are documented overlaps with the presumed Gaulish substratum. Similarly, Germanic peoples lived in neighbouring western areas of the Roman Empire. Therefore, these languages too could have influenced the pronunciation of Latin on the borders of the Roman Empire.

Current historical sociolinguistics (Conde Silvestre 2007; Hernández Campoy and Conde Silvestre 2012) has analysed similar situations of multilingualism and variable contact between peoples and languages. The relevance of language contact in language change has long been recognized. Its role can thus no longer be denied when considering the structural differences detectable among Romance languages (Marotta 2020).

The progressive expansion of Rome into Gaul produced an ever greater verbal interaction between the invaders and the indigenous populations. This daily contiguity could easily give rise to multilingualism. Due to the common lack of education and the spontaneous acquisition of Latin, the majority of Celtic people may have displayed imperfect bilingualism, or *subélite bilingualism* (Adams 2003: 14), although in this context 'bilingualism' should be interpreted as a quite abstract label that covers a wide range of speakers (literate and non-literate) and communicative situations (from the military environment to trade).

Therefore, an influence from other speech rhythm on the Romance idioms spoken in the area where Celtic peoples lived cannot be excluded a priori, due to the presumed but perfectly probable bilingualism of the speakers (*contra* Loporcaro 2011a: 107f.; Filipponio 2015). Although there is unfortunately no strong empirical evidence, the hypothesis based on the influence of Gaulish languages in speaking Latin in the areas where Gaulish people lived cannot be excluded in principle. In a closed-corpus language, absence of proof cannot constitute proof of non-existence *tout court*.

As a matter of fact, the prosodic patterns of ancient and modern Celtic languages do not appear to be in contrast with the assumption of a stress timing for Celtic languages. As far as Gaulish is concerned, the issue on nature and position of lexical stress has been debated for a long time (see Lambert 1994; De Bernardo Stempel 1994; 1995; Eska 2004; Motta and Nuti 2009). However, nowadays there is widespread agreement on the intensive nature of stress as well as on the assumption of an ancient stage with initial stress, although the double accentuation for some toponyms further complicates the picture; for instance, *Bourges* (< *Bitúriges*) vs *Berry* (< *Bituríges*); *Nîmes* (< *Némausus*) vs *Nemours* (< *Nemáusus*; De Bernardo Stempel 2007). It seems even more complicated to trace the historical path of unstressed vowels in the search of confirmations on presumed syncope and deletion processes, due to the scarcity of data and to their exclusively epigraphic source as well. However, living Celtic languages exhibit the features characteristic of stress timing, as recent experimental findings on Irish have shown (Dorn et al. 2012).

In conclusion, although Romance languages sound different from each other, there are no very noticeable differences in rhythm between a large number of them. At the same time, a rather clear demarcation line can be traced between the Gallo-Romance domain and the north-western dialects of Italy on the one hand, and the rest of the Romània on the other.[8] It does not seem to be accidental that the first group of languages share both the Gaulish substratum and adjacency with Germanic languages. The long-standing linguistic contact between Latin, Celtic, and Germanic speakers might have produced language interference. In particular, Celtic and Germanic languages being stress-timed, the bilingualism or diglossia of speakers could have favoured the introduction of new articulatory habits, resulting in innovation both on the segmental and prosodic levels.[9]

5.9 'Western' versus 'Eastern' Romance

A traditional classification splits the Romance languages into two main branches geographically determined. The eastern group includes Romanian, Corsican, Sardinian, and all the varieties of Italo-Romance south of the La Spezia-Rimini Line (cf. Wartburg 1950; Lausberg 1969). The

---

[8] Portuguese holds a special place: it is a stress-timed language that shares many traits with northern Romance. And it might not be a coincidence that Lusitania was inhabited by Celtic populations before the arrival of the Romans.

[9] It is worth remembering that Martinet (1955) resorted to the category of stress to underline the contrast between Latin, with a melodic accent, and Germanic and Celtic languages, which had an intensive stress.

western group includes the Gallo-Romance and Gallo-Italian varieties, Occitan, Francoprovençal, Romansh, and the Ibero-Romance varieties. Typical features of the western languages are the maintenance of final -s and the lenition of intervocalic consonants. As discussed above, this classification is problematic.

Some inconsistencies have already been highlighted in the previous paragraphs. Let us briefly summarize the main topics:

(a) Sardinian does not fit into the schema of the eastern varieties, because of the failure to merge /ĭ, ŭ/ with /ē, ō/, respectively, and the lack of palatalization;
(b) since eastern languages are considered more conservative, one may ask why -s has been retained in Spanish, for instance, but not in Italian;
(c) French is classified as a western variety, but it has lost final -s, although it may still survive in the context of *liaison*;
(d) processes of consonant weakening in intervocalic position also occur in eastern varieties; for instance, *gorgia toscana* and lenition in central dialects of Italy; similarly, rhotacization of /d/ in Neapolitan (e.g., PEDEM > Nap. [ˈpɛːrə] 'foot';
(e) apocope is generalized in French and Gallo-Italian, but not in Spanish or Catalan, although all these varieties should belong to the same western group;
(f) Romanian, traditionally classified as an eastern variety, lacks consonant gemination, unlike Italian.

Nowadays, levels of mutual intelligibility are higher between some western and eastern languages (e.g., between Italian and Spanish) than between languages belonging to the same group (e.g., between Italian and Romanian, or between a northern Italian dialect and Spanish). There is also a much higher morphological, orthographic, and phonetic similarity between Spanish and Italian than between Spanish and French.

Such a dichotomic classification is also problematic with regard to syllable structure. Romanian, Italian, and southern Italo-Romance dialects (eastern varieties) present a syllable structure very similar to that of Spanish and Catalan (western varieties). On the other hand, French, Gallo-Romance varieties, Gallo-Italian dialects (and Portuguese) show a different and much more complex syllable structure.

An alternative classification of Romance languages could follow the vertical (north-south) instead of the horizontal axis (east-west), as already suggested by Cremona (1970), and now discussed in Marotta (2020). In particular, the new vowel quantity occurs in northern Romance, i.e., in French varieties and Gallo-Italic dialects as well as in some Ræto-Romance dialects. These latter varieties exhibit a more dynamic force that could be due – not exclusively, but also – to the long-standing contact with Celtic and Germanic languages, which exhibit very different phonological and prosodic patterns.

Selected References

Below you can find selected references for this chapter. The full references can be found online at the following page: www.cambridge.org/Romancelinguistics

Blevins, J. (1995). 'The syllable in phonological theory'. In Goldsmith, J. (ed.), *The Handbook of Phonological Theory*. Cambridge: Blackwell, 206–44.

Brandão de Carvalho, J., Scheer, T., and Ségéral, P. (2008) (eds). *Lenition and Fortition*. Berlin: Mouton de Gruyter.

Dauer, R. (1983). 'Stress-timing and syllable-timing reanalyzed', *Journal of Phonetics* 11: 51–62.

Giannini, S. and Marotta, G. (1989), *Fra grammatica e pragmatica. La geminazione consonantica in latino*. Pisa: Giardini.

Hayes, B. (1995). *Metrical Stress Theory. Principles and Case Studies*. Chicago: University of Chicago Press.

Ledgeway, A. (2016a). 'Italian, Tuscan, and Corsican'. In Ledgeway, A. and Maiden, M. (eds), *The Oxford Guide to the Romance Languages*. Oxford: Oxford University Press, 206–27.

Leumann, M. (1977), *Lateinische Laut- und Formelehre, I*, Munich: Beck.

Loporcaro, M. (2011a). 'Syllable, segments e prosody'. In Maiden, M., Smith, J. C., and Ledgeway, A. (eds), *The Cambridge History of the Romance Languages. Vol 1. Structures*. Cambridge: Cambridge University Press, 50–108.

Marotta, G. (1999b). 'The Latin syllable'. In Hulst, H. van der and Ritter, N. A. (eds), *The Syllable. View and Facts*. Berlin/New York: Mouton de Gruyter, 285–310.

Marotta, G. (2008). 'Lenition in Tuscan Italian (*gorgia toscana*)'. In Brandão de Carvalho, J., Scheer, T., and Ségéral, P. (eds), *Lenition and Fortition*. Berlin: Mouton de Gruyter, 235–72.

Marotta, G. (2012). 'Piedi metrici e sillabe orfane nella prosodia dell'italiano'. In Schafroth, E. and Selig, M. (eds), *Testo e ritmi. Zum Rhythmus in der italienischen Sprache*. Frankfurt am Main: Lang, 89–103.

Schmid, S. (2016). 'Segmental phonology'. In Ledgeway, A. and Maiden, M. (eds), *The Oxford Guide to the Romance Languages*. Oxford: Oxford University Press, 471–83.

6

Sandhi Phenomena

Max W. Wheeler and Paul O'Neill

6.1 Introduction

We take sandhi to be primarily a morphological phenomenon. Adaptation to different sandhi contexts gives rise to allomorphy (paradigmatic variation). Such adaptation generally reflects natural phonological processes which tend to reduce the markedness of sequences of phonological elements. We acknowledge that Romance also attests sub-phonemic alternations in sandhi environments, and we draw attention to some such cases, but they belong rather to phonology in general than to sandhi in particular. Probably the most striking feature of Romance sandhi alternations is the readiness with which they may become morphologized or lexicalized. This outcome may arise from subsequent sound change that makes the original motivated alternation opaque, or from levelling of allomorphic alternation that makes the distribution of allomorphs opaque. Occasionally, a morphologized/lexicalized alternation may be (partly) remotivated, as is famously the case with *rafforzamento fonosintattico* 'phonosyntactic strengthening' (Section 6.4.3.2) in standard Italian. But the phenomena of elision (Section 6.2.2) and *liaison* (Section 6.4.3.1) in modern French exemplify morphophonemic arbitrariness with very extensive incidence.

Words (including clitics) in Romance may begin with either a consonant (C) or a vowel (V), and may end with either a consonant or a vowel. So we find the following sandhi contexts: (i) V.#C, (ii) V.#V, (iii) C.#V, and (iv) C.#C. Of these, only (i) V.#C results in a sequence which is not to some degree phonologically marked. That is, V.#C is consistent with the least marked type of syllable structure CV.(CV.CV...) that all languages have – and V#C is not immune from phonological processes, though such will not be limited to the sandhi context (e.g., *gorgia toscana*: *la#casa* [la.hasa] 'the house'; see Section 6.3). We consider in turn each of the other basic types of word contact, and review what types of markedness-reduction processes each might be expected on general grounds to give rise to. One general observation to be made is that Romance does not favour insertion (epenthesis) to make sequences less marked. Nothing like r-insertion (*Cuba*[ɹ] *and America* in non-rhotic English) occurs in Romance to avoid hiatus. Cases are found of vowels inserted to avoid codas, but curiously only in Sardinia. In the Catalan of Alghero, epenthesis of [i] breaks up C.#C contacts not tolerated internally, so, e.g., *tot tapat* 'all covered' [ˌto.t i taˈpat], *cent voltes* 'a hundred times' [ˌsen.t i ˈvɔltas], *animals petits* 'small animals' [aniˌmal.ts i paˈtits], but *diun coses* 'they say things' [ˌdiwŋ. ˈkɔzas], where [ŋ.k] is an acceptable internal syllable contact (Lloret and Jiménez 2007). In Sardinian, underlying word-final consonants are quite rare, and mostly inflexional; C.‖ is avoided by paragoge of a vowel that copies the vowel preceding the consonant. Several examples may be seen in the data in (36) below.

V.#V: Such a structure violates constraints penalizing hiatus. As well as the familiar Optimality Theory constraint ONSET ('syllables have onsets') we suggest a more specific constraint **HIATUS ('no V.V'), for reasons to be mentioned shortly. Broadly speaking, Romance languages deal with such structures in the same way: stressed vowels are not altered (FAITHFULNESS TO PROSODIC HEADS is active); an unstressed vowel is deleted next to (or absorbed into) another vowel of the same quality; schwa [ə] (or [œ] in French]) is deleted next to a vowel of any other quality; other unstressed vowel sequences become diphthongs (synizesis/synaeresis); hiatus is retained between two stressed vowels or between a stressed vowel and an unstressed vowel of different quality other than schwa. In many languages (French, Catalan, English), schwa is the vowel minimally opposed to zero, and liable to be elided provided adjacent consonants are syllabifiable. Avoidance of hiatus in sandhi is discussed in Section 6.2.

C.#V, as it stands, is a marked structure that violates two syllable structure markedness constraints: NOCODA ('syllables do not have codas'), and ONSET. Typically in Romance, this markedness is resolved by resyllabification – the word-final consonant becomes the onset of the following syllable. The consequent misalignment (.C#V) between word structure and syllable structure is tolerated. But in French, *liaison* without *enchaînement* is a possibility (Encrevé 1988); a word-final consonant is pronounced, but remains in coda position before an initial vowel. In several Romance languages, the consonant in a .C#V (or C.#V) structure may be liable to lenition. This is the case, for example, in those Romance languages that preserve Latin final -<s> and retain a voicing contrast in fricatives, namely, French, Occitan, Catalan, and Portuguese. In these languages lenition (voicing of fricatives) may apply similarly to other word-final fricatives before a following vowel (or voiced continuant).

C.#C gives rise to more alternation in Romance than either of the other marked structures just mentioned. NoCODA is violated; there are good, grounded, typological reasons why a preconsonantal coda (C.C) is a 'worse', or more marked, structure than a coda otherwise (that is, C.‖). The phonetic features of a coda consonant are always less readily perceptible than those of an onset consonant – it is transition between consonant and vowel that gives the best perception cues. Before another consonant the features of a coda consonant tend to be masked by anticipatory co-articulation of that following consonant. Put another way, a preconsonantal coda consonant is phonologically weak. In Romance, a coda consonant may be subject to deletion, or to various kinds of weakening (and neutralization): assimilation, of place, manner, or laryngeal feature; shift along the sonority hierarchy stop–fricative–sonorant/approximant–glide. When the coda is itself complex, all of the coda elements are liable to weakening or deletion. A deleted coda may leave traces of its former character in the following word-initial onset. Hence *rafforzamento fonosintattico* 'phonosyntactic strengthening' in central and southern Italo-Romance varieties and Sardinian (Section 6.4.3.2). While some Romance languages retain a wide range of phonologically motivated allomorphy involving variation in word-final consonants before an initial consonant (Catalan: Section 6.4.1, south-western Occitan: Section 6.4.2), in others, the reflexes of this structure have become lexicalized – final consonant deletion or liaison in French (Section 6.4.3.1), lexicalized word-initial *rafforzamento fonosintattico* in central and southern Italo-Romance (Section 6.4.3.2). Lexicalization also seems to be taking place in western Andalusian Spanish (Section 6.4.3.3).

‖#C: We briefly mention a couple of historical processes of initial epenthesis, (i) the insertion of a mid or high front vowel before an initial #sC cluster (Lat. SPERARE 'hope' > Sp. *esperar* 'hope; wait'), and (ii) the insertion of /a/ before initial #[r]- in Gascon (Lat. REM 'thing' > Gsc. *arren* 'nothing') and Campidanese Sardinian (*radio* 'radio' [arˈraðiu]) (Sampson 2010). It has been claimed that such epenthesis originated in a strictly sandhi environment, namely, C#sC, C#r-, but Sampson argues that the historical evidence does not support such an idea (of generalization from a post-consonantal environment).

C#‖: Though, in the general case, as we have suggested, an utterance-final coda consonant has better perceptual cues than a preconsonantal coda, there are some sounds, or some alternations, where the utterance-final variant may, in fact, be weaker. Such is the case for [ɾ], where a tap without a transition to a following sound is quite difficult to detect, leading to loss in this environment sooner, or rather, than elsewhere (Catalan, Andalusian Spanish, Brazilian Portuguese, Occitan, to some degree in French, before the unconditioned change [r] > [ʁ]). In both Catalan and French, loss of final /r/ is lexically conditioned, but is more widely found in polysyllables than in monosyllables. A parallel case is final /n/, or rather, its reflexes: Vn# > alternation Ṽ.n#V ~ ṼN.#C ~ Ṽ.#‖. In the utterance-internal environments, nasality, partly transferred to the preceding vowel, is supported by the retained presence of an articulated nasal consonant. In utterance-final position, nasality, in the vowel alone, is liable to go unperceived, whence loss here sooner than elsewhere (Catalan, Lengadocian Occitan).[1]

6.2 Vowel Sandhi

We illustrate vowel sandhi with two examples involving elision. In the first (Section 6.2.1), from eastern continental Catalan, the conditions governing elision, glide formation (in the case of unstressed high vowels), or the retention of hiatus are all phonological or syntactic. In the second, from standard French (Section 6.2.2), elision, which at one time was phonologically motivated, has become opaque, through what are synchronically lexical exceptions.

6.2.1 Elision of [ə] in Eastern Continental Catalan

In eastern continental Catalan that is primarily considered here there are three unstressed vowels [ə], [i], and [u]. In V.#V sandhi contexts, [ə] may be subject to elision, or diphthong formation with one of the other unstressed vowels (i.e., [əj], [əw], [jə], [wə]); [i] and [u] may be subject to deletion (adjacent to [i] and [u], respectively), or glide formation. Or, with each of them, hiatus may be retained. We focus here on the treatment of [ə], for brevity, and to make a more direct comparison with French. The data are largely from Recasens (1993), and the interpretation from Wheeler (2005: ch. 4).

6.2.1.1 Stressed Vowel Followed by an Unstressed Non-high Vowel [ə]

As a result of vowel reduction in unstressed syllables, the only unstressed non-high vowel in initial position is [ə], spelled <a> or <e>. The possibilities in the case of input ˈV#ə are hiatus or elision. When the lowest, most prominent, vowel [ˈa] is followed by a word beginning with [ə], elision is obligatory (1a). With the other low vowels [ˈɛ] and [ˈɔ], marginally less prominent than [ˈa], elision also seems to be practically obligatory (1b).

---

[1] We use *utterance* here with deliberate vagueness. Though the processes in question always apply at the edge of an utterance, they may also be found at the edge of an intonational phrase, or a phonological phrase, in ways that vary between and within languages (or between varieties, or speakers).

(1) a. *està atordit* 'is stunned' [əs.ˈta .tuɾ.ˈðit]
         mesurar alçària 'measure.INF height' [mə.zu.ˈra l.ˈsa.ɾjə]
     b. *cafè amarg* 'bitter coffee (lit. coffee bitter)' [kə.ˈfɛ. ˈmark]
         això anima 'that encourages' [ə.ˈʃɔ. ˈni.mə]

What appears to be problematic about the realization of [ˈa.ə], [ˈɛ.ə], and [ˈɔ.ə] is that a stressed vowel of high perceptual prominence is followed by the unstressed vowel of minimum prominence [ə]. Perceptually it is as if the prominent vowel overwhelms the non-prominent vowel, or obscures its presence entirely. Because such sequences are hard to perceive, speakers may not take the trouble to make the sequence at all, despite loss of semantic information in some cases.

In the case of the less prominent stressed vowels followed by [ə], however, other considerations may come into play, favouring hiatus.

(2) *actor enèrgic* 'energetic actor (lit. actor energetic)' [ək.ˈto .ə.ˈnɛr.ʒik]
     no animes 'not encourage.2SG.PRS.IND' [ˈno .ə.ˈni.məs]

(3) *actor esplèndid* 'splendid actor (lit. actor splendid)' [ək.ˈtos.ˈplɛn.dit]
     collir espàrrecs 'pick.INF asparagus' [ku.ˈʎis.ˈpa.rəks]

In (2), elision of [ə] in an open syllable would lead to a stress clash e.g., *actor enèrgic* [ək.ˈto .ˈnɛr.ʒik] – more particularly, a clash of adjacent stressed moras. In (3), however, with [ə] in a closed syllable, clash of adjacent stressed syllables with a mora between the heads, is preferable to hiatus. Other considerations, too, may favour or disfavour hiatus.

(4) a. *corder anyal* 'lamb less than one year old' [kuɾ.ˈðe .ə.ˈɲal], cf. *any* 'year'
         setí arnat 'moth-eaten satin (lit. satin moth-eaten)' [sə.ˈti. ər.ˈnat], cf. *arna* 'moth'
     b. *sentir avidesa* 'feel.INF greed' [sən.ˈti .ə.βi.ˈðɛ.zə], cf. *àvid* 'greedy'
     c. *actor alpinista* 'mountaineering actor (lit. actor mountaineering)' [ək.ˈtol.pi.ˈnis.tə], cf. *Alp* 'Alp'
     d. *tabú acceptable* 'acceptable taboo (lit. taboo acceptable)' [tə.ˈβuk.səp.ˈtab.blə]
         tauló allargat] 'long plank (lit. plank long)' [təw.ˈlo.ʎər.ˈɣat] rather than **[təw.ˈlo .ə.ʎər.ˈɣat]

In (4a–b), a word-initial [ə] corresponds to a stressed vowel in the base word. Elision is disfavoured. However, despite the stressed base *Alp* in (4c), elision takes place because **[ək.ˈto. əl.pi.ˈnis.tə] would fall foul of a LAPSE constraint against more than two moras intervening between the head syllables of prosodic words. (CLASH and LAPSE constraints together favour stress on alternate syllables.) Finally, hiatus is more likely after a monosyllabic major lexical item (5); though elision in (5b) shows that elision is reckoned better than a three-syllable lapse between stresses.

(5) a. *fi estranya* 'unusual end (lit. end unusual)' [ˈfi .əs.ˈtra.ɲə]
         té animals 'has animals' [ˈte .ə.ni.ˈmals]
         vi exquisit 'select wine (lit. wine select)' [ˈbi .əks.ki.ˈzit]
     b. *vi extraordinari* 'extraordinary wine (lit. wine extraordinary)'
         [ˈbiks.trəwr.ði.ˈna.ɾi]

6.2.1.2 Unstressed Non-high Vowel [ə] Followed by a Stressed Vowel

When a non-high unstressed vowel ([ə]) precedes a stressed one, as before, elision is blocked when a clash (one mora or none intervening) between phonological phrase heads would result, as in the examples of (6).

(6) *foca àrtica* 'arctic seal' ['fo.kə .'ar.ti.kə] (*foca*]$_N$ *àrtica*]$_A$)
rega arbres del jardí 'water.3SG.PRS.IND trees in the garden'
['rɛ.ɣə .'a.βɾəz .ðəl .ʒər.'ði] (*rega*]$_V$ *arbres*]$_N$ *del jardí*]$_{PP}$)
assenyalar-ne una 'point.out.INF one (of them)' [ə.sə.ɲə.'lar.nə .'u.nə]

Note that whereas hiatus between a preceding stressed low vowel and [ə] is highly disfavoured (cf. 1), when [ə] is *followed* by a stressed low vowel, hiatus is preferred to a stress clash.

When the first word is in specifier position, or is a preposition (thus not a phonological phrase head and not protected by CLASH constraints), elision is normal (7), reflecting the domination of ONSET over faithfulness constraints.

(7) *la primera hora* 'the first hour' [lə .pɾi.ˌme.'ɾɔ.ɾə]
onze anys 'eleven years' [ˌon.'zaɲs]
entre altres 'among others' [ˌen.'tɾal.tɾəs]

6.2.1.3 Contact between Unstressed Vowels

Having dealt with sequences of vowels one of which is stressed, we turn to contact between unstressed vowels. When unstressed vowels come into contact, the CLASH constraint is not relevant. Reducing two unstressed syllables to one unstressed syllable can never lead to a CLASH violation. However, reducing two unstressed syllables to one would often lead to a more harmonic outcome. In fact, when each of the adjacent vowels is [ə], elision/fusion is the regular result, as in *perdre alè* 'lose.INF breath' ['pɛr.ðɾə. 'lɛ], *escriptora aguda* 'penetrating writer.FEM (lit. writer penetrating)' [əs. kɾip.'to.ɾə.'ɣu.ðə], with elision/fusion reflecting the favouring of the antihiatus constraints over faithfulness.

When an unstressed high vowel ([i] or [u]) precedes an unstressed non-high vowel ([ə]), three possible outcomes need to be considered: hiatus ([i.ə], [u.ə]), a rising diphthong ([jə], [wə]), and elision of the non-high vowel [ə]. For each case, often two of the three alternatives occur in variation, while the third is ungrammatical. Where hiatus and a rising diphthong are both acceptable, hiatus generally belongs to a more formal or conservative style of pronunciation (reflecting relatively high ranking of constraints disfavouring glides in complex onsets, as also word-internally). When a non-high unstressed vowel ([ə]) precedes a high one, a falling diphthong ([əj], [əw]) or elision of [ə] are both possible. Bonet and Lloret (1998: 185) remark that elision is commoner, for example, in the Girona region than in the Barcelona region.

6.2.2 Elision in French

In Old and Middle French, word-final (unstressed) [ə] (later [œ]) was elided before a vowel-initial word, avoiding hiatus; the final [a] of the feminine singular definite article *la*, and the homophonous feminine singular direct object pronoun, were treated in the same way. In the case of the articles/pronouns, *le, la* 'the.M/FSG'; the personal pronouns *je* 'I', *se* 'self.3', *me* 'me', *te* 'you.SG'; the preposition *de* 'of, from'; the conjunction *que* 'that', the elision was, and is, represented with an apostrophe: *le + arbre → l'arbre* 'the tree', *la + étoile → l'étoile* 'the star', *me + embêter → m'embêter* 'annoy me (lit. me= annoy.INF)'; but elision will also always have occurred in, for instance, *quelque̸ obstacle* 'some obstacle'. No issue would have arisen, had word-initial /h/ not been lost in regular sound change, without the subsequent vowel-initial reflexes (8) triggering the expected elision of preceding [ə] (Burov 2012: 187–92; Tranel 1987: 93–96, 228f. – we retain Tranel's use of [r] rather than [ʁ] or [ʀ]).

(8)   *le hibou* 'the owl' [lœ .i.bu]
        la hauteur 'the height' [la .o.tœr]
        je hais 'I hate' [ʒœ .ɛ]
        se heurter 'to collide (lit. self= hit.INF)' [sœ .œr.te]
        quelque honte 'whatever shame' [kɛl.kœ .ɔ̃t]

At this stage of the language, elision has become lexicalized: it applies before most vowel-initial words, but not all. Hiatus after [œ] is no longer ungrammatical. Words that etymologically had no /h/- may be added to the exception list, e.g., *le onze août* [lœ .ɔ̃n.z ut] 'the 11th of August' (*onze* < UNDECIM); *le héros* [lœ .ero] (where the <h-> was merely orthographic already in Latin). As well as under-application of elision making it an opaque process, over-application does likewise: elision takes place in the case of most, but not all, words that begin with a glide (9).

(9)   a.   /j/: *n'avoir d'yeux que pour* 'to only have (lit. of) eyes for' [na.vwar. djø .kœ .pur]
             le match d'hier 'yesterday's match' [lœ. matʃ. djɛr]
             l'iode 'the iodine' [ljɔd]
   b.   /w/: *l'oiseau* 'the bird' [lwa.zo]
             l'ouate 'the cotton wool' [lwat]
             l'ouïe 'the hearing' [lwi]
             le vent d'ouest 'the west wind' [lœ vɛ̃. dwɛst]
             l'oindre 'to anoint him (lit. him= anoint.INF)' [lwɛ̃dr]
   c.   /ɥ/: *l'huile* 'oil' [lɥil]
             l'huître 'the oyster' [lɥitr]

Elision before some of the word types in (9) has a historical justification, in that they originally began with a falling, not a rising, diphthong: /oe/ in *oiseau*, /oï/ in *oindre*, /yj/ in *huile*; or with syllabic vowels in hiatus: /u.i/ in *ouïe*.

Others, though, are likely to have had a rising diphthong as soon as they had a diphthong at all: *yeux, hier*. Or a different interpretation might be that, at one stage of French, the sonority gradient from a glide to a vowel was not sufficient to count as a syllable onset. In any case, however, in modern French other glide-initial words, some but not all of which are recent borrowings, do not trigger elision (10):

(10) a. /j/: *le yaourt* 'yoghurt' [lœ .ja.ur(t)]
 le yogi 'the yogi' [lœ .jɔ.gi]
 b. /w/: *le watt* 'the watt' [lœ .wat] (N.B. minimal pair with *l'ouate* in 9b).
 le whisky 'whisky' [lœ .wis.ki]
 c. /ɥ/: *le huit* 'the 8' [lœ .ɥit]
 pour le huer 'in order to boo him' [pur .lœ .ɥe]

Both the vowel-initial words (8) and the glide-initial words (10) that reject elision are at least consistent in being treated as if they began with an onset consonant in other syntactic contexts in addition to these, namely, in rejecting liaison (Section 6.4.3.1), and in selecting the preconsonantal allomorphs of those words that have suppletive forms: *ce* rather than *cet* 'this', *les* [le] rather than [lez] 'the.PL', *du* rather than *de l'* 'of the', *vieux* rather than *vieil* 'old', etc. Nevertheless, 'being treated as if they began with a consonant' does not extend to rejecting resyllabification of a preceding word-final consonant as an onset ('*enchaînement*') (11).

(11) *le hasard* 'chance', but *par hasard* 'by chance' [pa .r a.zar]
 le hibou 'the owl', but *quel hibou* 'what owl' [kɛ .l i.bu]
 le onze 'the 11', but *deux mille onze* '2011' [dø .mi .l ɜz]

The morphologization/lexicalization of elision in French is the more remarkable given that the original distribution was so simply motivated on a straightforward markedness principle, and as its effect is so pervasive in incidence, in text and in the lexicon. Note in those varieties of French in which by general rule all final [œ] is lost except when the surrounding consonants cannot otherwise be syllabified, [œ] is retained before the anomalous initial vowels (8) and glides (10).

6.3 Inter-word Vowel–Consonant Contact: V.#C

The sandhi context V.#C is as unmarked as possible from the point of view of syllable structure. However, some Romance languages have an active lenition process in which initial consonants are treated the same as medial ones. Thus, in Galician, Spanish (but not Judaeo-Spanish, Hualde 2013: 243f.), Catalan, and south-western Occitan (Gascon and Lengadocian), voiced non-strident obstruents /b/, /d/, /g/ are pronounced as fricatives or approximants (β, ð, ɣ) between continuants (that is, vowels, glides, /r/, /ɾ/, /l/,

/ʎ/, /z/, /ʒ/), and pronounced as stops elsewhere. This areal phenomenon is shared with Basque.

(12) **Spanish**
 las bodas 'the weddings' [laz βoðas]
 la dicha 'happiness' [la ðitʃa]
 el gordo 'the fat one' [el ɣorðo]

The distribution of lenition here is markedly different from the earlier process affecting Latin obstruents in the transition to western Romance, when initial consonants were always preserved. The same kind of active lenition of /b/, /d/, /g/ is found also in Sardinian (see examples in 36), and there are comparable phenomena in several dialects of southern Italy; e.g., in Neapolitan /b/: [b] ~ [v], /d/: [d] ~ [ɾ], /g/: [g] ~ [ɣ] (Ledgeway 2009: 39). In Tuscan, also, while voiced obstruents may be variably lenited (with results as in south-western Romance just mentioned), voiceless stops are also lenited ('spirantized') in such contexts (13) giving rise to what is traditionally termed *gorgia toscana* 'Tuscan throat' (cf. Sorianello 2010).

(13) **Tuscan**
 la patata 'the potato' [la ɸaˈθaθa]
 la piega 'the fold' [la ˈɸjɛɣa]
 la tavola 'the table' [la ˈθavola]
 la crema 'cream, custard' [la ˈhɾɛma]

In south-western Romance the lenition alternations of voiced obstruents are automatic and sub-phonemic, and have no morphological consequences. The same would be true in the Italian and Sardinian varieties were it not for the fact that these varieties also attest *rafforzamento fonosintattico* (RF – see Section 6.4.3.2). In RF initial consonants are strengthened – typically geminated – after a lexical set of vowel-final words, a set which does not include the feminine singular definite article *la*. So we can find partly lexically conditioned morphological alternations such as (14).

(14) **Tuscan**
 in casa 'at home' [iŋ ˈkasa] – *la casa* 'the house' [la ˈhasa] – *da casa* 'from home' [da k.ˈkasa]

We consider this phenomenon (RF) more fully in the context of consonantal sandhi contacts C.#C.

6.4 Inter-word Consonant–Consonant Contact: C.#C

Only certain Romance languages have a large proportion of consonant-final words with a large variety of consonants. In standard Italian, and many Italian dialects (Ligurian, Venetian, and all those of the centre and south), few words are consonant-final. In Spanish and Portuguese there are somewhat more, though many consonants (obstruent stops, and labials) are excluded from final position. In the remainder, a wide range of word-final consonants occur.

6.4.1 Consonant Contacts in Majorcan Catalan

We consider first a case where allomorphic alternation in consonant-final words before initial consonants is both regular and extensive. The case is that of Majorcan Catalan, where a consonant of almost any place and manner can end a word; only voice contrast is neutralized in word-final position before a vowel or a pause (= citation form) (Bibiloni 2016: 152–69; Wheeler 2005: 207–49 with data from Dols 1993). First, final plosives and nasals are subject to place assimilation before a following consonant (15). (For /ɲ/ see below.)

(15)   Majorcan place (and voice) assimilation
    a. /p/ + /t/: *cap tros* 'no chunk' [ˌkat. ˈtrɔs]
        /p/ + /d/: *cap dit* 'no finger' [ˌkad. ˈdit]
        /p/ + /g/: *cap goma* 'no rubber' [ˌkag. ˈgomə]
        /t/ + /p/: *set parts* 'seven parts' [ˌsɛp. ˈpaɾs]
        /t/ + /b/: *set braços* 'seven arms' [ˌsɛb. ˈbrasos]
        /t/ + /k/: *set cases* 'seven houses' [ˌsɛk. ˈkazəs]
        /t/ + /g/: *set gàbies* 'seven cages' [ˌsɛg. ˈgaβis]
        /k/ + /p/: *puc passar* 'I can go by' [ˌpup. pəˈsa]
        /k/ + /b/: *puc beure* 'I can drink' [ˌpub. ˈbəwɾə]
        /k/ + /t/: *puc treure* 'I can take out' [ˌput. ˈtɾɛwɾə]
        /k/ + /d/: *puc dormir* 'I can sleep' [ˌpud. dorˈmi]
    b. /p/ + /s/: *cap sac* 'no bag' [ˌka. ˈtsak]
        /p/ + /z/: *cap zero* 'no zero' [ˌka ˈdzero]
        /p/ + /ʃ/ *cap xeringa* 'no syringe' [ˌka. tʃəˈɾiŋgə]
        /p/ + /ʒ/ *cap jardí* 'no garden' [ˌka. dʒəɾˈði]
        /k/ + /s/ *puc sortir* 'I can go out' [ˌpu. tsoɾˈti]
        /k/ + /z/ *duc zinc* 'I bring zinc' [ˌdu. ˈdziŋk]
        /k/ + /ʃ/ *puc xerrar* 'I can talk' [ˌpu. tʃəˈra]
        /k/ + /ʒ/ *puc jugar* 'I can play' [ˌpu. dʒuˈɣa]
    c. /n/ + /p/ *són petits* 'they are small' [ˌsom. pəˈtits] (= *som petits* 'we are small')
        /n/ + /b/ *són bons* 'they are good' [ˌsom. ˈbɔns] (= *som bons*)
        /n/ + /m/ *són molts* 'they are many' [ˌsom. ˈmols] (= *som molts*)
        /m/ + /t/ *som tots* 'we all are (lit. we.are all)' [ˌson. ˈtots] (= *són tots*)
        /m/ + /d/ *som dos* 'we are two' [ˌson. ˈdos] (= *són dos*)
        /m/ + /k/ *som quatre* 'we are four' [ˌsoŋ. ˈkwatɾə] (= *són quatre*)
        /m/ + /g/ *som grans* 'we are grown up' [ˌsoŋ. ˈgɾans] (= *són grans*)
        /m/ + /f/ *som feliços* 'we are happy' [ˌsoɱ. fəˈlisos] (= *són feliços*)
        /m/ + /v/ *som vius* 'we are alive' [ˌsoɱ. ˈviws] (= *són vius*)
        /m/ + /s/ *som set* 'we are seven' [ˌson. sɛt]
        /m/ + /l/ *som liberals* 'we are liberal' [ˌson. liβəˈrals]
        /m/ + /ʎ/ *som llests* 'we are clever' [ˌsonʲ. ˈʎets]
        /m/ + /n/ *som nous* 'we are new' [ˌson. ˈnows]

Obstruent stops and labiodental fricatives before labiodentals and sonorants are subject to place and manner assimilation (16). In (16c) the alveolar trill [r] is already reckoned a geminate, so is not duplicated in the transcription. In (16e) a final /f/, before a consonant, behaves just like a final /t/; only a selection of examples is given.

(16) a. /p/ + /f/ *cap flor* 'no flower' [ˌkaf. ˈflɔ]
/p/ + /v/ *cap vidre* 'no glass' [ˌkav. ˈviðrə]
/t/ + /f/ *set forats* 'seven holes' [ˌsɛf. ˈforats]
/t/ + /v/ *set vots* 'seven votes' [ˌsɛv. ˈvots]
/k/ + /f/ *sac foradat* 'bag with holes (lit. bag perforated)' [ˌsaf. forəˈðat]
/k/ + /v/ *puc venir* 'I can come' [ˌpuv. vəˈni]
b. /p/ + /l/ *cap licor* 'no liqueur' [ˌkal. liˈkor]
/p/ + /ʎ/ *cap lladre* 'no thief' [ˌkaʎ. ˈʎaðrə]
/t/ + /l/ *set làmines* 'seven plates' [ˌsɛl. ˈlaminəs]
/t/ + /ʎ/ *set lladres* 'seven thieves' [ˌsɛʎ. ˈʎaðrəs]
/k/ + /l/ *puc lamentar* 'I can complain' [ˌpul. ləmənˈta]
/k/ + /ʎ/ *puc llegir* 'I can read' [ˌpuʎ. ʎəˈdʒi]
c. /p/ + /r/ *cap rata* 'no rat' [ˌka. ˈratə]
/t/ + /r/ *set rates* 'seven rats' [ˌsɛ. ˈratəs]
/k/ + /r/ *puc riure* 'I can laugh' [ˌpu. ˈriwrə]
d. /p/ + /m/ *cap mà* 'no hand' [ˌkam. ˈma]
/p/ + /n/ *cap nin* 'no boy' [ˌkan. ˈnin]
/t/ + /m/ *set mans* 'seven hands' [ˌsɛm. ˈmans]
/t/ + /n/ *set nins* 'seven boys' [ˌsɛn. ˈnins]
/k/ + /m/ *puc mirar* 'I can look' [ˌpum. miˈra]
/k/ + /n/ *poc net* 'not very clean' [ˌpɔn. ˈnɛt]
e. /f/ + /p/ *agaf pomes* 'I pick apples' [əˌɣap. ˈpoməs]
/f/ + /t/ *agaf taronges* 'I pick oranges' [əˌɣat. təˈrɔnʒəs]
/f/ + /ʒ/ *agaf gelat* 'I choose ice cream' [əˌɣa. dʒəˈlat]
/f/ + /r/ *agaf roses* 'I pick roses' [əˌɣa. ˈrɔzəs]
/f/ + /m/ *agaf mores* 'I pick blackberries' [əˌɣam. ˈmorəs]
/f/ + /n/ *agaf nesples* 'I pick medlars' [əˌɣan. ˈnespləs]

There are some slightly unusual modifications in the case of word-final nasals. Before an alveolo-palatal sibilant, as well as assimilating place, /m/ and /n/ trigger affrication (17), a process also found word-internally. As seen in (15c), after a nasal there is no affrication of an alveolar sibilant.

(17) /m/ + /ʃ/ *hem xerrat* 'we have talked' [ˌənʲ. tʃəˈrat]
/m/ + /ʒ/ *som joves* 'we are young' [ˌsonʲ. ˈdʒovəs] (= *són joves*)
/n/ + /ʒ/ *en Joan* 'Joan'[2] [ənʲ. dʒuˈan]

In preconsonantal position the palatal nasal /ɲ/ splits into a palatal glide and a nasal that assimilates place (18).

---

[2] *En* is the 'personal article' used before masculine singular proper names.

(18) /ɲ/ + /d/ *lluny de tu* 'far from you' [ˌʎujn. də ˈtu]
/ɲ/ + /p/ *l'any passat* 'last year (lit. the year passed)' [ˌlajm. pəˈsat]
/ɲ/ + /k/ *any curt* 'short year (lit. year short)' [ˌajŋ. ˈkuɾt]

Internally, the same process is found before inflexional /s/, e.g., *estrenys* 'you.SG squeeze' [əsˈtɾəjns], which is anomalous in displaying a coda with three consonants, when Majorcan otherwise has a strict maximum of two consonants in a coda, so *camps* 'fields' (/kamp/ + /s/) is [ˈkans].

A final alveolo-palatal obstruent becomes a palatal glide before an initial consonant (19):

(19) /ʃ/ + C *peix frit* 'fried fish (lit. fish fried)' [ˌpej. ˈfɾit], *calaix petit* 'small drawer (lit. drawer small)' [kəˌlaj. pəˈtit]
/tʃ/ + C *vaig dir* 'I said (lit. go.AUX.1SG say.INF)' [ˌvaj. ˈði], *Puig Major* 'Great Hill (lit. hill great)' [ˌpuj. məˈʒo].

Final /s/ undergoes total assimilation before a liquid or a (palatal) glide (20a). Alveolar /s/ plus a sibilant merge as an affricate with the place of the onset consonant (20b). Before other voiced consonants /s/ becomes [ɾ] (20c). Before other voiceless consonants, /s/ is preserved.

(20) a. /s/ + /l/ *és logic* 'it is logical' [ˌəl. ˈlɔʒik]
/s/ + /ʎ/ *es llit* 'the bed' [ˌəʎ. ˈʎit]
/s/ + /r/ *ses rates* 'the rats' [ˌsə. ˈratəs]
/s/ + /j/ *es iogurt* 'the yoghurt' [ˌəj. joˈɣuɾt]
b. /s/ + /s/ *les set* 'seven o'clock' [lə. ˈtsɛt]
/s/ + /ʃ/ *es xat* 'the chat' [ə. ˈtʃat]
/s/ + /ʒ/ *dos joves* 'two young people' [ˌdo ˈdʒovəs]
c. /s/ + /b/ *és bo* 'it is good' [ˌəɾ. bɔ]
/s/ + /d/ *és dolent* 'it is bad' [ˌəɾ. ðoˈlent]
/s/ + /v/ *dus vi* 'you bring wine' [ˌduɾ. ˈvi]
/s/ + /m/ *és meu* 'it is mine' [ˌəɾ. mew]

Final liquids are largely resistant to modification before initial consonants, though /r/ variably assimilates to a following lateral: *per la casa* 'through the house': [pəl. lə ˈkazə] ~ [pəɾ. lə ˈkazə], *per llogar* 'for hire' [pəʎ. ʎoˈɣa] ~ [pəɾ. ʎoˈɣa].

Just to spell out again the degree of allomorphy these processes give rise to, *set* 'seven', for example, has the following 12 variants in the data given above: [sɛt, sɛp, sɛb, sɛk, sɛg, sɛf, sɛv, sɛl, sɛʎ, sɛr, sɛm, sɛn].

The Majorcan examples we have considered so far in this section have just one consonant in the word-final coda. Majorcan Catalan words can readily have complex codas with two consonants (not more), which are pronounced in phrase-final position, and before vowel-initial words, where the second coda consonant is resyllabified as an onset. Before a consonant-initial word, however, a coda must consist of at most one consonant.

That is, in Majorcan a pre-onset coda cluster constraint **CC]σC is active. The motivation is fundamentally perceptual. There are inadequate cues to the place and/or manner of a consonant, especially a stop, between two consonants. The context is somewhat less favourable than in a phrase-final CC cluster. Phrase-final clusters of CC]σ form are likely to be pronounced more emphatically, since phrase-final position is also that of nuclear stress, so there is likely to be more time for the speaker to achieve articulatory targets, and phrase-final position also allows more time for perception of the relatively weakly cued elements than in phrase-internal position.

The effect of this constraint in Majorcan is that deletion of a consonant from a coda cluster is quite extensive. In the general case, it is the middle consonant of the cluster CC.#C, the word-final one, that is deleted. Quite often this consonant realizes an inflexional morpheme. The remaining consonant is subject to the assimilation processes mentioned previously. The following examples (21) are taken in the main, again, from Bibiloni (2016).

(21) *plats grocs* 'yellow plates (lit. plates yellow)' [ˌplag.ˈgrɔts]
llocs deshabitats 'uninhabited places (lit. places uninhabited)' [ˌʎod. dəzəβiˈtats]
obr sa porta 'I open the door' [ˌɔ. tsə ˈpɔrtə]
ho arregl tot 'I arrange it all' [ˌə.w əˌret. ˈtot]
resolc problemes 'I solve problems' [rəˌzɔl. prɔbˈbleməs]
molts d'anys 'many years (lit. many of years)' [ˌmol. ˈdajns]³
ells canten 'they are singing' [ˌeʎ. ˈkantən]
porc negre 'black pig (lit. pig black)' [ˈpɔɾ. ˈnəɣɾə], cf. *porcs negres* 'black pigs (lit. pigs black)' [ˈpɔɾ. ˈnəɣɾəs]
temps de figues 'fig season (lit. time of figs)' [ˌten. də ˈfiɣəs]
ponts baixos 'low bridges (lit. bridges low)' [ˌpɔm. ˈbaʃos]
pens que sí 'I think so (lit. I think that yes)' [ˌpəŋ. kə ˈsi]
lluit sense por 'I fight without fear' [ˌʎuj. ˌsənsə ˈpɔ]

As in (18), /ɲ/ undergoes an unusual split so that both height and nasality are retained but sequenced (22a). The clusters /nk/⁴ and /nʃ/ (/nʒ/) are treated in the same way (22b).

(22) a. *anys difícils* 'difficult years (lit. years difficult)' [ˌajn. diˈfisils]
punys bruts 'dirty fists (lit. fists dirty)' [ˌpujm. ˈbruts]
b. *banc blau* 'blue seat (lit. seat blue)' [ˌbajm ˈblaw]
menj mel 'I eat honey' [ˌməjm. ˈmɛl]

---

[3] Note that here two underlying consonants are deleted, but *molts* is anyway [mols] in phrase-final position, by the general **CCC]σ constraint.

[4] Nicolau Dols and Gabriel Bibiloni (p.c.) inform us that /nk/ is not treated in this way where /k/ realizes an allomorph of 1SG.PRS.IND; here /k/ is simply deleted preconsonantally: *prenc nota* 'I take note' [ˌprənˈnotə], *venc llibres* 'I sell books' [ˌvənʲ. ˈʎiβrəs]. As far as we are aware, this is the only case in which a morphological consideration affects word-final consonant sandhi in Majorcan.

Whereas generally the outside consonant in a word-final cluster is lost, atypically, in the case of /-sC-/ clusters, and /-rn-/, the prefinal consonant goes. So we get forms as in (23).

(23) *he vist barques* 'I have seen boats' [eˌvib ˈbarkəs]
  bosc cremat 'burnt wood (lit. wood burnt)' [bɔk. krəˈmat]; *boscs cremats* 'burnt woods (lit. woods burnt)' [bɔk. krəˈmats]
  aquest nin 'this boy' [əˌken. ˈnin]
  gusts nous 'new flavours (lit. flavours new)' [ˌgun. ˈnɔws]
  carn freda 'cold meat (lit. meat cold)' [ˌkaɱ. frəðə]; *carns fredes* 'cold meats (lit. meats cold)' [ˌkaɱ. frəðəs]
  forn calent 'hot oven (lit. oven hot)' [ˌfoŋ. kəˈlent]

6.4.2 Consonantal Contact in Occitan

The treatment of C.#C sandhi in south-western Occitan (Gascon and western Lengadocian) is broadly similar to that in Majorcan Catalan (Burov 2012:204, 211, 230; Loporcaro 1997:73 n.). Here are some examples (24a–b).

(24) a. Aranese Gascon
  poc pan 'not much bread' [ˌpɔp. pan]
  eth pè 'the foot' [ɛp. ˈpɛ]
  eth mur 'the wall' [ɛm. ˈmyr]
 b. western Lengadocian
  lop gris 'grey wolf (lit. wolf grey)' [ˌlug. ˈgris]
  sèrp d'aiga 'water snake (lit. snake of water)' [ˌsɛr. ˈðajɣɔ]; cf. *sèrps d'aiga* 'water snakes (lit. snakes of water)' [ˌsɛr. ˈðajɣɔ]
  avèm pas de clients per la vendre 'we haven't clients to sell it to'
  [aˌβɛm. pa ðe kliˈem. per la ˈβendre]
  mieg nut 'half naked' [ˌmjɛn. ˈnyt]
  sap faire 'knows how to do' [ˌsaf. ˈfajre]
  taps longs 'long corks (lit. corks long)' [ˌtal. ˈluns]
  aquèl cat blanc dormís 'that white cat is asleep'
  [aˌkɛl. ˌkab. ˈblan. durˈmis]
  un còp me venguèt quèrre 'once she came to look for me' [yŋ.ˈkɔm. me βeŋˈgɛk. ˈkɛre]

A characteristic of eastern Lengadocian, shared with Provençal, is the simplification of geminates, internally and across boundaries. Hence an eastern Lengadocian variant of the last example of (24) would be [yŋ.ˈkɔ. me βeŋˈgɛ. ˈkɛre]. A significant consequence of this degemination process is that it derives allomorphs in which a word-final consonant is absent altogether. This is plausibly one of the routes by which other Occitan varieties, principally, Provençal, Lemosin, and Auvernhat, have lost all word-final obstruents, though Provençal retains /s/ after a stressed vowel and also inflexional /s/ marking second person singular, but not /s/ marking nominal plurals.

6.4.3 Lexicalization in C.#C Contacts

In the previous sections (6.4.1–2) we have described situations in which deletion in word-final codas is triggered by phonological context, namely, position before a consonant-initial word. We have not focused on the variants found in the other contexts, taking it for granted that, as is very generally the case, no deletion occurs there, though we could point out that, in Catalan and Occitan, voicing contrasts in final obstruents are neutralized everywhere: before vowels, as a rule, stops are voiceless and fricatives are voiced;[5] in phrase-final position, all obstruents are voiceless. We contrast this state of affairs with two cases in which original alternations in final-consonant words have become opaque, and lexicalized.

6.4.3.1 French *Liaison*

In French, *liaison* is the name given to the phenomenon whereby the final consonant (as represented by the orthography) of certain words is pronounced before vowel-initial words in certain contexts but not elsewhere. Which consonants, in which words, and in which contexts, is determined only to a small degree by phonological factors; the determining features are lexical, and partly morphological or syntactic. In this section, we attempt to give some account of how this situation came about. The original distribution – of alternants with and without final consonants – was determined, it is believed, by phonological context alone.

In old French, a word could end in any single consonant. A word could end in two consonants if the first was a nasal or /r/.[6] Modern French orthography generally reflects this state of the language: *champ* 'field', *plomb* 'lead', *font* 'source', *long* 'long', *vend* 'sells', though in modern French these words are open syllables [ʃɑ̃], [plɔ̃], [fɔ̃], [lɔ̃], [vɑ̃] (unusually a final consonant is retained, at least in phrase-final and prevocalic position, in *cinq* 'five' [sɛ̃k], and *donc* 'thus' [dɔ̃k]); *faubourg* 'suburb' [fobuʁ], *vert* 'green' [vɛʁ], *part* 'part' [paʁ], *porc* 'pig' [pɔʁ], *cerf* 'stag' [sɛʁ], *sers* 'serve.2SG. PRS.IND', (unusually both consonants are retained in *mars* 'March' [maʁs],

---

[5] The voicing of final (strident) fricatives before vowels is common to the western Romance languages that display word-final fricatives and have a voicing contrast in fricatives, i.e., Portuguese, Catalan, Occitan, French, Raeto-Romance, dialects of northern Italy, and Sardinian. Spanish and Galician will have shared this before merging voiced fricatives with voiceless fricatives generally.

[6] Other prefinal consonants had already been lost: coda /l/ was 'vocalized' (to [w]) and merged with the preceding vowel (UALET > *valt > vaut > [vo(t)] 'is worth'); preconsonantal /s/ was lost, at first lengthening the preceding vowel (GUSTU(M) > goust > goût 'taste'). A final nasal was lost after /r/ even before the orthography was fixed: CARNE(M) > chair 'flesh', UERME(M) > ver 'worm', FURNU(M) > four 'oven'.

Table 6.1. *French numeral allomorphy*

		_#C	_#V	_#||	Observations on redistribution
1	un	ɛ̃	ɛ̃.n	ɛ̃	
2	deux	dø	dø.z	**dø**	The _#C form is extended to the _#|| context, replacing *[døs].
3	trois	tʁwa	tʁwa.z	**tʁwa**	The _#C form is extended to the _#|| context, replacing *[tʁwas].
5	cinq	sɛ̃	sɛ̃.k	**sɛ̃k**	The _#V form is extended to the _#|| context, replacing [sɛ̃], cf. *tronc* 'trunk' [tʁɔ̃]. Some speakers extend [sɛ̃k] to the _#C context also.
6	six	si	si.z	sis	
7	sept	sɛt	sɛ.t	sɛt	The _#|| form is extended to the _#C context, replacing *[sɛ].
8	huit	ɥi	ɥi.t	ɥit	
9	neuf	**nœf**	nœ.f	nœf	*Neuf ans* '9 years' and *neuf heures* '9 o'clock' are pronounced with [nœ.v], doubtless original.[a] Before other words, beginning with vowels or consonants, the #|| form has been extended.
10	dix	di	di.z	dis	The _#|| form is extended to the preconsonantal context only in *dix-neuf* '19' [diznœf], with voice assimilation, and variably also in *dix-sept* '17' [di(s)sɛt].
20	vingt	vɛ̃	vɛ̃.t	**vɛ̃**	The _#C form is extended to the _#|| context, replacing [vɛ̃t]. However, [vɛ̃t] is used preconsonantally before other numerals: *ving*[t]*-deux* '22', *ving*[t]*-cinq* '25', *ving*[t]*-neuf* '29'.
100	cent	sɑ̃	sɑ̃.t	**sɑ̃**	As with *vingt*, the _#C form is extended to the _#|| context, replacing *[sɑ̃t].

[a] See n. 5.

ours 'bear' [uʁs], *parc* 'park' [paʁk], and variably *serf* 'serf' [sɛʁ(f)]). Morin (1986:168) proposes that, by late old French, word-final clusters were permitted only in phrase-final position, not before vowels. Between the twelfth and the sixteenth centuries, final consonants progressively disappeared, first in the weakest, preconsonantal coda position, then, generally, in phrase-final codas. Later, the range of contexts in which the remaining prevocalic alternants appeared began to shrink, giving the pattern of modern French liaison, grammatically and lexically conditioned. Morin (1986: 169) suggests that preconsonantal /s/ weakened to /h/, then remained as vowel lengthening, before disappearing altogether. This would parallel the historical treatment of preconsonantal /s/ within words.

The allomorphy of consonant-final numerals in modern French in Table 6.1 gives some idea of what the distribution may have been more generally in consonant-final words once a rule was introduced deleting a coda in preconsonantal position (cf. also Section 10.5.3). Even here, though, there has been a considerable amount of redistribution of allomorphs, short of complete levelling. We take it that the earlier regular distribution is that which can be observed for *un* '1', *six* '6', *huit* '8', and *dix* '10', that is, the final consonant is pronounced before a vowel (liaison context), and, except for /n/ (*un*), also in phrase-final position. The current distribution of allomorphs displays complex and inconsistent trends of analogical extension, and current variation indicates that the processes are ongoing. Although the trend with the French vocabulary as a whole has been in the direction of extending the range of the preconsonantal variants, that is, the vowel-final forms, contrary trends can be observed here, perhaps, due to the frequency of the phrase-final forms in counting.

Apart from the numerals *six*, *huit*, and *dix*, there are two other words that retain a prepausal form distinct from the preconsonantal form: *plus* 'more' [ply] _#C, [ply.z] _#V, and [plys] _#‖; and *tous* 'all.MPL' [tu] _#C, [tu.z] _#V, and [tus] _#‖.[7] In addition to the general patterns of liaison, to be considered shortly, a handful of other words retain allomorphs, now suppletive, that originated in sandhi alternations. *Œuf* 'egg' [œf] loses its [f] in the plural *œufs* [ø]; likewise, *bœuf* 'ox' [bœf] – *bœufs* [bø], *os* 'bone.SG' [ɔs], *os* 'bone.PL' [o]. Here the original preconsonantal allomorph occurred before plural /+s/, itself subsequently lost except in liaison environments; now [œf], [bœf], and [ɔs] have been extended to use word-finally before a consonant: *bœuf braisé* 'braised steak (lit. beef braised)', *os brisé* 'broken bone (lit. bone broken)'. *Beau* 'fine.MSG' [bo] has a prevocalic suppletive allomorph *bel* [bɛl], as in *un bel été* 'a beautiful summer', plural *beaux* [bo] ~ [bo.z]; and *vieux* 'old.MSG' [vjø] has a prevocalic allomorph *vieil* [vjɛ.j], as in *un vieil arbre* 'an old tree', plural *vieux* [vjø] ~ [vjø.z].

The conditions for the occurrence of liaison are outlined by Tranel (1987: 171) in the following words:

> The phonetic appearance of linking consonants is subject to various conditions that can be divided into four groups of factors: phonetic, syntactic, morphological, and stylistic. There is really only one absolute constraint concerning the appearance of linking consonants: it is of a phonetic nature. Liaison may occur only before a vowel-initial or a glide-initial word. Apart from this, liaison is an extremely variable phenomenon where stylistic factors combine with other factors to yield a considerable range of possibilities going from an extremely limited liaison system to a very dense one. As a rule, the more elevated the style, the more often liaison occurs; the more colloquial the style, the less often liaison occurs. Liaison also depends on the syntactic cohesion between words; the tighter the syntactic link between contiguous words, the more likely liaison is to occur; the looser the syntactic link between contiguous words, the less likely liaison is to occur. Finally, liaison tends to occur more readily if it signals a precise morphological mark (for example, the plural) than if it represents no particular grammatical information.

In contemporary standard French, liaison is almost entirely restricted to the consonants [n], [t], and [z], of which [t] and [z] often realize inflexional morphemes. Otherwise, there are just three words that may link final /ʁ/, two that may link final /p/, and one that may link final /g/ (25a–c) (Tranel 1987: 174f.).

---

[7] Many of the words that retain (prevocalic) liaison alternants belong to categories that are syntactically excluded from phrase-final position, such as, determiners, prenominal quantifiers, and prepositions.

(25) a. *léger* 'light': *un léger incident* 'a slight mishap' [ɛ̃ leʒe.ʁ ɛ̃sidɑ̃]
premier 'first': *au premier étage* 'on the first floor' [o pʁœmje.ʁ etaʒ]
dernier 'last': *un dernier avertissement* 'a final warning'
[ɛ̃ dɛʁnje.ʁ avɛʁtismɑ̃]
b. *trop* 'too (much)': *trop aimé* 'too much loved' [tʁo.p eme]
beaucoup 'much': *beaucoup aimé* 'much loved' [boku.p eme]
c. *long* 'long': *un long été* 'a long summer' [ɛ̃ lɔ̃.g ete]

In fact, in the case of *long* (25c), an archaic variant [lɔ̃k] – [ɛ̃ lɔ̃.k ete] – reflects the expected neutralization of voice (with stops realized voiceless) in word-final position. If it were not for the orthography, one might rather say that the feminine form of the adjective, *longue* [lɔ̃g], has taken the place of the masculine form in prenominal position (Morin 1986: 199). This distribution would thus parallel that found with *beau* 'fine' and *vieux* 'old' mentioned above, where the masculine prevocalic form is, in modern standard French, phonologically identical with the feminine form of the adjective.[8]

The syntactic contexts in which obligatory or preferred liaison takes place in standard French can be summarized as follows (after Tranel 1987: 189; Burov 2012: 155–58). The feature in common is close syntactic link with frequent collocation; but not all close syntactic links or frequent collocations demand liaison,[9] and liaison may be acceptable or preferred in some contexts not mentioned here.

(26) (i) In a noun phrase with a lexical noun, liaison occurs in the element or elements before it.
(ii) In a verb phrase, liaison occurs among the verb and the pronominal satellites around it, and among the pronouns themselves.
(iii) Liaison occurs with (most) monosyllabic prepositions, adverbs, and auxiliaries (*avoir/être* 'have/be') and their complements.
(iv) Liaison is standard in several fixed collocations.

(27) Examples of (26i):
un enfant 'a child' [ɛ̃.n ɑ̃fɑ̃], *aux étudiants* 'to the students' [o.z etydjɑ̃], *les autres enfants* 'the other children' [le.z otʁœ.z ɑ̃fɑ̃], *mes anciens étudiants* 'my old students' [me.z ɑ̃sjɛ̃.z etydjɑ̃]
ces instants 'these moments' [se.z ɛ̃stɑ̃], *quelques instants* 'a few moments' [kɛlkœ.z ɛ̃stɑ̃], *quelles affaires?* 'what matters?' [kɛl.z afɛʁ]
un gros arbre 'a thick tree' [ɛ̃ gʁo.z aʁbʁ], *de vieux amis* 'some old friends' [dœ vjø.z ami]

---

[8] *Bel* = *belle* [bɛl], *vieil* = *vieille* [vjɛj]; thus *long* = *longue* [lɔ̃g].
[9] For example, *quand* 'when' (relative adverb) takes liaison, *quand il travaille* 'when he is working' [kɑ̃.t il tʁavaj], but not *quand* 'when' (interrogative adverb), unless followed by *est-ce que*: *quand êtes-vous né?* 'when were you born?' [kɑ̃ ɛt vu ne], but *quand est-ce que vous êtes né* 'when were you born? [kɑ̃.t ɛskœ vu.z ɛt ne].

(28) Examples of (26ii):

ils arrivent 'they are arriving' [i.z aʁiv], *prends-en* 'take some' [pʁɑ̃.z ɑ̃], *nous en avons* 'we have some' [nu.z ɑ̃.n avɔ̃], *dont on a parlé* 'of which we spoke' [dɔ̃.t ɔ̃.n a paʁle], *vient-il?* 'is he coming?' [vjɛ̃.t il]

(29) Examples of (26iii):

dans un mois 'in a month' [dɑ̃.z ɛ̃ mwa], *en anglais* 'in English' [ɑ̃.n ɑ̃glɛ], *en écoutant* '(while) listening' [ɑ̃.n ekutɑ̃], *chez elle* 'at her house' [ʃe.z ɛl], *très intéressant* 'very interesting' [tʁɛ.z ɛ̃teresɑ̃], *moins autoritaire* 'less authoritarian' [mwɑ̃.z ɔtɔʁitɛʁ], *c'est impossible* 'it is impossible' [sɛ.t ɛ̃pɔsibl], *j'y suis allé* 'I went there' [ʒi sɥi.z ale].

(30) Examples of (26iv):

accent aigu 'acute accent' [aksɑ̃.t egy], *nuit et jour* 'night and day' [nɥi.t e ʒuʁ], *États-Unis* 'United States' [eta.z yni], *tout à coup* 'all of a sudden' [tu.t a ku], *de haut en bas* 'from top to bottom' [dœ o.t ɑ̃ bɑ], *de temps en temps* 'from time to time' [dœ tɑ̃.z ɑ̃ tɑ̃].

If the sketch of historical development given above is correct, in the French of ca. 1500, all consonant-final words will have had at least two variants – one before vowel-initial words, retaining the final consonant, and one before consonant-initial words lacking it. In later French, aside from the cases where liaison retains a prevocalic allomorph, one or other of the alternatives has been extended to all contexts. More often than not such an invariant form is the one with deletion of the original (old French) final consonant, but in many particular cases the consonant is retained. A few contrasting pairs are given in (31). The unpredictability is greatest among nouns; verbs and adjectives nearly always lost a final consonant. In words borrowed or formed in French after the Renaissance, an orthographic final consonant is generally pronounced.

(31) *broc* 'pitcher' [bʁo]   *bloc* 'block' [blɔk]
      clerc 'clerk' [klɛʁ]   *turc* 'Turk, Turkish' [tyʁk]
      clef 'key' [kle]   *nef* 'nave' [nɛf]
      nerf 'nerve' [nɛʁ]   *serf* 'serf' [sɛʁf] (or [sɛʁ])
      encens 'incense' [ɑ̃sɑ̃]   *sens* 'meaning' [sɑ̃s]
      tas 'pile' [ta]   *as* 'ace' [as]
      avis 'opinion' [avi]   *vis* 'screw' [vis]
      chaos 'chaos' [kao]   *rhinocéros* 'rhinoceros' [ʁinɔseʁɔs]
      sot 'stupid' [so]   *dot* 'dowry' [dɔt]
      chat 'cat' [ʃa]   *mat* 'matt' [mat]
      goût 'taste' [gu]   *août* 'August' [ut] (or [u])
      début 'beginning' [deby]   *brut* 'rough' [bʁyt], *but* 'goal' [byt] (or [by])

6.4.3.2 Initial Geminates from Coda Assimilation: *Rafforzamento Fonosintattico*

A striking morphophonological characteristic of central and southern Italo-Romance varieties (including standard Italian) and of Sardinian is the gemination, or strengthening, of initial consonants after specified vowel-final words (*rafforzamento*, or *raddoppiamento*, *(fono)sintattico* '(phono)syntactic strengthening/doubling', abbreviated here as RF; Marotta 2010), e.g., It. *da casa* 'from home' [da k.ˈkasa] vs *la casa* 'the house'[la ˈkasa] (cf. also Sections 1.2.2.4, 7.4.2).[10] The origin of this phenomenon is clear enough (Loporcaro 1997): the set of vowel-final words that trigger RF incudes those that, in Latin, (i) ended in a consonant, and (ii) were monosyllabic. A few of these are unstressed, and proclitic (32a). Compounds whose final part is one of these also trigger RF (32b).

(32) a. *a* < AD 'to': It. *a lui* 'to him' [a l.ˈlui]; Nap. *a Napule* 'to Naples' [a n.ˈnapulə][11]
che < QUID × QUOD 'that': *dice che vuole* 'she says she wants to' [ˈditʃe ke v.ˈvwɔle]; *i bambini che vedi* 'the children that you see' [i bamˈbini ke v.ˈvedi]
da < DE+AB: *da me* 'from me' [da m.ˈme], *da fare* 'to do' [da f.ˈfare]
e < ET 'and': *eppure* < *e + pure* 'and yet' [ep.ˈpure]
né < NEC 'neither/nor': *né caldo né freddo* 'neither hot nor cold' [ne k.ˈkaldo ne f.ˈfreddo]
o < AUT 'either/or': *ossia* < *o + sia* 'that is to say (lit. or be.it)' [os.ˈsia]
se < post-Imperial Lat. SED < SI × QUID (Loporcaro 197: 27): *se puoi* 'if you can' [se p.ˈpwɔj]
b. *come* < QUOMODO+ET 'like, as': *come noi* 'like us' [ˌkome n.ˈnoj]
qualche < QUALE+QUID 'some': *qualche giorno* 'some day' [ˌkwalke d.ˈdʒorno]; Nap. *quacche libbro* 'some book' [ˌkwakkə l.ˈlibbrə]

Others of the original triggers are stressed words (33). With a similar effect are some original consonant-final words that became monosyllabic by aphaeresis within Romance: *là* < (IL)LAC 'there', *lì* < (IL)LIC 'there', *qua* < (EC)CUM HAC 'here', *qui* < (EC)CUM HIC 'here', *ciò* < ECCE HOC 'this', e.g., Nap. *llà sotto* 'down there' [ˌlla s.ˈsottə].

(33) *che* < QUID: *che dite?* 'what are you saying?' [ˌke d.ˈdite]
dà < DAT: *dà molto* 'gives a lot' [ˈda m.ˈmolto]
di' < DIC: *dimmi* 'tell me'
è < EST: *è vero* 'it is true' [ˌɛ v.ˈvero]
fa' < FAC: *fammi un favore* 'do me a favour'
più < PLUS: *più morto che vivo* 'more dead than alive' Flo. [ˌpju m.ˈmɔrto he v.ˈvivo]; Nap. *cchiù doppo* lit. 'more after (= later)' [kˌkju d.ˈdoppə]

---

[10] Consonants that are inherently long/geminate in Italian: /ɲ/ [ɲ.ɲ], /ʎ/ [ʎ.ʎ], /ʃ/ [ʃ.ʃ], /ts/ [t.ts], /dz/ [d.dz] are unaffected, as is /s/ in an initial cluster /sC-/. Gemination by RF is noted orthographically only in cases of 'univerbation', where two originally separate words are conventionally written as one, as with *eppure*, *ossia*, in (32a). Though Italian linguists generally transcribe the long or geminate consonants with [ː] we prefer to write [C.C], which reveals the syllable structure. We do not mark vowel length: by default, a vowel in an open syllable before a consonant onset is long, otherwise short.
[11] Neapolitan examples are from Ledgeway (2009: 40–48).

sì < SIC 'thus'; *così* < (EC)CUM SIC 'so': *così male* 'so bad' [ko͜si m.ˈmale], *cosiddetto* 'so-called'

sta < STAT: *sta bene* 'it is good' [ˌsta b.ˈbɛne]

tre < TRES: *tre cani* 'three dogs' [ˌtre k.ˈkani]

At an early stage, a Latin final consonant in such contexts became totally assimilated to a following onset consonant. In Classical Latin this process was represented orthographically in the items listed here only with AD as a prepositional prefix: AD + FIGERE → AFFIGERE 'to attach', AD + SUMERE → ASSUMERE 'to take on'. But inscriptional evidence from the Imperial period confirms that the process was more widespread (Loporcaro 1997: 42, 121): <at tuos> for AD TUOS 'to(wards) your', <sud die> for SUB DIE 'just before/ just after the day'. In proto-Italo-Romance, in Loporcaro's interpretation (1997: 121) there will have been paradigms such as (34).

(34) a. _#C b. _#V c. _#‖
 /ˈdat#ˈpane/ 'gives bread' /ˈdat#ˈakwa/ 'gives water' /ˈnon#ˈdat/ 'does not give'
 [ˈda p.ˈpane] [ˈda(t) ˈakwa] [ˈnon ˈda(t)]

The evidence suggests that Latin word-final consonants were retained long enough in monosyllables, or the few stressed finals in polysyllables, to trigger RF effects, while word-final consonants elsewhere had already been deleted in Italo-Romance. The special status of monosyllables in this respect is consistent with what is observed more widely in Romance with Latin final <m> or <n>, which are often preserved in Romance as /n/, and lost elsewhere; e.g., It. *non* < NON 'not', *son(o)* < SUM 'I am', Sp. *quien*, Rom. *cine* < QUEM 'who(?)', Fr., Cat. *ton* < *tum < TUUM 'your.2SG', Occ. *ren*, Fr. *rien* < REM 'nothing', Sp. *tan* < TAM 'so'; but It. *nome*, Cat., Occ. *nom* < NOMEN 'name', It. *sciame*, Cat. *eixam* < EXAMEN 'swarm', and no sign of Latin final <m> in polysyllables.[12] When word-final consonants are deleted in contexts such as (34b, 34c), the geminate in contexts such as (34a) remains as a relic. It is no longer recoverable by speakers why *a* 'to, at', *se* 'if' and the other words of (32) and (33) trigger RF, but, for example, *di* 'of' < DE, *mi/me* < ME 'me', *ti/te* < TE 'you.2SG', *si/se* < SE '3.REFL.', *la* 'DEF.FSG' do not. (However, *e* 'and' retains a prevocalic variant *ed* in some contexts, e.g., It. *titoli ed esami* 'titles and examinations', and *a* 'to, at' a variant *ad*: *passare ad altro* 'change the topic (lit. pass.INF to other)'; other items with consonant-final variants are to be found in some Italo-Romance varieties: archaic Italian *o ~ od* 'or', *che ~ ched* 'that'.)

In Italo-Romance, the present tense paradigms of *dare* 'give', *stare* 'stand', *fare* 'do', *avere* 'have', *sapere* 'know', and *andare* 'go', influence one another

---

[12] However, IAM 'already' loses its nasal in all Romance varieties: Sp. *ya*, Fr *(dé)jà*, so Loporcaro may not be correct to include It. *già* among 'today's doubling monosyllables which can be traced back to a consonant-final etymon' (1997: 49).

in analogical reformations, giving rise to 3SG monosyllabic forms *fa* (as if from **fat*, for FACIT), *ha* (as if from **(h)at*, for HABET), *sa* (as if from **sat*, for SAPIT), and *va* (as if from **vat*, for VADIT), triggering RF just like the models *dà* (< DAT) and *sta* (< STAT). The fact that *ha* is one of the early RF triggers has an important morphological consequence through its role in forming the future tense, as in *farà* 'will do.3SG' (*fare* + *ha* 'do.INF has'), *andrà* 'will go.3SG' (*andare* + *ha* 'go.INF has'), *finirà* 'will finish.3SG' (*finire* + *ha* 'finish.INF has'). In our interpretation of the historical sequence of events, the third person singular future form contributes to expanding the set of RF triggers beyond monosyllables to include polysyllables with stressed final vowels.[13] Hence in standard Italian (35):

(35) *andrò piano* 'I will go slowly' [anˌdrɔ p.ˈpjano], *caffè forte* 'strong coffee (lit. coffee strong)' [kafˌfɛ f.ˈfɔrte], *città bella* 'beautiful city (lit. city beautiful)' [tʃitˌta b.ˈbɛlla]

In standard Italian, a further consequence is an almost complete remotivation of RF on phonological grounds: in this variety, RF is triggered by (a) all words with a stressed final vowel (including originally vowel-final monosyllables: *sto male* 'I am unwell' [ˌstɔ m.ˈmale]), and (b) the small original list of unstressed items (32), to which a handful of others with an unstressed final vowel are added, apparently through analogies which are not wholly clear: *ma* 'but' (< MAGIS), *tra* < INTRA and *fra* < INFRA 'between, within',[14] *sopra* 'above' < SUPRA, *contra* 'against' < CONTRA, and *dove* 'where' < DE + UBI. Southern Italo-Romance and Sardinian varieties lack this remotivation; in these, RF is triggered almost exclusively by words that had a final consonant in Latin. But since the lexical division is opaque, the list of trigger words can vary markedly between dialects, as items are analogically added to or removed from the list (Loporcaro 1997: 72–117). Or the remotivation is itself undermined by sound change: in Tuscan, word-final stressed diphthongs lose their glide element, but fail to trigger RF as other final stressed monophthongs do, giving e.g., Flo. *vorrei parlare* 'I would like to speak' [vorˈrɛ ɸarˈlare] alongside *vorrà parlare* 'she will want to speak' [vor.ˈra p.parˈlare] (Loporcaro 1997: 11).

The status of RF is somewhat different in Italo-Romance varieties of the far south of the peninsula and Sardinian, where, alongside vowel-final RF triggers such as *a* 'to, at', *e* 'and', *né* 'neither', corresponding to those in Italian, 3SG verb forms retain allomorphs with reflexes of Latin final <t>. Hence we may find alternations such as these (36a) in Logudorese Sardinian (Contini 1986: 531, from Nughedu, except the first example from Berchidda). And in Sardinian reflexes of plural -<s> are retained also,

---

[13] Alongside oxytone compounds formed within Italo-Romance such as *perché* 'why, because', *sicché* 'so that'.
[14] Loporcaro (1997: 24) includes *tra* and *fra* among words having a Latin final consonant, though he does not offer etyma, and they are usually traced to INTRA and INFRA.

where intervocalic [z] alternates with RF (36b). Note the grammaticalization of the contrast between lenition and RF to mark nominal number in (36c).[15]

(36) a. e b.ˈbenniðu 'he came'   ˈbenniðu ˈɛstɛ? 'did he come?'
fi p.pasˈtɔrɛ 'he was a shepherd'   pasˈtɔrɛ ˈviði? 'was he a shepherd?'
a s.siˈɣið a f.faeɖˈḍarɛ 'he continued speaking'   siˈɣiðu ˈaða? 'did he continue?'
ˈfaɣɛ t.ˈtempu m.ˈmalu 'the weather is bad'   ˈtempu m.ˈmalu ˈvaɣɛðɛ 'is the weather bad?'
b. ˈdua f.ˈfeminaza 'two women'   ˈsun ˈduaza 'they are two.FEM'
ˈbattɔ k.ˈkanɛzɛ 'four dogs'   ˈsun ˈbattɔrɔ
sɔˈz annɔzɔ 'the years'
c. sa t.ˈtanka d.dɛ anˈtoni 'Antoni's properties'   sa ˈðanka ðɛ anˈtoni 'Antoni's property'

Like French liaison, Italo-Romance RF illustrates how quite straightforward, phonologically well-motivated, sandhi phenomena can become opaque, and then suffer analogical lexical readjustments. In addition, in the standard Italian case, one might well say RF is linguistically superfluous. Speakers of standard Italian from those areas (northern Italy) whose local varieties lack RF tend to ignore it, without problems of comprehension, or of social stigma.

6.4.3.3 Aspiration of /s/ in Andalusian Spanish

In this respect it is illustrative to analyse the current changes under way in Andalusian Spanish due to the historical aspiration of /s/ in a coda. Currently this aspiration is mostly no longer present in C#|| contexts (*más* [ma] 'more') given its low perceptual salience and its potential to be confused with breathy voice which usually occurs at the end of utterances (O'Neill 2005). Aspiration appears more consistently in .C#V contexts, depending on the variety (e.g., *más agua* 'more water' [ma.ˈh a.ɣwa]). In C#.C contexts aspiration can modify the manner of articulation of following consonants and produce novel phonemic contrasts (O'Neill 2010). The developments from s#.C are generally that, in eastern varieties, all following consonants except fricatives are geminated, and voiceless stops are aspirated also. In western varieties the same holds true but the elongation of the consonants is much less (for the aspirated voiceless stops it is only variably present) and the consonants can be pronounced with breathy voice (nasals) or frication (laterals and spirants). While these changes are attested both within and between words (*caco* 'thief' [ˈka.ko], *casco* 'helmet' [ˈka.kʰo]; *dos comiendo* 'two (people) eating' [ˌdo. kʰo.ˈmjen̥].

---

[15] Note paragoge in phrase-final position in these examples, alternating with RF of a following initial consonant. Thus *cantat* 'sing.3SG' has three sandhi variants: [ˈkanta.ð] before a vowel, [ˈkanta] +RF before a consonant, and [ˈkantaða] before a pause (Loporcaro 1997: 114).

d̪o]), some interesting developments are occurring in the city of Seville. Certain lexical items (e.g., *más* 'more' and *dos* 'two') show consistent phonetic cues of aspiration for orthographic <s> across words, but such cues are only variably present after the plural marker (*perro* 'dog' vs *perros* 'dogs') and totally absent after the second person singular marker in the verb (*come* 'he eats' vs *comes* 'you eat'; see O'Neill in prep.). The phonological effects appear to be becoming opaque and lexicalized (*comiendo* 'eating' [ko.ˈmjen̪.d̪o], *dos comiendo* 'two (people) eating' [ˌd̪o. kʰo.ˈmjen̪.d̪o], *¿vienes comiendo?* 'are you eating now?' [ˌbje.ne. ko.ˈmjen̪.d̪o], *niños comiendo* 'children eating', mainly [ˌni.ɲo. ko.ˈmjen̪.d̪o] but also [ˌni.ɲo. kʰo.ˈmjen̪.d̪o]). Moreover, there is some evidence (Pons-Rodríguez in prep.) that, in the verb, post-aspiration is being morphologized (*¿qué comes?* 'what are you eating?' [ˌke. ˌkʰo.me] vs *¿qué come?* 'what is she eating?' [ˌke. ˈko.me]). This must have its origin in analogy with nouns in which the phonological sandhi effects may also be becoming morphologized (*el caco* 'the thief' [el. ˈka.ko], *los cacos* 'the thieves' [lo. ˈkʰa.ko]). The evidence for Andalusian Spanish is only preliminary and variable, but there are parallels with French liaison and especially Italo-Romance RF mentioned previously; the textual and lexical incidence of these phenomena remains very pervasive.

Selected References

Below you can find selected references for this chapter. The full references can be found online at the following page: www.cambridge.org/Romancelinguistics

Burov, I. (2012). *Les Phénomènes de sandhi dans l'espace gallo-roman*. Doctoral thesis, Université Michel de Montaigne – Bordeaux III, Bordeaux. https://tel.archives-ouvertes.fr/tel-00807535.
Contini, M. (1986). 'Les phénomènes de sandhi dans le domaine sarde'. In Andersen, H. (ed.), *Sandhi Phenomena in the Languages of Europe*. Berlin: Mouton de Gruyter, 519–50.
Dols Salas, N. A. (1993). *The Predictive Formalization of Consonantal Contacts in Majorcan Catalan (Empirical and Theoretical Bases)*. MPhil thesis, Department of Hispanic Studies, University of Sheffield.
Encrevé, P. (1988). *La Liaison avec et sans enchaînement: phonologie tridimensionnelle et usage du français*. Paris: Le Seuil.
Hualde, I. (2013) 'Intervocalic lenition and word-boundary effects', *Diachronica* 30(2): 232–66.
Lloret, M.-R. and Jiménez, J. (2007). 'Prominence-driven epenthesis: evidence from Catalan'. Ms. www.academia.edu/5683215/.
Loporcaro, M. (1997). *L'origine del radoppiamento fonosintattico. Saggio di fonologia diacronica romanza*. Basel/Tübingen: Francke.

Marotta, G. (2010). 'Raddoppiamento sintattico'. In Simone, R., Berruto, G., and D'Achille, P. (eds), *Enciclopedia dell'italiano*. www.treccani.it/enciclopedia/raddoppiamento-sintattico_%28Enciclopedia-dell%27Italiano%29/.

Morin, Y.-C. (1986). 'On the morphologization of word-final consonant deletion in French'. In Andersen, H. (ed.), *Sandhi Phenomena in the Languages of Europe*. Berlin: Mouton de Gruyter, 167–210.

Sampson, R. (2010). *Vowel Prosthesis in Romance. A Diachronic Study*. Oxford: Oxford University Press.

Sorianello, P. (2010) 'Gorgia toscana'. In Simone, R., Berruto, G., and D'Achille, P. (eds), *Enciclopedia dell'italiano*. www.treccani.it/enciclopedia/raddoppiamento-sintattico_%28Enciclopedia-dell%27Italiano%29/.

Wheeler, M. W. (2005). *Phonology of Catalan*. Oxford: Oxford University Press.

7

Effects of Stress

Judith Meinschaefer

7.1 Introduction

This chapter sets out to explore the effects of word stress on linguistic structure, effects which are visible in a variety of ways, at the level of sound structure as well as morphosyntactic structure, in synchrony as well as in diachrony. By stress, we understand more generally, as Gordon and van der Hulst (2020: 65) put it, 'increased prominence on one or more syllables in a word'. Prominence, in turn, is a perceptual term, relating to perceived 'strength' of a syllable in a word, or, again in a more general perspective, of a linguistic unit in the context of surrounding linguistic units. Within a broader theory of cognition, prominence may be considered the result of metrical structure, in music just as in language (Fitch 2013). According to Fitch, metrical structure or 'meter' relates to the categorization of events (be they linguistic or musical or of yet another quality) as strong or weak within a hierarchical tree structure consisting of heads and non-heads (Fitch 2013). The broader term 'metrical structure' is meant to encompass both effects of prominence and of non-prominence, as well as effects of metrical constituency. The effects of stress are almost ubiquitous in language, and this is what this article sets out to show. In what follows, we will consider the linguistic effects of metrical structure on various levels of linguistic structure.

While stress, or prominence, is abstract, in language it is embodied in sound substance. It is thus to be expected that many of its effects, and possibly its most visible effects, will be at the level of sound structure. In general, stressed syllables are produced with greater articulatory effort, hence they have a higher fundamental frequency or pitch, a longer duration and a greater amplitude or loudness (Dogil and Williams 1999; Fletcher 2010; Gordon and Roettger 2017). In Romance there is no evidence that the phonetic effects of stress present systematic differences with respect to other well-studied languages. Rather, the differences with respect to other linguistic families lie in the relative importance of the cues. In Romance, pitch appears to be the most important cue (e.g., Ortega-Llebaria and Prieto 2011), in contrast to the greater importance of intensity in Germanic languages (Fry 1955; Lieberman 1960). Although phonetic and phonological effects of stress are sometimes difficult to dissociate, in the present article we focus on phonology and morphosyntax, and do not systematically consider the phonetic effects of stress. These brief explanations about phonetic correlates of stress shall suffice; they serve as a background for the description of the phonological and morphosyntactic effects of stress that are the main topic of this article.

Yet another dimension of stress, namely that of rhythm, is likewise not considered here. The definition of metrical structure given above appears closely related to what is understood as 'contrastive rhythm' by some scholars, i.e., as the timing and grouping of sequences of stronger or weaker phonetic elements (Nolan and Jeon 2014). The term rhythm is also used to refer to secondary stress, a phenomenon much less studied than primary, or word stress. In recent decades many studies have been conducted on rhythmic properties of Romance languages in particular. Still, since much of this research focuses on gradient, stochastic, non-symbolic properties of sound structure, it will not be considered here. To date, whether rhythm defined in this way, which is clearly relevant for language acquisition and speech processing, has effects on linguistic structure as well, remains to be studied.

This article deals, first, with synchronic phonological and morpholexical phenomena in Romance languages and varieties that are conditioned by prominence or – more generally speaking – metrical structure. Some of these are exceptionless and automatic, but many others have already reached a stage of being lexicalized or morphologized to some degree. As a linguistic system evolves, a gradual loss of the conditioning context may eventually lead to diachronic change, either in the form of change of individual formatives (lexicalization/morphologization) or as change in the system (e.g., as change in inventories). Here, we also deal with this second type of effect of stress, visible in the diachrony of a linguistic system, while trying to distinguish between synchronic phonological effects on surface forms, i.e., systematic alternations, and diachronic effects on underlying representations, i.e., on linguistic inventories and systems, as far as this is possible.

An introduction to the basic tenets of metrical and prosodic theory which serve as the background for the following explanations as well as a brief description of assignment of word stress in Romance are given in Section 7.2. Phonological effects of stress are considered in Section 7.3, discussing effects of prominence first (Section 7.3.2), followed by effects of non-prominence (Section 7.3.3) and effects of metrical constituent structure (Section 7.4). How effects of stress shape the form of words is dealt with in Section 7.5.

7.2 Metrical Structure, Stress Assignment, and the Prosodic Hierarchy

7.2.1 Introduction

In this section we briefly sketch the basic tenets of metrical and prosodic theory as well as a few basic assumptions about word stress assignment in Romance languages and varieties. Romance data have figured prominently in the recent history of this field of research, beginning with Harris' early work on Spanish word stress (Harris 1973; 1983), Selkirk's analyses of French liaison (Selkirk 1972; 1974), and Nespor's and Vogel's studies on various phenomena of Standard Italian (Nespor and Vogel 1979; 1986; Vogel 1982). Reviews may be found in Selkirk (2011) and Elfner (2018).

7.2.2 Prosodic Structure

Prosodic structure, of which 'metrical structure' in its common understanding is just one sub-domain, is based on hierarchically organized constituency, in the same way as syntax. Stress, or 'prominence', is one of the crucial relations holding between prosodic constituents: some are 'stronger' than others. In fact, in most current frameworks prosodic structure can be inferred from syntactic structure, but it can at the same time be non-isomorphic to morphosyntactic structure, because constraints on phonological well-formedness interfere with requirements of isomorphism to syntax.

According to standard assumptions of prosodic hierarchy theory, the prosodic structure of natural language is structured on various levels that are stratified as depicted in (1).

(1) The prosodic hierarchy
    a.   Intonational phrase   ι
    b.   Phonological phrase   φ
    c.   Prosodic word   ω   ('π ... π) or (π ... 'π)
    d.   Foot   π   (σ σ) or (μ μ)
    e.   Syllable   σ   L(ight) – μ or H(eavy) – μμ
    f.   Mora   μ

The term 'stress' can refer to prominence relations on different levels of the prosodic hierarchy. Relevant for the present discussion are prominence relations (i) between elements of a foot, (ii) between feet in the prosodic word, and (iii) between the prosodic words in a phrase. The elements of a foot may be syllables or morae. By the term mora we understand those syllabic constituents that determine syllable weight: light syllables have one mora, heavy syllables have two; a short vowel weighs one mora, a long one two, and a coda consonant also weighs one mora. Feet whose prominence is leftmost are termed trochaic ('xx), and feet with rightmost prominence are termed iambic (x'x). The prominence relations between the feet in a (prosodic) word determine the location of word stress. Phrasal stress, in contrast, results from the prominence relations between the (prosodic) words in a phrase. The layers of metrical structure relevant to the present discussion are the layers of word, foot, and syllable or mora. Two of these layers on which prominence itself has been traditionally considered as especially important are the word and the phrase.

The assignment of prominence at the word level, i.e., of word stress, is not only based on the segmental and syllabic structure of the word, but interacts with its morphosyntactic structure, such as morphological boundaries and sometimes even with specific morphosyntactic features such as person, number, or lexical category. Prominence assignment at the phrase level, in turn, i.e., phrasal stress, cannot be computed directly from word-level prominence, but depends crucially on the information structure of a sentence. In this article, we focus on the first aspect, i.e., word stress. Research on phrasal stress is a relatively new phenomenon, but for the last few decades phrasal stress has been a very dynamic field of research. In the next section, we briefly consider regularities in the assignment of prominence in these two domains, before we proceed to look at the effects of stress on phonological and morpholexical structure.

7.2.3 Word Stress

Whether word stress in individual Romance languages is assigned in a rule- or constraint-based fashion or whether it is a lexical feature of individual forms, learned on an item-by-item basis in the course of language acquisition, continues to be a controversial issue, at least for certain languages (cf. also Section 5.6). Just to give an example, while most analyses of Spanish stress assume that there is a least some degree of regularity which can be captured in a formal mechanism, evidenced by a large body of research to which we come back below, a substantial number of scholars have claimed for Italian that word stress is largely lexicalized (e.g., Burzio 1994; Burzio and DiFabio 1994; Mazzola 1997; Bafile 1999; Marotta 1999; Giraudo and Montermini 2010; Loporcaro 2011b: 79). As for French, whether or not it has word stress at all, or only phrasal stress, continues to be the subject of controversy; cf. Bosworth (2017) and Özçelik (2017) for two recent – and controversial – analyses. As shown in the present chapter, Romance word stress has a variety of effects that go beyond the marking of prominence, an observation that holds not only for Spanish, but also for French and in particular for Italian, where we find complex processes of segment lengthening that are evidently conditioned by stress. It is an often-cited argument that such effects can be explained much better by the assumption that word stress is governed by rules or constraints and, in particular, that its assignment is based on metrical structure, rather than, for example, on the assignment of diacritic accent marks which merely indicate the stressed syllable.

The Latin stress system is well described in its details and has been the object of a variety of theoretical analyses (Mester 1994; Jacobs 1997; 2003a; 2003b; 2015; Kostakis 2017). In Latin, stress is predictable from segmental structure. It is generally uncontroversial that Classical Latin assigned stress to the penult (last syllable but one) or antepenult according to the weight of the penult (Kent 1932: 66; Allen 1973: 155). If the penult is heavy, it is stressed; if it is light, the antepenult is stressed. A syllable in Latin is heavy if it contains a long vowel or a coda consonant; otherwise, it is light. A final syllable is (almost) never stressed in words with more than one syllable (cf. Kent 1932: 66; Allen 1965: 85 for some exceptions), an observation that is generally accounted for by the assumption that in Latin the final syllable was extrametrical, i.e., invisible to the rules of stress assignment.

There has been much research on certain Romance languages, such as Spanish (cf. Hualde 2012 for an overview), and Italian (D'Imperio and Rosenthall 1999; Krämer 2009), but also Portuguese (see Magalhães 2016 for an overview), and Catalan (Wheeler 2005), but much less research on others, such as Romanian (Chițoran 2002). In this section, we can cite only the most important studies, at least for well-studied languages like Spanish, Italian, and French. It is relatively uncontroversial that in Romance stress is rightmost in the word, and in most varieties is it confined to a window of three syllables, counting from the right edge of the word (excluding enclitics in most varieties). In Italian and Romanian, certain suffixed forms may violate this generalization, depending, among other factors, on the prosodic properties of the base. Some Italian third person plural forms are stressed on the pre-antepenultimate syllable (Spagnoletti and Dominicy 1992), e.g., third person plural *índicano* 'they indicate',[1] cf. singular *índica* 'he/she/it indiates', while in other third person plural verb forms stress lies within the window, e.g., third person plural *divídono* 'they divide', and singular

---

[1] Here and in the following, an acute accent is used in orthographic representations to indicate the position of stress in the word. Note, however, that in most Romance languages and varieties exemplified here, stress is not indicated in the standard orthography, with the exception of Spanish and, to some extent, Italian.

divíde 'he/she/it divides'. The same holds for some, but not all, Romanian nouns ending in the suffix *-iță* (Chițoran 2002: 78), e.g., *véveriță* 'squirrel', but *actríță* 'actress'.

In French, stress is on the final syllable in all words, or on encliticized elements, e.g., *donne-le-moi* 'give.IMP.2SG=it=me!', pronounced as [dɔnlə ˈmwa], which has led some researchers to claim that in French the domain of stress assignment is the phonological phrase rather than the prosodic word. The question whether French has word stress, or whether stress is assigned exclusively at the phrasal level, will come up repeatedly throughout this chapter. It continues to be the object of controversial discussions; cf. Bosworth (2017) and Özçelik (2017) for two recent studies. If a French word ends in a 'mute e', also termed 'unstable e' or schwa, this vowel is never stressed (e.g., *corde* realized as [kɔʀd] or, depending on speaker, variety, and prosodic context, optionally as [kɔʀdə] or [kɔʀdœ] 'rope'; Tranel 1987: 101). However, the vowel <e> of a clitic such as the third person accusative pronoun *le* 'him, it', which is variably realized as [lə], [lœ], [lø], or [l], can bear phrasal stress, e.g., *dis-le* [diˈlœ] 'say.IMP.2SG=it').

For most varieties it is generally assumed that stress assignment is based on trochaic footing, i.e., the prominent syllable is leftmost in the foot, with the exception of French, which is sometimes claimed to employ iambic footing. In Latin, the final syllable was, with very few exceptions, never stressed. Modern Romance languages differ as to whether they have preserved unstressed medial and final syllables (such as Italian) or have deleted them (such as French); see also Section 7.3.3.2. Accordingly, it is controversial whether, for instance, Italian continues Latin extrametricality or not, but final extrametricality has never been proposed for languages like French. For other languages, extrametricality has sometimes been assumed as lexically specified to account for antepenultimate stress, such as in Spanish or Romanian.

Another controversial aspect concerns the weight-sensitivity of Romance stress. The Latin stress rules treat light syllables (i.e., open syllables with a short vowel) and heavy syllables (i.e., closed syllables or syllables with a long vowel) differently; hence, Latin clearly had a weight-sensitive stress system. For Spanish, the question of weight-sensitivity has been discussed in many studies; see Piñeros (2016) and Shelton and Grant (2018) for recent – and divergent – opinions.

Finally, for numerous varieties, it has been proposed that stress assignment in nominals and verbs is based on different rules or constraints, with stress assignment in verbs being heavily morphologized; see, for example, for Spanish the work by Harris and others (Harris 1987; 1989; Oltra-Massuet and Arregi 2005; Doner 2017); for Romanian see (Chițoran 1996; 2002; Iscrulescu 2006).

7.3 Phonological Effects

7.3.1 Introduction

Effects of prominence and effects of non-prominence may in general be considered as a form phonologization of the phonetic effects of stress: prominent vowels are longer, louder, and are produced with a higher articulatory tension, while the contrary holds for non-prominent vowels. We will also consider less immediate effects of stress, that is, effects of metrical constituency in a more general sense.

7.3.2 Effects of Prominence

7.3.2.1 Vowel Lengthening

All Romance languages and varieties have lost the Classical Latin length contrast in vowels (Lausberg 1969). Yet, on a phonetic level vowels in prominent positions are often lengthened, while those in non-prominent positions may undergo shortening or even deletion. Lengthening of open syllables under stress is found in various Romance languages and has been phonologized in some (see also Section 5.3.1). A few varieties have developed contrastive vowel length from sources other than open syllable lengthening. A detailed study of vowel length in Romance is available in Loporcaro (2015).

Some of these lengthening processes have received particular interest in previous research: stressed vowel lengthening in standard Italian as well as in Friulian (see Section 7.4.4), and, to some degree, in earlier stages of Gallo-Romance, not discussed here; see, e.g., Gess (2001).

As for standard Italian, stressed vowels in open syllables undergo lengthening, while all unstressed vowels are short, (2). Open syllable lengthening remains a productive synchronic alternation. Hence, vowel length is not contrastive in Italian (but consonantal length is).

(2)   Italian long vowels in stressed open syllables
      [miˈlaːno]   *Milano*   'Milan'   [milaˈneːse]   *milanese*   'Milanese'

More controversial is the claim that in Italian all stressed vowels undergo lengthening to the same degree (Chierchia 1986, taken over by, for example, Repetti 1991; Vogel 1994; Saltarelli 2003). Many phonetic studies tend to deny this, indicating that a stressed vowel in an open antepenult is shorter than a stressed vowel in an open penult (Farnetani and Kori 1990; Santen and D'Imperio 1999; Vayra, Avesani, and Fowler 1999; D'Imperio and Rosenthall 1999; Hajek, Stevens, and Webster 2007; Krämer 2009: 164; but see Canalis and Garrapa 2012 for a different finding). Diachronic observations on diphthongization support the claim that vowels undergo lengthening in penultimate, but not in antepenultimate position (Calabrese 1984; Vincent 1988), in that mid vowels in a stressed open penult often develop into diphthongs (3a, 3c; see Section 7.3.2.2), but those in a stressed open antepenult often do not, (3b, 3d); cf. Maiden (2016).

(3) Distribution of diphthongs in stressed syllables (Vincent 1988: 425)

	Latin	Italian		
a.	ˈPĔDEM	[ˈpjɛde]	piede	'foot'
	*ˈmɛle	[ˈmjɛle]	miele	'honey'
b.	ˈMĔDICUM	[ˈmɛdiko]	medico	'doctor'
	ˈPĔCORAM	[ˈpɛkora]	pecora	'sheep'
c.	ˈŎPUS	[ˈwɔpo]	uopo	'need'
d.	ˈPŎPULUM	[ˈpɔpolo]	popolo	'people'
	ˈŎPERA	[ˈɔpera]	opera	'work'

The available evidence from phonetic as well as diachronic studies thus favours assuming that only vowels in stressed open penultimate syllables are lengthened, but not vowels in stressed open antepenultimate syllables, at least not to the same degree. From a theoretical perspective, this appears plausible, if one assumes that Italian preserves Latin final syllable extrametricality (see Section 7.2.3), so that the penult can form a well-formed foot only if it is heavy, i.e., the vowel is long (or the syllable closed), (4a), while the antepenult forms, if heavy, a foot on its own, but if it is light, the foot consists of the (stressed) antepenult followed by the weak penult, (4b), so that there is no functional motivation for vowel lengthening.

(4) Italian vowel lengthening and final syllable extrametricality

		μ	(μμ)		μ	
a.	amico	[a	ˈmi:		<ko>]	'friend'
b.		μ	(μ	μ)	μ	
	amabile	[a	ˈma	bi	<le>]	'friendly'

The Italian type of open syllable lengthening can thus be considered as a kind of 'repair' process motivated by metrical well-formedness conditions. If we devote a special section to vowel lengthening centred around the Italian type, coming back to metrical repair processes in Section 7.4, this is motivated by the fact that we consider this type of phonological lengthening to enhance primarily the naturally occurring phonetic lengthening under stress, while other repair processes treated below are more abstractly phonological in nature, having a less concrete phonetic motivation in the effects of phonetic prominence on phonology. This holds in particular for vowel lengthening in Friulian, a phenomenon that has been the topic of numerous studies, or in Occitan, classified here as an instance of compensatory lengthening that is dealt with in Section 7.4.4.

7.3.2.2 Diphthongization

According to some scholars, a process closely related to stressed syllable lengthening is diphthongization in stressed syllables (cf. also Section 5.5.1). While the phenomenon is extremely complex (Lausberg 1969: 152, cf. Maiden 2016 for a concise overview), the textbook account is that proto-Romance mid-low vowels /ɛ/ and /ɔ/, going back to Latin ĕ and ŏ, developed into opening diphthongs. In systems such as Italian, diphthongization occurred only in stressed open syllables, while in systems such as Spanish syllable structure was not a conditioning factor; i.e., diphthongization occurred in closed syllables, too. Examples are given in (5).

(5) Romance diphthongization

	Italian	Spanish	
PĔ.TRAM	*pietra*	*piedra*	'stone'
CĔR.UUM	*cervo*	*ciervo*	'deer'
NŎ.UUM	*nuovo*	*nuevo*	'new'
PŎR.TUM	*porto*	*puerto*	'port'

The Romance variety which was to become standard French patterns with Italian; yet in French all diphthongs (except [jɛ]) developed later into monophthongs, giving rise inter alia to a system with front rounded vowels (Rheinfelder 1987: 24). In all Romance varieties diphthongization – as a productive phonological process – was restricted to stressed syllables, leading in the course of history to numerous morphophonological alternations that continue to shape the morphology of Romance languages (see Section 7.5.1).

Yet it remains controversial whether diphthongization is an effect of prominence or whether its origin is metaphonic. While Loporcaro (2011a) claims that the diachronic motive for diphthongization was open syllable lengthening under stress, Maiden (2016) argues that diphthongization is a result of the assimilatory raising process of metaphony, triggered by following high vowels. As pointed out by Maiden (2016), following Schürr (1970 and earlier work), the kind of opening diphthong exemplified in (5) is more consistent on phonetic grounds with the result of anticipatory assimilation processes relative to a subsequent high vowel; a prominence-induced lengthening of the syllable, in contrast, should lead to a closing diphthong, with a less sonorous second element, as a result of a decrease in articulatory tension in a lengthened syllable. At the same time, in most, but not all, Romance systems diphthongization has led to opening diphthongs, i.e., an articulatory gesture from closed to open, which, according to Loporcaro (2011a), is an unexpected result of metaphonic raising, for which one would expect a gesture from open to closed.

Despite the interest that the topic has aroused for many decades now, the intricacies of the complex interaction between lengthening, raising, and diphthongization remain to be explored adequately. Under both scenarios, diphthongization may count as an 'effect of stress' in the sense explored here. Even if its origin were metaphonic rather than related to (phonetic) lengthening, it could still be considered an indirect effect of prominence, as argued by Mascaró (2016). According to Mascaró, Italo-Romance metaphony is largely restricted to the stressed syllable because phonologically it corresponds to the linking of a floating feature to the stressed position, because, so the argument goes, prominent positions attract floating features.

7.3.3 Effects of Non-prominence
7.3.3.1 Introduction
In Romance, effects of non-prominence are at least as widespread and varied as effects of prominence, both with respect to historical change and to synchronically productive alternations. An obvious effect of non-prominence of vowels is deletion, which can occur in word-initial, word-medial, or word-final position. Vowels can also be reduced, i.e., be phonetically centralized, raised and/or devoiced. In the evolution of the Romance languages, processes of deletion and reduction have had far-reaching consequences, not only for the shape of individual lexemes, but also for the evolution of vowel systems and of inflexional systems, and, finally, for the stress systems themselves.

7.3.3.2 Vowel Deletion
7.3.3.2.1 Aphaeresis
Deletion of unstressed vowels in word-initial position, termed aphaeresis, appears to be a sporadic process, but it is sometimes even found in highly frequent words, e.g., Lat. APOTHĒCA > It. *bottega* 'small shop' (Lausberg 1969: 201). The reason for the general lack of systematic application of aphaeresis may be an effect of prosodic word-initial strengthening, whose functional motivation could lie in the importance of the beginning of the word for recognition. In certain Romance varieties, aphaeresis appears to be more systematic than in others, but in no variety does it seem to correspond to a fully productive process, at least not in lexical words. Examples of aphaeresis having led to a change in word forms are given in (6).

(6)   Aphaeresis
        Latin   Campidanese (Virdis 1978: 14–16)
        AMĀRI'TOSUM   mari'gòzu   'bitter'
        AE'STĀTEM   'stadi   'summer'
        EX'CUTERE   'skùdiri   'to shake off'
        Sp. apotecario   pote'kariu   'pharmacist'

Latin	Romansh (Mayerthaler 1982: 196)	
ᴇx'sūᴄᴛᴜᴍ	schetg	'dry'
ᴀᴇ'sᴛāᴛᴇᴍ	stat	'summer'
ᴀ'xᴜɴɢɪᴀ	'sunscha	'grease'
ᴀ'ᴄūᴛᴜᴍ	git	'sharp'

Much more frequent than aphaeresis is word-internal (syncope) and, in particular, word-final (apocope) deletion.

7.3.3.2.2 Syncope

A particular kind of word-internal vowel deletion, often termed syncope in the Romance literature, is post-tonic word-internal deletion in proparoxytona (cf. also Section 5.4.2). This was highly productive in many areas of the Romània already in late Latin (Lindsay 1894; Grandgent 1907) and proto-Romance (Meyer-Lübke 1890: 261–73), but to different degrees. Like Latin stress, syncope in Latin has been a prime example in formal analyses of rhythmic vowel deletion (Hartkemeyer 1997; Jacobs 2008; 2015).

As for modern Romance languages, even a superficial comparison of Italian words and their Spanish and French cognates shows that in the development of Spanish and French, post-tonic syncope has been far more productive than in the evolution of Italian (Meyer-Lübke 1890: 262; Lausberg 1969: 208), (7).

(7)
	Latin		Italian	Spanish	French
	ᴅɪ'ᴀʙᴏʟᴜᴍ	'devil'	['djavolo]	[di'aβlo]	['djɑbl]
	'ᴛᴀʙᴜʟᴀᴍ	'plank'	['tavola]	['taβla]	['tabl]
	'ʟɪᴛᴛᴇʀᴀᴍ	'letter'	['lɛt:era]	['letra]]	['lɛtʁ]
	'ᴘᴏᴘᴜʟᴜᴍ	'people'	['pɔpolo]	['pweβlo]	['pœpl]
	'ʀēɢᴜʟᴀᴍ	'rule'	['rɛgola]	['rːeɣla]	['ʁɛgl]

Post-tonic syncope (and apocope as well, see below) has been so productive in the former two languages that there are hardly any medial post-tonic vowels left. In French, final stress has been generalized across the board, without exception. In Spanish, too, proparoxytona amount to little more than ten per cent of the lexicon (Bárkányi 2002). In the history of Portuguese, in contrast, syncope has been much less productive than in Spanish (Williams 1934; 1962: 53). At the same time, in modern (European) Portuguese vowel deletion continues to be synchronically far more productive (Mateus and Andrade 2002: 134; Cruz-Ferreira 2009) than in many other Romance varieties. The same applies to Brazilian Portuguese (Kenstowicz and Sandalo 2016) and Catalan (Mascaró 2002). To give an example, while the diachronic process of syncope has affected a smaller number of lexemes in Portuguese as compared to Spanish, syncope can currently be observed as a productive synchronic alternation in certain varieties of Brazilian Portuguese, spoken e.g., in the north-east of Brazil (Silva 2015), but also in the south, (8).

(8)   Syncope in Brazilian Portuguese (Silva 2015: 25)
        máscara   ['maskɐɾɐ]   ['maskɾɐ]   'mask'
        pérola   ['pɛɾolɐ]   ['pɛɾlɐ]   'pearl'

Pre-tonic word-medial vowel deletion is likewise synchronically productive in many Romance varieties, while historically pre-tonic vowels have been more stable than post-tonic ones (Lausberg 1969: 195). It is particularly productive in the variety of European Portuguese spoken on the Azores (Silva 2009; Vigário 2016: 42), but also possible in standard Portuguese, (9a), as well as in Quebec French (Bosworth 2017), (9b). In both languages, high vowels are more prone to deletion than non-high vowels.

(9)   Pre-tonic vowel deletion
   a.   European Portuguese (Mateus and Andrade 2002: 134)
        fonologia   [funulu'ʒiɐ]   [fnulu'ʒiɐ]   'phonology'
        precisão   [pɾisi'zɐ̃w̃]   [pɾsi'zɐ̃w̃]   'precision'
   b.   Quebec French (Garcia, Goad, and Brambatti Guzzo 2017: 3)
        précipiter [presipi'te]   [prespi'te]/[presip'te]   'to hasten'

7.3.3.2.3 Apocope

In Latin the inflexional categories case, number, and gender were marked on nouns and adjectives by suffixes that often consisted of a single vowel, in some cases followed by a consonant. The five declension classes of Latin were primarily distinguished by vowel quality and quantity. In most modern Romance varieties, Latin word-final consonants were deleted (with the exception of /s/ in some western Romance areas). The deletion of word-final vowels, in contrast, has been very productive in certain varieties of Romance, but almost totally absent in others (10). In Italian (and Sardinian), most final vowels were preserved, so that modern Italian, despite having lost case distinctions, still has a nominal inflexional system whose three to six classes (depending on the classification adopted, see Dressler and Thornton 1996; Acquaviva 2009 for two diverging analyses) go back to the Latin nominal declension classes. In French, in contrast, apocope has been particularly productive, deleting all final vowels but /a/, which was reduced to [ə] and is nowadays not pronounced in most registers, with two obvious consequences: first, the thorough restructuring of the prosodic system, where all lexemes are assigned final stress, see Section 7.3.3, and second, the loss of nominal inflexion, including inflexional exponents of gender.

(10)   Apocope in Romance
	Latin	Italian	Spanish	French	
a.	'ROTAM, F	['rwɔta] ruota	['r:weða] rueda	[ʁu] roue	'wheel'
b.	'PŎRTUM, M	['pɔrto] porto	['pwerto] puerto	[pɔʁ] port	'port'
c.	UI'GINTĪ	['venti] venti	['bejnte] veinte	[vɛ̃] vingt	'twenty'
d.	CA'NĀLEM, M	[ka'nale] canale	[ka'nal] canal	[ka'nal] canal	'canal'
e.	UA'LŌREM, M	[va'lore] valore	[ba'loɾ] valor	[va'lœʁ] valeur	'value'

In Spanish, apocope was restricted to the vowel /e/, (10d, 10e), when preceded by a single coronal consonant (Menéndez Pidal 1999; Penny 2002). It was a productive post-lexical alternation in old Spanish (Moreno Bernal 2004), which developed into a morphological alternation in modern Spanish, where apocopated final /e/ surfaces in plural forms of nouns like *valor* SG ~ *valor-e-s* PL 'value' (Harris 1992; 1996; Colina 2003; Bermúdez-Otero 2013), but its distribution is no longer conditioned by stress or other prosodic factors.

Finally, while Italian has underlyingly preserved most final vowels, in modern Italian there is a productive alternation termed *troncamento* ('truncation'), which deletes an unstressed word-final /e/ (Nespor 1990; Meinschaefer 2006), as in *volere fare* > *voler fare* 'to want to do'. *Troncamento* presents considerable diatopic and stylistic variation, but it is also subject to grammatical constraints. In general, it is more common in central and northern Italian, and it is particularly characteristic of verse or poetry. There is evidence that, at least in standard Italian as spoken in Tuscany, *troncamento* is conditioned by metrical structure, being bounded to the phonological phrase and sensitive to the weight of the following prosodic word (Meinschaefer 2006). In some regional varieties and registers of Italian, *troncamento* may delete not only a final /e/, but also a word-final /o/ or /a/, depending on lexical and morphosyntactic features. To give an example, in Tuscan Italian deletion of /o/ is attested in highly frequent verb forms like *hanno* > *han* 'they have', *sono* > *son* 'I am', *abbiamo* > *abbiam* 'we have', but it does not occur on infrequent lexemes or on lexemes pertaining to formal registers, e.g., *censurano* > **censuran 'they censure' (Meinschaefer 2009).

We shall mention only in passing instances of apocope in hiatus, likewise frequently found in Romance; see Sampson (2016) for a brief overview. Vowel deletion in hiatus is, in numerous Romance varieties, particularly salient and often largely morphologized at the boundary between (cliticized) function word and following lexical word, (11a). It is primarily motivated by vowel coalescence, but in Italian, where it is optional in some regional varieties, but uncommon in others, it is also sensitive to the stress pattern of the following word (Garrapa and Meinschaefer 2010). Based on corpus data from Tuscan Italian, Garrapa and Meinschaefer show that deletion of the final vowel of a pronominal clitic followed by a vowel-initial verb, (11b), is less likely when the first vowel of the verb is stressed as compared to when it is unstressed, with an average deletion rate of 40 per cent.

(11) Vowel deletion in hiatus
    a.   Fr.   *le amour* > *l'amour*   'the love'
    b.   It.   *lo amava* > *l'amava*   'loved him (lit. him=love.PST.IPFV.3SG)'

With respect to vowel deletion in hiatus, a robust cross-linguistic generalization is that even in hiatus only unstressed vowels are deleted, while stressed vowels remain intact (Casali 1997).

7.3.4 Vowel Reduction

Vowel reduction in non-prominent position is a less extreme form of weakening than the deletion processes discussed above. In languages such as European Portuguese, some form of weakening of vowels in non-prominent position is categorical, but it may surface optionally as either reduction or deletion (Mateus and Andrade 2002: 134–36); the same holds for Quebec French. Like deletion, reduction occurs less frequently in pre-tonic than in post-tonic position (Maiden 1997; Mateus and Andrade 2002: 134). In Romance, vowel reduction may surface as a change in quality, often centralization or raising, or in the form of devoicing, most often in final position, but also in the form of glide formation, in particular in contact with other, more prominent vowels. While centralization and glide formation have, in many instances, led to changes in word forms and in inflexional systems, devoicing has, in the few varieties where it occurs, remained an optional process. The relevant phenomena are briefly illustrated in this section.

Reduction often takes the form of centralization, i.e., reduction to schwa ([ə]) or to [ɐ], but raising is also a common result. A cross-linguistically rather widespread outcome of reduction-induced changes in vowel quality, once the process becomes categorical and obligatory, is a ban on certain segments from non-prominent positions, found in many Romance varieties. So segmental contrasts may be neutralized in non-prominent positions. In Romance, this is particularly evident with respect to the inventory of vowels in stressed vs unstressed position.

To give a few examples, standard Italian has a seven-vowel system in stressed syllables, but only five vowels in unstressed syllables (Krämer 2009). The vowels /ɛ/ and /ɔ/ occur only in stressed positions; in non-prominent positions the contrast between mid-low and mid-high vowel is neutralized to mid-high [e] and [o]. The same holds for Portuguese and Catalan, though their vowel systems are more complex than the Italian system; cf. Vigário (2016: 47) for a brief overview. A comparative description of Romance vowel inventories in stressed and unstressed positions is given in Schmid (2016).

A complex type of neutralization is exemplified by Corsican, a variety related to Tuscan, in (12). In Corsican, all underlying mid vowels neutralize to high when unstressed, but in inflexional endings, mid-low [ɛ] is preserved.

(12) Corsican (Dalbera-Stefanaggi 2002: 33)
['frɛsku]   [fris'kura]   'fresh' ~ 'freshness'
['petra]   [pitri'kɔzu]   'stone' ~ 'stony'
['dolu]   [du'lɔrɛ]   'grief' ~ 'pain'
['sɔlɛ]   [su'lana]   'sun' ~ 'sunny side'

Examples from numerous other varieties could be added here. No such restriction is found in standard Spanish, which has a simpler five vowel system (Hualde 2005). As for French, according to some scholars this language does not have word stress, but only phrasal stress, so that all vowels other than those in phrase-final position should be unstressed. Yet, French neutralizes mid-low vowels to mid-high in certain forms, conditioned by prominence as well as syllable structure (Tranel 1987). Finally, devoicing of final vowels occurs in Portuguese in final position (Cruz-Ferreira 2009) as well as in Quebec French in any position (Bosworth 2017: 40), (13).

(13) Vowel devoicing in Quebec French (Garcia, Goad, and Brambatti Guzzo 2017)
précipiter   [presi̥pite]   [presipi̥te]   [presi̥pi̥te]   'to hasten'

7.4 Effects of Metrical Constituency

7.4.1 Introduction

In this section, we consider phonological phenomena which cannot be interpreted as direct effects of prominence or non-prominence, but which are rather conditioned by constraints on metrical well-formedness. First, we deal with processes of consonant gemination and vowel insertion. Both arguably serve to optimize or repair the form of the word-final foot in oxytonic words. Second, we describe clash resolution as aiming at an optimization of metrical structure, creating a more regular alternation of prominences. Third, we discuss compensatory lengthening as a process that preserves the metrical position of a segment following its deletion. While this brief introduction has presented the phenomena ordered according to their functional motivation (optimization of metrical structure, followed by preservation of metrical positions), in what follows we will first look at segmental phenomena, followed by clash resolution.

7.4.2 Consonant Gemination

A rather sporadic process is the lengthening of a consonant following the stressed vowel in proparoxytones, (14), found in a few Italian lexemes (Loporcaro 1997b: 41).

(14) | Latin | Italian | | |
|---|---|---|---|
| FĒMINAM | [ˈfemːina] | femmina | 'women' |
| LĒGITIMUS | [leˈdʒitːimo] | legittimo | 'legitimate' |

As argued in Section 7.3.2.1, stressed vowels do not lengthen in proparoxytones, any more than they diphthongize, because in this structure the stressed syllable can serve as the head of a well-formed foot even if it is light. The metrical effect of consonant gemination in (14) is, however, the same as that of vowel lengthening: the stressed syllable becomes heavy. While adding extra weight in these words is not a repair process in a strict sense, given that the metrical structure is well-formed even in the absence of consonant gemination or vowel lengthening, it might still be argued that gemination is an effect of stress: as claimed by Repetti (2000), in certain northern Italian varieties at least the preferred foot is the uneven trochee, see (15b), rather than the moraic trochee, (15a), as evidenced by patterns of vowel insertion in proparoxytona following syncope and apocope.

(15) Two types of trochaic feet built on heavy (H) and light (L) syllables
    a.   Moraic trochee   (L L) or (H)
    b.   Uneven trochee   (H L)

Scholars working on other Romance varieties have likewise argued for the uneven trochee as a licit or even preferred foot in varieties like French (Selkirk 1978; Bullock 1995), Italian (Bullock 1998), and Latin (Jacobs 2003b). Others have maintained that in the same languages the moraic trochee is preferred to the uneven trochee (Mester 1994; Bosworth 2017).

A different case of consonant gemination, i.e., central Italian *raddoppiamento fonosintattico* (RF; cf. Sections 1.2.2.4, 6.4.3.2), has likewise been claimed to serve as a metrical repair process (Basbøll 1989; Repetti 1991; Vogel 1994; 1999). As shown in (16), phonologically regular RF lengthens a word-initial consonant when the preceding word ends in a stressed open (light) syllable, associating the first half of the geminate with the stressed syllable of the preceding word, making this syllable heavy. RF does not apply in words with complex onsets.

(16) Italian *raddoppiamento fonosintattico* (RF)
    città bella 'beautiful city'
    H   (L) (H) <L>   H   (H) (H) <L>
    [tʃit ˈta ˈbɛl la] > [tʃit ˈtab ˈbɛl la]

Raddoppiamento fonosintattico has been generalized from Tuscany to central and southern Italo-Romance (cf. Loporcaro 1997b for an overview of the diatopic distribution in Italo-Romance), but – surprisingly – in Romance varieties other than Italo-Romance comparable processes of consonant gemination at word boundaries have not been discovered. Other scholars, however, have assumed that RF is not a metrical repair process, but a kind of compensatory lengthening, associating a metrical position left behind by a deleted final consonant to the preceding metrical foot (Loporcaro 1997a), thereby closing it. From a diachronic perspective, this scenario is plausible, as most oxytonic words in Italo-Romance have arisen from Latin words as a result of some sort of word-final truncation, often of a single consonant. Under both analyses, as a repair process as well as a compensatory lengthening, RF can be considered as conditioned by metrical structure. Section 8.4.4 deals in more detail with such processes of compensatory lengthening.

7.4.3 Vowel Insertion

Vocalic and syllabic paragoge, found in a few Italo-Romance varieties (Rohlfs 1966: 467–70; Giannelli 1997), can in a similar fashion be motivated as a metrical repair process: vocalic paragoge following a stressed word-final vowel, as exemplified in (17), adds an extra syllable to a monomoraic foot, formed by a single light syllable, thus preserving a bimoraic minimum (Repetti 1989; Sluyters 1990). A similar process, insertion of the syllable [ne] after word-final stressed vowels, (18), occurs in central and southern Italo-Romance varieties (Vignuzzi 1997: 315).

(17) Tuscan paragoge
    però   [pe'rɔe]   'however'
    andò [an'dɔe] 's/he went'

(18) Syllabic paragoge (Vignuzzi 1997: 315)
    sì   /'sine/   'yes'
    fa   /'fane/   'do.INF'

7.4.4 Compensatory Lengthening

A type of lengthening of stressed vowels, somewhat more complex than the open syllable lengthening found, for examples, in Italian, occurs in Friulian, where lengthening has been claimed to be compensatory rather than conditioned by metrical well-formedness (Hualde 1990; Morin 1992; Prieto 1992a). Yet it occurs primarily in stressed vowels. By compensatory lengthening we understand lengthening of a segment following the deletion of an adjacent segment, conceptualized as a reassociation of the timing slot of the deleted segment to the lengthened segment.

As can be seen in the Friulian data in (19a), vowel lengthening occurs in masculine forms, which were subject to apocope in earlier stages of the language, but not in the vowel-final feminine forms, where the unstressed final vowel has been reduced, but not deleted. Furthermore, comparison of (19a) and (19b) shows that in apocopated forms the vowel lengthens only in a closed syllable that goes back to a stressed open syllable in Latin, (19a), but not in a closed syllable that was already closed in Latin, (19b). Finally, stressed vowels in proparoxytonic forms show no lengthening, (19c).

(19) Friulian vowel lengthening (Prieto 1992a: 209–12)
    a.   Latin stress on open penult
            CRŪDUM   ˈkruːt   'raw.MSG'
            CRŪDAM   ˈkrude   'raw.FSG'
            FĪˈNĪTUM   fiˈniːt   'finished.MSG'
            FĪˈNĪTAM   fiˈnide   'finished.FSG'
    b.   Latin stress on closed penult
            ˈRUPTUM   ˈrot   'broken.MSG'
            ˈMĪLLE   ˈmil   'thousand'
    c.   Latin stress on antepenult
            ˈSPĪRITUM   ˈspirit   'spirit.M'
            ˈHŪMIDUM   ˈumit   'humid.MSG'

Clearly, lengthening in the examples in (19a) is not the result of constraints on surface forms: on the surface, we find stressed heavy syllables as well as stressed light syllables. Rather, lengthening occurs (i) only in syllables that were open in earlier stages, but (ii) only in case the relevant word forms underwent apocope.

As a first approximation, it can be said that the process is conditioned by metrical structure: apocope of the final vowel leaves behind a prosodic constituent, i.e., an empty mora, that is associated with the closest vocalic segment, i.e., with the preceding vowel. Hence, without apocope, no lengthening occurs, not even in stressed open syllables, because there is no empty mora to reassociate. If the syllable is already closed, i.e., associated with two morae, it cannot serve as an anchor for the empty mora, and lengthening does not occur.

From the perspective of a formal synchronic analysis, this phenomenon is rather complex. Synchronically, vowel length appears to be conditioned by the laryngeal features of the following obstruent (Baroni and Vanelli 2000; Iosad 2012; Torres-Tamarit 2014). A synchronic analysis of the phenomenon thus deviates largely from the type of metrical conditioning by stress which is the focus of the present article.

A Romance variety that presents both open syllable lengthening under stress (see Section 7.3.2.1) and compensatory vowel lengthening after consonant deletion is Limousin (Chabaneau 1876), a variety of Occitan. Here, non-high back vowels (but not front vowels) in a stressed open penult undergo lengthening, (20a); in addition, compensatory lengthening (20b) following deletion of /s/ (but not of /t/) is found (Javanaud 1981). While there are quite a few studies on compensatory vowel lengthening in Gallo-Romance (Morin and Ouellet 1991; Morin 1994; 1995; 2006; 2012; Gess 1998a; 1998b; 2001; 2006; 2008), the complex Occitan facts have hardly been studied in detail.

(20) Long vowels in varieties of Limousin (Occitan)
    a. Open syllable lengthening (Chabaneau 1876: 10)

ˈCAUAT	[ˈtsaːvo]	*chavo*	3SG.IND	'hollows'
DEˈMORAT	[deˈmoːʀo]	*demoro*	3SG.IND	'stays'

    b. Compensatory lengthening (Roux and Lévêque 2011: 59)

2SG.SBJV	ˈSCRĪBĀS	[ejˈkrivaː]	'write'
3SG.SBJV	ˈSCRĪBAT	[ejˈkriva]	
2SG.IND	ˈSCRĪBIS	[ejˈkrivej]	

Finally, compensatory lengthening of consonants in the form of gemination after consonant deletion, formally equivalent to total assimilation (Hayes 1989: 279), is also found in Romance, as in It. *notte* [ˈnɔtte] < ˈNOCTEM [ˈnokte(m)] 'night', *rotto* [ˈrotto] < RUPTUM [ˈruptu(m)] 'broken', but this process interacts less evidently with stress. We will not consider it here.

7.4.5 Clash Resolution

The avoidance of two immediately adjacent stressed syllables in a sequence of two words, sometimes termed 'clash resolution', appears to be a productive repair process in Italian and French, while clashes are tolerated more freely in Ibero-Romance, i.e., Catalan (Prieto 2011), Spanish (Prieto and van Santen 1996; Hualde 2010) and Portuguese (Madureira 2002; Barbosa and Arantes 2003). Accordingly, the phenomenon came into focus in research on Italian and French relatively early, while it has been confirmed in phonetic studies only much later that clash resolution is at most an optional phenomenon in Ibero-Romance. In Italian, clashes can be avoided by means of stress retraction, (21a), or destressing of the first stress in the clash configuration (Nespor and Vogel 1989). No clash occurs if either the first word is not stressed on the final syllable, (21b), or the second word is not stressed on the initial syllable, (21c).

(21) Stress retraction in Italian
    Examples (21a) to (21c) adapted from Nespor and Vogel (1979: 469)

a.	[meˈta ˈtɔrta]	[ˈmeta tɔrta]	'half (a) cake'
b.	[ˈpɔka ˈtɔrta]	no clash	'little (= not much) cake'
c.	[meˈta kkanˈtsone]	no clash	'half song'
d.	[meˈta kˈkorsa]	clash not resolved	'halfway'

As can be inferred from (21a) as opposed to (21d), stress retraction and *raddoppiamento* potentially apply in the same context, but exclude each other. Both processes require that the first word bear final stress, but stress retraction is subject to the additional condition that another stressed syllable immediately follow, (21a, 21d), while *raddoppiamento* potentially applies regardless of the metrical structure of the following word, (21c, 21d). According to Nespor and Vogel (1979: 479), stress retraction and *raddoppiamento* are in complementary distribution across varieties of Italian. However, they do not give any details to substantiate this claim.

French appears to prefer destressing of the first element to stress shift (Post 1999); the same holds for Ibero-Romance (Hualde and Nadeu 2014). In French, clash resolution interacts with unstressed vowel deletion (22), i.e., deletion of the schwa vowel [ə], in that a potential stress clash may block schwa deletion (Mazzola 1992; Hoskins 1993).

(22)　French schwa [ə] deletion in clash configurations (Hoskins 1993: 36)
    Deletion avoided   *porte-plume*   [ˈpɔʁtə#ˈplym]   'penholder''
    Deletion optional   *porte-manteau*   [ˈpɔʁt#mɑˈto] (preferred) or
                                                [ˈpɔʁtə#mɑˈto]   'coat rack'
    Deletion not avoided   *porte-cigarette*   [ˈpɔʁt#sigaˈʁɛt]   'cigarette case'

The distribution of schwa deletion in (22) clearly shows that the process is motivated by metrical well-formedness conditions, avoiding both clashes and lapses. As has been repeatedly shown in previous research, clash resolution is a domain-span rule: it applies within a phonological phrase, but not across a phrase boundary. Hence, as shown in (23), it is possible between noun and preceding modifier, but not between subject and predicate.

(23)　(Nespor and Vogel 1979: 469)
    Adj-N   *Non fermarti a metà porta.*   [meˈta ˈpɔrta] > [ˈmeta ˈpɔrta]
             'Don't stop halfway through the door.'
    S-V   *I bignè scottano.*   [i biɲˈɲɛ ˈskɔtːano]
             'The doughnuts are very hot.'

7.5 Morpholexical Effects

7.5.1 Alternations in Verb Roots

Alternations of the verb root are pervasive in Romance verbal inflexion, and some of these alternations are conditioned by the position of stress. In previous sections, the far-reaching reflexes of prominence and non-prominence on vowels have already been illustrated; the very same processes have contributed to the emergence of alternations in the form of verb roots, even in varieties that arguably have lost word stress altogether, such as French.

At the base of stress-conditioned patterns of root alternation in modern Romance lies the distribution of stress in the Latin verbal paradigm. In Latin, stress assignment was phonologically determined, so that in the present indicative and subjunctive stress was on the root (i.e., rhizotonic) in the singular forms and in the third person plural, but usually on the ending (i.e., arrhizotonic) in the first and second plural forms. Given that stressed and unstressed vowels are subject to different phonological processes, the outcome of this alternation between stress on ending and on root in proto-Romance has often been a vocalic alternation in the root. The resulting morphophonological alternations, following for the most part a distribution which is called the 'N-pattern' by Maiden (2003; 2018: 166–73), persists in many modern varieties; an example is given in (24).

(24) Indicative present forms of the Spanish verb *querer* 'want'

		stress on stem/root rhizotonic	stress on ending arrhizotonic
SG	1	quiéro	
	2	quiéres	
	3	quiére	
PL	1		querémos
	2		queréis
	3	quiéren	

Besides diphthongization, vowel raising and vowel reduction have likewise contributed to the creation of stem/root alternations. In most varieties, these alternations are synchronically no longer productive, and the correlation between, for instance, diphthong and stress is not biunique. Hence, in Spanish it is true that most diphthongs are found in stressed syllables, but diphthongs do surface in unstressed syllables, often in lexemes derived by particular affixes, such as the superlative or the diminutive; (25a); at the same time, by no means does every mid vowel become a diphthong when stressed; (25b).

(25) Distribution of diphthongs in Spanish
 a. *nuévo* 'new'   *novedád* 'novelty'   *nuevísimo* 'very new'
 b. *tensár* 'tighten' *ténso*   **tiénso*   1SG
    pensár 'think'   **pénso*   *piénso*   1SG

The 'N-pattern', originally conditioned by the alternation between rhizotonic and arrhizotonic stress, has been extended to other stem alternations, which are morpholexical rather than morphophonological in nature, which cannot be traced back to a phonological process conditioned by stress. Examples are the -ISC/ESC-augmentation in Italian (Carstairs-McCarthy 1989; Burzio and DiFabio 1994; Burzio 1998; Maiden 2003), see

(26a), and in other Romance varieties (Esher 2016; 2017), or Italian velar insertion (Lampitelli 2017) as well as clearly suppletive patterns of allomorphy, such as that found in the Italian verb *andare* 'go' (Carstairs-McCarthy 1989; Maiden 2018: 192–201); see (26b).

(26) a. -ISC-augmentation in Italian *finire* 'finish'

			stress on augment	stress on ending
SG	1		*fin-ísc-o*	
	2		*fin-ísc-i*	
	3		*fin-ísc-e*	
PL	1			*fin-iámo*
	2			*fin-íte*
	3		*fin-ísc-ono*	

b. Suppletion in Italian *andare* 'go'

			rhizotonic	arrhizotonic
SG	1		*vádo*	
	2		*vái*	
	3		*va*	
PL	1			*andiámo*
	2			*andáte*
	3		*vánno*	

Apart from 'N-pattern' distributions, stress-conditioned stem alternations have also been introduced and regularized in certain verbal sub-paradigms, where in earlier stages of the relevant varieties there was no comparable alternation. This holds in particular for what Maiden terms the PYTA forms (Maiden 2001; 2018: 44–48), i.e., forms of the simple perfect and, depending on the variety, certain other sub-paradigms. A case in point is Italian forms of the simple perfect of certain so-called irregular verbs. Many Italian verbs of the first conjugation possess (fully regular) perfect forms built on the present stem. In contrast to the present tense, though, these perfect forms are strictly arrhizotonic, i.e., stress is on the ending in all forms; see *parlare* in (27). Most verbs of the second and third conjugation class, however, have a distinctive root/stem alternant for the perfect. Crucially, this special stem surfaces only in some forms of the perfect sub-paradigm (first and third persons singular and third person plural) and it is always rhizotonic, while in the remaining forms of the perfect a different stem is used, and stress is arrhizotonic; see *dire* in (27). Thus, the perfect forms of these verbs show a biunique correlation between perfect stem and rhizotonic stress, on the one hand, and present stem and arrhizotonic stress, on the other. This alternation between forms built on the present stem and those built on the perfect stem is termed the 'E-pattern' (Maiden 2001; 2018: 289–91).

(27) Perfect of Italian *parlare* 'speak' and *dire* 'say'

		parlare, PRS.IND.1SG *parlo*	*dire*, PRS.IND.1SG *dico*	
		arrhizotonic	rhizotonic	arrhizotonic
SG	1	*parlái*	*díssi*	
	2	*parlásti*		*dicésti*
	3	*parlò*	*dísse*	
PL	1	*parlámmo*		*dicémmo*
	2	*parláste*		*dicéste*
	3	*parlárono*	*díssero*	

The complex patterns of root alternations summarized above have figured prominently in recent theoretical work on the formal analysis of morphophonological alternations. Three research strands can be distinguished. First, the focus has been on the question whether particular instances of these alternations should be analysed as phonological or morphological, i.e., whether it is possible to account for a given alternation on the basis of a single underlying lexical entry (Anderson 2008; 2013; Embick 2012; Lampitelli 2017) or whether it should be dealt with in terms of selection of one or the other alternant from a set of stored allomorphs; see, e.g., work by Maiden (2011; 2017) for analyses of the data covered by Anderson (2008; 2013) as morphological rather than phonological in nature. The latter direction, i.e., analysis as allomorphy, has in particular been adopted by researchers working in the framework of Optimality Theory, focussing on the question of how much parallelism between phonology and morphology is required by the formal mechanisms to allow for stress-driven allomorph selection (Bermúdez-Otero 2013; Wolf 2013), as well as on the role of constraints on paradigmatic uniformity (Burzio and DiFabio 1994; Burzio 1998; 2004); see Bonet and Lloret (2016) for an overview.

Second, the alternations sketched above have provided important arguments for the claim that morphology is an autonomous component of the grammar (cf. Chapter 11). In this line of research, the last two decades have witnessed an abundant production of philologically informed descriptions and analyses of patterns of root alternation in a wide range of synchronic and diachronic Romance varieties, showing in many instances that distributional patterns such as the 'N-pattern', the 'E-pattern', etc. are not only found in paradigms in which they have a phonological origin, but that they are analogically extended to other sub-paradigms, thus constituting abstract distributional patterns within morphological categories, or 'morphomes', in the sense of Aronoff (1994). Finally, some of the alternations described here, in particular the Spanish alternation between diphthong and monophthong, have also been studied in an analogical model of the lexicon, in particular with respect to the question how they appear in derived words (Eddington 1996; 1998; Carlson and Gerfen 2011a; 2011b).

7.5.2 Alternations in Function Words

Not only verbs but also function words often display intricate patterns of allomorphic alternation in Romance; one well-studied example is the allomorphy of the Italian definite article as in *il tavolo* 'the table.MSG', *l'amico* 'the friend.MSG', and *lo zio* 'the uncle.MSG'. Stress configurations, however, seem for the most part to be irrelevant in the distribution of allomorphs. We know of only one case in which stress in the host conditions allomorphic selection of the definite article. In (28), the Spanish noun *agua* 'water', having feminine gender, combines with the feminine form of determiners and adjectives (28a), with one exception: the definite article appears in the masculine form when it immediately precedes this noun, (28b). The same alternation is found in all Spanish nouns with a word-initial stressed /a/ (Eddington and Hualde 2008); see also Section 7.5.2.

(28) Spanish definite article allomorphy
    a.   *esta agua* 'this.F water', *la otra agua* 'the.F other.F water'
    b.   *el agua* 'the.M water'

Given the assumption that function words are universally prosodically invisible (Selkirk 1984), i.e., with few exceptions such as interrogative pronouns, they do not constitute prosodic words, the rarity of effects of stress in function word allomorphy may be plausible: since function words are prosodically subordinated to their host – they are clitics – they are not assigned prominence themselves, so that no conflicts will arise with regard to the metrical structure of their host. The Spanish example in (28) may have its functional motivation in a prosodic well-formedness constraint applying to the host: a stressed syllable attracts weight, i.e., it should have an onset (Gordon 2005; Topintzi 2011), which in (28) is provided by the final consonant of the masculine form, lacking in the feminine form.

7.5.3 Minimality Requirements on Lexical Words

For many languages it has been shown that prosodic words have a minimal size: they are subject to language-specific minimality constraints (McCarthy and Prince 1986; 1990). Lexical minimality is often defined with respect to metrical structure (Blumenfeld 2011). In many languages the prosodic word may not be smaller than a well-formed foot (Prince 1980), that is, it must consist of at least two syllables (in a language with a quantity-insensitive stress system) or of at least two morae (in a quantitative system). Under this metrical interpretation of minimality, we consider minimal word size constraints an 'effect of stress': words are subject to minimality conditions because as prosodic units, in order to be pronounceable, they must be assigned a metrical structure and they must be assigned prominence, i.e., word stress.

Word minimality conditions, and constraints on the canonical shape of morphemes more generally, can certainly be induced from observations about the statistical distribution of certain prosodic structures in the lexicon of a language, but they are also more directly observable in 'new' words, in particularly in formations that do not draw on lexical material, such as ludic formations, (29), or in child language at early stages of language acquisition, (30).

(29) Ludic formations
 a. Reduplication (Scullen 2002: 178)
  Fr. *gâteux*   *gagá²*   'foolish'
 b. Hypocoristics
  Sp. *Federíco*   *Fíco*   'Frederic' (Lipski 1995: 387)
  It. *Giuséppe*   *Péppe*   'Joseph' (Alber 2010)
 c. Truncation
  Sp. *profesór*   *prófe*   'teacher, professor' (Piñeros 2000: 292)

(30) Child language (Demuth and Johnson 2003: 219)
 Fr. *omnibus* [by'by] 'bus'

In contrast to lexical words, function words, being universally prosodically invisible (Selkirk 1984), are in general not subject to minimality conditions, but are rather prone to undergo further prosodic reduction both diachronically and in synchronic alternations.

As for Romance, it has been argued for some varieties that the minimal word is disyllabic: this holds for Spanish (Prieto 1992b) and Sardinian (Bolognesi 1998; Floricic 2011). For other languages it has been claimed that it corresponds to a bimoraic foot: Latin (Mester 1994), Italian (Repetti 1989; Bullock 1991; Vogel 1994; 1999; Thornton 1996), Catalan (Cabré Monné 1994), Hispano-Romance in general (Martínez-Gil 2010), and Picard (Halicki 2011). Still others, such as Portuguese, have so far hardly been examined from this perspective.

Coming back to what was said above, that the prosodic word is predicted to correspond to a disyllabic foot in languages with a quantity-insensitive stress system, but to a bimoraic foot in a quantitative system – the split observed within Romance, i.e., between languages with a disyllabic minimum and those with a bimoraic minimum, is in fact expected in the theory of metrical and prosodic structure adopted here. To be sure, this hypothesis awaits systematic testing in the Romance area, but in order to test it, more solid studies of the prosodic systems of individual varieties are needed. Even in the varieties of a well-studied language family like

---

[2] Etymology according to *Le Grand Robert* (2017), lemma *gaga*.

Romance, it is notoriously difficult to decide whether the stress system of a given language is quantity-sensitive or not. The Spanish stress system, for example, has been the topic of dozens of studies addressing this particular aspect; see Piñeros (2016) and Shelton and Grant (2018) for recent – and still controversial – views on the subject.

Let us illustrate yet another complication, drawing on observations about French. The French lexicon contains a considerable number of words consisting of only a light syllable, that is, of a syllable that cannot be parsed into a well-formed foot, such as [bo] 'beautiful', [gʁɑ̃] 'big', [bɛ̃] 'bath', [pje] 'foot', [mɛ̃] 'hand', etc. Numerous French lexemes are thus 'subminimal' words. At the same time, it has been shown that French ludic formations, but also French derived words and child language productions, do conform to a disyllabic template (Dressler and Kilani-Schoch 1993; Plénat 1993; Kilani-Schoch 1996); others assume that the template is a bimoraic foot (Scullen 1993). The case of French clearly shows that the relation between prosodic constituents and 'existing' lexical units is much more complex than claimed above.

In two cross-linguistic typological studies, Kiparsky (1991) and Kager (1995) show that, in fact, many languages tolerate subminimal words. At the same time, they draw a connexion between this observation and the well-known fact that languages also tolerate what is termed in metrical theory 'degenerate' feet, i.e., feet that are not binary, but monosyllabic or monomoraic: according to Kiparsky and Kager, there are, on the one hand, languages that do not impose a minimal word size and do allow word-final or word-initial stresses of a sort that can only be analysed by 'degenerate' feet (i.e., initial stress on a light syllable in iambic languages and final stress on a light syllable in trochaic languages). French is an example of the latter. On the other hand, many languages do impose a word minimum, while not tolerating peripheral stresses of the relevant type. They further show that the number of languages that do not fall into one of these two types is rather small. According to Kiparsky (1991), both phenomena are related to whether a language licenses catalexis or not, so that linguistic systems fall into two types: those that have catalectic elements (which may surface in the form of peripheral stresses and subminimal words), and those that do not. To date, we do not know whether French is a case in point; note also that some, but not all, scholars assume that French does not have word stress at all, and hence should lack prosodic words altogether. Yet, modern French shows 'effects of stress' at least in the form of vowel reduction, of clash resolution, and of stress-conditioned alternations in verb roots. To sum up, despite a relatively large body of research on prosodic minimality in Romance, the crucial theoretical implications still lack empirical support.

Selected References

Below you can find selected references for this chapter. The full references can be found online at the following page: www.cambridge.org/Romancelinguistics

Anderson, S. (2008). 'Phonologically conditioned allomorphy in the morphology of Surmiran (Rumantsch)', *Word Structure* 1: 109–34.

Basbøll, H. (1989). 'Phonological weight and Italian raddoppiamento fonosintattico', *Rivista di linguistica* 1: 5–31.

Chierchia, G. (1986). 'Length, syllabification and the phonological cycle in Italian', *Journal of Italian Linguistics* 8: 5–33.

D'Imperio, M. and Rosenthall, S. (1999). 'Phonetics and phonology of main stress in Italian', *Phonology* 16: 1–28.

Gess, R. (2008). 'More on (distinctive!) vowel length in historical French', *Journal of French Language Studies* 18: 175–87.

Hualde, J. I. (1990). 'Compensatory lenghthening in Friulian', *Probus* 2: 31–46.

Hualde, J. I. (2012). 'Stress and rhythm'. In Hualde, J. I., Olarrea, A., and O'Rourke, E. (eds), *The Handbook of Hispanic Linguistics*. Chichester: Wiley-Blackwell, 153–71.

Magalhães, J. (2016). 'Main stress and secondary stress in Brazilian and European Portuguese'. In Wetzels, W. L., Costa, J., and Menuzzi, S. (eds), *The Handbook of Portuguese Linguistics*. Chichester: Wiley-Blackwell, 107–24.

Nespor, M. and Vogel, I. (1989). 'On clashes and lapses', *Phonology* 6: 69–116.

Post, B. (1999). 'Restructured phonological phrases in French: evidence from clash resolution', *Linguistics* 37: 41–63.

Selkirk, E. (1978). 'The French foot: on the status of "mute" e', *Studies in French Linguistics* 1: 141–50.

Vigário, M. (2016). 'Segmental phenomena and their interactions: evidence for prosodic organization and the architecture of grammar'. In Fischer, S. and Gabriel, C. (eds), *Manual of Grammatical Interfaces in Romance*. Berlin: De Gruyter, 41–73.

8

The Notion of the Phoneme

Benedetta Baldi and Leonardo M. Savoia

8.1 Introduction

Phonemic analysis answers a question that modern reflexion on language has highlighted from the beginning, namely that a level of abstract constants which are systematically associated with phonetic properties is necessary to obtain adequate explanation.[1] In the structuralist paradigm distinctiveness plays a crucial role, insofar as it defines the phonetic constants of a language. Inherited from the Saussurean conception of the nature of linguistic systems (Saussure [1916] 1967), phonemics is founded on the idea that communicative efficiency is the principle regulating the internal organization of languages. As a consequence, structuralist approaches miss the difference between the internal properties of languages – sounds and meanings as constitutive components of linguistic expressions – and their use in utterances, in real referential and communicative interactions. This limit affects all structuralist tools of analysis, in the sense that the result of the enunciation is at the same time its organizing principle. In the case of the phoneme, its distinctive and oppositional nature has been the hallmark of structuralist reflexion on language: the distinctive properties of a phonic sequence are the means for guaranteeing its ability to signify. Actually, the distinctive capability seems rather a general property of linguistic communication, to the extent that it is necessary that two messages be minimally phonetically different in order to be recognized as distinct and potentially associated with different meanings. That is, distinctiveness seems an external, pre-theoretical mechanism that human languages include as a perceptual and operational

---

[1] Most of the data discussed in this contribution have been collected by the authors through field research and interviews with native speakers; in all other cases the source of the data is provided.

requirement. Saussurean theory incorporates this basic property, assigning it the role of the general principle organizing language systems. This explains the uncertain status of distinctiveness: it is a recognizable abstract device that guarantees communicative efficiency, the constitutive notion of the system; on the other hand, it occurs along the speech chain, mixed in with the other non-phonemic properties, among the non-distinctive properties of what Saussure calls 'parole'.

8.2 The Phoneme

European and American structuralism has sought to establish a connexion between phonetic properties and distinctive units, at first abstractly conceived in the Saussurean formulation. Trubetzkoy (1939) assumed that distinctive properties should occur and be recognizable in the phonetic segments of the speech chain. Likewise, Bloomfield (1933: 81) concludes that '[t]he phonemes of a language are not sounds, but merely features of sound which the speakers have been trained to produce and recognize in the current of actual speech-sound'. The idea is that phonemes must be recognizable in the phonetic sequence in a regular and systematic way, thus ensuring communicative effectiveness. Phonemes are understood as bundles of distinctive features specified in terms of phonetic primitives. Phonologists have proposed some requirements, rules, or procedures for identifying phonemes. Bloomfield (1933: 79, 81) relates phonemes to the regular presence in utterances of certain recognizable features. Two properties are taken over, i.e., the constant occurrence of specific features in the utterance and their recognizability. Trubetzkoy ([1935] 1968: 7, 9f.), in turn, formulates three rules to establish phonemes and their variants:

> Rule I: If two sounds in the same language occur in exactly the same phonetic environment and can be exchanged one with the other without effecting any change in the meaning of the word, then both sounds constitute only facultative phonetic variants of one and the same phoneme.
> Rule II: If two sounds occur in exactly the same phonetic position and yet cannot be exchanged one for the other without changing the meaning of the words concerned or without rendering the relevant word unrecognizable, then both sounds are phonetic realizations of two different phonemes.
> Rule III: If two acoustically or articulatorily related sounds in a given language never occur in the same phonetic environment, they are regarded as combinatory variants of one and the same phoneme.

Phonetic invariance and complementary distribution are the relevant requirements. American structuralism tried to regulate the correspondence between the phoneme, as a distinctive unit, and the phonetic continuum, by a set of requirements that must be satisfied in order to speak of phoneme: linearity, invariance, biuniqueness, local determinacy (Chomsky 1964). The linearity condition implies that the recoverability of the relevant features in utterances is necessary for the corresponding phonemes to be recognized. Moreover, the phonetic properties associated with a phoneme, possibly also with a sequence of allophones, must occur in the same sequence as that of the corresponding phonemes. Linearity is further restricted by invariance, requiring that any phoneme has a set of defining features, so that any occurrence of a phoneme implies the occurrence of its set of defining features. The biuniqueness condition states that each sequence of phones is represented by a unique sequence of phonemes and that each sequence of phonemes represents a unique sequence of phones. As Chomsky (1964: 84) shows, these strict requirements are problematic because an adequate phonemic analysis must take other information into account.

A striking effect of the phonemic paradigm is that it ultimately conceals the distribution of the phonetic segments. Requirements such as linearity and invariance are insufficient for phonemic representation, and distinctiveness understood as the conceptual tool for capturing the units of a system, pares what the speaker actually knows about her/his language to the bone. The upshot of the search for oppositional units is that the very things speakers need to recognize in order to interpret the phonetic sequences of their language are considered irrelevant to the organization of the system.

8.3 Conditions for Phonemes: Linearity, Invariance, and Biuniqueness

A preliminary issue concerns the phonetic content of phonemes. All approaches agree in connecting the identity of a phoneme with a set of defining properties (Bloomfield 1926; Trubetzkoy 1939; Harris 1951; Martinet 1955; 1961) – what Chomsky (1964) terms 'invariance'. We know that all phonologists provide ad hoc solutions or special treatments for cases in which this parameter is lacking or poses insoluble problems. Can complementary distribution alone identify phonemes in an adequate way? Chomsky (1964: 84) stresses that the notion of minimal pair is interesting only if defined 'in terms of a complete phonemic analysis', otherwise the commutation test is devoid of heuristic force. More precisely, it includes morphological information (cf. Chiari 2005), in that, for example, in many

Romance varieties we have at least two possibilities: the minimal pair involves the lexical base, as in It. [lun-a] 'moon' vs [lan-a] 'wool', or the inflexional elements, as in It. [mel-a] 'apple.FSG' vs [mel-e] 'apple.FPL'. Naturally, the two types of contrast reflect very different properties and functional mechanisms. The crucial point is that the commutation test and, specifically, the notion of 'minimal pair' are significant only if they are defined in terms of 'a completed phonemic analysis' (Chomsky 1964: 84).

A very common occurrence is that of irreducible allophones. In the Aromanian of some areas of southern Albania, immediately preceding the stressed nucleus of the word, *l velarized to [ɣ] before back vowels [ɔ o u] and [a], as in (1a); in the context of front vowels [l] is preserved, as in (1b). In intervocalic post-tonic position we find rhotacized outcomes, as in (1c), or [l] deriving from *ll, as in (1c'). Reasons of paradigmatic internal uniformity lead to retention of [ɣ] also before different vowels, as in (1a'). /l/ is preserved in protonic and in pre-consonantal position, as in (1d).

(1) **Libofshë (southern Albania)**
    a.   ['ɣɔrə] 'them', ['ɣoku] 'the ground'
        ['ɣui] 'him', [ɣuŋg] 'long', ['ɣupu] 'the wolf'
        [ɣa] 'to', [mi 'ɣau] 'I wash myself', ['ɣapti] 'milk'
    a'. [ɣarg] / [ɣɛrdz] 'broad.MSG / MPL'
        ['ɣənə] 'wool', [ɣəm] 'we wash'
    b. ['librə] 'book', ['limbə] 'tongue', ['lɛmə] 'wood'
    c. ['sɔri] 'the sun', [sari] 'the salt'
        [fi'tʃoru] 'the boy', [kuru] 'the arse'
    c'. [cjɛlə] 'skin' (< Lat. PELLEM)
    d. [lə'dzɛsk] 'I.read', ['dultsi] 'sweet'

It is true that [ɣ] occurs in contexts that exclude [l] and vice versa, but no feature is shared by these segments: one is a velar fricative, the other a lateral sonorant. Is complementary distribution sufficient to assign them to the same phoneme? Moreover, [r] encompasses both the original intervocalic *l, in (1c), and the original *r, in (2a, 2b). The residual presence of intervocalic [l] from *ll, in (1c'), precludes a strict complementary distribution.

(2) **Libofshë (southern Albania)**
    a. ['sɔra] 'the sister', [a'sɛra] 'yesterday'
    b. [roʃ] 'red.MSG', ['rɔta] 'the wheel'

[r] contrasts with [l]/ [ɣ] in initial position, occurring even before back vowels, as in (2b). If the procedure were decisive, we would conclude that /r/, /l/, and /ɣ/ are full-fledged phonemes, or, alternatively, /r/ neutralizes with /l/ before a back vowels, if we continue to deal with [ɣ] as an allophone of /l/.

The cost is to abandon the phonetic recognizability criterion, thus opening the way to an overpowerful procedure, that would ultimately assign to the same phoneme all segments in complementary distribution, even if devoid of defining properties (cf. Chomsky 1964).

We can connect posteriorization of *l to an intermediate phase in which the lateral takes on a back articulation. In the so-called 'Lausberg Zone', the Italo-Romance dialect area on the Calabrian-Lucanian border, a fricative uvular realization of *l retains the link with /l/, given that in contexts of phonosyntactic gemination (cf. Section 6.4.3.2) the coronal lateral surfaces, as shown by comparison of the data in (3a) and (3b), from Valsinni.

(3)   a. ɛi ʁaˈβɛtə   b. a llaˈβɛtə   (Valsinni, southern Basilicata)
          'you have washed'   '(s)he has washed'

In this case, the phonetic irreducibility remains even if the alternation ʁ / ll could be used to support the hypothesis of a 'crazy' phoneme comprising /ʁ + l/.

The overall effect is that the phoneme swallows up the real occurrences of phonetic properties relevant for the phonological and semantic recognizability of the sequence. This result is typical of phonemic treatments. Take metaphony in Sardinian: Jones (1990) proposes a vowel system for Logudorese varieties in which raised mid vowel outcomes are absent, as in (4):

(4)   /i/   /u/
           /ɛ/   /ɔ/
              /a/

Jones chooses to assume low-mid phonemes, although the degree of aperture appears to be irrelevant, given that low-mid outcomes precede non-high vowels whereas high-mid outcomes precede high vowels, giving rise to a typical complementary distribution, as in (5) from Siniscola:

(5)   **Siniscola (northeastern Sardinia)**
[urˈtɛɖɖɔzɔ] / [urˈteɖɖu] 'knife / knives'
[ˈlɛttɔzɔ] / [ˈlettu] 'beds / bed'
[ˈvɛttsa] / [ˈvettsu] 'old.F / old.M'
[apˈpɛrjɔ] / [apˈperizi] 'I open / you.SG open'
[ˈɔkrɔzɔ] / [ˈokru] 'eyes / eye'
[ˈnɔva] / [ˈnovu] 'new.FSG / new.MSG'
[ˈdrɔmmɔ] / [ˈdrommiti] 'I sleep / (s)he sleeps'

This distribution contrasts with that characterizing southern Sardinian varieties, where raising of final mid vowels neutralized the opposition between high and mid vowels in final position and created a new functional load between stressed high-mid and low-mid vowels. In the

Campidanese dialect of Orroli, in (6a), [i] from *-i, in *-is, *-it in the second and third persons singular of the present indicative of verbs of the Latin fourth conjugation, and the masculine singular inflexion [u] from *-u, trigger metaphony. On the contrary, in (6b), [i] from *-e / *-es, the singular and plural endings of one of the nominal inflexion classes, and from *-es / *-et, the present indicative second and third singular persons of the Latin second and third conjugations, and [u] from *-o- in masculine plural nouns and the first person singular present indicative do not trigger metaphony and combine with low-mid stressed vowels. Contexts with final -a are illustrated in (6c).

(6) **Orroli (southern Sardinia)**
 a. ['sreβ-izi] 'you serve'
  [si 'omr-iði] 'he goes to sleep'
  [mar'teɖɖ-u] 'hammer.MSG'
  ['betʃ-u] 'old.MSG'
  ['oɣ-u] 'eye.MSG'
  ['no-u] 'new.MSG'
 b. ['pɛrd-u] / ['pɛrd-izi] 'I lose / you.SG lose'
  ['srɛβ-u] 'I serve'
  [mi 'ɔmr-u] 'I go to sleep'
  ['kɔtts-u] / ['kɔ-izi] 'I cook / you.SG cook'
  [pɛ-i] / [pɛ-izi] 'foot.MSG / feet.MPL'
  [mar'tɛɖɖ-uzu] 'hammer.MPL'
  ['bɛtʃ-uzu] 'old.MPL'
  ['ɔɣ-uzu] 'eye.MPL'
  ['nɔ-uzu] 'new.MPL'
 c. ['bɛtʃ-a] / ['bɛtʃ-aza] 'old.FSG / FPL'
  ['nɔ-a] / ['nɔ-aza] 'new.FSG / FPL'
  [ar'rɔð-a] 'wheel.FSG'

In this dialect, according to Jones (1990), the phonemic inventory is as in (7):

(7) /i/   /u/
  /e/   /o/
   /ɛ/ /ɔ/
    /a/

The distribution of [e] and [o], the high-mid outcomes, remains restricted to contexts of (a subset of) final -i/-u, whereas they are excluded from the other possible contexts including final -a. Instead, [ɛ ɔ] occur in all tonic contexts, with -i, -u, -a, on a par with the other stressed vowels [i a u]. Crucially, there is no minimal pair in which the same inflexional high vowel occurs indifferently with low- and high-mid stressed vowels, so the difference between stressed low- and high-mid vowels is entirely morphologized. More precisely, we will never find a minimal pair such as CɛloCi/u... vs Ce/oCi/u..., where i/u have the same morphological status.

Now, in Sardinian varieties inflexional endings are distributed according to verb class, so that verbs in -i- have identical vocalic outcomes throughout the paradigm, preventing alternations between different persons. A different distribution characterizes the morphologization of metaphony in Italo-Romance varieties (Maiden 1991). In the Sicilian of Modica (Savoia 2015; Savoia and Baldi 2016a), neutralization of unstressed mid and high vowels has created a reduced system [i a u], such that metaphonic outcomes from /ɛ ɔ/, i.e., [je wo], and mid vowels [ɛ ɔ] occur in the same environments, specifically in combination with final [i], as in (8a) and (8b) from Modica. Note that final [u] excludes [ɛ ɔ], as in (8b), selecting only diphthongized outcomes. This may be connected to the fact that this system originally distinguished between the final or post-tonic *e* in the feminine plural, singulars of one class of nouns and adjectives, third person of the verb, and in other contexts, and the final/post-tonic *i* of the masculine plural, second person singular present, and first person singular of the perfect. As for original *o, for instance in the first person present of the verb, we must conclude that its merger with /u/ preceded metaphony, as in southern Calabrian dialects. Again, [je wo] are excluded in contexts where they are followed by [a].

(8) Modica (southern Sicily)[2]
   a. [ˈpɛri] 'foot.MSG'   b. [ˈpjeri] 'foot.MPL'
       [ˈlɛtta] 'bed.MPL'   [ˈljettu] 'bed.MSG'
       [ˈvɛttʃa] 'old.FSG'   [ˈvjettʃu] / [ˈvjettʃi] 'old. MSG / PL'
       [ˈvɛʃpa] / [ˈvɛʃpi] 'wasp.FSG / FPL'
       [ˈrrɔta] / [ˈrrɔti] 'wheel.FSG / FPL'
       [ˈɔva] 'egg.PL'   [ˈwottʃu] / [ˈwottʃi] 'eye.MSG / MPL'
                                          [wovu] 'egg.MSG'
       [ˈrɔssa] 'big.FSG'   [ˈrwossu] / [ˈrwossi] 'big. MSG / PL'
       [ˈɛriva] 'grass.FSG'   [ˈpjekura] / [ˈpjekuri] 'sheep.FSG / FPL'
       [ˈpɛddi] '(s)he.loses'   [ˈpjeddu] / [ˈpjeddi] / [ˈpjeddunu]
                                              'I.lose / you.lose / they.lose'
       [ˈpɛssi] / [ˈpɛssɨru] 'I./(s)he.lost / they.lost'
       [ˈrɔmmi] '(s)he.sleeps'   [ˈrwommu] / [ˈrwommi] / [ˈrwommunu]
                                              'I.sleep / you.sleep / they.sleep'
       [ˈrɔrmiri] 'to sleep'
       [mɔri] '(s)he.dies'   [ˈmwori] / [muˈrjemu] 'you.die / we.die'

The vowel system of Modica, like all other Sicilian systems, lacks high-mid vowels with phonemic function; [je wo] are restricted to the metaphonic contexts, in (8b), and could be treated as allophonic outcomes of low-mid vowels. Nevertheless, [ɛ ɔ] occur only before [i a], in (8a), where

---

[2] Western Sicilian dialects show a plural inflection -a in a subset of masculine nouns, generally specifying a collective or aggregate reading.

they are in complementary distribution with the diphthongs [je wo] and contrast with [i a u]. We might be tempted to assign [ɛ ɔ] phonemic status, but in the context of post-tonic [u], only [je wo] occur (as well as, of course, [i a u]). The result is that not only do [je wo] require a following high vowel, but also that [ɛ ɔ] admit only a following [i]. So we might conclude that the diphthongs are in turn phonemes, given that they contrast with [ɛ ɔ] before [i], associating with different interpretations, see (9a–b), while in contexts of [u] they are allophones of [ɛ ɔ]. This is a tangled situation. In any case, the morphological information is crucial, in that metaphonizing [i] is the plural inflexion of nouns or the second person singular of the verb, giving rise to paradigmatic alternations such as those in (9b). A hypothetical treatment in phonemic terms might assume that before [u] phonemes /je wo/ are introduced, as in (9c).

(9) a. /i/ /u/
      je ? wo ?
      /ɛ/ /ɔ/
           /a/
   b. /pɛr-i/ 'foot'   vs /pjer-i/ 'feet'
      /mɔr-i/ '(s)he dies' vs /mwor-i/ 'you die'
   c. /ɛ/, /ɔ/ → /je/, /wo/ in the context __ [u]

This distribution is reminiscent of the discussion in Halle (1959), resumed in Chomsky (1964), whereby the phonemic level of representation introduces unnecessary redundancy into the description. Specifically, we may find a situation in which the same property can be treated both as a phoneme and an allophone, contrary to the conditions on phonemes of linearity, invariance, and biuniqueness. Following Halle (1959), the phonemic level of representation is inadequate to uniquely capture a single level of representation and, therefore, needlessly complicates the representation.

Similar conclusions may be drawn from the alternation systems of many central-southern Italian varieties in which metaphony creates high-mid vowels, as allophones of the low-mid phonemes, that are independently present in the system. In the Abruzzese variety of Mascioni (L'Aquila), raising metaphony changes high-mid vowels to high, in (10), and low-mid to high-mid, in (11).

(10) metaphony of high-mid vowels in Mascioni
     ['veta]   'fingers'   vs ['vitu]   'finger'
     [joˈkea]   'I/(s)he played'   [joˈkii]   'you.SG played'
     ['roʃʃa]   'red.FSG'   ['ruʃʃu]   'red.MSG'
     ['roʃʃe]   'red.FPL'   ['ruʃʃi]   'red.MPL'
     ['roppo] 'I break'   ['ruppi]   'you.SG break'

<*****>

(11) metaphony of low-mid vowels in Mascioni
['sɛrpa] 'snake'   vs   ['serpi] 'snakes'
['pɛrdo] / ['pɛrde] 'I lose / (s)he loses'   ['perdi] / ['perdu] 'you.SG lose / they lose'
['prɛte] 'priest'   ['preti] 'priests'
['nɔa] / ['nɔe] 'new.FSG / FPL'   ['nou] / ['noi] 'new.MSG / MPL'
['krɔpo]/ ['krɔpe] 'I cover / (s)he covers'   ['kropi] / ['kropu] 'you.SG cover / they cover'

The high vowels and [a] occur freely in all contexts (12):

(12) **Mascioni**
[kruðu] / [kruða] / [kruði] / [kruðe] 'raw.MSG / FSG / MPL / FPL'
[rijo] / [riji] 'I laugh / you.SG laugh', ['itʃe] '(s)he says'
['jattu] / [jatti] 'cat / cats'
['vakka] / ['vakki] 'cow / cows'
['sale] 'salt'

Mid vowels, in turn, freely occur in contexts other than final [i u], in (13).

(13) **Mascioni**
['sete] 'thirst' / ['bejo] 'I drink'
['koʃe] '(s)he sews' / ['koʃo] 'I sew'
['mɛle] 'honey' / ['kɔre] 'heart'
['lɛo] 'I pull' / ['jɔko] 'I play'
['lɛa] '(s)he pulls' / ['jɔka] '(s)he plays'

This distribution can be interpreted in terms of a phonemic system including as a distinctive property the difference between high-mid and low-mid, as in (14):

(14)
/i/   /u/
/e/   /o/
/ɛ/   /ɔ/
    /a/

Naturally an important restriction emerges that excludes [ɛ ɔ] from the context of final [i u], so that we could assume that [ɛ ɔ] have a low functional load, compared with the more complete distribution of [e o]. Again the very intriguing question is that they are to be treated as phonemes to the extent that they have functional load contrasting with closed degree vowels.

In such a case, Trubetzkoy (1939) would speak of neutralization. But /e o/, while neutralizing with /i u/, still occur in metaphonic contexts as outcomes of metaphony of /ɛ ɔ/. Therefore, neutralization is inadequate to explain the distribution, because [e o] continue to occur in the context of final [i u]. So we cannot say that [e o] neutralize with [i u]: the latter are simply allophones of /e o/ changed to high vowels. A typical 'counterfeeding' distribution emerges, in the sense of Kiparsky (1982): a rule creates outcomes identical to those changed by another rule. In the case of Mascioni, metaphony of low-mids generates high-mid results, the very phonemes that metaphony of high-mids has eliminated by changing them to high vowels. A consequence of this distribution is that high-mid vowels are able to occur in metaphonic contexts, while those contexts exclude low-mid vowels. The latter are indeed absent in the context of a following high vowel.

Two generalizations can be stated, whereby metaphony of the high-mid vowels introduces an alternant coinciding with the phonemes /i/, /u/, in (15a). Metaphony of low-mid vowels might be treated as a type of neutralization between /ɛ/, /ɔ/ and /e/, /o/, respectively, but it is this result that makes /e/, /o/ distinctive with respect to /i/, /u/. So, metaphony comes to be interpreted in terms of two independent statements, with the further problem that in terms of the complementary distribution principle *i, u* are allophones of /e/, /o, as in (15b) for Mascioni.

(15) a. Metaphony of high-mid vowels: /e/, /o/ become /i/, /u/ in the contexts __X [i, u]
b. Metaphony of low-mid vowels: /ɛ/, /ɔ/ are neutralized as /e/, /o/ in the contexts __ X [i, u]

Biuniqueness and invariance are called into question by a system such as that of Mascioni, all in all a typical metaphonic paradigm, for which phonemic analysis cannot capture and formalize what the speaker has to know regarding the distribution of the mid vowels in the different contexts. Metaphony in Orroli and Modica exemplifies a common shift whereby metaphony, totally or partially, is governed by morphological information (a common result in Italo-Romance metaphony, cf. Maiden 1991). However, a phonological motivation is generally preserved in that the alternations reflect the phonetic classes of the vowels involved.

We conclude this point by considering the possibility that the same phonetic outcome covers two phonemes, creating the conditions that Bloch (1941) names *phonemic overlapping*, and which Kiparsky (1982) reformulated as *opacity* in the derivation. In the dialect of Venosa (Basilicata) the outcomes of raising metaphony from /e o/ undergo the same diphthongization that changes original /i u/ into /ai au/, respectively. The result is a complete overlapping, concealing the underlying starting point, as in (16a–b). In Venosa all final vowels weakened to [ə], so that metaphony is entirely morphologized, depending on the morphological properties of the words. This dialect differentiates the duration of stressed vowels according to syllable structure, whereby in open syllables, long vowels or diphthongs occur while in closed syllables and in proparoxytones we find short outcomes (Savoia and Carpitelli 2008).[3] The data in (16a–b) show the distribution of the diphthong, which characterizes both the metaphonic

---

[3] In these dialects stressed nuclei in antepenultimate position on a par with the ones in closed syllables show identical durational and timbre properties, selecting short and more open realizations (Rohlfs [1949] 1966; Savoia and Carpitelli 2008; Savoia 2015; Savoia and Baldi 2016b).

outcomes from /e o/ in (16a–b) and original /i u/ in (16a′–b′). (16c) attests the existence of high stressed vowels, corresponding to the results of metaphony from /ɛ ɔ/.

(16) **Venosa (northern Basilicata)**
 a. [ai]: [ˈmeːsə] 'month' vs [ˈmaisə] 'months'
 a′. [ˈrairə] '(s)he laughs', [ˈrɪrənə] 'they laugh'
 b. [au]: [nəˈpoːtə] 'nephew' vs [nəˈpautə] 'nephews'
 b′. [kausə] 'I sew', [ˈkʊsənə] 'they sew'
 c. [rɛndə] 'tooth' vs [ˈrində] 'teeth', [ˈpeːrə] 'foot' vs [ˈpiːrə] 'feet'
 [dɔrmə] 'I sleep' vs [ˈdurmə] 'you.SG sleep', [tʃiːlə] 'heaven'

Thus, [ai] and [au] involve only a subset of the high vowels, the phonemic /i u/ and the outcomes of /e o/, if we consider [i u] from low-mid vowels as metaphonic allophones, as in (17) from Venosa:

(17) m/e/sə → m/i/sə → m[ai]sə
 r/i/rə → r[ai]rə
 r/ɛ/ndə → r[i]ndə

The picture is that of a complete overlap between /i u/ and /e o/ in a subset of the contexts and, again, the split of metaphony between a phonemic and an allophonic rule. Biuniqueness, invariance, and local determinacy all seem to be circumvented. We may ask ourselves what phonemics encodes, insofar as its epistemic categories either make the description more complex or fail to capture crucial generalizations concerning the internal organization of the system.

Linearity is in turn called into question by processes that transfer distinctiveness from one element to another. Eastern Andalusian Vowel Harmony is a process that has the effect of realizing the properties of one morpho-phonemic segment on an adjacent element. Here word-final -s aspirates and variably deletes, -s > h (> ∅), final mid vowels open to [ɛ ɔ] and the low vowel is fronted to [æ], as in (18) (Hualde and Sanders 1995).

(18) **Eastern Andalusian**
 [ˈmono] 'monkey' vs [ˈmɔnɔ⁽ʰ⁾] 'monkeys'
 [ˈboka] 'mouth' vs [ˈbɔkæ⁽ʰ⁾] 'mouths'
 [ˈtjene] '(s)he keeps' vs [ˈtjɛnɛ⁽ʰ⁾] 'you.SG keep'

The aperture degree extends over the mid vowels inside the word, including the stressed vowel, so that all mid vowels of the word are low-mid or, otherwise, high-mid. As for the origin of this process, Hualde and Sanders (1995: 426) maintain, as an alternative to the most current explanation according to which 'the final aspiration … has influenced the preceding vowel by opening it', that the open outcomes have been forced by a pre-existing vowel quality distinction between final mid vowels, realized as very close and approximating high vowels (Hualde and Sanders 1995: 428) and mid lax vowels preceding *–s* in the plural forms in nouns and between second and third persons singular in verbs. Jiménez and Lloret (2007) connect the opening of final mid vowels with the reduction of *–s* to *–h*/∅. In these varieties the property [spread glottis] generally associated with fricatives (Halle and Stevens 1971) contributes to the raising of the first formant, thus favouring the occurrence of low-mid vowels. However, what is crucial is the phonemic status of *-s*: according to Jiménez and Lloret (2007) there are contexts that make it possible to assume that /s/ is present in the phonemic representation of forms such as those in (19). Thus, the phonemic content of /s/ is ultimately realized by the opening of the adjacent vowel, a classic case of violation of the linearity condition.

(19)   /monos/   →   ['mɔnɔh]   →   ['mɔnɔ∅]   'monkeys'

In dealing with similar processes, Chomsky (1964: 87f.) concludes that:

> It seems to me, then, that ... the definition of a phoneme as 'a bundle of [phonetic] distinctive features', 'a class of phones in free variation or complementary distribution', or a 'minimal term in a phonological opposition' can be maintained only if we are willing to tolerate such absurdities as the phonemic representations /kæ̃t/, /rayDɪr/, /ra·yDɪr/ for 'can't', 'writer', 'rider', and so on, in many other cases.

Actually, this type of distribution is not unusual, and it frequently shows up as a consequence of partially obscured phonetic processes. In many Sardinian varieties the final *-s*, generally the inflexion of plural or of the second person singular of the verb, interacts with the following initial consonant, giving rise to sandhi. The set of alternants may include the deletion of *-s* combined with gemination of the following unvoiced obstruent or the approximant lenited outcomes of the initial voiced consonants. In Sèneghe, central Sardinia, the final *-s* is preserved before unvoiced stops, as in (20a), but deleted before voiced consonants in (20b) and absorbed by the following fricative or sonorant, in (20c). The data in (20a', b', c') illustrate the occurrences of the relevant initial consonants in intervocalic contexts, where they are preceded by the singular form of the article, *sa*, *su*, or by the object clitic. Finally, (20c') exemplifies the occurrence of the voiced stops in absolute initial contexts or when preceded by a nasal.

(20)   **Sèneghe (central Sardinia)**
    a.   sɔs 'piskizi 'the fishes'   a'.   su 'βiski   'the fish'
          ɖɔs 'tiru 'them= I.pull'   ɖu 'ðiru   'it– I.pull'
          sas 'kambaza 'the legs'   sa 'ɣamba   'the leg'
    b.   sa 'βukkaza 'the mouths'   b'.   sa 'ukka   'the mouth'
          sɔ 'βattɔzɔ 'the cats'   su 'attu   'the cat'
          sa 'ðɛntɛzɛ 'the teeth'   sa 'ɛntɛ   'the tooth'
    b".   i'm bukka 'in mouth'
          # 'battu 'cat'

c.	sa f'femminaza 'the women'		c'.	sa 'vemmina the woman'	
	sa m'mãʒɔ 'the hands'			sa 'mãũ 'the hand'	
	sa n'nuɣizi 'the walnuts'			sa 'nuɣi 'the walnut'	

The /s/ may correspond to a voiced approximant, in (20a), whereby the distinctive import of /s/ falls entirely on the following consonant, which is realized as a lenited outcome, in (21). The intermediate representation must be treated as phonemic in order to preserve the linearity condition, in that this must be read as an instantiation of the phonemic import of the sequence. Otherwise (cf. Chomsky 1964), linearity is not satisfied and the distinctive role of the phonemic representation is lost.

(21) /sos battos/ → so /β/attos ? → [sɔ βattɔzɔ]

An interesting test for biuniqueness and linearity is Valencian harmony. Here a harmonic change affects post-tonic -a which becomes [ɛ] or [ɔ] when preceded by stressed [ɛ] or [ɔ] respectively (Jiménez 1998). So, in Canals, we find the alternations in (22a–b). If the stressed vowel is one of [i e a o u], post-tonic -a is retained, as in (22c) (Jiménez 1998: 138, 146).

(22) **Canals (Valencia)**
a.	terra	'land'	/tɛra/	→	[tɛrɛ]
b.	porta	'door'	/pɔrta/	→	[pɔrtɔ]
c.	kasa	'house'	/kasa/	→	[kaza]
	mira	'(s)he looks'	/mira/	→	[mira]
	suma	'sum'	/suma/	→	[suma]
	pera	'pear'	/pera/	→	[pera]
	tota	'all.FSG'	/tota/	→	[tota]

Thus, the phonemic aperture degree of the final vowel in (22a–b), is totally absorbed by the stressed nucleus, which assigns it its own distinctive properties, low-mid and front/back, leading to a sort of mirror-image distribution. More clearly, phonetic representation conceals /a/ under stressed [ɛ ɔ], as suggested in (23).

(23) /pɔrta/   'door'   →   /pɔrtɔ/,   if   ɔ = /a+ɔ/

As a consequence, linearity, biuniqueness, local determinacy, and invariance are all avoided or ignored.

8.4 Phonemes and Historical Changes

Some linguists draw on the structural conceptualization of sound systems to explain changes from Latin to Romance. Weinrich (1958) explains the reorganization of the consonantal systems of Romance varieties as determined by the necessity of avoiding phonemic merger between degeminated outcomes of original geminate obstruents and original simple intervocalic obstruents. Thus, a phonological chain determines simplification of geminates and weakening (lenition) of the original unvoiced intervocalic obstruent in the spirit of the Martinet (1955). We know that degemination and intervocalic lenition/weakening do not always go hand in hand, and in many central Italian, Corsican, or Sardinian dialects, voicing or lenition does not imply degemination; the same is true for Florentine, where 'gorgia', the fricativization of intervocalic obstruents, co-exists with the geminates. Indeed, not even degemination presupposes voicing or lenition, as in the case of Romanian and some Gascon varieties (Béarnais; Rohlfs 1935) and Aragonese, where degemination does not combine with lenition/voicing. Haudricourt and Juilland ([1949] 1970) conclude that degemination is a necessary but not sufficient condition for lenition/voicing and connect the preservation of unvoiced obstruents in Romanian and Béarnais to the influence of the substrate that would have modified the nature of original geminates in a very early period of Romanization.

Lausberg ([1969] 1971) assumes that weakening in intervocalic position of original simple consonants has favoured degemination, so that new simple unvoiced outcomes have occupied the intervocalic slots vacated by original unvoiced obstruents. As Tekavčić (1980) notes, a crucial point is the chronology that one reconstructs, in that degemination must follow voicing/lenition: otherwise we would expect that outcomes of original geminates should also undergo lenition (Hall 1976). Martinet (1955) assumes that degemination was a long and slow process, so that it could have influenced voicing without totally overlapping with degeminated and original simple obstruents. Tekavčić (1980) connects voicing with other weakening phenomena that affected original voiced obstruents, and with the reduced functional load that originally existed between /p, t, k/ and /b, d, g/ in internal position. Recently, Loporcaro (2011) reviewing the entire question observes that the 'philological evidence' supports the hypothesis that lenition precedes and then forces degemination.

The preceding discussion concerns an application of the phonological chain in the change processes postulated by Martinet (1955) as the interpretive key to complex reorganization phenomena in phonological systems. Martinet discusses some other types of hypothesized chains in Romance varieties, in particular the vocalic shift in some French and Portuguese dialects, where the change in the articulation of a vowel has determined or favoured the movement of other vowels. In São Miguel (Azores), displacement of original /u/ to /y/ has triggered that of /o/ to /u/, and subsequently of /ɔ/ to /o/ and of /a/ to /ɔ/ (24).

(24)   a   →   ɔ   →   o   →   u   →   y

The idea is that the phonemic slot vacated by one phoneme can or must be filled by another element according to the functional relations holding inside the system. Martinet (1955) appealed to the connexion between palatalization of /u/ and distinctive efficiency proposed in Haudricourt and Juilland ([1949] 1970) for French, whereby the back articulatory space is limited and, therefore, tendentially unstable. Consequently, back vowel phonemes may seek a more recognizable definition by enriching their phonological content, i.e., by combining rounding and fronting. This necessity allegedly drove original *u to change to /y/ in old French and other western Romance varieties.

Another intriguing problem is the palatalization of /k/ before original *a in French and Occitan varieties (Tagliavini 1964; Banfi 1996). The internal impulse for the palatalization of *k cannot be reconstructed with certainty; nevertheless, Haudricourt and Juilland ([1949] 1970) find the explanation of this process in the reorganization of the Francien system in which the assibilation of the old *ki, ke* groups left the sequence *kä / kɛ* free to change into *k'ä / k'ɛ*. At the same time, monophthongization of *au* to *o* in the north and the loss of the *w* in *kw* in the centre had changed the status of the palatalized element *k'* from a combinatory variant to a phoneme. On the one hand, it occurred freely before *o*, e.g., *chaud* [ʃo] 'warm.MSG', and on the other we again find *a* following the velar *k*, e.g., *quand* [kã] 'when'. So, phonemicization of the palatal is the result of the overall relations inside the system. The fact that palatalization of *ka is absent in some northern French varieties and discontinuous in Romansh and other northern Italian varieties (Ladin, Friulian), is explained in Wartburg ([1936] 1980) by the influence of Germanic contact. The conclusion of Haudricourt and Juilland ([1949] 1970) is that in Picard and Norman varieties the regression to k has been possible since the palatalized result had not yet reached phonemic status, but remained a combinatory variant.

Now, we may ask ourselves what the functional load of this new phoneme could be. We illustrate this issue with data from a peripheral domain, the Cadore varieties of Borca and San Vito di Cadore (Italy) in (25). (25a) illustrates the outcome in stressed syllables, (25a') the preservation of kwa, (25b) the pre-tonic syllable, (25c) the final syllable. (25c') shows the possibility of k- occurring before -a; likewise, tʃ- can occur before other vowels, in (25c, d), also deriving from other original consonants. Finally, original ga has several outcomes, j and dʒ, and, in turn, j can derive from other consonantal elements, as in (25f).

(25)   **Cadore (Veneto)**
    a.   tʃɛza / tʃaza SVi. 'house'
           tʃaŋ / tʃɛi 'dog / dogs'
           tʃauðo/ tʃɔuðo 'hot.MSG'

a'. kwanta 'how much'
   b. tʃaˈvɛl 'hair'
      tʃaˈmɛza 'shirt'
   c. botʃa 'mouth'
   c'. pwotʃa / pwotʃo 'few.FSG / MSG'
       pwoka / pwoko 'few.FSG / MSG'
   d. al tʃama 'he calls'
      vɛtʃa / vɛtʃo 'old.FSG / MSG'
   e. jal / dʒal SVi. 'cock'
      jate / dʒate SVi. 'cat'
      jamba 'leg'
   f. ðeˈnwojo 'knee'

The point is that the preservation of kwa excludes the occurrence of k in the original context -a, except for the post-tonic contexts, as in *pwoka* in (25c'), apparently determined by a morphological process levelling the lexical base. We do find tʃ- before the other vowels, but we do not find k before a, at least in non-morphologically relevant contexts, i.e., inside the base. This preserves the original complementary distribution invoked by Haudricourt and Juilland ([1949] 1970), so that phonemicization does not seem a necessary or significant motivation in explaining historical processes.

8.5 Features Theory and Generative Phonology

It is well known that an early critical change in the paradigm of phonology is the Jakobsonian theory of phonological features. Jakobson (Jakobson [1929] 1962: 8) connects the status of phoneme to the presence of a bundle of invariable features. The universal set of phonological properties proposed in Jakobson, Fant, and Halle (1952) delineates a new phonology to the extent that the same features characterize phonemic and phonetic units. The feature theory is an essential part of the new phonology conceived in Halle (1959; 1962) and fully formulated in Chomsky and Halle (1968) (see also Harms 1968; Hyman 1970). Features allow us to express the measure of simplicity of representations by capturing the link between naturalness and the generality of the description, where the latter is directly interpreted in terms of the number of formal symbols (features and others) (Halle 1962). Moreover, features are able to capture natural classes, i.e., segments undergoing the same processes since they share phonological properties.

In Halle (1959), features combine with the Sapirian theory that sounds have a representational level underlying the phonetic one, which states what the speaker knows about sounds and their relation with lexical and morphological elements, i.e., what we now name knowledge of language. Sapir (1921; 1925; 1933), unlike European linguists inspired by Saussure, assigns to the phoneme a psychological nature revealed by the ability of naive speakers to detect the more abstract information underlying the phonetic realization, encoding the unpredictable properties of the lexical unit (see, for instance, Sapir 1921: 45f.). Sounds of a system and sound processes can only be fully understood as a 'complex psychology of association and pattern'. Halle (1959), going beyond Jakobson, lays the foundations of a phonology that excludes as inadequate the structuralist notion of the phoneme, replacing it with an abstract underlying level of representation that fixes the unpredictable properties that characterize the mental storage of lexical elements. The use of an identical set of primitives in phonetic and underlying phonological representations raises some typical questions, that Bromberger and Halle (1989: 53) depict in the following terms:

> phonology is concerned with the relationship between representations that encode the same type of information – phonetic information – but do so in ways that serve distinct functions: articulation and audition, on the one hand, and memory, on the other.

In the phonological model proposed by Chomsky and Halle (1968), phonology is definitively treated as a component of the grammar, part of the theory of the linguistic knowledge of speakers. Phonemes are no longer the abstract units reached by means of a formal procedure, devoid of a clear theoretical status. Chomsky and Halle (1968: 11) abandon this label. The phonological component is the 'system of rules' that apply to the syntactic surface representation and assign it a phonetic interpretation. They distinguish the 'lexical representation', i.e., the representation of formatives provided by the lexicon (Chomsky and Halle 1968: 12). The lexical representations contain the underlying, unpredictable, properties of lexical units. Rules map the 'input representations of systematic phonemes' into phonetic representations: no linearity, invariance and biuniqueness conditions are required. Any decision on the morphemic level depends on simplicity metric and naturalness of the process. In other words, rules account for the distribution of the phonological properties and express generalizations on the surface level. They are a part of the linguistic knowledge of the speaker, his or her internal language, and specify the relation between lexical units, syntactic structure, and their phonological interpretation (cf. Harms 1968; Hyman 1970).

Metaphony and the other numerous harmonization phenomena that characterize Romance languages provide an important testing ground for phonological conceptualization. We have seen that they generally are too complex to be dealt with in terms of phonemic contrasts. In fact, they involve a complex kind of linguistic mastery including phonological, lexical, and morphosyntactic properties, which alone can explain the distribution of the alternants and their identification by the speaker, circumventing the conceptual difficulties and the partial irrelevance of the notion of phoneme.

In the case of metaphony in Siniscola in (5) a rule of the type in (26) may be sufficient, expressing the distribution of [low] in mid vowels, i.e., except [a], [+back, −round]; X is a variable over any possible sequence of consonants, including a null one

(26) [−high] → [−low] / $\left[\dfrac{\quad\quad\quad\quad\quad\quad\quad}{\alpha \text{ back}, \alpha \text{ round}} \right]$ X [+high]

A rule such as (26) expresses a constraint on the occurrence of the low- and high-mid vowels, limiting [e o] [−low] outcomes to the contexts where they are followed by [i u], [−low, +high]. A type of knowledge that in this dialect can be accounted for by only referring to the phonological context. Returning to the metaphonies investigated in Section 8.3, we would expect that the negligible functional load of the contrast between the two series of vowels in Campidanian varieties could lead to the loss of the difference between low- and high-mid stressed vowels, in the terms of Martinet (1955). This does not take place (Savoia 2015; Frigeni 2002; 2004). Campidanian varieties preserve these alternations confirming the idea that a different level of representation is involved that the generative phonological model brings to light. Thus, we may assume that the lexical/morphemic representations alternating in (13a) have high-mid underlying vowels, while those in (13b) have low-mid vowels. The mapping between underlying and surface representations is implemented by two rules of metaphony, respectively in (27a) and in (27b) from Mascioni, that change them into the corresponding metaphonic alternants:

(27) a. [+vocalic, −low] → [+high] / ___ X [+vocalic, +high]
     b. [+vocalic, +low] → [−low] / ___ X [+vocalic, +high]

This knowledge is based on completely neutralized representations, as illustrated in the derivation in (28).

(28)   /v e t/ + /a/   /v e t/ + /u/   /pɛrd/ + /o/   /pɛrd/ + /i/
                                  [−high]   [+low]
     a.   i   ....
                                  [+high]
     b.   ....   e
                                                                         [−low]
              ↓   ↓   ↓   ↓
              ['veta]   ['vitu]   ['pɛrdo]   ['perdi]

Crucial here is that there is a level of representation of the lexical units that includes the unpredictable phonetic properties that define morphemes. We may understand these properties as part of the (unconscious) knowledge of the speaker. To know metaphony means to connect a more or less complex system of alternants for any lexical base, one which is not necessarily transparent. Speakers need to recognize the relevant morphemes also in opaque or neutralized contexts, recovering the underlying basic form. Opaque alternations have two main effects: the processes/rules may require mutual ordering, as in (29), and a neutralizing rule may conceal the lexical difference among alternants, implying a certain degree of abstractness, as in (29)–(30). Anyway, the knowledge required of the speaker involves the relation between meaning and morphosyntactic properties. In a case such as Orroli, in which a process raises all post-tonic mid vowels to [+high], we need to assume that the metaphony rule applies before the raising rule, or, more correctly, to underlying non-raising forms, as in (31).

(29) Metaphony Rule (MR)
  ε, ɔ → e, o

  [−high] → [−low]/ $\left[\begin{array}{c} \underline{} \\ +\text{stress} \end{array} \right]$ X [+high, −low]

  Neutralization Rule (NR)
  e, o → i, u / ___ X #

  [−low] → [+high] / $\left[\begin{array}{c} \underline{} \\ -\text{stress} \end{array} \right]$ X #

The metaphony rule in (29) changes [−high] stressed vowels into [−low] if the following vowel is [+high]; it applies to the underlying representations, independently of the neutralization that maps mid vowels to high outcomes in post-/pre-tonic position, as illustrated by the alternations ['oɣu] / ['ɔɣuzu], ['srɛβu] / ['sreβizi] in (30).

(30)

	/srɛβ/ −/o/	/srɛβ/ +/is/	/ɔɣ/ +/os/	/ɔɣ/ +/u/
	[−high]	[−high]	[−high]	[+high]	[−high]	[−high]	[−high]	[+high]
MR	....		↓		......		↓	
			[−low]				[−low]	
NR	u				u			
	[+high]		↓		[+high]		↓	
	↓				↓			
	['srɛβu]		['sreβis]		['ɔyus]		['oɣu]	

Alternations such as those in (30), in which a segment preserves a phonetic property of a different segment no longer recognizable in the sequence, are reminiscent of the classic cases of abstractness discussed in Hyman (1970). Extrinsic order and opacity (Kiparsky 1982; Hyman 1970) entail a complex type of knowledge and have been at the centre of the debate about the degree of abstractness admissible in phonology.

Successive revisions of the original model of Chomsky and Halle (1968) have enriched the structural endowment of the theory, assuming an autosegmental representation (Goldsmith 1990), hierarchical organization of features (Clements 1985), and prosodic structure. In this vein, the fundamental tenets of Government Phonology (Kaye 1986–87; 1990; Kaye, Lowenstamm, and Vergnaud 1990; Harris 1994) constrain the format of phonological representations and the nature of possible processes in terms of phonetic interpretability. Furthermore, some proposals aim to redefine the nature of the underlying representations. Contrary to the underspecification model, Halle et al. (2000), Calabrese (1998), and Nevins (2010) argue for underlying representations fully specified in order to obtain a simpler and naturalistic interpretation of segments and processes. A different line consists in recourse to privative monovalent elements (Kaye, Lowenstamm, and Vergnaud 1985; Harris and Lindsey 1990; 1995; Backley 2011). This solution answers some descriptive and theoretical questions, by constraining the format of the rules and the treatment of the processes.

Calabrese (1995; 1998) treats metaphony as an autosegmental process sensitive to markedness constraints on possible combinations of features. The idea that not all bundles of features have the same degree of naturalness, so demanding readjustment rules, is connected to the morphological mechanisms proposed by Halle and Marantz (1993) in the Distributed Morphology model. A traditional problem of metaphony is that the outcomes of high-mid stressed vowels are generally [i u] before high final vowels, while the low-mid stressed vowels present different outcomes. If we assume a unique process, like Calabrese (1995; 1998), whereby [+high] is the metaphonizing trigger as in (31), the combination of [+high] with [−ATR], the feature specifying the intermediate degrees of height, is forbidden in these varieties and, generally, very expensive. So [+high, −ATR] derived as the metaphonic outcome from low-mid vowels [−high, −ATR], is avoided by changing [+high,−ATR] into [−high, +ATR] [e o], or into diphthongs splitting the two features between two positions, [ie]/[uo] as in the dialect of Arpino in (31) (discussed in Calabrese 1998; Parodi 1892) presenting a morphologized arrangement in which it is masculine singular, masculine plural, second person singular, etc., that trigger metaphony.

(31)   ˈnera / ˈnirɔ 'black.FSG / MSG'
       ˈsola / ˈsulɔ 'alone.FSG / MSG'
       ˈsɛntə / ˈsjɛntə 'I feel / you.SG feel'
       ˈkɔʎʎə / ˈkwɔʎʎə 'I pick / you.SG pick'

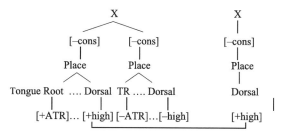

Figure 8.1

Spreading of [+high] is problematic when it links to the content of the low-mid vowels, such as those in Figure 8.1, where, in order to avoid the combination with [−ATR], a readjustment rule is required that either reverses the values of features to [−high, +ATR] or splits [+high] and [−ATR] into two separate segments [iɛ], [uɔ] (Calabrese 1995: 396).

As we see, the autosegmental model constrains the possible format of the rules, allowing only rules manipulating the specifications present in the structure. In these approaches the properties of underlying representations cannot be entirely obscured.

Let us consider height harmony in the Pasiego Cantabrian variety, described in Penny (1969), where, if the stressed vowel is [+high], pre-tonic [−low] vowels realize as [+high], as illustrated by the examples in (32a) (Harris and Lindsey 1995). Mid pre-tonic vowels are allowed only if the stressed vowel is in turn mid or low. On the contrary, a pre-tonic high vowel also occurs freely, if the stressed vowel is mid or low, as in (32b). This distribution suggests that harmony in (32a) cannot be explained in terms of the simple propagation of the height value [+/−high] from the stressed vowel, otherwise we would expect **senteré, **senterán. Rather, it is possible to see the assimilation in (32a) as the result of the propagation of [+high] alone (Vago 1988).

(32) **Pasiego Cantabrian**

	INF	1SG.FUT	2PL.FUT	3PL.FUT	
a.	bebér	beberé	bibirí:s	beberán	'drink'
	komér	komeré	kumirí:s	komerán	'eat'
b.	sintír	sintiré	sintirí:s	sintirán	'feel'

A different treatment can be tested, in which a more general mechanism is assumed. In Government Phonology, vocalic and consonantal segments are characterized by privative elements, such as [A] for aperture, [I] for palatality, [U] for roundedness and velarity (Backley 2011). The assumption of privative properties prevents phonological analysis from using feature changing rules such as (a) in Figure 8.2, insofar as privative elements force underlying representations either to have or not a specific property, as in (b) a   [–high] → [+high] / ___ X [+high, +stress]

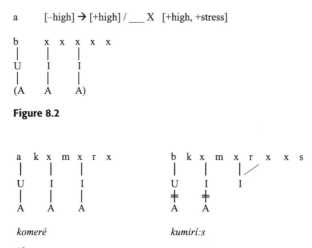

Figure 8.2

Figure 8.3

in Figure 8.2. The autosegmental format, in turn, excludes the insertion of phonological material not present in the representation.

Privative elements reduce the possible rules and the possible representations admitting only that elements are deleted (delinking) or spread (association). The result is that the underlying representations can only be a subset of the overall possible representations.

In keeping with Harris (1990), Harris and Lindsey (1995), mid vowels include two properties, or elements, so that Pasiego harmony can be treated as delinking, whereby [A] in a weak pre-tonic position is admitted only if present on the stressed vowel, as in Figure 8.3. The mechanism involved is licensing by the prosodic head in the domain. So raising in (b) is caused by the occurrence of a high stressed vowel; mid vowels [e o] [I/U, A] in a weak prosodically governed nucleus are allowed only if the head stressed vowel includes in turn [A], as in (a). Otherwise, in the weak positions [A] is delinked, as in (b).

Naturally we assume that mid vowels are present in the underlying lexical representation.

8.6 Approaches to Complex Phenomena: Phonology as Externalization

As we saw, Romance phenomena have provided phonological theory with processes that require types of interpretation involving something different from distinctiveness or, even, the traditional underlying representations of Chomsky and Halle (1968). A more sophisticated kind of knowledge seems to be involved. Following Calabrese (1998) and Nevins (2005), contrastiveness can be appealed to as a property driving harmonic processes. A harmonic distribution of aperture properties in the stressed and in the weak following vowel characterizes some central Sardinian varieties, such as that of Àllai (Savoia 2005; Loporcaro 2005). The occurrence of a low-mid vowel [ɛ]/[ɔ] in post-tonic position implies a low-mid vowel in stressed position, as illustrated in (33a), but the contrary is not true, given that stressed [ɛ]/[ɔ] can co-occur with [a] in post-tonic position but post-tonic [ɛ]/[ɔ] are excluded from the contexts in which the tonic vowel is [a], as in (33b). Vowels [i a u] freely co-occur, so that stressed [a] co-occurs with post-tonic [i a u], and correspondingly tonic [i]/[u] co-occur with post-tonic [I a u], as in (33b). Metaphony affects the height degree of stressed mid vowels requiring a [+ATR] if followed by post-tonic [i]/[u]. High-mid vowels [e]/[o] occur only in stressed position when followed by post-tonic [i u], as in (33c), according to the requirements of Sardinian metaphony discussed in Section 8.3.

(33) Àllai (central Sardinia)
    a.   ['kɛrdzɔ] / ['kɛrɛzɛ] 'I want / you.SG want'
        ['bɛttʃa] / ['bɛttʃɔzɔ] 'old.FSG / old.MPL'
        ['mɔvvɔ] / ['mɔvvɛzɛ] 'I move / you.SG move'
    b.   ['sannu] / ['sanna] / ['sannuzu] / ['sannaza] 'healthy.MSG / FSG / MPL / FPL'
        ['patti] 'part, portion'
        ['sikku] / ['sikka] / ['sikkuzu] / ['sikkaza] 'dry.MS / FSG / MPL / FPL'
        ['liddʒu] / ['liddʒizi] 'I read / you.SG read'
        ['suðru] / ['suðra] / ['suðruzu] / ['suðraza] 'deaf.MS / FSG / MPL / FPL'
    c.   [ap'perizi] 'you.SG open', ['bettʃu] 'old.MSG'
        ['morizi] 'you.SG die'

In these systems distributional constraints that relate the height degree of final vowels to the height degree of stressed ones let [−high, −ATR] combine both with final low-mid vowels and [a]. Consequently, this specification has a contrastive status. Likewise, metaphonic [−high, +ATR] is contrastive with respect to stressed [i u], since these latter admit final vowels [+high, +ATR], as suggested in (34) from Àllai. As for mid vowels, [−low, −ATR] vowels contrast with [−low, +ATR] ones.

(34)   i   u   [+high, −low, +ATR]
       ɛ   ɔ   [−high, −low, −ATR]
       e   o   [−high, −low, +ATR]
           a   [−high, +low, −ATR]

The distribution in (34) suggests that height properties of post-tonic vowels are licensed by the stressed vowel. Metaphony represents only one of the harmonic devices which govern the possible combinations of vowels in the domain of the stressed vowel. Moreover, this distribution raises an evident problem for the classical framework in generative phonology, suggesting that [a] and high vowels [i u] form the natural class of the vowels that exclude mid vowels in final position. On the contrary, the traditional feature composition proposed in Chomsky and Halle (1968) gathers [a] with low-mid as [−high, +low], excluding a natural class comprising [a] and [+high] vowels, [i u]. This difficulty maintains also in a model endowed with [ATR], as (37), where [a], [+low, −ATR], cannot be put together with [+high, +ATR] vowels [i u].

We may suppose that the relevant intuition is that harmony corresponds to a phase of an incomplete expansion of the neutralization in [+high] vowels discussed in Section 8.3. That is, in harmonizing dialects metaphonic contexts are safeguarded, given that post-tonic mid vowels are anyway preserved in the context of mid tonic vowels, while neutralization applies in the contexts where the stressed nuclei occur which are not involved in metaphony, i.e., [i a u]. In conclusion we will assume that the height properties of the final mid vowels are sensitive to those of the stressed vowel, including metaphony, in (35a) and the requirement whereby the mid final vowels have to be authorized (licensed) by the properties of the stressed vowel. Specifically post-tonic [ɛ ɔ] need to be preceded by the corresponding contrastive value in the tonic vowel [−low, −ATR], as in (35b). Hiatus contexts in the variety of Àllai relaxes (35b) and allows [i u] to co-occur with post-tonic [ɛ ɔ], as in [ˈniɛ] 'snow'.

(35) a. ATR metaphony
[+high] and [+ATR] in the stressed nucleus license [+high, +ATR] in the following vowel.
b. Harmony of low-mid vowels
Contrastive specification [−low, −ATR] in the stressed vowel licenses [−low, −ATR] in the following vowel.

This treatment fits with the crucial intuition (cf. Savoia and Maiden 1997; Walker 2005; Savoia 2015) that in metaphony and in other harmonic processes, the stressed vowel licenses the vocalic segments in its domain by subsuming a subset of their properties, in this case the aperture and height properties. As matters stand, all other combinations include high vowels in post-tonic position, and in the case of a tonic mid vowel, the application of (35a) generates the metaphonic result [e o]. Otherwise we have low-mid outcomes, as in Figure 8.4 from Àllai.

If we use the element model, the alternations of Àllai in (33) imply the alignment of elements. Unlike features, elements allow us to obtain a

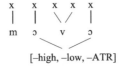

['mɔvvɔ] 'I.move'

Figure 8.4

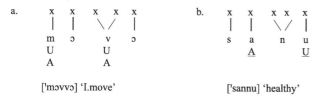

Figure 8.5

unified expression of the phenomenon. A low-mid vowel [I/ U, A] in final position is admitted in the context of a low-mid stressed vowel; thus, [A] in a complex expression in post-tonic position is legitimated by [A] in a complex expression in stressed position as in (a) in Figure 8.5. Otherwise, a post-tonic position licenses simple expressions [I]/ [U]/ [A], as in (b) in Figure 8.5.

A rethinking of the theoretical status of phonology has been proposed by Chomsky in recent years (Hauser et al. 2002). The central property of language coincides with syntax (Hauser et al. 2002), i.e., the 'basic compositional operation, Merge' along with the word-like atomic elements (Berwick and Chomsky 2016). Phonology and morphology are part of the system for externalization that 'convert internal syntactic objects to the entities accessible to the Sensory-Motor interpretive system' (Berwick and Chomsky 2016: 40, 82). Phonology is no longer the guarantor of the underlying distinctiveness, but coincides with the phonetic, morphophonological, and prosodic outcome of the process of externalization making syntactic objects and lexical elements interpretable for the speaker. Abstractness per se is not a theoretical problem. The true issue is to specify the morphophonological and phonological mechanisms and generalizations that relate morphemes, phonetic units, and syntactic objects.

The assumption that phonological units are directly defined by the processes they take part in seems able to capture their role in the externalization. Many distributional phenomena favour this interpretation. For instance, in the vowel systems of the Surselvan and Engadine Romansh varieties, here exemplified by Trun (Surselva), stressed [ɔ] corresponds to etymological *a in contexts where it is followed by a nasal in coda, __NC, including original geminate nasals, as in [ɔn] 'year', in (36a). Before a velar nasal in the word-final position, in intervocalic position and __ N [C, −voiced] the diphthongs [au]/[ɛu] occur, according to different varieties, as in (36a–b). In the other contexts [a] occurs, as in (36c).

(36) **Trun (Surselva)**
    a.   context __ N$_{coda}$]
        [jau ˈkɔntəl] / [nus kanˈtain] 'I.sing / we.sing', [ˈkɔmba] 'leg'
        [gʀɔnt] / [ˈgʀɔnda] 'big.MSG / FSG'
        [ɔn(s)] 'year/s', [fɔm] 'hunger'

b. context ___N
[mauŋ] 'hand', [cauŋ] 'dog', [sauŋ] / ['sauᵑna] 'healthy.M / F'
c. [naːs] 'nose', [bʀaːtʃ] 'arm', [ˈaːla] 'wing'

Descriptively, these outcomes can be dealt with by assuming that nasals spread a velar resonance. Stressed nuclei in the contexts where the nasal is not a coda, subsume the resonance properties of the nasal, changing to [ɔ]. The association of element [U] (Backley 2011) with the velar configurations is particularly clear in the contexts where the diphthong is realized in the presence of a velar or (pre)velarized quality of the final or intervocalic nasal, as in (36b) (Savoia and Baldi 2017).

The question is how this assimilation can be analysed in a coherent theoretical framework. We may think that the phonological potential of segments is involved in fixing the organization of the sequence. More precisely, there are languages in which (a part of) the phonological properties of the string are instantiated by the tonic vowel, at least in certain contexts. This is true of the Romansh varieties such as that of Trun, where nasality is doubled and implemented by the stressed vowel. As for the content of nasals, according to Harris and Lindsey (1995) it includes an inherent acoustic low-frequency configuration expressed by [L]. In our varieties this low-frequency property is interpreted by [U] in the vowels. The difficulty is evident: neither elements nor features are able to express the link between rounding/velarization and nasality in a natural way. We can tentatively assume that a low-frequency formant [Lf1] is involved in the harmonizing process; more precisely, [Lf1] will have slightly different sensorimotor interface level interpretations according to its role in the string. The [Lf1] element of the nasal is shared and, in this way, legitimized, by the stressed vowel including [A] giving rise to a (high) back vowel. The different solutions depend on the different prosodic domains where the stressed nucleus acts as a licenser. For instance, in the diphthongs, the [U] element is realized as a segment inside the nucleus, as in Figure 8.6 for Trun.

The phonosyntactic import of alternations has been generally overshadowed in structuralist treatments, focusing on distinctive efficiency, as well as in generative phonology, insofar as what is explored are the word-domain processes. Nevertheless, phonosyntactic phenomena uncover the strict linkage between syntactic properties and phonological externalization, in that sentence phonology also contributes to depicting the Conceptual-Intentional level of interpretation (Manzini and Savoia 2016).

tʃ [A]   x   x   Ø
 \ |
  [Lf1,U]   [tʃauŋ] 'dog'

Figure 8.6

This type of process has always had an ancillary role, understood as a marginal mechanism in comparison with the word-domain processes, usually a function of the word-internal inflexion, and consequently distinctive. More to the point, there is continuity between word-internal and phonosyntactic processes, in the sense that the latter context is only a subset of the former, the same sound-meaning relation valid in the former also holding for the latter. So a unified treatment is necessary to achieve at least descriptive adequacy. Propagation of *u* is a good example, providing grounds for a strongly different consideration of the underlying representation, substantially indifferent to the traditional constraints on the phonological representations. Here the process becomes the true object of analysis, rather than the nature of the representation. Propagation is the assimilatory process (left-to-right) characterizing many southern Italo-Romance varieties in which a stressed [−round] vowel [i ɛ a] and, in some grammars, also pre-tonic [a], copy the content of a [+back, +round] vowel (typically [u]) occurring in the preceding word-internal and syntactic context (Rohlfs 1966; Piccillo 1971; Mocciaro 1978; Tuttle 1985; Savoia 1987; 2001; Schirru 2008; 2013; Savoia and Baldi 2016b; 2018).

In the Calabrian variety of Cerchiara (37), harmonic spreading creates sequences such as [uæ], and takes place both in open and in closed syllables, regardless of the nature of the intermediate consonant. Word-internal contexts are illustrated in (37a), phonosyntactic contexts in (37b) and (37c) respectively for D-N and Cl-V. Stressed nuclei other than [æ] may also be involved, cf. [uɛ] in (37b). The outcome of metaphony does not undergo propagation, as in (37d).

(37) **Cerchiara (northern Calabria)**
    a. [purˈtuæßə] / [purˈtuæmmə] '(I) brought / (we) brought'
    b. [u ˈnuæsə] 'the nose'   b'. [ˈnæɐsə] 'nose'
    c. [m u ˈðuæjə] '(you) me= it= give'   c'. [kə mə ˈðæɐjə] 'what (you) me give?'
        [u ˈfuættsə] '(I) it.M= do' [a ˈfættsə] '(I) it.F= do'
    d. [kuˈtʃiːmə] '(we) cook'

In Saracena, unstressed [u] spreads to stressed /a/ in open syllables when the two nuclei are adjacent, yielding [ɔː], for instance word-internally in (38a) or in phonosyntactic contexts in (38b). In (38a') no harmony is triggered in the absence of [u] and the usual long palatalized outcome [ɛː] occurs; in (38b') the closed syllable blocks propagation.

(38) **Saracena (northern Calabria)**
    a. [stuˈtɔːmə] 'we.extinguish'   cf. [ˈstuːtə] 'I extinguish'
    a'. [caˈmɛːmə] 'we.call'
    b. [u ˈnɔːsə] 'the nose'   [ˈnɛːsə] 'nose'
        [u ˈcɔːmə] 'I him= call'   [a ˈcɛːmə] 'I her= call'
    b'. [u/a ˈfattsə]   'I it.M/F= do'

In Stigliano in (39) (Savoia 1987), spreading affects all stressed vowels and also pre-tonic [a]. The outcomes of the harmony for stressed /a/ are [ɔː] in (39a), [wɔː] following a velar consonant in open syllable and [wa] in closed syllable, in (39b, b′, c). For pre-tonic [a] the outcomes are [wɔ] after velar consonant and [ɔ] in other contexts, cf. (39d–e). For other stressed vowels we find the simple insertion of a [w u] segment, in (39f).

(39) **Stigliano (southern Basilicata)**

a.	[lə ˈnɔːsə] 'the nose'	cf.	[ˈnaːsə] 'nose'
	[səˈdɔːvə] 'I sweated'		[ˈseudə] 'I sweat'
b.	[lə ˈkwɔːnə] 'the dog'		[ˈkaːnə] 'dog'
b′.	[təkˈkwɔːvə] 'I touched'		[ˈtɔkkə] 'I touch'
c.	[lə ˈlwaskwə] 'I him= leave'		[la ˈlaskwə] 'I her= leave'
c′.	[addəmˈmwannə] 'I ask'		
d.	[lə kwɔˈnɔskə] 'I him= know'		[la kaˈnɔskə] 'I her= know'
e.	[lə sɔˈpeimə] 'we it= know'		[saˈpeimə] 'we know'
f.	[lə ˈdwiʃtə] 'the finger'		[ˈdiʃtə] 'finger'

Thus, propagation has the representation in Figure 8.7, in which the phonological content of pre-tonic [u] is copied in the nuclear space of the stressed vowel, where it creates a rising diphthong, as in Cerchiara, in (a) in Figure 8.7, or combines with the content of the host nucleus, giving rise to [ɔ], as in Saracena in (b) in Figure 8.7. Following Walker (2005) and Kaun (1995), we may think that the harmonizing effect makes this domain, i.e., the pre-tonic span, phonetically interpretable.

Propagation allows for morphosyntactic constraints, as detailed in Rizzi and Savoia (1993) and Manzini and Savoia (2016). The various contexts triggering this harmony include, in addition to the word-internal contexts, the masculine determiners, in particular the articles u/lə/nu/nə, and the masculine singular object clitics u/lə, as illustrated in (37)–(39). Propagation can be induced also by other syntactic contexts, with differences among dialects, as the first person singular and third

Figure 8.7

person plural ending -u of the auxiliary and copula, the negation [ɔn], the masculine singular ending -u of prenominal adjectives and other morphosyntactic combinations. If we consider the morphosyntactic distribution of spreading in the varieties of Saracena, Cerchiara, and Stigliano, the schema in (40a) obtains. Following the generalizations in Rizzi and Savoia (1993) and Manzini and Savoia (2013), the relevant contexts are assigned '+' if propagation is systematic, '+/−' if it is variable and '−' if it does not apply. In (40b) examples are provided for the syntactic contexts not illustrated in (37)–(39).

(40) a.

		Saracena	Cerchiara	Stigliano
i.	D-N/Adj	+	+	+
ii.	Q-N/Adj	+/−	+	−
iii.	Adj-N	+	+	−
iv.	Cl-V	+	+	+
v.	Neg-V	−	+	−
vi.	Modal/copula/auxiliary-V	+/−	+	−

b. Stigliano
    i. [kədd ˈuautə ˈfuɪʎʎə]   'that other son'
  Cerchiara
    ii. [ccu ˈggruænnə]   'more big, bigger'
    iii. [nu ˈbbuɛllə ˈkuænə]   'a fine dog'
    v. [ɔnˈn uæddʒə ˈßuɪstə]   'not I.have seen (= I did not see)'
    vi. [l ˈamu ˈfuættə]   'it= we.have made (= we have made it)'
       [su gˈguæβətə]   'they.are tall'
  Saracena
    ii. [ccu sˈsɛːnə]/ [ccu sˈsɔːnə]   'more= healthy'
    iii. [nu bˈbɛllu ˈkɔːnə]   'a fine dog'
    v. [ˈsɪɲɲu ˈnɔːtə]   'I.was born'
       [u βuˈlimə fɔːl fɛː]   'it= we.want do (= we want to do it)'
       [su sˈsɛːnə/ sˈsɔːnə]   'they.are healthy'

According to Manzini and Savoia (2016), propagation essentially shows agreement on the properties (features) of gender/nominal class and number inside the clause. The sole type of agreement relation that is irrelevant for propagation is *subject–predicate*, NP [$_{VP}$ V... The point seems to be that since agreement between subject and verb does not involve the nominal class, the syntactic mechanism underlying propagation must involve the properties of nominal class. In the structures in (41a–b), from Saracena, inflexions are analysed as introducing referential properties (lexical categories) associated to the nominal/adjectival root. The subscript letters indicate the argumental properties of the noun or verb roots.

(41) a.

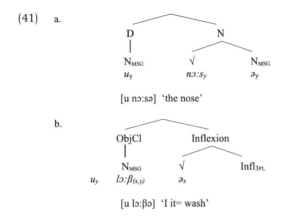

[u nɔ:sə] 'the nose'

b.

[u lɔ:βə] 'I it= wash'

Agreement can be understood as the identity of a set of phi-feature clusters interpreted as a single argument discontinuously instantiated, e.g., the features of the article and the nominal inflexion (Manzini and Savoia 2016), leading to the interpretation of the sentence. Therefore, the phenomena of propagation that we are concerned with can be seen as phonological constructs that externalize syntactic information, namely those concerning inflexional/agreement properties. It is no accident that propagation, on a par with other harmony processes, allows extension and amplification over a phonological domain of a perceptually vulnerable property, and relevant for interpretation (Kaun 1995; Walker 2005; Nevins 2010).

8.7 Concluding Remarks

We have seen from Romance data that the traditional structuralist notion of the phoneme is inadequate to capture the internal mechanisms that drive the processes. Functional notions such as phonemic load and the organization of the system suggest some motivations, which do not seem however to be conclusive. Indeed, the notion of phoneme generally obscures the system of morphological and syntactic relations, on which the grammar of a language is constructed. We saw that taxonomic procedures of phonemics raise many problems, given that the logical necessity of a regular and predictable correspondence between phonetic and phonemic representation is weakened by many usual phenomena. Complementary distribution and the notion of minimal pair are unsatisfactory insofar as they are constrained at least by morphological requirements, which may substantially influence the distribution of the phonemes.

Generative phonology pursues a different conception of phonology, as a part of the knowledge of the speaker, the Internal Language. In the current picture of linguistic knowledge, phonology is part of the externalization processes that translate syntactic hierarchical objects into the 'sequential format' including word formation and phonological organization, accessible to the production and perception systems. Phonological processes translate lexical information into sequences interpretable at the Sensory-Motor interface, possibly partially modifying the lexical content of morphemes and words, thus contributing to the variation across languages. (Berwick and Chomsky 2016; Chomsky, Gallego, and Ott 2019).

Selected References

Below you can find selected references for this chapter. The full references can be found online at the following page: www.cambridge.org/Romancelinguistics

Calabrese, A. (1998). 'Metaphony revisited', *Rivista di linguistica* 10: 7–68.
Chomsky, N. (1964). *Current Issues in Linguistic Theory*. The Hague: Mouton.
Halle, M. (1962). 'Phonology in generative grammar', *Word* 18: 54–72.
Harris, J. and Lindsey, G. (1995). 'The elements of phonological representation'. In Durand, J. and Katamba, F. (eds), *Frontiers of Phonology*. London: Longman, 34–79.
Haudricourt, A. and Juilland, A. ([1949] 1970). *Essai pour une histoire structurale du phonétisme français*. The Hague/Paris: Mouton.
Hualde, J. I. and Sanders, B. (1995). 'A new hypothesis on the origin of the Eastern Andalusian vowel system', *Annual Meeting of the Berkeley Linguistics Society* 21(1): 426–37. http://dx.doi.org/10.3765/bls.v21i1.1386.
Kiparsky, P. (1982). *Explanation in Phonology*. Dordrecht: Foris.
Loporcaro, M. (2005). 'Typological remarks on Sardinian: 1. Vowel harmony 2. Sardinian in a correlative typology of the Romance languages', *Sprachtypologie und Universalienforschung*, 58: 210–27.
Maiden, M. (1991). *Interactive Morphonology: Metaphony in Italy*. London: Routledge.
Savoia, L. and Baldi, B. (2016a). 'Armonie vocaliche e metafonia nelle varietà siciliane', *Bollettino Centro di studi filologici e linguistici siciliani* 27: 201–37.
Savoia, L. and Baldi, B. (2016b). 'Propagation and preservation of rounded back vowels in Lucanian and Apulian varieties', *Quaderni di linguistica e studi orientali* 2: 11–58.
Vago, R. (1988). 'Underspecification in the height harmony system of Pasiego', *Phonology* 5: 343–62.

9

Typologically Exceptional Phenomena in Romance Phonology

Eulàlia Bonet and Francesc Torres-Tamarit

9.1 Introduction

The goal of this chapter is to survey a set of phonological phenomena in Romance that might be considered exceptional from a cross-linguistic, typological perspective.[*] A phonological phenomenon may either be rarely documented within Romance but relatively common in other languages, or hardly attested in the world's languages but present to some degree in Romance. We offer a panoramic overview of such phenomena and, in most cases, briefly explore their consequences for phonological theory.

Typological studies and phonological theory have always gone side by side. On the one hand, the central task of phonological theory is to determine the range of cross-linguistic variation. Phonology is eminently typological in this respect. If we think of Optimality Theory (OT), still the mainstream framework in phonology, the description of individual systems in terms of language-particular rankings of universal but violable constraints is inseparable from claims about phonological typology. The recent development of software tools that calculate factorial typologies in OT make it possible for analysts to investigate computationally the typological predictions of their analyses. On the other hand, typologists are interested in the relative distribution of grammatical properties, that is, in their cross-linguistic frequency. Some phonological theories integrate functional

---

[*] We would like to thank Stephen Anderson, Travis Bradley, Walcir Cardoso, Franco Fanciullo, Rob Jelier, Mark Jones, Ioan Mascaró, Andrew Nevins, Diana Passino, Douglas Pulleyblank, Lori Repetti, Paolo Roseano, Patric Sauzet, Donca Steriade, Maria del Mar Vanrell, Xulio Viejo Fernández, Marina Vigário, and Leo Wetzels for kindly answering our questions and for giving us wise advice on where to look to find phonological rarities in Romance. We acknowledge support from MCIN/AEI/10.13039/501100011033 (Project PID2020-113971GB-C22), and E. Bonet also acknowledges support from the Catalan Government (research group 2017 SGR 634). Both authors contributed equally to this work and are responsible for any errors.

considerations into their models in order to explain the observed relative distribution of phonological properties. Another current line of research attempts to explain the prevalence of certain phonological patterns as a result of learning biases, explored from either experimental or computational approaches. The fact that the relationship between phonological theory and typology is a topic of current interest is evidenced by the publication within a two-year period of one monograph by Gordon (2016) and another by Hyman and Plank (2018), both entitled *Phonological Typology*.

In addressing the wide array of topics concerning Romance phonology covered in this chapter from the perspective of phonological typology, we have not only evaluated the phenomena in relation to the notion of markedness as it is found in phonological theory, but also referred, when possible, to their relative frequency cross-linguistically as well as their geographical distribution. We have consulted three online databases for this comparison: *PHOIBLE* Online (Moran et al. 2014), an archive of cross-linguistic phonological inventories of 1,672 languages, the *World Atlas of Language Structures*, *WALS Online* (Dryer and Haspelmath 2013), a database of grammatical properties of 2,679 languages, and the *World Phonotactics Database* (Donohue et al. 2013), a database of phonotactic restrictions including phonotactic data on over 2,000 languages and segmental information for an additional 1,700.

Section 9.2 is devoted to phoneme inventories, Section 9.3 reviews aspects related to syllabic structure, Section 9.4 covers several segmental processes, while Section 9.5 addresses various issues related to autosegmental features.

9.2 Phoneme Inventories

9.2.1 Front Rounded Vowels

Few languages of the world have front rounded vowels. In *WALS Online*, out of 562 languages, 37 have one or more front rounded vowels (23 high and mid; 8 high only; 6 mid only). According to PHOIBLE Online, between 1 and 4 per cent of the inventories of the world's languages include front rounded vowels, with the higher percentage (4 per cent) corresponding to inventories with the short high front rounded vowel /y/. Within Europe, front rounded vowels are more common in northern languages, such as Dutch, German, Northern Frisian, Norwegian, Swedish, Finnish, Estonian, or Breton. But in Romance languages front rounded vowels are found in other varieties beyond the well-known case of standard French, with /y/, /ø/, /œ/, and the nasalized /œ̃/. Schmid (2016) reports the presence of /y/ and /ø/ in the Romansh varieties of Vallader and Puter and in the Ladin variety of Marèo (the same vowels being present in Ligurian, a Gallo-Italic variety). Occitan has /y/ and, as observed in Roseano and Finco (2021), the Ladin variety of

Moena has /ø/. Canadian French has, in addition to /y/, /ø/, /œ/, and nasalized /œ̃/, the lax high front rounded vowel /ʏ/, in words such as *lune* 'moon'. While Portuguese does not generally have front rounded vowels, /y/ and /ø/ are present in southern varieties of continental Portugal and in one of the Azores islands, São Miguel (sporadically in another island, Terceira). This fact has been studied by Krämer (2017), who observes that these vowels can also appear in unstressed position and in diphthongs such as [øw] and [øj].

9.2.2 Galician *Geada*

In Galician, as in Spanish or Catalan, there is a complementary distribution between the set of non-continuant voiced obstruents [b d g] and the voiced continuants [β ð ɣ]. The former set appears in word-initial position after a pause, and after homorganic laterals and homorganic nasals. The set of voiced continuants appears in all other contexts, that is, after vowels and continuant sonorants (see Mascaró 1992 for a general overview of this process of spirantization in Basque, Catalan, and Spanish). In the so-called *geada* dialects of Galician, however, there is a gap in the series of the continuant voiced allophones [β ð ɣ]: the voiced velar continuant [ɣ], typical of other dialects of Galician, is replaced by the voiceless velar fricative [x]. In word-initial position, after a pause or not, *geada* dialects also exhibit [x] instead of the voiced velar stop [g]. Therefore, in this position the contrast is only between /k/ and /x/, not between /g/, /k/, and /x/. In post-nasal contexts, *geada* dialects are subdivided into three more specific varieties: the largest variety has [g] after velar nasals, another variety keeps [x] in that context, and there is still another variety that has [k] in post-nasal contexts. The data on *geada* dialects are taken from Colina (2013) and illustrated in (1) (see also Martínez-Gil 2004).

(1)   Geada dialects of Galician
    a.   Word-initial position
        gato   ['xato]   'cat'
        grilo   ['xrilo]   'cricket'
    b.   Post-vocalic and post-sonorant context
        agua   ['axwa]   'water'
        algo   ['alxo]   'something'
        cargar   [kar'xar]   'to load'
    c.   Post-nasal context
        (i) [ŋg]-dialects
        longo   ['loŋgo]   'long'
        (ii) [ŋx]-dialects
        longo   ['loŋxo]   'long'
        (iii) [ŋk]-dialects
        longo   ['loŋko]   'long'

In [ŋg]-dialects, [x] and [g] stand in complementary distribution, the latter being restricted to post-nasal contexts. For [ŋx]- and [ŋk]-dialects, there is simply no [g]. The absence of /g/ is clear for [ŋx]- and [ŋk]-dialects, and it can easily be maintained for [ŋg]-dialects, in which [g] is just an allophone of underlying /x/. This situation is exceptional within Romance languages, which generally have the voiced velar stop /g/ as a contrastive sound, and this is further supported by the distribution of phonemic inventories across languages. Only 32 languages out of a sample of 567 languages from *WALS Online* lack the voiced velar stop /g/ (Maddieson 2013a). This represents 5.6 per cent of the total geographically and genetically balanced sample of languages in the atlas. In *PHOIBLE Online* 775 inventories are reported not to have /g/. This represents more than a third of the inventories, but this does not mean that as many as 775 languages do not have /g/, since *PHOIBLE* often includes more than one inventory per language. Therefore, the percentage of languages lacking /g/ is smaller, and the lack of /g/ in *geada* dialects of Galician represents a quite exceptional pattern both within Romance languages, which generally have the six stops in their phonemic inventory (i.e., /p t k b d g/; but see Asturian in Section 9.2.3), and across the world's languages.

According to Maddieson (2013a), languages without /g/ have a wide but scattered geographical distribution, for which Gordon (2016: 21) gives a theory-external, aerodynamic explanation, as 'ease of voicing is correlated with frontness of the constriction ... Velars ... inhibit voicing since the small cavity behind the velar constriction triggers a rapid equalization of the pressure below and above the glottis thereby eliminating the pressure differential necessary to sustain voicing' (Gordon 2016: 21; see also Maddieson 2013a).

In *geada* dialects, not only is /g/ lacking as a contrastive segment, but the voiced velar fricative (or approximant) [ɣ] is also missing. There exists a cross-linguistic preference for voiceless fricatives over their voiced counterparts. Among those languages lacking one of the members of a voiceless–voiced fricative pair, more than 60 per cent of the total of 317-language sample in Maddieson (1984) lack [ɣ] and have [x] (Gordon 2016: 46f.). In this respect, *geada* dialects constitute a quite robust pattern.

9.2.3 The Voiced Velar Stop in Asturian

Asturian displays a situation similar to that described for *geada* dialects of Galician. According to the *Gramática de la Llingua Asturiana* (2001), the phoneme /g/ is generally realized as a voiced velar fricative [ɣ] in all contexts, including word-initial position after a pause, and even after velar nasals (e.g., *fungar* 'to blow one's nose' is the only example found in the grammar, p. 39). García Arias (2003) also reports that the behaviour of /g/

seems different from the other voiced stops /b d/ because its realization is generally fricative, even word-initially. Both authors seem to imply that the realization of /g/ as a fricative is the general situation, but it is not clear whether this realization is categorical. However, according to Muñiz Cachón (2002; 2003), the variety of Spanish spoken in Asturias is also described as completely lacking a stop pronunciation of the phoneme /g/ in favour of a voiced uvular fricative [ʁ], as opposed to the voiced velar fricative [ɣ] described in the *Gramática* for the Asturian language. If /g/ is always realized as a fricative, then Asturian, and the variety of Spanish spoken in Asturias described in Muñiz Cachón (2002; 2003), lack the phoneme /g/ entirely, and it makes little sense to talk of a phoneme or a contrastive sound /g/. With respect to the fricative realization in post-nasal contexts, García Arias (2003) does not provide any example of such a sequence morpheme-internally (cf. *fungar*, the only example given in the *Gramática*), but reports on a development that might explain the striking realization as a fricative of /g/ after velar nasals. Nasals in word-final coda position neutralize in favour of the velar nasal [ŋ] in Asturian. Across word boundaries and before vowel-initial words, nasal velarization is not blocked by resyllabification, and gives rise to sequences such as [uŋ 'ilo] 'a thread'. According to García Arias (2003), such a sequence can be reinterpreted by some speakers as containing a post-nasal voiced velar fricative [ɣ] (e.g., *un guilo* 'a thread'). The extent to which such post-nasal realizations have been generalized to morpheme-internal position is unknown to us. To sum up, Asturian, together with the *geada* dialects of Galician and a variety of Spanish spoken in Asturias, exhibit lack of contrastive /g/, a feature which is highly exceptional within the family of Romance languages, and a typologically rare but still attested pattern in the world's languages.

9.2.4 Spanish *Ceceo*

Peninsular Spanish, excluding most varieties of Andalusian, exhibit a contrast between /s/ and /θ/. The pronunciation of /s/ in Andalusian Spanish is different from the rest of Peninsular Spanish varieties. In non-Andalusian varieties of Peninsular Spanish, /s/ is a voiceless apico-alveolar fricative, while in Andalusian it is predorso-dental, subject to variation (see the website *El español hablado en Andalucía*, http://grupo.us.es/ehandalucia/). In south-western Andalusia, minimal pairs found in varieties of Peninsular Spanish such as *seta* ['seta] 'mushroom' and *zeta* ['θeta] '(the letter) Z', pronounced with a voiceless interdental fricative, are neutralized and pronounced with a sound closer to the interdental fricative of non-Andalusian Peninsular Spanish, transcribed as [θ̬] in Hualde (2005: 156) (['θ̬eta] 'mushroom' and 'zed'). This pronunciation is usually referred to as *ceceo*, as opposed to *seseo*, a phenomenon typical of the north and east of Andalusia and Latin American Spanish, in which there is simply no interdental fricative in the system (both *seta* and *ceta* are pronounced as [ˈseta], that is, with the predorso-dental fricative typical of Andalusian). *Ceceo* is stigmatized in urban Andalusia, while *seseo* enjoys some prestige, and some speakers exhibit either *ceseo* or *seceo*, in a random confusion of the two sounds. From a typological perspective, a system like that described for *ceceo* is typologically exceptional in that there is no voiceless alveolar fricative, but a voiceless interdental (or advanced dental) fricative instead. From a typological perspective, the sound /θ/ is not among the 25 most common consonants in the world's languages (Maddieson 1984). This dental non-sibilant fricative occurs in 43 of the languages surveyed in *WALS Online*, or 7.6 per cent of the languages. The areal distribution of this sound is spread worldwide, and is present in diverse language families. In *PHOIBLE Online* only 87 inventories are reported to exhibit /θ/, representing 4 per cent of the total of 2,155 inventories included in the database. We wrote a Python code to check whether all 70 languages (not inventories) exhibiting /θ/ are exhaustively contained in the set of 1,351 languages that have /s/. Only 21 of those 70 languages exhibit /θ/ but no /s/, that is, 30 per cent of the languages that have /θ/ lack /s/. In total, such a system only represents 1.2 per cent of the languages included in *PHOIBLE Online*. In this respect, *ceceo* dialects of Andalusian Spanish exemplify an extremely exceptional typological pattern in the world's languages. A possible explanation is that what has been described as a voiceless interdental is just a language-particular phonetic implementation of a much more abstract unit /s/, defined as the only non-dorsal fricative in the system that happens to receive a more advanced articulation. This hypothesis finds independent support in those dialects of Andalusian Spanish that distinguish /s/ from /θ/, the latter being a true interdental fricative.

9.2.5 Retroflex Consonants in Sardinian and Italo-Romance Varieties

Whereas retroflex consonants are very common in languages spoken in India and surrounding countries, in Australia, and parts of central Africa, within Romance languages only a very small subset of languages exhibit them. These are southern Corsican, Sardinian, and the Italo-Romance varieties of the far south of the Italian peninsula (Sicily, southern Calabria, and Salento). As reported by Schmid (2016: 479f.) and Loporcaro (2011: 142f.), in both southern Corsican and Sardinian, the (intervocalic) Latin geminate lateral -LL- developed into a geminate voiced retroflex stop /ɖ:/, e.g., [ˈnuɖːa] 'nothing' < Lat. NULLA(M), [ˈbiɖːa] 'village' < Lat. UILLA(M), [ˈpuɖːu] 'rooster' < Lat. PULLU(M), for Sardinian (the last three examples are taken from Mensching and Remberger 2016); [ˈiɖ:a] 'she' < Lat. ILLA(M) for Corsican. The same retroflex outcome is found in Calabrian dialects, although in southern Calabrian a geminate retroflex lateral is found (e.g., [kaˈvaɭ:u] 'horse' < Lat. CABALLU(M)). The geminate retroflex lateral is also present in word-initial position in Campidanian Sardinian, corresponding to word-initial L- in Latin (e.g., [sa ˈɭ:uʒi] 'the light'), but also in intervocalic position morpheme-internally (e.g., [ˈsɔɭ:i] 'sun') (see Frigeni 2005 for more details on the synchronic realizations of the etymological intervocalic -L- in Campidanian Sardinian). In southern Italian dialects, however, the outcome of the Latin geminate lateral was a voiced retroflex affricate [ɖ:ʐ]; these dialects also exhibit the voiceless counterpart retroflex affricate [ʈ:ʂ], as well as the singleton [ʈʂ] derived from the Latin complex onset -TR- (e.g., [ˈmaːʈʂi] 'mother' < Lat. MATRE(M)). The same complex onsets preceded by a fricative element, Latin -STR-, developed into retroflex pronunciations in Corsican (e.g., [ˈnoʂʈru] 'our' < Lat. NOSTRU(M)). For Sicilian the same cluster has been transcribed as lacking the stop element (e.g., [ʂʈ]), and for Calabrian as a geminated singleton [ʈ:]. In several northern varieties of central Friulian /d/ is pronounced as a retroflex [ɖ] (Roseano and Finco 2021). Finally, in the Spanish varieties spoken in the highlands of Colombia, Ecuador, Peru, and Bolivia, and in the north of Argentina and Chile, the cluster /tɾ/ in Spanish is pronounced as a retroflex [ʈɻ] with a devoiced retroflex rhotic (e.g., [eŋkon ˈʈɻo] '(s)he found').

According to Jones (2004), the diachronic path of the voiced retroflex stop in Italian, Sardinian, and Corsican dialects finds its origin in the misperception of a velarized lateral as a retroflex lateral. Both velarized and retroflex laterals are characterized acoustically by a low frequency distribution of energy in the spectrum. This sound change finds independent support in a number of other languages (see Jones 2004 for more details). Jones hypothesizes that at a later stage the retroflex lateral was pronounced with a flap of the tongue tip. This flap was later reinterpreted as occlusion, [ɖ].

According to the data available in PHOIBLE Online, only 7.9 per cent of the world's languages exhibit the voiced retroflex stop /ɖ/. A slightly higher percentage of languages have its voiceless counterpart /ʈ/. Retroflex fricatives, the retroflex rhotic and nasal, and the retroflex lateral are even less common. Interestingly, the voiceless retroflex affricate /ʈʂ/ is only represented in PHOIBLE Online by 2.5 per cent of the languages and its voiced counterpart [ɖʐ] is even more exceptional, being present only in 0.5 per cent of the languages.

9.2.6 Palatal Stops in Raeto-Romance

Palatal and postalveolar fricatives and sonorant consonants are not unusual in Romance (e.g., [ʃ, ʒ, ɲ, j, ʎ]). Palatal stops, however, are much less common. According to Maddieson (1984), the vast majority of the world's languages contrast stops at three places of articulation: bilabial, dental/alveolar, and velar. If affricates are excluded, the next most common place of articulation is palatal, and then uvular (see also Gordon 2016: 45f.). According to *PHOIBLE Online*, the voiceless palatal stop /c/ is present in 304 inventories out of 2,155 inventories surveyed in the database (14 per cent), and the voiced palatal stop /ɟ/ is reported for 277 inventories (13 per cent). Therefore, palatal stops are quite exceptional among the world's languages. A four-way contrast for oral stops is exclusive to the Raeto-Romance varieties (but see Schmid 2016 and citations therein for the presence of palatal stops in conservative Alpine Lombard dialects and southern Italian dialects). As stated in Roseano and Finco (2021), central Friulian has a four-way distinction among oral stops, which also contrast in voicing (i.e., /p b t d c ɟ k g/) (e.g., /ˈcaze/ 'house', /ˈcike/ 'cigarette butt', /ˈcuc/ 'dummy, pacifier (for babies)', Roseano p.c.). The palatal stops /c ɟ/ can also be pronounced as palatal affricates (e.g., c͡ç ɟ͡ʝ). In some innovative varieties of Friulian, these palatal stops are pronounced as postalveolar affricates (/ˈcaɲ/ 'dog' and /ˈɟat/ 'cat' receive the pronunciations [ˈt͡ʃaɲ] and [ˈd͡ʒat], Roseano and Finco 2021). In most varieties of Ladin /c ɟ/ were lost and replaced by affricates or fricatives. In Badiot-Marèo, one can find minimal pairs such as /ˈcamp/ 'field' vs /ˈt͡ʃamp/ 'left', /ˈcɛːr/ 'dear' vs /ˈt͡ʃɛːr/ 'certain'. For Romansh, there is no agreement on whether palatal stops are in fact palatal affricates /c͡ç ɟ͡ʝ/. Roseano and Finco report, however, minimal pairs from previous sources such as /canˈtar/ 'to sing' vs /t͡ʃanˈtar/ 'to sit' in Vallader, /ˈfaca/ 'done.FSG' vs /ˈfat͡ʃa/ 'face' in Sursilvan, /ˈfac͡ça/ vs /ˈfat͡ʃa/ in Surmiran (Anderson 2016, who includes the two palatal affricates /c͡ç ɟ͡ʝ/ in his phonemic inventory for Surmiran). For a recent study on palatals (and postalveolars) in Raeto-Romance, see Schmid (2018). Another Romance variety with palatal stops is the palatalizing variety of Majorcan Catalan (Recasens and Espinosa 2006; Ramírez Martínez 2017). In this Majorcan variety, velar stops have two allophonic variants: the velar stops [k g] before back vowels, and the palatal stops [c ɟ] before front vowels, but also before the low vowel and schwa, and in word-final position. Palatalization before /a/ is probably due to the more fronted articulation of the vowel (Recasens and Espinosa 2006). Ramírez Martínez (2017) suggests that Majorcan Catalan could represent a middle stage in the palatalization process that took place in French (k > kʲ > c > /t͡ʃ/ > /ʃ/, as in *cheval* 'horse' < Lat. CABALLUM).

9.2.7 Glottal Stops in Campidanian Sardinian

We have already reported that the Latin intervocalic geminate lateral gave rise to a voiced retroflex stop /ɖː/. In Sarrabus, a small eastern area on the coast of southern Sardinia, and in some villages in the eastern area (Frigeni 2005: 21), the Latin intervocalic singleton lateral developed into a voiceless glottal stop /ʔ/ (e.g., [ˈmaʔu] 'bad' < Lat. MALU(M); Mensching and Remberger 2016). Mensching and Remberger further state that the Latin intervocalic -N- also gave rise to a glottal stop, with concomitant nasalization of the preceding vowel (e.g., [ˈmãʔu] 'hand' < Lat. MANU). In other varieties of Campidanian Sardinian, the Latin geminate lateral in intervocalic position developed into other sounds including /β/ or /w/, the voiced uvular fricative /ʁ/, a labialized /gʷ/, and the velar lateral /ʟ/ (Wagner 1941; Virdis 1978). Although some Spanish varieties lacking /x/ or /χ/ include the voiceless glottal fricative /h/ in their phonemic inventory, no Romance language displays the phoneme /ʔ/, Sarrabus Sardinian being the only exception. The glottal fricative [h] is also the outcome of s-aspiration in Andalusian and Latin American Spanish. Nicaraguan Spanish has been reported to exhibit a glottal stop as an allophonic realization of the deleted /s/ in word-final position before vowel-initial words (Chappell 2015). The glottal stop is not typologically rare, but its presence in Romance as a contrastive sound is very exotic.

9.3 Syllabic Structure

9.3.1 Word-Initial and Word-Medial Consonant Clusters

In word-initial position Latin permitted only obstruent-liquid clusters (excluding tl- and dl-), as in BLANDUS 'nice', TRIBUS 'tribe', which have rising sonority, in accordance with the Sonority Sequencing Principle (Clements 1990), and prohibited all other sonority-offending clusters such as obstruent–obstruent clusters (only present in loanwords from Ancient Greek), and sonorant-obstruent clusters, with falling sonority, also referred to as sonority reversals. Obstruent–nasal clusters, although rising in sonority, were also banned in Latin (a violation of the Minimal Sonority Distance principle). Typologically, this is the most restrictive pattern and the unmarked one. Romance languages such as Spanish, standard Italian, or Romanian conform to this pattern. Here we abstract away from word-initial /sC/ clusters, which can easily be accommodated as cases of extrasyllabic initial consonants.

Some Romance languages are less restrictive with respect to the type of clusters they allow in onset position, both word-initially and word-medially; in most cases these consonant clusters arise from unstressed vowel deletion. Following the terminology in Passino (2013a), some languages are of the 'anything goes' type, while others have a 'hybrid' pattern. The first pattern can be illustrated with European Portuguese, where vowel deletion (especially of schwa and /u/) can result in consonantal clusters with several consonants, as shown by examples such as *empedernir* [ẽpdɾnír] 'petrify' or *desprestigiar* [dʃpɾʃtiʒjár] 'depreciate', the latter with six consonants in word-initial position. For this type of case, Mateus and Andrade (2000) present an analysis with empty syllable nuclei corresponding to the position of the deleted vowels, and use examples like *desprestigiar* to argue that the two [ʃ] must be in coda position (see Section 9.4.12). The presence of this realization of the fricative, though, could be attributed to faithfulness to the form with all the vowels, in an Optimality-theoretic account using output-output constraints. Some varieties of contemporary French also have an 'anything goes' pattern according to Passino (2013a) (e.g., *reprend* [χpʀɑ̃] 'take again', *lever* [lve] 'raise'). French vowel deletion and the resulting consonant clusters have been the subject of much debate, especially with regard to the role of syllable structure and sonority-related constraints (see Côté 2000; 2006; Eychenne 2006 and references therein).

Emilian, a Gallo-Italian variety, is an example of the hybrid type of language described in Passino (2013a) that tolerates obstruent–obstruent and obstruent–nasal clusters (e.g., zbdɛːl 'hospital' < *ospiˈtale, dmaŋ 'tomorrow' < DE+MANE), but prohibits sonority reversals (i.e., sonorant-obstruent clusters), which are repaired through word-initial epenthesis (e.g., alvaːr < *leˈvare 'remove'; see also Passino 2013b). The appearance of such word-initial cluster types is due to a diachronic process of schwa deletion in both pretonic and posttonic positions. The same situation is also reported in Passino (2013a) for Piedmontese, another Gallo-Italian variety, and Vimeu Picard, a Gallo-Romance language. Abruzzese, an upper southern Italian dialect area, displays a slightly different pattern. Obstruent–obstruent clusters and obstruent–nasal word-initial clusters are not permitted, but initial geminates and homorganic nasal–obstruent clusters are possible (e.g., ttækkə 'attack', mbʊːtə 'funnel'; Passino 2013a: 185).

Passino (2013a) highlights the fact that all obstruent–obstruent clusters attested so far in Italo-Romance varieties are voiced and that such clusters behave phonologically as single segments in some languages. No obstruent–obstruent cluster with non-matching voicing specifications is attested in Romance. The word-initial homorganic nasal–obstruent clusters of Abruzzese and other southern Italian varieties could be compared with prenasalized plosives, which behave phonologically as single segments, and are characteristic of Bantu languages, and found in other language families in East and South Asia, South America, and Oceania. Only 17.7 per cent of the languages surveyed in the *World Phonotactics Database* (Donohue et al. 2013) exhibit prenasalized plosives (i.e., 667 of a total of 3,776 languages). Unfortunately, the distribution of obstruent–obstruent, obstruent–nasal clusters and sonority reversals is not available in the *World Phonotactics Database*, and no information about this is available from *WALS Online*. Passino (2013a) cites the Slavonic languages Serbian,

Croatian, and Slovenian as examples of languages that allow obstruent–obstruent clusters but also repair sonority reversals by epenthesis or by making the liquid sonorant syllabic (in Croatian) (see also Scheer 2005). See Section 9.4.11 for sonority-offending consonant clusters due to metathesis in Campidanian Sardinian.

9.3.2 Final Consonantal Clusters with Rising Sonority in Insular Catalan

Catalan allows word-final codas with up to three consonants with falling sonority, leaving /s/ and /z/ aside. In insular Catalan (Balearic Islands; Alghero, in Sardinia), however, final codas with rising sonority are found in verbs in the first person singular present indicative, never in other categories, which are subject to schwa epenthesis instead. For instance, the noun *filtre* [fíltrə] 'filter' ends in an epenthetic schwa, while the cognate standard Catalan verb form *filtro* 'I filter' is realized as [fíltɾ]. Some analyses of this puzzling pattern have related the absence of an overt first person singular-related morph, a Ø-morpheme, to the generation of an empty syllabic nucleus that attracts the unaffiliated consonants to its onset (see, for instance, Dols and Wheeler 1996). Lloret (2004) shows that these final clusters behave like codas, not like onsets, and argues for an analysis framed in Optimal Paradigms (McCarthy 2005) in which epenthesis is outranked by the need to have a constant verbal stem. Pons-Moll (2007) also appeals to paradigmatic pressures, but in this case epenthesis is blocked to avoid syncretism with the third person singular, which ends in an inflexional schwa.

9.4 Segmental Processes

9.4.1 Vowel Devoicing

Voiceless vowels, contrasting with voiced vowels, are very rare in languages of the world (Ladefoged and Maddieson 1996), but vowel devoicing is a fairly common phenomenon, especially in unstressed syllables when the vowel is adjacent to a voiceless consonant. Few Romance languages have been reported to have vowel devoicing, but among them are Canadian French and Andean Spanish (also Brazilian Portuguese in very limited environments; see Meneses and Albano 2015 and references therein). In Canadian French, vowel devoicing affects only high vowels, /i, y, u/, when they are surrounded by voiceless consonants; it is a gradual and variable process. According to Gendron (1966), there is more devoicing in medial syllables than in the initial syllable, and /u/ is the least affected vowel of the three high vowels. An important point of debate has been whether vowel devoicing and vowel deletion, also present in French, are part of the same phenomenon or are different. Although both of them target high vowels, vowel deletion can occur in the context of either voiced or voiceless consonants. For discussion, see Dumas (1972; 1987), Cedergen and Simoneau (1985) or Bayles (2016). Vowel devoicing in Andean Spanish has been thoroughly studied in Delforge (2009). She concludes that devoicing (also called vowel reduction in the literature) is a gradient process independent of speech rate which can affect high vowels as well as /e/ especially when followed by an *s* in coda position; most often this *s* is the plural marker. She also argues that vowel devoicing is a contact phenomenon influenced by Quechua and provides an Optimality-theoretic analysis of it using gestural-alignment constraints.

9.4.2 Diphthongization of Long Vowels in Canadian French

While vowel length was contrastive in all positions in Latin, in Romance languages it remains contrastive in stressed position in some varieties of northern Italy; only in oxytones in Friulian and in oxytones and paroxytones in Cremonese, for instance. Most Italo-Romance dialects have long vowels limited to open syllables (see Loporcaro 2015 for an overview and discussion). In French there are two main sources for long vowels, which appear generally in closed stressed syllables. One of them is the presence of a so-called *consonne allongeante* or 'lengthening consonant' following the vowel. These are /v, z, ʒ, r/ and the cluster /vr/ (e.g., *vivre* [viːvr] 'to live', *vise* [viːz] 'aim.PRS.IND.1/2SG', *paire* [pɛːr] 'pair', *rêve* [rɛːv] 'dream.PRS.IND.1/3SG', *rage* [raːʒ] 'anger'). Other vowels are said to be inherently long, in most cases as the result of compensatory lengthening due to the historical loss of a consonant, mainly *s*; nasalized vowels are always long. Some minimal pairs include *b[ɛ]tte* 'Swiss chard' vs *b[ɛː]te* 'beast' or *f[ɛ]tes* 'done.FPL' vs *f[ɛː]te* 'party, holiday', although length is only marginally contrastive. Two differences between the vocalic system of Canadian French and that of standard French are relevant to the present discussion (see Walker 1984 for a comparison between these two varieties of French): (a) Canadian French has a tense–lax distinction in high vowels, with the lax realization being found in closed syllables with non-lengthened vowels (as in *jupe* [ʒʏp] 'skirt'), while standard French has only tense vowels (but see Storme 2017a for a more detailed description and analysis of tense and lax vowels in European French); and (b) in Canadian French long vowels are usually diphthongized, with an offglide. Diphthongization of long vowels is a well-known feature of English, but it is unusual in Romance, where rising diphthongs arose from Latin short mid vowels in languages like Spanish or Italian (see, for instance, Loporcaro 2016 for diphthongization of this type). According to Dumas (1981) all long vowels can be diphthongized, as shown in (2). The offglide in the diphthongs always agrees in roundness and frontness with the vowel.

(2) Diphthongized vowels in Canadian French (Dumas 1981)
ɪⁱ ʏʸ ʊᵘ
ɛⁱ œʸ ɔᵘ
aⁱ aʸ ɑᵘ
   ɑᵘ

Although the potential for high long vowels to diphthongize is debated, McKenzie and Sankoff (2009) conclude that they are indeed diphthongized, although the effects are clearer with mid vowels. Some examples of words containing diphthongized vowels appear in (3).

(3) Words with diphthongized vowels (adapted from Walker 1984)
[ij]: *vire* 'ledge' [yɥ]: *pur* 'pure' [uw]: *rouge* 'red'
[ej]: *neige* 'snow' [øɥ]: *jeûne* 'fast' [ow]: *chaude* 'hot.FSG'
[ɛj]/[aj]: *père* 'father' [œɥ]: *beurre* 'butter' [ɔw]: *port* 'port, harbour'
[ɑw]: *pâte* 'pastry, dough'
[ɛ̃j]: *crainte* 'fear' [œ̃ɥ] *défunte* 'deceased.FSG' [ɔ̃w]: *ombre* 'shade'
[ɑ̃w]: *lente* 'slow.FSG'

McKenzie and Sankoff (2009; 2010) have observed that while short vowels have a very stable realization, long, diphthongized vowels have a less steady realization, which can vary depending on age and social class, with a tendency to a lowering of the vowel.

Walker (1984) suggests that the presence of diphthongization is a way to increase the difference between short and long vowels. Short vowels are weakened through laxing, devoicing, or deletion, while long vowels are strengthened through diphthongization. For the interaction between diphthongization and harmony see Poliquin (2006).

9.4.3 Gliding of High Vowels and Palatalization in Romanian

Romanian, like many other languages in the world, has consonant palatalization before front vowels. However, besides very few cases of velar palatalization word-internally (e.g., [gʲol] 'lake'), the suffixes that consist of the vowel /i/ (i.e., the plural marker in nouns and adjectives and the second person singular marker in verbs) always trigger palatalization; palatalization surfaces only when the suffix is deleted, and hence the palatalized consonant is always word-final. These /i/ suffixes, along with the suffixes that have the high vowel /u/, trigger a complex pattern of alternations that has been studied most prominently in Steriade (1984) and Chițoran (2002) (see Steriade 2008 and Bermúdez-Otero 2018 for related issues). These /i/ affixes are realized as a vowel, [i], in some contexts including stems ending in a consonant cluster with rising sonority (e.g., /akr-i/ [ˈakri] 'sour.MPL') or before other suffixes or clitics (e.g /vataf-i-lor/ [vaˈtafilor] 'supervisor.PL.DAT');

they are realized as a glide [j] when the stem ends in a vowel (e.g., /bo-i/ [boj] 'oxen'); and they are realized as palatalization (in most views) when the stem ends in one consonant (e.g., /lup-i/ [lupʲ] 'wolves'; /vataf-i/ [vatafʲ] 'supervisors') or in a consonant cluster with falling sonority (e.g., /plimb-i/ [plimbʲ] 'you walk'). The patterns of palatalization in the context of various consonants are given in (4). For each pair, the first consonant is that found without the suffix, while the second one is that found in the context of plural or second person singular.

(4) Palatalization with suffix /i/ in (standard) Romanian (based on Chițoran 2002: 187 (228))
    a.   /i/ after labial obstruents
         [p]-[pʲ], [b]-[bʲ], [f]-[fʲ], [v]-[vʲ]
    b.   /i/ after coronal obstruents
         [t]-[tsʲ], [d]-[zʲ], [ts]-[tsʲ], [tʃ]-[tʃʲ], [dʒ]-[dʒʲ], [s]-[ʃʲ], [ʃ]-[ʃʲ], [z]-[ʒʲ], [ʒ]-[ʒʲ]
    c.   /i/ after velar obstruents
         [k]-[tʃʲ], [g]-[dʒʲ]
    d.   /i/ after sonorants and the glottal fricative
         [m]-[mʲ], [n]-[nʲ], [r]-[rʲ], [l]-[j]/[lʲ], [h]-[hʲ]

Labial obstruents, (4a), sonorants, and the glottal fricative, (4d), generally show only secondary palatalization: the consonant is maintained and a secondary place of articulation is added to it. Coronal obstruents, (4b), and velar obstruents, (4c), however, surface with full palatalization, since the consonant changes its primary place of articulation (in cases like [d]-[zʲ], (4b), manner changes instead). What at first sight is typologically unusual about this pattern is that full palatalization in Romanian always co-occurs with what Bateman (2007: 59) calls a 'secondary release'. Generally, for an /s/+/i/ input one would expect to find either secondary palatalization, [sʲ], or full palatalization, [ʃ], but not a combination of both, [ʃʲ]. It is obvious that this combined palatalization must be related to the absence of [i] in the surface form; for an input such as /pas-i/ 'steps', the output is [paʃʲ], not **[paʃi] or **[pasʲi]. Steriade (1984) does not assume secondary palatalization for Romanian; in her analysis, /i/ is subject to a word-final rule of High Vowel Desyllabification, which has the effect of integrating the vowel as a coda to the previous syllable keeping its X-slot; that is, it becomes a glide. In her analysis, an input like /lup-i/ 'wolves' has a phonetic form [lupj], without palatalization, while /pas-i/ 'steps' would result in a form [paʃj], with full palatalization of the last consonant of the stem. While this analysis avoids having to postulate the existence of simultaneous full and secondary palatalization on one and the same consonant, it has to assume that Romanian allows final codas with rising sonority, as would be the case with [paʃj] or [lupj]. In Chitoran's (2002) OT-framed proposal candidates such as [lupj] are ruled out by highly ranked syllable-related constraints, with the set of ranked constraints favouring the output with palatalization, like [lupʲ]. Chițoran accounts for the details of secondary and total assimilation within the feature-geometric model by Clements (1991) and Clements and Hume (1995). It is unclear how she would integrate the different operations of linking and delinking into her general OT proposal.

As observed by Ladefoged and Maddieson (1996) and Bateman (2007), the fact that in palatalization the primary place of articulation is maintained with labial consonants, (A1a), is to be expected because two different articulators are involved, while in coronal and velar consonants (as in 4b–c), full palatalization is a more common outcome because the same articulator is involved, namely the tongue body. Very few languages in the world have been reported to have full palatalization with labial consonants. In Judaeo-Spanish, for instance, dorsals and velars can fully palatalize regressively, but not labials (see Bradley 2015). However, the Moldovan dialect of Romanian, discussed in Bateman (2007), seems to have full palatalization of labial consonants, as illustrated in (5).

(5) Full palatalization with labials in Moldovan (Bateman 2007: 92)

	Singular	Plural	
p → kʲ	plop	plokʲ	'poplar'
f → ʃ	kartof	kartoʃʲ	'potato'

With evidence drawn from Moldovan itself but also from other Romance languages, Bateman (2007) argues that these alternations do not arise synchronically but are the end result of different steps which did not involve labial palatalization as such. She adopts insights by Ionescu (1969) and Avram (1977), for whom a high glide [j] was inserted after labials preceding [i], the glide later hardened and the labial consonant finally dropped. Synchronically, then, these alternations must be treated as allomorphy.

9.4.4 Glide Strengthening in Romansh

A process of glide hardening similar to that in Bolognese is found in some varieties of Surmiran and in Puter and Vallader Romansh (Anderson 2016), in which [ɛi] and [ɔu] yield [ɛk] and [ɔk], respectively, in closed syllables. In these varieties, front glides alternate with voiceless velar stops in closed syllables (e.g., [ˈpɛirər] 'pear tree' cf. [pɛkr] 'pear', [flɔkr] 'flower'; Anderson 2016: 173f.). Such a strengthening process yields sonority-rising clusters in coda position, which is a typologically marked syllabic configuration (see Section 9.3.2 for final clusters with rising sonority in insular Catalan). A similar process is found in Faroese (Anderson 1974).

9.4.5 Velar Nasals in Northern Italian Dialects and Galician

In Venetian and most northern Italian dialects, place contrasts in nasals are neutralized in favour of velar nasals not only in absolute word-final position (e.g., ˈmaŋ 'hand', piˈroŋ 'fork'), but also in non-final, preconsonantal positions (e.g., kaŋˈtaɾ 'to sing', iŋˈvɛrno 'winter') (Zamboni 1974). Final velarization of nasals is a common place neutralization process in the world's languages. In the *World Phonotactics Database*, 40.7 per cent of 1,393 languages surveyed for this feature are reported to have velar nasals in coda position. However, the *Database* does not distinguish between word-final and word-internal nasal codas, so it is difficult to extract a conclusion from this percentage. Lack of place assimilation in preconsonantal coda position is quite exceptional in the context of the Romance languages. In Piedmontese, velar nasals also surface as the first member of a complex coda (e.g., ˈdʒeŋt 'people') and, more interestingly, in intervocalic onset position (e.g., ˈsmaŋa 'week', Schmid 2016: 483).

In Bolognese, intervocalic historical /n/ gave rise to a velar nasal in coda position in paroxytones except after historically stressed /a/ (e.g., [ˈloŋna] < Lat. LUNA 'moon', [maˈteŋna] < Lat. MATUTINA 'morning', but [ˈlɛːna] < LANA 'wool'; Hajek 1991). Velar nasals are also present in coda position after loss of earlier /n/ (e.g., [iŋporˈtæŋt] < ĩːporˈtãːt < *importante* 'important'). Interestingly, non-low vowels before nasals underwent a historical process of diphthongization which is still observable from the orthography of Bolognese (e.g., *louna* 'moon', *vein* 'wine'). Hajek (1991) integrates diphthongization into the historical changes that yielded [ŋ]: LUNA(M) > luːna > lũːna > lũw̃na > lõw̃na > [loŋna]; UINU(M) > vĩːnu > vĩːn > vĩj̃n > vẽj̃n > vẽj̃ > [veŋ]. Nasalized long vowels diphthongized and later the off-glides hardened to [ŋ]. Hajek (1991) shows that the alternation between nasalized glides and velar nasals can easily be accommodated into an autosegmental analysis based on features shared between glides and the velar nasal. Despite the naturalness of the historical changes and the hardening of nasalized glides (also found in synchronic alternations in the Ligurian dialect of Cairo Montenotte, e.g., lyjna/lyŋna 'moon'; Parry 2005), the result of these historical processes is a quite exceptional outcome consisting of a velar nasal in word-internal coda position that does not agree in place with a following coronal nasal in onset position, where homorganicity would be expected.

Galician also presents velar nasals in intervocalic onset positions, but at a morpheme boundary, in the feminine forms of the indefinite article and its derivatives (e.g., ˈuŋa 'a / one(F)', niŋˈguŋa 'none(F)'; Colina and Díaz-Campos 2006: 1248). García Arias (2003: 32) reports interesting data from Asturian, which can frequently generalize a velar nasal in word-initial position before /t/ (e.g., ŋˈtos 'then', ŋtaˈmo '(s)he started', ŋtaˈmar 'to undertake').

Although the *World Phonotactics Database* reports that 42.4 per cent of the 1,863 languages surveyed for this feature exhibit velar nasals in onset position, none of these belong to the Indo-European group (Italo-Romance dialects are not surveyed in this *Database*), and are concentrated in sub-Saharan Africa, Asia, Australia, and, in a lesser proportion, in South America.

9.4.6 Nasal Place Neutralization towards [m] in Spanish

In standard Spanish, nasal consonants assimilate in place to the following consonant and they are realized as a coronal [n] in word-final position, an unmarked pattern for codas that can be accounted for with constraints such as CODACONDITION (Itô 1989; McCarthy 2008); this, applied to place, forbids a place specification on a coda consonant unless linked to a following consonant (the coda consonant cannot have its own place specification). A consonant [ŋ] in final position is also fairly common in Spanish and other languages (see Section 9.4.5). In Yucatán Spanish, words such as *pan* 'bread' can surface with final [n] or [ŋ], as expected. However, they can also surface with final Ø (as in Catalan, for instance; see Section 9.4.7) and, most interestingly, as a bilabial [m]. The realization of nasals in Yucatán Spanish has been studied fairly recently in Michnowicz (2008). The data he collected from Mérida shows, following the main lines of some previous studies, that in absolute final position [n] is the most common realization (61 per cent), followed by [m] (25 per cent), then [ŋ] (9 per cent), very common in surrounding areas, and finally Ø (5 per cent). In some cases [m] is found also in word or phrase internal position, as in *mayormente* [majormemte] 'mostly' or *saben como* [saβemkomo] '(they) know how', where [m] appears next to a consonant with a different place of articulation (coronal [t] and dorsal [k], respectively). Through several multivariate statistical (VARBRUL) analyses, Michnowicz (2008) found that for absolute final nasals unstressed syllables tend to favour [n] while stressed syllables favour [m]. Social factors also influence the use of each consonant, with [n] being found more often in Spanish monolinguals and [m] in Mayan–Spanish bilinguals, the contact with Mayan having been posited as the origin of [m] in final position. Older speakers prefer [n], while middle age and younger speakers prefer [m]. With respect to gender, while [n] is equally found in men and women, [m] is more present in women while [ŋ] is more present in men. Fifty-two per cent of higher-class Mayan–Spanish bilingual women favour [m]. Michnowicz (2008) suggests that the increase in the use of final [m] might be due to it being a salient feature of regional identity. A well-suited framework to model the variation found in Yucatán Spanish final nasals would be Stochastic Optimality Theory (Boersma and Hayes 2001).

9.4.7 Word-Final Deletion of /r/ and /n/ in Catalan

In Catalan, /r/ and /n/ delete when preceded by a stressed vowel and in absolute word-final position (e.g., rə'mo cf. rəmu'rɛtə 'noise / noise.DIM'; ku'zi cf. ku'zins 'cousin/s') (Mascaró 1976; Bonet and Lloret 1998). The process of /r/ deletion has a number of lexical exceptions depending on the dialect. However, the process of /n/ deletion is general in the native vocabulary of the language, with a few exceptions. Both processes seem to be typologically exceptional because coronal nasals and rhotics are sonorant with default place of articulation. Blevins (2006), for instance, states that nasals are among the most common sounds in word-final coda position. Some languages, such as Manam (Oceanic) restrict all possible codas to nasals, for example. The process of /n/ deletion seems to contradict the notion of markedness: labial and palatal nasals are allowed in coda position, as are all non-coronals, although the coda position is generally the locus of neutralization phenomena and loss of marked phonological features. One possible interpretation of the facts is suggested in Jiménez and Lloret (2011), according to whom coronal nasals, although typologically unmarked, are perceptually weaker than labial and dorsal nasals. Therefore, deletion of a coronal nasal could come at a lesser cost (see also Bonet et al. 2004; 2005; Faust and Torres-Tamarit 2017). Deletion of word-final /r/ after stressed vowels is even more intriguing, given that in Catalan all other sonorants except /n/, and all obstruents, surface faithfully as such in coda position.

9.4.8 Campidanian Sardinian Lenition

Campidanian Sardinian exhibits an interesting case of phonologically derived environment effect by which underlyingly voiceless stops undergo a process of voicing and spirantization in word-initial position when they follow a vowel belonging to the preceding word. Underlyingly voiced stops, however, do not spirantize and surface as such in the same context. Some examples from Bolognesi (1998) appear in (6).

(6) Campidanian Sardinian lenition
    a. Lenition of voiceless stops
        [piʃːi] ~ [belːu βiʃːi] '(beautiful) fish'
        [polonia] ~ [sːa βolonia] '(the) Poland'
        [komputːɛ] ~ [sːu ɣomputːɛ] '(the) computer'
    b. No lenition of voiced stops
        [bĩu] ~ [sːu bĩu] '(the) wine'
        [dɔmu] ~ [sːa dɔmu] '(the) house'
        [gatːu] ~ [sːu gatːu] 'the cat'

Phonologically derived environment effects such as that described for Campidanian Sardinian are also referred to as saltatory alternations

(Hayes and White 2015). In a saltatory alternation, the alternating underlying segment skips an intermediate form, and the underlying segment that is identical to that intermediate form does not alternate. The Campidanian Sardinian data have attracted the interest of many phonologists (for more details, see Łubowicz 2002; Hayes and White 2015; Storme 2017b).

Saltatory alternations should not be confused with counterfeeding chain shifts, in which segments derived by the application of one process are not affected by another process that targets underlying segments that are identical to the segment derived by the first process. Saltatory alternations have been attested for languages other than Campidanian Sardinian (see Hayes and White 2015; Storme 2017b). It is difficult to assess such a process as typologically exceptional, but it seems clear that phonologically derived environment effects are not the unmarked situation, and this is why their modelling is challenging for both rule-based theories of phonology and OT. Within Romance, Campidanian Sardinian is the only language that exhibits a saltatory alternation involving lenition of stops.

9.4.9 Intervocalic Fortition in Salentino

Stops in intervocalic position are usually the target of lenition processes, which include voicing and spirantization. In Salentino, however, a process of intervocalic fortition, morpheme-internally and across words in initial position, has been reported (Fanciullo 1976). This process has lexical exceptions and is therefore not systematic. The voicing contrast is maintained after consonants (and after consonantal empty skeletal positions in contexts of *raddoppiamento fonosintattico* — see Section 6.4.3.2). This situation is certainly typologically exceptional (e.g., *piscuèttu* It. *biscotto* 'biscuit', *ápisu* It. *abisso* 'abyss', *puffettinu* It. *buffet* '(small) sideboard', *tilori* It. *dolore* 'pain', *nutu* It. *nodo* 'knot', *li tiénti* It. *i denti* 'the teeth'; *konna* It. *gonna* 'skirt', *akostu* It. *agosto* 'August', *cratu* It. *grado* 'degree'; Fanciullo 1976). After consonants and under *raddoppiamento fonosintattico* the voicing contrast is maintained (e.g., *nna* [Ø]*arca* 'a boat' cf. *'n* [b]*arca* 'in (a) boat', *ttre* [bb]*arche* 'three boats'; *nnu* [t]*ente* 'a tooth' cf. *ttre* [dd]*ienti* 'three teeth'; *nnu* [k]*addu* 'a rooster' cf. *ttre* [ɡɡ]*atte* 'three cats'; Ledgeway 2016: 253). According to these data, the process of intervocalic devoicing may be considered synchronically active.

One possible interpretation for this particular system of voicing alternations could be that consonants with less sonority (voiceless stops are less sonorous than voiced stops) are preferred in onset position. This constraint would take precedence over the fact that onset positions, as opposed to coda positions, license voicing contrasts (Lombardi 1995). In the context of *raddoppiamento fonosintattico*, geminates would preserve the voicing contrast because their length might reinforce faithfulness to underlying contrasts. A phonetically grounded explanation for the maintenance of the voicing contrast after consonants, as opposed to in intervocalic positions, seems harder to find.

Salentino is the only Romance language reported to display such a distributional pattern of voicing contrasts in stops. Furthermore, intervocalic devoicing does not seem to be a natural, phonetically grounded synchronic process, and is presumably unattested as a synchronic phonological process (see Gouskova et al. 2011; Begus 2015).

Descriptions of Salentino can be found in Fanciullo (1976) and Mancarella (1998). There is still a need for more detailed phonetic studies on individual grammars of Salentino that could shed some light on its phonological system, followed by a thorough phonological analysis of the actual lexical distribution of voiceless and voiced stops in a speaker's grammar. Is intervocalic fortition in Salentino a surface-true, static generalization over the lexicon for any individual grammar? Is it a productive, synchronic process? How many lexical exceptions are there? Does this process coexist with spirantization in any individual grammar? Future work on voiced stops in Salentino seems very promising.

9.4.10 Final Affrication of /ʒ/ in Catalan

Catalan has alternations with [t͡ʃ] in word-final position and [ʒ] in intervocalic position word-internally (e.g., *boig* [bɔt͡ʃ] 'mad.MSG' vs. *boja* ['bɔʒə] 'mad.FSG', *bogeria* [buʒə'riə] 'madness'). The classical generative analysis of these alternations (Mascaró 1976; Wheeler 1979) assumed an underlying /ʒ/ (e.g., /bɔʒ/) which became an affricate d͡ʒ in word-final position and devoiced to [t͡ʃ] (devoicing being a process that affects all obstruents in word-final position). Interpreted in this way, the process of final affrication is fairly atypical because it only applies to the voiced postalveolar fricative (not to /ʃ/) and because it constitutes strengthening in an unusual position (word-finally). The alternation becomes more natural if surface [ʒ] is interpreted as the result of lenition in intervocalic position. This line of analysis has been pursued by Wheeler (2005) and, more recently, by Bonet and Lloret (2018), both within OT.

9.4.11 Campidanian Sardinian Rhotic Metathesis

In the Sestu variety of Campidanian Sardinian described in Bolognesi (1998), an intricate pattern of rhotic metathesis is attested that yields sonority-offending initial clusters. Rhotics are allowed in coda position only in a small set of words, all of which are vowel-initial (e.g., 'ɔrku 'ogre', 'arɡu 'sour'; Bolognesi 1998: 419). However, when these words are preceded by a determiner, the final vowel of the determiner is deleted and the rhotic surfaces in word-initial position following the last consonant of the determiner. This phenomenon produces highly marked sonority-offending initial clusters (e.g., sː rɔkːu 'the ogre', sː raɣu 'the sour one'; Bolognesi 1998: 419). We see in these examples that the consonant left in onset position geminates if it is a voiceless obstruent, and spirantizes if it is a voiced consonant. The avoidance of a rhotic in coda position can also be observed morpheme-internally by comparing the Sestu forms with other dialects without metathesis (e.g., mratsːu 'rotten (of cheese)'; cf. martsːu in Porru Campidanian Sardinian; mraʒini 'margin' but marʒini in Porru; Bolognesi 1998: 419). Sonority-offending sonorant-rhotic initial clusters always involve a non-coronal sonorant (the clusters *lr and *nr are unattested). Rhotics are prohibited not only in coda position but also as the second members of complex onsets in non-initial positions. Rhotic metathesis operated in these cases morpheme-internally, and thus no morphophonological alternations are available (e.g., ˈkraβa cf. ˈkaβra in more usual Sardinian 'goat', Bolognesi 1998: 420). This type of rhotic metathesis is restricted to affecting adjacent syllables. If the immediately adjacent syllable is onsetless, or would produce an ill-formed coronal sonorant-rhotic cluster, the rhotic deletes (e.g., maˈistu cf. *maˈristu (< maˈistru) 'school teacher', kaˈnista cf. *kaˈnrista (< kaˈnistra) 'small basket', ɔlˈlastu cf. *ɔlˈlrastu (< ɔlˈlastru) 'wild-olive tree', ˈnostu cf. *ˈnrostu (< ˈnostru) 'our'). The fact that forms where metathesis skips over a medial syllable are unattested seems to give support to this observation (e.g., *mraˈistu, *kraˈnista).

As said, the surface forms obtained after the application of rhotic metathesis in Sestu Campidanian Sardinian are typologically exceptional because they produce sonority-defiant sonorant-sonorant initial clusters, similar to the cases obtained after the application of unstressed vowel deletion in Emilian dialects and Abruzzese (see Section 9.3.1).

Algherese Catalan has several processes of rhotic metathesis similar to those described for Sestu Campidanian Sardinian (Torres-Tamarit et al. 2012). The most interesting is the second type of rhotic metathesis, which can be interpreted as a prominence effect in the sense that a marked structure, a complex onset containing a rhotic as its second member is dispreferred in a non-prominent position and is displaced to the left edge of the stem (e.g., *freber* instead of *febrer* 'February', *probe* instead of *pobre* 'poor'; Torres-Tamarit et al. 2012: 356). This phenomenon has also been reported in the Occitan dialect of Bagnères-de-Luchon (e.g., *brespes* cf. **besprass* 'vespers', *trende* cf. **tendro* 'tender'; Grammont 1933). This specific type of metathesis is referred to as *misplacement* by Buckley (2011) because the affected segment is shifted over more than one intervening segment. Algherese Catalan provides additional interesting data. The migration of the rhotic cannot exceed more than one syllable (e.g., *cogombre* > *cogrombe* 'cucumber' cf. **crogombe*; *catedral* > *catredal* 'cathedral' vs **cratedal*).

Although such a phenomenon is termed non-local or non-continuous in Buckley (2011), there is some kind of locality involved, in the sense that a form like *******cratedal*, in which the rhotic lands on the leftmost syllable, is not attested.

9.4.12 Palatalization of /s/ in Coda Position in Portuguese

In Portuguese, there is a contrast in onset position between alveolar and palatal sibilants, which can be voiced or voiceless (e.g., *selo* [ˈselu] 'seal' or *chá* [ˈʃa] 'tea' in word-initial position; *caça* [ˈkasɐ] 'hunt' or *acha* [ˈaʃɐ] 's/he finds' in word-internal position; Mateus and Andrade 2000: 10f.). However, in European Portuguese and, optionally, in the Carioca variety of Brazilian Portuguese the contrast between alveolar and palatal sibilants is lost in coda position and a palatal realization [ʃ]/[ʒ] is systematically found instead (e.g., *lápis* [ˈlapiʃ] 'pencil(s)', *rasca* [ˈʀaʃkɐ] '(of) bad quality', or *Lisboa* [liʒˈboɐ] 'Lisbon', with voicing assimilation). See Azevedo (1981) and Massini-Cagliari, Cagliari, and Redenbarger (2016) for a more precise description of the areas where /s/ palatalization is found in Brazil.

Palatalization of word-final /s/ is blocked when followed by a word that begins with a vowel (*dois patos* [ˈdojʃˈpatuʃ] 'two ducks', but *duas almas* [ˈduɐz ˈalmɐʃ] 'two souls'; Mateus and Andrade 2000: 144). Therefore palatalization is a post-lexical phenomenon that applies across words after resyllabification. Voicing before a vowel and palatalization before a consonant are used as evidence by Frota (2000) to show that the domain of palatalization is the Intonational Phrase.

What makes sibilant palatalization in Portuguese a typologically exceptional phenomenon is the fact that it applies in coda position, where one would expect either an assimilated consonant or an alveolar consonant, [s] or [z], a more unmarked place of articulation for consonants than [ʃ] or [ʒ] (see, for instance, Itô 1989 for restrictions on codas, and Hume 1996 for coronality as an unmarked place of articulation). Mateus and Andrade (2000) assume a special rule that assigns the feature [−anterior] to *s* in coda position, where the unmarked place of articulation is [+anterior]. If this is the case, one could think that in early stages of acquisition sibilants are realized as [s] or [z] in coda position. The acquisition of the phonology of Portuguese has been studied in Costa (2010), Freitas (2017), and Matzenauer and Costa (2017) (see also references therein). Almeida, Costa, and Freitas (2010) report one child who produces the palatal sibilant in coda position without going through a stage with an alveolar sibilant in that position. Nevertheless, the transcriptions of another child, in Costa (2010), show a stage with [ʃ] and [ʒ] in onset position but [s] and [z] in coda position. More studies of children addressing this specific issue would help us discern a statistically more significant trend.

9.4.13 Onset Clusters in Ribagorçan Catalan

Latin word-initial clusters comprising a consonant followed by L gave rise to various outcomes in the Romance languages. PL (as in PLANU(M) 'flat'), CL (as in CLAUE(M) 'key'), or FL (as in FLAMMA(M) 'flame'), as well as BL and GL, remained unchanged in Catalan and French. In Italian, the initial consonant of the cluster was maintained but the lateral became a palatal glide [j]. In standard Spanish the result was a single palatal lateral [ʎ] (with other realizations in those varieties that later lost the palatal lateral altogether). In Portuguese the cluster became a single consonant, namely the postalveolar or palatoalveolar fricative [ʃ], realized as an affricate [t͡ʃ] in Galician when the initial consonant was voiceless. Other changes can be found, but the most marked is the maintenance of the first consonant with palatalization of the lateral: [pʎ], [kʎ], [fʎ] (and also [bʎ], [gʎ]). This realization is mainly found in Ribagorçan Catalan (partly in Aragon, partly in Catalonia) and surrounding areas, and in varieties of Occitan and Gascon. The palatal lateral is not a very common segment in the languages of the world, present only in 5 per cent of the inventories in *PHOIBLE*, and having the palatal lateral as the second element in a cluster is even less common. The palatal realization of the second element of the Latin clusters has been claimed to be an intermediate step for other outcomes found in Romance languages. See Bateman (2007), Recasens (2017), and references therein for discussion.

9.5 Suprasegmentals

9.5.1 Plural Morphemes and Low Tone in Occitan

Tone as a lexical property is absent in the Romance languages, while it is present in many African and South-East Asian languages, for instance (see Maddieson 2013b), and in Europe it exists in some Germanic languages. Sauzet (2011), however, hints at the possibility that tone is used to mark plurality in one variety of Occitan, spoken in Sant Julian de Cremsa (Saint-Julien-de-Crempse), in the Périgord area (Dordogne department). The data employed to suggest this idea come from the recordings made for the *Atlas linguistique et ethnographique du Languedoc occidental* (Ravier 1978–93). In this variety of Occitan, in plural noun phrases, plurality is marked segmentally only on the determiner, not on the noun, the plural definite article surfacing as [low] when masculine and preceding a consonant and [lej] when feminine and preceding a consonant; a sigmatic element, /z/, appears when masculine or feminine are followed by a vowel. It seems that when the noun is plural, the noun phrase surfaces with a final low tone, while the tone is higher when the noun phrase is singular. Sauzet suggests an analysis in which the plural morpheme has a corresponding morph with both segmental and suprasegmental material (low tone). The idea of tone being used to mark plurality must be taken cautiously, though, as Sauzet himself does. One first concern, which he expresses, is that it would seem that the phenomenon is not systematic. And, the very few examples he gives prompt several other queries: (i) Can one rule out the differences perceived being attributed to intonation rather than tone? (ii) Would the low tone be present only with masculine nouns or also with feminine nouns? (iii) Is the phenomenon also found with other determiners? (iv) Would the tonal difference be found in more complex noun phrases, with prenominal or postnominal adjectives? This is potentially a typologically exceptional phenomenon within Romance, but more systematic work should be done, both with the materials in Ravier (1978–93) and, if possible, with new fieldwork with native speakers, to test Sauzet's findings.

9.5.2 Moraic Verbal Morphemes in Friulian

Several Romance languages have short and long vowels, sometimes with a complex and opaque distribution, as is the case in Friulian, where a vowel is lengthened if followed by a word-final underlyingly voiced obstruent, which undergoes final devoicing (for a recent analysis see Torres-Tamarit 2015). The variety of Friulian spoken in the lower valley of Gorto has an additional pattern of vowel lengthening described and discussed in Roseano (2015). The stressed vowel is long only in the first person singular present indicative and first, second, and third persons singular and third person plural of the present subjunctive, only in first conjugation verbs and always in the verb root. Moreover, this lengthening takes place only when the stem ends in a single consonant (therefore no lengthening in forms like *i cjànt-i* 'I sing-PRS.IND.1SG') and stress falls in the last vowel of the stem (therefore no lengthening in forms like *i liber-i* 'I liberate-PRS.IND.1SG'). For the verb *cjatâ* 'find', for instance, there is a long vowel in the forms *i cjât-i* 'I find-PRS.IND.1SG', *i cjât-i* 'I find-PRS.SBJV.1SG', *tu cjât-is* 'you find-PRS.SBJV.2SG', *al cjât-i* 'he find-PRS.SBJV.3SG' and *a cjât-in* 'they find-PRS.SBJV.3PL'. Roseano (2015) attributes the lengthening in these forms to a floating mora with morphological status, an instance of non-concatenative morphology, not common in Romance. By a series of steps, this floating mora ends up linked to the stressed vowel of the root. According to Roseano (2015) this lengthening started historically in verbs with a final voiced obstruent in the stem, which around the fifteenth century lacked the inflexional vowel in the first person singular present indicative and first, second, and third persons singular of the present subjunctive; hence at that point it was a regular instance of phonological lengthening before voiced obstruents. This lengthening was kept when inflexional vowels were added and, by analogy, a long vowel was introduced in verbs whose stem did not end in a voiced obstruent and also in the third person plural present indicative. A synchronic analysis of this lengthening has to incorporate the fact that the affected verbs all belong to the first conjugation (and may be newly created verbs). The reason why, within the subjunctive, lengthening appears only in all forms of the present, except first and second persons plural, and is absent in non-present forms can easily be related to the fact that only stressed vowels can be lengthened, and that this lengthening can only affect the root. However, under this line of analysis, the presence of length in the first person singular present indicative, but not in other rhizotonic forms of the same tense, must be attributed synchronically to some other, unrelated factor (Lampitelli, Roseano and Torres-Tamarit 2021).

9.5.3 Truncated Vocatives

Truncation refers to a morphological process of word formation that shortens surface forms and is guided by prosodic templates, which correspond to categories of the prosodic hierarchy, usually feet. Alber and Arndt-Lappe (2012) study the typology of templatic truncation from a survey of 91 patterns of 27 languages. They find that 62.5 per cent of truncation patterns yield shortened forms that correspond to the size of metrical feet. Monosyllabic truncation is much less frequent (28.4 per cent). Finally, they find that 9 per cent of these patterns correspond to what they refer to as variable templates. A group of languages from the western Mediterranean, Algherese Catalan, Corsican, Sardinian, and southern Italo-Romance varieties, exhibit a pattern of vocative truncation that yields surface forms of variable size (Vanrell and Cabré 2011; Alber and Arndt-Lappe 2012; Cabré and Vanrell 2013; D'Alessandro and van Oostendorp 2016; Cabré et al. in press). As can be seen in (7), truncated vocatives in Sardinian preserve the base form from the left edge of the name up to the stressed vowel, excluding also the coda consonant from the stressed syllable. Vocative truncation is not a templatic process *stricto sensu*, since it is not guided by any prosodic requirement drawn from the Prosodic Hierarchy. Nor does vocative truncation correspond to a subtractive pattern, which consists in deleting a prosodic unit from the base, usually a syllable or mora.

(7) Vocative truncation in Sardinian (Cabré et al. in press)
Bèrtulu → Bè'
Giarònimu → Girò'
Isperàntzia → Isperà'
Giusepalbèrto → Giusepalbè'

Alber and Arndt-Lappe (2012) describe the variable size of truncated vocatives as a doubly anchored pattern that refers to the left edge of the stem and the stressed syllable. Such a pattern of variable truncation is not attested outside of Romance, and is characteristic of Algherese Catalan, Corsican, Sardinian, and southern Italo-Romance varieties.

Selected References

Below you can find selected references for this chapter. The full references can be found online at the following page: www.cambridge.org/Romancelinguistics

Bateman, N. (2007). *A Cross-linguistic Investigation of Palatalization*. Doctoral thesis, University of California, San Diego.

Bolognesi, R. (1998). *The Phonology of Campidanian Sardinian*. Doctoral thesis, University of Amsterdam.

Colina, S. (2013). 'Galician geada: in defense of underspecification in Optimality Theory', *Lingua* 133: 84–100.

Dumas, D. (1981). 'Structure de la diphtongaison québécoise', *Canadian Journal of Linguistics* 26: 1–61.

Fanciullo, F. (1976). 'Il trattamento delle occlusive sonore latine nei dialetti salentini', *L'Italia dialettale* 39: 1–82.

García Arias, X. L. (2003). *Gramática histórica de la lengua asturiana*. Oviedo: Academia de la Llingua Asturiana. Llibreria Llingüística.

Loporcaro, M. (2016). 'Metaphony and diphthongization in southern Italy: reconstructive implications for sound change in early Romance'. In Torres-Tamarit, F., Linke, K., and van Oostendorp, M. (eds), *Approaches to Metaphony in the Languages of Italy*. Berlin/Boston: De Gruyter Mouton, 55–87.

Massini-Cagliari, G., Cagliari, L. C., and Redenbarger, W. J. (2016). 'A comparative study of the sounds of European and Brazilian Portuguese: phonemes and allophones'. In Wetzels, W. L., Menuzzi, S., and Costa, J. (eds), *The Handbook of Portuguese Linguistics*. Malden: Wiley-Blackwell, 56–68.

Michnowicz, J. (2008). 'Final nasal variation in Merida, Yucatan', *Spanish in Context* 5: 278–303.

Sauzet, P. (2011). 'Los morfèmas de plural nominal a Sant Julian de Cremsa: [-w] e lo ton bas'. In Rieger, A. (ed.), *Actes du 9e Congrès de l'Association Internationale d'Études Occitanes*. Aachen: Shaker, 827–47.

Schmid, S. (2018). 'Palatal and postalveolar obstruents in six Italo- and Rhaeto-Romance varieties'. In Recasens, D. and Sánchez Miret, F. (eds), *Production and Perception Mechanisms of Sound Change*. Munich: Lincom, 91–110.

Vanrell, M. and Cabré, T. (2011). 'Troncamento e intonazione dei vocativi in Italia centromeridionale'. In Gili Fivela, B., Stella, A., Garrapa, L., and Grimaldi, M. (eds), *Contesto comunicativo e variabilità nella produzione e percezione della lingua. Atti del 7° convegno de l'Associazione Italiana di Scienze della Voce, 26–28 gennaio 2011, Lecce*. Rome: Bulzoni, 200–11.

Part Three

Morphology

10

Phonological and Morphological Conditioning

Franck Floricic and Lucia Molinu

10.1 Introduction

It has long been recognized that phonology/phonetics and morphology interact in such a way as to make it difficult to draw any clear dividing line between these subfields.* In this connexion, we might mention at least two Romance linguists – Georges Millardet (1923) and Clemente Merlo (1946) – who repeatedly pointed out that the whole structure of language is grounded on phonetics. From this point of view there is nothing exceptional in the notion that phonetics/phonology may provide the system with the very substance of morphological oppositions. The number and the range of the morphological processes attributable to phonetic principles in the Romance domain are so wide that we can only select a few typical phenomena here. It must be clear as well that it is not always evident to what extent a given morphological alternation is phonologically driven: whether we are dealing with a purely phonological phenomenon or whether we should recognize some lexical conditioning in the choice of the allomorphs (see Haspelmath and Sims 2010: 26); on the debate concerning the limits and contours of 'morphophonemics' see Martinet (1965). If in some cases the phonetic impulse for a morphological alternation is still transparent, in others the trigger is no longer available or can only be identified following a diachronic reconstruction process. What we are left with thus is a morphological alternation that leaves on the 'surface' no trace of its triggers (see Maiden 2005). Nonetheless, some resultant distributional patterns may extend far beyond their propagation point, and such

---

* We would like to thank Aitor Carrera, Ana Cano, and Ioana Chiţoran for their remarks concerning Aranese, Asturian, and Romanian data. We are particularly grateful to Adam Ledgeway and Martin Maiden for their careful reading of our contribution. Of course, all remaining errors are ours.

distributional regularities become what Aronoff (1994: 25) or Maiden (2005) call 'morphomic'.

10.2 Allomorphy of the Definite Article

The fact that 'the phonetic constitution of the word gives a powerful impetus to the whole lexicon' (Millardet 1923: 122) can be observed in many sectors of morphology. One of these is the shape of the definite articles found in Romance. In Castilian, for example, the masculine form of the article is selected before a feminine noun beginning with the stressed vowel ['a]- (cf. Nevins 2011: 2360): cf. *el chico* 'the boy.M', *la casa* 'the house.F', *la amiga* 'the friend.F', but *el agua* 'the water.F', *el alma* 'the soul.F'. As illustrated by examples such as *la amiga*, hiatus between two identical vowels is allowed while the (masculine) allomorph selection is not required either before adjectives (cf. *la alta velocidad* 'the high speed'), proper names, place names, or acronyms in ['a]- (e.g., *la Ana, la Alba, la Ávila, la Apa* (*Asociación de Padres de Alumnos*)). From this point of view, it is clear that the singular determiner distribution in Castilian cannot be reduced to dissimilation constraints (see also the discussion in Section 7.5.2).

A more complex situation is found in Aranese as shown in Table 10.1 (see, e.g., Barnils 1913: 53; Coromines 1991: 13;51; Carrera 2007: 79f.).

The unmarked feminine singular form of the article is *era* (< ILLAM 'that'), which can be reduced to *ra*. Before a word beginning with *á-* / *a-*, the final vowel of the determiner is deleted (cf. er 'aiɣu̯a, er a'βeʎa). In the

Table 10.1. *The article in Aranese (Canejan-Bausen)*

	FSG	FPL
before vowel	er a'βeʎa 'the bee'	ez a'βeʎes
	er 'aiɣu̯a 'the water'	ez 'aiɣu̯es
	er i'madʒe 'the image'	ez i'madʒes
before consonant	'era ɣa'ria 'the hen'	ez ɣa'ries
	'era 'muska 'the fly'	ez 'muskes
	'era 'pɛi̯ra 'the stone'	es 'pɛi̯res
	'era 'hɛsta 'the party'	es 'ɛstes
	MSG	MPL
before vowel	edʒ 'andʒe 'the angel'	ez 'andʒes
	edʒ 'ɔme 'the man'	ez 'ɔmes
	etʃ ur'madʒe 'the cheese'	es ur'madʒes
	etʃ ym 'the smoke'	es yms
before consonant	et ʃi'βau̯ 'the horse'	e ʃʃi'βau̯s
	eʃ ʃi'βau̯	
	ek kaŋ 'the dog'	es kas
	ep putʃ 'the chicken'	es puts
	en nas 'the nose'	ez 'nazi
	et sau̯'met 'the donkey'	es sau̯'mets

case of 'era 'hɛsta, it must be pointed out that the noun 'hɛsta has an initial laryngeal fricative ('hɛsta < FESTAM) which can be reduced to zero and whose underlying effect is to block deletion of the final vowel of the determiner (cf. Fr. *le hasard* [ləazaʁ] 'the chance'). In the plural, the feminine article is [ez] before a vowel and before voiced consonants or [es] before voiceless consonants. On the other hand, the masculine singular article is edʒ (< etʃ < et < ILLUM 'that') before a vowel but etʃ / et before a voiceless consonant or an underlying laryngal fricative (cf. etʃ ym 'the smoke'). However, due to pervasive assimilation phenomena, the final consonant of the article may assimilate to that of the following word, hence expressions such as ek kaŋ 'the dog', ep putʃ 'the chicken' (cf. Coromines 1991: 61) – very similar patterns are reported in the Gascon variety of Bethmale (cf. Schönthaler 1937). In the plural, the form of the masculine article is the same as that of the feminine: ez (es < els < ILLOS 'those') before a vowel or a voiced consonant, and es before an unvoiced consonant or an underlying laryngal fricative. Observe that the kind of assimilation illustrated by examples such as ek kaŋ 'the dog', ep putʃ 'the chicken', is reminiscent of Italian *raddoppiamento fonosintattico* (see Sections 6.4.3.2, 7.4.2, and 7.4.5) and is attested in other Occitan varieties. In the Languedocian dialect of Allez-et-Cazeneuve, for example, the plural marker -s can either weaken in coda position, or it can assimilate to the following consonant, as illustrated in Table 10.2.

Table 10.2. *Plural -s in Allez-et-Cazeneuve*

	FSG	FPL
before vowel	l a'gaso 'the magpie'	laz a'gasos
	l a'graul̯o 'the crow'	laz a'graul̯os
	'l aul̯ko 'the goose'	laz 'aul̯kos
before consonant	la 'pato 'the paw'	la$_p$ 'patos
		las 'patos
	la 'kraβo 'the goat'	la$_h$ 'kraβos
	la fru'mit 'the ant'	la$_f$ fru'mit
	la dēn 'the tooth'	la$_z$ dēn
	la 'βako 'the cow'	lab 'bakos 'the cows'
		'kau̯ko$_b$ 'bakos 'some cows'
		'kau̯koz 'bakos 'some cows
	MSG	MPL
before vowel	l a'ɲɛl 'the lamb'	luz a'ɲɛl
	ỹn eu̯ 'an egg'	luz ɛu̯ 'the eggs'
before consonant	lu tsa'βal 'the horse'	lut tsa'βal
	lu pjɛl 'the hair'	lu$_p$ pjɛl
	lu pɔr 'the pig'	lup pɔr
		lup pu̯ɔr
	lu te'su 'the pig'	lus te'sus
	lu βeu̯ 'the ox'	lu$_z$ 'beu̯
		lu$_b$ 'beu̯

The definite article here shows polymorphism due to the nature of the phonological class to which the initial segment of the noun belongs. Before vowels, the situation is rather simple: the article is [l] in the masculine and in the feminine singular and laz in the feminine plural: l a'ɲɛl 'the lamb', 'l au̯ko 'the goose', laz 'au̯kos 'the geese'. In the masculine plural, vowel-initial nouns trigger the allomorph luz (e.g., luz a'ɲɛl 'the lambs', luz ɛu̯ 'the eggs'). With consonant-initial nouns, the situation is more complex: the sigmatic forms lus (masculine) and las (feminine) are used before voiceless stops (cf. lus te'sus 'the pigs'; las 'patos 'the paws'). Before voiced stops, a sonority assimilation takes place, hence expressions such as lu_z bɛu̯ 'the oxen', la_z dẽn 'the teeth'. However, various options may be available in the same context: lu_z bɛu̯ and lu_b bɛu̯ are both attested in the plural, and the latter shows a phenomenon of total assimilation which leads to (quasi) gemination. The same observation holds for coexisting pairs such as las 'patos / la_p 'patos 'the paws' for which one may argue that total assimilation of [s] is obtained through a stage of debuccalization (cf. la_h 'kraβos 'the goats'). Note, however, that the assimilation process leading to gemination is much more general than the (plural) definite article: it can occur with other final consonants in a string $word_1$ + $word_2$, thus resembling Italo-Romance *raddoppiamento fonosintattico*: ỹm pi'lɔd de 'pɛi̯ro 'a pile of stones' (e.g., ỹm pi'lɔt 'a pile'), es trõm 'mĩnso / trɔd des'tretso 'she is too thin / too narrow' (cf. trɔp 'too'). It also occurs between past participles and the initial consonant of the following word, due to assimilation with the participial marker -t (e.g., lu mar'tsãn a 'ki ɛi bẽn'dyl la 'bako 'the trader to whom I sold the cow', n a pa_h pu'yf 'fa a'kel tra'βal '(s)he could not do this work').

10.3 Subject Clitic Allomorphy

Subject clitics are not attested in all Romance languages (see further discussions in Sections 4.2, 17.5.1.1, and 21.2.1). French has often been set apart in the Romance domain for having subject clitics, even though the latter are also attested, for example, in Francoprovençal and Raeto-Romance varieties, in the dialects of northern Italy, and in some Occitan dialects. The question of whether the subject clitic paradigm of colloquial French should be integrated into the verb paradigm as a verb affix is still a matter of debate (cf., among others, Meillet 1921: 69f., 177f.; Bally 1944: 300f.; Luís 2004; Culbertson 2010; see also Section 4.2). The paradigms in Table 10.3, adapted from Floricic (2016: 2673), illustrate the distribution of the subject clitic with consonant-initial verbs.

In the first person singular, the consonant of the subject clitic ʒə may show devoicing when the schwa disappears: ʃtuʁn 'I turn' (see Klausenburger 2000: 83). The third person singular and plural, which have

Table 10.3. Paradigms of Fr. baisser 'lower', tourner 'turn', refuser 'refuse'

	A. baisser			B. tourner			C. refuser		
	subject clitic	verb stem	ending	subject clitic	verb stem	ending	subject clitic	verb stem	ending
1SG	ʒ	b ɛ s		ʒ	t u ʁ	n	ʒ	ʁ e f y z	
2SG	t	b ɛ s		t	t u ʁ	n	t	ʁ e f y z	
3SGa	i	b ɛ s		i	t u ʁ	n	i	ʁ e f y z	
3SGa	ɛ	b ɛ s		ɛ	t u ʁ	n	ɛ	ʁ e f y z	
1PLa	ɔ̃	b e s		ɔ̃	t u ʁ	n	ɔ̃	ʁ e f y z	
1PLb	n u	b e s	ɔ̃	n u	t u ʁ	n ɔ̃	n u	ʁ e f y z	ɔ̃
2PL	v u	b e s	e	v u	t u ʁ	n e	v u	ʁ e f y z	e
3PLa	i	b ɛ s		i	t u ʁ	n	i	ʁ e f y z	
3PLb	ɛ	b ɛ s		ɛ	t u ʁ	n	ɛ	ʁ e f y z	

the same etymon as the definite article discussed in the preceding paragraph, show a gender opposition. Interestingly, the final lateral of the clitic may be deleted in informal speech (cf. ibɛs 'he lowers' / ɛbɛs 'she lowers'), even though this phenomenon is less frequent in the feminine, probably because the third person singular and third person plural have the same exponent: the orthographic differentiation between the two numbers is no longer available in speech. First person plural *nous* 'we' has been given along with *on* 'we (lit. one)' because in informal contexts the latter, which is a generic third person singular, is much more frequent.[1]

With vowel-initial verbs on the other hand, the schwa of the first person subject clitic ʒə is obligatorily deleted, while the high front vowel of the second person singular ty is optionally deleted, as illustrated in Table 10.4.

Due to syllabification constraints, the full variants *il* [il] and *elle* [ɛl] in the third person singular are required before a vowel (cf. ilekut 'he listens', ilɛm 'he likes', iloz 'he dares'), while in the plural the same constraint is satisfied by the plural marker -z which obligatorily surfaces in *liaison* contexts (cf. Section 6.4.3.1), hence the optionality of the lateral consonant. In the first and second person plural, the same segment appears before a vowel-initial verb, even though it has etymologically no connexion with plurality marking (cf. nuzekutɔ̃ 'we listen', vuzekute 'you listen'). Two options are available to account for the clitic variation: either two allomorphs – nu and nuz / vu and vuz – are selected according to the context; or a floating segment is syllabified when phonologically required. If we take French subject clitics to be some kind of affix, a possible analysis of expressions such as nuzekutɔ̃ 'we listen', vuzekute 'you listen', would be to assume that we are dealing with some kind of circumfixation phenomenon.

10.4 Possessive Allomorphy

The case of possessive adjectives is not very different from that of the definite article and will be discussed more briefly. It is well known that French has special rules governing the selection of possessives according to the phonetic environment. As illustrated in Table 10.5, some kind of mismatch arises between the form of the possessive singular and gender marking, in the sense that before a vowel, gender contrast is neutralized in favour of the masculine allomorph.

The selection of *mon* [mɔ̃n] 'my.MSG' before a feminine noun provides the noun with an onset recycling the underlying nasal consonant of the possessive (cf. *mon équipe* [mɔ̃nekip] 'my team' vs **[maekip] / **[mekip]). In the plural, gender oppositions are neutralized both before a consonant (with

---

[1] In some contexts the use of *nous* would even sound odd, thus, *on y va?* 'shall we go?', rather than *nous y allons?*

Table 10.4. Paradigms of French vowel-initial écouter 'listen', aimer 'love', oser 'dare'

	A. écouter			B. aimer			C. oser		
	subject clitic	verb stem	ending	subject clitic	verb stem	ending	subject clitic	verb stem	ending
1SG		ʒ e k u t			ɛ m			o z	
2SG	t (y)	e k u t		t (y)	ɛ m		t (y)	o z	
3SGa	i l	e k u t		i l	ɛ m		i l	o z	
3SGa	ɛ	e k u t		ɛ	ɛ m		e	o z	
1PLa	n uz	e k u t		n uz	ɛ m		n uz	o z	
1PLb	ɔ̃ n	e k u t	ɔ̃	ɔ̃ n	ɛ m	ɔ̃	ɔ̃ n	o z	ɔ̃
2PL	v uz	e k u t	e	v uz	ɛ m	e	v uz	o z	e
3PLa	i (l)	e k u t		i (l)	ɛ m		i (l)	o z	
3PLb	ɛ (l)	e k u t		ɛ (l)	ɛ m		e (l)	o z	

Table 10.5. *French possessives*

lexeme	MSG	MSLF	MSLF	FSG
MON	mon bateau	mon avion	mon équipe	ma fille
	'my boat'	'my plane'	'my team'	'my daughter'
	[mɔ̃bato]	[mɔ̃navjɔ̃]	[mɔ̃nekip]	[mafij]
lexeme	MPL	MSLF	MSLF	FPL
MES	mes bateaux	mes avions	mes équipes	mes filles
	'my boats'	'my planes'	'my teams'	'my daughters'
	[mebato]	[mezavjɔ̃]	[mezekip]	[mefij]

Table 10.6. *Masculine possessives in Cabranes*

	MSG		MPL	
	prenominal	postnominal	prenominal	postnominal
'my son(s)'	el mio fiyu [ɛl'mjo'fiju]	el fiyu míu [ɛl'fiju'miu]	los mios fiyos [lɔz'mjɔs'fijɔs] [lɔz'mjɔ'fijɔs]	los fiyos míos [lɔs'fijɔz'mios]
'your son(s)'	el to fiyu [ɛl'to'fiju]	el fiyu tuyu [ɛl'fiju'tuju]	los tos fiyos [lɔs'tɔs'fijɔs] [lɔs'to'fijɔs]	los fiyos tuyos [lɔs'fijɔs'tujɔs]
'his son(s)'	el so fiyu [ɛlso'fiju]	el fiyu suyu [ɛl'fiju'suju]	los sos fiyos [lɔs'sɔs'fijɔs] [los'so'fijɔs]	los fiyos suyos [lɔs'fijɔs'sujɔs]

Table 10.7. *Feminine possessives in Cabranes*

	FSG		FPL	
	prenominal	postnominal	prenominal	postnominal
'my daughter(s)'	la mio fiya [la'mjo'fija]	la fiya mía [la'fija'mia]	les mios fiyes [lez'mjɔs'fijes] [lez'mjo'fijes]	les fiyes míes [les'fijez'mies]
'your daughter(s)'	la to fiya [la'to'fija]	la fiya tuya [la'fija'tuja]	les tos fiyes [les'tɔs'fijes] [les'tɔ'fijes]	les fiyes tuyes [les'fijes'tujes]
'his daughter(s)'	la so fiya [la'so'fija]	la fiya suya [la'fija'suja]	les sos fiyes [les'sos'fijes] [les'so'fijes]	les fiyes suyes [les'fijes'sujes]

mes [me]) and before a vowel (with *mes* [mez]). An interesting and more complex pattern is reported in the Asturian dialect of Cabranes, where the shape of the possessive differs according to two orthogonal distinctions (cf. Canellada 1944: 24): pre- vs postnominal possessives and masculine vs feminine possessives, as illustrated in Tables 10.6 and 10.7.

In prenominal position the possessive neutralizes gender distinctions, generalizing the variants ['mjo] / ['to] / ['so], while the 'heavier' variant in postnominal position preserves gender contrasts (cf. ['miu] vs ['mia] in the singular and ['miɔs] vs ['mies] in the plural). In other varieties as well – for example that of Trubia baxa – the prenominal possessive has two variants for both genders (cf. ['mjo] / ['mi] in the first person singular, ['tu] / ['to], in the second singular, etc.; see Suárez García 2016: 135). A striking feature of the dialect of Cabranes is the competing options available in the plural of prenominal forms. As illustrated by examples such as [lɔz'mjɔs'fijɔs] / [lɔz 'mjɔ'fijɔs], agreement may not be marked on the various dependent elements of the noun phrase, but only on the article and the head noun. Such a pattern is reminiscent of Brazilian Portuguese and Latin American Spanish where [s] reduction is also attested inside the NP (see, e.g., Poplack 1980; Navas Sánchez-Élez 1997; Pomino and Stark 2009).

10.5 Stem Allomorphy

10.5.1 Verb Allomorphy

As pointed out in Maiden, Floricic, and Esher (forthcoming), stem allomorphy distinguishes Romance from Latin, where such a phenomenon was relatively uncommon. In the verb domain, stem alternation mainly involves: (i) palatalization and gemination due to the effects of a proto-Romance [j] / [w] immediately following the root; (ii) palatalization of root-final velars before following front-vowel inflexional endings; (iii) various types of differentiation of vowel quality according to whether the root was stressed or unstressed.

The verb paradigms in Table 10.8 show that in the Asturian dialect of Somiedo, the verbs ten'tar 'try' and pru'βar 'test' have a stem alternation due to diphthongization of the Latin stressed vowels ĕ and ŏ (see Cano

Table 10.8. *Differentiation of the root according to whether it is stressed or unstressed in Asturian (Somiedo)*

1SG	2SG	3SG	1PL	2PL	3PL
'tjentu 'I try'	'tjentas	'tjenta	ten'tamus	ten'taðes / ten'tais	'tjentan
'prweβu 'I test'	'prweβas	'prweβa	pru'βamus	pru'βaðes / pru'βáis	'prweβan
'pjensu 'I think'	'pjensas	'pjensa	pen'samus	pen'saðes / pen'sais	'pjensan
'kwerru 'I run'	'kwerres	'kwerre	kur'remus	kur'reðes / kur'reis	'kwerren
'komu 'I eat'	'komes	'kome	ku'memus	ku'meðes / ku'meis	'komen
'bolbo 'I (re)turn'	'bolbes	'bolbe	bul'bemus	bul'beðes / bul'beis	'bolben
ku'noθu 'I know'	ku'noθes	ku'noθ	kunu'θemus	kunu'θeðes / kunu'θeis	ku'noθen

González 2009: 54, 155–57, 170–72, 177): in the first and second persons plural, the complex of theme vowel + inflexional ending forms a syllabic trochee which attracts stress, hence the reduced stems tenˈt- / pruˈβ- as opposed to the non-reduced stems ˈtjent- / ˈprweβ- of the singular and of the third person plural.

In the case of penˈsar (< PENSARE) and kurˈrer (< CURRERE), however, the diphthong found in stressed syllables is not etymological and is the result of an extension of regular diphthongization. As illustrated by verbs such as ku ˈmer 'to eat', [o] raises to [u] in unstressed syllables, whence the first and second person plural kuˈmemus and kuˈmeðes / kuˈmeis.

Another, extensively studied, source of differentiation is that of the effect of late Latin j (see, e.g., Maiden 2018a: 84–91) and of w on the shape of the root. As for j, one of its principal effects is to palatalize the preceding consonant, as illustrated by the old Occitan present indicative and present subjunctive paradigms in Table 10.9 (cf. Anglade 1921: 329, 348, 352).

First person singular forms have a palatalized stem derived from the iotacization of the first front vowel when unstressed and in hiatus position (cf. DOLEO 'I suffer', *vɔljo 'I want', TENEO 'I hold', UENIO 'I come'). And the same palatalized stem appears throughout the subjunctive paradigms, even though in some cases (cf. *tenga, venga*, etc.), a velar segment has pervaded the whole conjugation, thus leading to a double paradigm (on the question of the 'velar insert', cf. Fanciullo 1998; Maiden 1992; 2001; 2018a: 112–15; Floricic 2018a).

Table 10.9. *Old Occitan present indicative and present subjunctive paradigms*

		1SG	2SG	3SG	1PL	2PL	3PL
IND		duelh 'suffer'	dols	dol	dolem	doletz	dolon
		dol	dol				
SBJV		duelha	duelhas	duelha	dolham	dolhatz	duelhan
		dolha	dolhas	dolha			dolhan
IND		vuelh 'want'	vols	vol	volem	voletz	volon
		vuolh	vol				
		velh					
SBJV		vuelha	vuelhas	vuelha	volham	volhatz	vuelhan
		vuolha			vulham	vulhatz	
		volha					
IND		tenh 'hold'	tenes	ten	tenem	tenetz	tenon
		tenc	tens				
SBJV		tenha	tenhas	tenha	tenham	tenhatz	tenhan
		tenga	tengas	tenga	tengam	tengatz	tengan
IND		venh 'come'	vens	ven	venem	venetz	venon
		venc					
SBJV		venha	venhas	venha	venham	venhatz	venhan
		venga	vengas	venga	vengam	vengatz	vengan

Table 10.10. *Gemination triggered by labiovelar glides*

	1SG	2SG	3SG	1PL	2PL	3PL
TENUI 'I held'	'tɛnni	te'nesti	'tɛnne	te'nemmo	te'neste	'tɛnnero
UOLUI 'I wanted'	'vɔlli	vo'lesti	'vɔlle	vo'lemmo	vo'leste	'vɔllero
PLACUI 'I pleased'	'pjakku̯i	pja'tʃesti	'pjakku̯e	pja'tʃemmo	pja'tʃeste	'pjakku̯ero
TACUI 'I fell silent'	'takku̯i	ta'tʃesti	'takku̯e	ta'tʃemmo	ta'tʃeste	'takku̯ero
NOCUI 'I harmed'	'nɔkku̯i	no'tʃesti	'nɔkku̯e	no'tʃemmo	no'tʃeste	'nɔkku̯ero

On the other hand, the glide w is historically responsible for stem differentiation in Italian, especially in the formation of the Latin -u̯i perfects, as illustrated in Table 10.10, where the labiovelar glide triggers gemination of the preceding consonant provided stress falls on the root (cf. Alkire and Rosen 2010: 150f.).

Stem differentiation within the paradigm of these perfects (cf. 'tɛnni < TENUI vs te'nesti < *tennesti < TENUISTI) might be reminiscent of the *Lex mamilla*, a phonological process which refers to the degemination that occurs with a concomitant change in stress position. The following stress patterns played a crucial role in the overall verb structure of Italian present indicative and 'strong' perfect. It will be observed that the only difference between the two patterns (present vs perfect) lies in the stress shift of the second person singular. A stress shift which is due to the existence of a heavy (disyllabic) ending, as exemplified in Table 10.11.[2]

Table 10.11. *Stress shift due to the existence of a heavy (disyllabic) ending*

σ'	σ			σ'	σ	
σ'	σ			σ	σ'	σ
σ'	σ			σ'	σ	
σ	σ'	σ		σ	σ'	σ
σ	σ'	σ		σ	σ'	σ
σ'	σ	σ		σ'	σ	σ

---

[2] Incidentally, Maiden (2018b: 220) (who labels the root allomorph the 'PYTA' root) points out that '[t]he Italo-Romance PYTA root only occurs where the morphological material to its right is unstressed, and this is clear where stress has moved historically from root to ending'. Maiden argues that the peculiar pattern of root-allomorphy exhibited by the Italo-Romance preterite can be interpreted in purely morphological terms: the analogical pressure from originally imperfective forms contributes to level the distinction of the root between originally imperfective (the non-PYTA root) and perfective (the PYTA root) verb-forms; but in stressed roots this process is blocked because (a) replacement of the PYTA root by the non-PYTA root would create blur, i.e., synonymy among inflexional affixes; (b) high frequency of the PYTA root with respect to other continuants of the Latin perfective, and in particular the high frequency of the third person singular, protects the stressed root from the analogical pressure of the non-PYTA root and favours the mutual association of PYTA root with unstressed ending, thus avoiding replacement of the unstressed ending by a stressed ending.

It must be borne in mind, however, that (a) degemination correlated with stress shift is not a 'law' and many examples can be adduced for which the root geminate is maintained despite stress displacement (see the Montalese Tuscan forms 1. èbbi, 2. ebbésti, 3. èbbe, (...) 5 ebbéssi, 6. èbbano – Nerucci 1865: 29; Rohlfs 1968: 312). By the way, second person singular forms such as vollesti 'you wanted', attested in the Tuscan dialect of Seravezza (Pieri 1904: 174), show that an extension of the geminate root from the first and third persons is always possible;[3] (b) the stress pattern itself may act as a mould to which many verbs conform and this accentual pattern can be strengthened by the accentual pattern of the present indicative; (c) in other cases, the inherited accentual pattern has been preserved, hence for example in Sicilian 1. 'vinni, 2. vi'nisti, 3. 'vinni, 4. 'vinnimu, 5. vi'nistivu, 6. 'vinninu (Rohlfs 1968: 311); (d) as observed by Tekavčić (1981: 268), no phonetic account can explain Italian forms such as volesti 'you wanted' (< UOLUISTI): the stressed vowel is the thematic vowel found in the present indicative of regular second conjugation verbs, probably under the pressure of first conjugation perfects where the thematic vowel surfaces through the paradigm.

Of course, this is not to say that the geminate of all the first singular perfects is a phonetically regular outcome of the corresponding Latin form. It was pointed out by many authors (among others, de Lollis 1885: 420f.) that a handful of verbs with a regular geminate may have served as a model which extended to whole series of perfects – de Lollis also refers to the need to differentiate the perfect and the present forms. Such a view is in keeping with Malkiel's (1990: 109) observation, according to which the canonical form $C_1VC_2C_2V$ 'crystallized as an identifiable *morphological scheme* – endowed with the power to attract miscellaneous formations adrift in the lexicon'. From this point of view, reconstructed forms such as *vɛnuit would be unnecessary and all we would have to assume is the existence of a morphological schema or template that served as a model (see Magni 2001).

Palatalization of root-final consonants before following front-vowel inflexional endings is another source of variation of verb stems. As shown by the Romanian examples in Table 10.12, the second singular exponent /i/ in the present induces palatalization of the preceding consonant (see Bourciez 1910: 175; Rosetti 1964: 207f., etc.).[4]

A verb such as a pur'ta 'bear, wear' is interesting for many reasons: leaving aside the stem variation triggered by the final palatal vowel

---

[3] The opposite tendency to extend the weak stem in the first singular is also attested, hence vincei 'I won', facei 'I made', etc. (Wahlgren 1920: 147f.). The resistance of forms like volli 'I wanted', feci 'I made', etc. (and the marginality of forms like facei) is probably connected to their cognitive salience and their high frequency. Note that Maiden (2018b) interprets forms such as vollesti as displaying retention of an original lengthened consonant, rather than as a result of analogical extension.

[4] Chiţoran (2002a: 11) assumes that synchronically in Romanian 'word-final consonants are palatalized in the presence of a front vowel morphological marker, for example the desyllabified inflexional marker /-i/'.

Table 10.12. *Second person singular allomorphy in Romanian*

	1SG	2SG	3SG	1PL	2PL	3PL
a kɨn'ta 'sing'	kɨnt	kɨntsʲ	'kɨntə	kɨn'təm	kɨn'tatsʲ	'kɨntə
a pur'ta 'wear'	port	portsʲ	'po̯artə	pur'təm	pur'tatsʲ	'po̯artə
a 'pjerde 'lose'	'pjerd	pjerzʲ	'pjerde	'pjerdem	'pjerdetsʲ	pjerd
a 'krede 'believe'	'kred	'krezʲ	'kredə	'kredem	'kredetsʲ	kred
a 'zitʃe 'say'	'zik	'zitʃ	'zitʃe	'zitʃem	'zitʃetsʲ	zik
a ve'dea 'see'	vəd	vezʲ	'vede	ve'dem	ve'detsʲ	vəd

Table 10.13. *Non-palatalization of the velar in Italian* -are *verbs*

INF	1SG	2SG	3SG	1PL	2PL	3PL
dimenticare 'forget'	di'mentiko	di'mentiki	di'mentika	dimenti'kjamo	dimenti'kate	di'mentikano
praticare 'practice'	'pratiko	'pratiki	'pratika	prati'kjamo	prati'kate	'pratikano
pagare 'pay'	'pago	'pagi	'paga	pa'gjamo	pa'gate	'pagano
vincere 'win'	'viŋko	'vintʃi	'vintʃe	vin'tʃamo	vin'tʃete	'viŋkono
tingere 'dye'	'tiŋgo	'tindʒi	'tindʒe	tin'dʒamo	tin'dʒete	'tiŋgono
tacere 'fall silent'	'tattʃo	'tatʃi	'tatʃe	tat'tʃamo	ta'tʃete	'tattʃono

(cf. the forms of second person singular portsʲ, krezʲ, pjerzʲ), the stressed o in the third person singular changes to o̯a historically due to final -ə (or -e, -a in other cases) (cf. Lausberg 1976: 215f.).[5] In the first and second persons plural, stress shift entails vowel reduction in the pretonic syllable, hence purt-. In verbs such as a 'zitʃe 'say', palatalization of the velar consonant before a front vowel leads to the creation of two allomorphs zik- and zitʃ-, the first covering the first person singular and third person plural present indicative cells (cf. Hualde and Chiţoran 2016: 30). Furthermore, two different kinds of palatalization are at work here: one turning the dental stop into an affricate and then into a fricative before high front vowels or j (cf. DEUS > *djeu > dzeu > zeu 'God'; DICO > dzic > zic), and the other turning the velar stop [k] into an affricate before high front vowels or j (cf. among others Puşcariu 1937: 152, 234f.; Sala 1976: 51f., 165, 226).[6]

Palatalization of velar consonants before front vowels gave rise in Italian to stem alternations for which it is not simple to formulate clear synchronic rules. As can be seen in Table 10.13, the same phonological

---

[5] In cases such as im'plora 'implores', a'proba 'approves', a'kordə 'grants', we are dealing with loanwords or recent verbs and no diphthongization takes place (Chiţoran 2002b: 233).

[6] This example illustrates the fact that the palatalization process can even extend to assibilation (see Jensen 1997: 158; Bonfante 1998: 18). Cazacu (1970: 122f.) observes that in sixteenth-century texts, 'dʒitʃe is attested in writings from Transylvania and Maramureş (the initial affricate dʒ instead of dz is taken to be due to regressive assimilation). The forms 'dʒitʃe and 'zitʃe appear in texts from northern Transylvania and Moldova and from Wallachia, respectively. The term 'iotacization' used among others by Pop (1952) to refer to the effect of i / e on a preceding root ending in a coronal is in some sense too restrictive. By the way, Iancu (1970) uses indifferently 'palatalization' and 'iotacization'.

Table 10.14. *Italian* fuggire *'flee'*, leggere *'read'*

PRS.IND	PRS. SBJV	PRS.IND	PRS. SBJV
'fuggo	'fugga	'lɛggo	'lɛgga
'fuddʒi	'fugga	'lɛddʒi	'lɛgga
'fuddʒe	'fugga	'lɛddʒe	'lɛgga
fud'dʒamo	fud'dʒamo	led'dʒamo	led'dʒamo
fud'dʒite	fud'dʒate	led'dʒete	led'dʒate
'fuggono	'fuggano	'lɛggono	'lɛggano

context – [k] + the high front vowel [i] – does not trigger palatalization of the velar in the case of the second person singular present indicative of *-are* verbs (cf. di'mentiki 'you forget', 'pratiki 'you practice', 'paɡi 'you pay'), while it does in the *-ere* verbs (cf. 'vintʃi 'you win', 'tindʒi 'you dye', 'tatʃi 'you are silent').

A verb form such as prati'kare 'practice' is derived from the adjective *pratico* 'practical, experienced' whose masculine plural form is 'pratitʃi with palatalization, thus showing that synchronically there is no phonological explanation for the different treatment of these forms. The *raison d'être* of such a distribution lies in relative chronology: Latin k + i or e leads to tʃ in Italian and other Romance languages and this is the regular outcome in forms such as 'vintʃi 'you win' (< UINCIS), 'vintʃe '(s)he wins' (< UINCIT) (cf. Lausberg 1976: 277–79; Tekavčić 1972: 275f.). On the other hand, di'mentiki and 'paɡi presuppose a historically underlying form *de'mentikas / *'pakas and the final *-i* – whatever its origin – could not palatalize the preceding velar given that it arose after the palatalization of velars took place.

A rather different situation shows up with Italian verbs such as *fuggire* 'escape', as shown in Table 10.14.

As observed by Gorra (1895: 84), old Tuscan had 'fuddʒo, 'fuddʒi, 'fuddʒe, etc., and 'fuddʒa in the present subjunctive, with an affricate through the whole paradigm. The crucial point is that stem uniformity and stability has been broken in favour of what Maiden calls a U-pattern (the arbitrary label given to a distributional pattern including the present subjunctive and the first person singular and third person plural of the present indicative: see, e.g., Maiden 2018a: 84). Given the importance of morphological uniformity and stability in terms of mental processing and reproduction, the impetus for restructuring the paradigms must have been strong and deep enough to achieve such a reconfiguration. From this point of view, paradigm-internal stem stability may be superseded by strong high-level constraints: in this case, it has long been assumed that inter-paradigmatic pressure of similar forms might bring about paradigm restructurings. In particular, the whole series of stem alternations such as 'lɛggo / 'lɛddʒi, 'pjaŋgo / 'pjandʒi 'I / you cry' has been taken to be responsible for its adoption by forms that did not contain it etymologically (cf. Rohlfs 1968: 260). Such extension/diffusion is

Table 10.15. correr 'run' or pendre 'take' in Azanuy

PRS.IND	PRS. SBJV	PRS.IND	PRS. SBJV
corgo	corga	prengo	prenga
corres	corgas	prens	prengas
corre	corga	pren	prenga
correm	corgam	prenem	prengam
correz	corgaz	prenez	prengaz
corren	corgan	prenen	prengan

not limited to Italian and can be found in various other Romance varieties (cf. Maiden 2001: 43f.). In the data from the dialect of Azanuy (Huesca) in Table 10.15 taken from Giralt Latorre (1992–93: 147), it can be seen that the velar insert extends to verbs such as *correr* 'run' or *pendre* 'take' where they are of course not etymological.

The originality of the situation described by Giralt Latorre (1992–93: 146f.) thus lies in the fact that the propagation of the 'velar insert' extends to the whole paradigm of the subjunctive, but it is limited to the first cell of the present indicative, where it contributes to hypercharacterize the first person singular and where it contributes to the creation of a L-pattern (an arbitrary label describing a pattern of paradigmatic distribution comprising the forms of the present subjunctive and that of the first person singular present indicative: see, e.g., Maiden 2005: 146–51; O'Neill 2015). Plaza Boya (1990: 192) also reports in the Valle de Benasque forms such as *beigo* 'I drink', *caigo* 'I fall', *tiengo* 'I hold', *biengo* 'I come', *salgo* 'I go out', *muelgo* 'I grind', *fuigo* 'I run away', *sallgo* 'I go out', etc. restricted as well to the first person singular of the paradigm. In his description of the verb inflexion in Benasques, Saura Rami (2000: 149 n. 8) points out that the -go forms (cf. *escriugo* 'I write', *riugo* 'I laugh', *beugo* 'I drink', *deugo* 'I must', *creugo* 'I believe', etc.) coexist with the 'regular' forms (cf. *escribo*, *rido*, *bibo*, *debo*, *credo*, etc.).

10.5.2 Nominal Allomorphy

Of course, what holds for palatalization in verb morphology also holds in the nominal domain. The regular Italian outcome of Lat. AMICI is a'mitʃi 'friends', with palatalization of the root-final velar. But many examples can be given of nouns whose plural ends in -ki / -gi and not in -tʃi / -dʒi: e.g., *buchi* ['buki] 'holes' or *laghi* ['lagi] 'lakes' (cf. Celata and Bertinetto 2005). And the situation is even more complex if we consider other dialects of Italy. Carlo Salvioni pointed out that forms such as *fungio* ['fundʒo] 'mushroom' attested from the north to the south of the Peninsula had ousted older *fungo* ['fuŋgo] under the pressure of the plural *fungi* [fundʒi], thus eliminating stem alternation on the grounds of a cognitive and frequency-based unification

Table 10.16. *Brazilian Portuguese plural formation*

SG	PL	
o gato [o ˈgato] 'the cat'	*os gatos* [oz ˈgatos]	
a casa [a ˈkazɐ] 'the house'	*as casas* [as ˈkazɐs]	
um rosto [ˈrosto] 'a face'	*uns rostos* [ˈrɔstes]	*uns rosto* [rosto]
o cão [ˈkẽw̃] 'the dog'	*os cães* [ˈkẽjs]	*os cão*
a mão [ˈmẽw̃] 'the hand'	*as mãos* [mẽw̃s]	*as mão*
o leão [leˈẽw̃] 'the lion'	*os leões* [leˈõjs]	*os leão*
o sal [ˈsaw] 'the salt'	*os sais* [ˈsajs]	*os sal*
o mel [ˈmɛw] 'the honey'	*os meis* [ˈmɛjs] / *meles* [ˈmɛlis]	
o papel [paˈpew] 'the paper'	*os papeis* [paˈpejs]	*os papel*
o pôster [ˈposteh] 'the poster'	*os pôsters* [ˈpostehs] / *pôsteres* [posˈteɾis]	
o museu [muˈzew] 'the museum'	*os museus* [muˈzews]	*os museu*
o jornal [ʒohˈnaw] 'the newspaper'	*os jornais* [ʒohˈnajs]	*os jornal*
o nível [ˈnivew] 'the level'	*os nívels* [ˈnivejs]	*os nível*
o barril [baˈhiw] 'the barrel'	*os barris* [baˈhis]	*os barril*
o réptil [ˈhɛptʃiw] 'the reptile'	*os répteis* [ˈhɛptʃeis]	*os réptil*
o sol [ˈsɔw] 'the sun'	*os sóis* [ˈsɔjs]	*os sol*
o gol [ˈgow]'the goal'	*os gols* [ˈgows]	*os gol*
o futbol [futʃiˈbow] 'the football'	*os futbols* [futʃiˈbows]	
o mês [ˈmes] 'the month'	*os mêses* [ˈmezis]	*os mês*
o mal [ˈmaw] 'the harm'	*os males* [ˈmalis]	*os mal*
o país [paˈis] 'the country'	*os países* [paˈizis]	*os país*
o rapaz [haˈpas] / [haˈpajs] 'the boy'	*os rapazes* [haˈpazis]	
o lápis [ˈlapis] 'the pencil'	*os lápis* [ˈlapis]	

process (cf. Goidanich 1893: 57 and Tuttle 1995 and the references therein). Maiden (1995: 82f.), however, points out that, leaving aside two or three examples, the Tuscan variety which led to modern Italian generally preserves the velar, thus supporting the idea that the Italian nouns could not derive from forms endowed with the inflexional marker -i. According to Maiden (1998: 99f.), some Italian nouns showing palatalization of the velar such as ˈfiziko ˈfizitʃi, ˈsindako ˈsindatʃi, kiˈrurgo, kiˈrurdʒi, etc. are learnèd forms.[7]

An interesting case of stem allomorphy in plural formation is offered by Brazilian Portuguese – it will be clear, from the examples in Table 10.16, that the phenomenon under discussion could equally be analysed in the paragraph dedicated to affix allomorphy. As illustrated by the following table, if the more general way to express plurality is to add *-s* to vowel final singular forms (cf. Cristófaro-Silva 2002: 278; Becker, Clemens, and Nevins 2011; 2017: 320), several other 'cas de figure' may be found.[8] For example, in the plural of *um rosto* [ˈrosto] 'a face' (< Lat. ROSTRUM 'beak, snout'),

---

[7] Plural nouns such as *asparagi* 'asparagus', *amici* 'friends', *porci* 'pigs' do not belong to this lexical stratum. See Maiden (2000) for an attempt to explain the historical origins of the palatalized and non-palatalized plurals in Italian. Ascoli (1892–94: 284–86) analysed the It. *narice* 'nostril' and Cst. *nariz* 'nose' as derived from the nominative plural NARICAE (cf. the secondary nominative singular NARICA).

[8] According to Becker, Clemens, and Nevins (2017: 320), there are two plural suffixes (allomorphs) in complementary distribution: -[s] after vowel and glides, and -[is] after consonants.

plurality is co-expressed by the adjunction of the inflexional marker -s and lowering of the back vowel, hence *rostos* ['rɔstos] (cf. Cristófaro-Silva 2002: 290; Cristófaro-Silva, Almeida, and Guedri 2007: 210).[9]

With singular nouns in -s, the plural is different according to whether they are monosyllabic, polysyllabic, or oxytonic. If stress is non-final, the plural remains unchanged with respect to the singular (cf. *lápis* ['lapis] 'pencil' > *lápis* ['lapis] 'pencils'). On the other hand, monosyllabic and (polysyllabic) oxytonic nouns show a particular behaviour: -*is* is added after the final sibilant which undergoes voicing in intervocalic position (cf. [pa'is] 'country' > [pa'izis] 'countries', ['mes] 'month' > ['mezis] 'months', etc.).

The situation is much more complex with *-ão* nouns, due among other things to several diachronic paths and to the synchronic coexistence of multiple options (cf. Da Silva Huback 2007: 30–39). As a matter of fact, these nouns can give rise to three kinds of plural: *-ões* (*balão* 'ball' – *balões*), *-ães* (*capitão* 'captain' – *capitães*); *-ãos* (*irmão* 'brother' – *irmãos*) (cf. Huback 2013: 88f.). Such a distribution is partly due to the fact that some *-ão* nouns continue Latin nouns in *-anem* / *-anes* (cf. CANES > *cães > cãis), nouns in *-anum* / *-anus* (MANUS > *mãos, germanos* > *irmãos*, etc.), nouns in *-onem* / *-ones* (LEONES > *leões > leõis*), etc.[10] By the way, the nasal consonant may surface in derivation contexts, thus providing evidence for its presence at an underlying level. This situation is probably responsible for some kind of opacity that led to multiple coexisting patterns. Interestingly, Huback (2013) points out that in the Houaiss dictionary, the relative frequency of the endings *-ões*, *-ãos*, and *-ães* overwhelmingly favours *-ões*, hence its adoption by forms that succumb to its power of attraction.

Another important series of plurals includes stems with final -*l* that vocalizes in -*w* in the major part of Brazilian varieties, and thus conflates with -*w* forms such as *museu* [mu'zew] 'museum'. Becker, Clemens, and Nevins (2017: 320) hold the view that most -*w* final nouns change [w] to [j] in the plural (cf. *papel* [pa'pew] 'paper' > [pa'pejs], *jornal* [ʒoɦ'naw] 'newspaper' > [ʒoɦ'najs], *sal* ['saw] 'salt' > ['sajs], *mel* ['mɛw] 'honey' > ['mɛjs], etc.).[11] The plural suffix -/is/ is taken to attach to the stem, the [i] of the suffix fusing with the -*w* of the stem.

---

[9] Cf. as well alternations in number and gender such as *ovo / ovos* 'egg/s' ['ovu / 'ɔvus], *novo / nova* 'new (M/F)' ['no.vu / 'nɔ.va]) (cf. Alkire and Rosen 2010: 231f.; Holt 2016: 464). Similar metaphonetic patterns can be found in Sardinian, as witnessed by contrasts such as ['bettʃu / 'bɛttʃus] 'old (SG/PL)', ['ottu / 'ɔttus] 'vegetable garden/s', ['oɣu / 'ɔɣus] 'eye/s' in Campidanian (cf. Bolognesi 1998: 21; Molinu 2017: 350–52).

[10] Alkire and -/ Rosen (2010: 216) mention that '[i]n the 1300s and 1400s, word-final stressed /ã/ and /õ/ merged with final /-ão/ from Latin –ANU'. But they point out that earlier plural forms were maintained, hence the existence of singular nouns such as ['kẽw̃] 'dog', whose plural is ['kẽjs] 'dogs', and not **['kẽw̃s] (cf. ['mẽw̃] 'hand' vs ['mẽw̃s] 'hands').

[11] For nouns such as [saw] 'salt' > [sajs], the following scenario can be hypothesized, whereby the lateral first deletes in intervocalic position: *sales* > **saes* > *sais* > sajs (cf. Da Silva Huback 2007: 49). The lateral consonant in final position velarized in the singular much later from a diachronic point of view.

In cases such as *réptil* ['hɛptʃiw] 'reptile', the [i] preceding the ending is assumed to change into [e], hence ['hɛptʃejs] 'reptiles'. For oxytonic nouns such as *barril* [ba'hiw] 'barrel', the velar glide is simply deleted, hence [ba'his] 'barrels'. The examples listed above show that nouns such as *gol* [gow] 'goal' or *futbol* [futʃi'bow] 'football' form their plural by simply adding the -*s* morpheme, hence [gows] 'goals', *futbols* [futʃi'bows] 'footballs', etc. According to Nevins (2012: 233) the *height* of the vowel is one of the major factors determining whether a [w]-final singular will choose [js] in the plural (the lax and lower vowels [ɛ, ɔ, a] favour the -[js] plural, whereas the higher vowels favour the -[ws] plural).

10.5.3 Adjectival Allomorphy

A well-known case of adjectival allomorphy is the alternation found in French before vowel-initial and consonant-initial nouns. Some examples are given in Table 10.17, with data partly taken from Bonami and Boyé (2005).

In all these examples (except the last two) the adjectival form selected before a vowel-initial (masculine) noun coincides with that of the feminine –[12] leaving aside here non-alternating adjectives such as *joli* [ʒoli] 'nice'. Needless to say, this complex phenomenon has given rise to much discussion. Even the data are not so clear as they seem. Bonami and Boyé (2005) take adjectives such as *chaud* 'hot' to be problematic in prenominal position (cf. ***un chaud entretien* 'a vivid discussion'), but a noun phrase such as *un chaud été* [œ̃ʃodete] 'a hot summer' seems perfectly possible, with or without the final consonant of the adjective. Interestingly, it is possible to find on the web many examples such as *un vive intérêt* (for *un vif intérêt* 'a vivid interest') or *un vive émoi* (cf. *un vif émoi* 'an intense emotion'), thus showing that in the same context the masculine or the feminine form of the adjective may be used (cf. as well adjectives such as *fort* [fɔʁ], for which liaison is possible either with the masculine or with the feminine form: *un fort accent* 'a strong accent' [œ̃fɔʁaksɑ̃] / [œ̃fɔʁtaksɑ̃]). The asymmetry between prenominal and postnominal adjectives manifests itself in the optionality of liaison (or in its exclusion) in the latter case: *un rat immonde* [œ̃ʁatimɔ̃d] 'a filthy rat' or *un lit agréable* [œ̃litagʁeabl] 'a pleasant bed' sound very odd in French. As observed in Floricic (2016: 2664), 'the distinction between what

---

[12] In the case of *grand avion* [gʁɑ̃tavjɔ̃], the surfacing consonant in liaison is a relic of that found in old French, where *grand* 'great', *chaud* 'hot', *froid* 'cold' were written *grant*, *chaut*, *froit*. It is hard to explain why the 'feminine-like' allomorph does not surface with adjectives such as *gros* 'big', *bas* 'low', *doux* 'sweet', *faux* 'false'. As shown by the last example in Table 10.17, the adjectival form selected in pre-nominal position before a vowel is the same as that selected before a feminine noun (i.e., *grosse, basse, douce, fausse*), except that the final consonant of the adjective is voiced. Besides [gʁozavjɔ̃] (**[gʁosavjɔ̃]), there are NPs such as *faux ami* [fozami] (**[fosami]), *doux effet* [duzefɛ] (**[dusefɛ]), *bas instinct* [bazɛ̃stɛ̃] (**[basɛ̃stɛ̃]).

Table 10.17. *Adjectival allomorphy before nouns in French*

lexeme	MSG	FLMS	FSG
VIEUX	vieux bateau 'old boat' [vjøbato]	vieil avion 'old plane' [vjɛjavjɔ̃]	vieille auto 'old car' [vjɛjoto]
NOUVEAU	nouveau bateau 'new boat' [nuvobato]	nouvel avion 'new plane' [nuvɛlavjɔ̃]	nouvelle auto 'new car' [nuvɛloto]
BEAU	beau bateau 'nice boat' [bobato]	bel avion 'nice plane' [bɛlavjɔ̃]	belle auto 'nice car' [bɛloto]
PETIT	petit bateau 'small boat' [pətibato]	petit avion 'small plane' [pətitavjɔ̃]	petite auto 'small car' [pətitoto]
PREMIER	premier saut 'first jump' [pʁəmjeso]	premier amour 'first love' [pʁəmjɛʁamuʁ]	première femme 'first woman' [pʁəmjɛʁfam]
GRAND	grand bateau 'large boat' [gʁɑ̃bato]	grand avion 'large plane' [gʁɑ̃tavjɔ̃]	grande auto 'large car' [gʁɑ̃doto]
GROS	gros bateau 'big boat' [gʁobato]	gros avion 'big plane' [gʁozavjɔ̃]	grosse auto 'big car' [gʁosoto]

Weil calls the "ascending construction" which "binds more closely the ideas that have been put into relation with one another" vs the "descending construction" which 'tends more to detach them from one another' manifests itself as well in the phonetic reduction of the Adj in Adj-N compounds. Complex expressions such as *tilapin* 'small rabbit', *titœuf* 'small egg', or *titrain* 'small train' show up with a truncated form of the adjective *petit* [pəti] 'small' and show greater internal cohesion' (cf. **un œuf ti). Needless to say, the same kind of asymmetry can be observed in other Romance languages. The reduced form of the adjective in Italian noun phrases such as *un bell'uomo* 'a nice man' or *un bel dipinto* 'a nice painting' is not available in postnominal position (cf. **un uomo bel / *un uomo bello*; **un dipinto bel / *un dipinto bello*).[13]

The distributional pattern just mentioned can also be observed with other nominal modifiers. Numerals such as *six* 'six' and *dix* 'ten' are spelled out as [si] or [sis] / [di] or [dis] before an unvoiced consonant but as [siz] / [diz] before a vowel or a voiced consonant (cf. also Table 6.1): *dix patrons* [di(s)patʁɔ̃] 'ten bosses', *dix amis* [dizami] 'ten friends', *dix ballons* [di(z)balɔ̃] 'ten balls'. On the other hand, if the numeral is used as an autonomous element, the

---

[13] Of course, the formal variation of the adjective can be neutralized in certain phonetic environments: in expressions such as *un bello sguardo* / *uno sguardo bello* 'a nice look', the form of the adjective is the same, due to the fact that the adjective is followed by an s + consonant sequence that triggers the full form of the adjective.

variant [dis] is the only one available: cf. *j'en ai dix* [dis] (**[diz], **[di]) 'I have ten of them'.

An interesting case of stem variation is offered by the formation of feminine and plural adjectives in the borderline varieties of La Litera (Huesca), between Aragon and Catalonia. In the examples in Table 10.18, Giralt Latorre (1998: 45f.) observes that the feminine adjectives are built by adding the ending *-na* to the masculine stem when stressed on the final vowel. In the same way, the masculine plural is obtained adding *-ns*.

On the other hand, it is possible to assume that, at an underlying level, the nasal consonant is still present and surfaces when non-final (see Bonet and Lloret 1998: 99). By the way, Giralt Latorre (1998: 46) observes that in the case of *bòn* 'good', the presence or absence of the final consonant depends on its position in the noun phrase: *un dia bò* 'a good day' ~ *un bòn dia*, *un traballador bò* 'a good worker' ~ *un bòn treballador*.

10.6 Affix Allomorphy

Affix allomorphy has been widely explored in recent years, especially with respect to phonological constraints responsible for affix variation. There seems to be much more variation among derivational affixes than among inflexional affixes. An oft-mentioned case is that of negative prefixes. In Italian, the shape of the negative prefix IN- is conditioned by the nature of the following consonant. As illustrated in Table 10.19, a place assimilation

Table 10.18. *Feminine and plural adjective formation in La Litera*

MSG	MPL	FSG
comú 'common'	*comuns*	*comuna*
plla 'flat'	*pllans*	*pllana*
fi 'fine'	*fins*	*fina*
tardà 'late'	*tardans*	*tardana*
català 'catalan'	*catalans*	*catalana*
bò 'good'	*bòns*	*bòna*

Table 10.19. *Place assimilation in Italian*

in + capace 'unable'	>	*incapace* [iŋkaˈpatʃe]
in + trovabile 'unfindable'	>	*introvabile* [introˈvabile]
in + possibile 'impossible'	>	*impossibile* [imposˈsibile]
in + violabile 'inviolable'	>	*inviolabile* [iɱvjoˈlabile]
in + lecito 'illicit'	>	*illecito* [ilˈletʃito]
in + maturo 'immature'	>	*immaturo* [immaˈturo]
in + razionale 'irrational'	>	*irrazionale* [irrattsjoˈnale]
in + utile 'useless'	>	*inutile* [iˈnutile]

process takes place, whereby the initial consonant of the base assimilates the nasal consonant of the prefix.

As can be seen, a velar stop initial base triggers velarization of the nasal consonant of the prefix, hence the variant [iŋ] of the adjective *incapace* 'unable'. In the same way, the labial stop of the base *possible* 'possible' triggers labialization of the nasal consonant, hence the variant [im] of the adjective *impossible* 'impossible'. The same (partial) assimilation process occurs with the preposition *in* 'in', whose nasal also assimilates to the following consonant: *in casa* [iŋ'kaza] 'at home', *in pace* [im'patʃe] 'peacefully', *in Belgio* [im'bɛldʒo] 'in Belgium'. In other cases, however, the assimilation process is not partial but total: total assimilation occurs with the sonorants [l, r] and with the labial nasal [m], hence forms such as *illecito* [il'letʃito] 'illicit', *irrazionale* [irrattsjo'nale] 'irrational' or *immaturo* [imma'turo] 'immature'. Observe that before vowels, the default apico-alveolar nasal stop is used, hence forms such as *inutile* [i'nutile] 'useless'. In still other cases, it is quite difficult to identify the shape of the allomorph. The adjective *ignoto* 'unknown' is derived from the basic form *noto* 'known', but the expected negative adjective should be **innoto, and not *ignoto* [iɲ'ɲoto] 'unknown' – a similar alternation is illustrated by the forms *nudo / ignudo* 'naked', even though in this case the palatalized form cannot be said to be negative. The adjective *ignoto* is a learnèd form and can hardly be analysed as containing an allomorph [iɲ] which is unattested in Italian.

Given the cross-linguistic preference for suffixation (cf. Kilani-Schoch and Dressler 2005: 37), we shall unsurprisingly find much more instances of allomorphy among suffixes. Many Romance examples can be adduced to illustrate this kind of variation. In Castilian, we can mention in this respect abstract nouns in *-ad*, *-dad*, *-tad*, *-edad*, *-idad* (<-TATEM), as illustrated in Table 10.20.

It is not easy to account for this distribution in terms of synchronic phonological rules. The variant *-dad* has been argued to be more basic: it is attached to many adjectives ending either with a vowel or with a consonant (cf. *bueno* 'good' > *bondad* 'goodness'; *igual* 'equal' > *igualdad* 'equality'). In the case of *umildad* 'humility', the selection of the variant *-ad* could be due to some kind of dissimilation constraint that prevents adjacency of identical elements (cf. **umildedad). According to Varela Ortega (2018: 31),

Table 10.20. *Castilian -dad, etc.*

umilde 'humble'	>	*umildad* 'humility'
leal 'loyal'	>	*lealtad* 'loyalty'
cruel 'cruel'	>	*crueldad* 'cruelty'
luminoso 'bright'	>	*luminosidad* 'brightness'
falso 'false'	>	*falsedad* 'falsehood'

Table 10.21. *Diminutive formation in Campidanian Sardinian*

'manu 'hand'	mani'ʒɛdda 'small hand'	**ma'nɛdda
'fatʃi 'face'	fatʃi'ʒɛdda 'small face'	**fa'tʃɛdda
'kɔru 'heart'	kɔri'ʒɛddu 'small heart'	**ko'rɛdːdu
dʒe'nuɣu 'knee'	dʒenu'ɣeddu 'knee'	**dʒenuɣi'ʒeddu
'femina 'woman'	femi'nedda 'small woman'	**femini'ʒedda
'mariɣa 'jar'	mari'ɣɛdda 'small jar'	**mariɣi'ʒɛdːda

Table 10.22. *Diminutive formation in Logudorese Sardinian*

mi'nɔre 'small'	mino'reddu 'very small'	**minori'ɣeddu
an'toni 'Antoni'	anto'neddu 'Antoni-DIM'	**antoni'ɣeddu
a'dziɣu 'few'	adzi'ɣeddu 'very few'	**adziɣi'ɣeddu
'bentu 'wind'	benti'ɣeddu 'small wind'	**ben'teddu
'fidzu 'son'	fidzi'ɣeddu 'small son'	**fi'dzeddu
'rassu 'fatty'	rassi'ɣeddu 'chubby'	**ras'seddu

bisyllabic and vowel final adjectives seem to favour the allomorph *-edad* (*sol-edad*, *brev-edad*, *fals-edad*), while those with three or more syllables and those ending with a consonant seem to favour *-idad* (*atroc-idad*, *debil-idad*, *comic-idad*, *fogos-idad*). But if phonological constraints can be put forward to account for abstract nouns such as *falsedad* (cf. **falsdad), these very constraints cannot be invoked to explain formations such as *débil* 'weak' > *debilidad* 'weakness': **debildad was perfectly possible with the allomorph *-dad*.

Another case of suffix allomorphy subject to prosodic constraints is offered by the diminutive suffix -eddu/a alternating with -iʒeddu/a in Campidanian Sardinian (cf. among others Bolognesi 1998: 280–84), as exemplified in Table 10.21.

Bolognesi (1998: 280f.), from whom the preceding examples are taken, holds that affix selection is conditioned by the Binarity Principle at work in Campidanian phonology: -iʒeddu/a is selected when the word consists of two syllables, while the allomorph -eddu/a is required when the word consists of three or more syllables. Similar data are reported by Molinu (1999) for Logudorese Sardinian, as illustrated in Table 10.22.

In this case too, the diminutive suffix *-eddu* has two allomorphs -eddu /-iɣeddu whose alternation is conditioned by the size of the stem (not by the 'word') and it satisfies the prosodic tendency to prefer binary structures. As a result, these diminutive formations contain four syllables and two trochaic feet.

The French suffix *-esque* offers another kind of phonologically driven allomorphy. The examples in Table 10.23 show that some speakers resort to *-este* in lieu of *-esque* after a velar consonant stem ending (cf. Plénat 2011: 149, 187–90).

Table 10.23. *French suffix -esque / -este*

alambic 'still'	>	alambiqueste
algue 'seaweed'	>	algueste
almanach 'almanac'	>	almanacheste
Amigues 'family name'	>	amigueste
anachronique 'anachronistic'	>	anachroniqueste
Anelka 'family name'	>	anelkeste
Zing [name of a forum]	>	zingueste
astérisque 'asterisk'	>	astérisqueste

Table 10.24. *Italian imperfect indicative*

dare 'give'				amare 'love'				temere 'be afraid'				partire 'go out'			
✓	TV	T	P/N	✓	TV	T	P/N	✓	VTV	T	P/N	✓	TV	T	P/N
'd-	a	v	o	a'm-	a	v	o	te'm-	e	v	o	par't-	i	v	o
'd-	a	v	i	a'm-	a	v	i	te'm-	e	v	i	par't-	i	v	i
'd-	a	va	Ø	a'm-	a	va	Ø	te'm-	e	va	Ø	par't-	i	va	Ø
d-	a	'va	mo	am-	a	'va	mo	tem-	e	'va	mo	part-	i	'va	mo
d-	a	'va	te	am-	a	'va	te	tem-	e	'va	te	part-	i	'va	te
'd-	a	va	no	a'm-	a	va	no	te'm-	e	va	no	par't-	i	va	no

According to Plénat (2011: 150), such a distribution can be accounted for by holding that a dorsal consonant (/k/, /g/, or /ŋ/) is changed into the unmarked coronal obstruent /t/ because of a dissimilation constraint, contra Pichon (1940; 1942), who suggested that a suffixal substitution was taking place.

A rarely discussed case of temporal affix alternation is that of the imperfect indicative in Italian (cf. Klausenburger 2000: 53–55), exemplified in Table 10.24.

A possible analysis of the distribution illustrated in Table 10.24 is to assume that the imperfect indicative exponent has two allomorphs [va] and [v] whose distribution is conditioned by the following segment: [v] when it is followed by a vowel, [va] when it is followed by Ø (final position) or by a consonant (cf. Touratier 1987: 276). From this analysis it follows that in the third person singular, the final vowel of, say, *amava* '(s)he loved' is not an inflexional marker but it is part of the tense marker. That a third person form should have a zero marker is unsurprising (cf. Dokulil 1958; Kuryłowicz 1962; 1964; Koch 1995).

10.7 Conclusion

Meillet (1904: 462) pointed out that all development of grammatical forms is dominated by a principle which is not formulated with enough generality and enough rigour, but which is the essential foundation of all research carried in this field: every function tends to be filled by a form which is unique, which is well defined, and always identical under all conditions in a given language. And Meillet continues his brilliant demonstration by observing that if there were no accident due to causes which lay outside morphology, the constant action of this tendency would necessarily lead to the realization of an ideal language where not only would there exist no anomaly, but the existence of several equally regular inflexions would not occur either. In other words the action of a purely morphological principle should lead to unification processes that bring about unity, coherence, and uniformity. But this unification tendency is regularly disrupted by phonetic processes that break down unity and uniformity. It is clear as well that very frequent forms may function as 'leaders' that act as the centre of attraction for analogical propagation (cf. Floricic 2018a). Such 'leaders' may contribute to reshaping and reorganizing whole paradigms (cf. among others the role of verbs such as DICERE 'say'). Frequency also has the effect of leaving in place elements that resist any formal alignment: in an ideal (morphological) world, the imperfect indicative of It. *essere* 'to be' should be **eravo, **eravi, **erava, *eravamo*, etc., or *ero*, *eri*, *era*, **eramo, etc. Instead, the paradigm of the imperfect indicative of this verb (viz. *ero*, *eri*, *era*, *eravamo*, *eravate*, *erano*) is clearly asymmetric and defective, the -*va*- exponent appearing only in the first and second persons plural – we leave open the question as to whether this kind of example should be analysed as an instance of multiple exponence.

Selected References

Below you can find selected references for this chapter. The full references can be found online at the following page: www.cambridge.org/Romancelinguistics

Becker, M., Clemens, L., and Nevins, A. (2017). 'Generalization of French and Portuguese plural alternations and initial syllable protection', *Natural Language & Linguistic Theory* 35: 299–345.

Cristófaro-Silva, T. (2002). 'Organização fonológica de marcas de plural no português brasileiro: uma abordagem multirrepresentacional', *Revista da Abralin* 11: 273–306.

Dokulil, M. ([1958] 1994). 'On morphological oppositions'. In Luelsdorff, P. A., Panenová, J., and, Sgall P. (eds), *Praguiana 1945–1990*, Amsterdam/Philadelphia: Benjamins, 113–30.

Hualde, I. and Chiţoran I. (2016). 'Surface sound and underlying structure: the phonetics–phonology interface', In Fischer, S. and Gabriel, C. (eds),

Manual of Grammatical Interfaces in Romance. Berlin/New York: De Gruyter, 23–40.

Maiden, M. (2001). 'Di nuovo sulle alternanze "velari" nel verbo italiano e spagnolo', *Cuadernos de Filología Italiana* 8: 39–61.

Martinet, A. (1965). 'De la morphonologie', *La Linguistique* 1: 1–30.

Nevins, A. (2011). 'Phonologically conditioned allomorph selection'. In van Oostendorp, M., Ewen, C., Hume, E., and Rice, K. (eds), *The Blackwell Companion to Phonology.* Chichester: Wiley-Blackwell, 2357–82.

O'Neill, P. (2015). 'The origin and spread of velar allomorphy in the Spanish verb: a morphomic approach', *Bulletin of Hispanic Studies* 92: 489–518.

Salvioni, C. (1900). 'A proposito di amiś', *Romania* 29: 546–58.

Tekavčić, P. (1972). 'Sull'alternanza morfematica nel verbo italiano', *Linguistica* 12: 269–300.

Touratier, C. (1987). 'Morphologie du verbe italien dans une perspective contrastive', *Cahiers d'Etudes Romanes* 12: 267–82.

Tuttle, E. (1995). 'On placing northern Italian noun singulars from plurals of the type amís "friend" within a theory of optimality and markedness', *Romance Philology* 48: 389–415.

11

The Autonomy of Morphology

Louise Esher and Paul O'Neill

11.1 Introduction

The word 'autonomy' has different but important nuances. Of the several definitions in the *Oxford English Dictionary* the following stand out as the most relevant: (i) 'the fact or quality of being unrelated to anything else, self-containedness; independence from external influence or control, self-sufficiency' and (ii) 'the condition of a subject or discipline (e.g., biology) of having its own laws, principles, and methodology which are not simply deducible from or reducible to those of a more fundamental subject (e.g., physics)'. In the context of the autonomy of morphology, according to the first definition morphology would be conceived as existing in a vacuum with little or no interaction with, or interference and control from, phonology, syntax, and semantics. Such a definition of the autonomy of morphology is entirely untenable, as attested by cases of morphosyntactic agreement and the phenomenon referred to by Zwicky (1985a; 1985b; 1992) as 'shape conditions' on the phonological form of certain classes of words; the triggers of which can both lie outside the syntactic word and be of a morphophonological nature. Floricic and Molinu, this volume (cf. Sections 10.2, 10.4), discuss a number of such examples in Romance, e.g., the neutralization of gender contrasts in possessive adjectives in French depending on whether the following noun begins with a vowel or consonant (*ma fille* 'my daughter', *mon fils* 'my son', but *mon équipe* 'my team', even though *fille* and *équipe* are both feminine nouns) and the similar phonological environment which determines the form of the definite article in Aranese and Spanish. In the latter language *la* alternates with *el* before feminine nouns which begin with stressed /a/ with the exception of proper names, placenames, and acronyms (*el águila* 'the eagle' vs *la aguja* 'the needle', but *la Ana que conozco* 'the Ana whom I know' and *la Ávila moderna* 'the modern Ávila' – all feminine nouns, but the last a placename and the penultimate a personal proper name). Morphology, therefore, certainly does interact with, and is intimately related to, semantics, syntax, and especially phonology, since in spoken languages morphological alternations are often expressed via phonological alternations. These intimate and pervasive interactions, however, have unfortunately led some more reductive theories of language to presuppose that all morphological phenomena can be derived from other linguistic principles. Thus, proponents of Distributed Morphology (e.g., Halle and Marantz 1993; Marantz 1997; Embick and Noyer 2007) advocate the Single Engine Hypothesis (Marantz 1997; 2001) whereby a 'single engine' (syntax) is responsible for both word structure and phrase structure (see also Arad 2003). This theory therefore denies the autonomy of morphology, as encapsulated in the second definition, in which morphology undoubtedly interacts with phonology, syntax, and semantics but it has an existence independent of these systems and is not conceptually irreducible to them. In this chapter we defend this definition of the autonomy of morphology, and whenever we use the term 'autonomy' we do so in accordance with this second definition. After a brief overview of the origins of the concept of the autonomy of morphology and the main ways that it has been applied to the Romance languages, we provide a typological overview of the canonical cases which support the autonomy of morphology and conclude with some theoretical observations and reflections.

11.2 Origins of the Autonomy of Morphology

The conception of the autonomy of morphology is not new, since morphology as a distinct system was central to the work of both nineteenth-century European linguists and American Structuralists (see Scalise and Guevara 2005). However, in early versions of Generative Grammar (Chomsky 1957) morphology did not exist as an autonomous generative system; all complex words were constructed in accordance with phrase structure rules and transformations. The rules of syntax manipulated not only simplex words but also individual morphemes. The relationship between words such as Sp. *llegar* 'to arrive' and *llegada* 'arrival', *destruir* 'to destroy' and *destrucción* 'destruction' was given a purely syntactic explanation whereby nominal phrases such as *la llegada del rey* 'the king's arrival' or *la destrucción de la ciudad (por Nerón)* 'the destruction of Rome (by Nero)' were the result of nominal syntactic transformations on syntactic verbal phrases of the type [The king$_{NP}$ arrive$_V$]$_S$ and [Nero$_N$ destroy$_V$ Rome$_N$]$_S$. The fact that verbal forms 'destroy' and 'arrive' in English did not produce the nominalizations **destroyation* and **arrivation* and that in Spanish *destruir* and *llegar* produced *destrucción* and *llegada* and not **destruida and **llegación was handled by a potentially omnipotent phonology. Thus morphology as an autonomous component of the grammar did not exist and was entirely deducible from, or reducible to, rules pertaining to syntax and/or phonology. However, Chomsky (1970) drew attention to the English distinction between derived nominals (*Nero's destruction of Rome*) and gerundive nominals (*Nero's destroying of Rome*), and it was considered useful to distinguish theoretically between these two sorts of nominalization because they differ in the following important and systematic ways (for a full discussion see Anderson 2016: 602f.):

- their formal uniformity: derived nominals have a great many distinct shapes. Compare, e.g., 'laughter', 'marriage', 'construction', 'belief', 'doubt' with their related verbs 'laugh', 'marry', 'construct', 'believe', 'doubt'; English gerundives are always formed by stem plus '-ing', e.g., 'laughing', 'marrying', 'constructing', 'believing', 'doubting';
- their semantic uniformity: derived nominals such as Eng. 'recital', 'transmission', 'inflation', 'generation', are commonly the locus of semantic idiosyncrasy, while the gerundives are semantically uniform ('reciting', 'transmitting', 'inflating', 'generating');
- the internal structure of their projected phrases: derived nominals can take articles, adjectives, quantifiers, and plural forms, and their complements appear in prepositional phrases (e.g., 'those first four completely unmotivated criticisms/**criticizings of my book which you had the temerity to raise'); gerundive nominals cannot, but do accept adverbs (e.g., 'John's pointedly denying/**denial that he took a bribe').

Both types of nominalization were accounted for by rules of syntax, but Chomsky reassessed this assumption on the basis of the evidence above and proposed the *Lexical Hypothesis*, whereby derivational morphological processes were not subject to the rules of syntax but entered the syntax directly from the lexicon as nominal forms. The result was that the lexicon was no longer merely 'an appendix of the grammar, a list of basic irregularities' (Bloomfield 1933: 274) which provided the syntax with words but could have internal computation for derivational (but not inflexional) morphology; crucially, for the present aims, the rules of this computation were different from those of phrase syntax and thus the lexicon was autonomous, according to the definition (ii) above. This autonomy of the lexicon will pave the way for the autonomy of morphology.

O'Neill (2016: 239–41) conceptualizes the *Lexical Hypothesis* as a line drawn between some processes of word formation and phrase formation, diagrammatically represented in Figure 11.1.

The left of the line in Figure 11.1 was the autonomous domain of the lexicon, the right was the domain of syntax. O'Neill (2016) notes how the publication of Chomsky (1970) resulted in intensive research on the exact

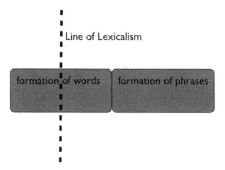

Figure 11.1 Conceptualization of the *Lexical Hypothesis*

nature of this autonomous component, its interaction with other components of the grammar and, in particular, where this 'Line of Lexicalism' fell within the formation of complex words. Proponents of what has been called the *Weak Lexical Hypothesis* (Chomsky 1970; Aronoff 1976; Anderson 1982; 1992; Scalise 1988) considered inflexional morphology to fall to the right of the Line and thus to be governed by rules of syntax. By contrast, proponents of the *Strong Lexical Hypothesis* had inflexional morphology falling to the left of this line. Halle (1973) considered that all morphological phenomena ought to take place in the lexicon and be separate from the rules governing phrase formation. Subsequent developments up until the present day have been characterized as '[a] tug-of-war with regards to the "Line of Lexicalism" and the linguistic phenomena which fall to the left and right of this line, and are therefore subject to rules of word structure or phrase structure respectively' (O'Neill 2016: 245). Scholars have also proposed a number of rules, conditions, and constraints, conceptualized as border controls, regarding this line and the interaction between both components: *Principle of Lexical Integrity* (Anderson 1992: 84; Bresnan 2001: 92), *Generalized Lexicalist Hypothesis* (Lapointe 1980: 8), *Word Structure Autonomy Condition* (Selkirk 1982: 70), the *Syntactic Atomicity Thesis* (Di Sciullo and Williams 1987: 49), the *Limited Access Principle* (Lieber and Scalise 2006: 128), and also the *Principle of Morphology-Free Syntax* and the *Principle of Syntax-Free Morphology* (Zwicky 1987: 654). Underlying all these principles and hypotheses is the view that certain types of word structure are governed by an autonomous component: the lexicon.

Within other frameworks, however, this component is termed the 'morphology' (e.g., *Network Morphology*: Brown and Hippisley 2012). There are various reasons for the differences in nomenclature: the polysemy of the term 'lexicon', its overlap or not with the concept of 'morphology' (Anderson 1982; Jensen and Stong-Jensen 1984), the historical and theoretical associations identified with the adjective 'lexical' (Aronoff 1994: 16–22; Carstairs-McCarthy 2010: 38–45), and the desire to call the component which controls morphology 'morphology', just as syntactic and phonological processes are governed by components termed 'syntax' and 'phonology', respectively. Irrespective of the nomenclature, the common assumption is entirely in keeping with our definition of the autonomy of morphology: that there exists a component responsible for the production of complex words (but not always of all words,[1] depending on the theory) and that the rules and mechanisms of this component function differently from the rules which govern phrase structure. Indeed this view has been characterized as '[t]he near-universal conclusion of linguists' (Carstairs-McCarthy 2010: 19). A notable exception, however, is Distributed Morphology (see Section 11.1).

11.3 Autonomy of Morphology from Phonology and Semantics and the Notion of the Morphome

As for the autonomy of morphology from phonology and semantics, many linguistic theories, especially those in the generative tradition, have also sought to reduce morphological alternations to alternations of meaning or alternations derivable by phonological rules (especially early generative phonology). In recent times, the strongest opposition to this tendency and that which has had the greatest impact on Romance linguistics has been Aronoff (1994), a work entitled *Morphology by Itself*. Here Aronoff introduced the concept of the 'morphome' which served as theoretical inspiration for numerous academic outputs on the historical development of the Romance languages by a number of linguists, including a comprehensive monograph on the evolution of the Romance verb (Maiden 2018) from a morphomic perspective.

Morphomes, also referred to as autonomous morphological structures, specifically denote a function which determines the recurrent and systematic appearance of form in different morphosyntactic, semantic, and phonological contexts. Morphomes also suppose the existence of 'a morphomic level' or, more simply stated, an autonomous morphological component of the grammar which is responsible for the production of all morphologically complex words and which mediates between the syntax/semantics and the phonology (Aronoff 1994: 25) but has mechanisms which are independent

---

[1] Even within theories that accept the autonomy of morphology, there has been much debate over the extent and nature of this autonomy, and in particular what words are governed by morphological or syntactic structures (for an overview, see Scalise and Guevara 2005; Lieber and Scalise 2006: 128; Booij 2009; O'Neill 2016); of particular contention have been clitics (for morphological interpretation of special clitics, see Zwicky 1977; Luís 2004; Luís and Otoguro 2004; Anderson 2005; Luís and Spencer 2005) and compounds (considered morphological by Booij 2005 and Ralli 2010, but syntactic by Anderson 1992; Lieber 1992; Aronoff 1994; Di Sciullo 2005). However see Bağrıaçık and Ralli (2017) for a non-binary view of clitics.

of them. Thus, morphemes are formalizations of the workings of an autonomous morphology and its interactions with other parts of the grammar. Morphemes are responsible for all morphology, even the cases in which there is a transparent and regular relationship between meaning and form (see also Smith 2013; Maiden 2018: 3f.), such as Spanish plural marking on nouns whereby, in the great majority of cases, /s/ is concatenated to the end of a noun and general phonological principles explain the corresponding allomorphs (*gato* ~ *gatos* 'cat ~ cats', *perro* ~ *perros* 'dog ~ dogs', *autobús* ~ *autobuses* 'bus ~ buses').

Although morphemes specifically refer to mapping functions and are relevant to all types of morphology, since the coining of the term it has been used in a wide array of contexts, with differences in meaning (see O'Neill 2014a: 31 for an overview, and Luís and Bermúdez-Otero 2016). Currently, the most widespread usage of 'morpheme' and of the adjective 'morphomic' is reserved for distributions without an extramorphological correlate, (e.g., the contrast between 'morphomic' and 'motivated' splits drawn by Corbett 2016), that is, as Aronoff (1994: 25) puts it, for those cases which 'truly earn their name'. These are cases where there is a systematic recurrence of the same form, be it the distribution of stem allomorphy within a set of lexemes or the different inflexional endings of a whole conjugational class, which cannot be aligned with any conceivable coherent semantic, syntactic, or phonological generalization. In these structures the discontinuous relationship between form and meaning is most apparent, and they constitute the robust pillars of evidence for the autonomy of morphology; they are canonical morphemes, morphemes in the narrow sense (Bermúdez-Otero and Luís 2016). In the rest of this chapter we provide a typological overview of these canonical morphemes in the Romance languages in accordance with the nuanced distinctions between morphemes proposed by Round (2015). Our discussion will be restricted to the inflexional morphology of the verb since this reflects the focus of existing research and is the domain which presents the clearest cases in favour of the autonomy of morphology. Due to restrictions of space it is not possible to enter into and disprove the complex explanations for such phenomena being phonologically or semantically motivated. We refer readers to the individual studies mentioned and the arguments against such functional conditioning therein. Our aim is to give a sense of the magnitude of evidence from the Romance languages which supports the autonomy of morphology, as defined in this chapter.

11.4 A Typology of Morphomic Structures in Romance

Round (2015) proposes that there exist three types of morphomic structure, which are identified on the basis of shared exponence, and are differentiated from each other by the type of objects which they manipulate.

Inflexional classes (or RHIZOMORPHOMES) group lexemes together by similarity of exponence, while paradigmatic stem distributions (or METAMORPHOMES) group paradigm cells together, and MEROMORPHOMES group inflexional formatives (Round 2015: 29f.). In the interests of clarity and consistency, Round's terminology will be used throughout this section, though this approach diverges from the usage of many authors (notably Maiden 2018: 3 n. 4), who use the label MORPHOMES for the structures here termed metamorphomes.

This section illustrates the morphomic structures thus far described for Romance, discussing how the patterns themselves emerge and change, what changes they are observed to induce in the distribution of inflexional material, and how they interact with each other. The examples are chosen to reflect the focus of existing research which has tended thus far to concentrate on metamorphomes (at the time of writing, no developed analysis of meromorphomic phenomena is available for Romance); coverage is thus illustrative rather than exhaustive.

11.4.1 Metamorphomes

11.4.1.1 The Concept at Issue

The inflexional paradigm is typically considered to be structured in terms of implicational relationships between its constituent cells (e.g., Ackerman et al. 2009; Stump and Finkel 2013; Bonami 2014; Blevins 2016; Stump 2016): certain pairs or groups of cells reliably share exponents with each other, and the forms which realize them are thus to some extent interpredictable. Recurrent groupings of cells function as abstract templates, holding true across multiple lexemes which may have diverse phonological realizations; for instance, in many Romance languages it is true that the synthetic future shares a stem with the synthetic conditional, whatever the lexeme at issue and whatever phonological form its stem may take (Maiden 2018: 263–66). These abstract templates are termed metamorphomes.

The metamorphomes so far identified for Romance are based principally on historical comparative observations of the distribution of stem allomorphy: the constituent cells of a metamorphome typically share one or more stem exponents, and the metamorphome may act as a template for morphological analogy distributing novel allomorphy or redistributing existing allomorphy (Maiden 2001; 2003; 2005; 2009a; 2009b; 2011a, b; 2013b; 2016a; 2016b; 2018; see also the studies collected in Maiden et al. 2011; Cruschina et al. 2013). The diachronic productivity of the patterns offers evidence of their psychological reality for speakers (Maiden 2018: 14–17).

In a synchronic description, the paradigmatic distribution of stem forms may be represented using a stem space diagram, which divides the paradigm into PARTITIONS, areas of perfect interpredictability between stem

Table 11.1. *Paradigmatic distribution of four Romance metamorphomes affecting finite forms: the N-pattern, the L/U-pattern, PYTA, and Fuèc*

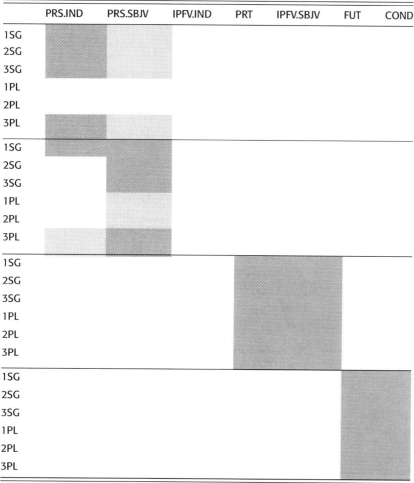

forms (Pirrelli and Battista 2000; Bonami and Boyé 2002; 2003; Montermini and Bonami 2013). While some partitions correspond to metamorphomes (e.g., the set of future and conditional cells), not all do, and the two notions are conceptually distinct. Partitions are defined synchronically based on perfect interpredictability of stem forms, and a given cell may only be assigned to one partition; metamorphomes may be defined diachronically as well as synchronically, based on perfect or partial interpredictability of exponents not limited to stems, and a given cell may participate in multiple metamorphomes.

Table 11.1 diagrams four of the metamorphomes commonly found across Romance languages. These metamorphomes have been given deliberately opaque and arbitrary labels, reflecting their inherent synchronic arbitrariness (for discussion see, e.g., Maiden 2018: 7, 266), such as the 'N-pattern', comprising singular and third person plural forms of the present indicative and in some cases present subjunctive (Maiden 2009a); the 'L-pattern', comprising the first person present indicative and all present subjunctive forms (sometimes excepting the first- and second person plural present subjunctive), and, in a variant termed the 'U-pattern', also the third person plural present indicative (Maiden 2009a; 2012; 2018: 84–166); 'PYTA', comprising all reflexes of Latin *perfectum* forms, usually the preterite and imperfect subjunctive (Maiden 2001); and 'Fuèc', comprising the synthetic future and conditional (Esher 2013). The labels assigned to the patterns are deliberately chosen as opaque, as a means of referring to each abstract distribution independently of any associated functional or phonological content (Maiden 2018: 7). The history and behaviour of these patterns is discussed in Sections 11.4.2.1–2.

At present, the established cases of Romance metamorphomes all involve exponents associated with lexical roots or stems; furthermore, Maiden (2013b; 2018: 256–60) presents evidence from Daco-Romance that the formal coherence of a metamorphome may disintegrate if its constituent cells diverge in lexical meaning. Basing himself on these observations, Maiden (2018: 310f.) argues that the fundamental function of the Romance patterns is to provide a reliable means of distributing arbitrary formal differences for a lexical same. However, it should be noted that a requirement to involve exponents of lexical material is not inherent to the definitions proposed by Aronoff (1994), Blevins (2016: 106), or Round (2015: 30, 48f.): none of these definitions restrict the notion of metamorphome to applying to a particular type of exponent (note also the notion of morphomic suffix developed by Stump 2016: 121–33). There is, furthermore, some evidence that patterns of identity between inflexional desinences, such as the systematic identity between conditional and non-first-conjugation imperfect indicative desinences in many Ibero- and Gallo-Romance varieties, may also be considered metamorphomic (Esher 2018).

11.4.1.2 Source of Four Common Romance Metamorphomes

As stated above, in accordance with the definitions of Aronoff (1994), all paradigmatic distributions of exponents are morphomic functions, including those which align perfectly with morphosemantic, morphosyntactic, or phonological criteria. A consequence of this view is that metamorphomes are necessarily present within any inflexional paradigm, and thus that most 'novel' metamorphomes do not arise *ex nihilo*; instead, they typically represent modification of an existing metamorphome. Changes in the shape of metamorphomes may result from reassignment of existing paradigm cells from one distribution to another (usually via sound change), addition of cells to the paradigm (via grammaticalization), or loss of cells from the paradigm (due to syntactic change). All three processes are attested in the history of the Romance verb.

In Latin, the verb paradigm can be divided into three sets of cells, based on the distribution of stem allomorphy: *infectum* forms, *perfectum* forms, and 'third stem' forms (Aronoff 1994). These are abstract systematic distributional patterns, reliably predictive but not uniquely defined by any phonological property or morphosyntactic/morphosemantic feature value: the 'third stem' is one of the first metamorphomes identified in the literature, while the *perfectum* and *infectum* groups do not correspond exactly to the natural classes of forms with (respectively) perfective and imperfective aspect (see Aronoff 1994: 55–58; Maiden 2013b: 495; Meul 2013: 30f.).

The Romance metamorphome PYTA comprises the surviving reflexes of Latin *perfectum* forms. In general, the constituent cells of this set continue to share a stem, but the number of constituent cells has reduced considerably as many of the synthetic forms realizing *perfectum* categories have fallen out of usage (often replaced by periphrases of the form auxiliary + perfective participle). While Portuguese retains reflexes of the Latin perfect indicative, pluperfect subjunctive, pluperfect indicative, and future perfect indicative/perfect subjunctive, few Gallo-Romance varieties retain reflexes of the Latin pluperfect indicative beyond the mediaeval period (for those that do, see Chabaneau 1876: 211; Allières 1997; Sibille 1997), the perfective past indicative is no longer in common use in the spoken Catalan of Catalonia (Alsina 2016: 375) or in certain Occitan varieties (Massourre 2012: 234), and in modern French no reflexes of *perfectum* forms are now natively acquired (Esher 2017). At the same time, the semantic values associated with individual categories are also liable to change: in Gallo-, Italo-, and Ibero-Romance, the modern reflex of the Latin pluperfect subjunctive, though usually termed 'imperfect subjunctive', is in practice aspect-neutral and not exclusively past (Maiden 2011a: 179), while the reflex of the pluperfect indicative commonly occurs as a conditional or 'imperfect subjunctive', and in Daco-Romance the Latin perfect subjunctive and future perfect merged as a conditional (Maiden 2016c: 109). The overall result is a functionally disparate array of tense/aspect/mood categories: a 'canonical' (in the terms of Corbett 2009) or 'overt' (Smith 2013) metamorphome, the constituent cells of which do not correspond to any natural class. Witness the verb paradigm for Pt. *saber* 'know' in Table 11.2, in which the allomorph *soub-* occurs exclusively and consistently in the four highlighted PYTA cells.

The N- and L-/U-patterns (exemplified in Table 11.3) all involve cells which were previously contained within the set of *infectum* forms. These patterns result from the morphologization of novel phonological alternations which arose through regular sound change. In the case of the N-pattern, the relevant changes are the shift from phonologically predictable stress to lexically assigned stress, and the context-sensitive differentiation of stressed and unstressed vowels, particularly affecting mid vowels

(Maiden 2018: 167–71). These changes introduce a contrast between the root-stressed cells (singular and third person plural forms in the present; also the second person singular imperative) and the other reflexes of *infectum* forms (principally the imperfect indicative, and the first and second person plural in the present): prosodic in all lexemes, and segmental in lexemes with the relevant stem vowels. In the case of the L-/U-patterns, two segmental changes are involved: firstly, the palatalization or affrication of consonants before yod, which affects present subjunctive forms, the first person singular present indicative form and also (in some Italo-Romance

Table 11.2. *Paradigm of Pt.* saber *'know'*

	PRS.IND	PRS.SBJV	FUT	COND	INFLECTED INF
1SG	sei	saiba	saberei	saberia	saber
2SG	sabes	saibas	saberás	saberias	saberes
3SG	sabe	saiba	saberá	saberia	saber
1PL	sabemos	saibamos	saberemos	saberíamos	sabermos
2PL	sabeis	saibais	sabereis	saberíeis	saberdes
3PL	sabem	saibam	saberão	saberiam	saberem
	IPFV.IND	PRT	PST.PRF	IPFV.SBJV	FUT.SBJV
1SG	sabia	soube	soubera	soubesse	souber
2SG	sabias	soubeste	souberas	soubesses	souberes
3SG	sabia	soube	soubera	soubesse	souber
1PL	sabíamos	soubemos	soubéramos	soubéssemos	soubermos
2PL	sabíais	soubestes	soubéreis	soubésseis	souberdes
3PL	sabiam	souberam	souberam	soubessem	souberem
	IMP	INF	GER	PST.PTCP	
2SG	sabe	saber	sabendo	sabido	
2PL	sabei				

Table 11.3. *Reflexes of Latin* infectum *forms for It.* portare *'carry' and Cat.* veure *'see'*

	PRS.IND	PRS.SBJV	IPFV.IND		PRS.IND	PRS.SBJV	IPFV.IND
1SG	ˈporto	ˈporti	porˈtavo	1SG	veig	vegi	veia
2SG	ˈporti	ˈporti	porˈtavi	2SG	veus	vegis	veies
3SG	ˈporta	ˈporti	porˈtava	3SG	veu	vegi	veia
1PL	porˈtjamo	porˈtjamo	portaˈvamo	1PL	veiem	vegem	vèiem
2PL	porˈtate	porˈtjate	portaˈvate	2PL	veieu	vegeu	vèieu
3PL	ˈportano	ˈportino	porˈtavano	3PL	veuen	vegin	veien

After Maiden (2018: 86, 169).

varieties, those which retained 3PL -IUNT) the third person plural present indicative form; and secondly, the palatalization or affrication of velars before front vowels, which affects all present indicative forms except the first person singular and, in varieties with 3PL -ENT, the third person plural (Maiden 2018: 84–90); note that this second change also applies throughout the imperfect indicative. Although these two changes are distinct, they produce identical distributions in which the root-final consonant of the present subjunctive, first person singular present indicative, and (where relevant) third person plural present indicative contrasts with the root-final consonant in the other reflexes of *infectum* forms. For both the N- and the L-/U-patterns, speakers appear to reanalyse the alternation as a morphological generalization in which two groups of cells systematically contrast (N-pattern cells vs other *infectum* cells; L-/U-pattern cells vs other *infectum* cells); the issue of overlap between the two patterns is discussed further in Section 11.4.1.3.

The history of Fuèc combines two mechanisms. The Romance synthetic future and conditional do not continue Latin synthetic forms, but instead arise through the grammaticalization of periphrases combining a lexical infinitive with the auxiliary HABERE 'have'. The appearance of these categories adds new cells to the inflexional paradigm; among attested Romance metamorphomes, Fuèc is thus the closest to an entirely novel metamorphome. However, it is important to recall that the future and conditional forms originate sharing a stem with the infinitive, from which they are subsequently differentiated by a series of sound changes, including deletion of unstressed vowels and consonant epenthesis (e.g., TENERE HABET > Cat. *tindrà* 'hold/have.FUT.3SG' vs INF *tenir*, *vo'lere HABET > Cat. *voldrà* 'want.FUT.3SG' vs INF *voler*), or assimilation (e.g., TENERE HABET > It. *terrà* 'hold.FUT.3SG' vs INF *tenere*, *vo'lere HABET > It. *vorrà* 'want.FUT.3SG' vs INF *volere*).

Overall within Romance, reassignment of cells following regular sound change is particularly prevalent and may further modify the patterns identified by Maiden: established patterns can merge or change shape, and new patterns can arise. An example of merger is attested in Catalan and Occitan in which the results of regular sound change in a limited number of verbs (in addition to analogical changes whereby other verbs adopted similar types of allomorphy) led to the forms of the PYTA and L-pattern all coinciding on the same velar allomorph (see Wheeler 2012). This purely accidental formal similarity was subsequently reanalysed as being systematic and hence in these languages the two metamorphomes have generally merged, albeit with much dialectal variation, and for some lexemes the past participle is also included in the enlarged metamorphome as displayed in Table 11.4 for Cat. *moure* 'move'. Note also that the allomorphy in these cells is characterized by a root-final velar consonant (Wheeler 2011; Esher 2016).

Table 11.4. *Cat.* moure 'move'

	PRS.IND.	PRS.SBJV	FUT	COND
1SG	moc	mogui	mouré	mouria
2SG	mous	moguis	mouràs	mouries
3SG	mou	mogui	mourà	mouria
1PL	movem	moguem	mourem	mouríem
2PL	moveu	mogueu	moureu	mouríeu
3PL	mouen	moguin	mouran	mourien
	IPFV.IND	IPFV.SBJV	PRT	
1SG	movia	mogués	moguí	
2SG	movies	moguessis	mogueres	
3SG	movia	mogués	mogué	
1PL	movíem	moguéssim	moguérem	
2PL	movíeu	moguéssiu	moguéreu	
3PL	movien	moguessin	mogueren	
	IMP	PST.PTCP	GER	INF
2SG	mou			
2PL	moveu	mogut	movent	moure

More commonly, the results of regular sound change modify the shape of individual patterns. The deletion of many final consonants in French causes syncretism between the singular forms of the present indicative but differentiates these from the third person plural form, splitting the N-pattern: this example is of interest because it illustrates a metamorphomic pattern which applies not merely to stems, but to entire wordforms (Esher 2017). Reassignment of cells after sound change can thus involve merger of previously unrelated forms and cells, as well as splits in established patterns. A striking example is found in Occitan dialects of the Limousin region, where a series of sound changes involving the loss of final consonants and the rise of distinctive vowel length causes near-exceptionless syncretism of second person singular with second person plural, and of first person plural with third person plural; among the consequences of these syncretisms is the defection of the second person singular and third person plural present indicative forms from the N-pattern to the set of historically non-root-stressed *infectum* reflexes (Hinzelin 2011; Esher 2020).

11.4.1.3 Behaviour of Metamorphomes

Comparative historical study of verb inflexion shows that the sets of cells which constitute metamorphomes also function as domains for analogical change and levelling of morphophonemic alternations.

Consistently, analogical changes affecting one constituent cell of a metamorphome also affect the others ('coherence', Maiden 2005): for instance, levelling of a distinctive PYTA root in some Gallo-Romance varieties applies equally to the preterite and the imperfect subjunctive (Maiden 2018: 50f.; for similar developments in Spanish and Portuguese see Maiden 2001; O'Neill 2009); the analogical spread of a velar thematic element through Catalan verbs affects all L-pattern and PYTA forms (Wheeler 2011; Maiden 2018: 108f.); levelling of thematic vowels in the Occitan variety of Nice affects all members of Fuèc (Esher 2013). In a number of Romance varieties, levelling of thematic vowels exclusively within the domain of PYTA is attested not only in the class of verbs which display distinctive allomorphy in PYTA, but also in regular verbs which lack any type of allomorphy (O'Neill 2014a: 58–64); this evidence suggests that the set of lexemes sensitive to metamorphomes could extend far beyond those lexemes which display distinctive allomorphy in the relevant cells. Metamorphomes also act as domains for incursive suppletion (see Section 12.3.2): Romance verbs meaning GO typically conflate reflexes of UADERE 'walk hastily', IRE 'go', and AMBULARE 'walk', with continuants of IRE ordinarily becoming confined to Fuèc and continuants of UADERE restricted to the N-pattern; in some Galician varieties, *coller* 'catch, gather' occurs in the PYTA (and sometimes also L-pattern) cells of *caber* 'fit into' (Maiden 2018: 53f.); and in Romansh the N-pattern cells of *dueir* 'must' are occupied by forms of its synonym *stueir* (Maiden 2011b). Note that Anderson (2010) instead analyses *dueir* as defective; metamorphomic defectiveness is robustly attested in Ibero-Romance (for the N- and L-patterns, Maiden and O'Neill 2010; O'Neill 2009; 2010), and in French (for PYTA, Boyé and Cabredo Hofherr 2010; Stump 2016: 162). In some cases, coherent analogical changes increase similarity of exponents across lexemes for a given metamorphome ('convergence', Maiden 2005): thus in Castilian, PYTA forms tend to become characterized by a high vowel (Maiden 2001), while, as illustrated above in Catalan and Occitan, PYTA and the L-pattern commonly present a velar thematic element.

The repeated sensitivity of analogical change to metamorphomes indicates that these patterns are of psychological reality in diachrony (Maiden 2018): if speakers had not internalized a morphological generalization about relationships of mutual implication between the constituent cells of a metamorphome, there would be no reason for innovative analogical changes to conform to metamorphomic templates (as opposed, for instance, to sets of cells with a morphosyntactic or morphosemantic correlate).

The inventory of phenomena which can be analogically distributed or redistributed according to established metamorphomic templates also includes periphrastic forms (Cruschina 2013) and, in some cases, person desinences (Maiden 2009b; O'Neill 2014a; Esher 2018); the distribution assumed by the latter is the intersection of the relevant morphosyntactic

Table 11.5. *Present-tense forms of Pt.* dever *'owe',* mover *'move',* beber *'drink' and the -ir verbs* servir *'serve',* dormir *'sleep',* vestir *'dress'*[a]

	IND	SBJV	IND	SBJV	IND	SBJV
1SG	d[e]vo	d[e]va	m[o]vo	m[o]va	b[e]bo	b[e]ba
2SG	d[ɛ]ves	d[e]vas	m[ɔ]ves	m[o]vas	b[ɛ]bes	b[e]bas
3SG	d[ɛ]ve	d[e]va	m[ɔ]ve	m[o]va	b[ɛ]be	b[e]ba
1PL	devemos	devamos	movemos	movamos	bebemos	bebamos
2PL	deveis	devais	moveis	movais	bebeis	bebais
2PL/3PL	d[ɛ]vem	d[e]vam	m[ɔ]vem	m[o]vam	b[ɛ]bem	b[e]bam
	IND	SBJV	IND	SBJV	IND	SBJV
1SG	sirvo	sirva	durmo	durma	visto	vista
2SG	s[ɛ]rves	sirvas	d[ɔ]rmes	durmas	v[ɛ]stes	vistas
3SG	s[ɛ]rve	sirva	d[ɔ]rme	durma	v[ɛ]ste	vista
1PL	servimos	sirvamos	dormimos	durmamos	vestimos	vistamos
2PL	servis	sirvais	dormis	durmais	vestis	vistais
2PL/3PL	s[ɛ]rvem	sirvam	d[ɔ]rmem	durmam	v[ɛ]stem	vistam

[a] Grey cells = L-pattern, lighter grey = reduced N-pattern.

features and the metamorphomic distribution (e.g., all second person singular forms within PYTA).

It can also happen that two metamorphomes overlap in distribution ('clash', Maiden 2018: 288; O'Neill 2018: 32–41; forthcoming); for example, the first person singular present indicative, as well as the singular and third plural forms of the present subjunctive, are constituent cells of both the N-pattern and the L-pattern. In such cases, multiple templates are available for analogy: not only the original metamorphomes, but also their intersection. The results are various: the different metamorphomes can merge producing a larger 'NandL' metamorphome, as attested in Savognin Romansh (cf. O'Neill forthcoming, but see Anderson 2008; 2011 for an alternative perspective) and Aragonese varieties (Saura Rami 2003: 221–40). One pattern can take precedence over the other: in Portuguese non-first-conjugation verbs, the L-pattern wins out over the N-pattern, which becomes relegated to the second person singular and third person forms of the present indicative; hence the robust patterns of alternation illustrated in Table 11.5 for these classes of Portuguese verbs with root mid vowels (O'Neill 2014b; forthcoming).

Alternatively, the different patterns can be aligned with different types of allomorphy; this is played out most noticeably in certain central varieties of Ibero-Romance in which the N-pattern is the domain of diphthongization and distinctive root allomorphy, and the L-pattern that of velar allomorphy and distinctive desinences (see O'Neill 2018: 31–36 for a discussion of this pattern). As for the intersection of these patterns, in some Romance varieties, analogies affecting the present subjunctive align the first and second person plural forms on the other L-pattern forms, prosodically as well as segmentally: in these varieties, the relevant forms have effectively been reassigned such that they are unambiguously members of the L-pattern alone. In other varieties, the etymological distinctive L-pattern alternant is evicted from the first and second person plural forms; here, the L-pattern is reduced to a subset of the N-pattern, again resolving the ambiguity. Interestingly, both cases are attested in the Asturian variety of Alto Aller (Rodríguez-Castellano 1952): the first and second persons plural present subjunctive forms of certain lexemes share both the rhizotonicity (root-stress) and allomorphy of the other L-pattern forms (*váyamos* 'go.PRS.SBJV.1PL', *téngamos* 'have.PRS.SBJV.1PL', *véngamos* 'come.PRS.SBJV.1PL', *séamos* 'be.PRS.SBJV.1PL'; Rodríguez-Castellano 1952: 146) whilst other lexemes share neither; for discussion and exemplification in other Romance varieties see Maiden (2012) and O'Neill (forthcoming).

A striking result of clash is found in Italo-Romance, where the domain of the characteristic PYTA roots has been reduced to a subset of preterite forms (first and third person singular, third person plural, and in numerous varieties of southern Italy also first person plural). The relevant forms comprise the intersection of PYTA with the set of root-stressed forms (as stress is lexically specified, it may be considered to have an arbitrary, metamorphomic distribution); the characteristic root has been restricted to rhizotonic forms, resulting in a more consistent relationship between stress placement and stem allomorphy (Maiden 2001; Esher 2015). A parallel may be drawn between this example and Enger's (2014) notion of reinforcement, in which exponents of inflexional class are aligned with each other so that one reliably predicts the other; in both cases, the key motivation for change appears to be increased consistency and predictability of patterning.

11.4.2 Rhizomorphomes (Inflexional Classes)
11.4.2.1 The Concept

Inflexional classes, termed RHIZOMORPHOMES by Round (2015), constitute another of the phenomena identified as morphomic by Aronoff (1994), who defines an inflexional class as 'a set of lexemes whose members each select the same set of inflectional realizations' (1994: 64). Like metamorphomes, rhizomorphomes involve systematic relationships between the inflected forms of a lexeme, and thus facilitate reliable inferences about inflexional exponents, constraining the complexity of the inflexional system (a function formalized as the 'No Blur Principle', Carstairs-McCarthy 1994; and the 'Low Conditional Entropy Conjecture', Ackerman and Malouf 2013; 2015). Canonically, rhizomorphomes are 'morphology-internal', without extra-morphological motivation (Corbett 2009: 5f.), though in practice the distribution of lexemes across classes may align partially or entirely with such a correlate (Corbett 2009). While rhizomorphomes are ordinarily considered to be classes of lexemes, Stump (2016: 92–95) presents arguments for treating them as classes of stems; for critical discussion of Stump's approach see Bach (2018).

11.4.2.2 Exponents of Rhizomorphomes

Conjugational class distinctions in Latin are traditionally identified according to the form of inflexional desinences and the identity of thematic vowels (Maiden 2011a: 201–03), and this approach is commonly continued in descriptions of Romance varieties, which define conjugations on the basis of thematic vowels (e.g., infinitive endings Cat. *-ar*, *-re*, *-ir*; It. *-are*, *-ere*, *-ire*). In modern Romance varieties, distinctions made by these means are fewer and more limited in scope: a given tense-aspect-mood (TAM) category may display identical desinences across all conjugational classes (e.g., the imperfect indicative in French, the present subjunctive in Catalan, the preterite and imperfect subjunctive in central Occitan), or may make only a two-way distinction (e.g., the imperfect indicative in Castilian and Romanian distinguishes between first- and non-first-conjugation forms). The greatest differentiation is typically found in the infinitive and past participle, where 'the conjugation-marking vowel is liable to be seen as an inherent, and arbitrary, element of the lexical stem' (Maiden 2011a: 209) as opposed to an exponent of morphosyntactic/semantic features (see also Bach and Esher 2015 for differential behaviour of the infinitive compared to the finite members of the inflexional paradigm).

Recent theoretical work in inflexion has tended to identify inflexional classes on the basis (instead or additionally) of stem distribution patterns; an early forerunner of this type is Sharp's (1976) proposal for Occitan. For French, Stump and Finkel (2013: 182–224) propose 72 conjugational types, as opposed to the traditional three; Bonami et al. (2008) find empirical support for two of the three traditional types, but point out that the third is a conflation of at least 61 different patterns and not treated as a single type by speakers. Such analyses highlight a typological change which has occurred within Romance, namely 'an innovatory tendency to manifest conjugational distinctions ... within the lexical root' (Maiden 2011a: 215). The tendency is particularly acute in French, where sound change has largely eliminated conjugational distinctions in inflexional desinences, and thus conjugational distinctions are almost entirely made by stem exponents. It is also worth mentioning the rise of new categories such as the synthetic future and conditional, in which the inflexional desinences (deriving from present and imperfect indicative forms of Lat. HABERE 'have') are necessarily identical across conjugations, while a thematic vowel from the erstwhile lexical infinitive remains as a stem formative: CANTARE HABET, FINIRE HABET > Cat. *cantarà* 'sing.FUT.3SG', *finirà* 'sleep.FUT.3SG'.

Originally meaningful elements which undergo semantic bleaching may be redeployed as exponents of rhizomorphemes (a type of refunctionalization, in the terms of Smith 2011). An example of this development is the 'augment' (Maiden 2003; Meul 2013), a thematic element originating from an ingressive infix -SC- (e.g., FLORERE 'be in bloom' vs FLORESCERE 'come into bloom', Maiden 2018: 178); while the ingressive meaning is lost, the formative itself is retained, with a new and systematic distribution. Within the inflexional paradigm, the augment generally assumes a distribution corresponding to existing metamorphomes (e.g., Cat. *-eix-* has an N-pattern distribution); within the lexis, it is commonly generalized across the majority of fourth-conjugation lexemes. The paradigmatic extension of the augment is typically accompanied by the neutralization of inherited inflexional class distinctions made by desinences or thematic vowels (Meul 2013: 104–22; Esher 2016: 294–98): for example, in the Occitan variety of Nice, *finisserai* 'finish.FUT.1SG' [with the augment and the theme vowel /e/ common to the first and third conjugations] replaces etymological *finirai* 'finish.FUT.1SG' [with the distinctive fourth-conjugation theme vowel /i/], but neither **finissirai nor **finerai is found. This correlation may be interpreted as indicating that the augment now has a key role as an exponent of inflexional class.

The case of the augment is notable since it offers evidence not only for the psychological reality of rhizomorphemes (as a template for the distribution of exponents) but for the functional value of these structures: total neutralization of conjugational class distinctions is theoretically possible, yet in practice the distinction is actively maintained, indicating that it is of some advantage to speakers. This observation concurs with the results of Ackerman and Malouf's (2015) iterated learning experiment, which show that constrained inflexional classes emerge as an adaptive response to system complexity, essentially improving the learnability of the system.

Other Romance examples illustrate the development of a reliable correlation between properties of the stem, and the traditional conjugational distinctions based on desinences and thematic elements; conjugation class is here exploited as a productive distributional template. In Ibero-Romance, 'non-first-conjugation verbs are distributed between conjugations according to characteristics of the height of the root vowel' (Maiden 2011a: 210); in Portuguese this is the height of the root vowel found in the L-pattern cells (Maiden 2018: 273–77) as attested by the examples in Table 11.5 above in which, with very few exceptions, all second-conjugation verbs with mid vowels in their roots display /e/ in the L-pattern forms while fourth-conjugation verbs (third conjugation in Ibero-Romance terminology) display /i/. Likewise, in Castilian, the presence of a high vowel in the root is associated with fourth-conjugation desinences, while the presence of a mid vowel is associated with second-conjugation desinences, and both tendencies have historically been strengthened by analogical changes modifying the root vowel or shifting the lexeme from one conjugation to the other (O'Neill 2011). Defectiveness in Castilian is also associated chiefly with fourth-conjugation (-*ir*) lexemes (O'Neill 2010). With the exception of N-pattern forms in varieties such as Spanish and Portuguese, there is a tendency for lexemes with first-conjugation desinences to be associated with invariant roots (Maiden 2011a: 210): although the sound changes described in Section 11.4.1.2 for the L-/U-patterns would be expected to cause similar alternation patterns in first-conjugation lexemes, few cases are known, and in both French and Italian, most first-conjugation lexemes which historically presented N-pattern vowel alternation have undergone analogical levelling which eradicates it (Maiden 2018: 277–81). In these cases, '[s]peakers have reanalysed a *contingent* association with conjugation class … as an *inherent* characteristic of that class' (Maiden 2018: 281); the result favours reliable inferences about inflexional forms. Overall, these phenomena again recall Enger's (2014) notion of reinforcement, in which two separate inflexional cues are aligned with each other so that each reliably predicts the other.

A final point to be made concerns the interaction of rhizomorphomes and metamorphomes. It is notable that where exponents of rhizomorphomes undergo analogical extension, their spread through the paradigm is constrained by metamorphomic patterns. This is true of heteroclisis (Stump 2006: 278) in Daco-Romance, which originates within the N-pattern, and may subsequently extend to other paradigm cells, but is systematically resisted by PYTA (Maiden 2018: 55–58, 221–25); and likewise of the paradigmatic extension of the augment in varieties of Occitan, where the augment may spread to all or no PYTA cells, and all or no Fuèc cells, but never differentiates between cells within an established metamorphome (Esher 2016). Conversely, exponents of metamorphomes, such as the thematic velar consonant characteristic of PYTA and the L-pattern in Occitan and Catalan (Wheeler 2011), may be extended to additional lexical items, but their spread appears constrained by rhizomorphomic patterns, proceeding one class at a time and affecting members of a given class simultaneously (Esher 2016). Within an approach which treats rhizomorphomes as classes of lexemes, these facts indicate that the two types of morpheme are orthogonal and sensitive to each other (Esher 2016); note that within an approach which treats rhizomorphomes as a property of stems (Stump 2016), the sensitivity of rhizomorphome exponents to metamorphomes is automatically expected (since stem distribution follows metamorphomic templates, any property of stems must also do so).

11.5 Theoretical Reflections and Considerations

In the foregoing, much evidence has been provided for morphomes and their psychological reality in Romance. The morphomes discussed are canonical in the sense that they, on the whole, defy any functional explanation and justification in terms of morphosemantics, syntax, or phonology. It is clear therefore that morphology ought to be considered autonomous from syntax, semantics, and phonology since there are certain characteristics of morphology (metamorphomes, rhizomorphomes) which are not simply deducible from or reducible to other grammatical principles. However, there are still a number of theories which either seek to deny any autonomy to morphology or severely limit its scope. Why?

In our opinion the answer lies in ingrained assumptions about the basic units of storage and a theoretical reductionist tendency to relate phenomena, wherever possible, to a single coherent system and organizing principle. Given that both phrasal structure and word structure could be considered as governing the ordering of smaller elements into larger meaningful structures (however see below for a criticism of this approach to morphology), be these words or phrases, it therefore seems a 'superfluous complication' (Anderson 2015: 13) to have two extremely similar processes which are subject to different rules or principles. The fact of the matter is, however, that this is how language works; there are two systems and one cannot be derived from or subsumed under the other. Carstairs-McCarthy (2010: 20–22) and Anderson (1992: 22–37; 2015) exemplify this point with reference to the contrasting ordering of grammatical arguments involved in an event when these arguments appear as morphological constituents within words in languages with a rich morphology as opposed to phrasal constituents in the syntax (see O'Neill 2016: 251 for a summary). Morphology and syntax share many properties but they are conspicuously not one and the same thing, as the discussions of meromorphomes and rhizomorphomes illustrate.

Likewise, regarding the autonomy of morphology from semantics and phonology, it could seem an unnecessary measure to propose that there are different systems which predict the different phonetic shapes in which a lexeme can appear, especially when the different shapes do not correspond to any additive or contrastive meaning, unlike the cases of singular vs plural nouns or first person plural vs second person plural verb forms (Sp. *gato* 'cat' vs *gatos* 'cats'; *cantamos* 'we sing' vs *cantáis* 'you.PL sing'). However, we have seen that the semantics and the phonology cannot explain the particular PYTA distribution of the Portuguese allomorph *soub-* in Table 11.2, or the other examples of metamorphomes and rhizomorphomes discussed above. The phonology and the semantics cannot explain why inflexional endings which express exactly the same meaning are different depending on conjugational class or why lexemes in certain conjugational classes have certain phonological characteristics (e.g., presence of a high vowel, lack of root allomorphy).

Regarding the ingrained assumptions about basic units of storage, within theories of morphology there is much disagreement around how best to account for the internal structure of words and the discrepancy in opinions often depends on assumptions about what is memorized: individual and biunique morphemes which form words via deterministic symbolic rules or whole words situated within complex networks, which are governed by probabilistic structures. Is the frequent Spanish word *perros* 'dogs' produced by a deterministic rule which combines the memorized lexical morpheme PERRO with the memorized grammatical morpheme –s to produce a word which is the sum of its parts (PERRO+PLURAL), or is this word's plural simply present in the mind due to its frequency? In the latter case, its internal structure and plural meaning would be explainable on the basis of its mental connexions with other similar words and their plural meanings: *gatos* 'cats', *patos* 'ducks', *cachorros* 'puppies', *humanos* 'humans'.

Blevins (2006; 2016) terms models of the first type 'constructive', and those of the second 'abstractive'. It is within morphological theories of the constructive type that the concept of the morpheme was first introduced and for which morphemes are the most controversial. Constructive models typically 'isolate recurrent bases and exponents within a system, encapsulate each of these elements in an individual rule or entry that represents their grammatical properties, and then derive surface word forms from these simple elements by rules or other combinatoric principles' (Blevins 2006: 533). Models of morphology which advocate morphemes as the basic units of storage and meaning, such as Item-and-Arrangement or Item-and-Process approaches, of which Distributed Morphology (Halle 1990; Halle and Marantz 1993; Embick and Noyer 2007) is merely a continuation, are obviously of the constructive type. Within such theories, meaning is mentally represented as lexical or grammatical morphemes, whose distribution, arrangement, and phonetic realization are due to a combination of syntactic/semantic/phonological and lexical conditioning. It is not only morphemic theories which are constructive, however, but also some realizational 'Word and Paradigm' models (Matthews 1991; Anderson 1992; Corbett and Fraser 1993; Aronoff 1994; Stump 2001; Brown and Hippisley 2012) which have the word as the basic unit of storage. These realizational models 'adopt the perspective of formal language theory, in which a "language" is a set of expressions or structures and a "grammar" is a device for enumerating these sets' (Blevins 2016: 16). Thus, they associate inherent lexical features with memorized roots and/or stems, and formalize the generalizations and patterns present in the morphological system by way of deterministic symbolic rules and constraints. Thus, words are constructed on the basis of a lexical root and the concatenation of other phonological formatives indirectly associated with certain grammatical features or the combination of the lexical root and certain morphosyntactic features can trigger a rule selecting a particular stored and indexed root for the lexeme.

Abstractive models of morphology (Skousen 1989; Baayen et al. 1997; Eddington 2000; 2006; Bybee 2001; Baayen et al. 2003; Blevins 2006; 2016) assume, with Word and Paradigm realizational theories, that the minimal meaningful unit and basic element of lexical storage is the word, and that complex word forms are stored in their entirety in the lexicon. However, they also hypothesize that words are related to one another on the basis of formal and semantic characteristics and that this particular organization 'provides generalizations and segmentation at various degrees of abstraction and generality whereby units such as morpheme [...] arise from the relations of identity and similarity that organize representation' (Bybee 2001: 7). For example, in abstractive models of morphology, the formatives *-e* and *-mos* in the Spanish or Portuguese word *comemos* 'we eat', would not be stored in isolation from the root *com-* and associated with the morphosyntactic feature-combination first person plural present. Rather, given the frequency of the form *comemos*, the word would be stored and the internal structure *com-e-mos*, in which /e/ is the conjugation vowel and *-mos* associated with first person plural would be abstracted from comparisons with other verbs (*bebemos* 'we drink', *respondemos* 'we reply', *aprendemos* 'we learn') which have the same structure and are also associated with first person plural present tense meanings, and are likewise morphologically related to other verb forms displaying the same conjugation vowel (e.g., infinitives *beber, responder, aprender*).

In models of morphology in the post-Bloomfieldian tradition, abstractive theories are, at first sight, challenging in the context of highly inflected languages such as the Romance languages since they seem to advocate the mass storage of whole word forms. This mass storage seems highly redundant and falls short of what Bloomfield (1933: 238) would term 'scientific compactness'. Notions of economy would seem to dictate that regular morphologically complex words should be rule-generated along the lines of various constructive approaches (Aronoff 1976; 1994; Scalise 1984; Anderson 1992; Matthews 1991; Beard 1995; Stump 2001; Ackema and Neeleman 2004) or models which advocate dual processing (Pinker 1991; Prasada and Pinker 1993; Clahsen et al. 1997; Clahsen 1999; Bybee 2001: 29; see Lavric et al. 2001 for discussion).

However, Blevins (2016: 70) has pointed out that theoretical compactness 'has no established relevance to language acquisition or use'. And that 'there is at present no evidence that the language faculty imposes memory demands that strain the storage capacity of the human brain, or that linguistic notions of "compactness" would be relevant to reducing this load'. Indeed, cognitive scientists working outside the field of language have suggested that the most realistic models of memory are ones 'in which marvels are produced by profligate use of capacity' (Landauer 1986: 493) as opposed to economy of storage (see also Hay and Baayen 2005: 343).

Regarding dual models of processing, Sims (2016: 16) notes that 'such a strict division between regular and irregular inflection has proven untenable under the accumulated weight of evidence that regular inflected forms also often exhibit properties that are indicative of cognitive storage and access of inflected forms as a single unit'. Indeed she makes the claim that 'independently and in parallel to the formal morphological literature, psycholinguistic investigations of the lexicon and lexical access have similarly established strong evidence for words as representational units,[2] and the need for an associative (i.e., paradigmatically orientated) network of connections between lexical entries'.

In this respect, it is interesting to analyse the formalization of the autonomous morphological component operating on the basis of functions (be they of the morphomic or paradigm function kind). The distribution of allomorphy within a paradigm, which metamorphomes embody, is only a problem in constructive theories in which the minimal units of storage are lexical roots/stems and grammatical morphemes. Taking the specific example of Pt. *saber* 'know' in Table 11.2, once the root allomorph *soub-* is extracted from the whole word forms there arises what Blevins (2006) terms the 'Humpty Dumpty problem' – how to put the parts back together after artificially sundering them. This becomes even more complicated in Portuguese, since one not only has to explain the meaningless distribution of the root allomorphy, but the fact that the conjugation vowel is the mid-open [ɛ] and not the mid-closed [e], typical of all other second-conjugation verbs. Blevins (2006: 534) notes that '[a] constructive orientation is clearly reflected in Aronoff's characterization (Aronoff 1994: 167) of the "third stem" in Latin "in terms of which forms are built on it"'. Indeed, the morphomic enterprise was, amongst other things, inspired by the impossibility of assigning a coherent meaning or coherent phonological environment to roots/stems within metamorphomes; this problem, however, is symptomatic of constructive theories which assume that stems are minimal units upon which other forms are built.

---

[2] Moreover, she notes that even the psychological models of morphological processing that acknowledge some type of morphemic representation in the lexicon (e.g., the race models/parallel dual-route models of morphological processing; Baayen et al. 1997; Baayen and Schreuder 2003; Hay and Baayen 2005: 344), admit that these parts of words do not exist in lieu of, but alongside, whole word forms and any type of morphemic representations owe their very existence to the paradigmatic relations they establish with whole-word representations.

In an abstractive model these generalizations naturally follow from the principles governing storage. The whole concept of metamorphomes merely corresponds to the situation whereby a subset of cells in the paradigm are more cohesive and have a greater interpredictability or diagnostic function with respect to the other cells. These cells therefore form their own cohesive unit, whereby once the form in any of these cells is heard and memorized, the other forms are automatically known. In abstractive theories, prediction of forms is crucial and such predictions can be based on patterns which are formally cohesive and predictive albeit not functionally so.

Most constructive theories, however, depend upon a common semantic or phonological factor to predict the distribution of allomorphy. Such factors are not available for metamorphomes, hence the need of morphomic functions or other contrivances to specify the purely paradigmatic distribution of the allomorphy. In an attempt to formalize the PYTA metamorphome for Portuguese and Spanish in accordance with the principles advanced in Aronoff (1994), O'Neill (2014a: 25) concluded that 'the introduction of a morphomic level merely constitutes an incorporation of a partial paradigmatic dimension into a constructive model of morphology' and that such a theory 'does not present significant advantages over abstractive theories as regards the formalisation of the synchronic facts and presents disadvantages as regards the motivation of diachronic tendencies'. That is, constructive models which suppose that roots are stored independently from their inflexional endings and from other roots, cannot explain in a straightforward way the cases of analogical spread or levelling, or the tendency of lexemes in a morphome to converge on a particular phonological form. In abstractive theories these developments would be expected given the cohesive and connected relationships between sets of words.

How does this theoretical discussion, however, contribute to our understanding of the autonomy of morphology? It does so by placing the problem of accepting the autonomy of morphology within certain constructive theories of morphology which rely on outdated notions of mental storage and computation. Abstractive theories assume that grammatical structure (i.e., not just morphology) emerges from stored forms within a rich, dynamic lexicon. However, not all stored forms or groups of forms are the same types, there are different patterns and models which can be conflicting and contrasting. Moreover, abstractions of different generalities and scope can be arrived at: for the segment, the word, the phrase, and the entire language. It may be true that there is a single component or device which governs all aspects of grammar; one based on human abilities of memorization, pattern detection, categorization, and analogy (Hofstadter and Sander 2013). However, there must also exist autonomous subcomponents, since the linguistic data show that there are phenomena regarding the structure and forms of words which have nothing to do with the structure of phrases and have nothing to do with common meanings and the sound rules of the language. Interestingly, some of these phenomena (e.g., metamorphomes and rhizomorphomes), are in no way necessary for human communication. However despite this fact they are constantly reinforced by the results of human communication; that is, in language change.

Selected References

Below you can find selected references for this chapter. The full references can be found online at the following page: www.cambridge.org/Romancelinguistics

Anderson, S. (1992). *A-morphous Morphology*. Cambridge: Cambridge University Press.
Aronoff, M. (1994). *Morphology by Itself*. Cambridge, MA: MIT Press.
Baerman, M., Brown, D., and Corbett, G. (eds) (2015). *Understanding and Measuring Morphological Complexity*. Oxford: Oxford University Press.
Blevins, J. (2016). *Word and Paradigm Morphology*. Oxford: Oxford University Press.
Blevins, J. and Blevins, J. (eds) (2009). *Analogy in Grammar*. Oxford: Oxford University Press.
Carstairs-McCarthy, A. (2010). *The Evolution of Morphology*. Oxford: Oxford University Press.
Cruschina, S., Maiden, M., and Smith, J. C. (eds) (2013). *The Boundaries of Pure Morphology*. Oxford: Oxford University Press.
Luís, A. and Bermúdez-Otero, R. (eds) (2016). *The Morphome Debate*. Oxford: Oxford University Press.
Maiden, M. (2018). *The Romance Verb. Morphomic Structure and Diachrony*. Oxford: Oxford University Press.
Maiden, M., Smith, J. C., Goldbach, M., and Hinzelin, M.-O. (eds) (2011). *Morphological Autonomy. Perspectives from Romance Inflectional Morphology*. Oxford: Oxford University Press.
Sims, A. (2016). *Inflectional Defectiveness*. Cambridge: Cambridge University Press.
Stump, G. (2016). *Inflectional Paradigms*. Cambridge: Cambridge University Press.

12

Suppletion

Martin Maiden and Anna M. Thornton

12.1 Definitions of Suppletion

Well-known Romance examples of suppletion appear in the inflexional paradigm of the verb GO: It. *vado* 'I go' vs *andiamo* 'we go', Fr. *vais* '(I) go' vs *allais* '(I) went' vs *irai* '(I) will go', where the exponence of the meaning 'go' seems to be entirely different in different parts of the paradigm (compare this with It. *canto* 'I sing' vs *cantiamo* 'we sing', or Fr. *chante* '(I) sing' vs *chantais* '(I) sang' vs *chanterai* '(I) will sing'). A widely accepted definition of suppletion is that it is a relation between two linguistic signs X and Y in language L in which the semantic difference between X and Y is maximally regular in L, while the phonological difference between them is maximally irregular (cf. Melčuk 2000), and 'not morphologically predictable' (Aronoff and Fudeman 2005: 168).

Suppletion is a non-canonical phenomenon, in the sense of Corbett (2007). Particularly in inflexional paradigms, one expects a regular semantic opposition to be expressed by an equally regular phonological opposition. Suppletion is sometimes described as a 'limiting case' of allomorphy (Bauer 1988: 94; also Spencer 1991: 8), where morphologists have to 'admit defeat' in their search for regularities (Bauer 1988: 41). Bloomfield (1933: 215) describes alternations such as *good* ~ *better* (cf. It. *buono* ~ *migliore*) by stating that the underlying form 'suffers' suppletion. Dressler (1985) calls suppletion a 'scandal' for the theory of Natural Morphology, and predicts that it will be rare within, and across, languages. Actually, Corbett (2007: 11) observes that 'it occurs frequently', since in a genetically and areally differentiated sample of 34 languages, only four revealed no suppletion in their inflexional morphology (see Brown et al. 2003).

As Melčuk (2000) argues, suppletion can be viewed as applying not only to inflexional morphology, but also to derivational morphology and even to idioms. He considers as examples of derivational suppletion Russian *četyre* 'four' vs *sorok* 'forty', and as a case of suppletion in idioms Russian *sukin syn* 'son of a bitch', lit. 'bitch.ADJ son' with plural *sukini deti* lit. 'bitch.ADJ children', rather than **sukini synovja with the expected plural of the word for 'son'. In fact, it may be helpful simply to ignore traditional divisions between 'inflexional' and 'derivational' morphology (and 'idioms') and view suppletion as an extreme discrepancy between unity of meaning, on the one hand, and the disunited forms expressing that meaning, on the other. This state of affairs is likely to be at its most striking in inflexional morphology, if one and the same lexical meaning is expressed by completely different forms, and possibly less extreme in derivational morphology, where often, but not necessarily (since there are cases of transposition where base form and derived form is identical), there is some degree of difference of lexical meaning between base and derived form. The difference between It. *vado* 'I go' and *andiamo* 'we go' exhibits an extreme contradiction between unity of lexical meaning and difference of form, while that between It. *due* 'two' and *secondo* 'second' might be argued to be less extreme and less surprising, because in addition to the meaning 'two' present in both, there is additional lexical semantic content in the meaning 'in numerical order' in *secondo*.

Another issue is whether the label 'suppletion' must be limited to irregular alternations affecting exponents of lexical meaning (roots or stems) or can apply to alternation purely between grammatical affixes, as argued by Haspelmath (2002: 29) and Melčuk. In inflexion, this amounts to recognizing affixes in different inflexional classes as suppletive alternants of the same grammatical entity (for example, *-ă* and *-e*, both realizing third person singular present in Romanian forms such as *cântă* 'sings' vs *simte* 'feels', would be considered suppletive). As Corbett (2007: 15) observes, this choice is only possible if one subscribes to 'lexical' theories of inflexional realization, where affixes have lexical entries, as do stems; if one adopts a 'word-and-paradigm' approach in which whole word-forms, and their place in inflexional paradigms, are the basic object of analysis (see, e.g., Stump 2001 and Blevins 2016), it makes less sense to view affixes as suppletive alternants in their own right. Besides, if affixes with the same morphosyntactic content belonging to different inflexional classes are considered an instance of suppletion, in most inflexional languages suppletion will 'take in a substantial proportion of inflectional morphology', as Corbett (2007: 15) points out.

A further issue is whether suppletion should be limited to instances in which the suppletive alternants derive diachronically from distinct lexemes (as in the different forms of GO in Romance), or should be used also for alternants which have become uniquely distinct phonologically due to sound change, such as Srs. *ditgel* 'I say' ~ *schevel* 'I was saying', both from forms of Lat. DICERE 'say'. Since diachronic information is unavailable to speakers (Corbett 2007: 13), 'etymological considerations should play no role' in defining the notion of suppletion (Mel'čuk 2000: 514); therefore, we discuss both the type arising from sound change and the type resulting from the entry of forms of one lexeme into the paradigm of another, called 'incursion' by Juge (1999: 184) and Corbett (2007: 13).

Suppletion is gradable. Mel'čuk (2000: 517–19) observes that three factors involved in recognizing a suppletive relation are gradable: (a) regularity of the semantic relation between X and Y; (b) irregularity of the formal relation between X and Y; (c) similarity of the signifiers between X and Y. Semantic relations are more regular in inflexion than in derivation, making it easier to recognize suppletion in inflexion. The degree of regularity or irregularity that can be recognized in the formal relation between X and Y depends on various factors, including the level of abstraction of the phonological representations adopted. A pertinent factor is whether a given formal difference is observable in only one pair of items (i.e., it is 'unique': Mel'čuk 2000: 518, Corbett 2007: 27), or whether it has parallels elsewhere in the language; the more isolated the relation, up to uniqueness, the stronger the suppletion. The question is how great the difference between two signifiers must be for us to recognize a suppletive relation; a related issue is how to measure that distance. Some authors seem to require 'total modification' (Matthews 1991: 139) or 'no resemblance' (Bloomfield 1933: 215) between two signifiers, while Mel'čuk (2000: 513) maintains that the condition that two elements have no phonemes in common is neither necessary nor sufficient for recognizing a suppletive relation. A distinction is generally made between strong suppletion, where the two elements have nothing phonologically in common, and weak suppletion, where there is a phonological resemblance, albeit not derivable by synchronically productive phonological rules (as in It. SG *dio* 'god' ~ PL *dei*, SG *bue* 'ox' ~ PL *buoi*; cf. Dressler 1985). Crocco Galèas (1991), examining a corpus of Italian placenames and the ethnonyms derived from them, proposes a scale with four degrees of strength of suppletion in terms of phonological proximity: 'very weak or phonological', 'weak or schematic', 'strong or sub-morphemic', 'very strong or total', with many sub-types (Table 12.1).

It is very difficult to set clear boundaries between the degrees, but the fact that suppletion, and particularly phonological similarity between the elements in suppletive relation, is gradable emerges clearly from these examples, and from those examined below.

Mel'čuk (2000: 518) calls formally strong suppletion 'genuine', and formally weak suppletion 'quasi-suppletion'. Other terms used to present this distinction are 'full' or 'total' vs 'partial' suppletion. Corbett (2007: 15–17) and Spencer (1991: 8) treat as 'total' suppletion those cases in which 'there is absolutely no phonological connection between the two forms' (Spencer 1991: 8), and as 'partial' suppletion those in which there is 'partial

Table 12.1. *Degrees of suppletion between Italian placenames and ethnonyms*

	base (placename)	derivative (ethnonym)
very weak	Faedo	faetano
weak	Subiaco	sublacense
strong	Padova	patavino
very strong	Napoli	partenopeo

phonological similarity' (Corbett 2007: 16), and even 'a fairly strong resemblance' (Spencer 1991: 8) between the elements.

It is preferable to use the terms 'strong' vs 'weak' rather than 'full' or 'total' vs 'partial' for these cases, because 'total' and 'partial' lend themselves to interpretation in a different sense. We can distinguish cases of fused exponence of lexical and grammatical elements, and cases where a suppletive stem combines with a morphologically regular affix: e.g., It. *è* (ɛ) 'is' could be analysed as fusion of lexical and inflexional material in a monophonemic wordform, while PRT *fu-i* 'I was' shows a suppletive stem and a regular ending expressing person and number. These two situations could easily be labelled 'total' vs 'partial' suppletion, taking 'partial' to mean that only part of an inflected form (the stem) is suppletive.

The Romance data are cross-linguistically typical in showing suppletion almost exclusively in basic, high-frequency lexemes, such as GO, COME, or GIVE.[1] In the theoretical literature there is a tradition of arguing, broadly, that this reflects 'economic' advantages of storing clearly distinct forms (cf. Werner 1987; Fertig 1998; Nübling 2001), and that the cognitive prominence of some high-frequency lexemes favours maximal differentiation of alternating forms (cf. Markey 1985: 63; Bittner 1988: 420; also Blevins 2016: 201 for suppletion as an advantageous form of 'discriminative irregularity'). Such insights may help explain the diachronic persistence of suppletions once they emerge, but the Romance languages do not appear to have particular fresh perspectives to offer, beyond the fact (see our discussion of Istro-Romanian below) that when suppletion occurs in non-basic vocabulary it may be a response to structural pressures to fill emergent 'gaps' in the grammatical system. While we survey the various degrees and types of suppletion in this chapter, we focus on an issue on which the comparative-historical Romance data throw light: under what historical circumstances can diachronically unrelated and completely different words come to constitute 'one and the same' word, occupying complementary parts of the paradigm of one and the same lexeme?

---

[1] The definition of 'basic' is elusive, and frequency cannot always be reliably assessed for a particular language. Indeed there are cases in the literature on suppletive words that are not obviously 'high frequency' (see, e.g., Corbett 2007: 34).

12.2 Typology and Distribution of Romance Suppletions

12.2.1 Introduction

This section is a descriptive overview of types of suppletion in Romance languages, to which we refer in the theoretically oriented discussion of the ensuing sections. While this illustration is not a comprehensive survey of *tokens* of suppletion in Romance, it is close to being a comprehensive survey of *types*, and therefore permits useful theoretical generalizations about the nature of suppletion, testable against and comparable with languages outside Romance.

12.2.2 Ordinal vs Cardinal Numerals

The relation between cardinal and ordinal numerals is addressed from a typological perspective by Stolz and Veselinova (2013), who define cardinals as those 'used in attributive quantification of nouns (e.g., "four days")' and ordinals as those that 'typically identify the position a given member of a set occupies relative to other members of the same set (e.g., "the fourth day")' (see Chapter 15, this volume, for in-depth discussion of Romance counting systems). From a sample of 321 languages, the most common scenario that they identify (over a third of the languages), is that the ordinal 'first' is suppletive, while ordinals for 'second' upwards are derived from the corresponding cardinals. This situation is represented by Romanian (Table 12.2) and almost by French, which has two forms for 'second', regularly derived *deuxième*, from *deux* 'two', and suppletive *second*; these alternate freely in most contexts, but only *deuxième* is used in compound numerals (*vingt-deuxième* 'twenty-second', **vingt-second), and some fixed expressions such as *de seconde main* 'second-hand' require *second*.

Most Romance languages, like Latin, belong to the second most common type (19 per cent of languages in Stolz and Veselinova's sample), where 'first' and a small set of consecutive higher ordinal numerals show suppletion. Table 12.3 shows masculine singular forms of low numerals in Latin and some Romance languages.

Strong suppletion holds for 'first' and 'second' in Latin and most other languages. The ordinals 'third', 'fourth', and 'fifth' represent various degrees of weak suppletion. Comparison of Romance languages shows no implicational hierarchy in the strength of suppletion among the ordinals between 'third' and 'ninth'. One might expect a decrease of strength of

Table 12.2. *Suppletion in Romanian ordinal numerals*

'one'	un	'first'	prim (or întâi)
'two'	doi	'second'	al doilea
'four'	patru	'fourth'	al patrulea
'nine'	nouă	'ninth'	al nouălea

Table 12.3. *Suppletion in Romance ordinal numerals*

	'one'	'first'	'two'	'second'	'three'	'third'	'four'	'fourth'	'five'	'fifth'
Lat.	UNUS	PRIMUS	DUO	SECUNDUS	TRES	TERTIUS	QUATTUOR	QUARTUS	QUINQUE	QUINTUS
Pt.	um	primeiro	dois	segundo	três	terceiro	quatro	quarto	cinco	quinto
Sp.	uno	primero	dos	segundo	tres	tercero	cuatro	cuarto	cinco	quinto
Occ.	un	primièr	dos	segond	tres	tresen	quatre	quatren	cinc	cinquen
Fr.	un	premier	deux	deuxième/second	trois	troisième	quatre	quatrième	cinq	cinquième
Srs.	in	emprem	dus	secund	treis	tierz	quater	quart	tschun	tschunavel
It.	uno	primo	due	secondo	tre	terzo	quattro	quarto	cinque	quinto

Table 12.4. *Suppletion in Romance ordinal numerals*

	'seven'	'seventh'	'nine'	'ninth'
Lat.	SEPTEM	SEPTIMUS	NOUEM	NONUS
Cat.	set	setè	nou	novè
Fr.	sept	septième	neuf	neuvième
It.	sette	settimo	nove	nono

suppletion as the numbers increase, but we find that 'fifth' is commonly less phonologically related to 'five' that 'fourth' is to 'four'; besides, it is often the case that 'ninth' is more irregular (and suppletively) related to 'nine' than 'seventh' is to 'seven', as shown by Table 12.4.

The languages differ in the amount of weak suppletion they display in the relation between low cardinal numbers and related ordinals: French has regularly derived ordinals for the whole series (with a small phonological distance between *neuf* and *neuvième*), while Spanish at the other extreme has some irregularity in all ordinals in the series. French, Catalan, and Occitan display a single suffix in all ordinals between 'third' and 'tenth', while the other languages have numerous suffixes (It. *quar-to, sett-imo, ott-avo*, Pt. *terc-eiro*, Sp. *nov-eno*), which could be considered to present cases of affixal suppletion.

Not all Romance varieties have indigenous synthetic ordinal numerals, and all Romance ordinal systems seem to be, to some extent, of learnèd origin – therefore tending towards suppletion with respect to the cardinal numbers. Some varieties of Sardinian have no morphological ordinals, using instead periphrases. Thus Nuorese (Pittau 1972: 87–89) has cardinals *unu* 'one', *duos* 'two', *tres* 'three', *battor* 'four', *kimbe* 'five' but ordinals *su 'e unu, su 'e duos*, etc. (lit. 'that of one', 'that of two') and also an innovatory set of forms which, partly by dint of being loans from Italian, are suppletive: *primu* 'first', *sicundu* 'second', *tertzu* 'third', *cuartu* 'fourth', etc. Indeed, there is a notable tendency across Romance for ordinals to be borrowings from Latin, contributing to their synchronically suppletive status: this is true, for example, of Sp. *segundo*, Fr. *second* [səgõ], Rms. *secund* 'second', which are not the expected native phonological reflexes of Lat. SECUNDUS, and are at least semi-learnèd borrowings.

Table 12.5. *Suppletive comparatives in Latin and some Romance languages*

	'good'	'better'	'bad'	'worse'
Lat.	BONUS	MELIOR	MALUS	PEIOR
Pt.	bom	melhor	mau	pior
Cat.	bo	millor	mal	pitjor
Fr.	bon	meilleur	(mauvais)	pire
Srs.	bien	meglier	mal	(mender)/pir
It.	buono	migliore	(cattivo) Olt. *malo*	peggiore

12.2.3 Comparatives and Superlatives

A lesson to be learned from the history of Romance comparative and superlative constructions is that what are normally described as suppletive forms sometimes reflect underlying differences in lexical meaning between the alternating forms: these may be 'different lexemes'. Comparatives and superlatives in Latin were usually formed synthetically, with the suffixes -IOR/-IUS and -ISSIMUS; only some phonologically defined bases (adjectives whose stem ended in a vowel) formed their comparatives periphrastically, e.g., IDONEUS 'apt', MAGIS IDONEUS 'more apt'. The Romance languages have generalized the analytic construction; the descendants of MAGIS or PLUS + adjective are used for the comparative (Ro. *mai înalt*, It. *più alto*, etc., 'higher, taller') and the superlative is formed by adding a definite determiner to these constructions (Ro. *cel mai înalt*, It. *il più alto*, etc., 'the highest'). However, most Romance languages have also inherited certain forms which were suppletive comparatives in Latin. Table 12.5 illustrates the forms.[2] Most (not all, e.g., Romanian) preserve synthetic comparative forms in the words for 'good' and 'bad'.

Caution is in order in claiming that descendants of Latin synthetic comparatives are also suppletive synthetic comparatives in Romance. Whereas in Latin comparatives (and superlatives) were systematically expressed by synthetic means, this morphological means is exceptional in Romance and restricted to a handful of high-frequency, basic words which tend to be, in any case, semantically estranged from their (historical) base forms. These facts may lead us to analyse them as independent lexical items, possibly with inherent comparative meaning. Some languages also show remnants of MAIOR (the weakly suppletive comparative of MAGNUS 'big'), and of MINOR (comparative of PARUUS 'small'), where the base forms have generally (and still suppletively) been replaced by other words: e.g., Pt. *grande ~ maior*; *pequeno ~ menor*; Cat. *gran ~ major*; *petit ~ menor*; Fr. *grand ~ majeur*; *petit ~ moindre*; It. *grande ~ maggiore*; *piccolo ~ minore*. Analytic comparatives from the alleged base adjectives of these synthetic forms are also used, to a different extent in different languages. There is typically some lexical semantic estrangement between

---

[2] A similar situation obtains with certain adverbs, such as BENE 'well' ~ MELIUS 'better', MALE 'badly' ~ PEIUS 'worse', which have descendants such as It. *bene ~ meglio*, *male ~ peggio*, Fr. *bien ~ mieux*, *mal~ pis*.

base adjective and synthetic comparative. French *majeur* is actually of learnèd origin (the old French continuant of MAIOR, namely *maire*, persists as the word for 'mayor'), while *moindre* generally persists in the sense 'lesser, least, slightest', and '(physically) smaller' is analytically expressed as *plus petit* lit. 'more small/little'. In Surselvan, indeed, the reflex of Latin MINOR, *mender*, has largely intruded into the semantic space of *pir* 'worse', while also retaining the sense of 'smaller/smallest' (cf. Spescha 1989: 284). If Giurgea (2016) is correct in analysing *mare*, the ordinary Romanian word for 'big', as a continuant of Latin comparative MAIOR (cf. also Vegliote *maur* 'big'), then we have an example of a Latin synthetic comparative losing its comparative value altogether. Further evidence that the synthetic suppletive comparatives are losing their inherent comparative value comes in popular analytic forms such as Fr. *plus meilleur* lit. 'more better' or It. *più meglio* lit. 'more better', where the comparative value is marked by *plus/più*.

A corpus-based study of the distribution of synthetic and analytic comparatives (and superlatives) would allow us better to assess the semantic relation between the suppletive synthetic comparatives and their bases;[3] it is certainly debatable whether descendants of the Latin suppletive comparatives are genuine suppletive (and, irregularly, synthetic) comparative/superlative forms, standing in a relation of overabundance with analytic forms,[4] or whether they have become distinct, inherently comparative/superlative adjectives. Further examples of the frequent lack of semantic parallelism between a base and its purported synthetic comparative/superlative come, for example, from Italian, where 'good friend' can be expressed by both *grande amico* lit. 'big friend' and *buon amico* 'good friend', and *grande amico* is the more frequent,[5] but 'best friend' is *miglior amico*, while *maggior amico* lit. 'bigger/biggest friend', which would be the expected comparative/superlative of *grande amico*, is not in common usage. A second indication comes from the observation that a single descendant of a Latin synthetic suppletive form appears to stand in a relation of overabundance with different analytic forms from different bases in different contexts (e.g., It. *vino più buono/migliore* 'better/best wine', *alunno più bravo/migliore* 'better/best pupil', *film più bello/migliore* 'better/best film', etc., cf. Santilli 2014), or even in the same context: Pt. *irmão menor* 'younger brother' alternates with *irmão mais novo* lit. 'brother more new/young' (the most normal way of expressing the concept), but also with *irmão mais jovem* lit. 'brother more young', *pequeno irmão* 'little brother', (BrPt.) *irmão caçula*.[6] Occasionally the purported comparatives can actually co-occur with their alleged bases,

---

[3] For a first attempt to analyse Italian *migliore/più buono* see Santilli (2014).

[4] On overabundance see Thornton (2011; 2012; 2019a; 2019b).

[5] The frequency of the phrases discussed in the text has been assessed from several available corpora, such as the OPUS2 parallel corpora (www.sketchengine.eu) and Google Books Ngram viewer (for Spanish, French, and Italian).

[6] From the Kimbundo word *ka'zuli*, 'the last member of a family'.

contributing different components of meaning (e.g., from a text found on the Internet, Sp. *cuando le llevas por varios años a tu pequeño . . . hermano menor* 'when you are several years older than your little . . . younger brother').

12.2.4 Inflexional Morphology of Personal Pronouns

Corbett (2005: 2) observes that personal pronouns offer 'the commonest instance' of suppletion, particularly if same-person pronouns are considered members of the same paradigm, showing number inflexion like nouns. However, forms meaning 'I' and 'we' are often not considered members of the same paradigm, because first person plural pronouns do not usually refer to a group of speakers, and therefore are not 'real' plurals of the first person singular. But Corbett (2005) argues that the frequent associative uses of first person plural pronouns are expected, since pronouns, and particularly first person pronouns, are at the top of the animacy hierarchy, where an associative meaning of the plural is most common; he further shows that in many languages the formal means of exponence of 'plural' in personal pronouns are the same as for nouns. Therefore, when there is a formal difference between the stems of pronouns with the same person value and different number values, that may be considered suppletion. Romance personal pronouns (Tables 12.6 and 12.7; see further Cappellaro 2016) may also inflect for case, and the different case forms are commonly suppletive (as also in Latin).

Both types of Latin strong suppletion between first person singular and first person plural pronouns, and between different case forms mainly in the first person singular, persist in Romance. Second person pronouns also show strong suppletion between singular and plural, and somewhat weaker suppletion between different case forms within the singular, as in Latin: initial [t] (or continuants thereof) appears in all second person singular case forms.

A further area of suppletion is between strong and clitic pronouns, with cases of strong suppletion as in Fr. 1SG *moi* ~ *je*, and of weaker suppletion as in It. 1SG *me* ~ *mi*, 2SG *te* ~ *ti* (the second form is the clitic). Altogether, the greatest

Table 12.6. *First person tonic pronouns*

	1SG SUBJECT	1SG NON-SUBJECT	1PL SUBJECT	1PL NON-SUBJECT
Lat.	EGO	ACC ME, DAT MIHI	NOS	ACC NOS, DAT NOBIS
Pt.	eu	mim comigo 'with me'	nós	nós connosco 'with us'
Sp.	yo	mí < MIHI conmigo 'with me'	nosotros	nosotros
Cat.	jo	mi	nosaltres	nosaltres
Srs.	jeu	mei	nus	nus
It.	io	me	noi	noi
Nuo.	deo	mene[a]	nóis	nois
Ro.	eu	ACC mine, DAT mie	noi	ACC noi, DAT nouă

[a] See Pittau (1972: 81) for other variants of this form, such as *mimmi*, used after the preposition *a* 'to', and *mecus* used after *kin* 'with', and parallel forms for the second person singular.

Table 12.7. *Second person tonic pronouns*

	2SG SUBJECT	2SG NON-SUBJECT	2PL SUBJECT	2PL NON-SUBJECT
Lat.	TU	ACC TE / DAT TIBI	UOS	ACC UOS / DAT UOBIS
Pt.	tu	ti < TIBI	vós	vós
		contigo 'with you'		convosco 'with you'
Sp.	tú	ti	vosotros	vosotros
		contigo 'with you'		
Cat.	tu	tu	vosaltres	vosaltres
Fr.	toi	toi	vous	vous
Srs.	ti	tei	vus	vus
It.	tu	te	voi	voi
Nuo.	tue	tene	bóis	bois
Ro.	tu	ACC tine / DAT ţie	voi	ACC voi / DAT vouă

suppletion is found in first- and second person pronouns, and the least in third person object clitics, which tend to have regular paradigms (e.g., It. MSG *lo* ~ FSG *la* ~ MPL *li* ~ FPL *le*).

In the relation between strong and clitic pronouns we also encounter incursive suppletion, as in It. 1PL *noi* (< NOS) ~ *ci* (< ECCE HIC 'lo here' or HINC(E) 'hence'). Italian 2PL *voi* ~ *vi* possibly also reflects incursion (*voi* < UOS, *vi* < IBI 'there'; Vincent 1988: 290), but these display a phonological similarity in initial /v/, qualifying as more weakly suppletive than the first person plural forms.

Romance third person tonic pronouns are particularly interesting for a typology of suppletion, because they show both strong suppletion resulting from incursion, and strong suppletion between forms descending from the same Latin lexeme. As Cappellaro (2016) observes, dedicated third person pronouns did not exist in Latin, which used demonstratives for reference to non-participants in the speech act. Romance third person pronouns developed from the Latin distal demonstrative ILLE and the anaphoric IPSE. Some languages exploited only one of these, such as Nuorese Sardinian, with the forms *issu* ~ *issa* ~ *issos* ~ *issas*, from IPSE, and Portuguese, with *ele* ~ *ela* ~ *eles* ~ *elas*, from forms of ILLE. Others incursively combined descendants of both, as in Neapolitan (Ledgeway 2009: 272) *isso* ~ *essa* ~ *lloro* (see further Cappellaro 2016). Finally, even in languages where third person pronouns all descend from the same Latin demonstrative they may appear quite strongly suppletive because of phonological development: It. 3MSG *egli* and *lui* and 3PL *loro* all descend from different number and case forms of ILLE, but their phonetic resemblance is minimal, so that synchronically they constitute very strong suppletion, although of non-incursive origin.

12.2.5 Inflexional Morphology of Verbs, Nouns, and Adjectives

Verb suppletion is present throughout Romance, occurring everywhere in BE (Table 12.8), and almost everywhere in GO (Table 12.9)[7] (except central

---

[7] See Aski (1995: 403f.).

Table 12.8. *BE (etyma: ESSE, FUISSE (suppletive perfective of ESSE) 'be'; FIERI 'become'; STARE 'stand'; SEDERE 'sit')*[a]

	(a) Romanian			(b) Italian			(c) Catalan			(d) Portuguese		
	PRS	SBJV	IPFV	PRT	PRS.IND	IPFV.IND	PRT	PRS.IND	IPF.IND	PRT	PRS.IND	IPF.IND	PRT
1SG	sunt	fiu	eram	fusei	sono	ero	fui	sóc	era	fui	sou	era	fui
2SG	ești	fii	erai	fuseși	sei	eri	fosti	ets	eres	fores	és	eras	foste
3SG	este / e	fie	era	fuse	è	era	fu	és	era	fou	é	era	foi
1PL	suntem	fim	eram	fuserăm	siamo	eravamo	fummo	som	érem	fórem	somos	éramos	fomos
2PL	sunteți	fiți	erați	fuserăți	siete	eravate	foste	sou	éreu	fóreu	sois	éreis	fostes
3PL	sunt	fie	erau	fuseră	sono	erano	furono	són	eren	foren	são	eram	foram
INF	fi				essere			ésser			ser		
PTCP	fost				stato			estat			sido		

[a] The forms in *fu-/fo-* continue FUISSE, those in *fi-* continue FIERI, those in *(e)st-* in Italian and Catalan continue STARE, while Pt. *ser*, *sido* continue SEDERE. Other forms continue Lat. ESSE.

Table 12.9. *GO (etyma: IRE 'go'; UADERE '"go" making an "impressive … showy advance"';[a] AMBULARE (or possibly *ambi'tare) 'walk'; FUISSE 'have been')*[b]

(a) Calvello, Lucania, southern Italy[c]

	1SG	2SG	3SG	1PL	2PL	3PL
PRS.IND	'vakə	'vajə	'vajə	'jammə	'jatə	'vannə
IPFV.IND	'jivə	'jivə	'jivə	'jivmə	'jivətə	'jivnə

(b) Italian

	1SG	2SG	3SG	1PL	2PL	3PL
PRS.IND	vado	vai	va	andiamo	andate	vanno
PRS.SBJV	vada	vada	vada	andiamo	andiate	vadano
IPFV.IND	andavo	andavi	andava	andavamo	andavate	andavano

(c) Surselvan Romansh[d]

INF	ir

	1SG	2SG	3SG	1PL	2PL	3PL
PRS.IND	mondel	vas	va	mein	meis	van
PRS.SBJV	mondi	mondies	mondi	meien	meies	mondien
IPFV.IND	mavel	mavas	mava	mavan	mavas	mavan

(d) French

	1SG	2SG	3SG	1PL	2PL	3PL
PRS.IND	vais	vas	va	allons	allez	vont
IMP		va		allons	allez	
IPFV.IND	allais	allais	allait	allions	alliez	allaient
FUT	irai	iras	ira	irons	irez	iront

(e) Portuguese

	1SG	2SG	3SG	1PL	2PL	3PL
PRS.IND	vou	vais	vai	vamos	ides	vão
IPFV.IND	ia	ias	ia	íamos	íeis	iam
PRT	fui	foste	foi	fomos	fostes	foram
FUT	irei	irás	irá	iremos	ireis	irão

[a] Adams (2013: 812f.).
[b] These etyma respectively yield forms in *i-* (*j-*), *v-*, *a-*, and *fu-* (*fo-*).
[c] Gioscio (1985).
[d] Spescha (1989: 465). Forms in initial *m-* continue AMBULARE: see Maiden (2018: 195).

Sardinian, and Romanian). Suppletion occurs locally in verbs meaning MUST (Table 12.10), GIVE (Table 12.11), FIND (Table 12.12), TAKE (Table 12.13), FIT (Table 12.14), PULL (Table 12.15), WANT (Table 12.16), SAY (Table 12.17), DRINK (Table 12.18), FALL (Table 12.19), HEAR (Table 12.20), EXIT (Table 12.21), COME (Table 12.23), and HAVE. A special case is Istro-Romanian, which often suppletively distinguishes imperfective from perfective aspect (Table 12.22). In nouns and adjectives, suppletion is very rare: some examples are French EYE (Table 12.24), or singular *œuf* [œf] 'egg' and its plural (under certain circumstances) *œufs* [ø],[8] Megleno-Romanian SMALL (and BIG) (Table 12.25), and nouns that form different forms of their paradigm with distinct derivational affixes in some northern Italo-Romance varieties (Table 12.26), and in Romanian (Table 12.27).

[8] For the relevant circumstances, see Swiggers (1985).

Table 12.10. *MUST (etyma: DEBERE 'must, owe'; *esto'pere 'must, be necessary') Surmiran Romansh (Savognin)*[a]

	1SG	2SG	3SG	1PL	2PL	3PL
PRS.IND	stó	stóst	stó	duágn	duéz	stón
PRS.SBJV	stóptga	stóptgas	stóptga	stóptgan	stóptgas	stóptgan
IPFV	duéva	duévas	duéva	duévan	duévas	duévan

[a] Signorell (1999).

Table 12.11. *GIVE (etyma: DARE 'give'; DONARE 'give, grant, bestow')*[a]

(a) Limone (Liguria-Piedmont border, Italy)[b]						
	1SG	2SG	3SG	1PL	2PL	3PL
PRS.IND	dau	das	da	du'naŋ	du'na	daŋ
(b) Modica (Sicily) ([d] > [r])[c]						
	1SG	2SG	3SG	1PL	2PL	3PL
PRS.IND	'ruɲɲu	'runi	'runa	'ramu	'rati	'rununu

[a] Schmid (1949: 118–29, 140–46); Maiden (2006).
[b] Schädel (1903: 108).
[c] Leone (1980: 142, 144).

Table 12.12. *FIND (etyma: AD+FLARE 'sniff out'; *tro'pare 'find') South-eastern Sicily*[a]

	1SG	2SG	3SG	1PL	2PL	3PL
PRS.IND	'trwɔvu	'trwɔvi	'trɔva	'ʃamu	'ʃati	'trɔvunu

[a] Leone (1980: 38f.).

Table 12.13. *TAKE (etymon: LEUARE 'raise') in Romanian*

	1SG	2SG	3SG	1PL	2PL	3PL
PRS	iau	iei	ia	luăm	luați	iau
IPFV	luam	luai	lua	luam	luați	luau

Table 12.14. *FIT (etyma: CAPERE 'take'; COLLIGERE 'gather in') in Larouco, Province of Ourense, Galicia*[a]

	1SG	2SG	3SG	1PL	2PL	3PL
PRS.IND	'koʎo	'kaβes	'kaβe	kaβemos	'kaβejs	'kaβeŋ
PRS.SBJV	'koʎa	'koʎas	'koʎa	'koʎamos	'koʎajs	'koʎaŋ
IPFV.IND	ka'βia	ka'βias	ka'βia	kaβiamos	kaβiajs	ka'βian
PRT	ko'ʎiŋ	ko'ʎitʃes	ko'ʎew	ko'ʎemos	ko'ʎestes	ko'ʎeron

[a] ALG maps 209–20.

Table 12.15. *PULL (etyma: TRAHERE 'pull'; *ti'rare 'pull') in Romansh (Prez)*[a]

	1SG	2SG	3SG	1PL	2PL	3PL
PRS.IND	tir	'tiras	'tira	tarʲaɲ	tarʲais	'tiran
IPFV.IND	tarʲeva					

[a] Decurtins (1958: 31f.).

Table 12.16. *WANT ((a) etymon: *vo'lere 'want'; (b) etyma: *vo'lere, Sl. voliti 'want')*

(a) Cascinagrossa, Liguria (Italy)[a]						
INF	au'rai					
	1SG	2SG	3SG	1PL	2PL	3PL
PRS.IND	voi	vo	vo	au'roma	au'ri	von
(b) Romanian						
	1SG	2SG	3SG	1PL	2PL	3PL
PRS	vreau	vrei	vrea	vrem	vreți	vor
IPFV	voiam	voiai	voia	voiam	voiați	voiau

[a] Castellani (2002).

Table 12.17. *SAY (etymon: DICERE 'say') in Surselvan Romansh*[a]

	1SG	2SG	3SG	1PL	2PL	3PL
PRS.IND	ditgel	dias	di	schein	scheis	dian
IPFV.IND	schevel					

[a] Spescha (1989: 486).

Table 12.18. *DRINK (etymon: BIBERE 'drink') in Lugo (Romagna, Italy)*[a]

	1SG	2SG	3SG	1PL	2PL	V3PL
PRS.IND	biv	biv	bev	dbē	dbi	bev
FUT	dbi'ro					

[a] Schürr (1956: 473) (also Pelliciardi 1977: 133).

Table 12.19. *FALL (etyma: CADERE 'fall'; *kasi'kare 'fall') in Casacalenda (Molise, Italy)*[a]

INF	kɛ'di					
	1SG	2SG	3SG	1PL	2PL	3PL
PRS.IND	'kaskə	'kjeskə	'kaskə	kɛ'demə or kɛs'kamə	kɛ'detə or kɛs'katə	'kaskənə

[a] Vincelli (1995). Cf. also Pelliciardi (1977: 135).

Table 12.20. *HEAR (etyma: SENTIRE 'feel'; INTENDERE 'understand') in Modica, Sicily*[a]

	1SG	2SG	3SG	1PL	2PL	3PL
PRT	nˈtisi	sinˈtisti	nˈtisi	nˈtisimu	sinˈtistru	nˈtisiru

[a] Da Tos and Benincà (2010: 71).

Table 12.21. *EXIT (etyma: EXIRE 'go out'; It.* uscio *'doorway' < OSTIUM) in Italian*

	1SG	2SG	3SG	1PL	2PL	3PL
PRS.IND	esco	esci	esce	usciamo	uscite	escono
IPFV.IND	uscivo	uscivi	usciva	uscivamo	uscivate	uscivano

Table 12.22. *Istro-Romanian suppletive aspectual distinctions*[a]

IPFV	PFV	
bɛ	poˈpi	'drink'
mənˈka	poiˈdi	'eat'
matʃira	zmeˈʎi	'grind'
aˈra	zoˈri	'plough'
muˈʎa	zmoˈtʃi	'wet'
uˈska	osuˈʃi	'dry'
duˈrɛ	zaboˈli	'hurt'
durˈmi	zasˈpi	'sleep'

[a] See Kovačec (1963: 25–28, 37; 1966: 70f.; 1968: 108f.); also Hurren (1969). The forms in Table 12.22 are given in the infinitive; the etyma of imperfective forms are Romance, those of the perfective Croatian.

Table 12.23. *Suppletion in imperative of COME (etyma: UENIRE; Gk. ἔλα [ela];*[a] *AMBULARE 'walk')*

Megleno-Romanian[b]

	1SG	2SG	3SG	1PL	2PL	3PL
PRS	vin	viɲ	ˈvini	vinim	viˈnits	vin
IMP		ˈjela			viˈnits	

Gallo (AIS point 712)[c]

	1SG	2SG	3SG	1PL	2PL	3PL
PRS	ˈvɛŋgu	ˈvieji	vɛ	məˈnimə	məˈnitə	ˈvɛɣunə
IMP		ˈɣannə			ɣanˈnatə	

[a] ἔλα is the second person singular imperative of the verb COME in Greek.
[b] Capidan (1925: 162, 171).
[c] Cf. maps 1655, 1695; also Maiden (2007: 152f.).

Table 12.24. EYE (etymon: OCULUM 'eye') in French

SG	PL
œil [œj]	yeux [jø]

Table 12.25. SMALL and BIG (etyma: *'miku 'small' + MINUTUS 'chopped small, fine-grained' and MAIOR[a] 'larger, major' + *matju'katu 'knobby')[b] in Megleno-Romanian

	SG		PL	
	M	F	M	F
(a)	mik	'mikə	mìnuts	mìnuti
(b)	'mari	'mari	mətʃkats	mətʃkati

[a] While this etymology is controversial (we follow here Giurgea 2016), it is uncontroversially different from that of the plural.
[b] See Maiden (2014).

Table 12.26. Derivationally related lexemes containing diminutive suffixes of different origin (etyma of the suffixes: *-'inu; *-'ettu (plural *-'itti))[a]

(a) Val Verzasca, Val Leventina, Vallemaggia (Canton Ticino)[b]		(b) Val d'Ossola (Piedmont)[c]	
SG	PL	SG	PL
ʎuˈriɲ 'kid'	ʎuˈrit	skaˈliŋ 'step'	skaˈlit
baˈziɲ 'kiss'	baˈzit	uˈdʒiŋ 'earring'	uˈdʒit
buˈʃiɲ 'calf'	buˈʃit	kydʒaˈrin 'teaspoon'	kydʒaˈrit

[a] Contini (1937); Rohlfs (1968: 43; 1969: 453 n. 3).
[b] See AIS maps 43, 58, 1081, 68.
[c] ALI maps 667, 344, 268, 497.

Table 12.27. Derivationally related lexemes containing diminutive suffixes of different origin (etyma of the suffixes: -ELLA; Sl. *-'ika) in Romanian[a]

	SG	PL	SG	PL
NOMINATIVE-ACCUSATIVE	rândunică 'swallow'	rândunele	viorică 'violet'	viorele
GENITIVE-DATIVE	rândunele	rândunele	viorele	viorele

[a] Cf. Maiden (1999).

12.3 General Determinants and Conditions of Suppletion as Reflected in the Romance Data

12.3.1 Sound Change as Determinant of Suppletion

The suppletions of Section 12.2.5 form two diachronic classes: those combining more than one etymon, and a minority with only one etymon

(Tables 12.13, 12.16a, 12.17, 12.18, 12.24) (see also It. *egli* vs *loro* in Section 12.2.4). The former reflect 'incursion', and are discussed in Section 12.3.2; the others reflect the effects of successive sound changes acting on forms of a single historically underlying lexeme, resulting in allomorphy so extreme that, synchronically, no phonological connexion between allomorphs is discernible. It is these latter that we examine first.

All Romance languages inherit in the verb 'be' (Table 12.8) forms of the Latin imperfective verb originally containing [s].[9] Already in Latin the change [s] > [r] in intervocalic position had taken place in the [s]-root: cf. ESSE (INF); SUM (PRS.IND.1SG); EST (PRS.IND.3SG) vs ERAT (IPFV.IND.3SG). This effect is inherited at least partially in Romance, and further sound changes may exacerbate it: e.g., Pt. *sou* (PRS.IND.1SG); *é* (PRS.IND.3SG); *era* (IPFV.IND.3SG). Romanian *lua* is an example of suppletion arising from the operation of sound changes on a single, invariant root form (Table 12.13). In most of the paradigm the root is *lu*-, but the singular and third person forms of the present and of the subjunctive have an allomorph in *i-* ([j]-). This suppletion actually reflects the accumulated effects of sound changes on the entirely regular Latin verb LEUARE. The verbs WANT in Cascinagrossa (Table 12.16a), SAY in Surselvan (Table 12.17), and DRINK in Romagnol (Table 12.18) owe their modern, unique suppletions almost entirely to sound change: all three have in common phonological differentiation according to whether stress did or did not fall on the root: deletion of the vowel of the lexical root when unstressed, creating complex novel consonant clusters, in turn precipitating adjustments such as vowel prosthesis (Cascinagrossa), assimilation (Surselvan), and dissimilation (Romagnol). The example in Table 12.24 also has a phonological explanation (see, e.g., Price 1971: 69). In the pronominal system, the suppletive Romanian feminine direct object clitic pronouns SG *o* ~ PL *le* (e.g., *O văd* 'her=I.see' ~ *Le văd* 'them.FPL=I.see') both emerge, via sound change, from the Latin feminine accusative demonstrative SG ILLAM ~ PL ILLAS; the French masculine and feminine plural stressed third person pronouns, *eux* [ø] vs *elles* [ɛl], are phonologically regular reflexes of Lat. M.PL ILLOS ~ F.PL ILLAS.

12.3.2 Incursive Suppletion and Its Causes

Corbett (2007: 13) writes:

> within diachrony I distinguish two origins of suppletion: incursion, where outside forms invade a paradigm, and suppletion introduced by sound change, where an originally unified paradigm is split by internal changes (Juge 1999). These are also called COMBINATORY versus DISSIMILATORY suppletion (Plank 1996). Some require the combination of forms with

---

[9] The history of the Latin form is complex (cf. Sihler 1995: 494f.).

different etymologies (incursion) and do not count the second type (sound change) as suppletion. This is not a distinction available to speakers, and it has no part in a synchronic typology ...

We surveyed above suppletion produced by sound change;[10] our focus is now the emergence of 'incursion'[11] – where forms belonging to the paradigm of one lexeme appear in some cells of the paradigm of an originally distinct lexeme – a phenomenon on whose diachronic emergence the Romance data can throw light.

The term 'suppletion' carries a significant, and misleading, implication, being ultimately derived from Latin SUPPLERE, 'to make (a receptacle) full with additional supplies of liquid' (*Oxford Latin Dictionary*). Now 'filling' presupposes a 'void' – the existence of 'empty cells', or 'defectiveness', somewhere in the paradigm. *Incursive* suppletion trivially involves *diachronic* defectiveness, in that 'something is missing' because the etymon whose reflexes appear in some cells of the inflexional paradigm of a lexeme is not continued (i.e., is defective) in some other cells of that paradigm. Synchronically, incursive suppletion is, as Corbett says, indistinguishable from phonologically induced suppletion, for which there was never any void in the paradigm. Defectiveness has at best a very limited role in determining suppletion (see also Corbett 2007: 13f.), but suppletion *can* sometimes arise in response to it. The Latin verb BE lacked a past participle, but the rise in early Romance of periphrastic perfective verb-forms comprising auxiliary + past participle (cf. Sections 19.3.2–3) created pressure for every verb to have its own past participle. For Italian and Catalan (and most Italo- and Gallo-Romance varieties), the 'missing' form was 'borrowed' from a verb semantically close to ESSE, namely STARE 'stand, be (stationary)', whence the respective past participles *stato*, *estat* (Table 12.8). In both languages the continuant of STARE still exists, its past participle remaining *stato*, *estat*, but it would be absurd to suppose that this verb still 'fills' a gap in the paradigm of BE, for that gap was filled centuries ago: the two verbs simply continue to share a form. A spectacular example of diachronic suppletive 'gap-filling' occurs in Istro-Romanian (Table 12.22): historically, Romanian varieties, like other Romance languages, do not morphologically distinguish imperfective and perfective aspect (outside the past indicative): but Istro-Romanians' bilingualism in Croatian – a Slavonic language characterized by robust (indeed, sometimes suppletive) morphological aspectual distinctions throughout the verb paradigm – created a structural need for distinctive aspectually perfective forms throughout the paradigm of virtually all Istro-Romanian verbs. The required perfective forms are often created by

---

[10] Also labelled 'pseudo-suppletion' by Rudes (1980: 660), 'phonological suppletion' by Börjars and Vincent (2011: 241).
[11] Also labelled 'true' suppletion by Rudes (1980: 662), 'proper suppletion' by Börjars and Vincent (2011).

borrowing a Croatian lexeme for the perfective, the inherited Romance lexeme continuing to express imperfective (see, e.g., Sala 2013: 222f.). Such structurally conditioned gap-filling does not necessarily result in suppletion, however: old Italian also 'invented' an analogical past participle for BE, (es) suto, based on infinitive essere, while Istro-Romanian also forms perfectives non-suppletively (e.g., by using a native Istro-Romanian form differentiated by, say, a Croatian prefix: e.g., IPFV laˈtra ~ PFV zalaˈtra 'bark').

The most puzzling and problematic aspect of incursive suppletion in inflexional paradigms is how originally distinct lexemes ever became conflated into the inflexional paradigm of a single lexeme. How and why would speakers cobble together bizarre allomorphies from different lexemes? After all, there is a principle known as 'Humboldt's Universal', formulated by Vennemann (1978: 259), which states that '[s]uppletion is undesirable, uniformity of linguistic symbolization is desirable: both roots and grammatical markers should be unique and constant'. This notion that speakers prefer an ideally iconic one-to-one relation between form and meaning, often taken as self-evident, underpins semiotically based theories such as Natural Morphology (see, e.g., the studies in Dressler 1987), where the optimal and natural relation between signans and signatum is assumed to be of that kind. The general validity of the notion is also implicit in Clark's (1987; 1993) experimentally grounded 'principle of contrast', which states that children acquiring their native language tend to assume that 'every two forms contrast in meaning'; synonyms are therefore avoided; it follows that forms not contrasting in meaning tend to be rejected (see especially Clark 1993: 115, 119–22). There are countless cases in Romance (and elsewhere) where that principle apparently operates by eliminating all but one variant: for example, in the history of French or Catalan, reflexes of Lat. DARE 'give' have been wholly eliminated by those of Lat. DONARE, originally meaning 'grant, bestow' (cf. Fr. donner 'give'). Maiden (2004; 2006) suggests that incursive suppletion in inflexional paradigms is generally motivated by avoidance of synonymy, and that one strategy by which speakers deal with emergent lexical synonymy is to assign to the co-existing lexemes distinctive, purely morphological, meanings, allocating them to complementary subdomains within inflexional paradigms which are already recurrent loci of allomorphy (of any kind) within the language. These 'distributional domains' will be addressed in Section 12.3.3.

That synonymy is 'avoided' does not mean that it cannot exist, indeed we shall see that synonymy is apparently a precondition for the emergence of many examples of suppletion; but at least in the acquisition process speakers seem to disfavour it and have strategies (including suppletion) for avoiding it. Now 'synonymy' can perfectly well exist if the synonyms initially belong to different linguistic systems, but language contact can cause them to coexist in the minds of speakers. It is surely plausible that frequent exposure to distinct forms that mean the same thing, but remain distinguished by the fact that they belong to different varieties, can produce synonymy once speakers cease to perceive clearly that they belong to different systems. Consider Table 12.11: Romance languages generally inherited Lat. DARE for 'give', but in Gallo-Romance (with Catalan) this verb has been replaced by reflexes of DONARE (cf. Schmid 1949: 118–29, 140–46). Independently, both in north-western Italy at the frontier between Gallo-Romance and Italo-Romance varieties, and in Sicily and Calabria most probably through contact of indigenous varieties with Norman French in the Middle Ages (see Maiden 2006), these two verbs came into contact. Thus, in Limone, on the Liguria-Piedmont border (Schädel 1903: 108), and adjacent to the Occitan speaking area, we find reflexes of DARE in the singular and third person cells of the present tense, but apparently DONARE elsewhere in the paradigm. A similar distribution appears in Occitan dialects of the Po valley in northern Italy (Zörner 2008: 158f.). In the southern Italian dialects, the distribution of the etymologically distinct lexemes in suppletion is reversed, DONARE appearing in singular and third person cells of the present, DARE elsewhere. We assume that there must have been a phase in which forms from the two lexemes were used synonymously and interchangeably, i.e., a phase in which overabundance, rather than defectiveness, occurred; then one of the two synonymous forms was discarded (but cases in which overabundance between weakly suppletive forms has persisted for centuries have been documented, cf. Thornton 2012; 2019b).

Note that for incursive suppletion to emerge it does not have to be that every sense of one lexeme is mirrored in the other. Nor need there be 'complementary distribution' in the suppletive distribution of forms of one lexeme and those of the other (although there usually is): incursive suppletion may be 'overlapping' and 'directional', in that one of the suppleting lexemes retains a full inflexional paradigm including meanings not found in the emergent suppletive paradigm, yet still shares forms with the other. Maiden (2006: 91–93) reviews evidence that in old Sicilian incursion of DONARE into DARE was 'asymmetrical', the former suppleting the latter, while itself surviving with a complete paradigm of its own preserving the meaning 'donate'. The determining factor for suppletion is not, therefore, 'global' synonymy between lexemes but rather the systematic and recurrent existence of contexts where the semantic distinction between the lexemes is effaced. If reflexes of DONARE were repeatedly used in contexts with a meaning indistinguishable from that of reflexes of DARE, regardless of whatever additional senses DONARE had, the stage was set for suppletion. This consideration is valid not only for contact-induced suppletion, but for other sources of the phenomenon, considered later.

There are other examples of suppletion arising from contact between Italo- and Gallo-Romance. FIND is expressed in many languages

(Table 12.12) by a reflex of AD+FLARE (e.g., Pt. *achar*, Ro. *afla*), which also occurs in Puglia, Basilicata, Calabria, and Sicily; most of Italy, with Gallo-Romance and Raeto-Romance, has the type represented by It. *trovare* (see Maiden 2006: 91). Almost certainly reflecting contact with Norman French in Sicily (Leone 1980: 36–39, 91f.), we find suppletive incursion of *tro'pare into AD+FLARE. Da Tos and Benincà (2010: 71) also illustrate incursive suppletion in Modica in Sicily (Table 12.20), such that reflexes of INTENDERE are suppletively integrated into the preterite of SENTIRE 'hear'. The use of a reflex of INTENDERE to mean 'hear' is attested elsewhere in Italo-Romance (notably in the past participle in southern Italian dialects) and in Sardinian, but it is also characteristic of Gallo-Romance (cf. Fr. *entendre* 'hear'), and possibly in this case, again, contact with (Norman) French favoured the emergence of synonymy with two verbs meaning 'hear', and then of suppletion.

In Table 12.19, 'fall' suppletively combines reflexes of CADERE and *kasi'kare, in a Molisan dialect. These verbs coexist widely in central and northern Italy, and in Italian *cadere* and *cascare* are virtually synonyms, the differences being connotational not denotational (*cascare* carries a heavier expressive charge).[12] In any case, the region from which our example comes lies on the southern periphery of that in which reflexes of innovatory *kasi'kare are regularly found; dialects to the south uniformly show only reflexes of CADERE.[13] So the *kasi'kare type may be an innovation spreading southwards, among speakers for whom the distinct connotations of these verbs may be opaque. The result is suppletion. Other examples of language contact as a generator of suppletion appear in Ro. *vrea* 'want' (< proto-Romance *vo'lere), where the current standard imperfect (*voiam* etc.) is the imperfect of another verb of the same meaning, *voi*, from Sl. *voliti* (Table 12.16). There is also a suppletive distribution of reflexes of *pi'ljare (*pigliare*) and PRAEHENDERE (*prendere*) 'take' in Tuscan, such that the latter is the source of the past participle of *pigliare* (*preso*): this fact is ascribed by Jaberg (1959: 30) to Tuscan's position between northern Italo-Romance, where reflexes of PRAEHENDERE persist, and central and southern Italo-Romance where TAKE is expressed by reflexes of *pil'jare. Where reflexes of CAPERE and COLLIGERE 'fit' integrate into a suppletive paradigm in various Galician dialects (Table 12.14), this is apparently an effect of dialect mixing, given that various Ibero-Romance dialects have replaced the reflex of CAPERE with that of COLLIGERE. In fact, *ALG* maps 209–20 show numerous cases in Galicia where either verb may still be used with the same meaning. Finally, while in Gallo-Romance the verb HAVE continues HABERE 'have', Ibero-Romance with Catalan has replaced HABERE with TENERE 'hold'. The

---

[12] See www.accademiadellacrusca.it/it/lingua-italiana/consulenza-linguistica/domande-risposte/cadere-cascare.
[13] See, e.g., *AIS* maps 220, 394, 1621, 1622.

Atlas linguistique et ethnographique du Languedoc occidental shows that in the Occitan of Rodome and Paziols,[14] bordering on the Catalan area, TENERE penetrates some present tense cells of the verb meaning HAVE, reflexes of Latin HABERE apparently surviving elsewhere in the paradigm: e.g., Paziols PRS.IND 1SG ˈteni 2SG ˈtenes 3SG tɛ̃n 1PL aˈβɛ̃n 2PL aˈβɛts 3PL ˈtenũn; IPFV 1SG aβˈjo.

Another, language-internal, determinant of synonymy (and, potentially, suppletion) depends on interactions between the lexical meaning of different lexemes and grammatical meanings defining specific cells of their paradigms. The reflex of DEBERE, namely *dueir*, is discontinued in some cells of the present indicative and present subjunctive in Surmiran (Table 12.10),[15] where it is supplanted by a continuant of proto-Romance *estoˈpere (namely *stueir*), a verb ultimately formed from the Latin impersonal expression EST OPUS 'it is necessary'. This is a matter of 'directional', 'overlapping' incursion, since *stueir* retains a full paradigm of its own, as an independent verb. These verbs generally have slightly different meanings, mirroring the German distinction between *sollen* 'must, be morally obliged' (= *dueir*) and *müssen* 'must, be necessary' (= *stueir*), and we should bear in mind that Romansh speakers have long been bilingual in German. Maiden (2011a; 2011b; 2017; 2018: 215–17) appeals to the tendency to avoid 'face-threatening' situations where the use of a verb of moral obligation imposes a duty which the subject of the verb might fail to meet, with consequent shame or humiliation. This risk is most acute if the relevant verb is used in present (rather than past or counterfactual) tense-forms, and Romansh accordingly replaces present forms of *dueir* with those of *stueir* 'must necessarily'. Maiden further argues, crucially, that resultant frequent use of *stueir* in lieu of *dueir* particularly in the present tense tended to blur the semantic distinction between the two in that part of the paradigm, creating a kind of 'paradigmatically local indistinctness', and ultimately favouring suppletive integration of forms of *stueir* into some cells of the paradigm of *dueir*. It is true that this explanation suggests that suppletion ought to occur particularly in the *second person* present, both singular and plural. That this is not the distribution which has emerged reflects different, and additional, paradigmatic organizational forces, which will be discussed in Section 12.3.3.[16]

Ledgeway (2009: 641–49) describes for the history of Neapolitan the emergence of a suppletive distinction in the verb HAVE between the reflex of TENERE 'hold' with imperfective meaning vs the reflex of HABERE 'have'

---

[14] Thanks to Louise Esher for drawing attention to these unpublished data.
[15] This example has been the object of debate between Anderson and Maiden. Anderson (2008; 2010; 2011; 2013) essentially posits defectiveness: *dueir* lacks a phonologically appropriate alternant for root-stressed cells of the paradigm, so forms of *stueir* fill the gaps. For counterarguments see Maiden (2011a; 2017; 2018: 212–15).
[16] Maiden (2011a; 2017) gives more details.

with perfective meaning. This, too, may be a case of semantically induced overlap between lexemes and certain cells of the inflexional paradigms, the original sense of 'hold' or 'possess' inherent in TENERE predisposing this verb to occupy cells with imperfective or durative meaning.

The case of SMALL and BIG in Megleno-Romanian (Table 12.25) is similar, but here the generator of 'local' synonymy is the relation between lexical meaning and the meaning PLURAL. In fact, adjectives indicating size, especially SMALL, are a locus of suppletion for number cross-linguistically, including Danish and Swedish, and Middle Cornish and Middle Breton (cf. Nurmio 2017). Briefly, the modern Danish and Swedish lexemes meaning SMALL continue old Scandinavian *lítil* 'small' in the singular, but the unrelated *smár* in the plural. Börjars and Vincent (2011: 250; also 255) observe that the latter may also be used with singular nouns, and in this case the nouns 'are often collectives and the adjective has a distributive meaning ... or it means "consisting of small parts"'. This (and the fact that the reflex of *smár* has meanings which that of *lítil* lacks, such as 'mean-spirited'), leads them to challenge the view that incursive suppletion is driven by avoidance of synonymy. They suggest (Börjars and Vincent 2011: 262) that

> the development of a suppletive relation is driven by a semantic asymmetry. In particular, one of the members in the asymmetric pair will have a more general meaning, we refer to this as the dominant element, and another will have a partly overlapping but also more specific meaning, the recessive member of the pair. The dominant element forms the basis for the new suppletive paradigm, with the recessive lexeme providing the suppletive forms. In other words, the suppletive pattern resolves the asymmetry in favour of the more general item. This in turn means that suppletion always involves semantic 'loss' or 'generalization'.

However, invocation of mere 'asymmetry', rather than synonymy, as a condition for suppletion seems an undesirable weakening of the theory. In fact, all incursive suppletions observable in the Romance languages can plausibly be accounted for in terms of synonymy, and the case of the word for SMALL, cited by Börjars and Vincent is, on closer examination, an excellent example of how synonymy is relevant to the emergence of the phenomenon. The Megleno-Romanian data are remarkably similar to the Scandinavian: the lexemes furnishing the plural of the word for SMALL (miˈnut) and for BIG (məʧˈkat) refer to 'part size', and can be applied to collective and mass nouns in the singular with meanings, respectively, of 'having small parts, chopped up fine' and 'having large parts, coarse-grained, lumpy' (for etymological details and semantic development, see Maiden 2014; also Nurmio 2017: 138f.). Indeed, Nurmio shows that there is a strong cross-linguistic correlation, in the typologically rare cases of number suppletion in adjectives for SMALL, such that the plural involves a word originally meaning 'consisting of small parts'. Maiden (2014) argues that, contrary to Börjars' and Vincent's belief, the meaning of these size adjectives provides powerful evidence *for* the determining role of synonymy. *Specifically in the plural*, an adjective meaning 'having small/large parts', may be significantly ambiguous, overlapping in meaning *just in the plural* with the simple meaning small/large. This is because that adjective can apply either to each element of a plurality (each element is fine-/coarse-grained) or it can apply to the plurality overall (the plurality is fine-/coarse-grained). In the latter sense we have emergent synonymy, since saying that a plurality is fine-/coarse-grained is tantamount to saying that each of its components is 'small/big': thus in Megleno-Romanian, miˈnut and məʧˈkat may be synonymous with mik and ˈmari, but only in the plural. Nurmio (2017: 150) suggests that Maiden's view is

> not incompatible with Börjars and Vincent, since they look at the whole lexeme as opposed to treating the singular and plural separately. If we look at the paradigms of *liten* and *små* as a whole there is indeed partial overlap (mostly in the singular) but full synonymy can occur in the plural cell of the paradigm.

The crucial difference remains, however, that in Maiden's view it *must* be the case that for some cell(s) of the paradigm there exists genuine synonymy: 'semantic overlap' is a likely context for the emergence of such synonymy – indeed it is hard to see how synonymy could ever emerge between words that did not show some prior semantic overlap – but it remains insufficient to determine suppletion.

The verb BE also shows effects of 'paradigmatically local' synonymy. Perfective forms, at least in contexts indicating 'destination reached', can become indistinguishable from the meaning 'go (to)'. Indeed, sometimes BE seems more natural than GO in such contexts: e.g., Eng. 'Are you going there? No, I've already been', or Fr. *Ça va?* lit. 'Does it go? (= How are things?)', to which the natural response using the present is *Ça va*, but in the perfect is *Ça a été* lit. 'it has been'. It is almost certainly this fact which explains how in Portuguese and Spanish the preterite (a perfective form) of *ir* 'go' came to be suppletively expressed by the preterite of the verb BE (compare Tables 12.8d and 12.9e).[17]

Table 12.23 suggests that introduction of other etyma into the imperative of the verb COME may also be explicable by appeal to synonymy, in some cases favoured by language contact. But the propensity of imperatives to suppletion may have a special status, as argued by Maiden (2006: 56f.; 2007:

---

[17] The verb BE also appears in pluperfect and non-present subjunctives because these tenses systematically share the root allomoph of the preterite (see, e.g., Maiden 2018: 62–67).

154f.), in that imperatives (especially of the second person singular) seem in certain respects morphologically 'detached' from the rest of the paradigm, possibly being acquired before other forms, and having broadly the status of interjections (see also Veselinova 2006: 144f.), standing apart from the verb with which they are associated. So much so that one even finds in Daco-Romance (Maiden 2006: 54–56) verbs that only exist as imperatives and might better be described as something like 'inflected interjections'.

Finally, the data in Tables 12.26 and 12.27 are probably to be viewed synchronically not as suppletion in a derivational diminutive suffix, with SG -ʹin ~ PL -ʹit, but rather as suppletion within lexemes, where singular and plural share a root but bear different derivational affixes.[18] There is no evidence that there has ever been a clear denotational distinction between the suffixes, and it is famously a characteristic of evaluative derivational suffixes that they can coexist without clear semantic distinction (cf. Beard 1995). In the history of Italo-Romance, for example, reflexes of *-ʹettu (plural *-ʹitti) and those of *-ʹinu seem for centuries to have jostled for position as the more productive diminutive suffix. Our suggestion is that the resultant synonymous coexistence of derived forms with one or the other suffix has been systematically resolved in such a way that the reflex of *-ʹinu is assigned to the singular, and that of *-ʹettu to the plural, as in Val d'Ossola SG urˈdʒiŋ 'earring' ~ PL urˈdʒit.[19]

It is not possible to show for every incursive suppletion that what historically underlies it is synonymy between originally different lexemes, but we submit that in all the Romance examples listed there are contexts leading to overlap such that distinct forms can no longer be clearly mapped onto distinct meanings. For example, it is easy to imagine scenarios – especially at a time when most human beings or animals 'going' anywhere went on foot – in which the distinction between AMBULARE 'go on foot' and IRE 'go' would become effaced in actual usage. We maintain that synonymy is a crucial and recurrent factor in the emergence of incursive suppletion. In some cases, the existence of synonymy peculiar to specific areas of the

---

[18] In this respect these examples are different from the typical examples of suppletion in which two lexically identical forms simply seem to be different 'words'. These are historically 'different words' in that they are originally rival, derivationally-formed, lexemes. See also the discussion in Maiden (2018: 175–92) of paradigmatic fusion of originally derivationally related sets of verb-forms, again constituting a kind of suppletion, despite phonological similarities. A different type of example, with a rather similar historical status, is It. SG *dio* 'god' ~ PL *dei*. This is not obviously 'suppletive', in that its (unique) alternation is no more extreme than, say MSG *mio* 'my' ~ MPL *miei*, or SG *bue* 'ox' ~ PL *buoi*, both of which have a phonological explanation in diachrony – although they might also be considered 'weakly suppletive'. *Dio* and *dei* have a common etymon in Latin DEUS, but they are 'different words', and therefore arguably 'suppletive', in that while *dio* is 'popular', *dei* is a learnèd borrowing from Classical Latin. The suppletive difference was also to some extent motivated by the fact that in a monotheistic society a plural of 'God' was inconceivable, and therefore 'gods' must be something different, pagan 'gods'. Since, however, *dio* can also mean any kind of 'god' (including a pagan one), there is semantic overlap.

[19] For additional specific reasons why *-ea* was replaced by *-ică* in Romanian, see Maiden (1999: 324–36).

12.3.3 The Paradigmatic Distribution of Suppletion

In principle, one might have as many different paradigmatic arrangements of suppletion as the number of cells in the paradigm and the number of different lexemes in play would permit. Assuming a paradigm with 40 cells, and two lexemes, the potential distributions would number in the trillions. Moreover, suppletions for the same pairs of etyma could vary erratically from dialect to dialect. Remarkably, then, the distributional patterns in Section 12.2.5 are practically the only ones found in Romance.[20] In verbs, most incursive suppletions are arranged in such a way that one lexeme occupies all the singular and third person cells of the present and imperative, while the other occupies all or most of the complementary cells of the paradigm. This is true (reasons of space do not allow presentation of full paradigms) of Tables 12.9a, 12.9b, 12.9d, 12.10, 12.11, 12.12, 12.13, 12.15, and 12.19.[21] Table 12.14 shows present subjunctive and first person singular present indicative as a suppleting domain. Finally, Table 12.20 shows first person singular, third person singular, first person plural, and third person plural of the preterite as a domain for suppletion: the example is not isolated, for in some dialects of Calabria (see, e.g., Maiden 2018: 290), the reflex of DONARE penetrates that of DARE in exactly those cells.

It is no accident that all our examples of *phonological*, non-incursive, suppletion (Tables 12.13, 12.16a, 12.17, 12.18) also distinguish the singular and third person forms of the present (and imperative) from the rest of the paradigm. These cases are purely the result of sound change, and are extreme examples of a type of phonologically caused allomorphy which permeates practically all Romance languages (see also Section 11.4.1.2), reflecting the historically regular effects of alternating stress. Typically, albeit with significant exceptions, in Latin as in Romance, stress fell on the root of the verb just in the singular and third person of the present tense and imperative, and on the ending everywhere else in the paradigm. In the history of Romance, vowels were typically subject to reduction and even deletion in unstressed syllables, but tended on the contrary to undergo various kinds of differentiation (including diphthongization) when stressed: consequently, recurrent, and varied, patterns of allomorphy

---

[20] The verb BE is a special case.
[21] The present subjunctive in some of our examples (e.g., Table 12.10) deviates from this distribution. The reasons lie beyond the scope of this chapter. Suffice it to say here that when this happens, it is also true of other kinds of allomorphy originally induced by sound change.

Table 12.28. *Preterite of* HAVE *in S. Michele di Ganzaria (Sicily, AIS map 1700, point 875)*

1SG	2SG	3SG	1PL	2PL	3PL
ˈɛppi	aˈvisti	ˈɛppi	ˈɛppimu	aˈvistivu	ˈɛppinu

rapidly arose in the verb in virtually all Romance languages (see, e.g., Maiden 1992; 2018: 167–73).

Most incursive suppletions in the Romance verb have simply 'slotted' into a recurrent existing pattern of allomorphy, and particularly those given above. In Table 12.14, the fact that *coller* 'fit' has invaded the paradigm of *caber* in the cells of the present subjunctive and first person singular present indicative precisely replicates a recurrent characteristic of Galician (and many other Romance languages), caused originally by palatalization of root-final velar consonants, such that the relevant cells became phonologically differentiated from the rest of the paradigm (cf. Maiden 2018: 84–91). The pattern seen in Table 12.20 replicates a characteristic and idiosyncratic Italo-Romance pattern of root allomorphy (cf. Maiden 2017), such that just the first person singular, third person singular and plural, and (locally) first person plural, display a special and unique root-allomorph: this is what we see, for example, in the preterite of 'have' in S. Michele di Ganzaria in Table 12.28.

Finally, the fact that future (together with the conditional, e.g., Fr. *irais* '(I) would go') is the sole locus of reflexes of Lat. IRE 'go' in French (Table 12.9d), is because the French future (and conditional) is a common locus of special, but phonologically induced, allomorphy (e.g., INF *venir* 'come', *avoir* 'know', FUT.1SG *viendrai*; *aurai*). In short, incursive suppletions, although they have no connexion in origin with sound change or other internal sources of allomorphy, nonetheless seem to 'seek out' and follow the distributional patterns of these latter. This, we suggest, is a crucial aspect of the role played by synonymy avoidance in incursion: speakers resolve synonymy by assigning the synonymous lexemes a kind of intra-morphological 'meaning', aligning them precisely with systematic, independently motivated patterns of allomorphy. Whether, and to what extent, this is true for the histories of other language families, awaits further research.

12.3.4 The Role of Phonological Resemblance in Determining Incursive Suppletion

Suppletion canonically involves semantic identity between forms that are completely different phonologically. Yet it is striking how many examples of incursive suppletion show some phonological similarity,[22] notably but not exclusively in their initial segments: consider Tables 12.11, 12.14, 12.15, 12.16b, 12.19, 12.25. Such resemblances occasionally occur because the lexemes are distant cognates (thus CADERE and *kasiˈkare, DARE and DONARE, and *voˈlere and Sl. *voliti*), but at the synchronic stage preceding the emergence of suppletion these resemblances are accidental. A corollary of the observation that suppletion is favoured where there is imperfect lexical identity between forms may indeed be that it is also favoured where there is incomplete phonological distinction between lexemes. This, too, is an issue deserving wider cross-linguistic investigation.

12.4 Conclusion

The Romance languages appear typologically unremarkable in respect of suppletion, and they confirm the general picture that suppletion seems limited to high-frequency, semantically basic terms.[23] What the Romance comparative-historical evidence suggests, however, is that incursive suppletion is driven by a tendency to avoid synonymy (especially liable to involve lexemes of low semantic specificity, and favoured by language contact). One manifestation of this is the allocation of synonymous lexemes to complementary subdomains of inflexional paradigms, those domains usually being defined by existing, and mostly phonologically caused, patterns of root allomorphy.

Of course, the Romance facts raise at least as many questions as they answer: 'why do speakers resort to suppletion in any given case, rather than simply eliminate variation?', and 'what determines the allocation of forms of one lexeme to one set of cells, and those of its counterpart to the complementary set, rather than the reverse?' The answers may arise from parallel investigations in other language families.

Selected References

Below you can find selected references for this chapter. The full references can be found online at the following page: www.cambridge.org/Romancelinguistics

Aski, J. (1995). 'Verbal suppletion: an analysis of Italian, French and Spanish to go', *Linguistics* 33: 403–32.

---

[22] Phonological similarities are less surprising in phonologically induced suppletions.

[23] The Istro-Romanian examples in Table 12.22, where incursive suppletion is argued to be a response to 'structural pressure' to create novel distinct grammatical forms, is an exception, in that lexemes of relatively specific semantic content (e.g., 'grind', or 'plough') are involved. It may be that suppletion arising from defectiveness in this way is not inherently restricted to basic vocabulary.

Börjars, K. and Vincent, N. (2011). 'The pre-conditions for suppletion'. In Galani, A., Hicks, G., and Toulas, G. (eds), *Morphology and Its Interfaces*. Amsterdam: Benjamins, 239–65.

Corbett, G. (2007). 'Canonical typology, suppletion, and possible words'. *Language* 83: 8–42.

Dressler, W. (1985). 'Sur le statut de la suppléance dans la Morphologie Naturelle', *Langages* 78: 41–56.

Fertig, D. (1998). 'Suppletion, natural morphology and diagrammaticity', *Linguistics* 36: 1065–91.

Juge, M. (1999). 'On the rise of suppletion in verbal paradigms', *Berkeley Linguistics Society* 25: 183–94.

Maiden, M. (2004). 'When lexemes become allomorphs: on the genesis of suppletion', *Folia Linguistica* 38: 227–56.

Maiden, M. (2014). 'Two suppletive adjectives in Megleno-Romanian'. *Revue Romane*. 49: 32–51.

Melčuk, I. (2000). 'Suppletion'. In Booij, G., Lehmann, C., & Mugdan, J. (eds), *Morphologie. Ein internationales Handbuch zur Flexion und Wortbildung/ Morphology. An International Handbook on Inflection and Word-Formation*. Berlin/New York: Walter de Gruyter, 510–22.

Nurmio, S. (2017). 'The development and typology of number suppletion in adjectives', *Diachronica* 34: 127–74.

Rudes, B. (1980). 'On the nature of verbal suppletion', *Linguistics* 18: 655–76.

Veselinova, L. (2006). *Suppletion in Verb Paradigms*. Amsterdam: Benjamins.

13

Inflexion, Derivation, Compounding

Chiara Cappellaro and Judith Meinschaefer

13.1 Introduction

There is a long tradition of scholarly literature on the distinction between inflexion and word-formation (the latter comprising derivation and compounding), and particularly on the distinction between inflexion vs derivation on the one hand (for a review see Booij 2000; 2006; Hacken 2014; Štekauer 2015a) and derivation vs compounding on the other (see Hacken 2000; Olsen 2014). There are two basic conceptions of the nature of this distinction, i.e., the view that inflexion and word-formation (derivation in particular) can be conceived as (i) neatly discrete categories or as (ii) non-discrete categories or processes which are defined on the basis of 'prototypical' properties (Štekauer 2015a) that are found at two opposite poles of a continuum. The aim of this chapter is to discuss how data from Romance languages highlight the problems presented by the traditional idea of a sharp distinction between discrete categories corresponding to inflexion and derivation (and compounding).

It is generally agreed that an important criterion for distinguishing between inflexion and word-formation is the 'function' that inflexional and word-formation processes have, in the sense that inflexion involves the creation of different wordforms of the same 'lexeme',[1] while derivation and compounding involve the creation of new lexemes (see, e.g., the discussion in Baerman 2015). In turn, by compounding we understand the

---

[1] Lexeme (cf. Matthews 1991) is a technical term that indicates, within a lexeme-based theory of morphology (as opposed to a morpheme-based theory, see Blevins 2016 for a recent discussion), 'a (potential or actual) member of a major lexical category, having both form and meaning but being neither, and existing outside of any particular syntactic context' (Aronoff 1994: 11). Following Matthews, it is customary to use one wordform (the citation form) in small capital letters to indicate the abstract lexeme (for verbs, it is the infinitive – cf. CANTARE, for nouns it is the singular form – cf. STORIA).

formation of a new lexeme from two (or more) lexemes, while derivation is usually understood as the formation of a new lexeme on the basis of a lexeme and an affix.

For example, It. *cantiamo* 'sing.PRS.1PL', *cantavamo* 'sing.PST.IPFV.1PL', and *cantare* 'sing.INF' are all inflected forms of one and the same 'word' or 'lexeme' (CANTARE) – a relationship that is prototypical of inflexion. On the other hand, It. *cantatore* 'he who sings' (CANTATORE) is an instance of derivation from an existing lexeme (CANTARE) plus a derivational affix (-/tore/). Moreover, the noun *cantastorie* 'story-teller' (CANTASTORIE) is formed by the combination of the two lexemes CANTARE 'to sing' and STORIA 'story' and is a prototypical example of compounding.

However, a neat functional distinction (in the sense of 'function' discussed above) is not always viable because determining what the lexical relatedness between forms is (same vs distinct lexeme) can be challenging. While matters are uncontroversial for the examples given above, it is much less clear whether Sp. *rápido* 'fast.MSG', *rápida* 'fast.FSG', *rápidos* 'fast.MPL', and *rápidamente* 'fast.ADV' are all forms of the same lexeme, or whether the adverb *rápidamente* is a 'new' lexeme that is different from its adjectival base lexeme *rápido*.

From a formal rather than 'functional' point of view, the morphological mechanisms that are available in inflexion may also be available in derivation (and compounding). For example, the wordforms *cant-iamo*, *cant-avamo*, *cant-are* vs *canta-tore* are constructed through the same formal means of suffixation. The fact that with respect to form and constituency there appear to exist but few differences between inflexion, derivation, and compounding once again highlights the difficulties of assuming a neat distinction.

Ultimately, the distinction between inflexion, derivation, and compounding, however it is to be drawn, relates to the question whether they are located in different modules of grammar. A classic view is the 'Split Morphology' hypothesis (Perlmutter 1988), which assumes that inflexion and word-formation are separated in the grammar. On this view, inflexion is the part of morphology relevant to syntax (Anderson 1982), while word-formation is located in the lexicon. Many scholars have argued that such a strict distinction is untenable; we will not repeat the arguments here (see, for instance, Booij 1994). Still, for a long time the discussion has been characterized by modular theoretical models such as Lexical Phonology and Morphology (Kiparsky 1982) or lexicalist approaches such as Lexical Functional Grammar (Bresnan 1982) and Head-driven Phrase Structure Grammar. More recently, with the advent of parallel, non-modular models such as Optimality Theory, even in its stratal version (see Kiparsky 2015 for an overview), or Construction Grammar and Morphology (Booij 2009; 2010; 2012) and Parallel Architecture (Booij and Audring 2017; Jackendoff and

Audring 2018), the discussion has become less orthodox. An exception is Distributed Morphology (Halle and Marantz 1993) – see McGinnis-Archibald (2016) for an introduction – a strictly non-lexicalist theory which nevertheless makes strong assumptions about modularity and the derivational nature of grammar which also have implications for the distinctions between inflexion and word-formation. Yet, Distributed Morphology's conception of the division of labour between syntax and morphology does not coincide with traditional views. In this chapter, we will not discuss any of these proposals; rather, the focus lies on drawing attention to phenomena found in modern Romance varieties as well as processes of language change that pose challenges to the idea that inflexion, derivation, and compounding may reside in distinct modules of the grammar. In what follows, we employ the classical term 'Split Morphology' to refer, in an imprecise but easily recognizable fashion, to any such assumption.

The structure of the chapter is the following. Section 13.2 outlines some of the basic characteristics of inflexion, derivation, and compounding in Romance languages. Section 13.3 explores issues with form and constituency. Section 13.4 focuses on inflexion and derivation, while Section 13.5 discusses the interaction between inflexion, derivation, and compounding in 'conversion'.

13.2 Basic Characteristics of Inflexion, Derivation, and Compounding in Romance

13.2.1 Introduction

A recent overview of the basic characteristics of inflexion in Romance can be found in Maiden (2016b). As regards word-formation, see the discussion in Rainer (2016) for derivation and Forza and Scalise (2016) for compounding, but also the chapters dedicated to individual Romance languages in Müller et al. (2015). In this section we refer to the selected features that will be fundamental for our discussion in the rest of this chapter.

13.2.2 Inflexion

Romance varieties (both standard languages and non-standardized dialects) are typologically fusional, like Latin. Words are generally segmentable into a lexical root and an inflexional desinence or suffix.[2] Pan-Romance features

---

[2] However, despite sub-word segmentability, a morpheme-based analysis is generally untenable for Romance as much as it is for Latin (Matthews 1972), given the pervasive presence of cumulative exponence and stem allomorphy, for example, or uninflectability (morphological invariance), zero exponence, empty morphs, and syncretism.

Table 13.1. *Italian noun* divano *'sofa.(M)SG'*

	SG	PL
	divan-o	divan-i

Table 13.2. *Italian adjective* buono *'good.MSG'*

	SG	PL
M	buon-o	buon-i
F	buon-a	buon-e

Table 13.3. *Romanian noun* fată *'girl.(F)SG'*

	SG	PL
NOM≡ACC	fată	fete
GEN≡DAT	fete	fete

in the verb are person, number, tense, and mood. For example, the It. wordform *amo* 'I love' can be segmented into a lexical root /am/- and a suffix -/o/ which is an exponent of first person, singular number, present tense, and indicative mood (see also Figures 3.1 and 3.2).

In Romance, nominal[3] categories show the inflexional features number and gender,[4] while case is only relevant in Daco-Romance to different degrees according to the type of nominal (determiner, quantifier, noun bearing definite article, or bare noun) and gender/number combination (see Pană Dindelegan 2013: 230f.): for bare nouns and adjectives, for example, case is relevant only in relation to feminines, as illustrated in Table 13.3.

In addition, Romance personal pronouns mark the feature person, and generally (but not always) case: on the one hand we have object clitic pronouns which always show case distinctions, and on the other we have Romance third-person tonic pronouns which typically show no case distinctions (cf. Cappellaro 2016; Pescarini 2016).

---

[3] 'Nominal' refers here to nouns and noun-like elements such as adjectives and determiners (excluding personal pronouns).

[4] Gender, following the theoretical premise that '[g]enders are classes of nouns reflected in the behavior of associated words' (Hockett 1958: 231), is inherent and non-overt on nouns, thus, strictly speaking, not marked on nouns. This is reflected in Corbett's suggestion to gloss gender on nouns by '( )' (cf. Leipzig Glossing Rules in Corbett 2012: 11).

13.2.3 Derivation

Affixation (prefixation and suffixation) is the most widespread derivational strategy found in Romance languages. Derivation without affixes, or 'conversion', is also a widespread Romance strategy and is discussed in detail in Section 13.5.

Suffixes can change the part of speech of the derivational base (the 'input' of derivation), while prefixes generally do not do so. Input and output of suffixal derivation, excluding adverbial derivation, behave symmetrically in that nouns, adjectives and verbs are both potential input and output categories. Examples below (Figures 13.4–13.6) are from Rainer (2015) for Spanish, Floricic (2015) for French, Grossmann (2016) for Romanian, and Pöll (2016) for Portuguese.

Table 13.4. *Nominal output examples*

	< N (denominal)	< A (deadjectival)	< V (deverbal)
Fr.	sarkozyste 'sarkozyst' < Sarkozy + /-iste/	grandeur 'greatness' < grand 'great'+ /-eur/	atterrissage 'landing' < atterrir 'to land' + /-age/
Pt.	ferreiro 'blacksmith' < ferro 'iron' + /-eiro/	fineza 'delicacy' < fino 'refined' + /-eza/	lavagem 'washing' < lavar 'to wash'+ /-agem/
Ro.	pizzar 'pizza-maker' < pizza + /-ar/	cretinitate 'stupidity' < cretin 'stupid'+ /-itate/	fertilizator 'fertilizer' < fertilizar 'to fertilize' + /-tor/
Sp.	desamor 'aversion' < /des-/ + amor 'love'	absolutez 'absolute' < absoluto 'absolute' + /-ez/	comedor 'dining room' < comer 'to eat' + /-dor/

Table 13.5. *Adjectival output examples*

	< N (denominal)	< A (deadjectival)	< V (deverbal)
Fr.	magique 'magic' < magie 'magic'+ /-ique/	simplet 'simple-minded' < simple 'simple' + /-et/	pensif 'pensive' < penser 'to think'+ /-if/
Pt.	familiar 'familiar' < família 'family' + /-ar/	apolítico 'unpolitic' < /a-/ + político 'political'	conservador 'conservative' < conservar 'preserve' + /-dor/
Ro.	spitalicesc 'hospital' < spital 'hospital' + /-icesc/	neclar 'unclear' < /ne-/ + clar 'clear'	vorbăreț 'talkative' < vorbi 'to talk' + /-ăreț/
Sp.	mujeriego 'womanizer' < mujer 'woman' + /-iego/	azulito 'blueish' < azul 'blue' + /-ito/	adulón 'flattering' < adular 'flatter' + /-ón/

Table 13.6. *Verbal output examples*

	< N (denominal)	< Adj (deadjectival)	< V (deverbal)
Fr.	caraméliser 'to caramelize' < caramel 'caramel' + /-TV-ser/	utiliser 'to use' < utile 'useful' + /-TV-ser/	sautiller 'to hop' < sauter 'to jump' + /-TV-ller/
Pt.	planejar 'to plan' < plano 'plan'+ /-ej-ar/	atualizar 'to actualize' < atual 'actual' + /-iz-ar/	coexistir 'to coexist' < /co-/ + existir 'to exist'
Ro.	încununa 'to crown' < /în-/ + cununa 'crown'	(se) încreți 'to curl' < /în-/ + creț 'curly'	reclădi 'rebuild' < /re-/ + clădi 'to build'
Sp.	gandulear 'to laze about' < gandul 'lazybones' + /-e-ar/	rigidizar 'to make more rigid' < rigid 'rigid' + /-iz-ar/	precocinar 'precook' < /pre-/ + cocinar 'to cook'

Another point of interest in derivation is the semantic function of the derivational process (the function of creating agentive, state, personal, or instrumental nouns, for example) and the richness of the affixal inventory found in Romance languages.

13.2.4 Compounding

Romance compounds are generally left-headed when the head is present, although even within one and the same variety there can be variation in the position of the head, as exemplified with Catalan in (1) below (cf. Forza and Scalise 2016: 524). Presence of a head classifies a compound as endocentric, while absence of a head classifies a compound as exocentric (see Scalise and Bisetto 2009: 38f.).

(1) Catalan compound structures
    a.   head in left position: *filferro* 'iron wire' < *fil* 'wire' + *ferro* 'iron'
    b.   head in right position: *malcostumar* 'to spoil' < *mal* 'bad' + *costumar* 'to treat habitually'
    c.   two heads: *fisicoquímic* 'physico-chemical' < *físic* 'physical' + *químic* 'chemical'
    d.   no head: *aigua-sal* 'pickle' < *aigua* 'water' + *sal* 'salt'

Romance languages display subordinate, coordinate, and attributive compounds (cf. Scalise and Bisetto 2009), as exemplified in Table 13.7 with Italian (cf. Forza and Scalise 2016: 525).

Moreover, there are pan-Romance types of compounds (see Table 13.8 for some examples) but also language-specific types such as N-i-Adj>N in Spanish and Sardinian (e.g., Sp. *cuellilargo* 'long-necked.MSG' < *cuell(-o)* 'neck' + *i* + *largo* 'long', Srd. (NCpd) *cambilongu* 'long-legged.MSG' < *camb(-a)* 'leg' + *i* + *longu* 'long') or VV>V in Romanian (e.g., *furlua* 'to take "accidentally on purpose"' < *fura* 'to steal' + *lua* 'to take', cf. Forza and Scalise 2016: 533). In general, with this Romanian exception, the output is generally either a noun or an adjective.

Table 13.7. *Subordinate, coordinate, and attributive compounds*

grammatical relations between constituents	examples	characteristics
subordination	It. *lavapiatti* 'dish washer' < *lavare* 'to wash' + *piatti* 'dishes'	the non-head is a complement
coordination	It. *divano-letto* 'sofa bed' < *divano* 'sofa' + *letto* 'bed'	there is no internal hierarchy
attribution	It. *cassaforte* 'safe' < *cassa* 'box' + *forte* 'strong'	the non-head is an attribute

13.3 Distinctions in Form and Constituency

13.3.1 Introduction

As already mentioned, mechanisms that are generally available in inflexion are also available in derivation, such as suffixation, for example, in the Italian wordforms *cant-iamo*, *cant-avamo*, *cant-are* vs *canta-tore*. Other formal means that are common in one can also be found in the other, such as cumulative exponence, empty morphs, and suppletion (see examples below).

Cumulativeness: consider how in Romanian, but not in Italian (for comparison in Table 13.9(b)), a derivational diminutive affixal segment, namely *-ic-* (of Slavic origin) in *viorică* 'violet', is also a marker of case (NOM/ACC) and number (SG) (cf. Maiden 1999; 2015: 70).

Empty morphs (form without meaning). For inflexion, consider the empty affix *-isc-* (from Lat. -SC- discussed in more detail in Section 13.4.3.3)

Table 13.8. *Romance compounds*

VN>N	Fr. *tire-bouchon* 'corkscrew' < *tirer* 'to pull' + *bouchon* 'cork'
	It. *portalettere* 'postman' < *portare* 'to carry' + *lettere* 'letters'
	Ro. *papă-lapte* 'milk-sop' < *păpa* 'to eat' + *lapte* 'milk'
	Sp. *abrelatas* 'can opener' < *abrir* 'to open' + *latas* 'cans'
VV>N	It. *bagnasciuga* 'water's edge' < *bagnare* 'to wet' + *asciugare* 'to dry'
NN>N	It. *bagnomaria* 'bain-marie' < *bagno* 'bath' + *(M)aria* 'Maria'
	Pt. *mapa mundo* 'map of the world' < *mapa* 'map' + *mundo* 'world'
	Ro. *câine-lup* 'wolfhound' < *câine* dog' + *lup* 'wolf'
	Sp. *perro-pastor* 'sheep dog' < *perro* 'dog' + *pastor* 'shepard'
NAdj>N	It. *camera oscura* 'darkroom' < *camera* 'room' + *oscura* 'dark'
	Pt. *sangue-frio* 'sang-froid'< *sangue* 'blood' + *frio* 'cold'
NAdj>Adj	Cat. *camacurt* 'short-legged' < *cama* 'leg' + *curt* 'short'
AdjN>N	It. *cortometraggio* 'short film' < *corto* 'short' + *metraggio* 'length'
	Pt. *alto-relevo* 'high relief' < *alto* 'high' + *relevo* 'relief'
	Ro. *prim-ministru* 'prime minister' < *prim* 'first' + *ministru* 'minister'
	Sp. *buenaventura* 'good fortune' < *buena* 'good' + *ventura* 'fortune'
AdjAdj>Adj	Cat. *agredolç* 'sweet and sour' < *agre* 'sour' + *dolç* 'sweet'
	Fr. *vert-bleu* 'green-blue' < *vert* 'green' + *bleu* 'blue'
	It. *chiaroscuro* 'light-dark' < *chiaro* 'light' + *scuro* 'dark'
	Sp. *blanqui-azul* 'white-blue' < *blanc(-o)* 'white' + *i* + *azul* 'blue'

Table 13.9. *Derivational diminutive affix*

a. Ro. *vior-ic-ă* 'violet'

SG	PL	
vior-ic-ă	*vior-ele*	NOM≡ACC
vior-ele	*vior-ele*	GEN≡DAT

b. It. *violett-a* 'violet'

SG	PL
viol-ett-a	*viol-ett-e*

in Italian third conjugation verbs (in 2b but not in 2a). For derivation, consider the empty affix -icc- in the diminutive Italian form *libr-icc-ino* 'little book' in (2d) < *libr(-o)* + *icc* + diminutive suffix /-in(-o)/ as opposed to *tavolino* 'little table' in (2c) < *tavol(-o)* + diminutive suffix /-in(-o)/.

(2) **Italian**
    a. *dorm-ire* 'to sleep' > *dorm-e*.PRS.3SG
    b. *fin-ire* 'to finish' > *fin-isc-e*.PRS.3SG
    c. *tavol-o* 'table' > *tavol-in-o* 'little table'
    d. *libr-o* 'book' > *libr-icc-in-o* 'little book'

Suppletion: consider Italian examples of suppletion in N>Adj derivation in (3a–c) as opposed to regular, non-suppletive N>Adj derivation in (3d–e) (see also Dressler 1985b).

(3)   a. It. *sogn-o* 'dream' > *onir-ic-o* 'of, pertaining to dreams'
       b. It. *chies-a* 'church' > *ecclesia-stic-o* 'of, pertaining to the church'
       c. It. *cas-a* 'house' > *dom-estic-o* 'of, pertaining to a house'
       d. It. *palazz-o* 'palace' > *palazz-esc-o* 'of, pertaining to a palace'
       e. It. *alberg-o* 'hotel' > *albergh-ier-o* 'of, pertaining to a hotel'

In this section, we focus on the differences between inflexion, derivation, and compounding at the morphophonological level. If inflexion and word-formation pertain to different modules of the grammar, it appears possible that inflected, derived, and compound words differ in at least some respects as to the phonological alternations that apply to them and as to how closely or loosely their components are linked. In this section, three aspects of such potential distinctions are considered: first, the question is addressed whether morphophonological alternations apply in the same way to inflected, derived, and compound words, or whether any systematic differences can been detected with respect to the domain of application of such alternations; second, whether inflected, derived, and compound words present any systematic differences as to their prosodic structure; third, whether the degree of bonding between formatives, as diagnosed by the possibility of ellipsis in coordination, differs between the three morphological types. It will become clear that morphological surface structure, i.e., whether the formatives involved are suffixes, prefixes, or roots, is more important than the process they express, be it inflexion, derivation, or compounding. More precisely, at least with respect to prosodic constituency (Section 13.3.3) and ellipsis in coordination (Section 13.3.4), suffixed inflected and suffixed derived words pattern together, differing from prefixes as well as from compounds. A few compounds pattern with the majority of suffixed forms, while a few derivational suffixes pattern together with the greater part of compounds.

13.3.2 Morphophonological Alternations

In general, the same morphophonological alternations apply in inflexion, derivation, and compounding. At the same time, at least in certain cases, the distribution of alternants seems to correlate with the distinction between inflexion, derivation, and compounding. Here, we mention only two major morphophonological alternations which are found in most Romance varieties: diphthongization (Maiden 2016a) and palatalization (Repetti 2016). Romance diphthongization refers to an alternation between a diphthong in a stressed syllable and monophthong elsewhere, such as Italian [ɔ]~[wɔ] and [ɛ]~[jɛ], see (11a). Note that the open vowel [ɔ] surfaces only in syllables bearing (primary or secondary) stress; in unstressed syllables it is reduced to [o], as in Table 13.10(a) *cuocitore/cocitore*. Romance palatalization is an alternation between a palatal consonant (fricative or affricate) and a non-palatal stop, such as It. [k]~[tʃ], depending on the frontness/backness of the following vowel, as illustrated in Table 13.10(b). In most varieties both alternations are no longer fully productive but have left their traces in an intricate distributional patterning in inflexion and word-formation. There are not many systematic studies of these alternations with respect to the distinction between inflexion and word-formation. Spanish diphthongization has been studied under this perspective in an analogical framework by Eddington (1996; 1998) and by Carlson and Gerfen (2011a; 2011b); the distribution of Italian palatalization in inflexion and derivation is investigated by Celata and Bertinetto (2005) and by Dressler (1985a).

In this section we consider only velar palatalization in Italian (Dressler 1985; Celata and Bertinetto 2005; Krämer 2009: 56–62), with the aim of exemplifying its intricate patterning across inflexion, derivation, and compounding. It will become clear that a neat distinction between palatalization in inflexion and in word-formation is impossible. Since Italian is one of the Romance varieties to preserve inflexion in the nominal domain, with singular nominals often ending in a non-front vowel [o, a] and plural

Table 13.10. *Italian diphthongization and palatalization*

a. Italian dipthongization			
V.PRS.3SG	V.PST.IPFV.3SG	derived noun	compound
[ˈkwɔtʃe]	[koˈtʃeva]	[kwo/kotʃiˈtore]	[ˌkwɔtʃiluˈmake]
cuoce	coceva	cuocitore/cocitore	cuocilumache
'cook'		'cook.agent'	'snail cooker'

b. Italian palatalization				
N.MSG	N.MPL	N.FPL	derived noun	derived adjective
ami[k]o	ami[tʃ]i	ami[k]e	ami[tʃ]izia	ami[k]evole
'friend'			'friendship'	'friendly'

Table 13.11. *Palatalization in the Italian verb* vincere *'win'*

1SG.PRS.IND	2SG.PRS.IND	3SG.PRS.IND	SG.PRS.SBJV
vin[k]o	vin[tʃ]i	vin[tʃ]e	vin[k]a

Table 13.12. *Italian palatalization in inflexion, derivation, and compounding*

a. Palatalization in Italian inflexion and word-formation			
MSG	MPL	derived noun	derived noun
ami[k]o	ami[tʃ]i	ami[tʃ]izia	ami[tʃ]issimo
'friend'		'friendship'	'most friendly'
b. No palatalization in Italian inflexion of the base noun, but in word-formation			
MSG	MPL	derived verb	derived noun
cuo[k]o	cuo[k]i	cuo[tʃ]ere	cuo[tʃ]itore
'cook'		'to cook'	'cooker'
c. No palatalization in Italian inflexion, but optional palatalization in word-formation			
MSG	MPL	derived noun	compound
fun[g]o	fun[g]i	fun[dʒ]/[g]icolo	fun[dʒ]/[g]icoltore
'mushroom'		'relative to mushroom-growing'	'mushroom-grower'

nominals often ending in a front vowel [i, e], this alternation is particularly pervasive.

As for Italian, palatalization of velar stops is found in both nominal and verbal stems. In inflected and derived nominals (i.e., nouns and adjectives), velar stops palatalize only before /i/, but not before /e/, see Table 13.10(b), while in inflected verbs both /e/ and /i/ are triggers for palatalization (Table 13.11). Verbs of the -/a/-class never palatalize, those of the -/e/-class always show palatalization, (Table 13.11), and there is variation in verbs of the -/i/-class (Krämer 2009: 59). Crucially, whether a stem undergoes palatalization in inflexion does not determine whether it does so in derivation or compounding; cf. the Italian examples in Tables 13.12(a–c).

The few stems that present optional alternation in inflexion may likewise optionally alternate or not in word-formation, as illustrated in Table 13.13.

Similar alternations in Spanish are considered by Elordieta (2014), following García-Bellido (1987), as evidence for a two-level morphological model. The data presented here show, however, that these matters are rather complex. The patterns of application or non-application of palatalization and other morphophonological alternations in inflexion and word-formation remain to be studied, both with respect to individual varieties as well as from a comparative Romance perspective. The main question is whether potential differences derive from the prosodic structure of the relevant forms, dealt with in the following section, or whether inflexion, derivation, and compounding pertain in fact to different modules of the

Table 13.13. *Italian inflexion and word-formation*

a. Optional alternation in Italian inflexion, alternation in word-formation			
MSG	MPL	derived noun	derived adjective
chirur[g]o	chirur[g]/[dʒ]i	chirur[dʒ]ia	chirur[dʒ]ico
'surgeon'		'surgery'	'surgical'
b. Optional alternation in Italian inflexion and in word-formation			
MSG	MPL	derived noun	derived noun
intona[k]o	intona[k]/[tʃ]i	intona[tʃ]ino	intona[k]ino
'plaster'		'plasterer'	'plaster.DIM'
c. Optional alternation in Italian inflexion, no alternation in word-formation			
MSG	MPL	derived noun	derived noun
traffi[k]o	traffi[k]/[tʃ]i	traffi[k]io	traffi[k]ino
'traffic'		'traffic.PEJ'	'profiteer'

grammar, and whether at least some morphophonological alternations do not apply in the same way in these modules. It is to be expected that studying the distribution of morphophonological alternations across these modules will provide deeper insights into the architecture of grammar.

13.3.3 Prosodic Constituency

It has often been argued that inflected, derived, and compound words have different prosodic structures (Nespor and Vogel 1986; Peperkamp 1997), i.e., that they differ with respect to whether their morphological constituents are part of the same prosodic word, of different prosodic words, or whether they form more complex prosodic structures. In fact, under the assumption that derivation and compounding differ with respect to whether one or two lexemes are involved, we expect that compounds consist of two prosodic words, in contrast to derived words. In Romance, prosodic word structure can be diagnosed *inter alia* by means of segmental wrules or constraints, such as voicing of intervocalic /s/ in Italian (Table 13.15(a)), vowel raising in Portuguese or centralization in Catalan (Table 13.15(c)), the distribution of the flapped vs the trilled rhotic in Spanish (Table 13.15(b)), or, as a criterion valid across many varieties, the presence of a diphthong vs a monophthong (Table 13.14).

The general pattern observed in Romance complex words is as follows: Inflected words, always formed by suffixation, pattern together with derived words formed by suffixation: they are simple prosodic words, with no prosodic boundary intervening between stem and affixes (Table 13.14(a–b)), with few exceptions (see below). This is evidenced in Table 13.14 by the fact that stress is assigned regularly to the penultimate syllable, so that it shifts to the right when a disyllabic inflexional ending or derivational suffix is attached (Table 13.14(a.iii–iv)), or when the suffix is (exceptionally)

Table 13.14. *Suffixed words: no prosodic boundary between stem and suffix*

	i	ii	iii	iv
a. Spanish inflected	(piéns-o)ω 'think-1SG'	(piéns-an)ω 'think-3PL'	(pens-ámos)ω 'think-1PL'	(pens-ába)ω 'think-PST.IPFV.1/3SG'
b. Italian derived	(buón-o)ω 'good-M.SG'	(bon-tà)ω 'good-ness'		
c. Spanish derived	(fuért-e)ω 'strong-SG'	(fort-ific-ár)ω 'strengthen'		

Table 13.15. *Prefixed words*

	no ω-boundary	ω-boundary between prefix and stem	
a.	Italian (Peperkamp 1995; Nespor and Vogel 2007: 125) consonant-final[a] [dizoˈnɛsto] (dis-onesto)ω 'dishonest'	vowel-final [asoˈtʃale] a-(sociale)ω 'antisocial'	
b.	Spanish (Elordieta 2014: 40) monosyllabic [diˈrekto] (directo)ω 'direct'	polysyllabic [semiˈrːekto] semi-(recto)ω 'half-straight'	[ˈrːekto] (recto)ω 'straight'
c.	unstressed Portuguese prefix *pro-* (Vigário 2003: 228f.) [prumuˈver] (pro-mover)ω 'promote' Catalan prefix *pre-* (Castellví 2016) [prəsəˈdi] (pre-cedir)ω 'precede'	stressed [prɔkumuˈniʃte]] pro-(comunista)ω 'pro-communist' [prekristiˈa] pre-(cristià)ω 'pre-Christian'	

[a] In Italian, consonant-final prefixes are prosodified differently from vowel-final prefixes only when the stem is vowel-initial (Peperkamp 1995).

stressed (Table 13.14(b–c)). At the same time, the stem loses its primary stress, as shown by the fact that the stem vowel is a monophthong (Table 13.14(a.iii–iv), (b.ii), (c.ii)), when stress is to its right.[5]

Words derived by means of prefixes are different. In some Romance varieties, two classes of prefixes can be distinguished: prefixes that are like suffixes in forming a single prosodic word with the stem, and prefixes that are separated from the stem by a prosodic boundary. The property

---

[5] Here and in the following, an acute accent is used in orthographic representations to indicate the position of stress in the word. Note, however, that in most Romance languages and varieties exemplified here, stress is not necessarily marked in the standard orthography.

Table 13.16. *Italian compounds*

a.	[tokːaˈsana] (tocca)_ω_ touch	(sana)_ω_ healthy	'cure all'
b.	[pɔrtaomˈbrɛlːi] (porta)_ω_ carry	(ombrelli)_ω_ umbrellas	'umbrella stand'
c.	(boca mouth (balon ball	manga)_ω_ sleeve mano)_ω_ hand	bocamanga 'cuff' balonmano 'handball'
d.	a+fono idro+vora commedio+grafo	[ˈafono] [iˈdrɔvora] [komːeˈdjɔgrafo]	'voiceless' 'water pump' 'comedy writer'

Nespor and Vogel (2007: 125).

distinguishing the first class of prefixes from the second class may be segmental structure (consonant-final vs vowel-final; Table 13.15(a)), syllabic structure (monosyllabic vs disyllabic; Table 13.15(b)), or metrical structure (unstressed vs stressed; Table 13.15(c)). Note that in languages such as Portuguese and Catalan, one and the same prefix can sometimes be pronounced either as unstressed or stressed (Table 13.15(c)).

Finally, the two elements of compound words appear generally to be separated by a prosodic word boundary, as shown by, for example, the observation that in Italian intervocalic /s/-voicing does not apply (Table 13.16(a)) and that the first member retains a mid-vowel, see Table 13.16(b) and *cuocilumache* in Table 13.10(a), which in Italian is found only in a position bearing stress. The prosodic structure of compounds is, however, a more complex matter (Fábregas 2004; Elordieta 2014). According to Hualde (2007) and Rao (2015), the intonational patterns of the Spanish compounds in Table 13.16(c) as well as their stress patterns indicate that the two stems constitute a single prosodic word.

Another case in point are neoclassical formations, illustrated in Table 13.16(d). The term neoclassical formation refers to combinations of forms taken from Latin or Greek that often pertain to the domain of technology and science. A recent overview is available with the study of Eins (2015). The status of neoclassical formations as derived vs compound formations remains controversial, given that the nature of the constituent forms may be heterogeneous (Amiot and Dal 2007); see Table 13.16(d). In prosodic respects, at least in Italian such formations appear to pattern like words derived by suffixation, shown by the fact that they have a single primary stress, often on the first element (Peperkamp 1997: 134). The prosody of neoclassical formation has so far hardly been studied.

Table 13.17. *European Portuguese*

['bɛlu]	[bə'leze]	[bɛ'liɲu]	[bɛle'mẽtə]	[bɛ'lisimu]
belo	beleza	belinho	belamente	belíssimo
'beautiful'	'beauty'	'beautiful.DIM'	'beautifully'	'most beautiful'

Finally, it has often been pointed out that certain Romance suffixes diverge from the general pattern: in some varieties, there are a handful of suffixes that appear to be separated from the stem by means of a prosodic boundary. This is exemplified in Table 13.17, where a prosodic boundary between stem and affix is indicated by the observation that the stem vowel does not undergo raising when the stressed suffixes *-inho*, *-mente*, or *-íssimo* are suffixed, contrary to what happens with most other stressed derivational suffixes such as *-eza*.

To date, the exact prosodic structure of prefixed and compound forms remains controversial; cf. Brambatti Guzzo (2018) for a recent study arguing once more for a revision of the prosodic hierarchy on the basis of Romance prefixed and compound words, following earlier work by Vigário (2003; 2010).

13.3.4 Morphological Ellipsis in Coordination

Not only do inflected, derived, and compound forms appear to differ with respect to prosodic constituency, but there also appear to be systematic differences with respect to morphosyntactic constituency, as diagnosed with respect to the possibility of such forms in ellipsis in coordination, see (4) below. As has been shown in the preceding paragraphs, these contrasts are orthogonal to the distinction between inflexion, derivation, and composition. Again, constituency, i.e., whether the formatives involved are suffixes, prefixes, or stems, appears to matter more than whether inflexion or word-formation is involved.

The phenomenon in question is generally assumed to diagnose the degree of bonding between different morphological formatives as well as their prosodic and morphosyntactic independence. Hence, it may be taken as a diagnostic for whether a formative is 'free' or 'bound', which is sometimes considered an important criterion in delimiting derivation and compounding (Bloomfield 1935). Current terms are 'suspended affixation', in particular with reference to Turkish (Lewis 1967; Kabak 2007), 'Gruppeninflexion' (Spencer 2005: 83) to denote similar phenomena that have long been studied in Indo-European comparative linguistics, 'broken forms' (Pounder 2006), 'coordination reduction' (Kenesei 2007), 'deletion under identity' (Zwicky 1985), 'word-part ellipsis' (Chaves 2008), 'morphological ellipsis', 'affix suspension', and 'affix sharing'. Ellipsis in coordination has also been used as a diagnostic in research on clitic forms (Zwicky 1985; Monachesi 1999). In contrast to Turkish and, to some degree, Germanic, as well as a few other languages, including Tocharian, Ossetic, and Japanese, there seems to be little systematic research on morphological ellipsis in Romance (but see Nespor 1985; Vigário and Frota 2002; Chaves 2008). Yet observations about the behaviours of specific formatives such as adverb forming -MENTE, and diminutive or superlative affixes have long been discussed in the research literature on Romance morphology.

In general, morphological ellipsis is possible in (certain) compounds as well as with stressed prefixes, but not with unstressed prefixes (Vigário and Frota 2002), see (5)–(6). Varieties that do not distinguish stressed and unstressed prefixes may allow morphological ellipsis with prefixes in general, such as French (7), or may allow it with some, but not with other prefixes, such as Italian (8).

(4) Compounds
  a. Spanish (Torner 2005)
    países   centro__   y   sur   americanos
    countries centre__   and south American
  b. French (Kenesei 2007)
    les   avec__   et   les   sans   maillots
    the   with__   and   the   without swimsuits

(5) Stressed prefixes (Vigário and Frota 2002)
    European Portuguese   pr[ɛ]-__   e   p[ɔ]s-tónica
                          'pre- __   and   posttonic'

(6) Unstressed prefixes (Vigário and Frota 2002)
    European Portuguese   **pr[i]-__   ou   p[u]s-fácio
                          'pre-__   or   postface'

(7) French prefixes
    les   anti-__   et   les   pro-nucléaires
    the   anti__   and   the   pro-nuclears
    'the protesters for and against nuclear energy'

(8) Italian prefixes (Kenesei 2007)
  a. pre-__   o   postbellico
     'pre-__   or   postwar'
  b. **s-__   o   infortunato
     'non-__   or   unfortunate'

In Romance compounds, morphological ellipsis is possible only under identity of the second element, which can be elided in the first co-ordination member (cf. (4); Vigário and Frota 2002). Under identity of the first element, however, this element cannot be elided in the second coordination member (9). In this respect, Romance differs from Germanic (10).

(9) Romance
    a. French (Kenesei 2007)
        **les   porte-   avions   et   __ -hélicoptères
        the   carry   planes   and   __-helicopters
        'aircraft carriers and helicopter carriers'
    b. Brazilian Portuguese (Brambatti Guzzo 2018)
        **tira-   manchas   e   __-odores
        remove   stains   and   __-odours
        'stain remover and odour remover'
    c. European Portuguese (Vigário and Frota 2002)
        **um   vestido   verde-   seco   e   __ -garrafa
        a   dress   green   dry   and   __-bottle
        'a dark green and a bottle-green dress'

(10) Germanic
    a. German   Herrenmäntel und ____-Schuhe
                      'men's coats and shoes'
    b. English   newspaper production and ____ processing

While morphological ellipsis appears to be generally impossible in Romance verb–noun compounds (9a–b), it has been claimed (Brambatti Guzzo 2018) that even closely related varieties appear to differ with respect to whether these compounds allow suspended affixation or not (11).

(11) Morphological ellipsis in VN-compounds
    a. European Portuguese
        corta-__   e   pisa-   papéis (Vigário and Frota 2002)
        cut-__   and   tread   paper
        'paper knife and paper weight'
    b. Brazilian Portuguese
        **lava-__   e   seca-   roupa (Brambatti Guzzo 2018)
        wash-__   and   dry-   clothing
        'washing machine and laundry dryer'

Morphological ellipsis is likewise possible with certain suffixes, but clearly impossible with many others (12).

(12) Suffixes
    a. European Portuguese
        alegre__   ou   triste-mente (Santos and Vigário 2016: 136)
        happy__   or   sad-ly
        **acampa__   ou   acantona-mento (Santos and Vigário 2016: 136)
        camp__   or   cantonment

b. Spanish
**un problema observa__ y analiz-able (Torner 2005)
a problem observ and analysable

Suffixes which allow morphological ellipsis, i.e., primarily -MENTE, are often argued to constitute independent prosodic words (e.g., Vigário 2010; Brambatti Guzzo 2018). In addition to the prosodic status of the stranded formative (prosodic word or not), other factors are relevant in morphological ellipsis, such as the weight of intervening phonological material (13a; Vigário and Frota 2002) or syntactic locality (13b; Chaves 2008).

(13) European Portuguese (Vigário and Frota 2002)
    a. ?Os rapazes trabalharam não só lenta__ mas também cuidadosa-mente.
        'The boys worked not only slowly, but also carefully.'
    b. **O homem agiu rápida ou agiu lenta-mente? (Chaves 2008)
        the boy acted rapid__ or acted slow-ly?
        'Did the man act rapidly or did he act slowly?'

Systematic differences between Romance languages have been discussed in particular with respect to adverb formations in -MENTE (Torner 2005; Kenesei 2007; Chaves 2008). Morphological ellipsis with -MENTE is possible in Spanish (14a), Catalan (14b), and Portuguese (12a), but not in modern Italian (Chaves 2008). In Catalan, it is the final occurrence of -MENTE that undergoes deletion (14b) (cf. Torner 2005; Chaves 2008), rather than the non-final occurrence(s), as in Spanish and Portuguese (12a, 14a).

(14) Morphological ellipsis with -MENTE in Romance
    a. Yo estoy física_, técnica_ y psicológicamente preparado. (Chaves 2008: 300)
        'I am physical(ly), technical(ly), and psychologically prepared.'
    b. Yo estic físicament i psicològica_ preparat. (Chaves 2008: 300)
        'I am physically and psychological(ly) prepared.'

Ellipsis with -MENTE, eliding the non-final occurrence(s), as in Spanish and Portuguese, is also marginally attested in early stages of old French (Karlsson 1981: 58; Ledgeway 2012: 18) and old Tuscan (Karlsson 1981: 123).

Observations about the acceptability of ellipsis under coordination with certain formatives, but not with others, are thus revealing, on the one hand, with respect to whether a given formative is bound like a prototypical affix, free like a prototypical lexeme, or something in between, and thus whether a specific word-formation pattern should be considered as derivation or as compounding. On the other hand, such observations may, finally, lead to a better understanding of the differential interaction between inflexion, derivation, and compounding as pertaining to different modules of the grammar with (presumably) syntactic processes like coordination and ellipsis.

13.4 Issues and Challenges: Inflexion and Derivation

13.4.1 Introduction

Most scholars agree that distinguishing between inflexion and derivation is not only highly desirable but necessary for both theoretical and analytical-descriptive reasons (cf. Baerman 2015). The distinction relies on one core 'functional' motivation rooted in the theoretical notion of 'lexeme', i.e., inflexion creates wordforms of one and the same lexeme while derivation creates new lexemes.[6] Orthogonally, the distinction can be based on the identification of key properties or characteristics that are prototypical or canonical (Corbett 2010) of either inflexion or derivation (discussed in Section 13.4.2).

The general debate has also focused on whether inflexion and derivation (word-formation more generally) belong to two separate grammatical components (cf. Split Morphology hypothesis, see Section 13.1) or whether they should be kept together in one morphological component (cf. Booij's 1994; 1996; 2006 theory of 'inherent' vs 'contextual' inflexion, with inherent inflexion having strong similarities with derivation). However, many scholars remain non-committal with regard to this issue.

Booij's work on inherent vs contextual inflexion has been particularly influential on how we now conceive of inflexion and derivation. He observed that not all the morphosyntactic features realized in inflexional paradigms have the same status. Number, for example, can in some languages or in sub-parts of a language system (as in the case of Italian) be 'inherent' and lexically specified. Gender, on the other hand, is eminently 'contextual' or determined by the syntax. Booij concludes, contrary to the 'Split Morphology' hypothesis, that inherent inflexion shares some of the properties we associate with derivation. In Booij's own words:

> We might distinguish between two types of inflection, inherent inflection and contextual inflection. An example of inherent inflection is the formation of plural nouns. In most contexts, the use of the plural form of a noun is not required by syntactic context, but a purely semantic choice based on what the language user wants to convey. The choice of specific finite forms of verbs, and of case forms of nouns, on the other hand, is governed mostly by syntactic context and then qualifies as contextual inflection. Participles and infinitives also qualify as cases of inherent inflection. The crucial observation is that it is only inherent inflection that can feed word-formation processes such as derivation and compounding (Booij 1994; 1996). This suggests that inherent inflection is halfway between derivation and contextual inflection. (Booij 2006: 660)

---

[6] From a purely 'formal' point of view, in fact, there is no morphological mechanism that is available to inflexion but not derivation, as emphasized in Section 13.3.

Table 13.18. *Portuguese inflexional wordforms*

a. Portuguese definite article

	SG	PL
M	*o*	*o-s*
F	*a*	*a-s*

b. Portuguese adjective 'new'

	SG	PL
M	*nov-o*	*nov-o-s*
F	*nov-a*	*nov-a-s*

13.4.2 Typical Properties Illustrated with Romance Data

We briefly touch here upon the most relevant prototypical properties of inflexion and derivation. This is by no means an exhaustive treatment (for which see Hacken 2014).

A first characteristic property of derivation (at least since the pioneering work of Scalise 1984; Haspelmath 1996) is that it can change the syntactic category of the base.

However, there are problems with this view in that, on the one hand, derivation may, but does not have to, change the syntactic category of the base, as the phenomena of conversion and prefixation well illustrate (cf. Section 13.5.3). On the other hand, there may be cases where forms that are considered as belonging to one inflexional paradigm can take on different syntactic roles. Consider, for example, Romance non-finite verb forms such as infinitives and participles which can assume the syntactic functions of nouns and adjectives.[7] For the past participle, see the Romanian examples below where the past participle occurs in verbal (15a) and adjectival (15b) function (cf. Pană Dindelegan 2013: 209).

(15) **Romanian**
    a.   Uşa   este   închisă   cu   atenţie   de   infermieră.
        door.the.F is   closed.PTCP.FSG with attention by nurse
        'The door is carefully closed by the nurse.'
    b.   Uşa   a   rămas   închisă.
        door.the.F has remained closed.PTCP.FSG
        'The door remained closed.'

A second important property is so-called syntactic relevance, or the claim that inflexional (but not derivational) morphology is 'what is relevant to the syntax' (Anderson 1982). In the examples from standard Portuguese in Tables 13.18–19, it is the syntax that compels the selection of inflexional wordforms (agreement patterns).

---

[7] Recall how in Booij's (1994; 1996) discussion, infinitives and participles are also treated as 'inherent inflection'.

Table 13.19. *Standard Portuguese 'the new pupil(s)'*

o_{MSG}	novo_{MSG}	aluno_{MSG}
a_{FSG}	nova_{FSG}	aluna_{FSG}
os_{MPL}	novos_{MPL}	alunos_{MPL}
as_{FPL}	novas_{FPL}	alunas_{FPL}

Table 13.20. *Non-standard Brazilian Portuguese 'the new pupil(s)'*

o_{MSG}	aluno_{MSG}	novo_{MSG}
a_{FSG}	aluna_{FSG}	nova_{FSG}
os_{MPL}	aluno_{MPL}	novo_{MPL}
as_{FPL}	aluna_{FPL}	nova_{FPL}

Table 13.21. *It.* parlare *'speak' and* chattare *'chat (online)' vs* andare *'go'*

	PRS.IND	PRS.IND	PRS.IND
1SG	parl-o	chatt-o	vad-o
2SG	parl-i	chatt-i	va-i
3SG	parl-a	chatt-a	va
1PL	parl-iamo	chatt-iamo	and-iamo
2PL	parl-ate	chatt-ate	and-ate
3PL	parl-ano	chatt-ano	va-nno

However, we do find data showing how syntactic rules can fail to operate. For example (see Table 13.20), in 'popular' non-standard Brazilian Portuguese (cf. Stark and Pomino 2009: 118, citing data from Scherre 2001), when the adjective is postnominal, noun and adjective do not show overt number agreement.

Productivity (thus predictability) is another typical property associated with inflexion but not with derivation: if a regular mechanism exists such that within an inflexional paradigm form x is synchronically related to form y (for example lexical root + desinence, It. *parl-are* 'to speak' > *parlo* 'speak-PRS.1SG' and *parl-iamo* 'speak-PRS.1PL'), then this mechanism should apply to all items in that (word-)class. As illustrated in Table 13.21 below, for the verb *chatt-are* 'to chat (online)', a recent borrowing from English, the present indicative form *chatt-o* 'chat-PRS.IND.1SG' and *chatt-iamo* 'chat-PRS.1PL' follow such a productive pattern. While even in inflexion we can find unpredictable irregularities, as in the forms *vad-o* 'go-PRS.IND.1SG' and *and-iamo* 'go-PRS.1PL' of *and-are* 'to go'.

On the other hand, we do not expect a mechanism for derivation such as N>A (lexical root + derivational suffix, i.e., It. *libr-ai(-o)* < *libr(-o)* 'book' + agentive suffix /-ai(-o)/), to apply necessarily to all nouns (cf. 16b).

Table 13.22. *Defectiveness. Sp.* partir *'part' vs* blandir *'brandish'*

	PRS.IND	PRS.SBJV	PRS.IND	PRS.SBJV
1SG	parto	parta	Ø	Ø
2SG	partes	partas	Ø	Ø
3SG	parte	parta	Ø	Ø
1PL	partimos	partamos	blandimos	Ø
2PL	partís	partáis	blandís	Ø
3PL	parten	partan	Ø	Ø

cf. Maiden and O'Neill (2010).

Table 13.23. *Syncretism: It.* BUONO *'good' vs* VERDE *'green'*

		SG	PL
M		buon-o	buon-i
F		buon-a	buon-e
		SG	PL
M		verd-e	verd-i
F		verd-e	verd-i

(16)   It. LIBRO 'book' and PENNA 'pen'
   a.   *libr-o*   >   *libr-aio* 'book-seller'
   b.   *penna*   >   **penn-aio 'pen-seller'

Thus, obligatoriness is yet another typical property of inflexion as opposed to derivation. The claim here is that 'in inflexion, the set of wordforms is predetermined in the sense that a member of any word class has certain duties to perform (marking features). ... Derivation for its part has no preset list of job duties, and thus no binding obligations' (Baerman 2015: 2f.). However, phenomena such as defectiveness (non-semantically motivated paradigmatic gaps) in Table 13.22 or syncretism in Table 13.23 show how this principle can fail to operate in inflexion as well.

As regards the order of affixes, the assumption is that, in wordforms which include both inflexional and derivational affixes, inflexional endings are farther from the root than derivational suffixes (cf. the Universal 28 of Greenberg 1963). However, there are examples (see 17–18) which challenge the validity of this assumption as a defining property.

(17)   Portuguese diminutives
   a.   *pão*.SG   ~   *pães*.PL   'bread, loaf'
   b.   *pãozinho*.SG   ~   *pãezinhos*.PL   'small bread (= roll)'

(18)   French adverbs in *-ment* (< MENTE)
   a.   adjective: *amical*.MSG / *amical-e*.FSG 'friendly'
   b.   adverb: *amical-e-ment* 'friendly'

The issue of semantic regularity in inflexion (vs semantic idiosyncrasy in derivation) is also an important analytical parameter but has its limitations. Morphosyntactic features that are realized in inflexion tend not to have semantic correlates, but this is not always the case. Number, for example, can be correlated with differences of lexical meaning. See, for example, the Italian noun *osso* 'bone' in (19b), which, as opposed to *tavolo* 'table' (19a), in the plural does not mean more than one bone but the whole set of bones or the skeleton (cf. discussion in Section 13.4.3.2).

(19) Italian nouns with regular (19a) and idiosyncratic semantics (19b)
    a.   *tavolo*.SG ~ *tavoli*.PL   ('one table' ~ 'more than one table')
    b.   *osso*.SG   ~ *ossa*.PL   ('bone' ~ 'the whole set of bones, i.e., skeleton')

13.4.3 Two Case Studies

13.4.3.1 Introduction

The following two Romance case studies highlight analytical and theoretical problems, from a synchronic and a diachronic perspective, for the view that inflexion and derivation are 'split'. For reasons of space we limit our discussion to these two case studies, but we refer the reader to two other important challenging issues in Romance for a general understanding of inflexion and derivation, that is (a) Romance evaluative morphology (diminutive, pejorative, and augmentative suffixes): since Scalise's influential work on Italian (1984), the problem of evaluative forms has not been satisfactorily accounted for in either inflexional or derivational terms (Stump 1993; Dressler and Merlini Barbaresi 1994; Bauer 1997; Maiden 1999; Fortin 2011; Štekauer 2015b; Gaeta 2015; Grandi and Körtvélyessy 2015 on the notion of 'third morphology'; see especially Chapter 14, this volume); and (b) the issue of so-called Romance 'double participles' (or 'weak' vs 'strong' participles): see for example It. *asciugato* 'dry.PST.PTCP.MSG' versus *asciutto* 'dry.MSG' or 'dry.PST.PTCP.MSG' and the discussion of the problematic analysis of *asciutto* as inflexional or derivational and its theorical implications in Bentley 2018. See also Loporcaro, Pescia, and Ramos (2004) for Portuguese, and Bentley and Ledgeway (2014; 2015) for Italo-Romance.

13.4.3.2 Synchrony: Italian Ambigeneric Nouns with -a Plural

Number marking on Italian nouns can be analysed in terms of inflexional classes (D'Achille and Thornton 2003) where the co-variation of singular and plural desinence is basic or, as often presented in grammar books, in terms of pluralization rules on the basis of singular nouns (Maiden and Robustelli 2007).

Table 13.24. *Standard Italian inflexion class system*

Inflexion class		SG	PL	GLOSS	GENDER
1	o/i	libro	libri	'book'	M
2	a/e	casa	case	'house'	F
3	e/i	cane	cani	'dog'	N
		noce	noci	'walnut (fruit)'	F
		cantante	cantanti	'singer'	F, M
4	a/i	poeta	poeti	'poet'	M
5	o/a	uovo	uova	'egg'	MSG/FPL
		braccio	braccia	'arm'	MSG/FPL
6	Invariant	re	re	'king'	M
		gru	gru	'crane'	F
		città	città	'city'	F

D'Achille and Thornton (2003: 212).

Table 13.25. *Italian* UOV-O *'egg'*

	SG	PL
MSG/FPL	uov-o	uov-a

There is a small class of ambigeneric nouns (MSG/FPL), arbitrarily designated inflexion class 5 and shaded in Table 13.24, which have an -*o* desinence in the singular associated with masculine gender (-*o* being the typical desinence associated with MSG values in the nominal system) and -*a* desinence in the plural associated with feminine gender (-*a* being the typical desinence associated with FSG values in the nominal system). This is a closed and non-productive class in Italian made up of about two dozen nouns whose origin lies in the survival of Latin neuter plural forms (second and third declension) which ended in -A (or -ORA). These plural forms, presumably on the basis of formal identity of plural -a with feminine singular -a, have been assigned feminine gender regardless of the gender of the corresponding singular forms (cf. Maiden 2016c with reference to Romanian ambigenerics).

The synchronic analysis of these nouns is controversial. In the inflexional-class-analysis they are indeed fully inflexional and have the expected paradigm structure in Table 13.25. Acquaviva (2008), however, has proposed that we should conceive of -*a* plurals as inherently plural and fully derivational lexemes with the paradigm structure in Table 13.26: '[w]e must therefore conclude that a seemingly straightforward paradigmatic relation like *uovo uova* 'egg' 'eggs' involves two minimally distinct nouns: a singular only *uovo* and a plural only *uova*, functionally 'the' plural of *uovo* but morphologically a distinct noun.' (Acquaviva 2008: 48f.)

Table 13.26. *Italian* uov-o *'egg' vs* uov-a *'eggs'*

	SG	PL
M	uov-o	–
	SG	PL
F	–	uov-a

Table 13.27. *Italian* mur-o/-i *'wall/-s' and* mur-a *'walled perimeter'*

	SG	PL
M	mur-o	mur-i
	SG	PL
F	–	mur-a

This derivational analysis of Italian -*a* plurals is justified by both their semantic idiosyncrasy (they do not mean 'more than one' but 'not one' according to a number of semantic categories involving the notion of weak differentiation),[8] and their behaviour as non-productive, non-obligatory and often involving so-called 'doublets'. For example, the noun *muro* 'wall' (MSG), alongside the form *mura* (FPL) meaning 'walled perimeter', displays a regular plural form *muri* (inflexion class 1) with the more regular semantics of 'walls' in the sense of 'more than one wall' (see Table 13.27). In this case we would have to posit two lexemes (a regular noun *muro/muri* and a *plurale tantum* noun *mura* derived from the same root as *muro*).[9]

Number is an inflexional category in Italian but has derivational properties on some words. As Acquaviva argues (2008: 5),

> [t]his is the original insight encapsulated in Booij's (1994; 1996) concept of 'inherent inflection'. ... [P]lural has indeed different morphosemantic properties as an ingredient of a lexical base (lexeme or stem), or of the grammatical context for such a base; however, and this is crucial, the *same plural forms may fulfil either function*. [emphasis ours]

13.4.3.3 Diachrony: Latin -SC-

The Latin formative -SC- and its development in Romance (cf. Maiden 2003; Meul 2013) well illustrates the empirical challenges that a diachronic analysis can pose to the Split Morphology hypothesis. In some areas of the Romània, in

---

[8] 'In a nutshell, plural does not mean "many" but "not-one", and its precise semantic value on a noun depends on how the noun defines "one"' (Acquaviva 2008: 79).

[9] Thornton (2011) however claims that a unified analysis of all -*a* plurals may not be ideal. She presents corpus data and proposes that some -*a* plurals are better analysed as inflexional forms belonging to 'non-canonical' paradigms (in the sense of Corbett 2007) with either overabundance or overdifferentiation.

fact, changes occur that involve a 'migration' (cf. Rainer 2016: 513f.) of -SC-reflexes from the domain of derivation to that of inflexion. However, if inflexion and derivation sat in two separate components of grammar we would not expect such migratory movements, just as we would not expect two genetically different organisms to metamorphose into one another.

In Latin, this derivational affix was associated with inchoative and ingressive meaning. See, for example, the minimal pairs in (20).

(20) a. RUBERE 'to be red'   a′. RUB-ESC-ERE 'to turn red'
      b. FLORERE 'to blossom'   b′. FLOR-ESC-ERE 'to begin to blossom'
      c. DORMIRE 'to sleep'   c′. CON-DORM-ISC-ERE[10] 'to fall asleep'

The augment was limited to the *infectum* aspect (which indicates that an action is unfinished and non-completed as opposed to the *perfectum*) and it could be argued that, since aspect is an inflexional category in Latin, -SC- did not fully conform to the prototypical properties we associate with derivation, and thus 'the derivational capacity of the infix, viz. the creation of a new lexical-aspectual category of verbs, is curtailed by the inflexional constraints, viz. its limitations to the *infectum*' (Meul 2013: 6).

In some parts of the Romània (Iberian Peninsula, Sardinia, and many dialects of southern Italy) the augment has become an integral part of the lexical root and has been extended to all tenses, as illustrated by Sp. *parecer* 'seem' (from PARESCERE and not PARERE) in (21). This is not problematic and is a change (loss of meaning but preservation of form) that had in fact already occurred in the history of Latin in lexemes such as GNOSCO 'I recognize', CRESCO 'I grow', DISCO 'I learn' where the occurrence of -SC- was fossilized (cf. Vermandere and Meul 2016: 264).[11]

(21) a. present indicative: *parezco, pareces, parece, parecemos, parecéis, parecen*
      b. imperfect indicative: *parecía*
      c. past participle: *parecido*
      d. infinitive: *parecer*

It appears (for Spanish see, for example, Lavale Ortiz 2013: 789f. and Pena Seijas 1993) that the availability in the system of derivationally related forms such as *noche* 'night' > *anochecer* 'to become dark', *caro* 'dear' > *encarecer* 'to endear' (nominal base + prefix + *ec-er*) is, in synchrony, the basis for the analogical development of denominal verbs (causative or transformative meaning) of the type *penumbra* 'half-light' > *empenumbrecer* '(cause to) become half-lighted' or *gay* 'gay' > *engayecer* '(cause to) become

---

[10] In this case the change in meaning is conveyed by the affix in co-occurrence with a prefixed preposition.
[11] There is also evidence suggesting that -SC- semantic content was fading in later Latin (cf. Haverling 2000). The co-occurrence of the augment with prefixed prepositions (20c′), a phenomenon that is also referred to in the literature as 'parasynthesis', is interesting and could be interpreted as a sign of a more general tendency for -SC- weak (ened) semantic contribution.

Table 13.28. *Italian* finire 'finish'

	PRS.IND	PRS.SBJV
1SG	finisco	finisca
2SG	finisci	finisca
3SG	finisce	finisca
1PL	finiamo	finiamo
2PL	finite	finiate
3PL	finiscono	finiscano

more gay', *rock* > *enrockecer* '(cause to) become more "rock"', as exemplified in (22). This is also not problematic for the Split Morphology hypothesis, since in these cases the derivational nature of the -SC- reflex is preserved.

(22) a. Era cosa curiosa ver cómo todo se iba empenumbreciendo poco a poco durante el eclipse, hasta que casi se hizo oscuro (quoted in Lavale Ortiz 2013: 795)
'It was strange to see how everything was slowly growing dimmer during the eclipse, until it became almost completely dark.'
b. Los más locos llevan tiempo diciendo que forma parte de un plan para engayecer a la gente ya desde niños (Twitter, September 2018)[12]
'For a while now the crazies have been saying that this is all part of a plan to make people gay from childhood.'
c. Antes de enrockecer su discurso en una potente *Canción de la esperanza* (Rayén Castillo Salazar, January 2016)[13]
'Before bringing on the rock with a powerful rendition of the *Canción de la esperanza*'

What seems to be problematic, however, is a type of change found in other areas of the Romània (Gallo-Romance, Italo-Romance, Daco-Romance), where the augment -SC- develops the intramorphological meaning of conjugation marking and acquires a distinctive 'morphomic' pattern of distribution, the so-called 'N-pattern' (Maiden 2003; 2018: 167–73) illustrated in Tables 13.28–29 with Italian and Romanian.

Assuming in fact that this change of function occurred gradually, and that at no point in time was the augment completely functionless (as proposed by Vermandere and Meul 2016, who challenge the applicability of 'exaptation' (Lass 1990) to the -SC- development in Romance), the migration from the domain of derivation to that of inflexion is damaging for the Split Morphology hypothesis.

---

[12] https://twitter.com/Evocid/status/1042126238620499969.
[13] www.pressreader.com/spain/la-vanguardia-1%C2%AA-edici%C3%B3n/20160125/282527247451294.

13.5 The Interaction of Inflexion, Derivation, and Compounding in 'Conversion'

13.5.1 Introduction

By 'conversion' we understand the syntactic recategorization of a form, i.e., a change in lexical category, that does not coincide with the attachment of a derivational affix. In traditional Romance studies, it has sometimes been assumed that certain formatives which would otherwise be considered as inflexional may function – in such examples – as derivational affixes in the sense that they signal or bring about a change in lexical category (cf. Haspelmath 1996 for a more recent version of this view). In this section, we reconsider the most important Romance examples involving a change in lexical category – of individual words as well as of phrases – in the absence of overt derivational morphology (cf. Castellví 2016 for a classification which is similar to the one adopted here). As will become clear from the phenomena considered in this section, derivation interacts with inflexion and compounding in complex ways.

13.5.2 Derivation without Affix

A process which is rather common in Romance is derivation without overt affixation, as illustrated in Table 13.30. In the Romance tradition, in those varieties where the resulting word has an inflexional affix, this inflexional

Table 13.29. *Romanian a păți 'suffer'*

	PRS.IND	PRS.SBJV
1SG	pățesc	pățesc
2SG	pățești	pățești
3SG	pățește	pățească
1PL	pățim	pățim
2PL	pățiți	pățiți
3PL	pățesc	pățească

Table 13.30. *Derivation of deverbal nouns without affixation*

	verb	noun	
Spanish	cambi-ar	cambi-o	'to change ~ change, N'
Italian	arriv-are	arriv-o	'to arrive ~ arrival, N'
French	combatt-re	combat	'to fight ~ fight, N'

formative has sometimes been considered the formative bringing about the category change in traditional approaches (Thiele 1993; Gather 1999).

In these formations, verb and noun share the same stem. There are two possibilities for formally analysing the derivation of such forms: on the one hand, one can assume that the root or stem is assigned – in the absence of an overt derivational affix – to a different lexical category; on the other hand, one can assume that no category change is necessary because roots are not inherently specified as belonging to a particular syntactic word class. Hence, the syntactic distribution of roots is not subject to any lexical restriction, though its distribution may be subject to semantic restrictions. The first alternative has often been postulated in structuralist approaches (cf. Bergenholtz and Mugdan 2000 for an overview); the second is adopted in many current approaches within the framework of Distributed Morphology (McGinnis-Archibald 2016), going back to American structuralist work (Nida 1949; Hockett 1958). The basic claim underlying the second approach, i.e., that lexical information – in many cases – does not include word class membership, but derives either from semantics or from syntax, is still the subject of discussion (Baker and Croft 2017). Under both analyses, instances of derivation without affix do not pose a challenge to the question pursued here, namely whether inflexion and word-formation can be considered as distinct.

The formation of deverbal nouns without affix is fully productive in Spanish, and at least moderately productive in Italian, Catalan, and Portuguese. In standard French, it is unproductive, but it is productive in French argot, with the peculiarity that all formations have feminine gender, as in *épater* V 'amaze' > *épate* N (F) 'show', *cavaler* V 'run' > *cavale* N (F) 'escape', *lansquiner* V 'urinate' > *lansquine* N (F) 'rain'. The derivation of denominal and deadjectival verbs without overt derivational affix is likewise very productive in many Romance varieties; however, these verbs are mostly prefixed forms, presenting additional complexities, and are considered in Section 13.5.5. More interesting with respect to the architecture of the grammar are possibly what may be termed 'true conversions', i.e., forms in which a fully inflected word (rather than a root or stem) is assigned to a different lexical category, considered in the following two sections.

13.5.3 Word-Level Conversion as Derivation

The examples of conversion given in (22) present parallels with derivation without affixation, but differ from this process in that inflexional formatives of the base category are retained, though the word-internal constituent structure is lost (23a) – and in few cases reinterpreted as a (different) formative of the new category, as in (23b).

(23) Conversion from verb to noun
    a.   French
          ri]$_{\text{VSt}}$ re]$_{\text{V}}$ > le rire]$_{\text{NSt}}$]$_{\text{N}}$ 'to laugh' > 'laugh, N'
    b.   Italian
          dov]$_{\text{VSt}}$-ere]$_{\text{V}}$ 'modal verb expressing necessity'
          > il dover]$_{\text{NSt}}$-e]$_{\text{N.MSG}}$ ~ i dover]$_{\text{NSt}}$ -i]$_{\text{N.MPL}}$ 'duty, homework, SG ~ PL'

In (23b), the verbal inflexional affix -/e/, which is part of the infinitive ending, is retained, but reinterpreted as a nominal inflexion, so that in the plural the noun *dovere* surfaces with the regular nominal plural inflexion -/i/. To be sure, historically the infinitive desinence is a fossilized case ending of a verbal noun, probably a locative in origin (Ernout 1953: 171; Weiss 2009: 445). Yet, under a synchronic perspective the nominal plural inflexion is unexpected in *doveri*, because the base of the conversion is the inflected word *dovere*, rather than a hypothetical stem *dover-*. In fact, in most Romance varieties the internal morphological structure of the inflected base of infinitive nominalizations is lost in conversion, as in (23a). In Romanian, however, many infinitive nominalizations, in contrast to supine nominalizations, present the Italian pattern illustrated in (23b) (Cornilescu et al. 2013: 707). Whether the process is cross-linguistically unusual is unclear to date.

Adjectives, too, may be converted into nouns (24). In Romance, the inflexional exponents that combine with nouns are generally the same as those which combine with adjectives; yet, in most Romance varieties there is more than one form class for nouns and adjectives. A converted noun always retains the form class of the base adjective, but – adjectives not being inherently specified for gender – it is assigned default masculine gender. Its interpretation is that of a quality noun; hence, it is a mass noun and cannot be pluralized.

(24) Conversion from adjective to noun
    a.   Italian
          buono]$_{\text{Adj}}$ > il buono]$_{\text{N}}$ 'good' > 'good, quality noun'
          verde]$_{\text{Adj}}$ > il verde]$_{\text{N}}$ 'green' > 'green, quality noun'
    b.   Spanish
          bueno]$_{\text{Adj}}$ > lo bueno]$_{\text{N}}$ 'good' > 'good, quality noun'

In Spanish, however, deadjectival conversions are not assigned default masculine gender, as may be inferred from the observation that the resulting forms do not select the masculine definite article *el*, but the 'neuter' definite article *lo*, which occurs exclusively in this context. All other 'neuter' forms in standard Spanish are pronouns (Ojeda 1984; Klein 1988; Harris 1991; Pomino and Stark 2009). Similar observations can be made for Asturian (Loporcaro 2018: 166).

13.5.4 Syntactic Conversion

The cases exemplified in (25) may be not so much a question of morphological derivation, as merely a syntactic recategorization. This type of syntactic conversion is in general quite productive with uninflected words, but it is also found with phrases.

(25) a. Fr. pour, PREP 'pros' contre, PREP 'cons'
le pour et le contre 'the pros and cons'
b. Sp. sí, ADV 'yes' no, ADV 'no'
el sí y el no '"yes" and "no"'
c. It. non so che 'I do not know what'
un nonsoché 'a certain something / je ne sais quoi'

In these examples, a word or a sequence of words is inserted into a syntactic position where an inflected word (in the sense of 'syntactic atom') with a different lexical category feature is expected to occur. Now, if we limit our understanding of 'morphological' to that which cannot be accounted for by the principles of syntax, such unexpected instances of insertion in syntax are, in fact, not a matter of morphology, be it inflexion or word-formation, but a matter of syntax. Nevertheless, not only the syntactic distribution, but also the semantic structure of the forms in (25) is affected by conversion, in that, e.g., the argument structure of the converted prepositions *pour* and *contre* is lost in the converted forms *le pour* and *le contre*. This semantic change goes beyond a mere syntactic recategorization and cannot in any principled way be seen as its consequence. Hence, processes affecting lexico-semantic properties of lexemes, typically observed in derivational morphology, appear to be relevant to syntactic conversion, as well.

In compounding, however, syntax does interact with morphology, as shown in the [NN]$_N$ compounds in (26), where a word that is not an adjective (*antifurto*, *coupe-feu*) combines with a head noun to yield an attributive compound. This structure is rather productive in many current Romance varieties; its status as morphological or syntactic has been the object of discussion (Montermini 2008; Masini 2009; Bisetto 2015).

(26) It. sistema antifurto
system anti-theft 'alarm system'
Fr. porte coupe-feu
door cut-fire 'fire door'

While Romance appears to lack the kind of phrasal compounds found in Germanic, as in Eng. *over-the-fence gossip*, the non-head elements of [NN]$_N$ compounds can have phrasal syntax, as in It. *città luogo di provincia* 'provincial capital town' (Bisetto 2015: 404). Such constructions are clearly a challenge for the assumption that compounding is morphological rather than syntactic; they have been interpreted by some scholars as evidence that at least some compounds are built in syntax (Fradin 2003; 2011). Finally, let us note that contrary to word-level conversion, which straddles the boundary between inflexion and derivation, what is termed here 'syntactic conversion' is not relevant to the delimitation of inflexion from word-formation, though it may be relevant to the question whether compounding is a matter of morphology or of syntax.

13.5.5 Formations without a Base

In Romance languages one finds, as in other languages, morphologically complex words without a base, i.e., whose base is neither an attested nor a possible word. Here, we discuss primarily derived verbs that are traditionally termed 'parasynthetic' formations. These verbs are noteworthy in that an intermediate step in the derivation, expected to correspond to a potential word, is neither attested nor well-formed. At the same time, as was the case for other phenomena considered here as conversion, there is no overt derivational affix.

Depending on the theoretical framework chosen, these formations may be considered as the result of complex interactions of different inflexional and word-formation processes, possibly including a step of (root- or stem-) conversion. From a semantic perspective, the interpretational processes that can be observed in these formations, in particular with respect to the contribution of the prefix, resemble those found in compounding more than those found in prototypical derivation, whose effect is often not much more than a change of lexical category. In fact, in traditional approaches prefixation is sometimes considered as compounding rather than as derivation (Darmesteter 1875), cf. Amiot (2005) for a reassessment on the basis of French data.

Traditional Romance linguistics denotes as 'parasynthetic' those formations which are derived by means of the 'simultaneous use of prefixation and suffixation' (Serrano-Dolader 2015: 525), (27), meaning that one can neither claim that the suffix nor that the prefix is attached first, since the intermediate step of the derivation is unattested (indicated here by *).

(27) It. [in]-tron-[izz]-are 'enthrone' tron-o 'throne' *tron-izz-are
      Sp. [a]-carr-[e]-ar 'carry' carro 'cart' *carr-e-ar
      Fr. [dé]-rat-[is]-er 'remove rats' rat 'rat' *rat-is-er

In many such forms, however, there is no overt derivational suffix (28). In traditional accounts, the verbal inflexional ending of these forms is sometimes considered as a derivational suffix that serves the function of changing the word class from noun to verb (Thiele 1993; Gather 1999).

(28) It. im-bocc-are 'put to the mouth' bocc-a 'mouth' *bocc-are
     Sp. a-rruin-ar 'to ruin'   ruin-a 'ruin'   *ruin-ar

In more recent research, two other options have been explored: first, the category-changing function has been ascribed to the derivational prefix (29a; Corbin 1987); second, an intermediate verbal formation derived by stem/root-conversion from the nominal base has been assumed, corresponding to an unattested, but possible word, which serves as the base for (fully regular) prefixation (29b; Scalise 1986: 147–51). It is this second kind of analysis that underlies the heading of 'formations without a base' that has been chosen here, assuming a 'missing step' in the derivation.

(29) a. Prefix has a derivational, category-changing function
         [bocc]$_{NSt}$ a > [im [bocc]$_{NSt}$]$_{VSt}$ are
     b. Conversion followed by prefixation
         [bocc]$_{NSt}$ -a]$_N$ > # [[[bocc]$_{NSt}$]$_{VSt}$ a-re]$_V$ > im-[boccare]$_V$
         'mouth' > 'put into the mouth'

An analysis in Construction Morphology is developed by Masini and Iacobini (2018). In a current model such as Distributed Morphology, in which roots are in any case category-less and the exponents of information relating to lexical category, i.e., derivational affixes, can also be phonologically empty, the challenge lies in an appropriate semantic characterization of these forms rather than in a morphosyntactic structural description.

Besides so-called parasynthetic denominal verbs, Romance displays a few other formations with similar properties. Deadjectival verbs constitute a case fully parallel to denominal verbs (30).

(30) Adjectival verbs
     a. It. im-bianc-are 'whiten'   bianco 'white'
     b. Fr. en-ivr-er 'intoxicate'   ivre 'drunk'
     c. Sp. a-cort-ar 'shorten'   corto 'short'

In addition, there are a few minor patterns with very limited productivity, exemplified with French examples in (31a–b).

(31) a. Adjectives
         Fr. in-chavir-able 'uncapsizable'   chavir-er 'capsize'   *in-chavir-er,
                                                                    ??chavir-able
     b. Nouns
         Fr. en-col-ure 'neck'   col 'collar'   *encol, ??colure

The (productive) patterns exemplified in (32) have been analysed by some scholars as 'parasynthetic compounds', mostly on semantic grounds (Bisetto and Melloni 2008; Melloni and Bisetto 2010). While they may formally look like prefixed nouns or adjectives, their semantic interpretation is more similar to that of Romance exocentric compounds (see Section 13.2.4).

(32) It.   sottotetto N   'attic'
            under roof
      Fr.   anti-bruit A   'noise-reducing'
            anti-noise
      It.   sopra-renale A   'suprarenal
            above renal

What the forms discussed in this section show is that in the formation of new lexemes, processes of inflexion, derivation, and compounding may interact in complex, non-sequential, and non-modular ways. In many cases, a modular separation of inflexion, derivation, and compounding can only be maintained at the price of assuming zero exponents in derivation and composition, as well as unattested and unacceptable lexemes as intermediate steps in the derivation.

Selected References

Below you can find selected references for this chapter. The full references can be found online at the following page: www.cambridge.org/Romancelinguistics

Acquaviva, P. (2008). *Lexical Plurals. A Morphosemantic Approach*. Oxford: Oxford University Press.
Baerman, M. (2015). 'Introduction'. In Baerman, M. (ed.), *Oxford Handbook of Inflection*. Oxford: Oxford University Press, 1–8.
Booij, G. (2006). 'Inflection and derivation'. In Brown, K. (ed.), *Encyclopedia of Language and Linguistics*. Oxford: Elsevier, 654–61.
Dressler, W. (1985a). *Morphonology. The Dynamics of Derivation*. Ann Arbor: Karoma.
Forza, F. and Scalise, S. (2016). 'Compounding'. In Ledgeway, A. and Maiden, M. (eds), *The Oxford Guide to Romance Languages*. Oxford: Oxford University Press, 524–37.
Hacken, P. Ten (2014). 'Delineating derivation and inflection'. In Lieber, R. and Stekauer, P. (eds), *The Oxford Handbook of Derivational Morphology*. Oxford: Oxford University Press, 10–25.
Karlsson, K. E. (1981). *Syntax and Affixation. The Evolution of MENTE in Latin and Romance*. Tübingen: Niemeyer.
Müller, P. O., Ohnheiser, I., Olsen, S., and Rainer, F. (eds) (2015). *Word-Formation: An International Handbook of the Languages of Europe*. Berlin: de Gruyter.

Olsen, S. (2014). 'Delineating derivation and compounding'. In Lieber, R. and Štekauer, P. (eds), *The Oxford Handbook of Derivational Morphology*. Oxford: Oxford University Press, 1–31.

Rainer, F. (2016). 'Derivational morphology'. In Ledgeway, A. and Maiden, M. (eds), *The Oxford Guide to the Romance Languages*. Oxford: Oxford University Press, 513–23.

Scalise, S. and Bisetto, A. (2009). 'The classification of compounds'. In Lieber, R. and Štekauer, P. (eds), *The Oxford Handbook of Compounding*. Oxford: Oxford University Press, 34–53.

Štekauer, P. (2015a). 'The delimitation of derivation and inflection'. In Müller, P. O., Ohnheiser, I., Olsen, S., and Rainer, F. (eds), *Word-Formation: An International Handbook of the Languages of Europe*. Berlin: de Gruyter, 218–34.

14

Evaluative Suffixes

Antonio Fortin and Franz Rainer

14.1 Introduction

Evaluative morphology has long been a favourite topic of philologists and linguists due to its semantic and pragmatic versatility and the many etymological problems presented by single suffixes. It was not until the 1980s, however, that it started to have an impact on linguistic theorizing, with Romance data playing an especially disruptive role. Jaeggli (1980) sparked off a series of articles on how to deal with the complex allomorphy of Spanish diminutives in a rule-based framework such as generative grammar, and Scalise (1984: 132f.) argued that the problems posed by the data necessitated nothing less than a revision to the architecture of grammar. The research that has accumulated over the last forty years eventually made it possible to dedicate a whole handbook to the question of evaluative morphology (Grandi and Körtvélyessy 2015).

Romance evaluative morphology, in particular, presents a number of challenges to linguistic theorizing (cf. also Section 27.2.3.1). We may take a few notable examples that were already raised in the 1980s. First, when considered against the criteria applied in delimiting derivation and inflexion, Romance evaluative affixes fall somewhere between the two (Scalise 1984: 133), while also apparently falsifying Greenberg's (1963) Universal 28 and, more strongly, a principled distinction between the two, as proposed by the Split Morphology Hypothesis (Anderson 1982), an issue that we discuss further in Section 14.4.3. Second, Spanish evaluative affixes prompted significant weakenings of influential hypotheses regarding category assignment in word-formation. Di Sciullo and Williams (1987: 27 n. 2) observe that the weakening of the various proposed feature percolation conventions of the 1980s were all 'actually responses to the same data ... namely, the Spanish diminutives reported by Jaeggli (1980)'. Third, the categorial promiscuity of Romance evaluative affixes (Section 14.2.2) presents prima facie irrefutable evidence against the Unitary Base Hypothesis (Aronoff 1976; Scalise 1984), which states that word-formation rules may apply to one, and only one, syntactically or semantically defined type of base. Fourth, Rainer (1986) shows that recursive diminutive application (Section 14.2.8) in Romance languages falsifies constraints on the iteration of word-formation rules, such as that proposed by Lieber (1981: 171–73), which prohibits them from applying to their own output.

We would like to suggest a somewhat different perspective on these problems and on the import of Romance evaluative morphology to linguistic theory, which will require a reconsideration of the apparently crucial counterexamples that it has posed in recent decades. Zwicky and Pullum (1987: 330) distinguish 'plain morphology', or the ordinary processes of word-formation and inflexion, from 'expressive morphology', which includes the conscious manipulation of morphology, often for jocular effect, in ways which reflect 'regularities of sociolinguistic competence, poetic form, and language games', rather than grammar. On the basis of this distinction, they argue that 'it may be inappropriate to use [expressive morphology] as the sole basis for arguments that support revisions to the general theory of grammar.' However, they explicitly exclude Spanish diminutives from expressive morphology because, they argue, they do not have a 'significant number of the [relevant] criterial properties' (Zwicky and Pullum 1987: 338). These properties are: (i) pragmatic effect; (ii) promiscuity with regard to input category; (iii) promiscuity with regard to input basehood; (iv) imperfect control; (v) alternative outputs; (vi) interspeaker variation; (vii) special syntax. Contrary to Zwicky and Pullum's and other authors' assessment of evaluative morphology, Romance evaluative suffixes satisfy all of these criteria. Thus, if evaluative morphology can be shown to be a species of expressive morphology, then the apparent counterexamples that it poses to otherwise reasonably robust generalizations lose their force.

The productivity and frequency of evaluative affixes vary considerably among the Romance languages, so we will mostly focus on those data, languages, and dialects which, in our opinion, pose the most interesting problems for linguistic theory.

14.2 Zwicky and Pullum's Criteria for Expressive Morphology

14.2.1 Introduction

Napoli and Reynolds (1995) argue that Italian evaluative suffixes exhibit just one of the aforementioned characteristics, namely (ii), promiscuity with regard to input category, and, therefore, that they do not qualify as expressive morphology. From that, they conclude that evaluative morphology can and should provide crucial evidence for or against hypotheses related to plain morphology. However, we shall see that Romance evaluative suffixes exhibit all the properties of expressive morphology.

14.2.2 Pragmatic Effects

'Expressive morphology is associated with an expressive, playful, poetic, or simply ostentatious effect of some kind' (Zwicky and Pullum 1987: 335). Napoli and Reynolds (1995: 152) argue that Italian evaluative affixes do not meet this criterion, because 'they do not elicit a particular pragmatic effect, such as a chuckle'. However, this presupposes a rather restrictive and idiosyncratic definition of pragmatic effects, one which views them as a very specific kind of performative speech act. Rather, it is virtually a definitional characteristic of evaluative affixes, that they have pragmatic effects. Alonso (1954) argued that the basic meaning of Spanish evaluative affixes is pragmatic and affective or playful, and Dressler and Merlini Barbaresi (1994) proposed that Romance diminutives and augmentatives carry an invariant autonomous pragmatic marker [non-serious], which has the effect of lowering the speaker's commitment to the illocutionary force of a speech act. This kind of pragmatic effect can be seen clearly in Italian and Spanish requests, where the use of a diminutive on the thing requested acts as a linguistic hedge, making the utterance less of a demand and therefore less of an imposition, and thus a gentler and politer way of asking for something.

(1) Potrei averne una fett-ina? (It., Dressler and Merlini Barbaresi 1994: 17)
could.1SG have=of.it a slice-DIM
'Could I have a little piece of it, please?'

(2) Hazme un cafecito, porfa. (Sp.)
Make.IMP.2SG=DAT.1SG a coffee.DIM please
'Would you make me a nice cup of coffee, please?'

In the Spanish of eastern Bolivia (3; cf. Iglesias Recuero 2001: 279) and Brazilian Portuguese (4), imperatives can be diminutivized, with the effect of turning a brusque order into an affectionate request:

(3) ¡Pasámelo! 'Pass it to me' → ¡Pasamelito!
'pass.IMP.2SG=DAT.1SG=it.DIM' (Bolivian Sp.)

(4) Dorme! 'Sleep!' → Dormezinho! 'sleep.IMP.2SG.DIM' (BrPt.)

Moreover, the pragmatic feature [non-serious] is also evident in the fact that it is inappropriate to use evaluative affixes in formal situations, throughout the Romance languages, perhaps universally (Wierzbicka 1991: 105; Dressler and Merlini Barbaresi 1994: 213–18).

14.2.3 Promiscuity with Regard to Input Category

Napoli and Reynolds (1995) show how Italian diminutives violate the Unitary Base Hypothesis, which states that word-formation rules may apply to one, and only one, syntactically or semantically defined type of base (Aronoff 1976; Scalise 1984). Lázaro Mora (1999: 4650f.) observes that Spanish evaluative suffixes can combine with any category of lexical base, though with differing frequency and productivity. As well as canonically modifying nouns and adjectives, Romance evaluative suffixes can attach to proper names, adverbs, verbs, prepositions (though somewhat marginally), pronouns, and numerals.

(5) Nouns
   a. Sp. *perr-it-o* dog-DIM-M.SG 'little dog'
   b. It. *ragazz-in-o* boy-DIM-M.SG 'little boy'
   c. Fr. *maison-ette* house-DIM.F.SG 'little house'

(6) Adjectives
   a. Sp. *pequeñ-ita* small-DIM.F.SG 'very small'
   b. Cat. *dolc-et* sweet-DIM.SG 'sweet' (endearing)
   c. Ro. *frumuş-el* pretty-DIM.SG 'pretty' (endearing)

(7) Proper names (hypocoristics)
   a. Sp. *Miguel-ito* Miguel-DIM.M 'little Miguel'
   b. Sic. *Sant-uzza* Santa-DIM.F 'little Santa'
   c. Fr. *Jeann-ette* Jeanne-DIM 'little Jeanne'

(8) Adverbs
   a. Sp. *despac-ito* slowly-DIM 'nice and slowly / quietly'
   b. Glc. *amod-iño* slowly-DIM 'nice and slowly'
   c. It. *indietr-ino* behind-DIM 'a bit behind'

(9) Verbs
   a. It. *salt-icchi-are* jump-DIM-INF 'to jump about'
   b. Sp. *dormid-ito* sleeping-DIM.M 'sleeping sweetly/soundly'
   c. Pt. *correnḍ-inho* running-DIM 'running' (endearing)

(10) Prepositions
   Sp. *hast-ita* 'until-DIM' (Martín Zorraquino 2012: 128)

(11) Pronouns
   a. Pt. *poqu-inho/pouco-zinho* little-DIM 'tiny amount'
   b. Ro. *nimic-uța* nothing-DIM 'absolutely nothing'
   c. Sp. *todos* 'everyone' > *tod-it-os* all-DIM-M.PL 'everyone' (endearing)

(12) Numerals
   a. Andean Sp. *una* one.F > *un-ita* one-DIM.F 'only/exactly one'
   b. BrPt. *dois* two > *dois-inhos* two-DIM.PL 'just two'

Although the validity of the Unitary Base Hypothesis with regard to ordinary word-formation rules is also the subject of debate, it cannot plausibly accommodate the promiscuity of Romance evaluative affixes, if we assume them to be part of plain morphology.

14.2.4 Promiscuity with Regard to Input Basehood

This criterion relates to the fact that rules of expressive morphology, unlike ordinary derivational rules, can apply to inflected forms and compounds. For example, the affix *-(e)teria* can be attached to an inflected form X, to yield a word meaning 'retail outlet selling X' (e.g., American Eng. *drygoodsteria*) and expletive infixation can be applied to compounds (e.g., *Madison Square fucking Gardens*) and syntactic phrases (e.g., *kick the frigging bucket*). Stump (1990) shows that diminutives outside inflexion are common in Breton, and Bobaljik (2005) does the same for Itelmen diminutives. Although this property is not widespread in Romance evaluative affixes, not only do Portuguese diminutives such as those in (4) display it, but so do other Romance varieties, as we see in Section 14.4:[1]

(13) Pt. *animal-zinho* animal-DIM 'little animal' > *animai-zinho-s* animal.PL-DIM-PL (cf. *animal* 'animal' > *animais* 'animals')

14.2.5 Imperfect Control

The criterion of imperfect control relates to McCawley's (1978) observation that speakers vary in their ability to effectively produce examples of certain expressive morphological phenomena. Building upon earlier work, Eddington (2002: 414) shows that, beyond dialectal

---

[1] Napoli and Reynolds (1995: 158) argue that, even if diminutives do satisfy this criterion, so do other, non-evaluative, derivational processes in Italian. However, they only give examples involving compounding, which is not self-evidently relevant to their point.

variation in diminutive-formation in Spanish, 'individuals also demonstrate some degree of uncertainty regarding the diminutive form of certain words'. For example, there is a morphophonological alternation in diminutives of words ending in *-e*, which are typically formed by attaching *-cito/a* for bisyllabic bases, or *-ito/a* for bases with three or more syllables:

(14) **Spanish**
    a. ≤ Bisyllabic: *madre* 'mother' > *madre-cit-a* mother-DIM-F 'dear mummy'
    b. Trisyllabic: *comadre* 'godmother' > *comadr-it-a* godmother-DIM-F 'dear godmother'

However, Prieto (1992: 174) has found that speakers tend to vacillate between these allomorphs of the diminutive if the base has three or more syllables:

(15) **Spanish**
    a. *chocolate* > *chocolat-it-o/chocolate-cit-o* chocolate-DIM-M
    b. *estuche* 'case, small box' > *estuch-it-o/estuche-cit-o* case-DIM-M
    c. *comadre* 'close female friend' > *comadr-it-a/comadre-cit-a* friend-DIM-F

Furthermore, for certain bases that end in unstressed *-or* or *-ar*, elicitation of their diminutive forms results in a degree of uncertainty with some speakers (Jaeggli 1980; Crowhurst 1992; Prieto 1992).

(16) **Spanish**
    a. *azúcar* 'sugar' > *azucar-(l/c)it-(o/a)* sugar-DIM-M/F / *azuqu<ít>a(r)* sugar<DIM>
    b. *Óscar* > *Oscar-(c)it-o* Oscar-DIM-M / *Osqu-ít-ar* Oscar<DIM> 'little Oscar'
    c. *Víctor* > *Victor-(c)it-o* Victor-DIM-M / *Vict-ít-or* Victor<DIM> 'little Victor'

14.2.6 Alternative Outputs

Perhaps related to the previous criterion, the property of alternative outputs reflects the fact that many speakers have 'alternative forms derived from the same source by the same rule' (Zwicky and Pullum 1987: 337) such as, for example, the relative position of the infixed expletive in *abra-bloody-cadabra* versus *abraca-bloody-dabra*.

Crowhurst (1992) reports that some native speakers of Mexican Spanish accept both *-it-* and *-cit-* diminutive forms with certain bases: for example, *pie-cit-o/pie-cecit-o* foot-DIM-M, *dient-it-o/diente-cit-o* tooth-DIM-M. Eddington's (2017) corpus-based study of dialectal variation in Spanish diminutives found that, with bisyllabic words either containing /je, we/ in the stem or ending in /jo, ja/, two allomorphs of the diminutive exist within a single dialect, as with *viejo* 'old' > *viejito/viejecito*, *pueblo* 'town' > *pueblito/pueblecito*, *dulce* 'sweet' > *dulcito/dulcecito*, and *rubio* 'blonde' > *rubiecito/rubito*. Native speaker informants of Chilean, Uruguayan, and Andalusian Spanish confirmed the acceptability of both variants, which indicates alternative forms within individual idiolects.

14.2.7 Interspeaker Variation

This criterion relates to the observation that there can be variation between speakers, regarding the outputs of expressive word derivation. For example, McCawley (1978) found that, while two subjects agreed that the 'correct' way to insert *fuckin* into *discovery* is *dis-fuckin-covery*, one subject judged that form to be 'grossly unnatural', preferring *dis-fuckin-scovery* (which, in turn, was judged to be grossly unnatural by the other two subjects). However, the extent to which these conflicting judgements reflect dialectal differences is unclear, since McCawley does not consider this possibility.

Nevertheless, Crowhurst (1992), Prieto (1992), and Eddington (2002; 2017) document variability between diminutive forms in Spanish, both intra- and inter-dialectally, with regard to the choice of suffix. We saw examples of this variability above, as illustrated by the allomorphs of the diminutive, *-it-* and *-cit-*. Crowhurst (1992) suggests that speakers of Sonoran Mexican Spanish who diminutivize, say, *diente* 'tooth' as *dientito*, have a minimal word template composed of two bisyllabic feet, while speakers who prefer *dientecito* do not.

14.2.8 Special Syntax

Ideophones and some English expressive word-formation processes can result in words that have special syntactic properties. For example, *shm*-reduplication creates nouns that can only be used as interjections (Zwicky and Pullum 1987: 9f.):

(17) a. Kalamazoo Shmalamazoo! (I hate that place.)
　　 b. **Let's not talk about Kalamazoo Shmalamazoo.
　　 c. **Is Kalamazoo Shmalamazoo in Michigan?

It should be noted that not all expressive morphology exhibits this property. For example, expletive infixation does not affect the syntactic properties of the base.

(18) a. That food was fan(-freakin-)tastic.
　　 b. Let's not talk about Kalama(-fucking-)zoo.

This suggests that Romance evaluative affixes simply have more in common with expletive infixation than with *shm*-reduplication, in this regard. Furthermore, evaluative suffixes in several Romance languages can be attached recursively to certain kinds of bases. Potts (2007) identifies repeatability as one of the criteria of expressives in that, unlike descriptive terms, they can be repeated in a single utterance, without redundancy.[2]

---

[2] Fortin (2011) shows that Romance evaluative affixes satisfy all of Potts' criteria for expressives, which strengthens the case that they should be viewed as expressive morphology.

(19) a. #I'm angry! I forgot my keys. I'm angry! They are in the car. I'm angry!
     b. Damn damn damn! I left my damn keys in the damn car! Damn!

Similarly, multiple evaluative affixes can be attached recursively to their bases, in many Romance languages.

(20) a. It. *fett-ina-ina-ina* slice-DIM-DIM-DIM; *piant-ic-ina-ina-ina* plant-DIM-DIM-DIM
     b. Cat. *petit-on-et* small-DIM-DIM (Bernal 2015: 209)
     c. ORo. *mit-it-el-uș* small-DIM-DIM-DIM (Uță Bărbulescu and Zamfir 2016)
     d. Sp. *chiqu-it-it-...-it-ito* small-DIM-DIM-...-DIM-DIM

In all cases, the effect is to intensify both the descriptive meaning of the affix – in these examples, the meaning [small] – and the endearment or contempt that an appreciative or pejorative diminutive can convey, respectively, with no redundancy whatsoever.[3] This kind of formal behaviour is certainly unique to evaluative suffixes, and a kind of 'special morphology'.

Finally, the Italian diminutive suffix can, in certain regional varieties, be used as a standalone adjective, with restricted configurational properties:

(21) **Italian**
     a. ... come si fa a non amare un **gattino ino ino** che sta sul palmo di una mano?[4]
        how one does to not love a **cat.DIM DIM DIM** that stands on palm of a hand
        '... how can one not love a little kitty-cat that fits in the palm of your hand?'
     b. ... il suo centrino era così **ino-ino-ino-ino-ino-ino** ...[5]
        the his doily was so **DIM-DIM-DIM-DIM-DIM-DIM**
        '... his doily was so tiny ...'

Given that evaluative affixes appear to systematically exhibit typological aberrancy of various kinds, Napoli and Reynolds (1995: 152) argue that, if they can be shown to belong to expressive morphology rather than plain morphology, then they cannot falsify morphological generalizations involving plain morphology. As Zwicky and Pullum (1987: 338) put it: 'this is our modest conclusion – it may be inappropriate to use [expressive morphology] as the sole basis for arguments that support revisions to the general theory of grammar'. Napoli and Reynolds (1995) go on to argue that Italian evaluative affixes are not expressive morphology. However, as we have seen here, Romance evaluative affixes satisfy Zwicky and Pullum's criteria, and should therefore be viewed as expressive morphology. Following this line of argument, Fortin (2011) suggests that prima facie counterexamples to typological universals that involve evaluative affixes ought to be reconsidered in this light.

---

[3] Rainer (1986: 206f.) argues that iterated evaluative affixation is not interpreted compositionally but, rather, as intensification of the meaning of the affix. We propose an account of the meaning of evaluative affixes in Section 14.3, from which this observation follows naturally.

[4] https://maghetta.it/2013/06/11/biscotto-morbido-al-cioccolato-di-santin-con-crema-al-caffe/.

[5] www.ilgiornale.it/news/interni/laddio-casini-centrino-torno-nel-centrodestra-terzo-polo-988041.html.

14.3 Evaluative Affixes in Semantic and Pragmatic Theory

14.3.1 Introduction

The accurate and comprehensive description of the range of meanings expressed by Romance evaluative affixes has been the source of much conflicting literature due to its sheer variety and complexity, which is without equal elsewhere in Romance morphology. However, general surveys of Romance languages, and even specialist studies of evaluative morphology, have often glossed over many aspects of their meaning. The first ever grammar of Spanish, Antonio de Nebrija's *Gramática de la lengua castellana*, published in 1492, covers only the literal, 'small' meaning of the diminutive suffix, and briefly mentions that the augmentative can have an appreciative or pejorative function.[6] Jaeggli (1980: 143), in his seminal study of the morphology and syntax of Uruguayan Spanish diminutives, states that the 'semantics of diminutives is fairly coherent' and that a diminutive form of a noun X means '(a) little, small, or not very important [X]'. Similarly, Stump (1993: 1) limits the meanings of all evaluative affixes, universally, to 'diminution, augmentation, endearment, or contempt'. These descriptions alone already point to far more variety and heterogeneity of meaning than we find in other kinds of morphology. However, they are remarkably incomplete descriptions, as we will now see.

14.3.2 Heterogeneous Meanings and Uses of the Diminutive

As the examples in (22) show, the diminutive alone 'can express a bewildering variety of meanings' (Jurafsky 1996: 534) that go well beyond the limited set of functions listed above.

(22) Latin American Spanish diminutives
    a. Diminution: *perr-it-o* dog-DIM-M 'small dog'
    b. Pejoration: *actric-it-a* actress-DIM-F 'mediocre actress'
    c. Appreciation: *niñ-it-o* boy-DIM-M 'dear/cute little boy'
    d. Hypocorism: *Miguel-it-o* Miguel-DIM-M 'little Miguel'
    e. Intensification: *ahor-it-a* now-DIM-FV 'immediately, right now'
    f. Attenuation: *ahor-it-a* (Caribbean Sp.) now-DIM-FV 'in a little while, not right now'
    g. Exactness: *igual-it-o* the.same-DIM-M 'exactly the same'
    h. Approximation: *azul-ill-o* blue-DIM-M 'bluish'

Furthermore, diminutives are used in several Romance languages to mitigate the illocutionary force of a speech act. As we saw in examples

---

[6] Of course, it could be argued that the meanings of Spanish evaluative affixes are bound to have changed in the intervening centuries. However, a striking number of the connotative meanings that evaluative affixes have in present-day Spanish, are attested in works of medieval Spanish literature, prior to Nebrija's grammar (García Gallarín 2000: 5f.).

(1)–(4) above, a diminutive can 'soften' a directive speech act, thus making the request less of an imposition.

Lenz (1935: 213f.) observes that, in Chilean Spanish, a street beggar might ask for *una limosn-it-a* a.F donation-DIM-F, with the diminutive functioning as a device for *captatio benevolentiae*. Thus, Romance evaluative affixes can take scope over whole utterances or speech acts. We will return to so-called sentence diminutives and the issue of the positional mobility of Romance evaluative affixes in Section 14.4.1.

A further apparently universal property of diminutive and augmentative affixes is that, if a size-related interpretation is possible when they attach to uncountable nouns, this results in an individuating or partitive meaning:

(23)   Individuating/partitive diminutives:
    a.   Cat. *aigü-eta* water-DIM 'small bottle of water'
    b.   Sp. *pan-cito* bread-DIM 'bread roll'
    c.   It. *gess-etto* chalk-DIM 'piece of chalk'

Interestingly, the description of the semantics and functions of Latin American Spanish evaluative suffixes given in Bello (1847) is more comprehensive with respect to twenty-first-century usage than some much more recent theoretical works. Bello (1847: 43–45) observes that the diminutive indicates smallness, with connotations of affection or compassion, hypocorism, youth (as in the designations of young animals and plants), or insignificance, with connotations of disdain, mockery, or contempt, and notes the extension of diminutives to adverbs, gerunds, and participles. He does not describe the meanings of these extensions in any detail. In the case of diminutivized adverbs, he states that the only function of the suffix is stylistic, in that (he argues) diminutives inherently introduce an informal or familiar register. In diminutivized verbal forms, he views the suffix as exclusively adverbializing, e.g., *corriendo* 'running' (V) → *corriendito* (Adv).[7] Finally, he decries what he sees as the excessive and unnecessary use of the diminutive, particularly in Chilean Spanish. In fact, given their interpersonal uses and usefulness, the productivity and frequency of evaluative affixes across all varieties of Spanish has not declined, as Eddington (2017) shows.

Beyond the issue of the heterogeneity and complexity of the semantics of Romance evaluative affixes, it is also the case that evaluative/expressive meaning (which, by definition, is non-propositional) is problematic for logical or formal semantic approaches, which have traditionally focused on the truth conditions of declarative sentences. Both the 'bewildering'

---

[7] In many varieties of present-day Spanish, diminutivized verbs can remain verbs, as we see in Section 14.4.2.4.

range of possible, and at times seemingly contradictory, meanings expressed by individual evaluative affixes (Jurafsky 1996), and the fact that they combine denotational and connotational meanings, means that formal semanticists and logicians have largely avoided tackling them. However, recent developments in formal semantic theory, due to Potts (2005; 2007) have expanded the logical toolkit to include expressive (or, more-generally, 'use-conditional') meaning, formalized independently of descriptive meaning. This multidimensional semantic analysis has been applied to Spanish and French evaluative affixes, with promising results.

Given the catalogue of problems that Romance evaluative suffixes have posed for morphology, semantics, and pragmatics (not to mention lexicography), we will suggest that the explanation for their typological aberrancy must be functional, rather than grammatical. As we will see, an adequate account of the senses and uses of evaluative affixes will have to consider their irreducibly bipartite meaning, with semantics and pragmatics playing independent roles. We propose that, while the semantic component of Romance evaluative affixes conforms to general grammatical principles, the affective and expressive component is sui generis, and that this accounts for its apparent anomalousness.

14.3.3 Semantic versus Pragmatic Accounts

Broadly, accounts of the meaning of evaluative affixes have fallen into two camps: those who take a semantic, size-related meaning as basic, and those who stress the priority of pragmatics over semantics. Jurafsky's (1996) influential paper falls into the former category, and Dressler and Merlini Barbaresi (1994) is the most thoroughgoing example of the latter. What these approaches have in common is that they aim to derive all functions, both semantic and pragmatic, from a prior, primitive sense or function.

Jurafsky aims to give an explicit account of the universal, diachronic, and synchronic semantics and pragmatics of the diminutive, within a cognitivist theoretical framework, and identifies various characteristics of diminutives that have long resisted explanation. First, and as we have seen, the diminutive can express a 'seemingly unlimited range' and 'bewildering variety' of meanings, some of which appear to be contradictory, as the attenuating and intensifying uses of Spanish diminutive -it- show. Second, despite this heterogeneity of meanings, the senses and pragmatic uses of the diminutive are remarkably consistent across genetically unrelated languages, as Jurafsky's (1996: 534–41) survey shows. This crosslinguistic regularity must be accounted for. Third, existing mechanisms of semantic change such as metaphor, conventionalization of inference, and generalization/bleaching are able to handle some of the senses, but not ones such as 'approximation' or 'exactness' (1996: 535).

Following Wierzbicka (1984), Jurafsky traces the meanings and functions of the diminutive to a prototypical sense 'child', and derives them using Lakoff's (1987) Radial Category which is an explicit representation of a polysemous category with a prototypical, central sense, and a network of peripheral conceptual extensions. Thus, diminutives arise from semantic or pragmatic links with children via the aforementioned historical mechanisms, plus a novel method of diachronic change, lambda-abstraction-specification, which takes a predicate and replaces it with a variable which ranges over predicates. Lambda-abstraction-specification accounts for the quantificational (individuating/partitive) and second-order predicates like approximation, exactness, and linguistic hedges.[8]

In contrast, Alonso (1954: 161) strongly rejects what he calls the 'old idea' that the affective functions of the diminutive are somehow derived from a semantic, size-related meaning – for example, by drawing a connexion between small things and cute or worthless things and, from there, to the appreciative and pejorative uses of the diminutive, respectively. For Alonso, the basic function of the Spanish diminutive, both synchronically and diachronically, is pragmatic, evaluative, and affective, rather than literally diminutive and semantic. Citing the wealth of affective and playful meanings that the diminutive can convey, he points out that it is rarely used, on its own, to indicate reduced size; rather, an adjective is typically included for that purpose: Sp. *una caj-ita pequeña* a box-DIM small 'a cute little box'. He adduces common examples like *añito* year.DIM and the kinds of non-nominal diminutives we have seen, for which no size-related meaning makes any sense (even metaphorically, in many cases), as evidence that the affective meaning is prior. Furthermore, following the Germanist Ferdinand Wrede, Alonso argues that the diminutive suffix serves to foreground the object or event that it marks. He thus characterizes the primary sense of the diminutive as the convergence of two interpretations: one which interprets it as the highlighting of an object in consciousness ('individualización interesada') and another which interprets it as an affective sign (Alonso 1954: 163).

More recently, Wolfgang Dressler and Lavinia Merlini Barbaresi have developed a theory of Morphopragmatics, which they and others have applied in great detail to evaluative affixes, principally in Italian and German. Like Alonso, they 'oppose the previous *communis opinio* whereby all pragmatic meanings of diminutives and augmentatives would derive from "small" and "big" respectively, or from some other morphosemantic meaning' (Dressler and Merlini Barbaresi 2001: 43) and reject Jurafsky's proposal that all meanings of the diminutive can be traced back to the

---

[8] Prieto (2015) adopts Jurafsky's proposal of the diminutive as a radial category, but argues that its prototypical sense is not 'child', but 'smallness' or 'littleness'.

semantics of 'child'. Instead, they view the pragmatic meanings as prior, with the semantic meanings supervening upon them.

In contrast to Alonso's basic pragmatic functions, however, they posit an invariant pragmatic feature [fictive] which, in the case of diminutives and augmentatives, is specified as the feature [non-serious]. They argue that most pragmatic functions of evaluative affixes derive from this feature, and adduce a wealth of evidence to show that those functions are autonomous from their denotational meanings. For example, they note that diminutives and augmentatives can often carry the same pragmatic effect, even though their semantics are in opposition (Merlini Barbaresi 2006: 333):

(24) **Italian**
    a.   Mangi   come un maial-ino.
          you.eat like a   pig-DIM
          'You eat like a little piggy.'
    b.   Mangi   come un maial-one.
          you.eat like a   pig-AUG
          'You eat like some huge pig.'

The evaluative suffixes in both cases are linguistic hedges that mitigate what could otherwise be received as an insult.

14.3.4 Romance Evaluative Affixes in Formal Semantics

Fortin (2011) and Fradin (2012) were the first attempts at unitary formal semantic accounts of Romance evaluative affixes. The crucial development which permitted this was Potts' (2005; 2007) multidimensional semantics, which was originally designed to handle supplemental expressions (like parentheticals, non-restrictive relative clauses, and appositives), but was subsequently generalized to expressives and use-conditional meaning generally (Potts 2005; Gutzmann 2015).

It should be noted that the umbrella term 'semantics' is somewhat misleading in this context, since the formalism models truth-conditional and use-conditional meaning as independent dimensions. Thus, as a synchronic account, the multidimensional analysis obviates the controversial issue of whether the denotational, pragmatic, or connotational (affective) meaning is basic. That said, the formalism of Fortin (2011) predicts that, while the presence of the denotational meaning of an evaluative affix depends on the kind of base it attaches to, the pragmatic meaning is always present. This does not mean that the pragmatic meaning is prior, but it does suggest a certain compatibility with the morphopragmatic approach.

The basic intuition is that the meaning of evaluative affixes consists of two separate parts, one descriptive, the other expressive. Fortin (2011) formalizes the descriptive dimension of the Spanish diminutive and augmentative suffixes as relative gradable adjectives, in the sense of Kennedy (1997). It thus predicts, for example, that the descriptive meaning 'small' of the diminutive (or its allosemes, 'young' and 'insignificant') should only be available if it attaches to a word that denotes an individual, or where an individuating interpretation is possible. For example, a diminutive can attach to a count noun N, to yield the meaning 'small N' – as in Sp. *perrito* dog.DIM 'small dog' – and to a mass noun N, to yield the meaning 'small unit of N' – as in Cat. *agüeta* water.DIM 'small (bottle of) water', but where a mass noun cannot be individuated, only the expressive meaning is available. This accounts for the individuating function of evaluative affixes, noted in example (11). The expressive dimension is modelled using Potts's (2007) expressive index, a triple <a I b> where *a* is typically the speaker, *b* is the object of *a*'s affect, and I is a real-number interval [−1, 1]. This encodes use-conditional meaning along three independent parameters:

(i) a speaker-oriented attitudinal relation *att*, between a speaker *a* and an object *b*;
(ii) the positive or negative bias of *att* as the midpoint *m* of I, where $m = 0$ encodes neutral affect;
(iii) the intensity of *att* as the width *w* of I, where $w = 1$ encodes neutral intensity.

This is to say that the expressive index conveys that individual *a* (typically the speaker) has the attitude I towards *b*. The required manipulations of the interval I are achieved by an algebraic operator, AFF, which shifts the midpoint of I leftwards and rightwards to reflect negative and positive affect, respectively, and narrows and widens the width of I to indicate intensification and attenuation, respectively. Note that *b* is any contextual object, broadly understood, so it can include individuals, words, situations, utterances, and speech acts. This accounts for both affective and illocutionary functions of evaluative affixes, since both can be precisely modelled as manipulations of an interval I: one where *b* is (say) an individual or situation, the other where *b* is a speech act. For example, one could model *a*'s moderately intense appreciation of an individual *b* with the expressive index <a [−0.2, 0.6] b> (where $m = 0.2$ and $w = 0.8$), and *a*'s downgrading of the illocutionary force of a speech act *b* with the index <a [−0.753, 0.753] b> (where $m = 0$ and $w = 1.506$). Crucially, pure (non-emotive) intensification and attenuation is straightforwardly modelled as the narrowing and widening, respectively, of a symmetrical interval, such that $m = 0$.

Although this approach is not designed to account for the diachronic development of the meanings of evaluative affixes, it has some features which make it attractive for their synchronic analysis. First, as a formal and explicit system, it makes precise predictions about what kinds of meanings should and should not be possible, without resort to potentially questionable metaphorical associations. Second, since **I** is an interval of real numbers, it can model infinitely gradable affects and intensities, and is thus an adequate formalism for capturing the 'seemingly unlimited range' of meanings that evaluative affixes can convey (Jurafsky 1996: 537). Third, the independence of the truth-conditional and use-conditional dimensions has several desirable consequences: (i) the meanings of evaluative affixes can be accounted for without having to postulate a single, basic meaning, and then deriving all the others from it; (ii) the formalism correctly predicts that the adjectival meaning can be applied only once, whereas the expressive meaning can be iterated (Rainer 1986: 206f.); (iii) the commonalities between diminutive and augmentative suffixes noted by Dressler and Merlini Barbaresi (1994) follow from the fact that they both manipulate expressive indices, the differences between them arising from their contrasting adjectival meanings; (iv) it accounts for the fact that the affective meanings of evaluative affixes satisfy Potts' (2007) criteria for expressives, including the fact that they cannot be embedded nor negated (Fortin 2011: 25–36).

We turn in what follows to a set of data that, up to now, has not attracted the attention it deserves, neither from Romanists nor from general linguists.

14.4 Diminutives outside Verb Inflexions in Romance

14.4.1 Positional Mobility of Evaluative Suffixes in Latin and Romance

In order to fully appreciate the data that will be the focus of Sections 14.4.2–3, some preliminary observations concerning the surprising mobility of Latin and Romance evaluative suffixes will be helpful. The issue was first addressed in Skutsch (1908: 37) under the label 'Enallage der Deminution' ('enallage of diminution'). Skutsch argued that in Latin expressions such as *aureolus anellus* 'golden-DIM ringlet' (Pl. *Epidicus* 640) or *puer bimulus* lit. 'boy two-year-old-DIM' (Catullus 17, 12–13) the diminutive suffix attached to the adjective did not modify its base but rather the head noun of the phrase. Soon afterwards, a hint at comparable positional mobility of diminutives in Romance appeared in Spitzer (1918: 107–10), who observed that in Portuguese the diminutive suffix *-inho* placed on a participle often conferred an affective note to the whole sentence. This same phenomenon can also be observed in Spanish. In (25), in fact, the diminutive suffix *-it-* does not modify the past participle it is attached to, but expresses the writer's attitude of commiseration towards the dwarves referred to by the elliptic phrase *Los tres* 'The three':

(25) Los   tres   ca-id-it-o-s   en el   suelo. (Sp., De Bruyne 2000: 259)
     the   three   fall-en-DIM-M-PL   on the   floor
     'The three poor creatures, lying on the floor.'

The 'landing site', to use Dressler and Merlini's (1994) term, need not be an adjective or a participle, by the way. In the following utterance, for example, overheard in conversation in Zaragoza (Spain), -it- ended up attached to the preposition *hasta*:[9]

(26) Estoy   hast-ita   las   mismísimas   narices. (Sp., Martín Zorraquino 2012: 128)
     be.PRS.1SG   until-DIM   the   very   noses
     'I am fed up to the back teeth.'

14.4.2 Diminutive Suffixes outside Verbal Inflexion

The diminutive suffixes that are going to be presented here have several traits in common: they are placed on verbs, outside the verbal inflexions, but have scope over the whole utterance; they are all very productive and strongly affective, pertaining to child-directed speech or other substandard, mostly rural/popular registers. In the literature, if mentioned at all, they are normally treated as curiosities and relegated to incidental remarks or footnotes. The fact that such highly similar constructions have arisen independently from Romania to Brazil, however, would seem to warrant a closer examination.

14.4.2.1 Romanian

Romanian is the only Romance language for which a (short) article on the phenomenon is available (Cazacu 1950). In this language, the diminutive suffixes *-ică*, *-iță*, and *-uță* are occasionally added to inflected verbs in child-directed or rural speech:

(27) **Romanian (C. Manolache; Cazacu 1950: 92)**
   a. Păpiță!   Păpică!   (← Pap-ă!)
       eat.IMP.DIM   eat.IMP.DIM   eat-IMP
       'Eat, my dear!' 'Eat, my dear!' 'Eat!'
   b. Mă   rog   matale, mă   rog-uță   matale
       me=   ask.PRS.1SG   sir   me=   ask.PRS.1SG-DIM   sir
       'I pray you, sir.'

One intriguing fact about these examples is that all three diminutives end in *-ă*. This highly polyvalent ending *-ă* realizes feminine gender in *-uță* (cf. *fiu* M 'son' → *fiuț* vs *casă* F 'house' → *căsuță*), and also in *-iță*, which in diminutive function only attaches to feminine bases (cf. *babă* 'old woman'

---

[9] Unfortunately, the exact semantic or pragmatic value of the suffix is not commented upon in the source.

→ *băbiță*). The suffix *-ică*, by contrast, appears in this form also with masculine bases (cf. male first name *Ion* → *Ionică*). The *-ă* therefore is a mere class marker in this latter case, unrelated to gender.[10] The fact that *-ă* at the same time realizes the second person singular of the (first conjugation) imperative may have facilitated the transfer of the diminutive on verbs in examples like those in (27a). In example (27b), it is more difficult to explain why the diminutive takes the form *-uță* instead of the unmarked masculine ending *-uț*, since the first person of the verb *a ruga* 'ask', viz. *rog*, does not end in *-ă*. Șerban (2013–14: 28) writes that, with parts of speech other than nouns and adjectives, normally *-uț* is added if the word ends in a consonant and *-uța* if it ends in a vowel, 'but that there are also exceptions like *roguță < rog*'.

14.4.2.2 Italian (Dialect of Lucca, Tuscany)

Hasselrot (1957: 233) brought sentence (28), taken from Nieri (1902), to the attention of Romanists. In this sentence, the diminutive suffix *-ino* is attached to the participle of a periphrastic perfect. On the function of the suffix, Hasselrot said: 'the suffix does not diminutivize the word to which it is attached but gives an affective touch to the whole sentence: "Have you eaten, my dear?"'[11] This function must be strictly separated from the diminutive-iterative function that we find in Italian, as well as in other Romance languages, when the diminutive suffix is attached directly to the verb stem, inside inflexional endings, as in *mangi-ucchi-are* 'to nibble' (← *mangiare* 'to eat'). In this latter case, the diminutive suffix directly affects the semantics of the verb.

(28) Hai   mangi-at-ino? (It.)
      have.2SG   eat-en-DIM
      'Have you eaten, my dear?'

14.4.2.3 Occitan (Gévaudan Dialect)

In order to highlight the exuberance of diminutives in Occitan as opposed to standard French, Charles Camproux, the great specialist of the Gévaudan dialects, adduced sentence (29) where the diminutive suffix *-on* is attached to a verb in the imperative form (*Traversa!* 'Go across!'). Formally, the ending *-a* is polyvalent: it represents both the imperative ending and the feminine form of the suffix *-on*. Note that there is no verb **traversonar* in this dialect. With respect to the function of the suffix, Camproux (1951: 185) added: 'the suffix attached to the imperative is meant to underline the tender concern of the mother').

---

[10] On these three diminutive suffixes, cf. Pușcariu (1899: 38–52, 66–77).
[11] Here and below all quotes in languages other than English have been translated into English by the authors.

(29) An-em ! pichot travers-on-a ! (Gvd., Camproux 1951: 184f.)
    go-HOR.1PL little.boy go.across-DIM-IMP.2SG
    'Come on, little boy, go across!'

14.4.2.4 Spanish

Spanish has a greater variety of relevant constructions than any of the languages seen so far. In example (30), taken from the Academy dictionary of 1770, the diminutive suffix -*ito* is attached in its unmarked masculine form to *Acabóse*, a sentence that already had an idiomatic status at the time.[12]

(30) Acab-o-s-ito.   (← Acabóse.) (Sp., DRAE, 1770; Spitzer 1961: 260)
    finish-PRT.3SG-REFL-DIM finish.PRT.3SG=REFL
    'It's definitively over.' 'It's over.'

A diminutive suffix – Ara. -*ico* – attached to a verb in the first person singular is reported from the colloquial Spanish of Zaragoza. The ending -*o* represents at the same time the first person singular present indicative and the unmarked masculine form of the suffix.

(31) Te   lo   jur-ic-o. (coll. Zaragoza Sp., Martín Zorraquino 2012: 128)
    you.DAT= it.ACC= swear-DIM-PRS.IND.1SG
    'I really swear.'

The diminutive attached to the participle of the periphrastic perfect, which we have already encountered in the dialect of Lucca, is also attested for the dialect of Andalusia. Faitelson-Weiser (1980: 197), to whom we owe example (32), commented on the function of the diminutive suffix as follows: '[t]he semantic effect is to express the tender commiseration of the singer'.

(32) ¿Quién le   ha pega-íto   a   mi padre [...]? (And., folk song)
    who   him= has beaten-DIM DOM my father
    'Who has beaten my poor father?'

The most frequent constellation in Spanish is constituted by the attachment of the diminutive suffix to gerunds used in a clearly verbal function, as part of progressive periphrases (33a–b) or subordinate clauses (33c).

(33) **Spanish**
   a. Está   *durm-ie-nd-ito.* (Leopoldo García Ramón, *La neña* 1891: 413)
      is.PRS.IND.3SG   sleep-TV-GER-DIM
      '[Our angel] is sleeping softly.'

---

[12] The Academy dictionary classified *acabosito* as a jocular adverb.

b. Nos pid-e el cuerpo ir *cant-a-nd-illo* nuestras
us= ask.PRS.IND.3SG the body go.INF sing-TV-GER-DIM our
coplillas preferíah!¹³
songs favourite
'Our body asks us to continually sing our favourite songs!'
c. *compr-a-nd-ito* algo de ropa para mis niños¹⁴
buy-TV-GER-DIM something of clothes for my children
'buying some clothes for my children'

14.4.2.5 Brazilian Portuguese

This use of diminutives had already been noted as a peculiarity of some varieties of Brazilian Portuguese by Leite de Vasconcellos (1883: 19), whence it found its way into Wagner (1952: 473), who considered such forms 'a proliferation due to the play instinct'. As in Spanish, we find the diminutive suffix on all kinds of gerunds and past participles in verbal function:¹⁵

(34) **Brazilian Portuguese**
a. Est-á dorm-ind-inho. (Folha de S.Paolo, 8/05/07; said of a baby or child)
be-PRS.IND.3SG sleep-GER-DIM
'[Our angel] is sleeping.'
b. Ele vem bajul-a-nd-inho a Ana todos os
he come.PRS.IND.3SG suck.up-TV-GER-DIM DOM Ana all the
dias. (Guimarães and Mendes 2011: 374)
days
'[This crawler] has continually been sucking up to Ana.'
c. O nosso clube vai ser com-id-inho com batatas.¹⁶
the our club go.PRS.IND.3SG be.INF eat-EN-DIM with potatoes
'Our club will be beaten [lit. pleasurably be eaten with potatoes].'

Some varieties of Brazilian Portuguese, however, go well beyond the Spanish usage. In (35) the diminutive suffix is attached to the infinitive in a clearly verbal construction:

(35) Quero est-a-r-zinho com ela. (BrPt., Raul Bopp, poem)¹⁷
I want stay-TV-INF-DIM with her
'I want to stay with my darling.'

While in (34) the form of the diminutive suffix was *-inho*, in (35) it is *-zinho*, which here represents an allomorph of *-inho* required by the stem ending in /r/ (*estar*). For the same reason we find *-zinho* in (36), where *quer* represents the third person singular:

---

¹³ Folk song, Andalusia.
¹⁴ American Spanish. www.pictaramweb.com/u/eduardonieves4550.
¹⁵ Guimarães and Mendes (2011: 375 n. 13): '"diminutivized gerunds" exist in some dialects but not in others'.
¹⁶ Homepage of Sporting Football Club. www.supersporting.net/sevilha-duplica-ordenado-para-levar-andre-geraldes-de-alvalade/.
¹⁷ https://labirintto.wordpress.com/poema-de-sete-faces/.

(36) Não quer-zinho comé nada (BrPt., *Leite de Vasconcellos* 1883: 19)
　　　not　want.PRS.IND.3SG-DIM　eat.INF　nothing
　　　'[Our angel] does not want to eat anything.'

This same allomorph is also required after stems ending in a stressed vowel, such as *está* (third person singular) and *estou* (first person singular):

(37) **Brazilian Portuguese**
　a.　Est-á-zinh-o　　　doente. (Leite de Vasconcellos 1883: 19)
　　　be-PRS.IND.3SG-DIM-M　sick
　　　'The poor creature is sick.'
　b.　agora　est-ou-zinh-a　　　lind-a　e　bel-a　na minha
　　　now　be-PRS.IND.1SG-DIM-FSG　pretty-FSG　and　beautiful-FSG　in　my
　　　humilde　residencia [sic]. (blog)[18]
　　　humble　home
　　　'Now I stay comfortably at my humble home.'

However, *-zinho* also exists as an independent suffix that can be attached outside unstressed inflexional affixes.[19] This latter use of *-zinho* can be observed in the examples under (38), where it attaches the first person of the present indicative (38a), the imperative (38b), and even the imperfect subjunctive (38c).

(38) **Brazilian Portguese**
　a.　Não poss-o-zinho　　　ir　　longe. (José Veríssimo; Maurer Jr 1969: 245 n. 9)
　　　not　can-PRS.IND.1SG-DIM　go.INF　far
　　　'I fear I cannot go far.'
　b.　Dorm-e-zinho　um pouco! (Dalcidio Jurandir, *Os habitantes*)[20]
　　　sleep-IMP.2SG-DIM　a　little
　　　'Sleep a little, my dear!'
　c.　Que tev-esse-zinho　　　pena[21] (José Veríssimo; Maurer Jr 1969: 245 n. 9)
　　　that　have-IPFV.SBJV.3SG-DIM　sorrow
　　　'That the poor creature was sorry'

This behaviour is entirely parallel to what we find in the nominal and adjectival domain (cf. *casa* 'house' → *casazinha*, alongside *casinha*; *sério* 'serious' → *seriozinho*). In most examples, the suffix appears in the masculine singular form (*-zinho*). It remains unclear, however, whether this is due to agreement with an implicit masculine controller or represents a case of emergence of the unmarked (the *-o* therefore is not analysed in the glosses).

---

[18] https://ask.fm/CesaraAyres/best?page=4.
[19] The relationship between these two types of *-zinho* has caused much controversy in Portuguese linguistics: while some linguists interpret them as allomorphs of one and the same morpheme, others see two independent suffixes synchronically. The treatment above presupposes this latter view, which cannot be defended here due to space limitations.
[20] doczz.com.br/doc/729961/os-habitantes.
[21] The standard form for the third-person past subjunctive of *ter* 'to have' is *tivesse*.

Example (37b) is more telling in this respect, because *estouzinha* shows unequivocal agreement with the unexpressed feminine gender of the subject of the sentence, just like the two adjectives *linda* and *bela*. This behaviour also recalls what we find in the nominal domain, where -*zinho* realizes the gender of the base noun (cf. *uma foto* F 'a photograph' → *uma fotozinha* F).

14.4.3 Lessons for General Linguistics

Most straightforwardly, the data adduced in Section 14.4.2 can be added to the already substantial pool of examples that contradict Greenberg's Universal 28,[22] which says: '[i]f both the derivation and inflection follow the root, or they both precede the root, the derivation is always between the root and the inflection.' (Greenberg 1963: 93). If, as is standardly assumed, evaluative morphology in Romance is part of derivational morphology (Weber 1963: 27–35), the order 'verbal inflexion inside diminutive suffix' is, of course, incompatible with Greenberg's claim.

Counterexamples to Universal 28, however, have wider theoretical ramifications because some theories of the architecture of grammar credit themselves with being able to derive it as a theorem. Such theories of Split Morphology (cf. Anderson 1982), as we have seen in the introduction, divide morphology into two neatly separate halves, derivation and inflexion. By locating derivation in the lexicon and inflexion after syntax, whose features it is bound to realize morphologically, the ordering relation 'derivational morphemes inside inflexional morphemes' in morphologically complex words in fact falls out automatically. What looks like an asset, however, turns into a liability with the accumulation of counterevidence to Universal 28.

In the face of empirical problems with Universal 28, some authors have proposed to divide morphology in a less dichotomous way. Scalise (1984: 133) proposed to split morphology into three parts, derivation, evaluative morphology, and inflexion. It is easy to see that this move does not escape the impact of our counterexamples, in which evaluative suffixes are located after inflexional ones. The same observation applies to Dressler's (1989) proposal to split both derivation and inflexion into a prototypical and a non-prototypical subpart aligned in the order PD < NPD < NPI < PI, and to dispense with the ordering requirements among immediately adjacent subparts. As a consequence, non-prototypical inflexion (NPI) would be allowed to feed non-prototypical derivation (NPD), among which Dressler also counts evaluative morphology. However, since the inflexion in our data also comprises prototypical categories such as person agreement, even this relaxation is of no avail in accounting for our data, whatever its other

---

[22] A comprehensive collection of such examples is missing. For further Romance examples, cf. Rainer (1996).

merits may be. Booij's (1993) similar proposal to split inflexion into contextual and inherent, and to allow inherent inflexion to feed derivation, suffers the same fate.

The problem of affix order, however, has also been tackled from another angle over the last decades. Linguists have tried to discover general principles that underlie the ordering of affixes. Such an approach, by the way, is necessary also in the kind of model mentioned in the last paragraph in order to determine affix order inside components or subcomponents. What research (overviews in Stump 2001; Manova and Aronoff 2010; Rice 2011; Mithun 2016) has made clear is that affix order is determined by an array of factors whose combination varies from language to language. From a synchronic viewpoint, scope and relevance are the driving semantic forces, but they can be overruled by formal factors. In the Athapaskan language Slavey, for example, the diminutive and augmentative suffix is placed outside the inflexional possessive suffix as a consequence of a phonological principle that places shorter suffixes inside longer ones (Rice 2011: 183f.), although scope considerations would suggest the opposite order (we say *my small/big shoes*, not: ***small/big my shoes*). But not only system-related factors are relevant in synchrony, for language processing has also been shown to influence affix order: less parsable/productive affixes tend to be located inside more parsable/productive ones, at least in English. Not all affix order, however, is synchronically motivated. Sometimes the order simply has to be stipulated and coded in templates or position classes as a brute fact. Mithun (2016) rightly insists that the synchronic perspective should be supplemented by a diachronic analysis: what is arbitrary in synchrony may find a straightforward explanation when the history of the language is taken into account. In diachrony, the order of grammaticalization of affixes is a major explanatory factor, but reanalysis and analogical extension, among other factors, may later blur the picture.

Let us now have a look at our data against this background. From a synchronic point of view, the data seem compatible with the principles of scope and relevance. This latter term is defined as follows in Bybee (1985: 4): '[t]he semantic relevance of an affix to a stem is the extent to which the meaning of the affix directly affects the meaning of the stem'. Manova and Aronoff (2010: 122) consider it the opposite of *scope*: '[t]he suffix with the broadest scope is the most general (i.e., least relevant) and is thus placed farthest away from the base, whereas the most relevant suffix has the narrowest scope and is thus the closest to the base'. This characterization squares very well with the function of the diminutives in our data, which give an affective overtone to the whole utterance or express a certain attitude towards the addressee, but do not affect the semantics of the verb itself. In some cases, an expression detached from the sentence, such as 'my dear', seems to be the most adequate gloss. For affixes with such a wide scope, the final position is a perfect landing site. This final position is also quite natural from a processing standpoint: all suffixes are highly productive and semantically transparent in context, and hence should occur at the periphery.

But how did the suffixes end up in this final position? We are not dealing with a case of externalization in the sense of Haspelmath (1993): the suffixes were never used in this function in a position close to the verb stem. Their 'migration' towards the end of the verb has certainly to be understood in the context of the general positional mobility of 'sentence diminutives' in Romance languages sketched in Section 14.4.2. The use of inflected verbs as landing sites was an innovation that arose independently in different languages and was facilitated by the fact that some of the verbal constructions that were first affected by this kind of use contain constituents that functioned already routinely as landing sites, notably past participles and gerunds. In the case of gerunds, the intermediate step was constituted by gerunds used as adverbs, such as Sp. *callandito* 'silently', lit. 'being.quiet.DIM', *corriendito* 'fast', lit. 'running.DIM', which could regularly receive the diminutive suffix just like other adverbs. The use of diminutives on imperatives, as in BrPt. *Dormezinho!* 'Sleep, my dear!', may have been facilitated by functionally equivalent diminutives on orders such as *Quietinho!* 'Be quiet!'. Hasselrot's (1957: 277 n. 3) hunch that in Brazilian Portuguese diminutivized pronouns might have served as intermediate steps (*Luizinha está doente* 'Luise.DIM is sick' > *Elazinha está doente* 'she.DIM is sick' > *Estázinha doente* 'she.is.DIM sick') seems less compelling, but cannot be dismissed outright. Once diminutive suffixes were used on some verb forms, they could be extended analogically to other verb forms that had fewer similarities to non-verbal diminutive forms. As already mentioned above, the polyvalence of some endings such as *-o*, *-a*, or *-ă*, which occur both on nouns, adjectives, adverbs, and verbs, may also have facilitated the transfer to the verbal domain. These remarks about how the curious behaviour of our diminutives may have come about must, of necessity, remain speculative. Verbal diminutives of this kind, unfortunately, are sparsely attested in the literature (and also on the Internet), since they are typical of child-directed speech and of substandard varieties, mostly dialects.

If we look at our diminutives from this functional perspective, they turn out to be less erratic than it might seem at first glance. Since, at the same time, we have found them to be intractable in models of grammar based on 'components', this fact can also be taken as an argument against such models. The ordering relation 'derivation inside inflexion' is certainly the normal case, in Romance as well as cross-linguistically, but this generalization, to the extent that it is true, seems to follow automatically from the different principles that have been found to determine affix order, just like the exceptional cases described in Section 14.4.2. It need not be stated separately in a grammar.

14.5 Conclusion

We have sought to show that Romance evaluative suffixation is not only a fascinating phenomenon in itself, that has rightly attracted a great deal of attention from Romance scholars in the past and in the present, but also keeps in store important challenges and lessons for general linguistics. The theoretical relevance that one is willing to concede to the data depends to some extent on whether Romance evaluative suffixation is considered 'plain' morphology or not. In Section 14.2, we argued that Romance evaluative morphology shares many properties with expressive morphology and that consequently theoretical claims limited to plain morphology are not necessarily affected by counterexamples coming from this area. In Sections 14.3 and 14.4, by contrast, we showed that the prima facie aberrant behaviour of evaluative suffixes with regard to meaning and affix order both reflect a deeper rationale. The apparent rampant polysemy of evaluative suffixes begins to look a lot less chaotic if analysed in a formal framework such as Potts' two-tiered semantics, an analysis that can also account for several 'anomalous' properties that evaluative affixation shares with expressive morphology, such as iterability. The unexpected placement of diminutive suffixes after verbal inflexional endings, in turn, has been argued to comply with deep principles underlying affix order in natural languages and to be fundamentally a consequence of the peculiar affective-pragmatic use of diminutives as 'sentence diminutives' in some Romance varieties.

Selected References

Below you can find selected references for this chapter. The full references can be found online at the following page: www.cambridge.org/Romancelinguistics

Alonso, A. (1954). *Estudios lingüísticos: temas españoles*. Madrid: Gredos.
Bello, A. (1847). *Gramática de la lengua castellana destinada al uso de los americanos*. Santiago de Chile: Imprenta del Progreso.
Camproux, C. (1951). 'Déficience et vitalité de la dérivation', *Le Français moderne* 19: 181–86.
Cazacu, B. (1950). 'Despre unele forme verbale cu sufixe diminutivale', *Studii și cercetări lingvistice* 1: 91–98.
Dressler, W. and Merlini Barbaresi, L. (1994). *Morphopragmatics. Diminutives and Intensifiers in Italian, German, and Other Languages*. Berlin: de Gruyter.

Eddington, D. (2017). 'Dialectal variation in Spanish diminutives: a performance model', *Studies in Hispanic and Lusophone Linguistics* 10: 39–66.

Hasselrot, B. (1957). *Étude sur la formation diminutive dans les langues romanes*. Uppsala: Lundequist.

Maurer, T., Jr. (1969). 'Um sufixo de comportamento original: o diminutivo em -zinho'. In Barbadinho Neto, R. (ed.), *Estudos em homagem a Cândido Jucá (filho)*. Rio de Janeiro: Simões, 233–46.

Napoli, D. J., and Reynolds, B. (1995). 'Evaluative affixes in Italian'. In Booij, G. and van Marle, J. (eds), *Yearbook of Morphology 1994*. Dordrecht: Springer, 151–78.

Stump, G. (1993). 'How peculiar is evaluative morphology?', *Journal of Linguistics* 29: 1–36.

Wagner, M. L. (1952). 'Das "Diminutiv" im Portugiesischen', *Orbis* 1: 460–76.

Zwicky, A., and Pullum, G. (1987). 'Plain morphology and expressive morphology'. *Proceedings of the Thirteenth Annual Meeting of the Berkeley Linguistics Society* 1987: 330–40.

15

Counting Systems

Brigitte L. M. Bauer

15.1 Introduction

Numerals are parts of speech that offer a means of counting and therefore are at the cross-roads of linguistics, cognitive sciences, arithmetic, archaeology, and anthropology.* Yet counting is not necessarily language-bound nor is it necessarily numerical. Infants, for example, are able to recognize (change in) quantity (Peucker and Weißhaupt 2013) and anthropologists have found that speakers of languages with few or no numerals are able to identify quantity (Harrison 2007: 187). Moreover, in the early stages of the agricultural revolution in the Near East (fourth millennium B.C.), food production and cattle were quantified with non-numerical tokens.

Today's counting system in Romance is numerical and decimal, with a few numerals in certain varieties that feature a base '20' (vigesimals). The Romance decimal counting system can be traced back to Latin and proto-Indo-European. The types of numeral in Romance and their evolution, their formal characteristics – combining inherited, innovative, and borrowed features – the potential effects of language contact, spontaneous innovations, and finally the strength of the decimal system that spreads at the expense of non-decimal phenomena, underscore the importance of Romance data for linguistic analysis.

This chapter examines the typology and diachronic development of counting systems in Romance and starts with a brief section (Section 15.2) on early systems of recording quantity that linger on in early Romance

---

* I am most grateful to the editors for their excellent comments and suggestions on an earlier version of this chapter. I am also obliged to Denise Schmandt-Besserat (University of Texas at Austin), Asli Özyürek (Max Planck Institut für Psycholinguistkk at Nijmegen), and Marie-Anne Sallandre (Université Paris VIII) for answering my questions about numerals in early writing and (French) Sign Language respectively.

languages. Section 15.3 explains the fundamental characteristics of numerical counting systems in general, including 'base' and 'arithmetical operation', before focusing on these concepts in Romance and on how they are formally expressed. Subsequently, Section 15.4 discusses the different types of numeral in Romance in the light of their Latin forerunners, revealing a major difference between the two systems. Section 15.5 assesses the potential effects of language contact in two deviant numeral formations in Romanian. Vigesimals and the role of borrowing vs internal parallel development will be analysed in Section 15.6. Section 15.7, finally, discusses the prominence of the decimal system in Romance. The chapter offers a linguistic account of numerals, focusing on insights that Romance data can provide for general topics in linguistic theory. For the formation of numerals in Romance per category starting with the lower digits, see Bauer (2021).

15.2 Early Systems of Quantification

In addition to the widespread decimal numeral system, languages in today's Europe – but many more in the past – may feature measure systems whereby each commodity has its own units of quantification and conversion factor. These early systems typically measure distance (length), volume (liquid and dry), weight, and area (for details, see, e.g., Justus 1999a; Gyllenbok 2018; Rowlett 2018; Zupko 2018). They are custom-based, using bases such a body parts (e.g., *foot*, *digit*, etc.), readily available practical items (e.g., *stones*, *containers*, *amphoras*), or in measuring distance, for example, the length a person could cover walking or ploughing, e.g., Lat. PASSUS 'step'; Eng. *furlong* (based on the length of a ploughed furrow). A measure unit may be subdivided into smaller units, which each had its own conversion factor and often came from the same semantic field such as body parts, e.g., Lat. PES 'foot' equalling 16 DIGITI 'fingers', 4 PALMI 'palms' or 12 UNCIAE 'twelfths' (later POLLICES 'thumbs'), with 1 GRADUS 'step' equalling 2.5 PEDES 'feet' and 1 PASSUS 'pace' equalling 5 PEDES, or the early French system of length where 1 *toise* was equal to 6 *pieds* 'feet', 12 *pouces* 'inches' (lit. thumbs), and 864 *lignes* 'lines' (Berriman 1953: 136). Early French volume units include 1 *muid* (< Lat. MODIUM 'bushel') equalling 4 *quarteaux* 'quarters', 12 *setiers* (< Lat. SEXTARIUS) 'sixths', 36 *veltes* (< OGer. V(i)ertel 'quarter'), 48 *minots* (Grk. *mina*+DIM), 144 *pots* 'pots, jars', and 576 *quarts* 'quarts' (Berriman 1953: 136), with factors 3, 4, and 12.

The principle of base units and conversion factors varying according to the commodity is a pivotal aspect of the unit system and goes back to the token system, which was prenumerical. Tokens were small tridimensional objects in the Near East (fourth millennium B.C.) that in size and shape convey a quantity of a given agricultural commodity. Their emergence has been connected to the agricultural revolution and the related storage of foods (Schmandt-Besserat 2019:16). In this system of quantification, each unit stood for a given quantity and nine units of a given commodity, for example, were rendered by nine tokens. This one-on-one system continued to be used when the two-dimensional tablets came about around 3200 B.C.: numerals followed later (Schmandt-Besserat 1992: 129–39, 189–94).

The unit system is well-represented in the early Romance languages – often going back to a Roman system – but features numerous local characteristics and variations, not only in absolute terms, but also in terms of conversion factors, which may vary from village to village (for overviews, see Berriman 1953; Klein 1974; Bowden 1990; Rowlett 2018; Zupko 2018). With attempts at standardization generally unsuccessful, the unit system continued to prevail until the French Revolution, which initiated a process of pervasive decimalization, not only in French but also in the other Romance languages. An occasional measure noun may survive (e.g., Sp. *gruesa*, Pt. *grosa*, Fr. *grosse* [< late Lat. GROSSA (GROSSUS) 'thick'] 'gross, twelve dozen, 144'). Other measure nouns are identified in today's dictionaries as old-fashioned measure terms – if included at all – and are no longer in use. Occasionally they may refer to a small quantity today, but typically not a precise quantity (e.g., Fr. *pouce* 'small quantity', but literally 'thumb [hence also inch]').[1] In this respect, the Romance languages differ fundamentally from certain other languages, such as English where early measure terms continue to be used (e.g., *yard*, *pint*, and the *pound*, but also the American system of agricultural weights, NASS 2013).

15.3 Numerical Counting

As a rule of thumb, when languages count 'beyond around "20"' (Comrie 2003: 32) their higher numerals are based on arithmetical operations. These operations require a so-called 'base' and they generate compound forms, be they transparent or not. Consequently, while the Romance numerals '1' through to '10' are monomorphemic, the numerals beyond '10' are compounds – etymologically at least – the result of combining of two or more numerals, which are in an arithmetic relation.

---

[1] Fr. *pouce*, It. *pollice*, etc. are used today in the context of the diagonal measurement of television and computer screens in accordance with the anglophone practice of measuring in inches.

15.3.1 Bases and Arithmetical Operations

Romance languages are profoundly decimal, which means that the number '10' (and its powers) acts as a base, the recurring numerical unit used in the arithmetical operations that generate higher numerals, cf. the following Romance examples: It. *sette* '7', *diciassette* 'ten.and.seven' > '17' (with *-a-* < Lat. AC 'and'), *settanta* 'seven.[TIMES].ten' > '70', *settantasette* 'seven.[TIMES].ten.[PLUS].seven' > '77', *settecento* 'seven.[TIMES].hundred' > '700', *settemila* 'seven.[TIMES].thousand'> '7000', *sette miliardi* 'seven.[TIMES].billion' > '7 billion',[2] and so forth.

The most widespread bases in the languages of the world are '5' (quinary), '10' (decimal), '12' (duodecimal), '20' (vigesimal), and '60' (sexagesimal; see Greenberg 1978 for numerous examples). Among them, the decimal and duodecimal systems may be consistent, and the quinary and the vigesimal are rarely pure.

While the Indo-European numeral system is decimal, certain languages also feature numerals with a different base, such as Breton where the regular series of teens (TEN.[PLUS].DIGIT) is interrupted by *tric'hwec'h* 'three.[TIMES].six'> '18' or Wel. *deunaw* 'two.[TIMES].nine'> '18' (Greene 1992: 545, 550). Other instances include elements of a base-four and a base-five system formation in certain Celtic languages, reflecting earlier prenumerical systems (Justus 1999a), the formal break in certain Germanic languages between '12' and '13' and '60' and '70' (see Bauer 2021), and the concept of 'long hundred',[3] referring to '120' rather than '100' (Justus 1999b). Because of the importance of numerals other than '10', the decimal system in Indo-European may not have been original or may not have been the only one in origin (see Polomé 1958; Lehmann 1970; Gamkrelidze and Ivanov 1994: 746–54; Justus 1999a; Luján 1999).

Across the languages of the world, the arithmetical operations underlying the numeral systems include (1) addition, (2) multiplication, (3) division, and (4) subtraction. In numerals based on addition, the appropriate numeral is added to the base; it follows the base in certain languages but precedes it in others (see Section 15.3.3 and examples under (1)). In operations of multiplication, the base is multiplied by the appropriate number, as in the following examples:

---

[2] The capitals between brackets refer to the underlying arithmetical operation, [TIMES] being multiplication and [PLUS] being addition. A dot indicates that the composing elements are in immediate juxtaposition, as in It. *settanta* 'seven.[TIMES].ten' > '70'; a blank means that the elements are separate, as in It. *sette miliardi* 'seven [TIMES] billion'; a hyphen identifies a hyphen in the spelling of the numerals, as in Fr. *dix-sept* 'ten-[PLUS]-seven' > '17'.

[3] There are indications that there was a distinction in early Germanic between 'hundred' '100' and 'long hundred', which had the value of '120' (Justus 1999b).

(1) **Addition**
    Fr.   *dix-huit*   'ten.[PLUS].eight'   >   '18'
    Ger. *achtzehn*   'eight.[PLUS].ten'   >   '18'
    Ger. *vierundzwanzig*   'four.and.twenty'   >   '24'

(2) **Multiplication**
    It.   *duecento*   'two.[TIMES].hundred'   >   '200'
    Eng. *four hundred*   'four.[TIMES].hundred' >   '400'

Addition and multiplication are the most common and widespread arithmetic operations underlying numerals in the languages of the world. Subtraction but especially division cross-linguistically are rare and they may be found in a variety of languages of Africa and the Americas (see Seiler 1990: 198). In the process of subtraction, the appropriate number is subtracted from a higher numeral, as in Yoruba *àrúndínlógbòn* (*àrún-dínl-ógbòn*) '5.decrease.30' > '25' (Ẹkundayọ 1977: 438).

In numerals based on division, the base is divided by the appropriate element, which takes the form of a fraction ('multiplication by a fraction' Greenberg 1978: 261), as in a number of Celtic languages, e.g., Wel. *hanner cant*, Scottish Gaelic *leith cheud* 'half hundred' > '50' (Greene 1992: 533–46) or Dan. *halvtredsindstyve* (> *halvtreds*; Ross and Berns 1992: 616):

(3)   halvtredsindstyve   (Dan.)
      half.third.times.twenty '50'

While bases may reflect areal distribution (see Comrie 2003: 36f.), arithmetical operations do not seem to do so. Yet with the strong predominance of the decimal system in the languages of the world as a whole, addition and multiplication are the most widespread arithmetical operations underlying numerals. This observation is in line with Greenberg's conclusion that division and subtraction are 'marked' processes (Greenberg 1978: 258–61; Seiler 1990). The typical occurrence of special markers in subtractive numerals seem to support this observation, as opposed to additive and multiplicative numerals, where mere juxtaposition or a connector suffice. Moreover, formations based on division tend to include fractions, which are often marked numerals (see Section 15.4).

15.3.2 Bases and Arithmetical Operations in Romance/Latin

The Romance numeral system is quasi-exclusively based on addition and multiplication and it is thoroughly decimal, as reflected in a number of phenomena. First, '10' and its powers (100, 1000, 1,000,000, etc.) function as recurring bases in teens, decads, hundreds, and the higher numerals.

Their presence may not always be transparent as a result of (regular) phonological change. Fr./Pt. *quinze* '15', for example, is completely opaque and the link with numerals '5' (Fr./Pt. *cinq/cinco*) and '10' (Fr./Pt. *dix/dez*) has been lost. Etymologically, however, the link is clear in the original Lat. QUINDECIM [five.[PLUS].ten] including a reduced form of QUINQUE '5' and the base DECEM '10'. In addition, numerals may have serialized, becoming suffixes in the process, e.g., PIE **dekmt-* '10' has serialized in Latin (Lat. -GINTA) and as such plays an important role in the inherited decads in Romance (e.g., French decads above '30', which all end in *-ante* or It. *quaranta* '40', *cinquanta* '50'; for the distribution of *-anta* vs *-enta* and for Fr. *vingt* and *trente* and equivalents in other Romance languages, see Price 1992: 460f; Bauer 2021).[4] Moreover, the counting between the decads does not exceed 'nine', with each new decad (a product of '10') being referred to with a new lexeme (Sp. *treinta y nueve* '39', but *cuarenta* '40'; see Table 15.1).

The powers of '10' act as a base as well, which may be accounted for by referring to the rule of thumb that the multiplier does not exceed the base. Consequently, the base '10' is used in the range 20–99, but not beyond. Following the system inherited from Latin, the next numerical entity after It. *novanta* (< Lat. NONAGINTA 'nine.[TIMES].ten' > '90') therefore is a new independent word for hundred, *cento* (Lat. < CENTUM) instead of **diecanta. *Cento* acts as additive and multiplicative base for numerals beyond '100', cf. It. *duecento* 'two.[TIMES].hundred', *centouno* 'hundred.[PLUS].one', *seicentotrentasette* 'six.[TIMES].hundred.[PLUS].thirty.[PLUS].seven' > '637', and so forth.

While the Romance languages are decimal, a few languages and dialects use vigesimals, featuring a base twenty instead of ten:

(4)   Fr. *quatre-vingts*   four-[TIMES]-twenties   '80'
      Fr. *quatre-vingt-dix*   four-[TIMES]-twenty-[PLUS]-ten   '90'
      Sic *tri bbintini*   three [TIMES] twenties   '60'
      Sav. *si-ven*   six-[TIMES]-twenty   '120'

These numerals will be discussed in detail in Section 15.6.

Overall the Romance languages – with a few well-defined exceptions – do not feature numerals based on division, nor formations based on subtraction. There is one reported example in the literature of subtraction in Romance: isolated dialectal instances in Lazio of numerals of the type *centə minə quínici* 'hundred minus fifteen' > '85' (Rohlfs 1969: 314; for an instance of division-based numerals, see Section 15.6.2). Conversely, in Latin subtraction was more widespread: '18' and '19' were referred to by UNDEUIGINTI (UN-DE-UIGINTI) 'one.from.twenty' and DUODEUIGINTI 'two.

---

[4] The trend to create uniform patterns in numerals is strong, e.g., Romanian teens in *-spe* (Lombard 1974: 102; Price 1992: 460).

Table 15.1. *Formation of cardinals in some standard Romance languages*

Lat.	It.	Pt.	Sp.	Fr.	Ro.
1 unus/una/unum	un(o)/una	um/uma	un(o)/una	un/une	un(u)/(una)/o
2 duo/duae/duo	due	dois/duas	dos	deux	doi/două
3 tres/tria	tre	três	tres	trois	trei
4 quattuor	quattro	quatro	cuatro	quatre	patru
5 quinque	cinque	cinco	cinco	cinq	cinci
6 sex	sei	seis	seis	six	șase
7 septem	sette	sete	siete	sept	șapte
8 octo	otto	oito	ocho	huit	opt
9 nouem	nove	nove	nueve	neuf	nouă
10 decem	dieci	dez	diez	dix	zece
Teens					
Lat.	It.	Pt.	Sp.	Fr.	Ro.
11 undecim	undici	onze	once	onze	unsprezece
12 duodecim	dodici	doze	doce	douze	doisprezece
13 tredecim	tredici	treze	trece	treize	treisprezece
14 quattuordecim	quattordici	catorze[1]	catorce	quatorze	paisprezece
15 quindecim	quindici	quinze	quince	quinze	cincisprezece
16 sedecim	sedici	dezasseis[2]	diez y seis / dieciséis	seize	șaisprezece
17 septemdecim	diciassette	dezassete[3]	diez y siete / diecisiete	dix-sept	șaptesprezece
18 duodeuiginti	diciotto	dezoito	diez y ocho / dieciocho	dix-huit	optsprezece
19 undeuiginta	diciannove	dezanove[4]	diez y nueve / diecinueve	dix-neuf	nouăsprezece
Decads					
Lat.	It.	Pt.	Sp.	Fr.	Ro.
20 uiginti	venti	vinte	veinte	vingt	douăzeci
30 triginta	trenta	trinta	treinta	trente	treizeci
40 quadraginta	quaranta	quarenta	cuarenta	quarante	patruzeci
50 quinquaginta	cinquanta	cinquenta	cincuenta	cinquante	cincizeci
60 sexaginta	sessanta	sessanta	sesenta	soixante	șaizeci
70 septuaginta	settanta	setenta	setenta	soixante-dix	șaptezeci
80 octoginta	ottanta	oitenta	ochenta	quatre-vingts	optzeci
90 nonaginta	novanta	noventa	noventa	quatre-vingt-dix	nouăzeci

[1] In BrPt. *quatorze* or *catorze*.
[2] In BrPt. *dezesseis*.
[3] In BrPt. *dezessete*.
[4] In BrPt. *dezenove*.

from.twenty'. These formations are decimal, but they differ from the other numerals in that the appropriate numbers '2' and '1' respectively are subtracted from the next counting unit, UIGINTI '20'.

This type of structure entails higher numerals as well, cf. Lat. DU(O) DETRIGINTA '28', DU(O)DEQUADRAGINTA '38', UNDEOCTOGINTA '79' (Coleman 1992: 397). Yet subtraction in Latin does not exceed the decads, and therefore '98' and '99', for which the next unit is CENTUM '100', are rendered by additive NONOGINTA OCTO and NONOGINTA NOUEM. In addition to this limited formation, subtraction is also attested in compounds, albeit rarely so. The Latin weight measure DEUNX (< DE + UNC-) 'less a twelfth' conveys 11/12 of a pound.

Formally, the operation of subtraction is conveyed by a preposition (DE 'from'), absent in the other Latin numerals. This is consistent with typological patterns, by which subtraction needs more than 'mere sequence' (Greenberg 1978: 258f.).

The origins of these subtractive numerals are as yet unknown. On the basis of similar formations in Sanskrit (e.g., *ekonaviṃśati* [< *ekan-na-viṃśati*] 'one.not.twenty' > '19') and Old English (e.g., *twā lǣs twentig* 'two less twenty' > '18'), Coleman suggests that these may be 'inherited variant(s)', provided the Sanskrit form is 'older than its attestation suggests' (Coleman 1992: 397).

With time, these formations had been replaced in Latin already by analytic ones based on addition – in line with the other formations – [DECAD + DIGIT], as reflected in Fr. *dix-huit*, *dix-neuf*, Cat. *divuit* '18', *dinou* '19', and with a connector OSp. *di(e)z y ocho*, and It. *diciannove* with a reflex of Lat. AC 'and' > -*a*-.

The arithmetical operation of division is not found in Romance nor Latin numerals. Yet the process underlies compounds in Latin of the type [FRACTION + NOUN], such as SESTERTIUS, which continues SEMIS TERTIUS (lit. 'half third') 'the third one half', a coin worth 2.5 asses (Menninger 1958: 78). This type of formation is characterized both by the presence of a fraction and overcounting – including the next quantitative unit, a common feature of numerals based on division. The Romance languages feature reflexes of Lat. MEDIUM 'middle' (not SEMIS 'half') (e.g., Pt. *meio*, It. *mezzo*, Fr. *mi-*, Ro. *miez*), but they typically occur in combination with nouns, rather than numerals and do not form numerical compounds, e.g., Fr. *midi* 'midday', *minuit* 'midnight', *mi-juillet* 'half(way through) July', Pt. *meia hora* 'half hour', Ro. *miezul nopții* 'midnight' (see Price 1992: 484).

15.3.3 Order of Meaningful Elements

The relative place of the components determines their arithmetical value and arithmetical operation: Fr. *quatre* '4' in initial position in *quatre-vingts* '80 (lit. four-twenties)' functions as a factor, while in *vingt-quatre* '24 (lit. twenty-four)', it functions as an addendum (cf. 5 vs 6):

(5) Fr. *quatre-vingts* four-[TIMES]-twenty

(6) Fr. *vingt-quatre* twenty-[PLUS]-four

In Romance, compound numerals based on addition typically have the base numerals in initial position, cf. Sp. *cuarenta y ocho* 'forty and eight' > '48'. In operations of multiplication, the factor systematically comes first, cf. Fr. *deux cents*, It. *duecento* 'two [TIMES] hundred(s)' > '200'. Yet there is some variation, as the next paragraphs will demonstrate.

There is an important distinction across the Romance languages between the lower inherited forms and the higher innovative ones. The inherited teens – now partly opaque in certain languages – are synthetic and characterized by the sequence [DIGIT.[PLUS].TEN], e.g., It. *tredici* or Fr. *treize* '13', from Lat. TREDECIM (< TRES '3' + DECEM '10'). By contrast, the innovative forms in this category feature the reverse sequence, and may or may not include a connector (see Table 15.1), cf.:

(7) a. It. *diciassette*, Sp. *diez y siete/diecisiete*, Pt. *dezassete*, BrPt. *dezessete*, Srd. *dekasette*, or Fr. *dix-sept* '17'
 b. It. *diciannove*, Pt. *dezanove*, BrPt. *dezenove*, Sp. *diez y nueve/diecinueve*, or Fr. *dix-neuf* '19'

Latin already featured early attestations of the modern formations, such as *decem (ac/et) novem* (Caes., *B.G.* 1.8.1; 2.4.9; *CIL* 5,4370; see also Coleman 1992: 397 and below).

For unknown reasons, the analytic break is at '16' in certain Romance languages, but at '17' in others. The breaks are very systematic: if the cut-off occurs after '15' then all numerals higher than '15' feature analytic structure, and all up to '15' are synthetic, following typological regularity (Greenberg 1978: 272f.). Moreover, it is striking that there are no Romance varieties – as far as we know – where there is optionality between the break starting at '16' or '17', with alternation between the competing forms.

In the Romance decads, which are also inherited, the base occurs in final position as well: serialized Lat. -GINTA survives in the Romance languages, which therefore continue this structure ([DIGIT.[TIMES].TEN]). The formations are opaque as such, but the serialized suffix is a distinctive feature, providing good examples of 'serialized products' comparable to the decads in *-ty* in English (Greenberg 1978: 269; for details, see Price 1992).

For the numerals between the decads, the sequence in Romance parallels those of the innovative teens [DECAD BASE.[PLUS].DIGIT], a sequence that Latin already favoured (e.g., UIGINTI SEX 'twenty six').

Moreover, there is a connector in certain additive formations, but its occurrence is not systematic cross-linguistically, language-internally, or historically. For the numerals between the decads, Spanish and Portuguese, for example, consistently use a connector ('and'), where Italian does not, and French varies: Fr. *et* 'and' appears in the first numerals of each decad, but not in the others (cf. *quarante et un* 'forty and one' vs *quarante-*[PLUS]*-six* 'forty-six', but *quatre-vingt-un* '81 (lit. four-[TIMES]-twenty-[PLUS]-one)'). A split pattern is also found in Catalan and Occitan, where numerals '21' through '29' have a connector 'and', but asyndetic forms are used elsewhere. Similarly, higher numerals may show variation in certain modern Romance languages. For numerals above 'hundred', for example, a connector may be added in Italian, e.g., *centodue* '102 (lit. hundred.[PLUS].two)' co-existing with more archaic *cento e due* and emphatic *mille e uno* 'thousand and one' co-existing with unmarked *milleuno* 'thousand.[PLUS].one' (Maiden and Robustelli 2007: 189).

Historically as well there is variation. Earlier varieties may feature a connector, e.g., OFr. *dis e set* 'ten and seven (= 17)' (11th-c. *La vie de St. Alexis* 271), where today these forms are asyndetic. Spanish data further show that the analytic forms with a connector in earlier stages in certain regions also included '12' and '13', etc.: OSp. *diez e dos/ dizedós* 'ten (and) two' > '12' and *dizetrés* 'ten.and.three' > '13' (Menéndez Pidal [1904]1973: 243).

In Latin, the numerals between the decads were analytic. In certain Romance languages they form one word, in others two words, with or without a hyphen. Yet the corresponding ordinals in Latin typically feature double marking (e.g., UIGINTI TRES '23' vs UICESIMUS 'twentieth' TERTIUS 'third', underscoring the independence of the two elements. In Romance the trend is towards single marking at the end of the compound, as in: Fr. *trente-sixième*, Srs. *trentasisavel* 'thirty.sixth' (example from Price 1992: 478; see Bauer 2021). This explains learnèd Latinized It. *vigesimo terzo* lit. 'twentieth third' (with double marking) as opposed to regular Italian *ventitreesimo* 'twenty-third' (Tekavčić 1972: 264), cf. learnèd Sp. *decimocuarto* lit. 'tenth.fourth'.

The connector most widely used cross-linguistically in Romance are reflexes of Lat. ET 'and', with additional instances of AC 'and', as in It. *diciassette* '17', *diciannove* '19', which continues non-standard Lat. DECEM AC SEPTEM/NOUEM; with variation in certain Italian dialects (Rohlfs 1969: 312). Williams reports the replacement in the fifteenth century of the conjunction *-e-* by *-a-* (found in modern European Portuguese), which he identifies as a preposition, without excluding the (more logical) possibility of *-a-* going back to Lat. AC (e.g., *dezasseis*; Williams 1962: 135). This would imply the long-term survival of both Lat. AC and ET and eventually the choice of reflexes of AC over ET. Here as well, there is diachronic variation, which to date needs further analysis.

The internal word order of numerals and the presence of a connector is a bone of contention. Greenberg argues that there is a correlation between the internal order of numerals and the typological patterning of the languages in question. The regression of [DIGIT.[PLUS].BASE] formations parallels the well-documented change in word order in Latin/Romance (Bauer 1995; 2011: 549–53; 2017: 302–04).

It has also been suggested that additive compounds do not need a connector when the base comes last (e.g., Lat. UNDECIM 'one.[PLUS].ten' > '10'), but that a connector appears when the sequence is the reverse (e.g., Lat. DECEM ET OCTO 'ten and eight' > '18'). Yet the data do not corroborate this assumption. First, while Latin favours asyndetic base-last teens, the connector is not systematically present in the numerals where the base comes first, cf. non-standard Lat. DECEM ET NOUEM vs DECEM NOUEM '19', but also standard Lat. UIGINTI SEPTEM 'twenty [PLUS] seven' > '27' and similar examples. Usage of connectors indeed was not always systematic in Latin.

While Lat. UIGINTI UNUS 'twenty [PLUS] one' and similar numerals are asyndetic, numerals above 'hundred' feature ET 'and' (e.g., CENTUM ET UNUS 'hundred and one)' > '101', CENTUM ET QUINDECIM 'hundred and fifteen' > '115'. Yet the connector is absent in more complex numerals, as in Lat. CENTUM UIGINITI UNUS '121 (lit. hundred [PLUS] twenty [PLUS] one)' (similarly MILLE ET UNUS '1001 (lit. thousand and one)', but MILLE CENTUM UNUS '1101 (lit. thousand [PLUS] hundred [PLUS] one)').

Moreover, data outside Latin/Romance, do not support the hypothesis either, and the use of connectors in base-final numerals is widespread, e.g., Ger. *dreiundvierzig* '43 (lit. three.and.forty)', Dch. *vierenveertig* '44 (lit. four.and.forty)', and so forth. Moreover, English features *fourteen*, but the reverse *forty-four* features no connector either. The data therefore do not point to a correlation between word order and the presence or absence of a connector. There is however a systematic trend in that compounds in which the base comes second, tend to become synthetic. This pattern is widespread in Romance, in other morphological processes as well (e.g., adverb formations in *-ment(e)*, see Bauer 2006).

15.4 Types of Numeral

The Romance languages distinguish several types of numeral. Among them, the formation of cardinals is most consistent within any given language and across the daughter languages. Historically speaking, we notice overall an increase of analytic and even periphrastic constructions and a change in type of numeral since Latin. In addition, grammatical marking on numerals has decreased.

15.4.1 Latin vs Romance Numerals

The Latin numerical system (see Table 15.2) was rich and systematic – even if perhaps not all forms are attested in the documents – including cardinal and ordinal numerals, but also distributives ('how many each time?'), and multiplicatives ('how often'), which may be adjectives – a limited formation – or adverbs. Each type of numeral had its own morphological marker, which is used throughout the entire paradigm: cardinals, ordinals (-[S]IMUS), distributives (-NO), and multiplicatives (-PLEX, -IE[N]S; Meillet and Vendryes 1924: 86). There are of course exceptions, such as e.g., Lat. PRIMUS 'first' from a stem PRIM- instead of UN- (It. *primo*, OFr. *prin*, Ro. *prim*) or Lat. SECUNDUS 'second', the gerundive of SEQUI 'follow' (OFr. *sëont*, Egd. *seguon*, and other reflexes, see Price 1992: 475). Cross-linguistically, numerals '1' and '2' often feature deviant formations, especially as non-cardinals (Greenberg 1978: 286–88). Moreover, there are several additional

Table 15.2. *Formation of Latin numerals*

Cardinals	Ordinals	Distributives	Multiplicative adverbs	Multiplicative adjectives
4 quattuor	quartus	quateni	quater	quadruplex
6 sex	sextus	seni	sexies	Ø
10 decem	decimus	deni	decies	decemplex
12 duodecim	duodecimus	duodeni	duodecies	Ø
15 quindecim	quintus decimus	quini deni	quinquies decies/quindecies	Ø
20 uiginti	uicesimus	uiceni	uicies	Ø
26 uiginti sex	uicesimus sextus	uiceni seni	uicies et sexies	Ø
70 septuaginta	septuagesimus	septuageni	septuagies	Ø
100 centum	centesimus	centeni	centies	centuplex
300 trecenti	trecentesimus	treceni	trecenties	Ø
1000 mille	millesimus	singula milia	millies	Ø
Etc.	Etc.	Etc.	Etc.	

formations in Latin, which have a distinct marker, but typically are defective (e.g., 'proportional numerals' such as DUPLUS 'double').

Reflecting a general trend in numeral systems in the languages of the world (Greenberg 1978: 286–88), cardinals are the unmarked elements in both Latin and Romance, from which the other numerals are derived. Non-cardinals indeed are secondary formations and have a higher degree of formal complexity: they are marked by affixes (often more than one, each covering part of the paradigm) or analytic elements that are added to the corresponding cardinal numeral, which functions as a morphological base.

Overall, numeral formations in Romance are less consistent than in Latin. Examining cardinals, ordinals, approximatives, distributives, and multiplicatives in Romance in that order, we note a progressive decline in terms of productive inherited forms and suffixes (on suppletion in Romance numerals, see Section 12.2.2). While cardinals, ordinals, and approximatives overall are primarily synthetic forms with their own morphological marking, the other numeral formations in Romance are primarily periphrastic. Among the synthetic formations, cardinals tend to be regular, with identifiable – if opaque – suffixes and patterns that recur across Romance (see Table 15.1). Ordinals and approximatives tend to feature several morphological markers both cross-linguistically and language-internally, such as ordinal markers in French which were originally marked by *-ain* (< Lat. -ENUS), e.g., OFr. *setain* '7th' in contrast to Mod.Fr. *-ième* (< *-isme*, of uncertain origin; for discussion, see Price 1992: 479f.). Similarly, the suffix marking approximatives varies from language to language, cf. reflexes of Lat. -ENA (Sp. *docena* 'dozen'), Lat. -ANA (Fr. *quinzaine* 'about 15'), Lat. -INA (It. *decina* 'about 10'), Lat. -ARIUM (It. *centinaio* 'about a hundred'). These suffixes, all inherited, are distributed across the daughter languages. Inherited suffixes may also have developed new functions, such as the old French ordinal suffix *-ain*, which came to mark approximatives. Similarly in Spanish, Catalan, old Occitan, and early northern Italian dialects the Latin suffix for distributives in -ENUS came to mark ordinals, as in OSp. *cuatreno* '4th', OPt. *onzeno* '11th', OGsc. *oitén* '8th', and so forth (for an overview, see Menéndez Pidal 1973: 246f.; Rohlfs 1969: 316f.; Hualde 1992: 337; Price 1992; Bauer 2021).

Yet while the Romance languages may feature synthetic forms in the examples above, there are exceptions. In Romanian, for example, the expression of approximatives is analytic, featuring a cardinal and an adverb (e.g., Ro. *cam cinci mii* 'around five thousand'; Stan 2016: 348). Similarly, ordinals are partially analytic (for details, see Stan 2016: 349).

Analytic ordinals are rather rare: in Sardinian, for example, ordinals take the form of a demonstrative + preposition + cardinal (Price 1992: 480 quoting Salvioni 1899: 234f.).

The other formations typically are analytic structures, such as adverbial multiplicatives, that feature elements such as 'times', e.g., Sp./Pt. *vez*, Fr. *fois*, and so forth. Similarly, distributives are rendered by periphrastic constructions, which developed in the individual languages, e.g., It. *una trentina di casi per milione di abitanti* '30 cases for every million inhabitants' (Maiden and Robustelli 2007: 197) or Fr. *vous avez deux tartines chacun* 'you have two slices of bread and butter each' (for details, cf. Price 1992).

15.4.2 A Systemic Difference

Given that many languages of the world merely have cardinals (Greenberg 1978), the full-fledged numerical paradigms of Latin are noteworthy. Put more succinctly: why does Latin have extensive paradigms for distributives and multiplicatives, which tend to be rare?

For distributives part of the answer is in the observation that distributives originally were collectives, reflecting an important grammatical feature in early Indo-European (Brugmann 1907; Postgate 1907). Hence the use of Lat. *boues bini* (Pl. *Persa* 2.516) 'a yoke of oxen' rather than 'two oxen'. Moreover, part of the answer, resides in the role distributive-collectives and multiplicatives play in the formation of the higher numerals.

The Latin and Romance numerical systems differ fundamentally in that the decimal system in Latin never reached its full potential. That happened only when – centuries later – the higher powers of ten came to be implemented in the numerical system (e.g., 'million', 'billion').

Since the highest base in Latin was MILLE 'thousand' (with plural MILIA), base numerals did not extend beyond MILLE MILIA '1,000 000', and the formation of cardinals stopped there. Instead, collective-distributives and multiplicatives were used to form numerals beyond that range, as illustrated in the following example:

(8) [MULTIPLICATIVE + NUMERAL + MILIA + ET ...]
     quadragiens   centum   milia   et   sexaginta tria   milia
     forty.times   hundred   thousands and   sixty   three thousands
     '4,063,000' (Lat., Aug., *Res gestae diui Augusti* 8)

The second strategy involves distributive-collective CENTENA in combination with MILIA and often a multiplicative:

(9) [MULTIPLICATIVE + DISTRIBUTIVE + MILIA]
     ter   et   triciens   centena   milia
     three.times   and   thirty.times   hundred.at.a.time   thousands
     '3,300,000'

While overt marking of multiplication in numerals is rare cross-linguistically, with most examples coming from North America, a 'clear type' of marking is the use of a multiplicative, which then functions as multiplier (Greenberg 1978: 268).

15.4.3 Grammatical Marking on Numerals

In terms of 'parts of speech', numerals in Romance behave as adjectives, nouns, and pure numerical elements, which are invariable. Historically, the adjectival behaviour of numerals is probably an acquired feature in Indo-European, where decads, hundreds, and thousands were originally nouns (Bauer 2017: 173f.). As adjectives, numerals may feature gender, case, and number marking. Yet while the numerals '1' through '3' inflected for case, gender, and number in Latin,[5] grammatical marking in the modern Romance languages is generally limited to '1', which is marked for gender (e.g., Sp. *un(o)/una*; Srs. *in/ina*). The daughter languages differ as to the marking of 'one' in compounds, cf. Fr. *trente et une voitures* lit. 'thirty and one.F cars.F' vs It. *trentun macchine* 'thirty.one.M cars.F'.[6] Case marking on 'one' is only found in languages that feature case, such as old French (e.g., OFr. *uns* 'one.NOM.MSG' vs *un* 'one.OBL.MSG').

For '2' there is masculine/feminine gender marking in a limited number of standard languages today (Pt. *dois/duas*; Cat. *dos/dues*, Ro. *doi/două*), and in many modern Romance dialects (for an overview, see Rohlfs 1969: 309–11; 1970; Price 1992: 449f.). Moreover, in the early forerunners of the standard languages 'two' was marked for gender (e.g., OSp. *do(u)s/dues*) and for case if this was a relevant feature, e.g., OFr. *dui/dous* 'two.NOM.MSG/OBL.MSG', OOcc. *dui/dos* 'two.NOM.MSG/OBL.MSG' (Menéndez Pidal 1973: 242; Jensen 1986: 51; Buridant 2000: 222).

---

[5] Lat. UNUS/UNA/UNUM '1(M/F/N)', DUO/DUAE '2(M,N/F)', and TRES/TRIA '3(M,F/N)'.
[6] Feminine marking is limited to nouns in the singular: *trentuna lira* 'thirty.one.F lira.F' (Maiden and Robustelli 2007: 190).

Marking of 'three' is limited to gender and attested in certain early Romance languages and dialects (e.g., old Venetian) and a number of contemporary Italian dialects. Moreover, reflexes of Lat. TRES/TRIA (M,F/N) are distributed over the dialects, with those of TRES being most widespread. Gender marking in modern Romanian is limited to the context of 'all three', *toate trele* vs masculine *toți trei* (Price 1992: 450; Beyer, Bochmann, and Bensert 1987: 137f.). The compound forms including Ro. *tus-*, a reduced from of *toți,* are also of interest in this context, cf. *tustrei* 'all three.M' vs *tustrele* 'all three.F' (Stan 2013: 325f.). Case marking is found in OFr. *troi/trois* 'three.NOM/OBL', OOcc. *trei/trois* 'three.NOM/OBL', early Italian dialects *trei/tres* 'three.NOM/OBL' (forms from Buridant 2000: 223).

As nouns, numerals in Romance may combine with articles or govern a partitive even if for certain numerals this usage has disappeared with time (Bauer 2017: 173f., 248–53). They may be marked for number, although this is not a consistent pattern across the daughter languages, cf. Fr. *deux cents euros* 'two hundred.PL euros' (with liaison), but It. *duecento* 'two.hundred' and Fr. *deux cent trois* 'two [TIMES] hundred [PLUS] three', both without number marking (cf. earlier It. *duecenti*'two.hundreds'). In contemporary Spanish, Portuguese, Sardinian, and Romanian, 'hundred' is marked for number in the plural: Sp. *trescientos* 'three hundreds' (*ciento* '100'), Pt. *quinhentos* 'five hundreds', Srd. *battokentos* 'four.hundreds', Ro. *două sute* 'two hundreds' (cf. *sută* 'hundred') (Price 1992: 471f.; Beyer, Bochmann, and Bensert 1987: 137). Note that in Spanish and Portuguese, 'hundred' is also marked for gender, e.g., Pt. *oitocentas mesas* 'eight.hundred.FPL tables.F'. Similarly number marking for other numerals varies cross-linguistically, e.g., 'thousand' is invariable in French, Romansh, and Ibero-Romance, but Romanian has *o mie* '1000' vs *două mii* '2000' and Italian *mille* '1000' vs *tremila* '3000', with dialects featuring regular reflexes of Lat. *milia* (Rohlfs 1969: 315; Price 1992: 472f.; Beyer, Bochmann, and Bonsert 1987: 137f.).

In French, we find plural marking of *vingt* '20' in vigesimal compounds, when *vingt* is in final position (e.g., *quatre-vingts* '80', but *quatre-vingt-deux* '82'; see Section 15.6). The question is whether final *-s* is a mere orthographical convention or whether there is more to it. Additional research is needed to answer this question and should include the role of liaison between the numeral and the following noun, especially in the light of the spread in contemporary French of liaison to numerous new contexts.

15.5 Potential Effects of Language Contact: Romanian Teens and Decads

Even if the concrete results may vary in the individual languages because of regular phonological change, the formation of cardinals in Romance is quite consistent, with three major exceptions: Romanian teens, Romanian decads, and vigesimals, which will be discussed in Section 15.6. These formations are systematic, covering substantial segments of the paradigm and therefore more than mere isolated forms. Here focus will be on the Romanian numerals.

15.5.1 Romanian Teens

In contrast to the sister languages, the Latin numerals have been replaced in Romanian by formations that feature a former preposition:

(10) **Romanian**

unsprezece	'11'	< un + spre + zece	< Lat. UNUS + SUPER + DECEM
doisprezece	'12.M'	< doi + spre + zece	< Lat. DUO + SUPER + DECEM
douăsprezece	'12.F'	< două + spre + zece	< Lat. DUAE + SUPER + DECEM
treisprezece	'13'	< trei + spre + zece	< Lat. TRES + SUPER + DECEM
cincisprezece	'15'	< cinci + spre + zece	< Lat. QUINQUE + SUPER + DECEM
optsprezece	'18'	< opt + spre + zece	< Lat. OCTO + SUPER + DECEM
nouăsprezece	'19'	< nouă + spre + zece	< Lat. NOUEM + SUPER + DECEM

In these formations, which have reduced forms in the spoken and sometimes written language, whereby -spreceze has been shortened to -șpe (e.g., treișpe '13', see Lombard 1974: 102), the component elements are inherited Latin forms, but the structure is not Latin with the arithmetical operation of addition being rendered by a reflex of the Latin preposition SUPER 'on top of'. Typologically, marking addition with an element 'upon' is 'widespread', but 'far less' common than the conjunction 'and' (Greenberg 1978: 265). There has been no change in word order: sequence [DIGIT.TEN] was also found in Latin, albeit as an asyndetic formation.

Moreover, the numeral for '12' is remarkable both from a Romanian and Romance perspective, in that it is the only one to include a masculine and feminine form; the numeral '11', by contrast (with a reflex of Lat. UNUS 'one'), shows no gender variation.

The Romanian teens have variously been ascribed to language contact (Slavonic, Albanian), or identified as an areal feature, or interpreted as a Romanian-specific phenomenon.

Indeed, since the earliest times, teens in Slavonic include a preposition (*na* governing a locative) for all formations, with [DIGIT + PREPOSITION NA + NOUN-LOC] being pan-Slavonic:

(11) *pętь   na   desęte (pan-Slavonic, Comrie 1992: 764)
      five   upon   ten.LOC
      'fifteen'

Forms in the individual languages show partial fossilization and reduction (for details, see Comrie 1992): *na desęte*, for example, has often been reduced into an opaque form such as *na*, as in certain Bulgarian dialects with forms such as *dvana* 'twelve'. Moreover, in most Slavonic languages, including Bulgarian, the first part of '11' and '12' is a masculine nominative-accusative singular, whereas for '13', the form is etymologically a feminine/neuter nominative-accusative (Comrie 1992: 764–71). These patterns in Slavonic do not account, however, for the gender distinction in Romanian '12' nor its absence in '11'. A final consideration is the precise timing: how does the fossilization in Slavonic relate to the potential time of the borrowing?

Another, less-known hypothesis argues that the Romanian teens are a borrowing from Albanian. Albanian formations indeed include a preposition (*mbë* 'on') and potentially an inflected form of '10', as in: [DIGIT + MBË + DJËT], in which *ðjét* 'must be an old inflected locative' (Hamp 1992: 918). Hamp argues that the formations in Romanian are the result of Albanian influence, in accordance with the borrowing practice for decads (see below).

Others argue that Romanian teens parallel those in Armenian, for example (e.g., Iordan and Manoliu 1972: 269; Price 1992: 460), positing a feature original to the area. This hypothesis is rather problematic. Teens in Armenian are indeed compounds, including [DIGIT [PLUS]TEEN], but while the numerals '17' through '19' include a connector, the others do not. Moreover, the connector is not a preposition, but rather a conjunction (*ew* 'and'), cf. Arm. *me-tasan* '11 (lit. one-[PLUS]-ten)' vs *ewt'n ew tasn* '17 (lit. seven and ten)' (Winter 1992: 348–52).

A final interpretation links the formations to Latin numerals of the type NOUEM AC/ET DECEM 'nine and ten', which was allegedly extended to '11' and '12' in the east (Price 1992: 460). Above we saw that in old Spanish, as well, lower analytic teens have been found, showing that it is a distinct possibility. Yet additional data are needed to substantiate this hypothesis, the more so since it does not address the occurrence of a preposition, which is a distinctive feature of the Romanian formations.

The deviation from the regular patterns in Romance and the strong structural parallels with the Slavonic formations indeed suggest that language contact may have been at play. More research, however, is required into the precise timing and the status of the source language at the time of potential borrowing (for details about the timing of the Romanian teens, see Stan 2016: 347). The Romanian forms, which are transparent and which feature distinct inherited Latin compositional elements, suggest that the Slavonic forms must have been highly transparent at the time of borrowing.

15.5.2 Romanian Decads

The Romanian formation of decads is generally assumed to be exceptional. Price, for example, states that 'Romanian stands alone in having entirely abandoned the Latin forms for the decads' above '10' (Price 1992: 463). The forms in question are: *zece* '10', *douăzeci* '20', *treizeci* '30', *patruzeci* '40', *cin(ci) zeci* '50', *şaizeci* '60', *şaptezeci* '70', *optzeci* '80', and *nouăzeci* '90' (Beyer, Bochmann, and Bensert 1987: 137).

Yet there are important parallels with Latin: the decads are based on multiplication and the sequence of composing elements is identical in the two languages, namely [DIGIT.TEN]. Moreover, the digits in Romanian are inherited from Latin. The *zece/zeci* 'ten/tens' part, however, requires further clarification. Formally, it goes back to Lat. DECEM, but it features a plural in Romanian decads from '20' on, which implies that it is a noun; it is a feminine noun, witness *douăzeci* '20', with feminine *două-* 'two.F'. This observation has been and still is reason to assume Slavonic influence: in Slavonic indeclinable PIE **dekmt-* took the form of a noun. Accordingly, Slavonic indeed has structures that parallel the ones in Romanian, as in OCSl. *trbi deşate*: the 'tens' are nouns, either masculine (most frequently) or feminine, with gender agreement with the first element. Yet the pattern is different for the higher decads: the 'ten'-element from '40' on takes the form of a genitive plural, as reflected in Common Slavic *deşetъ*, cf.: **pętъ deşetъ* 'five ten.GEN.PL'> '50', **sedmъ desętъ* '70' (for details, Comrie 1992: 773–75; for reflexes in the later languages, see Comrie 1992: 774–80).

The occurrence of the feminine form *două* in Ro. *douăzeci* '20' is reason for Hamp to assume that *zece* is feminine and that the pattern therefore cannot be a calque from Slavonic: '*zece* (fem.) [must be added] to the inventory of "autochthonous" elements of Romanian, and [we must] derive it as a borrowed grammatical feature from an early Albanian dialect' (Hamp 1992: 917). In Albanian as well, indeclinable PIE **dekmt-* appears as a noun, but is consistently feminine (Hamp 1992: 917). Hamp argues that the Slavonic cognate was masculine (Hamp 1992: 917), but data from Comrie (1992) show that while typically masculine in Slavonic, feminine forms are attested as well. Consequently, in order to appreciate the full implications of the Slavic and Albanian hypotheses, further research is needed into the timing and contact situation for both contact languages, but also other languages in the area. Research should also consider the possibility of analogy: in contrast to the other Romance languages, Romanian 'hundred' (*două sute* 'two.F hundreds.F') and 'thousand' (*două mii* 'two.F thousands.F') were feminine as well, and their grammatical patterns may have had analogical effects on the decads.

15.6 Vigesimals: Language Contact or Internal Development?

While by far most numeral systems in the languages of the world are decimal, the second largest group of numeral systems is vigesimal.

From Comrie's (2005) total corpus of 196 languages, 125 are identified as decimal and 42 as either 'pure vigesimal' or 'hybrid vigesimal-decimal'. Vigesimal systems occur all over the globe, in small and large languages, in isolates, and in numerous, if not all, language families, but distinctly not in all members of any given family. Both pure and hybrid vigesimal systems are found in languages in isolation or in proximity to other languages (see, for example, Comrie 2005: 530f.). In the Caucasus, for instance, we find a concentration of hybrid vigesimal systems and a few pure systems, but in New Guinea there are several isolated vigesimal languages (Comrie 2003: 37; see the map in Comrie. 2005: 531). Hybrid systems may reflect residues of earlier situations. We know, for example, that '[p]re-Colombian Meso-America was largely vigesimal' (Comrie 2005: 531), as reflected in Classical Mayan. With the Spanish Conquest, *ciento* '100', and with it other decimal numerals, infiltrated the numeral system.

Attested in French and a number of Romance dialects today, vigesimal forms were much more prominent in earlier times. Yet they are exceptional formations in Romance (and Indo-European, for that matter) for two reasons: they are characterized by the base '20' and not inherited from Latin.

If vigesimal forms typically co-occur with other bases in any given counting system, they are most commonly attested alongside a decimal system, as in Romance. The French vigesimals are of particular interest because they include full vigesimals and so-called semi-vigesimals. Full vigesimals explicitly feature a base '20', as in:

(12) **French**
    a.   quatre- vingts
            four   twenties   > '80'
    b.   quatre- vingt- un
            four-   twenty- one > '81'

Moreover, the counting between the units is based on twenty, with the unit changing when twenty is reached, as the following French examples illustrate:

(13) **French**
    a.   quatre- vingt- dix
            four   twenty ten   > '90'
    b.   quatre- vingt- dix- neuf
            four   twenty ten nine > '99'
    c.   cent
            hundred   > '100'

Semi-vigesimals do not include an explicit base 'twenty', but the counting occurs in units of twenty, such as:

(14) soixante-dix (Fr.)
      'sixty-ten'   > '70' [SEMI-VIGESIMAL]

Soixante-dix '70 (lit. sixty-[PLUS]-ten)' is semi-vigesimal, because it features a decimal numeral (*soixante* 'sixty') but the counting extends beyond '70'. In a decimal system, '70' should have been a new full decad, as in Belgian and Swiss French *septante* '70'. Beyond '70', counting in French completes the unit of twenty, as the following examples illustrate:

(15) **French**
      soixante-douze
      'sixty-twelve'   > '72' [SEMI-VIGESIMAL]
      soixante-dix-neuf
      'sixty-ten-nine'   > '79' [SEMI-VIGESIMAL]
      quatre-vingts
      'four-twenties '   > '80' [VIGESIMAL]

15.6.1 Vigesimals in Romance

Vigesimal forms have been found, today and in the past, in what is today France, Belgium, Switzerland, Spain, Portugal, and Italy. In Italy, vigesimal forms are primarily attested in southern dialects, as in Sicily, where they are most strongly established and most widespread (Rohlfs 1952: 43), with instances like *du vintini e ddèci* '30 (lit. two score and ten)', *quattru vintini* '80 (lit. four score)'(Rohlfs 1969: 313), or in the dialect of Noto *ru vintini riči* '50 (lit. two score [PLUS] 10)' (Rösler 1910: 205). Moreover, vigesimals are found in Abruzzo, Apulia, and in Calabrian dialects, where they were until recently 'much in use' (Rohlfs 1969: 378), e.g., Sal. *tre bbintine* '60 (lit. three score)', *quattru intine* '80 (lit. four score)', *tría ventine* '60 (lit. three score)', etc. Vigesimal forms have also been found in Tuscany and close to Naples, e.g., Tsc. *tre ventine* '60 (three score)', Ptl. *quattə vəndanə* '80 (lit. four score)' (Rohlfs 1952: 243; 1969: 313f.; 1971: 131f.). Instances also include higher numerals, e.g., Sal. *quínnici vintine/ quindice intine, quínnici vintini* '300 (lit. fifteen score)'. In terms of usage, vigesimal forms in Italy were traditionally used in the context of counting, e.g., fruits, eggs, and other agricultural products, architectural elements (such as pillars), and in reference to age (see Jaberg and Jud 1929: maps 301–02; Rohlfs 1969: 314).

The Iberian Peninsula overall does not provide many instances, possibly because of a lack of systematic research. A few scattered examples have been reported, such as NEuPt. *quarto vezes vinte* '80 (lit. four times twenty)' in use in the corn industry in Trás-os-Montes (northern Portugal), Leo. *dous veintes* '40 (lit. two twenties)', or Berceo's *tres vent medidas de farina* '60 measures of flour' (Menéndez Pidal 1973: 244; Rohlfs 1952: 243; Reichenkron 1958: 177f.).

Vigesimal forms in France include both full and semi-vigesimals, with dialectal *septante* 'seventy' and *nonante* 'ninety' in the east, as attested in Gilliéron and Edmond (1902; maps 1113, 1114, 1239, and 1240) and confirmed by Grevisse and Goosse (2016: 838). In Belgium and Switzerland the semi-vigesimals are replaced by *septante* '70' and *nonante* '90'; moreover, certain Swiss areas prefer *huitante* '80' to *quatre-vingt(s)* 'four-twenty/-ties' (Price 1992: 464). Learnèd and Latinized *octante* (< Lat. OCTOGINTA or Lat. OCTO '8' with the Romance suffix *-ante*) has been marginalized or quasi disappeared.

Yet in Belgium, where '70' and '90' today are decimals, dialectal data are revealing: the dialect of La Gleize, for example, today features *sèptante* '70' and *nonante* '90', and *catru-vints* '80', but also residues of vigesimal forms in the archaic language (Remacle 1952: 274). Other dialects, in Belgium, Switzerland, and France present similar patterns, showing that vigesimal forms were much more widespread in the past (for further details and discussion, see Bauer forthcoming).

In addition to dialectal data that suggest (an earlier) wide use of vigesimal forms in the French-speaking areas, early documents also confirm that picture. While old French was solidly decimal, featuring *setante* '70', *uitante* '80', and *nonante* '90', vigesimal forms start to appear from the twelfth century onwards, as in Villehardouin: *quatre vinz et .XVII. anz* '97 years' (*La conqueste de Contantinople* 1, Faral [1872] 1973). Around 1260 the French king founded a hospital for the blind in Paris, *L'hospice des Quinze-Vingts* 'Hospice of the 300 (lit. fifteen-[TIMES]-twenties)', referring to the number of beds it offered. Moreover, Nyrop reports instances from the Middle Ages covering numerals up to *dis huit vins* '360 (lit. ten [PLUS] eight [TIMES] twenties)'. He identifies examples of *cinq-vingts* '100 (lit. five-[TIMES]-twenties)' and *sept vingts* '140 (lit. seven [TIMES] twenties)' in the sixteenth century and of *six-vingts* '120 (lit. six-[TIMES]-twenties)' in the seventeenth century (Nyrop 1903: 343–44; Reichenkron 1958: 169). Yet it is clear that the decline had set in by the sixteenth century. The contexts of these uses typically entail money (as in counting coins), years in reference to age, units of length (e.g., steps, miles), animals, persons, or psalms (Huguet 1967: 479f.).

Moreover, sources note a sociolinguistic trend: while the decimal numerals have been identified by contemporaries as being used by 'learnèd men', 'the people' prefer *soixante dix* '70 (sixty [PLUS] ten)' and *qatre vins* '80 (four [TIMES] twenties)', which reflect a way of counting that is 'more accepted and more approved' (Meigret [1550] 1980: 42; Palsgrave quoted from Reichenkron 1958: 168). The situation in contemporary French established in the early nineteenth century, with a few (semi-)vigesimal forms surviving as residues of an earlier more prominent system (see Bauer forthcoming).

Other early Romance varieties also feature vigesimal forms. For medieval Occitan, for example, Jensen reports instances of *setanta* '70' and *nonanta*

'90', as well as *quatre vint et ueit vetz* '88 (lit. four [TIMES] twenty and eight) times' (Jensen 1986: 55). In contrast to modern Catalan, vigesimal forms are found in earlier stages, including in the early twentieth century such vigesimal forms as *vint y deu* '30 (lit. twenty and ten)', *dos vints* or *vint y vint* '40 (lit. two [TIMES] twenties, twenty and twenty)', which are today reported to have died out (Alcover 1925–26).

15.6.2 Formal Characteristics of Vigesimal Forms in Romance

Vigesimal and decimal forms in Romance are linguistically similar in that they are based on addition and multiplication and that the pattern for complex numerals is basically the same: [FACTOR.[TIMES].BASE]. The factor takes the form of a cardinal. Moreover, the sequence [FACTOR.[TIMES]. TWENTY] acts as a base for the numerals that are added: cardinal numerals, with or without a connector. The difference is the base itself, '20' instead of '10' and accordingly, the factors include numerals '1' through '20' and the addenda include '1' through '19'.

The corpus of Romance vigesimal forms that is to date available shows that the formations across the various languages parallel each other, with a few significant differences. First, with a few exceptions, the arithmetical operation is not formally expressed, e.g., Fr. *quatre-vingts* '80 (lit. four-[TIMES]-twenties)', Sal. *du intine* '40 (lit. two score)', Wal. (La Gleize) *noûv vints* '180 (lit. nine [TIMES] twenties)'. I have found only one exception to this trend: the example from the corn industry in Trás-os-Montes in northern Portugal where *vezes* 'times' explicitly conveys the underlying arithmetical operation, e.g., *quarto vezes vinte* '80 (lit. four times twenty)' (Menéndez Pidal 1973: 244). Typologically, 'overt expression of the operation of multiplication is relatively infrequent' (Greenberg 1978: 268).

Moreover, Romance vigesimal forms typically feature a cardinal numeral '20', except for the Italo-Romance formations, which systematically include a collective noun such as It. *ventina*. This characteristic is exclusive to the dialects of Italy, reflecting, according to Rohlfs (1969: 314), the characteristic way of counting throughout. For this hypothesis to be true, one should be able to find numerous collective numerical nouns in Italo-Romance, for which there is currently very little evidence (see, for instance, Ledgeway 2009: 220f). It is noteworthy that Romance languages feature few, if any, number nouns, in contrast to Germanic (see below).

In addition, for the odd decimals (e.g., '70', '90', ...) the vast majority of vigesimal forms favour the structure [FACTOR [TIMES] TWENTY [PLUS]. DIGIT/TEEN], e.g., Fr. *quatre-vingt-dix-huit* '98 (lit. four-[TIMES]-twenty-[PLUS]-ten-[PLUS]-eight)', Sav. *dou-vent-e-dis* '50 (lit. two-[TIMES]-twenty-and-ten)', Abr. (Teramo) *tre vendanə e ddicə* '70 (three score and ten)', Sic. *vintini e ddèci* '30 (lit. score and ten)'. One exception to this strong trend can be identified in the dialect of Bagnes (Switzerland): *sà vẽ vàtse e demyï* lit. 'six [TIMES] twenties cows and half (= '130 cows)' (Bjerrome 1957: 68). This last example is based on division, with halving of the last unit (viz. *vẽ* 'twenty') which is added to the vigesimal base of '120'. In addition, the process of division entails, *ipso facto*, overcounting because 'half' implies half of the next unit. This is a remarkable feature, because overcounting is not found elsewhere in Romance, in contrast to certain Germanic languages, where it is a relatively widespread phenomenon (for details, cf. Ross and Berns 1992: 612–20; Einarsson 1945).

It is noteworthy that the French varieties spoken in Belgium and Switzerland prefer *septante* 'seventy' and *nonante* 'ninety' to the vigesimal variants; they therefore do not use vigesimal counting, moving from *quatre-vingt-neuf* '89 (lit. four-[TIMES]-twenty-[PLUS]- nine)' to *nonante* at '90', thus avoiding semi-vigesimals such as *soixante-dix-neuf* '79 (lit. sixty [PLUS] ten [PLUS] nine)'.

While vigesimal forms in Romance cover a wide variety of numerals, up to '380', they typically do not exceed '400'. The formations are consistent, covering a series from 2.20 up to 19.20. Yet for a few numbers one may find either a different type of numeral or a choice: for example, dialects may offer a choice for '100' between *cinq vingts* 'five twenties' and *cent* 'hundred', or simply prefer *cent* (*deux cents* 'two [TIMES] hundreds', etc.) over a vigesimal formation.

15.6.3 Vigesimals in Other Languages

In addition to Romance, vigesimal forms are found in a number of other Indo-European branches, including Indo-Aryan, Albanian, Celtic, and Germanic. They are also found in Basque, a non-Indo-European language in contact with Romance. These formations have been discussed elsewhere (Bauer 2004), and I here refer to a number of characteristics that are relevant to the vigesimals in Romance.

In all languages, vigesimal forms are innovative and secondary, with the possible exception of Basque, where the documents are too recent to provide relevant data. Moreover, vigesimal formations often exist within a decimal system: Basque vigesimal forms cover '19' through '99' (Trask 2003: 126–28); Indo-Iranian dialects extend up to '400', which acts as a base for higher numerals (for details, see Edel'man 1999: 224f.). Insular Celtic languages feature full-fledged vigesimal paradigms, but speakers of Welsh tend to use English decimal numerals (Hurford 1975: 136) and certain Breton dialects prefer a decimal system 'patterned on that of French' (Greene 1992: 550).

Moreover, Celtic and Germanic evidence shows that vigesimal forms are the result of a medieval development, with 'Insular Celtic offer[ing] an exceptionally clear picture of the penetration of the vigesimal system into languages which had inherited a decimal system' (Greene 1992: 499). The change can be traced in medieval documents in the various Celtic languages (for details, see Pedersen 1913; Lewis and Pedersen 1974; Greene 1992; Broderick 1993: 241–44; Gillies 1993: 180f.).

There is considerable formal variation across the various languages, including structures of the type [DIGIT.[TIMES].20] (e.g., Alb. *dizét* 'two.[TIMES].twenty (= 40)', *trezét* 'three.[TIMES].twenty (= 60)', sometimes with an element specifying the operation (e.g., Dan. *fiyrsinttiughæ* 'four.times.twenty (= 80)', today abbreviated to *firs*; middle Dch. *vierwerf twintich* 'four.times.twenty (= 80)'). The odd decads may have continued vigesimal counting (e.g., Pashto *dwa šəle aw las* 'two twenties and ten (= 50)'), decimal marking (e.g., Alb. *nëndëðjétë* '9.[TIMES].10 (= 90)' vs *katrëzét* '4.[TIMES].20 (= 80)'), or overcounting, as in Pashto (e.g., *dwa nim šəle* 'two half twenties (= 50)' (Edel'man 1999: 223) or Dan. *halvtredsinstyve* 'half.third.times.twenty (= 50)', which is based on division (fraction).

Moreover, Germanic languages typically include so-called vigesimal number nouns, namely nouns of non-numeral origin that convey numerical value, e.g., Eng. *score* '20' or Dch. *snees* '20'. These nouns either reflect counting habits or storage practices. Dch. *snees*, for example, refers to the habit of putting (20) fish or onions on a string (see Bauer 2004), whereas Eng. *score*, a borrowing from Scandinavian, refers to a counting practice whereby notches are cut in a piece of wood to keep track of quantities, with a deeper notch for each quantity of twenty.

The etymology of all Germanic number nouns is not clear, but examples show that they typically occur in the contexts of elements that are counted on a regular basis: eggs, fruits, sheaves, years, coins. Similarly, with the exception of modern Celtic languages where vigesimal forms have ousted decimals, the usage of vigesimal forms in the other languages as well is closely connected to practices of counting, as in sheep husbandry in Basque (Araujo 1975) or 'household purposes' in Indo-Aryan, in counting livestock, fruits, knitting, and so forth (Edel'man 1999: 222).

Certain languages provide data as to the sociolinguistics of numerals, whereby vigesimal forms typically reflect the non-learnèd language, as in Indo-Aryan dialects where vigesimal formations are used in 'rural dialects and colloquial speech' and decimal numerals typically reflect 'formal speech' and 'literary style' (Edel'man 1999: 221f.). Similarly, the history of medieval Irish until today relates competition between the earlier decads advocated by the literary standard and the vigesimal system prevailing in the spoken language (Greene 1992: 530; Mac Eoin 1993: 118f.).

In conclusion, data from the relevant languages show that vigesimal forms there as well were an innovation, that they originated in non-standard varieties, that they are connected to counting practices, and that, in Germanic and Celtic, they emerged during the Middle Ages.

15.6.4 Origins of Vigesimal Forms in Romance

Since vigesimals were not inherited, discussion about their origins has centred around borrowing (cf. Section 28.3), with focus either on French vigesimals or vigesimals in western France and in southern Italy. Traditionally three hypotheses have been put forth, identifying a Gaulish, Scandinavian, and Basque origin respectively. Recently a fourth analysis has been added, identifying an internal development.

The Gaulish interpretation exclusively takes the French vigesimal forms into account, ascribing them to Gaulish substrate influence. It is a rather persistent explanation that is popular in the linguistic literature, including influential handbooks (e.g., Bourciez 1956: 27; von Wartburg 1961: 445; Posner 1996: 89; Buridant 2000: 224; Grevisse and Goosse 2016: 840). Yet there is no evidence for vigesimal forms in Gaulish, and in all likelihood there were none. Another presumed basis for the Gaulish hypothesis is the occurrence of vigesimals in modern Celtic languages. Yet as pointed out earlier by Rösler (1910: 196), the occurrence of vigesimals in Insular Celtic today does not say anything about the situation in much earlier Gaulish, a Continental Celtic language spoken on the European mainland.[7] Moreover, we now know that vigesimal forms in Insular Celtic were the result of a medieval development, posterior to Gaulish. Finally, if vigesimal forms were a Gaulish substrate feature, they should have existed in old French. Yet pre-twelfth-century French is fully decimal, as noted above.

The most important advocate of the Scandinavian hypothesis is Rohlfs (1952; cf. also Rösler 1929; Price 1992: 466f.), who attempts to correlate the vigesimals in France and southern Italy, assuming a Scandinavian borrowing, potentially via Norman French and ascribed to Viking settlements in the relevant areas.

This hypothesis is based on the importance of Sicily, and to a lesser extent mainland southern Italy, as a centre of vigesimal formations, the assumed high concentration of vigesimals in western France, and the occurrence of vigesimals in various Germanic, especially Scandinavian languages. Yet this interpretation is challenged by the precise timing of vigesimal forms in Germanic, the occurrence of vigesimals in areas that have not been under Viking rule or influence (e.g., Savoy), and the (quasi-)absence of them in areas where the Vikings have been influential, such as the Channel Islands or Palermo, the centre of Viking occupation in Sicily, as Reichenkron pointed out (1958: 164, 175f.; Jaberg and Jud 1929: maps 298–304). Finally, in light of a potential shared origin, the structural difference between the Italian and French vigesimal forms needs to be accounted for as well.

---

[7] This specification is relevant, as (later) Breton is an Insular Celtic language on the European mainland and features vigesimals (see more below).

The third hypothesis ascribes vigesimal formations to Basque, which indeed has a well-developed vigesimal system at least from the sixteenth century. There is no information about earlier relevant stages. On the basis of vigesimal counting practices in California (Araujo 1975), we know that Basque vigesimal counting is indeed transferable. Yet, if vigesimal forms in Romance originated in Basque, one might perhaps expect to find vigesimals in all languages geographically adjacent to Basque and not elsewhere, which is not the case (for a full discussion of these hypotheses, see Bauer 2004).

A final interpretation (cf. Bauer 2004) relates data from Romance to numerals in other Indo-European languages. On the basis of the occurrence of vigesimals in these languages, their structural features, and the timing of their emergence, Bauer (2004) concludes that vigesimal forms emerged spontaneously in Romance, Celtic, and Germanic during the Middle Ages at roughly the same time, in the eleventh and twelfth centuries. Their emergence is partly related to major changes in society, such as the dramatic increase of agricultural production, the spread of the use of money and monetary systems based on '12' and '20',[8] and the increase in commercial activities at higher levels (for details, see Bauer 2004). The concepts of '12' and '20' were rather well-known in Indo-European society. While the Indo-European numeral system was distinctly decimal, numerous linguistic and cultural phenomena suggest that other numerical units were relevant as well. I here refer to the Germanic counting system with its breaks after '12', '60', and '120' ('long hundred'), the numerous number nouns referring to '12', but especially '20' (Eng. *score*), the concept of twelve months, the twelve hour system, the role of '12' in Christianity, the twelve-day winter night ('twelfth night'; Haudry 1988), and the role of '60' in the time system. Finally, vigesimals, relating to already existing patterns, provide not only a way of counting, but more specifically a way of counting in units (hence the collectives in Italian) that are useful in terms of storage and economic handling (for further data and discussion, see Bauer 2004).

15.7 Decimal System in Romance

This chapter has identified major diachronic phenomena and trends in the history of numerals in Latin and Romance, which materialize in the individual languages each in their own way. Several of them have affected the numerical system at its core. First, the history of Latin–Romance counting systems is marked by a shift away from primarily synthetic formations

---

[8] Charlemagne's monetary system was based on units of twelve and twenty, namely 1 *livre*, 20 *solidi*, and 12 *denarii*. Cf. the UK pound until decimalization in 1971: 12 *pence* made one *shilling*, and 20 *shillings* made one *pound*.

covering a wide range of numerals to analytic and periphrastic expressions, especially in the category of non-cardinal numerals.

Moreover, the general loss of case and the partial loss of gender parallels the development of numerals from adjectival and nominal elements marked for case, gender, and number, respectively, into increasingly invariable numerical elements, even if modern Romance languages still feature grammatical marking on both low and high numerals.

A third trend pertains to the pervasive spread of decimals, which is manifest in three areas. First, the base '10' has been extended to higher powers, with the implementation of OFr. *milion* (< It. *mili-one* 'thousand-AUG'; Dressler and Merlini Babaresi 1994: 437; Meyer-Lübke 1894: 495–501), which serves as a model for many other formations (Bauer 2021). As a result, usage of multiplicatives and distributives-collectives as found in Latin high numerals became obsolete and the decimal system reached its full potential.

The spreading of decimals is also manifest in the history of vigesimals, a secondary Romance formation, which today have disappeared in the vast majority of Romance varieties. Residues remain, but their future may be uncertain (see Section 15.6.3 for Celtic). Psychological studies have shown that young children when learning how to count do not 'simply memoriz[e] an arbitrary number', but are aware of the (decimal) structure of complex numerals (Cheung, Dale, and Le Corre 2016: 2712). That awareness may impact on the acquisition of vigesimal forms.

The existence of (non-)official directives in France indeed suggests that (mixed) vigesimals are not easy to learn. Since the 1940s, directives from the Ministry of Education in France have advocated the use of Fr. *septante*, *octante*, and *nonante* in counting lessons (Grevisse and Goosse 2016: 838). Similarly, internet guidelines today recommend that in order to memorize '70', '80', and '90', one should use Fr. *septante*, *octante*, and *nonante* 'because the digit at the beginning is clearer (*sept* in *septante*)' (Réussite-des-enfants 2018). Alternatively, decads are explained to French children in terms of units of '10', with '70' corresponding to seven groups of ten, and so forth (Caprais 2018). Although no details are provided, the difficulty may ultimately reside in the counting up to twenty, exceptional within the system, rather than the decads themselves, which many (adult) speakers see as one unit, without being aware of its etymology.

Moreover, French sign language in France features no vigesimals: the numerals '60' through '100' are rendered as decimals. The decads are products of seven, eight, and nine and a sign referring to '10', and the counting between the units does not exceed '9'.[9] It is noteworthy that sign

---

[9] I am grateful to Marie-Anne Sallandre for providing me with videos showing the relevant numerals in French Sign Language.

languages may feature vigesimals, but that so far no link has been found with the counting system of the spoken variety or neighbouring languages (Zeshan et al. 2013: 371f., 374–77).

Finally, the spread of decimals is manifest in the extension of the decimal system since the French Revolution to all types of measurement, the early ones (weight, distance, area, and volume) and the ones that were added later (temperature, pressure, etc.). In this respect, the Romance languages have been very categorical: the pre-decimal measure systems and terminology have disappeared not only from French, but from all Romance languages. As a result, the Romance languages today have basically no abstract number nouns.

One of the trends that Comrie has identified in numerical systems of the world is the spread of decimal systems at the expense of other bases, which he ascribes to the fact that the most widespread languages, e.g., English, happen to be decimal (2003: 40). Yet there may be more to it than that: scale of material and cognitive production has reached levels that necessitate an abstract counting system where base and conversion factors are identical throughout the system. The decimal system with its powers – hundred, thousand, million, etc. – is thoroughly consistent and in itself does not need arithmetical calculation, because the arithmetic operations involving '10' are exceptionally straightforward. That widespread and important international languages are decimal is in likelihood important, but the characteristics of the decimal system itself are probably conclusive in its spread.

Selected References

Below you can find selected references for this chapter. The full references can be found online at the following page: www.cambridge.org/Romancelinguistics

Bauer, B. (2004). 'Vigesimal numerals in Romance: an Indo-European perspective'. In Drinka, B. (ed.), *Indo-European Language and Culture in Historical Perspective: Essays in Memory of Edgar C. Polomé. General Linguistics* 41, 21–46.

Bauer, B. (2017). *Nominal Apposition in Indo-European. Forms, Functions and Its Evolution in Latin-Romance.* Berlin: Mouton de Gruyter.

Bauer, B. (2021). 'The formation of numerals in the Romance languages'. In Loporcaro, M. and Gardani, F. (eds), *The Oxford Encyclopedia of Romance Linguistics.* Oxford: Oxford University Press. https://doi.org/10.1093/acrefore/9780199384655.013.685

Coleman, R. (1992). 'Italic'. In Gvozdanović, J. (ed.), *Indo-European Numerals.* Berlin: Mouton de Gruyter, 389–445.

Comrie, B. (2003). 'Numeral systems in the languages in Europe and North and Central Asia: preliminary results from the WALS database'. In

Suihkonen, P. and Comrie, B. (eds), *Collection of Papers, International Symposium on Deictic Systems and Quantification in Languages Spoken in Europe and North and Central Asia*. Izhevsk: Udmurt State University, 32–41.

Greenberg, J. (1978). 'Numeral systems'. In Greenberg, J. (ed), *Universals of Human Language. 3. Word Structure*. Stanford: Stanford University Press, 251–95.

Klein, H. A. (1974). *The Science of Measurement. A Historical Survey*. New York: Dover.

Menéndez Pidal, R. (1973 [1904]). *Manual de gramática histórica española*, 14th ed. Madrid: Espasa-Calpe.

Price, G. (1992). 'Romance'. In Gvozdanović, J. (ed.), *Indo-European Numerals*. Berlin: Mouton de Gruyter, 447–97.

Rohlfs, G. 1969. *Grammatica storica della lingua italiana e dei suoi dialetti. 3. Sintassi e formazione delle parole*. Turin: Einaudi.

Schmandt-Besserat, D. (1992). *Before Writing*. Austin: University of Texas Press.

Zeshan, U., Delgado, C., Dikyuva, D., Panda, C., and de Vos, C. (2013). 'Cardinal numerals in rural sign languages: approaching cross-modal typology', *Linguistic Typology* 17: 357–96.

Part Four

Syntax

16

Argument Structure and Argument Realization

Víctor Acedo-Matellán, Jaume Mateu, and Anna Pineda

16.1 Introduction

Argument structure can be defined from a semantic or a syntactic perspective. On the semantic side, argument structure is a representation of the central semantic participants in the eventuality (event or state) expressed by the (verbal) predicate.[1] On the syntactic side, argument structure is a hierarchical representation of the arguments required by the predicate that determines how they are expressed in the syntax.

There are currently two different theoretical approaches to argument structure: the projectionist one, which is typically adopted in lexicalist frameworks (see Levin and Rappaport Hovav 2005 and Wechsler 2015, among others), and the constructivist/neo-constructivist one, which is assumed in non-lexicalist frameworks (see Borer 2005 and Acedo-Matellán 2016, among others). According to the former perspective, the syntax of argument structure is claimed to be projected from the lexical meaning of the (verbal) predicate. According to the latter perspective, by contrast, argument structure is provided with a configurational/syntactic meaning that is independent from the conceptual contribution of the lexical (verbal) root and is constructed outside the lexicon.

In the paradigmatic projectionist proposal put forward by Levin and Rappaport Hovav (1995), two levels of lexical representation are postulated: event structure and argument structure. The former is a lexical-*semantic* level that provides a structural semantic decomposition of lexical meaning (e.g., see (1a) for the lexical-semantic structure of the verb *break*, which can be read as *the action of x causes y to become broken*), whereas the latter is a

---

[1] For reasons of space, in this chapter we will basically deal with what is known as *verbal* argument structure (for a recent overview, see Marantz 2013).

lexical-*syntactic* level that encodes the number of arguments selected by a predicate and the hierarchy that can be established among them (e.g., compare the external argument x and the internal argument y in (1b)). x will then be projected in syntax as a DP subject external to the verbal phrase, while y will be projected internally to it as a DP object.

(1) a. [[X ACT] CAUSE [Y BECOME <BROKEN>]]
    b. X<Y>

In projectionist frameworks argument structure alternations have been claimed to affect event structure via morphosemantic operations and/or argument structure via morphosyntactic operations. For example, according to Sadler and Spencer's (2001) lexicalist framework, the active–passive alternation in (2), which is analysed in (3), only affects the lexical-syntactic level of argument structure, i.e., (1b). In (3b), the suppression of the external argument is notated by means of parentheses: *(x)*. The suppressed external argument can be expressed in the syntax with an adjunct PP (*per en Marc* 'by Marc').

(2) **Catalan**
    a. En Marc va trencar el vas.
        DET Marc AUX.PST.3SG break.INF the glass
        'Marc broke the glass.'
    b. El vas va ser trencat (per en Marc).
        DET glass AUX.PST.3SG be.INF broken (by DET Marc)
        'The glass was broken (by Marc).'

(3) a. [[X ACT] CAUSE [Y BECOME <BROKEN>]] : event structure
       X<Y> : argument structure
       En Marc va trencar el vas
       Subject   Object   : syntax
    b. [[X ACT] CAUSE [Y BECOME <BROKEN>]] : event structure
       (x)<Y> : argument structure
       El vas va ser trencat (per en Marc)
       Subject   Oblique   : syntax

On the other hand, in the Minimalist Program the formation of argument structures and argument structure alternations should be treated entirely within the syntax proper (i.e., outside the lexicon) via the same Merge and Move operations which construct any syntactic constituent (see Harley 2011 for an overview of some minimalist approaches to argument structure). As a result, the notion of 'mapping' from lexicon to syntax or the 'linking' of arguments used in projectionist accounts of argument realization has no meaning in this second approach; instead the mere syntax of argument structure narrows down possible semantic interpretations of predicates and arguments. For example, proponents of minimalist neo-constructionist approaches claim that the structural meaning in (1a) that corresponds to (2a) can be read off a syntactic configuration such as that depicted in (4). The dynamic light verb (cf. Chomsky's 1995 causative little v) subcategorizes for a Small Clause (SC) whose inner predicate is the result state TRENCAT 'broken' and its internal subject is *el vas* 'the glass'. The idiosyncratic or encyclopaedic meaning is provided by the root √TRENC-, which is incorporated into the null light verb providing it with phonological content (see Hale and Keyser 1993).[2]

(4)   [$_{VoiceP}$ Marc [$_{vP}$ V$_{DO}$ [$_{SC}$ el vas √TRENC-]]]

In some current syntactic approaches to argument structure the alleged primitive predicate CAUSE in (1a) has been claimed to be read off a syntactic configuration where an activity verb selects a Small Clause (e.g., Zubizarreta and Oh 2007; Cuervo 2015). The external argument *Marc* is argued to be introduced by an upper functional head called *Voice* (Kratzer 1996; Harley 2013). Following Marantz (2013), the set of argument-introducing heads can be divided into Voice and so-called applicative heads (see Section 16.4), on the one hand, and prepositional heads, on the other. The Voice and applicative heads place the added argument syntactically above the phrase to which they add an argument. In contrast, prepositions add an argument below the phrase to which they attach (e.g., see Svenonius 2007). Finally, as for the passive alternant in (2b), in a non-lexicalist proposal such as that put forward by Embick (2004), the syntactic formation of the eventive passive involves an additional functional phrase Asp(ectual)P just above an agentive VoiceP (see Embick 2004 for details).

In Section 16.2 we deal with the well-known distinction among intransitive verbal predicates (unaccusatives vs unergatives) in the context of Romance linguistics. In Section 16.3 we offer a review of the crucial role of the Romance clitic *se* in argument structure and argument realization. Section 16.4 provides an overview of datives in various Romance languages. In Section 16.5 we show why these languages have a prominent place in the huge literature on the so-called lexicalization patterns. Section 16.6 contains some concluding remarks.

16.2 Unaccusativity and Unergativity

One of the most important hypotheses formulated in the syntactic literature on argument structure is the so-called *Unaccusative Hypothesis*, initially formulated by Perlmutter (1978) in the Relational Grammar framework and later developed by Burzio (1981; 1986) in the Government and

---

[2] See also Mateu (2002), Mateu and Espinal (2007), Ramchand (2008), and Acedo-Matellán and Mateu (2014), among others, for the important distinction between syntactically relevant structural/compositional meaning and syntactically irrelevant conceptual/idiosyncratic meaning.

Binding framework (cf. also Section 17.4.2). According to this hypothesis, intransitive verbs (or clauses; see Perlmutter 1978) can be classified into two classes on the basis of the status of their argument: the argument of *unergatives* is just like the subject of transitives, whereas the argument of *unaccusatives* is more like an object in important respects, though it may look like a subject on the surface. Two different D(eep)-structure configurations are attributed to them by Burzio (1981; 1986): unergative verbs such as It. *telefonare* 'phone', *lavorare* 'work', *dormire* 'sleep', etc. occur in the syntactic frame in (5a), while unaccusative verbs such as It. *arrivare* 'arrive', *uscire* 'go out', *morire* 'die', etc. enter into the configuration in (5b), where [$_{NP}$ e] expresses an empty NP subject. An important single split is represented in (5): unergatives have an external argument (i.e., the NP is *external* to VP), while unaccusatives have their argument internal to VP.

(5) a. [NP [$_{VP}$ V]]
    b. [[$_{NP}$ e] [$_{VP}$ V NP]]

Perlmutter (1978) and Burzio (1981; 1986) argue that the grammatical behaviour of unaccusative verbs/clauses, which can be diagnosed by means of morphosyntactic tests such as BE-selection (cf. also Sections 4.3.1, 18.3, 21.2.2.2) or *ne*-cliticization in Italian (see below for other 'unaccusativity diagnostics'), can be explained in a uniform way by postulating an underlying structure in which their surface subject originates in an internal argument position (see 5b). Burzio argues that the pattern of auxiliary selection in Italian is parallel to that of the distribution of *ne*-cliticization, and that it reflects the different D-structure configurations of unaccusative verbs (see 5b) vs unergative ones (see 5a). Unaccusative verbs select the auxiliary *essere* 'be', while non-unaccusatives (i.e., both unergatives and transitives) select the auxiliary *avere* 'have'. Burzio (1986: 30) points out that '*ne*-cliticization is possible with respect to all and only direct objects' and defines unaccusative verbs as those verbs whose subject can be replaced by the direct object clitic *ne*. Two related facts are then accounted for: first, the contrast between unergatives (e.g., *telefonare* 'phone') in (6a) and unaccusatives (e.g., *arrivare* 'arrive') in (6b) (note that Burzio renamed Perlmutter's unaccusatives as 'ergatives') and, in addition, the parallelism between the unaccusative subject in (6b) and the transitive object in (6c). As expected, *ne*-cliticization fails if the pronominalized NP is in subject position (see, e.g., 6d and 6e). Finally, as pointed out by Perlmutter, it seems more convenient to use 'unaccusative' as applied to structures (or clauses) rather than to verbs; for example, the passive construction can also be analysed as unaccusative (cf. 6f and 6b).[3]

---

[3] Related to *ne*-cliticization in Italian, French, and Catalan, another test that has been put forward as an unaccusative diagnostic in Spanish (see Treviño 2003) is that the partitive phrase *de todo* 'of everything' can only occur as subject of unaccusatives (i.a) and object of transitives (i.b). In contrast, unergatives do not admit it (i.c).

(6) **Italian**
    a.   **Ne   hanno   telefonato   tre.
          PART= have.3PL phone.PTCP three
          (cf. *Hanno telefonato tre ragazze*)
              have.3PL phone.PTCP three girls)
          'Three of them have phoned.'
    b.   Ne   sono   arrivate   tre.
          PART= are.3PL arrive.PTCP.FPL three
          (cf. *Sono arrivate tre ragazze*)
              are.3PL arrive.PTCP.FPL three girls)
          'Three of them have arrived.'
    c.   Ne   hanno   comprato tre.
          PART= have.3PL buy.PTCP three
          (cf. *Hanno comprato tre macchine*)
              have.3PL buy.PTCP three cars)
          'They have bought three of them.'
    d.   **Tre ne   sono   arrivate.
          three PART= are.3PL arrive.PTCP.FPL
          'Three of them have arrived.'
    e.   **Tre ne   hanno   {comprato due macchine / telefonato}.
          three PART= have.3PL buy.PTCP two cars phone.PTCP
          'Three of them have {bought two cars/telephoned}.'
    f.   Ne   saranno   comprate   molte (di macchine).
          PART= be.FUT.3PL buy.PTCP.FPL many (of cars)
          'Many of them will be bought.'

Burzio (1986: 55f.) formulates the following rule in (7) for *essere* 'be' assignment:

(7)   The auxiliary will be realized as *essere* when a binding relation exists between the subject and a nominal contiguous to the verb (where 'a nominal contiguous to the verb' is a nominal which is either part of the verb morphology, i.e., a clitic, or a direct object).

Despite its important merits, Burzio's syntactic account based on distributional arguments and binding principles has been said to be problematic due to some shortcomings (see, for example, Centineo 1996 for a critical review). For example, consider the relevant data in (8b) and (8d), taken from

Spanish
(i)   a.   {Llega / cae / queda / muere...} de todo.
          arrives falls remains dies   of everything
    b.   {Compra / mata / construye...} de todo.
          buys   kills   builds   of everything
    c.   **{Duerme / brilla / suena...} de todo.
          sleeps   shines rings   of everything

Lonzi (1985) and revisited by Levin and Rappaport Hovav (1995: 276f., ex. 106–07). These data have been claimed to be counterexamples to Burzio's (1986) claim that ergative (i.e., unaccusative) verbs are the only monadic verbs that admit *ne*-cliticization of their argument. Following Lonzi (1985), Levin and Rappaport Hovav (1995: 275) point out that a variety of verbs that take the auxiliary *avere* 'have' do permit *ne*-cliticization, but only when they are found in a simple tense; *ne*-cliticization is not possible when these verbs are found in a complex tense in which the auxiliary is expressed. Levin and Rappaport Hovav (1995: 277) conclude that 'phenomena said to involve "surface unaccusativity" [...] are not unaccusative diagnostics strictly speaking, but rather to a large extent receive their explanation from discourse considerations'.

(8) **Italian**
   a. **Di ragazze, ne hanno lavorato molte nelle fabbriche di Shanghai.
      of girls, PART=have.3PL work.PTCP many in.the factories of Shanghai
   b. Di ragazze, ne lavorano molte nelle fabbriche di Shanghai.
      of girls PART=work.3PL many in.the factories of Shanghai
      'There are many girls working in the factories of Shanghai.'
   c. **Di ragazzi, ne hanno russato molti nel corridoio del treno.
      of boys PART=have.3PL snore.PTCP many in.the corridor of.the train.
   d. Di ragazzi, ne russavano molti nel corridoio del treno.
      of boys, PART=snored.3PL many in.the corridor of.the train
      'There were many boys snoring in the corridor of the train.'

One could claim that Levin and Rappaport Hovav's (1995) remark on Italian only holds for imperfective tenses, since these can be regarded as the most appropriate for expressing habitual activities. However, the following triplet from Centineo (1996: 230f. n. 6) shows that this is not the case, since in the synthetic preterite these alleged unergative verbs are also compatible with *ne*-cliticization; see (9c).

(9) **Italian**
   a. Ce ne nuota tanta di gente, in quella piscina.
      there= PART= swims much of people in that pool
      'Lots of people swim in that swimming pool.'
   b. ??Ce ne ha nuotato molta di gente in quella piscina.
      there= PART= has swum much of people in that pool
   c. Ce ne nuotò molta di gente in quella piscina.
      there= PART= swam much of people in that pool
      'Lots of people swam in that swimming pool.'

Note that the ungrammaticality of (8a, 8c) and (9b) is actually predicted by Burzio's (1986) correlation between *ne*-cliticization and unaccusativity. Indeed, there is some evidence that points to the fact that the constructions in (8) and (9) are unaccusative. *Avere* would not then be the expected auxiliary in (9b) if the Italian existential construction in (9) turns out to be unaccusative. In this sense Centineo's (1996: 231 n. 6) remark can also be said to be relevant: 'it must also be added that some of the native speakers consulted about these data attempted to use *essere* as the auxiliary for <(9b)>.' Still, if one assumes that the construction in (9) is unaccusative, one wonders why *essere*-selection is not possible. This requires further research.

Furthermore, as pointed out by Rigau (1997), Catalan also offers evidence for the unaccusative status of existential constructions like (8b) and (8d). A well-known generalization in Romance is that bare NP plurals cannot be postverbal subjects of unergative verbs in free inversion contexts (e.g., see 10b) and are only possible as postverbal subjects of unaccusatives (e.g., Cat. *Venen nois* lit. 'come boys (= there come some boys)') or as direct objects of transitive verbs (e.g., Cat. *Les drogues maten nois* 'Drugs kill boys'). Given this, the existential construction in (10c) should be unaccusative. As expected, the postverbal bare subject in (10c) is pronominalized by partitive *ne*; see (10d).

(10) **Catalan**
   a. Els   nois   canten.
      the   boys   sing.3PL
   b. **Canten nois.
      sing.3PL boys
   c. (En aquesta coral) hi   canten   nois.
      in   this   choir   LOC=   sing.3PL   boys
      'There are boys singing (in this choir).'
   d. (En aquesta coral), (de nois) n'hi   canten   molts.
      in   this   choir   of boys   PART=LOC=   sing.3PL   many.
      'There are many boys singing (in this choir).'

Rigau (1997) and Mateu (2015) argue that in existential constructions like (10c) or (10d) the obligatory locative marker *hi* 'there' can be analysed as a quirky subject (see also Torrego 1989; Masullo 1992a; and Fernández Soriano 1999 for related locative and dative constructions in Spanish). However, things turn out to be more complex. For example, Italian examples like the ones in (11), taken from Maling, Calabrese, and Sprouse (1994), do not involve any surface locative element. These authors point out that (11a) is possible only on a very specific reading, namely, many people are calling in one specific place relevant to the speaker. A similar comment could be said to be appropriate for (11b). Alternatively, temporal phrases like *la domenica* 'on Sunday' in (11a) or *domani* 'tomorrow' in (11b) can be claimed to play an important role as well. The relevant conclusion seems to be that a spatio-temporal element is compulsory in the syntactic structure in order to license these existential constructions.

(11) **Italian**
  a. Ne   telefonano molti,   di   tifosi, la   domenica!
     PART= phone.3PL   many   of   fans   on   Sunday
     'Lots of fans ring on Sundays!'
  b. Domani   ne   parleranno   molti.
     tomorrow PART= will.speak.3PL many
     'Tomorrow many of them will be speaking.'

As pointed out by Rigau (1997; 2005) and Mateu and Rigau (2002), a clearer piece of evidence for the unaccusativity of the existential constructions in (10c) and (10d) can be found in some north-western varieties of Catalan where there is no agreement between the indefinite argument *nois* 'boys' and the verb (cf. also Section 26.4.3); see (12b). Indeed, the lack of agreement in (12b) would be unexpected if the bare plural NP were the subject/external argument of an unergative verb/construction (cf. the unaccusativity of the example in 13b).

(12) **North-western Catalan**
  a. Els   nois   canten.
     the   boys   sing.3PL
  b. (En   aquesta coral)   hi   canta   nois.
     in   this   choir   LOC= sings   boys
  c. (En   aquesta coral), (de nois) n'hi   canta molts.
     in   this   choir   of boys PART=LOC= sings many

(13) a. Venen   nois. (CCat.)
        come.3PL   boys
     b. Ve   nois. (NWCat.)
        come3SG   boys

Drawing on Hale and Keyser's (1993) configurational theory of argument structure, Mateu and Rigau (2002) claim that the syntactic analysis of the agentive unergative structure in (12a) is the one depicted in (14a), whereas that of the existential unaccusative structure in (12b) is the one shown in (14b).

(14) a. [$_{vP}$ Els nois [$_v$ V$_{DO}$ √CANT-]]
     b. [$_{vP}$ √CANT-V$_{BE}$ [$_{PP}$ hi [P$_{CCR}$ nois]]]

Following Hale and Keyser (1993), the formation of unergative verbs can be argued to involve incorporation of a nominal (or a simple root, e.g., √CANT- '$s[o]ng$'), which occupies the complement position in (14a), into an agentive null light verb (v_{DO}). The formation of the unaccusative argument structure in (14b) is quite different, since a null light verb v_{BE} subcategorizes for a Small Clause-like PP as complement. The preposition that expresses a Central Coincidence Relation (P$_{CCR}$) in (14b), which can be claimed to be crucial when dealing with possessive relations (see Hale and Keyser 2002: ch. 7 and Real-Puigdollers 2013, among others), is conceived of as a birelational element that relates a possessor (*hi* 'there') with a possessee (*nois* 'boys').[4] The same sort of element has been argued to be involved in impersonal existential constructions with HAVE such as Fr. *il y a*, Sp. *hay*, and Cat. *hi ha* 'there is' (see Rigau 1997, among many others, for the proposal that HAVE = BE + P). The main difference between these constructions and (14b) is that the latter involves an additional conflation of the root √CANT- with the null light verb. For two prominent SC-based analyses of existential constructions, see Hoekstra and Mulder (1990) and Moro (1997), among others.

It is important to point out that, besides syntactic accounts, there are also semantic approaches to unaccusativity. For example, a very influential approach is that pioneered by Antonella Sorace and her colleagues, who take systematic linguistic variation to suggest that unaccusativity is determined by a semantic notion whose components are organized along a (proto)typicality scale ranging from core to periphery. Sorace (2000; 2004) argues that a more nuanced descriptive approach than a simple two-way split (unaccusative vs unergative) is needed in order to account for the attested variation. In particular, she shows that in Italian some intransitive verbs (e.g., telic change of location verbs like *arrivare* 'arrive' or agentive process verbs like *lavorare* 'work') select an auxiliary more categorically than other verbs (e.g., atelic change of state verbs like *fiorire* 'blossom' or continuation of state verbs like *durare* 'last'). The former are called 'core' verbs, while the latter are called 'non-core' verbs. To account for these facts, Sorace puts forward the A(uxiliary) S(election) H(ierarchy) in (15; cf. also Section 4.3.1). According to her, verbs at the BE end of the ASH are core unaccusatives and express telic change, whereas verbs at the HAVE end are core unergatives and express agentive activity in which the subject is unaffected. In contrast, intermediate verbs between the two extremes incorporate telicity and agentivity to lesser degrees, and tend to have a less specified (basically stative) event structure. Furthermore, core verbs are claimed to be those on which native grammaticality judgements are maximally consistent, and are acquired early by both first and second language learners. In contrast, intermediate verbs are shown to be subject to cross-linguistic differences and exhibit gradient auxiliary selection preferences.

(15) Auxiliary Selection Hierarchy (ASH)
    CHANGE OF LOCATION   selects BE   least variation
    CHANGE OF STATE
    CONTINUATION OF A PRE-EXISTING STATE
    EXISTENCE OF STATE
    UNCONTROLLED PROCESS
    CONTROLLED PROCESS (MOTIONAL)
    CONTROLLED PROCESS (NON-MOTIONAL)   selects HAVE   least variation

---

[4] See Rigau (1997; 2005) for the claim that the locative clitic *hi* 'there' acts as an impersonalizer in (14b).

Sorace claims that the cross-linguistic variation found, for example, between Italian and French depends on the location of the relevant cut-off point along the ASH in (15). In particular, the main cut-off point in Italian can be claimed to be drawn just below the lexical-semantic class expressing 'existence of state' (e.g., It. *esistere* 'exist' selects BE), whereas the main cut-off point in French can be drawn further up in the scale in (15) (e.g., Fr. *exister* 'exist' selects HAVE).

Sorace's work on the ASH has influenced other accounts such as the O(ptimality) T(heory) proposals by Legendre and Sorace (2003) and Legendre (2007). These OT accounts are especially valuable since the authors try to argue for a unified analysis of the morphosyntactic ingredients (e.g., the reflexive clitic) and the semantic factors (e.g., telicity, stativity, or control) involved in auxiliary selection in French. In order to deal with systematic BE-selection in reflexive constructions the authors posit a constraint against linking morphosyntactic reflexives as unergatives. This crucially outranks all the semantic constraints, ensuring that reflexives will always select BE, no matter what their semantics. Despite their descriptive merits, the formal limits on the semantic ingredients involved in auxiliary selection are not provided by Sorace (2000; 2004).[5] See Loporcaro (2015) for a recent criticism of semantic approaches to auxiliary selection such as those put forward by Sorace (2000; 2004) and Aranovich (2003).

Finally, besides the two important unaccusativity diagnostics reviewed above (auxiliary selection and *ne*-cliticization), it should be noted that there are other tests that have also been claimed to be relevant when distinguishing unaccusatives from unergatives. For example, unaccusatives can enter into absolute participle constructions, whereas unergatives cannot (see, for example, Legendre 1989; cf. 16a and 16b). The well-formedness of (16a) and (16c) shows a parallelism between the subject of unaccusatives and the direct object of transitives: *el dictador* 'the dictator' is the internal argument in (16a) and (16c), but not in (16b), where it is the external argument.[6]

---

[5] Sorace (2000: 861) is aware of this non-trivial problem, noting that 'there are some important questions that I do not attempt to address. First, the reader will not find an explanation of why particular semantic components are more crucial to the selection of particular auxiliaries than others.' For an attempt to solve this problem, see Mateu (2002; 2009), who claims that meaning components like the ones in (15) are relevant precisely because these notions can be filtered into the abstract *relational* semantics associated with the unergative and unaccusative syntactic argument structures as they are understood in Hale and Keyser's (2002) proposal of l(exical)-syntax.

[6] See also De Miguel (1992) for the claim that a further aspectual restriction is relevant in Spanish: only telic unaccusative verbs (e.g., *llegar* 'arrive', *desaparecer* 'disappear') can enter into these participial constructions, whereas atelic unaccusative verbs (e.g., *existir* 'exist', *permanecer* 'remain') cannot: cf. Sp. *Una vez {desaparecidos/**existidos} los dinosaurios, . . .* 'Once the dinosaurs disappeared/existed, . . .'

(16) **Spanish**
    a.   Una vez muerto el dictador, ya hubo más libertad.
        one time die.PTCP the dictator, already existed more freedom
        'Once the dictator was dead, there was already more freedom.'
    b.   **Una vez hablado el dictador, no hubo más libertad.
        one time speak.PTCP the dictator, not existed more freedom
    c.   Una vez depuesto el dictador, ya hubo más libertad.
        one time oust.PTCP the dictator, already existed more freedom
        'Once the dictator was ousted, there was already more freedom.'

To conclude this section, it is worth pointing out that an important theoretical debate revolves around whether unaccusativity (and argument structure, in general; see Section 16.1) is a property of verbs, as argued by proponents of projectionism, or rather of constructions/structures, as argued by proponents of neoconstructionism/constructivism (see Levin and Rappaport Hovav 2005; Marantz 2013; Mateu 2014; Acedo-Matellán 2016: ch. 2), for relevant discussion of these two theories of the lexicon–syntax interface).

16.3 The Clitic SE

In this section we deal with the clitic SE, concentrating on its use in alternations: the transitive–unaccusative alternation usually called *causative alternation*, the transitive–transitive or intransitive–intransitive alternations (*telic* or *aspectual* SE), and, very briefly, the object/oblique alternation (*antipassive* SE).

In Romance languages, the anticausative counterpart in the causative alternation often features the clitic SE, as in (17). This change of state unaccusative variant alternates with the transitive counterpart, as in (18):

(17) La copa de vi s' ha trencat. (Cat.)
     the glass of wine SE has break.PTCP
     'The wine glass has broken.'

(18) Un convidat ha trencat la copa de vi. (Cat.)
     a guest has break.PTCP the glass of wine
     'A guest has broken the wine glass.'

The theoretical relevance of the morphological marking of anticausatives has been and still is a widely discussed topic in Romance linguistics. Several notions have been claimed to be involved in the presence or absence of SE, such as low/high spontaneity (a notion that has also been connected to a verb's *causalness*, in the sense that verbs with a relatively low spontaneity are more likely to be used as causatives, and less likely as anticausatives), external/internal causation, or telicity.[7] As a matter of fact, in the examples above one can see that the verb 'break' denotes a telic event which has a low degree of spontaneity, since in order for something to break an external force is needed (external causation); therefore its anticausative use is somehow less expected and Romance languages tend to mark it, as in (17). At the same time, Cat. *trencar* 'break' has a high degree of causalness, and thus its causative use is not marked in (18) – on the contrary, the prediction is that Romance verbs with a poor degree of causalness, such as 'grow', which designates an atelic, generally internally-caused event and thus expectedly used as intransitive (19), will be marked when used causatively, as shown by its embedding under 'make' in (20).

(19) Les plantes han crescut. (Cat.)
the plants have grow.PTCP
'The plants have grown.'

(20) El sol fa créixer les plantes. (Cat.)
the sun makes grow.INF the plants
'The sun makes the plants grow.'

All in all, it seems that, even if some cross-linguistic tendencies exist and languages normally use the marked and unmarked variants according to certain semantic distinctions, SE does not have the same semantic effect on all verbs, as many differences and mismatches across and within languages still remain. The Romance family is not an exception to this. For example, Balearic Catalan dispenses with the clitic with some verbs (21b), which do need the clitic in other dialects (21a). Similar variation is found in Spanish (22), either dialectal or idiolectal, depending on the case. Finally, variation is also found in French, apparently linked to slightly different meanings, as shown in (23):

(21) a. Ella s' ha engreixat més que tu. (Cat.)
she SE has fatten.PTCP more than you
'She has put on more weight than you.'
b. Ella ha engreixat més que tu. (Bal. Cat.)
she has fatten.PTCP more than you
'She has put on more weight than you.'

---

[7] See Abrines (2016), Fontich (2021) for Catalan; Mendikoetxea (1999) for Spanish; Labelle (1992), Labelle and Doron (2010), Doron and Labelle (2011) for French; Folli (2002; 2014) for Italian; and Haspelmath (1993; 2006; 2008), Alexiadou (2010), Haspelmath et al. (2014), and Heidinger (2015) for a cross-linguistic perspective.

(22) María (se) adelgazó   mucho aquel verano. (Sp.)
      María (SE) lose.weight.PRT much that summer
      'María lost a lot of weight that summer.'

(23) **French**
   a. Les branches de l' arbre ont   cassé.
      the branches of the tree have   break.PTCP
      'The branches of the tree have broken.'
   b. Le vase s' est   cassé.
      The vase SE is   break.PTCP
      'The vase has broken.'

Another interesting case in point are French prefixed anticausatives, which are normally marked with SE regardless of any other semantic consideration. Compare, for example, *s'agrandir* 'extend' vs *grandir* 'increase', both of them expressing atelic change of state events but only prefixed *s'agrandir* being marked with SE.

In view of examples such as the ones above, Schäfer (2008), Martin and Schäfer (2014), and Alexiadou, Anagnostopoulou, and Schäfer (2015) argue against such a systematic connexion between the conceptualization of events and the presence of SE, and consider instead that the presence of SE on an individual anticausative verb is to a large extent idiosyncratic (i.e., lexically stored).

The discussion of the morphological marking of anticausatives is also connected to another issue of theoretical relevance: the derivational relation, if any, between the causative and the anticausative alternants. Two major approaches exist (for an overview see, for example, Haspelmath 1993 and Alexiadou, Anagnostopoulou, and Schäfer 2006). Under a *causativization* hypothesis, the intransitive (anticausative) alternant is the basic one, whereas the causative form is derived by adding an external argument to a predicate which would be monadic (Lakoff 1968; 1970; Dowty 1979; Williams 1981; Brousseau and Ritter 1991; Pesetsky 1995). On the contrary, the *detransitivization* perspective considers the anticausative alternant to be inherently dyadic (i.e., bieventive predicate), although it lacks the explicit external argument as a result of the lexical process of detransitivization (Levin and Rappaport Hovav 1995; Reinhart 2000; 2002; and also Chierchia 1989/2004). All in all, it is again the case that languages show huge variation in this regard, so that neither account seems to be better than the other in general terms. However, if we focus on Romance languages, the fact that anticausatives are generally marked (with SE) could suggest that the transitive alternant is the basic one in these languages: that is to say that under a derivational approach to the causative alternation, the derived counterpart will be more complex, since it requires an additional operation, and in this regard the frequent morphological marking (qua morphological complexity) of Romance anticausatives would match with their alleged derived status.

Many authors have observed that, beside its appearance in anticausative constructions, which marks them as intransitive, SE is also involved in alternations involving either two transitive (cf. 24) or two intransitive alternants (cf. 25):[8]

(24) La Llúcia {ha/s'ha} menjat un albercoc. (Cat.)
 the Llúcia {has/SE=has} eat.PTCP an apricot
 'Llúcia has {eaten/eaten up} an apricot.'

(25) {Han/se han} caído dos hojas. (Sp., based on Cuervo 2015: 408)
 {have/se=have} fall.PTCP two leaves
 'Two leaves have {fallen/fallen off}.'

As pointed out by De Cuyper (2006: 131), facts like those in (24) and (25) pose a prima facie obstacle for a unifying analysis of SE, since they challenge the early claims that the reflexive pronoun is a valency-reducing morpheme withholding accusative case and the subject theta-role (cf. Burzio 1986: 408). To circumvent this problem, early studies considered this kind of SE optional (see De Cuyper 2006: 132–35), a position that no one would defend nowadays. Other authors have on the contrary investigated what SE could teach us about the nature of case. For example, Rigau (1994) argues that in SE-constructions like that in (24), SE absorbs partitive case, which would explain why in these constructions the object must bear accusative case: in Rigau's terms, it cannot be a non-definite, i.e., a mass singular or a bare plural, a claim later subsequently questioned (e.g., Barra Jover 1996; Todolí 1998). More recently, Armstrong (2013) argues, for a subset of cases like (24) in Spanish, that SE is licensed by incorporation, rather than case.

Case assignment is, however, not the main issue that constructions like (24) and (25) invite us to explore. Most authors have rather focused on the contribution that SE makes to the aspectual interpretation of the predicate, both in transitive and in intransitive cases, which is why this SE has often been dubbed *aspectual* or *telic*. The latter label is due to the claim that SE-constructions such as those in (24) and (25) are obligatorily telic (partly

---

[8] With respect to the extension of aspectual SE, at least in transitive cases like (24), De Cuyper (2006: 130f.) reports that it is found in Spanish, Catalan, Italian, Romanian, and, although more dialectally and diastratically constrained, also in French, though it is absent from Galician and Portuguese. This distribution partly explains why most studies on aspectual SE have been carried out on Spanish and, to a lesser extent, Italian. The preponderance of Spanish will be reflected in the works surveyed here.

disputed: see Armstrong 2013; MacDonald 2017), and, relatedly, that the internal argument must be definite, specific or bounded:

(26) La Llúcia s' ha menjat {un albercoc / **melmelada d' albercoc}
 the Llúcia SE= has eat.PTCP an apricot jam of apricot
 en un minut. (Cat.)
 in one minute
 'Llúcia has eaten up {an apricot/**apricot jam} in one minute.'

The endeavour to provide a natural structural analysis of telicity and other semantic dimensions of aspectual SE has shed considerable light on the structure of the VP, and is in tune with the increased attention that the formalization of the syntax–semantics interface has received in the last two decades within generative syntax. While the first analyses emphasized the lexical nature of the association between the verb and aspectual SE (Nishida 1994; Zagona 1996; De Miguel and Fernández Lagunilla 2000), other analyses emerging in the wake of minimalism applied the mechanism of feature-checking to formalize the telicizing effect of SE (Sanz 2000; Sanz and Laka 2002). As more articulated proposals on the syntactic representation of event structure became available (Travis 2000; Borer 2005; Ramchand 2008; MacDonald 2008), authors came up with new ways of accommodating SE in the configuration while explaining the aspectual effects and other semantic effects, like agentivity/non-agentivity (Folli and Harley 2005; De Cuyper 2006; Boneh and Nash 2011; Armstrong 2013). For instance, Folli (2001: 127f.) observes that, added to certain intransitive and aspectually ambiguous sentences like (27a), SE (It. *si*) renders them obligatorily telic, as shown in (27b). She then proposes that *si* is a lexicalization of an eventive head, V, encoding the notion of process, while the verb (*fuso* 'melted') lexicalizes a lower eventive head of resultative semantics, providing an end result for the event and, thereby, telicity (see 28, from Folli 2001: 133, an analysis of 27b):

(27) **Italian**
 a. Il cioccolato è fuso in / per pochi secondi.
 the chocolate is melt.PTCP in during few seconds
 'The chocolate has melted in/during a few seconds.'
 b. Il cioccolato si è fuso in / **per pochi secondi.
 the chocolate SE is melt.PTCP in during few seconds
 'The chocolate has melted down in/*during a few seconds.'

(28) [$_{VP}$ il cioccolato [$_{V'}$ V = si [$_{RvP}$ il cioccolato [$_{Rv'}$ Rv = fuso]]]]

Other analyses in which SE realizes an eventive V-type head are Folli and Harley (2005), Basilico (2010), Cuervo (2015), and Armstrong (2013), while Boneh and Nash (2011) make use of an applicative head (see Section 16.4) to analyse the SE-transitive cases in French.

Alternatively, other authors, such as MacDonald (2004), De Cuyper (2006), and Armstrong (2013) (for the classical SE-transitive cases involving ingestion verbs, like 26), propose that SE occupies a low argumental position in the abstract representation of the predicate. For instance, MacDonald (2004) analyses SE (in this example, Sp. *me* 'me') as the complement of a null locative preposition merged under the verb:

(29) a. Me comí la paella. (Sp., from MacDonald 2004: 1)
SE.1SG ate.1SG the paella
'I ate the paella up.'
b. [vP v [VP [*la paella*] [v· V = *comí* [PP P = ∅ [*me*]]]]] (MacDonald 2004: 5)

These latter analyses, and also, in a different way, that of Folli and Harley (2005), are particularly interesting in that they allow a comparison between the expression of notions like resultativity in Romance and Germanic, thus making a valuable contribution to a general theory of the VP. In particular, the claim is made, though not in Folli and Harley (2005), that the locus hosting SE in Romance corresponds to that hosting resultative particles (De Cuyper 2006) or goal PPs (MacDonald 2004) in Germanic, which allows to account for a cluster of shared properties: resultativity itself, unselectedness of the internal argument (De Cuyper 2006; see Section 16.5 n. 13), or even blockage of idiomatic interpretations (MacDonald 2004).

Considerably less attention has been given to SE in object-oblique alternations of the following kind taken from Rigau (1994: 30):

(30) En Pere {lamenta això /es lamenta (d' això)}. (Cat.)
the Pere regrets that SE regrets of that
'Pere regrets that.'

What is an object in the SE-less alternant is presented as an oblique, introduced by *de*, in the corresponding alternant with SE, yielding a kind of *antipassive* construction (Masullo 1992b; Legendre 1994; Kempchinsky 2004).[9] Assuming that argument and event structure are kept the same in both alternants, the discussion about antipassive SE has revolved rather on case. Authors such as Burzio (1986), Masullo (1992b), and Rigau (1994) have argued that antipassive SE absorbs accusative case, forcing the internal argument to be licensed by a preposition. More recent, minimalist works, like Basilico (2005), Armstrong (2016), and MacDonald (2017), have focused on a unification of antipassive SE with other kinds, often making use of a Late Insertion of the SE exponent.

---

[9] Verbs like Cat. *queixar-se* 'complain' do not alternate, but are grouped together with the SE-alternants of alternating verbs (Kempchinsky 2004; Armstrong 2016).

16.4 Datives

Datives in Romance are interesting from different points of view, such as their availability to be clitic-doubled and the associated semantic and structural effects, their (apparent) formal coincidence with Differential Object Marking (DOM), their alleged subject-like properties in a number of contexts, and their alternation with accusative marking in certain cases. We discuss these aspects below.

One first point has to do with clitic doubling. In some Romance languages, such as Spanish (31), Catalan (32) or Romanian (33), dative arguments can be clitic-doubled; but this is not an option in other languages such as Portuguese (34) or French (35) (see Jaeggli 1982 for an overview). There are also some Romance varieties, such as Trentino (36) (Cordin 1993) or the Spanish varieties spoken in Río de la Plata, Chile, and Caracas (37) (see Parodi 1998; Senn 2008; Pujalte 2009), where clitic doubling of dative arguments is compulsory:[10]

(31) (Le) dimos el libro al presidente. (Sp.)
 DAT.3SG= gave.1PL the book to.the president
 'We gave the book to the president.'

(32) (Li) vam donar el llibre al president. (Cat.)
 DAT.3SG= AUX.PST.1PL give.INF the books to.the president
 'We gave the book to the president.'

(33) Mihaela (îi) trimite o scrisoare Mariei. (Ro., based on Diaconescu and Rivero 2007: 213)
 Mihaela DAT.3SG= send.3SG a letter Maria.DAT
 'Mihaela sends a letter to Maria.'

(34) O João deu(**-lhe) o livro à Maria. (Pt., based on Torres Morais and Salles 2010: 182f.)
 the João gave.3SG=DAT.3SG the book to.the Maria
 'João gave the book to Maria.'

(35) Jean (**lui) a donné le livre à Marie. (Fr., based on Fournier 2010: 120)
 Jean DAT.3SG= has give.PTCP the book to Marie
 'Jean has given the book to Marie.'

(36) **(Le) dimos el libro al presidente. (LAmSp.)
 DAT.3SG= gave.1PL the book to.the president
 'We gave the book to the president.'

(37) **(Ghe) dago el regal al Mario. (Trn., based on Cordin 1993: 130)
 DAT.3=give.1SG the present to.the Mario
 'I'm giving the present to Mario.'

---

[10] For many speakers of European Spanish the clitic-less variant of cases like (31) is very marginal or ungrammatical.

Some theoretical implications of dative clitic doubling have to do with the categorical status of the doubled dative phrase (see Jaeggli 1982 and subsequent works), as well as with the type of ditransitive construction we are dealing with. Spanish has played an important role in these discussions. As a matter of fact, it has been extensively argued that Spanish clitic-doubled datives (38) are case-marked DPs, whereas non-doubled ones (39) are PPs (Masullo 1992c; Demonte 1995; Cuervo 2003; Ormazabal and Romero 2013; but see also Kayne 2005).

(38) Dimos el libro al presidente. (Sp.)
gave.1PL the book to.the president
'We gave the book to the president.'

(39) Le dimos el libro al presidente. (Sp.)
DAT.3SG= gave.1PL the book to.the president
'We gave the book to the president.'

The analysis of clitic-doubled datives as DPs, and not PPs, is connected to the existence of double object constructions in Romance and, by extension, of a dative alternation as the English one, composed of a *to*-dative prepositional construction where the goal argument is a PP (40) and a double object construction where the dative argument is a DP (41).

(40) The teacher gave a book to her student.

(41) The teacher gave her student a book.

The double object pattern in (41) was traditionally considered absent in Romance (Kayne 1984; Holmberg and Platzack 1995), where only the prepositional pattern (40) was clearly found, but nothing similar to (41) in terms of word order or lack of preposition could be identified (cf. also Section 1.2.2.1). However, after challenging the assumption that double object constructions had to be superficially identical to the one in English, and focusing instead on the structural and semantic properties of the pattern, authors were able to identify the pattern in a greater number of languages, including the Romance family and, in particular, Spanish (Strozer 1976; Masullo 1992c; Demonte 1995; Romero 1997; Bleam 2003). These authors established a parallelism between Spanish clitic-doubled ditransitives (40) and the English double object construction (41), on the one hand, and Spanish non-doubled ditransitives (38) and the English prepositional construction (40), on the other hand. More recently, on the basis of Pylkkänen's (2002) work on applicatives, Cuervo (2003) argues further in this direction, and similar claims are made for Romanian, another clitic doubling language (Diaconescu and Rivero 2007). However, the existence of clear-cut structural and semantic contrasts between doubled and non-doubled ditransitives in Spanish has been challenged by Pineda (2013; 2016; 2020a), who argues instead that the double object pattern (with an applicative head) exists in this language (and Catalan, another clitic doubling language) regardless of the presence or absence of the clitic. Actually, assuming Pylkkänen's applicative analysis of ditransitives, double object constructions have also been claimed to exist in non-doubling Romance languages, such as Portuguese (Torres Morais and Salles 2010) and French (Fournier 2010). Whereas in doubling languages the clitic is taken to be the spell-out of the applicative head, in non-doubling languages this head is assumed to remain always phonologically silent.

The discussion about whether dative and differentially marked objects constitute a homogenous class is a long-standing one. One of the cross-linguistically robust, yet puzzling uses of dative morphology is to signal certain classes of structural (direct) objects, normally including animates, specifics, definites, or a combination thereof (Givón 1984; Bossong 1991; Lazard 2001; de Swart 2007; Manzini and Franco 2016, among others). This picture is the most common one in those Romance varieties featuring DOM (with Romanian being an important exception), as illustrated by Spanish (42) (see Ormazabal and Romero 2010; 2013). The animate definite object in (42a) must take a marker which is homophonous with the dative *a* (42c), under DOM (see Moravcsik 1978; Comrie 1979; 1981; Croft 1988; 1990; Bossong 1991; 1998; Aissen 2003; López 2012, among others):

(42) **Spanish**
    a.   He   encontrado **(a)   la   niña.
         have.1SG find.PTCP   DAT/DOM the girl
         'I have found the girl.'
    b.   He   encontrado (**a)   el   libro.
         have.1SG find.PTCP   DAT=DOM the book
         'I have found the book.'
    c.   Les   regalé   un libro a   los estudiantes.
         DAT.3PL=offered.1SG a   book DAT the students
         'I offered a book to the students.'

The same picture is seen in many other languages, such as Indo-Aryan varieties, Guaraní, Tigre, Yiddish, Basque varieties that have DOM, and Arabic varieties – but there are also languages where differentially marked objects and datives are not homophonous: this is the case in Romanian, as mentioned above, where dative is inflexional or introduced by *la* 'at, to', whereas DOM is introduced by *pe* 'on'. Beyond Romance, this pattern is also found in Farsi, Hebrew, Turkish, Palauan, and Kannada, among others. An important question is whether this well extended syncretism signals a common syntactic source of dative and the differential marker of objects, or is simply a matter of surface opacity. Under some accounts proposed for Romance languages, the homomorphism has a structural nature, for example DOM and (certain types of) datives occupy the same (licensing) position (López 2012) or encode the same relation (Manzini and Franco 2016). Various contributions have also pointed out important structural differences between datives and differentially marked objects (see Ormazabal and Romero 2007 for Spanish, and Bárány (2018) for a cross-linguistic picture), motivating a morphological solution to the syncretism. Yet, a mixed explanation is proposed under other analyses: differential objects are accusatives structurally but require additional marking due to their complex featural make-up (Irimia 2018).

Dative-marked arguments of psychological (and other) verbs have been considered in some languages an instance of quirky subjects akin to the Icelandic type described, for instance, in Zaenen, Maling, and Höskuldur Thráinsson (1985) and Sigurðsson (1989). In particular, in the Romance family such an analysis has been proposed for Italian (see Belletti and Rizzi 1988; Cardinaletti 2004) and Spanish (see Masullo 1992a; 1993; Campos 1999; Fernández Soriano 1999), among others. Within these approaches, the fact is highlighted that the dative-marked argument exhibits a number of subject-like properties, and therefore it is to be analysed as a quirky (non-nominative) subject. An example of a Spanish psychological verb is provided below, showing that the dative-marked argument (*a tu hija*), and not the nominative one (*el futbol*), appears in preverbal position, as subjects usually do in Romance.

(43) A tu hija le gusta el futbol. (Sp.)
 to your daughter DAT.3SG=pleases the football
 'Your daughter likes football.'

However, the identification of such configurations with quirky subject constructions has been called into question by a number of authors (see, for example, Gutiérrez Bravo 2006 for Spanish) arguing that preverbal oblique (dative) arguments actually lack many of the defining characteristics of quirky (or non-nominative) subjects of the Icelandic type.

Dative case marking alternates with accusative case marking in a number of contexts across Romance languages. A well-known example is that of the experiencer argument of psychological verbs, which in languages such as Spanish (see Gómez Torrego 1993; Fernández-Ordóñez 1999; Mendívil Giró 2005; Marín and McNally 2011) and Catalan (see Cabré and Mateu 1998; Rosselló 2008; Royo 2018) displays a case alternation. This variation is normally linked to different word orders and to different thematic relations between the arguments. Catalan examples below illustrate the dative-marked experiencer (44), in a stative unaccusative configuration (OVS order), and the accusative-marked one (45), in a transitive causative configuration (SVO order):

(44) A la Maria li preocupa aquesta situació. (Cat.)
to the Maria DAT.3SG=worries this situation
'Maria is worried about this situation.'

(45) Aquesta situació preocupa la Maria. → Aquesta situació la preocupa. (Cat.)
this situation worries the Maria this situation ACC.FSG=worries
'This situation worries Maria. → This situation worries her.'

Interestingly, in Romanian, although there is no such alternation, many of these psych-predicates typically occur with accusative experiencers (see Nicula 2013):

(46) L-a interesat foarte mult. (Ro.)
ACC.MSG=has interested very much
'It interested him very much.'

Dative/accusative alternations in Romance languages are also found with a variety of agentive verbs, such as 'help', 'call on the phone', 'rob' or 'pay'.[11] Examples of the alternation in several Romance languages and varieties are provided below:

(47) **Catalan**
    a. El Joan {truca/telefona} a la seva filla. → Li {truca/telefona}.
       the Joan phones to the her daughter DAT.3SG=phones
    b. El Joan {truca/telefona} la seva filla. → La {truca/telefona}.
       the Joan phones the her daughter ACC.FSG=phones
       'Joan calls his daughter on the phone. → He calls her on the phone.'

(48) **Spanish (Nueva Gramática de la Lengua Española 2009: 16.9q)**
    a. Le telefonearías para entrenarla en llamarte Tito.
       DAT.3SG=phone.COND.2SG for train.INF=ACC.FSG in call.INF=you Tito
       '(When you returned to Europe,) you would call her to train her in calling you Tito.'
    b. Al día siguiente la telefoneó para invitarla al cine.
       at.the day following ACC.FSG= phoned.3SG for invite=ACC.FSG to.the cinema
       'The following day he phoned her to invite her to the cinema.'

(49) **Asturian (Xulio Viejo, p.c.)**
    a. ?Telefonée-y.
       phoned.1SG=DAT.3
       'I phoned him/her.'

---

[11] See Fernández-Ordóñez (1999) and Sáez (2009) for Spanish; Ramos (2005) and Morant (2008) for Catalan; Ledgeway (2000; 2009) for Neapolitan, Altamurano, Cosentino, Trebisaccese, and Sicilian; Troberg (2008) for French (in a diachronic perspective); Andriani (2011) for Barese; and Pineda (2016) for a comprehensive Romance view including Catalan, Spanish, Asturian, and Italo-Romance varieties.

b.   Telefonéelu,   telefonéela
        phoned.1SG=ACC.MSG   phoned.1SG =ACC.3FSG
        'I phoned him, her.'

(50) **Barese (Andriani 2011: 50f.)**
   a.   'Ngə   so'   təlefonátə.
        DAT.3=be.1SG   phone.PTCP
        'I have phoned her.'
   b.   La   so'   təlefonátə.
        ACC.3FSG=be.1SG   phone.PTCP
        'I have phoned her.'

(51) **Neapolitan (Ledgeway 2000: 30)**
   a.   Nce   telefunaje   a   socrama.
        DAT.3=phoned.1SG   to   mother-in-law
        'I phoned my mother-in-law.'
   b.   'A   telefunaje   a   socrama.
        ACC.3.FSG=phoned.1SG   DOM   mother-in-law
        'I phoned my mother-in-law'

Different analyses have been proposed for this alternation, sometimes reducing it to case-confusing phenomena (*laísmo/loísmo/leísmo*), sometimes proposing two different structures for the dative option and the accusative one, and yet sometimes assuming an 'underlying' ditransitive structure behind agentive verbs, e.g., *help someone = give help to someone* (following Torrego 2010), and analysing the alternation as an ongoing syntactic change from a structure with a dative-assigning head towards a transitive one, namely *transitivization* (see Pineda 2015; 2020b).

16.5 Lexicalization Patterns

Since Talmy (1975; 1985; 1991; 2000), the term *lexicalization pattern* refers to a language-dependent distribution of certain semantic notions in lexical elements. Talmy (1991; 2000) focuses primarily on the variation concerning the semantic notion of path or transition:

(52) a. We dance$_{Motion+Manner}$-d out$_{Path}$ together.[12]
     b. Sort$_{Motion+Path}$ -iguèrem   amassa   (en dançant$_{Manner}$). (Occ.)
         go.out   -PST.1PL   together   dancing

---

[12] From A. Golden's *Memoirs of a Geisha*, New York: Knopf, 1997.

Example (52) shows one same conceptual scene as expressed in English and Occitan: some people coming out from somewhere while dancing. In English-type languages the semantic notions of Motion and Manner (i.e., how the change of location took place) can be expressed in the verbal root. The Path of motion is expressed in a different morphosyntactic element, what Talmy (2000: 101f.) calls the *satellite*: here the particle *out*, although, as will be shown, later work has generalized the expression of path in these languages to directional PPs. In Occitan-type languages, the Motion and the Path are expressed through the same exponent, i.e., the verbal root, while the Manner of motion has to be expressed separately, as an adjunct. In fact, a 'direct' translation of (52a) into Occitan is ungrammatical:

(53) **Danc_{Motion+Manner} -èrem   defòra_{Path} amassa. (Occ.)
       dance   -PST.1PL out   together

In Talmy's framework, the two main patterns of lexicalization of the path of motion are, thus, the satellite-framed pattern (cf. 52a) in which the Path is typically encoded in an element morphologically different from the verbal root, and the verb-framed pattern (cf. 52b) in which the Path is encoded in the verbal root.[13]

Crucially, already Talmy extended the typology to understand differences in the expression of change of state:

(54) a.   Der Hund hat den   Schuh   kaputt-gebissen. (Ger., Talmy 2000: 247)
           the dog   has the.ACC shoe.ACC   broken-bite.PTCP
      b.   El   perro destrozó el   zapato (a   mordiscos). (Sp.)
           the dog   destroyed the shoe   to   bites
           'The dog bit the shoe to pieces.'

In satellite-framed German the verb may express an event concomitant to a change of state ('destroying through biting'). In verb-framed Spanish this component is, again, expressed in an adjunct, and the verb must encode the transition itself.

While other semantic notions have been explored in relation to their lexicalization patterns in different languages, we will concentrate on the

---

[13] De Cuyper (2006) makes the interesting proposal that Romance aspectual SE (see Section 16.3) functions as a satellite. As such, SE may license, in some cases, unselected objects (see Sp. *se* in i.a), much in the same way, De Cuyper argues, as Germanic prepositional-like satellites (cf. Dch. *op* 'up' in i.b):

(i) a. Juan **(se) bebe   su   fortuna. (Sp., De Cuyper 2006: 180)
         Juan SE   drinks his fortune
     b. Jan drinkt zijn fortuin **(op). (Dch.)
         Jan drinks his   fortune up
         'Juan/Jan drinks away his fortune.'

kind of variation illustrated in (52) and (54),[14] which has received, since the 1970s, massive attention in the literature of different theoretical persuasions, because it impacts on central aspects of the expression of argument and event structure (for recent reviews, see Acedo-Matellán and Mateu 2015; Levin and Rappaport Hovav 2019). The contribution of research on Romance to our understanding of the nature of this typology has been decisive, since these languages have been taken as the paradigm of verb-framed systems. Moreover, it is significant that most Romance varieties – including less studied ones, like Aragonese (see, e.g., Ibarretxe-Antuñano, Hijazo-Gascón, and Moret-Oliver 2017) or Raeto-Romance (see, e.g., Berthele 2006) – have been drawn upon to bear on the issue. In what follows, we will mention the main advances made with respect to this kind of cross-linguistic variation and based on research on Romance.[15]

The first qualification of Talmy's generalizations on the expression of directed motion cross-linguistically was due to an observation by Aske (1989) on Spanish. The next example, based on Aske's (1989: 3), shows that manner of motion verbs are allowed to be combined with directional expressions, provided that they encode an unbounded path (cf. *hacia* 'towards'), as opposed to a bounded one (cf. *a* 'to'):[16]

(55) La   botella flotó   {hacia / **a} la   cueva. (Sp.)
      the   bottle   floated {towards to}   the cave

Aske's observation – replicated elsewhere in Romance (cf. Fong and Poulin 1998 for French, and Stringer 2002 for French and Italian) – indicates that the directional expressions that cannot be combined with manner of motion verbs in verb-framed languages are the ones that induce telicity in the predicate, i.e., those that may change its event structure (cf. *The bottle floated into the cave in/#for five minutes*), and thus that they should be merged VP-internally (cf. Klipple 1991). Klipple (1997) implements this idea by proposing that a node expressing direction/aspect within the VP may be *conflated*, i.e., morphologically bundled, with a preposition in languages like English, while it conflates with the verb in French. This proposal suggests the importance of prepositional systems in understanding the typology (an

---

[14] Another semantic primitive related to two main lexicalization patterns is possession, distinguishing between so-called BE- and HAVE-languages (Harves and Kayne 2012). See Real-Puigdollers (2013: 315–69) for a theoretical analysis and an application to measure verbs in Romance.

[15] We leave out of the discussion the case of creation predicates claimed to involve a manner co-event, like *bake a cake*, i.e., 'create a cake through baking' (Levin and Rapoport 1988). Mateu (2003; 2012) observes that Romance disallows this kind of predicate, and in the latter work proposes to analyse this cross-linguistic variation through Snyder's (2001) *Compounding Parameter* (see below). Acedo-Matellán (2010: 148–55) argues that this cross-linguistic variation is reducible to the satellite-verb vs framed typology.

[16] Other authors (Folli 2001; Fábregas 2007; Beavers, Levin, and Tham 2010) have claimed, however, that Romance may combine manner of motion predicates with expressions encoding a bounded path like PPs headed by *hasta* 'up to, until' in Spanish. It is unclear, however, whether *hasta*-like prepositions really encode paths of motion (see Gehrke 2008: 223 and Real-Puigdollers 2013: 95–101).

aspect much exploited later: see, for example, Folli 2008; Real-Puigdollers 2010; 2013), and also indicates that it could be a purely morphological phenomenon. This proposal has been followed by other authors. For instance, Mateu (2002) and Mateu and Rigau (2002), for Catalan, Spanish, and Sardinian, and working with Hale and Keyser's (1993; 1998) theory of Lexical Syntax, propose that a Path node is specified to be conflated with a null light verb in Romance, which precludes this verb from combining with any other element encoding Manner (cf. the ungrammaticality of 53), and yields the collection of monomorphemic path verbs typical of Romance, such as Glc. *sa-ír* 'go out', Ro. *a intr-a* 'go in', etc., and also verbs of change of state (cf. 54b). In satellite-framed languages the absence of this requirement explains that movement and path are typically expressed separately, as in *go in/out/up/*etc., and that manner verbs can also be combined with path or resultative expressions (cf. 52a or 54a). Interestingly, Mateu (2002) applies this kind of approach to an analysis of the so-called locative alternation in Germanic and Romance (example from Acedo-Matellán and Mateu 2015: 119):

(56) a. Sue sprayed the sheets with perfume.
 b. Sue sprayed perfume onto the sheets.

(57) **Catalan**
 a. La Sue ruixà els llençols de perfum.
  the Sue sprayed the sheets of perfume
 b. **La Sue ruixà perfum sobre els llençols.
  the Sue sprayed perfume on the sheets

While satellite-framed languages liberally allow verbs like *spray* to be used in change of state alternants (56a) or in change of location alternants (56b), Romance usually disallows the latter kind of construction (see 57b), since these languages do not admit the combination of a manner of motion verb (Cat. *ruixar* 'spray') with a directional expression.[17] More recently, Acedo-Matellán (2010; 2016) implements the idea of the obligatory conflation of v and Path in Distributed Morphology terms as operations that take place at PF.

Other authors have proposed syntactic accounts of the typology, exploring both the macroparametric and the microparametric approaches to variation (Baker 2008). In Sugisaki's (2003) macroparametric approach locatives PPs may be dominated or not by a light *p* head inducing a goal

---

[17] For other works on the locative alternation, see Demonte (1991) and Lewandowski (2014) on Spanish; Munaro (1994) on Italian; Hirschbühler and Labelle (2009) on French; and Mateu (2017) on Catalan.

interpretation. Verb-framed French is negatively specified for the parameter, whereby sentences like *The boat floated under the bridge*, which license a directional interpretation in English, do not in French. Also macroparametric are the proposals in Zubizarreta and Oh (2007) and Gehrke (2008). These authors, however, follow Snyder (1995; 2001) and Beck and Snyder (2001), among others, rather than Talmy, in the description of the variation. Gehrke (2008), for instance, puts the focus on the ability of languages to create complex predicates with an accomplishment interpretation (see 52a or 54a), through Snyder's (1995) seminal *Compounding Parameter*, rather than on the lexical or syntactic properties of the element encoding path. Among the microparametric accounts, Real-Puigdollers (2010; 2013) proposes an analysis in terms of phase theory (Chomsky 2000), as understood in works like Marantz (2007): in verb-framed Romance, the functional head Path is defective, and has therefore to be spelled out with the previous functional head, v. In satellite-framed languages, Path is not defective, so v can be spelled out independently, and may therefore express manner of motion. Beyond the morphological facts, the proposal crucially captures some previously unnoted syntactic differences between Romance and Germanic. Folli and Harley (2016; 2020) propose that, in verb-framed Italian, the light verb carries a feature that makes it attract the functional head expressing Res(ult) (cf. Ramchand 2008). Res lexicalizes with v, yielding, again, the kind of change of location/state verbs encountered in Romance.

Analyses in the Ramchandian-nanosyntactic tradition (Folli and Ramchand 2005; Fábregas 2007; Folli 2008; Romeu 2014) treat the variation at the lexicon–syntax interface, although denying any notion of parameter. It is rather the (non-)existence of particular lexical items that explains the differences. Folli and Ramchand (2005), for instance, propose that Italian does not have any preposition like Eng. *to*, able to lexicalize the feature +R(esult). As a result, Italian must use verbs endowed with this feature, such as *andare* 'go' or *correre* 'run', to lexicalize such configurations.

The observation that manner verbs such as It. *correre* 'run', which encode 'forward motion' (cf. Nichols 2008), admit being used in expressions of bounded directed motion spawned yet another refinement of the typology (Fong and Poulin 1998; Folli 2001; Folli and Ramchand 2005; Fábregas 2007; Zubizarreta and Oh 2007; Real-Puigdollers 2010; 2013). For instance, Mateu and Rigau (2010) and Mateu (2012), partly in response to claims in works such as Iacobini and Masini (2007), point out that the Germanic-like combinations of verb and particle found in Italic and Raeto-Romance varieties, and also in Catalan, Spanish, and French, are all possible because the verb, which may encode some notion of manner, also encodes directionality/resultativity, the particle specifying rather than introducing path/result (example from Mateu and Rigau 2010: 259):

(58) Gianni è   corso   / **danzato   via. (It.)
      Gianni is run.PTCP.MSG dance.PTCP.MSG   away

Romance has also been prominent in diachronic studies of the expression of directionality/resultativity. Talmy (1991; 2000) claimed that Latin was a satellite-framed language, using verbal prefixes as satellites, and this claim is explored in depth in Acedo-Matellán (2010; 2016) and Acedo-Matellán and Mateu (2013). The development towards verb-framed Romance has been dealt with in different works, notably those devoted to old French. Dufresne, Dupuis, and Tremblay (2000), Dufresne, Dupuis, and Longtin (2001), and Dufresne, Dupuis, and Tremblay (2003) claim that old French verbal prefixes still codified path/transition.[18] More recently, Troberg and Burnett (2017) have qualified the claim, arguing that in old French the prefixes have lost the locative interpretation that they had in Latin and have become mere markers of aspect. These same authors explore the adjectival resultative constructions of old French such as *abattre mort* 'strike down dead'. Interestingly, they are argued to be, unlike those in Germanic, of the *weak* type (Washio 1997; see Acedo-Matellán and Mateu 2015), i.e., the verb already encodes result, and the adjective merely helps specifying it. Thus, old Romance turns out not be very different from modern Romance (see the remarks on example 58).

16.6 Concluding Remarks

Descriptive and formal studies on argument structure in Romance are both abundant and influential, and they have greatly fostered the advancement of our understanding of this area of natural language. In this chapter we have surveyed what we believe are the most significant contributions: unaccusativity diagnostics, approaches to the causative alternation and other event structure alternations involving the clitic SE, explorations of events of transferal based on the grammar of dative clitics as well as other relevant aspects of dative-marked arguments, and several refinements made to Talmy's typology.

Several other interesting issues have been left out, for space reasons: light verb constructions (see, e.g., Acedo-Matellán and Pineda 2019), cognate objects (see, e.g., Gallego 2012; Real-Puigdollers 2013: 231–313; Melloni and Masini 2017), other constructions with SE: reflexives, causatives, reciprocals, middles, and passives (see, e.g., Mendikoetxea 1999; Bartra Kaufmann 2008; Labelle 2008; Pescarini 2015), and the argument structure

---

[18] Kopecka (2004: 246f.) claims that modern French prefixed verbs like *é-pépin-er* 'de-seed' also represent the satellite-framed pattern, the prefix counting as a satellite. See Acedo-Matellán and Mateu (2013) for a different position.

of other lexical categories, e.g., nominalizations and adjectival predicates (see, among others, Sleeman and Brito 2010; Oltra-Massuet 2013; Fábregas 2016; Meinschaefer 2016).

Selected References

Below you can find selected references for this chapter. The full references can be found online at the following page: www.cambridge.org/Romancelinguistics

Acedo-Matellán, V. and Mateu, J. (2013). 'Satellite-framed Latin vs verb-framed Romance: a syntactic approach', *Probus* 25: 227–65.
Acedo-Matellán, V. and Pineda, A. (2019). 'Light verb constructions in Basque and Romance'. In Ortiz de Urbina, J., Fernández, B., and Berro, A. (eds), *Basque and Romance. Aligning Grammars.* Leiden: Brill, 176–220.
Belletti, A., and Rizzi, L. (1988). 'Psych-verbs and θ-theory', *Natural Language & Linguistic Theory* 6: 291–352.
Borer, H. (2005). *Structuring Sense, Vol. 2: the Normal Course of Events.* Oxford: Oxford University Press. http://dx.doi.org/10.1093/acprof:oso/9780199263929.001.0001.
Hale, K. and Keyser, S. (2002). *Prolegomenon to a Theory of Argument Structure.* Cambridge, MA: MIT Press.
Levin, B. and Rappaport Hovav, M. (2005). *Argument Realization.* Cambridge: Cambridge University Press.
Mateu, J. and Rigau, G. (2010). 'Verb-particle constructions in Romance: a lexical-syntactic account', *Probus* 22: 241–69.
Pineda, A. (2016). *Les fronteres de la (in)transitivitat. Estudi dels aplicatius en llengües romàniques i basc.* Barcelona: Institut d'Estudis Món Juïc.
Real-Puigdollers, C. (2013). *Lexicalization by Phase: The Role of Prepositions in Argument Structure and Its Cross-linguistic Variation.* PhD dissertation, Universitat Autònoma de Barcelona.
Rigau, G. (1997). 'Locative sentences and related constructions in Catalan: *ésser/haver* alternation'. In Mendikoetxea, A. and Uribe-Etxebarria, M. (eds), *Theoretical Issues at the Morphology–Syntax Interface.* Bilbao/Donosti/San Sebastián: Euskal Herriko Unibertsitatea, Gipuzkoa Foru Aldundia, 395–421.
Sorace, A. (2004). 'Gradience at the lexicon–syntax interface: evidence from auxiliary selection and implications for unaccusativity'. In Alexiadou, A. Anagnostopoulou, E., and Everaert, M., (eds), *The Unaccusativity Puzzle. Explorations of the Syntax–Lexicon Interface.* Oxford: Oxford University Press, 243–68.
Talmy, L. (2000). *Toward a Cognitive Semantics, Vol. 2: Typology and Process in Concept Structuring.* Cambridge, MA: MIT Press.

17

Agreement

Roberta D'Alessandro

17.1 Introduction

The term 'agreement' usually refers to a relation between two or more items in a sentence or a phrase.[1] This relation can be explicitly (i.e., morphologically) marked, or not. According to Steele (1978: 610), '[t]he term agreement commonly refers to some systematic co-variance between a semantic or formal property of one element and a formal property of another'. The term co-variance, however, does not explicitly take into account the fact that agreement usually takes place between a core element and one or more dependent elements. The definition we will be using in this chapter is therefore the following:

Agreement is a syntactic dependency relation 'cross-linking' two or more elements. This relation is very often made explicit by means of a marker of some kind on one or all the elements between which it is established.

 This definition draws a distinction between a syntactic dependency, called agreement, and its marking, usually also called agreement in the literature. This chapter will consider both the syntactic and the morphological aspects of agreement.

 Romance languages have played a substantial role in the development of the theory of agreement as we know it today. In Romance, agreement systematically obtains between the nominative subject and the finite verb and between the article, adjectives, and the noun within a DP. Other typical Romance phenomena, such as clitic doubling or subject clitics, are also considered agreement. Furthermore, some unusual agreement patterns are found in

---

[1] This research was funded by the European Research Council (ERC CoG 681959_MicroContact), which is hereby gratefully acknowledged. A CC BY licence is applied to the Author Accepted Manuscript arising from this submission.

Romance, such as the inflected infinitive in Portuguese and Sardinian, some anti-agreement-like effects in central Italo-Romance, impersonal *si* agreement patterns resembling quirky subject agreement (D'Alessandro 2004), and agreement with adverbials and topic-oriented agreement in some upper-southern Italo-Romance dialects (D'Alessandro 2017). In this chapter mostly core agreement facts will be discussed. For exceptional agreement patterns, the reader is referred to D'Alessandro and Pescarini (2016). The aim of this chapter is to highlight the milestones of the theory of agreement that have been established on the basis of Romance data.

I have selected only some of the agreement facts that have inspired contemporary syntactic theory: starting from Phrase Structure Rules (PSR), which have been the basis for computational agreement systems, through the Government and Binding period, where Romance data were at the core of the theory, to Minimalism, Romance data have offered food for thought and challenges for those trying to develop a theory of agreement.

The chapter is organized as follows. Section 17.2 presents the first PSR on agreement; Section 17.3 is dedicated to participial agreement and the birth of specifier-head (spec-head) agreement; Section 17.4 considers agreement in the Minimalist Program drawing on examples from a revised analysis of participial agreement, unaccusative agreement as the basis of long-distance agreement, agreement under c-command, and finally the theoretical mechanism of Agree. Section 17.5 switches to morphological agreement, and the tests used to distinguish between agreement morphemes and pronominals based on an analysis of subject clitics.

17.2 Phrase Structure Rules for Agreement

The early stage of generative grammar, transformational grammar, was characterized by a computational approach to language data. Since then, agreement has been at the core of the development of syntactic theory and is today not considered just a relation between elements, but, rather, the engine of syntax.

Katz and Postal (1964) and Postal (1966) exploited the intuition, also expressed in Chomsky (1957), that agreement is a transformation crosslinking two elements. This transformation consists in attaching an affix to all elements that enter an agreement relation. In 1966, Postal put forward a theory of agreement grounded on the idea that PSR copy agreement morphemes from the head to the dependent elements. In an NP, for instance, the affix is specified on a noun, and it gets copied to all other elements in the NP. These PSR were developed on the basis of Spanish because of its morphological transparency. One of the examples studied by Postal (1966: 46) is in (1).

(1)   un-o-s   alumn-o-s   (Sp., Postal 1966: 46)
       one-M-PL   pupil-M-PL
       'some pupils'

In (1), the affixes attached to a N that undergo copying express gender and number. Not all affixes have the same explicit morphology: the affix can assume different morphological shapes, even if its value is constant. A masculine singular affix on a noun can have a different morphophonological realization from the affix on that noun's determiner, as illustrated in (2) from Cosentino:

(2)   chiss-u   cane (Cos.)
       this-MSG   dog.MSG
       'this dog'

In (2), the masculine singular ending is underlyingly the same masculine singular value on the noun and on the determiner, but its phonetic realizations on the noun and on the adjective are different. Postal's proposal obviously concerned the morpheme as an abstract entry, not its phonetic realization. Postal proposed the following PSR for agreement (also called concord) in a phrase like (1):

(3)   R56[1]   NP → Article Noun (Adjective)

       R57   Noun → Noun   Stem Affix

       R58   Affix → Gender   (plural)

       R59   Noun Stem → Noun Stem Fem, Noun Stem Masc

       R60   Gender → $\begin{cases} \text{M in Noun Stem Masc} \_\_\_ \\ \text{F} \end{cases}$
                                                              (Postal 1966: 46)

(3) can be read as follows:

- Rule 56: rewrite an NP as an Article plus a Noun;
- Rule 57: rewrite the Noun as a Stem plus an Affix, ... and so on.

In addition, he states that the grammar must contain the following agreement transformation:

(4) $T_{agreement}$
       Article, Noun Stem, Affix, (Adjective)
       1   2   3   4
       1 ... 4 → Article + Affix, Noun Stem, Affix, (Adjective + Affix)

This rule describes the internal structure of a noun phrase. The transformation takes an affix of a Noun and attaches it to the Article and to the Adjective (if there is one). Note that attaching an affix to several elements can be decomposed into two operations: first, make a copy of the Affix; then, attach it to the relevant elements. This two-step concept of agreement is not made explicit in Postal (1966), but was made explicit soon afterwards by Chomsky (1965). It is very important, as it is what underlies the formulation of Agree in the Minimalist Program (Chomsky 1998/2000). The tree diagrams for the transformation representing agreement within the Spanish NP *unos alumnos* 'some pupils' (masculine plural) are reproduced in (5) and (6):

(5)
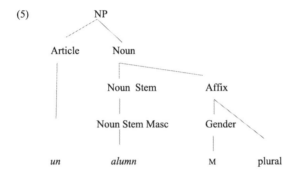

(6)
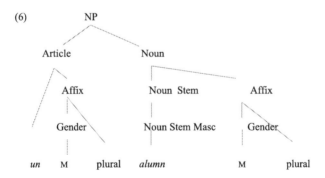

Chomsky refers to Postal's analysis in *Aspects* (Chomsky 1965), proposing a transformational mechanism for agreement, assigning a specification to every feature, according to the specification of the most prominent element. He states, for instance, that a grammar must contain transformational rules that assign to an article all the feature specifications of the noun it modifies. The copy mechanism is made more explicit in Chomsky's version of the agreement transformation. The rule he proposes reads as follows:

(7) 'Article → $\begin{bmatrix} \alpha \text{ Gender} \\ \beta \text{ Number} \\ \gamma \text{ Case} \end{bmatrix}$ / __ ... $\begin{bmatrix} + \text{N} \\ \alpha \text{ Gender} \\ \beta \text{ Number} \\ \gamma \text{ Case} \end{bmatrix}$

where Article ... N is an NP' (Chomsky 1965: 175)

This rule means that an article will take the α affix for Gender, the β affix for Number, and the γ affix for Case if it appears before a Noun that carries an α affix for Gender, and so on. Observe that English, the language on which Chomsky based his theories in the early years, does not express gender morphologically. The reason why gender is included in the transformation is, arguably, the fact that Postal developed his rules on the basis of Romance.

17.3 Spec-Head Agreement

The Government and Binding era that followed the publication of Chomsky's *Introduction to Government and Binding* (Chomsky 1981, henceforth GB) introduced several changes to the theory of agreement. There is a far-reaching change in the whole understanding of grammar that we cannot reproduce here. As far as agreement is concerned, one of the key concepts underlying the new system is the *Mirror Principle*, formulated by Baker (1985), according to which morphology reflects syntax. The definition is given in (8):

(8) *The Mirror Principle* (Baker 1985: 376)
     Morphological derivations must directly reflect syntactic derivations (and vice versa).

In (1978), Emonds, building on Kayne's (1975) observations regarding auxiliary deletion, clitic placement, and other phenomena in French, concludes that in this language auxiliaries and verbs are the same category, while in English they are not. Building on this observation Pollock (1989) brings the theory forward, proposing a rule of finite verb movement (the same movement that auxiliaries undergo) for French, but not for English (cf. also Sections 1.2.3.2, 20.2.1, and 21.2.3). Pollock examines French and English finite verbs, such as those in (9)–(11), and concludes that the verb in French moves to receive its inflexion. Given that negation and frequency/temporal adverbs occupy a fixed position in the clause, the difference between English and French with respect to the position of the verb must be due, according to Pollock, to movement in French, and lack thereof in English.

(9) **English and French (Pollock 1989: 367)**
    a.   **John likes not Mary.
    b.   Jean (n') aime pas Marie.
        Jean NEG like.PRS.IND.3SG NEG Marie

(10) a.   **Likes he Mary?
     b.   Aime-t-il Marie?
        like.PRS.IND.3SG=he Marie

(11) a.   **John kisses often Mary.
     b.   Jean embrasse souvent Marie.
        Jean kiss.PRS.IND.3SG often Marie
     c.   John often kisses Mary.
     d.   **Jean souvent embrasse Marie.
        Jean often like.PRS.IND.3SG Marie

In (9), the finite verb precedes the negation in French (where negation is represented by *pas*), but not in English. Example (10) shows that the finite V raises as far as the vacant C(omplementizer) position in interrogative sentences in French but not in English. Example (11) shows that the finite verb precedes the temporal adverb *souvent* 'always' in French, but not in English. Pollock took these data to show that the finite verb moves like an auxiliary in French but not in English, thus supporting Emonds' generalization. Pollock also observed that different positions are needed for V-movement with infinitival *be* and *have* in French (cf. *Ne pas être* 'NEG NEG be.INF' vs *N'être pas* 'NEG be.INF NEG') in French. An extra head is thus required to host the infinitival verb. This generalization, together with the considerations about the hybrid categorial status of Infl, which encoded both verbal inflexion and nominal inflexion and was therefore an exceptional mixed category, led to the postulation of a separate Agr(eement) position to which the verb can move in Romance.

The idea of verb movement and the existence of different heads to which the verb can move is synthesized in Belletti's (1990) *Generalized Verb Movement*. She undertakes a thorough comparative study of verbal morphology as well as syntax in Romance, concluding that finite verbs are assembled in the syntax through head movement of the verb through dedicated (inflexional) projections, and according to the *Mirror Principle* in (8). Consequently, the proposed structure for Italian sentences like (12) is, according to Belletti, as in (13).

(12)   Gianni non ha parlat-o. (It., adapted from Belletti 1990)
        Gianni NEG have.PRS.IND.3SG talk.PTCP-MSG
        'Gianni did not speak.'

(13)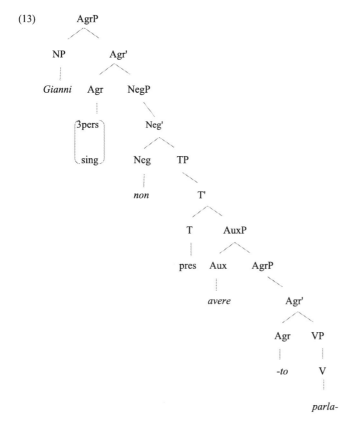

The verb head-moves successive-cyclically to incorporate morphemes on every functional head, acquiring the necessary inflexion. Belletti proposes a more elaborate structure than Pollock, introducing two Agr heads: a higher one, which is the head that contains subject agreement inflexion, and a lower one, which contains participial agreement inflexion.

Belletti's model is also adopted in early Minimalism, given its strong descriptive adequacy. In her model, Belletti tacitly assumes movement of the subject to the specifier position of the higher Agr projection licensing the person/number formative for nominative assignment. This assumption has solid roots in Kayne's proposal for object agreement, which we review hereafter, and from which the whole Spec-head agreement theory stemmed. Kayne's theory is also entirely based on Romance data.

17.3.1 Agreement in a Spec-Head Configuration

We have just seen that, according to Belletti, nominative case is assigned in the specifier position of the Agr projection. The reasons for this assumption stem from different concepts that emerged more or less during the same period within the GB framework. A specifier-head (henceforth Spec-head) relation is obtained under Government: a head governs whatever falls under the maximal projection that it heads, and in particular, a head also governs its associated specifier position. That the Spec-head relation was important was a generally held notion in the early 1990s. However, the assumption that this would be the only way for two syntactic items to agree with each other was only developed after the publication of a key paper by Kayne (1989). This article is the milestone of agreement in the GB framework, and is entirely based on Romance data. Kayne's (1989) work examines participial agreement in French and Italian (see further the discussion in Sections 18.3 and 21.1). He considers the following agreement alternation:

(14) French (Kayne 2000: 25)
    a.   Paul a   repeint /   **repeintes   les chaises.
         Paul have.PRS.IND.3SG repaint.PTCP.MSG repainted.PTCP.FPL the chairs.F
         'Paul has repainted the chairs.'
    b.   Paul les a repeintes.
         Paul them= have. PRS.IND.3SG repaint.PTCP.FPL
         'Paul repainted them.'

The agreement alternation we see in (14a–b) is quite straightforward: whenever the DP object is post-verbal, the past participle fails to agree with it, as shown by the ungrammaticality of *repeintes* in (14a). If the object moves and appears before the participle, the participle agrees with it. From this, Kayne concludes that there is a correlation between movement and agreement, a concept which provided the basis for agreement theory until very recently. In particular, Kayne proposes that agreement stems from the movement of the object into the specifier of an Agr projection. The participle moves to this Agr head in languages like French and Italian (but not in Spanish, where the participle is incompatible with Agr) and enters into a Spec-head relation with the object, therefore yielding agreement between the two.

Kayne only discusses the lower Agr projection, the one that connects with the object. The idea that a specific syntactic configuration is the only configuration in which agreement can take place was very appealing in the GB framework, and therefore the Spec-head configuration was immediately extended to all kinds of clausal agreement (as well as some cases of intra-DP agreement).

The general structure adopted for agreement, until early Minimalism, is the following:

(15)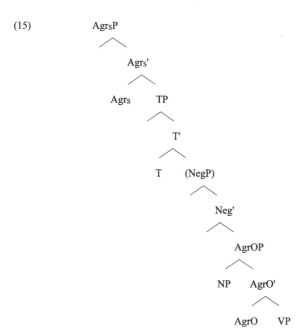

The higher Agr and the lower Agr have become AgrS (agreement with the subject) and AgrO (agreement with the object) respectively.

While Kayne capitalized on the clitic nature of the moved object to justify obligatory movement out of the VP for the object, movement for the subject was linked to the Extended Projection Principle, which was formulated in many ways, but which was basically a requirement for SpecIP, the canonical preverbal subject position, to be filled (Williams 1980; Chomsky 1981; 1982; Rothstein 1983; Lasnik 2001, and many others). Furthermore, A-movement of the subject is required for it to receive nominative case: the Infl head governs the NP subject and assigns nominative case to it in SpecIP.

In a sentence like (16), the subject has to move to SpecIP obligatorily. If SpecIP has to be independently filled, and if the I(nfl) head is split into Infl proper and Agr, movement of the subject through Agr is an obligatory requirement. This causes agreement between the subject and the finite verb to emerge.

(16) Li   bregands m'   an   cremat   l'   ostau!   (Prv., Ledgeway 2012: 432)
     the   brigands me=have.PRS.IND.3PL   burn.PTCP   the=house
     'The brigands have burnt my house down!'

Finally, while nominative was assigned under government and in a Spec-head configuration, accusative was still assigned to the complement of the V head under government, and not in a Spec-head configuration.

In order to unify case assignment, Chomsky (1993) proposes that accusative too is assigned in a Spec-head configuration, and that the object always moves to SpecAgrOP to get accusative case. Kayne's Spec-head agreement, based on Romance data, soon became the only way to represent agreement in GB. Overt agreement started to be separated from cases of covert agreement through an appeal to overt movement through Agr, in a way that we will discuss in the next section.

17.4 Agreement in the Minimalist Program

17.4.1 Participial Agreement Revisited

Chomsky (1998/2000) puts forward a new conceptualization of agreement, according to which the relevant syntactic relation for agreement to take place is closest c-command, and no longer Spec-head. Agreement is obtained through an operation, called Agree. The definition of the operation Agree is as follows:

> [t]he φ-set we can think of as a probe that seeks a goal, namely 'matching' features that establish agreement. ... Locating this goal, the probe erases under matching. ... The erasure of uninterpretable features of probe and goal is the operation we called Agree. ... Matching is a relation that holds of a probe P and a goal G. Not every matching pair induces Agree. To do so, G must (at least) be in the domain D(P) of P and satisfy locality conditions. More generally, uninterpretable features render the goal active, able to implement an operation. The operations Agree and Move require a goal that is both local and active. (Chomsky 2000:122)

Syntactic agreement is therefore defined as a locality sensitive operation, and does not happen as a consequence of movement. It is, in fact, completely independent of movement. In this new framework, agreement is conceptualized in terms of structural precedence rather than a specific configuration like Spec-head.

D'Alessandro and Roberts (2008) propose to capture Kayne's intuition regarding agreement by considering domains within which agreement can apply, rather than movement of the agreeing elements. In this section, their analysis of participial agreement in Italian is reviewed.

We start with the observation that past participle agreement in standard Italian is associated with promoted internal arguments, namely:

- internal arguments that are moved or linked to subject position: unaccusatives (17a), passives (17b), and impersonal-passives (17c);
- reflexive constructions (18), which are also argued to also involve promotion of the 'antecedent' of the reflexive (Kayne 1989);
- object clitics (19).

(17) **Italian (D'Alessandro and Roberts 2008: 478)**
    a.   L-e   ragazz-e sono   arrivat-e.
         the-FPL girls-FPL be.PRS.IND.3PL arrived. PTCP-FPL
         'The girls have arrived.'
    b.   L-e   ragazz-e sono   stat-e   arrestat-e.
         the-FPL girls-FPL be.PRS.IND.3PL be.PTCP-FPL arrest.PTCP -FPL
         'The girls have been arrested.'
    c.   Si   sono   vist-e   l-e   ragazze.
         REFL=be.PRS.IND.3PL see.PTCP-FPL the-FPL girls-FPL
         'We have seen the girls/the girls have been seen.'

(18) L-e   ragazze si   sono   guardat-e   allo   specchio.
     the-FPL girls-FPL REFL=be.PRS.IND.3PL look.PTCP-FPL at.the mirror
     'The girls looked at themselves in the mirror.'

(19) L-e   abbiamo   salutat-e.
     them-FPL have.PRS.IND.1PL greet.PTCP-FPL
     'We greeted them.'

If the object stays *in situ*, agreement does not obtain:

(20) **Abbiamo   salutat-e   l-e   ragazz-e. (It.)
     have.PRS.IND.1PL greet.PTCP-FPL the-FPL girls-FPL
     'We greeted the girls.'

In light of this theoretical development, the data of French and Italian participial agreement are quite difficult to explain. If we adopted Agree *tout court*, we would predict agreement with post-verbal objects in modern Italian, contrary to fact. The past participle c-commands the object *in situ* in a simple transitive clause, and it has the relevant features to match the object. In a sentence like (17), the past participle is in the right configuration to Agree with the feminine singular object. We also know that the participle assigns accusative case to the object, so according to this new definition the past participle should show overt agreement with the object, but it does not.

(21) **Ho   mangiat-a   l-a   mel-a. (It.)
     have.PRS.IND.1SG eat.PTCP-FSG the-FSG apple-FSG

The relevant part of the structure is presented in (22):

(22)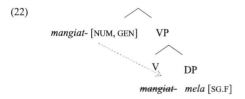

D'Alessandro and Roberts build on the distinction between Agree, which is a syntactic operation taking place in narrow syntax, and morphological insertion of inflexional material, which takes place at Phonological Form (PF), the module where morphological insertion takes place. The idea is that only if two elements that have entered into an Agree relation are Spelled-Out together (Chomsky 1995) do they belong to the same phonological phrase, and can therefore receive the same morphological specification. They propose a condition on the morphophonological realization of agreement (D'Alessandro and Roberts 2008: 482), according to which:

(23) a. Given an Agree relation A between Probe P and Goal G, morphophonological agreement between P and G is realized iff P and G are contained in the complement of the minimal phase head H.
b. XP is the complement of a minimal phase head H iff there is no distinct phase head H' contained in XP whose complement YP contains P and G.

In sum, (23) means that the domain in which agreement can take place at PF is mapped directly from syntax. If the participle and the object are in the same phonological domain, they 'see' each other's values, and they can receive the same agreement. In the case in which they belong to two different domains, they will not be able to retrieve the information about agreement on the other element, and a default ending will be inserted.

For transitive verbs, the external argument (viz. the subject) is inserted in SpecvP and v hosts the participle. At Spell-out, if the object has not moved to the same domain as the participle, it will belong to a different phonological phrase than the past participle. Given the condition on morphophonological realization of agreement in (23), it will not be possible to insert the same ending on the participle as the object. A default ending (masculine singular) will then be inserted on the participle.

Consider now the contrast between the following examples, where spell-out domains corresponding to phonological phrases are represented:

Italian

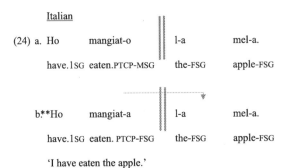

(24) a. Ho   mangiat-o   l-a   mel-a.
     have.1SG eaten.PTCP-MSG   the-FSG   apple-FSG

b. **Ho   mangiat-a   l-a   mel-a.
    have.1SG eaten. PTCP-FSG   the-FSG   apple-FSG

'I have eaten the apple.'

In (24), *la mela* belongs to a different phonological domain than *mangiato*. This is the reason why the participle cannot receive a feminine singular specification, but must receive the default ending instead.

In the case of unaccusative verbs, *v* is generally argued to be defective. Specifically, this means that the sentence in which it occurs constitutes a single phase, inasmuch as there is only one domain for the whole sentence and not a lower phase in the *v*(erb) phrase. We therefore expect agreement between the internal argument (which is also the surface subject with unaccusative verbs) and the participle independently of their position. This prediction is indeed borne out:

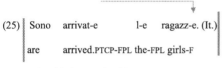

(25) Sono arrivat-e l-e ragazz-e. (It.)
    are arrived.PTCP-FPL the-FPL girls-F

'The girls have arrived.'

Passives and reflexives basically work the same way: if the participle (probe) and the nominal (goal) surface in the same phonological phrase, they will carry the same (*mutatis mutandis*) ending. If not, the participle will be assigned a default ending.

Object clitics trigger overt, morphologically realized agreement, because they move to the Spell-out domain of the participle, which means that they will belong to the same phonological phrase as the past participle: they will trigger overt morphological agreement with the participle. In other words, the idea developed in D'Alessandro and Roberts (2008) is that what matters is whether the past participle and the element it agrees with end up in the same phonological domain or not. If they do, we see overt morphological agreement. If they do not, we see default agreement.

However, the case of old (Tuscan) Italian is somewhat problematic for this analysis, since participles do agree with the *in situ* internal argument, as in example (26).

(26)   mio padre ha offert-i duomila march-i (OTsc., *Novellino* 18, 15–16)
      my father have.PRS.IND.3SG offer.PTCP-MPL two.thousand marks-MPL
      'my father has offered two thousand marks'

One possible explanation for this pattern comes from word order: in older stages of the language, and importantly still at the time of the writing of the *Novellino* (viz. the fifteenth century), from which this example is taken, word order was rather different from that of modern Italian. In particular, many elements could be scrambled in front of the past participle (see Franco 2009; Benincà and Poletto 2010), suggesting that the participle itself occupied a lower position in the clause. See for instance the following sentences from thirteenth-century Tuscan:

(27) […] i   nimici   avessero   già   il   passo
        the   enemies   have.PST.SBJV.3PL   already the   pass
        pigliato (OTsc., Bono Giamboni, *Orosio* 2, 9, 15–16)
        take.PTCP
        'the enemies had already taken the pass'

Given this, it is possible to argue that in old (Tuscan) Italian the past participle surfaces in the same Spell-out domain as the internal argument, as it stays low, possibly in the head of the lexical VP. Note that the object has moved in this particular sentence, but that was not always the case: the object could follow the participle in old Italian. Moreover, the participle could be preceded by a number of other elements, like adverbs and quantifiers, that can no longer appear pre-participially in modern Italian. Poletto (2014) shows that this correlation is borne out, inasmuch as when we get the order DP + participle we always get participial agreement, but when the order is past participle + DP agreement becomes optional/variable (see also Egerland 2010 for similar conclusions).

There are other exceptions to the agreement generalization, in addition to the old Italian data we just saw. In some Italo-Romance dialects it is possible to have participial agreement with an *in situ* internal argument as long as the argument is plural, as in (28), an example of 'omnivorous' participial agreement to which we will return in greater detail below.

(28) So   magnitə   ddu   melɔ. (Ariellese)
     be.PRS.IND.1SG eat.PTCP.PL   two   apples
     'I ate two apples.'

French agreement patterns are basically the same as those of Italian, but they also present some divergence from Italian. In French, agreement also obtains between the past participle and moved wh-objects:

(29) Je me demande   combien   de   tables   Paul a
     I   me=ask.PRS.IND.1SG   how.many of   tables.F   Paul have.PRS.IND.3SG
     repeint-es. (Fr., Kayne 2000: 26)
     repaint.PTCP-FPL
     'I wonder how many tables Paul has repainted.'

In (29), the wh-object *combien de tables* has been moved and agreement with *repeintes* obtains. This kind of agreement is not possible in standard Italian, but it was in older stages of the language. Below follow examples of standard vs old (Tuscan) Italian:

(30) Mi chiedo   quanti   tavoli   Paul abbia   ridipint-o/
     me=ask.PRS.IND.1SG   how.many   tables-M   Paul has.PRS.SBJV.3SG   repaint.PTCP-MSG/
     **ridipint-i. (It.)
     repaint.PTCP-MPL
     'I wonder how many tables Paul has repainted.'

(31) le   pietre ... avevano   perdut-a   loro virtude (OIt., *Novellino* 1, 41–42)
     the   stones-F have.PST.IPFV.IND.3PL lose.PTCP-FSG their power-F
     'the stones ... had lost their power'

Modern spoken French is arguably losing participial agreement completely and is moving towards the Spanish-style system. In any case, in standard written French, agreement between a wh-object and a participle is obligatory, as in old Italian. Furthermore, in French gender agreement of the participle with first and second person clitic pronouns is obligatory, and not optional as in Italian, where, for example, *ti ho vista*-FSG and *ti ho visto*-MSG are both accepted when referring to a female referent. Finally, unlike in Italian, modern French does not show agreement in causative constructions, as illustrated in (32):

(32) **French (Belletti 2017: 38)**
   a. Un   pantalon   a   été   fait   faire
      a.M   pair.of.trousers.MSG have.PRS.IND.3SG be.PTCP make.PTCP.MSG   make.INF
      (par Marie).
      by   Marie
      'a pair of trousers has been caused to be made (by Marie)'
   b. Une   jupe   a   été   fait(**e)   faire
      a.F   skirt.FSG have.PRS.IND.3SG be.PTCP make.PTCP.MSG(FSG) make.INF
      (par Marie).
      by   Marie
      'a skirt has been caused to be made (by Marie)'

Compare (32) with their Italian counterparts in (33):

(33) **Italian**
   a. Un   pai-o   di pantaloni è   stat-o   fatt-o
      a.M   pair-MSG of trousers be.PRS.IND.3SG   be.PTCP-MSG   make.PTCP-MSG
      fare   da Maria.
      make.INF by Maria
   b. Una   gonna   è   stat-a   fatt-a   fare
      a.F   skirt.FSG be.PRS.IND.3SG   be.PTCP-FSG   make.PTCP-FSG make.INF
      da Maria.
      by Maria

The difference between French and Italian agreement patterns remains an open issue.

17.4.2 Unaccusatives

As we saw, in *Minimalist Inquiries* (1998/2000) Chomsky takes the step of finally dissociating agreement from movement formally as well, through the formulation of Agree.

A theory of agreement based on structural precedence, like c-command, can very straightforwardly account for agreement in inversion constructions, or with post-verbal subjects in Romance. Take, for instance, the example from Romanian in (34): the subject of unaccusatives is underlying generated as the object but it does not appear to have moved given its post-verbal position. Yet, it shows agreement with the finite verb. Under the Spec-head theory of agreement, the only way to analyse this simple sentence was to postulate the presence of a silent expletive subject (pro) in the pre-verbal subject position (SpecIP) which formed a representational chain with the *in situ* subject (cf., among others, Belletti 1982; Rizzi 1982).

(34) Astăzi se   nasc   mulți   băieți. (Ro.)
      today REFL=be.born.PRS.IND.3PL   many   boys
      'Today many boys are being born.'

With Agree, this agreement pattern follows straightforwardly: the finite verb searches for (probes for) a DP, finds the THEME subject in its c-command domain, and then Agrees with it.

17.5 Morphological Agreement

So far we have treated agreement in syntactic terms alone. We now turn to the other definition of agreement, namely the morphological one. In the introduction, we gave the first definition of agreement as 'co-variance of a semantic or formal property of one element and a formal property of another' (Steele 1978: 610). This definition focuses more on the marking of an agreement relation between two elements than on the agreement relation itself. Morphological agreement refers in fact to the marking of agreement on syntactic items rather than to the syntactic operation or the structural configuration that holds between them. A second meaning of 'morphological agreement' refers instead to the full inflexional paradigm of a lexical entry such as, for instance, the whole set of declensional endings of a noun in Latin, or the whole set of finite verb conjugational suffixes in Romanian. This definition is further removed than the previous one from the syntactic, operation-like definition we have considered in the first part of this chapter. The set of all morphological inflexional elements characterizing a verb, a noun, or an adjective, is also called 'agreement'. This particular meaning is what we refer to when we talk about 'rich agreement': a language has rich verbal agreement if it has a large set of non-syncretic endings for the finite verb, for instance. Rich agreement has had a very important role in linguistic theory, and for this reason it will be discussed in this chapter.[2]

---

[2] Romance languages offer an important empirical basis also regarding generalizations on the verb roots. See, for instance, Maiden (2004; 2012; 2018).

Romance languages have had a large impact on our understanding of morphological agreement. Some aspects for which Romance data have been of fundamental importance are the classification of clitics, and in particular the difference between agreement clitics and subject pronouns.

17.5.1 Rich Agreement and Null Subjects

It is usually assumed, in traditional grammars, that if a language has a rich agreement paradigm, then it will be pro-drop (cf. also Section 1.2.3.1). By rich agreement we mean here that the language has a number of inflexional verbal morphemes, and that there are at least some differentiated inflexional morphemes in the paradigm. A definition of rich agreement has recently been given by Koeneman and Zeijlstra (2014) and is reproduced in (35):

(35) A language exhibits rich subject agreement if and only if agreement involves at least the same featural distinctions as those manifested in the smallest (subject) pronoun inventories universally possible. (Koeneman and Zeijlstra 2014: 574)

For our purposes, it is not necessary to define rich agreement too precisely. We will use the working definition of rich agreement as 'dedicated, differentiated inflexional morphology'.

The observation that rich agreement 'licenses' null subjecthood has been around since the beginning of modern linguistic thinking. The underlying intuition is that if you can retrieve the information about the subject from the verb inflexion, you do not need to express the subject overtly. This correlation has been observed in several languages. In Brazilian Portuguese, for instance, where the rich agreement paradigm has been radically reduced, witness Table 17.1 (cf. Nuñes 2011: 17), null subjects are also more restricted. As for overt subjects, first and second person pronouns are almost always overt, while third person subjects are still omitted, but much less so than in European Portuguese.

Table 17.1. *Verb agreement paradigm in (colloquial) Brazilian Portuguese, present indicative of* cantar *'sing'*

eu (I)	*canto*	Person: 1; Number: SG
você (you.SG) *ele* (he) *ela* (she) *a gente* (we)	*canta*	Person: default; Number: default (= 3SG)
vocês (you.PL) *eles* (they.M) *elas* (they.F)	*cantam*	Person: default; Number: PL (= 3PL)

However, despite the fact that first person singular has a dedicated form, first and second person pronouns are almost never omitted. This suggests that the one-to-one correspondence between presence of inflexion and absence of an overt subject is not so straightforward.

Several scholars have attempted to analyse the structural conditions for pro-drop and its relation with agreement. Barbosa, Duarte, and Kato (2005) performed an extensive study of some newspaper interviews, to check subject omission in European Portuguese and Brazilian Portuguese. Following Lammoglia Duarte (1995), they identified four main patterns of subject drop:

(36) Pattern I: the antecedent of the null subject is the subject of the matrix clause.
Pattern II: the antecedent is the subject of the previous adjacent sentence.
Pattern III: the antecedent is the subject of a previous, non-adjacent sentence.
Pattern IV: the antecedent is in the previous adjacent sentence, but is functionally distinct from the null subject. (Duarte and Varejão 2013: 107)

The results of the inquiry are summarized in Table 17.2.

Table 17.2 shows that overt subjects do not correlate only with the loss of agreement. Diachronically, the gradual disappearance of pro-drop might have correlated with an impoverishment of the inflexional system, but synchronically the distribution of overt subjects depends on structural, as well as featural, reasons.

Another example of a former pro-drop language which is no longer pro-drop is French, whose inflexional system today is heavily impoverished, with the simultaneous emergence of obligatory subject clitics. Roberts (1993), building on Vance (1989), proposes that the loss of pro-drop in French is due to both the loss of agreement inflexion and the loss of nominative assignment under government. This also explains why null subjects are lost in inversion structures during the sixteenth century. Together both causes led to the complete disappearance of null subjects in French.

Table 17.2. *Null (vs overt) subjects in transcribed interviews according to structural context*

Pattern	European Portuguese	Brazilian Portuguese
I	39/40 (97%)	18/23 (78%)
II	49/55 (89%)	28/48 (58%)
III	20/28 (71%)	07/28 (25%)
IV	16/24 (67%)	10/23 (43%)

Adapted from Barbosa, Duarte, and Kato (2005: 24), in Duarte and Varejão (2013: 108).

Within the generative framework, the correlation between null subjecthood and agreement inflexion was first formalized by Taraldsen (1980), followed by Rizzi (1982), and then Rizzi (1986), who, with different formulations, proposed the null subject parameter, linking null subjecthood, rich agreement, inversion, and *that*-trace effects in languages (see also Chomsky 1981). The idea is that languages with rich agreement have a rich Infl head that can license an empty pronominal category (viz. pro) that is present only in null-subject languages. More specifically, Rizzi proposes that Infl in null-subject languages governs the subject and it is rich enough to license the subject if empty by virtue of an empty pronominal on Infl coindexed with the empty subject. Consequently, the difference between (37a) and (37b) is that in Italian Infl is rich while in English it is not.

(37) a. __ Verrà. (It.)
come.FUT.3SG
b. **__ will come. (Eng.)

While a correlation between null subjecthood and rich verbal agreement systems seems plausible, many scholars have noted several exceptions. Chinese, Japanese, and Korean are, for instance, pro-drop languages, but lack agreement inflexion altogether (Huang 1984). Notice however that these languages are now considered topic-drop languages, and are not in the same group as the pro-drop languages. According to Huang, then, languages with no agreement (no Agr) can also license null subjects. A middle way between these two views is offered by Jaeggli and Safir (1989), who propose the Morphological Uniformity Hypothesis, according to which null subjects are permitted in all and only languages with morphologically uniform inflexional paradigms (see D'Alessandro 2015 for a thorough discussion of the Null Subject Parameter).

Rich agreement corresponds, for Rizzi and Taraldsen, to the presence of agreement morphology on the Infl head. Such a view is also assumed, with some substantial modification, by Alexiadou and Anagnostopoulou (1998). They compare the null-subject status of Germanic, Celtic, Greek, and Romance languages, and propose that a full agreement paradigm has a separate lexical entry to that of the verb. In particular, they take rich agreement to be pronominal, insofar as each of the endings of a rich verbal agreement paradigm has pronominal status. Default or impoverished agreement is instead totally dependent on its host, and therefore does not constitute a separate lexical entry from the verb. If rich agreement attached to the verb root is pronominal, it carries a D-feature with which it can satisfy the requirement on Infl (viz. the Extended Projection Principle) that each clause must have a subject. This means that pro-drop languages do not need a subject to satisfy the Extended Projection

Principle: they can satisfy it via verb movement. This approach captures the correlation between being a pro-drop language, having rich agreement, and having movement of the verb to Infl.

A direct consequence of having languages with a D-feature that can satisfy the Extended Projection Principle is that subjects in the canonical preverbal position, SpecIP, have a different status than their corresponding subjects in non-pro-drop languages. More precisely, preverbal subjects in rich agreement languages are said to be in a left-peripheral positions (viz, in an A'-position) outside of the sentential core (IP), and are therefore not in SpecAgrP within the sentential core (which is the landing position of the subject in early Minimalism, as we saw in the previous section). Alexiadou and Anagnostopoulou further demonstrate that subjects in rich agreement languages with verb movement to Infl do indeed not surface in a canonical preverbal subject position, but are rather topicalized. To support their claim, they present empirical evidence that subjects in null-subject languages are topics, and in a clitic-left dislocation configuration. The first piece of evidence they offer is that in Romance (as well as in Greek and many other languages) subjects can precede adverbs and *if*-clauses. For instance, Italian allows sentences like (38):

(38) ieri   dopo aver   mangiato ha   fatto
     yesterday after have.INF eaten   have.PRS.IND.3SG   make.PTCP
     una passeggiata. (It.)
     a   walk

From the comparison between the Italian sentence in (38) and its English counterpart it appears evident that Italian, a null-subject language, offers the possibility of having the subject very far from the verb (in Infl). The same does not hold for English, where the subject must occur closer to the finite verb. Alexiadou and Anagnostopoulou (1998) further remark that this generalization does not hold for Spanish, where the subject must occur closer to the finite verb as in English.

A second piece of evidence they offer comes from binding facts. Alexiadou and Anagnostopoulou first introduce the generalization, originally put forward in Montalbetti (1984) that overt personal pronouns cannot be bound variables in null-subject languages, as shown in (39) for Catalan:

(39) **Tots els estudiants_i es   pensen   que ells_i
     all the students   REFL= think.PRS.IND.3PL that they
     aprovaran. (Cat., Alexiadou and Anagnostopoulou 1998: 509)
     pass.FUT.3PL

If the subject appears in post-verbal position, binding is possible, as in (40). Following Solà (1992) and Barbosa (1994), Alexiadou and Anagnostopoulou conclude that this is the case because only subjects in post-verbal position are in an A-position, unlike those in preverbal position.

(40) Tots els jugadors$_i$ estan   convençuts   que guanyaran
     all   the players   be.PRS.IND.3PL persuade.PTCP that win.FUT.3PL
     ells$_i$. (Cat., Alexiadou and Anagnostopoulou 1998: 510)
     they
     'All the players believe that they will win.'

If these generalizations are true, when a language loses rich agreement it will lose its null-subject status and have to express the subject overtly. Subject clitics are often pressed into service, together with expletive subjects, in this function. Their status is, however, not completely straightforward, and several scholars have shown that there are several kinds of subject clitic. One of the most debated issues is whether they are pronominal or simply inflexional. We will return to this in the next section.

17.5.1.1 Agreement and Subject Clitics

Contrary to what intuition might suggest, the presence of subject clitics does not entail non-null-subjecthood. If this were the case, we would expect subject clitics to be overt pronominals, always overtly expressed.

If subject clitics were overt pronominals, and therefore counted as 'subjects', we would expect them to be more frequent in languages with little or no verbal inflexion (as in the case of Brazilian Portuguese). This generalization is not borne out, as we shall see below. If, on the other hand, they were inflexional, agreement elements, we might expect them to replace agreement inflexion completely. This is also not the case.

Whether subject clitics are inflexional or pronominal elements is discussed extensively by Rizzi (1986). Before looking at Rizzi's diagnostics, let us first have a look at the distribution of subject clitics, and their co-occurrence with inflexion (see further the discussions in Sections 4.2, 10.3, and 21.2.1).

Roberts (2010), but see also Kayne (1975), presents a classification of languages according to the distribution of subject clitics and verbal inflexion. He identifies four language types:

(41) a. SCL [+ agr] V [+agr]
     b. SCL [+agr]   V [−agr]
     c. SCL [−agr]   V [+agr]
     d. SCL [−agr]   V [−agr]

In (41) [+agr] indicates a full set of morphological person/number distinctions. A full set can contain at most one zero exponent and one syncretism, and V [+agr] indicates a null-subject language. A language like (41a) is a fully redundant null-subject system in which clitics and the verb endings co-vary. An example of such a language is Florentine in (42):

(42) **Florentine (Roberts 2010)**
(E) parlo	Si parla	I speak	we speak
Tu parli	Vu parlate	you.SG speak	you.PL speak
E parla	E parlano	he speaks	they.M speak
La parla	Le parlano	she speaks	they.F speak

Languages of type (41b) are non-null-subject systems in which the verbal inflexion is unable to identify a null subject, and the pronominal paradigm is fully realized. One such language is French:

(43) **French (Roberts 2010)**

Je dors	(dɔʁ)	I sleep
Tu dors	(dɔʁ)	you.SG sleep
Il/elle dort	(dɔʁ)	he/she sleeps
Nous dormons	(dɔʁ.mɔ̃)	we sleep
Vous dormez	(dɔʁ.me)	you sleep
Ils/elles dorment	(dɔʁm)	they.M/F sleep

Languages with (41c) are null-subject systems with fully differentiated verb inflexion but syncretism and gaps in the clitic paradigm. One example is Comasco, a northern Italian dialect:

(44) **Comasco (Roberts 2010)**
    a. dorm-i
        sleep-1SG
        'I sleep.'
    b. ta   dorm-at
        SCL.2SG sleep-2SG
        'You sleep.'
    c. al/la   dorm-a
        SCL.3SG.M/F sleep-3SG
        'He/She sleeps.'
    d. dorm-um
        sleep-1PL
        'We sleep.'
    e. dorm-uf
        sleep-2PL
        'You sleep.'
    f. dorm-an
        sleep-3PL
        'They sleep.'

The last group of languages (41d) show a full set of forms that together form a single, complementary (or near-complementary) pattern.

(45) **Carrara (Roberts 2010)**
    a. a   dorm
        SCL sleep
        'I sleep.'
    b. t   dorm
        SCL.2SG sleep
        'You sleep.'
    c. i/al   dorm
        SCL.3M/F sleep
        'He/She sleeps.'

d. a durm-in
   SCL sleep-1PL
   'We sleep.'
e. durm-it
   sleep-2PL
   'You sleep.'
f. i/al   dorm-n
   SCL.3M/ F sleep-3PL
   'They sleep.'

Roberts (2010) treats subject clitics as agreement inflexion. In fact, most subject clitics in Italian varieties are inflexional, not pronominal, as shown by Rizzi (1982). He proposes a number of diagnostics to distinguish between pronominal and inflexional subject clitics. His first observation is that subject clitic paradigms are often defective, while the absence of a subject pronoun is quite rare. Second, subject clitics are (almost always) obligatory in coordinated structures, while pronouns can be omitted in the second conjunct of coordination. Even in non-null-subject languages, like English, the subject can be omitted in the second conjunct, as shown in (46):

(46) You eat and laugh.

In the case of subject clitics in most Italian varieties such omission is not possible. In the Bergamascan dialect of Grumello del Monte, for instance, it is not possible to omit the subject clitic from the second conjunct, as shown in example (47). Observe that the clitic paradigm is defective, and Grumellese lacks a first person subject clitic.

(47) **Grumello del Monte (Manzini and Savoia 2005, I: 152)**
   a. mang-e   e   bi-e
      eat.PRS.IND-1SG and   drink.PRS.IND-1SG
      'I eat and drink.'
   b. ta   mang-et   e   ta   bi-et
      SCL.2SG eat.PRS.IND-2SG and SCL.2SG drink.PRS.IND-2SG
      'You eat and drink.'
   c. al   mang-ia   e   l   bi:-f
      SCL.3SG eat. PRS.IND-3SG and SCL.3SG drink.PRS.IND-3SG
      'He eats and drinks.'

In French, by contrast, coordinated subject clitics can be omitted, since, unlike those found in Italo-Romance dialects, they are pronominal, as shown in (48).

(48) Il   mange   et   boit. (Fr.)
     he=   eat.PRS.IND.3SG and drink.PRS.IND.3SG
     'He eats and drinks.'

The second observation concerns the fact that, while inflexional subject clitics can co-occur with negative quantifiers, subject pronouns cannot. In (49), for instance, the subject clitic can co-occur with *nigy* 'nobody':

(49) nigy   i   ve   (Grumello del Monte, Manzini and Savoia 2005, I: 62)
      nobody   SCL.3PL come.PRS.IND.3
      'Nobody comes.'

This is again not possible in French, where subject clitics are pronominal in nature:

(50) **Personne   il   ne   fait   cela. (Fr.)
      nobody   he=   NEG   do.PRS.IND.3SG that
      'Nobody does that.'

Finally, agreement markers may follow preverbal negation, but pronouns cannot. In (51) negation precedes the subject clitic, which is therefore an agreement marker, whereas in (52) we are dealing with a genuine pronoun, as in (50), with the result that negation can only follow the pronoun.

(51) No   el   magna. (Ven.)
      NEG   SCL.3SG   eat.PRS.IND.3SG
      'He doesn't eat.'

(52) Il   ne   mange   pas. (Fr.)
      he=   NEG   eat.PRS.IND.3SG NEG
      'He doesn't eat.'

The facts reviewed in this section show that clitics come in at least two forms: pronominal and agreement-like. While French subject clitics are, for instance, pronouns, in northern Italian dialects they are agreement markers. The implication from this conclusion is that while northern Italian varieties are pro-drop languages with rich inflexion, instantiated by subject clitics, languages such as French are genuine non-pro-drop languages (Rizzi 1986; Brandi and Cordin 1989).

Many studies have focused on subject clitics especially in relation to establishing their underlying, base positions and their surface positions. However, given that they are phonologically reduced, it is quite difficult to find evidence for their original, underlying position. One further important aspect of the debate on clitics that we should finally mention here is the theory advanced by Roberts (2010) that subject clitics represent the spell-out of an Agree relation with T, the inflexional core of the sentence. According to Roberts, dislocation is only apparent inasmuch as subject clitics are inflexional, ultimately the spell-out of a subset of features of the subject on T. As such they are the result of an Agree operation and have nothing to do with pronouns and case.

Selected References

Below you can find selected references for this chapter. The full references can be found online at the following page: www.cambridge.org/Romancelinguistics

Barbosa, P. (1994). 'A new look at the null subject parameter', paper presented at *Console III*, Venice.

Barbosa, P., Duarte, I., and Kato, M. (2005). 'Null subjects in European and Brazilian Portuguese', *Journal of Portuguese Linguistics* 4: 11–52.

Belletti, A. (1982). 'Morphological passive and pro-drop: the impersonal construction in Italian', *Journal of Linguistic Research* 2: 1–34.

D'Alessandro, R. (2015). 'Null subjects'. In Fábregas, A., Mateu, J., and Putnam, M. (eds), *Contemporary Linguistic Parameters*. London: Bloomsbury Press, 201–26.

D'Alessandro, R. (2017). 'When you have too many features: auxiliaries, agreement, and clitics in Italian varieties', *Glossa* 2(1): 50. http://doi.org/10.5334/gjgl.102.

D'Alessandro, R. and Pescarini, D. (2016). 'Agreement restrictions and agreement oddities in Romance'. In Fischer, S. and Gabriel, C. (eds), *Manual of Grammatical Interfaces in Romance*. Berlin: De Gruyter, 267–94.

D'Alessandro, R. and Roberts, I. (2008). 'Movement and agreement in Italian past participles and defective phases', *Linguistic Inquiry* 39: 477–91.

Duarte, M. E. and Varejão, F. (2013). 'Null subjects and agreement marks in European and Brazilian Portuguese', *Journal of Portuguese Linguistics* 12: 101–23. http://doi.org/10.5334/jpl.69.

Kayne, R. (1989). 'Facets of Romance past participle agreement'. In Benincà, P. (ed.), *Dialect Variation and the Theory of Grammar*. Dordrecht: Foris, 85–103 (Reprinted in: Kayne, R. (2000). *Parameters and Universals*. Oxford: Oxford University Press, 25–38).

Lammoglia Duarte, M. E. (1995). *A perda do princípio 'Evite Pronome' no português brasileiro*. Doctoral thesis, UNICAMP, São Paulo.

Ledgeway, A. (2012). 'From Latin to Romance: configurationality, functional categories and head-marking', *Transactions of the Philological Society* 110: 122–42.

Maiden, M. (2012). 'A paradox? The morphological history of the Romance present subjunctive'. In Gaglia, S. and Hinzelin, M.-O. (eds), *Inflection and Word Formation in Romance Languages*. Amsterdam: Benjamins, 27–54.

18

Alignment

Sonia Cyrino and Michelle Sheehan

18.1 Introduction

The term alignment is used in the typological literature to characterize the morphosyntactic behaviour of arguments and their relationship to the predicate (see, for example, Dixon 1972; 1994; Harris and Campbell 1995; Siewierska 1996; 2013; Comrie 2013). Different arguments can 'align' with each other based on any morphosyntactic criteria, but the term usually refers to case, agreement, and word order. For ease of reference, we adopt the typological terms used to refer to arguments: transitive subjects (A=Agent), intransitive subjects (S=Subject), and objects of transitives (O=patientive) (see Comrie 1978; Dixon 1994).[1] These labels allow us to categorize patterns as 'nominative–accusative', where A and S behave alike (as in the Swahili subject and object marking pattern in (1)), or 'ergative-absolutive', where S and O behave alike (as in the Dyirbal case pattern in (2)):

(1) Swahili; Niger Congo; Africa
    a. A-   li-   ni-   on-a.
        S.MRK.NCLI- PST- O.MRK.1SG- see-FV
        'S/he saw me.'
    b. A-   li-   on-a.
        S.MRK.NCLI- PST-see-FV
        'S/he saw.'

---

[1] Further distinctions are made for ditransitives (Dryer 1986), but we put this distinction to one side here to focus on intransitive/monotransitive alignment patterns.

(2) **Dyirbal; Pama-Nyungan; Australia (Dixon 1972: 142, 67)**
    a.   Balan   dugumbil   **baŋgul**   yaṛa-**ŋgu** munda-n.
        NCLII.there.ABS woman.ABS NCLI.there.ERG man-ERG take-NON.FUT
        'Man took woman.'
    b.   Bayi   yaṛa   walmaɲu.
        NCLI.there.ABS man.ABS got.up
        'Man got up.'

There are also instances of neutral case/agreement alignment, for example in languages which lack verbal/case inflexion so that all arguments trivially pattern alike (e.g., Mandarin), and patterns of 'tripartite' alignment, where A, S, and O all pattern differently in terms of case and agreement (e.g., Nez Perce; Deal 2010).

Some languages force the need for two kinds of intransitive subjects: henceforth S_A and S_O. This is because intransitive subjects often behave differently, yielding what has variously been called an *active–inactive*, *agentive–patientive*, *active–stative*, or simply *split-S* alignment (we adopt the final term here, using it interchangeably with the term *split-intransitivity*). The European isolate Basque displays split-S alignment in its case, agreement, and auxiliary selection (see Ortiz de Urbina 1989; Laka 1993; Baker 2018):

(3) **Basque; isolate; Basque country (Baker 2018: 171f.)**
    a.   Gizon-a-**k**   exte-a-Ø   saldu **du**.
        man-DEF-ERG house–DEF-ABS sold   has
        'The man has sold the house.'
    b.   Gizon-a-**k**   ikasi   **du**.
        man-DEF-ERG studied has
        'The man has studied.'
    c.   Gizon-a-Ø   etorri da.
        man-DEF-ABS came   is
        'The man has come.'

The intransitive subject in (3b) has the same (ergative) case as the transitive subject in (3a), whereas that in (3c) has the same unmarked (absolutive) case as the direct object in (3a). What is interesting is that this division of intransitive subjects appears not to be arbitrary but rather based on their thematic properties: intransitive subjects which are more agentive pattern like transitive subjects, and intransitive subjects which are more patientive pattern like transitive objects. As we shall see below, however, the precise division between S_A and S_O is subject to substantial cross-linguistic variation.

Within the Romance family, Latin and its descendants are considered to display basic nominative–accusative alignment, since in case and agreement markers on (pro)nouns and verbs A and S pattern alike and are formally distinguished from O, as shown in (4) (see, for instance, Ledgeway 2012; Migliori 2016).

(4) **Classical Latin**
    a.   Iugurtha [...]   Adherbalem   necat (Sall. *BI* 26)
        Jugurtha.MSG.NOM Adherbal.MSG.ACC murder.PRS.IND.3SG
        'Jugurtha murders Adherba.l'
    b.   Quintus   frater [...]   laborat (Cic. *Att.* 7, 18, 4)
        Quintus.MSG. NOM brother.MSG.NOM labour.IND.PRS.3SG
        'My brother Quintus is working hard.'
    c.   Cluilius,   Albanus   rex,   moritur (Liv. I, 23, 4)
        Cluilius.MSG.NOM Alban.SG.NOM king.MSG.NOM die.PRS.IND.3SG
        'Cluilius, the Alban king, dies.'

However, Latin also has a split-S alignment in certain paradigms of the verbal system (Cennamo 2009; Ledgeway 2012; Migliori 2016, among others), as seen in (5), where the verb, in the *perfectum*, shows the alternation of synthetic (5a) and analytic (5b) forms, respectively, reflecting the split system (La Fauci 1988; 1991; 1998; Ledgeway 2012). In the synthetic form, the O is marked with accusative (5a), whereas in the analytic form (5b), S with subscipt O is marked nominative and agrees in gender/number and case with the perfect passive participle:

(5) **Classical Latin**
    a.   quid   enim   uiderunt? (Cic. *Agr.* 2, 95)
        what.ACC indeed see.PST.PFV.IND.3PL
        'What indeed did they see?'
    b.   Stoicus,   qui   Athenis   nuper   est   mortuus (Cic. *Off.* 2.86)
        Stoic.NOM who.NOM Athens.LOC recently is die.PFV.PTCP.NOM.MSG
        'a Stoic philosopher who recently died in Athens'

This split-S alignment continues in a variety of guises into later Romance varieties. In fact, the in-depth investigation of phenomena such as auxiliary selection, past participle agreement, and *se/si* passives in Romance languages has proven central to advances in our understanding of split-intransitivity. In what follows, we discuss these phenomena in some detail, highlighting microvariation within the Romance family and discussing their importance for our broader understanding of alignment.

This chapter is organized as follows. In Section 18.2, we focus on the diachrony of alignment in Romance, as a backdrop for the following sections which take a synchronic perspective. In Section 18.3, we turn to auxiliary selection, considering both frequent and rarer patterns, as well as purported implicational hierarchies in this domain. Section 18.4 explores the alignment of past participle agreement, again charting both frequent and rare splits. Section 18.5 discusses alignment in SE-passives, which again display properties of split-S alignment in a restricted domain. Section 18.6 turns to word order in Romance, assessing the extent to which this is sensitive to the S_A/S_O distinction. Finally, Section 18.7 briefly discusses two other potentially relevant phenomena: INDE-cliticization and absolute participles/participial adjectives. As we shall see, in many of these cases, the Romance language family displays a remarkable array of alignment patterns which raise interesting challenges for theories of split-intransitivity and alignment more generally.

18.2 On the Diachrony of Alignment in Romance

As noted above, it is by now well established that a single language can display multiple different alignment patterns, sensitive to syntactic context (Moravcsik 1978; Dixon 1994). This can be observed in the transition from Classical Latin to Romance, where it has been argued that, although we see a prevalence of basic nominative–accusative alignment, the picture is not so clear cut (Zamboni 1998; Ledgeway 2012). In fact, Ledgeway (2012) claims, following the extensive work of La Fauci, that there was not an uninterrupted continuity from Latin to Romance with respect to nominative–accusative alignment, but that the existence of split-S alignment in the transition can be verified in the developmental behaviour of several distinct phenomena. Ledgeway argues, moreover, that Romance languages can be divided into two groups, northern and southern varieties, according to the path along which these phenomena developed. In this section, we review some of these traits.

In Latin, as noted above, at least two distinct alignment kinds can be detected. On the one hand, Latin has been considered to present predominantly nominative–accusative alignment (La Fauci 1988; 1991; 1998; Zamboni 2000; Ledgeway 2012), most clearly in the nominal domain, where A and S are systematically marked with nominative, whereas a structural direct object (O) is marked with accusative case, as shown in (4) above. Additionally, the verb system in the tenses of the *imperfectum* also operates according to a nominative–accusative alignment. As can be seen in (6), the finite verb agrees in person/number with the nominative subject and not with the accusative object (examples from Ledgeway 2012: 315):

(6) **Classical Latin**
    a. is [...]   capite   uelato   uictimam   caedet (Liv. 10.7.10)
        he.NOM head.ABL covered.ABL victim.ACC slay.FUT.3SG
        'with veiled head he slays a victim'
    b. populus   minutus   laborat (Petr. *Sat.* 44)
        people.NOM small.NOM suffer.PRS.IND.3SG
        'poor folk suffer'

c. magnus   numerus   hostium   cadebat (Caes. B.G. 5.34.2)
   great.NOM   number.NOM   enemies.GEN   fall.PST.IPFV.3SG
   'a great number of the enemy fell'

However, several authors have also noticed that Latin, especially in the transition to Romance, also shows signs of split-intransitivity (La Fauci 1988; 1991; Zamboni 2000; Ledgeway 2012), as seen in (5). In fact, this same kind of alignment can be observed in several Latin constructions. One of them is the so-called extended accusative (see Plank 1985), where nominative case is replaced by accusative for some verb classes, namely: verbs denoting change of state (7a), change of location (7b), anticausatives (7c), passives (7d), and impersonals (7e) (Cennamo 1999: 139):

(7) **Late(r) Latin**
   a. nascitur   ei   genuorum   contractionem   et
      be.born.PRS.IND.PASS.3SG   he.DAT   knees.GEN   contraction.ACC   and
      claudicationem (*Chiron* 516)
      limping.ACC
      'There arises contraction of its knees and limping'
   b. si sequenter   ipsum   currit (*Lex Alamannorum* 94 E codd. A; MGH leg. sect. I: V, 154)
      if subsequently   himself.ACC   run.PRS.IND.3SG
      'if subsequently he himself runs'
   c. ille   heres,   cui   talem   seruum   in   porcionem
      that.NOM   heir.NOM   who.DAT   such.ACC   servant.ACC   in   share.ACC
      uenit (*Lex Curiensis* 2, 23, 5; MGH leg.V, 320)
      come.PRS.IND.3SG
      'that heir, to whose share such a servant falls'
   d. sardam   exossatur (*Apicius* 9, 10)
      pilchard.ACC   fillet.PRS.IND.PASS.3SG
      'the pilchard is filleted'
   e. cum   factum   fuerit   missam (*Itinerarium Egeriae* 32, 2)
      when   done.PFV.PTCP.N   be.PFV.SBJV.3SG   service.ACC
      'when the service is over (lit. one ends the service)'

In these examples, there is no marker for nominative.[2] Instead, the intransitive subject (S) is marked in the same way as the transitive object, making it an S_O, in another instance of split-S alignment.

Cennamo (1999) shows that the development of Latin reflexives *se/sibi* (see below) into Romance impersonal and passive markers was concomitant with this split-intransitivity. Constructions with pronoun *se* with reflexive, reciprocal, and, more rarely, middle denotation could be found in different stages of Latin, but the impersonal, middle, and passive *se* can

---

[2] In example (7a), we observe a plural coordinated post-verbal subject but third person singular verb agreement. This might indicate the possibility for a null (expletive) 3SG subject (see the translation), and that could explain the accusative O.

be considered an innovation. Cennamo argues that this use arose through the existence of a split-intransitive alignment in late stages of Latin. The reflexive pronouns *se* (accusative and ablative) and *sibi* (dative), mark reflexive (8) and dative of interest (9) constructions in Latin (Cennamo 1999: 114f.):

(8) **Latin**
istae ueteres, quae se unguentis unctant (Pl. *Most.* 274)
these.NOM old.NOM.PL who.NOM REFL ointments.ABL smear.PRS.IND.3PL
'these old ladies, who smear themselves with ointments'

(9) si sibi nunc alteram (sc. fidicinam) ab legione abduxit (Pl. *Epid.* 90a)
if REFL now another.ACC lyre.singer from army.ABL bring.away.PST.PFV.3SG
'If he has now brought back with him (lit. 'for himself') from the army another one.'

According to Cennamo, *se* also occurs to mark anticausatives (10):

(10) neque herba nascetur neque lutamenta
neither weed.NOM be.born.FUT.PASS.3SG nor plasters.NOM
scindent se (Lat., Cato *De Agri Cultura* 128)
break.up.FUT.3PL REFL
'neither weeds will grow, nor the plasters will crack'

Other forms were also possible, though marginal (Cennamo 1999; 2000), and they appeared especially in idiomatic expressions, the so-called pleonastic reflexives. *Sibi* was used either optionally, lacking syntactic or semantic meaning (11), or in conjunction with a possessive adjective (12):

(11) **Latin**
Quid igitur sibi uolt pater? (Ter. *Andr.* 375)
what then REFL want.PRS.IND.3SG father.NOM
'What then does my father want?'

(12) ita nunc ignorans suo sibi seruit patri (Pl. *Capt.* 50)
so now unaware.NOM his.DAT REFL serve.PRS.IND.3SG father.DAT
'so now he is serving his father unaware'

Over time, the reflexive *se* became a marker of external causation and acquired a passive value. At this point, the reflexive appears in middle constructions and, later, it is used with certain intransitive (unergative) verbs, as its cognate still is in modern Romance varieties (see Section 18.6).

Cennamo (1999) shows that pleonastic *se/sibi* became markers of split-intransitivity in that they differentiated unaccusatives from unergatives. On the one hand, *sibi* occurred with verbs of change of state and location, the sole argument being thus marked as S with subscript O. On the other hand, *se* occurred with anticausatives, intransitive verbs of mental process, and speech act verbs, and later it was also found with activity verbs. She relates this pattern to the loss of the *r*-morphology that earlier characterized middle and passive verb forms (see below). As pointed out in Cennamo (1998: 82), it was possible for the *r*-morphology to alternate with the analytic patterns showing *se* and *sibi* together with an active verb form. That is to say that the Latin middle/passive verb forms that earlier were characterized by *r*-morphology were replaced in later Latin with the pleonastic reflexives.

In Romance languages, this kind of split-intransitivity seems to have been lost, that is, the distinction between the two types of transitive/intransitive uses of *se/sibi* dies out due, according to Cennamo (1999), to convergence of the dative and accusative forms of the reflexive in most Romance languages, with the major exception of Romanian. In European Portuguese, Spanish, and Italian, however, there are instances of constructions with *si* in which the transitive verb agrees in number with the direct object, displaying what might be described as an ergative pattern, as O patterns with S_A in this respect.

Another well-discussed aspect of Latin grammar are (semi-)deponent verbs, verbs ending in *-r* ('the *r*-morphology' mentioned above, see, among others, Pinkster 1992; Gianollo 2000; Migliori 2016). These verbs are described in the literature as 'passive in form, active in meaning' (cf. Flobert 1975; Tuttle 1986: 250). Included in the deponents were verbs of emotion, verbs of entreating, verbs of fulfilling of (bodily or official) function, and verbs of change of state of position (movement). In other words, deponent verbs belong to verbal classes with distinct syntactic properties: unaccusative (change of state and movement) verbs, experiential verbs, perception verbs, reciprocals (Gianollo 2000; 2005; 2010; Migliori 2016), that is, those verbal classes which express an event/state lacking an agent.

The *imperfectum/perfectum* contrast in Latin expresses an aspectual opposition, that is, unaccomplished and accomplished events, respectively. The endings of all verb classes are the same for the active voice for both the *imperfectum* and the *perfectum* paradigms. However, different endings occur with passive constructions and the so-called deponent verbs. The latter never have the endings for the regular active voice paradigm, but they do not have passive meaning. For that reason, Gianollo (2000: 237f.) considers *r*-morphology as an unaccusative conjugation, signalling the presence of a 'non-prototypical subject', that is, a subject that has properties of O.

Interestingly, no synthetic perfect is attested for passive constructions and for deponent verbs. It has been argued by Migliori (2016) that the *r*-morphological marker signalled split-intransitivity in the Latin verbal paradigm (active/inactive split, in her terms). This is seen in passive (13a) (Migliori 2016: 23) and deponent constructions (13b) (Migliori 2016: 29).

(13) **Classical Latin**
    a.   alter   filius [...]   necatur (Cic. *Clu.* 28, 16)
          other.MSG.NOM son.MSG.NOM murder.PRS.IND.3SG
          'The second son is (being) murdered'
    b.   eodem   anno   Q. Fabius   Maximus
          same.ABL.SG year.ABL Q. Fabius.NOM.SG Maximus.NOM.SG
          moritur (Liv. XXX 26, 7)
          die.PRS.IND.3SG
          'In the same year Q. Fabius Maximus dies'

The generalization is, then, that the *r*-morphology (occurring in the *imperfectum*) is similar to the passive analytic forms (occurring in the *perfectum*) since in both cases no A is present (Migliori 2016). In this way, it is possible to say that split-intransitivity, that is, the existence of agreement with S_O, is triggered by the presence of *r*-morphology. In forms where no *r*-morphology is present, the language exhibits a nominative–accusative alignment.

Flobert (1975), among other studies, shows that, although deponent verbs have been present during the whole history of the Latin language, their number slowly increased. Whereas in pre-Classical Latin (until 169 BCE), he reports 270 deponent verbs, in the beginning of the Romance era (end of the eighth century CE), the number reaches 884. More importantly, besides increasing in number, their behaviour also changes: they turn into a new class of transitives by means of a morphological change (namely, *a*-prefixation; Gianollo 2005). Their *perfectum*, since it was formed periphrastically, came to be formed with a 'transitive auxiliary', HABERE 'have'. Therefore, the loss of deponents may also have contributed to the rise of auxiliary HABERE.

The path of the two auxiliaries (ESSE 'be' and HABERE 'have') in analytic verbal forms in Latin alignment is another important consideration. Latin had some periphrastic (analytic forms) with verbs ESSE 'be' (14a) (for *perfectum* passive and deponent verbs), but also, less frequently with HABERE 'have' (14b) (Pinkster 1987; Cennamo 2008):

(14) **Classical Latin**
    a.   natus est nobis nepos (Ter. *Hec.* 639)
          born   is   to.us   nephew
          'a nephew has been born to us'
    b.   de   Caesare   satis   hoc   tempore   dictum
          about Caesar.ABL enough this.ABL time.ABL say.PFV.PTCP.N
          habeo (Cic. *Phil.* 5, 52)
          have.1SG
          'I have said enough of Caesar at present'

The periphrasis with HABERE was initially attested only with transitive verbs. This fact has been understood in terms of a gradual loss of lexical content from the verb 'to have', denoting possession, in a resultative construction where the object could occur with the past participle (Pinkster 1987: 197):

(15) qui   eum   uinctum   habebit (Lat., *Lex XII Tabularum* 3, 4)
     who.NOM   he.ACC   defeat.PFV.PTCP.MSG.ACC   have.FUT.3SG
     'who shall hold him in bonds.'

In addition to activity verbs, such as DICERE 'say' (14b) and UINCERE 'defeat' (15), stative verbs, such as PERSPICERE 'perceive, examine', are also found with HABERE (Cennamo 2008). From the sixth century CE, HABERE is established as a temporal auxiliary, according to the literature. However, as pointed out by Cennamo (2008), Migliori (2016) and others, in addition to the auxiliarization function of HABERE, this verb is used as a marker of A subjects in contrast to the other auxiliary ESSE, which was used with all S arguments. As we will see below, the rise of periphrastic tenses and auxiliary selection in Romance languages can be seen as a consequence of this situation in Latin.

Traditionally, periphrastic tenses in Romance have been described as the result of a grammaticalization process. The lexical verb HABERE ('have, possess') becomes an auxiliary by losing its original lexical meaning but maintaining its grammatical (tense) component in the periphrasis thus formed. At the same time, an adjectival/stative/resultative participle that occurs together with these former lexical verbs gains (or keeps) its lexical meaning and is reanalysed as verbal, in the sense that it is now responsible for the argument structure of the newly formed analytic tense which denotes anteriority (cf. Vincent 1982; Salvi 1987):

(16) epistulam   scriptam   habeo (Lat.)
     letter.ACC.FSG   write.PFV.PTCP.ACC.FSG   have.1.SG
     'I have the letter written' = 'The letter in my possession is written.'

We saw above that ESSE + participle was an 'analytic tense' in Latin, occurring both with passives/unaccusative and deponent verbs in the *perfectum*. The HABERE + participle analytic tense is late. Indeed, see the extensive discussion in Adams (2013) who convincingly argues that there are no examples of perfective HABERE in Classical Latin and very few in later stages of the language. Cennamo (2008: 124f.) shows that the analytic structure of the perfect tense in deponents spreads to other non-deponent (i.e., intransitive first and then transitive) verbs from the imperial age on:

(17) **Latin**
  a. sorores   una   die   obitae   sunt (*CIL* VI 17633)
      sisters.NOM   same.ABL   day.ABL   die.PFV.PTCP.FPL.NOM   be.PRS.IND.3PL
      'The sisters died on the same day'

b. praeteritus est dies (Plin. *Ep.* 10, 46)
go.PFV.PTCP.MSG.NOM be.PRS.IND.3SG day.NOM
'The day is over'
c. cogniti sunt Romulides (*Agnell.* 81, p. 333, 25)
learn.PFV.PTCP.MPL.NOM be.PRS.IND.3PL Romans.NOM.MPL
'the Romans (have) learnt'
d. certati sunt cursu (Hygin. *Fab.* 273, 12)
compete.PFV.PTCP.MPL.NOM be.PRS.IND.3PL race.ABL
'They (have) had a race'
e. lacrimatus est (Vetus Latina, *Johannes* (a) 11, 35)
cry.PFV.PTCP.MPL.NOM be.PRS.IND.3SG
'He was in tears'

Migliori (2016), following La Fauci (1997: 24) and Ledgeway (2012: ch. 7), presents a detailed description of the rise of the HABERE + past participle periphrasis in Romance (cf. also Section 19.3.2). She shows that the presence of the perfective periphrasis with ESSE + past participle (cf. Section 19.3.3), and the fact that Latin showed a split-S alignment in its verbal system, as seen above, gave rise to the innovative periphrasis. Drawing on the seminal work of La Fauci (1997), she shows that there are several contexts in Latin in which ESSE and HABERE alternate in the same construction (Migliori 2016: 125). Consider the following:

(18) **Latin**
a. Perspectum mihi est
   know.PFV.PTCP 1SG.DAT be.PRS.IND.3SG
b. Perspectum habeo
   know.PFV.PTCP have.PRS.IND.1SG
   'I know, I am convinced'

This periphrasis expanded through the whole Latin system and later into Romance because of the functional use of HABERE for A subjects.

Related to the rise of periphrastic tenses with HABERE + participle in Romance in analogy to the existing ESSE + participle structure is the development of different possibilities for auxiliary selection found in Romance. In fact, as will be seen in Section 18.3, there is significant variation across Romance varieties in this domain. While Italian preserves a split-S pattern (19), Spanish has generalized the use of *haber* 'have' to unaccusative verbs (20), re-establishing a nominative–accusative pattern:

(19) **Italian**
a. Ha dormito.
   has slept
   'He has slept.'

b. È svenuto.
   is fainted
   'He has fainted.'

(20) **Spanish**
   a. Ha trabajado.
      has worked
      'He has worked.'
   b. Ha llegado.
      has arrived
      'He has arrived.'

In other varieties, patterns of auxiliary selection are more complex, a point to which we return in Section 18.3.

Perfect participles in Latin show agreement licensed by **S with subscript O** but contemporary Romance past participle agreement has spread differently across different languages (see Section 18.4). It can also be considered a parallel development with the rise of a split auxiliary system. In many Romance languages where participle agreement is possible, there is gender and number agreement with S in ESSE + participle (21a), but no agreement between the A and the participle in HABERE + participle periphrasis (21b) (Ledgeway 2012: 326f.):

(21) **Majorcan Catalan**
   a. Ma mareta   s' és aufegada.
      my mother.DIM self=is suffocated.FSG
      'My poor mother has suffocated.'
   b. Vui   fer   lo que ha fet   (**feta)   aquesta.
      I.want do.INF the what has done.MSG done.FSG this.one.FSG
      'I want to do what she has done.'

This is not the only attested pattern, however, since some Italo-Romance varieties do actually display agreement with A arguments (see Section 18.4).

Finally, another area where Split-Intransitivity can be detected in the development of Latin to Romance is in the domain of word order. It is widely assumed that Classical Latin had free word order, though some authors argue that different orders were the result of pragmatic principles (or information structure; see, for example, Devine and Stephens 2006). The oldest texts, however, showed, according to Bauer (1995: 89), that the unmarked order had the verb in final position. Later, VO order begins to occur in some texts and gradually becomes predominant (Ledgeway 2012: 225–29).

The subjects of unaccusative and passive verbs (that is, S_O) could occur in a post-verbal position (22), a situation already noted in Classical Latin

(Ledgeway 2012: 232). Transitive (A) subjects and S_A subjects, on the other hand, were always pre-verbal (see also Adams 1976):

(22) **Latin**
    a.   uenerat   iam   tertius dies (Petr. *Sat*. 26)
        come.PLPL.3SG already third day
        'the third day had come already'
    b.   relinquebatur   una per   Sequanos uia (Caes. *B.G.* 1.9.1)
        remain.PST.IPFV.PASS3SG one through Sequani road
        'there remained one other line of route, through the borders of the Sequani'

This indicates that, at the level of the sentence, we appear to have a split-intransitive alignment already in (at least late stages of) Latin, though as we shall see in Section 18.6, matters are more complex than this in modern Romance varieties.

At the beginning of this section, we pointed out that the literature has shown that, since Classical Latin, there have been two kinds of alignment prevalent in Romance languages. Ledgeway (2012) argues that nominative–accusative alignment was most evident in the nominal system, but a split-S pattern was also present in the verbal system and in sentence-level grammar. This pattern was carried over to some phenomena in the transition to early Romance, and modern varieties preserve these reflexes to varying degrees. In the next five sections we discuss synchronic alignment in Romance, beginning with phenomena already discussed in relation to Latin (auxiliary selection, past participle agreement, word order, and SE-passives) before turning to other phenomena such as INDE-cliticization, bare plurals, and absolute participles.

18.3 Auxiliary Selection

As noted above, while some Romance varieties have since generalized HABERE 'have' (Spanish, Catalan) or replaced both with a novel auxiliary (Portuguese), many Romance languages inherited from Latin the use of both HABERE 'have' and ESSE 'be' auxiliaries in the analytic perfect/past tense (French, Italian, Sardinian, old Spanish, old Catalan, etc.), henceforth referred to as HAVE and BE (for further discussion, see also Sections 4.3, 18.3, and 21.2.2). While, in many cases, the choice of auxiliary follows a split-S alignment, there are low-level differences between languages regarding where exactly we find HAVE vs BE. In fact, a consideration of a wide range of dialects in addition to the major standard languages reveals a bewildering array of variation in this domain. We first review frequent kinds of splits in Section 18.3.1, before turning to rarer splits and their relation to alignment in Section 18.3.2.

18.3.1 Frequent Patterns

Perlmutter (1978; 1989) famously proposed that intransitive verbs should be split into two classes: unaccusatives with an S_O argument and unergatives, with an S_A argument.[3] In Italian, auxiliary selection with intransitive verbs is said to reflect this distinction. This is particularly apparent with verbs like *continuare* 'continue' in which either the A or the O argument can be suppressed in intransitive contexts. Where O is suppressed, leaving S_A, the auxiliary is *avere* 'have' (23b); where A is suppressed, leaving S_O, the auxiliary is *essere* 'be' (23c):

(23) Italian (Perlmutter 1989: 78, citing Rosen 1988)
    a.   Ugo **ha** continuato la   lotta.
          Ugo has continued the struggle
          'Ugo continued the struggle.'
    b.   Ugo **ha** continuato.
          Ugo has continued
          'Ugo continued.'
    c.   La   lotta   **è** continuata.
          The struggle is continued.FSG
          'The struggle continued.'

While in many Romance varieties, there is, undeniably, a thematic basis to auxiliary selection with intransitive verbs, there is nonetheless a great deal of cross-linguistic variation in this domain. A wealth of research has clearly established that it is not possible to determine, based on this diagnostic, a stable cross-linguistic semantic class of unaccusative verbs (see Sorace 2000). For example, the use of BE is much more limited in modern French than it is in Italian, and even more so in Canadian French (Sankoff and Thibault 1977). How to deal with this cross-linguistic variation in split-intransitivity is one of the major challenges arising from the study of Romance alignment.

Sorace (2000) claims, however, that this variation is systematic and subject to what she calls an Auxiliary Selection Hierarchy (ASH; Table 18.1, cf. also Section 4.3.1).

Verbs of the thematic/aspectual types towards the top of the hierarchy are more likely to occur with HAVE, and those towards the bottom to occur with BE in both Romance and Germanic languages. Moreover, verbs which show variable behaviour in a single language, occurring with either HAVE or BE, tend to be on the cusp between the HAVE/BE division. For example, in French, all change of location verbs select BE, but whereas change of state verbs display variability. Consider, by way of example, *échapper* 'escape'

---

[3] Perlmutter (1989) claims that this idea actually goes back to Sapir (1917). Burzio (1986) reformulates Perlmutter's core ideas in Government and Binding Theory.

Table 18.1. *The Auxiliary Selection Hierarchy*

HAVE	Semantic verb class	example
⇑	Controlled process (non-motional)	work, play, talk ...
	Controlled process (motional)	swim, run, walk ...
	Uncontrolled consecution	tremble, skid, cough ...
	Existence of state	be, belong, sit ...
	Continuation of pre-existing state	stay, remain, last ...
⇓	Change of state	rise, decay, die ...
BE	Change of location	come, arrive, fall ...

Based on Sorace (2000: 863).

which can occur with either auxiliary subject to a subtle semantic effect according to Sorace (2000: 867, translations altered):

(24) **French**
La   cause de ce   phénomène   a   jusqu'à présent
The   cause of this phenomenon   has   until at present
échappé à   toutes les   recherches.
escaped to   all   the   investigations
'The cause of this phenomenon has so far eluded all investigations.'

(25) Son   secret lui   est   échappé.
     his   secret him.DAT=is   escaped
     'He let his secret out.'

With the exception of *rester* 'remain', all stative and higher verbs select HAVE in French, however.

In Italian, change of state and change of location verbs overwhelmingly select BE, but continuation of pre-existing state and existence of state verbs are much more variable in their behaviour according to Sorace (2000: 868, translation altered):

(26) Il   presidente è / ha   durato in   carica due anni. (It.)
     the   president   is   has lasted in   post   two years
     'The president lasted for two years in post.'

Sorace further shows how other factors such as telicity and agentivity can affect auxiliary selection for verbs towards the middle of the ASH.

Support for the ASH comes not only from present-day Romance varieties, but also from older stages of Romance (see Aranovich 2003; Rosemeyer 2014 on old Spanish; Mateu 2009 on old Catalan) as well as other Indo-European languages, notably Germanic languages. More recently, it has been shown that a similar hierarchy applies to split-S phenomena in other domains/languages (see Baker 2018 on Basque and Georgian).

As Perlmutter (1989) and many others since have noted, however, reflexives behave somewhat unexpectedly in this context, requiring BE in Italian

Table 18.2. *Reflexive auxiliary hierarchy*

	Unacc.	Reflexive				Trans/Unerg
		Inherent	Dir. trans.	Indir. unerg.	Indir. trans.	
It.	BE					HAVE
Log.	BE					HAVE
ORmc.	BE					HAVE
OFlo.	BE					HAVE
Lec.	BE					HAVE
Sp.						HAVE

Loporcaro (2015: 61).

wherever they surface with a clitic SE object (see also Bentley 2006; Loporcaro 2007; 2015):

(27) Giorgio si è alzato. (It.)
    Giorgio SE= is raised
    'Giorgio got up.'

The thematic status of these verbs remains controversial. In terms of auxiliary selection and non-suppression of S under causatives, they pattern like unaccusatives, but according to other diagnostics, they behave like unergative/transitive verbs (see Siloni 2008). As noted in Sections 18.6–7, however, not all of these diagnostics are sensitive to basic thematic distinctions.

As Loporcaro (2007) notes (cf. also Section 4.3.2), moreover, with respect to auxiliary selection, the behaviour of reflexives across Romance varieties is quite variable (see also Alboiu et al. 2004 for an overview of the controversial status of reflexives with respect to Alsina's 1996 unaccusativity diagnostics).

Thus, while in standard Italian, all SE-reflexives require BE, other Italo-Romance varieties display minimally different patterns (Table 18.2). Logudorese Sardinian, for example, behaves like standard Italian except with indirect transitive reflexives, where the reflexive functions as a dative indirect object (Loporcaro 2015: 62):

(28) Maria z a ssamuna:ðu zal ma:nɔs. (Log.)
    Maria REFL= has washed the hands
    'Maria washed her hands.'

In old Florentine, on the other hand, only inherent reflexives require BE, with all other reflexives surfacing with HAVE (Loporcaro 2015: 64):

(29) **Old Florentine**
    a. io mi **sarei** brusciato
      I me=be.COND.1SG burnt
      'I would have burnt myself.'

b. La donna che [...] ci s' **hae** mostrata
    the woman that us=REFL=has shown.FSG
    'The woman that showed herself to us'
c. poscia che tanti speculi fatti s' **ha**
    after that so.many mirrors made REFL=has
    'After he has made (for himself) so many mirrors.'

The purported difference between (29a) and (29b–c) is that (29a) involves what Loporcaro calls a retroherent or inherent reflexive, lexically reflexive rather than derived from a transitive.

Finally, in Leccese, and in Vallader (Raeto-Romance), reflexives always take HAVE:

(30) **Vallader (Loporcaro 2007: 191, citing Ganzoni 1983)**
   a. ella s' **ha** lavada.
       she REFL=has washed.FSG
       'She has washed herself.'
   b. Dora e Mengia s' **han** scrittas suvent
       Dora and Mengia REFL=have written.FPL often
       'Dora and Mengia have often written to each other.'

Loporcaro (2007; 2011; 2015) claims that this variation undermines a semantic approach to auxiliary selection of the kind proposed by Sorace, and favours a syntactic account of the kind originally proposed by Perlmutter (though one in which class membership varies across languages).

18.3.2 Rarer Patterns

In addition to the patterns just discussed, which can be assimilated to split-S basic alignment patterns (see Loporcaro 2011; Baker 2018), we also find rarer kinds of splits in auxiliary selection (see Ledgeway forthcoming; 2019 for a recent overview, which builds on Ledgeway 2000; 2012; Loporcaro 2007). In some varieties, HAVE/BE are in free variation with a certain class of predicates and, in other cases, their distribution is sensitive to the person/number features of the subject, either across the board, or with a particular class of verbs. Consider eastern Abruzzese, where auxiliary selection depends wholly on the person features of the subject (Table 18.3). BE surfaces with first/second person subjects and HAVE with third person subjects (Ledgeway 2012: 296):

(31) **Arielli (eastern Abruzzo)**
   a. So /si scritto.
       am are.2SG written
       'I/you have written.'

b. A   scritto.
    have.3 written
    'S/he has/they have written.'

Table 18.3. *Person-based auxiliary selection in Abruzzo*

	1SG	2SG	3SG	1PL	2PL	3PL
L'Aquila	BE	BE	HAVE	BE	BE	HAVE
Vasto	HAVE	BE	BE/HAVE	HAVE	HAVE	HAVE
Introdacqua	HAVE	BE	HAVE	HAVE	HAVE	HAVE
Notaresco	BE	HAVE	HAVE	HAVE	HAVE	HAVE

Loporcaro (2007: 184, citing Giammarco 1973).

This is not the only attested pattern, however. Even within Abruzzese, there are many different splits, as Table 18.3 from Loporcaro (2007, citing Giammarco 1973) shows (see also Ledgeway 2000; D'Alessandro and Ledgeway 2010; D'Alessandro and Roberts 2010).

These facts are interesting because it has long been known that case/agreement alignment are also often sensitive to nominal features including person (see Silverstein 1976; Dixon 1994; Garrett 1990; Coon and Preminger 2017). As has previously been noted, these person-sensitive patterns of auxiliary selection can thus be considered an instance of differential subject marking (de Hoop and de Swart 2008).

In other varieties, variability or person-based sensitivity is limited to a subset of verb types. Take, for example, Maceratese, in which most unaccusatives and reflexives take BE, as in standard Italian, with the exception of indirect transitive reflexives, which allow either auxiliary in free variation (Paciaroni 2009).

(32) **Maceratese**
      Essa s ɛ rlaata / essa s a rlaato   le   ma. (Mac.)
      she SE=is washed.FSG she SE=has washed.MSG the.FPL hands.F
      'She washed her hands.'

In more complex cases, person-sensitivity and verb-type-sensitivity interact. In Altamurano, for example, in the present perfect, HAVE/BE are in free variation with first/second person subjects. With third person singular subjects we find BE with unaccusative predicates and HAVE with transitives/unergatives, while third person plural subjects always require HAVE. In the pluperfect HAVE/BE are in free variation with all verb classes, whereas in the counterfactual HAVE and BE are contrasted according to an epistemic vs optative distinction (Ledgeway forthcoming, citing Loporcaro 1988). This is also the case in Trentino dialects like Valsuganotto in which all reflexives and first and second person singular subjects require BE while third person subjects take HAVE (Ledgeway 2012: 326, citing Loporcaro and Vigolo

Table 18.4. *Variable auxiliary selection (Loporcaro 2011a)*

	Unacc.	Reflexive				Trans./Unerg.
		Inherent	Dir. trans.	Indir. unerg.	Indir. trans.	
Mar.	BE				BE/HAVE	HAVE
Agn. A	BE			BE/HAVE		HAVE
Agn. B	BE				BE/HAVE	HAVE
Cvl.	BE		BE/HAVE			HAVE
Vals.	BE			BE/HAVE		HAVE

1995: 98), but unaccusatives and transitives behave differently, allowing only BE or HAVE, respectively, regardless of person:

(33) Valsuganotto
    a. Me **son** spaurá / zbará lavá (le man).
        me=am frightened / shot washed the hands
        'I got scared/shot myself/washed myself (my hands).'
    b. El s **a** spaurá / zbará lavá (le man).
        he SE=has frightened / shot washed the hands
        'He got scared/shot himself/washed himself (his hands).'

These patterns are partly summarized in Table 18.4 from Loporcaro (2011a).

Ledgeway (2000) notes further, that, in some varieties, auxiliary selection is also sensitive to tense/finiteness/mood (see, for example, Ledgeway 2003 on Neapolitan, and Ledgeway 2019; forthcoming). Space limitations preclude a full discussion of these facts here, but these factors have also been noted to influence case/agreement alignment in unrelated languages (see Tsunoda 1981; DeLancey 1981; Coon 2013). In this way too, then, the variation attested within Romance appears to mirror broader typological trends in certain respects but also presents new theoretical challenges given the level of complexity involved.

In sum, as Loporcaro (2011a) notes, alignment in Romance auxiliary selection is far from simple. Even languages such as Italian and French provide strong evidence for split-S alignments in Romance, and once we move beyond the standard Romance languages, auxiliary selection displays a vast array of variation which is reminiscent of broader typological patterns, but which also often exceeds many such systems in terms of complexity.

18.4 Past Participle Agreement

18.4.1 Frequent Patterns

Discussions of Romance active past participle agreement have often focused on standard French and Italian (see further the discussions in Sections 17.3.1, 17.4.1, and 21.1). In these two languages, the past participle can agree with S_O or O. In Italian, objects promoted to subject trigger agreement (regardless of their position), whereas objects can trigger agreement only when cliticized to a pre-verbal position:

(34)   **Italian**
    a.   Maria è partita/*-o.
        Maria is left.F/MSG
        'Mary has left.'
    b.   Maria è stata assunta/**-o.
        Maria is been.FSG hired.F/MSG
        'Mary has been hired.'
    c.   Li ho visti/**-o.
        them.MPL=have.1SG seen.MPL/MSG
        'I have seen them.'
    d.   Ci/vi ha viste/-i/-o.
        us/you.PL=has seen.FPL/MPL/MSG
        'S/he has seen us/you.'

As these examples illustrate, moreover, agreement with subjects is obligatory in Italian (34a–b). With clitics, agreement is obligatory with third person objects but optional otherwise and in decline, with non-agreement becoming the more frequent option (Belletti and Rizzi 1996; Ledgeway p.c.). French patterns minimally differently from standard Italian. First, French allows past participle agreement with objects promoted via wh-movement (in questions or relative clauses) (Obenauer 1994). Second, in French, past participle agreement with objects, with the HAVE verb is often not present in spoken/informal registers, whereas agreement with subjects, with the BE verb, is obligatory (as in Italian) (Blanche-Benveniste 2006; Belletti 2017).[4] As Stark (2018) notes, in spoken corpora, omission of agreement with subjects/BE is rare and often immediately corrected, whereas omission of agreement with objects/HAVE is more frequent and uncorrected:

(35)   **Spoken French (Stark 2018: 5)**
    a.   … c' est des choses qui qui seraient | _ | qui
        it is some things.FPL which which be.COND.3PL which
        seraient plus permis | euh plus permises
        be.COND.3PL more allowed.M er more allowed.FPL
        'These are things that would no longer be allowed, er no longer be allowed.'

---

[4] For reasons of parsimony, we are skipping over many important details here. Some of the most interesting work on French past participle agreement has focused on contexts where it is blocked. Kayne (1989), for example, notes that it is blocked in instances of wh-movement where an expletive subject intervenes:

    i.   Quelle chaleur atroce il a fait(*e)! (Fr.)
        what heat terrible it has done(.FSG)
        'What a terrible heat!'

b. ... j'avais   des   bottes   rouges aussi mon dieu je sais
       I had   some   boots.FPL red.FPL also my god I know
       même pas où   je les   ai   mis
       even not where I them=have   put.M
       'I also had some red boots, my God, I don't even know where I have put them.'

These basic patterns are another instance of split-S alignment in Romance, as S_O once again behaves like O and unlike S_A in triggering past participle agreement, though, in French and Italian, S_O triggers agreement obligatorily whereas O does so only in restricted contexts and subject to the idiosyncrasies just discussed.[5] A consideration of the patterns in Spanish and Portuguese, which have lost auxiliary BE with unaccusative verbs, suggests that past participle agreement with subjects is a distinct phenomenon from agreement with objects. In these languages, past participles agree with objects promoted to subject in passives only, but not elsewhere, suggesting that past participle agreement with subjects is mediated by the presence of the auxiliary BE.[6] In (non-Balearic) Catalan, however, which has also lost BE except in passives, we also find optional agreement with a subset of cliticized objects (Muxí 1995), suggesting that at least in some cases, S_O and O pattern together regardless of auxiliary selection. An additional problem is that there are a number of dialects of north-western Puglia and south-eastern Basilicata which use HAVE, alongside BE in specific contexts, as a passive auxiliary and yet still have participle agreement with passive HAVE (see Ledgeway 2021).

18.4.2 Rarer Patterns

In standard French and Catalan, then, only a subset of displaced objects trigger past participle agreement. Once again, a consideration of less well-studied varieties highlights that this is not the only possible pattern, however. In Altamurano and Occitan, for example, past participles agree also with in situ objects, something which is possible only in very formal registers of modern standard Italian (La Fauci and Rosen 2010):

---

[5] An additional idiosyncrasy concerns the fact that event indirect object clitics can trigger agreement in the absence of a direct object clitic. This is the rule in Italian, e.g., *si sono scritt**i*** lit. 'self= are written.MPL (they have written to one another)', and usually even in the presence of a non-cliticized direct object e.g., *Maria s'è lavat**a*** *le mani* lit. 'Maria self=is washed.FSG the.FPL hands.F' (Maria washed her hands)', although some speakers also accept here *lavat**e*** 'washed.FPL', but *Maria se le è lavat**e*** lit. 'Maria self= them.F= is washed.FPL (Maria washed them)'. In this way, past participle agreement can be said to allow either a secundative or indirective ditransitive alignment in typological terms (see Dryer 1986).

[6] Ledgeway suggests that this could actually be phrased in terms of a distinction between lexical unaccusatives vs derivational unaccusatives (passives).

(36) pəppɪn   a   ssølto /   **sseltə   la   šummwεnd. (Alt.)
    Peppino has released.F released.M the.FSG mare.F
    'Peppino let the mare loose.'

More surprisingly, in some Romance dialects, we even find agreement with A/S$_A$, something which is impossible in the standard Romance languages discussed above. For example, in eastern Abruzzese, the past participle agrees with any plural argument whether it is A/S$_A$ or O/S$_O$, as shown by the following examples from D'Alessandro and Roberts (2010: 45)

(37) **Arielli (eastern Abruzzo)**
   a. Giuwanne e   Mmarije a   **pittate/pittite   nu mure.
      Giovanni and Maria   have.3 painted.SG/PL   a   wall
      'Giovanni and Maria have painted a wall.'
   b. Giuwanne a   **pittate/pittite   ddu mure.
      Giovanni have.3 painted.SG/PL   two walls
      'Giovanni has painted two walls.'

While they often co-occur, this phenomenon is independent of the phenomenon of person-sensitive auxiliary selection (discussed above) (Manzini and Savoia 2005: ch. 5). In broader typological terms, this pattern of agreement is reminiscent of what is called *eccentric agreement* by Hale (2001) and *agreement displacement* by Béjar and Rezac (2009). This refers to contexts where agreement is determined by the features of both A and O. Indeed, theoretical accounts of this phenomenon, such as that proposed by D'Alessandro and Roberts (2010) often assimilate the two phenomena.

18.5 SE-Passives

Many Romance varieties have a periphrastic passive formed with an auxiliary verb (usually *be*) and a perfective participle (cf. Sections 19.4 and 27.2.3.3), as mentioned in Sections 18.3–4 (see 38b).[7] Even more widespread, however, is a passive formed with the clitic *se/si* (38a; cf. also Section 19.4.4).[8]

(38) **Spanish**
   a. Las casas   se   alquilaron (**por turistas)
      the houses.FPL   REFL=   rented.3PL by   tourists
   b. Las casas   fueron   alquiladas   (por turistas)
      the houses.FPL   were   rented.FPL   by   tourists
      'The houses were rented (by tourists).'

---

[7] There are many Romance varieties which lack a periphrastic passive, however (see Ledgeway 2021).
[8] This SE clitic is also used to mark reflexives, anticausatives, impersonals, and middles, but we abstract away from these other constructions here (see Schäfer 2017 for a comparison of these kinds of constructions).

The SE-passive generally disallows the expression of the demoted A argument, as shown in (38a), though overt by-phrases have been reported in SE-passives in Canadian French and Romanian as well as in some varieties of Italian and Spanish (Schäfer 2017 for discussion). Another property of SE-passives is that they are usually restricted to third person themes (D'Alessandro 2007). Old Romanian is an exception to this, however (see Zafiu et al. 2016).

In tensed clauses, SE occurs with all the major verb classes, even unaccusatives/raising verbs:

(39) **Italian (Cinque 1988: 522)**
    a.   Spesso si   arriva in ritardo.
          often   REFL=arrived in lateness
          'Often one arrives late.'
    b.   Spesso si   risulta non essere in regola.
          often   REFL=results NEG be.INF in order
          'One often turns out not to be in order.'

As noted by Burzio (1986), and discussed at length by Cinque (1988), however, in Italian, SE-passives are not possible in non-finite control clauses, in contrast with periphrastic passives:

(40) **Italian (Cinque 1988: 523 n. 5)**
    a.   **Loro vorrebbero   [[invitarsi]].
          they want.COND.3PL invite.INF=REFL
    b.   Loro vorrebbero [[essere invitati]].
          they want.COND.3PL be.INF invited.MPL
          'They would like to be invited.'

Under raising verbs, on the other hand another instance of split-S alignment surfaces: SE-passives in this context are possible only with transitive/unergative verbs:[9]

(41) **Italian (Cinque 1988: 525)**
    a.   Sembra non essersi   ancora scoperto il vero colpevole.
          seems NEG be.INF=REFL yet   discovered the true culprit
          'The true culprit seems not to have been discovered yet.'
    b.   Sembra non essersi   lavorato a sufficienza.
          seems NEG be.INF=REFL worked at sufficiency
          'There doesn't seem to have been sufficient work done.'
    c.   **Sembra essersi   arrivati troppo tardi.
          seems be.INF=SE arrived too   late

As Cinque notes, this split-S alignment is common for periphrastic passives, being observed in German, Dutch, and French, for example. In Italian,

---

[9] Note also that SE-passives become acceptable in non-finite contexts where they have a middle-type (generic) reading. Cinque shows this middle construction to have different properties from the SE-passive.

French, and Spanish, SE-passives thus display a split-S alignment, limited to a specific domain. European Portuguese displays a different pattern, as Cinque (1988: 532) observes, probably because it has inflected infinitives:

(42) Parece ter-se chegado. (EuPt.)
    seems have=REFL arrived
    'Someone seems to have arrived.'

Romanian is also different. As Dobrovie-Sorin (1988) shows, SE can occur only with unergative verbs in Romanian:

(43) **Romanian (Dobrovie-Sorin 1988: 405)**
  a. **Nu se este niciodată mulțumit
     NEG REFL= is never satisfied
     'One is never satisfied'
  b. Nu se poate dormi cu atâta zgomot.
     NEG REFL= can sleep with so.much noise
     'No-one cannot sleep with so much noise.'

In addition to SE-passives, in which the verb agrees with a promoted O argument, some Romance languages also have impersonal SE constructions which involve default third singular agreement with different properties (see D'Alessandro 2007 for discussion).

18.6 Word Order

Basic word order in null subject Romance languages such as Spanish, European Portuguese, Romanian, and Italian remains controversial. This is true mainly because these Romance null subject languages use word order to encode information structure in subtly different ways (see, amongst many others, Belletti and Shlonsky 1995; Zubizarreta 1998; Belletti 2004; Cruschina 2012; and Chapter 26, this volume). What is of relevance to alignment, however, is the basic word order attested with intransitive predicates in out-of-the-blue contexts. Whereas the majority of unergative verbs require SV order in this context, most unaccusative verbs permit also VS order (free inversion):

(44) **European Portuguese**
  a. O que é que foi?
     the what is that was?
     'What happened?'
  b. Chegou alguém.
     arrived someone
     'Someone has arrived.'
  c. #Dançou alguém.
     Danced someone
     'Someone has been dancing.'

It has long been pointed out, however, that the availability of free inversion does not really track the unergative/unaccusative divide. Or, put more neutrally, the split-intransitivity attested in relation to word order is a different split than that attested with other grammatical phenomena (see Baker 2018 for the claim that this is true more generally of unaccusativity diagnostics). In Italian, for example, there are unergative verbs which permit free inversion (45) as well as unaccusative verbs which disallow it (46), and the same is true of Spanish and Portuguese (Benincà 1988; Pinto 1997; Corr 2016; Bentley and Cruschina 2018).

(45) **Italian (Benincà 1988)**
    a.   Ha   telefonato Maria.
          has   phoned   Maria
          'Maria has phoned (here/us).'
    b.   Ha   bussato il   postino.
          has   knocked the postman
          'The postman has knocked (here/at our door).'

(46) **Italian (Pinto 1997: 21)**
    a.   [Che è successo?]   #È   impallidito Berlusconi.
          what is happened   is   turned.pale Berlusconi
          ['What happened?'] 'Berlusconi has turned pale.'
    b.   [Che è successo?]   #Si   è   stufata Penelope.
          what is happened   REFL is bored   Penelope
          [What happened?] 'Penelope has got bored.'

Pinto claims that the relevant factor here is the possibility of a covert deictic argument oriented towards the speaker (see also Sheehan 2010; Corr 2016), but Bentley and Cruschina (2018) point out some empirical challenges for this proposal:

(47)   [Che è successo?] È morto uno sconosciuto. (It.)
        what is happened is died   an   unknown
        ['What happened?'] 'An unknown person has died.'

It is not clear how (47) can be oriented to the speaker. It therefore remains unclear what exactly determines the possibility of verb–subject word order in out-of-the-blue contexts in Romance, but this is not straightforwardly tied to the S_A/S_O distinction (see Bentley and Cruschina 2018 for a novel proposal).

18.7 Other Phenomena

18.7.1 INDE-Cliticization
Another property which displays a sensitivity to split-intransivity is INDE-cliticization. Italian, Catalan, and French all retain a partitive clitic deriving

from INDE which usually indexes only O arguments. Languages such as Spanish and Portuguese no longer have such a clitic. As is to be expected, with intransitive verbs, indexing of S_O is possible, whereas indexing of S_A is generally not:

(48) **Italian (Perlmutter 1989: 72–74)**
    a. Giorgio ne ha comprate due.
         Giorgio NE= has bought.FPL two
         'Giorgio bought two of them.'
    b. Ne sono cadute due.
         NE have fallen two
         'Two of them fell.'
    c. **?Ne hanno gridato due.
         NE have.3PL shouted two
         'Two of them shouted.'

As Perlmutter (1989: 75) notes, however, this is not a diagnostic of thematic objecthood, but rather of grammatical objecthood. In causative constructions, external S_A arguments of unergatives can undergo INDE-cliticization onto the higher causative (or perception) verb:

(49)   Ne farò gridare due. (It.)
      NE make.FUT.1SG shout.INF two
      'I will make two (of them) shout.'

It has also been noted, moreover, that in Italian at least, not all reflexive verbs permit INDE-cliticization, despite requiring BE (Cinque 1988: 576 n. 62):

(50)   **Non se ne spaventano troppi, di bambini, qui. (It.)
      NEG SE= NE= frighten.3PL too.many of children here
      'Not too many get frightened, of the children, here.'

This suggests that INDE-cliticization, while it often aligns with other split-S phenomena, is not actually tracking the S_A/S_O distinction.

18.7.2 Absolute Participles and Participial Adjectives

Another aspect of Italian grammar which displays a split-S alignment is the use of participles. Both participial absolutes and participial adjectives can be formed only with transitive or unaccusative verbs and not with unergatives:

(51) **Italian (Perlmutter 1989: 67–69)**
    a. Perduti i soldi, Giorgio cercava mezzi di sussistenza.
         lost the money Giorgio searched means of subsistence
         'Having lost his money, Giorgio was looking for some means of subsistence.'
    b. Uscite le donne, gli uomini hanno cominciato a discuterne.
         left the women, the men have started to discuss=NE
         'With the women gone, the men began to discuss them.'
    c. **Starnutito all'improvviso, Giorgio non sapeva cosa fare
         sneezed unexpectedly, Giorgio NEG knew what do.INF

(52) a. Le arance mangiate dai bambini.
       the oranges eaten.FPL by.the children
       'The oranges eaten by the children.'
   b. Le persone rimaste sono tutte ubriache.
       the people remained are all drunk
       'The people who remained are all drunk.'
   c. **Le persone parlate
       the people spoken

Note that reflexives have been claimed to behave like unergatives on the second of these diagnostics (Siloni 2008):

(53) **I ragazzi baciatisi ieri sono miei alunni. (It.)
     the children kissed=SE yesterday are my pupils

Again, evidence from causatives shows that this is not wholly determined by thematic roles, however, as a participial absolute can be formed on an S_A argument in this context:

(54) Fatto parlare Nino, ... (It.; Davies and Rosen 1988)
     made speak Nino
     'Nino having been made to speak, ...'

Once again, then, this shows that what is relevant here is not thematic status as O, but rather a derivational notion of grammatical objecthood.

18.8 Conclusion

In this chapter, we have discussed the different manifestations of alignment in Romance. It has been our aim to pinpoint that, both diachronically and synchronically, Romance languages make a significant contribution to our understanding of alignment from a broader cross-linguistic perspective. What emerges is the overwhelming diversity of alignment in Romance varieties, once we look beyond case/verbal agreement and particularly once we consider non-standard dialects and how they confirm that multiple alignment types can be manifest in a single language.

Selected References

Below you can find selected references for this chapter. The full references can be found online at the following page: www.cambridge.org/Romancelinguistics

Alboiu, G., Barrie, M., and Frigeni, C. (2004). 'SE and the unaccusative-unergative paradox'. In Coene, M., de Cuyper, G., and D'Hulst, Y. (eds), *Antwerp Working Papers in Linguistics: Current Studies in Comparative Romance Linguistics* 107: 109–39.

Cennamo, M. (2000). 'Patterns of active syntax in late Latin pleonastic reflexives'. In Smith, J. C. and Bentley, D. (eds), *Historical Linguistics 1995: Selected Papers from the 12th International Conference on Historical Linguistics*. Amsterdam: Benjamins, 35–56.

Cinque, G. (1988). 'On *si* constructions and the theory of *arb*', *Linguistic Inquiry* 19: 521–81.

D'Alessandro, R. and Roberts, I. (2010). 'Past participle agreement in Abruzzese: split auxiliary selection and the null-subject parameter', *Natural Language & Linguistic Theory* 28: 41–72.

Gianollo, C. (2010). 'I verbi deponenti latini e l'unità della flessione in *-r*'. *Incontri Triestini di Filologia Classica VIII, 2008–09*. Trieste: Edizioni Università di Trieste, 23–49.

Ledgeway, A. (2012). *From Latin to Romance. Morphosyntactic Typology and Challenge*. Oxford: Oxford University Press.

Loporcaro, M. (2007). 'On triple auxiliation in Romance'. *Linguistics* 45: 173–222.

Migliori, L. (2016). *Argument Structure, Alignment and Auxiliaries between Latin and Romance. A Diachronic Syntactic Account*. Utrecht: LOT.

Perlmutter, D. (1989). 'Multiattachment and the Unaccusative Hypothesis: the perfect auxiliary in Italian', *Probus* 1: 63–119.

Pinto, M. (1997). *Licensing and Interpretation of Inverted Subjects in Italian*. UiL OTS Dissertation Series. Utrecht: LED.

Sorace, A. (2000). 'Gradients in auxiliary selection with intransitive verbs', *Language* 76: 859–90.

Vincent, N. (1982). 'The development of the auxiliaries *habere* and *esse* in Romance'. In Vincent, N. and Harris, M. (eds), *Studies in the Romance Verb*. London: Croom Helm, 71–96.

19

Complex Predicates

Adina Dragomirescu, Alexandru Nicolae,
and Gabriela Pană Dindelegan

19.1 Outline and Scope

This chapter first discusses the various meanings associated with the concept of 'complex predicate' and sets up a battery of reliable syntactic diagnostics for the identification of a complex predicate, which will be invoked throughout the analysis of the Romance empirical data.

We then address the shift from Latin syntheticity to the greater analyticity of the Romance languages, one of the most striking developments of which in the verbal domain is the emergence and subsequent profusion of a whole series of periphrastic verb constructions, which often add to and complement the older synthetic structures inherited from Latin to offer explicit marking of categories which were previously not distinctly marked, e.g., synthetic FECI 'do.PST.PFV.1SG (= I did)' > Ro. *făcui* alongside analytic *am făcut* 'have.PRS.1SG do.PTCP (= I did/have done)'; synthetic SCRIBO 'write.PRS.IND.1SG (= I write/am writing)' > It. *scrivo* 'I write/am writing' alongside *sto scrivendo* 'stand.PRS.IND.1SG write.GER (= I am writing)'. The transition from the morphologically oriented structures of Latin to the increasingly syntactically oriented structures of Romance (Ledgeway 2012: 11) involves the grammaticalization of verbs such as HAVE, BE, WANT, OWE, COME, GO, MAKE, HOLD, STAND, FOLLOW, and the transfer of many inflexional categories from the lexical verb to the auxiliary/first component of the monoclausal complex predicate.

Taking stock of the set of syntactic diagnostics used to classify a given structure as a complex predicate, we turn to the analysis of the Romance facts, which are extremely well documented both in diachrony and in synchrony, and which can be used as a series of fruitful case studies to throw light on the diachronic and synchronic relationship between inflexion and periphrasis from a wider cross-linguistic perspective.

19.2 Delimitations and Diagnostics

19.2.1 What Is a Complex Predicate?

A large set of constructions with distinct properties has been considered to constitute complex predicates, this notion often being applied in a vague and underspecified manner. In a very broad sense, any predicate structure that 'consists of more than one piece is complex' (Svenonius 2008: 47). Under this broad understanding, even auxiliary-verb constructions have been included in the class of complex predicates (Abeillé and Godard 2002; 2003; Müller 2006; 'verbal complex' in Monachesi 2005), a fact which, in a certain respect, captures the intuition that Romance auxiliaries represent a heterogeneous set of elements, which share fewer morphosyntactic properties than do English or other Germanic auxiliaries (Green 1987: 257; Ledgeway 2012: 119).

A coarser definition restricts the notion of complex predicate to constructions based on restructuring (Rizzi 1978) – defined in Cardinaletti and Shlonsky (2004: 524) as an operation by which 'the scope of operations associated with a lower predicate [cliticization, auxiliary selection] is extended to the domain of a higher predicate' – and other related constructions such as: periphrastic causatives, verb–particle constructions, resultatives, *consider* + predicate combinations (in Amberber, Baker, and Harvey 2010), along with serial verb constructions and light verb constructions (in Svenonius 2008), and constructions with motion verbs, copula verbs, and perception verbs (in Abeillé and Godard 2002: 404; 2003: 125–27).

The common intuition, to which we return below, is that complex predicates are monoclausal, this property variously being obtained either via clause union (Aissen and Perlmutter 1976) or restructuring (Rizzi 1978; 1982), i.e., as an operation by which an underlying biclausal structure becomes a simple sentence (cf. also Pesetsky 2019 in this respect), or via direct selection of a complement of a smaller size than a CP (Wurmbrand 2001).

Other authors stress the fact that, monoclausality notwithstanding, there are subtler differences between different types of complex predicates. In Baker and Harvey (2010), there are two types of complex predicate, distinguished on the basis of the relation established between the component units: complex predicates based on *merger* (the units share conceptual structure), the result being a predicate structure 'whose range classes with the range of predicate structures found in monomorphemic predicates' (Baker and Harvey 2010: 13; cf. also Sheehan 2016: 981 on Romance causatives) and complex predicates based on *coindexation*, an operation which extends the conceptual structure of the predicate (e.g., perception verbs and *faire*–infinitive verbs, which do not obey the condition of the unique argument structure, Labelle 2017).

This chapter adopts a broad notion of complex predicates and focuses on monoclausal periphrases whose component units are verbal in nature. Examples of particular interest include auxiliary-verb constructions (passive periphrases, resultative perfects, periphrastic futures and conditionals) and monoclausal constructions with aspectual, modal, causative, and perception verbs, typically complemented by a non-finite form.

19.2.2 Diagnosing Monoclausality

From a formal perspective, the monoclausal nature of the complex predicate ensures that its components share one single extended projection, a property which derives the syntactic diagnostics variously proposed in the literature. The complex nature of these formations, in conjunction with monoclausality, explains why, in some aspects, complex predicates pattern with prototypical words, but in others, with prototypical phrases (Amberber, Baker, and Harvey 2010: 3); however, from a narrow syntactic perspective, only one of the component verbs, the bearer of TAM[1] (and phi-feature) information, serves as a syntactic head of the complex predicate (Svenonius 2008: 55).

The following linguistic phenomena have been generally used to diagnose monoclausality:

(i) negation expressed exclusively on the higher head and disallowed in the embedded domain, illustrated with an Ibero-Romance aspectual periphrasis (Ledgeway 2012: 127):

(1) O   seu   país   non   está (**non) buscando construir
    the   his   country   not   is   not   seeking   build.INF
    unha   bomba   nuclear. (Glc.)
    a   bomb   nuclear
    'His country is not trying to build a nuclear bomb.'

(ii) clitic climbing, illustrated with a Fr. *faire*–infinitive construction (Abeillé, Godard, and Sag 1998: 2; cf. also Section 20.4.2):

(2)   Paul le   fera   lire   aux   élèves
      Paul 3MSG.ACC=   make.FUT.3SG   read.INF   to.the   students
      de terminale. (Fr.)
      of sixth.form
      'Paul will make the sixth-form students read it.'

---

[1] With certain periphrastic formations, TAM marking is shared between the two components; for example, in active HAVE/ BE + participle constructions, aspect is formally marked on the participle; however, the auxiliary, which is the head of the formation from a narrow syntactic perspective, bears most of the grammatical information, marking, among other things, mood, tense, and phi-feature values.

(iii) *se/si*-passive adjoined to the higher head (Burzio 1986), illustrated with a Romanian 'semi-auxiliary' modal configuration (Guţu Romalo 2005):

(3) Romanele nu se pot scrie
 novels.DEF not PASS=can.IND.PRS.3PL write.INF
 peste noapte. (Ro.)
 over night
 'Novels cannot be written overnight.'

(iv) in certain languages the choice of perfective auxiliary of the lower verb is determined by the argument structure of the higher verb; e.g., in Italian, both in a prototypical restructuring configuration (4a), and in a compound passive (4b), the selection of auxiliary BE is determined by the unaccusative nature of *andare* 'go' and *stata* 'been' (Frank 1996):

(4) a. Mario ci sarebbe proprio voluto andare. (It.)
 Mario there be.COND.3SG really want.PTCP go.INF
 'Mario would have really wanted to go there.'
 b. Maria è stata accusata. (It.)
 Maria be.AUX.PASS be.PTCP.FSG accuse.PTCP.FSG
 'Maria has been accused.'

Other phenomena taken to be sensitive to complex predicate formation (e.g., past participle agreement, reflexivization) are tied to more particular language-specific rules and cannot be taken as general tests of complex predicate formation (this is also the case of auxiliary selection, discussed above). It is also important to highlight that there are numerous structures which, despite showing a certain degree of cohesion, do not make up complex predicates, but rather admit a biclausal analysis: Romanian causatives, modals, and perception verbs followed by the subjunctive, certain Spanish verbal periphrases, and future periphrases of the Fr. *aller* 'go' type or Ro. future *o* + subjunctive are all constructions in which clitic climbing, one of the characteristic signatures of monoclausality (but cf. Cinque 2004), does not apply (Abeillé and Godard 2003: 125–27). The question of which combination permits or requires clitic climbing is also subject to variation in Romance, with particular language-specific and construction-specific options (e.g., clitic climbing occurs in French with causatives and perception verbs, but not with other classes of verbs) (Legendre 2007: 294). Furthermore, Cinque (2004) stresses the fact that a given verb may be associated with two distinct syntactic configurations in the very same language: witness (5) below, where It. *volere* 'want' may occur both in a restructuring (5a) and a non-restructuring (5b) configuration, as testified by the presence (5a) or absence (5b) of clitic climbing.

(5) a. Lo   volevo   [vedere subito]. (It.)
        3MSG.ACC=want.IPF.1SG see.INF immediately
        'I wanted to see it immediately.'
     b. Maria vorrebbe   già   averlo
        Maria want.COND.3SG already have.INF=3MSG.ACC
        già   lasciato. (It.)
        already left.
        'Mary would already want to have already left it.'
     b.' **Maria lo   vorrebbe   già   aver
        Maria 3MSG.ACC=want.COND.3SG already have.INF
        già   lasciato. (It.)
        already left.

When restructuring/complex predicate formation does not apply, the properties of the lower verb do not extend to the higher verb; for example, only when clitic climbing applies does the higher verb reflect the auxiliary selection properties of the lower verb (compare 6a and 6b) (Burzio 1986; Frank 1996). There are, of course, notable and important exceptions, e.g., *andare/venire* 'go/come' always take auxiliary BE, while *finire/cominciare* 'finish/start' always take the auxiliary HAVE irrespective of clitic climbing (Adam Ledgeway, p.c.).

(6) a. I   ragazzi si   sarebbero   voluti   vedere
        the children REFL=be.COND.3PL want.PTCP.PL see.INF
        più   spesso. (It.)
        more often
     b. I   ragazzi avrebbero   voluto   vedersi
        the children have.COND.3PL want.PTCP see.INF=REFL
        più   spesso. (It.)
        more often
        'The children would have wanted to see each other more often.'

Last but not least, while auxiliary-verb constructions and other monoclausal constructions have in common two of the core features which identify a complex predicate (clitic climbing and negation on the first verb), they exhibit major differences with respect to other important features; the review in Ledgeway (2012: 119–50) is summarized in Table 19.1:

Table 19.1. *Auxiliary-verb constructions vs other monoclausal constructions*

auxiliary-verb constructions	other monoclausal constructions
morphophonological reduction	–
adjacency (excl. Fr)	no obligatory adjacency
clitic forms	the same form as the lexical verb
no VP-ellipsis	VP ellipsis
no stress	stress (in answers)

19.3 Auxiliaries

19.3.1 Introduction

In auxiliary-verb constructions, also labelled 'verbal complexes' (Ramat 1987; Monachesi 2005), the auxiliary is the bearer of TAM information, and the argument structure of the entire complex is that of the lexical verb. In contrast to Latin, where only the perfect passive and (semi-)deponent auxiliary ESSE 'be' is systematically used (see Ledgeway 2012: 34 n. 9 on the apparent auxiliary usage of other verbs, e.g., UELLE 'want', POSSE 'can', DEBERE 'must'), the Romance languages are characterized by a profusion of analytic, auxiliary-based constructions which replace or often add to and complement the existing synthetic structures (Green 1987: 263; Ledgeway 2012: 11, 33), an empirical development reflecting the emergence of (a) dedicated structural position(s) hosting auxiliaries to the left of the VP (Ledgeway 2012: 33; 2017). A significant number of originally lexical verbs develop into a wide range of auxiliaries, following the parameters generally underlying such processes of grammaticalization: phonetic attrition, morphological specialization, morphosyntactic decategorialization, and semantic bleaching. The emergence of auxiliaries also triggers a redistribution in the marking of grammatical values (Vincent 1987; Danckaert 2016: 132), i.e., large-scale transfer of many inflexional categories from the lexical verb to the auxiliary (Ledgeway 2012: 119).

19.3.2 Auxiliary-Verb Constructions Based on HABERE 'Have'

The Latin verb HABERE underwent multiple grammaticalization paths, the most productive and best studied of which is the compound past, a pan-Romance development. The emergence of the HABERE periphrases (the compound past and the doubly compound structures, the future, and the conditional) occurred at different moments in the Latin-to-Romance transition, or even within the history of the Romance languages themselves.

The literature documents two main points of view with respect to the emergence of the HABERE compound past: some authors (Thielmann 1885; Benveniste 1962; Harris 1982; Salvi 1987; Pinkster 1987) consider that it developed in late Latin, while others (Ledgeway 2012; Adams 2013; Roberts 2013; Haverling 2016; Legendre 2017) argue that it is a Romance-specific development. The latter represents the more plausible scenario; Adams (2013: 646) stresses the fact that Latin periphrases which on the surface look like perfects are open to interpretations in which HABERE has full lexical value, hence there is a long period of ambiguity before grammaticalization took place. Also relevant in this respect is the fact that HABERE did not have a fixed position but could either precede or follow the participle and complements could also intervene between the auxiliary and the participle in early Romance – e.g., old French (Buridant 2000: 375–77), early Italian (Rohlfs 1969: 330), and even sixteenth- and seventeenth-century Romanian (Nicolae 2019).

The emergence of the Romance compound past has been traced back to the reanalysis of an originally resultative aspectual periphrasis (7a) as a present perfective periphrasis (7b) (details below) (Ledgeway 2012: 130; Haverling 2016: 200).

(7) a. [VP [THEME [LOC in ea prouincia] pecunias magnas
                in that province.ABL money.ACC.FPL big.ACC.FPL
    [AP collocatas]] habent] (Lat., Cic. Leg. Man. 18; in Ledgeway 2012: 130)
    placed.ACC.FPL have.IND.PRS.3PL
    'they have large sums invested in that province'
  b. [IP [VP [LOC in ea prouincia] [THEME pecunias
             in that province.ABL money.ACC.FPL
    magnas] collocatas] habent]
    big.ACC.FPL placed.ACC.FPL have.IND.PRS.3PL
    'they have invested large sums in that province'

The Romance developments do not immediately replace the Latin synthetic perfect; and still today in many parts of the Romània the synthetic perfect is very strong, unlike its compound competitor, e.g., in large parts of Spanish and Portuguese-speaking Latin America, European Portuguese, southern Calabria, and Sicily; rather, the periphrasis acquired new values, ranging from present resultative (8) and iterative (9), and canonical present perfect (10) to punctual perfective (11), all variously preserved in different diachronic and diatopic Romance varieties (Harris 1982; Salvi 1987; Squartini and Bertinetto 2000; Adams 2013; examples compiled by Ledgeway 2012).

(8) Non m' ha chiamatu. (SCal., in Alfonzetti 1998)
    not me=has.AUX.PST.3SG call.PTCP
    'I don't know what's happened to him' [because he hasn't rung me]

(9) Aquí también ha hecho frô. (Pal., in Leal Cruz 2003: 132)
    here too it.has.AUX.PST do.PTCP cold
    'Here too it continues to be cold.'

(10) Siempre la he escuchado con atención,
     always 3FSG.ACC= have.AUX.PST.1SG listen.to.PTCP with attention
     pero nunca más. (EuSp., in Penny 2000: 159)
     but never more
     'I have always listened to her attentively, but never again.'

(11) La France a   déclaré   la guerre en 1939. (spoken Fr.)
     the France has.AUX.PST.3SG declare.PTCP the war in 1939
     'France declared war in 1939.'

There are two main factors which favoured the grammaticalization of HABERE as a perfective auxiliary: semantic bleaching of HABERE, from expressing an action with a durative value (initially a near synonym of TENERE 'keep') to expressing a relation, i.e., possession (Salvi 1987: 229); and subject coreference between the locative subject of HABERE and the agentive/experiencer subject of the participle, causing the subject of transitive and unergative participles to be reanalysed as the subject of the entire structure (Ledgeway 2012: 131f.) (unaccusatives and passives occur with ESSE 'be', see Sections 19.3.3, 19.4). With HABERE losing the ability to host its own thematic subject, the argument structure of the participle is extended to the entire construction (the *Heir-Apparent Principle* of Harris and Campbell 1995); the participle becomes the lexical head of the extended projection of the simplified structure, and thematically empty HABERE becomes a placeholder for the mood and tense values of the entire construction. From a strictly syntactic point of view, one of the crucial steps in the development of the compound past is structural simplification (Roberts 2013), i.e., the removal of the thematic subject of HABERE.

Furthermore, in late Latin and in Romance there emerges an entirely new system for the future and the conditional, based on Latin periphrases involving the infinitive and the present indicative of HABERE (CANTARE HABEO 'sing.INF have.PRS.1SG', which gave rise to the Romance inflexional future Fr. *chanterai*, It. *canterò*, Sp. *cantaré* 'I will sing') and the infinitive and the imperfect of HABERE (CANTARE HABEBAM 'sing.INF have.PST.IPFV.1SG', which is the origin of the Romance conditional: Fr. *chanterais*, Sp. *cantaría*) and, more rarely, the perfect of HABERE (CANTARE HABUI 'sing.INF have. PFV.1SG' yielding the Tuscan/modern Italian conditional *canterei* 'I would sing') (Pinkster 1987: 25f.; Vincent 1987: 245f.). The grammaticalization process involving futures and conditionals is radically different from that leading to compound past forms in two respects: first it emerged much earlier[2] from structures where HABERE is placed after the lexical verb (as it reflects a head-final ordering, this was taken as evidence for the claim that future and conditional auxiliaries grammaticalized earlier than compound past auxiliaries, see Adams 1991; Ledgeway 2012: 33 n. 7),[3] and, secondly, the final result is a novel synthetic form (in contrast to the compound past,

---

[2] Cf. also the controversial example involving DARAS 'you will give' (juxtaposed to NON DABO 'I will not give') in seventh-century Fredegarius, identified by Krusch (1888: 85) (see Alkire and Rosen 2010: 165).

[3] Cf. early examples such as (i) given in Adams (1991: 148–54), ambiguous between possibility and futurity:

(i) si enim sustuleris istam tertiam, remanere habent duae (Pompeius 129.26)
     'For if you take away the third [last syllable], two [syllables] will have to remain.'

which remained an analytic form all over Romance). The 'new' synthetic future emerged in all the Romance varieties, except Sardinian, Romanian, and Dalmatian (Ledgeway 2012: 134f.).

Moreover, periphrastic future forms, which already existed in Latin from the classical period (Pinkster 1987: 211) are attested in all the Romance languages. Sometimes, they are based on the auxiliary 'have', as in Abruzzese (*ajja cantà, hî da cantà, a da cantà, avem a cantà, avet a cantà, anno da cantà* – Ledgeway 2012: 135) and in Romanian (*am să cânt, ai să cânți, are să cânte, avem să cântăm, aveți să cântați, au să cânte* 'have.IND.PRS.1SG-3PL COMP.SBJV sing.SBJV.1SG-3PL'). However, these periphrastic formations do not show the same degree of morphosyntactic cohesion as analytic formations of the compound past type; for example, the Romanian HAVE-future behaves incongruously with respect to the monoclausality diagnostics in that the clausal negator surfaces on the higher verb, HAVE (12a), while clitic climbing is impossible with the clitic surfacing in the domain of the lower verb (12b); furthermore, periphrastic formations based on the past imperfect of HAVE with a future in the past interpretation are also possible (13) (Zafiu 2013: 40f.).

(12) a. Nu am să (**nu) cânt. (Ro.)
    not have.IND.PRS.1SG COMP.SBJV not sing.PRS.1SG
    'I'm not going to sing.'
  b. (**L-)am să-l cânt. (Ro.)
    it=have.IND.PRS.1SG COMP.SBJV=3MSG.ACC sing.PRS.1SG
    'I'm going to sing it.'

(13) Aveam să cânt. (Ro.)
    have.IND.PST.IPFV.1SG COMP.SBJV sing.PRS.1SG
    'I was going to sing.'

19.3.3 Auxiliary-Verb Constructions Based on ESSE 'Be'

Although the grammaticalization of ESSE had been under way since Latin (when it was used as a perfective passive and as a periphrastic future auxiliary, Green 1987: 259f.), the paths taken by ESSE in Romance are less numerous than those involving HABERE (for the Romance analytic passive, see Section 19.4). On the one hand, verbs semantically incompatible with HABERE, i.e., unaccusatives, were absorbed into the ESSE perfective periphrasis for (semi-)deponents and passives (Aranovich 2009: 21), with which they have in common their co-occurrence of an Undergoer subject (Ledgeway 2012: 133), a construction such as LAPSUS SUM (lit. slipped I.am, 'I have slipped') being constructed on the model of the passive AMATUS SUM (lit. loved I.am, 'I have been loved') (Burton 2016: 165). These facts gave way to the well-known phenomenon of auxiliary selection in Romance varieties such as Italian (Burzio 1981; Centineo 1986; Van Valin 1987),

French (Sorace 2000; 2004), old Spanish (Lamiroy 1999; Mackenzie 2006; Stolova 2006), and old Romanian (Dragomirescu and Nicolae 2013); this includes mixed systems which appear to illustrate the gradual phasing out of the proto-Romance active/inactive alignment and the return to the nominative/accusative alignment (Loporcaro 2007: 173–85). On the other hand, in a language such as Romanian, the auxiliary 'be' grammaticalized as an irrealis marker (Avram and Hill 2007), which occurs in the structure of the perfect subjunctive (*să fi citit* COMP.SBJV be.IRREALIS read.PTCP 'should have read'), the perfect conditional (*aş fi citit* AUX.COND.3SG/PL be.IRREALIS read.PTCP 'I would have read'), the future perfect (*voi fi citit* AUX.FUT.1SG be.IRREALIS read.PTCP 'I will have read'), the perfect infinitive (*înainte de a fi vorbit* before of to be.IRREALIS talk.PTCP 'before I/you etc. would have talked'), and the presumptive (*voi fi citind* AUX.FUT.1SG be.IRREALIS read.GER 'I would be reading').

19.3.4 Auxiliary-Verb Constructions Based on Other Verbs

Except for the analytic forms with HABERE (Section 19.3.2), other future periphrases are based on proto-Romance *voˈlere 'want' (Ro. *voi cânta, vei cânta, va cânta, vom cânta, veţi cânta, vor cânta*; Friulian, southern Italian dialects), UENIRE (AD) 'come to' (Srs. *vegnel a cantar, vegns a cantar, vegn a cantar, vegnin a cantar, vegnis a cantar, vegnen a cantar*), DEBERE 'owe; must' (in Sardinian), IRE/AMBULARE/VADERE 'go' (Sp. *voy a cantar, vas a cantar, va a cantar, vamos a cantar, vais a cantar, van a cantar*; and in French, Occitan, and (Brazilian) Portuguese) (Ledgeway 2012: 122–24, 134f.).

Other verbs enter periphrases expressing different temporal and aspectual values (Green 1987: 259f.; Ledgeway 2012: 122–24, 134f.; 2017: 847): UENIRE 'come' expresses different values, from iterative aspect (14a) to past tense (14b), while TENERE 'hold, keep' expresses iterative aspect (14c) or the present perfect (14d); STARE 'stand' and SEDERE 'sit', along with ESSE, may occur in passive, progressive, and present perfect periphrases (see Section 19.4.5).

(14) a. L' ai tornat a veire. (Lgd., in Ledgeway 2012: 122)
3MSG=have.AUX.PST.1SG returned to see.INF
'I saw him again.'
b. Vaig anar al mercat
go.AUX.PST.1SG go.INF to.the market
ahir. (Cat., in Ledgeway 2012: 123)
yesterday
'I went to the market yesterday.'
c. Lo tenh de velhat (Occ., in Ledgeway 2012: 123)
3MSGACC=hold.AUX.PRS.3SG of watched
'She keeps watching him.'

d. El ga invecià tanto. (Ven., in Ledgeway 2012: 123)
     he have.AUX.PST.3SG aged a.lot
     'He has aged considerably.'

Many of the periphrastic structures occurring in Romance (e.g., the *vo'lere, TENERE, and STARE periphrases) do not have forerunners in Latin texts (Pinkster 1987: 195, 211).

19.3.5 TAM Make-up of Auxiliaries

Cross-Romance comparative considerations indicate that the division of labour in the marking of TAM categories in the analytic cluster varies across the Romance languages, and that the degree of the morphological richness of a given auxiliary differs from one Romance variety to another (Giacalone Ramat 2000: 125; Nicolae 2015: 82–84; 2019: 31f., cf. also Fleischman 1983: 183). Consider, for example, the contrast between the analytic paradigms with the grammaticalized descendants of HABERE in (standard) French (15) and (standard) Romanian (16).

(15) a. J'ai mangé (Fr.)
        I.have.IND.PRS.1SG eat.PTCP
        'I have eaten/I ate'
     b. J'avais mangé (Fr.)
        I.have.IND.IPF.1SG eat.PTCP
        'I had eaten'
     c. J'aurai mangé (Fr.)
        I.have.IND.FUT.1SG eat.PTCP
        'I will have eaten'
     d. (que) j'aie mangé (Fr.)
        that I.have.SBJV.PRS.1SG eat.PTCP
        '(that) I have eaten'
     e. J'aurais mangé (Fr.)
        I.have.COND.1SG eat.PTCP
        'I would have eaten'

(16) Eu am mâncat (Ro.)
     I have.IND.PRS.1SG eat.PTCP
     'I have eaten/I ate'

The contrast in (15)–(16) reveals that Romanian HAVE is unable to undergo tense variation (Dobrovie-Sorin 1994; Avram and Hill 2007; Giurgea 2011; Nicolae 2015), but does, however, possess an unambiguous mood specification (indicative), while its French counterpart undergoes tense, mood, and aspect variation. Thus, Romanian auxiliaries are mood-oriented, while French auxiliaries are tense-oriented (also marking mood and aspect values), a microparametric distinction which also accounts for the distinct nature of the multiple-auxiliary paradigms in these two languages: Romanian possesses multiple auxiliary structures in which auxiliaries encode mood-oriented information (17) (indicative/conditional and irrealis), while in French doubly compound structures auxiliaries have tense-oriented values (18).

(17) Voi / Aş fi trimis (Ro.)
AUX.FUT.1SG AUX.COND.1SG be.IRREALIS≡INF send.PTCP
'I will / would have sent'

(18) J'avais eu / J'ai eu envoyé (Fr.)
I=have.AUX.IPFV.1SG have.PTCP I=have.AUX.IND.PRS.1SG have.PTCP send.PTCP
'I had sent'

19.4 The Periphrastic Passive

19.4.1 Synthetic vs Analytic

The history of the passive represents another illustration of one of the most significant typological changes in the transition from Latin to Romance, namely the passage from Latin predominantly synthetic structures (AMATUR '(s)he is loved') to Romance chiefly periphrastic structures (Fr. *Il est aimé*, Ro. *El este iubit*, It. *Lui è amato*, Sp. *Él es amado* 'He is loved') (Danckaert 2017: 217). The Romance periphrases are descendants of Latin constructions used for perfective paradigms (Danckaert 2017: 216; Ledgeway 2021a: §1). The synthetic passive, restricted in Latin to imperfective paradigms (Danckaert 2017: 216; Ledgeway 2021a: §1), was fully replaced in Romance by analytic formations made up of a descendant of ESSE or another auxiliary + a passive past participle, this representing a 'functional extension of an already existing periphrasis of the classical language' (Ledgeway 2012: 16).

19.4.2 Frequency and Distribution

It is common in the Romance literature to refer to the 'unpopularity' of the passive, especially in informal registers. While it is true that in some non-standard varieties of Italy the canonical passive is inexistent or very rarely used (see Ledgeway 2021a: §§2.1–2 and references), it is equally true that in some contexts and under certain pragmatic conditions, especially in the standard languages, the passive has a wide distribution and a significant frequency. Overall, the usage of the passive is much more nuanced.

The considerable differences in usage depend on different factors: (i) type of register (formal vs informal register; written vs oral register – the formal and written registers resort to the passive much more often, see also Cennamo 2016: 975); (ii) pragmatic conditions (the choice of the passive is tied to a given pragmatic context; for example, a particular way of formulating a question might influence the selection of the passive); (iii) semantic and syntactic-semantic type of verb (i.e., weak transitive verbs are rarely or never used in the passive; the ungrammaticality of the passive with stative, modal, measure verbs, or unergative verbs with an internal object is well documented); (iv) lexical restrictions of the Agent and of the Patient/Theme (the [+human] vs [–animate] feature bears upon the selection of the passive); for details on the frequency and distribution of the passive, see Ledgeway (2021a: §§2.1–2).

19.4.3 Participle Agreement

Irrespective of other variables (auxiliary selection, participle agreement in the compound past, overt realization of the Agent, etc.), there is a constant feature of analytic passives across Romance: the passive past participle undergoes number and/or gender agreement with the clausal subject (19a–d). Brazilian Portuguese is exceptional in this respect: as a general tendency of agreement weakening, for some speakers, the participle does not undergo number agreement with preverbal subjects, and gender and number agreement with postverbal subjects (Ledgeway 2021a: §7.1).

(19) a. Deputaţii sunt aleşi de popor. (Ro.)
b. Les députés sont élus par le peuple. (Fr.)
c. I deputati sono eletti dal popolo. (It.)
d. Los diputados son elegidos por el pueblo. (Sp.)
the deputies.M(.DEF.MPL) are elected.MPL by(.)the people
'Members of parliament are elected by the people.'

19.4.4 The Reflexive Passive

Alongside the periphrastic passive, the Romance languages also make use of the reflexive passive (cf. also Section 18.5); this construction is particularly productive in Romanian and Italian (D'Alessandro 2007; Maiden and Robustelli 2007: 285f.; Adams 2013: 711), but also occurs in the other Romance varieties.

Without being equivalent in all occurrences, the auxiliary-based passive and the reflexive passive are used in parallel, with distinct features depending on the syntactic construction and stylistic register. The reflexive passive is specialized for the third person, singular and plural, with non-animate passive subjects and constructions with an unexpressed Agent (20); as for the linguistic register, it is preferred in popular and colloquial varieties.

(20) a. Cărțile   se   citesc. (Ro.)
        book.PL.DEF REFL.3 read.PRS.3PL
        'Books are read.'
    b. Si   distrusse   Dresda. (It.)
        REFL.3   destroy.3SG Dresden
        'Dresden was destroyed' (Maiden and Robustelli 2000: 285)

19.4.5 Inventory of Passive (Semi-)Auxiliary Verbs

In most Romance varieties, the passive periphrasis is based on ESSE, irrespective of the auxiliary/auxiliaries employed for the perfect.

Exceptionally, in southern Italian dialects spoken in the Pugliese province of Bari and in south-eastern Lucania, HABERE is used as a passive auxiliary, in free variation with ESSERE and UENIRE (Loporcaro 1988; Cennamo 2016: 975; Ledgeway 2021a: §3.4); this represents an extension of the free variation of ESSERE and HABERE from active constructions. A different situation is found with a southern Calabrian dialect from Polia, where, in the absence of this free variation with active forms, *avire* 'have' generalized, being used also in the passive (Marchese 2016, in Ledgeway 2021a: §3.4).

Besides the exceptional selection of HABERE, the Romance languages show considerable variation in the choice of the passive auxiliary. In French, Italian, and Romanian (Abeillé and Godard 2003), prototypical ESSERE occurs with a full paradigm and with identical forms in the passive (21a) and in the copulative (21b) usage; note that Romanian also has a third usage of 'be' as a perfective/irrealis auxiliary (cf. Avram and Hill 2007) in which it is invariable (21c).[4]

(21) a. Profesorul   trebuie   să
        teacher.SG.DEF must.PRS.3SG COMP.SBJV
        fie   plătit. (Ro.)
        be.SBJV.3   pay.PTCP
        'The teacher must be paid.'
    b. Profesorul   trebuie   să
        teacher.SG.DEF must.PRS.3SG COMP.SBJV
        fie   bătrân. (Ro.)
        be.SBJV.3   old
        'The teacher must be old.'

---

[4] In old Romanian, perfective/irrealis BE also occurred with variable forms, and had identical forms with copulative and passive BE (Nicolae 2015: 120, n. 5):

(i) să   fim   noi   iubit   pre   Dumnezeu (ORo.)
    COMP.SBJV   be.SBJV.1PL   we   love.PTCP   DOM   God
    'for us to have loved God'

c. Profesorul   trebuie   să
   teacher.SG.DEF   must.PRS.3SG   COMP.SBJV
   fi   plătit   pentru serviciile   cerute. (modRo.)
   be   pay.PTCP   for   services.DEF   required
   'The teacher must have paid for the required services.'

Alongside prototypical *essere* 'be' (22a), Italian also employs *venire* 'come' (22b) and *andare* 'go' (22c), the former for the dynamic passive, the latter for a deontic passive (Ledgeway 2016: 226). Their occurrence in compound tenses (hence their combination with another auxiliary) is ungrammatical. *Venire* incorporates a dynamic value (i.e., in contrast to *La porta è aperta* 'the door is open(ed)', which is ambiguous between a stative and a dynamic reading, *La porta viene aperta* 'The door gets opened' is unambiguously dynamic; Maiden and Robustelli 2007: 284); the *andare* passive is characterized by more complex restrictions (see Maiden and Robustelli 2007: 282f.).

(22) a. Il   topo   è   mangiato   dal   gatto. (It.)
        the   mouse.M   is   eat.PTCP.MSG   by   cat
        'The mouse is eaten by the cat.'
     b. Il   libro   viene letto   dal   ricercatore. (It.)
        the   book.M   comes read.PTCP.MSG   by.the researcher
        'The book is read by the researcher.'
     c. Queste   medicine   vanno   prese
        these   medicines.F   andare.IND.PRS.3PL   take.PTCP.F.PL
        ogni   mattina. (It.)
        every   morning
        'These medicines should be taken every morning.'

Catalan mainly uses the auxiliary *ser* 'be' (23a) (Alsina 2016: 379); with restrictions similar to those found in Italian, a UENIRE auxiliary is also employed as a dynamic passive (23b), its choice being also dialectally constrained (Wheeler, Yates, and Dols 1999: 512; Ledgeway 2021a: §3.3).

(23) a. Han   estat   descrits   els   simptomes
        have.3PL be.PTCP   described.PTCP.MPL   the   symptoms.MPL
        (per un doctorand). (Cat.)
        by   a doctoral.student
        'The symptoms were described by a doctoral student.'
     b. Lus   premits   venian   distribuits. (Alg.)
        the   prizes   come.PST.IPFV.3PL   distribute.PTCP.MPL
        'The prizes were being handed out.'

Spanish employs two BE verbs, *ser* (24a) and *estar* (24b), with different aspectual properties, *estar* incorporating a resultative aspectual value.

Furthermore, the presence of the Agent is preferred with *ser* but disfavoured with *estar*.

(24) a. Los   terroristas   fueron   arrestados
        the   terrorists.MPL   be.PRT.3MPL   arrest.PTCP.PL
        por   la   policía. (Sp.)
        by   the   police
        'The terrorists were arrested by the police.'
     b. Los   terroristas   están   arrestados. (Sp.)
        the   terrorists.MPL   be.IND.PRS.3PL   arrest.PTCP.MPL
        'The terrorists are under arrest.'

Besides the canonical BE-passive, which belongs to the formal register (Jones 1993: 124), Sardinian also features a WANT-passive similar to that found across the dialects of southern Italy (Ledgeway 2000; 2021b), and a modal passive with *kérrere* 'want' (25), used in all registers (Jones 1993: 124; Mensching and Remberger 2016: 286f):

(25) Sa   mákkina   keret   accontzata
     the   car.FSG   want.IND.PRS.3SG   repair.PTCP.FSG
     dae   unu   meccánicu. (Srd.)
     by   a   mechanic
     'This car needs to be repaired by a mechanic.'

Romansh varieties feature an analytic passive based on the auxiliary *neir* 'come' (< UENIRE) (Anderson 2016: 177):

(26) La   proposta   vign   acceptada. (Rms.)
     the   proposal.FSG   come.IND.PRS.3SG   accept.PTCP.FSG
     'The proposal is accepted.'

Besides the grammaticalized BE construction in (27), in non-standard registers Romanian also employs *veni* 'come' (28) in constructions with a modal necessity value (Iordan 1950; Pană Dindelegan 2003: 133–39; Dragomirescu and Nicolae 2014). Like Sardinian and southern dialects of Italy, Romanian features a construction based on a deontic modal, *a trebui* 'must' (29), used with a full paradigm (see also Cabredo Hofherr 2017: 244).

(27) Copiii   sunt   lăudați   de   părinți. (Ro.)
     children.DEF.M   be.IND.PRS.3PL   praise.PTCP.MPL   by   parents
     'The children are praised by their parents.'

(28) a. Cratița   în   care   se   coace   cozonacul   vine
        pan.DEF.F   in   which   REFL=   bakes   cake.DEF   comes
        unsă   cu   unt. (Ro.)
        smear.PTCP.FSG   with   butter
        'The pan in which the pound cake is baked has to / must / ought to be / is smeared with butter.'

b. Celălalt bec vine slăbit. (Ro.)
the.other bulb.MSG comes loose.PTCP.MSG
'The other bulb must be loosened.'

(29) Cartea / cărțile trebuia / vor trebui
book.F.DEF books.FPL.DEF must.PST.IPFV AUX.FUT.3PL must.INF
citită / citite de elevi. (Ro.)
read.PTCP.FSG read.PTCP.FPL by students
'The book(s) were to be read / will have to be read by the students.'

Among the sub-Danubian varieties, the *veni* 'come' and *rămâne* 'remain' passives occur occasionally in Istro-Romanian (30) (Sârbu and Frățilă 1998: 66). Given the circulation of these passives in areas of contact with Venetan, it is presumed that Venetan might have played a role in the existence of these constructions, yet it is hard to decide whether language contact is the sole source for these constructions (Dragomirescu and Nicolae 2014: 79).

(30) a. Ie vire ucis. (IRo.)
he comes kill.PTCP
'He is killed.'
b. Ie ramas-a ucis. (IRo.)
he remain=have.AUX.PST.3SG kill.PTCP
'He was killed.'

In several Romance languages (Fr., Ptg., Sp., It., Cat., and Ro.), especially in the journalistic and literary styles, the verb 'see' accompanied by the reflexive pronoun is used in passive structures, followed by a participle or an infinitive (31) (Giacalone Ramat 2017: 170–73; Ledgeway 2021a: §3.5).

(31) a. Il se voyait envahir / envahi
he REFL=see.PST.IPFV.3SG overrun.INF overrun.PTCP
par un sentiment d' échec. (Fr.)
by a feeling of failure
'He was being / was taken over (lit. saw himself to invade / invaded) by a sense of failure.'
b. El s-a văzut abandonat și
he REFL=have.AUX.PST.3SG abandon.PTCP and
uitat de Dumnezeu. (Ro.)
forget.PTCP by God
'He saw himself abandoned and forgotten by God.'

19.4.6 The Double Passive

A special construction attested across non-formal varieties of modern Spanish, but deemed absent from the other Romance languages, is the 'double passive' (32a–b) (Bosque and Gallego 2011). The construction consists of a cluster made up of two verbal complexes: a passive periphrasis with the lexical verb and the auxiliary *ser* 'be', and a doubling periphrasis made up of a tensed form of *ser* and an aspectual verb. Bosque and Gallego (2011) analyse this construction as a type of syntactic doubling, and stress the expletive nature of some of the components (the low auxiliary and the high, aspectual, participle). A similar phenomenon is found in colloquial French with the aspectual verbs *finir* 'finish' / *commencer* 'begin' (32c); here, the passive reading of the infinitival complement is formally marked on the aspectual verb (Ledgeway 2021a: §2.3).

(32) a. La ermita fue empezada a ser
       the hermitage be.PRT.3SG start.PTCP.FSG to be.INF
       construida en el siglo XIV. (Sp.)
       build.PTCP.FSG in the century 14
       'The hermitage was started to be built in the fourteenth century.'
    b. El misil fue acabado de ser armado ayer. (Sp.)
       the missile be.PRT.3SG finish.PTCP of be.INF arm.PTCP yesterday
       'The missile was finished being armed yesterday.'
    c. La maison est finie de construire. (Fr.)
       the house be.PRS.ind.3SG finish.PTCP.FSG of build.INF
       'The house has finished being built.'

19.4.7 The Position of Constituents in the Passive Periphrasis

The preferred word order in Latin passive ESSE-constructions places the auxiliary in postposition (participle > ESSE), but the reverse word order is also possible (ESSE > participle) (Ledgeway 2012: 223). In a statistical analysis, Bauer (2006: 294) convincingly demonstrates that the ESSE > participle word order gradually extends in the history of Latin. In accordance with the passage from a head-final to a head-initial grammar, the word order ESSE > participle continues to gradually surpass the reverse word order in the diachrony of the Romance languages (for the word order preferences of late Latin, see the percentages in Danckaert 2017: 226). For example, the patterns with pre-auxiliary participles (33) were much more frequent in old Romanian than in modern Romanian, where the auxiliary + participle word order, productive since old Romanian (34), has generalized.

(33) Deaci dzise se aducă Pavelu.
     do say.PST.PFV.3SG COMP.SBJV bring.SBJV.3SG Paul
     Adusu fu el de ceia … (ORo.)
     bring.PTCP be.PST.PFV.3SG he by those
     'So he meant to bring Paul. He was brought by those …'

(34) nu sunt dumnedzei ceia ce-su
not be.IND.PRS.PL gods those who=be.IND.PRS.3PL
cu mârule fapți (ORo.)
with hands.DEF make.PTCP.MPL
'They are not gods who are made with the hands.'

On the basis of word order evidence, the recent literature documents an attempt towards reconsidering the emergence of the Romance analytic passive (e.g., It. *sono amato* 'I am loved'). Thus, according to this hypothesis, based on the word order difference between the Latin pattern (AMATUS EST 'he has been loved') and its Romance counterparts, which feature the word order auxiliary > participle, the analytic passive does not descend from a Classical Latin structure, but rather represents a new formation, not older than the fourth century CE (Danckaert 2017).

19.4.8 Monoclausal Properties

In contrast to tense and mood auxiliaries, which present many syntactic and morphophonological signs of decategorialization (grammaticalization), the periphrastic passive formation has greater autonomy, ensuring, among other features, the possibility of employing multiple (semi-)auxiliaries in the passive (this represents one of the reasons why the term 'semi-auxiliary' is more appropriate than 'auxiliary' with reference to the analytic passive). This also accounts for the fact that, in the absence of a broader linguistic or extralinguistic context, these periphrases are systematically ambiguous: constructions like (35a) may be read either as passives (35b) or as [copula + predicative] constructions (35c).

(35) a. Pâinea este coaptă. (Ro.)
bread.DEF.FSG is bake.PTCP.FSG
'The bread is baked.'
b. Pâinea este coaptă cu grijă. (Ro.)
bread.DEF.FSG is bake.PTCP.FSG with care
'The bread is carefully baked.'
c. Pâinea este foarte coaptă, aproape arsă. (Ro.)
bread.DEF.FSG is very bake.PTCP.FSG almost burn.PTCP.FSG
'The bread is well baked, almost burned.'

Also, there are significant differences in the behaviour of the passive auxiliaries: the BE-auxiliary behaves in all aspects like a copula verb, while auxiliaries based on motion verbs exhibit clear signs of grammaticalization, the most important of which is the loss of the motion semantics. Using for illustration material from Romanian, the diagnostics below synthesize the monoclausality vs autonomy properties for the analytic BE-passives.

Diagnostics for monoclausality:

(i) negation expressed exclusively on the auxiliary:

(36) Nu mi-au   fost   date   cărțile. (Ro.)
      not 1SG.DAT=have.PRS.IND.3PL   be.PTCP   give.PTCP.FPL   books.DEF.FPL
      'The books were not given to me.'

(ii) (dative) clitic climbing (accusative clitics are excluded by default in the passive):

(37) Mi-au   fost   date   cinci   cărți. (Ro.)
      1SG.DAT=have.PRS.IND.3PL   be.PTCP   give.PTCP.FPL   five   books.F
      'Five books were given to me.'

(iii) occurrence of the passive in restructured modal configurations (see Section 19.6):

(38) a. Cartea   poate   fi   citită   de elev. (Ro.)
          book.DEF.FSG   can   be.INF read.PTCP.FSG   by pupil
          'The book can be read by the pupil.'
      b. Cartea   îmi   poate   fi   furată   oricând. (Ro.)
          book.DEF.FSG   1SG.DAT=   can   be.INF steal.PTCP.FSG   any time
          'My book can be stolen from me at any time.'

Diagnostics for autonomy:

(i) semantically, passive BE behaves like any other copula;
(ii) passive BE has a full paradigm (like existential BE): it shows no sign of morphophonological erosion and may co-occur with other (TAM-expressing) auxiliaries (39);

(39) (Aș   fi   dorit)   să   fi   fost
      have.AUX.COND.1SG be.INF   wish.PTCP   COMP.SBJV   be.INF   be.PTCP
      ajutat   de prieteni. (Ro.)
      help.PTCP   by friends
      'I would have wanted to have been helped by friends.'

(iii) full constituents may be interposed between passive BE and the participle (40a), and the participle may be even topicalized (40b), giving rise to the word order participle > passive auxiliary;

(40) a. A   fost   și   astăzi   lăudată. (Ro.)
          have.PRS.IND.3SG   be.PTCP   also   today   praise.PTCP.FSG
          'She was praised today as well.'
      b. Știut   este   că ... (Ro.)
          know.PTCP   is   that
          'It is known that ...'

(iv) passive BE may be replaced by other auxiliaries (41a) or be elided (41b).

(41) a. Crațița   este / rămâne / trebuie / vine   unsă
       pan.DEF.FSG is   remains must   comes smear.PTCP.FSG
       cu   unt. (Ro.)
       with butter
       'The pan is/remains/must be/comes smeared with butter.'
   b. Obligată   de părinți, a   renunțat   la facultate. (Ro.)
      force.PTCP.FSG by patents have.PRS.IND.3SG give.up.PTCP at faculty
      'Forced by her parents, she gave up university.'

19.5 Aspectual Periphrases

In Romance, aspectual values are often (but not always) syncretic with temporal values (Bertinetto and Squartini 2016: 939; Maiden 2016: 501f.), but there also exist numerous verbs which lexically encode aspect, and aspectual periphrases with verbs having different meanings, which show a complex predicate behaviour. These aspectual periphrases are made up of a verb (such as CONTINUE, BE, STAND, GO, HOLD, etc.) bearing the inflexional information and a lexical verb in the infinitive or the gerundive.

Verbs lexically encoding aspect in Romance have a different behaviour. Similarly to other classes of verbs, in standard Italian, clitic climbing is not obligatory with aspectuals (Rizzi 1982: 4),[5] hence their complex predicate status is contextual (42); in Romanian, negation and clitic climbing are obligatorily hosted by the aspectual verb when it is followed by a supine (43a) (Dragomirescu 2013: 196f.), but when the second verb is in the infinitive (43b) or the subjunctive (43c–d) the construction receives a biclausal analysis, as negation may occur either on the higher verb (43c) or on the lower verb (43d) (with scope differences), and clitic climbing is disallowed (43b).

(42) a. Gianni continua   a / sta   per raccontargli
        Gianni continue.PRS.IND.3SG to stay.PRS.IND.3SG for tell.INF=3DAT
        stupide storie. (It., in Rizzi 1982: 4)
        stupid stories
   b. Gianni gli   continua   a / sta   per raccontare
      Gianni DAT.3=continue.PRS.3SG to stay.PRS.IND.3SG for tell.INF
      stupide storie. (It., in Rizzi 1982: 4)
      stupid stories
      'Gianni is continuing / going to tell him stupid stories'

---

[5] In actual usage, clitic climbing is always obligatory in the regional Italian of southern speakers, but usually absent in the speech of northern speakers, this distribution reflecting the options found in the dialects spoken in each area in turn (Adam Ledgeway, p.c.).

(43) a. Cărțile   nu le   termină   de citit. (Ro.)
       books.DEF.F   not 3FPL.ACC=finish.PRS.IND.3   of read.SUP
    b. Cărțile   (**le) nu   termină   a   le   citi. (Ro.)
       books.DEF.F 3FPL= not finish.PRS.IND.3 to 3FPL= read.INF
       'He doesn't finish reading the books.'
    c. Nu continuă   să   vină   la ore. (Ro.)
       not continue.PRS.IND.3   COMP.SBJV   come.SBJV.3   to hours
       '(S)he doesn't keep on attending classes'
    d. Continuă   să   nu   vină   la ore. (Ro.)
       continue.PRS.IND.3   COMP.SBJV not come.SBJV.3   to hours
       '(S)he keeps on not attending classes.'

Aspectual (progressive) BE-periphrases are specific to Gallo-Romance, Italian, and Sardinian (44a) (Bertinetto and Squartini 2016: 947–50; Andriani 2017: 197). Romanian also possesses an imminential periphrasis made up of *fi* 'be' and the subjunctive (44b), which disallows clitic climbing (and allows for negation both on the higher and on the lower predicate, with scope differences), therefore not qualifying as a complex predicate. Squartini (1998: 27–29) indicates that the aspectual BE-periphrases with a gerund/present participle are also attested in Catalan (*estar*), French (*être*), Galician (*estar*), Portuguese (*estar*), and Spanish (*estar*). Imminential and proximative periphrases may also be found in Catalan, French, Italian, Portuguese, and Spanish (Bertinetto and Squartini 2016: 951).

(44) a. So   travallande. (Srd., Jones 1993: 83)
       be.IND.PRS.1SG   work.GER
       '(I) am working.'
    b. Era   să   te   lovesc. (Ro.)
       be.IPFV   COMP.SBJV   2SG.ACC=   hit.PRS.1SG
       'I almost hit you.'

Aspectual (progressive) STAND-periphrases are specific to Italo-Romance and Ibero-Romance, where they represent a widespread option for expressing progressive aspect (45a–b); diachronically, in many Romance varieties (but not in all of them; cf. standard European Portuguese and Romanesco) the infinitive was replaced by the gerund in these constructions (Andriani 2017: 198f.). The infinitive is still an option in certain varieties, being introduced by the non-finite subordinator *a* 'to' (46a–b). The infinitival STAND-periphrasis (alternating with the gerundial one) is also attested in Neapolitan, western Abruzzese, Laziale, and Tuscan varieties (see Andriani 2017: ch. 5 for an overview).

(45) a. Ma non vedi   che   sto
       but not see.IND.PRS.2SG   that   stand.IND.PRS.1SG
       guidando? (It., Andriani 2017: 199)
       drive.GER
       'Can't you see I'm driving (right now)?'

b. Istan   fakende   su mándicu. (Srd., Jones 1993: 84)
    stand.IND.PRS.PL make.GER   the food
    'They are preparing the meal.'

(46) a. Tu   duorme   e   Ninno tuo   stacə
        you   sleep.IND.PRS.2SG and Ninno your stands
        a penarə. (Nap., Rohlfs 1969: 133)
        to suffer.INF
        'You're sleeping and your Ninno is suffering.'
     b. Estou   a falar   com
        stand.IND.PRS.1SG to speak.INF with
        você. (EuPt., Mendes Mothé 2006: 1554)
        you
        'I'm speaking to you.'

The GO-andative periphrasis with infinitives is specific to certain Italian varieties, where it is found in an early grammaticalization stage, without (yet) encoding temporal and aspectual information (Andriani 2017: 205) (47); this type of structure underwent further grammaticalization as an intentional future in Ibero-Romance (48). Go is also attested in progressive constructions with the gerund in Catalan (*anar*), French (*aller*), Galician (*ir*), Italian (*andare*), Occitan (*anar*), Portuguese (*ir*), Romansh (*ir*), and Spanish (*ir*) (Squartini 1998: 27–29; Bertinetto and Squartini 2016: 949f.).

(47) a. Vado   a dormire. (It., Andriani 2017: 205)
        go.IND.PRS.1SG   to sleep.INF
        'I'm going to sleep.'
     b. [...] chesto che   te   vaco
             this   that to-you go.IND.PRS.1SG
        a dì? (Nap., Ledgeway 2009: 454)
        to say.INF
        '[you'll certainly be surprised at] what I'm going to tell you?'

(48) a. ¿Dónde van   a estar a las dos? (Sp., Zagona 2002: 33)
        where go.IND.PRS.3PL to be   at the two
        'Where are they going to be at two (o'clock)?'
     b. Vou   (**a) compra-lo   diario (Glc., Pérez Bouza 1996: 72)
        go.IND.PRS.1SG   to   buy=the   newspaper
        'I'm going to buy the newspaper.'

Other verbs which may be part of aspectual (progressive) gerundial periphrases have been recorded by Squartini (1998: 27–29): COME (Cat. *venir*, Gal./Pt. *vir*, It. *venire*, Sp. *venir*), WALK (Glc., Pt., Sp. *andar*), and CARRY (Glc. *levar*, Sp. *llevar*).

19.6 Modal Complex Predicates

Unlike auxiliaries (Section 19.3), but similarly to aspectuals (Section 19.5), modal verbs (reflexes of proto-Romance *poˈtere 'be able', Lat. DEBERE/ HABERE DE-AB 'must', proto-Romance *voˈlere 'want', Lat. QUAERERE 'seek, require') selecting an infinitive or a non-finite complement do not generally show signs of morphophonological erosion, yet they pass to variable degrees the generally accepted complex predicate diagnostics (Section 19.2).

Clitic climbing has been extensively investigated across Romance. In modern Romance, the availability of clitic climbing with modals ranges from impossible in French (49a), heavily preferred in Occitan (49b), optional in Spanish (49c), Catalan (49d), and Italian (49e) (with a preference for clitic climbing in the spoken language) to obligatory in Neapolitan (49f) and Romanian (non-finite configurations) (50) (Rizzi 1982: 4; Picallo 1990: 285f.; Motapanyane and Avram 2001: 152–54; Abeillé and Godard 2003: 127, 129f.; Guțu-Romalo 2005: 161f.; Ledgeway 2012: 120f.).

(49)   a.   Nous   pouvons   les   aider. (Fr.)
                we   can.PRS.IND.1PL   3.MPL=help.INF
                'We can help them.'
       b.   Los   anam   (los)   ajudar. (Lgd.)
                3MPL=go.PRS.IND.1PL   3MPL=help.INF
       c.   Los   vamos   a   ayudar (los). (Sp.)
                3MPL= go.PRS.IND.1PL   to   help.INF=3MPL
                'We are going to help them.'
       d.   El   Pere   ho   deu   explicar   (-ho). (Cat.)
                the   Pere   3NSG.ACC=must.PRS.3SG   explain.INF=3NSG.ACC
                'Pere must explain it.'
       e.   Mario lo   vuole /   sa   risolver(lo)   da solo
                Mario 3MSG.ACC=wants   knows   solve(=3MSG)   by himself
                (questo   problema). (It.)
                this   problem
                'Mario wants to / can solve it by himself (this problem).'
       f.   'E   gghjammo   a   aiutà. (Nap.)
                3MPL.ACC   go.IND.PRS.1PL   to   help.INF
                'We are going to help them.'

(50)   a.   Îi   pot   (**îi)   ajuta. (Ro.)
                3MPL.ACC=can.IND.PRS.1SG   3MPL.ACC=help.INF
                'I can help them.'
       b.   Le   trebuie   (**le)   date   cărți   fetelor. (Ro.)
                3PL.DAT=must   3PL.DAT=give.PTCP.FPL   books   girls.DEF.DAT
                'Books must be given to the girls.'

c. Îl   are de   (**îl)   citit. (Ro.)
      3MSG.ACC= has K.SUP 3MSG.ACC= read.SUP
      '(S)he has to read it.'

Romanian modals present a more complex picture, as they may take a wider range of complements: they can select either a non-finite complement – a bare short infinitive (50a) (the modal *putea* 'can, be able', in a diachronically stable construction, Hill 2012), a participle or a prepositionless supine (50b) (the modal *trebui* 'must, have to') or a supine (50c) (*avea* 'have', in its modal usage) – or a subjunctive clausal complement (51) (a Balkan Sprachbund property, cf. Sandfeld 1930: 173–80). The subjunctive configuration is unambiguously biclausal (Nicolae 2013: ch. 4), as shown by impossibility of clitic climbing and by the availability of negation in the embedded domain. Reflexes of *voˈlere/QUAERERE may also take a finite clausal complement and, in Spanish and Neapolitan, a participial complement (52) (Ledgeway 2012: 121).

(51) (**Îl)   pot   să   nu   (îl)
     3MSG.ACC= can.IND.PRS.1SG COMP.SBJV not 3.MSG.ACC=
     citesc. (Ro.)
     read.SBJV.1SG
     'I can NOT read it.'

(52) a. Quería   que preparasen   todo   / preparado
     b. Vuleva   ca   preparassero   tutta cosa / preparata
        want.PST.IPFV.3SG that prepare.PST.SBJV.3PL everything   prepare.PTCP
        todo (Sp.)
        tutta cosa (Nap.)
        everything
        'He wanted for them to prepare everything / everything prepared.'

The availability of negation in the embedded domain is also subject to variation: while in languages such as French (53a) and Spanish (53b) (Zagona 2002: 195) the clausal negator may freely occur in the embedded domain, in Romanian non-finite configurations (53c) (Nicolae 2013: ch. 4) and in Neapolitan (53d) (Ledgeway 2000: 168) negation exclusively occurs in the domain of the modal verb:

(53) a. Il   peut   ne   pas dire   toute la   vérité. (Fr.)
        he   may.PRS.IND.3SG not not say.INF all   the truth
        'He may not say all the truth.'
     b. La   cámara no   puede   leer   el   nivel de la   carga. (Sp.)
        the camera not can.IND.PRS.3SG read.INF the level of the charge
        'The camera cannot read the level of the charge.'

c. Nu poate (**nu) spune tot adevărul. (Ro.)
not can.PRS.IND.3SG not say.INF all truth.DEF
'He cannot say all the truth.'

d. Dubbeto 'e num puté venì. (Nap.)
doubt.IND.PRS.1SG of not be.able.INF come.INF
'I doubt that I won't be able to come.'

Therefore, there appears to be a strong correlation between clitic climbing and the availability of negation in the embedded non-finite domain: languages (/configurations) with obligatory clitic climbing (Romanian, Neapolitan) disallow negation in the embedded domain, while languages(/configurations) in which clitic climbing is blocked (French) or optional (Spanish, Italian) freely allow the negator to occur in the embedded domain. This shows that in the former type of languages, the modal verb and its non-finite complement make up a monoclausal configuration, ensuring that complex predicate formation is obligatory.

Of the Romance languages which show auxiliary selection, only in Italian (54a) and Occitan (54b) (but not in French and Neapolitan) is the auxiliary which surfaces on the modal verb sensitive to the transitive/unaccusative nature of the embedded infinitive (Ledgeway 2012: 121):

(54) a. Non mi sono potuto addormentare. (It.)
b. me soi pogut pas dormir. (Lgd.)
not myself=am been.able not fall.asleep.INF
'I couldn't fall asleep.'

To sum up, modal verbs show variable degrees of concatenation with their non-finite complement across Romance; while the tight monoclausal nature of the [modal verb + infinitive/non-finite complement] complement is evident in Romanian and Neapolitan, the same is not true of the other Romance languages, in which optional or impossible clitic climbing and the availability of negation in the embedded domain testify to a looser concatenation of the modal verb and the infinitive.

19.7 Causative Complex Predicates

19.7.1 Introduction

Most of the Romance languages, except for modern Daco-Romance (Benucci 1993: 53), feature causative constructions with the Romance reflexes of Lat. FACERE 'make, do' (55a), LAXARE 'let' (55b), and MANDARE 'command' (55c) followed by an infinitive (examples from Sheehan 2016: 981).

(55) a. La ragazza fece cadere la caraffa. (It.)
the girl made fall.INF the carafe
'The girl made the carafe fall.'

b. Elle a   laissé entrer   le petit garçon. (Fr.)
   she have.AUX.PST.3SG let enter.INF the little boy
   'She let the little boy enter.'
c. O   Presidente da   Assembleia mandou votar   a   lei
   the president of.the assembly   ordered vote.INF the law
   aos   deputados. (EuPt.)
   to.the deputies
   'The President of the Assembly made the members of parliament vote through the law.'

Complex predicate formation is diagnosed using the same tests as those used for auxiliaries; however, in contrast to auxiliary-verb constructions, causative constructions (and constructions with perception verbs, see Section 19.8) contribute to the argument structure of the new overall construction/periphrasis with an external argument, and may also add an adjunct (Labelle 2017: 309).

The constructions in (55) are characterized by E(xceptional) C(ase) M(arking) on the subject of the infinitive (which surfaces with the accusative – or with the dative, see Section 19.7.2.1 – instead of the nominative). When the subject is cliticized, it raises to the first verb, leading to restructuring (55b becomes 56a); negation is also hosted by the first verb (56b). Therefore, constructions such as (55) do not match the complex predicate diagnostics (Section 19.2.2), whereas those in (56) do.

(56) a. Elle l'a   laissé   entrer. (Fr.)
        she 3MSG.ACC=have.AUX.PST.3SG   let.PTCP   enter.INF
        'She let him enter.'
     b. Elle ne l'a   pas laissé   entrer. (Fr.)
        she not 3MSG.ACC= have.AUX.PST.3SG NEG let.PTCP enter.INF
        'She did not let him enter.'

19.7.2 Facere **Causatives**

The causative structure with FACERE had been attested since classical and postclassical times, and it proliferated in early Romance. There is, however, a significant difference between the Latin biclausal construction and the Romance monoclausal one (Vincent 2016).

There is major diachronic variation across the Romance languages. In Portuguese and Spanish it appears that clitic climbing, which was previously obligatory, has become optional quite recently, so that Spanish and Portuguese causative constructions have gradually undergone a change from monoclausality to biclausality (Davies 1995; Sheehan 2016: 993). By contrast, while modern Romanian disallows the FACERE causative as a complex predicate (because the verb *face* 'make' selects a subjunctive clausal complement), old Romanian attests the Romance monoclausal infinitival construction (Nedelcu 2016: 244) (57).

(57) Şi   va   fi   ceriul   nou şi   pământul
    and AUX.FUT.3SG be.INF sky.DEF.NOM new and land.DEF.NOM
    nou, cari   eu le-am   făcut   a
    new which   I   3FPL.ACC=have.PRS.1SG make.PTCP to.INF
    trăi   naintea   mea (ORo.)
    live.INF in.front.of my
    'And the sky and the land that I made come to life in front of me will be new.'

Since the pioneering work on French by Kayne (1975), the literature on causatives has distinguished two types of monoclausal FACERE constructions: *faire-infinitif* and *faire-par* (see also Guasti 2006; Ciutescu 2013). Both these types are also attested in Italian, in some varieties of Spanish, and, to a lesser extent, in European Portuguese and Catalan (Sheehan 2016: 985), with subtle semantic differences: in French, Italian, and Spanish, the *faire-infinitif*, unlike the *faire-par*, involves a sense of obligation exerted on the subject of the second verb (Folli and Harley 2007: 212), whereas in the *faire-par* construction the subject of the first verb has to be an agent (not a cause), and therefore it is obligatorily animate.

19.7.2.1 The *Faire-infinitif* Construction

In this structure, illustrated in (58), the subject of the embedded verb surfaces in the dative when the verb is transitive; clitics and negation attach to the first verb (Labelle 2017: 306).

(58) a. Il fera   boire   un peu   de vin
        he will.make drink.INF   a bit   of wine
        à son enfant. (Fr., Sheehan 2016: 987)
        to his child
        'He'll make his child drink a bit of wine.'
    b. On   la   lui   laissa   réparer. (Fr., Labelle 2017: 307)
       one 3FSG.ACC=3SG.DAT=let.PST.PFV.3SG repair.INF
       'He was allowed to repair it.'
    c. La   hizo   funcionar. (Sp., Labelle 2017: 307)
       3FSG.ACC=make.PST.3SG function.INF
       'He made it work.'

The Romance languages show variation with respect to clitics; for example, the reflexive clitics (*se/si* Zubizarreta 1985: 274) may attach to the embedded verb in French and Spanish (59a–b), but not in Italian (59c):

(59) a. On a   fait   se   raser
       we have.PRS.IND.3SG make.PTCP 3REFL=shave.INF
       Pierre. (Fr., Zubizarreta 1985: 274)
       Pierre
       'We made Pierre shave himself.'
    b. Le   hicimos   lavarse   las manos   a Pedro. (Sp.)
       3MSG.ACC=made.PST.PFV.1PL wash.INF=3REFL the hands   to Pedro
       'We made Pedro wash his hands.'

c. **Mario ha   fatto   accusarsi   Piero. (It.)
    Mario have.PRS.IND.3SG make accuse.INF=3REFL Piero
    'Mario made Piero accuse himself.'

19.7.2.2 The *Faire-par* Construction

In the *faire-par* construction, the subject of the embedded verb is realized as an adjunct PP introduced by the same preposition as the *by*-phrase in the passive construction (60) (Labelle 2017: 319). In Brazilian Portuguese and Catalan, this construction seems to be possible when the prepositional phrase is suppressed (Sheehan 2016: 985)

(60) a. Elle fera   manger cette pomme par Jean. (Fr., Kayne 1975: 235)
         she make.FUT.3SG   eat.INF that   apple by Jean
         'She'll have that apple eaten by Jean.'
     b. Gli   fecero   sparare addosso da un agente. (It., Burzio 1986: 270f.)
         CL.DAT.3SG   make.PST.PL   fire.INF upon   by an agent
         'They had him fired upon by an agent.'

It is a monoclausal construction allowing clitic climbing of the embedded objects, including datives (60b); the reflexive/passive clitic *se* cannot be hosted by the embedded infinitive (61) (Labelle 2017: 326).

(61) **On   fait /   laisse   se   laver
     IMPS   make.PRS.IND.3SG let.PRS.IND.3SG   3REFL=   wash.INF
     avant de   s'asseoir   à table. (Fr., Zubizarreta 1985: 264)
     before of   3REFL=sit.INF   at table
     (intended) 'We make / let wash oneself before sitting down at table.'

19.7.3 LAXARE Causatives

LAXARE causatives with ECM complements are permitted in French, European Portuguese, Spanish, and (marginally) in Italian. In these structures, clitic climbing is permitted, the subject of the infinitive surfaces to its right, and when the embedded infinitive is transitive its subject appears in the dative (Sheehan 2016: 984):

(62) a. J' ai   laissé   lire   le livre
         I have.PRS.IND.1SG let.PTCP read.INF   the book
         à Jean. (Fr., Sheehan 2016: 984)
         to Jean
         'I have let Jean read the book.'
     b. Je le   lui   ai
         I 3MSG.ACC= 3SG.DAT=   have.PRS.IND.1SG
         laissé   lire. (Fr.)
         let.PTCP   read.INF
         'I have let him read it.'

19.7.4 MANDARE Causatives

MANDARE is the source of the canonical causative verb in European Portuguese, where it allows both restructuring/complex predicate formation (63a) and ECM constructions (63b).

(63) European Portuguese (Sheehan 2016: 984)
    a. O   João   mandou   à   Ana   procurar   o   livro.
         the João   order.PST.PFV.3SG to.the Ana   fetch.INF   the book
    b. O   João   mandou   procurar o   livro   à   Ana.
         the João   order.PST.PFV.3SG find.INF   the   book to.the Ana
       'João made Ana find the book.'

19.8 Complex Predicates with Perception Verbs

Most of the Romance languages (except for modern Daco-Romance) feature monoclausal constructions with 'see' and other perception verbs which select an infinitival complement with a preverbal subject. Perception verb constructions have many features in common with causative constructions. The subject of the embedded verb is exceptionally case marked (with the accusative) (64a) and may surface as an accusative clitic hosted by the main verb (Labelle 2017: 300) (64b). Just as in the case of modal verb configurations in certain languages (Section 19.6), there is variation: clitics and negation may also surface on the embedded verb (64c) (Labelle 1996: 91).

(64) a. Jean a   vu   Marie   réparer   la voiture. (Fr.)
         Jean have.AUX.PST.3SG seen Marie.ACC repair.INF the car
       'Jean saw Marie repair the car.'
    b. Jean l'   a   vue   réparer   la voiture. (Fr.)
         Jean 3FSG.ACC=have.PRS.IND.3SG seen.FSG repair.INF the car
       'Jean saw her repair the car.'
    c. J'ai   cru   voir   Pierre ne pas
         I have.PRS.IND.1SG believe.PTCP see.INF Pierre not NEG
         s'arrêter   au   feu rouge. (Fr.)
         3REFL=stop.INF at.the light red
       'I thought I saw Pierre fail to stop at the red light.'

In Romanian, perception verbs are followed by a gerund (Nicula 2012), in constructions with subject-to-object raising (and negation on the first verb) (65a); evidence for subject-to-object raising comes from the availability of the passive voice (65b), a context in which the raised subject bears nominative and acts as the subject of the passive verb. Note that there is no clitic climbing in this construction (cliticization of the embedded subject on the perception verb in (65a) is the effect of subject-to-object raising).

(65) a. Nu îl văd pe Ion lovind-o. (Ro.)
not 3MSG.ACC=see.IND.PRS.1SG DOM Ion hit.GER=3FSG.ACC
'I do not see Ion hitting her.'
b. El nu a fost văzut
he(NOM) not have.PRS.IND.3SG be.PTCP see.PTCP
lovind-o. (Ro.)
hit.GER=3FSG.ACC
'He has not been seen hitting her.'

Across Romance, these constructions behave differently (Sheehan 2016: 982f.). In Spanish, Italian, French, Catalan, Galician, and European Portuguese (to a lesser extent) the perception verb and its complement make up a complex predicate. French, Spanish, European Portuguese, Catalan, and Romanian display ECM complements where the lexical verb is a gerund(ive); these constructions involve Exceptional Case Marking; ECM complements do not generally display restructuring phenomena such as clitic climbing, though the subject of the embedded verb behaves like an argument of the matrix perception verb and must be expressed on the matrix verb when it is realized as a clitic.

19.9 Conclusions: What Romance Languages Tell Us about Complex Predicates

The concept of complex predicate is, to a certain degree, fuzzy, yet it brings under the same umbrella a variety of syntactically and semantically distinct constructions, which have in common monoclausality (mainly diagnosed by clitic climbing and the exclusive realization of negation on the high verb).

The examination of the empirical data has shown that the distinction between complex predicates based on merger and complex predicates based on coindexation (Baker and Harvey 2010; see Section 19.2.1) holds with respect to the Romance languages too: on the one hand, in complex predicates with auxiliaries, modals, and aspectuals, the argument structure of the formation reflects the argument structure of lexical verbs, hence auxiliary/modal/aspectual verbs are 'athematic' predicates (which 'do not assign either an external or internal argument but, rather, inherit their argument structure directly from their non-finite verbal complement', Ledgeway 2007: 121), but rather mere placeholders for TAM values; on the other hand, complex predicate formations with causatives and perception verbs are characterized by an argument/conceptual structure distinct from that of the component verbs.

Morphophonological erosion affects only a subclass of complex predicate constructions, those with (non-passive) auxiliaries. By contrast, modals and aspectuals (as well as passive auxiliaries) do not generally undergo morphophonological erosion/weakening, yet they share with auxiliaries the fact that they are devoid of thematic properties; the term 'semi-auxiliary' appears to be an appropriate label for this class of fully inflecting, yet athematic, verbs.

Furthermore, modal and aspectual semi-auxiliaries may also occur in biclausal configurations and preserve their athematic nature; identity of subject between the higher and embedded predicates (technically obtained via subject raising or obligatory control) gives the appearance of a more cohesive structure, yet a complex predicate formation is not at play, given biclausality.

The diachronic paths taken by the various types of Romance complex predicates are also diverse. Some of the formations undergo grammaticalization, the most extreme case being that of the western Romance futures and conditionals; in this case, a new synthetic system was created on the basis of analytic formations with postverbal auxiliaries. Other complex predicates are extremely stable form a diachronic point of view: the Romanian modal complex predicate made up of the verb *putea* 'can, be able' plus a bare infinitive did not undergo any significant change in the five centuries of the attested history of Romanian (Hill 2012). Opposite diachronic developments are also attested. For example, rather than undergoing further structural simplification, the Spanish and Portuguese causative constructions appear gradually to revert to a biclausal structure, as shown by the fact that previously obligatory clitic climbing has quite recently become optional. Global changes affecting the syntax of a given language may have local effects on the grammar of complex predicates: the replacement of the infinitive by the subjunctive in Romanian (a more general Balkan Sprachbund phenomenon) has led to the replacement of the infinitival monoclausal causatives attested in old Romanian with subjunctive biclausal causatives, the only option in modern Romanian.

To sum up, the phenomena investigated point to the fact that 'complex predicate' is a heteroclite concept in any accepted sense, as every construction in its turn features different properties and has non-converging diachronic developments.

Selected References

Below you can find selected references for this chapter. The full references can be found online at the following page: www.cambridge.org/Romancelinguistics

Adams, J. N. (2013). *Social Variation and the Latin Language*. Cambridge: Cambridge University Press.

Cardinaletti, A. and Shlonsky, U. (2004). 'Clitic positions and restructuring in Italian', *Linguistic Inquiry* 35: 519–57.

Cennamo, M. (2016). 'Voice'. In Ledgeway, A. and Maiden, M. (eds), *The Oxford Guide to the Romance Languages*. Oxford: Oxford University Press, 967–80.

Cinque, G. (2004). 'Restructuring and functional structure'. In Belletti, A. (ed.), *Structures and Beyond: The Cartography of Syntactic Structures, III*. Oxford: Oxford University Press, 132–91.

Ledgeway, A. (2021a). 'Passive periphrases in the Romance Languages'. In Gardani, F. and Loporcaro, M. (eds), *The Oxford Encyclopedia of Romance Linguistics*. Oxford: Oxford University Press. Advance online publication. https://doi.org/10.1093/acrefore/9780199384655.013.639.

Monachesi, P. (2005). *The Verbal Complex in Romance: A Case Study in Grammatical Interfaces*. Oxford: Oxford University Press.

Rizzi, L. (1978). 'A restructuring rule in Italian syntax'. In Keyser, S. J. (ed.), *Recent Transformational Studies in European Languages*. Cambridge, MA: MIT Press, 113–58.

Roberts, I. (2013). 'Some speculations on the development of the Romance periphrastic perfect'. *Revue roumaine de linguistique* 58: 3–30.

Salvi, G. (1987). 'Syntactic restructuring in the evolution of Romance auxiliaries'. In Harris, M. and Ramat, P. (eds), *Historical Development of Auxiliaries*. Berlin: Mouton de Gruyter, 225–36.

Sheehan, M. (2016). 'Complex predicates'. In Ledgeway, A. and Maiden, M. (eds), *The Oxford Guide to the Romance Languages*. Oxford: Oxford University Press, 981–93.

Svenonius, P. (2008). 'Complex predicates and the functional sequence', *Tromsø Working Papers on Language and Linguistics: Nordlyd* 35: 47–88.

Vincent, N. (1987). 'The interaction of periphrasis and inflection: some Romance examples'. In Harris, M. and Ramat, P. (eds), *Historical Development of Auxiliaries*. Berlin: Mouton de Gruyter, 237–56.

20

Dependency, Licensing, and the Nature of Grammatical Relations

Anna Cardinaletti and Giuliana Giusti

20.1 Introduction

Dependency is a general term that refers to different structural relations. We highlight three very general classes of phenomena that are often captured by this term: (i) the structural relation between a lexical head (e.g., V, N, A) and the functional structure projected by it such as the relation between a verb and an auxiliary or between a noun and a determiner; (ii) the local selectional relation between a lexical head and the constituents that are combined with it to satisfy its argument structure, as in the case of the verb and the direct and indirect objects; (iii) the structural relation created by two different constituents that share the same referential index. In the last-mentioned case, we observe two major types: a constituent is displaced, as in the case of the subject of a passive clause or a *wh*-constituent; or two constituents share the same referent but have different functions in the clause (or in different clauses), as is the case of pronouns and their antecedents.

This chapter is structured as follows. Section 20.2 presents head–head dependencies. In so doing, it deals with parallels between clauses and nominal expressions in the linearization of the lexical head with its functional structure. Section 20.3 is devoted to head–argument dependencies, namely the encoding of the major grammatical relations: the subject in the clause, direct and indirect objects in the predicate, and the possessor in the nominal expression. The dependencies dealt with in the first two sections are 'local'. Sections 20.4–5 focus on the structural relations between two full-fledged phrases, one dependent for its interpretation on the other, which may be quite 'distant'. A long-distance dependency can be created by the displacement of one and the same constituent triggered by some functional feature (associated with the constituent itself or the position to which it moves, or with both). Section 20.4 considers the different types of long-distance dependency created by displacements. Section 20.5 considers long-distance dependencies created by pronouns.

20.2 Parallels between Nominal Expressions and Clauses

Investigation of Romance languages has contributed significantly to the development of the generative framework since the late 70s. In the late 80s, the application of X-bar theory was extended to functional heads, and the observation that functional features are hierarchically rigidly ordered was mainly based on Romance facts (cf. also Section 1.2). This investigation, applied to both sentences and nominal expressions, also made it possible to uncover structural parallelisms between the two domains (cf. also Section 1.2.4.5.2), which had gone unnoticed before.

20.2.1 Split IP, Split CP, and Verb Movement

Chomsky (1986) applied X-bar theory to the structural representation of auxiliaries and complementizers. The extension of the X-bar schema to functional heads on the one hand placed greater attention on functional words and features and on the other hand made it possible to uncover language variation in the linearization of the head with respect to its modifier dependents, which is captured in generative grammar through head-to-head movement. The empirical evidence from Romance languages confirmed the power of this model, but at the same time the need for a richer articulation of sentence structure.

Assuming Chomsky (1986), Pollock (1989) explained the difference between English and French in verb positions (cf. also Sections 1.2.3.2, 17.3, and 21.2.3), i.e., after or before negation (1), adverbs (2), and floating quantifiers (3), in terms of the impossibility vs obligatoriness of Verb movement to Infl, respectively:[1]

(1) a. John [Infl does] not [V like] Mary.
    b. Jean (n') [V+Infl aime] pas [V aime] Marie. (Fr.)

(2) a. John [Infl] often [V kisses] Mary.
    b. Jean [V+Infl embrasse] souvent [V embrasse] Marie. (Fr.)

(3) a. My friends [Infl] all [V love] Mary.
    b. Mes amis [V+Infl aiment] tous [V aiment] Marie. (Fr.)

---

[1] In (1) and throughout the chapter, material in strikethrough indicates the base-generated position of moved elements.

The French-internal contrast displayed in (4) shows that Chomsky's (1986) CP-IP-VP model is insufficient. An extra functional head between the adverb *souvent* and the negation *pas* is necessary to host infinitival verbs, which appear before *souvent* but after *pas* in (4):

(4) **French**
    a. Souvent paraître / Paraître souvent triste pendant son voyage de noces, c'est rare.
       often seem / seem often sad during one's honeymoon, that is rare
      'To often look sad during one's honeymoon is rare.'
    b. Ne pas paraître / **Ne paraître pas triste pendant son voyage de noces, c'est normal.
       NEG not seem / NEG seem not sad during one's honeymoon, that is normal
      'To not look sad during one's honeymoon is normal.'

Pollock proposed to split Infl into two heads, each encoding one of the inflexional features attributed to Infl: T and Agr(eement).

On the basis of Italian data, Belletti (1990) argued for a refinement of the ordering of Tense and Agreement, based on Baker's (1985) *Mirror Principle* (cf. also Section 17.3): in inflected words, Agreement morphemes follow Tense morphemes, hence they should be higher in the structural hierarchy. The AgrP-TP-VP model was generally adopted, even if criticized by Chomsky (1995), who denies the existence of Agr projections and claims that phi-features do not play any role at LF and are thus uninterpretable.

Belletti (1990) also showed that infinitives and past participles can appear higher in Italian than in French and extended the analysis to more adverb classes than Pollock had proposed. This prompted further research in the functional organization of sentence structure.

Ten years later, Cinque's (1999) detailed investigation of adverbs led to an explosion of functional heads in the inflexional domain of the clause. Adverbs are inserted as specifiers of functional projections encoding aspectual, mood, and modal features. Many more functional projections were therefore assumed. As a consequence, the verb was argued to have more movement possibilities, appearing before or after many adverbs of the functional hierarchy. This is the case of Italian, where verb movement is optional up to the position between habitual and repetitive adverbs, i.e., up to the highest position of low adverbs (Cinque 1999: 180 n. 80; 214 n. 7). In (5), the grammatical positions of the verb are indicated by √, the ungrammatical positions by **; some examples are provided in (6):

(5) ... ** saggiamente **di solito/solitamente || √ di nuovo √ spesso/raramente √ rapidamente √ ...
      wisely usually again often/rarely rapidly

    (6) a. Gianni lo merita di nuovo / raramente.
           Gianni ACC.MSG=deserves again rarely
          'Gianni deserves it again / rarely.'

b. **Gianni lo   merita   solitamente / francamente / probabilmente.
   Gianni ACC.MSG= deserves usually   frankly   probably

The microvariation observed in verb placement, both language-internally with regard to different verbal forms (e.g., finite vs non-finite in French) and cross-linguistically among different Romance languages, has been recently investigated by Schifano (2018), who suggests that the morphological shape of paradigms devoted to the expression of Tense, Aspect, and Mood determines whether the licensing is achieved through movement (syntactic strategy) or not (morphological strategy).

As argued by Cardinaletti (2007), (5) summarizes the verb placement possibilities in declarative sentences. In questions, the verb may precede *di solito/solitamente* and higher adverbs (cf. Rizzi 2001). The different verb placement in declarative and interrogative sentences is well-known from the study of English and other Germanic languages. Since the late 70s (Emonds 1976; Besten 1983; Thiersch 1978), auxiliaries and finite verbs have been claimed to raise in questions to a position preceding the subject, identified with C°. The fact that in Romance, subject–verb inversion is only found with pronouns (*Est-il* / **Est Jean parti?* 'is=he/is Jean left?') suggests that V-movement targets heads lower than C° (cf. Sportiche 1993/98; Kayne 1994), subject to microvariation (Cardinaletti 2014).

Mainly on the basis of Italian, Rizzi (1997) shows that Chomsky's (1986) CP-IP-VP tripartition is also insufficient for the CP layer and suggests a split CP (cf. also Section 1.2.3.3). More structural positions are needed to host different complementizers and topicalized and/or focalized elements, which may occur between the complementizer and the subject in the so-called clausal left periphery. The functional hierarchy arrived at by Rizzi (1997) is in (7a), where the Force head hosts finite complementizers (It. *che* 'that', Fr. *que* 'that', etc. found in finite complement and relative clauses), and the Fin head hosts infinitival complementizers (e.g., It. *di* 'of'). TopP is reserved for topics (and can be recursive, and indicated by ^{REC}Top), while FocP is the projection hosting focalized and *wh*-constituents. Rizzi (2001) further refines the articulation of the CP layer as in (7b), where two more projections are assumed. IntP hosts interrogative complementizers (e.g., It *se* 'if') and *wh*-words for 'why', which have a peculiar behaviour in Romance languages (Korzen 1985 for French; Contreras 1989 for Spanish; Shlonsky and Soare 2011 for Romanian), while WhP hosts *wh*-elements introducing embedded clauses, which may follow foci:[2]

---

[2] More Italian facts supporting Rizzi's serialization, in particular the occurrence of (Familiar) Topics after Foci, are discussed by Cardinaletti (2016b).

(7) a. Force ^{REC}Top Foc ^{REC}Top Fin IP
    b. ... Force ... Int ... Foc ... Wh ...

Finally, an IP-internal articulation of discourse-related positions immediately above VP, the so-called low periphery, is suggested by Belletti (2001; 2004) to host postverbal foci and topics.

Rizzi's proposal has been challenged by De Cat (2007a; 2007b) for French, López (2009) for Spanish, and by Kempchinsky (2013) for western Iberian languages (Asturian and Portuguese). They suggest that for these languages, which have fewer fronting possibilities than Italian, a much simpler left periphery should be adopted. De Cat suggests adjunction of the topic(s) to TP, López analyses topics and foci as multiple specifiers of FinP, and Kempchinsky assumes a Discourse Shell projection (following Emonds 2004).

20.2.2 The Adjectival Hierarchy and the Position of N

The possibility of adjectives in prenominal and postnominal position in Romance (cf. It. *una simpatica ragazza* 'a nice girl' / *una ragazza simpatica* lit. 'a girl nice') raises the question of how the modifier–noun dependency is represented in syntactic structure. The competing hypotheses are multiple and regard the possibility of directly inserting the adjective and the noun in either AN or NA order or derive one order from the other by movement. In the former case, alternatives concern the directionality of insertion and the nature of adjectives as specifiers or heads of dedicated functional projections, or adjuncts. In the latter case, alternatives concern whether N moves as a head (Cinque 1994) or carries along part of its projection (Cinque 2010), or whether adjectives move to dedicated positions (Demonte 1999; 2008).

The hypothesis that nominal structure parallels clausal structure assumes N-movement into functional heads as well as the proposal that adjectives are specifiers of hierarchically ordered functional heads (Cinque 1994; cf. also Section 1.2.4.5.2). In (8a), we observe the order Speaker-oriented > Subject-oriented > Manner > PP in an event nominal, with the adjectives inserted as specifiers of hierarchically ordered functional heads (X, Y, Z) and the lexical N moving through Z to Y. In (8b), the same relative order of adverbs and V is displayed by a perfectly parallel clause:

(8) a. [la [$_{XP}$ probabile [$_{YP}$ goffa [$_N$ reazione] [$_{ZP}$ immediata [N] [$_{NP}$ [N] [$_{PP}$ alla tua
       the   probable   clumsy   reaction   immediate   to.the your
       lettera]]]]]] (It.)
       letter
       'the probable clumsy immediate reaction to your letter'

    b. [$_{XP}$ Probabilmente avranno [$_{YP}$ goffamente [$_V$ reagito] [$_{ZP}$ subito [$_{VP}$ [¥] [$_{PP}$ alla tua
            probably   have.FUT.3PL clumsily   reacted   immediately   to.the your
       lettera]]]]]. (It.)
       letter
       'Probably, they will have clumsily immediately reacted to your letter.'

Object-denoting nominals also display hierarchically ordered adjectives, which include Evaluating > Size > Colour > Material, and intermediate N-movement. Most Romance languages behave like Italian in favouring an ANA order. There is, however, cross-Romance variation in the position of N. In (9a), we observe in French and Ladin (Cinque 1994) the same order found in Italian (8a). In Wallon (9b), N is quite low, following a colour adjective (cf. Bernstein 1991, from Remacle 1952). In Sardinian (9c), N is quite high preceding evaluative adjectives (cf. Jones 1993). In Romanian (9d), N is generated with the definite article and can precede a demonstrative set in a projection higher than the Evaluating adjective (Dobrovie-Sorin 1987; Grosu 1988; Giusti 1994; Cornilescu 1994):

(9) a. [DP un [XP joli [YP gros   [N ballon] [ZP rouge [N] [NP [N]]]]]] (Fr.)
       [DP una [XP bella [YP granda [N palla] [ZP cotchna [N] [NP [N]]]]]] (Lad.)
        a   nice   big   ball   red
       'a nice big red ball'
    b. [DP one [XP bèle [ZP bleûve [N cote] [NP [N]]]]] (Wal.)
        a   nice   blue   dress
    c. [DP una [XP bella [N mala] [YP manna [ZP rubia [N] [NP [N]]]]]] (Srd.)
        a   nice   apple   big   red
       'a nice big red apple'
    d. [DP [N+D băiatul] [KP acesta [N băiat] [XP frumos [N băiat]]]] (Ro.)
                boy.the   this   handsome
       'this handsome boy'

All examples in (9) display the hierarchy Evaluating > Size > Colour. The different positioning of the head N supports the proposal that there is a functional head for each adjectival modifier where the head N could appear, according to a parametric choice of the language.

Demonte (1999; 2008) proposes an alternative approach to the strict functional hierarchy, noting that in Spanish the order of prenominal adjectives is not as strict as the literature suggests for Italian. Demonte points out four classes of possible prenominal adjectives: (i) modal and epistemic modifying the denotation assignment function, (ii) intentionally oriented (intensifiers, restrictive, and evaluative) modifying central properties, (iii) circumstantial modifying a temporal interval, and (iv) non-restrictive adjectives expressing a distinctive property. She also points out that sequences of adjectives in prenominal position can only display one qualitative adjective (iv) and a variable number of members of the other three classes, as in (10).

(10)   **Spanish**
       a. **mi alto simpático amigo   **QUAL > QUAL > N
          'my tall nice   friend'
       b. mi posible futura amplia vivienda MOD.EP > CIRCUM > QUAL > N
          'my possible future spacious house'

Demonte then observes that classes (i) and (ii) can co-occur in either order, with class (iv), as in (11)–(12):

(11) Spanish
    a.   el   presunto delgado asesino MOD.EP > QUAL > N
         'the alleged   thin   murderer'
    b.   el   delgado   presunto asesino QUAL > MOD.EP > N
         'the thin   alleged murderer'

(12) a.   mi   única divertida colega INT.OR > QUAL > N
         'my only   funny   colleague'
      b.   mi   divertida única   colega QUAL > INT.OR > N
         'my funny   only   colleague'

Finally, Demonte observes that adjectives of classes (i)–(iii) can co-occur with another adjective of the same class in either order, again with different scope interpretations, as in the pairs in (13)–(15):

(13) Spanish
    a.   la   supuesta   falsa declaración MOD.EP > INT.OR > N
         'the supposedly false statement'
    b.   la   falsa supuesta declaración INT.OR > MOD.EP > N
         'the false supposed statement'

(14) a.   el   presunto supuesto asesino $MOD.EP_x$ > $MOD.EP_y$ > N
         'the alleged   supposed murderer'
      b.   el   supuesto presunto asesino $MOD.EP_y$ > $MOD.EP_x$ > N
         'the supposed alleged   murderer'

(15) a.   mi   verdadero único   amigo $INT.OR_x$ > $INT.OR_y$ > N
         'my true   only/unique friend'
      b.   mi   único   verdadero amigo $INT.OR_y$ > $INT.OR_x$ > N
         'my only/unique true   friend'

Following insights by Corver (1997a; 2007b), Demonte argues that all adjectives start as the predicate of a small clause complement of a null nominal head N coindexed with the NP subject of the small clause. Potentially gradable adjectives are associated with an uninterpretable feature to be checked by a higher head Deg(ree). SpecDegP is then available for movement of the NP subject of the predication, which can recursively contain a predicate AP:

(16) el [DegP [NP sombrero rojo] [A+Deg bellísimo] [NP N [SC NP [A] (Sp.)

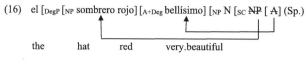

    the   hat   red   very.beautiful

'the very beautiful red hat'

Adjective movement to Deg accounts for prenominal qualitative adjectives with non-restrictive interpretation, while their base generation as predicates of a small clause accounts for the restrictive interpretation of qualitative adjectives in postnominal position. The free ordering in prenominal position in (11)–(15) is accounted for by the assumption that modal (class i) and circumstantial (class iii) adjectives can be adjoined to NP or DegP.

Against a universal hierarchy and in favour of right-/left-adjunction, Lamarche (1991) and Bouchard (1998; 2002: 124) observe that in (17), *malhonnêtes* has scope over *chinois* as expected in a right-adjunction proposal, and unexpected in the N-movement hypothesis in (9), while *présumés* is triply ambiguous, due to different possibilities of adjunction, as depicted in the glosses:

(17) **French**
    les présumés professeurs chinois malhonnêtes
    the alleged   professors   Chinese dishonest
    (i)   les [présumés [[professeurs chinois] malhonnêtes]]
         'the alleged dishonest Chinese professors'
    (ii) les [[présumés [professeurs chinois]] malhonnêtes]
         'the dishonest alleged Chinese professors'
    (iii) les [[[présumés professeurs] chinois] malhonnêtes]
         'the dishonest Chinese alleged professors'

Laenzlinger (2005) and Cinque (2010) derive the mirror order of postnominal adjectives following Kayne's (1994) antisymmetric proposal, which bans right-adjunction as well as head movement. They assume that each functional projection is dominated by an AgrP, whose specifier can host the NP and the portion of structure pied-piped along with it.

The predicate/adnominal divide is defined by Cinque (2010) as indirect/direct modification. Cinque claims that indirect modification is a reduced relative clause (IP) inserted hierarchically higher than direct modification (XP); the whole projection of direct modification will then be moved in the dotted line between D and NumP, as shown in (18):

(18)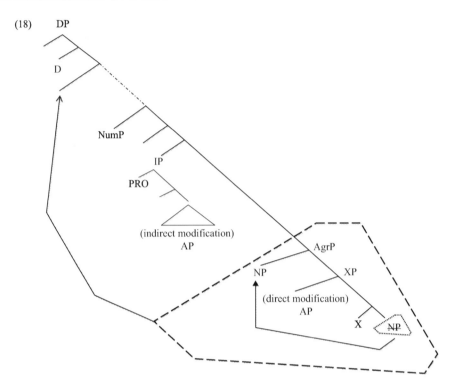

As a consequence of mandatory movement of the highest AgrP in the direct modification spine to the left of IP, indirect modification is linearized at the left of direct modification in N-final languages, such as English, and at the right of postnominal modification in ANA languages such as all Romance varieties, which also display some direct modification adjectives in postnominal position. Thus, adjectives that can be ambiguously interpreted as direct or indirect modification are prenominal in Germanic and postnominal in Romance. The Italian sentences in (19a–b) provide an example of the different semantic readings obtained from the direct vs indirect modification dependencies:

(19) **Italian**
    a.   Individual-level vs stage-level readings
        i. Le invisibili stelle di Andromeda sono molto distanti. (unambiguous)
          the invisible stars of Andromeda are   very   far
          'Andromeda's stars, which are generally invisible, are very far away.' (individual-level)
          #'Andromeda's stars, generally visible, which happen to be invisible now, are very far away.'
          (stage-level)

ii. Le stelle invisibili di Andromeda sono molto distanti. (ambiguous)
the stars invisible of Andromeda are very far
'Andromeda's stars, which are generally invisible, are very far away' (individual-level) or
'Andromeda's stars, generally visible, which happen to be invisible now, are very far away' (stage-level)

b. Restrictive vs non-restrictive readings
i. Le noiose lezioni di Ferri se   le   ricordano   tutti. (unambiguous)
the boring lessons of Ferri REFL= ACC.FPL= remember.PRS.IND.3PL all
'Everybody remembers Ferri's classes, all of which were boring.' (non-restrictive)
#'Everybody remembers just those classes by Ferri which were boring.' (restrictive)

ii. Le lezioni noiose di Ferri se   le   ricordano   tutti. (ambiguous)
the lessons boring of Ferri REFL= ACC.FPL= remember.PRS.IND.3PL all
'Everybody remembers Ferri's classes, all of which were boring.' (non-restrictive)
'Everybody remembers just those classes by Ferri which were boring.' (restrictive)

Prenominal orders apparently contradicting the hierarchy are explained by Giusti's (1996) proposal that DP can be split to host discourse features (arguably contrast, Giusti 2006), like the clausal CP. Language variation is centred on which elements can be hosted in the nominal left periphery. The Italian nominal left periphery only hosts contrasted topical adjectives, which can occur at the left of a prenominal possessor as in (20b–c), where (20b) apparently violates the hierarchy displayed by the unmarked order in (20a):

(20) **Italian**
a. le   sue lunghe trecce bionde
    the   her long   braids blond
b. le   BIONDE sue lunghe trecce ~~bionde~~
    the   blond   her long   braids
c. le   LUNGHE sue ~~lunghe~~ trecce bionde
    the   long   her   braids blond
    'her long blond braids'

Giusti (2005) proposes that the Romanian nominal left periphery can host a contrasted topical adjective, moved to the left of the cardinal *trei* and inflected with the suffixal article in (21b) or a contrastively focused demonstrative in turn preceded by the noun carrying the suffixal article in (21c). Note that the demonstrative is the highest element in the unmarked order (21a). Its focalization is therefore obtained by filling the highest head of the DP with an inflected N (21c). Only one displaced position is possible in these utterances, which are only appropriate in marked contests and certainly have borderline acceptability, but contrast sharply with the severely ungrammatical (21d–e):

(21) **Romanian**
a. [[$_{DP}$ aceste [$_{FP}$ trei [$_{FP}$ amabile [$_{NP}$ scrisori]]]] primite ieri]
   these   three   nice   letters   received yesterday

b. ??[[DP+KON AMABILELE [FP trei [FP amabile [NP scrisori]]]] primite ieri]
   nice.the   three   letters   received yesterday

c. ??[[DP scrisorile [FocP ACESTEA [FP trei [FP amabile [NP scrisori]]]]] primite ieri]
   letters.the   these   three   nice   received yesterday

d. **scrisorile ACESTEA AMABILE trei primite ieri
   letters.the these   nice   three received yesterday

e. **AMABILELE ACESTEA trei scrisori primite ieri
   nice.the   these   three letters received yesterday

Giusti and Iovino (2014; 2016) extend the split-DP hypothesis to Latin. The Latin nominal left periphery only hosts a single element, which can be an adjective of any category (22a–c), a genitive (22d), or an adjective extracted from an embedded genitive (22e):

(22) **Latin**
a. [LP [AP uetere] [DP illa [FP [AP uetere] [NP disciplina]]]]
   old.ABL.FSG   that.ABL.FSG   discipline.ABL.FSG
   'that old discipline' (Cic. Clu. 76)

b. [LP [AP tres] [DP illi [FP [AP tres] [NP fratres]]]]
   three   those.NOM.MPL   brothers.NOM.MPL
   'those three brothers' (Cic. Fam. 9,21,3)

c. [LP [AP Picentium]   [[AP nouorum]   [[AP Picentium]   [N sociorum]]]]
   Picene.GEN.MPL   new.GEN.MPL   allies.GEN.MPL
   'of new Picene allies' (Liv. 10,11,7)

d. [LP [DP2 Caesaris]   [DP1 hic [NP [DP2 Caesaris] [N' [PP per   Apuliam
   Caesar.GEN.MSG   this.NOM.MSG   through Apulia ACC.FSG
   ad   Brundisium]   cursus]]]]
   to   Brundisium.ACC.MSG   march.NOM.MSG
   'this march through Apulia to Brundisium of Caesar's' (Cic. Att. 8,11,7)

e. Sed abiit [LP [DemP2 huius] [DP1 [NP tempus] [DP2 [DemP2 huius] [NP querellae]]]]].
   but has.gone.away this.GEN.FSG   time.NOM.NSG   regret.GEN.FSG
   'But the time of this regret is far away.' (Cic. Cael. 74)

The split-DP analysis provides a framework to account for the parametric change from Latin to Romance (Giusti 2014). Latin is an apparently free order language without articles and with ease of extraction from the nominal expression because the DP-projection in the split-DP is lower than the left periphery. Romance languages, which all display articles, have a more restricted order than Latin, and a much more restricted possibility of extraction, because the DP-projection in the split-DP is higher than the left periphery.

20.3 Encoding and Licensing of Grammatical Relations

The encoding of grammatical relations such as subject, direct and indirect objects, oblique complements, and circumstantials theoretically concerns major areas of the research in syntax, morphology, semantics, and pragmatics that aims to explain word order alignments, agreement (on the selector), case assignment (on the dependent) and the different semantic and pragmatic phenomena arising with these phenomena.

The rich morphology on verbs, different classes of personal pronouns, variation in word order found with different classes of verb and different semantic and pragmatic interpretations are all empirical properties that characterize Romance languages and have inspired competing analyses set in different approaches. In this section, we provide a brief sketch of some of these phenomena and their accounts.

Grammatical relations are encoded by either DPs (subject, direct object) or PPs (indirect objects, oblique complements and circumstantials). No other modern Romance language except Romanian displays morphological case on DP internal elements. Abstract Case on DPs is supported by the morphological case realized on corresponding clitic pronouns which are attested in the different Romance languages.[3] Northern Italian dialects, northern Tuscan dialects, Provençal, and Raeto-Romance varieties display nominative clitic pronouns (Renzi and Vanelli 1983); accusative and dative clitic pronouns are attested in almost all Romance languages (with few exceptions, see Loporcaro 2010: n. 25 and Paoli 2009; 2014); locative and genitive/partitive clitic pronouns are less widespread and found today in Catalan, French, and Italian.

The properties of Romance clitic pronouns were described in detail by Kayne (1975), who recognized two morphologically and syntactically different series of pronouns, clitic and strong pronouns. Cardinaletti and Starke (1999) show that clitic pronouns also differ from weak pronouns and propose that natural languages may possess not two, but three pronominal classes. The rich Romance clitic system leads to the following generalization: clitic pronouns only realize arguments of the verb because they need to be extracted, and only arguments allow extraction (Cardinaletti 2015; 2016a). Non-arguments, such as temporal (23a) (from Cinque 1990: 119) and causal adjuncts (23b) and frame locatives (23c) (from Rizzi 1990: 127 n. 9), are never realized by clitic pronouns:

(23) a. Rimarrò tre settimane. a'.**Spero di rimanerle in allegria.
stay.FUT.IND.1SG three weeks hope.PRS.IND.1SG of stay.INF=3PL in joy
'I will stay three weeks.' 'I hope to stay them being jolly.'
b. Telefono per questo motivo. b'.**Ci telefono.
phone.IND.PRS.1SG for this reason there=phone.IND.PRS.1SG
'I phone for this reason.' 'I phone for this.'
c. Gianni è felice a casa dei genitori. c'.**Gianni ci è felice.
Gianni is happy at home of.the parents Gianni there=is happy
'Gianni is happy at their parents' house.' 'Gianni is happy there.'

---

[3] Strong and weak pronouns display residual manifestations of morphological case (cf. Italian strong subjects *io* 'I' and *tu* 'you' vs objects *me*, *te*; weak subject *egli* 'he' vs object *lui* 'him'; French weak subjects *je* 'I', *tu* 'you', *il* 'he', *ils* 'they').

Finally, consider null realizations of the arguments of the verb. Null subjects, found in most Romance languages (except modern French and Brazilian Portuguese, Duarte and Figueiredo Silva 2016),[4] and null objects, which are less frequent, require licensing in accordance with parametrization. Null subjects are licensed by rich inflexion (Rizzi 1982), null objects are either *pros*, licensed by the verb (Italian, Rizzi 1986) or a null clitic (French, Tuller 2000; Brazilian Portuguese, Cyrino and Matos 2016), or variables bound by null topics (European Portuguese, Cyrino and Matos 2016).

Grammatical relations are licensed structurally: in unmarked word order, subjects are preverbal and objects are postverbal. Romance languages also allow different postverbal positions for the subject, and show intricate language variation in this clausal space.

20.3.1 Encoding the Subject

Subjects are licensed in a high position within the sentential core, namely SpecTP, where nominative Case and agreement features are checked. Romance languages provide evidence for a richer 'subject field', composed of the projections TP and SubjP, which encode different subject features: phi-features at the basis of subject–verb agreement and the subject-of-predication feature, respectively (Cardinaletti 2004). The crucial empirical evidence is provided by those cases in which preverbal subjects of predication are not DPs, but dative or locative PP arguments of unaccusative verbs, as in Italian (24) (Belletti and Rizzi 1988; Cardinaletti 1997), or locative PPs, as in Brazilian Portuguese (25) (Quarezemin and Cardinaletti 2017):

(24) **Italian**
 a. [SubjP A Gianni [TP è [VP a Gianni piaciuto il regalo]]].
   to Gianni is   pleased the present
   'Gianni liked the present.'
 b. [SubjP Su Gianni [TP è [VP su Gianni caduta una grande disgrazia]]].
   on Gianni is   fallen a big misfortune
   'A misfortune befell Gianni.'

(25) [SubjP Naquela loja [TP pro_GEN vendem [VP naquela loja livros]]]. (BrPt.)
   in.that store   pro_GEN sell.PRS.IND.3PL   books
   'In that shop, they sell books.'

Further evidence is provided by French Complex Inversion (Kayne 1983). The clitic subject pronoun adjoins to Subj, the auxiliary adjoins to it, and the strong subject occupies SpecSubjP (see Kayne 1994: 139 n. 15 and Sportiche 1999 for similar analyses):

---

[4] The analysis of northern Italian dialects as pro-drop languages is debated, cf. Poletto (2000) and Cardinaletti and Repetti (2010) for different analyses, and the discussions in Sections 4.2.1, 17.5.1.1, and 21.2.1.

(26) Quand [SubjP Pierre / lui a-t-il [TP il a [VP il téléphoné]]]? (Fr.)
    when   Pierre   he has=he   telephoned
    'When did Pierre / he call?'

The canonical subject position is thus preverbal. With (in)transitive verbs, this is the case in all Romance languages. Language variation is found with unaccusative verbs, with which the unmarked subject position is postverbal with the exception of French (Burzio 1986). Postverbal subjects are also licensed with transitive and intransitive verbs when they are narrow foci. To capture the correlation with null subjects (Rizzi 1982), Belletti (2005) interprets postverbal subjects as the result of subject movement to clause-internal SpecFocP, followed by verb-raising to an aspectual head above the subject and movement of referential *pro* to the preverbal subject position (DP and *pro* are generated as constituents of one single nominal expression, called 'big DP' as happens in doubling structures, cf. Torrego 1995; Uriagereka 2005):

(27) [TP pro Ha [AspP parlato [FocP Gianni [VP Gianni parlato]]]]. (It.)
           has   spoken   Gianni
    'Gianni spoke.'

If the 'doubling + low periphery' hypothesis is not adopted, these cases require a different way of licensing the subject, via either covert movement to the preverbal subject position or the Agree relation suggested by Chomsky (2000; 2001), a dependency-creating operation between the Infl-Probe and the subject Goal.

Finally, Spanish and Romanian also allow postverbal subjects in the wide-focus order VSO, as in (28a) from Ordóñez (1997: 31) and (28b) from Laenzlinger and Soare (2005: 41), where an extra subject position is assumed (Ordóñez 1998; 1999; 2007; Zubizarreta 1998):

(28) a. Ayer   ganó Juan la lotería. (Sp.)
         yesterday won Juan the lottery
         'Yesterday Juan won the lottery.'
     b. A   citit Ion cartea. (Ro.)
         has read Ion book.DEF
         'Ion read the book.'

The possibility of VSO is often correlated with the differential object marking (DOM) found in Spanish and Romanian (see Section 20.3.2): Languages that allow VSO have DOM (Belletti 2004; Gallego 2013). The reverse is not true: southern Italian dialects (Ledgeway 2016), Catalan (Escandell-Vidal 2007; 2009; Benito Galdeano 2017) and Portuguese (Schwenter 2014) have (some instances of) DOM, but they do not license VSO.[5]

---

[5] In Italian (Cardinaletti 2001) and European Portuguese (Costa 2004: 119–24), VSO is a legitimate order when both the subject and the object are focused with a pair-list reading. In such cases the subject is taken to be VP-internal.

20.3.2 Encoding Objects

In Romance languages, direct objects are distinguished from indirect and prepositional objects through the absence vs presence of a dependent marker. In this respect, they are similar to subjects. In fact, nominative and accusative are often called direct cases, to be distinguished from all other functions that are marked with indirect/oblique cases.

In Nichols' (1986) typology of head- vs dependent-marking languages, following insights by Vincent (1997), Ledgeway (2011: 434–37) notes that Romance languages are of a mixed type. Head-marking appears in the form of subject-agreement on verb-morphology (cf. Section 20.2.1) and as object (rarely subject) clitics affixed on the selecting head V. It is well-known that both series of pronouns in all Romance languages also display dependent marking in the form of case-morphology (cf. Section 20.4.2). In full DP-objects, eastern Romance presents a residue of oblique case mainly on determiners (29a). But prepositions are abundantly used to distinguish indirect objects, while direct objects are generally prepositionless. Note that in both Romanian and Spanish, the dative dependent of a double object predicate is optionally doubled by a clitic, which can be considered head-marking:

(29) a. (Le)-am dat bomboane băieților / ?la băieți. (Ro.)
DAT.3PL=have.PRS.IND.1SG given sweets boys.the.DAT.PL to boys
'I gave given the boys sweets' (Dragomirescu and Nicolae 2016: 920)
b. Pablo (le) mandó un diccionario a Gabi. (Sp., Cuervo 2003)
Pablo DAT.3SG=send.PST.PFV.3SG a dictionary to Gabi
'Pablo sent a dictionary to Gabi.'

There are many apparent exceptions to the bare direct object / marked indirect object generalization. Direct objects in Spanish, Romanian, and some Italo-Romance varieties can be marked by a preposition, as in (30)–(31):

(30) a. Atacamos a Pepe. (Sp., Fábregas 2013: 5)
attack.PRS.IND.1PL *a* Pepe
'We attack Pepe.'
b. L-am văzut pe Ion. (Ro., Dobrovie-Sorin 1987: 200)
ACC.3SG=have.PRS.1SG seen *pe* Ion
'I saw Ion.'

(31) a. Appo vistu a Juanne. (Srd., Jones 1995)
have.PRS.IND.1SG seen *a* Juanne
'I saw Juanne.'
b. Emu infattatu à Petru. (Cor., Ledgeway 2016: 226)
have.PRS.IND.1PL met *a* Petru
'We met Petru.'

This phenomenon is known as the prepositional accusative or differential object marking (DOM; cf. also Section 23.2.4.1). It is quite widespread across languages (Bossong 1985; 1991) and the preposition presents different forms across Romance languages, mainly AD > *a* 'to, at', but also (SU)PER > *pe* 'on' in Romanian, sometimes IN MEDIO (AD) > *ma/me* 'to' in central Italy, and DE+AB > *da* 'from' in Sicilian Gallo-Italic varieties (A. Ledgeway p.c.). Typological and functional linguistics have established that differentially marked direct objects are high in one or all the hierarchies in (32) regarding the interpretation of NPs, while canonically (un)marked direct objects are low (cf. Levin 2019, and references therein). The direct object of a transitive verb has greater chances of being differentially marked the lower the verb is in the transitivity scale (Hopper and Thompson 1980; Tsunoda 1985; Herslund 2002):

(32) a. Animacy scale: First/second > Third pronoun > Name > Human > Animate > Inanimate
   b. Definiteness scale: Pronoun > Proper name > Definite > Indefinite specific NP > Non-specific NP
   c. Affectedness scale: ACTION > PERCEPTION > PURSUIT > KNOWLEDGE > FEELING

Variation across languages, constructions, and even speakers involves not only the point(s) of the hierarchies which discriminate the two opposites, but also many other properties of individual languages with which DOM interacts, making DOM a privileged object of theoretical studies.

The lexical properties of the verb class and the morphosyntactic properties of the nominal expression are the most important factors that interact with DOM. This leads many linguists to argue that 'transitivity' is a clausal, not just a verbal property (Delbeque 2002; Cennamo 2003).

From the point of view of historical linguistics, Sornicola (2011: 36–40) notes that verbs such as HELP, PRAY, CALL, LISTEN can select a dative object in many old and modern Romance languages, including French, a language which normally does not display DOM. The direct/prepositional object alternation is claimed to have started from the co-existence of these intransitive bi-argumental verbs with fully transitive verbs. The preposition *a* may have then appeared on strong (dative) pronouns as an expletive, in order to maintain the bisyllabic structure derived from Lat. MIHI, TIBI, surfacing as OSp. *miue, teue,* C/SItR. *mene, tene* and *mia, tia,* most of which were otherwise being lost, and then extended to accusative pronouns. Note, that Lat. AD 'to (wards)' itself selects accusative. According to Sornicola, the need to distinguish objects with topical or animacy features from subjects may have helped the propagation of the phenomenon rather than being triggered by it. Von Heusinger and Kaiser's (2011) corpus search on [+human] objects of transitive verbs across three different periods of Spanish confirms the hypothesis that spread of DOM on human objects depends on the level of Affectedness of the predicate and relative degree of 'agency' of the object. This is also confirmed by Fiorentino (2003) for different stages of Neapolitan.

Data from the development of the locative preposition *pe* 'on' in Romanian go in a different direction. According to Mardale (2009), Hill (2013), and Hill and Mardale (2017), *pe* bleaches into a differential object marker through an intermediate stage as a topic marker. The hypothesis is that *pe* was projected in the left periphery of the nominal expression (cf. Section 20.3.2) with features checked at the left periphery of the clause. This proposal is in line with Brugè and Brugger's (1996) proposal that Spanish *a* heads a projection (KP) above DP which is overt when KP is accusative. Null K is possible in object position either when the DP is not [+animate] or when it is assigned partitive case, which is the case displayed by genitive clitic *ne* in Italian according to Cardinaletti and Giusti (1992; 2016).

Generative approaches have implemented different versions of Larson's (1998) VP-shell hypothesis and its development into the *v*P-phase (Chomsky 2001; 2008; Gallego 2010) to account for the correlation between the semantic interpretation of the marked direct object and the occurrence of the *a*-marker (cf. Ordóñez 1998; 2007; Torrego 1998; Cuervo 2003; Belletti 2004; Leonetti 2004; Ledgeway 2011; López 2012).[6] The split *v*P structure presents a functional head above the lexical VP (little *v*) assigning the theta role to the external argument and at the same time assigning structural accusative case to the internal argument. The issue is here whether accusative *a* and dative *a* are markers of the same structural dependency (as argued by Manzini and Franco 2016 for Italo-Romance; Gallego 2010 and Torrego 2010 for Ibero-Romance) or whether there are two *a*-markers occurring in different positions (Torrego 1998; López 2012). This issue does not arise in Romanian due to the locative origin of *pe*.

The split *v*P hypothesis permits one to analyse clitic doubling as an overt marker of agreement between the case-assigning *v* and the targeted DP. The considerable microvariation found with the occurrence of the doubling clitic is expected on the hypothesis that parameters are features associated with functional heads. In this line of research, the iteration of *v*-heads and the parametrization of a D-feature that can be absent or present in *v* and, if present, can be complete or incomplete, can capture many apparently unrelated facts that characterize Romance languages (for overviews cf. D'Alessandro and Roberts 2008; Fábregas 2013; Mardale 2017; Gallego 2018, and references therein). Among these, we mention the following three facts.

(i) The dative/accusative alternation found in causative constructions in Italian and French suggests that the *a*/*à*–marker serves to differentiate

---

[6] In simple terms, a 'phase' is a derivational domain, which enjoys phonological, semantic, and syntactic autonomy.

the embedded initiator subject of a transitive predicate from the main causer subject of the causative event, as in (33a). The subject of an embedded intransitive is instead assigned accusative when the embedded predicate is monoargumental (regardless of whether it is unaccusative or unergative), as in (33b):

(33) **Italian**
    a. Maria ha fatto bere il vino **(a) Gianni.
        Maria has made drink.INF the wine to Gianni
        'Maria made Gianni drink the wine.'
    b. Maria ha fatto bere (**a) Gianni.
        Maria has made drink.INF to Gianni
        'Maria made Gianni drink.'

Note that the accusative clitic *lo* in (34a) either resumes the patient role of transitive 'drink' as in (33a) or the agent role of unergative 'drink' in (33b). The dative subject of transitive 'drink' can also be cliticized, as in (34b):

(34) **Italian**
    a. Maria lo ha fatto bere.
        Maria ACC.MSG=has made drink.INF
        'Maria made him drink.' / 'Maria had it drunk.'
    b. Maria glielo ha fatto bere.
        Maria DAT.SG=ACC.MSG=has made drink.INF
        'Maria made him drink it.'

(ii) The dative/accusative alternation is also found on the experiencer objects of unaccusative verbs (Belletti and Rizzi 1988; Folli and Harley 2007; Torrego 2010; Piñeda and Royo 2017):

(35) **Italian**
    a. La storia interessa (a) Maria.
        the history interests to Maria
        'History interests Maria.'
    b. La storia le/la interessa.
        the history DAT/ACC.FSG=interests
        'History interests her.'

(iii) Accusative Goals alternating with the more canonical dative can be passivized (Ledgeway 2000: 30f.; Andriani 2011: 53f.; Piñeda and Royo 2017), showing that they are exactly parallel to canonical direct objects:

(36)   a. Maragall ha estat telefonat personalment pel president. (Cat.)
          Maragall has been phoned personally by.the president
          'Maragall was called in person by the president.'
      b. Maríjə ha státə tələfonátə (dò marítə). (Bar.)
          Maria has been phoned (of.the husband)
          'Maria was telephoned (by her husband).'

    c. Socrama   fuje telefunata. (Nap.)
        mother-in-law=my was   phoned
        'My mother-in-law was telephoned.'

The three properties above are related to the presence of a functional feature (an applicative, following insights by Pylkkänen 2002; cf. Cuervo 2003 for Spanish, Diaconescu and Rivero 2007 for Romanian). This functional feature is mingled with *v* but subject to parametric variation as regards the precise point in which it is projected.

20.3.3 Possessives

In addition to PPs (37a) and genitive DPs (37b; cf. Grosu 1988), arguments of nouns may be realized by possessives. Romance languages provide evidence that possessives may be of different grammatical categories: determiners as in French and Spanish (38a), adjectives as in Italian (38b), and genitive personal pronouns as in Italian and Romanian (38c) (Cornilescu 1994; Cardinaletti 1998):

(37) a.   la   maison de Jean / la   casa   di Gianni / la   casa   de Juan (Fr./It./Sp.)
          the house   of Jean   the house   of Gianni   the house   of Juan
          'Jean's/Gianni's/Juan's house'
     b.   portretul   regelui (Ro.)
          portrait.DEF   king.DEF.GEN
          'The king's portrait'

(38) a. sa   (belle)   maison / su   (hermosa)   casa (Fr./Sp.)
         her/his.FSG   beautiful   house   her/his.FSG   beautiful   house
         'his/her (beautiful) house'
     b. la   sua   (bella)   casa (It.)
         the his/her.FSG beautiful   house
         'her/his beautiful house'
     c. la   loro   (bella)   casa /   elegantul   lui /   ei /   lor   apartament (It./Ro.)
         the they.GEN   beautiful   house   elegant.the   he.GEN   she.GEN   they.GEN   apartment
         'their beautiful house / her/his/their elegant apartment'

The categorial realization does not have an impact on the grammatical relations encoded by possessives. While with common nouns (38) possessives realize a possessive relation, with deverbal nouns they realize either the theme or the agent of the noun:

(39) a.   sa   description /   su   descripción (Fr./Sp.)
          his/her.FSG   description   his/her   description
          'his/her description'
     b.   la   sua   descrizione (It.)
          the his/her.FSG   description
          'her/his description'

    c.   la   loro   descrizione / descrierea   lui (It./Ro.)
        the they.GEN description description.the he.GEN
        'their/his description'

Cinque (1980a; 1980b) suggests that possessives realize the subject of the noun phrase, thus establishing a parallelism between nominal expressions and clauses. The realization of the theme of the noun as a possessive is constrained if the agent is also present; the ungrammatical sentence in (40b) contrasts with (40a), where the possessive realizes the agent; the possessive can be the theme of the noun only if the noun is turned into a passive (40c) (cf. Milner 1977 for French and Cornilescu 1994 for Romanian):

(40) **Italian**
    a.   la sua descrizione dell' evento
        the his description of.the event
        'his description of the event'
    b.   la sua descrizione di Gianni (** with the intended reading 'its description by G.')
        the its description of Gianni
        'its description of Gianni'
    c.   la sua descrizione da parte di Gianni
        the its description by part of Gianni
        'its description by Gianni'

The occurrence of possessives immediately after the determiner (38b–c) suggests that (i) they are licensed in a position parallel to the clausal subject position and (ii) the licensing of prenominal possessives 'can be compared to structural case-assignment to an argument' (Picallo 1994: 269). Let us call this projection Poss(essive)P (Sportiche 1990/98: 217).

Strong possessive adjectives as in Spanish and Italian may however stay in their NP-internal thematic positions, usually occupied by PPs and DPs (37) (Cardinaletti 1997; Brugè 2002):

(41) a.   la casa   suya (Sp.)
       b.   la casa   sua (It.)
           the house his/her(Sp. /their).FSG
           'his/her(/their) house'

Postnominal possessives are analysed as in (42a) (in situ possessives end up postnominal due to N-movement to F, Cinque 1994). The prenominal and the thematic position of possessives are transformationally related (cf. Langacker 1968; Kayne 1975; Belletti 1978). The derivation of (38b) is (42b):

(42) a.   [$_{DP}$ la [$_{POSSP}$ ... [$_{FP}$ casa [$_{NP}$ sua ~~casa~~]]]]
       b.   [$_{DP}$ la [$_{POSSP}$ sua ... [$_{FP}$ casa [$_{NP}$ ~~sua~~ ~~casa~~]]]]

Some central Italian dialects (e.g., Ancona, Marche (43a)) and all modern southern Italian dialects (e.g., Lanciano, Abruzzo (43b)) with the exception of Sicilian and extreme southern Calabrian only allow postnominal possessives (Cardinaletti and Giusti 2019), paralleling VSO languages in which the subject does not raise. Possessive movement to prenominal subject position is thus subject to language variation as is the case of subject movement to preverbal subject position:

(43) a. [DP el [POSSP [FP ca' [NP mio ca']]]] (Anc.)
b. [DP lu [POSSP [FP canə [NP mé canə]]]] (Lnc.)
      the   dog   my

20.4 Long-Distance Dependencies

Long-distance dependencies are instantiated either by 'movement' or by co-reference. In this section, we present cases of the former type.

In a theory that strives for economy, movement is a costly operation; it therefore only obtains when needed. There are three types of long-distance movement: A-movements create a link between the highest argument of the predicate phase and the subject of the clause, satisfying some version of the 'Extended Projection Principle' which requires a proposition to have a subject. Clitic movement displaces an element that is at the same time a phrasal constituent and a head from its initial position (where it is interpreted as a constituent) to a head position. A'-movements create discourse structures such as different clause types (interrogative, exclamative, jussive, etc.), with displacements of different amounts of structures.

20.4.1 A-Movements

At many points in this chapter, we have had recourse to the notion 'subject'. The subject is the external argument of the predicate, which comes into a special dependency relation, often called agreement, with T(ense). The dual nature of subject as a dependent of both V and T is captured in the generative literature by the so-called VP-internal subject hypothesis first proposed by Koopman and Sportiche (1991), according to which the subject originates in SpecVP (or SpecvP, in more recent terms), where it receives its theta role locally assigned by v/V but no case. For this reason, it moves to SpecTP where it is assigned nominative by a finite T. The hypothesis has the theory-internal advantage of keeping structural relations such as theta role and case assignment local. It is empirically supported by Sportiche's (1988) analysis of floating quantifiers. Notably, quantifiers can be found in a long-distance dependency with the quantified nominal expression only if the nominal expression moves leaving the quantifier in place, as is the case of the subject in (44a) and the clitic object in (44c), but not the object in (44b):

(44) Italian
    a. {Tutte} Le bambine {**tutte} hanno {tutte} mangiato {tutte} un panino {tutte}.
        {all} the girls {all} have {all} eaten {all} a sandwich {all}
        'All the girls have eaten a sandwich.'
    b. La bambina ha mangiato {tutti} i panini {**tutti}.
        The girl has eaten {all.MPL} the sandwiches.MPL {all.MPL}
        'The girl has eaten all the sandwiches.'
    c. La bambina li ha mangiati {tutti} li.
        the girl ACC.MPL= has eaten.MPL {all.MPL}
        'The girl has eaten them all.'

When the external argument is absent, as is the case of a passive predicate, the internal argument moves to the subject position to receive case. In a theory of economy, this is only possible if the passive verb is unable to assign accusative case to its internal argument. Most Romance languages signal this non-canonical subject-T dependency with auxiliary BE (which was already present in Latin in passive compound tenses), which agrees for the person features of the subject, as usual.[7] Central Romance languages also display gender and number agreement on the past participle:

(45) Italian
    a. Le torte sono state mangiate.
        The cakes.FPL are been.FPL eaten.FPL
        'The cakes have been eaten.'
    b. I panini sono stati mangiati.
        the sandwiches.MPL are been.MPL eaten.MPL
        'The sandwiches have been eaten.'

This was analysed by Kayne (1989a) as evidence for local movement through the specifiers of past participle projections (cf. Section 19.3.1). In a theory of Spec-head agreement, Belletti (2001) proposed an Agr projection above each participial head. In the more recent theory of phases, D'Alessandro and Roberts (2008) propose that this is derived by the defective character of the passive *v* and the consequent need to extend the lower phase (the *v*P) to the higher phase (the CP). The argument is built on independent evidence provided by Belletti (2001: 30) that active past participles have to move across a low manner adverb such as *bene* 'well', while passive past participles can but do not have to. Note that the active past participle does not agree with the feminine singular features of the object (46a), while it must agree when the object is promoted to subject in (46b):

---

[7] In many Ladin varieties, the auxiliary is not BE, but COME. Some dialects of eastern Basilicata and north-western Puglia optionally use HAVE alongside 'BE'. See Ledgeway (2021).

(46) **Italian**
    a.   Hanno {**bene} accolto {bene} la sua interpretazione solo loro.
           have {well} received {well} the his.FSG performance.FSG only they
           'Only they have well received his performance.'
    b.   La sua interpretazione è sempre stata {bene} accolta {bene}.
           the his.FSG performance.FSG is always been.FSG {well} received.FSG {well}

According to D'Alessandro and Roberts, the obligatory movement of the active past participle in (47a) is evidence that the lower *v*P is an independent phase; it assigns accusative to its internal argument (DP2), which is interpreted in *v*P independently of the upper CP-phase. In the case of a passive past participle in (47b), the internal argument (DP1) needs to remain in the computation of the CP-phase, where it is interpreted as the subject of the clause. For this reason, the participle may remain in place where it can therefore follow *bene*. But for the internal argument to be interpreted as part of the upper phase, the past participle must move into the *v*P which is dependent on the passive auxiliary BE. For this reason, the relationship with its internal argument must be overt:

(47) a. [$_{CP}$ C [$_{TP}$ T+*v*Aux.HAVE [$_{vP}$ Aux.HAVE [$_{vPrtP}$ DP2 *v*PTCP [$_{VP}$ V DP1]]]   transitive *v*P

    b. [$_{CP}$ C [$_{TP}$ T+*v*Aux.BE +*v*PTCP [$_{vP}$ *v*Aux.BE+*v*PTCP [$_{vPrtP}$ *v*PTCP[$_{VP}$ V DP1]]]   passive *v*P

This is also the case with unaccusative verbs (48a) and *se/si* constructions (48b), which are characterized by the extension of the phase because they only have a DP1 internal argument that is interpreted as the clausal subject sharing person features with T and number and gender features with *v*PTCP:

(48) **Italian**
    a.   Sono arrivate tre ragazze.
           are arrived.FPL three girls
           'Three girls arrived.'
    b.   Si sono visti tre ragazzi.
           REFL= are seen.MPL three boys
           'Three boys were seen.'

20.4.2 Clitic Movement

Cliticization shares properties with A-movement. It is TP-internal (clitic pronouns target a position to the right of preverbal subjects 49) and local (clitic pronouns never move out of embedded clauses 50):

(49) a.   Jean la voit ~~la~~ / Gianni la vede ~~la~~. (Fr./It.)
           Jean ACC.FSG= sees   Gianni ACC.FSG= sees
           'Jean/Gianni sees her.'

b. Jean l'   a   vu/vue le/la / Gianni l'   ha   visto/vista lo/la. (Fr./It.)
   Jean ACC= has   seen.M/FSG   Gianni ACC= has   seen.M/FSG
   'Jean/Gianni saw him/her.'

(50) **Italian**
   a. Gianni ha deciso [CP di dirlo lo   a Maria].
       Gianni has decided   to say.INF-CL.ACC.M.SG to Maria
   a'. **Gianni lo   ha deciso [CP di dire lo a Maria].
       Gianni ACC.MSG= has decided   to say.INF   to Maria
       'Gianni decided to tell Maria (it).'
   b. Gianni ha deciso [CP che lo   dirà lo   a Maria].
       Gianni has decided that CL.ACC.M.SG say.FUT.3SG to Maria
   b'. **Gianni lo   ha deciso [CP che dirà lo   a Maria].
       Gianni ACC.MSG= has decided   that say.FUT.3SG to Maria
       'Gianni decided that he will tell Maria (it).'

Mandatory past participle agreement as in French and Italian (49b) led to the view that cliticization is decomposed into two steps: DP-movement triggering agreement on the past participle (Kayne 1989a), followed by cliticization proper, i.e., head movement to the inflected auxiliary (Sportiche 1990/98; Belletti 1999; Cardinaletti and Starke 1999):

(51) [TP Jean [T' l'a [AgrOP la vue [VP Jean vue la]]].

The proposal by Kayne (1989b) that clitic pronouns are heads is supported by the observation that they undergo movement together with their hosts. In French interrogatives (52a) (Kayne 1975) and Italian hypotheticals (52b) and gerunds (52c) (Rizzi 2000: 108), the verb moves to a position to the left of the subject taking the object clitic pronoun along:

(52) a. [SubjP [Subj L'   as] [TP tu [l'as] [VP vu le]]? (Fr.)
                  ACC= have   you   seen
        'Did you see him?'
     b. [CP [C L'   avesse] [TP Gianni l'avesse [VP programmato lo in anticipo]]] ... (It.)
             ACC= had   Gianni   programmed   in advance
        'If Gianni had planned it in advance, ...'
     c. [CP [C Avendola] [TP Gianni [avendola] [VP restituita la al   direttore]]] ... (It.)
              having=ACC.FSG Gianni   given.back   to.the director
        'Since Gianni gave it back to the director, ...'

Romanian shows that cliticization also applies to adverbs which appear between clitic pronouns and finite verbs (53a) and are taken along by imperative verb movement to C' (53b) (Dobrovie-Sorin 1994):

(53) **Romanian**
   a. Îl   mai   văd.
      ACC.MSG= again see.PRS.1SG
      'I am seeing him again.'

b. [CP [C Mai   spune-]   [TP mi   ~~mai spune~~]]
       again   tell.IMP.2SG   =me.DAT
   'Tell me again!'

An alternative analysis of cliticization is put forward by Sportiche (1996/ 98), who takes clitic pronouns to realize functional heads in the clausal skeleton (CliticVoices), into whose specifier a null object is moved to establish a specifier-head relation with the clitic head, the so-called Clitic Criterion:

(54) [TP Gianni   la   vede [CliticVoiceP *pro* ~~la~~ [VP ~~Gianni~~ vede ~~*pro*~~]]]. (It.)
          Gianni   ACC.FSG=   sees
      'Gianni sees her.'

In Sportiche's analysis, one and the same structure accounts for simple cliticization, as in (54), and clitic doubling, where clitic pronouns co-occur with argument XPs: either direct objects (55) (River Plate Spanish and Romanian; Jaeggli 1982; Dobrovie-Sorin 1990; 1994), or indirect objects (56) (Spanish, Demonte 1995; and Italian):

(55) a. Lo   vimos   a   Juan. (Sp.)
          ACC.MSG=   see.PST.PFV.1PL   to Juan
          'We saw Juan.'
      b. L-   am   văzut   pe   Ion. (Ro.)
          ACC.MSG=   have.PRS.1SG   seen   ACC   Ion
          'We saw Ion.'

(56) a. Le   entregué   las   llaves   al   conserje. (Sp.)
          DAT.MSG=   give.PST.PFV.1SG   the   keys   to.the   janitor
          'I gave the keys to the janitor.'
      b. Gliele   ho   date   a   Gianni. (It.)
          DAT=ACC.FPL=   have.PRS.IND.1SG   given.FPL   to   Gianni.
          'I gave them to Gianni.'

Doubling DPs/PPs are taken to raise to the specifiers of CliticVoices by covert movement. (57) shows the syntactic and LF-representation of (55a):

(57) a. Syntax: [CliticVoiceP lo [VP vimos a Juan]].
      b. LF: [CliticVoiceP a Juan lo [VP vimos ~~a Juan~~]].

As observed above, cliticization is a local movement. Apparent instances of long-distance clitic movement are found in clitic-climbing contexts in Italian (58) (and all Romance languages except French and some northern Italian dialects, Kayne 1991; Egerland 2009; cf. also Section 19.2.2):

(58) **Italian**
    a. Voglio   farlo   ~~lo~~.   a.′ Lo   voglio   fare ~~lo~~.
        want.PRS.IND.1SG do.INF=ACC   ACC= want.PRS.IND.1SG do.INF
        'I want to do it.'   'I want to do it.'
    b. Comincio a farlo ~~lo~~. b.′ Lo   comincio a fare ~~lo~~.
        start.PRS.IND.1SG to do.INF=ACC   ACC= start.PRS.IND.1SG to do.INF
        'I am starting to do it.'   'I am starting to do it.'
    c. Vado   a farlo ~~lo~~. c.′ Lo   vado   a fare ~~lo~~.
        go.PRS.IND.1SG to do.INF=ACC   ACC= go.PRS.IND.1SG to do.INF
        'I am going to do it.'   'I am going to do it.'

Clitic climbing is reduced to TP-internal movement by enriching grammar with either a restructuring rule applying in the presence of modal, aspectual, and motion verbs, by which these verbs and the lexical verb create a complex V (Rizzi 1978), or the base generation of these verbs as functional heads in the clausal skeleton (Cinque 2004; 2006). When clitic climbing applies, restructuring verbs indeed lose their argument structure and behave like functional verbs (Cinque 2004; Haegeman 2006). (59) is a schematic representation where FP stays for the functional projections associated with the lexical verb, subject to rigid ordering restrictions, and clitic indicates the landing site of clitic climbing as in (58a′–c′):

(59)   [$_{CP}$ ... [$_{TP}$ clitic [$_{FP}$ V$_{restr}$ [$_{FP}$ ... [$_{VP}$ V$_{lex}$]]]]]

To account for enclisis as in (58a–c), a low clitic position above VP must be assumed, as schematized in (60) (Cardinaletti and Shlonsky 2004):

(60)   [$_{CP}$ ... [$_{TP}$ clitic [$_{FP}$ V$_{restr}$ [$_{FP}$ ... [$_{FP}$ clitic [$_{VP}$ V$_{lex}$]]]]]]

An argument for the existence of two clitic positions is provided by (61): auxiliary *essere* 'be', selected by the unaccusative verb *andare*, not only occurs with proclisis (61a) but also with enclisis (61b). Since *essere* is only possible with restructuring verbs (cf. *Gianni ha / **è detto [di andare a Roma]* 'Gianni has / **is said to go to Rome'), both (61a) and (61b) are restructuring contexts, where *ci* occupies the high and the low clitic position, respectively:

(61) **Italian**
    a. Gianni ci   è voluto [$_{VP}$ andare ~~ci~~].
        Gianni LOC= is wanted   go.INF
    b. Gianni è voluto [$_{FP}$ andarci   [$_{VP}$ ~~andare ci~~]].
        Gianni is wanted   go.INF=LOC
        'Gianni wanted to go there.'

Another argument comes from (62), where two links of the clitic chain are spelled out: one on the infinitival verb and the highest one in the functional domain (Kayne 1989b: 257 n. 37):

(62) ?Gianni li   vuole [FP vederli   [VP vedere li]]. (It.)
    Gianni ACC.MPL= wants   see.INF=ACC.MPL
    'Gianni wants to see them.'

In addition to proclisis and enclisis, European Portuguese (in future and conditional tenses), Spanish and Italian dialects (in positive imperatives) also display mesoclisis. A lively debate between morphological and syntactic accounts continues (Vigário 1999; Harris and Halle 2005; Kayne 2010; Manzini and Savoia 2011; Arregi and Nevins 2018).

20.4.3 A'-Movements

A'-movement differs from A-movement in targeting a position to the left of the subject, SpecFocP in Rizzi's (1997) articulated CP-structure (63), and allowing long-distance dependencies (64).

(63) **French**
    Qui   [a-t-elle a vu qui]?
    Whom   has=she   seen
    'Who did she see?'

(64) Qui   crois-tu [CP qui qu'[TP elle a   vu qui]]?
    whom   think-you   that   she has seen
    'Who do you think that she saw?'

Romance languages have much contributed to the understanding of the properties of A'-movement. First, while in most Romance languages *wh*-movement is mandatory, French shows that *wh*-movement may be optional (cf. also Sections 1.2.2.1, 24.2.2). Alongside (63), (65) is also possible:

(65) [TP Elle a   vu   qui]? (Fr.)
         she has seen whom
    'Who did she see?'

Shlonsky (2012) convincingly argues that the *wh*-phrase in (65) is in situ and that Chomsky's (2001) Agree is not sufficient to account for the parallel behaviour of *wh* in situ and moved adjuncts (both are banned in negative complements and *wh*-islands). Movement to SpecFocP of a null operator (Mathieu 1999) or the *wh*-feature (Chomsky 1995) should also be involved.

Second, *wh*-movement is not necessarily contingent on verb/auxiliary movement to C°, as is the case in Germanic languages (Besten 1983). Alongside (63), (66) is also possible (cf. Rizzi 1996):

(66) Qui [TP elle a   vu qui]? (Fr.)
    whom   she has seen
    'Who did she see?'

Third, subject extraction may take place from either the thematic subject position (as in Italian (67), cf. Rizzi 1982: ch. 4) or the preverbal subject position (as in French (68)), in which case the subject trace in SpecTP is licensed by the agreeing complementizer *qui* (Rizzi 1990: 56), instead of *que* 'that':

(67) Chi credi [CP chi che [TP abbia [VP chi visto Maria]]]? (It.)
who think.PRS.IND.2SG that have.SBJV.3SG seen Maria
'Who do you think saw Maria?'

(68) **French**
a. Quelle fille crois-tu [CP quelle fille **que/qui [TP quelle fille a [VP quelle fille vu Marie]]]?
which girl think=you that has seen Marie
'Which girl do you think has seen Marie?'
b. L' homme [CP que [TP je crois [CP homme **que/qui [TP homme viendra [VP viendra homme]]]]]
the man that I think that come.FUT.3SG
'The man that I think will come'

Fourth, Romanian shows that multiple *wh*-fronting may be compatible with a single Foc projection in the left periphery (Rizzi 1997), in that it involves remnant movement of a structural chunk containing the *wh*-constituents (Laenzlinger and Soare 2005):

(69) [FocP [XP Cine ce] [TP a scris [XP cine a scris ce]]]? (Ro.)
Who what has written
'Who wrote what?'

Constituents with different types of discourse-related features, such as foci and topics, also enter A'- dependencies. While the former have quantificational properties being sensitive to weak cross-over (70a) and incompatible with clitic pronouns (71a) on a par with *wh*-phrases (70b)–(71b), the latter do not: topics are insensitive to weak cross-over (70c) and resumed by clitic pronouns (71c) (Rizzi 1997):

(70) **Italian**
a. ??GIANNI_i sua_i madre ha sempre apprezzato(, non Piero).
Gianni his mother has always appreciated not Piero
'It is Gianni who his mother has always appreciated(, not Piero).'
b. **Quale_i ragazzo sua_i madre apprezza?
which boy his mother appreciate?
'Which boy does his mother appreciate?'
c. Gianni_i, sua_i madre lo ha sempre apprezzato.
Gianni, his mother ACC.MSG= has always appreciated
'Gianni, his mother always appreciated him.'

(71) a. IL TUO LIBRO (**lo) ho comprato(, non il suo).
the your book ACC.MSG= have.PRS.IND.1SG bought not the his
'I bought YOUR book(, not HIS).'

b. Cosa (**lo) hai comprato?
   what ACC.MSG= have.PRS.IND.2SG bought
   'What did you buy?'
c. Il tuo libro, lo ho comprato.
   the your book ACC.MSG= have.PRS.IND.1SG bought
   'I bought your book.'

A'-movement may also target topics which are not resumed by clitic pronouns and which are sensitive to weak cross-over, as in Italian resumptive preposing (Cinque 1983; 1990; Cardinaletti 2009):

(72) Il presidente giurò di non avere avuto contatti con esponenti del governo
The chairman swore to not have.INF had contacts with members of.the government
straniero e [la stessa cosa] giurò anche il suo segretario. (It.)
foreign and the same thing swore also the his secretary
'The Chairman swore that he had had no contacts with members of the foreign government and his secretary did as well.'

While movement is commonly assumed to account for the dependency between fronted *wh*-, focalized, and resumptive preposing elements and their base-generated positions, there is an ongoing debate on the analysis of clitic left-dislocation as in (70c)–(71c): via syntactic movement to the left periphery out of a clitic doubling configuration (Sportiche 1996/98; Cecchetto 2000; Belletti 2005; López 2009; Kempchinsky 2013) or base generation in the left periphery, with a dependency being created with the clause-internal clitic (Cinque 1990 for Italian; De Cat 2007a; 2007b for French).

Finally, Romanian shows that when they have a definite interpretation, *wh*-phrases may also enter doubling configurations with clitic pronouns on a par with topics and do not therefore qualify as syntactic quantifiers (Dobrovie-Sorin 1994):

(73) Pe care (băiat) l- ai văzut? (Ro.)
   which (boy) ACC.MSG= have.PRS.2SG seen
   'Which (boy) did you see?'

20.5 Pronominal Dependencies

Dependencies between pronouns and their antecedents are licensed representationally. Depending on the type of pronouns involved, they are called binding and control dependencies.

20.5.1 Binding

While reflexive pronouns require their antecedents to be in one and the same clause (74a), the antecedents of personal pronouns occur in a superordinate clause (74b) or in the discourse (74c). Clitic pronouns found in

Romance languages behave like reflexive and personal pronouns, respectively (75), and are subject to binding theory too:

(74) **Italian**
    a.   Maria ha detto [che Gianni$_i$ apprezza se stesso$_i$].
         Maria has said that Gianni appreciates himself
    b.   Maria$_i$ ha detto [che Gianni apprezza solo lei$_i$].
         Maria has said that Gianni appreciates only her
    c.   Cosa pensi di Maria$_i$? Gianni apprezza solo lei$_i$.
         what think.2SG of Maria? Gianni appreciates only her
         'What do you think of Maria? Gianni appreciates only her.'

(75)   a.   Maria ha detto [che Gianni$_i$ si$_i$ apprezza].
         Maria has said that Gianni REFL= appreciates
         'Maria said that Gianni appreciates himself.'
    b.   Maria$_i$ ha detto [che Gianni la$_i$ apprezza].
         Maria has said that Gianni ACC.FSG= appreciates
         'Maria said that Gianni appreciates her.'
    c.   Cosa pensi di Maria$_i$? Gianni la$_i$ apprezza.
         What think.PRS.IND.2SG of Maria? Gianni ACC.FSG= appreciates
         'What do you think of Maria? Gianni admires her.'

Italian displays two types of reflexive elements: clause-bound *se stesso* as in (74a) and subject-oriented, non-local *sé*, as in (76) (Giorgi 1990):

(76)   Quel dittatore$_i$ pensava che i libri di storia
         That dictator thought that the books of history
         avrebbero parlato a lungo di sé$_i$. (It.)
         have.COND.3PL told for long of self
         'That dictator thought that history books would talk about him for a long time.'

Among Romance reflexives, French *lui-même* is peculiar in being possible with object antecedents and logophoric antecedents (Zribi-Hertz 1989; 1990).

Finally, differently from clitic pronouns (77a), strong personal pronouns may be co-referential with a DP in one and the same clause (77b):

(77) **Italian**
    a.   **Gianni$_i$ lo$_i$ apprezza.
         Gianni ACC.MSG= appreciates
    b.   Gianni$_i$ apprezza solo lui$_i$.
         Gianni appreciates only him
         'Gianni only admires himself.'

In (77b), the two elements co-refer by referring independently of each other to one and the same individual, a situation sometimes called 'accidental co-reference.' Since Romance languages display different morphological paradigms for personal pronouns, they show that this situation only arises when pronouns have a referential index, as is the case of strong pronouns (Cardinaletti and Starke 1999: 224 n. 57).

20.5.2 Control Constructions

Null subjects of infinitival clauses (called PRO) are dependent on DPs in the superordinate clause in order to be interpreted. This dependency is called 'control' (cf. also Sections 1.2.2.2, 2.6.2):

(78) Gianni$_i$ ha promesso a Maria [di PRO$_i$ partire]. (It.)
Gianni has promised to Maria of leave.INF
'Gianni promised to Maria to leave.'

Partial control is possible in Romance languages with verbs selecting a (hidden) comitative argument (Sheehan 2014). See the European Portuguese example (79a). The analysis is the same as English (79b), where exhaustive control, derived by movement, combines with a null comitative object *pro* (replacing a *with*P) (Boeckx, Hornstein, and Nunes 2010: 185):

(79) **European Portuguese**
    a. O João$_i$ preferia [PRO$_{i+}$ reunirse mais tarde].
        the João prefer.IND.PST.3SG meet.INF=REFL more late
        'João preferred to meet later on.'
    b. The chair hoped [~~the chair~~ to meet *pro*$_{comitative}$ at 6].

The subject of a control infinitive can be co-referential with the object of the matrix verb. Interestingly, clitic climbing in this case is not allowed, as shown by the Spanish example in (80):

(80) a. **Maria lo convenció a Juan$_j$ [de PRO$_j$ comer].
        Maria ACC.MSG= convince.PST.IND.3SG a Juan de eat.INF
    b. Maria convenció a Juan$_j$ [de PRO$_j$ comerlo].
        Maria convince.PST.IND.3SG a Juan de eat.INF=ACC.MSG
        'Maria convinced Juan to eat it.'

Terzi (1996) takes the contrast in (80) as evidence that restructuring involves coindexing the infinitival T with the matrix T. This is only possible in subject control infinitives because the two Ts check the same index through agreement. The contrast between subject and object control is also found in languages that lack infinitives. Among Romance languages, this is the case in Romanian and some southern Italian dialects in Apulia and Calabria. All these Romance varieties are *pro*-drop. The issue arises whether the null subject of the embedded subjunctive is a PRO parallel to control infinitives (Kempchinsky 1986; Landau 2004; Jordan 2009) or a *pro* parallel to finite clauses (cf. Dobrovie-Sorin 1994; 2001; Motapanyane 1994 for Romanian; Calabrese 1992 for Salentino; Cardinaletti and Giusti 2020 for different varieties of southern Italian dialects). Evidence for the former hypothesis is the fact that co-reference is mandatory, and not optional as would be expected with a *pro* (cf. example (81) taken from Jordan 2009: 134):[8]

(81) **Romanian**
    a.   Mara$_i$ a   încercat PRO$_i$ să scrie   o scrisoare.
        Mara has tried   să write.PRS.3SG a letter
        'Mara tried to write a letter.'
    b.   **Mara$_i$ a   încercat Ana/*pro$_j$ să scrie   o scrisoare.
        Mara has tried   Ana   să write.PRS.3SG a letter

A second piece of evidence for the PRO hypothesis, adduced by Terzi (1996), is the contrast in Salentino (82), where, in the absence of the complementizer, the clitic may (but need not) climb to the matrix T:

(82) **Salentino**
    a.   Karlu   voli   (ku) lu   kkatta lu.
        Carlo   want.PRS.IND.3SG ku ACC.MSG= buy.PRS.3SG
    b.   Karlu lu   voli   (**ku) lu   kkatta lu.
        Carlo ACC.MSG= want.PRS.IND.3SG   buy.PRS.3SG
        'Carlo wants to buy it.'

Cardinaletti and Giusti (2020) propose that Salentino has two different structures: one with the complementizer *ku* parallel to Romanian *să* in (81a), which does not allow clitic climbing (83a), the other is parallel to the 'Inflected Construction' found with motion verbs in Sicilian (Cardinaletti and Giusti 2001; 2003; Cruschina 2013; Di Caro 2019; Del Prete and Todaro 2019), which is a monoclausal complex event construction and, as such, displays obligatory clitic climbing (83b) (see also Ledgeway 2013; 2015):

(83) a.   **Mara$_i$ a   încercat-o   să scrie ө
        Mara has tried=ACC.FSG să write.PRS.3SG
        'Mara tried to write it.'
    b.   U   vaju   a {**u} accattu u   gnignorno
        ACC.MSG= go.PRS.1SG a   buy.PRS.1SG every.day

20.6 Conclusions

In this chapter, we have presented the major contributions provided by the linguistic literature analysing different types of dependencies in Romance languages. All of these analyses aim to relate the relative richness in inflexional morphology to variation in word order, argument marking, agreement, and the realization of pronominal reference.

---

[8] The subject position preceding *să* reflects Terzi's hypothesis that *să* is a T-marker. It could however be following *să*, if *să* is taken to be a low complementizer, according to Rizzi's (1997) split-CP system, as argued for by Hill and Alboiu (2016). This is also the stance taken by Cardinaletti and Giusti (2020) for the Salentino data.

Selected References

Below you can find selected references for this chapter. The full references can be found online at the following page: www.cambridge.org/Romancelinguistics

Belletti, A. (1990). *Generalized Verb Movement*. Turin: Rosenberg & Sellier.
Cardinaletti, A. (2004). 'Toward a cartography of subject positions'. In Rizzi, L. (ed.), *The Structure of CP and IP. The Cartography of Syntactic Structures, II*. Oxford/New York: Oxford University Press, 115–65.
Cardinaletti, A. and Starke, M. (1999). 'The typology of structural deficiency: a case study of the three classes of pronouns'. In van Riemsdijk, H. (ed.), *Clitics in the Languages of Europe*. Berlin/New York: Mouton, 145–233.
Cinque, G. (1994). 'On the evidence for partial N-movement in the Romance DP'. In Cinque, G., Koster, J., Pollock, J.-Y., Rizzi, L., and Zanuttini, R. (eds), *Paths towards Universal Grammar. Studies in Honor of Richard Kayne*. Georgetown: Georgetown University Press, 85–110.
Costa, J. (2004). *Subject Positions and Interfaces: the Case of European Portuguese*. Berlin: Mouton de Gruyter.
Dobrovie-Sorin, C. (1994). *The Syntax of Romanian. Comparative Studies in Romance*. Berlin/New York: Mouton de Gruyter.
Giusti, G. (2006). 'Parallels in clausal and nominal periphery'. In Frascarelli, M. (ed.), *Phases of Interpretation*. Berlin/New York: Mouton de Gruyter, 163–84.
Koopman, H. and Sportiche, D. (1991). 'The position of subjects', *Lingua* 85: 211–58.
Ledgeway, A. (2011). 'Syntactic and morphosyntactic typology and change'. In Maiden, M., Smith, J. C., and Ledgeway, A. (eds), *The Cambridge History of the Romance Languages. Vol. 1. Structures*. Cambridge: Cambridge University Press, 382–471.
Picallo, C. (1994). 'Catalan possessive pronouns: the avoid pronoun principle revisited', *Natural Language & Linguistic Theory* 12: 259–99.
Pollock, J.-Y. (1989). 'Verb-movement, Universal Grammar, and the structure of IP', *Linguistic Inquiry* 20: 365–424.
Rizzi, L. (1997). 'The fine structure of the Left Periphery'. In Haegeman, L. (ed.), *Elements of Grammar*. Dordrecht: Kluwer, 281–337.

21

Parametric Variation

Adam Ledgeway and Norma Schifano

21.1 Introduction

A comparison of the grammars of Latin and Romance reveals both some 'big' changes in the passage from the parent language to the daughter languages, as well as a series of 'smaller' changes both in the Latin–Romance transition and the subsequent developments that have given rise to considerable differentiation across Romance. In early Government-Binding theory, Universal Grammar (UG) was treated as a small set of abstract principles subject to parametric variation (Chomsky 1981), largely coinciding with the main typological classes recognized by traditional descriptive linguistics (Koopman 1984; Travis 1984; Baker 1996; cf. also Section 1.2.2.2). Consequently, 'big' changes have traditionally been modelled in terms of macroparameters which include at least the following major dimensions of linguistic variation:

(1)   a.   Head directionality (Tesnière 1959; Chomsky 1981; Hawkins 1983; Travis 1984)
      b.   Configurationality (Hale 1981; 1982; 1983; Ledgeway 2012: chs 3, 5)
      c.   Nominative/ergative alignment (Comrie 1978; Dixon 1994)
      d.   Polysynthesis (Baker 1996)
      e.   Topic/Subject prominence (Li and Thompson 1976; Huang 1982)

Of these macroparameters, only the first two are relevant to Latin–Romance developments. In relation to the head parameter, at least in its earliest attestations, Latin was predominantly head-final, whereas modern Romance is head-initial, with Classical Latin representing a transitional stage in which both conservative head-final and innovative head-initial orders are found (Adams 1976; Ledgeway 2012: ch. 5). In terms of structural organization, Latin has also been argued to exhibit a non-configurational syntax in which relationships between individual linguistic items are signalled lexocentrically through the forms of the items themselves, whereas in Romance relationships between related linguistic items are encoded by their fixed positions relative to each other (Vincent 1988: 53f., 62f.; 1997: 149, 163; 1998: 423f., Ledgeway 2011: §3; 2012: ch. 3). Consequently, in Latin not only is it difficult to establish fixed orders for individual heads and their associated complements or modifiers within their given phrase, but even adjacency between semantically related items is not a requirement (Marouzeau 1949: 42; 1953: 62; Pinkster 1990: 184–86; Oniga 2014: 223–24; Powell 2010), as shown by the fact that there are frequent discontinuous structures. In Romance, by contrast, all elements appear to have pre-established positions and the languages do not readily license hyperbaton.

Over recent decades, however, much work has radically departed from this macroparametric view with a shift of focus on to predominantly surface-oriented variation (cf. Kayne 1996; 2000; 2005a; 2005b; Manzini and Savoia 2005), an approach well suited to modelling 'small' diachronic changes. This has led to the proliferation of a remarkable number of local, low-level microparameters interpreted as the (PF-)lexicalization of specific formal feature values of individual functional heads such as D, v, Infl/T, and C (Borer 1984; Chomsky 1995) in accordance with the Borer–Chomsky Conjecture (Baker 2008b). In this respect, the emergence in Romance of articles and clitics, auxiliaries, and a host of finite and non-finite complementizers, all generally absent from Latin but nonetheless exhibiting significant microvariation across Romance (cf. Ledgeway 2012: chs 2, 4; 2016a), provides us with a rich empirical base from which to study microparametric variation.

Any account of the Latin–Romance transition and Romance-internal variation must therefore make reference to changes of both a macro- and microparametric order. Approaches narrowly couched in terms of macroparameters alone, in which each category may pattern in just one way or another in relation to a handful of linguistic options (cf. 1a–e), seriously limit possible dimensions of linguistic variation and hence of diachronic change. Indeed, on this view the rise and fall of (late) Latin and Romance reflexes of split intransitivity (cf. discussion in Section 21.2.2.2) within an otherwise predominantly nominative-accusative alignment are entirely unexpected (cf. La Fauci 1988; 1997; Ledgeway 2012: ch. 7; Rovai 2012). On the other hand, exclusively microparametric approaches in which each category may vary freely independently of all others place a costly burden on UG, which must specify an inordinate number of highly local and ultimately random dimensions of possible linguistic variation, despite most of these proving entirely irrelevant to the observed diachronic changes. Microparametric approaches therefore seriously increment the acquisitional task of the child who has to set each value in isolation from the next, on the basis of the primary linguistic data alone, and at the same time exponentially multiplies the number of parametric systems and, in turn, the number of possible grammars predicted by UG (Roberts 2012).

Thus, while macroparametric approaches lead us to expect successive stages of languages to rigidly fall into one of a few 'pure' types, microparametric approaches lead us *a priori* to expect wildly 'mixed' types. As observed by Roberts (2010a: 24–25), neither scenario correctly captures the relevant facts about the Latin–Romance transition. Rather, what we find is a bimodal distribution of macro- and microparametric properties (cf. Baker 2008b) whereby all Romance varieties tend towards the same basic linguistic 'type', namely head-initial, configurational, accusative, non-polysynthetic (with strong analytic tendencies), and subject-prominent, but which at the same time allow some degree of low-level deviation from some of these core patterns. For example, although operating in terms of a core nominative-accusative orientation, Romance varieties display widespread but variable reflexes of split intransitivity (Bentley 2006). Similarly, alongside core subject-prominent structures a number of Romance varieties also show specific kinds of topical non-nominative subjects with unaccusatives, paralleling in many respects topic-prominent structures (cf. Cardinaletti 2004: 122–26, 136f.; Avelar 2009; Avelar and Galves 2011; de Andrade and Galves 2014).

In what follows, we assume therefore a theory that combines some notion of macroparameters alongside microparameters (Baker 1996; 2008a; 2008b). Following ideas first proposed by Kayne (2005b: 10) and further developed by Roberts and Holmberg (2010) and Roberts (2012), progress in this direction has recently been made by the Rethinking Comparative Syntax research group (cf. http://recos-dtal.mml.cam.ac.uk/); their central idea is that macroparameters should be construed as the surface effect of aggregates of microparameters acting in unison, ultimately as some sort of composite single parameter. On this view, macroparametric effects obtain whenever all individual functional heads behave in concert, namely are set identically for the same feature value, whereas microparametric variation arises when different subsets of functional heads present distinct featural specifications. Conceived in this way, parametric variation can be interpreted in a scalar fashion and modelled in terms of parametric hierarchies along the lines of (2).

(2)   Does p characterize L?

- No = Macroparametric setting
- Yes → All functional heads?
  - Yes = Macroparametric setting
  - No → Extended to naturally definable class?
    - Yes = Mesoparametric variation
    - No → Restricted to lexically definable subclass?
      - Yes = Microparametric variation
      - No → Limited to idiosyncratic collection of individual lexical items?
        - Yes = Nanoparametric variation

Macroparameters, the simplest and least marked options that uniformly apply to all functional heads, are placed at the very top of the hierarchy, but, as we move downwards, variation becomes progressively less 'macro' and, at the same time, more restricted, with choices becoming progressively more limited to increasingly smaller subsets of features (namely, no F(p) > all F(p) > some F(p), for F a feature and p some grammatical behaviour). More specifically, functional heads increasingly display a disparate behaviour in relation to particular feature values which may, for example, characterize: (i) a naturally definable class of functional heads (e.g., [+N], [+finite]), a case of mesoparametric variation; (ii) a small, lexically definable subclass of functional heads (e.g., pronominals, proper nouns, auxiliaries, unaccusatives), a case of microparametric variation proper; and (iii) one or more individual lexical items, a case of nanoparametric variation.

By way of example, consider the principal patterns of agreement of the Romance active past participle exemplified in (3a–g),[1] modelled in the parametric hierarchy in (4) (cf. Ledgeway 2013: 189–92; forthcoming).[2]

(3)   a.   A   sopa,   tinha-a   comido. (Pt.)
            the.FSG   soup.FSG   have.PST.IPFV.1SG=it.F   eat.PTCP.MSG
            'As for the soup, I had eaten it.'
     b.   seme   magnate   lu   biscotte /
            be.PRS.1PL   eat.PTCP.SG   the.MSG   biscuit.MSG
            so   magnite   li   biscutte. (Arl.)
            be.PRS.1SG   eat.PTCP.PL   the.MPL   biscuits.MPL
            'We have eaten the biscuit. / I have eaten the biscuits.'
     c.   Avètz   presas   de   fotòs? (Occ.)
            have.PRS.2SG   take.PTCP.FPL   of   photos.FPL
            'Did you take any photos?'

---

[1] Cf. Smith (1999), Loporcaro (1998; 2016), Manzini and Savoia (2005, II: 553–96), Ledgeway (2012: 317f.). See also the discussions in Sections 17.3.1, 17.4.1, and 18.4.

[2] The original base and intermediate positions of displaced items are indicated in the examples below with strikethrough.

d. La clé que j'ai prise. (Fr.)
   the.FSG key.FSG that I=have.PRS.1SG take.PTCP.FSG
   'The key which I took.'
e. Li/Ci hanno visti. (It.)
   them.M/us= have.PRS.3PL see.PTCP.MPL
   'They saw us.'
f. Los/Nos as vistos/vistu. (Srd.)
   them.M/us= have.PRS.2SG see.PTCP.MPL/MSG
   'You have seen them/us.'
g. Els/Les he llegit/llegides. (Bcl.)
   them.M/F= have.PRS.1SG read.PTCP.MSG/FPL
   'I've read them.'

(4)   (a) Does active v_{PTCP} probe φ-features of DP?

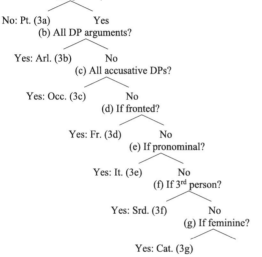

Assuming active participle agreement to be the surface reflex of an underlying Agree relation for φ-features (in gender and/or number) between the functional head v_{PTCP} and a given nominal, we can recognize at least seven different microparametric specifications for v_{PTCP}. The simplest and least constrained system is exemplified by Ibero-Romance varieties such as Portuguese in (3/4a), where v_{PTCP} simply never displays any agreement, failing to enter into an Agree relation with any DP. Its mirror image is the pattern of participial agreement found in the eastern Abruzzese dialect of Arielli (3/4b) where the participle, and hence v_{PTCP}, simply agrees with any plural DP, be it the internal or external argument (D'Alessandro and Roberts 2010). In this respect, we note that Portuguese and Ariellese represent rather simple and relatively unmarked options, in that v_{PTCP} in these varieties either indiscriminately fails to probe all DP arguments or, on the contrary, systematically probes all (plural) DP arguments. Occitan varieties, on the other hand, are slightly more constrained, though still liberal by general Romance standards, in that v_{PTCP} only probes a subset of DP arguments, namely those marked accusative (3/4c), whereas in French there is the further proviso that the DP$_{ACC}$ must have also undergone fronting under A- or A'-movement as with unaccusatives or relativization (3/4d). In all four cases we are dealing with mesoparametric variation, in that the four options can be subsumed within a naturally definable class insofar as they exclusively make reference to a single functional head [D], in turn further specified for the feature [+ACC] in Occitan and French (presumably un(der) specified in the case of Portuguese and Ariellese) and the relevant A/A'-movement feature in French.

We observe, however, a shift from meso- to microparametric variation as we move down the hierarchy to Italian, insofar as the relevant class of triggers for participial agreement is no longer represented *tout court* by a naturally definable class of functional heads (viz. [D]), but now makes reference to a small and lexically definable subclass of Ds, namely pronominals. Thus, in Italian v_{PTCP} only agrees with fronted nominals when represented by pronominal clitics (3/4e), an option taken a stage further in Sardinian dialects (3/4f) and, in turn, Barcelona Catalan (3/4g) where there are further requirements that the pronominal clitic be third person and feminine, respectively. In these two latter cases, we are entering nanoparametric territory inasmuch as the relevant generalizations hold of just a handful of individual lexical items.

In light of these assumptions about parametric variation, we examine below some case studies in Romance microparametric variation in the sentential core (Section 21.2) and the left periphery (Section 21.3) which show how minimal differences among otherwise highly homogenous systems can be used to investigate microvariation along the diachronic and synchronic axes in order to better understand what precisely may vary and how such variation may be implicationally structured in relation to the predictions of parametric hierarchies like (2).

21.2 Sentential Core

21.2.1 Subject Clitics

In an area extending from southern France and southern Switzerland to northern Italy and northern Tuscany, there exists a highly heterogeneous class of atonic subject pronouns (cf. also Sections 4.2, 10.3, and 17.5.1.1) which can only be separated from the finite verb by another clitic (Benincà 1983) and which display a distinct syntactic behaviour with respect to the corresponding tonic series, as shown by a number of well-known tests (Kayne 1975: 84–87). Mainly, but not exclusively, derived from weakened forms of originally nominative tonic subject pronouns (Vanelli 1984; 1987; Poletto and Tortora 2016: 783), subject clitics represent one of the richest areas of Romance-internal microvariation, offering the linguist a significant testbed for investigating parametric variation. In northern Italian varieties, subject clitics have variously been interpreted as: (i) the spell-out of Agr, namely the inflexional marking of person and number on the finite verb (Brandi and Cordin 1981; 1989: 229; Rizzi 1986: 393); (ii) the instantiation of unvalued person and number φ-features (Roberts 2010b: 305); and (iii) the lexicalization of various heads of the higher functional field, including not only IP but also the CP domain, in recent cartographic approaches (Poletto 2000). According to various authors, the subject clitics of northern Italy differ from the subject clitics of French (and presumably from those of Francoprovençal too; cf. Poletto 2006: 166 n. 10) in that, while in the northern Italian varieties they are heads (viz. non-autonomous items), in French they behave as full XPs or weak pronouns (in the sense of Cardinaletti and Starke 1999) when in canonical preverbal subject position (Brandi and Cordin 1981; 1989; Rizzi 1986; Poletto 1996: 269; 2006: 175; Poletto and Tortora 2016: 773f.), with important implications for the analysis of such varieties in relation to the Null Subject Parameter. In particular, should they be considered on a par with languages like Italian and Spanish in which pronominal subjects are left unexpressed in the unmarked case and recovered by means of the verb's rich inflexional agreement, in these varieties realized precisely through the subject clitic, or should they be considered on par with languages like English in which the subject has to be overtly marked through the realization of a subject pronoun?

In northern Italian varieties, the object of study of the present section, the notion of subject clitic proves spurious (Rizzi 1986: 393; Poletto 1996: 296), encompassing at least (i) four distinct syntactic typologies (person, number, deictic, and invariable), each encoding distinct person feature compositions and corresponding to different positions (Poletto 2000; Poletto and Tortora 2016: 775–79) and (ii) three morphological types (vocalic, consonantal, consonantal + vocalic; Poletto 2000: 12f.; Manzini and Savoia 2005, I: 128). The heterogeneity of subject clitics is further corroborated by the exceptional number of gaps and syncretisms exhibited by their paradigms. Although all northern Italian varieties present subject clitics, one or more persons often lack a clitic altogether or share a form with other cells of the paradigm (Poletto 1997: 138; Manzini and Savoia 2005, I: 69–196; Roberts 2010b: 306; Poletto and Tortora 2016: 774).

Despite this exceptional variation, a number of structured implications have been identified, highlighting how variation is always limited (Benincà 2014: 187). Examples of implicational scales include the types of subjects which require doubling by a clitic (phonologically null subjects > tonic pronouns > full noun phrases > quantifier phrases > other; Poletto and Tortora 2016: 783f.), the relationship between clitics and verbal inflexion (if the verbal inflexion is not distinct for some persons, the subject clitic will be; Renzi and Vanelli 1983; Poletto 1997: 138; Manzini and Savoia 2005, I: 118; Roberts 2010b: 306f.), and the person hierarchy (the occurrence of clitics for certain persons in declarative SV(O) clauses without a lexical subject and with a non-auxiliary verb implies the presence of subject clitics for others; Renzi and Vanelli 1983). The latter implicational scale proves of particular interest for a parametric approach to microvariation. Descriptively, it can be summarized as in (5), where the intended implication is that if a variety has only one clitic, it will be second person singular, if it only has two clitics, they will be second singular and third person singular, and so on:[3]

(5) 2 > 3 > 6 > 5 > 4 > 1

Consequently, the distribution of subject clitics across the relevant Romance varieties gives rise to the six microparametric options in (6), which can be modelled by the parametric hierarchy in (7):

(6) a. 2sg
     b. 2sg/3sg
     c. 2sg/3sg/3pl
     d. 2sg/3sg/3pl/2pl
     e. 2sg/3sg/3pl/2pl/1pl
     f. 2sg/3sg/3pl/2pl/1pl/1sg

(7) (a) Is the subject clitic system restricted to Participants?

    Yes: (6a)   No
                 (b) Is Individuation restricted to singular?

        Yes: (6b)   No
                     (c) Is Individuation extended to plural?

            Yes: (6c)   No
                         (d) Is Participant extended to Addressee?

                Yes: (6d)   No
                             (e) Is Participant maximally specified
                                 and/or underspecified for Addressee?

                    Yes: (6e)   No: (6f)

---

[3] See Manzini and Savoia (2005, I: 118) for critical remarks on (5). A further dimension of variation within this scale concerns the obligatory vs optional nature of the clitic, with the 2 > 3 > 6 series being obligatory in contrast to 5 > 4 > 1, which prove optional when available (Renzi and Vanelli 1983: 129). Here, we also gloss over possible syncretisms between persons (Manzini and Savoia 2005, I: 69–196).

Adopting Harley and Ritter's (2002) feature geometric analysis of person (formalized as Participant, viz. Speaker vs Addressee) and number (formalized as Individuation, viz. Group vs Minimal), question (7a) identifies varieties where only discourse participants are marked by a subject clitic, namely second singular (viz. 6a), first singular being morphologically null when unmarked (Harley and Ritter 2002: 489) and third persons being excluded as discourse independent (Harley and Ritter 2002: 487). This option is exemplified by the dialect of Sarre (Aosta):

(8)   tø   'drymmɔ. (Sarre, Manzini and Savoia 2005, I: 116)
       SCL.2SG= sleep.PRS.IND.2SG
       'You sleep.'

Question (7b) describes varieties where subject clitics also include non-discourse participants, viz. third persons (cf. 6b), but are restricted to the default number of Individuation, viz. singular (or 'Minimal' in the terminology of Harley and Ritter 2002: 489), as in the dialect of Varese Ligure (La Spezia), where subject clitics are available for second and third persons singular only:

(9)   ti   'dɔrmi   /   u   'dɔrme. (Varese Ligure, Manzini and Savoia 2005, I: 100)
       SCL.2SG= sleep.PRS.IND.2SG SCL.3SG= sleep.PRS.IND.3SG
       'You/he sleep/s.'

When Individuation is extended to the marked plural number ('Group' in the terminology of Harley and Ritter 2001: 490), as in (7c), we obtain the next option in Renzi and Vanelli's (1983) typology, namely varieties where the subject clitic system includes second and third singular, as well as third plural (viz. 6c), as in Venetian (10), while inclusion of the second plural (viz. 6d) is naturally captured by the extension of Participant to Addressee (7d), as exemplified by the dialect of Ala di Stura (Turin) in (11):

(10)   ti   magni   / el   magna   (Vnt., Poletto 2006: 179)
       SCL.2SG= eat.PRS.IND.2SG SCL.3SG= eat.PRS.IND.3SG
       / i   magna.
       SCL.3PL= eat.PRS.IND.3PL
       'You/he/they eat(s).'

(11)   at   'dyɔrs   /   u   'dyɔrt   (Ala di Stura, Manzini and Savoia 2005, I: 108)
       SCL.2SG= sleep.PRS.IND.2SG SCL.3SG= sleep.PRS.IND.3SG
       / u   dyr'mis   / u   'dyɔrmunt.
       SCL.2PL= sleep.PRS.IND.2PL SCL.3PL= sleep.PRS.IND.3PL
       'You/he/you/they sleep(s).'

Finally, question (7e) draws a distinction between those varieties where the subject clitic series extends to the first person plural only (viz. 6e), either inclusive or exclusive (cf. discussion of maximal specification for Participant and underspecification for Addressee, respectively, in Harley and Ritter 2002: 490), as in Pomaretto (Turin) (12), and those varieties where the full series, including first person singular, is available (cf. 6f), witness Cairo di Montenotte (Savona) in (13):

(12) ty   'dørme   /   a   dørm   /   nu   'dørməŋ   /
     SCL.2SG=   sleep.PRS.IND.2SG   SCL.3SG= sleep.PRS.IND.3SG   SCL.1PL= sleep.PRS.IND.1PL
     u   dyr'mɛ   /   i   'dørməŋ. (Pomaretto, Manzini and Savoia 2005, I: 113)
     SCL.2PL=   sleep.PRS.2PL   SCL.3PL= sleep.PRS.3PL
     'You/he/we/you/they sleep(s).'

(13) a   pòrl   /   t   pòrli   /   u   pòrla   /
     SCL.1SG=   speak.PRS.IND1SG   SCL.2SG= speak.PRS.IND.2SG   SCL.3SG= speak.PRS.IND.3SG
     a   parluma   /   i   pòrli   /   i   pòrlu. (Cai., Parry 2005: 167)
     SCL.1PL=   speak.PRS.1PL   SCL.2PL= speak.PRS.IND.2PL   SCL.3PL= speak.PRS.IND.3PL
     'I/you/he/we/you/they speak(s).'

In conclusion, once Renzi and Vanelli's (1983) person-based scale is formalized within Harley and Ritter's (2002) feature geometric analysis of person, the attested implications can be successfully captured by a parametric hierarchy like (7) in which the typologically most marked options are naturally located at the bottom of the hierarchy.

21.2.2 Auxiliary Selection

Numerous dimensions of meso- and microvariation characterize the choice of auxiliary in the formation of Romance active perfective periphrases with the past participle (for bibliography, see Ledgeway 2012: 292–99, 311–17, as well as the extensive discussion in Sections 4.3 and 18.3), as illustrated by the five broad dimensions of mesoparametric variation in hierarchy (14) taken from Ledgeway (2019, in press).

(14)   (a) Does L present auxiliary alternation?
           /   \
No: Pescolanciano (15a)   Yes:
    Cat. (15b)   (b) Sensitive to mood?
                           /   \
                  Yes: Ro. (16)   No
                                        (c) Sensitive to tense?
                                       /   \
                              Yes: Slc. (17)   No
                                                  (d) Sensitive to person?
                                                 /   \
                                         Yes: Arl. (18)   No
                                                         (e) Sensitive to argument structure?
                                                        /
                                                Yes: Occ. (19a–b)

Question (14a) draws the broadest distinction between those varieties which do not show any alternation and all others that display varying patterns of alternation between auxiliaries BE and HAVE. Clearly, the simplest option is represented by varieties which generalize one auxiliary (cf. Tuttle 1986: 267–76; Manzini and Savoia 2005, II: 759–809; Ledgeway 2012: 341f.), be that BE as in many central-southern Italo-Romance dialects (15a) or HAVE as in many Ibero-Romance and (extreme) southern Italian varieties (15b).

(15) a. (mə) 'sɔŋgə / (tə) si / (ts) ε... mə'nuːtə
    me= be.PRS.1SG you.SG= be.PRS.2SG self= be.PRS.3SG come.PTCP
    maɲ'ɲɛɐtə (/laˈvaːtə). (Pescolanciano)
    eat.PTCP wash.PTCP
  b. (M') he / (t') has / (s') ha...
    me= have.PRS.IND.1SG you.SG= have.PRS.IND.2SG self= have.PRS.IND.3SG
    vingut / menjat (/ rentat). (Cat.)
    come.PTCP eat.PTCP wash.PTCP
    'I/you/(s)he have (has) come/eaten/washed.'

21.2.2.1 Tense and Mood

If, however, a variety does present auxiliary alternation, then as indicated in (14) this variation can, in order of complexity, be determined by mood, tense, person, and argument structure. Beginning with mood and tense, we find varieties such as: (i) Romanian, where auxiliary choice is dictated by the realis (⇒ HAVE) vs irrealis (⇒ BE) mood distinction (Avram and Hill 2007; Ledgeway 2014), with (inflected) HAVE uniquely licensed in the present indicative (16a) and (invariable) BE in the subjunctive (16b), perfect infinitive (16c), and future and conditional perfect (16d) and (ii) the Campanian dialect of San Leucio del Sannio (Iannace 1983: 72–80, 88f.; Ledgeway 2012: 342f.), where auxiliary distribution proves sensitive to tense distinctions, with present perfect and the future-oriented conditional perfect/pluperfect subjunctive (henceforth 'counterfactual perfect') aligning with HAVE (17a) and the pluperfect indicative with BE (17b).

(16) **Romanian**
  a. (M-)am / (te-)ai / (s-)a...
    me=have.PRS.1SG you.SG=have.PRS.2SG self=have.PRS.IND.3SG
    /venit /mâncat (/spălat).
    come.PTCP eat.PTCP wash.PTCP
    'I/you/(s)he have (has) come/eaten/washed.'
  b. Nu cred să (se) fi venit /mâncat (/spălat).
    not believe.PRS.1SG that self=be come.PTCP eat.PTCP wash.PTCP
  c. Înainte de a (se) fi venit /mâncat (/spălat).
    before of to self= be come.PTCP eat.PTCP wash.PTCP

d. (Se)   vor   /ar   fi   venit   /mâncat   (/spălat).
      self= will.3PL   would.3PL   be   come.PTCP eat.PTCP   wash.PTCP
      'I don't believe that they have ... / Before having ... / They will/would
      have ... come/eaten/washed.'

(17) S. Leucio del Sannio
  a. (M')   èggio   ditto   / muorto   (/lavato)
      me=   have.PRS.1SG   say.PTCP   die.PTCP   wash.PTCP
      // Si   nun   èsse   muorto.
          if   not   have.SBJV.3SG   die.PTCP
      'I have said/died/washed // If he hadn't died.
  b. (M')   èra   ditto   / muorto   (/lavato).
      me=   be.PST.IPFV.1SG say.PTCP   die.PTCP   wash.PTCP
      'I had said/died/washed.'

Auxiliary distribution in both varieties represents the surface reflex of a simple distinction between naturally definable instantiations of an auxiliary functional head (viz. T$_{Aux}$): in Romanian, auxiliation differentially marks a binary [±realis] distinction, whereas in Sanleuciano the alternation spells out a binary [±past] temporal distinction in that [+past] licenses BE in the pluperfect while the [–past] specification on T$_{Aux}$, uniting the present and counterfactual,[4] licenses HAVE in the present and counterfactual perfects. Although both mesoparametric options make reference to a binary featural opposition, sensitivity to mood is placed higher than tense in (14) on the assumption that, while the most primitive modal distinction involves a simple binary contrast between realis and irrealis, tense involves, following Vikner's (1985) neo-Reichenbachian analysis, the three binary temporal relations T$_{Past}$ (= R$_1$...S) > T$_{Future}$ (R$_2$...R$_1$) > T$_{Anterior}$ (E...R$_2$) (cf. Cinque 1999: 81–83), according to which [+past] arises from the combination of the values R$_1$_S; R$_1$,R$_2$; E,R$_2$. Furthermore, the observation that all (Romance) verbs have to be specified at the very least for mood, while not all verbs are specified for tense, leads us to assign a more basic status to mood over tense.

21.2.2.2 Person and Argument Structure

Below the modal and temporal dimensions in (14b–c) follow person and argument structure. The former accounts for varieties such as Ariellese (18) where, in the present at least, a simple binary person split obtains according to a [±discourse participant] distinction (cf. Benveniste

---

[4] We interpret the superficial past tense morphology found in counterfactuals as 'fake' (cf. Iatridou 2000; Ritter and Wiltschko 2014).

[1950]1966: 228) yielding BE in 1/2 persons and HAVE in 3 persons (D'Alessandro and Ledgeway 2010; D'Alessandro and Roberts 2010).

(18) So / si / a / seme / sete /
be.PRS.1SG be.PRS.2SG have.PRS.3SG be.PRS.1PL be.PRS.2PL
fatecate /-chite / 'rrevate /-ite. (Arl.)
work.PTCP.SG/-PL arrive.PTCP.SG/-PL
'I/you/(s)he/we/you/they have (has) worked/arrived.'

In other varieties, such as Lengadocien Occitan, we find a conservative binary active-stative split (Ledgeway 2012: 319–23; cf. also Section 18.2), where HAVE surfaces in conjunction with A/S$_A$ (transitives/unergatives) subjects (19a) and BE with SO (unaccusatives) subjects (19b).

(19) **Lengadocien**
  a. Avètz fach bon viatge?
     have.PRS.IND.2PL make.PTCP good trip
     'Did you have a good journey?'
  b. Soi vengut amb los amics.
     be.PRS.IND.1SG come.PTCP with the friends
     / Lo volcán s' es endormit.
     the volcano self= be.PRS.IND.3SG fall.asleep.PTCP
     'I came with friends. / The volcano has become dormant.'

As discussed in Ledgeway (2019, in press), auxiliary systems based on person and argument structure distinctions frequently blend these with modal and temporal restrictions to produce increasingly marked and complex proper subsets of person and verb class combinations. For example, in the Lazio dialect of Pontecorvo (Manzini and Savoia 2005, II: 701-03) a [±present] temporal restriction limits the person split to the present perfect (20a), with generalization of BE in the pluperfect and counterfactual (20b). Similarly, the active-stative split found in many early Romance varieties is frequently suspended in [−realis] contexts (Nordahl 1977; Ledgeway 2003; Stolova 2006), where all instances of S$_O$ may exceptionally align with have on a par with A/S$_A$ (21).

(20) **Pontecorvo**
  a. su / si[5] / a... par'lacə / və'nucə.
     be.PRS.1SG be.PRS.2SG have.PRS.3SG speak.PTCP come.PTCP
     'I/you/(s)he have (has) spoken/come.'
  b. 'ɛrə / 'irə / 'ɛra... / sa'ria / sa'rissə
     be.PST.IPFV.1SG be.PST.IPFV.2SG be.PST.IPFV.3SG be.COND.1SG be.COND.2SG
     / sa'ria ... par'lacə / və'nucə.
     be.COND.3SG speak.PTCP come.PTCP
     'I/you/(s)he had // would have spoken/come.'

---

[5] 2SG si causes lengthening of the initial consonant of the following participle, not indicated in (20a).

(21) el   sieruo   que es   fuydo
      the   servant that be.PRS.IND.3SG flee.PTCP
      / si... ladrones... ouissen   entrado (OSp.)
        if   thieves   have.PST.SBJV.3PL   enter.PTCP
      'the servant who has fled / if ... thieves had entered'

Crucially, however, the relevant lower-level modal and temporal contrasts introduced into such systems do not override the fundamental person or verb class distinctions, but are embedded within the categories of person and argument structure to introduce more fine-grained person and verb class combinations. It is for this reason that person and argument structure are positioned lower than mood and tense in (14), in that mood and tense as independent determinants of auxiliary variation are not constrained, at least in Romance, by person and argument structure, whereas person and argument structure as independent dimensions of auxiliary selection are frequently augmented by the incorporation of mood and tense restrictions. By the same token, argument-structure-driven auxiliation may, in turn, incorporate restrictions on person in addition to those on tense and mood. In this way, the hierarchy in (14) correctly models the subset and inclusiveness relations implicit in Romance auxiliary systems, including so-called cases of triple auxiliation (Loporcaro 2007) where, for example, person-based systems may embed modal and temporal restrictions (cf. 20a–b) but not those relating to argument structure, whereas active-stative splits may variously overlay modal, temporal, and personal restrictions. For example, in the Pugliese dialect of Minervino Murge (Manzini and Savoia 2005, III: 27f.), in the present all verb classes show free variation in all persons except the third, where BE is only an option (alongside HAVE) with unaccusatives (22a), whereas transitives/unergatives only license HAVE (22b):

(22) **Minervino Murge**
  a. 'sɔ(ndə)~ 'jaɟɟə /   si~a /   jɛ~ɔ
      be.PRS.1SG~have.PRS.1SG   be.PRS.2SG~have.PRS.2SG be.PRS.3SG~have.PRS.3SG
      / 'simmə~'a'vimmə /   'sɛitə~a'vɛitə/ /   'sɔndə~'jɔnnə
      be.PRS.1PL~have.PRS.1PL   be.PRS.2PL~have.PRS.2PL be.PRS.3PL~have.PRS.3PL
      mə'nɛutə.
      come.PTCP
      'I/you/(s)he/we/you/they have (has) come.'
  b. 'sɔ(ndə)~ 'jaɟɟə /   si~a /   ɔ
      be.PRS.1SG~have.PRS.1SG   be.PRS.2SG~have.PRS.2SG have.PRS.3SG
      / 'simmə~a'vimmə /   'sɛitə~a'vɛitə /   'jɔnnə
      be.PRS.1PL~have.PRS.1PL   be.PRS.2PL~have.PRS.2PL have.PRS.3PL
      dər'mɛutə.
      sleep.PTCP
      'I/you/(s)he/we/you/they have (has) slept.'

21.2.2.3 Diachronic Considerations

The most conservative pattern of auxiliation of the five mesoparametric options in (14), that determined by argument structure (cf. Vincent 1982; Bentley 2006), is situated at the bottom of the hierarchy. Consequently, all deviations from this mesoparametric pattern involve a movement up the hierarchy towards one of the other four less marked and conceptually simpler options but, significantly, no movements downwards. There is also no *a priori* reason to assume that movement up the hierarchy must proceed stepwise, witness Romanian where the shift from an original active-stative split to a (finiteness-/)mood-driven system (cf. 16a–b) involves a saltational change, with no evidence of auxiliary variation having first passed through intermediate person- and tense-driven splits (Dragomirescu and Nicolae 2009; Ledgeway 2014). That said, movements up the hierarchy might be motivated by earlier downward microparametric shifts within a given mesoparametric network. This is the case with HAVE-generalization found in many modern Ibero-Romance and southern Italo-Romance varieties where in medieval texts the first extensions of HAVE to unaccusative syntax are licensed uniquely in irrealis modal contexts (cf. 20), from where Ledgeway (2003) demonstrates that it gets a foothold in the system before progressively spreading to realis contexts yielding the generalized extension of HAVE witnessed today (cf. 15b). Arguably, the rise of a modally determined extension of HAVE to unaccusative syntax represents a microparametric change, involving a downward movement within the mesoparametric network dedicated to argument structure which ultimately provides the necessary impetus to trigger the mesoparametric change targeting the top of the hierarchy.

One final dimension of variation that we have not yet discussed in relation to (14) is the possibility that the core reflex of unaccusativity, viz BE-selection, becomes lexically fossilized and today limited to a synchronically opaque, small number of intransitive predicates. This nanoparametric state of affairs, in which a once productive auxiliary distinction has all but fallen out of the system, accurately describes many *langue d'oïl* varieties, including French (and especially Canadian varieties; cf. Sankoff and Thibault 1977; King and Nadasdi 2005). As a consequence, these varieties have witnessed a striking decline in the number of unaccusatives that today may still select BE, precariously surviving in association with specific predicates as a lexical idiosyncrasy (Benveniste 1965: 181; Guiraud 1969: 40f.; Giancarli 2011: 373f.).

21.2.2.4 Summary

In conclusion, we have seen how modelling Romance auxiliary systems in terms of a parametric hierarchy, whose structural organization makes some strong predictions about markedness relations between different linguistic choices, can be profitably used, especially when earlier stages of (non-standard) languages are not documented, to understand the direction of change in auxiliary systems, what precisely may change, and how such diachronic variation may be implicationally structured. Particularly striking is the observation that the original active-stative split (cf. 14e),

Table 21.1. *Typologies of Romance verb-movement*

Typology	Varieties
High	French, Romanian
Clause-medial	northern regional Italian, NIDs
Low	European Portuguese, southern regional Italian, SIDs
Very low	Spanish, Valencian

which historically underlies all Romance languages and situated at the bottom of our hierarchy, proves diachronically extremely unstable and has frequently been subject to further microparametric variation. The effects of such variation have been in many cases to gradually eradicate one of the two auxiliaries to the advantage of a single auxiliary producing diachronically more stable, less marked, higher-level parametric options.

21.2.3 Verb-Movement

After a long wave of studies on the Romance vs Germanic contrast in verb-movement (cf. the position of the verb with respect to the adverb highlighted in bold in Fr. *il pleure* **toujours** vs Eng. *He* **always** *cries*), traditionally interpreted as a binary dichotomy between movement and non-movement languages, respectively, recent cartographic studies have revealed a much more nuanced picture with different Romance languages exhibiting different degrees of verb-movement across the clausal spine (for relevant bibliography, see Schifano 2018: §1.1; see also discussion in Section 20.2.1). By combining one of the traditional diagnostics for verb-movement, namely adverb placement, with Cinque's (1999) fine-grained hierarchy of functional projections and related adverbs, it is possible to identify at least four different typologies of Romance verb-movement (Schifano 2015a; 2015b; 2016; 2018): (i) high movement to the higher adverb space (HAS) above adverbs such as PROBABLY (23); (ii) clause-medial movement to the HAS between adverbs such as GENERALLY and INTENTIONALLY (24); (iii) low movement to the lower adverb space (LAS) between adverbs such as STILL and ALWAYS (25); (iii) very low movement just outside the verb phrase (viz. *v*-VP) to a position between adverbs such as ALMOST and COMPLETELY (26), as summarized in Table 21.1 (Schifano 2018: chs 2–3):[6]

(23) **French**
Antoine confond **probablement** (**confond) le poème avec un autre.
Antoine confuse.PRS.3SG probably the poem with an other
'Antoine is probably confusing the poem with another.'

---

[6] Here we restrict our attention to the placement of the present indicative lexical verb. See Schifano (2015a; 2018) for patterns of movement with other verb forms.

(24) **Northern regional Italian**
 a. Gianni (**confonde) **generalmente** confonde queste due poesie.
    Gianni generally confuse.PRS.3SG these two poems
    'Gianni usually confuses these two poems.'
 b. Gianni parla **apposta** (**parla) con un accento napoletano.
    Gianni speak.PRS.3SG intentionally with an accent Neapolitan
    'Gianni speaks with a Neapolitan accent on purpose.'

(25) **European Portuguese**
 a. A Maria (**se recorda) **ainda** se recorda desta história.
    the Maria still self= remember.PRS.3SG of.this story
    'Maria still remembers this story.'
 b. O João vê **sempre** (**vê) este tipo de filmes.
    the João see.PRS.3SG always this type of films
    'João always watches this type of film.'

(26) **Spanish**
 a. Sergio (**se equivoca) **casi** se equivoca.
    Sergio almost self= err.PRS.3SG
    'Sergio almost makes a mistake.'
 b. Entiendo **completamente** (**entiendo) lo que dices.
    understand.PRS.1SG completely the which say.PRS.2SG
    'I completely understand what you are saying.'

Moving beyond traditional formulations of the Rich Agreement Hypothesis, which seeks to establish a link between verb-movement and morphological richness (e.g., Koeneman and Zeijlstra 2014), it is possible to show that the attested typologies are not arbitrary choices of the individual languages but, rather, the predictable outcome of a precise interplay between morphology and syntax in the licensing of the interpretation of the verb. Assuming that the clausal spine consists of three fields, namely a high mood-related field, a clause-medial tense-related field, and a low aspect-related field (Tortora 2002; Cinque 2004: 688; Holmberg and Roberts 2013; Nicolae 2013; Schifano 2015a: 89; 2018: 134f.), Romance verb-movement can be reinterpreted as targeting either the mood-field (yielding high movement), the tense-field (yielding clause-medial movement), the aspect field (yielding low movement), or a position at the bottom of the aspect-field (yielding very low movement).

The specific field targeted by each language can then be predicted if we assume that the driving force behind verb-movement is the requirement that the verb's TAM interpretation be licensed. This licensing can be achieved either through a morphological strategy, namely inherent licensing via the presence of dedicated synthetic paradigms devoted to the expression of mood, tense, or aspect (henceforth 'paradigmatic instantiation', PI), or a syntactic strategy, namely overt verb-movement to the relevant field (Schifano 2015a: 90–93; 2018: 136–39). By way of illustration, consider mood. In a clause-medial language like (northern regional) Italian, the modal interpretation of the verb is licensed through the morphological strategy, as mood is paradigmatically instantiated in this variety, witness its synthetic and largely non-syncretic paradigms devoted to the expression of values like realis/irrealis and declarative/conditional, viz. indicative (27a), subjunctive (27b), and conditional (27c). As a consequence, the verb does not need to overtly reach the high mood-related field (cf. syntactic strategy), yielding clause-medial movement.

(27) **Italian**
    a.   lavorate
           work.PRS.IND.2PL
    b.   lavoriate
           work.PRS.SBJV.2PL
    c.   lavorereste
           work.COND.2PL
           'you (would) work'

Conversely, in a high-movement language like Romanian, mood is not paradigmatically instantiated, witness its analytic subjunctive (28b) and conditional (28c). This means that, in order to license its modal interpretation, the Romanian verb needs to move overtly to the mood-field in accordance with the syntactic strategy, thereby yielding high verb-movement.

(28) **Romanian**
    a.   lucrați
           work.PRS.2PL
    b.   să   lucrați
           SBJV work.PRS.2PL
    c.   ați   lucra
           AUX.COND.2PL work.INF
           'you (would) work'

On a par with the other Romance parameters reviewed in this chapter, the different typologies of verb-movement identified above can be insightfully modelled in terms of a parametric hierarchy. To do so, we first need to identify the relevant formal features involved in verb-movement. Following Schifano (2015a; 2018), we argue that such features are [M(ood)], [T(ense)], and [Asp(ect)], which appear (in finite clauses): (i) on the lexical head V; and (ii) on the corresponding fields of the I-domain, viz. [M] in the mood-field, [T] in the tense-field, and [Asp] in the aspect-field. We assume that these features are always interpretable on V (i.e., can be read by the

Table 21.2. *Correlation between PI and (un)interpretability*

Typology	PI of TAM	Interpretability
high	mood [–PI]	[uM]
clause-medial	mood [+PI]; tense [–PI]	[iM]; [uT]
low	mood [+PI]; tense [+PI]; aspect [–PI]	[iM]; [iT];[uAsp]
very low	mood [+PI]; tense [+PI]; aspect [+PI]	[iM]; [iT]; [iAsp]

Schifano (2018: 166).

computational system), but not necessarily on the corresponding fields, a variability which is the formal element responsible for the attested typologies. In particular, we argue that the lack of PI with a given category gives rise to a scenario where the feature on the field is u(ninterpretable), while a strong degree of PI implies the i(nterpretability) of the corresponding feature, as summarized in Table 21.2.[7]

Assuming with Adger and Svenonius (2011: 37) that uninterpretability forces feature matching (a type of feature copying process) and that feature matching entails movement, we obtain a correct formalization of the Romance verb-movement typologies. In clause-medial and (very) low-movement languages, where mood is [+PI], the mood-field bears [iM] and no feature matching and hence no verb-movement to the high field is observed; similarly, in the (very) low-movement languages, tense is [+PI], hence the tense-field bears [iT] and no feature matching and verb-movement to the clause-medial field is attested either. Conversely, when the feature on the field is uninterpretable, the field becomes a Probe looking for a Goal with a matching feature. This is the case for high-movement languages where mood is [–PI], hence the mood-field bears [uM] which is matched and checked against the corresponding interpretable feature on V, resulting in the verb's displacement to the higher field. Similarly, in clause-medial languages tense is [–PI], such that [T] is uninterpretable on the tense-field which, for the purposes of feature matching, must therefore probe a corresponding interpretable feature on V causing it to move to the clause-medial field. Finally, in low-movement languages aspect is [–PI], hence the aspect-field bears [uAsp] triggering low movement to allow feature matching.

---

[7] Cf. Schifano (2018: 139–52) for a thorough assessment of the PI of TAM in a selection of Romance languages belonging to the four typologies.

Having formalized the attested variation, the different microparametric options can be modelled by the hierarchy in (29) (Schifano 2018: 177):

(29)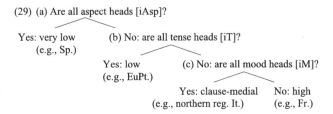

Question (29a) asks whether all aspect heads bear [iAsp], which can be inferred by looking at the degree of PI of aspect in the relevant language, the Yes-branch leading to very low movement varieties like Spanish. Note that, because of the effects of the Head Movement Constraint on Romance verb-movement (which requires the displaced verb to pass through all intermediate head positions), if a category is [+PI], all the higher categories are [+PI] too. In terms of features, this implies that if the feature of a given field is interpretable, the corresponding feature of the higher fields is interpretable too. Accordingly, although (29a) does not ask about tense and mood, the interpretability of the corresponding features in very low-movement languages follows automatically (Schifano 2018: 168–75). A negative answer to (29a) leads to the assessment of tense (29b), whose heads are interpretable in low movement languages like European Portuguese, and mood (29c), which bears [iM] in clause-medial varieties like northern regional Italian, but [uM] in high movement languages like French.

In conclusion, the rich Romance-internal evidence reviewed here highlights the importance of adopting a fine-grained view of the clausal domain, leading to the identification of microparametric options which would otherwise go unnoticed. We have also shed new light on the debated relationship between morphology and (verb-)movement, showing how the morphological shape of verb paradigms, rather than a broadly 'rich' morphology, determines the attested internal variation.

21.2.4 Negation

Across Romance, three main syntactic patterns of negation can be identified: (i) preverbal, as in European Portuguese, Spanish, Catalan, Italian, central/southern Italian dialects, north-eastern and some north-western Italian dialects, eastern Romansh, and Romanian (30a); (ii) discontinuous, consisting in both a preverbal and obligatory non-emphatic postverbal marker, as in standard French and many northern Italian dialects (30b); (iii) postverbal, as in Aragonese, northern Catalan dialects, and several

Gallo-Romance varieties, including spoken French, northwestern Italian dialects, and western/central Romansh (30c):[8]

(30) a. **Nu** a mâncat. (Ro.)
   NEG have.PRS.IND.3SG eat.PTCP
   'S/he didn't eat.'
   b. **No** la dorm **no**. (Livo, NID, Manzini and Savoia 2005, III: 134)
   NEG SCL.3FSG= sleep.PRS.IND.3SG NEG
   'She doesn't sleep.'
   c. Ou farai **pas**. (Gvd., Oliviéri and Sauzet 2016: 346)
   it= do.FUT.1SG NEG
   'I will not do it.'

While the preverbal negator is invariably derived from Lat. NON 'not' across standard Romance (Poletto 2016a: 834), three main typologies of postverbal negators (including optional emphatic ones) can be identified in accordance with their etymology: (i) minimizers, e.g., It. *mica* < MICA(M) 'crumb'; (ii) n-words for 'nothing', e.g., Prv. *ren* < REM 'thing'; (iii) clause-final negators from NON, e.g., BrPt. *não*.[9] According to Poletto (2008; 2016a; 2016b) and Garzonio and Poletto (2009; 2018), the etymological origin of negators correlates with their syntactic distribution, as described by Zanuttini (1997), who identifies four possible positions across Romance in accordance with their distribution with respect to adverbs and non-finite verb forms: (i) NegP1, hosting the preverbal negator and located below C (cf. also Poletto 2000; 2016a: 834); (ii) NegP2, hosting the minimizer class and located in the LAS before ALREADY (cf. Cinque 1999); (iii) NegP3, hosting the quantifier class, following ALREADY but preceding NO LONGER; and (iv) NegP4, hosting the pro-sentence class, following ALWAYS. As for the syntactic status of negative markers, empirical evidence such as placement with respect to clitics and interaction with verb-movement suggests the existence of two types of preverbal negator, one which is clitic and the other which is an independent head position (Zanuttini 1997; Cinque 1999: 121; Benincà and Poletto 2005: 241–44), while postverbal negators are generally analysed as adverbs with phrasal status (Zanuttini 1997; Rowlett 1998; Cinque 1999: 120f.).

In addition to microvariation in form and position, one of the most studied aspects of negation in Romance, and beyond, has been the apparent correlation between the three structural types described above and the three diachronic stages attested cross-linguistically, traditionally known

---

[8] Cf. Schwegler (1990: ch. 6), Molinelli, Bernini, and Ramat (1987: 165f.), Bernini and Ramat (1996: 17–21), Parry (1997: 179; 2013: 78f.), Zanuttini (1997), Manzini and Savoia (2005, III: 127–55), Poletto (2016a: 836f.), Benincà (2017: 190f.). The picture is more complex in Brazilian Portuguese, for which see Schwegler (1983: 317; 1987) and Dubert and Galves (2016: 436).

[9] Cf. Cinque (1999: 120f.), Benincà and Poletto (2005: 247f.), Manzini and Savoia (2005, III: 127–334), Poletto (2008), Garzonio and Poletto (2009; 2018), Parry (2013: 93), Poletto (2016a: 838).

as Jespersen's Cycle (cf. also Section 23.7.3) and exemplified in (31) from French (Poletto 2016a: 836), where the preverbal negator of earlier stages of the language (Stage I) is obligatory reinforced by a postverbal adverb in the modern language (Stage II), eventually left as the only the marker of negation in the contemporary colloquial register (Stage III):

(31) a. Je ne dis. (OFr.)
I NEG say.PRS.IND.1SG
b. Je ne dis pas. (ModFr.)
I NEG say.PRS.IND.1SG NEG
c. Je dis pas. (coll. Fr.)
I say.PRS.IND.1SG NEG
'I do not say.'

Over the decades, various aspects of Jespersen's Cycle have been discussed and reformulated, also in the light of new empirical evidence. Topics of debate include the exact number of stages (van der Auwera 2009) and triggering factors (Parry 2013: 94f.). The object of study of the present section regards, however, another puzzle surrounding the negative cycle, namely its Romance-internal distribution. As noted from the outset, obligatory non-emphatic postverbal negators (cf. Stages II and III) are concentrated in a continuous geographical area which includes some eastern Ibero-Romance and several Gallo-Romance varieties, leaving about half of the Romània stranded at Stage I (Schwegler 1983: 318), where postverbal reinforcers may only be added under specific pragmatic conditions (cf. Cinque 1976; 1991).[10] In order to account for this particular distribution, different proposals have been advanced in the literature, including German adstratum influence (e.g., Lockwood 1968: 208) and reduced use of postverbal emphatic constructions (e.g., Schwegler 1983: 323). In what follows, we suggest a novel hypothesis which links the attested distribution, viz. Stage I vs Stage II–III varieties, to the typologies of verb-movement described in Section 21.2.3 above. In particular, we start from the observation that varieties where non-emphatic postverbal negators are attested (cf. Stages II–III) coincide with the high and clause-medial typologies of verb-movement, as summarized in Table 21.3, suggesting a correlation along the lines of (32):

(32) If a variety is at Stages II–III, it exhibits clause-medial or high verb-movement.

Starting from the varieties which are at Stages II–III, we observe that these include French and northern Italian dialects such as Milanese, exhibiting high and clause-medial verb-movement, respectively (Schifano

---

[10] Here we gloss over Brazilian Portuguese, where all the three stages are attested (cf. n. 8).

Table 21.3. *Verb-movement and negation typologies*

Verb-movement	Negation — Stage I	Stages II–III
High	Romanian	French, Occitan, Gascon
Clause-medial	northern regional Italian, NIDs (e.g., Teolese)	(northern regional Italian), NIDs (e.g., Milanese)
Low	European Portuguese, southern regional Italian, SIDs	*
Very low	Spanish, Valencian	*

2018: 13–15, 62f.), as well as Occitan and Gascon, which also show high verb-movement just like French (Ledgeway 2020). Note that the correlation in (32) is not bi-directional – if a variety exhibits clause-medial or high verb-movement, it does not follow that it must be at Stages II–III – as shown by the fact that Romanian, northern regional Italian, and a northeastern Italian dialect like Teolese (Padua) all belong to Stage I, despite their high and clause-medial verb-movement (Schifano 2014; 2018: 13–15, 63–66).[11] Conversely, all the varieties which belong to the (very) low verb-movement typologies have not moved beyond Stage I (although they do allow optional emphatic postverbal negators, see discussion below), as predicted by (32). In what follows, we review a number of theoretical and empirical arguments which indicate that such a correlation is not accidental.

21.2.4.1 Correlation between Verb-Movement and Jespersen's Stages

Starting from theory-internal reasons, (32) finds formal justification in the licensing requirements of the postverbal negators. As discussed above, postverbal negators of the minimizer class (NegP2) represent the grammaticalization of nouns denoting a minimal unit. Likewise, those belonging to the quantifier class (NegP3) are originally derived from quantifiers, most of which are themselves the output of the univerbation of a negator plus a quantity or generic noun (e.g., Brg. *nutta* > NE + GUTTA(M) 'not drop', Garzonio and Poletto 2018; It. *niente* > NE(C) ENTE(M), 'not thing', Parry 2013: 80 n. 5).[12] The claim that all negative adverbs are still essentially nominal is also independently supported by Manzini and Savoia (2005: 206,

---

[11] See below for further comments on northern regional Italian.
[12] The clause-final negators in NegP4 represent an apparent exception, in that they do not share the same nominal nature as those in NegP2/NegP3. However, they should not be equated with prototypical postverbal negators since, unlike the latter, they are sentence-final pro-sentence markers, generally related to focus (Poletto 2016a: 838) and, as such, do not share the same licensing requirements. The prediction is that low movement varieties should then be able to make use of such negators, a case in point being Brazilian Portuguese which can use a NegP4 marker in non-emphatic contexts (cf. n. 8), despite its very low verb-movement (Schifano 2018: 70–73).

209, 216–18), who locate such adverbs within a nominal string. Acknowledging their nominal nature, we claim that postverbal negators have to be licensed as elements carrying a NEG(ation) feature and that such licensing is achieved by moving the verb through the head of their associated functional projection on its way to its landing site. This licensing mechanism explains why the varieties which exhibit (very) low verb-movement, namely varieties where the verb does not cross the LAS such as Spanish (Section 21.2.3), have not moved beyond Stage I, since in such varieties the NEG feature of postverbal negators cannot be licensed.

Looking at the empirical evidence, an interesting case in point is found in the northern Catalan dialect of Roussillon (Rossellonès), where postverbal *pas* is used non-emphatically as the sole marker of sentential negation (Gómez Duran 2011: 299–307; Llop Naya 2017: 57):

(33) La   Maria vindrà   **pas**. (Ros., Gómez Duran 2011: 301)
      the   Maria come.FUT.3SG   NEG
      'Maria will not come.'

The prediction made by (32) is that Rossellonès should feature a higher instance of verb-movement than the other varieties of Catalan which have not moved beyond Stage I, such as Valencian Catalan, which only exhibits preverbal negation and belongs to the very low verb-movement typology (Section 21.2.3). This seems to be confirmed by the adverb placements discussed by Gómez Duran (2011: 343), who observes that in Rossellonès adverbs can occupy a position which is not allowed in other dialects of Catalan. In particular, she reports that adverbs can appear immediately after the inflected verb in Rossellonès, as exemplified by (34a), where the low adverb *sempre* 'always' appears between the auxiliary and the past participle, suggesting a higher placement of the auxiliary than in Valencian (34b):[13]

(34) a. Nosaltres hi   havíem   **sempre** anat   amb la nostra. (Rou., Gómez Duran 2011: 366)
        we   LOC= have.PST.IPFV.1PL   always   go.PTCP with the ours
        'We had always gone there with ours.'
     b. El seu home **sempre** ha   (**sempre) estimat   (sempre)
        the her man always   have.PRS.IND.3SG   love.PTCP always
        una altra dona. (Vlc., adapted from Schifano 2018: 79)
        an other woman
        'Her man has always loved another woman.'

Some evidence in favour of (32) also comes from non-standard Romance varieties of Italy. Over recent decades, colloquial varieties of Italian have witnessed an increase in the use of postverbal strategies of negation where different

---

[13] Further research is needed to support Gómez Duran's (2011) observation about adverb placement in Rossellonès. See discussion in Schifano (2018: 26–29, 68f., 75–80) regarding the possibility for the AUX-PTCP complex in Valencian to precede *sempre*, which should not be interpreted as the output of high verb-movement, and for the claim that the movement typology of Romance auxiliaries coincides with that of lexical verbs.

n-words which require preverbal *non* in standard Italian are used as the sole non-emphatic negator, suggesting a gradual shift towards Stage III (35) (Molinelli 1984; Molinelli, Bernini, and Ramat 1987; Bernini and Ramat 1996). Crucially, such patterns are only attested in the northern colloquial varieties where the typology of verb-movement is high enough to license Stage III negation, while they have not developed in the low movement southern regional varieties of Italian (Schifano 2018: 8f., 11–13), as predicted once again by (32):

(35) Ma   c'era   **niente** da   fare. (It., Cremona, Bernini, and Ramat 1996: 21)
      but   LOC=be.PST.IPFV.3SG   nothing   by   do.INF
      'But there was nothing we could do.'

Similar evidence comes from some northeastern Italian dialects. When discussing the presuppositional negator of the *mica/mancu* type, Poletto (2016a: 835f.) observes that in several northeastern Italian dialects this type of negator is used in contexts in which presuppositional *mica* is not allowed in colloquial standard Italian (e.g., relative clauses; cf. Cinque 1976; 1991). Although in such varieties this negator is not yet obligatory, Poletto takes this pattern to represent a further development of negative marking in these varieties, in the direction of a postverbal non-emphatic negator of the French type (cf. also Garzonio and Poletto 2009). Again, the fact that this gradual shift should be happening in the north, where precisely we find clause-medial verb-movement, but not in the south, where we find low verb-movement, lends further support to (32).

Finally, our proposed correlation between verb-movement and negation typologies may provide an independent account for the cross-Romance lack of complete instances of Jespersen's Cycle, as discussed by different authors (e.g., Benincà 2017: 192) who have variously attempted to explain it (Poletto 2016a: 837; Garzonio and Poletto 2018).[14] According to the approach developed here, one of the possible driving forces behind a switch from Stage III back to Stage I could be a change in verb-movement, whereby a clause-medial or high verb-movement language, where postverbal negators are licensed (cf. 32), becomes a (very) low movement variety. Once the verb no longer moves high enough to license postverbal markers, a switch to Stage I follows automatically. However, following the notion of paradigmatic instantiation (Section 21.2.3), we expect such a change in verb-movement – and hence in negation typology – to be very rare cross-linguistically, given that a morphological enrichment of the paradigms dedicated to the expression of TAM is highly unlikely.[15]

---

[14] See Benincà (2017: 192–94) for some apparent cases of complete cycles.
[15] By enrichment, we mean a scenario whereby a language develops new synthetic and non-syncretic paradigms devoted to the expression of TAM (or reduces the analyticity and/or syncretisms of the existing ones).

Before concluding, a comment about emphatic presuppositional negation is in order, inasmuch as the patterns attested in many (very) low verb-movement varieties seem to present evidence against (32). Across many southern Italian dialects, there are (at least) three syntactic patterns for the expression of presuppositional negation: (i)–(ii) a preverbal presuppositional negator co-occurring (36a) or not (36b) with the standard negation; and (iii) a postverbal presuppositional negator occurring with standard negation (36c) (Ledgeway 2017):

(36) a. Stativi tranquilli, **un** vi **mancu** fazzu
be.IMP.2PL=yourselves quiet NEG you= NEG$_{PRESUPPOSITIONAL}$ make.PRS.1SG
pagà. (NCal., Ledgeway 2017: 110)
pay.INF
'Don't worry, I won't charge you for it after all.'

b. **Neca** ci vonsi jiri. (Mus., Ledgeway 2017: 107)
NEG$_{PRESUPPOSITIONAL}$ there= want.PST.PFV.3SG go.INF
'In any case, he didn't want to go there.'

c. Sta schersi? – **Nu'** sta scherzu **filu**. (Lec., Ledgeway 2017: 117)
PROG joke.PRS.2SG NEG PROG joke.PRS.1SG NEG$_{PRESUPPOSITIONAL}$
'Are you kidding? – I'm not kidding.'

Patterns like (36a) and (36c) appear to represent a potential problem for (32) in that they instantiate cases of NegP2 (cf. *mancu* and *filu*, viz. the type which normally requires licensing in Stage II languages) in (very) low verb-movement varieties (Ledgeway and Lombardi 2005; 2014; Schifano 2018: 17–23). Despite appearances, such patterns do not, however, invalidate (32), since presuppositional negators are not pure sentential negative markers in such dialects, given their obligatory occurrence with the real NegP1 negator (Cinque 1999: 220 n. 35) and their optional emphatic use linked to specific pragmatic conditions. As such, these varieties do not qualify as Stage II. Similarly, because the negator *neca* appears alone in preverbal position in (20b), we take this pattern to instantiate Stage I, such that (32) does not apply.

In conclusion, the evidence reviewed above suggests a strong correlation between the verb-movement typologies independently attested across Romance and negation typologies which stem from the licensing requirements of postverbal negators. From a parametric perspective, this implies that the Romance negation parameter hierarchy is simply parasitic on that for verb-movement, with Stage II–III microparametric options represented by the Yes and No branches of (29c). This is a pleasing result since it allows us to assume a simpler architecture of the grammar, without the need to postulate additional parameters and associated mechanisms and explanations to account for the specific behaviour of microvariation in sentential negation. Rather, the observed variation in the licensing of Romance sentential negation now follows straightforwardly from the independently motivated parametric options in verb-movement into which it can ultimately be subsumed.

21.3 Left Periphery

Building on parallels with Romance nominal structures (cf. Ledgeway 2015), we explore below some major dimensions of microvariation in the development of the Latin-Romance C-system, as formalized in hierarchy (37).

(37) (a) Does C grammaticalize definiteness? (= realis complementizer)

    No: Lat. AcI (38)   Yes: Romance (40)
                     (b) Does C grammaticalize indefiniteness? (= irrealis complementizer)

      No: Lat. AcI (38)   Yes: Romance (40)
                      (c) Strong C?

        No: modern Romance   Yes (= V2)
(f) Does C probe V? (= V-to-C mvt)   (d) Satisfied by Merge?

No   Yes (46a–i)   Yes: medRom. *si* (44b),   No (= (e) Move:
                      Gsc. *que* (45)   medRom. V-to-C mvt (44a)

21.3.1 Grammaticalization of (In)definiteness on C

Focusing on complement clauses, we exploit the traditional intuition that these are nominal (whence the traditional label 'noun clauses'), as evidenced by the fact that Romance complementizers typically continue D elements (cf. various Romance reflexes of Lat. QUID / QUOD / QUIA > *chelque / colcu / c(h)a/că*). Consequently, C(omplementizer) is merely a descriptive label for a particular set of occurrences of D(eterminer) binding a propositional variable with sentential content restricted by the embedded sentence (cf. Manzini and Savoia 2003; 2011). We therefore expect parallels in the distribution and development of articles and complementizers, an expectation borne out in the Latin-Romance transition. Assuming realis and irrealis complements to be associated with definite and indefinite eventive arguments (Manzini 1996; Baker and Travis 1997), we take the C position to variously license propositional definite and indefinite descriptions. Thus, in the same way that the lack of (in)definite articles in the nominal domain highlights Latin's failure to grammaticalize the marking of (in)definiteness on D, the absence of an overt complementizer in the core Latin complementation pattern, the accusative and infinitive construction (AcI), highlights a parallel behaviour in the clausal domain where C fails to mark the definite/indefinite nature of realis/irrealis complements. Consequently, a negative setting for our first question (37a) regarding the grammaticalization of definiteness marking on C presupposes, as with articles, a corresponding absence of indefiniteness marking on C (37b), with both realis and irrealis complements introduced by null C heads in the AcI construction:

(38) [_CP_ [_TP_ EUM   OMNIA   SCIRE]   Ø]   DICO/UOLO. (Lat.)
               him.ACC   everything   know.INF   Ø_COMP_   say/want.PRS.IND.1SG
      'I say that he knows / I want him to know everything.'

By contrast, Romance varieties present positive settings for options (37a–b), although displaying significant microvariation in how the (in)definiteness properties of (ir)realis complements are grammaticalized through the C-system, the details of which can be captured in terms of Chomsky's (2007; 2008) and Ouali's (2008) proposals about feature transfer between C and its complement T (viz. the sentential inflexional core) through the operations KEEP, SHARE, and DONATE. More specifically, the positive branches to questions (37a–b) can each be further decomposed and expanded into the increasingly marked microparametric options in (39) (see discussion in Ledgeway and Lombardi 2014; Colasanti 2018):

(39) (a) Does C grammaticalize (in)definiteness?

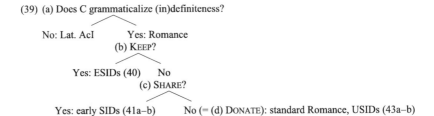

    No: Lat. AcI   Yes: Romance
                        (b) KEEP?

              Yes: ESIDs (40)   No
                                  (c) SHARE?

                        Yes: early SIDs (41a–b)   No (= (d) DONATE): standard Romance, USIDs (43a–b)

There arise then three possibilities. A positive answer to (39b) yields the least marked option (viz. KEEP) which ensures that the featural opposition is not transferred down to the verb under T, but surfaces on the C head alone in the lexical choice of the complementizer. This describes the modern dialects of the extreme south of Italy (40), which formally distinguish between realis and irrealis complements through a dual finite complementizer system (Ledgeway 2016b: §63.3; cf. also Sections 1.2.3.3.1, 1.2.4.4).

(40) Nci   dissi   a lu figghiolu ca/'u   si   ndi   vaci. (Bovese)
      to.him= say.PST.PFV.3SG   to the son   that_Realis/Irrealis_ self=   therefrom= go.PRS.3SG
      'He_i told [his son]_j that he_{i/k}'s leaving/that he_j should leave.'

More complex options characterize varieties which answer negatively to the KEEP option in (39b). The first involves the extension of marking of (in)definiteness from C such that it is inherited by T (viz. SHARE), thereby surfacing on all relevant functional heads (cf. polydefiniteness in the Romanian nominal group). Consequently, in varieties specified positively for (39c) (in)definiteness marking surfaces both in the shape of the complementizer and on the embedded verb in a classic indicative/subjunctive opposition (Ledgeway 2004; 2005; 2006):

(41) **Old Salentino**
  a. significano ca illo fece dissobediencia
     mean.PRS.IND.3PL that_Realis he make.PST.PFV.3SG disobedience
     'they mean that he was disobedient'
  b. commandao cu doy fossero uno
     command.PST.PFV.3SG that_Irrealis two be.PST.SBJV.3PL one
     'he commanded that two should be one'

However, the formal instantiation of SHARE on T is not limited to morphological reflexes, but may surface syntactically through variable verb movement (Ledgeway 2009; Ledgeway and Lombardi 2014). Such is the case in modern Salentino (42a–b), where, despite the loss of the subjunctive, the relevant definite/indefinite distinction on T is manifested through its ability to attract the finite verb, as revealed by the higher position of the irrealis verb with respect to adverbs (Schifano 2018):

(42) **Modern Salentino**
  a. Ticu ca **già** sta paca.
     say.PRS.1SG that_Realis already PROG pay.PRS.3SG
  b. Speru cu (**già) sta paca già.
     hope.PRS.1SG that_Irrealis PROG pay.PRS.3SG already
     'I say/hope he's already paying.'

Finally, a variety which is specified positively for microparametric option (37a) grammaticalizing the marking of (in)definiteness in the C-system, but specified negatively for both the KEEP and SHARE options in (39b–c), is left with no other option but complete transfer of the relevant (in)definiteness feature solely on T. We thus naturally derive the effects of the DONATE option simply from the negative specification of the SHARE option (= 39d). Typically, such marking on T surfaces in a morphological indicative/subjunctive contrast on the verb as found in most (standard) Romance varieties (43a), or, in the dialects of upper southern Italy (43b), through the syntactic reflex of variable V-movement (Ledgeway 2009; 2012b; Ledgeway and Lombardi 2014).

(43) a. Le digo que se calla/-e. (Sp.)
        him=say.PRS.1SG that self=silence.PRS.IND.3SG/-SBJV.3SG
     b. Cci dicu ca **sempe** sta / (**sempe) stessa
        him=say.PRS.1SG that always stay.PRS.3SG stay.SBJV.3SG
        sempe cittu. (Cos.)
        always silent
        'I tell him_i that he_j keeps quiet/that he_i should keep quiet.'

21.3.2 Weak/Strong C

On a par with the weak/strong D parameter (cf. Guardiano and Longobardi 2005), we assume a weak/strong dimension of parametric variation for the C head (cf. 37c) which, if strong, must be associated with (a) V(-feature) overtly in the syntax. Given the overt marking for (in)definiteness in Romance embedded contexts observed in Section 21.3.1, the weak/strong nature of Romance C can only be established by considering its behaviour in root contexts. On these criteria, most modern Romance varieties qualify as weak C languages, inasmuch as there is no systematic association in the syntax between V and [+declarative] root C. By contrast, medieval Romance varieties, and some modern Ladin varieties, are strong C languages, in that root C is characterized by a V2 constraint which imposes generalized V-to-C movement with variable fronting of one or more constituents to the Topic-Focus field (8a; Salvi 2004; Benincà 2013; Poletto 2014; Wolfe 2018; cf. also Section 1.2.4.1). However, alongside this Move option (viz. 39e), the system also makes available the less costly (external) Merge option (viz. 39d), whereby the strong V-feature requirement on C is satisfied by direct lexical insertion of the functional head *sì/si* (44b; Ledgeway 2008).

(44) **Old Neapolitan**
  a. [FocP [Spec sì fuorti cuolpi] [C-FinP li donava [TP li donava sì fuorti cuolpi]]]
     such strong blows him= give.PST.IPFV.3SG
  b. [FocP [Spec spissi cuolpi mortali] [C-FinP sì [TP le dava spissi cuolpi mortali]]]
     many blows mortal sì to.him= give.PST.IPFV.3SG
     'Such strong / Frequent blows he inflicted upon him.'

The Merge option also characterizes many modern Gascon varieties (45), also strong C languages since they obligatorily lexicalize [+declarative] root C with *que* 'that' (Ledgeway 2012: 167f.; 2020; cf. also Section 1.2.3.3.1). Just as in medieval Romance, the strong specification of C predicts that the EPP feature also appears on C, rather than on T, in Gascon where preverbal subjects are always left-peripheral never surfacing between *que* and the finite V.

(45) [TopP Ta pay [C-FinP qu' [TP (**ta pay) èy arribat.]]] (Gsc.)
     your father that your father be.PRS.IND.3SG arrived
     'Your father has arrived.'

Although most other modern Romance varieties are weak C languages (cf. 37c), C may still probe V (and hence license V-to-C movement) under particular marked conditions (37f), as reflected, among other things, in (simple/complex) subject-verb inversion and enclisis of object clitics. Following Rizzi and Roberts (1989) and Rizzi (1990), this more constrained type of V-to-C movement represents a synchronic residue of generalized V2 movement, today licensed in a restricted number of non-veridical polarity contexts tied to specific types of illocutionary force (cf. also Sections 24.2.2–5 and 24.3.2.2):

(46) a. Cossa fa- lo? (interrogative; CVen.)
 what do.PRS.IND.3SG=he
 'What's he doing?'
 b. ¡Cuán rápido habla Bruno! (exclamative; Sp.)
 how quick speak.PRS.IND.3SG Bruno
 'How quickly Bruno speaks!'
 c. Ti falet unu lampu! (optative; Srd.)
 you=strike.PRS.SBJV.3SG a lightening.bolt
 'May you be struck by lightning!'
 d. Tivesse Célia chamado, ... (hypothetical; Pt.)
 have.PST.SBJV.3SG Célia call.PTCP
 'Had Célia called, ...'
 e. Ducă-se pe pustii! (jussive; Ro.)
 take.SBJV.3=self on desert
 '(S)he/They should clear off!'
 f. Non si muova nessuno! (exhortative; It.)
 not self=move.PRS.SBJV.3SG nobody
 'Nobody move!'
 g. Dût-il m'en coûter cent fois plus, ... (concessive; Fr.)
 must.PST.SBJV.3SG=it me=thereof=cost.INF hundred times more
 'Even if it were to cost me a hundred times more, ...'
 h. Sedi-al rivat o no sedi-al rivat (disjunctive; Frl.)
 be.PRS.SBJV.3SG=he arrive.PTCP or not be.PRS.SBJV.3SG=he arrive.PTCP
 'Whether he's arrived or not'
 i. Fes-li un petó! (imperative; Cat.)
 do.IMP.2SG=to.her a kiss
 'Give her a kiss!'

Thus, while generalized V2 movement triggered by a semantically uninterpretable V-feature in declarative contexts is systematically lost in weak C varieties, V-to-C movement is retained just in those contexts where movement plays a role in interpretation licensing the observed non-veridical polarity values (cf. Munaro 2004). Nonetheless, the distribution of such semantically-driven V-to-C movement is not uniform across Romance, revealing often unpredictable degrees of productivity and attrition. Conflating some of the traditional labels above, we distinguish here between interrogative, exclamative, optative (subsuming hypothetical, concessive, jussive, (ex)hortative), and imperatival illocutionary forces whose distribution is modelled according to the microparametric choices in subhierarchy (47).

(47) (a) Does C probe V? (= V-to-C mvt)

No: Merge option (48)   Yes
                (b) Extended to all marked force types?

        Yes: GaR.   No
                    (c) Restricted to optative, exclamative, imperative?

            Yes: It., Ro.   No
                        (d) Restricted to exclamative, imperative?

                Yes: IbR.   No
                          (e) Restricted to imperative?

                    Yes: SIDs   No ⇒ nanoparametric variation
                                          Fr. focused adverbs (48a); C-drop (49b)

The positive setting for option (47b) identifies those liberal Gallo-Romance varieties such as French and especially north(east)ern Italian dialects (cf. Poletto 2000: chs 3, 5) which continue to license V-to-C movement across all marked clause types. Nonetheless, in French some of these cases of V-to-C movement are not particularly productive even in higher registers, and often subject to restrictions related to verb class (functional>lexical), mood (irrealis>realis) and grammatical person (3/2>1). In such behaviours are visible some often well-advanced and ongoing morphosyntactic and lexical restrictions on a once fully productive movement operation which in lower registers is now predominantly replaced, except for imperatives, by the Merge option (cf. negative specification of 37f/47a):

(48) **French**
    a.   [CP Mange-t- [TP il ~~mange~~?]]
            eat.PRS.3SG =he
    b.   [CP Est-ce qu' [TP il mange?]]
            Q   he=eat.PRS.3SG
       'Does he eat?'

This weakening of the Move option is even more evident in those varieties singled out by the positive specifications of options (47c–d) such as Italian/Romanian and Ibero-Romance, respectively, which have both lost semantically-driven V-to-C movement with polar interrogatives, but continue to display it with (some types of) exclamatives and imperatives, though differing with respect to the availability of such movement in optatives. In these varieties too non-declarative illocutionary force is in many cases more readily licensed through the Merge option (cf. negative specification of 47a) with lexicalization of C by various complementizers and particles (Ledgeway 2012: 175f.; Corr 2017) such as Sardinian interrogative *a* and Portuguese/Spanish optative *oxalá/ojalá*. Finally, option (47e) identifies varieties such as southern Italian dialects where V-to-C movement has all but disappeared from the grammar except for imperatives, the clause type in which V-to-C movement proves most resilient across Romance (Rivero 1994; Graffi 1996).

We conclude by noting two cases of nanoparametric variation in the distribution of Romance V-to-C movement, relics of a syntactically driven V2 constraint whose synchronic licensing displays all the hallmarks of a non-productive and lexically idiosyncratic phenomenon. The first regards (complex/simple) subject–verb inversion as a result of V-to-C movement in formal registers of French triggered by a handful of focused adverbs (49a), whereas the second case concerns the phenomenon of C-drop in irrealis clauses (49b), the result of V-to-C movement (cf. Poletto 2000: 118–33; Ledgeway 2016b: §63.2.1.4; see also the discussion in Section 1.2.4.4). In both cases, the nanoparametric nature of the phenomena is variously underscored by the idiosyncratic nature of the triggers, by considerable distributional irregularities, and by varying degrees of optionality and idiosyncratic and idiolectal instability.

(49) a. Aussi conclut-on … (Fr.)
therefore conclude.PRS.IND.3SG=one
'One therefore concludes …'
b. Dedueixo (que) sigui una bona ocasió. (Cat.)
deduce.PRS.IND.1SG that be.PRS.SBJV.3SG a good occasion
'I deduce (that) it is a good opportunity.'

To conclude, the discussion in this section has highlighted how there are significant 'deep' parallels in the dimensions of microvariation characterizing the functional structure and organization of the Romance nominal and clausal groups which go beyond mere surface accidental similarities. In particular, we have seen that there is no need to posit separate parametric choices for these two domains, inasmuch as observed synchronic and diachronic variation across both domains can be readily captured in terms of a single set of higher- and above all lower-level parametric options. This parallelism constitutes a welcome finding in that it points to how the available parametric space, as we also saw to be the case with variation in verb-movement and sentential negation (cf. Section 21.2.4), can be further constrained and redefined in terms of a set of common transcategorial principles and options.

References

Below you can find selected references for this chapter. The full references can be found online at the following page: www.cambridge.org/Romancelinguistics

Baker, M. (2008b). 'The macroparameter in a microparametric world'. In Biberauer, T. (ed.), *The Limits of Syntactic Variation*. Amsterdam: Benjamins, 351–74.

Cinque, G. (1999). *Adverbs and Functional Heads. A Cross-Linguistic Perspective*. Oxford: Oxford University Press.

Guardiano, C. and Longobardi, G. (2005). 'Parametric comparison and language taxonomy'. In Batllori, M., Hernanz, M.-Ll., Picallo, C., and Roca, F. (eds), *Grammaticalization and Parametric Variation*. Oxford: Oxford University Press, 149–74.

Ledgeway, A. (2012). *From Latin to Romance. Morphosyntactic Typology and Change*. Oxford: Oxford University Press.

Ledgeway, A. (2015). 'Parallels in Romance nominal and clausal microvariation', *Revue roumaine de linguistique* 60: 105–27.

Ledgeway, A. (2019). 'Parameters in the development of Romance perfective auxiliary selection'. In Cennamo, M. and Fabrizio, C. (eds), *Historical Linguistics 2015. Selected Papers from the 22nd International Conference on Historical Linguistics, Naples, 27–31 July 2015*. Amsterdam/Philadelphia: Benjamins, 343–84.

Loporcaro, M. (1998). *Sintassi comparata dell'accordo participiale romanzo*. Turin: Rosenberg & Sellier.

Manzini, M. R. and Savoia, L. (2005). *I dialetti italiani e romanci. Morfosintassi generativa* (3 vols). Alessandria: Edizioni dell'Orso.

Poletto, C. (2000). *The Higher Functional Field*. Oxford: Oxford University Press.

Poletto, C. (2016a). 'Negation'. In Ledgeway, A. and Maiden, M. (eds), *The Oxford Guide to the Romance Languages*. Oxford: Oxford University Press, 833–46.

Poletto, C. and Tortora, C. (2016). 'Subject clitics: Syntax'. In Ledgeway, A. and Maiden, M. (eds), *The Oxford Guide to the Romance Languages*. Oxford: Oxford University Press, 772–85.

Schifano, N. (2018). *Verb Movement in Romance: A Comparative Study*. Oxford: Oxford University Press.

Zanuttini, R. (1997). *Negation and Clausal Structure*. Oxford: Oxford University Press.

Part Five

Semantics and Pragmatics

22

Word Meanings and Concepts

Steven N. Dworkin

22.1 Traditional Approaches to Lexical Change

From its very beginnings as an organized scholarly discipline, Romance linguistics has devoted much attention to the diachronic study of the lexicon of the Romance languages.* At the outset such work took the shape of etymological investigations into the origins of individual lexical items, as can be seen in the writings of the so-called founding father of the field Friedrich Diez (1797–1876), who in the period from 1836 to 1853 authored the first pan-Romance historical grammar (his three-volume *Grammatik der romanischen Sprachen* 1836–44) and the first pan-Romance etymological dictionary, his *Etymologisches Wörterbuch der romanischen Sprachen* (1853; fifth edition, 1887). Etymology as the search for and identification of individual word origins dominated research into the historical examination of the lexicon until the first two decades of the twentieth century. At that time, as a result of the efforts of such leading scholars of the Romance lexicon as Hugo Schuchardt, Jakob Jud, and Walther von Wartburg, Romance etymology evolved into the preparation of complete lexical biographies, covering all formal and semantic facets of a given word's or word family's evolution. This wider perspective ideally included all relevant formal and semantic changes undergone by the word under study, its relationship in the lexicon to its synonyms and antonyms and, if appropriate, the circumstances leading to its demise or obsolescence. This approach was continued and refined in the second half of the century by such specialists as Kurt Baldinger, Yakov Malkiel, and Max Pfister, to name but three outstanding examples. Consequently, the sub-discipline traditionally known as

---

* I wish to thank Victor Celac and Ion Giurgea for their help with the Romanian material presented here. I take full responsibility for any errors of fact or interpretation.

etymology gradually transformed itself into diachronic lexicology, in which identification of a given lexical item's immediate origin in the language at issue was but the first step.

Students of Romance diachronic lexicology have a singular advantage over specialists in the history of the lexicons of other language families. Romanists have at their disposal an abundant documentation of various written registers of the source language, Latin (for an overview, see Chapter 3, this volume). Although these registers are not faithful reproductions or transcriptions of the numerous regional and social oral varieties of Latin that underlie the Romance languages (cf. Section 2.3), they provide a treasure trove of authentic lexical items that often reflect the realities of the spoken language. Some of the Romance vernaculars (French, Occitan, Italo-Romance varieties, Spanish) have a documented history that goes back in some cases nearly or over a thousand years, a situation that allows the lexicologist to witness empirically, trace, and analyse many of the relevant formal and semantic changes. Consequently Romanists have found themselves in the privileged position of being able to share with colleagues working on other languages insights into the causes and nature of lexical change. The lessons learned from the observation of documented Romance phenomena have the potential to throw light on processes of lexical change in other families for which the sole approach to the linguistic past is often comparative reconstruction or internal reconstruction.

Over the last few decades the study of lexical change has undergone major changes in focus both within and outside the Romance domain. Traditionally, Romance diachronic lexicology has focused, from an onomasiological perspective, on the formal and content-level semantic history of nominal, verbal, adjectival, and adverbial bases. Research along these lines has enabled Romanists to make important findings concerning both lexical commonalities and stability and important differentiations (often regional) among the Romance languages (cf. Rohlfs 1979; Stefenelli 1992; Dworkin 2016). The study of lexical semantic change traditionally dealt with such processes as a word's acquisition of new meanings or the loss of earlier meanings and the consequent broadening or narrowing of a word's semantic scope, or the acquisition by a word of positive (amelioration) meanings or negative meanings (pejoration); cf. for one broad overview from a Romance perspective, though now dated, see Ullman (1959). Although etymology and diachronic lexicology are no longer central disciplines in historical Romance linguistics, there is still much work to be done at the levels of individual Romance languages and of the Romance family as a whole with regard to these traditional approaches to diachronic lexicology. There is a sizeable residue of words whose origins remain unknown or, at least, controversial. Identifying a word's etymological starting point and its original meaning(s) is an essential first step in tracing the further steps in its semantic evolution. Traditional approaches to Romance etymology or diachronic lexicology have tended to ignore questions pertaining to the genesis and history of neologisms resulting either from borrowings or from internal creations employing the derivational resources of the languages at issue (e.g., suffixation, prefixation, compounding); for discussion of these issues, see Buchi and Dworkin (2019) and Dworkin (2019).

Leaving aside language-specific cultural factors, the various cognitive processes at play in lexical and semantic change (metaphors, metonymy) occur across languages and language families. Within the domain of Romance linguistics, the work of Peter Koch and his students (see especially Blank 1997; Blank and Koch 1999; 2003; and Mihatsch and Steinberg 2004) has demonstrated the role of such cognitive processes, especially with regard to the lexical semantic evolution through conceptual metaphor of terms designating body parts, fruits and the corresponding tree names, and of temporal and spatial adverbs. Work dealing with the Romance languages has offered abundant illustrations of such conceptual metaphor changes as SPACE > TIME (e.g., Lat. CURTUS 'short (in length)' > Fr. *court*, Sp. *corto* 'short (space and time)', CONTAINER > HEAD, e.g., Lat. TESTA 'pot' > Fr. *tête*, It. *testa*, Lat. CONCHA 'shell' > Srd. *konka* 'head', TAKE, GRASP > UNDERSTAND, e.g., Lat. COMPRAEHENDERE 'to seize, grasp' > Fr. *comprendre*, Sp. *comprender*, Lat. CAPERE 'to seize, capture' > It. *capire* 'to understand'. Such developments repeat themselves throughout the history of the Romance languages; cf. such developments as Fr. *piger* and *saisir*, Sp. *pillar* 'to seize, grasp' > 'to understand'. Dworkin (2006; 2011) and Stolova (2015: 94–100) offer an overview, with relevant bibliography, of such work in the Romance domain.

22.2 Grammaticalization and Pragmatic-Semantic Change

This chapter will examine a different facet of the diachronic study of word concepts and meanings in the Romance languages. Over the last several decades specialists in general historical linguistics, understood as the cross-linguistic study of the phenomena and processes of language change, have explored the interface between what, on the surface, appears to be syntactic change and certain semantic phenomena affecting the lexical item at issue. They have examined facets of language change associated with syntax but with consequences for the semantic status of the items involved, such as recurrent paths of grammaticalization, the less common phenomenon of degrammaticalization, as well as lexicalization, subjectification, pragmaticization (understood here as the genesis of pragmatic and discourse markers), and the creation of lexical items with evidential functions. Do these processes constitute various manifestations of grammaticalization, understood as a decrease in or loss of a word's autonomous lexical status, accompanied by an increase in its use as a grammatical or pragmatic marker (e.g., as a pronoun, preposition, conjunction, discourse marker) or bound morpheme (inflexional or derivational affix), or are they separate, but often related and overlapping processes? This question seems particularly pertinent with regard to grammaticalization, degrammaticalization, and lexicalization. In many instances they have a lexical starting point, since they involve a change in the semantic status and scope of the nouns, verbs, or adjectives involved. Hopper and Traugott (1993: 12) state that the syntactic process of grammaticalization in its early stages often, perhaps always, involves a shift in meaning. However, it is the syntactic shift that usually leads to the resulting semantic change. We have here a close link between lexical (manifested as semantic) and syntactic change. Brinton and Traugott (2005: 11–15) argue that there exist no clear-cut boundaries between lexical and grammatical categories. Traugott (1989: 31) operates with the dual concepts of lexical semantic change and grammatical semantic change, and speaks specifically of 'the semantics of grammaticalization' (cf. the discussion, with rich bibliography, on the question of grammaticalization versus lexicalization in Breban et al. 2012: 3–6).

Romanists working on issues of diachronic lexicology in the broad sense of complete word histories are beginning to focus their attention on the genesis and subsequent evolution of prepositions, grammatical particles, pragmatic and discourse markers, as well as the acquisition by some originally independent lexical items of evidential and/or subjectification functions. One may argue that all these categories represent different categories or manifestations of grammaticalization. The semantic phenomena identified here are crosslinguistic (and perhaps universal), although their formal and syntactic shapes may vary widely across languages and language families. They may not manifest themselves in all languages belonging to a given family. Some languages of the same family may show different degrees of grammaticalization (on Romance, see Lamiroy 2011; Fagard and Mardale 2012).

Such an approach to the study of the lexicon constitutes a fruitful meeting place for the activities of Romanists and for general linguists concerned with the historical evolution of the lexicon understood in its broadest sense. Although there is an abundant general linguistics literature on these topics, examples from the Romance languages and possible lessons to be derived by general linguistics from the analysis of the relevant Romance phenomena do not figure prominently in these many pioneering studies on grammaticalization and associated phenomena authored by non-Romanists, e.g., Traugott (1989), Traugott and Hopper (1993), Heine (2003a), Brinton and Traugott (2005), and Norde (2009), to name and to identify selectively a few of the most prominent scholars engaged in such research and their work.

This situation is gradually changing, as can be seen by such studies focusing on the Romance languages as Marchello-Nizia (2006), Ledgeway (2011), and in the essays gathered in Ghezzi and Molinelli (2014), and Loureda and Pons Bordería (forthcoming) to cite but a few recent examples. The Romance languages show significant commonalities and differences with regard to these processes and their impact on the lexicon. Rather than focusing on traditional approaches to lexical semantic change as described in the first section, this chapter will examine the workings of functional and semantic-pragmatic changes undergone by lexical categories such as nouns, verbs, adjectives, and adverbs as part of the syntactico-semantic processes by which they acquire grammatical functions, while sometimes (though far from always) losing completely their original status as independent lexical items. Although linguists working on other language families have done much valuable work on many of the issues to be presented here, the historical record of the Romance languages reveals an unparalleled wealth of diachronic, diatopic, and diastratic variation, in short a fertile empirical testing ground for assessing and shaping new ideas and perspectives about semantic change, structure, and variation observable in grammaticalization and related processes (cf. Section 1.2.1).

Although the study of grammaticalization goes back to the work of the French Indo-Europeanist Antoine Meillet ([1912] 1958) at the beginning of the twentieth century, modern approaches begin in the 1980s with the work of, among others, Christian Lehmann (1982; 1985; 1995) and Frans Plank (1984). One of the main features of this process was labelled 'semantic bleaching' or desemanticization of the affected lexical item, by which a member of a primary and open-ended grammatical category such as a noun, verb, adjective, or adverb, lost part or all of its semantic scope as an independent lexical item and took on the functions of a grammatical tool such as an auxiliary verb, preposition, or inflexional affix, all members of closed categories. This reduction in semantic scope was often accompanied by varying degrees of phonetic erosion. There may be a link between semantic bleaching and phonetic erosion. It seems reasonable to claim that the reduction of a word's semantic scope and its syntactic function allows speakers to feel no great need to preserve its phonetic integrity. However, as shown by the genesis of the adverbial suffix -*ment(e)* '-ly' (< Lat. MENTE (ABL. SG) 'with mind'), semantic bleaching does not necessarily lead to phonetic reduction. We shall see below that the grammaticalization processes involved in the genesis of discourse markers and lexical evidential markers did not lead to the phonetic erosion of the underlying nouns, verbs, or adjectives.

Within the Romance domain the 'textbook' examples of such extreme semantic and categorical weakening are (1) the reduction of the present indicative forms of the Latin verb HABERE 'have' to the status of inflexional suffixes in the future tense resulting from the evolution undergone by the Latin construction type AMARE HABEO 'love.INF have.PRS.IND.1SG (= I am obliged to love)' (cf. Fr. *aimerai*, Sp. *amaré*, Pt. *amarei*, It. *amerò* 'I will love'), (2) the creation of the compound past tenses in which the inflected forms of the local reflexes of HABERE 'have' (Fr. *avoir*, Sp. *haber*, OPt. *haver*, It. *avere*), and ESSE 'be' (Fr. *être*, It. *essere*, and Sp., Pt. *ser*),[1] are reduced to the status of auxiliary verbs (followed by the past participle of the main verb; for an overview, see Sections 19.3.2–3), and (3) the transformation of the Latin ablative MENTE 'mind' (< MENS) into the adverbial suffix seen in Fr. *-ment*, Sp., It., Pt. *-mente*. Certain semantic categories of verbs tend to lend themselves better than others to grammaticalization. Citing the specific examples of Fr. *aller* 'to go', *avoir* 'to have', *faire* 'to do, make', Marchello-Nizia (2006: 143) declares that words with wide semantic scopes are the best candidates to undergo grammaticalization. Grammaticalization does not occur uniformly over the Romance languages. Lamiroy (2011) has concluded that French is the most highly grammaticalized Romance language, followed by Italian, and Spanish and Portuguese; she did not include Romanian in her purview. Certain grammaticalization processes did not occur in this last-mentioned language, e.g., the creation of a synthetic future based on the local reflexes of the present indicative forms of HABERE or the formation of adverbials with a suffix derived from MENTE. Romanian does have future auxiliaries that result from different grammaticalization processes. Taking the grammaticalization of simple and compound prepositions observable in the evolution in the Romance languages, Fagard and Mardale (2012) concur that French is the most grammaticalized Romance language, followed by Italian, Spanish, Portuguese, and Romanian. One can legitimately question the validity and the feasibility of such comparisons, as the conclusions will vary according to the chosen linguistic features. This critique also holds for the observations made in Lamiroy (2011), reported above.

Just as in lexical semantic change when the acquisition or development of a new meaning does not necessarily lead to the elimination of earlier senses, in many instances the reduction in a form's lexical/semantic status as part of a change due to grammaticalization led to the continued coexistence of the original full meaning and the newer innovative grammatical meaning. One might be able to argue that speakers perceive such co-existing forms as one polysemous/polyfunctional entity rather than as two discrete homophones. This is not always the case in Romanian, in which the inflected form of various auxiliary verbs are different from the

---

[1] Lat. SEDERE 'to be seated' also played a role in the genesis of *ser*.

corresponding inflected forms of the lexical verb, e.g., lexical 3SG.PRS.IND *are*, 1PL.PRS.IND *avem*, 2PL.PRS.IND *aveți* versus their functional counterparts *a, am, ați* meaning 'to have'. In like fashion Cat. *anar* 'to go' displays the suppletive present indicative paradigm 1SG *vaig*, 2SG *vas*, 3SG *va*, 1PL *anem*, 2PL *aneu*, 3PL *van* when used as a lexical verb of motion, but uses the corresponding forms *và(re)ig, va(re)s, va và(re)m, và(re)u, va(re)n* as an auxiliary verb in a compound past tense (e.g., *jo vaig cantar* 'I sang'). Similarly, the continuants of Latin DEBERE 'owe, must' display a different paradigm in Sardinian according to their use as a full lexical verb (*devo, deves, deve*) or as an auxiliary (*deo, des, det*) in the future tense (Ledgeway 2011: 725; 2012: 135). In French and Italian, *avoir* and *avere* function as both a main verb indicating possession and as an auxiliary verb, whereas Portuguese also uses one verb, *ter* (< TENERE 'hold') for both roles. Only modern Spanish lexically distinguishes the main verb *tener* from the auxiliary verb *haber* (as a result of changes undergone by the latter verb in the late medieval language). In those Romance languages (French, Spanish, Portuguese) that have a fully developed 'go-future' comprising a form of the verb 'go' and the infinitive (Fr. *je vais manger*, Sp. *voy a comer*, Pt. *vou comer* '(I) go (to) eat.INF (I will eat)'), the verb 'go' has lost in this construction its concrete meaning of physical displacement for the purpose of carrying out the verbal action ('I am going from point X to point Y in order to eat'), but has gained a new abstract meaning of futurity or intention as part of the construction at issue while at the same time becoming a form of preverbal tense marker, which continues to exist alongside identical forms of *aller/ir* indicating 'motion' (cf. Section 19.3.4).

In the Romance languages other verbs of motion or location have undergone similar metaphorical concrete to abstract grammaticalization semantic changes and have become auxiliaries in so-called progressive constructions while retaining their meanings as full verbs (e.g., Sp. *ando buscando a mi hijo* 'I am looking for my son', *viene estudiando aquí desde hace tres meses* 'he has been studying here for three months', *sigo trabajando en la misma universidad* 'I continue to work at the same university'; cf. *andar* 'to walk', *venir* 'to come', *seguir* 'to follow, continue'; for recent discussion and further examples, see Bertinetto and Squartini 2016: 947–50). In Italian and the Surmiran variety of Romansh, the verb 'to come', respectively *venire* and *neir*, have grammaticalized as a passive auxiliary; in Surselvan Romansh, the descendants of UENIRE 'to come' are also grammaticalized as the auxiliary of the future (Ledgeway 2012: 135). In all cases the verbs in question have retained their full independent lexical meanings. Since the time of the earliest Romanian texts, the language has employed periphrases with grammaticalized *vrea* 'want' + the bare infinitive or an auxiliary form of 'have' + the *a-* infinitive or the subjunctive to express the future (Zafiu 2016: 39; Maiden et al. 2021: 372–374).

Semantic bleaching is often represented as a path or cline of the following nature: full lexical item > function word > grammatical marker / particle > grammatical affix, or content item > grammatical word > inflexional affix (Hopper and Traugott 1993: 7). Is the process of semantic bleaching the same when a content word becomes, say, a grammatical affix (as in the case of the passage of the noun MENTE to the adverbial suffix -ment[e]) as when a grammatical marker becomes further grammaticalized (e.g., the oft-cited example of the transformation of forms of the Latin distal demonstrative ILLE into the definite article in most Romance languages, the transformation of the reflexes of the Latin preposition DE into a partitive marker (e.g., Fr. *du pain*, It. *del pane* 'some bread'), or the recent further grammaticalization in French of the preposition *sur* 'on'.

It seems that nouns were less prone to semantic bleaching or reduction and phonetic erosion than verbs. Much further research would be needed to determine whether this situation holds in other language families. In most Romance languages, the reflexes of Latin CASA 'cabin, hut' have survived as the basic designation for 'house' (Sp., Pt., It. *casa*, Ro. *casă*). However, in Gallo-Romance, OFr. *chiese* (or the variant *chase*) 'house' became grammaticalized as the preposition *chies* 'at the house of' (cf. *enchies* 'next to, at the house of'), the forerunner of modern *chez* 'at the house of', and fell into disuse as an independent noun, giving way to *maison* 'house' < MANSIONEM 'abode, dwelling' (cf. the analysis stressing the interface of etymology and syntax proposed in Longobardi 2001). In like fashion the reduced form Cat. *ca* became a preposition with the meaning 'at the house of', and co-exists alongside the full noun *casa* 'house'; see also Vnt. *ca'*. The use of such articulated forms as *cal/can* 'at the house of' (< *ca* + *el/en* 'house + the. MSG') indicates that speakers of Catalan do not consider *ca* and *casa* to be variants of the same base. The French adverb *jadis* 'formerly', is a contraction of OFr. *ja a dis* 'already to days (= some days ago)', in which *dis* is the plural of early OFr. *di* 'day' (cf. *midi* 'midday').

From the time of the medieval language onward, Sp. *cabo* 'end' (< CAPUT 'head') functioned as both a full noun and became grammaticalized as part of compound prepositions *a cabo de*, *en cabo de*, both 'at the end of', *por cabo de* 'near', as well as a verbal prefix as in OSp. *cap: cabtener* 'to support', *caboponer* 'to enclose completely', *caboprender* 'to entrap'. Following a different path, Cat. *cap* 'head', which still retains that meaning as well as related secondary meanings, was grammaticalized as a negative polarity item *cap* 'not one'. Whereas the Latin accusative HOMINEM survived in Fr. *homme*, Sp. *hombre*, Pt. *homem* 'man', the nominative HOMO lives on in Italian and Romanian as the full noun *uomo* 'man' and *om* 'person', but as the indefinite pronoun Fr. *on* 'one'. In Lombard, HOMO grammaticalized as a first person plural affix, as in *mangium* 'we eat'. The phenomenon is found in other northern Italian varieties (Benincà, Parry, and Pescarini 2016: 194).

Although Sp. *merced* 'mercy, grace' continues as a full noun, the syntagm *vuestra merced* 'your grace/mercy' underwent such a degree of phonetic erosion that its nominal component became opaque, resulting in the shift to the pronominal address form *usted* (through several documented intermediate stages). These events occurred relatively late in the history of the language; the new pronoun is first recorded in the early seventeenth, but did not become integrated until the late eighteenth century. A similar process underlies the creation of the Portuguese second person pronoun *você* and Cat. *vostè* (cf. Section 25.3.2). A similar erosion took place in the evolution of Ro. *domnia ta* (singular), *domniile voastre* (plural) 'your lordship(s)' to the politeness pronouns *dumneata, dumneavoastră* (see Maiden et al. 2021: 151–155). In all the Romance languages the reflexes of the numeral UNUS/UNA 'one' also grammaticalized as the indefinite article while continuing to co-exist with the homophonous numeral. Calabrian formally distinguishes between the numeral *unu/una* and the aphaeresized indefinite article *nu/na* (Ledgeway 2011: 722).

The genesis of the postverbal element through grammaticalization in French discontinuous negation involved the semantic reduction of full nouns. Lat. PASSUS 'step, pace' generated Fr. *pas* 'step' which, first came to be used to reinforce the negator *non/ne* with verbs of motion (cf. Sections 21.2.4, 23.7.3). Over time, *pas*, so used, became grammaticalized as an obligatory element in French negation. The full noun *pas* is still used in French, but synchronically speakers do not associate it with the negator. The same holds for *rien* 'nothing', the reflex of Lat. REM, accusative of RES 'thing'. Originally a feminine noun in old French, *rien* became grammaticalized as an indefinite pronoun meaning 'something' in the medieval language. As a result of its use with the negator *ne/non* starting in the middle French period, *rien* acquired the negative meaning 'nothing'. Its replacement in the sense 'something' was *quelque chose*, literally 'some thing', which perhaps involved some loss of the semantic autonomy of the noun *chose* 'thing', a form that became grammaticalized in the fifteenth century (Marchello-Nizia 2006: 113). Unlike *rien*, *chose* retained its separate status as a full noun. In like fashion, the noun *personne*, originally 'person' also became grammaticalized as a negative polarity item, alongside the full noun *personne*. Other nouns originally indicating small quantities, minimizers, grammaticalized into markers of negative polarity, e.g., It. *mica*, Fr. *mie*, Lmb. *minga*, Ro. *nemic(ă), nimic* '(not even a) crumb', NLmb. *buca* 'morsel', Fr. *point*, Flo. *punto* 'point, stitch', Fr. *goutte* 'drop', Lmb. *negota/ nagott* '(not a) drop'. The Spanish negators *nadie* (an outgrowth of OSp. *nadi*) 'nobody' and *nada* 'nothing' result from the grammaticalization of the adjectivally-used Latin participles NATI and NATA (the latter in the phrase RES NATA lit. '[not] a born thing'), respectively masculine plural and feminine singular past participles of CLat. NASCI 'to be born'. If indeed It. *niente* 'nothing' does go back to NE + GENTE 'not people', the Italian negator shows a complete reduction of the nominal component of its putative etymon (see also OFr. *neient, nient*, Occ. *neen, nien*); the same holds true if *niente* goes back to NEC+ ENTE 'thing', as some specialists in Italian etymology suggest (cf. the discussion in Nocentini 2010: s.v. *niente*).

The semantic weakening or the severe reduction of the semantic scope and flexibility of nouns, adjectives, and verbs has led through grammaticalization to the creation of non-derived or non-suffixal adverbials in the Romance languages. In such cases as Fr. *enfin* 'finally, at last' (lit. 'in + end'), *toujours* 'always' (a reduction of OFr. *toz les jors* 'all the days, every day'), speakers could easily associate on the semantic level *fin* and *jours* with the corresponding full nouns meaning 'end' and 'days', whereas it seems less likely that they would associate the historically nominal element (Fr. *coup*, Occ. *cop* 'blow') of *beaucoup*, OOcc. *belcop* 'many' (of which the initial syllable continues *beau/bel* 'fine') and *maintenant* 'now' (originally 'immediately'), whose immediate source may be the present participle of the verb *maintenir* 'to hold up, maintain', with the nouns *coup* 'blow, strike' and *main* 'hand'. The French conjunction *or* 'now' (also *dorénavant* < OFr. *d'ores en avant* , *d'ore en avant* 'from now on') illustrates the complete semantic reduction of its nominal etymon Lat. HORA 'hour' as does the Portuguese concessive conjunction *embora* 'although, while (concessive)' < *em boa (h)ora* lit. 'in a good hour'. A different evolutionary path led to the creation of the verbal phrase *ir embora* 'to go away', older *ir em boa hora*, lit. 'to go in good hour'. Hummel (2019) cites examples of bare nouns that, in specific contexts, have acquired an adverbial function and have lost, when so used, the semantic value they had when functioning as lexical nouns, e.g., Sp. *pasarlo bomba* (lit. 'to pass=it + bomb') 'to have a good time', Fr. *boire nature* (lit. 'to drink nature'), 'to drink a product without additional ingredients'.

22.3 Prepositions and Prepositional Phrases

Almost all the simple prepositions in the Romance languages go back to morphologically simple Latin prepositions, e.g., Fr. *à* 'to', *contre* 'against', *de* 'of, from', *en* 'in', *entre* 'between', *par* 'by', *pour* 'for', *sous* 'under', *sur* 'on', Sp. *a* 'to', *contra* 'against', *de* 'of, from', *en* 'in', *entre* 'between', *para* 'for', *por* 'for, through, by', *sobre* 'above, on', It. *a* 'to', *contro* 'against', *di* 'of', *in* 'in', *per* 'for', *sopra* 'above, on', < Lat AB/AD, CONTRA, DE, IN, INTER, PER, SUB, SUPER. The semantic reduction of full lexical items such as nouns, verbs, adjectives, and adverbs through grammaticalization also plays a major role in the genesis and lexicalization of some simple (e.g., It. *fino* 'until' < Lat. FINEM 'limit, end') and, far more often, compound prepositions and prepositional phrases functioning as adverbials coined in the individual Romance languages. In some instances the original lexical item is no longer recognizable to speakers, e.g., Fr. *chez* (discussed above), Occ. *doumaci* 'thanks to'. In some instances the original noun has been thoroughly grammaticalized and is no longer recognizable as an independent nominal element to speakers, as is the case of Fr. *parmi* 'among', originally *par mi*, a prepositional phrase involving the preposition *par* 'by' and OFr. *mi* 'middle' cf. Fr. *malgré* 'in spite of'' with the noun *gré* that has lost its independent status and lives on only in set phrases such as *(de) bon gré* 'willingly'. Modern colloquial French shows instances of nouns such as *côté* 'side' and *question* 'question, matter' being used with prepositional value *côté mon travail* 'concerning my work', *question travail* 'as far the job is concerned'.

Opinions are divided as to whether Fr. *près* 'near' and *presque* 'almost' derive from the Latin adjective PRESSUM (participle of the verb PREMERE 'to press'; cf. It. *presso* 'near, in, at', *pressoché* 'almost') or from the related adverb PRESSE 'neatly' (cf. OSrd. *presse*). The Latin adjective SALUUM 'entire, intact, safe' underlies the preposition Fr. *sauf*, Sp., Pt., It. *salvo* 'except, saving'. The French temporal preposition *pendant* 'during, for' (that can also function as a conjunction *pendant que* 'while' and which also underlies *cependant* 'however', lit. 'this.pending') has its origin in the old French noun and adjective *pendant* (itself derived from the present participle *pendant* ← *pendre* 'to hang'; note also Fr. *durant* 'during' (< *durer* 'to last'), *moyennant* 'subject to, in consideration of' (< *moyenner* 'to average'). Old Romanian documents two prepositions that represent the grammaticalization of verbal gerunds: *alegând* 'except for', the present participle of *alege* 'choose, pick out', and *trecând* 'except for', from the present participle of *trece* 'pass (over)'. Neither has survived into the modern language (Nedelcu 2016: 424f.). Similarly, Italian prepositions such as *durante* 'during', *mediante* 'through, by way of', *nonostante* 'in spite of', *rasente a* 'close to, hard against' have their origins in verbal present participles. English and German have also created prepositions based on gerunds and participles (e.g., *during, pending, barring, notwithstanding*; Ger. *betreffend* 'regarding', *entsprechend* 'according to, corresponding to', *während* 'while, during'). The Romance languages offer scattered examples of prepositions derived from finite verb forms: Sp. *hace*, It. *fa* (used as a postposition) 'ago', derived from the third person singular of *hacer* and *fare* 'to do, make' respectively; also It. *tranne* 'except', derived from an imperative form of *trarre* 'pull' + clitic pronoun *ne* ('from it'), and originally meaning something like 'take out of it'. Historically, Fr. *hormis* 'except' is a compound involving the participle *mis* ← *mettre* 'to put, place' and the adverbial *hors* 'out of', originally *mis hors* (attested since the thirteenth century). It is unlikely that speakers of French associate the final syllable of *hormis* with the participle of the high-frequency verb *mettre*. With regard to prepositions and especially prepositional phrases created within French, Marchello-Nizia (2006: 126) claims that more than 50 per cent derive from nouns, 10–15 per cent from verbs, and circa 5 per cent from adjectives. This method of forming new prepositional phrases through grammaticalization and semantic weakening or reduction of the core noun, verb, or adjective is found, alongside prepositions inherited from Latin, across all the Romance languages. Hummel (2019) treats in great detail preposition + adjective phrases that function as adverbs, constructions that many Romanists prefer to analyse as lexicalizations, in which the semantic scope of its adjectival core is severely reduced in comparison to its use as an independent adjective.

Spoken Latin created a number of prepositions that welded together and lexicalized two or three function words. In the course of this process some of the elements in play underwent severe phonetic reduction and a loss of their individual grammatical semantic identity. Some examples: DE POST 'from after' > OSp. *depués* (mod.Sp. *después*), ousting the old Spanish preposition *pos/pues* (which continues to function as a discourse marker), OPt. *depós* (also *após*), It. *dopo* (cf. *poi* 'then'< POST), Ro. *după* 'after'; DE RETRO 'from behind' > It. *dietro* 'behind', OFr. *deriere* (> *derrière*), Oc. *deriere* (cf. OFr. *riere* < RETRO), and Sp. *alrededor* 'around' a further evolution of OSp. *alderredor* (*al* + *de* + *redor*) based on OSp. *redor* 'around' < RETRO.

In many cases of prepositions built on a nominal core, the noun is still transparent, although it has undergone a reduction in its semantic scope and has lost all morphological flexibility with regard to number marking, e.g., It. *accanto (a)* 'beside' (originally *a canto*) Fr. *face à*, Sp. *cara a*, It. *fronte a* 'facing', Sp. *camino a* 'in the direction of', Fr. *grâce à*, Sp. *gracias a* 'thanks to', *en lugar de* 'instead of', Ro. *în loc de*, Sp. *en vez de*, It. *invece di* 'instead of'. Speakers would have no difficulty in associating the core element of such prepositions with the original lexical nouns, namely It. *canto* 'side, corner', Fr. *face*, Sp. *cara*, both 'face', It. *fronte* 'forehead', Sp. *camino* 'road, path', Fr. *grâce*, Sp. *gracias*, both 'thanks', Sp. *lugar*, Ro. *loc*, both 'place', Sp. *vez* 'occasion, turn', It. *vece* 'stead, place'. Specialists seem divided as to whether the formation of such prepositional phrases involves grammaticalization or lexicalization, but, regardless of the label, the processes of semantic reduction seem to be identical. Prepositions (and other forms of adpositions) show different degrees of grammaticalization across the Romance languages (for examples and discussion, see Fagard and Mardale 2012: 317–20, with abundant examples from French, Spanish, Portuguese, Italian, and Romanian). Fagard and Mardale state, '[g]rammaticality is a matter of continuum rather than of discrete categories' (2012: 312).

22.4 Degrammaticalization (or Lexicalization?)

Most scholars working on grammaticalization have stressed the unidirectional nature of such processes. Whereas full content items such as nouns, adjectives, verbs, and adverbs could undergo semantic bleaching or erosion (and often phonetic reduction) on their way to becoming function words, grammatical and discourse markers, and, in extreme cases, affixes, it is claimed that the reverse process never happens, i.e., that a grammatical morpheme does not go back up the cline to become less grammaticalized or become a full lexical item. Several prominent linguists have challenged this view, offering what they claim to be relevant examples of semantic/functional changes in the opposite direction on the grammatical cline. Degrammaticalization is often viewed as a form of upgrading, with grammatical items assuming a less grammatical status, affixes turning into clitics and particles, but less often involving change from grammatical to full lexical status. As is so often the case in linguistic discussion, a technical term such as degrammaticalization is used in differing ways and with differing meanings (see Heine 2003b).

Opinions are divided as to whether such shifts are really instances of degrammaticalization or simply lexicalization phenomena. Certainly the dividing line between these categories is fuzzy, as is the frontier between grammaticalization and lexicalization. Indeed, different linguists have different understandings of the phenomena designated by these terms. Brinton and Traugott (2005: 57f.) declare that lexicalization as separation concerns the emancipation of bound morphemes into free morphemes. Some scholars (e.g., Norde 2009; Franco 2016: 161 n. 23) use these labels interchangeably, arguing that there is only one process, which degrammaticalization and lexicalization look at from different ends (see also Willis 2017). Regardless of the label employed in the analysis, the process involves forms of semantic-pragmatic change.

Most literature on this topic does not offer any examples from the Romance languages, a family in which instances of degrammaticalization seem to be rare. The history of French adverbial *très* 'very' is a possible good case of this phenomenon. In early old French texts *très* functioned as a preposition and as a prefix (cf. OFr. *tresqu'à* 'all the way to', *tresqu'en* 'all the way into') and as a verbal prefix indicating excess (OFr. *tresbattre* 'to beat severely', *trestrembler* 'to tremble violently') reflecting its origin in Lat. TRANS 'across, beyond'. It acquired its present adverbial functions in the fifteenth century (Marchello-Nizia 2006: 166–72). Similarly, Ro. *prea* 'too, too much' derives from the intensifying prefix *prea-*, of Slavic origin (e.g., *preasfânt* 'most holy'). As other seeming instances of degrammaticalization, note the use of Srd. *presse* as a noun with the meaning 'haste, hurry' (Wagner 1960–64: s.v. *presse*) from the adverb PRESSE, and the use in Italian of the plural *pressi* as a noun with the meaning 'vicinity'. These developments contrast with the genesis of It. *pressa*, OSp. *priessa* (modern *prisa*) 'haste' < PRESSAM. Might the Sardinian forms actually be examples of lexicalization? The same question would apply to the late medieval substantivization of Fr. *derrière* 'rear end', originally an adverb and preposition.

It would probably be best to view as lexicalizations those instances in which functional items acquire (temporary) nominal status, e.g., Fr. *les oui et les non*, Sp. *los síes y los nóes* 'the ayes and the nays', Sp. *los pros y los contras* 'the pros and the cons'. One might include here the lexicalization and univerbation in Spanish of the prepositional phrase *por venir* 'to/for come' as the noun *porvenir* 'future'. The same analysis may hold for (incipient) cases in which bound morphemes acquire status as free morphemes; note It. *gli ismi*, Sp. *los ismos* 'the isms'. Conner (2019) calls attention to sporadic instances in Spanish of the use of the prefixes *macro-*, *micro-*, *mega-*, and *pseudo-* as adjectives (with regular inflexion for gender and number): *los índices macros*; *las universidades pseudas* < *los macroíndices* 'the macro-indices', *las pseudouniversidades* 'the pseudo-universities', *lo macro y lo micro* perhaps best paraphrased as 'the macro aspect and the micro aspect'. He prefers the label 'debonding' (a concept discussed in detail by Norde 2009 and Willis 2017) for this process.

22.5 Discourse Markers and Semantic-Pragmatic Change

Elizabeth Traugott, by herself or with colleagues, has carried out much of the pioneering work on the semantic development of discourse and pragmatic particles and markers. The examples come mainly (though not exclusively) from English. Recent work by specialists in the Romance languages shows that these languages can provide many valuable insights into the semantic and functional evolution of these elements. Waltereit (2006) argues that discourse markers are historical relics of speakers' strategies for manipulating the structure of the discourse or the interaction. He seeks to illustrate this claim with an analysis of the evolution of Italian *diciamo* (< *dire* 'to say, tell') from a first person plural present indicative/imperative to its use as a discourse marker. Verbs and adverbs, more so than nouns and adjectives, constitute the principle lexical sources for Romance discourse and pragmatic particles and markers, a very heterogeneous word class or category, for which many different definitions appear in the literature (for a survey, with rich bibliography, see Fanego 2010: 197–201). Some linguists view discourse particles as a subclass of pragmatic markers. As in other instances of grammaticalization and lexicalization, there is observable here a development from items with rich morphological inflexion and a wide range of syntactic functions and semantic scope to reduced forms with no morphological variation, employed in fixed syntactic combinations that show procedural or contextual rather than conceptual or propositional meanings resulting from the weakening of the item's original semantic scope, as is the norm in grammaticalization. Fanego (2010: 200) holds to the view that grammaticalized items such as discourse particles or markers offer semantic layering, the simultaneous presence of different layers of meaning. Diachronically, many functional (pragmatic or discourse) markers develop through semantico-pragmatic change from propositional meetings and often co-exist with their (homophonous) lexical sources. All attention-getters (e.g., It. *guarda*, Fr. *regarde*, Sp. *mira*, Pt. *olha*, all meaning 'look'), the imperative forms of the respective verbs, exist in the lexicon of speakers alongside the original verbs of perception in their literal and metaphorical extended meanings. Some Romance expressions that function as the equivalent of the English politeness marker 'please' show the change undergone by full verbs, e.g., Fr. *s'il vous plaît* 'if it pleases you', *je vous en prie* 'I beg of you', Sp. *tenga la bondad de* 'have the goodness to', *haga el favor de*, (Eu)Pt. *faz favor* '(if you) please', in essence, verb-centred lexicalized clauses, It. *prego* 'I beg', Ro. *vă rog* 'I ask you'. Spanish, Portuguese, and Italian also employ as politeness markers the noun-based prepositional phrase *por favor* and *per favore*, lit. 'through (a) favour'. Spanish, French, and Italian have grammaticalized the third person singular of the present subjunctive of the verbs *être*, *ser*, and *essere* 'be', namely *soit/sea/ossia* (the last also involving the conjunction *o* 'or') as resumptive discourse markers; the corresponding forms in Portuguese and Romanian did not undergo this semantic-pragmatic change.

Adjectives do not often constitute the lexical source of pragmatic or discourse markers across the Romance languages; witness Sp. *bueno* 'good', *claro* 'clear', *seguro* 'sure', Fr. *bon* 'good', It. *ovvero* 'otherwise, indeed' (based on the conjunction *o* + the adjective *vero* 'true'), Pt. *pronto* 'ready' (see Soares da Silva 2006), Ro. *chiar* 'clear'. These forms when used as discourse particles or markers do not enjoy the full semantic scope of the adjective from which they derive, and they show no inflexion for gender and number as do their full-fledged lexical sources. Historically, it is difficult to determine in individual cases when these shifts may have taken place in the spoken language. Each marker has its own history. Ocampo (2006) documents the first instance of *claro* so used in a play from the early nineteenth century (1815), but of course it could have occurred much earlier in speech. He also does not consider the creation of discourse markers to be instances of grammaticalization. La Rocca (2013) and Garcés Gómez (2014) survey and discuss critically the various hypotheses proposed to account for the genesis of discourse markers in the Romance languages.

Likewise, nouns tend not to have undergone extreme semantic-pragmatic reduction or bleaching to form discourse markers. In those instances in which a noun historically underlies a discourse marker, there seems to be an intermediate adverbial stage in the grammaticalization process. The genesis of Fr. *alors*, It. *allora*, both 'now, then' as discourse markers constitutes a good example. Whereas speakers of old French may have continued to perceive a relationship between *alores* and the noun *ore(s)*, modern speakers would be unable to see at the synchronic level the connexion between the final segment of *alors* and the noun *heure* 'hour, time'. The same holds true for the lexicalized *dorénavant* < OFr. *d'ores en avant* and *désormais*, both 'henceforth, from now on'. In contrast, the link between *allora* and *ora* is still perceptible to speakers of Italian. Sp. *luego*, Pt. *logo* both 'then, next' historically go back to Lat. LOCO, an adverbial derived from the ablative singular of LOCUS 'place'. Prior to becoming a discourse marker (often in the combination *desde luego* 'of course'), Sp. *luego*, Pt. *logo* functioned as a temporal adverbial, a value retained in the leave-taking phrase *hasta luego, até logo* 'until the next time'. The French politeness marker *merci* 'thank you' has its origin in the noun *merci* (< accusative MERCEDEM) 'grace, favour', as used in the phrase *votre merci*. Reflexes of this Latin base seem not to have undergone a similar semantic development as a marker in Spanish, Portuguese, and Italian. In like fashion, Sp. *gracias*, It. *grazie* (morphologically plurals) have a nominal origin, Lat. GRATIAS, and represent the reduction of a phrase (Lat. GRATIAS AGERE, Sp. *dar las gracias*). Ro. *mulțumesc* ('I thank') and *mulțumim* ('we thank') 'thank you' is a lexicalization of the first person singular and plural of the verb *a mulțumi* 'to thank'. These nouns also underwent semantic reduction as part of the prepositions Fr. *grâce à*, Sp. *gracias a*, It. *grazie a*, Pt. *graças a*. Should Pt. *obrigado* lit. 'obliged; thank you' be viewed as an example of a similar semantic reduction (although, so used, it is still inflected for gender and number)? Many of the discourse markers that have a nominal centre appear in the form of prepositional phrases (see the Spanish examples, below).

Spanish discourse markers illustrate well many of the pragmatic-semantic factors involved in the genesis of members of this category across the Romance languages. Martín Zorraquino and Pórtoles Lázaro (1999) analyse from a synchronic perspective the semantics and diverse function of approximately seventy such items. There exist few corresponding diachronic studies of the evolution of these discursive elements. Some involve a further degree of grammaticalization of a functional grammatical element, e.g., *entonces*, *pues* both 'then, now'. Many involve lexicalization of a prepositional phrase with a semantic narrowing of the central element of the phrase (e.g., *por cierto* 'certainly', *a propósito* 'by the way', *por añadidura* 'in addition', *en cambio* 'on the other hand', *en fin* 'finally', *al fin y al cabo* 'in conclusion', *de hecho* 'indeed'). One marker, *por ende* 'therefore, consequently' (today restricted to the written language) preserves as its centre the obsolete so-called adverbial-pronoun *ende* (< INDE 'thence') abundantly employed in old Spanish to replace a prepositional phrase introduced by *de* 'from' (see Dworkin 2018: 40f.). In like fashion the present participle *obstante* of the rare verb *obstar* 'to hinder' lives on in the discourse marker *no obstante* 'nevertheless'.

The historical study of discourse and pragmatic markers and particles is very difficult due to a not surprising lack of written documentation of these elements. They are features of spoken dialogic interaction and are rarely recorded in early texts that tend not to reproduce spontaneous oral interaction between speaker and listener (with the possible exception of plays). As is well known in historical linguistics, absence from written sources does not indicate the absence of the element or construction from spontaneous speech. Discourse markers are clearly not a recent innovation. They are creations of each Romance language rather than inheritances from Latin. Only a handful of the discourse markers identified for written Latin, e.g., AT, AUTEM, ENIM, ERGO, IAM, IMMO, IGITUR, MODO, NAM, NEMPE, SCILICET, UTCUMQUE, have left reflexes in the Romance languages, e.g., IAM, which underlies Sp. *ya*, Pt. *ja*, OFr. *ja* (the forerunner of modern *déjà*), It. *già*, all meaning 'already' (for other Romance descendants, see Meyer-Lübke 1935, item 4572). The Latin marker MODO underlies Vgl. *mut*, OIt./SItR. *mo*, Cpd.(*a*)*moi*, ORo. *amu, acmu*, all 'now, just now' (Meyer-Lübke 1935, item 5630). Lexical items that became discourse markers in at least one Romance language did not necessarily acquire this new function in other sister languages. Similarities in the choice of discourse markers result from independent parallel cognitively motivated metaphoric concrete > abstract semantic changes experienced by the items in question rather than from common genetic inheritance.

I shall use Spanish discourse markers as a starting point for a selective comparative analysis of similarities and differences among the Romance languages in the use of common lexical material to generate discourse markers. The Latin preposition POST 'after, behind' is the source of OSp. *pos*, Sp. *pues*, Pt. *pois*, It. *poi*, Ro. *apoi*. I include as a member of this family Fr. *puis*, traditionally derived from *'*postjus*. Whereas Sp. *pues*, originally a preposition (cf. modern *después*, Pt. *depois* 'after'), It. *poi* became discourse markers, the same is not true for their French cognate. Although *pronto* became a discourse marker in Portuguese, functioning as a filler transmitting the idea of 'finished, complete', or 'prepared for', Sp., It. *pronto* did not undergo this shift.

Several scholars have argued that the genesis of discourse or pragmatic markers based on inflected verb forms is an instance of subjectification (see Section 22.6), as they come to express the speaker's subjective attitude toward the propositional content of the utterance. Company Company (2004) argues for this position with case studies drawn from Spanish. Examples of such markers from Spanish include *venga* lit. 'come', *mira* lit. 'look', *oye/oiga* lit. 'listen', *vaya* lit. 'go', *que va* lit. 'that it goes', *vale decir* lit. 'it.is.worth say.INF', *anda* lit. 'walk', *vamos* lit. 'let us go', *digamos* 'let us say', (*o*) *sea* lit. 'let it be'. Many of these Spanish markers have cognate equivalents in other Romance languages, e.g., It. *diciamo* lit. 'let us say', *vale a dire* lit. 'it is equivalent to saying', *guarda* lit. 'look', Fr. *allons* lit. 'let us go', *disons* lit. 'let us say', *soit* lit. 'let it be'. These markers are based on inflected verb forms (predominantly the imperative), and some (e.g., Sp. *venga, vaya, anda*) do not lend themselves to smooth translations into English when employed as discourse markers that express an emotional reaction.

22.6 Subjectification and Evidentiality

Subjectification encodes linguistically the speaker's stance or position with regard to the proposition contained in the utterance and/or to the interlocutor. I quote here the definition offered by Traugott (1989: 35): 'the historical pragmatic-semantic process whereby meanings become increasingly based on the speaker's subjective belief, state, or attitude toward what is said'. Some linguists employ the label 'stance'. Intersubjectification expresses the attitude or stance of the speaker with regard to the listener/interlocutor. (Inter)subjectification is a form of semantic change, once again, as in grammaticalization, involving a weakening of the item's original referential meaning. The linguistic elements involved are usually modal auxiliaries, speech act verbs, pragmatic markers, and modal adverbials created through semantic reduction processes associated with grammaticalization. Since discourse and pragmatic markers are often multifunctional, markers used to express subjectification can also carry out other discourse functions in other contexts. Cornillie (2007) analyses the subjectification over time of deontic and epistemic modals in Spanish, and concludes that epistemic modals have undergone a greater degree of subjectification than deontic modals. According to Cornillie, epistemic modals express a version of reality that is subjectively construed by the speaker. The dividing line between subjectification and evidentiality may at times be very thin. Traugott and Dasher (2002: 187) claim that discourse markers develop a semantic-pragmatic meaning reflecting the attitude or viewpoint of the speaker (subjectivity) and the speaker's stance regarding the interlocutor (intersubjectivity).

Aikhenvald (2004: 3) defines evidentiality as a linguistic category whose primary meaning is source and mode or type of information. To be considered as an evidential, a morpheme must have source of information as its central meaning. In many languages of the world, evidentiality is a separate grammatical category manifestly expressed through specific evidential morphemes. Such is rarely the case with the Romance languages or with most other European languages that do not code evidentiality by grammatical means or markers such as specific evidential affixes. Friedman (2018: 132) describes succinctly the possible evidential use of the admirative suffix *-ka* in Aromanian and of the inverted perfect in Megleno-Romanian. These constructions are calques on Albanian and Macedonian respectively. In fact, Aikhenvald (2004), who works with a rather restrictive definition of the category, denies that European languages possess evidentials. Evidentiality is not a discrete morphological category in the Romance languages, in which it can be manifested syntactically through certain uses of the future, conditional, and imperfect tenses or the subjunctive mood (Squartini 2005), or lexically (see below). It can be viewed as a semantico-pragmatic category (Haßler 2010). In the languages of the world there exists a grammatical-lexical continuum in the expression of evidentiality, a category that is very often difficult to distinguish from (and often overlaps with) epistemic modality. Squartini (2004) examines this issue with regard to Fr. *devoir*, Sp. *deber*, It. *dovere* 'must'. Many linguists working with data from various language families (including the Romance languages) recognize the close semantic interaction between evidentiality and epistemic modality; see Haßler (2010), Pinto de Lima (2014: 142f., and *passim*), and the essays in Cruschina and Remberger (2017). Izquierdo Alegría (2017), writing in Spanish, opts for the label *(para)evidencialidad* '(para)evidentiality'. Evidentiality, as a semantic category, can be divided into direct or indirect evidentiality. The former occurs when the speaker directly witnesses or hears of the event; the latter occurs when the speaker is informed by other sources of the event.

The Romance languages can express the semantico-functional domain of evidentiality through a variety of lexical means involving a functional semantic shift of certain full verbs and adverbials in a grammaticalization process by which these items become lexical evidential markers or, at least, evidential semantic extensions of the lexical item at issue: Fr. *sembler*, *paraître* 'to seem', Sp., Pt. *parecer*, It. *parere*, Ro. *părea* (also *parcă* 'it seems that' and *de parcă* + conditional 'as if' < *pare că* 'it.seems that'), (substandard) *mătincă* 'I believe, think that' < *mă tem că* 'I fear that' (Dincă and Cojocaru 2015) and the related adverbials Fr. *apparemment*, *visiblement*, Sp. *aparentemente*, Ro. *aparent*; note also Sp. *evidentemente* 'obviously', *visiblemente* 'clearly', etc. and their Romance cognates. The Romance languages have grammaticalized evidential markers with a series of fixed lexical expressions used for that purpose. In many cases the immediate source is the grammaticalization of speech-act verbs or verbs of perception as verbs that express some form of evidentiality or indication how the speaker (or writer) obtained the information in the proposition, or whether the information is firm or certain/reliable, or whether there may be some degree of uncertainty, as the source is hearsay or inference, e.g., Fr. *voyons* 'let's see', *à première vue* 'at first sight, at first glance', Sp. *por lo visto* 'as can be seen'. In certain contexts, speech act verbs can acquire semantic features of evidentiality that indicate some degree of uncertainty about the veracity or reality of the proposition (especially with regard to its future realization) without specifically identifying or commenting on the accuracy or reliability of the source of information, e.g., Fr. *on dit que*, Sp. *se dice que*, Pt. *diz-se que*, the lexicalized Sp. *dizque* (discussed in detail in Alcazar 2018), It. *si dice che*, Ro. *cică* (a semantic and phonetic reduction of *zice că* 'says that'). Pinto de Lima (2014) studies in detail, with specific regard to the Portuguese verbs *prometer* 'to promise' and *ameaçar* 'to threaten', how verbs of 'promising' and 'threatening', when used with a non-human subject, can undergo a restriction of their semantic scope so as to become exponents of evidentiality (as described above with regard to the Romance languages). The same seems to hold true for the corresponding verbs in other Romance languages, e.g., Fr. *promettre*, Sp. *prometer*, It. *promettere*, Ro. *promite*; Fr. *menacer*, Sp. *amenazar*, It. *minacciare*, Ro. *amenința* (as in Fr. *Il menace de pleuvoir*, Sp. *amenaza con llover* 'it is threatening to rain', Fr. *il promet de faire beau cet après-midi* 'the weather promises to be fine this afternoon'). Adverbs expressing a point of view can also acquire value as evidentials (again as understood in the context of the Romance and other European languages). Martín Zorraquino and Pórtoles Lázaro (1999) consider *claro* to be a discourse particle of evidentiality, an analysis with which Ocampo (2006) disagrees. Romanian offers an example of an evidential marker that results from the semantic-pragmatic reduction of a prepositional phrase with a nominal core, namely *pesemne*, possibly translatable as 'it appears that' < *pe semne* lit. 'on the signs'.

Some varieties of Campidanese Sardinian have developed, through processes of semantic-pragmatic change, evidential markers from earlier existential proforms with deictic value. The forms at issue are *ddoi/ddui*, outgrowths of ILLOC(QUE) 'thither'. As existential proforms they indicate a location different from that of the speaker (cf. It. *lì*). Bentley (2011: 26) presents examples of these forms used as evidentials indicating that the speaker is not an eyewitness to the action or state described by the verbal predicate in the utterance, e.g., *Ddui est su propriu probleme in Sicilia* '(It is reported that) there is the same problem in Sicily', *A cantu parit ddoi depit ai ni in cui* 'it seems that there is snow there' (Bentley 2011: 126). This use of *ddoi/ddui* has nowhere replaced their primary use as spatio-temporal existential deictics.

22.7 A Concluding Observation

Traditional Romance diachronic lexicology, or the historical study of word concepts and meanings, has focused on the search for and identification of the origin of the nouns, verbs, adjectives, and adverbs in question and their subsequent formal and semantic evolution over the recorded history of the individual languages. Although many leading Romanists engaged in such research, lexical history in its broadest sense, including the mechanisms of semantic change, was not considered a core component of traditional historical grammar, on the same level as diachronic phonetics/phonology, morphology, and syntax. With few exceptions (such as Yakov Malkiel 1968: 175–98; 1975), scholars working on issues in Romance diachronic lexicology made little, if any, effort to demonstrate explicitly how their findings might benefit linguists working on similar questions in other language families or on the nature of lexical change as a linguistic process. No attempt was made to describe or discuss the possible interface between syntactic and semantic change in the Romance languages.

With the rise in general historical linguistics of interest in the various processes that can be subsumed under the broad (though perhaps somewhat polysemous if not controversial) label of grammaticalization, scholars have begun to understand better the impact of such syntactic processes upon the semantic scope of individual lexical items involved in the changes at issue. They have begun to examine the nature of semantic-pragmatic change in contrast to change at the level of full lexical content. Many of the semantic-pragmatic changes identified and described in this chapter affect cognate lexical items in the different Romance languages. In many cases the very semantic nature of the lexical items paved the way for independent parallel cognitively motivated semantic-pragmatic changes. As I have attempted to show in summary fashion in this chapter, specialists in Romance synchronic and diachronic linguistics, over the last three decades, have been examining in depth these phenomena, either on a pan-Romance scale, or on the level of individual Romance languages. The bibliography on these topics has become enormous, especially with regard to grammaticalization, the genesis of discourse markers, and the mechanics of evidentiality and subjectification. Many of the individual examples presented in this chapter have been the subjects of recent detailed synchronic and diachronic studies. The analyses and findings resulting from work in Romance linguistics have much to offer to general diachronic linguistics in order to further our understanding of the nature of all facets of semantic change and its relationship to changes occurring at the other levels of linguistic analysis.

Selected References

Below you can find selected references for this chapter. The full references can be found online at the following page: www.cambridge.org/Romancelinguistics

Blank, A. and Koch, P., eds. (2003). *Kognitive romanische Onomasiologie und Semasiologie*. Tübingen: Niemeyer.
Brinton, L. and Traugott, E. (2005). *Lexicalization and Language Change*. Cambridge: Cambridge University Press.

Buchi, E. and Dworkin, S.N. (2019). 'Etymology in Romance'. In Loporcaro, M. and Gardani, F. (eds), *The Oxford Encyclopedia of Romance Linguistics*. Oxford: Oxford University Press. https://doi.org/10.1093/acrefore/9780199384655.013.441

Cornillie, B. and Izquierdo Alegría, D. (eds) (2017). *Gramática, semántica y pragmática de la evidencialidad*. Pamplona: EUNSA.

Cruschina, S. and Remberger, E.-M., (eds) (2017). *The Rise and Development of Evidential and Epistemic Markers. Special Issue of Journal of Historical Linguistics 7*.

Friedman, V. (2018). 'Where do evidentials come from?' In Aikhenvald, A. (ed.), *The Oxford Handbook of Evidentiality*. Oxford: Oxford University Press, 125–54.

Ghezzi, C. and Molinelli, P. (eds) (2014). *Discourse and Pragmatic Markers from Latin to the Romance Languages*. Oxford: Oxford University Press.

Loureda, O. and Pons Bordería, S. (eds) (forthcoming). *Discourse-Pragmatic Change in Romance*. Leiden: Brill.

Norde, M. (2009). *Degrammaticalization*. Oxford: Oxford University Press.

Stolova, N. (2015). *Cognitive Linguistics and Lexical Change. Motion Verbs from Latin to Romance*. Amsterdam/Philadelphia: Benjamins.

Traugott, E. and Dasher, R. (2002). *Regularity in Semantic Change*. Cambridge: Cambridge University Press.

Willis, D. (2017). 'Degrammaticalization'. In Ledgeway, A. and Roberts, I. (eds), *The Cambridge Handbook of Historical Syntax*. Cambridge: Cambridge University Press, 28–48.

23

Key Topics in Semantics: Presupposition, Anaphora, (In)definite Nominal Phrases, Deixis, Tense and Aspect, Negation

Chiara Gianollo and Giuseppina Silvestri

23.1 Introduction

Research on semantics across different languages and language families has focused on the variation in the language-internal organization, interpretation, and licensing of such categories as presupposition, anaphora, definite and indefinite nominal phrases, deixis, tense, aspect, and negation. This chapter undertakes a critical overview of the theoretical results and advances in these areas, assessing their implications for, and applicability to, these same categories in Romance whilst highlighting what new insights the rich body of Romance evidence has provided and can provide for the general theory. This chapter does not aim at an exhaustive review of the literature on these categories in Romance; rather, it discusses the global impact of the discussion of Romance data on our theoretical understanding, referring to foundational work and the most recent attempts to solve unsettled issues.

23.2 Presupposition

23.2.1 Introduction

In order to illustrate the morphosyntactic devices that trigger presuppositional readings in Romance varieties (Section 23.2.4), it is worth briefly sketching how presupposition is generally defined in semantics.

Traditionally, presupposition has been defined semantically (Schwarz 1977: 247), whereby, given two variables P and Q in the discourse context, P presupposes Q iff P's being true or false requires Q to be true. Presupposition can also be taken as a pragmatic notion (Stalnaker 1974), whereby P presupposes Q iff whenever the utterance of P is conversationally acceptable, the speaker of P assumes Q and believes the hearer to assume Q as well.

Thus, a Spanish sentence such as (1) has at least two main elements corresponding to presupposed knowledge:

(1) La Segunda Guerra Mundial fue el conflicto más desgarrador del vigésimo siglo. (Sp.)
'The Second World War was the most poignant conflict of the twentieth century.'

In order for this sentence to be felicitous from a pragmatic point of view, the speaker and the hearer have to share at least the same reference to reality conveyed by the two NPs, which denote two existing entities, i.e., *la Segunda Guerra Mundial* 'the Second World War' and *(d)el vigésimo siglo* '(of) the twentieth century'. If this condition of mutually identical assumption is not fulfilled, the utterance is pragmatically infelicitous, and the discourse participants have to resort to further strategies in order to make the referring context unambiguous (Lewis 1979; Heim 1982).

23.2.2 Presupposition and (In)definiteness

Existential presuppositions refer to entities expressed by the speaker and assumed to be existing in the real world. Such entities or individuals can be denoted by definite or indefinite NPs:

(2) a. Un bun prieten al meu a făcut cunoştinţă cu un actor. (Ro.)
'A good friend of mine met an actor.'
b. L'étudiant américain doit payer la taxe d'habitation. (Fr.)
'The American student must pay the residence tax.'

The two relevant indefinite NPs in (2a), i.e., *un bun prieten al meu* 'a good friend of mine' and *un actor* 'an actor', presuppose the existence of two individuals, i.e., a friend of the speaker and an actor.

In (2b) the definite NPs *l'étudiant américain* 'the American student' and *la taxe d'habitation* 'the residence tax' refer to entities which need to be previously known in their specifics in order for the sentence to be semantically successful. Under a presuppositional analysis of definite descriptions (Frege 1892; Strawson 1950; Heim 2011), the definite NPs in (2b) carry a presupposition of uniqueness (Heim 2011: 998f.), on top of the presupposition of existence of two entities (i.e., American student, residence tax). The definite NP denotes some unique entity that the speaker is referring to and the listener can identify as well. However, uniqueness is not part of the asserted content of definite descriptions, but of their conditions of use, i.e., of their presuppositional entailments.

If a given context does not satisfy the presupposition, it is not possible to attribute any truth value to the sentence. The relevant descriptions fail to denote (Heim 2011: 1014) and give rise to semantic indeterminacy:

(3) La dictadura italiana de 2017 terminó pronto. (Sp.)
    'The Italian dictatorship of 2017 soon ended.'

As a matter of fact, there was no Italian dictatorship in 2017. Hence, the presupposition is not fulfilled due to a non-existing entity.

23.2.3 Presupposition Autonomy and Triggers

Presuppositional entailments remain as necessary assumptions when the sentence is modulated according to some semantic and pragmatic parameters. In particular, a presupposition cannot be affected by change of modality (4a–b) nor by speech-act related modulations of the sentence, such as questions or exclamations (4b):

(4) a. Il nostro vicino ha adottato il cane di Gianni. (It.)
        'Our neighbour has adopted Gianni's dog.'
    b. Il nostro vicino vorrebbe adottare il cane di Gianni (? / !) (It.)
        'Our neighbour would like to adopt Gianni's dog (!) /
        Would our neighbour like to adopt Gianni's dog?'

Nor are presuppositions affected by negation (Horn 1989; see also Section 23.7). Sentential negation affects the conventional meaning of a sentence, i.e., the truth condition conveyed by the utterance, but leaves the presuppositions untouched:

(5) Mes collègues (ne) sont (pas) insupportables. (Fr.)
    'My colleagues are (not) unbearable.'

In (5) what is presupposed is the very existence of some colleagues of the speaker.

Presuppositions are generally associated with specific lexical items or are triggered by grammatical features and structures, other than (in) definite descriptions.

Among the relevant presupposition triggers, Romance languages show factive and change-of-state verbs (6a–b), iterative adverbs (6c), and epistemic modal particles (6d):

(6) a. Non mi sono accorta che Gianni è partito. (It.)
        'I did not realize that Gianni has gone.'
    b. ¡Por favor deja de fumar! (Sp.)
        'Please stop smoking!'

c. Marie m'a contacté de nouveau aujourd'hui. (Fr.)
   'Marie has contacted me again today.'
d. Afinal o Micha não é russo, é ucraniano.[1] (Pt., Amaral and Del Prete 2017: 6)
   Alla fine Micha non è russo, è ucraino. (It.)
   'Actually, Micha is not Russian, he's Ukrainian.'

Romance languages pair with several other languages in the use of such triggers which make the sentences presuppositional while the overall meaning of the utterances is left unaltered.

23.2.4 Presuppositionality and Case Marking

One important contribution of Romance languages to the understanding of presuppositionality concerns the case marking that in some Romance varieties may function as a presupposition trigger. In particular, in southern Italian dialects the strategy of differentially marking the accusative and the dative may ultimately depend on the speakers' semantic and pragmatic assumptions. For the interpretation of the relevant empirical evidence in Sections 23.2.4.1–2, we take a presupposition to be the piece of information that a speaker implicitly assumes to be already known by all discourse participants (Enç 1991; Diesing 1992).

23.2.4.1 Presuppositionality and Differential Object Marking

Many Romance languages display so-called differential object marking (DOM; Bossong 1982: 580; 1985), the phenomenon of language-internal variation in the morphological marking of direct objects (cf. also Section 20.3.2). In Romance DOM is generally realized through the marker *a* (< Lat. AD 'to(wards)'), with the exception of Romanian, where it is marked by *pe* (< Lat. (SU)PER 'on').[2] DOM is generally interpreted as the result of the activation of certain semantico-syntactic properties: animacy, i.e., an intrinsic property of nominals (Silverstein 1976; Dixon 1979; Lazard 1984; de Swart and de Hoop 2007: 606); definiteness, i.e., the structural realization of features related to referentiality (Lyons 1999; Aissen 2003); and discourse-related entailments, such as specificity and topicality (García-

---

[1] Amaral and Del Prete (2014) analyse *sempre* 'always, still' in European Portuguese as a presupposition trigger, in particular as a semantic element denoting truth persistence, in that the truth of a previous presupposed knowledge is confirmed:

(i) Sempre vou ao cinema no domingo à noite. (Pt., Amaral and Del Prete 2017: 2)
    'I'm *still* going to the movies this Sunday evening.'

Conversely, Pt. *afinal* and It. *alla fine* 'finally' convey semantic entailments related to truth non-persistence, whereby the truth of a previously proposition is disconfirmed.

[2] In the Gallo-Romance dialects of Sicily DOM is signalled by *da* < DE+AB (Rohlfs 1969: 8, 15; Manzini and Savoia 2005, II: 502); in some central Italian dialects by *ma/me* < IN MEDIO (AD) (Rohlfs 1969: 15). The markers *a, da, ma/me* also canonically mark dative in these same varieties (Rohlfs 1971: 333–35).

García 2005; de Swart and de Hoop 2007; Leonetti 2008; Iemmolo 2010). In the Romance domain, DOM is attested in Ibero-Romance (e.g., Campos 1999: 1529–45; Escandell-Vidal 2009), Romanian (Dragomirescu and Nicolae 2016: 920–23), several African varieties of French (Roberge 1990: 105–07), and Sardinian (Jones 1993: 65–68; 1995; La Fauci 1997: 51–53).

DOM is also widely present across Italo-Romance.[3] In some southern Calabrian varieties, DOM invariably marks the same semantic properties of the relevant NPs, namely referentiality, specificity, and humanness, and gives rise to a presuppositional interpretation of the entities involved (Ledgeway, Schifano, and Silvestri 2019a; 2019b). In such varieties DOM, which is realized through *a* 'to', is a presupposition trigger:

(7) **San Pantaleone, Calabria (Ledgeway, Schifano, and Silvestri 2019a; 2019b)**
    a.   Petru   mazzau   du   previti.
        Petru   kill.PST.PFV.3SG   two   priests
        'Petru killed two priests (= two priests not known to the discourse participants).'
    b.   Petru   mazzau   a   du   previti.
        Petru   kill.PST.PFV.3SG   to   two   priests
        'Petru killed two priests (= two specific priests known to the discourse participants).'

23.2.4.2 Presuppositionality and Greek-Style Dative

The Romance dialects of southern Calabria have extended the genitive preposition *di* 'of' to mark many values of the dative (Ledgeway 2013: 9–13; Ledgeway, Schifano, and Silvestri 2020), a phenomenon traditionally known as the *dativo greco* or 'Greek-style dative', as it mirrors the Greek pattern of genitive–dative syncretism in case marking. Speakers' use of the *dativo greco* is not arbitrary and conveys a marked pragmatic interpretation: the Greek-style marking of the dative involves a presuppositional interpretation of the Recipient:

(8) **Bova, Calabria (Ledgeway 2013: 11)**
    a.   La   machina,   nci   la vindu   a   nu studenti.
        the   car   to.him=it=I.sell   to   a   student
        'I'll sell the car to a student (= not known to me, any old student I can find).'
    b.   La   machina,   nci   la vindu   di   nu studenti.
        The   car   to.him=it=I.sell   of   a   student
        'I'm selling a student the car (= specific student known to me).'

In (8b) the RECIPIENT is realized with the genitival mark *di* and interpreted as referring to presupposed knowledge in that the existence and the identity of the student is assumed to be known. The same NP is marked

---

[3] DOM is attested in standard Italian as well (Berruto 1985; Benincà 1986; Berretta 1989; Zamboni 1991; Lorenzetti 2002).

with the dative *a* 'to' in (8a) and conveys a non-specific and non-presuppositional reading. Therefore, the *dativo greco* functions as a presupposition trigger for Recipient arguments.

23.3 Anaphora

23.3.1 Introduction

Anaphora is the interpretive dependence of one expression on the denotation of another expression in the linguistic context which has been introduced previously (anaphoric phenomena) or which will be introduced subsequently (forward-looking, cataphoric phenomena). Research into Romance languages has substantially contributed to the theoretical discussion of anaphora, and to our understanding of anaphoric phenomena. In this section we single out some particularly salient aspects concerning pronominal anaphora (Section 23.3.2) before discussing temporal anaphora (Section 23.3.3).

23.3.2 Pronominal Anaphora

The elaboration of theories of anaphora resolution (binding and coreference) as determined by an interplay of semantic and syntactic principles has greatly profited from the discussion of Romance data in contrast with the paradigmatic ones from English, and has had a fundamental impact on our understanding of language design (cf. recent comprehensive treatments such as Safir 2004; Büring 2005; Reinhart 2006: ch. 4; Reuland 2011; Rooryck and Vanden Wyngaerd 2011; Sportiche 2013). See also the discussion in Section 20.5.1.

23.3.2.1 Intrasentential Anaphora

In relation to intrasentential anaphora, classical Binding Theory, a pillar of generative approaches to syntax, has been radically rethought in the last decades: this rethinking was not just a revision of its formal implementation in accordance with the Minimalist paradigm, but emerged, more broadly, as a consequence of our improved understanding of how semantic and pragmatic factors interact with locality conditions on syntactic dependencies. The comparison of English with crosslinguistic data, crucially including Romance data, started early (Giorgi 1982; 1984; Pica 1984; Everaert 1986; Manzini and Wexler 1987; Burzio 1991; Reinhart and Reuland 1993) and led to a questioning of the strict divide and complementarity between bound anaphors and bound pronominals established by classical Binding Theory.

First, much attention has been devoted to the interplay between morphology and interpretation. Romance, unlike English but like German and Dutch, shows an item specialized for the [+anaphor] reflexive use only in the third person, whereas the first and second person forms can be used both as anaphors (9a) and as pronouns (9b); this obviously challenges feature-based theories of binding, which would force us to assume rampant homophony.

(9) **French (Pica 1984: 122)**
    a.   Je$_i$ me$_i$ vois.
          I   me= see.PRS.IND.1SG
          'I see myself.'
    b.   Je$_i$ demande à Paul de me$_i$ regarder.
          I   ask.PRS.IND.1SG to Paul of me= watch.INF
          'I ask Paul to watch me.'

The empirical generalization is clear: absence of Condition B effects (namely, a pronoun is free in its binding domain, violated by *me* in 9a) happens when a language lacks a dedicated reflexive pronoun. However, its formalization is still debated. The discussion of this issue and related ones, such as the difference in distribution and interpretation between '-self' forms and 'same' forms, as in It. *sé* (stressed third person reflexive form) vs *se stesso* ('him-/itself', cf. *stesso* 'same'), Fr. *lui* 'he/him' vs *lui-même* 'himself' (lit. 'he-same') – Kayne (1975: 344f.) – and the exemptions from Condition A (namely, an anaphor is bound in its binding domain) under certain conditions, has stimulated much comparative, diachronic, and acquisitional research (for an overview, cf. Rooryck and Vanden Wyngaerd 2011: 17–27, 42–44; Sportiche 2013).

Influential studies have dealt with the relationship between form and interpretation of anaphoric expressions beyond the anaphor vs pronoun distinction and intrasentential behaviour: they have often adopted decompositional views of functional elements with important semantic consequences. Cardinaletti and Starke (1994), on the basis of a Germanic–Romance comparison, propose to classify pronouns in terms of degrees of structural deficiency; Kayne (2000: ch. 8) focuses his decompositional analysis on person morphemes in French and Italian; Manzini and Savoia (2011: ch. 8) focus, instead, on case morphemes on pronouns; Déchaine and Wiltschko (2002) present the French pronominal system as a paradigmatic example of their threefold typology of pronouns based on internal structure.

Another aspect for which Romance evidence has played a fundamental role is the study of variation in binding domains and in the parametrization of locality conditions (for a summary, cf. Büring 2005: ch. 3). One cannot overstate the impact that syntactic research on these issues had on the semantic treatment of referential dependency relations. Early work on Italian, concerning, for instance, the role of mood in extending the binding domain (Napoli 1979) and the mixed character of Italian possessive *proprio* '(one's) own', behaving both as a short-distance (10a) and as a long-distance anaphor (10b) (Giorgi 1982; 1984), contributed to an expansion of the typology of anaphoric expressions and to the investigation of contextual conditions which they obey (e.g., subject-orientation, cf. 10c).

(10) **Italian (Giorgi 1982: 133, 134)**
    a.   Gianni$_i$ ama la propria$_i$ casa.
         Gianni loves the his.own house
         'Gianni loves his (own) house.'
    b.   Gianni$_i$ pensava che quella casa appartenesse
         Gianni thought that that house belonged
         ancora alla propria$_i$ famiglia.
         still to.the his.own family
         'Gianni thought that that house still belonged to his (own) family.'
    c.   Gianni$_j$ convinse Mario$_i$ che la propria$_{*i/j}$ casa era
         Gianni convinced Mario that the his.own house was
         andata in fiamme
         gone in flames
         'Gianni convinced Mario that his house had gone up in flames.'

This, in turn, led to a productive discussion of the points of contact between long-distance anaphors and logophoricity (cf. Hagège 1974 for a first appreciation of Latin data in this respect, and Charnavel 2017, Charnavel et al. 2017 for French).

Finally, Romance has figured prominently in research on the use of reflexive clitics with verbs: reflexive clitics, such as Fr. *se*, form reflexive verbs (Fr. *Jean se lave* 'Jean washes himself'), but also verbs where the clitic does not behave as a full argument, but is a marker of intransitivity (Fr. *Jean se fâche* 'Jean gets angry') and of a number of voice-related alternations. These facts, brought to the attention of theoretical linguists by Kayne's (1975) study of French syntax, have been subject to numerous attempts at unification, with Romance featuring in foundational work such as Cinque (1988), Kayne (1991), Dobrovie-Sorin (1998) and more recent research (Alexiadou and Anagnostopoulou 2004; Chierchia 2004; Reinhart and Siloni 2004; Labelle 2008; Schäfer 2017).

23.3.2.2 Discourse Anaphora

The study of intersentential discourse anaphora lies at the core of fundamental paradigm shifts in the semantic theorizing of the last decades, which have seen the development of Discourse Representation Theory and other frameworks for the study of the relation between discourse and semantic interpretation. The notion of discourse referent was introduced (Kamp 1981; Heim 1982), allowing for the principled establishment of the conditions of use of referentially dependent (pro)nominal expressions, and for an improved understanding of how the introduction and the management of referents in discourse work.

The specific contribution of Romance nominal anaphora to these research trends especially revolves around the significance of two structural properties for discourse organization: the presence of null subjects (i.e., the pro-drop nature of most Romance systems) and the sensitivity of word order to information structure. These properties have proven very helpful for the formulation of accessibility measures for referential antecedents.

Romance null subjects have figured in generalizations on the relationship between the status of the discourse referent (its degree of activation) and its linguistic form (Prince 1981; Givón 1983; 1992; Ariel 1990; 2001; Arnold 1998; Gundel et al. 1993; Gundel 2010). Various formulations of accessibility measures have been proposed, all resting on the general pattern of anaphora stated in (11):

(11) Reduced, semantically general anaphoric expressions tend to favour locally coreferential interpretations; full, semantically specific anaphoric expressions tend to favour locally non-coreferential interpretations (Huang 2006: 302)

Reduced expressions will therefore be anaphoric to highly accessible/highly activated referents, whereas fuller expressions have the potential to reactivate a distant antecedent, to switch from a close one or to introduce a new discourse referent altogether. General pragmatic principles, such as Grice's Maxim of Quantity, prevent the use of a fuller expression when a more reduced expression meets the contextual conditions. Accessibility is influenced by a number of factors (topic continuation, grammatical role, distance, clause type, etc.). An illustration comes from the contrast between null and overt subjects in a null-subject language like Italian (Carminati 2002):

(12) Marta$_i$ scriveva frequentemente a Piera$_j$ quando pro$_i$/lei$_{?i/j}$
 Marta wrote often to Piera when pro/she
 era negli Stati Uniti. (It., Carminati 2002: 78)
 was in.the US.
 'Marta often wrote to Piera when she was in the US.'

In (12), a null subject is obligatorily coreferent with the most accessible antecedent, the subject of the matrix clause, favouring topic continuity. An overt subject, instead, strongly favours coreference with the least accessible antecedent, the dative argument of the matrix clause (coreference with the subject is not completely excluded, but is marginal).

Romance data have informed research on the conditions of null-subject resolution, comprising work on crosslinguistic variation, as well as studies on L2 acquisition. Besides null subjects, other facts investigated in Romance include the referential differences between free and clitic forms of pronouns (clitic forms are only anaphoric, free forms can be topicalized or focused), the discourse properties of demonstratives (cf. different conditions of activation of Spanish demonstratives in Gundel et al. 1993: 286–89), the conditions licensing null objects in Brazilian Portuguese (Cyrino 1997), the forward-looking potential of some morphosyntactic strategies, i.e., their ability to signal upcoming relevance for a newly introduced referent (Chiriacescu and von Heusinger 2010 on Ro. *pe*).

This body of research naturally connects to the study of information structure and the link between discourse-referential properties and syntactic positioning of arguments: in particular, Romance data have been instrumental in the investigation of givenness and its relation to topicality and presuppositionality (on which cf. Section 23.2.3). Anaphoricity has been singled out as the feature distinguishing referential topics (familiarity topics in Frascarelli and Hinterhölzl 2007) from aboutness topics. See Cruschina (2011: ch. 1) on the importance of Romance evidence for the definition and classification of these notions.

23.3.3 Temporal Anaphora

Commenting on the origins of Discourse Representation Theory, Kamp and Reyle (2011: 872f.) state that the '[s]tarting point was the analysis of tense, and more specifically the question how to define the different roles of Imperfect (Imp) and Simple Past (PS) in French. The semantic effects these tenses produce are often visible through the links they establish between the sentences in which they occur and the sentences preceding them.' The French tense system is the object of foundational observations for the modelling of the discourse function of tense (Kamp and Rohrer 1983; Kamp and Reyle 1993: ch. 5). The classical contrast in (13) shows that the simple past (or 'preterite') in (13a) situates the event at a time following the reference point established in the previous discourse unit (Alain's eye-opening event); the past imperfect in (13b), instead, expresses a situation already holding at the point of Alain's eye-opening, and it is therefore anaphoric with respect to the reference time of that event.

(13) **French (Kamp and Reyle 2011: 873)**
 Quand Alain ouvrit (PRT) les yeux, il vit (PRT) sa femme qui était (IPFV) debout près de son lit.
 'When Alain opened his eyes he saw his wife who was standing by his bed.'

    a.   Elle lui sourit. (PRT)
         'She smiled at him'
    b.   Elle lui souriait. (IPFV)
         'She was smiling at him.'

In order to capture these and similar phenomena, a model was devised to represent the conditions on the anaphoric dependence of tense in terms of discourse relations, similarly to the treatment of (pro)nominal anaphora. This way, important parallelisms between tenses (and temporal adverbials) and pronouns emerged (cf. Partee 1973, who saw how Reichenbach's reference time could be considered the antecedent for anaphoric tense use).

23.4 (In)definite Nominal Phrases

23.4.1 Introduction

Among many semantically relevant issues on which Romance linguistics is contributing to the theoretical debate on definiteness and indefiniteness, we select the following for discussion: the distribution, functional load, and diachronic emergence of definite and indefinite articles in crosslinguistic perspective (Section 23.4.2); the inventory of indefinite pronouns and determiners (Section 23.4.3).

23.4.2 Articles: Distribution, Functional Load, Diachronic Emergence

The systematic comparison of the conditions of use of articles in Romance and Germanic languages carried out by work within the Principles and Parameters framework was instrumental in singling out the complex interplay between syntax and semantics in this domain. Aspects that have attracted much attention include the distribution of articleless bare nouns, crosslinguistic contrasts in the obligatoriness of articles, apparently expletive uses of articles, the interpretational ambiguity of (in)definite nominal phrases, and the expression of genericity. All these aspects bear on the mapping between the semantic and the morphosyntactic component, and have led to a number of influential proposals on the general architecture of language. Longobardi (1994; 2001) developed a syntactic parametrization based on the DP-hypothesis (Abney 1987; Szabolcsi 1994), in which he reduces crosslinguistic differences in the interpretation of bare nouns and in the distribution of overt (and covert) determiners to morphosyntactic properties related to the variable requirements of the DP-projection. Chierchia (1998) proposed instead a semantic parametrization according to which languages differ in the denotational properties of their NPs: in Chinese, for instance, NPs denote kinds and can be argumental, whereas in

Romance they denote predicates, and therefore need a D category to become arguments; Germanic represents the union of both types, with NPs being either argumental or predicative depending on the count/mass and the singular/plural distinction. The varying distributional constraints on bare nouns are dependent on this choice in the semantic component. This work sparked a still ongoing debate on the relation between the morphosyntax and semantics of nominal phrases and the universality of the DP-hypothesis.

Definite articles have numerous functions in the Romance languages (deictic, anaphoric, associative-anaphoric, endophoric, situational uniqueness), yielding properly object-referential, generic, weak readings, as well as apparently expletive cases. Indefinite articles can express specificity or plain existential import. Moreover, either article can appear in predicative nominals (cf. Leonetti 1999 for a treatment of Spanish articles that encompasses interpretive issues relevant across Romance).

One domain in which definite and indefinite articles overlap is the expression of genericity: the options in (14) are functionally comparable expressions of genericity that differ in the way the generic interpretation is attained: (14a) denotes a kind, (14b) a plural set contextually extended to encompass the whole species, (14c) a prototypical individual:

(14) **Spanish (Leonetti 1999: 874)**
    a.   El   guepardo es fácil de domesticar.
         the   cheetah   is easy to tame
    b.   Los guepardos son fáciles de domesticar.
         the cheetahs are easy   to tame
    c.   Un guepardo es fácil de domesticar.
         a   cheetah   is easy to tame
       'The cheetah is / Cheetahs are / A cheetah is easy to tame.'

A generally restricted option in Romance (but less so in Brazilian Portuguese, cf. Munn and Schmitt 2005) is the use of bare plurals to express genericity: in Italian and Spanish they are possible only under certain conditions depending on predicate type, modification, and syntactic position in the clause (Longobardi 2001). Bare plurals, in the Romance languages that allow them, more readily receive an existential interpretation, but even in this case they are subject to distributional constraints (contrast between pre- and postverbal position, cf. 15) that have been connected to Diesing's (1992) Mapping Hypothesis (Longobardi 2001):

(15) **Spanish (Suñer 1982)**
    a.   Llegaron estudiantes.
         arrived   students

b. **Estudiantes llegaron.
students arrived
'Some students arrived.'

French does not permit argumental bare nouns at all, a fact which has been attributed to the interplay with the expression of number morphology (Delfitto and Schroten 1991). Brazilian Portuguese, however, is special in also allowing singular bare nouns (16) (Munn and Schmitt 2005; Müller and Oliveira 2004; Cyrino and Espinal 2015).

(16) Criança lê revistinha. (BrPt., Munn and Schmitt 2005: 823)
child.SG reads comic.book.SG
'Children read comic books.'

A further much-investigated crosslinguistic difference concerns the presence of a plural form for the indefinite article: some languages, e.g., Spanish (17a), use a plural form of the indefinite article *un(o/a)*, other languages use the so-called partitive article (e.g., Fr. *des*, It. *dei* (MPL) / *delle* (FPL)), which is either obligatory (cf. 17b) or optional (cf. 17c).

(17) a. Amanda vino con unas amigas. (Sp., Leonetti 1999: 841)
b. Amanda est venue avec **(des) amies. (Fr.)
c. Amanda venne con (delle) amiche. (It.)
'Amanda came with some friends.'

The semantic and syntactic properties of the partitive article and the actual relation with partitivity in its diachronic development have been subject to in-depth investigation, with important consequences for our understanding of the interplay between indefiniteness, number, and the mass/count distinction (Chierchia 1997; Ihsane 2008; Stark 2008; 2016; Zamparelli 2008).

Discussion of article distribution in Romance extends to the use of the definite article with proper names in some varieties. Longobardi (1994) assumes the existence of N-to-D raising for proper names on the basis of the distribution exemplified in (18)–(19):

(18) **Italian**
a. Maria ci ha invitato alla festa.
Maria us=has invited to.the party
b. La Maria ci ha invitato alla festa.
the Maria us=has invited to.the party
'Mary invited us to the party.'

(19) a. La vecchia Maria ci ha invitato alla festa.
the old Maria us=has invited to.the party
b. **Vecchia Maria ci ha invitato alla festa.
old Maria us=has invited to.the party
'Old Mary invited us to the party.'

Both the optional definite articles accompanying proper names (18b) and the obligatoriness of the article if an adjective is intervening (19b) are problematic if one does not assume, with Longobardi, that definite articles may have a purely syntactic function besides their semantically motivated one. A similar conclusion is suggested by the above-mentioned link between the presence or absence of articles and other morphosyntactically expressed features, such as number.

Many of the facts reviewed above have also been discussed from a diachronic perspective: languages prohibiting bare nouns and/or admitting expletive uses of articles appear to have progressed quite far along the grammaticalization cline, which sees articles lose or bleach their semantic content to become pure markers of nominality (Lyons 1999: ch. 9). Thanks to their uninterrupted and rich documentation, Romance languages provide valuable material for the study of the emergence of determiners. Although Latin did not have articles, all the Romance languages independently develop a system of definite and indefinite determiners, whose source is respectively the system of deictic pronouns and the cardinal numeral 'one': Ledgeway (2012: 82–118) provides an overview of the differentiation across Romance. The Latin roots of this seemingly parallel innovation in the Romance daughter languages (cf. Section 23.7.3 for a further case) have been investigated in foundational work systematizing a number of observations in the literature (Harris 1978; Selig 1992; Vincent 1997a; Giusti 1998; Ledgeway 2012: 82–118). Recent attempts such as Hertzenberg (2015) demonstrate the advantages of the synergy between a quantitative analysis and the application of theoretically sophisticated models to historical data. Research on early Romance varieties (Carlier 2001; 2007; 2013; Stark 2002; 2006; Carlier and Lamiroy 2018) has focused on the diachronically progressing restrictions on the distribution of bare nouns and on the semantic-pragmatic conditions favouring the use of articles in the very fluid situation represented by medieval texts. While determiner-like uses of the definite article appear already established at an early age, the emergence of the indefinite article is slower and more difficult to detect in historical sources, also given the non-categorical difference between the meaning of the cardinal numeral and of the indefinite article (Leonetti 1999: 835–37).

23.4.3 Indefinites

The Romance languages display a rich set of indefinite pronouns and determiners, i.e., existentials that are further specialized, along a number of semantic dimensions, for certain contexts (specific, non-assertive, free-choice, negative polarity, etc.). The relations and overlaps between these various forms have been represented by means of a semantic map, which shows how languages variously divide up the functional space of existential quantification between items of their inventory (Haspelmath 1997). Haspelmath's maps (Haspelmath 1997) for Latin and some Romance languages show great variation of outcomes, but also some constants (Gianollo 2018). One, the presence of indefinites specialized for the scope of negation, will be presented in Section 23.7. Another consists in the loss, from Latin to Romance, of an unambiguously specific indefinite (Lat. QUIDAM 'a certain'). Romance expressions meaning 'a certain' can be used to convey a specific reading, either 'specific known' (the identity of the discourse referent is known to the speaker) (*certain* in 20a) or 'specific unknown' (the indefinite has existential import but the intended referent is not further identified/identifiable) (*certain* in 20b).

(20) French (Jayez and Tovena 2006: 237)
    a.   J'ai rencontré un certain diplomate, que je connaissais très bien.
          'I met a certain diplomat, whom I knew very well.'
    b.   On m'a parlé d'un certain diplomate, mais je ne vois pas qui c'est.
          'I have been told about a certain diplomat, but I can't see who he is.'

Spanish *cierto* (21) has the syntactic distribution of a determiner and occurs without the indefinite article in this use (Eguren and Sánchez 2007; Zamparelli 2003 for determiner-like properties of It. *un certo*):

(21) Me interesa mucho cierta teoría reciente sobre el origen del lenguaje. (Sp., Eguren and Sánchez 2007: 1)
     'I am very interested in a certain recent theory on the origin of language.'

However, expressions meaning 'a certain' can also have non-specific uses (Zamparelli 2003; Jayez and Tovena 2006; Eguren and Sánchez 2007), similar to those found for epistemic indefinites. Epistemic indefinites (e.g., Fr. *quelque*, Sp. *algún*, Ro. *vreun*) signal the speaker's ignorance or indifference with respect to the witness to the existential claim. Their semantic content constrains their distribution in interesting ways, which have been intensively investigated for Romance in the past few years and promise to disclose new insights on the interplay between semantic, pragmatic, and syntactic constraints as determinants of context-sensitivity (cf. Alonso-Ovalle and Menéndez-Benito 2015).

23.5 Deixis

23.5.1 Introduction

On the basis of the work on the semantics of deixis of the last decades, formal linguists draw a distinction between deixis, on the one hand, and indexicality on the other. Indexicality, which is the more comprehensive notion, refers to a context-dependent inherent property of certain linguistic expressions, including personal pronouns, a set of place and time adverbs or adverbial phrases. Deixis, by contrast, denotes a special subclass of context-dependent referential items, which express the identity of the speaker/writer and the addressee (person deixis), the spatial and temporal coordinates of the utterance (place and time deixis), and possibly other types of context-dependence, e.g., psychological proximity, speaker involvement, presupposition (Traugott 1989; Traugott and König 1991; see also Da Milano and Jungbluth, Chapter 25, this volume). Deictic items relate to the spatio-temporal context shared by a speaker and at least one addressee and convey reference of mutual orientation of the discourse participants (Lyons 1977: 637; Anderson and Keenan 1985; Da Milano 2005; 2007; Maienborn et al. 2012, among others). Romance languages prove crucial for the understanding of both deixis and indexicality. This section is primarily concerned with the main findings related to deictic expressions based on Romance diachronic and comparative evidence which contributed to the understanding of deixis as a category of human language. Given the rich and complex patterns of demonstratives, spatio-temporal adverbs, temporal and aspectual expressions, and the deictic components of personal pronouns, Romance varieties have been informing past and current theories about structure, change, variation, semantics and pragmatics in deictic expressions.

23.5.2 Spatial Deixis

A number of functional and formal interpretations of spatial deictic systems are available which contribute to the discussion of diachronic and diatopic variation in Romance. Spatial deixis in Romance languages is mainly expressed through its prototypical device, i.e., demonstrative systems, which encode basic concepts such as distal and proximal along with more complex semantic entailments, including speaker- or addressee-oriented, psychological proximity. The Romance demonstratives originate in the tripartite Latin system formed by HIC 'this, here' proximal/speaker-oriented, ISTE addressee-oriented, and distal ILLE (e.g., Meillet 1928; Benveniste [1946] 1994; Vincent 1999; Lüdtke 2009; 2015).

The ternary structures of demonstratives and spatio-personal adverbs in Classical Latin are not maintained in Romance languages. The developments of Romance demonstratives from the tripartite Latin system witness the loss of the speaker-oriented demonstrative HIC (Lüdtke 2009; 2015: 546), which was subject to phonetic erosion and instability, and resultant internal restructuring. The semantic entailment of HIC came to be covered by continuants of the addressee-oriented demonstrative ISTE (Vincent 1999; Ledgeway 2015: 77). As for the continuation of ISTE, which extends its reference to include and cover both speech participants (Ledgeway 2004;

2015; 2019; 2020; Ledgeway and Smith 2016), Romance languages show different outcomes: either they do not express the addressee-oriented deictic through demonstratives (as in Romanian) or they employ the continuant of the Latin non-deictic pronoun IPSE '-self' (as in European Spanish, European Portuguese, Sardinian). Romance varieties provide rich diachronic and synchronic evidence for two major types of person-based demonstratives, i.e., binary and ternary systems (Diessel 1999).

Previous typological groupings based on traditional descriptions (Rohlfs 1968: 205–09; Lausberg 1966: §§740–41; Tekavčić 1980: 188–99, 569–75; Lyons 1999: 109–11; Manoliu 2011: 479; Salvi 2011: 324) are drawn according to a neat divide between binary and ternary systems. Such criterion has proven inadequate against recent surveys stemming from diatopic microvariation (especially Ledgeway 2004; 2015; 2016; 2019; 2020; Ledgeway and Smith 2016). A person-based binary demonstrative system (Type B_1) is displayed by most northern Italian dialects (Ledgeway 2015: 76–78 and references therein): referents relating to the spatial, temporal, or psychological domain of the speaker, i.e., the deictic centre, are expressed though the outcome of (ECCU)ISTUM > (A)QUESTO (+1/+2 PER) and those associated with the non-discourse participants (−1/−2 PER) are marked by a reflex of (ECCU)ILLUM > (A)QUELLO: Mil. *g'hoo sto brasc che non ha forza* 'I've got this arm which doesn't have any strength'; Mil. *quel banchett l'è propi giò* 'that bench is very low'; Ver. *Tira via ste man!* 'Take these hands (of yours) away!'; Ver. *No vardarme co quei ochi* 'Don't look at me with those eyes of yours'. In type B_1 systems, the demonstrative is often reinforced by a spatial adverb: Vnt. *sta casa qua* 'this house here'; Vnt. *quea casa là* 'that house there'. Type B_1 systems are also displayed by other northern Romance varieties (Ledgeway 2020): Occitan, Gascon, Ladin, standard Italian, Vegliote, Romanian, Moldovan, Megleno-Romance.

Northern Italian dialects show another type of binary system (Type B_2): its organization involves, like Type B_1 system, a [±1PER] opposition. Yet, the spatial adverb conveys all the deictic force, so that the demonstrative is reduced to a definiteness marker, witness a mismatch between the original person value of the demonstrative and that of the locative, leading to the generalization of either (A)QUESTO or (A)QUELLO: Lig. *sta dona là* lit. 'this woman there'; Frl. *kel libri ka/la* lit. 'that book here/there'. Italo-Romance exhibits further binary systems. In particular, in one type of binary system (Type B_{3A} in Ledgeway 2004; 2015: 85–90), reference to the shared domain of first and second person continues to be marked by the inclusive term (A)QUESTO, with (A)QUELLO marking all referents not referring to this domain. Modern Neapolitan (Ledgeway 2004: 96–104) witnesses very clearly the binary opposition between *chisto* [−3 PER] and *chillo* [+3 PER]. The similarity with the standard Italian opposition It. *questo* versus *quello* is only apparent, as the Italian binary system makes reference exclusively to the speaker: *questo* [+1 PER] and *quello* [−1 PER] (Maiden 1995: 125; Vanelli 1995: 324; Maiden and Robustelli 2000: 83). Diachronically, French also exhibits this binary type, given the loss of the earlier *cist* ((ECCU)ISTE) versus *cil* dyad and the refunctionalization of the latter term as the pronominal variant (Ledgeway 2020). The relevant binary opposition was initially maintained in conjunction with the ambiguous adnominal *ce* 'this/that' combined with postnominal locatives *-(i)ci* 'here' and *-là* 'there', which became obligatory with the pronominal forms *celui-ci/-là* 'this/that one'. In modern French, however, *-là* has gained much of the semantic domain of *-ci*, such that the modern French one-term system has neutralized distance distinctions and expresses the distal term with *là-bas* (Ledgeway and Smith 2016): *Jeanne est là* 'Jeanne is there'; *cette fille là* 'this/that girl'; *cette fille là-bas* 'that girl over there'.

The formation of a specific type of ternary systems, i.e., Type T_1 in Ledgeway (2015; 2019; 2020), resulted from the loss of HIC and the reference to the deictic domain of the speaker being expressed through the original addressee-oriented term ISTE, which also inherited the deictic reference of HIC. The result is an inclusive first-person term ((A)QU)ESTO which readily marks inalienable referents related to the addressee. The second-person deixis could be marked by innovative (ECCU)IPSU > ((A)QU)ESSO forms if required in ambiguous contexts. Type T_1 systems are attested in large areas of southern Italy (Ledgeway 2015: 79–81), in some Occitan varieties, as well as in Ibero-Romance, i.e., European Spanish (*este* (+1/ +2 PER) vs *aquel* (−1/−2 PER) vs *ese* (+2 PER);[4] Valencian and Ribagorçan Catalan (*eist(e)* (+1/+2 PER) vs *aquell* (−1/−2 PER) vs *eix(e)* (+2 PER); Nogué-Serrano 2015: 209); and European Portuguese (*este* (+1/+2 PER) vs *aquele* (−1/−2 PER) vs *esse* (+2 PER); Topa Valentim 2015: 302). In another type of ternary demonstrative systems (Type T_2 in Ledgeway 2015; 2019; 2020), reference to the deictic sphere of the addressee is no longer marked by (AQU)ESTO (see Type T1), but has come to be marked by (AQU)ESSO: Abr. *šta case* (+1 PER) 'this house' vs *ssa mane* (+2 PER) 'that hand of yours' vs *cla case* 'that house' (−1/−2 PER) (Ledgeway 2020).

Type T_1 systems evolved so that reference to the deictic domain of the addressee is marked by (A)QUESTO and, consequently, (A)QUESSO becomes redundant. In view of its marginal function, (A)QUESSO may fall into disuse, leaving a new binary system (Type B2A in Ledgeway 2015; 2019; 2020) in which reference to the shared deictic domain of both discourse participants continues to be marked by the inclusive term (A)QUESTO (+1/+2 PER), with (A)QUELLO marking all referents falling outside this domain (i.e., −1/−2 PER). This type of system is found in Judaeo-Spanish and modern Catalan (Nogué-Serrano 2015: 208), as well as some varieties of

---

[4] Including Galician and Aragonese (Ledgeway 2019).

Sardinian (Blasco Ferrer 1988: 839). A further binary system (Type B_{3B} in Ledgeway 2015; 2019; 2020) results from the overlap of (A)QUESTO and (A)QUESSO which led to an increased use of (A)QUESSO at the expense of (A)QUESTO, resulting in the opposition of (A)QUESSO [−3 PER] versus (A)QUELLO [+3 PER]. This system is shown by a limited number of Latin-American Spanish varieties (Chile, Cuba, Ecuador, Venezuela).

Related to the complex entailments of deixis are other aspects of the syntax and semantics of the spatial deictic items. Romance evidence sheds light on the debate about the intrinsic definiteness of demonstratives and brings up cases of indefinite uses of demonstratives. In standard Italian *questo* can be used as an indefinite determiner (von Heusinger 2011): *Ero in un campo di grano con una mia amica e nel mezzo c'era quest'albero* (von Heusinger 2011: 447) 'I was in a wheat field with a friend of mine and in the middle there was this (= a) tree'.

The outcomes of Lat. HIC 'this/here', although they have disappeared from the Romance demonstrative system, survive in the formation of the cognate spatio-personal adverbial forms. The internal organization of demonstratives and spatio-temporal adverbs are not correlated (Benedetti and Ricca 2002; Ledgeway 2004: 107f.; 2019; Da Milano 2007: §4.3; Stavinschi 2009: 46–48; 2010; Ledgeway and Smith 2016). The adverb system generally exhibits more distinctions than those available within the demonstrative system (Benedetti and Ricca 2002: 16). Thus, while some Romance demonstrative systems can be interpreted as unary, there are no unary spatio-personal adverbs systems in Romance (Ledgeway and Smith 2016: 881), witness the case of modern French and northern Italian varieties where the unary and binary demonstrative systems are aligned with ternary spatio-personal adverb systems (*qui/qua* vs *lì* vs *là* in northern Italian dialects and *ici* vs *là* vs *là-bas* in French). Also noteworthy are the quaternary systems found in Tuscan and in northern Calabrian, where two person-oriented terms (+1 PER and +2 PER) are combined with two distance-based distinctions (see Ledgeway and Smith 2016: 895). Romance empirical evidence also shows how adverb systems often express more than the merely spatial deictic dimension (Vanelli 1992; Benedetti and Ricca 2002: 20), including but not limited to spatial concepts, precise or vague coordinates and size of the location (It. *qui/qua* or *lì/là*).

23.5.3 Temporal Deixis

Comparative documentation concerning the diachronic morphology of temporal deictics greatly benefits from observation of the onomasiological variation across Romance languages (Ledgeway and Smith 2016). In particular, extensive variation concerning the principal temporal adverbs can be found among dialects. Italo-Romance varieties exhibit a number of diachronic outcomes of the terms 'yesterday' (HERI) and 'tomorrow' (CRAS,

DE-MANE lit. 'of-morning'), to indicate the day before and the day after, respectively (Ledgeway 2015: 99–102). Among the new formations attested in Italo-Romance we mention the reflexes of NUSTERTIUS (< NUDIUS TERTIUS, 'day before yesterday') and/or DIES TERTIA ('third day'; Ledgeway 2015: 99), as in Vbc. *itérza* and *istérza*, respectively. As for the 'day after tomorrow', southern Italian dialects present innovative lexical formations from POS(T)-CRAS and suffixation through the diminutive (-*i*-) and augmentative (-(*u*)*o*-) suffixes to yield terms which indicate in three and four days' time, respectively (Rohlfs 1969: 265; Ledgeway 2015: 100): Vbc. *piscrajə* 'in two days', *piscriddə* 'in three days', *piscrunciə* 'in four days' (cf. Ro. *poimâine* 'in two days', *răspoimâine* 'in three days').

In Romance spatial items can be used as temporal deictic elements, as in French (Beyssade 2015: 172f.), where the combination of the adverbs *ici* roughly 'here' and *là* '(t)here' in the locution *d'ici là* only results in a temporal interpretation, e.g., *les travaux seront achevés d'ici là* 'The work will be completed by then' (Beyssade 2015: 175).

Temporal deixis is also encoded through the verb system that grammaticalizes tense distinctions along with aspectual contrasts. For the crucial contributions of the deictic entailments of tense and aspect based on of Romance evidence, see Section 23.6.

23.5.4 Person Deixis

Person deixis refers to any linguistic expression employed to encode the persons directly or indirectly involved in the utterance. Besides the morphological expressions of person (and number) through verb inflexion, Romance varieties grammaticalize reference to person through a series of tonic subject pronouns and separate series of tonic and clitic object pronouns, as well as adnominal and pronominal possessive pronouns. Romance languages also encode the absence of deixis through the third person pronoun, when it is used anaphorically.

In Romanian, personal pronouns can co-occur with the referring noun, giving rise to a pragmatically marked construction (Stavinschi 2015):

(22) **Romanian (Stavinschi 2015: 28)**
    a. Vine   el   tata.
        comes he father.DEF
        'The father comes.'
    b. Ies   ei   banii.
        come.out they money.PL.DEF
        'Money comes out.'

In Tuscan varieties reference to the inclusive first person plural is conveyed through the impersonal form of the third person pronoun *si*, often in conjunction with the tonic first person plural pronoun *noi* 'we', e.g., *(Noi) si va a Roma domani* 'We'll go to Rome tomorrow'. In a similar although more extended fashion, French employs *on* to express reference to first person plural (*On y va?* 'Shall we go?'), as well as first and second person singular and second person plural (Beyssade 2015: 177; Smith 2016: 311).

A few Romance varieties show a peculiar construction to express reference to the exclusive first person plural. Catalan and Italian dialects use the verb in the first person plural followed by the comitative adjunct ('with X') to refer to the speaker and a third individual involved in the context while excluding the hearer:

(23) a. perquè hi   vam   anar   amb   ta   mare (Cat., Nogué-Serrano 2015: 224)
        because there= we.go go.INF with your mother
        'because your mother and I went there together'
     b. Amə   cantatə chə   Maria. (Vbc.)
        we.have sung   with   Maria
        'Maria and I sang.'

In Romance personal pronouns and demonstratives are used in allocutive contexts in order to encode social and empathetic entailments and convey extra-grammatical information about speaker, addressee, and referent. In this respect, Romanian stands out in displaying multiple politeness distinctions which draw a pragmatic continuum in which formality and informality represent the two poles (Vasilescu 2013: 402f.; Stavinschi 2015: 35f.). For instance, in order to address the hearer, Romanian speakers make a four-degree distinction, broadly characterizable on the basis of formality gradient, namely, *tu* (informal) vs *dumneata* (more polite) vs *dumneavoastră* (formal) vs *Domnia Voastră* (very formal). Demonstratives in pronominal function can acquire a pejorative reading in Italian, e.g., *Quelli non capiscono proprio nulla* and Ro. *Ăia nu înțeleg absolut nimic* 'Those ones do not understand anything at all'.

Deixis is also relevant to the linguistic expressions of anaphora, in that the phenomenon of reference to parts of discourse is intrinsically deictic. Even though the distinction between some deictic categories, such as person and space within the discourse universe, and anaphora has represented a complex issue across linguistic theories (Lenz 1997), we believe that Romance varieties contribute with evidence to single out the independent nature of anaphora as we illustrated in Section 23.3.

23.6 Tense and Aspect

23.6.1 Introduction

The grammaticalization of tense distinctions through the verb system is a pan-Romance phenomenon (Ambrosini 1969; Rohlfs 1969: 41–58; Bertinetto and Squartini 1996; 2016; Cordin 1997; Ledgeway 1999; 2009;

Alfonzetti 1998; Ricca 1998; Loporcaro 1999; Poletto 2008; Vincent 2014; Schifano 2018).

From a semantic point of view, following Lyons' definition (Lyons 1977: 637), tense is part of the deictic system of a language, inasmuch as it encodes not only temporal identification of the event but also different viewpoints on the temporality, i.e., different aspectual perspectives. In these terms, temporality can be interpreted based on two main aspectual distinctions, namely, either as a situation anchored to a start-point and an endpoint (perfective aspect) or as unbounded with respect to a context with undefined boundaries (imperfective aspect). Hence, the semantic categories of tense and aspect in Romance varieties, although partly independent of each other, have been extensively discussed as strictly intertwined (Bertinetto and Squartini 1996; 2016). Empirical evidence from the Romance domain has crucially shaped the discussion about the nature of such co-dependence. Conceptually, Romance tense–aspect systems stem directly from the Latin paradigms in that the essential past/present/future division is preserved as well as a perfective/imperfective alternation in the past temporality. In the development from Latin to modern Romance, new formations such as compound tenses and synthetic future paradigms encode a range of aspectual, temporal, and modal values.

23.6.2 Imperfectivity and Perfectivity in Present and Past

In Romance the aspectual opposition between imperfectivity vs perfectivity is overtly expressed in the past temporality, where the imperfective past (usually labelled 'imperfect') contrasts with a past perfective form, which can have synthetic shape (i.e., simple past or Fr. *passé simple*, It. *passato remoto*, Sp./Pt. *pretérito perfecto simple/pretérito perfeito*, Ro. *perfectul simplu*) or analytic structure (Squartini 1998).[5]

The present is assumed to be the form that neutralizes aspectual and temporal distinctions towards an imperfect aspect and a temporality overlapping with the actual time of the utterance. It is also the atemporal or

---

[5] The neat correspondence between perfective aspect and morphological tense is not necessarily displayed in Romanian, where the analytic morphology of the past perfective may also convey the past imperfective reading:

Romanian
(i) Astăzi am văzut un film.
 today I.have seen a film
 'Today I have watched/I was watching a film.'

(ii) Copilul a fost fericit.
 child.DEF.MSG have.3SG been happy
 'The child was happy.'

omnitemporal tense, i.e., it expresses a situation anchored to no temporal point, as in (24).

(24)   El   universo se   expande. (Sp.)
          The universe self= expand.3SG
          'The universe expands.'

Yet Romance languages show that the present tense covers not only imperfective aspectual perspectives, but also perfectivity interpretations, as with performative verbs (Bertinetto 1997: 76):

(25)   Giuro   che   non so   nulla. (It.)
          I.swear that not I.know nothing
          'I swear that I know nothing.'

Moreover, its overlapping timing with the actual time of the utterance interacts with the actionality of the verb (Vendler 1957) as in (26), where the present of the durative action (i.e., activity 26a, accomplishment 26b, state 26c) contrasts with the non-durative action (achievement 26d):

(26)   a.   Maria frita   o   peixe. (EuPt.)
                Maria fry.3SG the fish
                'Maria is frying the fish.'
        b.   Els advocats reconstrueixen els fets. (Cat.)
                the lawyers they.rebuild   the facts
              'The lawyers reconstruct the facts.'
        c.   Eşti   mulţumită? (Ro.)
                you.are.SG satisfied.FSG
              'Are you content?'
        d.   L'   avion   décolle. (Fr.)
                the aeroplane take.off.PRS.3SG
              'The aeroplane is taking off.'

The aspectual value of (26a–d) is not only progressive, as the contexts depicted by these predicates can give rise to other imperfective readings (Bertinetto and Lenci 2012) such as habitual (26a–b) or permanent state (26c). The present covers also different temporal denotations, as it may express perspective or future reference, as in (26d), and a past reference within a narrative frame (see Bertinetto and Squartini 2016: 940).

Romance varieties show that the sharpest aspectual contrast lies between an ongoing, progressive situation (27a, 28a) and a situation captured as a temporally absolute and complete event (27b, 28b):[6]

---

[6] Also referred as 'aoristic aspect' (Bertinetto 1986; Thieroff 2000: 275).

(27) **French**
    a. Quand tu dormais, il *pleuvait*.
        when you sleep.2.SG.PST.IPFV it rain.3.SG.PST.IPFV
        'When you were sleeping, it was raining.'
    b. Quand tu dormais, il *a plu*.
        when you sleep.2.SG.PST.IPFV it have.PRS.IND.3SG rain.PTCP
        'When you were sleeping, it rained.'

(28) **Italian**
    a. Quando ho telefonato, Maria *mangiava*.
        when have.PRS.IND.1SG phone.PTCP Maria eat.PST.IPFV.3SG
        'When I phoned, Maria was eating.'
    b. Quando ho telefonato, Maria mi ha *risposto*.
        when have.PRS.IND.1SG phone.PTCP Maria me= have.PRS.IND.3SG answer.PTCP
        'When I phoned, Maria picked up.'

In (27a) the progressive aspect expresses a vague temporal relation between the two predicates *tu dormais* and *il pleuvait*. In (27b) the use of perfective suggests that the event of raining came to an end within the temporal frame of the first predicate and indicates a sequentiality of events.

In (28a) the progressive aspect affects the telic value of the predicate so that there is no inference of the actual accomplishment of the event nor of the alignment of events, whereas in (28b) the perfective aspect conveys telicity as well as sequentiality/consecutiveness.

As shown in (28a) the aspectual contrast conveyed by imperfect vs simple past cannot simply correspond to a durative vs punctual opposition: whereas the simple past in (28b) depicts a punctual, non-iterated event, the same tense in (27b) expresses that a durative event came to an endpoint. Simple past is aspectually more autonomous, whereas imperfect needs more temporal and discourse context for disambiguation (29b):

(29) **Catalan**
    a. Ahir Maria va trucar als seus amics.
        yesterday Maria AUX.PST.3SG phone.INF to.the her friends
        'Yesterday Maria phoned her friends.'
    b. Ahir Maria trucava als seus amics.
        Yesterday Maria phone.PST.IPFV.3SG to.the her friends
        'Yesterday Maria was phoning her friends.'

Simple past and compound past compete in some Romance varieties in the temporalization of the past situations (Harris 1982; for a detailed account of the temporal references of the two tenses see Bertinetto and Squartini 2016: 942f.). Even though the picture concerning the aspectual and temporal usage of the two tenses is extremely complex in Romance and relies on several dimensions of variation (Vincent 1982), some generalizations can be drawn. The present perfective or present perfect (cf. Fr. *passé composé*, It. *passato prossimo*, Sp. *perfecto compuesto*, Ro. *perfectul compus*), i.e., one way of expressing anteriority with respect to the time of the utterance through a compound form, also encodes the present relevance of the past situation:

(30) a. Esta mañana me he   levantado a las seis. (Sp.)
　　　　this morning me= have.PRS.IND.1SG lifted.PTCP at the six
　　　　'This morning I got up at six.'
　　b. Il direttore ha   appena rifiutato l' incarico. (It.)
　　　　the director have.PRS.IND.3SG just reject.PTCP the role
　　　　'The director has just rejected the role.'
　　c. Maria ha   sortit al balcó de casa. (Cat.)
　　　　Maria have.PRS.IND.3SG exit.PTCP at.the balcony of house
　　　　'Maria has gone out onto the balcony.'

Its original aspectual value in Latin, namely, the resultative, is mostly lost in Romance and only retained in the dialects of the far south of Italy (with the exception of some Salentino varieties) which only employ the simple past to express anteriority (31b):

(31) **Ragusano, Sicily**
　　a. Ci l' aju   scritta a littra.
　　　　there= it= have.PRS.IND.1SG write.PTCP.FSG the.FSG letter.FSG
　　　　'I have the letter written.'
　　b. Astamatina scrissi   a littra.
　　　　this.morning write.PST.PFV.1SG the letter
　　　　'This morning I wrote/have written the letter.'

The history of Romance shows a progressive shift away from an original resultative reading of the Latin compound forms towards a past temporal reference, a case of what Squartini and Bertinetto (2000) term 'aoristic drift' (see also Bertinetto and Squartini 2016: 944f.), a process that cyclically might be still occurring in varieties like modern French, modern Romanian, and northern Italo-Romance, where the compound forms are used to mark any past perfective event/state, rather than the synthetic preterite which has been lost. Modern Romance also shows innovative aspectual values of compound forms, such as durativity and/or iteration:

(32) **Portuguese (Teyssier 1976: 209)**
　　a. Este ano tem   sido fértil em acontecimentos.
　　　　this year have.PRS.IND.3SG be.PTCP fertile in events
　　　　'This year there have been many events.'
　　b. Aquele ano foi   fértil em acontecimentos.
　　　　that year be.PST.PFV.3SG fertile in events
　　　　'That year was full of events.'

Simplifying an ongoing change, we may say that the history of the Romance present perfect displays an original aspectual prominence (33a) that gives way to a temporal value (33b). In turn, the anteriority of such forms acquires other aspectual values (33c) that, eventually, are completely bleached to the advantage of a purely anterior punctual temporality (33d):

(33) a. HABEO FACTUM: resultative aspect; 'I have (something) done'
  b. Old and modern European Spanish *he hecho*: past tense with present relevance;
  c. Galician-Portuguese (*hei* >) *tenho feito*: durative/iterative aspect;
  d. French *j'ai fait*: past tense.

Nonetheless, all the same aspectual values of present perfect are expressed with simple past in many Latin-American Spanish varieties (Bertinetto and Squartini 2016: 942):

(34) a. Hoy lloré   mucho. (Mexican Sp.)
       today cry.PST.PFV.1SG much
       'Today I have cried a lot.'
  b. ¿Llegó   tu   madre esta mañana? (Colombian Sp.)
     leave.PST.PFV.3SG your mother this morning
     'Did your mother arrive this morning?'

Romance typology proves crucial for the understanding of linguistic change in terms of analyticity and syntheticity. In particular, the development of further compound past formations, including the so-called *temps surcomposés* ('doubly compound tenses') in French, Occitan, Francoprovençal, Romanian, northern Italian dialects, Raeto-Romance, and Sardinian and periphrases such as the GO past in Catalan and Occitan, is witness to the incessant shifting within a morphosyntactic continuum defined by the synthetic and the analytic pole (e.g., Bauer 1995; Vincent 1997b; Ledgeway 2011; 2012: ch. 2).

Since the morphosyntax and semantics of the remaining temporal formations and aspectual periphrases in Romance are too extensive to be covered here, we refer the reader to more comprehensive and extensive sources such as Dietrich (1973), Vincent (1982), Fleischman (1983), Squartini (1998), Bertinetto (2000), Dahl and Hedin (2000), Thieroff (2000), Ledgeway (2012), and Bertinetto and Squartini (2016: 945f.).

23.6.3 Tense, Aspect, and Modality: Imperfect and Future

The Romance imperfect is subject to a number of modal interpretations due to the fact that its own temporal connotation is vague with respect to the boundaries of the intended situation and its imperfective (i.e., continuous and progressive) aspect can be interpreted only according to discourse-related elements. The main modal shift that Romance imperfect exhibits is from *realis* to *irrealis* modality. In particular, it can be used to express the future-in-the-past (35) and, more importantly, it can convey hypotheticality and counterfactuality (Quer 2016: 965) in protases of present counterfactuals (as in French, 36a) and protases as well as apodoses of anterior counterfactuals (as in colloquial Italian, 36b, and colloquial Spanish, 36c):

(35)   Ho   immaginato   che   venivate   prima. (coll. It.)
       have.PRS.IND.1SG   imagine.PTCP that   come.PST.IPFV.2PL   earlier
       'I thought that you would come earlier.'

(36) a. Je serais   rassurée   s' il y   avait   quelqu' un. (Fr.)
        I be.COND.1SG   reassure.PTCP if it there= have.PST.IPFV.3SG   some   one
        'I would be reassured if there were somebody.'
     b. Se non leggevo   l'avviso,   andavo   alla
        if not read.PST.IPFV.1SG the announcement   go.PST.IPFV.1SG   to.the
        riunione sbagliata. (It.)
        meeting   wrong
        'If I had not read the announcement, I would have gone to the wrong meeting.'
     c. Si sabía   esto, no venía. (Sp.)
        if I.know.PST.IPFV.1SG this, not come.PST.IPFV.1SG
        'If I had known this, I would not have come.'

The Romance inflexional future undergoes modal reinterpretation,[7] due to its non-actual temporality which logically refers to a potential yet unreal situation. It follows that the temporal reference to a prospective event may be overridden to the benefit of an irrealis modal reading:

(37) a. Ieri   Gianni si   sarà   abbuffato   al   ricevimento. (It.)
        yesterday   Gianni self= be.FUT.3SG   gorge.PTCP   to.the   reception
        'Yesterday Gianni must have gorged himself at the reception.'
     b. Le   vrai   problème du   groupe   sera   cet   étudiant. (Fr.)
        the true   problem   of.the   group   be.FUT.3SG   this   student
        'The true problem of the group must be this student.'

In (37a) the future conveys a hypothetical modal interpretation, whereas in (37b) it expresses a conjectural stance.

23.7 Negation

23.7.1 Introduction

The investigation of Romance data has been pivotal in the theoretical discussion of the interpretation of negation and on the complexities of

---

[7] Romance languages express future eventualities in the verb system through different formations (Bertinetto and Squartini 2016: 951–53; Quer 2016: 964).

the form–meaning mapping in this domain. We will single out three aspects of the debate, where our understanding has been substantially enhanced by research on Romance languages: the challenge posed by the mismatch between the (multiple) morphosyntactic expression of negation and its interpretation in Negative Concord languages (Section 23.7.2); the semantic implications of the diachronic developments affecting the expression of sentential negation (Section 23.7.3); the nature and the structural prerogatives of pragmatically marked negation (Section 23.7.4).

23.7.2 Negative Concord

Romance evidence has been instrumental in establishing a theoretically grounded typology of negation systems. Bernini and Ramat (1996), in one of the earliest detailed crosslinguistic overviews, start by discussing the variety observed in Romance. Evidence from Romance languages is also at the core of foundational work on negation in the generative tradition, such as Pollock (1989), Laka (1990), Zanuttini (1991), Acquaviva (1993), Haegeman (1995), Déprez (1997), Rowlett (1998), and of ground-breaking comparative studies on negation at the syntax-semantics interface, such as Ladusaw (1992), Giannakidou (1998; 2000), Herburger (2001), and Zeijlstra (2004).

The fundamental challenge posed by Romance to the semantic analysis of negation is represented by the apparent mismatch between its form and its interpretation in Negative Concord systems: the fact that multiple expressions of negation contribute a single negation operator in sentences like (38) apparently runs against the principle of compositionality:

(38)   Maria non ha visto nessuno. (It.)
       Maria not has seen nobody
       'Maria didn't see anybody.'

An inextricably connected issue concerns the fact that indefinites like *nessuno* 'nobody' seem to oscillate between accompanying the sentential negative marker, cf. (38), and being carriers of negation themselves, as in (39):

(39)   a.   Nessuno ha richiesto il servizio. (It.)
            nobody has requested the service
            'Nobody has requested the service.'
       b.   A: Chi hai visto alla festa? B: Nessuno.
            who have seen at.the party   Nobody
            'A: Who did you see at the party?' B: 'Nobody.'

Residually in contemporary varieties (but much more frequently in earlier stages), these indefinites may even appear in contexts where no negation is present, as in (40), where they behave as negative polarity items (NPIs) licensed by the interrogative operator:

(40)   a.   C'   è   nessuno? (It.)
           there= is   nobody
           'Is there anyone here?'
     b.   Hai   visto   nessuno   dei   nostri   amici   alla   festa? (It.)
           have   seen   nobody   of.the   our   friends   at.the   party
           'Have you seen any of our friends at the party?'

These facts fostered a debate concerning the nature of these Romance indefinites, designated as 'n-words' (Laka 1990) in view of their ambiguous status between negative quantifiers and NPIs: n-words have been variously analysed as negative quantifiers, existential quantifiers, indefinite variables, and consequently various forms have been proposed for the licensing mechanism (quantifier absorption, pragmatic licensing, multiple or binary Agree; for a critical overview, see Penka 2011: ch. 2). In turn, the debate has had a decisive influence on broader theoretical work, investigating the dependencies between various types of indefinites and the negative operator and leading to innovative models of the syntax-semantics interface (Ladusaw 1992; de Swart 2010; Biberauer and Roberts 2011; Manzini and Savoia 2011: ch. 3; Penka 2011; Zeijlstra 2011; Chierchia 2013). The attempt to unify semantic and syntactic licensing through feature theory is recurrent in this work. On the one hand, a tighter, more principled correspondence is sought between syntactic and semantic requirements (±negative, ±affective, ±scalar, ±focus). On the other hand, the existence of uninterpretable counterparts of interpretable features is assumed in order to account for the apparent violation of compositionality: in Negative Concord languages, multiple morphosyntactic expressions of negation co-occur by virtue of their uninterpretable negative feature and license the same 'abstract aspect of clause structure' (Ladusaw 1992: 238), that is, the semantic operator of negation. Further important data from Romance discussed in this respect concern the source of the microvariation observed in Negative Concord systems (Vallduví 1994; Zanuttini 1997; Espinal 2000; Haegeman and Lohndal 2010; Parry 2013; Poletto 2016; Tubau et al. 2018) and the diachronic fluctuations in the history of Romance (Martins 2000; Ingham 2011; Hansen and Visconti 2012; Labelle and Espinal 2014; Larrivée 2014a; Poletto 2014: ch. 6). This body of research is increasingly providing insights as to how to best model the relation between the expression and the interpretation of negation.

23.7.3 Diachronic Developments

Diachronic investigations of negation from Latin to Romance are closely connected to the debate on Negative Concord introduced above. The main puzzle concerns why (and how) the Negative Concord grammars of the Romance varieties developed from the double negation system of Latin (cf. Section 21.2.4), where each morphosyntactic expression of negation corresponded to a semantic negation operator, cf. (41).

(41) Nemo   non benignus   est   sui   iudex (Lat., Sen. *De beneficiis* 2.26)
nobody.NOM not indulgent.NOM is himself.GEN judge.NOM
'Nobody is not an indulgent judge of himself.' (= Everyone is prejudiced in his own favour).

Here, as in other much-discussed cases, we witness seemingly independent, parallel developments in the Romance daughter languages for which one would like to find an explanation in terms of a common inheritance. These facts raise major questions for semantic research, such as those concerning the determinants of the licensing relation between negation and other elements in the clause, and those revolving around the pragmatic and structural factors triggering change in this domain.

There is a persistent intuition in the literature that strengthening phenomena affecting the expression of negation especially in colloquial Latin (cf. 42) may have led to systematic formal redundancy, which in the course of time would have been reanalysed as a form of Negative Concord (Ernout and Thomas 1953: 154f.; Posner 1984; Molinelli 1988; 1989; Schwegler 1990: ch. 6). Works such as Molinelli (1988; 1989), Schwegler (1990: ch. 6), Danckaert (2012: ch. 7), and Gianollo (2016; 2018), in addition, stress the correlation between the diachronic processes affecting negation and other co-occurring structural changes (synthetic to analytic, OV to VO).

(42) Neque   ego   homines magis asinos   numquam uidi (Lat., Pl. *Pseudolus* 136)
and.not I.NOM man.ACC more donkey.ACC never   see.PST.PFV.1SG
'And I never saw men who behave more like donkeys'

Negation-strengthening is also a much-discussed factor in relation to Jespersen's Cycle, i.e., the cyclical change affecting the form of the sentential negative marker (cf. Section 21.2.4). The formal renewal is not simply motivated as a repair strategy of morphophonological weakening, but emerges from the system-internal alternation between a plain and an emphatic way of expressing negation, whereby 'emphasis' is variously understood as the need for expressivity, exploited as an attention-capturing strategy, or the rejection of a proposition which is 'old' in the discourse (Detges and Waltereit 2002: 171–86; Kiparsky and Condoravdi 2006; Eckardt 2006: ch. 5; Schwenter 2006). A similar functional pressure would therefore underlie both changes affecting the interpretation and form of indefinites in the scope of negation and changes affecting the negative marker itself (cf. Willis, Lucas, and Breitbarth 2013; Gianollo 2018: ch. 5 for a formal implementation).

Negation-strengthening may take different forms, and is often understood as related to the semantics and syntax of focus (scalar or contrastive, depending on context). The elements used in this function have typologically recurrent sources (Horn 1978; cf. also Section 21.2.4), since they express minimal quantities (minimizers, cf. Fr. *mie* 'crumb', Sp. *gota* 'drop') or generic entities (generalizers, cf. Fr. *personne* 'person', Cat. *cap* 'head'). The abundance of these forms in the history of Romance fostered comparative work with major theoretical repercussions, revolving around the issue whether these elements are just subject to pragmatic licensing conditions or also take part in syntactic operations connected with their communicative function (Vallduví 1994; Eckardt 2006: ch. 5; Eckardt and Csipak 2013; Batllori 2016).

23.7.4 Pragmatically Marked Negation

Romance has offered much empirical material for the study of pragmatically marked negation, namely, realizations of negation whose interpretation contains additional components with respect to plain sentential negation. One type of pragmatically marked negation appears in denials (43) and corrections (44), which Repp (2009) interprets as denials with a substitution part.

(43) A: Estás   um pouco preocupado? (EuPt., Martins 2014: 638)
        be.PRS.IND.2SG a little worried
        'Are you a little worried?'
     B: Estou   lá/agora um pouco preocupado, estou
        be.PRS.IND.1SG NEG.MRK a little worried be.PRS.IND.1SG
        morto de preocupação.
        dead of worry
        'I'm not a little worried, I am worried sick.'

(44) Julia no es alta sino (**pero) baja. (Sp., Schwenter 2000: 294)
     Julia not is tall SINO/PERO short
     'Julia is not tall but short.'

Negation in denials (sometimes called 'external negation') does not target the propositional content, but elements of meaning like presuppositions, implicatures or the linguistic form of an item involved in the proposition (metalinguistic negation in Horn 1989). This special semantico-pragmatic status has been argued to correspond to a special syntactic position, higher than standard negation (Alonso-Ovalle and Guerzoni 2002; Repp 2009; Larrivée 2014b; Martins 2014). Some languages employ the same form for both standard negation and denials, other have special forms for denials (cf. Martins 2014 for European Portuguese).

Another type of pragmatically marked negation, so-called presuppositional negation, is found when the speaker is reacting to an explicit assertion with which s/he does not agree or to an implicit presupposition (cf. Section 23.2). It. *mica* (45) has been subject to detailed studies concerning its conditions of use (Cinque 1976; Penello and Pescarini 2008).

(45) Non è mica venuto alla fine, nonostante avesse promesso. (It.)
 not is MICA come at.the end although had promised
 'In the end he did not come, although he had promised to.'

Some Romance varieties are particularly telling with respect to the conditions governing the distribution of pragmatically marked negation, since they have two different negative particles used respectively for plain and pragmatically marked negation: a case in point is Piedmontese, with plain *nen* and marked *pa* (cf. Zanuttini 1997; Parry 2013).

A further type of reaction, involving the emphatic expression of (positive or negative) polarity, features the reduplication of the polarity expression and the presence of a complementizer in what has been analysed as a biclausal structure by Poletto and Zanuttini (2013) for Italian (46):

(46) No che non è venuto. (It.)
 not that not is come
 'No, he did not come.'

Emphatic reduplication in monoclausal structures is found in Portuguese (Schwenter 2005; Martins 2013; Larrivée 2014b):

(47) O João não comprou um carro não. (EuPt., Martins 2013: 118)
 the João not bought a car not
 'João did NOT buy a car.'

Pragmatically marked negation may become important in the diachrony of a language since some types may function as negation-strengthening devices, which, as seen in Section 23.7.2, may be drawn in to Jespersen's Cycle.

Selected References

Below you can find selected references for this chapter. The full references can be found online at the following page: www.cambridge.org/Romancelinguistics

Bertinetto, P. M. and Squartini, M. (2016). 'Tense and aspect'. In Ledgeway, A. and Maiden, M. (eds), *The Oxford Guide to the Romance Languages*. Oxford: Oxford University Press, 939–53.

Carlier, A. and Lamiroy, B. (2018). 'The emergence of the grammatical paradigm of nominal determiners in French and in Romance: comparative and diachronic perspectives'. *Canadian Journal of Linguistics* 63: 141–66.

Cruschina, S. (2011). *Discourse-Related Features and Functional Projections*. Oxford: Oxford University Press.

Gianollo, C. (2018). *Indefinites between Latin and Romance*. Oxford: Oxford University Press.

Labelle, M. and Espinal, M. T. (2014). 'Diachronic changes in negative expressions: the case of French', *Lingua* 145: 194–225.

Ledgeway, A., (2020). 'Rethinking microvariation in Romance demonstrative systems'. In Bárány, A., Biberauer, T., Douglas, J., and Vikner, S. (eds), *Syntactic Architecture and Its Consequences. II. Between Syntax and Morphology. Open Generative Syntax Series*. Berlin: Language Science Press, 451–90.

Ledgeway, A., Schifano, N., and Silvestri, G. (2019a). 'Differential object marking and the properties of D in the dialects of the extreme south of Italy', *Glossa: A Journal of General Linguistics* 4(1): 511–25.

Manzini, M. R. and Savoia, L. (2011). *Grammatical Categories. Variation in Romance Languages*. Cambridge: Cambridge University Press.

Martins, A. M. (2000). 'Polarity items in Romance: underspecification and lexical change'. In Pintzuk, S., Tsoulas, G., and Warner, A. (eds), *Diachronic Syntax. Models and Mechanisms*. Oxford: Oxford University Press, 191–219.

Poletto, C. (2016). 'Negation'. In Ledgeway, A. and Maiden, M. (eds), *The Oxford Guide to the Romance Languages*. Oxford: Oxford University Press, 833–46.

Traugott, E. and König, E. (1991). 'The semantics-pragmatics of grammaticalization revisited'. In Traugott, E. and Heine, B. (eds), *Approaches to Grammaticalization, I: Focus on Theoretical and Methodological Issues*. Amsterdam: Benjamins, 189–218.

24

Speech Acts, Discourse, and Clause Type

Alice Corr and Nicola Munaro

24.1 Introduction

This chapter considers how the Romance languages can contribute to our understanding of the encoding of discourse-oriented meaning, both structurally, at the level of the sentence, and interpretatively, at the level of the utterance. Ambiguity abounds in the application of the term 'discourse'; in particular, not all elements which may be considered 'discourse-oriented' involve meaning internal to the sentence codified within the CP layer (i.e., information structure packaging; cf. Chapter 26, this volume), but rather mediate between the sentence-external discourse context and the sentence-internal discourse context. This chapter focuses on the latter, viz. discourse-oriented meaning that interfaces between the sentence and the wider extra-sentential context.

24.2 Clause Type

In this section we explore some aspects of the morphosyntactic encoding of clause type in the Romance languages (cf. also Section 21.3.2). Basically, we distinguish the morphosyntactic notion of *clause type*, meant as the formal or grammatical structure of a sentence, from that of *illocutionary force*, a pragmatic notion which refers to the communicative function of a sentence. Although the two notions are often assumed to overlap (Sadock and Zwicky 1985), this is not always the case, so the distinction turns out to be both conceptually and empirically necessary (cf. also Siemund 2018). Converging evidence from the Romance languages suggests that the clause type to which a given sentence can be associated is codified through the lexicalization of dedicated functional slots within the left periphery of the clause (cf. Rizzi 1997 among others). Indeed, Romance languages provide an ideal testing ground for theoretical assessments of clause typing, as the relevant functional projections are hierarchically organized in a rigid sequence of layers and can be variously activated either by verb raising to the respective head positions or by the direct insertion of functional items, such as complementizers or clause-typing particles; alternatively, in interrogatives and exclamatives the relevant specifier can host the preposed *wh*-constituent.

In what follows we investigate the specific grammatical means employed by the Romance languages in the morphosyntactic marking of the five basic clause types: declarative, interrogative, exclamative, imperative, and optative.

24.2.1 Declaratives

A declarative clause, in its prototypical function, expresses an assertion, but this unmarked clause type can be used more widely to express different kinds of speech act. In general, declaratives are not distinctly marked as such either morphosyntactically or prosodically, and are therefore characterized by the unmarked basic SVO word order and by a flat intonational pattern. However, as pointed out by Giurgea and Remberger (2016), in Gascon (alone among Romance varieties) the declarative clause type is marked by specific grammatical means, namely by the obligatory presence of the declarative particle *que* 'that', which immediately precedes the finite verb (from which it can only be separated by preverbal clitics) and is almost exclusively found in affirmative sentences (cf. also Sections 1.2.3.3.1, 21.3.2):[1]

(1) Lo   Napoleon qu'   a   hèit   hòrt   un   bon   ahar. (Gsc.)
     the Napoleon that has made strong a   good affair
     'Napoleon made a very good deal.'

Other Romance languages display different strategies to stress emphatically the positive polarity value of a statement against possible contrary expectations, such as, for example, clause-initial *sí* 'thus, so' and *bien* 'well' in Spanish, with slightly different presuppositional entailments (cf. Hernanz 2010):

(2) **Spanish**
  a.   Sí   ha   cantado la   soprano.
       yes   has sung   the soprano
       'The soprano did sing.'

---

[1] The same particle may appear in subordinate clauses when the embedded clause is asserted; hence it is frequently attested in clausal complements of verbs of saying, knowing, and believing (which represent veridical contexts) provided that it is separated from the subordinating complementizer *que* by another constituent.

b. Bien ha cantado la soprano.
   well has sung the soprano
   'But the soprano sang.'

Another syntactic strategy performing a similar function is the emphatic reduplication of the verb or the verbal cluster attested, for example, in colloquial Italian or Portuguese:

(3) a. Gianni ha bevuto la birra, ha bevuto. (It.)
       Gianni has drunk the beer, has drunk
       'Gianni did drink the beer.'
    b. O gato comeu o rato comeu. (Pt.)
       the cat ate the mouse ate
       'The cat did eat the mouse.'

24.2.2 Interrogatives

Interrogative clauses are typically produced in order to elicit information from the addressee. Depending on the type of information requested by the speaker, we can distinguish between polar interrogatives and constituent interrogatives.

Polar interrogatives are produced to elicit the assignment of a truth value to the relevant propositional content. A polar interrogative may display the same word order of the corresponding declarative clause, in which case the interrogative interpretation is triggered only by the prosodic curve, with a final raising tone:

(4) Ion a citit cartea? (Ro.)
    Ion has read book.DEF
    'Has Ion read the book?'

In languages displaying subject clitic pronouns, (polar) interrogatives may be marked by the enclisis of the subject clitic pronoun onto the inflected verb, highlighting the activation of a left-peripheral slot where the interrogative reading of the utterance is encoded. This process is compulsory in the northern Italian dialects where subject-clitic inversion has been preserved (cf. Poletto 2000), while it is relegated to the formal register in French:[2]

---

[2] Furthermore, French displays an erstwhile cleft structure such that the polar interrogative clause is introduced by a copular inflected verb followed by the complementizer, which introduces the propositional content to which the addressee is asked to assign a truth value:

(i) Est-ce que vous allez à Paris? (Fr.)
    is=it that you go to Paris
    'Are you going to Paris?'

The reader is referred to Giurgea and Remberger (2014) for a comparative analysis of constituent fronting in polar interrogatives in some Romance varieties.

(5) a. Ghe-to magnà la torta? (Pad.)
       have=you eaten the cake
       'Have you eaten the cake?'
    b. Allez-vous à Paris? (Fr.)
       go=you to Paris
       'Are you going to Paris?'

In a few isolated Italo-Romance dialects spoken in northeastern Lombardy, (polar) interrogatives are characterized by a 'do support' strategy of the English type (see also Section 4.3.5), which features an inflected form of the verb *fà* 'do' followed by the infinitive of the lexical verb (cf. Benincà and Poletto 2004):

(6) Fé-t dàjel? (Monno, northeastern Lombardy)
    do=you give.INF=him=it
    'Do you give it to him?'

A similar phenomenon is attested in Sienese, a southern Tuscan variety where polar interrogatives display a sort of verbal reduplication to the effect that the lexical verb is preceded by an inflected form of the verb *fare* 'do', preceded, in turn, by the interrogative marker *che* (cf. Lusini 2013):

(7) Che facesti andasti al mare? (Sen.)
    what do.PST.PFV.2SG go.PST.PFV.2SG to=the seaside
    'Did you go to the seaside?'

In some central and southern Italo-Romance varieties (cf. Rohlfs 1969: §757), as well as in Catalan (cf. Prieto and Rigau 2007), polar interrogatives may display an explicit sentence initial interrogative marker:

(8) a. Ce sta cchiovi? (Sal.)
       PTC PROG rain.PRS.IND.3SG
       'Is it raining?'
    b. Cchi siti sula? (Sic.)
       PTC be.PRS.2PL alone
       'Are you alone?'

(9) Que plou? (Cat.)
    PTC rain.PRS.IND.3SG
    'Is it raining?'

On the other hand, embedded polar interrogatives are invariably introduced by the interrogative complementizer *se/si*.[3]

---

[3] However, in Spanish, Catalan, and Galician the interrogative complementizer *si* 'if' may be optionally preceded (though see Section 24.3.2.2) by the declarative complementizer *que* 'that' (cf. Suñer 1992), arguably lexicalizing the highest complementizer position of the left-periphery:

Constituent interrogatives, on the other hand, are uttered to elicit from the addressee the identification of a specific value for the variable introduced by the relevant *wh*-element. Ordinary *wh*-fronting to the sentence initial position is attested across Romance; in this case the *wh*-item is immediately followed by the inflected verb, possibly in accordance with the criterial condition on the well-formedness of interrogative clauses postulated by Rizzi (1996). Also in *wh*-questions French displays subject-clitic inversion in formal registers, a strategy that is instead mandatory in northeastern Italian dialects which still preserve enclitic subject pronouns:

(10) a. De quoi parle-t-il? (Fr.)
of what speaks=he
'What is he speaking about?'
b. Quant vegn-al? (Frl.)
when comes=he
'When is he coming?'

The linear adjacency between the *wh*-item and the inflected verb is preserved even in the presence of a lexical subject, which appears immediately after the inflected verb, or after the past participle in compound tenses (cf., among others, Torrego 1984; Ordoñez 1998; Barbosa 2001; Zubizarreta 2001):[4]

(11) a. ¿Qué compró Mara ayer? (Sp.)
what buy.PST.3SG Mara yesterday
'What did Mara buy yesterday?'

(i) a. Me preguntaron (que) si tus amigos ya te visitaron. (Sp.)
me=ask.PST.PFV.3PL (that) whether your friends already you=visit.PST.3PL
'They asked me whether your friends had already visited you.'
b. Els preguntaré (que) si volen venir a la festa. (Cat.)
them=ask.FUT.1SG (that) whether want.PRS.IND.3PL come.INF to the party
'I'll ask them whether they want to come to the party.'

According to Gonzàlez i Planas (2014), the absence/presence of the complementizer *que* 'that' corresponds to the *de re/de dicto* distinction.

[4] In *wh*-questions French features so-called Stylistic Inversion, in which the nominal subject appears exceptionally in postverbal position, following the past participle in compound tenses (cf. Kayne and Pollock 2001; Taraldsen 2001):

(i) À qui a téléphoné ton ami? (Fr.)
to whom has phoned your friend
'Whom did your friend call?'

The strict adjacency between *wh*-item and inflected verb can be relaxed when the interrogative clause is introduced by the *wh*-item corresponding to English 'why', which presumably occupies a structural position higher than other *wh*-items (cf. Rizzi 2001):

(ii) Perché Gianni è partito? (It.)
why Gianni is left
'Why has Gianni left?'

b. On ha anat el teu amic? (Cat.)
   where has gone the your friend
   'Where has your friend gone?'

In some northern Italian dialects the sentence initial *wh*-item can be immediately followed by the complementizer, in which case the inflected verb is generally preceded by the proclitic subject pronoun:

(12) a. Cossa che te fa? (Portogruaro, eastern Veneto)
        what that you= do
        'What are you doing?'
     b. Indo c a nemm? (Montagnola, northwestern Lombardy)
        where that we= go
        'Where are we going?'

In embedded interrogatives the *wh*-item follows immediately the matrix selecting predicate, but the position of the nominal subject is less restricted than in main contexts, as it can more easily intervene between the *wh*-item and the inflected verb (cf. Ambar and Veloso 2001):

(13) **Italian**
     a. Ho chiesto loro dove fosse andato Gianni.
        have.PRS.IND.1SG ask.PTCP them where be.PST.SBJV.3SG go.PTCP Gianni
     b. Ho chiesto loro dove Gianni fosse andato.
        have.PRS.IND.1SG ask.PTCP them where Gianni be.PST.SBJV.3SG go.PTCP
        'I have asked them where Gianni had gone.'

(14) **Portuguese**
     a. Não sei quando vai o Pedro a Lisboa.
        NEG know.PRS.IND.1SG when go.PRS.IND.3SG the Pedro to Lisbon
     b. Não sei quando o Pedro vai a Lisboa.
        NEG know.PRS.IND.1SG when the Pedro go.PRS.IND.3SG to Lisbon
        'I don't know when Pedro goes to Lisbon.'

In embedded questions northern Italian dialects display a high degree of variation with respect to the obligatoriness of the subordinating complementizer after the fronted *wh*-element. Some dialects do not insert any complementizer, others require the complementizer, in still others the insertion of the complementizer is optional (cf. Poletto and Vanelli 1993):

(15) a. I m an dmandè in dua fus andeda la Maria. (Carpi, Emilia)
        they=me=have asked where were gone the Maria
        'They asked me where Maria had gone.'
     b. An so minga cus (c) al faga Giani. (Ferrara, northern Emilia)
        NEG know.PRS.1SG NEG what (that) he=do.SBJV.3SG Gianni
        'I don't know what Gianni is doing.'

  c. Dime parché che te cori cussì! (Portogruaro, eastern Veneto)
    tell=me why that you=run so
    'Tell me why you are running like that!'

In some Romance languages *wh*-questions can employ a cleft structure, in which the sentence initial *wh*-item is followed by the copula and the complementizer, and the rest of the clause displays the ordinary declarative word order. This strategy is particularly common in Portuguese and French, where it can be considered the default question structure:

(16) a. Onde é que a Ana foi? (Pt.)
    where is that the Ana went
    'Where did Ana go?'
  b. Quand est-ce que tu pars? (Fr.)
    when is=it that you=leave
    'When are you leaving?'

In northern Italian dialects the cleft structure is particularly frequent when the questioned constituent is the subject of the clause:[5]

(17) a. Chi ze che ga magnà qua? (Vnt.)
    who is that has eaten here
    'Who ate here?'
  b. Chi l'è che l'à parlaa da mi? (Mendrisio, northwestern Lombardy)
    who it=is that he=has spoken of me
    'Who has spoken of me?'

In colloquial French and in (both European and Brazilian) Portuguese there is the possibility of leaving the *wh*-item in sentence-internal position (cf. also Sections 1.2.2.1, 20.4.3), a strategy currently referred to in the literature as *wh*-in situ (cf. Chang 1997; Cheng and Rooryck 2000; Mathieu 2004; Shlonsky 2012 for French, Ambar 2002 for European Portuguese, and Kato 2013 for Brazilian Portuguese):

---

[5] In many other dialects the clause initial *wh*-item can co-occur with the inflected copula (onto which the subject pronoun encliticizes), followed, in turn, by the complementizer:

(i) a. Andu è-l ch' andem? (Bagnolo S. Vito, southern Lombardy)
   where is=it that go.PRS.1PL
   'Where are we going?'
  b. Cui iz-al c al ven? (Frl.)
   who is=it that he=comes
   'Who is coming?'

In the languages in which cleft structures are attested in main *wh*-questions, they are also attested in embedded contexts. For a comparative analysis of cleft interrogatives structures in French and in the northern Italian dialects the reader is referred to Munaro and Pollock (2005).

(18) a. Jean a acheté quel livre? (Fr.)
    Jean has bought which book
    'Which book did Jean buy?'
  b. O Pedro viu quem? (Pt.)
    the Pedro saw whom
    'Whom did Pedro see?'

The structure in which the *wh*-item appears in sentence-internal position is interpreted as a real question, that is, as a genuine request for information.[6] Furthermore, *wh*-in situ is robustly attested across the northern Italian domain, with slightly different patterns across dialects and dialectal groups (cf. Munaro 1999); in some Lombard dialects both bare *wh*-items and complex *wh*-phrases can appear in sentence-internal position:

(19) a. Fé-t ndà ngont? (Monno, northeastern Lombardy)
    Do=you go.INF where
    'Where are you going?'
  b. Ta l metat induè? (Mendrisio, northwestern Lombardy)
    you= it= put.PRS.2SG where
    'Where do you put it?'
  c. T' è catà fö che libru? (Mendrisio, northwestern Lombardy)
    you= have found out which book
    'Which book did you choose?'

Both in French and in the northern Italian dialects, *wh*-in situ is generally disallowed in indirect questions, where the *wh*-item must be fronted to a left-peripheral position of the embedded clause, independently of the nature of the subordinating complementizer.[7] Within the Romance domain, only northern Italian dialects display cases of *wh*-doubling, i.e.,

---

[6] *Wh*-in situ is also attested in Spanish, but in this case there seem to be more severe contextual restrictions; in particular, when the *wh*-element appears in situ we have a different presupposition in the sense that the value of the variable is taken from a restricted set:

(i) ¿Invitaste a tu fiesta a quién? (Sp.)
   invited.PST.2SG to your party to whom
   'Whom did you invite to your party?'

Some scholars have proposed an analysis according to which Spanish in situ questions involve overt movement of the *wh*-element to the specifier of a functional projection in the left periphery, followed by remnant movement of the residual clausal material to a higher left-peripheral landing site (cf. Uribe-Etxebarria 2002; Etxepare and Uribe-Etxebarria 2005). The same analysis has been proposed for *wh*-in situ questions in some northeastern Italian dialects (cf. Munaro, Poletto, and Pollock 2001, Poletto and Pollock 2004).

[7] On the other hand, Portuguese allows for *wh*-in situ in embedded interrogatives, provided they are introduced by the interrogative complementizer *se*:

(i) O João quer saber se tu compraste o qué. (Pt.)
   the João wants know if you bought the what
   'João wants to know what you bought.'

doubling of the *wh*-item within the same simple clause, with a *wh*-item appearing in sentence initial position and a second one in sentence-internal position (cf. Poletto and Pollock 2009):[8]

(20) a. *Sa e-to   dito che?* (Ils.)
what=have=you said what
'What have you said?'

     b. *Cuma ta l'è   cüsinaa cumè?* (Mendrisio, northwestern Lombardy)
how you=it=have cooked how
'How did you cook it?'

     c. *Cusa al pésa   quantu   l   tò   sacch?* (Mendrisio, northwestern Lombardy)
what it=weighs how.much the your sack
'How much does your sack weigh?'

Finally, among the Romance languages only Romanian displays multiple *wh*-fronting, that is, simultaneous movement of both *wh*-items to a position of the left periphery (Rudin 1988; see also discussion in Section 1.2.2.1):

(21) **Romanian**
     a. *Cine ce   a   spus?*
who what has said
'Who said what?'
     b. *Cine cu   cine   vorbeşte?*
who with whom speaks
'Who is speaking with whom?'

Within the class of special or non-standard constituent questions, where the value of the variable is to be looked for outside the standard set, we can distinguish at least the three categories identified by Obenauer (2004; 2006), which require mandatory fronting of the *wh*-item to a higher left-peripheral position even in the varieties allowing for *wh*-in situ in standard questions. By way of example, surprise/disapproval questions, analysed by Munaro and Obenauer (2002), can be characterized as expressing the speaker's (negative) attitude towards the propositional content of the utterance, and in particular towards the specific value of the variable introduced by the *wh*-item: unlike in standard questions, in this case such a value is known to the speaker, who simply expresses his/her surprise, dismay,

---

[8] *Wh*-doubling is occasionally attested in embedded questions; in these cases the *wh*-item appearing in sentence internal position is generally optional, while the fronted *wh*-item is a clitic form:

(i) a. *I m'à   domandà sa   'l fa   (che).* (Ils., western Veneto)
they=me=have asked what he=does (what)
'They asked me what he's doing.'
     b. *So   mia 'ngo l'é   'ndà   ('ngont).* (Monno, northeastern Lombardy)
know.PRS.1SG NEG where he=is gone where
'I don't know where he has gone.'

annoyance, or disapproval concerning the whole event. In Bellunese, a northern Venetan dialect, surprise questions differ structurally from standard questions as they require the bare *wh*-item in sentence initial position:

(22) **Bellunese**
    a.   A-tu   invidà chi?
           have=you invited whom
           'Who have you invited?'
    b.   Chi   à-tu   invidà?!
           whom have=you invited
           'Who the hell have you invited?!'

The last question expresses an attitude of surprise about the choice of the invited person, the implication being that the person in question should not have been invited. Moreover, Obenauer (1994) noted that both in French and in Portuguese, where *wh*-in situ is attested in standard interrogatives, special questions require the mandatory fronting of the *wh*-item to a higher left-peripheral position, so that it will appear in sentence initially:

(23) **French**
    a.   Quand (diable) arrivera   le   train?
           when   (devil)   will.arrive the train
           'When (the hell) will the train arrive?'
    b.   Le train arrivera   quand (**diable)?
           the train will.arrive when   devil
           'When will the train arrive?'

(24) **Portuguese**
    a.   Por   onde   (diabo) eles   entraram?
           through where (devil) they entered
           'Where (the hell) did they enter from?'
    b.   Eles entraram por   onde   (**diabo)?
           they entered through where devil
           'Where did they enter from?'

24.2.3 Exclamatives

In the exclamative clause type the speaker signals that the whole propositional content or a part of it, namely the preposed (*wh*-)constituent, is noteworthy or remarkable to some extent, in the sense that the domain of quantification is widened to include values not contemplated in the speaker's initial expectations, so that an emotionally salient effect of surprise follows straightforwardly. Now, Romance languages provide some interesting clues in our understanding of the syntactic codification of this clause type.

Beginning with total exclamatives, where the speaker marks as noteworthy the entire propositional content, Italo-Romance presents structures in which the exclamative clause may be introduced by a discourse marker, as in the following examples from Emilian dialects, where the complex clause-initial interjection is obligatorily followed by the complementizer *se* 'if' or *che* 'that' and is clearly prosodically integrated within the rest of the clause:[9]

(25) a. Mo vaca s' l'è gnù èlt! (Modena, Emilia)
   INTJ if he=is become tall
   'He has become tall indeed!'
 b. Mo deg c' l'èra elegant, Luigi! (Reggio Emilia, Emilia)
   INTJ that he=was elegant, Luigi
   'Luigi was elegant indeed!'

Interestingly, total exclamatives may also display subject-clitic inversion in co-occurrence with an expletive negation, as in the following example, where the propositional content is presented as surprising according to the speaker's negative expectations (cf. Portner and Zanuttini 2000):

(26) No ga-lo magnà tuto! (Pad.)
   NEG has=he eaten everything
   'Surprisingly, he ate everything!'

As for constituent exclamatives, an important aspect to be considered is the potential overlapping with the interrogative clause type, given that both exclamatives and interrogatives feature the preposing of constituents belonging to the *wh*-paradigm to a functional position of the left

---

[9] On the other hand, standard Italian provides evidence for the existence of a different category of interjections that can either be followed by *se* 'if', as in (i.a), or be prosodically and syntactically independent, in which case they can either precede or follow their associated clause, as exemplified in (i.b) and (i.c) respectively:

(i) **Italian**
 a. *Caspita/Accidenti* se Gianni ha passato l' esame!
   INTJ if Gianni has passed the exam!
   'Gianni did indeed pass the exam!'
 b. *Caspita!/Accidenti!* Gianni ha passato l' esame!
   INTJ Gianni has passed the exam!
   'Surprisingly, Gianni has passed the exam!'
 c. Gianni ha passato l' esame! *Caspita!/Accidenti!*
   Gianni has passed the exam! INTJ
   'Gianni has passed the exam, surprisingly!'

It is tempting to differentiate between the two types of interjections capitalizing on a richly-articulated left-peripheral functional sequence, and, in particular, by assuming that independent interjections lexicalize a SpeechAct projection which dominates the Force projection where integrated interjections are merged (cf. Haegeman and Hill 2013; Haegeman 2014; Munaro 2019).

periphery.[10] Some Romance languages provide evidence that in exclamatives the inflected verb may target a lower clausal position than in interrogatives. Indeed, in many Italo-Romance varieties, *wh*-exclamatives can be descriptively characterized by the obligatory insertion of the complementizer *che* 'that' after the sentence initial *wh*-constituent (as opposed to its absence in the corresponding *wh*-interrogative, where subject-clitic inversion obtains):

(27) a.   Che   **(che)   te   me   dis! (Fas.)
           what (that)   you=   me=   tell
           'What you are telling me!'
      b.   Se   **(che)   tu   as   fat! (Palmanova, Friuli)
           what (that)   you=   have   done
           'What you have done!'

Moreover, in Romance languages we find evidence that the surface position of the preposed *wh*-constituent is arguably higher in *wh*-exclamatives than in *wh*-interrogatives; such evidence is provided, for example, by Paduan where in an exclamative clause the sentence initial *wh*-phrase can be followed by a left-dislocated constituent, which must instead precede the *wh*-phrase in the corresponding interrogative (as pointed out by Benincà 1996; 2001):

(28) **Paduan**
      a.   Quanti   libri,   a to   sorela,   che   te   ghe ghe   regalà!
           How.many   books   to your   sister   that   you=   her= have   given
           'How many books, to your sister, you have given!'
      b.   A to   sorela, quanti   libri   ghe ghe -to   regalà?
           to your   sister   how.many books   her= have =you   given
           'To your sister, how many books have you given?'

A further argument that suggests that the *wh*-phrase targets different surface positions in exclamatives and in interrogatives is provided by French and Portuguese; as discussed by Obenauer (1994), while in interrogatives *wh*-phrases are optionally subject to *wh*-fronting in these two languages, they must appear in clause-initial position in exclamatives, witness the following minimal pairs:

---

[10] In some cases, a given *wh*-item may specialize for the exclamative use, like the degree word *ce* 'what' in Romanian (cf. Giurgea 2015), or the item *comme* 'like, as' in French:

(i) a.   Ce   tare   vorbește! (Ro.)
          what   loud   speak.PRS.3SG
          'How loud (s)he's speaking!'
     b.   Comme   il est   attrayant! (Fr.)
          as   he=is   attractive
          'How attractive he is!'

(29) **French**
    a.   Avec quelle élégance il a pris le dernier obstacle!
         with what elegance he=has taken the last obstacle
    b.   **Il a pris le dernier obstacle avec quelle élégance!
         he=has taken the last obstacle with what elegance
         'With what elegance he took the last obstacle!'

(30) **Portuguese**
    a.   Quanto dinheiro o João ganhou!
         how.much money the João earned
    b.   **O João ganhou quanto dinheiro!
         the João earned how.much money
         'How much money João earned/won!'

The ungrammaticality of (29b) and (30b), as opposed to the possibility of having *wh*-phrases in sentence-internal position in their interrogative counterpart, again strongly suggests that the surface position of the preposed *wh*-constituent is different (and higher) in exclamatives than in interrogatives.

From a descriptive point of view, the syntactic encoding of the exclamative clause type in root contexts seems to be particularly rich in Spanish, where, as discussed by Gutiérrez-Rexach (2001), a wide variety of different patterns is attested in accordance with the type of introducing element, as exemplified in (31):[11]

(31) **Spanish**
    a.   ¡Vaya hermosa que es María!
         GO.SBJV.3SG pretty that is María
    b.   ¡Bien hermosa que es María!
         well pretty that is María
    c.   ¡Lo hermosa que es María!
         the pretty that is María
    d.   ¡Que hermosa que es María!
         what pretty that is María
         'How pretty María is!'

A detailed formal account of exclamatives introduced by *que* 'that' in Ibero-Romance is undertaken by Corr (2017), who proposes that

---

[11] A syntactic template unattested in other Romance languages is found in Catalan, which features the following peculiar exclamative type:

    (i)   Que n'ets de ximple! (Cat.)
         that of.it=are of foolish
         'How foolish you are!'

According to Villalba's (2003) analysis, the structure exemplified in (i) provides evidence for the presence of a null degree operator in exclamative constructions.

exclamative *que* provides evidence for the existence of a single morphosyntactic position dedicated to encoding exclamative meaning in the clausal syntax.

24.2.4 Imperatives

In positive imperatives the speaker conveys an order to be performed by the addressee, while in the case of negative imperatives s/he emphatically expresses a prohibition to perform the relevant action. In Romance languages two types of verbal imperative forms are attested, depending on the morphological properties of the verb: 'true' imperatives, that is, verbal forms that are specific to the paradigm of the imperative, like the ones exemplified in (32), and 'surrogate' imperatives, that is, verbal forms used as imperatives but morphologically identical to forms used in other paradigms for the same person, like the ones exemplified in (33):

(32) a. Kanta! (Srd.)
       sing.IMP.2SG
       'Sing!'
     b. ¡Hablad! (Sp.)
       talk.IMP.2PL
       'Talk!'

(33) a. Parleu! (Cat.)
       talk.IND.2PL
       'Talk!'
     b. Telefonate! (It.)
       telephone.IND.2PL
       'Telephone!'

This basic distinction is orthogonal to the positioning of object clitics with respect to the verbal form in positive imperatives, in the sense that in both true and surrogate imperatives the clitic is generally postverbal, that is, enclitic to the verbal head:[12]

---

[12] There are, however, cases of subjunctive forms used as imperatives exhibiting proclisis of the object clitic, as in the following example from Rivero (1994) where the clause is introduced by the complementizer *que* 'that':

(i) ¡Que me den   el libro! (Sp.)
    that me=give.SBJV.2PL the book
    'Give me the book!'

The same holds for cases in which a preverbal negation is present:

(ii) ¡No me den   el libro! (Sp.)
     NEG me=give.SBJV.2PL the book
     'Don't give me the book!'

(34) **Italian**
    a.   Fallo/Fatelo subito!
          do=it   at.once
    b.   **Lo fa/fate subito!
          it=do   at.once
        'Do it at once!'

(35) **Spanish**
    a.   ¡Denme   el libro!
          give.SBJV.2PL=me the book
        'Give me the book!'
    b.   **¡Me den   el libro!
          Me=give.SBJV.2PL the book

The distinction between true and surrogate imperative forms in Romance is particularly relevant in negative contexts. As discussed extensively by Zanuttini (1997), preverbal negative markers cannot occur when the verbal form is a true imperative, as exemplified in (36)–(37) with Spanish, while postverbal negative markers can occur in imperative clauses regardless of the verbal form employed:

(36) a. ** ¡No habla! (Sp.)
          NEG talk.IMP.2SG
    b. ** ¡No hablad! (Sp.)
          NEG talk.IMP.2PL
       'Don't talk!'

(37) a.   ¡No hables! (Sp.)
          NEG talk.SBJV.2SG
    b.   ¡No habléis! (Sp.)
          NEG talk.SBJV.2PL
       'Don't talk!'

(38) a.   Parla   nen! (Pie.)
          talk.IMP.2SG NEG
       'Don't talk!'
    b.   Vuza   no! (Mil.)
          shout.IMP.2SG NEG
       'Don't shout!'
    c.   Vous geinàs   pas! (Occ.)
          you=worry.IMP.2PL NEG
       'Don't worry!'

As pointed out by Zanuttini (1997), there are exceptions to this generalization, such as in the varieties exemplified in (39) where the preverbal negative marker is compatible with a true imperative form:

(39) a. Nu   kàska! (Rmg.)
          NEG   fall.IMP.2SG
          'Don't fall!'
      b. No   laóra! (Ampezzan)
          NEG   work.IMP.2SG
          'Don't work!'

The presence of a preverbal negation may also trigger the insertion of an infinitive (cf. 40) in which case the object clitic can be either proclitic or enclitic; we can also find a modal verb like STAY followed by the infinitive of the lexical verb (cf. 41), or, in the dialects of southern Italy, a gerund (cf. 42; see Rohlfs 1969: §722):

(40) **Italian**
      a. Non   mangiarlo!
          NEG   eat.INF=it
      b. Non   lo mangiare!
          NEG   it=eat.INF
          'Don't eat it!'

(41) a. No   stàit   a   crodi! (Frl.)
          NEG   stay.IMP.2PL   to   believe
          'Don't believe it!'
      b. No   sta   móverte!(Trn.)
          NEG   stay.IMP.2SG   move=yourself
          'Don't move!'

(42) a. Non   cadènnə! (Cal.)
          NEG   falling
          'Don't fall!'
      b. Nan   dɔcènnə! (Pgl.)
          NEG   saying
          'Don't talk!'

In Badiotto, a central Raeto-Romance dialect, a positive imperative must obligatorily be accompanied by a modal particle to be grammatical, while the particle can be missing in the corresponding negative imperative (cf. Poletto and Zanuttini 2003):

(43) **Badiot**
      a. Liél   ma/mo/pa/pö!
          read.IMP.2PL=it   PTC
      b. **Liél!
          read.IMP.2PL=it
          'Read it!'

(44) No   l   liét!
    NEG   it=   read.IMP.2PL
    'Don't read it!'

According to Poletto and Zanuttini (2003), the presence of the particle is required in positive imperatives in order to syntactically encode the notion of point of view, structurally linked to a modality projection which can be licensed in negative contexts by the preverbal negation itself. Surrogate imperative forms are attested throughout the southern Italian domain. In fact, there seems to be a tendency in this area to retain distinct marking for jussive (and optative) modality, as witnessed by the fact that the imperfect subjunctive is exceptionally retained precisely in jussive (and optative) clauses (cf. Rohlfs 1969: §609; Ledgeway 2003; 2009; D'Alessandro and Ledgeway 2010):

(45) a. Occhə lə mannə/mannèssə! (Abr.)
         that   it sends/send.SBJV.3SG
         'Let him send it!'
     b. S'assettassi! (Sic.)
         REFL=sit.SBJV.3SG
         'Please sit down!'

As pointed out by Colasanti and Silvestri (2019), in upper southern Italian dialects the imperfect subjunctive in jussive clauses is optionally introduced by the complementizer *ca*, which becomes mandatory when the speaker utters clause-initial speech act elements, such as an interjection:

(46) **Northern Campanian**
     a. (Ca)   facessə   u   bravə!
         (that) do.SBJV.3SG the good
         'He had better behave!'
     b. Oh, **(ca)   facessə   u   bravə!
         INTJ   that   do.SBJV.3SG the good
         'Hey! He had better behave!'

On the other hand, in extreme southern Italian dialects jussive clauses are obligatorily introduced by the particle *mi/mu/ma* followed by the indicative or by the complementizer *cu* followed variously by the subjunctive or the indicative:

(47) a. **(Mi)   veni   Mariu! (SCal.)
         PTC   comes   Mario
         'Mario had better come!'
     b. **(Cu)   begna   moi   lu   Mariu! (Sal.)
         that   come.SBJV.3SG   now   the Mario
         'Mario had better come now!'

24.2.5 Optatives

In optatives the speaker expresses his/her desire for the realization of a (mainly counterfactual) state of things which is beyond his/her control. Romance languages provide strong empirical evidence that this clause type also entails the activation of some functional projection within the left periphery. For example, in standard Italian optatives can be expressed by means of the present subjunctive optionally introduced by the declarative complementizer *che* 'that' or by the imperfect or pluperfect subjunctive optionally introduced by the hypothetical complementizer *se* 'if', or by the item *magari* 'if only':

(48) **Italian**
    a. (Che) il cielo li! benedica
        (that) the sky them=bless.PRS.SBJV.3SG
        'May heaven bless them!'
    b. (Se) avessimo il denaro!
        (If) have.PST.SBJV.1PL the money!
        'I wish we had the money!'
    c. (Magari) avessi ascoltato le sue parole!
        (if.only) have.PST.SBJV.1SG listen.PTCP the his words
        'I wish I had listened to his words!'

Furthermore, in at least some northern Italian varieties still displaying subject-clitic inversion (as well as in French), this strategy can be employed in optatives as an alternative to the insertion of a clause-initial complementizer to express a realizable or counterfactual wish of the speaker:

(49) a. Ti vessj-o dit la veretàt! (Frl.)
        you=had=I told the truth
        'If only I had told you the truth!'
    b. Rivàsse-lo in tempo! (Pad.)
        arrived=he in time
        'If only he arrived in time!'

(50) Puisse-t-il venir! (Fr.)
    could=he come.INF
    'May he come!'

Moreover, in the dialects of the extreme south of Italy optative clauses are often introduced by complementizers or by modal particles like *mu/mi/ma* (cf. Rohlfs 1969: §789):

(51) a. Chi ti vinissi na frève maligna! (Cal.)
        that you=came.SBJV.3SG a fever malign
        'May you catch a terrible fever!'

b. Na sula fiata cu tte pozzu 'asare! (Sal.)
    an only time that you=can.PRS.1SG kiss.INF
    'Would that I could kiss you just once!'

(52) **Southern Calabrian**
a. Lu focu mu ti mangia!
    the fire PTC you=eats
    'May you be swallowed up by the fire!'
b. Lu Signuri mu t'ajuta!
    the Lord PTC you=helps
    'May our Lord be with you!'

As discussed by Colasanti and Silvestri (2019), in optatives we find the same pattern observed above for jussives, namely the presence of a clause-initial complementizer, which is generally optional, becomes mandatory if the optative clause is introduced by an interjection:

(53) **Northern Calabrian**
a. (Chə) tə pəgghjissa nu lampə!
    (that) you=took.SBJV.3SG a lightning
    'May lightning strike you!'
b. Ih **(chə) tə pəgghjissa nu lampə!
    INTJ that you=took.SBJV.3SG a lightning
    'May lightning strike you!'

According to Sánchez López (2017), Spanish displays two fully productive optative structures, both of which contain a clause-initial item, either the complementizer *que/si* 'that/if' or the item *ojalá* 'if only', which arguably activates a left-peripheral position:[13]

(54) **Spanish**
a. ¡Que la suerte te acompañe!
    that the luck you=accompany.SBJV.3SG
    'May luck be with you!'
b. ¡Si al menos hubieses estado allí!
    if at least had.SBJV.2SG been there
    'If only you had been there!'

---

[13] A third peculiar syntactic strategy featuring the clause-initial *wh*-item *who* is shared by Spanish with Catalan and Galician (cf. Sánchez López 2016):

(i) a. ¡Quién fuera millonario! (Sp.)
        who were.SBJV.1SG millionaire
    b. Qui fos milionari! (Cat.)
        who were.SBJV.1SG millionaire
    c. ¡Quen fora millonario! (Glc.)
        who were.SBJV.1SG millionaire
        'If only I were a millionaire!'

(55) ¡Ojalá   haya   paz   entre   los   hombres!
      if.only have   peace among   the   men
      'Let there be peace among men!'

The presence of the complementizer *que* 'that' is optional in the Catalan optative construction introduced by *tant de bo* lit. 'so much of good':

(56) Tant   de bo   (que)   aprovis   l'   examen (Cat.)
      so.much   of good (that) pass.SBJV.2SG the exam
      'If only you passed the exam!'

Similar patterns are attested in Romanian, where optatives are introduced either by the clause-initial item *măcar* 'at least, if only' followed by the complementizer *de* 'if' and the conditional perfect or by the irrealis complementizer *să* followed by the subjunctive (cf. Grosz 2012):

(57) **Romanian**
   a.   Măcar   de-ar   fi   ascultat-o!
        if.only   if=opt   be   listened-her
        'If only he had listened to her!'
   b.   Ah, să   fi   ascultat John de Mary!
        oh, that be   listened John of Mary
        'Oh, if only John had obeyed Mary!'

24.2.6 Concluding Remarks

In this section we have investigated the grammatical means through which a given sentence is prototypically associated with one of the basic clause types. The attested cross-linguistic variation with respect to the morphosyntactic expression of clausal typing provides evidence – in a cartographic perspective – for the existence of several left-peripheral projections and associated positions which are responsible for this process and encode the speaker's subjective representation of the propositional content expressed by the clause (cf. Munaro 2010).

24.3 Speech Acts and Illocutionary Force

One of the key issues for linguistic theory is how form relates to interpretation at the level of the sentence. Speech act theory holds that language is fundamentally a medium for action: when we speak (or sign), our utterances effect actions that produce change. A *speech act*, or *illocutionary act*, is thus the communicative action effected through the production of an utterance, and the *illocutionary force* of an utterance is the communicative function attached to that expression.

Taking a traditional view of clause-type taxonomy, we can say that the communicative functions of the three main cross-linguistic clause types – declarative, interrogative, and imperative – are, respectively, an assertion, a question, and a directive. For example, in producing a sentence with an interrogative clause type, the speaker simultaneously performs a speech act whose purpose is to elicit information. However, as Section 24.2 demonstrates, not all interrogative clause types correspond to a genuine request for information.

Indeed, a neat clause-type (CT) to speech-act (SA) mapping is complicated by a number of empirical factors:

(i) a single (morphosyntactic) clause type can correspond to multiple speech acts:

(58) ¿Tienes fuego? (Sp.)
'Do you have a light?'
    a. Information-seeking question: 'Do you have a lighter in your possession?'
    b. Implicit request: 'Can you lend me your lighter?'
    c. Implicit command: 'Lend me your lighter.'

(ii) a single speech act can have multiple morphosyntactic realizations:

(59) **Galician**
    a. Debes devolverme o libro mañá.
       must.2SG give.back.INF=me the book tomorrow
       'You must give me the book back tomorrow.'
    b. {Devólveme / que me devolvas} o libro mañá!
       give.back.IMP.2SG=me COMP me=give.SBJV.2SG the book tomorrow
       'Give me back the book tomorrow!'
    c. Mañá devólvesme o libro.
       tomorrow give.back.PRS.2SG=me the book
       'Tomorrow you'll give me back the book.'

(iii) a single utterance may perform more than one type of communicative function simultaneously (60a), or may involve more than one clause type (60b–c):

(60) a. Ta inténdet, nè? (BrBgm.)
       SCL.2sg=understand.2SG QT
       'You understand, don't you?' (Paganessi 2017: 83)
    b. Apropiați-vă și nemica rușinându-vă. (ORo.)
       Approach.IMP.2PL=REFL and nothing be.ashamed.GER=REFL.2PL
       'Come close and don't be ashamed of anything' (Hill and Alboiu 2016: 98)
    c. Mougn èt t'taire! (Wal.)
       eat.IMP and you.SG=shut.up.INF
       'Eat and shut up!' (Hendschel 2001: 277)

(iv) speech acts are not limited to the canonical sentence centred around a predicate and subject (61a–b), and many do not have a specific clause type correlate at all (61a–c):

(61) a. SA: disagreement
       A: Nu-i şa? (IRo.)
       'Isn't it like that?'
       B: Ba, că   şa-i!
          PTC that thus=be.3SG
       'You are wrong, it *is* like that.' (Saramandu et al. 2011: 55)
    b. SA: bet
       A   que se agotan   las entradas antes de que lleguemos. (Sp.)
       PTC that REFL=run.out.3PL the tickets before de that arrive.SBJV.1PL
       'I bet they'll sell out of tickets before we get there.'
    c. SA: threat
       Te fazzu   ccògghiere li tienti te terra (Lec.)
       you=make.1SG   collect.INF the teeth of earth
       'I'll make you pick your teeth up from the floor.' (Ledgeway 2013: 203)

Such empirical observations provide persuasive evidence that illocutionary force can be decoupled from clause type; that speech acts are distinct from (syntactic) sentences; and that the range of (possible) illocutionary forces outnumbers the taxonomy of possible sentence types.

24.3.1 Theoretical Approaches to Speech Acts
24.3.1.1 The View from Speech Act Theory

Speech act theory has responded to these empirical issues by developing an account of utterance-level meaning independent from structural considerations. Traditional approaches framed illocutionary force and speech acts in terms of communicative conventions (Austin 1962 et seq.) or speakers' communicative goals or intentions (Searle 1965 et seq.). The intentionality component of earlier work, via which speakers attempt to change propositional attitudes between discourse participants (e.g., an assertion amounts to an act through which a speaker announces (i) their belief in a proposition *p*, and (ii) their desire/intention for the addressee to adopt that belief), is updated in more recent proposals that adopt a dynamic approach to the encoding of communicative functions.

In such dynamic models, propositions are put 'on the table' as proposals for changing the *common ground* (Stalnaker 1978), viz. the set of knowledge and assumptions shared between discourse participants; and speech acts constitute conversational moves which participants keep track of via a 'scoreboard' (Portner 2018; Beyssade and Marandin 2006a; 2006b) use data from French to propose a model of illocutionary force in which two types of conversational update – a proposal by the speaker to change the common ground, plus an appeal to the addressee to do the same – contribute to deriving either a 'simple' speech act, when the two updates align (Fr. *Ferme ta gueule, point barre!* 'Shut your mouth, period!'), or a 'complex' speech act when they do not (Fr. *Marie est venue, n'est-ce pas?* 'Marie has arrived, hasn't she?'). Such models also highlight the performative role of speech acts, following Austin's proposal that there is a performance (i.e., an action executed) underlying every sentence, whether or not it involves an explicit world-changing predicate (Fr. *Je vous déclare mari et mari* 'I pronounce you husband and husband').

24.3.1.2 The Role of Syntax

Syntactic approaches tend to assume a mapping between form and interpretation (e.g., Sadock 1974; Levinson 1983), and in that direction. Discussion of illocutionary force in syntactic theory has traditionally been restricted to root environments on the view that non-root environments, as dependent clauses, are not able to carry an independent communicative function but instead receive their illocutionary force via the independent (main) clause to which they are anchored. The locus of such information is generally agreed to be C, the head of the clause: (positive) imperatives, for example, are understood to involve V-to-C movement, a diagnostic of which in Romance is enclisis (Sp. *te lo comes* 'you.2SG=it=eat.2SG' → *¡Cómetelo!* 'eat. IMP.2SG=you.2SG.DAT=it!').

Discourse-oriented meaning in Romance is often associated with the verb surfacing in a higher position, a requirement that can alternatively be fulfilled by inserting other morpholexical material (e.g., Uriagereka 1995a; 1995b). Cartographic accounts (Rizzi 1997; Cinque 1999; Benincà 2001), which draw extensively on Romance data, have narrowed down the structural locus of illocutionary force to the highest position in the clausal functional structure. Within current theory, the consensus is that the highest position in clausal structure is Rizzi's (1997) Force Phrase, which, despite the name, is essentially a clause-typing position (Rizzi 1997: 283) whose head is left empty in matrix clauses, and lexicalized by a subordinator (*che/que/că* 'that') in subordinate clauses.[14]

More recently, illocutionary force has been explicitly represented in clausal structure by Coniglio and Zegrean (2012), who propose a 'split ForceP', divided into a higher, illocutionary projection, and a lower, clause-typing projection; and by the resurrection of the previously-abandoned syntactic 'performative' hypothesis. The latter assumed that the deep structure of root clauses involves an abstract marker (Katz and Postal 1964) or performative predicative (biclausal) structure (Ross 1970; Sadock 1974) encoding the relevant speech act value in the highest part of the sentence's structure. In the latest accounts, a dedicated 'speech act' domain (Speas and Tenny 2003; Haegeman and Hill 2013; cf. Section 24.3.3) above, or replacing, the CP has been proposed, promoting a distinction

---

[14] Extensive comparative Romance data across major and minor clause types (Section 24.2; Munaro 2010) suggests a further subdivision of the left periphery into a hierarchy of clause-typing projections (cf. also Section 21.3.2).

Table 24.1. *Possible intonational contours and corresponding communicative functions for Sp.* bebe la limonada *'s/he drinks the lemonade'*

Bebe	la limonada	Function
L+<H*	L+H* L%	Statement ('s/he drinks the lemonade') or command ('drink the lemonade!')
L+<H*	L* L%	Statement/command
L+H* L−	L* L%	Statement/command with emphasis on first word
L+<H* H−	L+H* L%	Statement/command with emphasis on second word; first word is topic
L+<H*	L+H* L!H%	Statement of the obvious
L*+H	L* H%	Information-seeking question
L+<H*	L+H* HL%	Confirmation question
L+<H*	L+¡H* L%	Echo question
L+H*	H* H%	Quiz question
L+<H*	H+L* L%	Insistent explanation/request

(Hualde and Prieto 2015: 389)

between discourse-oriented meaning internal to the sentence (i.e., information structure packaging; see further Chapter 28) in the CP, and discourse-oriented meaning that interfaces between the sentence and the wider structural context in a dedicated domain to its left (Corr 2017: 3).

24.3.1.3 The Role of Prosody

The relationship between prosody and meaning is well known, although how exactly prosody relates to pragmatics remains disputed (Büring 2013; Couper-Kuhlen 2015; Hirschberg 2017). In Romance, prosody plays a vital role in encoding illocutionary values: indeed, in the absence of any dedicated morphosyntactic marking or contextual cues, intonation alone can be used to convey the intended illocutionary meaning. Table 24.1 demonstrates the range of communicative functions encoded by various prosodic contours for a three-word utterance in Spanish. Notably, the mapping between function and prosody is non-isomorphic (Ohala 1983): witness how the first two intonational contours can each encode either a 'statement' or a 'command'.

Dialectal differences complicate the picture further, as described at length for Spanish in Hualde and Prieto (2015), such that the intonational marking that carries a certain meaning in one variety corresponds to a different function in another, an observation that extends across the Romance family (Frota and Prieto 2015: 417). Indeed, whilst some generalizations can be made (e.g., wide-focus statements in Romance exhibit two dominant nuclear contours, H+L* L% or L* L%, distributed geographically),[15] overall the picture for Romance is one of rich intonational variation.

---

[15] The nuclear pattern H+L* L% is typical of wide-focus statements in Friulian; northern Catalan and Algherese; Cisalpine Occitan; Portuguese; Romanian; Sardinian; and some varieties of Latin-American Spanish (Buenos Aires and Puerto Rico), whereas L* L% is the dominant pattern for Catalan, French, Occitan, and Spanish, as well as some European Portuguese varieties (Frota and Prieto 2015: 417).

Moreover, the extent to which intonation can be taken as a predictor of illocutionary function differs between Romance varieties. Frota and Prieto (2015: 405) conclude that differences in pragmatic meaning tend to be systematically encoded via intonation in polar interrogatives in Spanish, Catalan, Occitan, and Friulian, whereas no such systematicity is observed in this environment in Sardinian, Italian, and Portuguese. These authors also observe a division of labour between intonational and morphosyntactic strategies for the encoding of illocutionary meaning, such that those languages with greater use of morpholexical and syntactic strategies (e.g., Sardinian; Friulian) exhibit greater polyfunctionality in their intonational expression, whereas the reverse is true of languages (French; some Occitan varieties) with fewer such morphosyntactic markers (Frota and Prieto 2015: 409–11). From the syntactic perspective, prosodic minimal pairs create non-trivial differences in illocutionary meaning in Romance (Sp. ¡*Anda, que llegamos tarde!* 'C'mon, [that] we're late!' vs ¡*Anda que llegamos tarde!* 'As if we're late!'), supporting proposals for a *prosody-oriented syntax* encoding utterance (Giorgi 2014; Corr 2017), or more generally, discourse-oriented/speech act information (Bocci 2013; Frascarelli and Jiménez-Fernández 2016; Munaro 2019) in Romance.

24.3.2 Mapping Form to Function: Insights from Romance

A strong intuition persists that some sentences have a 'basic' meaning (i.e., direct speech acts, where clause type and illocutionary force align), even if they can be used with other interpretations (i.e., indirect speech acts, where clause type and illocutionary force diverge). Taking Romance imperatives as an illustration, Han (1998) argues that only clause type can be accounted for through syntax alone. Specifically, whereas positive imperatives in Romance can be encoded via a grammatical force indicator – in her account, an imperative operator with a [+directive] feature – no such direct mapping is possible in other (surrogate) imperative structures, e.g., negative imperatives (Sp. ¡*No lo leas!* 'not it=read.SBJV.2SG'). In the latter case, (obligatory) proclisis (Sp. **¡*No* {*léelo/leaslo*}! 'not {read.IMP.2SG=it/read.SBJV.2SG=it}!') is taken as a diagnostic for the lack of [+directive]. Han thus concludes that illocutionary force must be derived through other means.

This issue is complicated by the observation that 'basic' is not synonymous with 'most frequent'. Levinson (1983: 264) claims that 'the majority of speech acts are most frequently realised', an assertion supported by Romance data: Hualde and Prieto (2015: 374) maintain that the pragmatically neutral intonational pattern for a polar question in Madrid Spanish does not correspond to the most frequently used prosody for this sentence type.

In Romance, a number of instances of 'non-basic' illocutionary meaning are at least conventionalized; e.g., the use of an indicative declarative in place of an imperative to issue a polite but firm command (Fr. *Tu feras ce que je dis* 'you **will.do.2SG** that which I say'), or habitualized formulas that have undergone varying degrees of pragmaticalization (Frp. *S'el vos plét* 'if=it you=pleases'; It. *prego* 'please' < 'I.pray/ask'; Vâo. *gramasí* < *grant marsi* 'great thanks'). Moreover, some constructions only permit certain interpretations, as in the rhetorical interpretations of (62)–(63), encoded via the negative polarity item and the subjunctive, respectively:

(62) ¿Cuándo ha **movido un dedo** por ti? (Sp.)
      'When has s/he [ever] **lifted a finger** for you?'(Escandell-Vidal 2012: 639)

(63) ¿Quién dijo que **fuera** fácil? (Sp.)
      'Who said this **was.SBJV** going to be easy?' (ibid.)

In (63), whereas the use of the indicative (era 'was.INDIC') would admit a neutral reading, the subjunctive forces a rhetorical one, creating a minimal pair which demonstrates that morphosyntax can indeed play a role in encoding indirect speech acts.

Supporting this claim is the observation that ungrammatical structures can become grammatical when used to signal an appropriate communicative function, as demonstrated by the following Italo-Romance data from Han (1998: 15) and Portner and Zanuttini (2000: 196, 199), respectively:

(64) Chi   **(non) ha   baciato nessuno? (It.)
      Who   not   has kissed   nobody
      'Who has not kissed anybody?'

(65) **Italian**
      A: Hai   baciato Maria!
            have.2SG kissed   Maria
            'You've kissed Maria!'
      B: Ma   chi ha   baciato nessuno?!
            but who has kissed   nobody
            'But who has kissed anyone?!'

(66) **Paduan**
      a.   Vien-lo?   (**el vien?)
            come=SCL.3SG   SCL.3SG=come
            'Is he coming?'
      b.** No   vien-lo?   (No   (e)l vien?)
            NEG come=SCL.3SG   NEG   SCL.3SG=come
            'Isn't he coming?'

c. No   vien-lo   miga?
    NEG   come=SCL.3SG   NEG
    'He's not coming??'

The minimal pair in (64)–(65) shows that, in genuine information-seeking interrogatives, Italian requires the negative item *non* in order to license a postverbal negative constituent (here, *nessuno* 'no one'). The ungrammaticality of (64) contrasts with the felicity of its rhetorical counterpart in (65), which acts as Speaker B's denial of Speaker A's accusation/gossip, an interpretation reinforced by use of the adversative *ma* 'but'. Relatedly, the ban on clitic-verb inversion with negatives in Paduan is breached when the sentence includes a second postverbal negator *miga*, producing a pragmatically marked interpretation (66c), demonstrating that word order also systematizes pragmatic meaning in Romance.

24.3.2.1 The Role of Polarity

The above series of examples highlights the crucial role of polarity in encoding various illocutionary meanings, including emphatic affirmation (Ara. *¡Oy, ixe, si en dize de palabrons!* 'Gosh, this guy, he **sure does** say a lot of weird words!'; Nagore Laín 1986: 134); metalinguistic negation, where the speaker refutes the proposition of a previous utterance, including their own (e.g., Ro. *A murit şeful mafiei? A murit* **pe dracu'***!* 'The mafia boss has died? **Like hell** he's died!'); and positive and negative marking of (dis)agreement (67)–(68). The latter is formalized by Farkas and Bruce (2010) as involving the combination of relative polarity features [*same, reverse*],[16] and affirmation/negation [+,−], creating variation in polarity systems:

(67) **European Portuguese**
  Ele já terminou o curso?
  'Has he already finished the course?'
 a. [*same*,+]
  Terminou/sim/foi/já.
  'Yes, he has.' (lit. finish.PRT.3SG/yes/be.PRT.3SG/already)
 b. [*reverse*,−]
  Não.
  'No, he hasn't.' (Martins 2016: 588)

(68) **Romanian**
  Nu e cel mai frumos copil din lume?
  'Is he not the most beautiful child in the world?'

---

[16] Martins (2013) replaces the [*same/reverse*] opposition with [*confirmation/denial*].

a. [*reverse*,+]
   Ba da, este.
   'Yes, he is.'
b. [*reverse*,−]
   Ba nu, mie nu mi se pare frumos deloc.
   'No, I don't find him beautiful at all.' (Roelofsen and Farkas 2015: 408)

Such polarity-encoding elements are often polyfunctional, with the same item entailing different meanings according to context. Batllori and Hernanz (2013: 14), citing Rigau (2004; 2012), describe how the Catalan particle *pla* 'truly' has three main values: emphatic scalar quantification (Cat. *Tu* **pla** *ets un janfosca!* 'You are **even more of** an idiot [than he is]!'); emphatic negation (Cat. *No m'ho crec. En Pere* **pla** *ha anat al cine aquesta nit!* 'I can't believe it. Pere HASN'T gone to the cinema tonight'); and emphatic affirmation (Cat. *Aquest casement* **pla** *es farà* 'This marriage will **indeed** take place'). These interpretational differences appear to be syntactically encoded, as in the combination of polarity items with complementizers (Sp. *Hoy sí (que) ha llovido* lit. 'today **yes** (**that**) it.has rained (= But it has been raining today!)'), where the presence of the complementizer subtly changes the sentence's communicative value so that, unlike when the complementizer is absent, it can only be uttered to counter a previous assertion (Etxepare 2007: 125; Hernanz 2007).

Structural analyses of such items show that they (i) obey syntactic constraints, and (ii) represent a non-heterogeneous class, which in turn entails that different polarity items target different sentential fields. To demonstrate that metalinguistic negation is not merely pragmatic (Horn 1985; 1989) but is a syntactic phenomenon, Martins (2014) shows that European Portuguese has two types of metalinguistic negator. One is sentence-internal (EuPt. *Ele viveu* **lá** *sempre (**lá) em Paris (**lá)* '**Like hell/no way** he's always lived in Paris') and the other sentence-peripheral (EuPt. *Ele viveu (**uma ova) sempre (**uma ova) em Paris* **uma ova** '**Like hell/no way** he's always lived in Paris'), as confirmed by their systematically differing syntax, illustrated here by a complementary sentential distribution.

24.3.2.2 Word Order, Complementizers, and Verb Movement

Verb movement to a higher clausal position functions as an indicator of illocutionary force in a range of structures (cf. also Section 21.3.2), even where it flouts otherwise systematic word order patterns, such as narrative V1 in old Romance V2 systems (Sic. **Dichi**, *adunca, sanctu Gregoriu ki* … '**says.3SG** then Saint Gregory that …'; Wolfe 2015: 157). In Romanian, inverted word order, involving verb movement to Force in the left periphery (Hill 2013: 170), combines with overt pronoun usage to produce speaker-oriented 'affective' meaning (19th-c. Ro. *Stam* **eu** *şi mă chiteam în capul meu că* … 'there was **I** thinking to myself that …'; Ion

Creangă, Stavinschi 2015: 27). The emotional markedness of this strategy intensifies when the pronoun co-occurs directly before the (definite) noun to which it refers (Ro. *Vine el tata* 'comes he father.the'; SA: threat). In popular speech, the pronoun can lack agreement (Stavinschi 2015: 18), thereby functioning as an expletive (Ro. *Ei las, bre, că mi-a veni el apa la moară* 'Forget it, mate, [lit.] that to.me=will come he water.the.fsg to the mill (= circumstances will change in my favour)'; Vasiliu 1993: 129 apud Stavinschi 2015: 18).

Polarity is also proposed to play a role in Galician and European Portuguese monosentential verbal reduplication, understood to be derived by verb movement to a polarity-related position, Σ, and subsequently to a discourse-related position, C, where it is used to express denial in emphatic response assertions (Martins 2013):[17]

(69) **Galician**
 a. Aníbal non **sabe** destes assuntos.
  'Aníbal doesn't **know** of such matters.'
 b. [TopP Aníbal_j **sabe**_i destes assuntos [CP sabe_i [ΣP Aníbal_j [Σ· sabe_i [TP sabe_i destes assuntos]]]]].
  'Aníbal *does* **know** of such matters.'

Evidence from Romance word order also casts doubt on the generalization that illocutionary force is restricted to main clauses. For example, 'peripheral' vs 'central' adverbial clauses can be differentiated according to the presence vs absence of *main clause phenomena*, a category of discourse-oriented root-(like) operations (Emonds 1970; 1976; Hooper and Thompson 1973). However, these operations are sometimes permitted in central adverbial clauses (e.g., clitic left-dislocation in Fr. [*Si ce livre-là tu le trouves à la Fnac*], *achète-le* lit. '[If **that book=there** you find it at the Fnac], buy it (= If you find that book at the Fnac bookshop, then buy it!)'; Haegeman 2012: 188). In conservative Asturian, the encoding of speaker 'conviction' (Fernández-Rubiera 2010) overrides the status of the complementizer as an obligatory proclisis trigger in embedded environments:

(70) Digo {qu'ayúdame /   que me ayuda}
  say.1SG that=help.3SG=me that me=help.3SG
  (#)pero nun toi   seguru (Ast.) [OK with proclisis; # with enclisis]
  but   not be.1SG sure
  'I say that s/he helps me, (#)but I'm not sure (i.e., that s/he does)' (Fernández-Rubiera 2010: 87)

---

[17] Syntactic tests demonstrate that, unlike verb reduplication in other Romance languages (cf. Section 24.2), western Ibero-Romance verbal reduplication involves *monosentential* structures (Martins 2013).

Further evidence of the encoding of illocutionary force in embedded clauses are intensional/*de dicto* reported speech structures in Spanish and Catalan, which contrast with extensional/*de re* structures, codified through the presence vs absence of a clause-initial complementizer (González i Planas 2014; Corr 2017: 146f.):

(71) En Miquel ens va dir [que] quants aniríem a la festa,
 (#) però no me'n recordo, de quants va dir. (Cat.) [OK without COMP; # with COMP]
 'Miquel said to us [that] how many people were going to the party,
 (#) but I do not remember how many he said.' (González i Planas 2014: 41)

In the *de re* version (without the complementizer), *quants* 'how.many' refers to a specific number of attendees (known and stated by Miquel, even though the speaker cannot subsequently recall how many attended the party), whereas in the *de dicto* sentence (with the complementizer), the *wh*-item has no referent, and thus the speaker cannot provide a number of attendees because he is reporting Miquel's *request*, i.e., an illocutionary act, for this information.

Relatedly, Giorgi (2010) attributes the variation in the availability of double-access readings (Abusch 1997) in Romance to the representation of the speaker's co-ordinates in the embedded CP. In Italian, for example, a sentence with an embedded present tense such as *Gianni ha detto che Maria è*.PRS.3SG *incinta* 'Gianni said that Maria {is/**was} pregnant' is only felicitous if Maria is pregnant at the time of Gianni's *and* the present speaker's utterance, whereas in Romanian the equivalent sentence is felicitous whether or not Maria is still pregnant at the time of the utterance (Ro. *Ion a spus că Maria e*.PRS.3SG *însărcinată* 'Ion said that Maria {is/was} pregnant'). According to Giorgi, only one interpretation is possible in Italian because the speaker's co-ordinates are represented in the embedded CP, entailing that the embedded verb is indexicalized with respect to both the speaker and the matrix subject. By contrast, in Romanian the embedded clause's temporal value is dependent on the matrix subject, because the speaker's co-ordinates are represented only in the matrix, but *not* the embedded, CP.

The matrix/embedded distinction is further blurred in Romance by the observation that complementizers can introduce matrix clauses, including indicative declaratives (Abr. *Ca ha lassate da piove!* '[That] it.has.INDIC stopped raining!'; Prins 2014: 112), a phenomenon sometimes descriptively labelled as 'insubordination' (Evans 2007) due to such clauses' apparently subordinate form. Matrix-initial complementizers are associated with various illocutionary nuances, e.g., rhetorical responses (72a), quotation (72b), and surprise (72c), with some varieties permitting their use in out-of-the-blue contexts (72d):

(72) a. Ca quannu te l'avìa a ddiri? (Plm.)
           '[That] since when did I have to tell you that?' (Garzonio and Sorrisi 2013: 51)
      b. Que no te s'escucha ná. (Ext.)
           '[I said that] we can't hear you.' (Corr 2017: 150)
      c. Queus jorz, sire? Si nel savez? (OFr.)
           'What day, my lord? '[If] don't you know it?' (Rodríguez-Molina and Enrique-Arias 2018: 265)
      d. Context: the addressee is trying to switch on the coffee machine.
           Que está tancada (Cat.)/Que está estropeada (EuSp.)/(**Que) está estragada. (EuPt.)
           '(That) it's broken'.

In some cases, the complementizer forms a single constituent with an erstwhile verb (Sic. *Dicica* 'apparently' > *dici* 'say.3SG' + *ca* 'that'; e.g., *Dicica iddu ci cafuddava* 'Apparently he beat her up' Cruschina 2015: 16), adjective (Ro. **Sigur că** *va veni* '**Of course** {**it is certain that**} s/he's coming' Hill 2007: 61), or adverb (Fr. **Evidemment que** *c'est ennuyeux de vieillir* '**Of course** [that] ageing is annoying!'), encoding various types of speaker-oriented (here, evidential or epistemic) meaning. However, whilst some such examples are embeddable (e.g., Ibero-Romance quotative/evidential usages, cf. 71), formal analyses (Remberger and Cruschina 2008; 2017; Corr 2017) have shown that many instances of 'insubordinate' phenomena in Romance exhibit main-clause rather than dependent-clause syntax, displaying restrictions on embedding (Ro. *Spunea că* **sigur că** *va veni* 'S/he said that **it is certain** {**of course**} that s/he will come'; Hill 2007: 68), and V2-like word orders (Eon. *Oi ninín, vente cumigo, que téñote ofrecido* 'Hey kiddo, come with me, that I.have=**you** put.forward [for communion]', in Corr 2017: 231).

24.3.2.3 Disambiguating Discourse

Various types of morpholexical marker play a disambiguating role in signalling (on the part of the speaker) and identifying (on the part of the addressee) the appropriate illocutionary force for a given utterance, the most obvious illustration of which are discourse-oriented particles themselves. These can be obligatory (73a); 'optional' (73b);[18] and surface in dedicated positions clause-internally (73b), clause-peripherally (73c), or in both sites (73d):

(73) a. Lî-l   **(ma/mo/pö/pa)! (Bad.)
           read.IMP=it   PTC
           'Read it!'
      b. Chiama (pure) la polizia! (It.)
           Call.IMP PTC   the police
           'Call the police (if you feel like it)!' (Coniglio and Zegrean 2012: 235)

---

[18] In a pre-theoretical sense, i.e., the sentence remains grammatical when the item in question is absent.

c. Se cê quiser comprar as duas, eu fico mais feliz, **viu** (BrPt.)
   if you want.FUT.SUBJ.3SG buy.INF the two I stay.1SG more happy PTC
   'If you want to buy both, I'll be happier, y'know.' (Bossaglia et al. 2017: 261)
d. (Doar) de mâine cineva va veni (doar) cu o soluție. (Ro.)
   PTC from tomorrow someone will come.INF PTC with a solution
   'From tomorrow someone will (evidently) come up with a solution.' (Coniglio and Zegrean 2012: 236)

Such markers provide a further layer of modal or illocutionary meaning beyond the propositional content, steering the addressee towards the speaker's intended meaning and/or facilitating conversational progression. Their meaning is semantically underdetermined, giving rise to polyfunctionality and context-dependent interpretations whose precise contribution is invariably impossible to capture using descriptive paraphrases (Frl. *Dai, dai, vignìs al cine, mo, sù, i sai ch'i podeis vignì, dai!* 'C'mon, c'mon, come to the cinema, **c'mon c'mon**, I know you can come, **c'mon**!'; Roseano et al. 2015: 132). In Romance, many such particles are derived from communication, motion, or perception verbs, typically, although not necessarily, in imperative form (Sp. *¡Anda!* 'Wow/no way/c'mon!' < 'go.IMP.2SG' vs BrPt. *Viu* 'y' know' < 'see.PST.3SG'). Their meaning is bleached relative to their lexical counterparts (It. *Dai!* 'C'mon!' < 'give.2SG'), a difference which is reflected morphosyntactically (e.g., invariability/reduced verbal paradigm; incompatibility with/resistance to clitics, adverbs, embedding and negation).

In Romance, right-peripheral/utterance-final 'tags' perform a similar illocutionary role. Beyssade and Marandin (2006a; 2006b) show that an apparently polysemous sentence can be disambiguated by an appropriate tag: adding confirmative Fr. *n'est-ce pas* ('won't you?') or the polite request *s'il te plaît* ('please') to an ambiguous declarative such as Fr. *Tu rentreras à la maison demain* 'You will go home tomorrow' distinguishes it as a confirmation-seeking question and a directive respectively.

24.3.3 Syntactic Encoding of 'Speech Act' Information

The syntactic behaviour of discourse particles is interpreted by some as evidence that 'speech act' information is encoded in the clausal domain, supporting recent syntactic models of the performative hypothesis. Corresponding evidence is also found in the nominal domain, where vocatives are systematically distinguished from thematic nouns across Romance via various strategies (see also Section 25.3.3). Alongside prosody, the most common strategy for distinguishing vocatives in Romance is the impossibility of the definite article (e.g., Sp. *Oye (*el) hijo, ven pa'cá* 'Hey [*the] son, come over here'), though alternative mechanisms are attested across the language family, including the use of particles (Arn. *Ò hilh mèn* 'O my son'; Süils 2010: 83); phonetic truncation (Log. [ˈsi] vs [ˈsilvja] 'Silvia'; Floricic 2002: 157); inflexional marking (Ro. *Eleno!* 'Elena.**VOC**' vs *Elena* 'Elena.**DEF.FSG**'); and, less commonly, vowel quality (Ext. *Heu, Mário!* 'Hey, Máriu!' vs *(El) Máriu* '[the] Máriu'; Carmona García 2011: 86).

Nonetheless, a number of varieties retain the article in vocatives in apparent contradiction of this pan-Romance impossibility (Fr. *Asseyez-vous, les enfants!* 'Sit down, [**the**] children!'). Closer inspection of Romanian shows that the use of the definite article with the vocative can (Ro. *poete* 'poet.**VOC**' vs *poetule* 'poet.**the**.**VOC**' (derog.)), though does not have to (Ro. *Băiete!* 'boy. **VOC**!' / *Băiatule!* 'boy.**the**.**VOC**!'), produce a specific pragmatic interpretation.

The syntax of vocatives in Romanian also exhibits systematic differences from the syntax of thematic nouns. According to Hill (2013: 51), Romanian requires the definite article to surface word-finally on the first constituent in N-Adj/Adj-N combinations (*omul bun* 'person=**the** good'; *bunul om* 'good=-**the** person'), but this rule is contravened in vocative phrases where the definite article surfaces on the noun in Adj-N expressions (*stimate cititorule, publicațiile noastre îți stau la dispoziție* 'dear.**VOC** reader=**the**.**VOC**, our latest publications are at your disposal').[19]

Moreover, Italo- and Daco-Romance 'speaker-oriented' vocatives (cf. Section 25.3.3) provide evidence that vocatives are not restricted to encoding addressee information (Ro. *Dane, {mamă/tată}, vino-ncoace!* 'Dan, (lit. '**mum**'/ '**dad**'), come here!'; said by parent to child; Croitor and Hill 2013: 824). These vocatives can exhibit first- (Mes. *Dommi, nonnicedda mia!* 'Sleep. **IMP**, granny **my.FSG**', spoken by grandmother; Abbate 2010: 152) and second-person (Trp. *Va sùsiti ch'è tardu, a mamma tua* 'C'mon get.up.**IMP**, that it's late, **PTC** mother **your.FSG**', spoken by mother; Abbate 2010: 152) singular, but not plural (Cal. *Quatra, susativǝ mamma **vostra!* 'Guys, get.up. **IMP=REFL.2PL** mother **your.FPL**', spoken by mother), agreement on possessive adjectives. Since this agreement is restricted to singular referents, it has been proposed that the possessive adjectives agree with the utterance participants (i.e., SPEAKER/ADDRESSEE) themselves (Akkuş 2016; Corr 2017), rather than (first/second) person, which admits plural agreement.

Constraints on the sentential distribution of illocutionary-oriented items provide further evidence of their syntactic nature (Moro 2003; Hill 2014; Corr 2017). Namely, vocatives and discourse particles can occur in root environments but are banned in embedded contexts, yet are able to surface utterance-finally (BrPt. *Não se esqueça (João/olha,) que (**João/olha,) prometeu chegar cedo (, João/olha)* 'Don't forget (**João/okay**,) that (****João/okay**,) you promised to arrive early (, **João/okay**)'; Moreira 2013: 29). Their sentential

---

[19] Note that this is not quite empirically correct, as shown by examples such as Ro. *Dragilor noștri prieteni!* ('dear.MPL.**the**.VOC our friends!'), where the presence of the possessive requires the adjective to host the definite article (Adam Ledgeway, p.c.).

distribution also undermines the assumption that ForceP is the highest clausal position: vocatives and discourse particles can co-occur preceding the complementizer in matrix environments (Eon. *Ai papá* [ForceP *que* [TP *me leva el demo!*]] 'Arghh dad, (**that**) the devil is taking me away!'), entailing that these items are either stranded outside the functional structure of the clause, or that the latter must be extended beyond ForceP in order to account for these items' grammatically conditioned behaviour.

Recent accounts adopt (and modify) Speas and Tenny's (2003) proposal for a dedicated 'speech act' domain. Empirical evidence for an internally articulated domain is provided by the attestation of multiple, hierarchically-ordered discourse particles co-occurring in the same utterance across Romance, e.g., Ro. *Vai Dane* **hai** *că nu te cred* 'Ah, Dan.VOC, **c'mon**, [that] I don't believe you', where *vai* obligatorily precedes *hai*, according to Haegeman and Hill (2013: 380). Such conversation-oriented discourse particles are interpreted by Hill (2014) as offering the 'missing lexical evidence' for the postulation of dedicated head positions in the 'speech act' space and by Haegeman (2014) as corresponding to an internally articulated structure composed of a higher discourse-activating layer, and a lower, bonding layer.[20]

Their co-occurrence with vocatives, and associated ordering restrictions, e.g., Ro. ***Dane, vai hai că nu te cred* '**Dan.VOC PTC PTC** that not you=believe.1SG', further supports the internal subdivision of speech act structure. Additional evidence comes from the hierarchical ordering of addressee vs speaker-oriented vocatives, e.g., southern reg. It. *Dai va forza* {*Olimpia*_VocAddr/***a nonna*_VocSpkr} *dormi*, {*a nonna*_VocSpkr/***Olimpia*_VocAddr} 'C'mon **Olimpia**, go to sleep (lit. **to granny**)' (grandmother to grandchild), a distribution suggesting that the hierarchy of utterance participants is ADDRESSEE > SPEAKER, *pace* Speas and Tenny (2003), Hill (2007; 2014), and Moreira (2013); or that the order may be amenable to parameterization.

24.4 Conclusion

This chapter has presented an overview of the contribution of Romance languages to a number of the key issues associated with theories of discourse at the level of the sentence/utterance, such as the morphosyntactic expression of clause type, the codification of illocutionary force, and the mapping between form and function in the realization of speech acts. Discussion of the contribution of Romance to our understanding of sentence-*internal* discourse, i.e., information structure, is provided in Chapter 26 of this volume.

---

[20] See Wiltschko et al. (2015) for an alternative, non-cartographic structure developed along similar lines, and Corr (2017) for appraisal of these, and for the proposal of the Utterance Phrase as a cartographic alternative.

Selected References

Below you can find selected references for this chapter. The full references can be found online at the following page: www.cambridge.org/Romancelinguistics

Beyssade, C. and Marandin, J.-M. (2006b). 'The speech act assignment problem revisited: disentangling speaker's commitment from speaker's call on addressee'. In Bonami, O. and Cabredo-Hofherr, P. (eds), *Empirical Issues in Syntax and Semantics 6*. Paris: CSSP, 37–68.

Coniglio, M. and Zegrean, I. (2012). 'Splitting up force'. In Haegeman, L., Aelbrecht, L., and Nye, R. (eds), *Main Clause Phenomena: New Horizons*. Amsterdam/Philadelphia: John Benjamins, 190–229.

Corr, A. (2017). *Ibero-Romance and the Syntax of the Utterance*. Doctoral thesis, University of Cambridge.

Giorgi, A. (2010). *About the Speaker: Towards a Syntax of Indexicality*. Oxford: Oxford University Press.

Giurgea, I. and Remberger, E.M. (2016). 'Illocutionary force'. In Ledgeway, A. and Maiden, M. (eds), *The Oxford Guide to the Romance Languages*. Oxford: Oxford University Press, 863–78.

Haegeman, L. and Hill, V. (2013). 'The syntactization of discourse'. In Folli, R., Sevdali, C., and Truswell, R. (eds), *Syntax and Its Limits*. Oxford: Oxford University Press, 370–90.

Martins, A. M. (2014). 'How much syntax is there in metalinguistic negation?', *Natural Language & Linguistic Theory* 32(2): 635–72.

Moro, A. (2003). 'Notes on vocative case: a case study in clause structure'. In Quer, J., Schroten, M., Scorretti, P., Sleeman, and Verheugd, E. (eds), *Romance Languages and Linguistic Theory*. Amsterdam/Philadelphia: John Benjamins, 247–61.

Munaro, N. (2010). 'Towards a hierarchy of clause types'. In Benincà, P. and Munaro, N. (eds), *Mapping the Left Periphery*. Oxford: Oxford University Press, 125–62.

Rizzi, L. (1997). 'The fine structure of the left periphery'. In Haegeman, L. (ed.), *Elements of Grammar*. Dordrecht: Kluwer, 281–337.

Sadock, J. and Zwicky, A. (1985). 'Speech act distinctions in syntax'. In Shopen, T. (ed.), *Language Typology and Syntactic Description*. Cambridge: Cambridge University Press, 155–96.

Speas, P. and Tenny, C. (2003). 'Configurational properties of point of view roles'. In Di Sciullo, A. M. (ed.), *Asymmetry in Grammar*. Amsterdam: John Benjamins, 315–45.

25
Address Systems and Social Markers

Federica Da Milano and Konstanze Jungbluth

25.1 Introduction

Our knowledge of Romance languages in synchrony and in diachrony allows us to follow the wide range of address systems used at a particular time in one or several of them to express varying levels of politeness, social distance, courtesy, familiarity, or insult towards the interlocutor. The social relationships behind these choices involve heterogeneous factors, the most important among them being age, kinship, social and affective relations, and the nature of the communicative situation (formal, informal). The dependence of the address systems on the context of communication makes them deictic elements, i.e., forms that find their referent in the context and which are bound to the social norms in use. Their fundamental characteristic is in fact of a pragmatic nature: they depend on the system of rules that govern the behaviour of speakers both in the use of linguistic means and in the choice of non-verbal behaviours in their relationships.

European, particularly Romance, languages provide rich exemplification for the famous distinction between the so called T and V pronouns (referring to the Latin pronouns TU 'you.SG.FAM' and UOS > *[vos] 'you.SG.HON') developed by Brown and Gilman (1960; cf. Section 25.2) based on their study of Italian, French, Spanish, and German. One of the most important strategies for being polite is to avoid addressing people directly. Two particularly widespread honorific strategies to address a socially higher ranked interlocutor consist in using the plural form instead of the singular or the third person singular instead of the second person which, in the terms of Brown and Levinson (1987), are considered to be face saving devices. 'Face' refers to the 'public self-image that every member wants to claim for himself' (Brown and Levinson 1987: 61). Particularly among strangers and in strongly hierarchical marked relationships, the use of the second person pronoun by the less powerful interlocutor may threaten the face wants of the addressee. Using the third person singular form, the speaker does not address the interlocutor directly, but talks in a way which is conventionalized for referring to an absent third person. In so doing, the speaker does not force the interlocutor to behave in a certain way, but leaves it to the interlocutor to decide whether to interact at all, and if so, how. The Spanish morphosyntactically third person address pronoun *usted* (< *vuestra merced* 'your grace') may serve as an example. In an ongoing interaction on an unequal footing, this freedom of choice is understood as a form of courtesy or respect moderating the speech act which, in turn, urges the interlocutor to take the turn. The latter may be expressed with a similar effect by using the second person plural instead of the singular, a procedure well established in French. In the ongoing interaction framed by social distance simulating several people as possible interactors, the speaker again plays down the discourse force of the utterance, allowing the addressee not to reply.

Some of the Romance languages allow one to make ternary distinctions of politeness using second person pronouns. In several Romance languages gender is a feature of the second person pronoun. Furthermore, there are differences of use in rural and urban areas and between men and women in some places, particularly with regard to who might be considered as close or familiar and treated correspondingly.

In order to address people, call to them, call their attention in the conversation, or to take the turn after they have held it, languages use various methods: nouns (epithets), pronouns, and vocatives. While the pronouns and the corresponding verb forms represent the address system as organized in paradigms as part of grammar (Section 25.3.2), the nominal forms may develop into fine-grained inventories of social markers (Section 25.3.1). Sometimes certain collocations fuse as formulaic expressions. In contrast, vocatives are pragmatic items with no other function than to call someone to initiate a dialogue (Section 25.3.3; cf. 'attention-getter', Parrott 2010).

Our focus here will be on the change of address systems as languages are embedded and determined by the historical, cultural, and particularly social context at stages with which linguistic phenomena are bound up. Changes of social order in societies in remote times up to the present time have had a major impact on the use of address systems and their change (on Latin: Adams 2013), as has language contact due to population movements whether forced or unforced. There are several important factors influencing these changes involving processes of (de)grammaticalization and pragmaticalization. Indeed, there is a 'growing list of extra-linguistic variables associated with pronominal address [which] includes social position, relative authority, group membership, generation, age [...] sex, kinship, genealogic distance, mood, social context, language variety' (Pinkerton 1986: 690). It is precisely these features which turn second person pronouns into social markers (on 'person' as a universal category: Maillard 1994).

This chapter has a threefold objective: first, we shed some light on the complex architecture of address systems which Romance languages have developed over time out of their shared Latin heritage (Section 25.2); second, we aim to familiarize readers with some of the different kinds of address systems conventionalized in Romance languages (Section 25.3); and, finally, we foreground the processes of language change which led to the great variety of systems present in the post-Latin varieties today (Section 25.4).

25.2 From Latin to Romance: Expressing Politeness by Pronouns

In Classical Latin, any single interlocutor was addressed by one and the same pronominal form. In Latin TU 'you' is the pronoun referring to second person singular. Only in Late Antiquity did this social method of referring to a single interlocutor change when UOS-forms, i.e., second person plural forms, start being used as polite forms for addressing a single interlocutor. This use of the V-form must be understood as a *plurale maiestatis* or 'plural of majesty', i.e., the plural is used instead of the singular in order to express respect. According to Brunot (1922), this change is introduced during the 'tetrarchy', when four emperors formed the government, during the reign of Diocletian, who established this structure in 293 CE. His claim is that the plural used to refer jointly to the emperors became reanalysed as a form of respect referring to a single authority, later generalized for addressing any interlocutor of higher status. However, according to many studies (see, e.g., Norberg 1968; Grevisse 1975) the use of a plural pronoun for the emperor can be traced back to the reign of Emperor Gordian III around 240, and hence to an earlier period. They therefore deduce that the tetrarchy served only as an accelerator for a behaviour already in use (but see also Section 25.4). Today, the development is seen as a grammatical fossil of the pragmatic phenomenon of indirectness minimizing a (potentially) face-threatening act, namely direct address (Ashdowne 2016: 900). Interestingly, in the monasteries and among the literate members of society the use of the T-forms (second person singular forms) to address any single interlocutor was long maintained in Christian Europe due to the prestige of ancient translations.

In the history of Romance, the category of politeness is introduced when in Latin the originally second person plural UOS 'you.PL' begins to be used as a singular honorific instead of original singular TU, which comes to be marked contrastively as 'you.SG.FAM'. In old French the use of V-forms is evident from the earliest texts: the alternation of the forms is very subtle and is used to express a transitional attitude towards a particular situation. In the *Chanson de Roland*, an irritated Ganelon uses *tu* in addressing Roland: *tu n'ies mês hom ne jo ne sui tis sire* 'you$_{SG.FAM}$ are not my vassal, nor am I your$_{SG.FAM}$ lord', but later he says *jo ne vus aim nient* 'I do not love you$_{SG.HON}$ at all'. The changing use points to a relation on an equal footing and closeness in the first utterance. In contrast, in the second situation, the offended Ganelon is distancing himself from his antagonist. The interactive context triggers different forms of address and shows that relationships are never fixed for ever but the object of negotiation. In *La Mort le roi Artu*, the first great French prose text, the knights and the king use V-forms to each other, but Lancelot uses *tu* in addressing one of his squires: *Va t'en droit a Kamaalot et fai tant que tu saiches les noveles de madame la reïne* 'Betake yourself$_{SG.FAM}$ straight to Camelot and make sure you$_{SG.FAM}$ know the news of the Queen'. Coffen (2003) defines this behaviour as *flottement pronominal* 'pronominal floating'. However, again the situational context of sharing a secret evokes an intimacy which is reflected in the use of a T-pronoun between the confirmed pair of master and squire. Negotiations on relationships in discourse may trigger a changing use of forms of address also reported for the Spanishes of the Americas (Raymond 2016: 284; cf. *tratamientos circunstanciales* 'circumstantial treatments' – Real Academia Española 2009: 1250–51; Section 25.4).

There is evidence for the spread of the plural forms used as polite forms from French to Spain when in the twelfth century V-forms were presented as being used between the Cid and his peers: 'In the *Poema de mio Cid*, the king is addressed as *vos*, as is the Cid (by the king and others); the Cid addresses [his wife] Ximena and most of his relatives as *vos*, but uses *tú* to his younger kinsmen' (Penny 1992: 137). Indeed, the paradigm of second person pronouns in old Spanish encoded relations of distance, i.e., respect, or closeness between speakers. Accordingly, the address system included two terms only: TU > *tú* and UOS > *vos*. However, the latter still referred to the informal plural, and to the singular and the plural for expressing politeness in formal relations. On the one hand, Spanish speakers started to add *otros* 'others': *vos* > *vosotros* to unambiguously address a group of people in informal contexts. On the other hand, in relations towards noblemen showing multiple differences of hierarchical status the use of nominal forms such as *Vuestra merced* 'your grace', *Tu merced* 'your grace', *Vuestra señoría* 'your lordship', *Vuestra excelencia* 'your excellence', *Vuestra majestad* 'your majesty' gained usage, replacing the pronoun *vos* in this kind of context (Section 25.3.1). Among them the first composite became most frequent. The formulaic expression went through a series of contractions, e.g., *vuesarced*, *voacé*, *vucé*, *vuced*, *vested*, before finally conventionalized as *usted* (Penny 1992: 137–39). There is less evidence of the spread of the polite form to Italy: Dante uses *tu* to Vergil, although the latter is portrayed in the *Divine Comedy* as showing Dante how to become an epic poet of the modern world. With his choice of the T-form Dante brings them closer together: 'Dante is the new Vergil' (Stierle 1996: 62). However, when the poet Petrarch uses *voi* to his beloved Laura, he follows the practice of Provençal and Sicilian poets directing themselves to their ladies (Peterson 2016: 285). In so doing, he performs the expected social reference as part of societal etiquette of his time in that space. In contrast, when Petrarch writes love poems after her death using the T-form *tu*, he shows his affective involvement overcoming the former social distance. Both examples show that Tuscan had conventionalized diastratic and diaphasic variation in the use of their address forms at that time.

25.3 Forms of Address between Lexicon and Grammar in Use Today

25.3.1 Noun Phrase: Nominal Forms of Address

We now turn to the inventories of polite nominal forms of address (Section 25.3.1), followed by the paradigms of pronominal forms (Section 25.3.2), address systems based on oppositions including contracted former nominal collocations and formulaic expressions for expressing politeness, before concluding with a discussion of vocatives (Section 25.3.3) which have the function of addressing only. Finally, typological patterns and their changes are discussed (Section 25.3.4).

A nominal form used in Portuguese addressing the hearer is *o senhor* / *a senhora* 'lord / lady' (< Lat. SENIOREM 'elder'), a noun preceded by a determiner, expressing respect for elderly people and substituting a second person singular pronoun. This nominal phrase used in encounters by someone of a more humble social level with the interlocutor marks distance. In doing so, the speaker is factoring out the intimacy of the experienced proximity as part of the ongoing dialogue, minimizing the face-threatening act and showing humility with regard to the higher social status of the addressee (Section 25.2).

In the Romance languages spoken at the edges of the former Roman Empire, Romanian and Portuguese, there are still a multitude of nominal forms to address authorities of government, the supremes of judicial, executive, legislative, military, or ecclesiastic power, most of which are still expected to be used today in spoken and written discourse: Pt. *Vossa Excelência* for the President, ministers, or senators among others; *Magnificência* for the *rector* 'president' of a university; *Senhoria* for all other authorities; *Vossa Eminência Reverendíssima* for addressing a cardinal; *Dom* for bishops and *Padre* for priests; and several other distinctions of rank and power connected with social roles in these institutions beside a multiple of titles used in earlier times in the context of monarchies of different kinds. In Romanian we find nominal forms such as *Domnia/Alteța/Excelența Voastră*. However, today non-reciprocal usage referring to vertical relationships may be questioned, and forms expressing relationships on an equal footing are used instead. In Brazil, a television show host was asked why he did not address his guests by the nominal form *o senhor*. He justified his use of generalized informal pronoun *você* by claiming to follow prestigious French usage of *vous* (Malheiros Poulet 2008). Interestingly enough, in this social context the use of *o senhor* has changed and is no longer considered a form of respect but, rather, a social marker pointing to membership of a social class (cf. V-form *voi* used by Petrarch; Section 25.2).

In contrast, there are also new nominal forms coined among adults, co-workers, or academics for addressing people on an equal footing: for example in Brazil the colloquial nominal form, a bare noun *pessoal* 'guys, folks, people, all', homophonous with the adjective *pessoal* 'personal' [cf. *pessoa* 'person'] (Jungbluth and Vallentin 2015). This singular noun has the semantic function of plurality and is used in addressing a crowd, rather like the pronoun of the first person plural *a gente* (N:FSG) 'the people', replacing *nós* 'we', which has turned into a Brazilian standard form and become part of the pronominal paradigm. The impact of highly frequent address forms for language change in general affecting larger parts of grammar is noteworthy. For example, the reduction of verb forms may be exemplified by contrasting Brazilian and European Portuguese, where the membership of the paradigm is reduced by half. As the pronoun of second singular *tu* is replaced by a generalized use of third person singular pronoun *você*, the first person singular verb is only opposed to third person singular. This form is also used for expressing first person plural with an obligatorily preceding *a gente* 'the people > we'. The only verb form expressing plural is the third person, which may be also preceded by second person plural *vocês*.

Unlike Brazilian Portuguese, and beyond the simple twofold hierarchy of politeness, Romanian developed a notably rich inventory of address forms. In addition to the basic, informal, familiar address pronouns *tu* and *voi*, with corresponding verb forms, most of the forms are based on the Latin DOMINUS 'lord', DOMINA 'lady', which resulted in Ro. *domn* 'sir' and *doamnă* 'lady' and in the derived noun *domnie* 'lordship', the basis of address forms *dumneata* (originally 'thy lordship'), MSG *dumnealui* (originally 'his lordship'), FSG *dumneaei* (originally 'her lordship'), *dumneavoastră* ('your.SG lordship', historically PL; plural reference is still possible), PL *dumnealor* (originally 'their.M lordships'). *Dumneavoastră* 'your.SG lordship' followed by a second person plural verb form is used today for addressing in a respectful way the interlocutor and is limited to the standard language, not being established in the dialects of Romania. In the singular there is a term which in the standard language is intermediate between *tu* and *dumneavoastră*, namely *dumneata* (originally 'lordship.your.SG'), with colloquial variants such as *mata*, *matale*, all with a second person singular verb form. These forms are well established in dialect usage (Maiden 2016: 105). Iliescu and Popovici (2013) recognize a three-level system of politeness, low (*dumneata*; *mata*, *matale* + second person singular verb) – middle and close to the standard form (*dumneavoastră* + second person singular verb; also *dumnealui* and *dumneaei* + third person singular verb) – and high (*Domnia Voastră* + second or third person singular verb or, *Domniile Voastre* + second or third person plural verb, and *Domnia Sa* + third person singular verb). There is also a series for third person *el* ~ *dânsul* ~ *dumnealui/dumneasa* ~ *Domnia Sa*, although not all speakers perceive *dânsul* as a polite form. *Dânsul* is a compound dating from the end of the seventeenth century derived from the old forms *însul* (*însa*, *înșii*, *însele*), < Lat. IPSE, that were obligatorily combined with a preposition. The use of all of these forms is very frequent and important not only at the opening and closing of the conversation, but also during it, to address the interlocutors encouraging them to go on speaking and for further discourse organization purposes (Erfurt 1989). Quick changes of short turns and overlaps, paraphrasing, and ellipses, which recall phenomena of spoken language use and are labelled as co-constructions in pragmatic research on other languages (Dausendschön-Gay et al. 2015; Fernández-Villanueva and Jungbluth 2016; cf. discussion in Müller 2016), are claimed to be of a discourse-connecting nature in Romanian polylogues (cf. Slama-Cazacu 1982; Erfurt 1989). The main argument foregrounds their function of connecting the turns in a frame-semantic interface embedded in grids of communication built upon intonational and non-verbally expressed strings of references (Erfurt 1989: 160f.) which are prominent in dialogue, along with the well-known relations of cohesion and coherence. In so doing, the speakers manage to disentangle pairs of utterances belonging together and to discriminate them from other dialogues uttered more or less simultaneously in the ongoing polylogues. Vocatives (Section 25.3.3) and the choice of address forms play a prominent role in these discourse procedures.

25.3.2 Pronominal Forms: Address Systems

Address systems contrasting pronominal forms may show not only T/V oppositions of Latin origin, but may also integrate additional terms expressing three levels of politeness or further social differences (Section 25.2), and in some language varieties the choice is determined by the gender of the addressee, a phenomenon which is cross-linguistically rare. The latter may be shown for varieties in northern Italy, for gender agreement in Catalan, and by Portuguese varieties in early modern times and Kabuverdianu (Section 25.4).

Consider for example Italian, with the pronominal forms 2SG *tu*, 2PL *voi* (still used as a second person singular honorific in the south), and *Lei* (lit.'she', formally a third person singular feminine pronoun used as a second person singular honorific). When former feminine third person form *Lei* was integrated as a pronoun of address expressing respect for the interlocutor (Grand 1930), it became generalized and could lose the feature of gender. In passing, we just mention that use of its plural form *Loro* (3PL) as a form of address is considered old-fashioned today. And again, the tendency is to consider language contact, in this case Spanish influence, as being responsible for the integration of the third person singular form encoding respect in contrast to the unmarked second person singular. Speakers of Spanish make their choice among *tú* 'you.SG.FAM', *vosotros/-as* 'you.PL.FAM', and *usted* 'you.SG.HON', the last mentioned being used with a third person singular verb. The Italian poet Giacomo Leopardi considered this usage in Italian a *maledetto spagnolismo della terza persona* 'detestable Hispanism of [using] the third person', in a letter of 1829. Actually, this usage dates back to Latin. As noted above (Section 25.1), Roman emperors from the third century onwards began to use a plural pronoun (NOS 'we') referring to themselves (*plurale maiestatis*). Consequently, the second person plural form UOS was used by other people as an expression of deference to refer to the emperor (polite second person plural address still exists in French, with the polite form *vous*). With its increasingly widespread use, however, this form was no longer considered to be a sufficient expression of respect. Nominal forms – nominal phrases of an abstract noun determined by preceding possessive pronoun – such as *vestra maiestas* 'your majesty' and *vestra gloria* 'your glory' began to be used. During the Middle Ages in Italy, the nominal form *Vostra Signoria* 'your Lordship' was introduced, with increasing success. The transition towards the use of a third person pronoun (*Lei* 3.FSG, originally an object form which gradually replaced the subject form *Ella*), is thus explained as a matter of anaphoric reference: the feminine form of the pronoun is justified by the fact that it refers to a feminine noun (*Signoria* 'lordship.FSG').

When systems of three terms change (Brunet 2008), usually one of the polite forms is dropped. Today, standard Italian has two address pronouns, namely *tu* and *Lei*, whereas up until the nineteenth century, *voi* was used as a neutral, unmarked form in the singular, not as a form of maximum respect. However, the inherited second person distinction TU-UOS and associated pronominal and verb forms are faithfully maintained, especially in rural dialects, of southern Marche, southern Umbria, Abruzzo, Campania, northern Calabria, and Salento. In many of the remaining areas of southern Italy (Rome, Naples, Basilicata, northern Puglia, southern Calabria) UOS (> *voi, vui(e), vu(a), vu(e)*) today represents both the singular and plural form of polite and/or respectful address, often reinforced by an appropriate title (Ledgeway 2015:105–08).

The corresponding Spanish nominal form *Vuestra Señoría* 'your lordship', reserved for high-ranking people, has not become an object of language change (Section 25.4) as happened with the most common *Vuestra Merced* 'your grace', which is feminine as in Italian, and which became a gender-undifferentiated *usted*, with pronominal status. This development was paralleled in Portuguese with *Vossa mercê* > *você* (Section 25.3). However, in northern varieties in Italy the third person singular indirect forms of address display gender distinctions: M/F Pie. *chiel/chila*, Lmb. *Lü/Le(e)*, Rmg. *Lo/Li*, Vnt. *Lu/La* (Ledgeway 2015: 107).

As mentioned, French is considered to have just two forms, namely *tu* and *vous*; however, Judge and Healey (1985: 70) affirm that the use of third person singular forms *il, elle* occurs in 'certain somewhat exaggerated situations of politeness': e.g., *Et monsieur, qu'est-ce qu'il désire?* 'And sir, what would he like?'

Another system showing three levels of respect is used in some Catalan varieties: here the difference between rural and urban usage continues to be important. In the urban varieties of Catalan a two-term system is used contrasting *tu* 'you.SG.FAM' and *vostè* 'you.SG.HON'. Interlocutors usually apply either of these forms of address reciprocally. In contrast, children and adolescents in the countryside may still address their parents by a non-reciprocal *vostè* 'you.SG.HON' (with third person singular verb), the respectful form of address: *És que vostè és molt guapo/-a, pare/mare* (M/F) 'You are very smart.MSG/smart.FSG, father/mother'. The third person singular usage shows gender agreement depending on the sex of the addressee. In return, the parents address their children with *tu* 'you.SG.FAM' (and verb in second person singular). In the urban context reciprocal *tu* is routine in similar encounters. The paradigm may include another form of address: *vós* 'you.SG.HON' acquires singular honorific meaning (with second person plural verb), which is somewhat archaic, but frequent in the religious domain for praying to God or saints. In first encounters, *vós* points to large social, particularly age-related, differences distancing the interlocutors from one another (Nogué-Serrano 2008; 2015: 226–28). This usage as a social marker is confirmed by the authors of the style book of the Catalan Society for Audiovisual Media (*És a dir*) who favour a general use of *vostè*, but admit the use of *vós* for elderly people (Nogué-Serrano 2015). The choices among the three degrees of respect *tu-vós-vostè* are determined either by the social relationship indicating status, or they may refer to face, a social role and a functional variable which changes in accordance with the different communicative situations.

Spanish shows another very complex pronominal address system based on pronominal forms, as described by Luquet (2003: 1):

> [I]n this language there are three main systems referring to the addressee: the one that opposes *tú* and *usted*, in the singular, to *vosotros, vosotras* and *ustedes*, in the plural (system used in force for the most part in the Iberian Peninsula); the one which opposes *tú* and *usted* to *ustedes* (system in force in certain parts of Andalusia, in the Canary Islands, the Antilles and in most of Mexico, Colombia, Venezuela and Peru); the last one, which opposes *vos* and *usted* to *ustedes* (system in force in Argentina, Paraguay, and Uruguay, as well as in Costa Rica, Nicaragua, and Guatemala).

From a diachronic point of view, this distribution is explained in the following way: the Hispano-American areas further away from the government of the colonial power have kept the use of *vos*, while the centre of Mexico and Peru, as well as the Caribbean, have followed the Spanish trend of replacing *vos* by *tú* (Mexico: Vázquez Laslop and Orozco 2010; Escobar 2012). However, the boundaries between the two systems are often difficult to define clearly.

25.3.3 Vocatives

The function of vocatives is to call or address (cf. also Section 24.3.3). There are theoretical grounds not to consider the vocative a case form (Hjelmslev 1937: 4; Daniel and Spencer 2009).

In the Romanian paradigm, vocative is opposed to nominative-accusative and genitive-dative case forms in the singular (Blake 2004: 1087). Possibly continuing the Latin second declension vocative, the morphological vocative of the masculine singular is usually marked by -*e*. In contrast to Latin, singular nouns in -*ă* or -*a* have vocatives in -*o*, an ending of Slavonic origin: *Ana*, vocative: *Ano!*; *popă* 'priest', vocative: *popo!*. Romanian also has, most unusually, a vocative plural: alongside the nominative-accusative definite form (e.g., VOC *băieții!* 'boys.ADV.DEF.PL', *doamnele!* 'ladies.ADV.DEF.PL'), Romanian also employs the genitive-dative definite forms, e.g., *domnilor și doamnelor!* 'ladies.ADN.DEF.PL and gentlemen.ADN.DEF.PL' (Maiden 2016: 103).

A very peculiar case is represented by the Romanian inverse address ('alocuțiunea inversă': Beyrer 1979), a phenomenon is occasionally found in other Romance and non-Romance languages (southern varieties of Italy, Arabic, Slavonic languages spoken in the Balkans, among others). They normally include kinship terms (such as *mamă* 'mother', *maică* 'mother.DIM'; *tată* 'father', *taică* 'father.DIM') which are typically used in addressing family members, where the addressee's attention is secured or held by using the word that expresses the speaker's relation to the addressee. This use of reverse addressed forms may be exemplified by a mother calming her daughter. She affectionately addresses her child using the address form she expects to receive from her: *Lasă mamă că-ți fac alta* lit. 'Don't worry, mother [i.e., daughter], I'll make you another one' (Stavinschi 2015: 37). In so doing, she shows herself empathetic towards her daughter and helps her to take a step back from herself. This practice is not only common in the Balkans (Stavinschi 2015) but is also attested in southern Italo-Romance. That the Spanish formal address pronoun *usted* is used to console children who get hurt (Moyna 2016: 1) may have a similar motivation. Instead of a vocative, this usage allows the child to experience the distance expressed by the choice of this address form and to feel encouraged to distance herself from the pain (cf. using *vos* for consolation Johnson 2016: 131, 135f.).

25.3.4 Paradigms and Their Variation: Losses and Gains

Obviously, the selection of address forms is reflected in the selection of corresponding verb forms. Changes affecting the paradigm of the latter have an impact on that of the former. When references become ambiguous due to the loss of inflexional encoding of person, the use of address pronouns increases. Added to this, the combination between address pronouns and the verb forms is open to developing new combinations including apparent mismatches between pronouns of the second person with verb forms of the third person (see below). This change is in stark contrast to null subject languages such as European Portuguese, which continue the Latin situation, but is widespread in certain varieties of Latin America. Similar to (spoken) French where subject pronouns have become an obligatory part of the predicate, in Brazilian Portuguese the use of subject pronouns has also become obligatory, thereby revealing a different grammar with respect to European Portuguese patterns (Kilbury-Meissner 1982).

As we will see in more detail in Section 25.4, in American Spanishes the coexistence, in some regions, of the use of *vos* or *tú* (*voseo* and *tuteo*, respectively), had morphosyntactic consequences, mainly in the verb systems. In *tuteo* regions, the verb that accompanies *tú* is in the second person singular, the default case in accordance with European Spanish. Yet the verb form that accompanies *vos* with T function, varies significantly from one region to another. In contrast to second person singular forms (*tú*) *tomas/tienes/sales* '(you.SG) take/hold/go.2SG' and second person plural forms (*vosotros/-as*) *tomáis/tenéis/salís* '(you.PL) take/hold/go.2PL', in Central America, and more specifically in Venezuela and Colombia, *vos* may be coupled in the present indicative with the following representative verb forms *vos tomás/tenés/salís* 'you.PL take/hold/go.2PL', showing monophthongization of original -*áis*, -*éis*. In Argentina, Uruguay, and partially in Paraguay, *vos* can be associated with three different verb forms, as first noted by Ureña (1921).

> [T]he singular and the plural ones, corresponding, in one case, to the Castilian forms (*reís, vivís*) and, in the other case, with the archaic forms, in which the -*i*- of the modern diphthongs of the last syllable is missing (*pensás, tenés, querés*) ...; and, finally, old forms are used that can be considered either as simplified forms (*estabas ~ estabais*), or as forms of the singular, because they are in the educated language (*estabas, estarías, estuvieras*), or in the popular language of regions where *vos* is unknown: *mirastes, estuvistes*. (Zamora Vicente 1970: 401)

Returning to Brazilian Portuguese, *você* is followed by a third person singular verb form. Meanwhile, *tu* fell into disuse in most parts of Brazil; however, some traces are preserved in prayers and liturgical texts, as may be expected. However, *tu* is still used in some regions of the south and in some isolated pockets in northeast regions. And again, language contact or its absence due to migration movements in the past are considered to have had an impact on the (dis)continuity of the use of *tu* across Brazil (Coelho and Görski 2011). The lack of contact with speakers of other Brazilian regions in the remote northeast regions, particularly in the cities of Belém and São Luís do Maranhão, gave continuity to the use of *tu* (with second person singular verb), maintaining the European pattern.

The revival of the use of second person pronoun *tu* in Brazilian Portuguese in the south was consistently favoured by the influx of people of different European origins. Speakers of the still prestigious European Portuguese and the use of related second person pronouns in the multiple European (dialect) varieties originally spoken in Italy, Prussia, other parts of Germany, and Switzerland by the newcomers converged. These Brazilian varieties connect the address pronoun *tu* with third person singular verb forms, a practice which may be influenced by other familiar address forms derived from *vossa mercê* 'your mercy', e.g., *você/ocê/cê* (Scherre 2018) with a third person verb form, in the singular, *você fala* 'you speak.3SG', and in the plural: *vocês falam* 'you speak.3PL'. Although use of the address form *tu* accompanied by the third person singular verb form is considered substandard, at present *tu* is maintained or revitalized as the default pronoun for addressing relatives, friends, and friendly acquaintances in many parts of Brazil. In fact, recent studies confirm that Brazil is experiencing a kind of comeback of the use of *tu* in urban regions following the model of Rio de Janeiro and particularly among the younger generations (Paredes Silva 2011; Scherre 2018).

25.3.5 Typological Patterns of Address Systems

According to Coffen (2002), from a diachronic point of view we can distinguish, typologically, between a first stage, in which languages introduce a morphological or lexical distinction between an undifferentiated second person form and a more formal one, and a second stage, in which there is a tendency towards re-simplification. In this framework, she classifies Romance languages in the following way (also with internal diachronic shifts in the same language): languages with address systems with number distinctions (continuing the Latin pattern): singular vs plural; languages with address systems with person distinctions by including a third person singular form as second person pronoun performing indirect address; a mixed type, namely languages with multiple politeness distinctions (Portuguese and Romanian). Ashdowne (2016) distinguishes four typological patterns: Type I: opposition between a form as second person singular and a form as second person plural used strictly according to number (*tu/voi* in various areas of Italy: dialects of Abruzzo, southern Marche, southern Umbria, southern Puglia, and in parts of Campania and Calabria); Type II: use of the second person plural for V (e.g., French, Neapolitan, in Calabria, northern Puglia, Rome, Canton Ticino, Corsica, as well as some dialects of Tuscany); Type III: present-day V-forms represent reflexes of indirect address carried out by means of the third person (e.g., standard Italian, standard European Spanish, Catalan); Type IV: represented by the complexities of Portuguese. Also, some of the Latin American varieties of Spanish show ternary systems. According to *WALS*, multiple politeness distinctions are rare cross-linguistically, and most languages, in particular European languages, are restricted to binary distinctions. In reference to Romanian, Sorin and Giurgea (2013) observe:

> There are two facts which are considered as specific for the Romanian politeness paradigm: the presence of the third person pronominal forms, which are used either deictically or anaphorically ... and the existence of three degrees: non-politeness, intermediate politeness, characterized by singular agreement and singular doubling clitics. (Dobrovie-Sorin and Giurgea 2013: 283)

25.4 Changing Address Systems across Time

As Siewierska-Chmaj (2004) underlined, in Europe the use of non-singular number for respectful singular reference has been attributed to cultural diffusion, especially the influence of French in which the second person singular *tu* is used to express intimacy or more rarely condescension, and the second person plural *vous* to convey social distance or respect. Furthermore, deeper cognitive factors seem to be involved (Siewierska 2013). One possible explanation offered by Brown (1965) is that plurality is a natural metaphor for social power: in the light of subsequent research on cognitive metaphors and the metaphorical basis of grammar, this explanation seems to be more convincing than when it was originally advanced. Another possible explanation is offered by Brown and Levinson (1987) who consider the use of second person plural forms to be a type of impersonalizing device. It is possibly significant that other genetically and areally unrelated languages show a similar pattern, such as Amharic, Mande, Shona, Yoruba (in Africa); Bengali, Indonesian, Khasi, Malayalam, Nepali, Persian, Telugu (in south and south-east Asia); Eastern Pomo, Navajo (in the Americas); Djaru, Ngiyambaa (in Australia).

Driven by language contact with French with its V-form used for addressing people of higher social status, English speakers in contact with Normans started to use second person plural pronoun *you*. In Middle English, 2SG *thou* inherited from Old English and used for any interlocutor became restricted to dialogues among interlocutors standing on an equal footing. In contrast, respect could be expressed by using the originally second person plural form *you* for a single addressee. Contact among the cultures and the two languages and their varieties staying remaining diglossic (Schneider 2017; on language contact triggering the inclusion of new address terms, see Helmbrecht 2013), politeness became part of the English address system. Finally, the English system lost its ancient term *thou* and the related differentiation according to the status of the interlocutor and reverted to an egalitarian way of addressing people by using just one pronoun: *you* representing 'you.PL.FAM', 'you.SG.HON', and 'you.SG.FAM'. Simon (2003: 110; on German: Hickey 2003) usefully presents the rise and fall of the category 'politeness' by means of an instructive graph on the bottom of which a rhomboid form with six positions represents the basic person–number system. The vertical axis refers to the three persons, the first and the second anchoring the speech act in the *origo*, the latter present in the address system, and the third person which may be understood as non-person (Benveniste 1956). The horizontal axis contrasts the two numbers, singular and plural. Upgrading the dimension of respect above the positions of the second person the new category of 'politeness' is integrated flipped open above the basic system of personal pronouns. Changes of this kind are also detectable in other contexts of language contact, namely in the case of the multiple Spanish varieties spoken in the Americas. There is a very rich field of ongoing research focusing on the use of address pronouns and other means of expressing (im)politeness in the Spanishes of the Americas (Moyna and Rivera-Mills 2016; including Brazilian Portuguese: Lopes and Couto 2011; Lehmkuhl et al. 2018). In fact, the divergence from the European Peninsular patterns and later on from Latin American routines, some of them representing national norms, belong to two different migration movements.

First, after more than four hundred years under Spanish rule, there is a huge variety in the way forms of address are used in the different Spanish speaking countries of Latin America. As a general rule, the closer the relations to the Spanish colonizer were from the beginning (e.g., from the turn of the fifteenth to the sixteenth centuries) including interlocutors travelling to and from the cities of the New World back to Europe on a regular basis, the more closely they express themselves according to the courtly or bourgeois Peninsular norm of their time. This is true for the Vice-Kingdoms of New Spain, led by Mexico and its capital, and of Peru, prominently by the society of Lima (Moser 2015).

On the other hand, peripheral spaces such as Argentina show more divergence, which did not change after the country became a viceroyalty in the late eighteenth century. While the systems discussed above mirror the opposition between informal *tú* 'you.SG.FAM', and *usted* 'you.SG.HON' following European usage, the Spanish spoken west of the River Plate generalizes the use of *vos* 'you' (Fontanella 1987; Ferrari 2015; Bertoletti 2016). However, 'the standardization of *voseo* [the use of *vos*] in the Spanish of Buenos Aires occurred only in the second half of the twentieth century' (Ferrari 2015: 265), changing the address form *vos* into a national symbol, another form of social marker.

Speakers of Spanish in Uruguay as in Chile and in parts of Colombia (namely in Bogotá), conventionalized a paradigm of three pronouns of address: *tú*, *vos*, and *usted* (Moser 2015; Rivadeneira Valenzuela 2016): 'the existence of three distinct forms, something unusual in Romance and other European languages, has led to complex patterns of variation and change that have become traits of national, regional and social identity' (Le Page and Tabouret-Keller 1985; Edwards 2009; Moyna and Rivera-Mills 2016: 3). In contrast to Argentina, among Chileans *usted* 'you.SG' is the unmarked choice. However, '[i]n Chile, the pronoun *tú* ['you' singular, male, elite, formal] is used by speakers in the higher end of the socio-cultural spectrum and in more formal styles, while *vos* 'you' [singular, confidential] is reserved for strictly intimate situations' (Ferrari 2015: 264; glosses added). Note the accumulation of the features represented in the glosses. The data for the use of *tú* seems to be based on dialogues among men only, but the relevance of gender for this peculiar practice needs to be confirmed by future research. Another paradigm showing three levels of formality is used in Uruguay. While one of the pronouns expresses a confidential relationship among the interlocutors, i.e., intimate *vos* 'you' [singular, confidential], opposed to closeness *tú* 'you' [singular, familiar], and formal *usted* 'you'[singular, honorofic], 'in which *vos* and *tú* are distinguished on the basis of sociolect [or] register ..., even though *voseo* is catching on among the young (Di Tullio 2010)' (Ferrari 2015: 264; glosses added). In Colombia there is a copresence of different combinations of the pronouns of address revealing diatopic variation among regions, sometimes even being distinguishable at local level. And again, the gender of the interlocutors plays an important role. 'Based on the findings of a survey carried out in the city of Bogotá on young university students, [Bartens 2003] concludes that there are substantial differences across genders. Men range from distance *ustedeo* to *tuteo* to familiarity or closeness *ustedeo*' (Ferrari 2015: 274). Compare *usted de cariño* '*usted* of affection' (Kluge 2016: 331); 'polysemous' *usted* (Moser 2015); use of *usted* to calm children, see Section 25.3.1). 'Women use distance *ustedeo*, but in symmetrical familiarity relationships mostly *tú*' (Ferrari 2015: 274).

In order to understand the availability of the term *vos* (< Latin UOS) for the development of the address systems in Latin America, one has to take into consideration the first century of encounters there. 'By the fifteenth century, *vos* has become so close in value to informal *tú* that new deferential forms of address are experimented with, based on abstract nouns, imported from the lexicon, such as *merced* 'grace', *señoría* 'lordship', etc.' (Penny 1992: 124). In Spain in the Early Modern period, speakers finally decided on the first of these nouns preceded by the possessive pronoun *vuestra* 'your' (Penny 1992; 2000). Interestingly, this innovation of addressing powerful people with the nominal form *vuestra merced* 'your grace' was never adopted by the Judaeo-Spanish speech community (Penny 1992).

However, in the Americas use of the collocation *vuestra merced*, which might be considered a formulaic expression, became more and more frequent and developed into shorter forms such as *vuesarced* > *voacé* > *vucé* (Penny 1992: 124f.) and even *vo*. For this most shortened form, probably highly frequent in spoken language use, there is even written evidence in Mexican letters of the seventeenth century onwards (Sans-Sánchez 2016). While in some places, finally *vos* became part of the paradigm of forms of address, European Spanish conventionalized *usted* from the sixteenth century onwards. In a similar way, Portuguese developed intermediate forms based on *vossa merced* 'your grace' > *vossemecê* > *vosmecê* > *você* 'you.SG.HON', *você* representing modern usage.

In other parts of the lusophone world, in the fifteenth to seventeenth centuries along the coast of West Africa and up the *Rios de Guiné*, speakers of different European origin (some of them Portuguese) and Africans started to create intermediate forms based on the nominal forms *o senhor* 'mister', *a senhora* 'lady', respectively. Some sources indicate the use of respectful *Nha* 'you.FSG.HON' for addressing a woman leader (*a senhora* 'lady'; cf. *nhára:* Lang, Brüser, Santos, Dengler, and Blum 2002: 486; cf. *nháraship* Brooks 2003). Kabuverdianu spoken on the islands of Cape Verde provides evidence for its use (*Nha* Lang et al. 2002: 485) and for the contrasting form for addressing respectfully a powerful man *Nho* 'you.MSG.HON' (Lang et al. 2002: 486). Both forms must be considered as part of the emerging paradigm of pronouns of this lusophone variety which is used as lingua franca and subsequently as first language in the case of the African-European offspring born on the continent or on one of the islands (Brooks 2003; Dakubu 2012; Jungbluth

2018). In several places on the continent, matrilinear structures determined the social practice. From a typological point of view, introducing second person pronouns based on the gender of the addressee is not widespread and seems to be unique among the Atlantic Creoles, and unknown among the Asian varieties of Portuguese (Cardoso 2016; cf. Jungbluth 2015).

Unlike Latin, where respect is not expressed by the choice of pronouns, European Spanish introduced *usted* in the singular and *ustedes* in the plural as pronouns for addressing people viewed as being in positions of power with respect to the speaker. In the Americas, *ustedes* replaces the second person plural pronouns *vosotros* and *vosotras* for addressing males and females respectively, thereby neutralizing the distinction of gender in the plural. However, in the singular some varieties spoken in Uruguay, Chile, and parts of Colombia spell out the differences of power more precisely by integrating an intermediary level *vos* between *tú* and highly respectful *usted*.

Two stages of language change, from Latin to the Ibero-Romance languages and from there to the Spanish varieties of Latin America, show the inclusion of politeness as a category of the address system in different parts of Latin America. Other social differentiations may determine the choices from within paradigms contrasting three terms. Research has identified the related uses of *voseo, tuteo,* and *ustedeo* (Moser 2015). In all these uses changes are taking place which may lead to apparently 'polysemous' terms in terms of politeness, in that earlier distinctions disappear. In Mexico, for example, beside an honorific use of *usted* in formal contexts, semi-formal and even informal uses are also found (Moser 2015: 291). Beside more or less formal registers, where semi-formal contexts may be discerned, in the paradigms the following social features are conventionalized: 'confidence' is most frequently expressed, and sometimes gender and membership of a certain social class become important social markers. Thus:

Lat. TU 'you.SG' > Sp. *tú* 'you.SG.FAM' (Spain, Canary Islands) > *tú* 'you.SG.FAM' (Mexico and Central America; Antilles, Venezuela, Colombia) / 'you.SG.HON ([semi-]formal)' (Mexico: Guadalajara) / 'you' (singular, male, elite, formal) (Chile);

Lat. UOS 'you.PL' > OSp. *vos* 'you.SG.HON' > Sp. *vosotros* 'you.MPL.FAM'; *vosotras* 'you.FPL.FAM.' / *vos* 'you' (Argentina) / *vos* 'you.SG 'confidential' (Chile) / 'you.SG 'intimate' (Uruguay)/ *vos* 'you.FAM' (Costa Rica, Nicaragua, Guatemala, Paraguay);

OSp. *vuestra merced* 'your grace' > Sp. *usted* 'you.SG.HON' and *ustedes* 'you.PL.HON' (Argentina, Costa Rica, Nicaragua, Guatemala, Paraguay, Mexico, Peru, Chile, Uruguay, Colombia, parts of El Salvador and Honduras).

A third stage of change, roughly four hundred years later, takes place with migration from Latin America to the United States. Today, Spanish is recognized as the largest minority language of the USA. In the new neighbourhoods, speakers from different countries of South and Central America live and work side by side. The accommodation which takes place among speakers of different Spanish mother tongues, and in close contact with American English, shows once again the importance of prestigious forms. Their use in social settings does much for the image and prestige of the speaker. Interestingly, Argentinian *vos*, proudly used by those who originate from Buenos Aires and area who are known to be economically quite successful in their country of destination, is adapted by fellow residents of different origin (Sorenson 2016: 172f.). Short-term accommodation among individual speakers may end up as long-term accommodation among entire speech communities (Giles, Coupland, and Coupland 1991; Kerswill 2002: 680; Sorenson 2016: 191). In other places, migrants from El Salvador seek to pass as Mexicans by using *tú* instead of *vos* (Woods and Rivera-Mills 2012; cf. Benavides 2003), hoping thereby to mislead those in authority. People from Nicaragua who used *vos* in their homeland are observed to converge towards Cuban *tú* in the USA and Salvadoreans accommodate to Mexican *tuteo* ('Mexican-oriented Salvadoran immigrants' Woods and Shin 2016: 317–19), e.g., the generalized use of *tú* (Moyna and Rivera-Mills 2016: 238). Findings on the use of second person address in letters written in New Mexico show that its transfer to the US after 1848 is mirrored in new choices in favour of *usted*, three instances of plural *ustedes* having been discovered even for the period 1850–99 (Sanz-Sánchez 2016: 71), beside several instances of *tú*. In the seventeenth and eighteenth centuries, under Spanish dominion, neither of these pronouns were used, but the senders chose *Vuestra señoria* 'your.lordship' and *Vuestra merced* ('your.grace') instead. Thus:

> *tú* 'you.SG.FAM' (Mexico and Central America; Uruguay, Antilles, Venezuela, Colombia) / 'you.SG.HON ([semi-]formal)' (Mexico: Guadalajara) > 'you.SG.FAMI' USA Miami: Cuban and Nicaraguan speech community (Alonzo 2016); USA Texas: Mexican and El Salvadorean speech community;
> *vos* 'you' (Argentina) / *vos* 'you.SG (confidential)' (Chile, Uruguay); *vos* 'you. SG.FAM' (Argentina, Costa Rica, Nicaragua, Guatemala, Paraguay) > *vos* 'you' USA Texas: Argentinian and El Salvadorean speech community;
> *usted* 'you.SG.HON' and *ustedes* 'you.PL.HON' (Argentina, Costa Rica, Nicaragua, Guatemala, Paraguay, Mexico, Peru, Chile, Uruguay, Colombia, parts of El Salvador and Honduras) > USA, New Mexico: used by several Spanish speaking communities there.

These findings are in line with changes observed in many other languages of the world:

> The uneven distribution of politeness distinctions in pronouns across the languages of the world suggests that there are other conditioning factors that have to be taken into account. Language contact and the social and

cultural disposition to adopt linguistic means which are used to express politeness in neighboring languages that have a high prestige seem to be more important as a determining factor than the general functional background of polite language use. It is this social and cultural disposition of the adopting society which is responsible for the selection of certain forms as politeness forms. (Helmbrecht 2013)

As data from Romanian show (Section 25.3.3) neither the boundaries between Slavonic and Romance nor, looking at Middle English, between Romance and Germanic, constitute significant barriers.

25.5 Conclusion

Forms of address are by their very nature closely intertwined with personal interaction, and social markers play a major role in these encounters. The Latin paradigm of personal pronouns showing six forms – wherein the personal pronoun of second person singular, the T-form 'you', merely refers to any single interlocutor without distinction – could be considered as not being socially marked at all. However, when speakers start to use the second person plural pronoun, V-form 'you.SG.HON', to express respect towards a single interlocutor, this practice not only affects the second person plural pronoun, which becomes ambiguous for number, but also the former general second person singular pronoun, which receives an unprecedented social marker of familiarity. Instead of changing the pragmatics of personal pronouns of second person plural, some Romance languages used personal pronouns of third person singular in order to address their interlocutors showing respect: It. *Lei* / Sp. *usted* / Cat. *vostè*. In some languages, such as French, this usage of the third person singular form is also found, but it is still not conventionalized (Section 25.3.2).

What may be most striking is the fact that several Romance languages spoken in different continents started to integrate the gender of the addressee as a feature of the second person honorific pronoun: several varieties spoken in northern Italy (e.g., Lmb. *Lü/Le(e)*; Section 25.3.2), Portuguese-based Kabuverdianu *nho* : *nha* (Section 25.4). Other social markers, even combinations of them, may determine the choices people make among several terms. Interestingly, the pronouns may switch places with regard to grades of respect or confidence expressed. Whereas everyone uses *usted*, men of the upper class in their formal meetings in Chile use *tú* as an in-group marker of confidence, while women in Chile are observed to use *vos* in relations of confidence. In contrast, *vos* in Catalan is used for addressing older people (Section 25.3.2), while the more frequent pronouns *tu* and *vostè* are used for close or more distant relations, the latter expressing respect.

Forms of address have different functions. First, address forms in subject position do not always reduce or eliminate ambiguity, as exemplified by the high rate of the use of *vos* despite having non-ambiguous verb morphology compared to subjects in *tuteo* varieties (Erker and Guy 2012). Obviously, in some contexts, *vos* is treated as a form of recalling the addressee in order to reinforce his attention. Second, subtle differences may determine the use of second person forms. For example, Costa Ricans use *tú* with a referential function which is unmarked, whereas the address form *vos* expresses confidence among peer group members. In contrast, the use of *usted* must be considered neutral (Michnowicz et al. 2016; Quesada Pacheco 1996: §57.4). Third, it must be emphasized that usage in the capitals or other big cities often diverges from that of rural areas (Sections 25.3.2, 25.4). While people from Guadalajara consider *tú* to be formal, in other parts of Mexico it is considered informal (Moser 2015). Finally, cross-linguistic research on pronominal address shows that extra-linguistic variables play an important role, turning simple forms of address into social markers, and there are always some more added to the list of factors: social position, relative authority, group membership, generation, age, gender of speaker and of addressee, relationship between the interlocutors, kinship, genealogical distance, social network, etc. (Pinkerton 1986: 690; Rivera-Mills 2016).

Of course, social context and the language variety are important, aside from other linguistic factors such as semantic features of lexical items (Section 25.3.1), frequency of the forms, speech act type, and subject pronoun expression. Furthermore we should take into consideration also the 'discursive significance of forms of address ... not only as constituted by, but actively helping to constitute, the moment-by-moment negotiation of identity and context in the everyday lives of speakers' (Raymond 2016: 663).

There is much research on forms of address which displays spectacular differences of address systems even in closely related language varieties. Treating people on an equal footing may lead to a reduction of forms of address. As shown by the example of Cuba during Fidel Castro's leadership where members of the political movement and subsequently citizens of the nation, *los compañeros*, addressed each other usig *tú* (T), or the Sandinista Revolution in Nicaragua generalizing the use of *vos* (T), as well as trade unions such as the *comisiones obreras* ('workers' commissions') in Spain using *tú* (T) as a symbol of solidarity, political views may have a major impact on choices and frequencies of forms of address. Adolescents experience choices different from those which characterize the speech of older speakers (Sections 25.3.1, 25.3.2). Research has only just started (Section 25.4) on processes of divergence and convergence accelerated by repeated migration and their influence on the changes of address forms, and we still need to complete the picture of language use in plurilingual societies. It is without doubt fascinating 'how the ... choices (of address forms) work to shape identity and community both in the United States as well as in Latin America' (Rivera and Mills 2016: 336) and in other speech communities all over the world.

Selected References

Below you can find selected references for this chapter. The full references can be found online at the following page: www.cambridge.org/Romancelinguistics

Adams, J. (2013). *Social Variation and the Latin Language*. Cambridge: Cambridge University Press.
Brown, R. and Gilman, A. (1960). 'The pronouns of power and solidarity'. In Sebeok, T. (ed.), *Style in Language*. Cambridge, MA: MIT Press, 253–76.
Dakubu, E.K. (2012). 'The Portuguese language on the Gold Coast, 1471–1897', *Ghana Journal of Linguistics* 1: 15–33.
Ferrari, L. (2015). 'Spanish varieties of Latin America 1: South America'. In Jungbluth, K. and Da Milano, F. (eds), *Manual of Deixis in Romance Languages*. Berlin/Boston: De Gruyter, 258–78.
Helmbrecht, J. (2013). 'Politeness distinctions in pronouns'. In Dryer, M. S. and Haspelmath, M. (eds), *The World Atlas of Language Structures Online*. Leipzig: Max Planck Institute for Evolutionary Anthropology. http://wals.info/chapter/45.
Jungbluth, K. (2015). 'Creoles'. In Jungbluth, K. and Da Milano, F. (eds), *Manual of Deixis in Romance Languages*. Berlin/Boston: De Gruyter, 332–56.
Jungbluth, K. and Da Milano, F. (eds) (2015). *Manual of Deixis in Romance Languages*. Berlin/Boston: De Gruyter.
Jungbluth, K. and Vallentin, R. (2015). 'Brazilian Portuguese'. In Jungbluth, K. and Da Milano, F. (eds), *Manual of Deixis in Romance Languages*. Berlin/Boston: De Gruyter, 315–31.
Kluge, B. (2016). 'Forms of address and community identity'. In Moyna, M. and Rivera-Mills, S. (eds), *Forms of Address in the Spanish of the Americas*. Amsterdam/Philadelphia: John Benjamins, 325–33.
Ledgeway, A. (2015). 'Varieties in Italy'. In Jungbluth, K. and Da Milano, F. (eds), *Manual of Deixis in Romance Languages*. Berlin/Boston: De Gruyter, 75–113.
Lopes, C. R. S. and Couto, L.R. (eds) (2011). *As formas de tratamento em português e em espanhol: variação, mudança e funções conversacionais*. Niterói: Editora da UFF.
Siewierska, A. (2013). 'Gender distinctions in independent personal pronouns'. In Dryer, M. S. and Haspelmath, M. (eds), *The World Atlas of Language Structures Online*. Leipzig: Max Planck Institute for Evolutionary Anthropology. http://wals.info/chapter/44.
Stavinschi, A. (2015). 'Romanian'. In Jungbluth, K. and Da Milano, F. (eds), *Manual of Deixis in Romance Languages*. Berlin/Boston: De Gruyter, 17–44.

26

Information Structure

Silvio Cruschina, Ion Giurgea, and Eva-Maria Remberger

26.1 Introduction

This chapter sets out to explore the interplay between word order alternations and pragmatic-discourse factors that are traditionally subsumed under the concept of information structure, namely, the way in which information is updated and organized – 'packaged', metaphorically speaking – within a sentence according to contextual conditions and to the background knowledge of the interlocutors (see Halliday 1967; Chafe 1976; Lambrecht 1994). Focus and topic are central notions of information structure, fundamental to understanding syntactic and prosodic readjustment processes in many languages. Despite their central role in the analysis of different grammatical phenomena, and the significant advances in the last decades, several questions remain open, such as the relationship between focus and newness, as well as topic and givenness, the 'aboutness' nature of topics, the grammatical correlates of different types of focalization and topicalization constructions, the linguistic reflexes of different types of focus and topic, and the interaction between focus and topic, on the one hand, and subjects on the other.

The Romance languages have played a prominent role in the research on these issues. In fact, work on Romance has contributed extensively to our current empirical understanding of the grammatical phenomena related to information structure and to the theoretical analyses of the encoding of information-structure notions in the grammar and at the interfaces. With respect to these phenomena, the Romance family shows a broadly homogenous behaviour, but at the same time offers insights into a range of microvariation. In what follows, thus, we will present a few significant developments and achievements in the relevant research on the Romance languages with respect to the above-mentioned issues.

26.2 Focus, Focalization, and Focus Types

26.2.1 Introduction

Starting with Benincà (1988), Cinque (1990), and Rizzi (1990), an important topic in Romance – and especially Italian – linguistics has been the distribution of focus within the sentence and, in particular, the syntactic operation that brings the focus constituent to a sentence-initial, preverbal position, which we will refer to as focus fronting. A foundational article in this field is Rizzi (1997), which breaks up the earlier simple complementizer phrase CP into a sequence of functional projections that directly encode topic and focus features in the phrase structure (1) (for further refinements, see Rizzi 2001; 2004; cf. also Section 1.2.3.3). Under this view, the fronted focus moves to a dedicated left-peripheral focus position, namely the specifier of FocP (SpecFoc), in order to satisfy the Focus-Criterion (see also Brody 1995; Benincà 2001).[1]

(1) [ForceP Force [TopP XP [Top^{REC} [FocP YP [Foc [TopP ZP [Top^{REC} [FinP Fin [TP T ...]]]]]]]]]
     Credo [ForceP che [TopP a Gianni [FocP QUESTO, [TopP domani [FinP Ø [TP gli
     think.1SG   that to Gianni   this   tomorrow   CL.DAT=
     dovremmo   dire]]]]]]. (It.; adapted from Rizzi 1997: 295)
     should.1PL   say
     'I believe that to Gianni, THIS, tomorrow we should say.'

Raising to SpecFoc is a scope-marking phenomenon, implementing a focus-background partition (the complement of the Focus head constitutes the background).

Rizzi (1997) pointed out several syntactic differences between focus fronting and topicalization, which support a dichotomy between 'quantificational A'-dependencies' (focus fronting and wh-movement) and 'non-quantificational A'-dependencies' (i.e., topicalization; see also Section 26.3). Focus fronting is unique (whereas topic movement can be iterated), and does not show clitic resumption, which is often obligatory with topic movement.[2] Focus fronting competes with wh-fronting – focus fronting and wh-fronting are therefore incompatible with each other (whereas topics and wh-fronting can co-occur) – and similarly shows the so-called weak crossover effects (whereas topics do not). Bare quantifiers can be focus-fronted, but they cannot be left-dislocated by topic dislocation

---

[1] A 'Criterion' in the sense of Rizzi (1996; 1997; 2006) is the requirement that a phrase with feature [F] must be in a Spec-head configuration with a functional head carrying the same feature F. Criteria have been proposed for A'-movement (wh-movement, focus and topic fronting; but see Section 26.4.2 for the proposal for a Subject Criterion) and are tied to interpretation, indicating the scopal domain of a specific category (e.g., the phrase in SpecFoc is interpreted as focus and its complement as the background of a Focus-Background partition).

[2] This does not hold in Romanian, where definite, specific indefinite, and D-linked quantificational fronted objects are obligatorily clitic-doubled. See Dobrovie-Sorin (1990; 1994).

(this claim has been disputed by some scholars, see Section 26.3.4, examples 32–33).

Another line of studies has investigated the relation between focus and intonation (see Cinque 1993; Costa 1998; Zubizarreta 1998; Frascarelli 1999; 2000; Frota 2000). Syntax and prosody are brought together by Zubizarreta (1998), who proposes that Spanish and Italian, unlike Germanic languages, make use of movement in order to achieve the compliance between the 'nuclear stress rule' (default prominence assignment) and the requirement of placing prosodic prominence on the focus. Zubizarreta distinguishes two types of discourse-related movement operations: feature-driven movement to sentence-peripheral positions and prosodically conditioned movement (p-movement), which changes the basic order in the postverbal domain.[3] Zubizarreta's (1998) analysis relies on a distinction between 'neutral' or non-contrastive focus, which does not allow exceptions to the nuclear stress rule and thus may trigger p-movement, and contrastive/emphatic focus, which overrides the default prominence placement rule, allowing destressing of postfocal material (this type of focus is manifested in non-final in-situ foci and in fronted foci).

26.2.2 Focus and New Information

In Romance syntax, the notion of 'focus' has been used to account for certain marked word order patterns. Besides focus fronting, these patterns include certain non-canonical orders in the postverbal domain, in particular the postverbal placement of the subject (see Section 26.4.3). In order to understand the pragmatic conditions associated with these syntactic configurations, it is important to distinguish several notions: focus, new information, and several sub-types of focus.

Focus is traditionally described as 'new information' (the informative, non-presupposed part of an utterance), but there are reasons to distinguish between the notions 'new' (defined in opposition to 'given') and 'focus' (see Krifka 2006; Féry and Samek-Lodovici 2006; Selkirk 2008; Beaver and Clark 2008; Rochemont 2013; 2016). To take an example, in the second sentence of (2), the 'we went' part represents 'given' information, referring back to the trip introduced in the previous sentence. Nevertheless, there is no salient antecedent in the context for the open proposition 'λx.we went (to Italy) by using x'. Therefore, under Rooth's (1985; 1992) alternative-based theory of focus, as well as Schwarzschild's (1999) givenness-based theory of focus, this sentence does not contain a narrow focus on 'by car', although this is the only 'new' part (in Schwarzschild's system, the whole sentence

---

[3] For the idea that prosodic requirements – i.e., the focus-stress correspondence – may have a direct effect on syntactic structures and word order, see also Szendrői (2001; 2003) and Samek-Lodovici (2006).

qualifies as +F(ocus)). We may see that this observation correlates with the infelicity of using typically syntactic devices for marking narrow focus, such as focus fronting and clefts.

(2) a. Vara asta am călătorit în Italia. Am mers cu maşina.
summer.DEF this we.have travelled in Italy we.have gone with car.DEF
/ # Cu maşina am mers. (Ro.)
with car.DEF we.have gone
b. Cet été nous avons voyagé en Italie. Nous y sommes allés
this summer we have travelled in Italy we LOC= are gone
en voiture. / # C' est en voiture que nous y sommes allés. (Fr.)
in car it is in car that we LOC= are gone
'This summer we travelled to Italy. We went by car / # It's by car that we went.'

Conversely, given constituents may be under narrow focus, e.g., when they provide the answer (see *una calculadora* in 3b):[4]

(3) **Spanish**
a. ¿ María se compró una calculadora o un libro?
María REFL=buy.PST.3SG a calculator or a book
'Did María buy a calculator or a book (for herself)?'
b. María se compró **una calculadora**.
María REFL=buy.PST.3SG a calculator
'María bought a calculator (for herself).'

We will use the alternative-based definition of focus (Rooth 1985; 1992): 'focus indicates the presence of alternatives that are relevant for the interpretation of linguistic expressions' (Krifka 2007: 18). In this framework, sub-types of focus can be defined based on properties of the alternatives and the existence of certain presuppositions or implicatures (see Section 26.2.3).

The notion relevant for the postverbal placement of the subject in null-subject Romance languages, in sentences that are not all-new ('out-of-the-blue'), is novelty ('new') rather than focus, as can be seen in the possible continuation of the first sentence in (2a) given in (4). Here, the object is given and topicalized, but there is, again, no salient antecedent for the open proposition 'λx. x paid for the trip', therefore the postverbal subject is not a narrow focus:

(4) Călătoria ne-au plătit-o părinţii. (Ro.)
trip.DEF us.DAT=have.3PL paid=it parents.DEF
'Our parents paid for the trip.'

---

[4] In what follows, we mark narrow focus constitutents in bold face.

26.2.3 Focus Types and Focus Fronting

It has been observed that for focus fronting it is not sufficient that all the rest of the clause is given. Most studies make a distinction between information focus, which is not fronted, and contrastive focus, which may (although need not) be fronted (see Benincà 1988; Rizzi 1997; Frascarelli 2000; Belletti 2004; Bianchi and Bocci 2012; Bianchi 2013 for Italian; Zubizarreta 1998; 1999, López 2009 for Spanish; Göbbel 1998; É. Kiss 1998; Motapanyane 1998; Alboiu 2002 for Romanian; Costa and Martins 2011 for European Portuguese). The term 'information focus' does not clearly distinguish between 'focus' and 'new'. The criterion used for 'information focus' is the test of question–answer pairs (the sentence analysed is imagined as being the answer to a question). A sentence addressing a question raised in the previous discourse clearly displays focus in the alternative-based sense, having a salient antecedent. But the term 'information focus' can also extend to the new part of the sentences in (2)–(4), provided that discourse coherence is modelled by using implicit questions under discussion and information focus is defined in relation to such an implicit question (e.g., in the second sentence in (2), we can imagine a question under discussion 'how did you travel?'; in (4) – 'how did you pay for the trip?' or 'what can you tell me about the trip?').

Using the question–answer test, it appears that 'information' focus normally occurs postverbally, in sentence-final position (cf. 5–6). If the question is on the subject, answers containing a preverbal focal subject, such as that in (6), are judged as infelicitous in the given context, at least in Spanish, Italian, and European Portuguese (Zubizarreta 1998; 1999; Gutiérrez-Bravo 2008: 383; Belletti 2004: 21):

(5) **Spanish**
    Q ¿Qué compró Pedro?
        what bought Pedro
        'What did Pedro buy?'
    A1 Pedro compró **manzanas**.
        Pedro bought apples
    A2 #**Manzanas** compró Pedro.
        apples bought Pedro
        'Pedro bought apples.'

(6) **Italian**
    Q Chi ha parlato?
        who has spoken
        'Who spoke?'
    A1 Ha parlato **Gianni**.
        has spoken Gianni

A2   #**Gianni** ha parlato.
     Gianni has spoken
     'Gianni spoke.'

On the basis of this observation, Belletti (2001; 2004) proposes that the structure between the inflexional core of the sentence (IP) and the verb phrase (vP) – the so-called *v*P periphery – parallels that of the clause-external left periphery (cf. 1). In her analysis, the sentence-final new information focus targets a low focus position within this clause-internal periphery, which is also surrounded by topic positions that are specialized as landing sites for right-dislocated topics (see also Cecchetto 1999; Villalba 2000).

In French and Brazilian Portuguese, which are not null-subject languages and therefore have very restricted subject inversion, an information-focus subject can occupy the canonical preverbal position or – especially in the spoken languages – occurs in a cleft sentence (which is usually reduced, see 8A3; see Drijkoningen and Kampers-Manhe 2012; Kato and Martins 2016: 29f.):

(7)   **Portuguese**
      Q   Quem levou o meu laptop?
           who took the my laptop
           'Who took my laptop?'
      A1   Levou [o **ladrão**]$_{Focus}$ (EuPt./**BrPt.)
           took the thief
      A2   [O **ladrão**]$_{Focus}$ levou ele. (**EuPt./BrPt.)
           the thief took it
           'The thief took it.'

(8)   **French**
      Q   Qui dort?
           Who sleeps
           'Who's sleeping?'
      A1: **Jean** dort.
           Jean sleeps.
      A2   **Dort **Jean**.
           sleeps Jean
           'Jean is sleeping.'
      A3   C'est **Jean** (qui dort).
           it=is Jean who sleeps
           'It is Jean (who's sleeping).'

Interestingly, the cleft construction to mark information focus is not readily available for constituents other than subjects (9; Beyssade et al. 2004; Belletti 2005; 2007; 2009: 262):

(9) French
Q   Qu'est-ce-que tu   as   acheté?
    what   you= have   bought
    'What did you buy?'
A   **C'est **un livre** (que j'   ai   acheté).
    it=is   a   book   that I   have   bought

The contrastive type of focus, which allows focus fronting, is illustrated in (10):

(10) Cu trenul   merg   la mare,   nu   cu maşina. (Ro., Zafiu 2013: 575)
      by train.DEF go.1SG   to seaside not by car.DEF
      'It is by train that I go to the seaside, not by car.'

Using an alternative-based analysis of focus, 'contrastive focus' is defined as involving a closed set of contextually identifiable alternatives (É. Kiss 1998). If such contextually present alternatives are rejected, as in (10), the focus is corrective, a sub-type of contrastive focus.

Another special sub-type of focus which may license focus fronting is mirative focus (Cruschina 2012), which presents the sentence at hand as less expected than its focal alternatives. This type has first been proposed in order to account for the frequent use of focus fronting in Sardinian and Sicilian in non-contrastive contexts – along with focus fronting of new information focus (see 11; cf. Jones 1993; Cruschina and Remberger 2009; Remberger 2010; Cruschina 2012; 2015; 2016; 2021; Bentley 2008). Further studies have shown that this type is found, to various extents, in most Romance varieties (Cruschina 2012; 2019; Brunetti 2009; Jones 2013; Bianchi 2013; 2015; Remberger 2014; Bianchi, Bocci, and Cruschina 2015; 2016, Cruschina, Giurgea, and Remberger 2015; Jiménez-Fernández 2015a; 2015b; Giurgea 2015b; Cruschina and Remberger 2017):[5]

(11) a. **A machina** m'   arrubbaru! (Sic., Cruschina 2012: 71)
          the car   me= steal.PST.3PL
          'They stole my car!'
      b. **Unu figumoriscu** at   mandigadu   Giuanne! (Srd., Jones 2013: 81)
          a   prickly.pear   has   eaten   Giuanne
          'Gianni has eaten a prickly pear!'

---

[5] In the corpus-based studies by Sabio (1995; 2006) and by Abeillé, Godard, and Sabio (2008; 2009), cases of focus fronting similar to mirative focus have been described:

French
(i)   Tu   sais   ce   qui   est   arrivé? **Le candidat du patron**, ils   ont   refusé!
      you know   this that is   arrived the candidate of.the boss   they   have   refused
      'Do you know what happened? They refused the boss's candidate!'

(ii) **Trois heures** il   avait de   retard, le   train!
      three hours   it   had   of   delay   the   train
      'The train was delayed by three hours!'

(12) E   io che pensavo   che non avessero   nemmeno un soldo!
     and I   that think.IPF.1SG   that not have.SBJV.3PL   even   a   cent
     Indovina un po'?! **Alle** **Maldive** sono   andati in viaggio di nozze!
     guess   a   little to.the   Maldives   are.3PL gone   in journey of wedding
     'I thought they were penniless! Guess what! They went *to the Maldives* on honeymoon!' (It.; Bianchi, Bocci, and Cruschina 2016: 6)

Bianchi, Bocci, and Cruschina (2015; 2016) analyse the mirative import as the result of an association between the focus fronting operation and a conventional implicature that there is at least one focus alternative proposition that is more likely than the asserted proposition. This implicature explains the effect of surprise and unexpectedness that is often associated with focus fronting: a feature which distinguishes mirative focus from information and contrastive focus is the fact that the 'background' – the non-focused part of the sentence – is not necessarily given: indeed, mirative fronting can occur in out-of-the-blue contexts (cf. 11–12 above).

Further studies have shown that mirative focus fronting must be distinguished from another fronting operation that involves a similar prosodic marking (main stress on the fronted constituent), but is used to mark the sentence as exclamative (Cruschina, Giurgea, and Remberger 2015; Giurgea 2015b; see also Andueza 2011 for Spanish; Ambar 1999; Costa and Martins 2011 for Portuguese; in 13, capitals indicate the syllable associated with nuclear stress):

(13) [FruMOAsă rochie] a   cumpărat! (Ro.)
     beautiful   dress   has bought
     'What a beautiful dress (s)he bought! / That's a beautiful dress (s)he bought!'

This is a type of scalar exclamative, which must begin with a scalar word (an adverb or adjective; when adnominal, the adjective is placed DP-initially). Mirative focus fronting, on the other hand, does not interfere with sentence type: it may occur in declaratives (see 12) and also interrogatives (Giurgea and Remberger 2014; Bianchi and Cruschina 2016).

Besides these special types of focus where focus fronting is used, certain studies have argued that focus fronting can apply even if the focus is not contrastive or mirative, the only requirement being that the fronted constituent should be narrow focus rather than merely new (see Brunetti 2004; 2009 for Italian; Giurgea 2016 for Romanian). Regarding the question–answer test, Brunetti (2004) argued that the short answers, which are actually the most natural way of answering, involve focus fronting followed by deletion of the rest of the clause, due to the high degree of salience of the antecedent. Corpus research on Italian and Spanish (Brunetti 2009) and Romanian (Giurgea 2016) revealed that focus fronting can appear in answers, especially if the question is implicit or does not immediately precede the answer, or the answer uses a reformulation. Similarly, experimental data on different varieties of Spanish have recently shown that the preverbal position is not necessarily restricted to contrastive focus or emphasis, and that preverbal information foci are indeed accepted by native speakers (see Gabriel 2010; Hoot 2012; 2016; Vanrell and Fernández-Soriano 2013; 2018; Uth 2014; 2018; Heidinger 2015; 2018; Jiménez-Fernández 2015a; 2015b; Sánchez Alvarado 2018; Gutiérrez-Bravo, Sobrino, and Uth 2019).

A further special interpretive feature associated with non-mirative focus fronting is existential presupposition (there is a value for the focalized constituent for which the sentence is true), also known for English clefts (Akmajian 1970; Percus 1997): Bianchi and Cruschina (2016) note it for polar interrogatives, Giurgea (2016) argues that it is also present in declaratives, at least in Romanian:[6]

(14)   **Romanian**
    a.   Pe   ION   l-au   invitat?
         DOM Ion   him=have.3PL invited
         'Is it Ion they invited?' ⇒ 'There's somebody they invited.'
    b.   Pe   ION   l-au   invitat.
         DOM Ion   him=have.3PL invited
         'It's Ion they invited.' ⇒ 'There's somebody they invited.'

Some studies argued that verum focus can also be marked by special types of focus fronting, involving raising of the complex [V+T] head in Romanian and raising of a predicative phrase in Sardinian (see Giurgea and Remberger 2012b; 2014; Giurgea and Mîrzea-Vasile 2017; for Spanish, see also Leonetti and Escandell-Vidal 2009).

As for prosody, several studies have shown that distinctive prosodic properties may be associated with different types of focus, as well as with different focus domains, i.e., narrow vs broad focus (see Frota 2000; D'Imperio 2002; Hualde 2002; Donati and Nespor 2003; Avesani and Vayra 2003; 2004; Frascarelli 2004; Face and D'Imperio 2005; Bocci and Avesani 2006; 2011; 2015; Frota et al. 2007; Feldhausen et al. 2011; Beyssade et al. 2009; Estebas-Vilaplana 2009; Bocci 2013; Vanrell and Fernández-Soriano 2013; 2018; Prieto 2014; see Poletto and Bocci 2016 for an overview).

---

[6] Because N-words can be focus fronted, Giurgea (2016) proposes that the presupposition of focus fronting should be understood as a presupposition that at least one alternative is true, which, in affirmatives, amounts to an existential presupposition by virtue of the fact that all alternatives are affirmative.

26.2.4 Focus Types and Clefts

The focusing function of clefts has been acknowledged since the first analyses of clefts, even though their specific pragmatic characterizations may require the distinction of different information-structural sub-types (see, e.g., Dufter 2009). It is generally assumed that clefts do not simply encode a plain information focus but convey an exhaustive or contrastive interpretation (Lambrecht 2001; De Cesare 2017).[7] However, in French, cleft sentences can also be used for information focus, for focal subjects at least (cf. 8A3 above). A more direct relationship between postverbal focalization and clefts is proposed in Belletti (2005; 2007; 2009; 2012; 2015), who claims that the focal constituent of clefts targets the same syntactic projections for focus, depending on the pragmatic sub-type: information focus within the vP periphery, and contrastive focus within the CP.

Since they are both focus-marking devices, one may wonder what the relationship between focus fronting and clefts is: are they two alternative or two competing strategies for a similar pragmatic function? We find that the distribution and pragmatic characterization of focus fronting and clefts is not the same across Romance. On the one hand, Romanian lacks clefts altogether, resorting to focus fronting where other languages would use clefts. On the other hand, French and Portuguese prefer clefts: focus fronting in modern French is rather rare, being limited to specific registers (cf. n. 5); in Portuguese, the acceptability of contrastive focus fronting is subject to speaker variation (Costa and Martins 2011). Other Romance languages have both constructions at their disposal, but the specialization of either structure depends on many factors, including interpretation and register. To be sure, an important difference between the two consists in the fact that clefts are incompatible with mirative focus.

26.3 Topicalization Constructions and Types of Topics

26.3.1 Introduction

The notion of 'topic' is involved in several linguistic phenomena, pertaining to syntax, semantics, and phonology: certain marked word order patterns, involving displacement of a constituent ('topicalization'), certain dedicated constructions (e.g., *as for*-phrases), certain prosodic phenomena (see Jackendoff's 1972 'B-accent'), the presuppositional interpretation of definites (see Strawson 1964; Reinhart 1981), and anaphora resolution (see Reinhart 1981). The characterization of the notion of 'topic' involved in these phenomena remains largely controversial in the literature (see Roberts 2011 for a general overview). The pretheoretical notion of 'topic',

---

[7] On the issue of exhaustivity in focus fronting, see Brunetti (2004), Giurgea (2016).

which is essentially a discourse notion, as it can apply to portions of text/conversation larger than a single sentence – hence the name 'discourse topic' – is currently described using the notion of 'question under discussion', see Carlson (1983). But it is very often the case that the linguistic material that corresponds to the question under discussion does not coincide with the constituent syntactically marked as a topic – see (15), where the topicalized phrase (the object) represents only a part of the question under discussion, which is '?x. x informed Maria':

(15) **Romanian**
    a.   Cine   a   anunţat-o   pe   Maria?
        who   has informed=her DOM   Maria
        'Who informed Maria?'
    b.   Pe   Maria   a   anunţat-o   Ana.
        DOM Maria   has informed=her Ana
        'Maria was informed by Ana.'

As for the notion of 'sentence topic' – the notion relevant for displacement, as in (15), or for prosodic features such as B-accents – some studies define it using the notion of discourse topic, analysed as a case of question under discussion (see von Fintel 1994; van Kuppevelt 1995; Roberts 1996; Büring 1999; 2003). Against this view, an influential line of research, whose foundational article is Reinhart (1981), divorces sentence topic from discourse topic completely, defining sentence topic based on a notion of aboutness independent from both discourse topic and givenness. Following Strawson (1964), Kuno (1972), and Dik (1978) in considering the notion of aboutness as a primitive, Reinhart (1981) develops a formal implementation of this notion, viewed as a device for organizing the information which is exchanged and expanded during conversation (Stalnaker's 1978 'context set'): the topic provides a heading (or address) under which the information conveyed in the sentence is stored. The various propositions which have a referent as a topic thus build a sort of file card. Under this view, topics must be referential. For generic or quantificational noun phrases occupying topic positions, it is the kind or the set quantified over that is the aboutness topic. The only test for aboutness proposed by Reinhart is the possible paraphrase by '(S)he told about X that ...'. Topics trigger presuppositions of existence (Strawson 1964), but this does not mean that their existence must be given in the common ground of the conversation – they can be totally hearer-new (for a different view, see however Erteschik-Shir 1997; 2007). Reinhart's view was continued and further elaborated in Vallduví (1993), Erteschik-Shir (1997; 2007), Portner and Yabushita (1998), and Jacobs (2001).

The study of Romance languages has contributed to the debate concerning the nature of topics first of all because these languages have a rich array of dislocations which may be treated in terms of topicality (cf. also Section 27.2.3.2): thus, in addition to left-dislocation, they also have clitic right dislocation (ClRD).[8] Moreover, more than one dislocated phrase is allowed, in both peripheries, and left-dislocation may be accompanied by a resumptive clitic (ClLD) or not:[9]

(16) Catalan (Valldoví 1995: 128)
    a. El   ganivet$_1$, al   calaix$_2$, l$_1$'hi$_2$ FICAREM.
        the knife   in.the drawer   it=LOC=put.FUT.1PL
    b. L$_1$'hi$_2$ FICAREM,   el ganivet$_1$, al   calaix$_2$.
        it=LOC=put.FUT.1PL the knife   in.the   drawer
        'We'll put the knife in the drawer.'

Another phenomenon by which Romance has contributed to the general debate on the nature of topicality is the distribution of subjects, which is much more sensitive to pragmatic factors in null-subject Romance languages than in English. This issue will be discussed in Section 26.4. In what follows, we will concentrate on phrases which are indisputably topicalized, avoiding preverbal subjects, unless they precede a left-dislocated phrase, in which case they are certainly peripheral. The general conclusion that emerges from the study of Romance dislocations is that more than a single notion of 'topic' is involved in these phenomena.

26.3.2 Topic-Marking and Givenness-Marking

There is general agreement that, unlike left-dislocated phrases, right-dislocated phrases are necessarily given and cannot indicate topic shift (see Benincà 1988; Valldoví 1992; Lambrecht 1981; 1994; Villalba 2000).[10] In (17), we see a typical instance of topic shift; the preposed objects are D-linked (they are the two sons introduced in the first clause) but are not given (they are both discourse-new – they are not previously mentioned – and hearer-new – as the information about the existence of sons of Leo is conveyed by the first sentence, as new information). Moreover, they involve a partition of the discourse topic suggested by the first clause (Leo and his sons) into two sub-topics (the relation of Leo to Gianni and

---

[8] Except for Romanian, which seems to lack this construction.
[9] In Italian, given constituents can also appear to the right of the clause, after the nuclear stress, in a distinct intonational unit, without being accompanied by a clitic – the so-called 'marginalization'. Some authors analyse this construction as involving dislocation (Antinucci and Cinque 1977; Frascarelli 2000; Samek-Lodovici 2006; 2015), but Cardinaletti (2001; 2002) convincingly argues that marginalized objects are in situ.
[10] It has been noted that ClRD may sometimes introduce a discourse-new referent, but this referent is then presented by the speaker as shared knowledge (Berruto 1986; Benincà 1988; Ferrari 1999; Lambrecht 1981); for a weakening of the givenness requirement in questions, in Italian, see Crocco (2013).

his relation to Marco), which is characteristic of contrastive topics (see Büring 1999).

(17) **Italian (Frascarelli 2017: 476)**
Leo ha due figli.
Leo has two sons
'Leo has two sons.'
  a. Gianni$_i$, lo$_i$ incontra spesso, Marco$_j$, non lo$_j$ vede mai.
      Gianni him=meets often Marco not him=sees never
  b. #Lo$_i$ incontra spesso, Gianni$_i$, non lo$_j$ vede mai, Marco$_j$.
      him= meets often Gianni not him= sees never Marco
      'Gianni, he often meets while Marco, he never sees.'

An example where ClRD is acceptable is (18), where the object is previously mentioned and no contrast is involved:

(18) **Italian (Bocci 2013: 33)**
  a. È arrivato Marco. Sai chi l'ha invitato?
      is arrived Marco know.2SG who him=has invited
      'Marco has arrived. Do you know who invited him?'
  b. L'ha invitato Gianni, Marco.
      him=has invited Gianni Marco
      'Gianni invited him (, Marco).'

Given that in the case of topic continuity, the topic is normally realized as a weak pronoun or *pro*, topicalization is first of all a device used to signal topic shift (including contrastive topics, as in 17), something which probably holds across languages (see, e.g., Reinhart 1981 for English). From this perspective, the fact that the left periphery is used for topic shift and contrast in Romance is expected. It has been observed that even in an example such as (15), in which the preposed object is given and part of the question under discussion, the use of ClLD often suggests a contrast – here, between Maria and other people who were informed by somebody (see Arregi 2003; López 2009). Under this view, we may say that the function of ClRD is not to indicate topicality, but rather givenness. This idea is supported by the following observation: topicality, as argued in Reinhart (1981), is a relational notion, involving a split of the sentence into a Topic and a Comment. Therefore we expect topicalization to indicate overtly the scope of the topic, by making it a sister of the Comment (see Neeleman et al. 2009). However, this does not hold for right-dislocated phrases, as can be clearly seen in cases when the right-dislocated phrase is inside a syntactic island, and the new information (*conosco molta gente che gli vuole parlare* in 19), which should occur in the Comment, extends outside this island (a relative clause, see 19a; that topicalization obeys islands, and therefore the ClRD-ed phrase is inside the embedded clause, is shown by the impossibility of extracting it into the matrix by ClLD, see 19b):

(19) Italian (Frascarelli 2017: 494)
   a. Conosco [molta gente [che gli$_i$ vuole parlare, a Leo$_i$.]]
      know.1SG many people that DAT=wants talk.INF to Leo
      'I know many people who want to talk to Leo.'
   b. **A Leo$_i$, conosco [molta gente [che gli$_i$ vuole parlare.]]
      to Leo know.1SG many people that DAT=wants talk.INF

Another instance of topic position whose sister does not coincide with the Comment is the left-peripheral position below the fronted focus, a position available only in Italian and Catalan (cf. *el nen* 'the boy' in 20). Interestingly, this position does not support a contrast or shifted topic interpretation (see Frascarelli and Hinterhölzl 2007), leaving givenness as the only information-structural characterization of the concerned element:

(20) A DISNEYWORLD el nen portarem aquest estiu. (Cat.; Vallduví 1995: 132)
   to Disneyworld the boy take.FUT.1PL this summer
   'We'll take the boy to Disneyworld this summer.'

We may conclude that certain dislocations, in Romance, are not topic-marking devices but rather givenness-marking devices. Givenness, unlike aboutness, is defined on constituents independently on the relation with the rest of the sentence (see Reinhart 1981), so we expect that givenness-marking dislocations should not behave as scope-marking operations.

26.3.3 Different Types of Topics in the Left Periphery

We have seen that Romance languages allow multiple dislocations into the left periphery. Several studies (Benincà and Poletto 2004; Frascarelli and Hinterhölzl 2007; Bianchi and Frascarelli 2010) claimed that this is partly due to the existence of different types of topic positions, which are hierarchically ordered:

(21) Hanging Topics > Scene-Setting > Left Dislocated Topics > Listed Items > Focus ...
   (adapted from Benincà and Poletto 2004)

(22) Aboutness-shift Topic > Contrastive Topic > Focus > Familiar/Given Topic ...
   (Frascarelli and Hinterhölzl 2007; Bianchi and Frascarelli 2010)

Whereas Benincà and Poletto's classification includes syntactic properties, which will be discussed later (see Section 26.3.4), Frascarelli and Hinterhölzl's (2007) types are defined as distinct information-structural terms: aboutness topics (A-topics, cf. *această idee* 'this idea' in 23, *a mio fratello* 'to my brother' in 24) are defined as in Reinhart (1981); the preposed placement is correlated, in addition, with topic shift; C(ontrastive)-topics (cf. 17; *pe mine* 'on me' in 23) are defined as elements that introduce 'alternatives which have no impact on the focus value and create oppositional pairs with respect to other topics'; familiar topics, later labelled G(iven)-topics, (cf. *Marco* in 18b, *a Leo* 'to Leo' 19a, *el nen* 'the boy' in 20) are 'used to resume background information or for topic continuity'.[11] Bianchi and Frascarelli (2010) claim that these three types differ in the distribution in subordinate clauses: A-topics only occur in root-like embedded clauses, which are endowed with illocutionary potential, C-topics occur in subordinates with a propositional denotation, G-topics are unrestricted (thus, they are the only 'topics' allowed in certain adverbial clauses). They argue that the difference in acceptability of topic fronting in embedded clauses between English and Italian follows from the fact that English lacks G-topic fronting.

Here is an example of co-occurrence of left-peripheral topics:

(23) Această idee pe mine nu m-a convins. (Ro.)
 this idea DOM me not me=has convinced
 'This idea didn't convince me.'
 [Context: *this idea* refers to the previous sentence]

The sentence is understood as being about 'this idea', not about the speaker, so only the first topicalized phrase acts as an A-topic. This phrase is given, but it is new as a topic (in the imagined context, it refers back to the whole previous sentence, so it cannot be the topic of that sentence), so it qualifies as an 'aboutness-shift topic'. The second topicalized phrase, *pe mine*, is used to indicate a contrast between the speaker and other people, alluding to the fact that there are some people who have been convinced by that idea.

We have seen examples where the A-topic is given (example 23) or new but D-linked (example 17a). It can also be totally new, occurring at the beginning of a discourse:

(24) Sai? A mio fratello (gli) hanno rubato la moto. (It.; Brunetti 2009: 760)
 know.2SG to my brother DAT=have.3PL stolen the motorbike
 'You know what? My brother's motorbike was stolen.'

However, even here we have a link with the immediate context, by the speaker-referring possessive *mio* 'my' which occurs inside the definite description. It has been observed that new topics obey certain restrictions, being either familiar to the hearer or at least related to the context via their descriptive part (either explicitly as in 24, or via associative anaphora), so that the existence of the referent can be accommodated by the hearer (cf. Erteschik-Shir 2007 for topics in general, Benincà 1988; Brunetti 2009 for Italian; Giurgea 2017a for Romanian; Rizzi 2005; 2018 speaks of a D-linking condition; and López 2009 of an anaphoric feature; these latter conditions appear to be too strong).

---

[11] Furthermore, Frascarelli and Hinterhölzl (2007) claim that the three types of topics are prosodically distinct in Italian.

Frascarelli and Hinterhölzl (2007) claim that A-topics and C-topics are unique, whereas G-topics can be iterated. But it is not clear why more than one C-topic per clause should be impossible – actually, López (2009) claims that all left-dislocated phrases are contrastive.[12]

If A-topics are described along the lines of Reinhart (1981), phrases which mark them should be either referential or, at least, involve quantification over a set which functions as the actual A-topic. However, all kinds of non-referential phrases can be topicalized in Romance (non-specific indefinites, predicates, clausal projections, adverbs). Thus, under the threefold classification in (22), such phrases should either be C-topics or G-topics. However, Giurgea (2017b) proposes a different account: discussing Romanian, a language which lacks the Givenness-marking positions discussed in Section 26.3.2 (see the right-dislocated topics in 18, and 19a, and the topic below Focus in 20, see also n. 9), he argues that left-dislocation is used to indicate the connexion of the clause to the discourse topic, rather than mere givenness or aboutness: under this view, we do not expect any ban on non-referential topicalized phrases. Confirmation comes from the fact that non-referential topicalized phrases which are not contrastive are not always given, but may be merely context-linked (e.g., by containing a context-given part) or, exceptionally, even completely new. The latter obtains with elements which may indicate contextual relevance by themselves, without any link to the previous context, such as *interesant* 'interesting', *memorabil* 'memorable', *amuzant* 'funny' (see an attested example in 25). If topicalization is a means to indicate the dynamics of the discourse topic, such phrases are expected to be topicalized, as the discourse topic can always be enriched with the question under discussion 'what is worth of mentioning/interesting/amusing in the situation discussed?'

(25) Romanian (*Dilema*, n° 636, Giurgea 2017b)
Interesantă este distribuția pe rase a aderenței la noua lege.
interesting is distribution.DEF on races GEN adherence.DEF.GEN to new.DEF law
'What's interesting is the racial distribution of the adherence to the new law.'

Scene-setting constituents are often treated together with topics, but in fact they do not fit in the aforementioned typology of topics: the sentences they introduce are not about them, they do not need to be part of the question under discussion or to be given – deictic adverbs such as *domani* 'tomorrow' in (1) are arguably context-given, but scene-setting constituents can also be non-context-linked, see (26) (this example also shows a formal difference between topicalized locatives and scene-setting expressions, in Italian: the latter are not resumed by a locative clitic):

---

[12] For A-topics, multiple instantiation per sentence is allowed in Erteschik-Shir's (1997; 2007) system.

(26) **Italian (Frascarelli 2017: 488)**
[A Casal de'Pazzi], il traffico **(ci) sembra scorrevole.
at Casal de'Pazzi the traffic LOC=seems moving
'At Casal de'Pazzi, the traffic flow seems good.'

Some studies (Krifka 2007; Frascarelli 2017) treat these constituents, together with domain adverbials (e.g., *healthwise*), as 'frame-setting' expressions (Jacobs 2001), i.e., expressions that restrict the domain in which the following proposition should be evaluated along different dimensions. Giurgea (2017b) proposes that spatial and temporal adverbials which appear sentence-initially in all-new contexts have an 'anchoring' function:[13] as spatial and temporal locations are given in the shared world knowledge of the conversation participants, they can be used to anchor the new information in the common ground.[14]

26.3.4 Different Syntactic Constructions and Their Derivation

Romance ClLD must be distinguished from the Hanging Topic construction (HT).[15] In the latter, the topic phrase is clearly base-generated: it does not show prepositions or case marking, it can relate to an element inside a syntactic island,[16] it can be resumed by strong pronouns or epithets – the former two properties are illustrated in (27). Moreover, HT must be referential.[17]

(27) **Italian (Frascarelli 2017: 482)**
a. **A Luigi, Maria è andata via senza parlargli. (ClLD)
  to Luigi Maria is gone away without talk.INF=him.DAT
b. Luigi, Maria è andata via senza parlargli. (HT)
  Luigi Maria is gone away without talk.INF=him.DAT
  'Maria went away without talking to Luigi.'

The use of resumptive clitics with topicalized phrases varies across Romance along several parameters:

(i) Clitic inventory. Some languages have a larger array of clitics than others: a locative clitic and a 'partitive clitic' used for source PPs, genitives, bare NPs and plural/mass indefinites is only available in

---

[13] The term 'anchoring' has been used in the analysis of specific indefinites ('referential anchoring', see von Heusinger 2002).
[14] According to Klein (2008), sentences are evaluated with respect to a 'topic situation' (cf. Austin 1950), and topicalized expressions express parameters of the topic situation, helping the hearer to identify it (when this situation is not obvious from the context). As location in time and space are obligatory parameters of situations, it is expected that they may occur with a topic-like function.
[15] See Cinque (1983; 1990); Sauzet (1989); Villalba (2000); Benincà (2001); Delais-Roussarie, Doetjes, and Sleeman (2004).
[16] ClLD obeys island constraints, except for the wh-island, see Cinque (1990); Suñer (2006).
[17] Likewise, in the right periphery ClRD must be distinguished from afterthoughts, which are not syntactically integrated (cf. Lambrecht 1981; Ziv 1994; Villalba 2000; Crocco 2013).

Italo-Romance, Gallo-Romance, and Catalan, as well as in earlier stages of Spanish and Portuguese; a predicate clitic is available in these languages and, in addition, in Spanish and Portuguese; clitics for direct objects and datives are found everywhere;

(ii) Sensitivity to the type of movement. In Romanian, the use of clitics is not correlated with the type of displacement (topic, focus, or wh-) but only with specificity (direct object clitics occur iff the dislocated phrase is definite or a specific indefinite); in all the other languages, clitic resumption is characteristic of topicalization, being excluded with wh-movement and focalization (for some exceptions in Italian, see Benincà 1988; Benincà and Poletto 2004; Bocci 2007);

(iii) Specificity. Within languages that use ClLD for topics only, clitic resumption may still depend on specificity. Thus, Spanish does not use clitics with non-specific indefinites. Moreover, clitics may be obligatory or optional: with definite and specific direct objects, they are optional in Portuguese but obligatory everywhere else (the special behaviour of Portuguese is probably related to the fact that this language allows referential null objects; see Duarte 1987; Raposo 1998; Barbosa 2001);[18]

(iv) Syntactic category. In Italian and French, resumption is optional with PPs in general, including indirect objects; the construction without a clitic, called 'simple preposing', shows some interesting differences with respect to ClLD (Cinque 1990; Rizzi 1990; 2004; Cruschina 2010).

For dislocated subjects as in (23), one can assume a resumptive *pro* in null-subject Romance varieties, an assumption supported by the fact that non-null-subject Romance varieties such as French may occur with a resumptive weak pronominal subject in conjunction with topical subjects (see Lambrecht 1981 and de Cat 2007):

(28) [Context: Comment va ton frère? 'How is your brother?')
 Mon frère i-va bien. (coll. Fr., Lambrecht 1981: 63)
 my brother he=goes well
 'My brother is fine.'

Although it is generally agreed that ClLD instantiates a syntactic dependency (as opposed to HT),[19] there is an open debate on whether

---

[18] Certain registers of Italian allow the absence of clitic doubling for object topics where discourse-linking is not referential but resides in the descriptive part of the DP (e.g., *tale proposta* 'such a proposal'). This construction is known as 'resumptive preposing' or 'anaphoric fronting' (*anteposizione anaforica*) and shows a mix of focalization and topicalization properties (Benincà 1988; Cinque 1990; Benincà and Poletto 2004; Cardinaletti 2009; Leonetti and Escandell Vidal 2009). See, in particular, Cardinaletti (2009) for the idea that resumptive preposing targets an Aboutness-shift topic position but involves a type of movement characteristic of wh-items and foci.

[19] An exception is de Cat (2007), who claims that French dislocations are all HT-like, in that there is no evidence for a syntactic dependency (no islands or reconstruction). However, dislocated elements in French may contain prepositions, which cannot be interpreted in the surface position, and therefore must involve a dependency with the 'base' position.

movement of the topic phrase is involved (Cinque 1977; 1983; Rivero 1980; Dobrovie-Sorin 1990; 1994; Kayne 1994; Sportiche 1996; Cecchetto 2000; Villalba 2000; López 2009), or rather a different type of relation (chain formation without movement, according to Cinque 1990; chain formation mediated by an anaphoric operator Rizzi 1997;[20] 'Agree', according to Suñer 2006; Iatridou 1995 proposes base-generation in the periphery of the clause containing the clitic, and movement only for long-distance topicalization; in a similar vein, Zubizarreta 1998 proposes base-generation in the specifier of a functional projection in the clausal structure headed by the clitic). The facts invoked as arguments against movement are the presence of the clitic, the grammaticality with wh-islands, the absence of weak crossover effects, the impossibility of licensing parasitic gaps, and the free ordering and iteration of topicalized phrases (Cinque 1990).[21] The movement analysis is supported by the presence of prepositions and case markers in the dislocated phrase, which can only be licensed and interpreted in the base position (see 29–30),[22] by the possibility of dislocating parts of idioms, by the existence of island effects, and by reconstruction facts (see variable binding by a quantifier in 29 and fronting of an anaphor in 30):[23]

---

[20] Building on Lasnik and Stowell's (1991) analysis of English appositive relatives, Rizzi (1997) claims that in ClLD the base position is occupied by a 'null constant', instead of a variable (as in focus fronting and wh-movement). However, ClLD is possible with quantificational DPs, in which case it is not clear in what sense the trace can be considered a 'constant' (for Italian, see attested examples in Floricic 2013):

(i) Cada libro, **(lo) leyó Juan, y cada revista, **(la) leyó Pedro. (Arregi 2003: ex. 22)
    each book   it= read Juan and every magazine   it= read Pedro
    'Each book, John read, and each magazine, Pedro read.'

Arregi (2003) proposes that in ClLD, the clitic is interpreted as an individual (e-type) variable.

[21] Frascarelli (2004) argues for base-generation based on the absence of reconstruction for principle C of the binding theory (Chomsky 1981) in certain examples. However, in this type of example, absence of reconstruction for principle C has also been noticed for wh-movement in English by Lebeaux (1989), who analysed this phenomenon by assuming late adjunction (cf. Frascarelli 2004: n. 10). Suñer (2006) adds to these arguments the possibility of using epithets in the base position, in Rioplatense Spanish:

(i) A   mi mejor amiga, la vi   a   esa loca linda el jueves. (Suñer 2006: 130)
    DOM my best   friend her= saw.1SG DOM that crazy gal the Thursday
    'My best friend, I saw that crazy gal, on Thursday.'

However, it is not clear that such epithets cannot be analysed as parentheticals or afterthoughts. López (2009), in defence of the movement analysis, proposes that epithets are predicates, originating in a single constituent with the topicalized phrase, based on qualitative binominal constructions such as *ese tarugo de su hermano* 'that jackass of her brother'.

[22] Agree, proposed by Suñer (2006), can account for prepositions functioning as case markers (DOM and the dative preposition), but not for lexical prepositions which occur in ClLD, such as It. *in* 'in', *su* 'on', *sotto* 'under', Cat. *amb* 'with', *sobre* 'about'.

[23] It has been claimed that reconstruction targets a position lower than the preverbal subject but higher than the postverbal subject (cf. Zubizarreta 1998, who tests that with variable binding by a quantifier). Cecchetto (2000) reports principle C effects with a subject *pro* (cf. i.a), but not with a focalized postverbal (cf. i.b) or preverbal (cf. i.c) subject pronoun:

(29) A suo_i figlio credo che [ognuno_i di loro] finirà
      to his son   think.1SG that each of them end-up.FUT
      per lasciargli   un appartamento. (It., Cinque 1983, ex. 33)
      to leave.INF=3DAT an apartment
      'I believe that each of them will end up leaving an apartment to his son.'

(30) A sí misma, María no se quiere para nada. (Sp., López 2009: 219)
      DOM herself María not REFL= loves for nothing
      'María doesn't love herself at all.'

Note also that the correlation between topicalization and lack of weak crossover is not universal: thus, in Romanian, clitics are used with specific/D-linked wh-phrases and fronted foci, which correlates with absence of weak crossover effects (cf. Dobrovie-Sorin 1990; 1994).

The movement analysis of clitic dislocations impacts on the theory of clitics, which can no longer be viewed as mere alternative realizations of certain DPs or PPs. Some studies have proposed that clitics originate in a single constituent with the dislocated phrase, a so-called 'big DP' (Cecchetto 1999; 2000); others view the clitic as a verbal affix which agrees with the doubled phrase (López 2009), as a functional head in the verbal extended projection (Sportiche 1996), or as the spell-out of a lower copy, for antilocality reasons (Grohmann 2003).

The presence/absence of clitics depending on specificity is illustrated in the following contrast:

(31) **Romanian**
      a. Două probleme a   rezolvat fiecare. (∀ > 2)
         two problems has solved   each
      b. Două probleme le-a rezolvat fiecare. (2 > ∀)
         two problems them=has solved each
         'Two problems, everybody solved.'

In both cases, the topicalized phrase is D-linked – solving problems must occur in the previous discourse. The topicalized phrases may be analysed as

---

Italian (Cecchetto 2000: 96–99)

(i) a. L' opera prima di [uno scrittore]_i, pro_*i la scrive sempre (volentieri).
       the work first of a writer   (he) it= writes always with pleasure
       'The first work of a writer, he always writes (with pleasure).'
    b. L' opera prima di [uno scrittore]_i, la scrive sempre lui_i.
       the work first of a writer   it= writes always he
       'The first work of a writer is always written by the writer himself.'
    c. L' opera prima di [uno scrittore]_i, (solo) LUI_i la capisce veramente.
       the work first of a writer   only he   it= understands really
       'The first work of a writer is really understood only by the writer himself.'

Angelopoulos and Sportiche (2017) show that French ClLD displays reconstruction effects (contra de Cat 2007).

contrastive, realizing a partition in the discourse topic, but the sub-topics are distinct in the two examples. In (31a), what are contrasted are quantifiers: 'two problems' is contrasted with 'one problem', 'three problems', 'most problems', 'all problems' etc. To each alternative, a focus structure of the form {λx.how many students solved x} is associated. Correlatively, in (31a), the indefinite is non-specific and scopes below 'each'. In (31b), the contrast is between referents: 'two specific problems', contrasted with 'the other problems', or with other specific problems (cf. Rooth 2005). As in (31a), to each alternative, a focus structure of the form {λx.how many students solved x} is associated. Correlatively, in (31b), the indefinite is specific and scopes above 'each'.

The type of alternatives presented in (31a) arguably also underlies the bare quantifier fronting illustrated in (32):

(32) Algo   Juan sí   comió. (Sp., Arregi 2003: ex. 3)
     something Juan yes ate
     'Something Juan DID eat.'

As there is no D-linking or clitic resumption, this type (which has been documented for Italian, Spanish, Catalan, and Romanian) has been analysed as a *sui generis* type of movement (Cinque 1990; Quer 2002) or an instance of focalization (Zubizarreta 1998). However, the prosody (there is no focal stress on the quantifier; the nuclear stress tends to occur on the verb) and the possibility of intercalating a preverbal subject in Spanish and Romanian (see 32) show that this is not an instance of focus fronting. Arregi (2003) argues that in such cases the quantifier functions as a contrastive topic.[24] Building on this result, Giurgea (2015a) proposes an account for the fact that this construction is always accompanied by verum focus: he notes that the topic alternatives always yield stronger claims than the sentence at hand (e.g., in 32 they are 'whether John ate much', 'whether John ate all', 'whether John ate something specific', etc.); by highlighting these alternatives, the speaker insists on the fact that, although he is ignorant about these more informative possibilities, he is sure at least about the weaker claim he makes. Supporting evidence for the fact that the fronted quantifier corresponds to a weaker claim comes from negative contexts, where, as the implications are reversed, quantifiers such as 'all' and 'much' are used:

(33) Chiar   totul   NU ştie. (Ro.)
     exactly everything not knows
     '(S)he does NOT know everything.'

---

[24] Further evidence for a topic status comes from the possibility of using a resumptive clitic in Italian (keeping the non-specific, narrow scope reading), as shown and discussed in Floricic (2013):

(i) A quel prezzo **qualcosa lo** puoi   trovare. (It., Floricic 2013: 273)
    at that price something it= can.2SG find.INF
    'At this price, there is something you can find.'

Absence of resumptive clitics is also found with left-dislocated constituents placed between a fronted focus and the verb, in Italian and Catalan (G-Topics, see 20; cf. Benincà and Poletto 2004; Samek-Lodovici 2006). Samek-Lodovici (2006; 2015) analyses these constructions as involving multiple right-dislocated constituents (he assumes that the finite verb itself can be right-dislocated, as part of a remnant Tense Phrase).

26.4 Subject Placement

26.4.1 Introduction

Moving away from the predominant SOV order of Classical Latin, and through an alleged V2 stage in the medieval period, today most Romance languages show an unmarked SVO order (Benincà 2006; Ledgeway 2012: 69). However, several factors such as the argument structure of predicates, lexical-semantic properties of the verb, and the thematic prominence of arguments play a crucial role in the determination of the subject placement (see further Sections 16.2 and 18.6). In particular, the syntax of subjects in Romance tightly interacts with information structure. Most Romance varieties are null-subject languages with the 'free inversion' property (Rizzi 1982), which means that, despite their unmarked SVO nature, they allow postverbal subjects with any kind of verb, under conditions that are largely pragmatic. Not all postverbal subjects, however, are determined by information-structure properties: the postverbal subjects of wh-questions, for instance, must be attributed to independent syntactic constraints on preverbal subjects (see, e.g., Barbosa 2001; Cardinaletti 2007; 2009; Leonetti 2018). Right-dislocated postverbal subjects are also to be kept separate from postverbal subjects that result from subject inversion, inasmuch as they obey distinct contextual and pragmatic conditions (cf. Section 26.3.2).

Pragmatically determined subject inversion generally signals the non-topical status of the postverbal subject and is typically found in two contexts: in so-called thetic sentences, where the whole sentence contains new material (it is 'all-new', or 'broad focus') (cf. Section 26.4.3), and when the subject is a narrow focus or part of the new material of the clause (cf. Section 26.4.3; see also Section 26.3.2). In this section, we concentrate on the information-structure conditions and properties that license the postverbal placement of the subject in the clause (cf. Section 26.4.3). But before moving to these aspects, let us briefly review the existing theories about the status of preverbal subjects in Romance (cf. Section 26.4.2).

26.4.2 Status of Preverbal Subjects

The generalization that postverbal subjects are non-topical may lead to the conclusion that, unless fronted through focus fronting, preverbal subjects, at least in null-subject languages, are always topics sitting in a dedicated left-peripheral position. This has indeed been proposed by several authors (Contreras 1991; Solà i Pujols 1992; Dobrovie-Sorin 1994; Barbosa 1995; 2000; 2001; Olarrea 1996; Cornilescu 1997; Alexiadou and Anagnostopoulou 1998; Ordóñez 1998; Ordóñez and Treviño 1999; Alboiu 2002; Manzini and Savoia 2005). However, there is strong evidence that this generalization is too strong and cannot be true (Motapanyane 1994; Cardinaletti 1997; 2004; Goodall 2001; Costa and Duarte 2002; Hill 2002; Suñer 2003; Costa 2004; Rizzi 2005; 2018; Frascarelli 2007; Gutiérrez-Bravo 2007; López 2009; Villa-García 2013; Giurgea 2017a). First of all, there are certain preverbal environments in which only subjects are allowed: between hortative subjunctive *que* 'that' and the verb in Spanish (Villa-García 2013, see 34a vs b), between an auxiliary raised to the left periphery and the verb in Portuguese and in certain registers of Spanish (Suñer 1994). Only preverbal subjects and oblique experiencers are also admitted before a bare subjunctive (cf. 35a) and between a raised auxiliary and the verb in Italian (cf. 35b) (Cardinaletti 2004):

(34) **Spanish (Villa-García 2013, exs 11a, 7a)**
    a.   ¡Que Antonio no lo vea!
        that Antonio not it= see.SBJV.3SG
        'Antonio should not see it!'
    b.   ¡(De mi hija) que (**de mi hija) no hablen nunca más!
        about my daughter that about my daughter not speak.SBJV.3PL never more
        'About my daughter, they should never speak again!'

(35) **Italian (Cardinaletti 2004: 122)**
    a.   Credevo a Gianni piacessero queste storie.
        believed.1SG to Gianni pleased.SBJV.3PL these stories
        'I believed Gianni liked these stories.'
    b.   ?? Credevo a Gianni (gli) avesse dato questi libri.
        believed.1SG to Gianni 3.DAT= had.SBJV.3SG given these books

Even outside these specific environments, preverbal subjects do not obey the same constraints as topicalized phrases: they may be non-specific DPs such as narrow scope indefinites (36) or existential and negative quantifiers, as in (37) and (38), which are unrelated to the context via their descriptive part, in pragmatically neutral sentences, which is impossible for topicalized phrases (see Sections 26.3.3–4):[25]

---

[25] In (37), the presence of the second N-word (*nimic* 'nothing') guarantees that the negative subject is not focus-fronted. If that had been the case, the second N-word would have been given information, part of the background, and a double negation reading would have obtained (*NIMENI nu poate face nimic* 'NOBODY can't do nothing'; such a sentence may occur as a correction to a previous claim *Unii nu pot face nimic* 'Some people can't do anything').

(36) Un vigilante montaba guardia en cada esquina. (Sp., Suñer 2003: 345)
 a policeman stood guard in each corner (cada esquina > un vigilante)
 'A policeman guarded each corner.'

(37) Nimeni în lume nu poate face nimic pentru mine. (Ro., Giurgea 2017a: 291)
 nobody in world not can do nothing for me
 'Nobody in the world can do anything for me.'

(38) [context: 'What's happening?']
 Cineva taie lemne. / #Lemne taie cineva. (Ro., Giurgea 2017a: 291)
 somebody cuts woods woods cuts somebody
 'Somebody is cutting wood.'

A line of research on preverbal subjects and topics assumes a multifunctional specifier position in the preverbal field (labelled SpecTP in Zubizarreta 1998; Hill 2002; Sheehan 2007; Giurgea and Remberger 2012a; SpecFinP in Giurgea and Remberger 2014; Giurgea 2017a), which accommodates either A-bar moved phrases (topics, foci, wh-items) or subjects. In this view, the presence of non-topical subjects is explained by the existence of an EPP feature,[26] which is not specialized to subjects, as in English-type languages, but can associate with a peripheral attracting feature (a Top-, Foc-, or Wh-probe) or to a D-feature (in which case it attracts the closest argument). A similar hypothesis is that the EPP may associate either with T, attracting closest arguments, or with Fin, attracting peripheral phrases (Sheehan 2010). In this approach, it is assumed that a null element with a topic-like interpretation satisfies the EPP in all-new VS orders (see Section 26.4.3 for details).

In the cartographic framework, which assumes that each attracting feature is associated with a single dedicated head, preverbal subjects and oblique experiencers are currently assumed to sit in the specifier of a dedicated projection SubjP. Cardinaletti (1997; 2004) argues that such a position is specialized for strong subjects, as opposed to weak subjects (i.e., weak pronouns and *pro*) which sit in a lower position, called SpecAgrSP. She proposes that SubjP encodes a special feature called 'subject of predication'. Rizzi (2005; 2018) takes over this proposal and labelled this feature 'aboutness', claiming that the subject of predication is 'the argument "about which" the event expressed in the predicate is presented'.

In this theory, subjects of predication and (aboutness) topics share the aboutness feature, but are to be distinguished in that topics, unlike

---

[26] Extending the idea of an Empty Projection Principle responsible for the filling of the canonical subject positions (the 'classical EPP'), the term 'EPP' refers, in minimalist syntax, to a requirement that the specifier position of a certain head should be filled, via Move or Merge. Being associated with an unvalued feature that must enter an Agree relation with a goal, the EPP-feature triggers movement of the goal (cf. Chomsky 2000).

subjects, need to be linked to the discourse. Both subjects of predication and topics serve an information-structure function, insofar as they contribute to the update and organization of the information. However, the two notions subject of predication and (aboutness) topic belong to different levels of the grammar: the former is contextually and pragmatically determined (Lambrecht 1994), while subject of predication must be taken as a purely semantic-logical notion, which should be defined independently from contextual properties. This means that not all subjects are necessarily topics (cf. the non-referential phrases as in 37 and 38), and that not all topics are subjects: in general, aboutness topics are not limited to particular syntactic functions, whereas aboutness subjects of predication tend to coincide with nominative subjects, oblique experiencers, and locatives in locative inversion constructions (see Rizzi and Shlonsky 2006).

The dispute and controversies concerning the status of preverbal subjects in null-subject languages only concerns subjects in an immediately preverbal position. Subjects can also occur to the left of foci, wh-phrases, or topicalized phrases (see 23 above), in which case they clearly occupy a topic position in the left periphery. In French, the distinction between subject topics and subjects occurring in the canonical preverbal position is straightforward (de Cat 2007: 25, 75). In (39a), we see a non-topical subject in the canonical subject position; in (39b), where the subject is topic, it is dislocated and resumed by a weak pronoun in the canonical subject position (topic-marking by dislocation is very common in the colloquial language):

(39) French
 a. [Context: what happened?]
    Les voisins (#, ils) ont mangé mon lapin.
    the neighbours they have eaten my rabbit
    'The neighbours have eaten my rabbit.'
 b. Le malais, #(c') est difficile.
    the Malay it is difficult
    'Malay is difficult.'

26.4.3 Subject Inversion: Narrow Focus and Thetic Sentences

Subject inversion has been identified as a strategy to mark narrow focus in null-subject languages, generally in the presence of a topicalized constituent (see Section 26.2.3):

(40) Gardenese (Casalicchio and Cognola 2018: 81)
    [Context: Who has always bought the flour in the shop?]
    Te butëiga, la farina l'à for cumpreda la l'oma.
    in shop the flour it=has always bought the mum
    'It was always mum who bought the flour in the shop.'

Due to its focalization nature, this type of subject inversion is strictly dependent on information structure and is not sensitive to the type of predicate. The VS order, however, is also found in all-new contexts: in this case, the postverbal position is not related to focalization, but it has rather been linked to the presence of a silent aboutness argument, serving the function of topic or subject of the predication depending on the specific theory.

All-new sentences uttered as out-of-the-blue announcements or as answers to questions such as 'what happened?' are often considered to lack an aboutness topic. Following Brentano (1874), Kuroda (1972) introduces the distinction between categorical sentences, which have a topic-background partition, and thetic sentences, which lack such a partition: they are not about an entity or a class, but just denote the occurrence of an event.[27] As mentioned, null-subject Romance languages use VS orders in such sentences (41, taken from Corr 2016: 1). The conditions in which such orders can be used may lead to a better understanding of what thetic sentences are.

(41) a. Morrió el güelu. (Ast.)
die.PST.3SG the grandfather
'(My) grandfather died.'
b. Apareceu um cão. (Pt.)
appear.PST.3SG a dog
'A dog appeared.'
c. Llamó Lucía. (Sp.)
call.PST.3SG Lucía
'Lucía called.'

Across Romance, we find both syntactic and semantic constraints on VS orders in all-new contexts. Such constraints are rather strong in French, where VS is primarily limited to unaccusatives, either with an adverbial or the complementizer *que* 'that' before the verb,[28] or with an expletive subject pronoun (in which case the verb agrees with the expletive):

(42) **French (Marandin 2001)**
a. Alors sont entrés deux hommes.
then are entered two men
'Then two men came in.'
b. Il est arrivé trois hommes.
it is arrived three men
'There came three men.'

---

[27] See also Sasse (1987; 1995; 2006); Ladusaw (1994).
[28] See also Lahousse (2003; 2004; 2008).

VS is restricted to unaccusatives and certain unergatives such as *telefonar* 'phone' also in Brazilian Portuguese (Lobo and Martins 2017: 46). In null-subject Romance languages VS is also allowed – albeit to different degrees – with unergatives. Syntactic constraints are at play when an object is present: VSO is ruled out in Italian and Catalan,[29] is heavily constrained in European Portuguese, and freely available in Spanish (with some speaker variation),[30] as well as in Romanian (see Leonetti 2017 for an overview):

(43) a. Telefonou uns clientes. (BrPt., Lobo and Martins 2017: 46)
     phoned.3SG some clients
     'Some clients phoned.'
   b. A răsturnat pisica vasul. (Ro., Giurgea and Remberger 2012a: 63)
     has turned.over cat.DEF pot.DEF
     'The cat knocked over the pot.'
   c. Se comió el gato un ratón. (Sp., Zubizarreta 1999: 4233)
     REFL= ate the cat a rat
     'The cat ate a rat.'

Also interesting are the semantic constraints on all-new subject inversion. It has been noted that the sentence must report an episodic event (44a, 45): individual-level predicates (see 44a), generic sentences and iteratives (see 45) are excluded (cf. Bianchi 1993; Soare 2009; Giurgea and Remberger 2009; 2012a; Giurgea 2017). The requirement that the subject of individual-level predicates should be topical is also visible in colloquial French, see (39b).

(44) **Italian (Bianchi 1993: 60)**
   a. Sono disponibili alcune guide turistiche.
     are available some guides tourist.ADJ
     'Some tourist guides are available.'
   b. **Sono poliglotte alcune guide turistiche.
     are polyglot some guides tourist.ADJ
     'Some tourist guides are polyglots.'

(45) [Out-of-the-blue context]
     Cântă copiii (# în fiecare seară). (Ro.)
     sing.3PL children.DEF in every evening
     'The children are singing (/ sing every evening).'

The episodic reading that allows subject inversion arises from the anchoring of the proposition to the speech situation, which is thus placed

---

[29] VSO in Italian is only possible if either O, or both S and O are 'marginalized' (on marginalization, see n. 9, and Cardinaletti 2002).
[30] Ortega-Santos (2016: 48) reports that, in his dialect, VSO in 'what happened' contexts is not felicitous in the absence of some preverbal material.

in the relevant spatio-temporal location of the discourse. This supports the view that thetic sentences are not topic-less, but rather have the location of the reported eventuality as a topic (Gundel 1974; Erteschik-Shir 1997; 2007). Consequently, it has been proposed that thetic VS orders are licensed by a null stage topic, which satisfies the EPP feature (Lahousse 2008; 2011; Giurgea and Remberger 2012a; 2012b; Giurgea 2017; also É. Kiss 2002 for Hungarian). It has alternatively been proposed that it is the event argument itself (Bianchi 1993) or a situational argument that functions as the 'subject-of-predication', about which a specific bounded eventuality is predicated (Bentley and Cruschina 2018). An example where a situational topic is very plausible is (46), where VS is licensed by a context which makes reference to a situation:

(46) [Context: What is that tension in the air?]
    S-au   certat   frații. (Ro.)
    REFL=have.3PL quarrelled brothers.DEF
    'The brothers had a fight.'

Bentley and Cruschina (2018) further notice that thetic VS requires the eventuality to be bounded. This explains why not all change-of-state verbs are allowed, but only those that involve a specific final goal on a scale of change, via entailment or an implicature (the pragmagtic infelicity of example 47b must be understood with respect to an all-new context):

(47) **Italian**
    a.   Si   è   svuotato il   serbatoio.
         REFL= is emptied the tank
         'The tank has become empty.'
    b.   # Si   sono annoiati   i   bambini.
         REFL= are become-bored the kids
         'The kids have become bored.'

French, where the availability of VS orders is very limited, uses other strategies for marking the subject as non-topical in thetic sentences: so-called presentational constructions such as *il-y-a* clefts, i.e., clefts based on an existential construction. Thus, for a typical thetic sentence such as 'The phone is ringing', which imposes VS in null-subject Romance languages (see 48a), French uses (48b) (cf. Lambrecht 1994; 2000; de Cat 2007):

(48) a.   Sună telefonul. (Ro.)
          rings phone.DEF
     b.   Il y   a   le   téléphone qui sonne. (Fr.)
          it LOC=has the phone   that rings
          'The phone is ringing.'

Existential sentences are another type of presentational construction used to mark thetic sentences. Existentials may in turn alternate with VS, depending on definiteness of the grammatical subject (or 'pivot'). This distribution is found, for example, in Sardinian (cf. Jones 1993; Bentley 2004; La Fauci and Loporcaro 1997; Remberger 2009). Such an example is (49a), where the clitic is obligatory and the DP argument of the verb does not agree with the verb and must be indefinite – it is an existential pivot rather than a true subject. With definite arguments, the standard construction with subject inversion is the only possible way of marking theticity (see 49b). Note also the different auxiliary selection. Remberger (2009) correlates the differences between these constructions with different positions of the DP argument inside the vP domain:

(49) **Sardinian**
    a.   B'   at   arribatu   tres   pitzinnas.
          LOC=has   arrived   three   girls
          'There arrived three girls.'
    b.   (B')   est   arribatu   Zubanne.
          LOC= is   arrived   Zubanne
          'Zubanne has arrived (there).'

To conclude the discussion of VS orders in null-subject Romance languages, we should note that the restrictions presented above, characteristic of thetic sentences, do not apply to V-initial orders with subjects which are in narrow focus or part of the new information (see 50a, which has an individual-level predicate, and 50b, which is habitual):

(50) a.   Sabe   francês   [o   Paulo]$_{Focus}$ (Pt., Costa 1998: 141)
          knows   French   the   Paulo
          '*Paulo* speaks French.'
    b.   Aici   [fac   păsările   cuiburi]$_{New-Info}$ (Ro.)
          here   make.3PL   birds.DEF   nests
          'Here, birds are making their nests.'

Whereas for XP-V-S orders (as in 50b), one can assume that the EPP is satisfied by the fronted XP (especially when it is a topic), a different account is needed for V-initial orders in configurations with narrow focus (see Giurgea 2017a for some tentative suggestions).

Selected References

Below you can find selected references for this chapter. The full references can be found online at the following page: www.cambridge.org/Romancelinguistics

Belletti, A. (2004). 'Aspects of the low IP area'. In Rizzi, L. (ed.), *The Structure of IP and CP. The Cartography of Syntactic Structures, II*. Oxford/New York: Oxford University Press, 16–51.

Benincà, P. (2001). 'The position of topic and focus in the left periphery'. In Cinque, G. and Salvi, G. (eds), *Current Studies in Italian Syntax. Essays Offered to Lorenzo Renzi*. Amsterdam: Elsevier, 39–64.

Cruschina, S. (2012). *Discourse-Related Features and Functional Projections*. Oxford: Oxford University Press.

Cruschina, S. (2016). 'Information and discourse structure'. In Ledgeway, A. and Maiden, M. (eds), *The Oxford Guide to the Romance Languages*. Oxford: Oxford University Press, 596–608.

Cruschina, S., and Remberger, E.-M. (2017). 'Focus fronting.' In Dufter, G. and Stark, E. (eds), *Manual of Romance Morphosyntax and Syntax*. Berlin/Boston: de Gruyter, 502–35.

Giurgea, I. (2016). 'On the interpretation of focus fronting in Romanian', *Bucharest Working Papers in Linguistics* 18: 37–61.

Giurgea, I. (2017). 'Preverbal subjects and topic marking in Romanian', *Revue Roumaine de Linguistique* 62: 279–322.

Leonetti, M. (2017). 'Basic constituent orders'. In Dufter, A. and Stark, E. (eds), *Manual of Romance Morphosyntax and Syntax*. Berlin: Mouton de Gruyter, 887–932.

Remberger, E.-M. (2010). 'Left peripheral interactions in Sardinian', *Lingua* 120: 555–81.

Remberger, E.-M. (2014). 'A comparative look on focus fronting in Romance'. In Dufter, A. and Toledo y Huerta, À. O. (eds), *Left Sentence Peripheries of Spanish. Diachronic, Variationist and Comparative Perspectives*. Amsterdam/Philadelphia: Benjamins, 383–418.

Rizzi, L. (1997). 'The fine structure of the left periphery'. In Haegeman, L. (ed.), *Elements of Grammar*. Dordrecht: Kluwer, 281–337.

Zubizarreta, M. L. (1998). *Prosody, Focus and Word Order*. Cambridge, MA: MIT Press.

Part Six

Language, Society, and the Individual

27

Register, Genre, and Style in the Romance Languages

Christopher Pountain and Rodica Zafiu

27.1 Definitions

The terms 'register', 'genre', and 'style' have been employed in a number of often overlapping ways in the terminology of descriptive linguistics (Carruthers 2018: 337; Battye et al. 2009: 284). In this account, we will follow the spirit of the classic definitions given by Biber and Conrad (2009: 2).

27.1.1 Register

By 'register' we mean a linguistic variety which is associated with a particular situation of language use. Such a broadly drawn definition means that register is often taken to refer to any kind of diaphasic variation and that genre and even style are subsumed into it: this is the reason why register is the main focus of attention in this chapter. The objective discrimination of individual registers is usually made according to situation, and the linguistic study of register has consisted in correlating such situational variation with the use of characteristic vocabulary and grammatical structures; these linguistic features do not in themselves define register. Yet while the distinction between situation of use and linguistic features seems clear enough, it may be clouded by the fact that linguistic features are sometimes in themselves patently motivated by the situation of use: for example, verb-first position in Spanish headlines brings the subject of the verb, and hence the matter of greatest interest, into focus (for examples, see Pountain 2017: 194). There is also the risk that situational definitions of register result in categories which are too broadly conceived: 'journalistic' register, the discrimination of which is based on the situational use of language in newspapers and magazines, can be seen on the basis of linguistic analysis to include a number of clearly distinguishable subregisters such as news reporting, sports reporting, headlines, leaders, obituaries (again see Pountain 2017: 193–99). Most difficult of all to attribute to a particular register are texts in which there occur linguistic features which are known to be characteristic of different registers. The following is an extract from an opinion piece in Spanish criticizing hard adventure tourism:

(1) Pretenden tirarse por un barranco, o ir al Polo Norte, o hacer el pino en el asiento de una moto a doscientos por hora, y luego, pasado el subidón de adrenalina, contárselo a los amiguetes, tan campantes, y aquí no ha pasado nada. (Arturo Pérez-Reverte, *El Semanal*, 22 August 1999)

'They expect to launch themselves down a ravine, or go to the North Pole, or do a handstand on the seat of a motorbike going at 200 kilometres an hour, and then, once the adrenaline boost has gone, to tell the story to their mates in an offhand way: nothing happened.'

Amiguete (*amigo* 'friend' with the diminutive suffix *-ete*) and *campante* (an adjective meaning 'impassive, without batting an eyelid') are tagged as 'colloquial' by *DLE*; *aquí no ha pasado nada* is direct speech, the kind of thing the tourists might say; but the 'absolute' structure *pasado el subidón de adrenalina* is more typical of formal expository prose. The mixing of colloquial and expository registers in this piece hence precludes a simple assignment of the text to one particular register.

There has been a widespread assertion that register variation is characteristic of what Kloss (1967) calls *Ausbau* languages, that is to say, languages which have been developed as official and standardized languages for a large number of purposes (e.g., legal, administrative, journalistic, pedagogical, creative). Romaine (1994: 64) went so far as to say that 'much of the difference between developed and undeveloped languages is essentially one of register range'. The standard Romance languages clearly fall into this category (Pountain 2011b: 607–09), and are extensively documented over a number of centuries. They therefore have a significant contribution to make to the study of register variation and its history. Additionally, some scenarios in the Romance-speaking world show that register variation is not limited to texts written in the standard language: Sánchez-Muñoz (2010) shows that the phenomenon is also observable among heritage speakers of Spanish in the US, for whom Spanish is essentially a domestic language.

The Romance languages also offer a unique opportunity for the study of register across closely related languages, raising the interesting and relatively little explored question of the extent to which the 'same' register (as defined situationally) exhibits the same, or similar, linguistic features. Sanders (1994), for example, finds evidence of differences between French and English newspaper 'register'. There has also been interest in what has been termed 'regional pragmatic variation' within the Spanish-speaking world, which offers considerable scope for the investigation of differences among different diatopic variants of the same language: for an overview, see Placencia (2011).

27.1.2 Genre

By genre we understand types of text. (The term 'text types' is increasingly used to refer to the different ways of structuring content: narrative, descriptive, argumentative, etc.) As Biber and Conrad (2009: 2) suggest, of primary linguistic interest in the study of genre are the conventional structures used to construct the text, which can be organizational, presentational, or formulaic. Some genres, for example recipes, formal letters, and executive reports, appear to be more strictly conventionalized than others, such as poems or novels. Formulaic expressions can be very restricted ('frozen') and vary significantly from language to language, and even within the same language. This is particularly true of salutational and valedictory formulae in formal letters: a French text of this type is likely to begin simply with *Monsieur* (lit. 'sir' < 'my.sire'), while Spanish uses *Muy señor mío* (lit. 'very sir my') and Portuguese uses *Excelentíssimo Senhor* (lit. 'most excellent sir') (all equivalents of 'Dear Sir/Gentleman'). Within the Spanish-speaking world, an alternative formula *De mi consideración* (lit. 'of my consideration/esteem') appears to be restricted to the Southern Cone of South America and is unknown in Spain. But while such salutations appear to be idiosyncratic, other cross-language differences within genres can reflect more systematic features: the (polite and very general) *vous* imperative (e.g., *mélangez* 'mix!') is normally used in a French recipe (*Mélangez à l'aide d'une cuillère en bois* 'Mix using a wooden spoon'), while the infinitive (e.g., *mezclar* 'to mix') is more typical of the corresponding Spanish instruction (*Mezclar con una cuchara de madera*) so that the choice between the intimate but very generally used *tú* and the (hyper-)polite *usted* forms of address which are unavoidably evident in the Spanish imperatives ¡*Mezcla (tú)!* / ¡*Mezcle (usted)!* 'Mix!' is avoided. Domínguez García (2010) relates the variation observable among Spanish discourse markers to text types, concluding that *y* 'and' and *entonces* 'then' are characteristic of narrative, *pero* 'but', *porque* 'because', and *por ejemplo* 'for example' of argumentative, and *pues* 'so', *bueno* 'well', and *claro* 'of course' of conversational types.

27.1.3 Style

The term style is currently understandable in a number of different ways. It has been used in sociolinguistic research (Schilling-Este 2002) to reflect different kinds of linguistic production by the same speaker ('intra-speaker variation'): common styles identified by investigators in this 'attention to speech' approach are casual speech, careful speech, reading of continuous text, and reading of word lists; these clearly relate to the Hallidayan notions of tenor and mode to be discussed in Section 27.1.4. Another sociolinguistic usage is to do with the ways in which speakers manipulate linguistic variants with which they are familiar, either to accommodate to their interlocutors ('audience design') or to make a statement about themselves ('speaker design'). In the Romance tradition, the study of style, or 'stylistics', has been understood in two different ways. What is usually referred to in the Romance tradition as 'stylistics of language', pioneered by Bally, is much broader in scope than these sociolinguistic views of style, though it might be taken to include them: Bally's object of study was 'the affective value of the features of organized language, and the reciprocal action of those expressive features which combine to form the language's means of systematic expression' (Bally 1951: 1); his concerns are such phenomena as connotational and figurative meaning, and the syntagmatic and paradigmatic relations among words. The other way in which stylistics has been understood relates to literary discourse, and to language used as an essentially artistic medium. One of the main concerns of literary stylistics has been to define *écart* ('deviation'), or the ways in which literary language subverts and extends the standard language (Gueunier 1969); another is to refer to ways of writing which reflect 'aesthetic preferences, associated with particular authors or historical periods' (Biber and Conrad 2009: 2). It is literary stylistics with which we will be concerned in Section 27.4.

27.1.4 Some Dimensions of Register, Genre, and Style

Halliday (1978: 33) identified three parameters for the description of 'what is linguistically significant in the context of situation': field, tenor, and mode. These are useful in discussing register, genre, and style because they cut across all three of these categories. Field relates to the subject matter of a text and the whole activity of the speaker and participants in its setting: it is clear that not only does choice of lexis depend on field, but so does the frequency of particular grammatical features (so, in historical accounts and literary narratives, for example, third person past tenses will predominantly occur). Tenor concerns the relationship between the participants (speaker/writer and hearer/reader): the degree of formality of a text and the politeness strategies it contains are obviously dictated by its tenor. Mode relates to the medium of communication: writing and speech constitute broadly different modes. An example of how these notions can be deployed in illuminating the 'style' of a philologically problematic Romance text (the *Libro de la vida* of Santa Teresa de Jesús, which is often held up as an example of 'spontaneous' sixteenth-century Spanish) is given in Pountain (2016b).

27.2 Register

27.2.1 'Spoken' and 'Written' Language

The difference between 'spoken' and 'written' language has often been seen as fundamental in linguistics (Luzzati 1991: 3; see also Section 29.1.1). It is in fact not just a distinction of mode: the grammatical structuring of spoken language is represented as being fundamentally different from that of the written language, especially insofar as it is prone to performance 'error'. A short piece of spontaneous speech in Portuguese will illustrate this:

(2)   a.   Aqui, o futebol, o, o desporto,
Here, the football, the, the sport,
qualquer desporto que se pratica aqui é o
any sport which is.practised here is the
desporto amador, claro, embora no, no futebol
sport amateur, of.course, although in.the in.the football
que é a parte que eu mais estou ligado
which is the part that I most am connected
é o futebol, já se queira profissionalizar
is the football, now it.is.wanted to.professionalize
um pouco essa modalidade.
a little that type
(CRPC - Corpus de Referência do Português Contemporâneo, http://alfclul .clul.ul.pt/crpc/oral_portugal/pfpubl/pf1212pu.txt, consulted 28 September 2018)
'Here, football, sport, any sport which is played here is amateur sport, of course, although in, in football, which is what I'm most closely associated with, football, they're wanting to professionalize this kind [of sport] a bit.'

Here we can observe hesitations and repetitions (*o, o; no, no*) and the use of the filler *claro* 'of course' which are typical of spontaneous speech. The speaker refines the topic at first by the use of three noun phrases in apposition (*o futebol* 'football' – *o desporto* 'sport' – *qualquer desporto que se pratica aqui* 'any sport played here'), another common strategy in spoken discourse. In the relative construction *a parte que eu mais estou ligado* 'the one that I'm most connected with', the relativizer *que* would be preceded by the preposition *a* 'to' in standard written usage (viz. *a que* 'to which'). The syntax of *no futebol que é a parte que eu mais estou ligado é o futebol* (lit. 'in football, which is the one that I'm most associated is football') mixes the two constructions *no futebol, que é a parte [a] que eu mais estou ligado* ('in football, which is the one I'm most associated with') and *a parte [a] que eu mais estou ligado é o futebol* ('the one I'm most associated with is football'): in such 'performance errors', speakers appear to change their minds about the construction they are using at a mid-point. The equivalent sentence in the written standard, purged of repetition, hesitation and what are often regarded as syntactic solecisms by purists, might be:

(2) b. Aqui, qualquer desporto que se pratica
Here any sport which is.practised
é o desporto amador;
is the sport amateur
embora, o futebol, que é o desporto
although the football which is the sport
a que eu mais estou ligado,
to which I most am connected
já se queira profissionalizar um pouco.
now it.is.wanted to.professionalize a little
'Here, any sport which is played is amateur sport; although now they want to professionalize football a bit, which is the sport I'm most associated with.'

It is sometimes argued that the spoken language has its own grammatical structures which are different from those of the standard written language (Désirat and Hordé 1976: 59–62). However, we may contrast the contrary view of Blanche-Benveniste (1991), who considers that there is no significant difference between the structures of written and spoken French once paradigmatic structure is taken into account. Following her method of analysis, we can represent the structure of (2a) as:

(2) c. Aqui, o futebol, é o desporto amador
o(, o) desporto,
qualquer desporto que se pratica aqui
claro,
embora no(, no) futebol que é a parte que eu mais estou ligado,
a parte que eu mais estou ligado é o futebol,
já se queira profissionalizar um pouco essa modalidade.

The paradigmatic alternatives which here are overt can be likened to the prior consideration of alternatives in the process of planning which goes on in the production of formal written language, where only one is eventually selected (for further consideration of the relative construction, however, see Section 27.2.3.4).

The distinction between spoken and written register reflects the preoccupations of two major currents in Romance linguistics. The first is concerned with establishing the historical development of the standard Romance languages through written texts since these are in principle the only direct sources of knowledge of the languages prior to the possibility of the recording and transcription of speech (see such explicit accounts as Ayres-Bennett 1996 and Pountain 2001; on the problems of the interpretation of such documents see Romaine 1982 and Pountain 2011a). The second, dialect geography, has by contrast pursued the investigation of surviving spoken Romance varieties; in fact, a great premium was originally placed on using informants who were illiterate and hence immune from the 'contaminating' effects of the written standard (see Iordan and Orr 1970: 149).

There is a strong association between the written language and the standard. Written texts, especially literary, have often been viewed as representing the 'best' usage and have provided an authority for the standard language. The Florentine-based literary language of Dante, Petrarch, and Boccaccio was favoured as the literary standard by Bembo and was the basis for the national Italian standard imposed after unification (Maiden 1995: 6–10). The first dictionary of the Real Academia Española, explicitly called the *Diccionario de autoridades* 'Dictionary of authorities' (Real Academia Española 1963), took the usage of what the Academia regarded as the best writers of the Spanish Golden Age as its basis. In all Romance-speaking countries there is a strong concern that written texts should follow the standard, either through active legislation or by common accord (for a general account see Pountain 2016a). The spoken language, by contrast, has often been equated with non-standard forms and 'mistakes': indeed, the identification of 'mistakes' in written texts has been taken to provide evidence for the reconstruction of the spontaneous spoken language (see Pountain 2011a: 101f.).

27.2.1.1 The Identification of *français populaire*

This leads on to a discussion of one of the most celebrated issues regarding register in Romance linguistics and a concern which is not paralleled, for example, in English (Lepschy 2002: 50): the nature of what has been called *français populaire* (lit. 'popular French'). The matter has been particularly contentious within the French-speaking world because of the ideology of the standard which deflected attention from, and even hindered, the linguistic analysis of the spoken language (Gadet 2009: 115). In his pioneering study, Bauche (1920) defined *français populaire* as 'the language spoken fluently and naturally among the common people, the language which the man of the people learns from his father and mother and which he understands every day on the lips of his fellows' (Bauche 1920: 18). He opposed '*written* or *correct*, or *classical*, or *literary*, or *official language*' to '*spoken*, or *popular*, or *vulgar*, or *common language*' (Bauche 1920: 15), and he regarded *français populaire* as the real locus of French. He also praised its versatility and inventiveness, a view echoed by Guiraud (1978: 11f.), who saw the essential difference between cultivated French and *français populaire* as being that while development of the former is inhibited by normative rules, the latter undergoes natural processes of linguistic change. A simple example is the creation of the form *vous disez* 'you say' in *français populaire* (for *vous dites* in the standard language), which shows remodelling of this form of the verb *dire* 'say' by analogy with *lire* 'read' (*vous lisez* 'you read'). It is sometimes suggested that the spoken language foreshadows changes which will ultimately be accepted in the standard Guiraud (1978: 16), although there is of course no guarantee of this in cultures in which, as in French, normative pressures are strong.

The corresponding term has also been applied to other languages, notably Italian and Romanian, though not with exactly the same meaning. The label *italiano popolare* (lit. 'popular Italian') refers to the low-register sociolect of uneducated people who generally also speak local linguistic varieties (Berruto 1993: 58–68). *Româna populară* (lit. 'popular Romanian') had a predominantly positive connotation, the vernacular being viewed as the 'true' language, the traditional heritage, which was proposed as a model by nineteenth-century Romanticism and adopted as a guide for the 'democratic' style of writing used in the second half of the twentieth century (Zafiu 2009; 2018). It was also seen in abstract terms as being characterized by the common features of several (or even all) regional varieties (Vulpe 1969). Yet at the same time, as with *français populaire*, normativists have criticized many of the features of *româna populară* as being substandard.

27.2.1.2 The Boundaries of Spoken and Written Register

Despite the apparent clarity of this binary opposition, the distinction between spoken and written registers, even in terms of mode, is not hard and fast. Spoken language may be scripted or planned, that is to say, dependent on previously constructed written text; educated spoken discourse may be quite heavily informed by the speaker's experience of written texts. What purport to be representations of spontaneous speech, e.g., interviews in the press, may in fact have been substantially edited to accommodate the written standard. Cicurel (1994) describes the representation of speech in the written dialogue of novels and newspaper reports as a 'hybrid discursive genre', calling attention to how indications about the variety of spoken language used may be given in commentary (diegesis) or by approximation to spoken language (e.g., through the use of slang) (mimesis). The difference between such representations and authentic speech itself is shown by the need for transcriptional notation of the latter to indicate prosodic elements: pauses, hesitations, repetitions, overlap, breaks in construction, volume of the voice, etc. Despite our awareness of these problems in the present day, there has nevertheless been considerable interest within the history of the Romance languages in what is often referred to as 'the spoken within the written', since written texts may hold important evidence about the spoken language (and indeed are our only source of such knowledge prior to the availability of sound recordings): see especially Oesterreicher (1996) on some methodological problems in this regard.

The case of drama, especially prose drama, is particularly interesting in this respect, since this genre, like novelistic dialogue, purports to mimic actual speech. Pountain (2009; 2012; 2018) assesses the evidence for socially based linguistic variation in the prose dramas of the sixteenth-century Spanish playwright Lope de Rueda. At the same time it is clear that some theatrical representations of speech are conventionalized or caricatured. There has been much discussion of the Spanish Golden Age stage 'dialect' known as *sayagués*, put in the mouths of rustic characters. A stereotypical feature of the dialect of the rural Salamanca area on which *sayagués* is based is palatalization of word-initial /l/: thus *llugar* 'place' corresponds to Castilian *lugar*. However, as Penny (1991: 159) observes, Juan del Encina (1469–1529) also puts a form *collorado* 'red' (corresponding to Castilian *colorado*) into the mouth of one of his rustic characters even though this form is not actually found in the dialect itself (/l/ is not initial in this word). Désirat and Hordé (1976: 35) similarly point to what they label caricatures of local usages in classical French: in Act Two, Scene 1 of Molière's *Dom Juan*, for example, the peasants Pierrot and Charlotte converse entirely in a local variety, but in order to produce a comic effect.

27.2.1.3 Subregisters

The primary distinction made between written and spoken registers also obscures the many variations of register observable within what are perhaps more appropriately, given the foregoing discussion, characterizable as modes. The distinctions of style made by sociolinguists to which we referred in Section 27.1.3 reflect a continuum from 'careful' to 'spontaneous' speech, akin to the tripartite division made by Battye et al. (2009: 290) into *le français soigné* ('careful French'), *le français familier* ('informal French'), and non-standard French. Within written mode, there is a huge proliferation of subregisters, the distinctive linguistic features of which are often determined by their different fields and tenors: Gotti (2012) shows how linguistic features of legal documents, such as sentence complexity, anaphoric reference, and the use of conjunctions, are motivated by the need for legal documents to be unambiguous. The same linguistic features may be shared by different situationally defined registers: in Spanish, the use of nominalizations (e.g., *detención* 'arrest' in *tras su detención* 'after his arrest') instead of a verbal expression or clause (*después de haber sido detenido* 'after having been arrested' / *después de que lo detuviera [la policía]* 'after the police arrested him') is typical of both news reporting and formal administrative documents.

27.2.1.4 Jargons and Slangs

Bauche (1920: 18) and Guiraud (1978: 8) are both careful to distinguish *français populaire* from what they call *argot*. For Bauche, *argot* is 'an artificial language, created in order for speakers to understand one another without being understood by outsiders', i.e., a cryptolect, like the many criminal slangs in the Romance-speaking world, some of which are well documented: Spanish examples are *germanía* (Spain), *caliche* (Mexico), *coa* (Chile), and *replana* (Peru). Guiraud (1978) likewise refers to *argot* as belonging to a 'closed circle'. He also distinguishes *français populaire* from 'a technical language', by which we may understand use of the terminology of a specialized field of interest, not with the intention of concealing meaning, but rather of making semantic distinctions which are not available in the available lexicon of most speakers – what is often referred to as jargon.

However, within everyday spoken language we can also detect words, expressions, and constructions which would not generally be tolerated in formal written register. In modern Spanish *jeta* 'face' is restricted to colloquial usage (*cara* is the general term for this notion); in spoken Brazilian Portuguese *a gente* (lit. 'the people') is used as a first person plural pronoun instead of standard/written *nós*. Words such as Sp. *jeta* are often considered to belong to what we might distinctively call slang (as opposed to cryptolect or jargon). The linguistic definitions of such terms as *slang* and *jargon* offered here are essentially arbitrary, and do not correspond to their overlapping and often affective meanings observable in common usage; the same is true of Fr. *argot, jargon*, Sp. *argot, jerga, jerigonza*, Pt. *gíria, jargão*, It. *gergo*, and Ro. *argou, jargon*. Even originally more precise terms are prone to shift their meaning: *caló*, used in a Spanish context to denote the cryptolectic usage of Spanish gypsies, has become in Mexico a general word for what we are here labelling slang; elements of the *lunfardo* of Buenos Aires, originally a lower-class cryptolect, have also now passed into wider colloquial usage, which has raised its esteem. The interplay between cryptolect and common colloquial usage is also evident in the 'upward' promotion of a number of words from French *verlan* (the inversion of syllables within a word, originally with cryptolectic intent. The term itself is an inversion of *(à) l'envers* 'backwards', see Lefkowitz 1989): two which have become particularly common are *meuf* (from *femme*) 'woman' and *beur* (from *arabe*) 'Arab'. Some of the syntactic constructions which are characteristic of slang have been intensively studied comparatively within Romance linguistics:

for example, the deprecatory Fr. *ce fripon de valet* lit. 'this rascal of (a) servant' (Lombard 1931; Tuțescu 1969).

In Italian, *gerghi* are more anchored in local varieties (for their syntactic characteristics, see Trumper 2013: 671). An interesting common factor of Romance slangs is historically and sociologically motivated lexical borrowing: not only Sp. *caló*, but also French, Italian, and Romanian slangs have borrowed vocabulary from Romany, e.g., Fr. *michto*, Ro. *mișto* 'fine'; Fr. *gadjo*, It. *gaggio*, Ro. *gagiu* 'guy' (Leschber 1995; Colin and Mével 1990; Ferrero 1996). Trumper (2013: 673) also mentions the presence of some morphological features of Romany in southern Italian slangs. Although slangs are generally considered to be lexically determined, linguistic descriptions have also noted some characteristic morphosyntactic features, such as the preference for the suffixes *-oso, -osa* in Italian (*cerchioso* 'ring', Sanga 1994: 162) and the cognate *-os, -oasă* in Romanian (*bengos* 'lucky', Zafiu 2001: 228; 2010: 69). In modern urban slang there are cultural convergences due to internationalized urban culture as well as to the influence of North American English slang. For instance, truncation, well represented in French, Italian, and Spanish (e.g., Fr. *prof < professeur* 'teacher', *ado < adolescent* 'teenager', *dico < dictionnaire* 'dictionary', *fac < faculté* 'faculty, university', see Bauer 2011: 559), has also become very popular in informal Romanian in recent decades (e.g., *grădi < grădiniță* 'kindergarten', *plicti < plictisitor* 'boring', *șobi < șobolan* 'rat'). Taboo words (Fr. *les gros mots*, following Guiraud 1975), though excluded from neutral and high registers, are present in slang, regional spoken varieties, and in speech, and aggressive speech acts (swearing, insults), often used as attitude markers, are also characteristic of slang, e.g., the use in Brazilian Portuguese of the intensifying expressions *de cacete* (lit. 'of club/penis)') and *de caralho* (lit. 'of testicle'). Lagorgette and Larrivée (2004) provide an extensive bibliography of the study of insults in French; Alfonzetti and Spampinato Beretta (2012) have identified the dominant semantic fields, the syntactic patterns, and the paradigmatic values of the Italian insults found in a thirteenth- to fifteenth-century corpus.

27.2.2 Variation According to Register

Many features of linguistic variation according to register in the Romance languages have been identified. Some appear to be common to a number of languages beyond Romance. For example, when Cicurel (1994: 128) observes of French that 'the written language remains founded on a phrasal structure while the spoken language of conversation uses parataxis, dislocation, and the addition of elements by association of ideas', this is a phenomenon which is clearly very generally linked to the spoken mode, in which, as we have seen in (2a), material is often presented in the order in which it occurs to speakers and then refined and related syntactically. Indeed, this feature of spoken language lies behind a number of more particular features of Romance, especially dislocation itself (Section 27.2.3.2) and some aspects of relativization (Section 27.2.3.4). Spoken mode also universally favours ellipsis (definable as absence of material which is expected in the standard written language) when the relationship between elements is recoverable pragmatically. (3) serves as an invitation to take a beer, and as it stands does not constitute a logically formed conditional structure (there is beer in the fridge whether or not the interlocutor is thirsty); however, the interlocutor knows pragmatically that the presence of beer would not be mentioned unless an invitation were intended. It will be noted that the same applies to the English equivalent of the French example.

(3) Il y a   de la bière dans le   frigo, si vous avez soif.
     there is some beer   in   the fridge if you have thirst
     'There's some beer in the fridge, if you're thirsty.'

Lexical difference among registers also seems to be universal, although the detail is particular and beyond the scope of this article. For example, in French, there are such well-known standard/informal lexical pairs as *livre/bouquin* 'book', *voiture/bagnole* 'car', *bicyclette/bécane* 'bicycle', but these are not paralleled in the same way, or even at all, in other Romance languages. Hyperbole appears to be a universal strategy in expressions of pleasure or distaste in colloquial language, and it is noticeable that a number of Romance languages deploy learnèd borrowings in a similar way, such as Fr. *phénoménal*, Sp./Pt./Ro. *fenomenal*, It. *fenomenale*; Fr./Sp. *terrible*, Pg. *terrível*, It. *terribile*, Ro. *teribil*. However, even here there are particular and even local preferences: the colloquial Portuguese, especially Brazilian, use of *legal* (lit. 'legal') 'great, cool' is not paralleled elsewhere in Romance.

27.2.3 Some Particular Phenomena

Some specific features are shared quite widely among the Romance languages, even though they are realized in formally different ways. Comparison amongst the Romance languages also raises the question as to how far such features are universally exploited by other language groups: Schneider's (2003: 39–47) study of diminutives in German (cf. Section 27.2.3.1) suggests that while many languages share the same kind of morphologically productive resources with the Romance languages, there are likely to be pragmatic and cultural differences in their affective value.

27.2.3.1 Affective Suffixes

Diminutive and augmentative suffixes are used in Romance spoken registers to communicate a speaker's attitude and are multifunctional, their interpretation depending mainly on the meaning of the lexical base to which they are attached (for an overview, see Chapter 14, this volume). Affective suffixes in the spoken Ibero-Romance languages have been the subject of many studies (e.g., the data-rich Alonso 1951; Gooch 1967; Náñez Fernández 1973); in both Spanish and Portuguese, the diminutive suffixes can function as intensifiers: thus Pt. *andar devagarzinho* (to.walk slowly.DIM) can mean 'to walk very slowly' (Bechara 2009: 248). Cross-linguistic (including Romance) comparison has established a hierarchy of diminutivizable categories (Dressler and Merlini Barbaresi 1994: 132f.). Units of time easily accept such suffixes, particularly diminutive, e.g., It. *attimino* (*attimo* 'instant'), Ro. *anișor* (*an* 'year'). Romanian creates attitudinal diminutives for deictic adverbs (*acușica*, from *acu(și)* 'now'; cf. Mexican Sp. *ahorita* 'immediately; soon', from *ahora* 'now'), for pronouns (*nimicuța*, from *nimic(a)* 'nothing') and even for interjections (*aolică* from *aoleu* 'ouch!', Iordan 1975: 175); in Italian they can be created from indefinite pronouns (*qualcosina*, from *qualcosa* 'something'), numerals (*milioncino*, from *milione* 'million'), and exclamatives (*caspiterina!*, from *caspita!* 'oh gosh!') (Merlini Barbaresi 2004: 267); in both languages we find diminutives derived from greeting formulae: It. *buongiornino* (*buon giorno* 'good day'), Ro. *bonjurică* (*bonjur* 'good day'). With adjectives and manner adverbs, diminutive suffixes function as downgraders, indicating an overtone (It. *giallino*, Ro. *gălbior* 'light yellow; yellowish', from It. *giallo*, Ro. *galben* 'yellow') or a lesser degree of the denoted property (It. *benino*, Ro. *binișor* 'pretty well', from It. *bene*, Ro. *bine* 'well').

27.2.3.2 Dislocation

The readier availability of dislocation (movement of constituents to leftmost or rightmost positions in the sentence) and its versatility in spoken French has often been remarked on (Cicurel 1994: 128). Calvé (1985) observes that dislocation can be to the left (4a) or to the right (4b) and can be multiple (4c–d):

(4) a. <u>Sa sœur</u>, elle part demain. (Fr.)
     His sister she leaves tomorrow
     'She leaves tomorrow, his sister.'
   b. Je l' ai remis sur l'étagère, <u>ton livre</u>. (Fr.)
     I it.DO have put.back on the.shelf your book
     'Your book, I've put it back on the shelf.'
   c. <u>Jean</u>, <u>lui</u>, <u>la mécanique</u>, il connaît ça. (Fr.)
     Jean him the mechanics he knows that
     'He knows about mechanical things, Jean.'

d. Il la lui a donnée, à Jean, son père, sa moto. (Fr.)
    He it.DO him.IO has given to Jean his father his car
    'Jean's father, he's given him his car.'
    (examples from Calvé 1985: 230; the English translations attempt to reflect the register of the original French)

Left-dislocation also occurs in Spanish (for a convenient summary, see Pountain 2012: 139–41), where it also appears to be more frequent in the spoken language: Vigara Tauste (1992: 72) says that it is 'seems to be one of the most obvious and objective phenomena in colloquial syntax'. However, dislocation in Spanish has attracted interest more generally because word order in standard Spanish is syntactically flexible, certainly more flexible than in standard French (see, for example, the classic study of Contreras 1976). By contrast with French, the presence of a subject pronoun is not obligatory in Spanish, and the formal equivalent of (4a) (*su hermana, ella sale mañana*) is unnatural. It is also possible in Spanish to have left-dislocation of an object without an intonational juncture (5a–b); direct objects may be left-dislocated without recapitulation of a referring clitic pronoun (5c), and left-dislocation may take place from within a subordinate clause (5d):

(5) a. El libro lo dejó en la mesa. (Sp.)
         the book it.DO he left on the table
         'He left the book on the table.'
     b. A mi hermana le di un regalo. (Sp.)
         to my sister her.IO I.gave a present
         'I gave my sister a present.'
     c. Eso me (lo) dijiste ayer. (Sp.; Contreras 1976: 82)
         that me.IO (it.DO) you.said yesterday
         'You said that to me yesterday.'
     d. Pero ahora, nosotros las encuestas demuestran
         But now we the polls show
         que les podemos quitar la mayoría absoluta.
         that to.them we can take. away the majority absolute
         (Sp.; Vigara Tauste 1992: 85)
         'But now the polls show that we can take away their absolute majority.'

Examples of left-dislocation from spontaneous spoken Spanish may involve anacolutha, or 'loose' syntactic relationships between the dislocated element and the rest of the sentence:

(6) Ahora, también hay que contar con que la gente preparada
     now also it.is.necessary to count with that the people prepared
     y la gente con interés, también es muy reducido el número.
     and the people with interest also is very small the number
     (Esgueva and Cantarero 1980: 40)

'Now you also have to bear in mind that the number of people who are prepared and interested is very small.'
(Non-dislocated: [...] *también es muy reducido el número de (la) gente preparada y (la) gente) con interés*)

In Spanish, Verb–Subject order (without an intonational juncture) is frequent and cannot be considered to constitute right-dislocation. Hidalgo (2000: 140) says that right-dislocation (of the subject, with an intonational juncture) in Spanish has an affective function, as in (7), where *el pobre* is added as a humorous comment:

(7) Se parece mucho a su madre, <u>el</u> <u>pobre</u>.
     he is like much to his mother the poor
     'He looks very much like his mother, poor thing.'

Italian appears to behave more like French. Samek-Lodovici (2015: 78–84) claims that right-dislocation is 'extremely productive' in Italian, with many constituents being susceptible to the process (e.g., direct object in (8a) and prepositional complements in (8b)); more than one constituent can be dislocated at a time (8c), and clitic doubling is not always necessary with non-direct objects (*di Maria* is not doubled by *ne* in (8d); see Cruschina 2016: 601f.):

(8) a. Li   abbiamo mangiati, <u>i</u>   <u>funghi</u>. (It.)
         them we.have eaten   the mushrooms
         'We've eaten the mushrooms.'
     b. Ne   abbiamo parlato a lungo, <u>di</u> <u>Maria</u>. (It.)
         of.her we.had spoken at length of Maria
         'We had spoken at length about Maria.'
     c. Non glie=ne   ha   parlato, <u>Marco</u>, <u>della</u> <u>guerra</u>, <u>ai</u>   <u>bambini</u>. (It.)
         not them.IO=of.it he.has spoken   Marco   of.the   war   to.the children
         'Marco hasn't spoken to the children about the war.'
     d. Gianni gli   ha   già   parlato, <u>a</u> <u>Marco</u>, <u>di</u> <u>Maria</u>. (It.)
         Gianni him.IO he.has already spoken   to Marco of Maria
         'Gianni has already spoken to Marco about Maria.'

All these instances show intonational junctures. (In Romanian, left-dislocation of direct and indirect objects, with obligatory clitic resumption, is no longer exclusively associated with spoken register.) For further discussion, see also Section 26.3.

27.2.3.3 Passive

Correlation between the incidence of the formal equivalents of the English BE-passive and register is well established: e.g., Eng. *This letter was written by my sister* / Fr. *Cette lettre a été écrite par ma sœur* / Sp. *Esta carta fue escrita por mi hermana* / Pt. *Esta carta foi escrita pela minha irmã* / It. *Questa lettera è stata scritta da mia sorella* / Ro. *Această scrisoare a fost scrisă de sora mea*. This passive is more frequent in the standard written Romance languages than in the spontaneous spoken languages, where the reflexive passive (cf. Section 18.5), the active with left-dislocation of the object (see Sections 19.4 and 27.2.3.2–3), or the indefinite third person active (and in French the indefinite subject *on*) are more frequent (Cennamo 2016: 967). While indeed the form is particularly infrequent in speech, we can be more discriminating about its association with different written registers: Green (1975), having posed the question of how frequent the passive was in Spanish, concludes that 'only a certain amount can be said which does not require riders and modification according to the register involved' (Green 1975: 360), and shows that the Spanish *ser* 'be' passive is most frequent in journalistic reporting and lowest in creative writing; he also notes that expression of a agent introduced by *por* 'by' is infrequent even in reporting. In present-day Romanian, the passive periphrasis with *a fi* 'be' is associated with high registers, and with academic and legal texts (Dragomirescu 2013: 171).

27.2.3.4 Relativizers

In general, formal written language is characterized by the use of relativizers which make the syntactic function of the antecedent explicit, while in spontaneous spoken language less exact relativizers are employed (cf. Fiorentino 1999), for example:

(9) una excursión que hicimos para subir al Teide
    an excursion REL we.made to   go.up to.the Teide
    que   entonces no   había   telesilla
    which then   NEG there.was chairlift
    = [...] donde / en donde / en el que no   había   telesilla
            where / at where / on.REL   NEG there.was chairlift
    'an excursion we made to climb Teide, on which there was then no chairlift'
    (Cortés Rodríguez 1987: 307, cited Pountain 2008: 969)

It is easy to see that the precise sense of the relativizer *que* in (9) is pragmatically derivable from the context, and so the utterance is perfectly understandable. The spoken languages do, however, have a strategy for providing information about the function of the antecedent: the relative clause includes a resumptive pronominal mention, as in (10a–b). Such constructions tend to be castigated puristically and so are very clear markers of spontaneous spoken usage.

(10) a. Ali vai o homem que eu falei com ele (non-standard Pt.; Bechara 2009: 166)
       there he.goes the man REL I spoke with him
     = Ali vai o homem com quem eu falei (standard Pt.)
       there he.goes the man with REL I talked
       'There goes the man with whom I talked / who I talked to'
   b. Fata care am vorbit cu ea (non-standard Ro.)
       girl.the REL I.have talked with her
     = Fata cu care am vorbit (standard Ro.)
       girl.the with REL I.have talked
       'The girl with whom I talked / the girl I talked to'

In Romanian, clitic doubling of the direct object is obligatory, regardless of register (Stark 2016: 1038f.); where the non-standard spoken language differs from the written standard is in the absence of the differential object marker *pe* (lit. 'on') (Vulpe 1975), thus:

(11) Casa pe care am cumpărat-o (standard Ro.)
     house.the OBJ which I.have bought=it
     = Casa care am cumpărat-o (non-standard Ro.)
       house.the REL I.have bought=it
     'The house which I bought'

Conversely, the use of relativizers which are marked for number and gender, which can combine with prepositions, or which have a very specific function, is more frequent in formal written register. The development of forms deriving from Lat. QUALE(M) 'which' (Fr. *lequel*, Sp. *el cual*, Pt. *o qual*, Cat. *el qual*, It. *il quale*, etc.) may have been encouraged by this (see Pountain 2011b: 647f.); the relative adjectives Sp. *cuyo* and Pt. *cujo*, denoting a genitive relationship, despite also being apparently inherited in popular speech from Latin, are clearly associated with the standard language and formal register, and the same is broadly true of Sp. *quien* 'who(m)', which today is animate-referring, and has developed a plural form *quienes* (see Pountain 2008: 968). Standard Romanian has only recently lost number and gender inflexion on the nominative-accusative forms of the relativizer *care* 'which' (from QUALE(M) – *carele*, *carea*, *carii*), and case inflexion, illustrated by the dative-genitive forms *cărui(a)*, *cărei(a)*, *căror(a)*, is clearly restricted to formal registers.

The use of what is sometimes called the 'transition relative' (Blatt 1957: 56), i.e., use of a relative simply to signal anaphoric reference to a previous mention of a noun or noun phrase, is strongly associated with formal register:

(12) Tale è il principio che dobbiamo tener presente:
     such is the principle which we.should keep present

> il quale principio si fonda [...]
> REL principle REFL founds
> (Battaglia and Pernicone 1965: 269, cited in Pountain 2011b: 648)
> 'Such is the principle we should bear in mind; this principle is founded [...]'

27.2.3.5 Future Tense Functions

There is a widespread tendency in spoken registers of Romance for the expression of reference to future time to be indicated not by the synthetic future (Fr. *je sortirai*, Sp. *saldré*, Pt. *sairei*, etc. '(I) exit.FUT.1SG'), but by either the simple present (Fr. *je sors*, Sp. *salgo*, Pt. *saio* '(I) exit.PRS.1SG') or a paraphrase (Fr. *je vais sortir*, Sp. *voy a salir*, Pt. *vou sair* '(I) go.1SG (to) exit.INF'). Kahane and Hutter (1953: 21, cited in Fleischman 1982: 101) claim that the synthetic future is well-nigh absent in spoken Brazilian Portuguese.

The epistemic and evidential use of the future is also correlatable with the spoken and informal registers of the Romance languages. The epistemic future is more frequent and multifunctional in Italian than in French (Squartini 2001), and it is partially grammaticalized in Romanian (where it is sometimes described as a 'presumptive mood'). In Romanian (Zafiu 2013: 40f.) its association with the informal register is demonstrated by the fact that a part of its paradigm uses almost exclusively a colloquial variant of the future (*o fi* 'will be').

(13) O fi   deja   ora   opt. (Ro.)
      be.FUT.3SG already hour eight
      Saranno   già   le   otto. (It.)
      be.FUT.3PL already the   eight
      'It must be eight o'clock already.'

The evidential (hearsay) value of the conditional, or future in the past, which is common to several standardized Romance languages (Squartini 2008), is viewed as specific to journalistic register, even though it may also appear in other contexts (e.g., in academic writing) when it is necessary to report statements and to mark the speaker's lack of commitment to the truth of the assertion (in French, it is referred to as the *conditionnel journalistique* 'journalistic conditional', and similar designations are used in other languages). Kronning (2014) shows that this use of the conditional is frequent in French, Italian, and American Spanish, but less present in peninsular Spanish, where it is generally criticized as a Gallicism, though it has actually been attested since the sixteenth century. The same value (attested since the seventeenth century) is frequent in contemporary Romanian (Zafiu 2013: 53; 2016: 28; Popescu 2011). Its use in journalistic register is probably a simple consequence of the extended use of reported speech in mass-media discourse.

27.2.3.6 Morphological Variation

Morphological variation may also be related to register. In Romanian, some morphosyntactic innovations, such as various forms of loss of inflexion, are associated with sub-standard registers: prepositional structures are used instead of the genitive-dative inflected form (e.g., *la câțiva prieteni* 'to some friends' for *câtorva prieteni* 'some.GEN-DAT.PL friends', see Stan 2013: 270) and the inflexional masculine genitive-dative article *lui* is used in a prepositional way for some feminine nouns referring to persons (e.g., *lui prietenul* 'the.GEN-DAT friend.DEF.MSG' for *prietenului* 'friend.DEF.MSG.GEN-DAT' and *lui mama* 'the.GEN-DAT mother.DEF.FSG' for *mamei* 'mother.DEF.FSG.GEN-DAT', see Stan 2013: 264). Standard Romanian prefers inflexional markers that do not produce phonological alternations or, in general, structures which undergo less phonological alternation. In the colloquial language, a tendency to generalize the plural ending *-i* (triggering various forms of allomorphy) to feminine nouns ending in *-ă* (thus *coperți* for *coperte* as the plural of *copertă* 'cover': Pană Dindelegan 2009: 12–15) has become accepted as standard.

27.2.3.7 Discourse Phenomena

In Romanian, the distinctive morphological marking of proper names when used vocatively, e.g., *Ioane!* ('Ion!') corresponding to *Ion*, or *Anǎ!* or *Ano!* ('Ana!') corresponding to *Ana*, is considered colloquial (Croitor and Hill 2013: 805–10). Mazzoleni (1995: 384f.) notes that the difference between the Italian vocative markers also depends on register: *o* being the standard written form (e.g., *O Carlo, ascolta!* 'Oh Carlo, listen!') as opposed to a plethora of sub-standard regional varieties such as *ao* (Roman) and *oi* (Calabrian). Romanian interpellation markers are typically colloquial: on a scale of informality, *măi, bre* are less informal than *mă, fă, bă*. Address inversion (extensively described by Braun 1988: 265–96; e.g., Ro. *mamă* 'mother' addressed by a mother to her child) is also colloquial in Romanian and very frequent in central and southern Italian dialects (Renzi 1968; Mazzoleni 1997).

Discourse markers may also be register-sensitive. López Serena and Borreguero Zuloaga (2010) confirm the hypothesis that Spanish discourse markers are more frequent in oral discourse, especially in their interactional function, and that some markers are specific to informal conversation (e.g., *vale* 'OK', *oye* 'I say', lit. 'hear', *mira* 'look'). These authors consider that while the metadiscursive function of discourse markers is common to both spoken and written discourse, their cognitive function manifests itself more frequently in written register. For further discussion, see Section 24.3.3.

27.3 Genre

As with style (see Section 27.4), it is beyond the scope of this article to engage in the detail of the many genres observable in the Romance languages, even though it is clear that some genres are stereotypically associated with certain linguistic features. For example, texts belonging to legal genre are characterized by the use of nominalizations, generic terms, indefinite pro-forms, impersonal and passive constructions, and explicit connectives (for Italian see Mortara Garavelli 2001 and Serianni 2003: 107–22), and for Romanian see Irimia 1986: 213–43; Stoichiţoiu Ichim 2001: 82–98). As Bakhtine (1984: 265, cited in Adam 2001: 15) observes, '[t]he richness and variety of discourse genres are infinite, since the virtual variety of human activity is inexhaustible and each sphere of activity contains a repertory of discourse genres which continue to differentiate and increase as the sphere gets more complex'. Adam himself, looking at a number of instructional texts (recipes, assembly instructions, topographical guides, horoscopes, and magazine tip columns) argues that even such apparently homogeneous materials should not be viewed as instances of a single text-type or 'family'; for a similarly discriminated account of Spanish instructional texts and identification of their distinctive linguistic features, see Parodi (2010b). The so-called religious genre is also susceptible of over-generalization: sacred texts and liturgy tend to be more conservative, characterized by archaic syntax, such as the expression of the possessive by a definite article before the noun and the possessive following in the well-known traditional form of the Spanish Lord's Prayer (14).

(14) el   pan   nuestro de cada día
     the   bread our   of each day
     'our daily bread'
     (though now modernized to *nuestro pan de cada día*)

In Romanian, a phenomenon which is present almost exclusively in such texts is the placement of the article on the postadjectival noun rather than on the first constituent of the noun phrase (Cornilescu and Nicolae 2011):

(15) mare   mila   ta
     great   mercy=the   your
     'your great mercy'

Sermons, by contrast, are more accepting of colloquial features. In (16), the expression *boîte d'idiots* 'bunch (lit. box) of idiots' is associated with spoken French and would not normally be used in formal written language.

(16) Les non-sauvés voient cette boîte d'idiots et croient que nous sommes tous des idiots.
'Those who are not saved see this bunch of idiots and think we're all idiots.'
(www.moriel.org/teaching/sermons-in-french/a-chink-in-the-armour.html, accessed 7 February 2020)

Since the textual record is such a fundamental resource in the history of the *Ausbau* Romance languages, and since it could be argued that the majority, if not all, manifestations of written language belong to a particular genre characterized by 'a constellation of potential discourse conventions, sustained by previous knowledge' (Parodi 2010a: 25), it follows that attention to genre is crucial in understanding the philological record. Ayres-Bennett (2018) highlights the need to discriminate genre in the use of large-scale multi-genre corpora. In two case studies of French, one on the movement from singular to plural agreement of the verb with a noun phrase involving *la plupart* 'the majority, most' (e.g., *la plupart des gens aiment la musique* 'the majority of people like music') and one on the variation between *en après* (lit. 'in after' and *par après* (lit. 'by after') as alternatives to the simple *après* 'after' in Middle and Classical French, she demonstrates that genre is a significant variable; not only that, but she questions the assumptions commonly made about the proximity of particular genres to speech and the concomitant interpretation of changes as being 'from above' or 'from below'.

Kabatek (2005: 40) insists on the general relevance of discourse tradition (*tradición discursiva*) to the history of Castilian, seeing the extension of vocabulary and syntactic structure and the reduction of linguistic variation in the thirteenth century as being conditioned by the creation of a series of new discourse traditions, sometimes based on models from the textual tradition of other languages, which took place under the aegis of Alfonso X. He further claims (Kabatek 2008) that discourse tradition is an essential determinant of change which must be taken into account in historical linguistics in general. This volume brings together a number of studies which demonstrate the relevance of genre to certain syntactic changes. Only one or two can be mentioned here by way of illustration: Company Company (2008), for example, shows that the grammaticalization of Sp. *hombre* 'man' as an indefinite pronoun (compare the cognate Fr. *on*, Cat. *hom*) was limited to wisdom literature and did not spread further; however, the diffusion of adverbs in *-mente*, which was favoured in the same genre, was successful in becoming more generally established in the language. Pons Bordería (2008) identifies the grammaticalization of Sp. *esto es* 'that is' as stemming from legal texts which used this expression as an equivalent of Lat. *id est* and then spread to scientific texts and translations. Koch (2008) hypothesizes that the use of Sp. *vuestra merced* (lit. 'your mercy') as a polite second person form originates in aristocratic epistolary usage and then spreads into courtly speech, its oral use then propitiating its grammaticalization as, eventually, *usted* (cf. also Section 25.2). An interesting Romance-wide issue raised by Barra Jover (2008) is why the Romance languages may show differential developments in cases of syntactic change for which genre seems to be relevant. He shows that Fr. *ledit* 'the said, aforementioned' diffused into literary texts more readily than its Spanish counterpart *(el) dicho*, which remained limited to legal and administrative discourse, and attributes the differential development to the administrative background of many of the literary authors in the court of the Dukes of Burgundy in the fifteenth century.

Returning to a consideration of the modern languages, Fløttum, Jonasson, and Norén (2007) investigate the values of the French pronoun *on* 'one' in three genres, narrative fiction, conversation, and academic papers, concluding that in conversation *on* is more often equivalent to the first person plural *nous* 'we', while in academic papers it is either generic (referring to both reader and author) or the editorial *we* (referring only to the author); in narrative fiction its reference is variable.

27.4 Style

27.4.1 'Good' Style

In the *Ausbau* Romance languages there is inevitably an association of 'good' style with the standard language. Typical of the process of standardization is what Lodge (1994: 59f.) identifies as a confusion of the stylistic and social axes of variation, the standard being associated stylistically with formal written register and socially with the cultivated ruling classes (in the case of French, first the royal court and then the holders of economic power, the Parisian bourgeoisie). However, the notion of 'good' style also depends on purely linguistic features such as the avoidance of 'cacophony'. Words which rhyme or repeat the same sequences of sounds are to be avoided. In modern Romanian, the word *cacofonie* itself was, as a result of folk etymology, misinterpreted, a fact which gradually led to the banning of the phonological/orthographical sequence *-cac-*, considered to be partially homophonous with a series of taboo words such as *caca* (noun) / *căca* (verb) 'shit'. Thus the conjunction *ca* 'as' was reinforced to *ca și*, the older connective *precum* 'as' was favoured over *ca*, and the metalinguistic term *virgulă* 'comma' was inserted between *ca* and a following word beginning with *ca-/ că-/co-*; the sequence *că când* 'that when', which is homophonous with the gerund of *a căca* (viz. *căcând* 'shitting'), is similarly extended to *că atunci când* 'that then when'. 'Good' style in French, often referred to as *le bon usage*, has since the eighteenth century been associated with clarity, which may be interpreted as a pursuit of transparency between syntax and meaning, in particular, the avoidance of ambiguity and redundancy; the latter principle may account for why the dislocation which is so evident in spoken French (see Section 27.2.3.2) has been resisted in the standard language. Such concerns hark back to Classical precepts: Aisy (1685) listed a number of desirable syntactic features of French which contribute to Quintilian's notions of *emendata oratio* ('purity of language') and *dilucida oratio* ('clarity of language'), of which a few are:

> Parentheticals and long sentences are to be avoided.
> Anaphoric reference and the reference of relative pronouns must be clear.
> Clitics must attach to the verbs to which they pertain.
> *Pour* 'for' and an infinitive must not be separated.
> An auxiliary verb must not be separated from its participle.

In modern times, the mass media (newspapers, television) have been active in encouraging the pursuit of 'good' style: see, for example, *El País* (2014) and *Canal Sur* (2004).

27.4.2 Literary Style

As vehicles for creative literature, what may be referred to as 'artistic' style has also been cultivated in the Romance languages from some of their earliest manifestations (Judge 1994: 69). Again, there is a debt to the classics: exemplified lists of the classical rhetorical figures of speech such as metaphor, simile, synecdoche, etc., are routinely given in many grammars of the Romance languages (for a reference list, exemplified from Spanish, see Pountain 2017: 212f.). In truth, some of these devices are more ingrained in everyday linguistic usage than their identification with creative literary writers would suggest – metaphor and synecdoche are common processes of lexical semantic change – and their exploitation is not a distinctive characteristic of the Romance languages.

An important feature of literary writing (see Section 27.1.3) is what may be seen as the breaking of the rules of the standard language in the interests of artistic effect. In the Renaissance, authors writing in the Romance languages of western Europe often went in the direction of imitation of Latin. Spanish poets of the Golden Age cultivated hyperbaton, or the breaking of syntactic units, as in (17), the first line of Góngora's *Soledad primera*:

(17)   Era   del   año   la   estación   florida
       was   of.the   year   the   season   flowery
       'It was the flowery season of the year'
       (The normal order would be *Era la estación florida del año*)

This echoes the Latin possibility of preposing a genitive to the noun on which it is dependent (though not exactly its topicalizing effect: see Devine and Stephens 2006). Even outside the constraints of poetry, it is possible to identify in Golden Age Spanish a rhetorical style which is used in the discourse of upper-class speakers in prose drama, characterized by the placing of the verb in final position, the more extensive use of adjectives placed before the nouns they qualify, and the use of absolute constructions, all of which were normal features of Classical Latin (see Pountain 2011a: 112–15). In more recent times, departure from the standard has sometimes been quite blatant, with the subversion of both selectional restrictions and even the most fundamental rules of syntax. Désirat and Hordé (1976: 72) say of French Romantic literature: 'what immediately strikes the linguist is that the impression of disorder and syntactic dislocation is, in the full sense of the term, an "artistic effect" and that the starting point of this art is – but always and only from this strict syntactic point of view – the most classical syntax'. One of the most highly regarded works of Brazilian twentieth-century literature, João Guimarães Rosa's *Grande sertão: veredas*, is well known for the difficulties presented by the linguistic inventiveness of the author (see Marquezini 2006). In (18), which presents the intense relationship between the narrator, Riobaldo, and Diadorim, a fellow mercenary, Rosa, emulating colloquial usage overall, uses the unusual verb *desmisturar-se* 'unmix' as the opposite of *misturar-se* 'mix', and the three negatives before the verb in *ninguém nada não falava* lit. 'nobody nothing NEG said (= no one said anything)', the standard constructions being *ninguém falava nada* lit. 'nobody said nothing' or *não falava nada ninguém* lit. 'NEG said nothing nobody'.

(18) Diadorim e eu, nós dois. A gente dava passeios. Com assim, a gente se diferenciava dos outros — porque jagunço não é muito de conversa continuada nem de amizades estreitas: a bem eles se misturam e desmisturam, de acaso, mas cada um é feito um por si. De nós dois juntos, ninguém nada não falava. Tinham a boa prudência. Dissesse um, caçoasse, digo — podia morrer. (João Guimarães Rosa, *Grande sertão: veredas*, Rio de Janeiro: Livraria José Olympio, 1967, p. 25)

'Diadorim and me, the two of us. We used to go for walks. As such, we were different from the others – because mercenaries aren't much given to long conversations or close friendships: they might mix and unmix, on and off, but they all keep themselves to themselves. No one ever said anything at all, ever, about the two of us being together. They were pretty cautious. If anyone had said anything, even as a joke, they might have been killed.'

The stylistic preferences of prestigious authors may end up being very widely proliferated, so that they may become characteristic of a particular genre: what in French is called *style indirect libre* ('free indirect style') has found favour in narrative novelistic writing, probably because of its extensive use by Jane Austen in English and Gustave Flaubert in French (though it is not an exclusively modern phenomenon: see Cerquiglini 1984): in (19), Flaubert follows a description of Charles Bovary's boring personality with a question which follows the sequence of tense of reported speech (*Emma se demandait si un homme ... ne devait pas tout connaître* 'Emma asked herself whether a man ... should not know everything'), representing the thoughts of Emma Bovary about her husband.

(19) La conversation de Charles était plate comme un trottoir de rue ...
Un homme, au contraire, ne devait-il pas tout connaître, exceller en des activités multiples, vous initier aux énergies de la passion, aux raffinements de la vie, à tous les mystères? (Gustave Flaubert, *Madame Bovary*, Paris: Garnier-Flammarion, 1966, p. 76)

'Charles's conversation was as flat as a street pavement ... Should a man not rather know everything, excel in many different activities, introduce you to the forces of passion, to the refinements of life, to all mysteries?'

An important question for all historical linguists who habitually rely on written texts, especially literary works, for evidence of past states of the languages they are studying is how 'style' is to be interpreted philologically: for two practical examples from the history of Spanish, see the discussion of the 'style' of Santa Teresa de Ávila's *Libro de la vida* in Pountain (2016b) and the detailed case study of adjective position in the *Poema de Mio Cid* in Pountain (1996).

27.5 The Importance of Diaphasic Variation in the History of the Romance Languages

Latin diastratic and diaphasic variation is difficult to investigate, but what we do know suggests that it is of great relevance for an understanding of the emergence of the Romance languages. It has sometimes been assumed that the Romance languages derive from the spoken Latin which steadily evolved into the Romance vernaculars, rather than from written Latin, which was often highly contrived in style and conservative in its adherence to the precepts of Classical grammarians. However, Adams (2013: 841–53) has identified two directions of linguistic change: 'from below' (for example, ECCE 'behold' or variants such as *akku < ECCE HUM, where ECCE is followed by a demonstrative, which spread from informal spoken registers and provided the source for Romance demonstratives such as Cat. *aqueix* 'that (near addressee)' < *akku IPSE), and 'from above' (for example, the future periphrasis with HABEO 'have', which is first encountered in high registers of Latin).

27.5.1 'Learnèd' Influence

As shown by Pountain (2011b), for a long period the prestigious writers of the main western Romance languages were diglossic, continuing to use Latin for some text types but also as a model and source for lexical and syntactical borrowings. The situation was rather different for Romanian, where elaboration of the vernacular came relatively late and it was Old Church Slavonic and probably Byzantine Greek that were the prestige languages. Yet here too Latin became a model for some writers in the seventeenth and eighteenth centuries, and Latin word order was deliberately imitated in literary Romanian (Nicolae 2019: 68f.). The standardization of Romanian, despite taking place within a period of Romantic nationalistic ideology in which the vernacular was valued, none the less imported a large number of words (often of 'learnèd' Latin origin), collocations, and even syntactic patterns from French and Italian, which had the effect of increasing the distance between the vernacular and the standard written language (see Section 27.5.2). In all these routes of borrowing we must suppose that the point of entry into the host language was written register and cultured genres (see also Pountain 2006).

Romance lexical borrowings from Latin are often difficult to distinguish from inherited words, since they can generally be easily assimilated: see Reinheimer-Rîpeanu (2004a; 2004b), which also addresses the phenomenon of the downward migration of such words. The same can be said of some learnèd syntactic constructions which can be identified as calques from written Latin. Vincent (2007) investigates adjective position in old Italian texts, calling attention to the importance of the relation between register, genre, and style and adjective pre-position at different periods.

27.5.2 The Relative Distance between Registers

Even though, as we have seen, every *Ausbau* language has a register hierarchy, there are many differences between the Romance languages with respect to the relative distance and relationships of diastratic and diaphasic varieties. Contrasting cases are the strong elaboration and centralization of high register for both written and spoken French (though *le bon usage* is not completely hostile to variation: see Ayres-Bennett and Seijodo 2013) as opposed to focalization on the prestigious written form and the absence of a common spoken variety before national unification in Italy. As noticed by Dardano (2006: 1959), in Italy 'the lack of a common language is the prime cause of the high degree of formality of the traditional literary language'. Koch and Oesterreicher (2011) tried to measure the magnitude of the discrepancy on a scale of what they term 'immediacy' and 'distance' in French, Italian, and Spanish, one of their conclusions being that French displays the greatest distance between the extreme points on the axis (Koch and Oesterreicher 2011: 270f.). However, in the present-day Romance languages there appears to be a good deal of cross-influence between written registers and orality (especially due to popular mass-media and virtual communication) as a result of which standard varieties are losing prestige and 'high' registers are being brought closer to the colloquial (Sobrero 2005; D'Achille 2011: 261; Zafiu 2001: 45).

27.5.3 Attitudinal Factors

The modern Romance languages have also been shaped by puristic attitudes which have been taken on the basis of an awareness of diaphasic variation. For example, diminutives (see Section 27.2.3.1) have been both castigated in formal registers because of their affective values (Dressler and Merlini Barbaresi 1994: 409f.), but also praised for their expressivity: Manni (1737: 57) said that diminutives in Italian 'make our speech abundant, as well as delightful and expressive'.

Clitic doubling in Italian, associated with low-register varieties, was generally criticized as 'pleonastic' by sixteenth-century grammars (D'Achille 2011: 178), and is associated with various degrees of informality (Poletto and Sanfelici 2017: 821). Yet in Romanian such normative attitudes were only developed when the phenomenon was already very frequent and almost fully grammaticalized, and so nineteenth-century rationalist critiques (e.g., Budai Deleanu 2011) had no effect. Moreover, twentieth-century grammars accepted clitic doubling in the standard language and even recommended it, thus accelerating its use.

Features of the written language may similarly generalize in time and become prescriptively acceptable. An example is the suffix *-ment(e)* '-ly', which came to predominate in written Romance and subsequently became the main means of adverb formation in all the standard Romance languages with the exception of Romanian (Hummel 2017: 26f.); it appears originally to have been a feature of high registers of written Latin (Bauer 2011: 255) which eventually migrated downwards.

27.6 Conclusion

Because of their common ideological models and cultural traditions, the Romance languages show understandable similarities in the nature and even the detail of their diaphasic variation. More intriguing, perhaps, are the differences among and within them, the study of which is still only very partial. Realization of the importance of diaphasic variation in language change, especially with regard to the identification of textual traditions and the extraction of variational data from the available textual record in which the standardized Romance languages are rich, has opened up new and necessary challenges for Romance historical linguistics. A particularly urgent concern lies in incorporating sensitivity to such variation in the exploitation of the large corpora which have been created in recent years.

Selected References

Below you can find selected references for this chapter. The full references can be found online at the following page: www.cambridge.org/Romancelinguistics

Adams, J. (2013). *Social Variation and the Latin Language*. Cambridge: Cambridge University Press.
Ayres-Bennett, W. and Carruthers, J. (eds), *Manual of Romance Sociolinguistics*. Berlin/Boston: De Gruyter, 253–79.
Bally, C. (1951). *Traité de stylistique française*. Geneva/Paris: Georg/Klincksieck.
Beeching, K., Armstrong, N., and Gadet, F. (eds), *Sociolinguistic Variation in Contemporary French*. Amsterdam/Philadelphia: Benjamins, 115–20.
Coleman, J. and Crawshaw, R. (eds) (1994). *Discourse Variety in Contemporary French. Descriptive and Pedagogical Approaches*. London: Association for French Language Studies/Centre for Information on Language Teaching and Research.
Guiraud, P. (1978). *Le Français populaire*. Paris: Presses Universitaires de France.
Iordan, I. ([1944] 1975). *Stilistica limbii române*. Bucharest: Editura Științifică.
Koch, P. and Oesterreicher, W. (2011). *Gesprochene Sprache in der Romania: Französisch, Italienisch, Spanisch*. Berlin/New York: De Gruyter.
Oesterreicher, W. (1996). 'Lo hablado en lo escrito: reflexiones metodológicas y aproximación a una tipología'. In Kotschi, T, Oesterreicher, W., and Zimmermann, K. (eds), *El español hablado y la cultura oral en España e Hispanoamérica*. Frankfurt am Main/Madrid: Verwuert/Iberoamericana, 317–40.
Parodi, G. (ed). (2010b). *Academic and Professional Discourse Genres in Spanish*. Amsterdam/Philadelphia: Benjamins.
Pountain, C. (2017). *Exploring the Spanish Language*. London/New York: Routledge, chs 7–8.
Zafiu, R. (2001). *Diversitate stilistică în româna actuală*. Bucharest: Editura Universității din București.

28

Contact and Borrowing

Francesco Gardani

28.1 Introduction

Language contact describes that state of affairs in which speakers of different languages have some kind of linguistic interaction with each other. The circumstances under which this may happen differ in nature and extent and include individual multilingualism, societal multilingualism, and even mere exposure to other languages via, for example, the media or sacred texts. Thus, language contact is a phenomenon which is responsible for potential changes in language, viz. contact-induced change, whose extent may vary considerably depending on the degree of multilingual interaction itself (cf. also Section 2.5). The study of language contact is therefore of crucial importance to our understanding of the evolutionary dynamics of language. A fundamental process and result of contact-induced language change is borrowing. This has rightly been considered one of the principal sources of language change, along with sound change and analogy (see Anttila 1989; Bybee 2015: 248) and consequently it plays a decisive role in the field of contact linguistics. The Romance languages have the potential to contribute substantially to this area of investigation, since they have a wide geospatial distribution, a long history of contact with several typologically diverse languages, and are abundantly documented. As a matter of fact, the Romance linguistic landscape cuts across multiple possible contact setting types, including: contact between languages of one family (Romance) and a different one (non-Romance); contact between languages of the same family; settings in which a Romance language is the recipient language (RL); others in which a Romance language is the source language (SL); settings in which a SL is either a substrate (e.g., Semitic for Sicilian on the island of Pantelleria, see Section 28.3.3) or a superstrate (e.g., Latin/Romance for Greek in southern Italy in ancient and Byzantine periods) or an adstrate (English for modern Italian); locally circumscribed contact (e.g., Raeto-Romance and German); areal formation (e.g., Romance in the Balkans); long-term contact settings, such as those between Spanish and the indigenous languages of the Americas; short-term contact settings originating in migration (e.g., Romanian in contact with Italian in Italy); and finally, settings such as overseas explorations and colonial processes favouring the genesis of creoles (e.g., Portuguese-lexifier creoles). Of course, language contact also concerns and affects sign languages, for which the reader is referred to Quinto-Pozos and Adam (2015) and Zeshan and Webster (2020), for an overview and references. Given these facts, the empirical evidence for contact-induced change involving Romance is abundant, as reflected by an impressive body of published work, although this mostly deals with individual case studies (e.g., Drewes 1994; Breu 2008; Remberger 2011; Ralli 2012; 2013; Dal Negro 2013; Adamou, Breu, Scholze, and Shen 2016; Saade 2016; 2020).

Another reason why the Romance family qualifies as an ideal testbed for language contact studies is that the Romance languages are diverse enough among themselves to be appealing for cross-linguistic generalizations and at the same time, homogeneous enough to ensure comparability between a Romance 'common ground' and all possible sorts of contact languages. However, this great potential has remained largely untapped in one main respect: the Romance data have not been used in their entirety to test theories of contact-induced language change and in particular borrowing. The present chapter takes up this challenge and, by drawing on empirical evidence from a broad range of Romance varieties, aims to outline contact-induced grammatical change and provide a critical assessment of the state-of-the-art in research on borrowing as a key mechanism of contact-induced language change and variation.

This chapter is structured as follows. Section 28.2 is devoted to the effects that language contact can exert on grammar and details the difference between innovative and conservative effects, as well as that between addition and loss. Section 28.3 discusses borrowing as the basic mechanism leading to change, distinguishing between RL and SL agentivity, and between matter borrowing and pattern borrowing. The ensuing subsections are dedicated to phonological borrowing (Section 28.3.1), prosodic borrowing (Section 28.3.2), morphological borrowing (Section 28.3.3), and syntactic borrowing (Section 28.3.4). Section 28.4 discusses the upper limits of borrowing, specifically in terms of areal formation and mixed language genesis. Section 28.5 reviews a number of main predictors of grammatical borrowing by providing evidence, both for and against, involving Romance languages, and Section 28.6 critically addresses issues concerning the so-called borrowability hierarchies.

28.2 Effects of Language Contact

Language contact typically involves individual users, or a whole speech community, acquainted with at least two languages. The grammatical systems of these two languages might be incongruent, in one way or another, and to different degrees. What happens in this case? In principle, nothing needs to happen to languages in contact, in the spirit of Keenan's (2002) principle of 'inertia' (see also Roberts 2017 and for a critique of Longobardi's 2001 implementation, see Waldken 2012): '[t]hings stay as they are unless acted upon by an outside force or DECAY' (Keenan 2002: 327). Often, however, contact does affect at least one of the languages in contact. To take one concrete case, several Mayan languages have borrowed vocabulary items from Spanish, displaying consonantal clusters in word-initial position, for example *cruz* /krus/ 'cross'. In Mayan languages, however, word-initial consonantal clusters are not admitted. Therefore, two scenarios are possible: the RL either accepts the phonotactic rule of the SL, that is, the new word is taken over just as it is, or it accommodates the system-incongruent loanword to fit into its own phonological system: the latter scenario is 'phonological accommodation' (Lehiste 1988: 2), which is often accomplished by deletion, addition, or recombination of certain sounds. In the case of Sp. *cruz* in the Mayan RLs the second scenario obtained. Accordingly, Ch'ol accommodated the Spanish loanword as *rus* by deleting the initial consonantal segment, and Tzotzil rendered it as *kurus* by breaking the consonant cluster via vowel insertion (Campbell 1996: 98). Evidently, phonological accommodation (but also morphological accommodation, see Gardani 2013; 2019) is just an adjustment imposed by the existing phonological system and, importantly, it does not lead to any change in an RL. As we will see below, the real manifestation of change in an RL occurs whenever alien forms and patterns are added to the native stock and inventory or are eliminated from it. In other cases, when in an RL variables exist to realize a feature (for instance, when more than one form competes for one and the same output, see Gardani, Rainer, and Luschützky 2019) change can manifest itself through the fact that the weak competitors are maintained under the influence of an SL which has similar or parallel forms and structures, rather than being abandoned in favour of stronger competitors. In our Mayan-Spanish contact case, the alien phonotactic rule was not accepted into the native system, however a change did occur at the level of the lexicon, namely a new word became part of the lexical inventory of the RLs. It is noteworthy that language contact is often just an accomplice that 'could be considered to have, at best, a trigger effect, releasing or accelerating developments which mature independently' (Weinreich 1953: 25).

In the literature, one comes upon lists of several types of contact effects, such as, for example, convergence and divergence (Braunmüller and House 2009), language attrition (Schmid and Köpke 2019), language decay (Sasse 1992), language genesis (Lefebvre 2015), and language shift (Fishman 1964). All of these, however, practically boil down to representing varying degrees of two ontologically basic types of effects affecting an RL: innovative effects and conservative effects. Both the lexicon and the grammar can be subject to them. Contact-induced innovation occurs when an SL feeds an RL (addition) or when an SL bleeds an RL (loss).

Specifically, addition consists in a linguistic element (form, feature, pattern) of the SL being added to the RL, such as the introduction of novel grammatical oppositions. Such a case has seemingly been the phonemicization of voiced fricatives in early Middle English because of massive loanword imports from Anglo-Norman (Jagemann 1884: 67) and later central French: the phonematic inventory of Old English included the fricatives /f/, /θ/, and /s/, whereas their voiced counterparts [v], [ð], and [z] had allophonic status and only appeared in voiced environments (1c) (Minkova 2014: 90). Only in Middle English times, partly due to Romance input (1b), did a phonological opposition emerge, as minimal pairs such as native *ferry* vs borrowed *very* in (1a) bear witness (see further Minkova 2011 and Hickey 2016: 206).

(1) a. Early Middle English ferry   very
    b. Anglo-Norman   fer 'iron'   ver 'to see'
    c. Old English   wulf [wulf] 'wolf' wulfas [wulvas] 'wolves'

An RL can also lose a feature under the influence of an SL, because that feature does not exist in the SL. Loss can affect a concrete lexeme or formative or an abstract pattern, such as an agreement pattern. In a study on the linguistic effects of Swiss German-Romansh bilingualism in central Grisons, Weinreich (2011: 322) observed that bilingual children would produce sentences such as (2a), displaying the citation form of the adjective *cotschen* 'red' (/ˈkotʃan/). Those children thus failed to realize the mandatory Romansh rule which requires subject agreement on predicative adjectives to yield (2c), in which the adjective is marked feminine singular. The reason is that they replicated the Swiss German pattern (2b), in which this kind of agreement rule is absent.

(2) a. Romansh RL   /la   tʃaˈpetʃa   ɛ   ˈkotʃan/
                     DET.FSG   hat.F   is   red
    b. Swiss German /dr   huat   iʃ   roːt/
                     DET.MSG   hat.M   is   red
    c. Romansh   /la   tʃaˈpetʃa   ɛ   ˈkotʃna/
                     DET.FSG   hat.F   is   red.FSG
                     'The hat is red.'

Thus far, we have seen cases in which language contact has had innovative effects on an RL, in one or another way. However, language contact can also inhibit change, that is, it has conservative effects. It can promote the retention of a grammatical feature, preventing internal developments when variants that are otherwise recessive in varieties not affected by contact are maintained, or conversely, inhibit the emergence of a feature. Enrique-Arias (2010) has shown that contact with Catalan has produced a conservative effect on the varieties of Spanish spoken on the island of Majorca: he observes that a number of features attested in Majorcan Spanish are recessive in general Spanish. One such feature is strict negative concord requiring a preverbal negator even in the presence of a fronted negative polarity item (3a) (data from Enrique-Arias 2010: 106f.). Enrique-Arias shows that strict negative concord (as well as other features) was a possible variable of Spanish when the language was introduced into the island (cf. old Spanish in 3c), and convincingly argues that this feature has most likely been retained because of the existence of parallel structures in Catalan (3d).

(3) a. Majorcan Spanish En ningún momento no se ha planteado …
 in no moment NEG CL=has planned
 'She has at no point considered [resigning].'
 b. Standard Spanish Nadie (**no) ha venido.
 nobody NEG has come
 c. Old Spanish nadi no l diessen posada.
 nobody NEG=3MSG.DAT give lodging
 '[that] nobody should give him a place to rest.'
 d. Catalan Ningú no ha vingut.
 nobody NEG has come
 'Nobody has come.'

In a totally different sociogeographic context, the same old Spanish strict negative concord pattern was retained in Paraguayan Spanish (4a) due to contact with Guarani (4b), which employs it as a standard construction (Granda 1991).

(4) a. Paraguayan Spanish Nada no dije.
 nothing NEG say.PST.1SG
 b. Guarani Mba'eve nda-'ei.
 nothing NEG-say.PST.1SG
 c. Standard Spanish Nada dije / No dije nada.
 nothing say.PST.1SG NEG say.PST.1SG nothing
 'I said nothing.'

We have seen which general effects language contact can have on an RL. We have, however, not yet asked what mechanisms lead to innovative or conservative effects. As far as conservative effects are concerned, it appears clear that the existence of parallel structures, or identical forms, in the languages in contact has a stabilizing effect and can foster their maintenance. On the other hand, the absence of a feature in one contact language is mimicked in the other. As for innovative effects, however, change occurs mainly through the mechanisms of codeswitching and borrowing, the latter the topic of discussion in Section 28.3.

Note furthermore that while in this chapter I take an almost exclusively systemic perspective on language change (for a similar perspective, see also Sala 1998; 2013), other authors adopt an activity-oriented approach to contact-induced language change based on an understanding of language as the practice of communicative interaction, organized at the level of discourse, rather than in terms of a system. For example, Matras (2012: 22) claims that contact phenomena 'are the product of language-processing in goal-oriented communicative interaction' and enable, rather than interfere with, the communicative activity. According to Matras, the bilingual speaker has a more complex repertoire of communicative structures than the monolingual speaker, and is keen to exploit it in its entirety; on the other hand, a bilingual speaker has to select the options that are contextually appropriate and abandon those that are not on the basis of a 'selection and inhibition mechanism' (for a critique, see Gardani 2014).

28.3 Borrowing

Probably the most famous classification of mechanisms of lexical and grammatical transfer is the distinction between borrowing and substratum interference proposed by Thomason and Kaufman (1988): as they explain, borrowing is associated with situations of language maintenance, whereas interference is related to situations of imperfect learning and language shift. Simultaneously, van Coetsem (1988) formulated another dichotomy: borrowing vs imposition (see also van Coetsem 2000). While apparently similar, the two dichotomous pairs are, in fact, fundamentally different. Van Coetsem's two types of transfer are conceived in terms of agentivity, a concept which is based on the notion of linguistic dominance (Lucas 2015: 522 has criticized van Coetsem's (lack of) definition of 'dominance/dominant', while research on language control mechanisms – Costa, Branzi, and Ávila 2016 – provides supporting evidence for the psycholinguistic role of dominance). While the direction of transfer is obviously always from an SL to an RL, the agents of change can be speakers of either language. Borrowing occurs when the agents are dominant in the language *into* which they transfer (RL agentivity), while imposition occurs when agents are dominant in the language *from* which they transfer (SL agentivity).

However, in many contact situations RL agentivity and SL agentivity are complementary, and not exclusive. Van Coetsem's model contemplates a third scenario in which the distinction between the two transfer types is neutralized. Such a case has been identified by Winford (2005: 408) in the case of Asia Minor Greek famously described by Dawkins (1916). Winford claims that Greek-dominant bilinguals implemented RL agentivity, while Turkish-dominant bilinguals implemented SL agentivity, at the same time. In addition, at the level of intra-individual bilingualism, 'some bilinguals may have implemented both types simultaneously' (for discussion and examples, see van Coetsem 1990: 261–64).

Ideally, when studying cases of contact-induced change, one should have to detail the agentivity types at play in each specific case. It goes without saying that, whenever information concerning the dynamics of agentivity is available, it ought to be provided. Unfortunately, the dynamics of language contact are rarely documented in such a precise way as to allow us to know exactly what the mechanism was. Alternatively, one could resort to the differential linguistic outcomes of different contact settings, as predicted, for example, by Thomason and Kaufman (1988: 37–45). But these predictions are probabilistic and as such might produce circular judgements. For these reasons, I prefer to operate with 'borrowing' as an overarching term 'to refer to a process whereby a language acquires some structural property from another language' (Moravcsik 1978: 99), whatever mechanism of transfer was at play. While precise demarcations between codeswitching and borrowing are generally regarded as difficult to identify, I concur with Haspelmath (2009: 40) that '[c]ode-switching is not a kind of contact-induced language change, but rather a kind of contact-induced speech behavior'. Also, Meakins (2013: 187) has pointed to the artificial character of this differentiation, which is likely to mirror the separation between historical linguistics – focusing on language change – and contact linguistics – focusing on the bilingual individual.

The term borrowing is mostly associated with lexical borrowing, i.e., the borrowing of lexical material. No doubt this is the most evident and probably the most frequent type, and the literature on lexical borrowing is enormous (for a selection of inspired studies, see, for example, Hope 1971; Malkiel 1975; Miller 2006; 2012; Haspelmath and Tadmor 2009; Durkin 2014; Queiroz de Barros 2018). However, as the above examples have shown, borrowing may also affect the grammar of an RL. Grammatical borrowing refers to the adoption of grammatical elements and/or patterns of an SL in an RL, given a situation of contact between speakers of two languages. The elements and/or patterns can involve all levels of grammar, phonetics, phonology, prosody, morphology, morphosyntax, and syntax. In this sense, grammatical borrowing is complementary to lexical borrowing. In the following subsections, I will focus on specific subtypes of grammatical borrowing according to the areas of grammar affected by language contact. Before doing so, one central distinction (which, in fact, concerns both lexical and grammatical borrowing) has to be introduced, viz. matter borrowing vs pattern borrowing (adopting the terminology coined by Matras and Sakel 2007b; Sakel 2007).

Matter borrowing is the borrowing of an actual formative along with its meaning/function. It can be exemplified with the native Spanish number plural suffix -s (5b), which in Bolivian Quechua replaces the native suffix -*kuna* (5c) to encode nominal plural and which is obligatorily used on native Quechua bases (5a) (Bolivian Quechua data from Muysken 2012: 33f., based on Urioste 1964) in (5).

(5) a. Bolivian Quechua algu algu-s
    b. Spanish perro perro-s
    c. Quechua allqu allqu-kuna
       dog dogs-PL
       'dog' 'dogs'

Pattern borrowing is the borrowing of abstract structures or of rules. It can be exemplified with the periphrastic realization of the comparative in Molise Croatian (6a) according to an Italian model (6b), as opposed to synthetic comparative formation in Standard Croatian (6c) (Breu 1996: 26).

(6) a. Molise Croatian veče lip
    b. Italian più bello
       more pretty
    c. Croatian ljepši
       pretty.CMPR
       'prettier'

As we will see in Section 28.4, pattern borrowing represents the principal factor in the diffusion of structural traits and the development of linguistic areas.

28.3.1 Phonological Borrowing

As observed in Section 28.2, very often speakers of RLs accommodate system-incongruent loanwords to fit into the phonological systems of their languages. As Liberman, Harris, Hoffman, and Griffith (1957: 358) put it, 'a person who is newly exposed to the sounds of a strange language finds it necessary to categorize familiar acoustic continua in unfamiliar ways'. The same mechanism applies to everyday communication when we listen to speech: we cast many sounds to which we are exposed into 'one or another of the phoneme categories that [our] language allows' (ibid.). In fact, 'the main task of phoneme perception systems in the brain is to enable [a] perceptual equivalence' between related speech sounds (Binder 2016: 447). Psychological research (Kuhl 1991; Kuhl, Williams, Lacerda, Stevens, and Lindblom 1992; Feldman, Griffiths, and Morgan 2009) has demonstrated that listeners tend to cluster perceptual stimuli, i.e., speech sounds, into prototypes which act as 'perceptual magnets', a phenomenon that has been dubbed the 'perceptual magnet effect' (Kuhl 1991).

In situations of bilingualism and intensive language contact as well, speakers are continuously exposed to input from a second language. The conflict between incongruent phonological properties of languages in contact can be solved in terms of phonological adaptation, as in the Mayan/ Spanish case in Section 28.2, but it can also lead to the introduction of new phonological distinctions in an RL (for a recent collection of case studies on Romance-Germanic bilingual phonology, see Yavaş, Kehoe, and Cardoso 2017). On the basis of the assumption that language experience alters perception (Kuhl, Lacerda, Stevens, and Lindblom 1992), Blevins (2017) has hypothesized that external (i.e., foreign) phonetic prototypes may be internalized by RL speakers and act as new catalyzers in an RL. A paper by Egurtzegi (2017) provides an elegant analysis of phonological borrowing in terms of the role of the perceptual magnet effect. Modern Basque dialects normally only have five contrastive vowels (Michelena 1977: 47), /i, e, a, o, u/, but Zuberoan (Souletin) and the neighbouring Mixean variety of low Navarrese also have the front rounded high vowel phoneme /y/. See the following minimal pair (Lafon 1962).

(7) hun   vs hün
     'good'   'marrow'

Speakers of Zuberoan and low Navarrese have been in close and sustained contact with speakers of the Romance variety of Bearnese Gascon. Egurtzegi (2017) claims that /u/-fronting, which eventually led to /y/, is due to the influence of the neighbouring Gallo-Romance languages Gascon and French, which possess a /u/ vs /y/ contrast. Since /y/ is a perceptually salient vowel (Blevins 2017: 107), it might have acted as a prototype attracting tokens of the phonetically close /u/.

While this Basque case illustrates an additive effect of borrowing, the next case illustrates contact-induced phonological loss, more precisely a case of loss occurring in the context of language attrition. Standard Italian, just like most central and southern Italo-Romance varieties, presents a singleton vs geminate contrast, yielding minimal pairs such as *caro* 'dear' vs *carro* 'wagon'. Lucchese, the northern Tuscan variety spoken in Lucca, also displays distinctive consonantal length, but also shows an ongoing degemination process, which is variable in nature and mostly affects the alveolar trill (e.g., /ˈtɛrːa/ > [ˈtɛra] 'land') and sporadically, other consonants as well (e.g., /maˈtːone/ > [maˈtone] 'brick'). In a perception study conducted on 15 Lucchese-speaking immigrants in San Francisco (California), Celata and Cancila (2010) found that the weakening of the geminate opposition has gone far beyond the situation just described for the variety spoken in Lucca, apparently resulting in the loss – in perception – of the distinctive opposition, under the influence of English, which lacks distinctive consonant length. As a result, the test subjects were not able to discern between the pairs in (8a–c) (Celata and Cancila 2010: 192).

(8) a. [rː]-[r] caro lontano   carro lontano
              [ˈkaro lonˈtano]   [ˈkarːo lonˈtano]
              'distant relative'   'distant wagon'
    b. [sː]-[s] casa aperta   cassa aperta
              [ˈkasa aˈpɛrta]   [ˈkasːa aˈpɛrta]
              'open house'   'open box'
    c. [tː]-[t] in dote al matrimonio indotte al matrimonio
              [inˈdɔte al matriˈmɔnjo] [inˈdɔtːe al matriˈmɔnjo]
              'as dowry for the marriage' 'induced to marriage'

Thus far, we have seen the addition of a phonemic opposition (7) and the loss of a distinctive feature such as length (8), but as Campbell (1996: 99) has claimed, 'virtually all aspects of phonology can be borrowed'. As a matter of fact, phonological rules can be borrowed as well. A case in point is the French spoken at Quimper (Brittany), which is claimed to have borrowed a rule of stem-final devoicing from Breton (Vendryes 1921: 339; see also Campbell 2013: 79). In (9), a voiced fricative surfaces as voiceless in word-final position in Quimper French (9a); this devoicing does not occur, however, in standard French (9b). It does, however, occur in Breton (9c), the contact language of French in Quimper. In Breton, voiced obstruents surface as voiced before the plural suffix but are devoiced in word-final position (Ternes 1970: 127).

(9) a. Quimper French /yn ʃəˈmiːz nœv/   > [ʃəˈmiːs nœf]
    b. French   /yn ʃəˈmiːz nœv/   > [ʃəˈmiːz nœv]
                       'a new shirt'
    c. Breton   /korv/   > SG [korf] vs PL [korvew]
                       'body'

28.3.2 Prosodic Borrowing

Prosodic borrowing is the borrowing of categories, such as stress, rhythm, duration, prominence, and intonation (Lleó 2016). As such, it clearly can be classified as pattern borrowing. Judging from the scarcity of overview works on prosodic borrowing (a remarkable exception being the volume edited by Delais-Roussarie, Avanzi, and Herment 2015), it would seem that prosodic borrowing is an extremely rare phenomenon or, alternatively, that this field is grossly understudied. Appearances are deceptive, though.

Publications on single case studies are abundant (Petit 1997; Vella 2003; Colantoni and Gurlekian 2004; O'Rourke 2005; studies in Matras and Sakel 2007a; Gabriel and Lleó 2011) and the interest in this area of research is rapidly increasing: see, for instance, works by Elordieta and Irurtzun (2016) on pitch accent tonal alignment in declarative sentences in Lekeitio Spanish spoken in the Basque Country; Enzinna (2016) on Spanish-influenced rhythm in Miami English; Colantoni (2011) on early peak alignment and downstep in Buenos Aires Spanish, attributable to contact with Italian.

I present here a case studied by Sichel-Bazin, Buthke, and Meisenburg (2015). It concerns two Gallo-Romance languages, Occitan and French, which have been in a centuries-long diglossic situation in southern France. The authors studied accentuation, phrasing, and intonation patterns. To investigate accentuation and prosodic phrasing, they performed a qualitative analysis on recordings of summaries of fairy tales and a pilot quantitative analysis based on acoustic characteristics of summaries of fairy tales produced by two bilingual speakers speaking Occitan and southern French or Occitan and Italian, while two monolingual northern French speakers served as a control group. To investigate intonation, they used questionnaires and analysed three sentence types: biased statements of the obvious (such as Occ. *E ben es encenta de son òme!* 'She's pregnant by her husband, of course!'), yes–no questions, and wh-questions. The authors found evidence for bidirectional contact influence. As for accentuation and phrasing, Occitan has contrastive lexical stress and therefore one would expect accentuation to be related to the phonological word. However, Occitan has borrowed from French the accentual phrase, a prosodic unit on which the French accentuation system is based: the accentual phrase may contain lexical words and clitics, obligatorily has final pitch accent hitting its last full syllable, and has an optional tonal rise at its left edge (for details, see Jun and Fougeron 2002). As for southern French, it has a certain degree of lexical stress and is reminiscent of Occitan in its rhythmic patterns (Sichel-Bazin, Buthke, and Meisenburg 2015: 71). As for intonation, Sichel-Bazin, Buthke, and Meisenburg (2015: 95) observe that 'the degree of contact with Occitan, which correlates directly with the age of the speakers and the area they live in, has a clear influence on intonation in southern French'. Occitan and northern French share most contours in statements and questions. However, in statements of the obvious, they display different nuclear configurations, while southern French also uses the Occitan contour. In wh-questions, Occitan has falling contours, northern French has both rising contours (for wh-in-situ constructions) and falling ones (for wh-movement), while southern French 'tends to one or the other pole as a function of the intensity of contact with Occitan' (Sichel-Bazin, Buthke, and Meisenburg 2015: 71).

28.3.3 Morphological Borrowing

Morphological borrowing is generally thought to be a rare phenomenon (for a recent debate, see Matras 2015 vs Thomason 2015), an assumption reflected in virtually all borrowability hierarchies, as we shall see in Section 28.6. Most such scales assume that derivational affixes are more easily transferable than highly bound inflexional affixes, an asymmetry attributed by Weinreich to their different levels of entrenchment in the grammar: 'the fuller the integration of the morpheme, the less likelihood of transfer' (Weinreich 1953: 35). While, however, Meillet (1921: 86) claimed that 'there are no records that inflexions such as those in *j'aimais* [I=love.PST.IPFV.1SG], *nous aimions* [we love.PST.IPFV.1PL] have passed from one language to another', counter-evidence has come up precisely from Romance languages. Megleno-Romanian, for example, is an eastern Romance language spoken by a few thousand people in south-eastern Macedonia and northern Greece. In Megleno-Romanian dialects in close contact with Lower Vardar (south-eastern) Macedonian dialects (in particular the Gevgelija dialect), some first-conjugation verbs ending in the consonant cluster *muta cum liquida* display an exponent *-m* for the first person singular of the present indicative (10a), whereas other Megleno-Romanian varieties do not display it (10c). Probably, the exponent *-m* was borrowed from neighbouring south-eastern Macedonian (10b) (Capidan 1925: 159), although an alternative internal explanation of the phenomenon – in terms of a Megleno-Romanian conjugational restructuring – is also conceivable (see Friedman 2012: 327).

(10) a. Megleno-Romanian dialects antru-m
enter.PRS.1SG-1SG
b. Macedonian nos-am
carry-PRS.1SG
'I carry'
c. Megleno-Romanian antr-u
enter-PRS.1SG
'I enter'

As for derivational morphology, a well-known example is the borrowing of *-able* from French into English, cf. Fr. *lav-able* and Eng. *wash-able* (cf. Grant 2009; 2012). Cases of derivational borrowing are frequent, both in the Romance domain and cross-linguistically (Seifart 2013; 2017). As Gardani (2018; 2019) has recently shown, it appears that agent, patient, and instrument noun formatives are borrowed more frequently than other categories. To take one example, the Austronesian language Iloko, spoken in the north-west Luzon Island (Philippines), has borrowed from Spanish the agentive suffix *-ero* (F *-era*), which is used with both Spanish roots, e.g., *partera* 'midwife', and native roots, e.g., *karaykayéra* 'female raker' (from *karaykáy* 'foot of a bird; rake') (Rubino 2005: 346).

As we have seen in Section 28.3, borrowing can also entail the transfer of abstract structures, which are then instantiated with RL-native material. The Sicilian dialect of Pantiscu, spoken on the island of Pantelleria, 95 km off the Sicilian coast and 67 km from Tunisia, provides an elegant example of pattern borrowing. From the mid eighth century onwards, Pantelleria was prevalently Semitic-speaking (Tropea 1988: xli). Sicilian was introduced there no earlier than the seventeenth century and it was initially only spoken along the coast. Almost certainly, the Arabic-speaking population shifted towards Sicilian, imposing some Arabic linguistic traits onto Sicilian. One such trait was the realization of the pluperfect. A unique case in the Romance-speaking landscape is that in Pantiscu the pluperfect comes as a verbal periphrasis consisting of two finite forms (11a), unlike elsewhere in Italo-Romance where it is expressed by a periphrasis consisting of (finite) auxiliary + (non-finite) past participle (11c). The Pantiscu pluperfect pattern involves the third person singular imperfect of the auxiliary èssiri 'be', which is constant for all person–number cells, and the simple perfect inflected for person–number. Strikingly, this pattern largely matches the Semitic pattern, as the Maltese data in (11b) demonstrates. In Arabic, the first verb form is the imperfective past of the auxiliary kāna 'be', the second form is the perfective past of the lexical verb, and both forms inflect for person, number, and gender. In Pantiscu, the aspectual difference is rendered by the use of the imperfect of the auxiliary and the perfect of the lexical verb, while the former, era, unlike Maltese, is an invariable third person singular form extended to all person and number combinations (cf. also Brincat 2003: 104).

(11) a. Pantiscu èra scrissi
        be.PST.IPFV.3SG write.PFV.1SG
    b. Maltese kont ktibt
        be.PST.IPFV.1SG write.PST.PFV.1SG
    c. Italian avevo scritto
        have.PST.IPFV.1SG write.PST.PTCP
        'I had written'

The Romance-Semitic contact leading to the borrowing of the pluperfect pattern in (11) dates back centuries. As Loporcaro, Kägi, and Gardani (2018: 278) have observed, however, the effects of a new type of contact, that between Pantiscu and Italian, have started to manifest themselves. According to the data they collected in fieldwork in 2017, the Semitic-origin pattern is very well conserved in Pantiscu. However, while informants from the urban area tend to produce utterances such as (12a), which is clearly a calque on Italian (12b), informants from the rural areas reject the pan-Romance pluperfect in (12a) as ungrammatical.

(12) a. Pantiscu   Avía   putútu   kkattári   tuttikósa!
     b. Italian   Avevo   potuto   comprare   tutto!
                    have.PST.IPFV.1SG   can.PST.PTCP   buy.INF   everything
                    'I had been able to buy everything!'

28.3.4 Syntactic Borrowing

Syntactic borrowing is the borrowing of structural patterns and rules and qualifies as prototypical pattern borrowing. Harris and Campbell (1995: 120) wrote that '[s]yntactic borrowing is perhaps the most neglected and abused area of syntactic change'. As far as overview works are concerned, little has changed since then (for exceptions, see Bowern 2008; Lucas 2012; Andersen 2016). However, a sustained number of dedicated works on syntactic borrowing in single contact settings have been published, and the Romance languages have played an important role in providing analyses of relevance for the general theory, as we will see in this section (as well as in Section 28.4). Syntactic borrowing mainly encompasses clausal syntax, sentential syntax, and word order (cf. Muysken 1996: 121; Curnow 2001: 432–33; Aikhenvald 2006: 16), and the cases presented hereafter cover these three areas of syntax.

As for borrowing at the level of clausal syntax, a case in point is the innovative use of object clitic doubling in Nahuatl-influenced varieties of Spanish (Flores Farfán 2013: 219; Dakin and Operstein 2017: 9). Nahuatl is a non-configurational, agglutinative, head-marking language which makes extensive use of noun incorporation. A VP's object is obligatorily head-marked by means of an affix, as is visible in (13b), while this is not the case in Spanish (13c). However, it has been observed that in the variety of Spanish used by Nahuatl-Spanish bilinguals in Balsas, Guerrero, some Nahuas, when speaking Spanish, tend to insert an object clitic yielding constructions such as in (13a). Clearly, they impose a pattern of Nahuatl syntax onto their own variety of Spanish.

(13) a. Nahuatl-influenced Spanish   ¿Usted   los   vende   pescados?
                                      you   3MPL.ACC=   sell.PRS.3SG   fish.PL
     b. Nahuatl   ti-k-tlanamaka   peskaados?
                                      you-OBJ-sell   fish.PL
     c. Standard Mexican Spanish   ¿Usted   vende   pescados?
                                      you   sell.PRS.3SG   fish.PL
                                      'Do you sell fish?'

At the level of sentential syntax, we find several cases of borrowed comparative constructions (cf. Stolz and Stolz 2001; Stolz 2013). A particularly intriguing case is discussed by Chamoreau (2012a); it concerns the domain of comparative constructions of superiority in Purépecha, an endangered language isolate spoken in Mexico, which has stood in contact with Spanish for nearly five centuries. By comparing adverbial clauses of comparison in Purépecha with comparative constructions both in the pre-contact recipient language, Lengua de Michoacán, and in Spanish, Chamoreau (2012a: 68) convincingly demonstrates that a type of construction, consisting of a particle and a locative phrase (14), constitutes an innovation. It involves the Spanish-origin degree marker *mas* (Sp. *más* 'more') and the relator *ke* (Sp. *que* 'that, than'), followed by *entre* 'between'.

(14) Pedro   mas   sesi-e-s-ti   ke   entre   Xwanu.
      Pedro   more   good-PRED-AOR-ASRT.3   than   between   Xwanu
      'Pedro is better than Xwanu.'

In fact, this construction deviates both from comparative patterns in Spanish and the use of the locative preposition *entre* 'between' in Spanish. Chamoreau links this instance of creative borrowing to the cross-linguistic tendency 'to connect comparison with location and to express comparison through the locative type' (p. 70), a hypothesis which seems pertinent. The emergence of innovative hybrid structures such as the one just seen in Purépecha, is not rare in contact-induced change, as we will see in the discussion of Italo-Romance data in Section 28.4.

While the Purépecha case just discussed is limited to a specific type of comparative construction, a change with potentially far-reaching consequences for the syntax of the RL is found in Tetun Dili, an Austronesian language of East Timor with a history of long and intensive contact with Portuguese since the late 1700s, which led to a process of Lusification (Williams-van Klinken, Hajek, and Nordlinger 2002: 1). As observed by Hajek (2006), Tetun Dili has been shifting from parataxis towards an increasing use of hypotaxis realized by means of conjunctions and coordinators. While native mechanisms to express inter-clausal relations do exist in Tetun Dili, they are not obligatory and are generally omitted, and the comparative evidence shows that other East Timor languages (including conservative Tetun) prefer unmarked clause chaining. In Tetun Dili, the native inter-clausal chaining mechanisms have been reinforced, apparently by the use of Portuguese conjunctions and patterns, and the contact-induced hypothesis is supported by the fact that hypotaxis is especially frequent in higher registers. As the data in (15) show, native and borrowed forms and patterns can either be absent (*o´ hakarak, bele ba´ uma*), or appear as alternatives (*se o´ hakarak, ... or o´ hakarak karik, ...*), or coexist (*se o´ hakarak karik, ...*) (Hajek 2006: 172).

(15) (se)   o´   hakarak   (karik),   bele   ba´   uma. (Tetun Dili)
      (if)   you.SG want   (perhaps),   can   go   house
      'If you want, you can go home.'

Another clear example of syntactic borrowing at the level of sentential syntax is the innovative postposed relative clause in Basque (Jendraschek

2006: 152; Trask 1998: 320). Basque has a basic SOV word order and exhibits all the typological properties commonly associated with this word order pattern, such as having preposed modifiers and being exclusively postpositional (Trask 1998: 320). The only deviation from this virtually perfect SOV order concerns relative clauses. Generally, in Basque a finite relative clause precedes its head and does not involve any relative pronoun, while subordination is marked by a suffix -*n* on the finite verb, as in (16).

(16) lore-a-k   eman   dizki-o-da-n   neska hor   dago. (Bsq.)
     flower-DET-PL   give   PRS.3PL.ABS-3SG.DAT-1SG.ERG-REL   girl   there be.PRS.3SG
     'The girl I gave the flowers to is right here.'

However, a typologically divergent relativization pattern of the SVO type has emerged in certain parts of the country and gained ground, especially among uneducated speakers (Trask 1998: 320). It involves the use of a native Basque interrogative word *zein* functioning as a relative pronoun, while the pattern itself was borrowed from the Romance neighbours of Basque. This pattern is exemplified in (17): here, the head *neska* 'the girl' precedes the VP and the relative clause is introduced by the pronoun *zeini*. Interestingly, the subordinating suffix -*n* that we saw in (16), still occurs on the finite verb, suggesting that the innovative relative clause construction in (17) represents a transition stage between the genuine Basque construction and the Romance pronominal relativization strategy.

(17) neska zein-i   lore-a-k   eman   dizki-o-da-n (Bsq.)
     girl   which-DAT   flower-DET-PL   give   PRS.3PL.ABS-3SG.DAT-1SG.ERG-REL
     'The girl to whom I gave the flowers'

Often, word order has been viewed as the 'easiest sort of syntactic feature to borrow or acquire via language shift' (Thomason and Kaufman 1988: 55). Crucially, some authors have maintained 'that certain of the word order types ... come to exist only through foreign influence. Thus, contact and borrowing have important consequences for proposed universals of word order and even for the very definition of universals in general' (Harris and Campbell 1995: 137). Not surprisingly, the literature is full of examples. For Romance, most of them concern cases of contact with Spanish (e.g., Camacho 1999; Ocampo and Klee 1995; Odlin 1990) but not exclusively (e.g., Cognola 2011). A simple case of word order pattern borrowing is found in Alsace French, where it was induced by contact with German. Example (18) shows convergence between Alsace French (18a) and German (18b), in contrast with standard French (18c), as regards the placement of the non-finite verb at the end of the clause in declarative main clauses (Petit 1997: 1236f.).

(18) a. Alsace French Il   faut   ça   aussi écrire.
                    EXPL need.PRS.3SG this   also write.INF
     b. German   Man   muss   das   auch schreiben.
                    IMPR need.PRS.3SG this   also write.INF
     c. French   Il   faut   écrire   ça   aussi.
                    EXPL need.PRS.3SG write.INF this also
        'This has to be written too.'

Most of the time, changes in word order are introduced by means of single borrowed constructions and, if they are reinforced by borrowed constructions with similar typological types, they can lead to major typological change. To take one example, Hill and Hill (2004) have shown that the borrowing of the Spanish particle *de* 'of, from' has been instrumental in producing a word order shift in Malinche Mexicano, a modern variety of Nahuatl spoken in Tlaxcala and Puebla on the slopes of the Malinche Volcano. Sixteenth-century Nahuatl was a language with a word order type corresponding to Hawkins' (1983) type 6 (V-1/Po/NG/AN), that is, it was strongly verb-initial, with left-dislocation of arguments to a position before the verb clearly associated with topicalization, displayed a strong preference for Noun-Genitive order, a productive use of locative postpositions, and rigid adjective-noun order. Under the influence of Spanish, a prepositional non-rigid V-medial language, Malinche Mexicano has moved in the direction of Hawkins' (1983) word order type 2 (V-1/Pr/NG/AN), displaying an increasing use of prepositional structures, while reducing the use of postpositional locative suffixes. Seemingly, the starting point of this development was indigenous locative expressions with relational nouns in Locative-Noun order (i.e., prepositional order), with an adjunctor *in*. At some point, Sp. *de* started replacing *in* (or being cliticized to it) leading speakers to equate relational nouns with Spanish prepositions and to reanalyse *de* as a genitive marker (note that *den* in (19a, 19c) is *de* 'of' + *in* 'DET'). Subsequently, speakers started omitting possessive formatives on some elements, such as locative and possessive expressions, yielding (19a).

(19) a. Malinche Mexicano miec   omi-tl   den   micquē-tl
                          many   bone-ABS of.DET   dead.body-ABS
     b. Spanish   muchos huesos   de   un   muerto
                          many   bones   of   DET   dead
     c. Nahuatl   miec   in   ī-omi-yō   den   micquē-tl
                          many   DET   POSS.3SG-bone-COLL of.DET   dead.body-ABS
        'many bones of a dead person'

28.4 The Upper Limits of Borrowing

In Section 28.2, I said that the basic types of effects induced by language contact on an RL are innovative and conservative effects. Sometimes, these occur to such an amplified extent that they induce far more extreme changes. To these belong mainly the emergence of linguistic areas, typological change (see, for instance, Flores Farfán 2018 and Olko, Borges, and Sullivan 2018), creolization (see, for example, Sessarego 2017), and the emergence of mixed languages. In this section, I will briefly discuss cases pertaining to areal formation and bilingual mixed languages.

Current discussions of areality point to pattern borrowing as a main factor for the diffusion of structural traits and the development of linguistic areas (known by the German term *Sprachbünde*, singular *Sprachbund*, lit. 'language league'): see, for instance, Ross (2001), Donohue (2012), and chapters in Hickey (2017). *Sprachbünde* are characterized by a structural convergence of three or more languages which come to share a number of grammatical features, within a certain geographic area. Romance linguistics has contributed decisively to the concept of linguistic areas: one of the best known cases of a *Sprachbund* and, in fact, the first to attract the interest of researchers (Kopitar 1829), is the Balkan *Sprachbund* (Sandfeld 1930; Joseph 1983). In the Balkan *Sprachbund*, the shared elements include patterns of argument marking (such as clitic doubling, a tendency away from inflexional case marking, a recipient/possessor inflexional syncretism, and many more, cf. Lindstedt 2014).

As often it is not clear which is the source and which is the recipient of change, we do not yet know exactly how linguistic areas emerge. It appears, however, almost uncontroversial that *Sprachbünde* are the result of 'mutual reinforcement' of trends (Lindstedt 2000). One mechanism leading to such reinforcement is contact-induced grammaticalization (Heine 1994; Heine and Kuteva 2003; 2005), that is, a grammaticalization process is transferred from an SL to an RL. As a matter of fact, Romance languages are involved not only in the Balkan Sprachbund but also in the emergence of other possible linguistic areas – not Sprachbünde *stricto sensu* though – such as the Alps (cf. Seiler 2004) and the south of Italy (e.g., Höhn, Silvestri, and Squillaci 2017). It is in the context of studies on the influence of Greek on southern Italo-Romance varieties that the role of replica grammaticalization has received the attention it deserves (see Ledgeway 2013; Ledgeway, Schifano, and Silvestri 2018). As is well known (Rohlfs 1937; 1977), the centuries-long coexistence and linguistic contact between speakers of Italo-Romance varieties and speakers of Italo-Greek, viz. Greko in Calabria and Griko in Salento, have yielded a considerable amount of structural convergence. As Ledgeway (2013) neatly shows, in this area contact has often not resulted in the mere copying of forms or structures; rather, speakers have reanalysed existing Romance features and patterns, such as, for instance, dative and genitive, finite and infinitival complementation, determiner usage and verb movement to adjust to the Greek model. To take a concrete example, the syntax of Palizzese, a southern Calabrian variety, shows a convergence towards Greko (20b) in that it allows, besides infinitival complementation – as expected in an Italo-Romance language (20c) – also finite complement clauses such as in (20a), on the model of Italo-Greek (20b) (data from Squillaci 2017: 6f.). To be sure, in both southern Calabrian and Greko infinitival complementation has been maintained alongside competing finite *mi /na* clauses, in conjunction with a class of functional predicates (cf. 21 and see Ledgeway 2013, for a detailed discussion).

(20) a. Palizzese Vogghiu mi vaiu.
     b. Greko Θelo na pao.
        want.PRS.1SG PTC.IRR go.PRS.1SG
     c. Italian Voglio andare.
        want.PRS.1SG go.INF
        'I want to go.'

(21) Egò tus àcua platèttsi / na platèttsusi. (Greko)
     I them= hear.PST.1SG talk.INF / that talk.SBJV.3PL
     'I heard them talking.'

Another revealing example from contact between Italo-Romance and Italo-Greek shows that language contact can result in innovative hybrid patterns (cf. also the Purépecha case in 14). The same southern Calabrian variety, Palizzese, displays a genitive structure that apparently calques the Greek dative-genitive syncretism; in reality, however, as Ledgeway (2013: 193) has shown, this is not an autonomous genitive structure but rather 'a hybrid structure in which the indirect object is referenced in part through dative marking on the verbal head [*nci*] and in part through genitive marking on the nominal dependent [*da*]' (cf. example (22) from Squillaci 2017: 6f.). For in-depth discussion, see Ledgeway, Schifano, and Silvestri (2020).

(22) a. Palizzese nci desi u regalu da figghiola.
     b. Greko tis edoka to kaloma ti miccedda.
        to.her= give.PST.1SG DET gift DET.GEN girl
     c. Italian Ho dato il regalo alla bambina.
        have.PRS.1SG give.PTCP DET gift to.DET girl
        'I've given the gift to the girl.'

The second type of contact-induced phenomenon addressed in this section are mixed languages, which are a type of contact language that arises as the result of the fusion of two languages, normally in situations of bilingualism, and emerge in situations of severe social upheaval (Meakins 2013; 2016; Bakker 2017). Accordingly, mixed languages cannot be classified following the standard historical-comparative method. Mixed languages come in three main types: (a) grammar-lexicon mixes, (b) structural mixes, and (c) converted languages. Two Romance languages,

Spanish and French, are involved in the emergence of cases of (a) and (b) (for the third type such as Sri Lanka Malay, see the overview in Meakins 2013).

Media Lengua (Muysken 1997) is a mixed language spoken in Central Ecuador by a Quechuan group known as the Obreros. It qualifies as grammar-lexicon mix type, for its morphosyntactic frame is essentially Quechua, while around 90 per cent of the vocabulary is Spanish as the result of a relexification process. The pattern of Spanish stems with Quechuan suffixes is clearly visible in (23).

(23) Unu fabur-**ta** pidi-**nga-bu** bini-**xu-ni**. (Muysken 1997b: 365)
one favour-ACC ask-NOM-BEN come-PROG-1
'I come to ask a favour.'

Michif (Bakker 1997; 2017) is the mixed Cree-French language of the Canadian Metis which originated probably in the early 1800s out of mixed marriages between Plains Cree-speaking women and French Canadian fur traders. Michif qualifies as a structural mix for its great degree of structural mixing: the verbal system is Cree, the nominal system is French, and accordingly, its vocabulary is composed of mostly Cree verbs and mostly French nouns (cf. Meakins 2013: 173). The NP-VP split is clearly observable in (24) (Bakker 1997: 6).

(24) êkwa pâstin-am sa bouche **ôhi** le loup **ê-wî-otin-át**.
and open-he.it POSS.F mouth this.OBV DET.M wolf COMP-want-take-he.him
'And when the wolf came to him, he opened his mouth.'

28.5 Linguistic Factors Favouring Grammatical Borrowing

'A language accepts foreign structural elements only when they correspond to its tendencies of development' (Jakobson 1938: 54, in the translation provided by Weinreich 1953: 25). Many general claims, such as this, and universals concerning grammatical borrowing have been put forward in the contact literature, often in terms of the structural requirements necessary for borrowing even to occur. But this quotation from Jakobson is the quintessence of the most widespread belief in the language contact literature: structural compatibility between SL and RL favours borrowing while typological disharmony inhibits it (see Field 2002: 42; Sebba 1998; Weinreich 1953: 44; Winford 2005: 387). Intuitively, this proposal appears to go in the right direction: it should be easier to borrow patterns that are similar to, and thus compatible with, those native to an RL than structurally incompatible patterns. The areas of grammar in which structural compatibility between SL and RL are often considered relevant in the literature include word order, morpheme order, the existence of one and the same feature, and matches in terms of how this feature is realized (cf. Meakins and O'Shannessy 2012: 220). As far as the existence of a feature in both languages is concerned, a case in point is the borrowing in Mesoamerican languages of the Spanish diminutive suffixes -ito and -ita, discussed by Chamoreau (2012b). The author shows that Mesoamerican languages that lack grammatical gender distinctions realize diminutivization only by the suffix -ito. However, Yucatec Maya, which has a weak grammatical gender distinction (expressed by prefixes, for examples, in semi-pairs such as j-meenwaaj 'baker.M' vs x-meenjanal 'cook.F'), accepts both the masculine marker -ito and the feminine marker -ita and applies them to native lexical roots. In (25), -ita occurs on an adjective that agrees in gender with a noun denoting an intrinsically female human (Chamoreau 2012b: 84).

(25) Yucatec Maya bek'ech-ita u y-íits'in.
                    thin-DIM.F ERG.3SG POSS-younger.sister
                    'His younger sister is slender.'

Thus, in Yucatec Maya, the pre-existence of a grammatical gender distinction, though weak, seems to support the borrowing of gender marking formatives from Spanish. New research has, indeed, confirmed that structural compatibility plays an important role in borrowing (Law 2020; Mithun 2020; Ralli 2020; Souag 2020). However, many authors have expressed doubts about considering structural similarity a factor favouring borrowing, for 'borrowing and language contact can introduce structures to a language which are not harmonious with existing structures' (Harris and Campbell 1995: 150). Again, it is the Romance 'contactosphere' that provides counterevidence. For example, Flores Farfán (2008: 38f.) observes that Hispanicized varieties of Nahuatl are shifting towards more analytic structures under the influence of Spanish. The VP in (26a) marks the object by means of a dedicated formative, but the object NP is not incorporated, as one would expect from polysynthetic Nahuatl (26c). Example (26a) clearly represents a pattern converging towards Spanish (26b). As a matter of fact, this is becoming the default usage in highly Hispanicized speech, at least in bilinguals, whereas the polysynthetic structure in (26c) is characteristic of more conservative modern Nahuatl varieties.

(26) a. Hispanized Nahuatl _-ki-chiiwa   tlaxkahli.
                            3S-3O-make   tortilla
     b. Spanish   Ella   hace   tortillas.
                            she   make.PRS.3SG tortillas
     c. Nahuatl   _-tlaxkal-chiiwa.
                            3S-tortilla-make
                            'She makes tortillas.'

Even stronger claims about the unsuitability of structural similarity as a factor favouring borrowing were made by Babel and Pfänder (2014: 254), and Seifart (2015: 92) claims that structural similarity between a source language and a recipient language 'plays at best a minor role in determining the extent of affix borrowing'.

Another factor which has repeatedly been claimed to favour borrowing is the presence of functional gaps in an RL (see, among many others, Hale 1975; Heath 1978: 115). As Harris and Campbell (1995: 128) aptly note, the claim that the lack of shared structural similarity may trigger borrowing stands '[q]uite in opposition to the spirit of the structural-compatibility hypothesis', while being still 'akin to it in many ways'. The basic idea is that borrowing may exercise a therapeutic function in that it fills functional gaps. When a language A lacking some features or patterns comes into contact with a language B possessing them, the speakers of A may perceive these gaps and, once they become more familiar with B, adopt B as a model to fill those gaps. However, this claim has been met with scepticism, and some scholars have either dismissed it as untenable in theoretical terms (Brody 1987: 508) or shown that the existence of functional gap plays no role in facilitating the borrowing process (see, for instance, Gardani 2008: 88 and Thomason 2015: 42).

In studies focusing on morphological borrowing (Gardani 2012: 92), it was observed that such structural factors as morphotactic transparency, which obtains when the morphological segmentation of affixes is easily perceivable (cf. Dressler et al. 1987: 102), and biuniqueness, that is, the relational invariance between *signans* and *signatum* (cf. Dressler 1999: 404), do, in fact, have a boosting effect on inflexional borrowing.

At the current state of our knowledge, however, it appears reasonable to say that for all linguistic predictors claimed to boost or inhibit borrowing (for a wide-ranging list, see Aikhenvald 2006: 26–36), no definitive answers can be provided. Only statistical analyses based on large data sets will allow us to better understand the dynamics of grammatical borrowing.

28.6 Borrowability Hierarchies

Reasonably, one can agree with van Coetsem (1988: 3) that 'language has a constitutional property of stability; certain components or domains of language are more stable and more resistant to change (e.g., phonology), while other such domains are less stable and less resistant to change (e.g., vocabulary)'. As a matter of fact, one of the research questions which have most intrigued scholars of language contact is how different elements of language react to language contact and how prone they are to borrowing. In

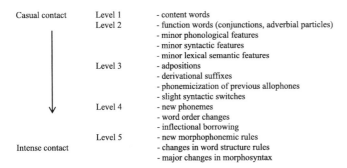

Figure 28.1 Thomason and Kaufman's (1988) borrowing scale

this context, a number of claims have been made concerning the resistance of grammar to borrowing in terms of rankings, often referred to as borrowability scales (e.g., Whitney 1881; Haugen 1950; Moravcsik 1978: 110–13; Thomason and Kaufman 1988: 74–76; Field 2002; Matras 2007; for useful overviews, see Matras 2009: 153–65 and Wohlgemuth 2009: 11–17), most of which are constructed on parts of speech (nouns, verbs, etc.) and distinctive analytic units (phoneme, morpheme, etc.). A far more promising approach, in my view, consists in investigating which modules and submodules of grammar (phonology, syntax, etc.) are more, or less, susceptible to borrowing. Probably, the proposal which best serves this goal is the famous borrowing scale by Thomason and Kaufman (1988: 74–76), summarized in Figure 28.1, which predicts the degree of borrowing based on the degree of contact intensity.

In a nutshell, the rationale behind each borrowability hierarchy is that the degree of resistance of grammar to borrowing covaries with their degree of systematicity (Tesnière 1939: 85). Driven by the basic conviction that 'lexicon, morphology, and syntax form a continuum of symbolic units serving to structure conceptual content for expressive purposes' (Langacker 1987: 35), Gardani (2008; 2012) has studied inflexional borrowing in a cross-linguistic sample by distinguishing between submodules of inflexion. Adopting the distinction theorized by Booij (1996) between inherent inflexion (i.e., independent from the syntactic context) and contextual inflexion (required by the syntactic context), Gardani demonstrates that formatives pertaining to the one or the other submodule display different degrees of borrowing frequency. Specifically, Gardani finds that inherent-inflexional formatives such as nominal plural are more highly borrowable than contextual-inflexional ones. The following example of borrowing of a Greek formative -*ades* (27b), rendered as V[dz], in Aromanian (27a) (Gardani 2008: 65), contrasted with Daco-Romanian (27c), is a case in point.

(27) a. Aromanian dumnidz-(á)dz
           god-PL
     b. Greek   psará-des
                  fisherman-PL
     c. Romanian dumneze-i
                  god-PL

Similarly, Matras (2007: 37–39, 60) has proposed tentative subhierarchies for phonology and syntax and has observed, for example, that prosody is more prone to borrowing than segmental phonology. Such detailed analyses, however, are exceptional in the literature and represent an urgent *desideratum*, to which the Romance data can contribute significantly.

28.7 Conclusion

This chapter has examined evidence drawn from the Romance-speaking world to show the enormous potential that the Romance languages have to contribute to contact linguistics. A number of diverse case studies were discussed, covering contact between a Romance and a non-Romance language, contact between two Romance languages, settings in which a Romance language is the RL and others in which a Romance language was the SL, cases of locally circumscribed contact and of areal diffusion. I have presented a selection of recent research in the field of grammatical borrowing and discussed claims and universals proposed in the literature regarding the principles of borrowing. The evidence at our disposal clearly confirms that '[n]o linguistic feature – be it a form, or a pattern – is entirely "borrowing-proof"' (Aikhenvald 2006: 2). However, I have argued that, given the current state of our knowledge, it is not possible to provide a serious, non-intuitive assessment of predictions concerning the differential borrowability of different submodules of grammar, for a statistical evaluation of large data corpora, both cross-linguistically and across Romance, is indispensable in order to attain this goal. This is the most urgent and promising line of research for the future.

Selected References

Below you can find selected references for this chapter. The full references can be found online at the following page: www.cambridge.org/Romancelinguistics

Adamou, E., Breu, W., Scholze, L., and Shen, R. (2016). 'Borrowing and contact intensity: a corpus-driven approach from four Slavic minority languages', *Journal of Language Contact* 9: 515–44.

Bakker, P. (1997). *A Language of Our Own: The Genesis of Michif, the Mixed Cree-French Language of the Canadian Metis*. New York/Oxford: Oxford University Press.

Enrique-Arias, A. (2010). 'On language contact as an inhibitor of language change: the Spanish of Catalan bilinguals in Majorca'. In Breitbarth, A., Lucas, C., Watts, S., and Willis, D. (eds), *Continuity and Change in Grammar*. Amsterdam/Philadelphia: Benjamins, 97–118.

Gardani, F. (2008). *Borrowing of Inflectional Morphemes in Language Contact*. Frankfurt am Main: Peter Lang.

Hill, J. H. and Hill, K. C. (2004). 'Word order type change and the penetration of Spanish *de* in modern Nahuatl', *STUF – Language Typology and Universals* 57: 23–48.

Muysken, P. (2012). 'Root/affix asymmetries in contact and transfer: case studies from the Andes', *International Journal of Bilingualism* 16: 22–36.

Quinto-Pozos, D. and Adam, R. (2015). 'Sign languages in contact'. In Schembri, A. and Lucas, C. (eds), *Sociolinguistics and Deaf Communities*. Cambridge: Cambridge University Press, 29–60.

Saade, B. (2020). 'Quantitative approaches to productivity and borrowing in Maltese derivation', *Morphology* 30: 447–67.

Sakel, J. (2007). 'Types of loan: matter and pattern'. In Matras, Y. and Sakel, J. (eds), *Grammatical Borrowing in Cross-Linguistic Perspective*. Berlin/New York: Mouton de Gruyter, 15–29.

Seifart, F. (2017). 'Patterns of affix borrowing in a sample of 100 languages', *Journal of Historical Linguistics* 7: 389–431.

Sessarego, S. (2017). 'Chocó Spanish double negation and the genesis of the Afro-Hispanic dialects of the Americas', *Diachronica* 34: 219–52.

Van Coetsem, F. (1988). *Loan Phonology and the Two Transfer Types in Language Contact*. Dordrecht: Foris.

29

Diamesic Variation

Maria Selig

29.1 Defining Diamesic Variation

29.1.1 'Spoken' and 'Written' Language

Only in the nineteenth century does the differentiation between 'spoken' and 'written language' come to be established in linguistic thought (cf. also Section 27.2.1). Prior to this, thinking about language meant thinking about an ideal or prescriptive kind of grammar, and this grammar was naturally authoritative for both kinds of speech: oral and written. The codified norm had to be observed during conversation at court just as much as in the composition of poetry or political treatises. Its polar opposite was the language of the illiterate, the inferiority of which was based on its lack of standardization. The difference between speaking and writing was secondary, being overshadowed by the much more significant differentiation between 'right' and 'wrong' language. The positive view on language change, developed by nineteenth-century linguistics, and the shift in perspective from the prescriptive to the descriptive entailed a re-evaluation of orality as the natural home of living and freely developing language. This also affected attitudes towards writing. Ferdinand de Saussure, for instance, said that 'writing obscures language' (Saussure [1916] 1972: 51f.). In 1905, the Latinist Franz Skutsch even spoke of the 'ice sheet of literature', which covers up the 'rushing stream of living language' (Skutsch 1905: 428).

The depreciation of writing and the conviction of orality's pre-eminence, however, did not prevent linguistic research from what Linell (2005) calls the 'written language bias'. Despite the demand to turn spoken language into an object of linguistic research, the models and categories that had evolved over centuries of scholarly engagement with written texts und codified standard languages remained in use.[1] Language continued to be defined as a homogenous system unconnected to speaking. Similarly, the notion that speaking was nothing but the more or less correct implementation of context-free rules continued to dominate linguistic theories for decades. It is true that there were also linguists who recognized the otherness of spontaneous communication in the phonic medium and who concluded that variety was inherent in strategies of verbalization. These linguists include among others Karl Bühler, whose work on the phenomenon of ellipsis also served to critique common syntax theories of his day (Bühler [1934] 1982: 154–79). Yet, quite clearly, only technological innovations enabling the conservation of spoken language provided the framework for thoroughly exploring the specifics of language use in spoken everyday language.

After decades of work on recordings and transcriptions of spoken communication, it is clear that linguistic forms of spontaneous oral interaction can be grasped only partly with the help of the categories and models provided by traditional grammar. Some linguists have discussed whether spoken language has a grammar of its own (Berruto 1985). Romance scholarship as a rule has not gone that far, but rather has opted for interpreting the newly discovered structures of spontaneous orality as a sign of the internal variation of (individual) languages. The discussion surrounding the linguistic characteristics identified as 'oral' thus amounts to the question of how linguistic variation can be accounted for in theoretical terms, and which model can render it adequately.

29.1.2 Diamesic Variation, the Architecture of Varieties, and Register Theory

Mioni (1983) presented one of the first attempts to integrate the differences associated with the media of communication into Romance models of linguistic variation. In the context of his studies on what he calls *italiano tendenziale* ('tendential Italian'), Mioni coined the term 'diamesic variation', which Berruto (1987: 19–27; 1993a; 1993b) subsequently popularized in his sociolinguistic studies on Italian. As the element *dia-* indicates, the definition of diamesic variation draws on Coseriu's (1981) model of the 'architecture' of varieties. Mioni, and Berruto after him, proposed to extend the spectrum of varieties, which Coseriu stakes out between the axes of diatopic (= regional), diastratic (= social), and diaphasic (= situational) variation, to include an additional, 'diamesic' dimension. However, this extension,

---

[1] This even applies to phonetics and phonology, two disciplines that testify to the new interest in spoken language at the beginning of the twentieth century: their segment-oriented approach clearly shows that they continue to be marked by alphabetic writing practices (Linell 2005: 58–65).

which adds a dimension of variation according to medium, is not without problems. Berruto (1987: 20) assumes that the diamesic axis extends between the poles of *'parlato-parlato'* ('spoken-spoken') and *'scritto-scritto'* ('written-written'). Nencioni (1976) had developed these doubly determined terms in order to clarify that the phonic or graphic exteriority type of linguistic signifiers does not simultaneously determine the selected variety. While written communication is prototypically connected to registers diaphasically indexed as 'high' (*'scritto-scritto'*), this connexion is by no means obligatory, as is evinced by graffiti, diary entries, or Internet communication (*'scritto-parlato'* = 'written-spoken'). Neither can phonic communication be unambiguously assigned to 'low' registers since it can range from spontaneous face-to-face interaction in the family (*'parlato-parlato'*) to festive ceremonies (*'parlato-scritto'* = 'spoken-written'). Berruto (1987: 22) writes that diamesic variation is not of the same kind as the other dimensions, but that it 'runs through them and is run through by them'. Thus, there seems to be a dialectical relation between communication media and linguistic variation: on the one hand, such media determine the exteriority type of linguistic signs; on the other hand, speaking and writing vary considerably, depending on the contexts in which the communication media are deployed, respectively. Media simultaneously create variation and are subject to variation.

The allusion to the interconnexion with other dimensions of variation immediately triggers the question of whether it makes sense to postulate a separate diamesic dimension at all. A solution such as the one Halliday proposes might also be conceivable: he combines the medial difference between speaking and writing ('mode') with the variation of the thematic fields ('field') and the variation of the social relations between the communication partners ('tenor'); jointly, the three factors determine the differentiation of 'register' (Halliday 1978; cf. also Biber 1995). However, even here in this register-based approach, the link between media and linguistic variation remains vague.

29.1.3 Three Dimensions of Diamesic Variation: Medial, Sociolinguistic, and Functional Aspects

The model of 'communicative immediacy' and 'communicative distance' developed by Koch and Oesterreicher (1985; 2001; 2007; 2011; 2012) significantly clarifies these issues. Koch and Oesterreicher, like Nencioni, insist that the terms 'spoken language' or 'written language' encompass several dimensions of linguistic variation that must strictly be kept apart. The first dimension pertains to the medial aspect of the 'realization' of linguistic signs. This variation is dichotomous and there are only two solutions, i.e., graphic or phonic signifiers. The phenomenon of 'medium transferability' (Lyons 1981: 11) shows that the contrast of the two exteriority types is not directly linked to the other dimensions of diamesic variation: typically oral strategies of verbalization such as 'hanging topics' (Fr. *le métro, tu vas n'importe où* '(with) the underground, you can go wherever you want') or non-standard forms such as Fr.*?bagnole* '(old) car' can be achieved without any problems either phonically or graphically. The variation in the materiality of the signs thus needs to be distinguished from the other dimensions of diamesic variation.

In determining these dimensions, Koch and Oesterreicher follow an approach proposed by Söll (1980: 17–29) and distinguish two further forms of variation. On the one hand, the sociolinguistic dimension of diamesic variation juxtaposes non-standard 'spoken' and standard 'written' varieties, focusing on the impact of historical processes of standardization. On the other hand, the functional dimension of diamesic variation pertains to the variation regarding the 'conception' of what is said/written (Söll 1980: 19): depending on the respective situational conditions, speakers/writers can choose different syntactic options; they can mix verbal, para-verbal, and non-verbal elements; or they can rely on context and use contextual ellipses or accept preliminary formulations. This third dimension of diamesic variation, that between a 'pragmatic' and a 'syntactic mode' (Givón 1979: 206–33; cf. also Sornicola 1981; Chafe 1982), is anthropologically, and not historically, conditioned, resulting from the possibility of shaping the conditions for verbal communication with variation and choosing those strategies that are suitable for the respective constellations.

Koch and Oesterreicher offer a model for this functional dimension of diamesic variation, which systematically connects pragmatic conditions with strategies of verbalization. They list the following parameters that determine the situational variation (2011: 7; cf. also Steger et al. 1974):[2]

(a)   Private–public sphere
(b)   Degree of familiarity between partners: familiar–non-familiar
(c)   Degree of emotional involvement: high–low degree of emotionality
(d)   Degree of involvement into the situation and the action: involved–not involved
(e)   Relation of reference and deixis to the speaker-hearer *origo*: close to–far from *origo*
(f)   Physical proximity of communication partner: face-to-face communication–space-time separation

---

[2] These social (a; b; c), cognitive (d; e; i; j), and processual (f; g; h) parameters are more abstract than the situational conditions used in register theory. For instance, 'Degree of fixation on a topic' in (j) revolves around the question of whether there is a fixed topic – and thus a cognitively more challenging topic development – within the communication or not, whereas register theory in this case differentiates only the range of topics. Similarly, the parameter 'Degree of dialogicity' in (h) captures the discourse-relevant conditions of turn-taking in conversations, independently of the nature of the social relations between the communication partners.

(g) Degree of cooperation: much–little speaker/hearer cooperation
(h) Degree of dialogicity: dialogic/polylogic–monologic
(i) Degree of spontaneity: low–high degree of planning
(j) Degree of fixation on a topic: free–planned topic development

Koch and Oesterreicher propose to structure this variation as a continuum between two poles, which represent the two extreme forms of functional diamesic variation (Koch and Oesterreicher 2011: 10, 13):

(i) Around the pole of 'communicative immediacy,' we find forms of communication that reveal a maximum of spontaneity and contextualization and that are realized by partners who know each other and who are in principle of equal standing. Correspondingly, this pole can be assigned strategies of verbalization characterized by the extensive usage of contextual information, preliminarity and flexibility, and expressivity and simple syntactic-semantic structures. The domain of communicative immediacy is prototypically related to non-standard varieties.

(ii) The counterpole of 'communicative distance' is the pole around which forms of communication revolve, which can increase the portion of explicitly verbalized information as well as the cognitive complexity of the verbalizations since the communication partners can or must communicate independently of the situation, and since the themes of the interaction are fixed and the partners do not interact as private persons but rather in institutional roles, etc. The communicative distance is prototypically connected to standard varieties.

Between these two poles lie intermediate forms, both in terms of situational context as well as with regard to the linguistic forms. With this continuum model, Koch and Oesterreicher explicitly refute the notion that 'spoken language' has a grammar of its own. Together with the language-of-distance forms, the linguistic forms of spontaneous and unplanned interaction are integrated into a coherent system providing variable solutions depending on which conditions of communication are in place.

29.1.4 Synchronic Variation and Processes of Standardization

Koch and Oesterreicher's model allows us to overcome the categorical and dichotomous opposition of 'spoken' and 'written language' and to structure diamesic variation by means of the continuum between communicative immediacy and communicative distance. At the same time, it shows that diamesic variation is not conditioned by mediality. Parameters such as the degree of monologicity, for instance, are regulated by the collocutors' communicative intent. Speech partners can also agree on the mode of turn-taking in the phonic medium as well, so that extended periods of interaction can be monologic. Neither the singer of tales nor the priest during his sermons need expect any interruption! With situational variation being accounted for in this way, i.e., independently of the medium, it becomes possible to recognize the specific character of the communication of distance in proto-literate societies. In these societies, too, there are forms and texts distinct from the forms of spontaneous everyday communication and which should be referred to as 'elaborated orality' (Koch and Oesterreicher 2011: 29).

Nevertheless, communication media play a central role in linguistic variation. It is obvious, for example, that the different planning possibilities provided by written communication determine the range of variation of the parameters (d), (e), (i), and (j), which regulate the cognitive depth of verbalization. Since writing is primarily used to communicate with partners who are at a distance in space and time, the usage of writing also regularly affects parameters (f), (g), and (h), which determine the processual aspects of communication. The usage of writing extends the anthropologically based variation into previously inaccessible strategies of planning and control.

Most of all, however, the written medium can prompt decisive changes in the *longue durée*. The extended usage of a variety both in the realms of communicative distance and in writing is a decisive factor in the three subprocesses of standardization, i.e., elaboration (Section 29.2.4), centralization (Section 29.2.5), and codification (Section 29.2.6): in societies that regularly use writing in situations of communicative distance, the new possibilities for planning and the visual reification of language and text contribute to the development of new cognitive functions of verbal communication as well as new complex lexical and syntactic structures. The possibility of archiving texts and the possibility of building stable communicative networks even across larger spatial distances favour the development of transregionally valid standard languages. Likewise, codification (i.e., the intensive reflexion on linguistic rules and the attempt to formalize them) is closely intertwined with writing – even if the example of Sanskrit grammarians shows that writing is by no means an indispensable prerequisite for normalization and grammaticography (Bright 1994).

For this reason, I will speak in what follows of 'standard languages' and 'written languages' without explicitly highlighting every time that these are language forms characterized by high frequency in situations of communicative distance by means of writing and by efforts at codification. The notion of 'spoken varieties' or 'vernacular varieties' will also be used as an abbreviation; it implies that these language forms are characterized by situations of communicative immediacy, a general lack of writing, and their distance from the standard. This terminological solution, however, must not conceal the fact that diamesic variation is not categorical and dichotomous, but rather must be analysed along the three dimensions of medial, sociolinguistic, and functional variation.

29.2 Effects and Consequences of Diamesic Variation

29.2.1 Written and Spoken Latin: The Sociophilological Approach

One of the most important areas in which linguists encounter the consequences of diamesic variation is written documentation of the older stages of a language. In most traditional societies, the usage of the written medium is closely intertwined with communicative distance. Written records never reflect the entire range of linguistic variation, but clearly privilege the standard variety over others. Written documentation is characterized by the conservative dynamics of the standard language, tending not to adopt any more changes once the processes of centralization and codification have been concluded. Therefore, the first phases of the processes of language change often cannot be verified despite good written documentation; only with social change and upheaval, and the concomitant triggering of restandardization and/or the textualizing of new varieties, do the results of language change become visible. Yet Latinists and Romanists have known for a long time that there are also exceptions to this rule. Extant Latin records document not only Classical Latin but also other, non-standard varieties (cf. also Section 2.4). At least since Hugo Schuchardt and his monumental *Vokalismus des Vulgärlateins* (Schuchardt [1866–68] 1975), it has been common practice in research on Latin-Romance developments to search systematically for 'sources of Vulgar Latin' in written documentation and to link the forms found there to developments in the Romance languages (cf. also Section 3.2.1).

Some scholars have interpreted the connexions between certain genres or groups of writers and non-Classical forms as if 'Vulgar Latin' were an independent variety or even a language of its own (cf. Pulgram 1975; de Dardel 1996). The forms labelled as 'Vulgar Latin,' however, are but an indicator of the internal variation of the Latin language. When citing the list of the 'sources of Vulgar Latin', which Väänänen (1981) mentions in his famous *Introduction au latin vulgaire*, what must be highlighted is its heterogeneity. Väänänen (1981: 14–20) names the following sources:

(1) Hints in the writings of grammarians (e.g., *Appendix Probi*)
(2) Glossaries
(3) Inscriptions, graffiti
(4) Letters by Cicero, the works of Plautus and Petronius
(5) Technical literature
(6) Historiography from the sixth century CE onwards
(7) Langobardic, Visigothic, or Merovingian legal texts

(8) Writings by Christian authors
(9) Reconstructions on the basis of historical-comparative analyses of Romance idioms

The significance of the last category (9), the reconstructed forms, cannot be discussed in detail at this point (but see the extensive discussion in Chapter 3, this volume). In a sense, they constitute the 'backbone' of Romance language research, since they demonstrate that the Romance languages do not seamlessly link up with the Latin written tradition and that Classical Latin did not occupy the entire variational space within the Latin language. One important break in Väänänen's list, however, needs further discussion, becoming evident when recontextualizing the 'sources' in the framework of a sociophilological approach (Wright 2002; 2016): in the first five categories, remoteness from the standard is clearly the result of situational or social factors and has to do with the grammarians' critical perspective regarding non-standard forms, the conditions of communicative immediacy in letters and similar genres, or the social background of the writers. The texts listed in categories (6) through (8), on the other hand, originate from situations of communicative distance in institutional contexts. They must have been intended as conforming to the standard language. Their categorization as sources of non-standard forms, then, is related to diachronic changes within the Classical Latin norm; these 'sources' will be treated in more detail in the next section (Section 29.2.2).

The remaining 'sources' document the synchronic variation in the Latin variational space, dating as far back as the first centuries of Latin language history. 'Sources' of non-standard forms include, for instance, texts by authors or scribes who did not belong to the dominating rhetorical culture (Adams 2013; 2016). The graffiti at Pompeii (Väänänen 1966), letters by legionaries such as those written by Claudius Terentianus (Adams 1977), or the tablets from the British legionary camp at Vindolanda (Bowman and Thomas 1983; 1994; 2003; Bowman, Thomas, and Tomlin 2010; 2011), as well as Latin inscriptions that could have originated from all classes of society, show that the usage of writing in Roman society was not limited to a small élite, but rather that the extent of literacy must have been relatively large at least until the end of the Roman imperial era. Väänänen (1981: 111, 113) cites the following forms found among the graffiti at Pompeii as examples of 'Vulgar Latin' (1–2):

(1) Amicus ave (Lat., *CIL* IV, 8783, Pompeii)
 friend.NOM.SG hello
 'Hello, my friend'

(2) Aiutor (cf. CLat. ADIUTOR) (Lat., *CIL* IV, 7069, Pompeii)
 helper.NOM.SG
 'Helper' (= proper name)

Example (1) shows that the reduction of the vocative form in the -o-declension, the only declension featuring a formal distinction between nominative and vocative in Classical Latin (viz. *-e* for the vocative singular, e.g., AMICE 'friend.VOC.SG'), must have begun during the first century CE at the latest; example (2), on the other hand, is not as easy to interpret: Väänänen takes it as evidence for the fact that intervocalic [j] had already developed into the affricate [dʒ], since in this graffiti <i> is used for the prescriptive <di>. Väänänen thus assumes that for the writer, <i> and <di> functioned as interchangeable spellings for [dʒ] (Väänänen 1981: 52). Yet, it would also be conceivable that the plosive closure [d] before [j] had been dissolved in the lexeme ADIUUARE 'to help' and in its derivative ADIUTOR, as the Italian continuations of this etymon prove (ADIUUARE > It. *aiutare*) (Stotz 1996, III: 235). Regardless of which solution is correct, this example shows that in quite a few cases, it is clear that the given forms are non-Classical, yet the interpretation of the deviations is not always unambiguous.

Two other types of 'sources' provide evidence for another important phenomenon: the writing of Latin does not always entail the use of the Classical norm, even when this norm has been mastered. The situations in which writing is used vary, and it is also used in areas marked by a higher level of communicative immediacy. Such 'sources' of 'Vulgar Latin' also include Cicero's (106–43 BCE) letters to friends and confidants, or the literary texts written by Plautus (254–184 BCE) or Petronius (†66 CE), in which the everyday language of the different classes is represented mimetically. Such language-of-immediacy texts (that is, texts imitating the language of immediacy) date back as far as the pre-Christian era and reveal characteristics that can be connected to the later development of the Romance languages. Väänänen (1981: 113) cites two passages in which a prepositional marker is used instead of bare case marking in the inflexional ending (3–4):

(3) hunc   ad carnuficem   dabo (Lat., Pl. *Capt.* 1019)
    DEM.ACC.MSG to henchman.ACC.SG give.FUT.1SG
    'I shall send this one to the henchman.'

(4) duos parietes   de eadem   fidelia   dealbare (Lat., Cic. *Fam.* 7,29,2)
    two wall.ACC.PL from same.ABL.SG bucket.ABL.SG paint.INF.ACT
    'to kill two birds with one stone'

Based on these and other examples, it is tempting to establish a sort of 'subsurface' continuity between the later Romance languages and the vernacular Latin of the Republic (cf. Section 2.4), from which the proverb quoted in Cicero derives and which Plautus represented in his œuvre. A more detailed analysis of the cited passages, however, shows that the prepositions do not yet 'replace' the case endings here, because their usage is semantically more restricted (Adams and De Melo 2016). In this respect, the cited passages do not anticipate the developments in the Romance languages but merely demonstrate that prepositional marking competed with case inflexion very early on.

Category (5), that is, technical texts for example, by Cato the Elder (234–149 BCE), Varro (116–27 BCE), or Vitruvius (first century BCE), documents the wide range of registers found in the Latin literary corpus. Vitruvius writes in his treatise on architecture that '[t]he architect cannot and must not be a grammarian like Aristarchus' (1,1,13). His remark shows that the linguistic norms for technical texts did not have to correspond to the strictly codified language of public oratory and literature. Over the centuries, technical texts thus remained a field of written text production in which following the rules of Classical Latinity was not absolutely necessary.

Moreover, it is clear that the question of whether the written documentation can be used for reconstructing the development of spoken varieties is not only relevant for research on 'Vulgar Latin.' Interest in the history of the spoken varieties of other periods has significantly increased over the past decades. This research has also shown that the written documentation is far more diverse than the image of the 'ice sheet' suggests. Ernst (2019), for instance, systematically looked for eighteenth-century French examples of written texts produced by members of the middle and lower classes and made them accessible for linguistic analysis. Within Spanish language history, the examples of the colonial literacy of the *reino de las Indias* ('kingdom of the Indies'), from the sixteenth through the eighteenth centuries, are significant in that they illustrate how poorly-educated soldiers and colonizers adopted writing (Oesterreicher, Stoll, and Wesch 1998; Oesterreicher and Schmidt-Riese 2014). Particularly in the context of overseas colonization, linguists have vigorously looked for documents that make tangible the varieties spoken by settlers, which shaped the linguistic dynamic in the new settlements. The sociophilological approach and the recontextualization of the texts prove crucial for accurately assessing the status of the documented forms in these research fields as well.

29.2.2 The Dynamics of Late Latin: Diglossia, Restandardization, and Polynormativity

The notion of 'Vulgar Latin' emerged because later Romance idioms do not connect seamlessly with the record of written Latin. Some forms are not documented in the written texts and must be reconstructed; in the case of others, important intermediate stages are missing between those recorded in Latin texts and those found in the first Romance language documents. It has already been mentioned that this gap is an indicator of the internal variation of the Latin language and does not reflect a side-by-side situation of two autonomous languages. The structural gap between the first Romance language documents and early medieval Latin, however, is so perspicuous that a normal standard-language variation cannot be inferred. In the Early Middle Ages, the Latin variational space must have been characterized by a pronounced structural tension between the spoken varieties and the written language, since the new textualizations are otherwise inexplicable. The question, then, is from what time these differences existed and how they affected communicative practice.

This question continues to be a subject of controversy in Latinist and Romance studies. Generally speaking, Latinists tend to situate the point in time when the Latin variational space split up rather late and to regard the communicative tensions created by such a structural heterogeneity as minor. Latinists consider the Latin of the Early Middle Ages as a still functional *viva vox* ('living speech') (Banniard 1992). Romanists, by contrast, would argue that the Romance languages had to adopt writing, since the communicative crisis into which the Latin standard language had plunged could not have been overcome otherwise (Lüdtke 1978). Considering how few Romance language texts were written between 800 and 1150 CE, it is evident that the first Romance language documents do not signify the dissolution of a crisis, but rather are first indicators of a practice that would stabilize only later, after 1150 (Frank-Job and Selig 2016). It is quite daring, however, to equate the Latin of the seventh through ninth centuries with a normally functioning standard language. The signs indicating that Latin had developed into a diglossia from about 600 CE onwards are unambiguous, even if this situation was handled flexibly and without a communicative breakdown (Selig 2008; Kabatek 2016).[3]

The concept of diglossia also fits well with the history of Classical Latin. It is noticeable that the literary norm and the varieties used in public political communication had been strongly codified since the time of Cicero (106–43 BCE). This purist tendency even gained momentum during the Roman imperial period, and authors such as Quintilianus ensured that the norm derived from Cicero's writings became an integral part of rhetorical instruction (Poccetti, Poli, and Santini 2006). It is debatable whether the reason for the later crises is to be located in this purist and conservative – if not archaizing – handling of the rhetorical norm. By contrast, it is undisputed that Christian authors, who understandably were interested in as broad a reception of their works as possible, state that the Latin of the *grammatici* ('grammarians') and the language usage of the *populus* ('people')

---

[3] It is even legitimate to use the term "diglossia" to refer to the period before 1150 as well, since the few extant Romance language documents do not challenge the dominance of Latin as the H-variety. Cf. Frank-Job and Selig (2016) for more detail on this.

diverged considerably from each other. Saint Augustine (354–430 CE) for instance formulated the famous dictum '[b]eing reprimanded by grammarians is preferable to not being understood by the people' (*Enarrationes in psalmos* 138,20).

Augustine proposes a recipient-oriented and thus flexible treatment of Classical Latin, a maxim to which he himself adhered. He uses Classical Latin in his theological writings, but in his sermons, he looks for compromises instead of insisting on a staunch adherence to the standard norms (Banniard 1992: 65–104). These compromises also encompass some developments that lead towards later Romance idioms. For this reason, the Christian authors are often referred to as 'sources of Vulgar Latin.' What Augustine, and later Saint Gregory the Great (540–604 CE) propose, then, resembles the polynormative approach taken by Vitruvius and the other authors of technical texts. The rhetoricians' purist norm is accepted in principle, but is set aside for certain areas of communication in which forms more closely related to non-standard varieties are chosen instead.

To refer to this non-purist, recipient-oriented norm, the Christian authors often use the term *rusticus* and *rusticitas*, which might be best translated as 'uneducated' or 'illiterate.' It is anything but a coincidence that the decrees of the Council of Tours (813 CE) use the phrase *lingua romana rustica* ('Romance/Roman language of/for the illiterates'). In late Latinity and during the Early Middle Ages, the term *rusticus* gradually became synonymous with the language of those who had no access to the traditional rhetoricians' culture. The term can thus also designate the forms that the representatives of the literate culture developed as compromises for communication with the other social classes – in Banniard's terms for 'vertical communication' (Banniard 1992: 38f.). Throughout Late Antiquity and the Early Middle Ages, the genres intended for the catechesis of laymen (e.g., sermons, the *vitae* of saints) reveal compromises through which the élite attempted to reduce the gap between their own education and the lay audience's *rusticitas*. In contrast with the opening dedications to ecclesiastical superiors, the narrative parts of such texts are mostly characterized by simpler syntactic and lexical forms. The field of administrative literacy, too, is marked by the predominance of recipient-orientation, and wherever comprehensibility is paramount, simpler forms based on the language-of-immediacy varieties are used (Sabatini 1965; Sornicola 2017).

Notwithstanding the clear tendencies to polynormativity, it remains unclear whether the early medieval authors were working on a restandardization, i.e., a renewal of the written-language norms via an approximation to the language-of-immediacy varieties (cf. Section 29.2.7). This question arises in light of the numerous non-Classical forms found in the historiographical writings from the Merovingian era, primarily in the *Chronica* of Fredegar (c. 660 CE) or in the *Liber Historiae Francorum* (726–99 CE). Several scholars have postulated that in Merovingian Latin, a three-case inflexion evolved, which can be regarded as an intermediate stage between Classical Latin case marking and the caseless inflexion system of nearly all modern Romance languages (Pei 1932; Taylor 1924; Vielliard 1927). However, in traditional-minded research – as well as in Väänänen's works – the deviations are interpreted as signs of a lack of proficiency in the Classical rules and as a contamination of the written language with the forms of spoken varieties. The question of which of these two views is correct will have to remain unanswered. The Merovingian era is characterized by the crisis of the rhetoric schools, and the development towards a situation of oligoliteracy (Goody and Watt 1968), characteristic of the Middle Ages, is already on the horizon. The increasing limitation of literacy to clerical circles rather supports the second interpretation, i.e., the attempt to preserve the Classical norms even though the conditions for the acquisition of these norms were not always in place. Yet the traditional depreciation of all Merovingian texts as faulty and incompetent is inadequate in any case. Polynormative rules apply to the individual genres that are represented within literacy; the question of whether the Latin is incorrect or whether there are new written-language norms thus has to be answered differently for the individual domains.

In this context, Sabatini (1965; 1968; cf. also Böhmer 2010) has drawn attention to a phenomenon of early medieval document literacy, the *scripta latina rustica* ('written Latin for the illiterates'). In deeds dating from the period between the sixth and twelfth centuries and originating primarily from southern Italy and northern Spain, caseless noun forms are used in those parts of the texts that are not dominated by traditional legal formulae. These forms essentially correspond to the later Romance language singular and plural forms. Moreover, there are new grapheme–phoneme correspondences that anticipate those of the first Romance language documents: e.g., in combination with <t> or <c>, <z> is used to represent [t͡s] (Lat. <Laczaro>, <Graczioso>); likewise, the grapheme <h>, which had lost its function in Latin, serves to disambiguate <c>, which had become ambiguous due to palatalization (Lat. <chi> for QUI [k] 'who' vs <cera> for CERA [t͡s] 'wax'; Sabatini 1968: 333f.). Another continuity between the examples of a *latinitas rustica* ('Latin for the illiterates') and the first Romance language documents becomes evident in the Strasbourg Oaths, in which a number of graphic solutions can be found that were already tested in the early medieval deeds (e.g., <u> for [o] <dunat> 'gives', <o> for [ə] <Carlo> 'Charles', etc.) (Sabatini 1968: 337, 341–44; Meisenburg 1996: 47–65). This observation, too, supports the idea of regarding the transition to the first Romance documents as an extended phase of experimentation marked by multiple attempts, rather than an abrupt change marking a striking caesura (Selig 1993; cf. also Finbow 2016: 682–84).

29.2.3 Spoken Varieties and Linguistic Change

A commonly held notion in linguistics is that linguistic change takes place within spoken varieties of a language, and that the codified written form plays no part in this quasi-natural transformation. However, this belief requires clarification. It is, for example, inaccurate to claim that written languages do not change; they do change when they come in contact with the innovations of the spoken varieties, but under the conditions definitive for written practice and the communication of distance (Section 29.2.2). The following section (Section 29.2.4) will elaborate on another clarification, i.e., the idea that the written language-of-distance practice also serves as a starting point for innovations. The current section aims to investigate in greater detail the notion of an innovative orality per se.

When orality or spoken varieties are associated with linguistic change, this always refers to varieties that are primarily or even exclusively connected to phonic use in situations of communicative immediacy and which are not exposed to the effects of codification. Yet these three dimensions are connected to the phenomenon of linguistic change in various ways. The norm-related aspect, i.e., the lack of integration into a codified discourse (Section 29.2.6), indubitably benefits the acceptance and diffusion of innovations. However, we cannot forget that the spoken varieties are (or were) partly anchored in small-scale, dense networks so that the focusing and norm-preserving effect of the constant exchange between the speakers can become important (cf. Blanche-Benveniste and Jeanjean 1987: 9–37).

The phonic medium and the missing reconnexion to (ortho)graphy also favour innovation. Numerous phonetic processes pertaining to the conditions of the communication of immediacy can come into effect: in the case of frequently used lexemes, shortened allegro forms evolve, which meet the speakers' need for a quick, unplanned formulation; under the conditions of phonic perception, inflexional endings are also subject to 'wear and tear' because the listeners identify signifiers very quickly at the beginning of the sound event. Further sound change processes that could manifest themselves profusely during the Latin-Romance development include: processes of consonantal strengthening at the beginning of a word; processes of vocalic strengthening (diphthongization) in stressed syllables; processes of consonantal weakening in the syllable coda; nasalization as a result of co-articulation processes; metatheses; haplologies; etc. The new forms lose their connexion to the full Latin forms over time and become autonomous as soon as they enter the medieval written language. Nonetheless, the connexions to the Latin etyma are never fully erased, as shown for example by the phenomenon of *cultismos/semi-cultismos* 'learnèd/semi-learnèd forms' (5–6) or the Latinizing graphic forms of the Renaissance (7).

(5) Sp. *fábula* 'fable' < Lat. FABULA 'story' vs Sp. *hablar* 'speak' < Lat. FABULARI 'to speak, chat' (Penny 2002: 39)

(6) Sp. *regla* 'rule, order' < Lat. REGULA 'lath; rule' vs Sp. *reja* 'ploughshare' < Lat. REGULA 'lath; rule' (Penny 2002: 39)

(7) Lat. TEMPUS 'time' > OFr. *tens* > Fr. *temps* [tã] 'time; weather' (Wartburg 1971: 155)

But it is most of all the third dimension, that of communicative immediacy, which favours linguistic change in spoken varieties. Many of the Latin-Romance developments have always been traced back to factors such as emotionality or drastic wording, factors closely connected to the communicative conditions of immediacy (Koch 1995). In the realm of lexical developments, it is widely accepted that the Romance forms can be explained through such universal tendencies. Väänänen (1981: 80), for instance, lists several examples for the replacement of neutral forms with more expressive lexemes (8).

(8) a. CLat. EDERE 'to eat' (> Ø) replaced by CLat. MANDUCARE 'to chew' (> e.g., Fr. *manger*, OOcc. *manjar*, Cat. *menjar*, Log. *mandicare*, It. *mangiare*, Ro. *a mânca* 'to eat')
b. CLat. FERRE 'to carry' (> Ø) replaced by CLat. PORTARE 'to transport' (> e.g., Fr. *porter*, OOcc. *portar*, Cat. *portar*, Log. *portare*, It. *portare*, RaeR. *portar*, Ro. *a purta* 'to carry, bear')
c. CLat. LOQUI 'to speak' (> Ø) replaced by CLat. FABULARI 'to chat' (> e.g., Pt. *falar*, Sp. *hablar*, Log. *faeddare*, OIt. *favellare* 'to speak')

The Romance forms going back to euphemistic usage (CLat. TUTARI 'to protect, look after' > Fr. *tuer* 'to kill') also testify to the expressive mechanism, since factors such as positive face or taboo ensure that 'less' is said than normally must be (Blank 1997: 331–33).

Factors such as affectivity or subjectivity have also been invoked as explanations for developments in the realm of morphology and syntax. The emergence of the article (Selig 1992: 185–99) or the development of the analytic perfect (Jacob 1995) have been mentioned in this context. Naturally, not all morphosyntactic developments can be connected to orality, but a certain type of change still takes shape which can be linked to the conditions of communicative immediacy: developments in which the Latin construction was discarded in favour of a verbalization pattern adding content-related aspects merely implied in the Latin construction. Such expressive clarifications mainly occur in those subject areas considered particularly significant for everyday concerns, e.g., the field of 'plans for action und hopes' (Koch and Oesterreicher 1996: 83–85). In order to counterbalance the uncertainty of future events, speakers develop strategies with which they can signal a higher degree of certainty: they use periphrases with auxiliary verbs, which signal modal attitudes such as 'obligation' or 'intention' (9):

(9) a. Lat. CANTARE HABEO 'sing.INF.ACT have.PRS.IND.1SG (= I have to sing)': Pt. *cantarei*, OFr. *chanterai*, It. *canterò*
   b. Lat. HABEO (AD) CANTARE 'have.PRS.IND.1SG (to) sing.INF.ACT (= I have to sing)': OLmb. *a cantare*, Sic. *aggiu kkantari*, Luc. *aǧǧ a kkantá*, Log. *app a kkantáre*
   c. Lat. HABEO DE CANTARE 'have.PRS.IND.1SG (of) sing.INF.ACT (= I have to sing)': Pt. *hei-de cantar*
   d. Lat. DEBEO CANTARE 'must.PRS.IND.1SG sing.INF.ACT (= I am obliged to sing)': Nuo. *deppo cantare*
   e. Lat. UOLO CANTARE 'want.PRS.IND.1SG sing.INF.ACT (= I want to sing)': Ro. *voi cânta* (cf. also Rohlfs 1968: 337; Fleischman 1982: 144f.)

Another expressive strategy is to emphasize the imminence of future events by associating the action with a movement whose goal is this future action (10):

(10) Lat. UENIO/UADO + AD + CANTARE 'come/go.PRS.IND.1SG (to) sing.INF.ACT (= I am going to sing)': Srs. *jeu végnel a cantar*, Fr. *je vais chanter*, Sp. *voy a cantar*, Pt. *vou cantar*

The development of these future tense forms also draws attention to the fact that the so-called 'Vulgar Latin' developments do not revolve around the direct replacement of the old form. The new periphrases emerge as a manifestation of expressive needs and remain initially connected to the conditions of expressivity. The innovations trigger linguistic variation, i.e., the coexistence of simple, non-expressive forms and more expressive periphrases. It is therefore not surprising that other forms of expressively reinforcing statements with a future reference can be found in Latin texts, such as the use of future perfect forms or the periphrasis -URUM ESSE (Väänänen 1981: 132f.). It was not only the forms that later persisted in the Romance languages that were involved in the development of the future tense. The expressive need became manifest in a number of more expressive 'satellite constructions,' and it was not until processes of grammaticalization had come to an end that the selection was limited to one construction (Koch and Oesterreicher 1996; cf. Detges and Waltereit 2002).

The issue of the relation between orality and linguistic change must also be discussed with respect to the substandard varieties of modern Romance national languages (dialects, sociolects, regional languages). We must determine how the latter's lack of involvement in processes of codification and the conceptual connexion to the communication of immediacy have influenced the development of these varieties. This question is even more pertinent with regard to the non-European forms of the colonial languages French, Spanish, and Portuguese, since the former's connexion to their respective standard varieties was broken off very early on. The question of how linguistic structures have been shaped by orality is highly relevant to creole languages as well (Ludwig 1996).

Pustka (2010) discusses a construction observable in the regional French on Guadeloupe, namely, *subordination sans subordonnant* ('subordination without a subordinator'). She lists the examples in (11)–(12).

(11) Alors c' est pour ça tu viens pas jouer
 so that= be.PRS.IND.2SG for that you.SG= come.PRS.IND.2SG NEG play.INF
 avec eux? (Fr. on Guadeloupe)
 with them
 'So that is why you don't go play with them?'

(12) Je pense il y a quand même en Guadeloupe des
 I= think.PRS.IND.1SG it= LOC= have.PRS.IND.3SG nevertheless in Guadeloupe some
 secteurs. (Fr. on Guadeloupe)
 sectors
 'I think there are nevertheless areas on Guadeloupe.'

Some authors have identified the phenomenon that Pustka observes as a creolism, since in Guadeloupean creole, subordination without an overt subordinator represents the basilectal form (13) (Pustka 2010: 159):

(13) Fó pa an di non. (Gua.)
 it.is.necessary NEG I= say.PRS NEG
 'I cannot say no.'

Yet constructions in which the subordinator *que* 'that' is missing are also attested in old French (14) and in *français populaire* 'popular French' (15) (Pustka 2010: 161f.).

(14) E or sai ben n' avons guaires
 and now know.PRS.IND.1SG well NEG= have.PRS.IND.1PL NEG
 a vivre (OFr., *Chanson de Roland*, v. 1923)
 to live.INF
 'And I know very well that we have only little time left to live'

(15) ?Il a dit i viendrait. (Fr., Bauche 1946: 123)
 he= have.PRS.IND.3SG say.PTCP he= come.COND.3SG
 'He said he would come.'

Varieties that have not yet been fully codified (such as the old French *scriptae*) or non-standard varieties (such as the *français populaire* or the *français régional* 'regional French' on Guadeloupe) tolerate structures that do not mark the subordination of the second predication explicitly with *que* 'that' since the context of the utterance is considered sufficiently disambiguating. In those cases in which the syntactic juxtaposition of the constructions within an intonation phrase suffices to signal subordination, Raible (1992) speaks of 'aggregative structures' and contrasts them with the more complex and semantically more explicit 'integrative structures' of the language of distance. It is striking that subordination without a subordinator occurs in the vast majority of cases after verbs of saying and thinking (Pustka 2010: 152–56). Studies on the use of this verb group in conversational research have yielded a wide range of constructions, from parentheses to simple parataxis, as well as explicit subordinations. The subordination without *que* 'that' belongs to a field that, due to its relevance for dialogic exchange, is much used and shows considerable constructional variance (Imo 2007).

When approaching the issue of the 'age' of spoken Latin or spoken French, we need to take into consideration that the syntactic variability between 'aggregative' and 'integrative' structures is anchored in the anthropologically founded conditions of communication of immediacy. The discussion has already been mentioned because research on 'Vulgar Latin' has found numerous parallels between old Latin texts and Romance innovations; similarly, research on contemporary spoken French has uncovered frequent parallels with old French constructions (Barme 2012: 14–17). These parallels become understandable upon recognizing that the functional 'syntax of oral language' (Drescher and Neumann-Holzschuh 2010) repeatedly and continuously takes effect under the specific conditions of the communication of immediacy and thus generates continuity between the aforementioned language stages. This clarification also impacts the discussion that ascribes to the overseas varieties of French, the *français marginaux* ('marginal varieties of French'), the capacity to continue, via 'supposedly optimizing restructuring' (Chaudenson, Mougeon, and Beniak 1993: 16), the developments that were artificially interrupted in the codified standard language. More intensive empirical research on linguistic change in non-standard varieties of the Romance languages still needs to be carried out in order to determine precisely the influence of functional diamesic variation, codification, and graphic mediality on the development of spoken varieties.

29.2.4 Inscripturation: Romance Vernacular Varieties and the Transition to Written Use

The transition of spoken varieties to written use requires the formation of new vernacular graphic traditions. In modern scenarios of language planning, this subprocess of standardization is often at the centre of discussions about identity among the speakers of the individual varieties in question. A well-known example is the long and difficult search for a shared graphic standard for the Raeto-Romance varieties (Darms 1989; Anderson 2016: 169). The search for new graphic standards, however, is only one aspect of the transition to written use. Other subprocesses include the extensive and intensive elaboration (i.e., the adoption) of new discourse traditions in the realm of communication of distance and the formation of new complex linguistic structures (Koch and Oesterreicher 2007: 185–96; 2011: 135–42). In the modern standardizations of Romance languages, these processes have taken place in a condensed time frame and through central regulation due to the planning of socio-technocratic experts. In medieval Romance language history, by contrast, extensive and intensive elaboration took place slowly, over the course of centuries.

Bossong (1979) has analysed the linguistic change triggered by the new functional requirements, using the translations of astronomical treatises from Arabic into thirteenth-century Spanish as an example. Arabic already provided linguistic and textual procedures with which the astronomical calculations could be rendered in writing in a concise and transparent manner. The old Spanish translations, in turn, are longer and, more importantly, ponderous, since in old Spanish – unlike Arabic – two requirements for complex textualizations had not yet been fulfilled: the development of an abstract technical vocabulary – Bossong speaks of 'universalization' – and the development of strategies for subordination and condensation – according to Bossong, the syntactic 'complexification' (Bossong 1979; 1982). The Alphonsine translations initiate these two processes for old Spanish, inspired by the contact with the then already elaborated Arabic. In old French, it is the translations of Aristotelian works by Nicole Oresme (about 1320–82), the most renowned member of the translation school of Charles V (1338–80), that significantly contributed to the intensive elaboration of French (Frank-Job 2008). Oresme set out from Latin structures and systematically formed verbal abstracta: for instance, with regard to semantics, these formations entailed the typification of verbal actions without any remnants of individualizing references (arguments, tense, aspect, etc.);[4] with regard to syntax, they allowed the subordination of nominal predications in superordinate sentence structures. An example (16) will illustrate these two dimensions of Oresme's language work:

(16) a. de chescune chose la   nature est trouvee par cognoissance
        of each   thing the nature is found   by knowledge
        en ses parties (OFr., Oresme, Le livre d'Yconomique d'Aristote 330a)
        in its parts
        'the nature of each thing is disclosed by a knowledge of its parts'
    b. de chescune chose la   cognoissance de ses parties
        of each   thing the knowledge   of its parts
        la fait   cognoistre (OFr., Oresme, Le livre d'Yconomique d'Aristote 330a)
        it= makes   know
        'a knowledge of the parts of any thing provides a knowledge of the thing'

---

[4] Cf. also the studies carried out by Schaffer (1982-83) and Fleischman (1977) on the nominalizations in old French that use calques of the Latin word formation suffixes -TUDO or -ATICUS.

Oresme condenses the frame *cognoistre les parties de X* ('to know the parts of X') into the nominal syntagma *la cognoissance de ses parties/en ses parties* ('the knowledge of its parts') and uses this condensation into a verbal abstractum in one case as subject (*la cognoissance de [...] la fait cognoistre* 'a knowledge of [...] provides a knowledge of it', 16a), in another as prepositional complement with an instrumental function (*[...] est trouvee par cognoissance de [...]* 'is disclosed by a knowledge of [...]', 16b). Moreover, Oresme systematically uses nominalizations, or other abstract nouns, to form prepositional periphrases (P+N+*de*), such as *a cas de* ('in the case of'), *a cause de* ('because of') or *par necessite de* ('by the need to'), which make it possible to signal the logical relation between the superordinated and subordinated frames (e.g., *a l'occasion d'icelles empirances* 'on the occasion of those deteriorations') (Frank-Job 2008: 590–96; cf. also Raible 1992).

By using the vernacular varieties in scientific genres, figures such as Ramon Llull (1232–1316) or the Italian *volgarizzamenti* contributed to the elaboration of the Romance vernaculars (Nadal and Prats 1983; Folena 1991). Efforts to develop linguistic forms complying with the conditions of the communication of distance, however, began even before the thirteenth and fourteenth centuries. True, genres like the *chansons de geste* or courtly literature dominated vernacular written text production at first and therefore, to speak of the orality of medieval Romance varieties is legitimate (Fleischman 1990; Selig 1997). Nevertheless, the functional conditions of the communication of distance favour from the outset the development of complex syntactic and lexical forms. Due to etymological kinship, the boundaries between Romance and Latin structures are porous, such that lexical loans or syntactic calques are easily realized. Romance language scholars speak of the 're-Latinization' of those Romance varieties that were used extensively in the written communication of distance as early as medieval times (Raible 1996). In the Strasbourg Oaths, for instance, the conjunctional paraphrases OFr. *in quant* (17a) and *in o quid* (17b) are formed as *ad hoc* solutions in order to make possible the insertion of comparative and final subordinate clauses:

(17) a. in quant Deus savir et podir me dunat (OFr., Strasbourg Oaths)
in as.much God knowledge and power me= give.PRS.IND.3SG
'as far as God will give me the wisdom and power'
b. in o quid il mi altresi fazet (OFr., Strasbourg Oaths)
in that which he= me= equally do.PRS.SBJV.3SG
'so that he may do the same for me'

The close contact with Latin has resulted in a considerable number of language contact phenomena. The major wave of Latinizing graphic forms that the Renaissance printers developed for French are well known and have been thoroughly researched (Beaulieux 1927; Catach 1968; Meisenburg 1996;

cf. (7)). There is also a considerable body of research on contact phenomena within the lexicon, i.e., learnèd or semi-learnèd terms (variously termed in Romance *cultismos/semicultismos*, *mots savants/demi-savants*, and *parole dotte/semi-dotte*; Bustos 1974; cf. (5), (6)). There has been less research done on contact phenomena in the realm of syntax, which appear mainly in the field of subordination. For instance, the elaboration of subordination through 'absolute constructions,' i.e., the combination of N + participle/gerund in the syntactic position of adverbial complements, is strongly influenced by Latin models. Especially in Italian, the option of this subordination, made possible through verbal nominalization, saw considerable elaboration (18). In translated texts, the orientation along Latin models encouraged writers to attempt to imitate Latin structures, such as the accusative-and-infinitive construction (19), even if the linguistic prerequisites were not in place. This overstretching of the structural means of Romance was not continued in the later stages of the respective languages (Raible 1996: 126).

(18) Sconfitti, morti e presi gli Aretini, frate Guittone iscrisse (OIt., *Cronica fiorentina* 136,7)
defeated dead and taken the Aretinians brother Guittone write.PST.PFV.3SG
'after the defeat of the Aretinians, Guittone wrote'

(19) a. docebat [...] patrum id superbia factum [...] (Lat., Liv. 1,9)
teach.PST.IPFV.IND.3SG father.GEN.PL that arrogance.ABL.SG make.PTCP.PST.ACC.SG
'he taught that it had happened because of the arrogance of their parents'
b. pour leur remonstrer le tout estre auenu par l' orgueil
for them.DAT= show.INF the all be.INF happen.PTCP by the arrogance
de leurs pères (MidFr., Antoine de La Faye, *Histoire romaine de Tite Liue padouan*)
of their fathers
'to show them that it had all happened because of the arrogance of their parents'

The Romance languages that have been involved in processes of standardization since the nineteenth century are faced with the same necessity of developing a differentiated vocabulary and complex syntax. Again, the contact with an already elaborated language is crucial. In Seychellois creole, for instance, just as in Oresme's case, prepositional periphrases are developed in order to make possible non-finite subordinations. The periphrases take up French models and transfer them into creole (e.g., Sey. *annacor avek* 'in accordance with' < Fr. *en accord avec* 'in agreement with'; Sey. *an relasyon avek* 'in relation to' < Fr. *en relation avec* 'in relation to'; Michaelis 1994).

29.2.5 *Scriptae*: 'Invisible Hands' and Linguistic Centralizations

The question of how the modern Romance national languages formed was one of the most important issues for the 'national philology' of the nineteenth and early twentieth centuries. The language histories from this period often still shape our perception of medieval standardization processes: nineteenth-century linguists assumed that the writers of the first

Romance documents textualized the local dialect they spoke (Beaulieux 1927). Therefore, scholars argued, medieval written tradition was marked by the use of a considerable number of dialects, one of which prevailed after a period of polycentric coexistence: the French standard language supposedly goes back to *francien*, the medieval dialect of the Île-de-France; Italian derives from the Tuscan of *Le Tre Corone* 'The Three Crowns' (viz. Dante, Petrarch, and Boccaccio); and Spanish continues medieval Castilian. However, the story of the rise of an individual dialect, ennobled by its use at the royal court or in literature – besides having certain ideological implications – is closely connected to the 'written language bias.' The hypothesis that medieval centralizations could only take place due to the 'roofing' (Kloss 1978) of one prestige dialect is linked to the idea that linguistic systems are homogenous and that the supraregional spread of a uniform 'national' norm could only result from a (Darwinian) struggle among – and the repression of most of – the medieval written dialects.

But there is strong empirical evidence that even the first Romance texts are the manifestation not of one local dialect, but of a kind of language mixture (cf. also Section 3.3). The Strasbourg Oaths are emblematic in this regard: in light of the co-presence of *oïl* (northern) and *oc* (southern) forms in these few lines, as well as of the numerous Latinisms, the attempt to pin down a dialectal origin for the oaths seems futile from the start (pace Castellani 1978). Likewise, the presence of linguistic forms stemming from different dialect areas in literary texts is absolutely normal, and even charters handed down in the original and untarnished by any interpolations on the part of copiers do not allow dialects to be scrutinized in their pure form. Remacle proved in an epochal work published in 1948 that the language of the original Wallon charters did not reflect a geographically clearly delimited dialect but was a *Schreibsprache*, a *scripta*: as in all other medieval written texts, the language of the deeds originated in a scriptorium; it did not, Remacle argued, represent a local spoken dialect but consisted of those elements that the scribes considered appropriate for the new written uses.

Yet the constructed character of the first textualizations does not imply that the scribes initiated a sort of standardization programme in order to create a vernacular written language. Such a notion (Cerquiglini 1991) is an obvious anachronism. The heterogeneity of the linguistic forms derives from the fact that the medieval scribes never intended to represent spontaneous everyday communication. With their texts, the scribes wanted to reach a more or less regional or even supraregional audience, and they wanted to write in a language that was appropriate for the respective occasions. As in processes of koinéization, they made a selection from among the forms at their disposal in order to distance themselves from explicit regional ascriptions (Selig 2017). They avoided forms whose link to small, local communication communities was overly explicit, and used supraregionally disseminated forms instead. Furthermore, they used Latinisms or forms from prestigious vernacular discourse traditions, but also conservativisms such as the use of the two-case declension in old French texts in order to express their desire to write language-of-distance texts of a certain prestige level and addressed to non-local recipients (Grübl 2015).

As soon as the second half of the twelfth century, vernacular literacy developed stable discourse traditions (Frank-Job and Selig 2016), and textualizations evolved into written-language traditions, which, for instance, were tied to specific chanceries (Gleßgen 2008; cf. Grübl 2013), communicative networks such as noble courts, or the thirteenth- and fourteenth-century urban landscapes in the northern parts of France and Italy. Yet the prerequisites for the formation of focused norms seem to emerge only gradually, not only in the realm of oral communication networks, but also in the realm of literacy. For medieval authors and scribes, the coexistence of Latin and vernacular language side by side was normal, as was the relative lack of norms regulating vernacular written text production. In the Luxembourg region, one and the same chancery, sometimes even one and the same scribe, would write for the local lower nobility or for the supraregionally operating high nobility; they adapted their linguistic choices by signalling the diverging communication radius of the document via the inclusion or the avoidance of regionalisms: local for the lower nobility or the respective urban population, supraregional for the networks of higher nobility (Völker 2003). Polynormativity does not only exist in France in this period; northern Italian written text production is also polynormative, even during periods when centralizing tendencies in favour of the Tuscan-based literary norm had already set in. Texts such as saints' lives or similarly catechetical texts remained associated with regionally marked linguistic forms; the orientation along the lines of a supraregionally unified norm, on the other hand, is characteristic of literary communication or chanceries, which increasingly addressed the issues of normalizing and standardizing vernacular written language (Wilhelm 2009; 2011).

The medieval transition to literacy and the centralization linked to it must thus be analysed as invisible-hand processes, characterized by polynormative tendencies and non-teleologic dynamics. The vernacular texts are a priori not geared towards reproducing local dialects; therefore, the stabilizing tendencies of communicative networks (courts, chanceries, cities) result in regional koinés characterized by the general instability of the still unfocused written communication practice. The processes of centralization advanced more vigorously in France and in Spain than in Italy, where there was no normalizing centre until the *Questione della lingua* ('language question') in the fifteenth and sixteenth centuries.

Nevertheless, it was the intellectuals of the Renaissance and the Baroque eras, and not medieval authors and scribes, who initiated the focusing of written-language vernacular norms in all Romance language areas.

29.2.6 Codifications: 'Grammatization' and 'Standard Ideologies'

Latin-Romance language history shows that the connexion between written language and codification is not a given. It is not until the early modern era that Romance varieties emerge as the subject of lexicographic and grammaticographic codifications. Whereas the birth of Anglo-Norman literature around 1150 is taken as the beginning of a consolidated Romance writing practice, and the emergence of the *Questione della lingua* ('language question') in the mid-fifteenth century is seen as the beginning of Romance codifications, three centuries passed until the first attempts were made to influence the spontaneous and unregulated processes of elaboration and centralization through explicit efforts at codification.

Specific social conditions trigger the discussions surrounding language as well as the ensuing codifications. The *Questione della lingua* in Italy was born of the discussion between intellectuals who turned away from Latin as the spread of printing opened up new markets for vernacular literature (Eisenstein 1983). In Italy, the *cortegiani* ('courtiers') also engaged the *Questione della lingua* early on, and both groups – courtiers and intellectuals – jointly sought after the best language form (Vitale 1978). Likewise, printers and editors played a decisive role in France in the discussions regarding *bon usage* ('correct usage') (Trudeau 1992), but the discussion around codification develops without close contact with (and in part even in sharp opposition to) the ruling political classes. It is not until the seventeenth century, after royal power had gained in strength, that Claude Favre de Vaugelas (1585–1650) influences the discussion surrounding *bon usage* at least temporarily in favour of a norm anchored in spoken courtly conversation and constantly renewing itself (*purisme rajeunisseur*; François 1912). In Spain, Elio Antonio de Nebrija (1444–1522) in turn exemplifies the fact that a strong central power can take an interest in the codification of the vernacular language very early on. His dictum, 'the language was always the companion of the empire', is well known. It is probably less well known that Nebrija also penned a much more successful Latin grammar (Lapesa 1981: 288–90; Lázaro Carreter 1985: 151–62). This is a significant indicator that Latin was still the predominant written language and lingua franca for early modern Europe and that there was a continuity between the Latin grammar tradition and the first attempts to codify the Romance vernacular languages.

The influence of the Latin tradition has often been a topic in research on the history of modern linguistics. It should be stressed that, together with grammaticographic and lexicographic concepts, the models developed by Classical and Medieval Latin tradition for theorizing about language, linguistic norms, and linguistic variation were taken over as well. Sylvain Auroux therefore refers to the efforts at codification during the Renaissance and the Baroque eras as the 'grammatization' of the Romance languages, as that point in time when the 'written language bias' begins to impact the perception of the Romance languages as well (Auroux 1994). The now clearly delimited and established standard languages transformed the coexistence of the vernacular varieties into a hierarchical 'top' (e.g., *bon usage* 'correct usage', *castellano drecho* 'correct Spanish') and 'bottom' (the regional and social dialects). Yet during the premodern era, the effects of codification remained limited to a small élite. Similar to the late Latin and medieval situation, many areas of written text production were not affected by standard language regulations (Sections 29.2.2, 29.2.5). Moreover, the norm laid down by premodern codifications was aligned so closely with the literary use of language that grammatical prescriptions could barely impact actual language use. What the grammarians did bring about, however, was the institutionalization of a normalizing discourse that anticipated modern standard ideologies. In the upper classes, self-monitoring and alignment with fixed language norms became a central social practice (Trudeau 1992). The rules for the use of the subjunctive, which were established by the French grammarians of the seventeenth and eighteenth centuries, therefore are more reminiscent of the attempt to bring *langue* 'language' and *logique* 'logic' closer together than of directives for an appropriate use of language (Wartburg 1971: 172–76).

29.2.7 Mass Literacy, Restandardization, and New Media

The rise of mass literacy during the twentieth century vastly changed the conditions for standard language varieties. The extreme codification that used to be characteristic of the three 'big' Romance languages – French, Italian, and Spanish – could easily be upheld as long as this norm was only valid for a small élite using the written language. With the introduction of general education, however, the standard norm also became binding on segments of the population which up until then had only rarely found themselves in situations of standard language communication. The changes that mass literacy entailed are well known: a new kind of diglossic situation, since the standard language communication practices taught in school had not been accessible to most speakers without additional schooling; the development of intermediate registers, documented by the partial adoption of the standard language on the part of those less literate; and the depreciation of regional varieties, both dialects of the standard language as well as autonomous regional languages, in practice as well as in their speakers' consciousness. Early on, these processes were a research topic for Romance linguistics; milestones include Leo Spitzer's studies on letters written by Italian soldiers during World War I (Spitzer 1922) or Henri Frei's monograph on *français populaire* 'popular French' (Frei 1929), for instance. They show how far removed the linguistic and discursive norms taught in school were from those speakers'/writers' communicative practice, and how strongly their standard language performance was impacted by dialectally or diastratically marked orality, which determined their everyday language use. Linguistic research generally took the part of the new speakers of the standard varieties. During the *bataille de l'orthographe* ('spelling battle') of 1900, for instance, a number of French linguists became involved in efforts to loosen the rules of the *orthographe grammaticale* ('grammatical spelling') and to facilitate the access to orthography through a stronger alignment with actual pronunciation (Catach 1985). The emergence of sociolinguistics is also closely connected to research on the spread of the standard language in new speech communities.

In Italy, dialectological research was already vibrant due to the marginal presence of standard Italian in the everyday language of all classes, and developed into sociolinguist dialectology. The dialectologist Manlio Cortelazzo coined the term *italiano popolare* ('popular Italian') to describe the intermediate registers originating from dialect speakers' contact with the standard language, and defined it as 'the type of Italian spoken by speakers who do not fully master the standard language and whose mother tongue is dialect' (Cortelazzo 1972: 11). The disapproval that this definition still conveys very soon gave way to an acceptance of the complex linguistic situation between standard language and dialects or regional languages. Concepts such as *italiano regionale* ('regional Italian') or *dialetto italianizzato* ('Italianized dialect') now provide a precise terminology for describing the architecture of the Italian language and the ways in which it has been impacted by contact phenomena (Jones, Parry, and Williams 2016).

It was also within Italian research that the concept of restandardization developed (*ristandardizzazione*). Based on an exact observation of the diverse registers that had emerged from the contact between standard language and spoken everyday varieties, the concept of *italiano dell'uso medio* ('average Italian') – an oral and written vernacular spoken in all of Italy and marked by only weak regional influence – developed, which Francesco Sabatini proposed as the new point of reference for Italian varieties (Sabatini 1985; cf. also Berruto 1987: 55–103; Mioni 1983). The linguistic forms proposed for inclusion into this 'restandardized' Italian partly stem from the realm of oral syntax, such as dislocations (e.g., It. *il libro, non l'ho letto* 'the book, I haven't read it') or the polyvalent subordinator *che* 'that' (e.g., It. *la valigia che ci ho messo i libri* lit. 'the suitcase that there I put the books' = 'the suitcase I put the books in'). There are also parallels to the Italian discussion about restandardization in French and Spanish, since the loosening of standard language norms is very closely tied to the social developments of the modern and post-modern eras (Cerruti, Crocco, and Marzo 2017).

The functional dimension of diamesic variation also manifests itself in the new forms of computer-mediated communication, such as chat groups and Instant Messaging. Computer-mediated communication does not always fall in the category of language of immediacy. However, many forms of chatting on social media or instant messaging are characterized by privacy, familiarity, high emotional involvement, strong cooperativeness, spontaneity, little or no topic fixation, etc. During processualization, the language-of-distance parameters produced by spatial separation are counterweighted by the speed with which communication can unfold in this medium. Computer-mediated communication thus demonstrates new patterns of expressive written communication (Berruto 2005). The intersection of the graphic and the phonic code in forms such as It. <x> = *per* 'by (in multiplication)' and 'for', <xé> = *perché* 'because', <3> = *tre* 'three', <3mendo> = *tremendo* 'terrible', emoticons and emojis, iconic sign repetitions (It. <Poverrrinaaa!> 'Poooor thing!'), or short forms (It. <intrsata> = *interessata* 'interested') show how the lack of the para- or non-verbal semiotic dimensions of face-to-face-communication is compensated for and how new linguistic practices related to diamesic variation emerge.

Selected References

Below you can find selected references for this chapter. The full references can be found online at the following page: www.cambridge.org/Romancelinguistics

Berruto, G. (1993b). 'Varietà diamesiche, diastratiche, diafasiche'. In Sobrero, A. (ed.), *Introduzione all'italiano contemporaneo: La variazione e gli usi*. Rome: Laterza, 37–92.
Cerruti, M. Crocco, C., and Marzo, S. (eds) (2017). *Towards a New Standard. Theoretical and Empirical Studies in the Restandardization of Italian*. Boston/Berlin: Mouton de Gruyter.
Drescher, M. and Neumann-Holzschuh, I. (eds) (2010). *La Syntaxe de l'oral dans les variétés non-hexagonales du français*. Tübingen: Stauffenburg.
Ernst, G. (2019). *Textes français privés des XVIIe et XVIIIe siècles*. Berlin: de Gruyter.
Frank-Job, B. and Selig, M. (2016). 'Early evidence and sources'. In Ledgeway, A. and Maiden, M. (eds), *The Oxford Guide to the Romance Languages*. Oxford: Oxford University Press, 24–34.
Grübl, K. (2015). 'Ce que les chartes nous apprennent sur la variation et le changement linguistique au Moyen Âge: l'exemple de la déclinaison bicasuelle de l'ancien français', *Revue de linguistique romane* 79: 5–38.

Kabatek, J. (2016). 'Diglossia'. In Ledgeway, A. and Maiden, M. (eds), *The Oxford Guide to the Romance Languages*. Oxford: Oxford University Press, 624–33.

Koch, P. and Oesterreicher, W. (2007). *Lengua hablada en la Romania: español, francés, italiano*. Madrid: Gredos.

Koch, P. and Oesterreicher, W. (2012). 'Language of immediacy – language of distance: orality and literacy from the perspective of language theory and linguistic history.' In Lange, C., Weber, B., and Wolf, G. (eds), *Communicative Spaces. Variation, Contact, and Change. Papers in Honour of Ursula Schaefer*. Frankfurt: Lang, 441–71.

Linell, P. (2005). *The Written Language Bias in Linguistics. Its Nature, Origins and Transformations*. London: Routledge.

Selig, M. (2017). 'Elaboración de las lenguas medievales, procesos de techamiento y normas lingüísticas: "dialectos" focalizados y variedades de elaboración inestables'. In Yañez Rosales, R. and Schmidt-Riese, R. (eds), *Lenguas en contacto, procesos de nivelación y lugares de escritura. Variación y contextos de uso*. Guadalajara/México: Universidad de Guadalajara, 27–49.

Wright, R. (2016). 'Latin and Romance in the medieval period. A sociophilological approach'. In Ledgeway, A. and Maiden, M. (eds), *The Oxford Guide to the Romance Languages*. Oxford: Oxford University Press, 14–23.

30

Social Factors in Language Change and Variation

John Charles Smith

30.1 Introduction

Sociolinguistic variation is an intrinsic feature of language. It has doubtless existed throughout history – indeed, it has been claimed that language itself may have evolved as a means of expressing and maintaining group identity (Dunbar 1996). In addition, sociolinguistic variation is a crucial aspect of language in the contemporary world, and uniformitarianism maintains that the same factors which govern language use and language change today must equally have been at work in the past.[1]

However, work on sociolinguistic variation for any period much before the present involves a good deal of conjecture. In the worst case, our main tools are surmise and the analysis of unsystematic metalinguistic comments, although we do sometimes have better data than these (see Nevalainen and Raumolin-Brunberg 2003 for an attempt to put historical sociolinguistics on a firmer footing), and sociolinguistic studies of earlier stages of a variety of languages, including Latin and Romance, have been undertaken with a degree of success. For instance, Adams (2013) gives an

---

[1] See Ringe, Warnow, and Taylor (2002: 60f.): 'The U[niformitarian] P[rinciple] holds that we can constrain our hypotheses about the structure and history of languages of the past only by reference to what we know of contemporary language structures, linguistic behaviour and changes in progress, since the recoverable information about any language or speech community of the past is always far more limited than what we can know about languages whose native speakers we can still observe; and, further, that we can extrapolate into prehistory (and across gaps in the historical record) only on the basis of what we know from the study of contemporary languages and the actually documented past. Positing for any time in the past any structure or development inconsistent with what is known from modern work on living languages is unacceptable, and positing for prehistory any type of long-term development that we do not observe in documented history is likewise unacceptable, unless it can be demonstrated that there has been some relevant change in the conditions of language acquisition or use between the past time in question and later periods which can be observed or have been documented.' See also further discussion in Roberts (2017).

account of the sociolinguistics of Latin; Wright coins the felicitous term 'sociophilology' in connexion with his analysis of late Latin and early Romance texts;[2] Banniard (2013), in his discussion of social factors in the transition from Latin to Romance, appeals to what he terms 'retrospective sociolinguistics'; and Lodge (2004) surveys what we can reasonably infer about the sociolinguistic history of Parisian French. Other relevant work will be discussed below. However, it was not until the work of Labov in the United States, beginning in the early 1960s (Labov 1963; 1966), followed by Trudgill's work in the United Kingdom (Trudgill 1974a), that variationist sociolinguistics became systematic, with rigorous collection and analysis of data.

30.2 Variation and Change

Variation and change stand in a complex symbiotic relationship, in that each is at once the fruit and the seed of the other. Labov (2010: 369) puts it pithily: '[c]hange is linked with (and opportunistically parasitic on) variation'. The language of a speech community does not generally change in a simple 'A > B' fashion (this view of change, still implicit in many accounts, is what we might term the 'metachronic fallacy'). Instead the change involves a period of variation, in which variants 'compete', as it were – thus 'A > A/B > B' ('B' may be the result of internal change or of borrowing). It follows, of course, that the new variant may be edged out by the old one, yielding the schema 'A > A/B > A' (on this type of 'failed change', see Postma 2010). However, the variation 'A/B' may also turn out to be stable, demonstrating that the relationship between change and variation is asymmetrical; as Weinreich, Labov, and Herzog (1968: 188) point out, '[n]ot all variability and heterogeneity in language structure involves change, but all change involves variability and heterogeneity'. The variants will often correlate with sociolinguistic variables, which may in turn account for how any change progresses. Meillet (1921: 17) stressed the essentially social nature of language change, going so far as to claim that the only variable factor one could invoke in order to account for language change was social change, of which language change was simply a consequence – sometimes direct and immediate, but more often indirect and delayed. Seen in this light, sociolinguistic variation is of crucial importance in helping us to a better understanding of what Weinreich, Labov, and Herzog (1968: 102) refer to as the 'actuation problem': 'why do changes in a structural feature take place in a particular language at a given time, but

---

[2] 'Sociophilology is a word which I invented in 1996 in order to refer to an approach to the linguistic study of texts from the past which attempts to combine traditional philological analysis with the insights of modern sociolinguistics' (Wright 2002: vii).

not in other languages with the same feature, or in the same language at other times?' (for a recent discussion of the actuation problem in general, see Walkden 2017). It may be that there is no answer to this question in a scientific sense (that is, the matter is impossible to predict), as Weinreich, Labov, and Herzog (1968: 99) themselves admit – but a sufficient understanding of the sociolinguistic context may, in some cases at least, enable us to answer the question in retrospect.

It is clearly impossible in a short chapter such as this to provide anything more than a succinct survey of some major issues, exemplified from Romance. For amplification, the reader is referred to the references given in the text. A recent overview of sociolinguistics with reference to the Romance languages is Ayres-Bennett and Carruthers (2018), with detailed analysis of particular aspects provided by the other papers in the same volume. A compendium of work on Spanish is Díaz-Campos (2011). Social deixis, register, language contact, and diamesic variation, all of which have a sociolinguistic dimension, will be touched on here, but are dealt with in detail in Chapters 25, 27, 28, and 29, respectively.

30.3 Social Variables

Language may vary according to time (diachronic variation, the subject matter of historical linguistics) and place (diatopic variation, the traditional preserve of dialect geography). Time and place may not be social in themselves, but in practice they are inseparable from sociolinguistic variation. Core social variables include age (see Eckert 1997); social class (diastratic variation; see Dodsworth 2011; Ash 2013; Diemer et al. 2013); sex or (social) gender (diagenic variation; see Wodak and Benke 1997; Eckert and McConnell-Ginet 2003; Queen 2013; Meyerhoff 2017); and ethnicity (diaethnic variation; see Fought 2013). In addition, we should consider variation according to style and register (diaphasic variation; see Carruthers 2018; Zafiu 2018) and medium (diamesic variation; see Roberts and Street 1997). Although these various factors can be analysed independently of one another, they are interrelated (see especially Labov 2001: 294–322), as will become obvious in what follows.

30.3.1 Time

Some scholars have in fact proposed a sociolinguistic typology of diachrony. Dixon (1997), discussing essentially the entire timespan of human language, puts forward a 'punctuated equilibrium' model of language change, in which languages remain relatively stable in times of social stability, but change rapidly in times of social upheaval. This view has found an echo in some work on Romance, especially on periodization. For instance, Ayres-Bennett (1996: 98) notes that Middle French is typically viewed 'as an era of linguistic instability paralleling the political upheavals of the age and as a period of transition between the heyday of Old French and the stability and fixity of Modern French' and that the Middle French period is 'marked by wars, epidemics and social and political upheavals'. Similar comments are to be found in Brunot (1966: 419f.), Wartburg (1958: 119), Martin and Wilmet (1980: 7), Zink (1990: 3), and Wunderli (1982: 7f.). However, it is far from obvious that there is a straightforward correlation between social turmoil and rapid language change. To take another example from French, the period of the French Revolution was a time of great social upheaval, yet the language which emerged from it as *le français national* was essentially the same as the 'surnorme' ('supernorm') of the *ancien régime* which had preceded it. As Lodge (1993: 216) notes, '[i]t is paradoxical that since the Revolution of 1789 the French state has sought in the name of democracy and egalitarianism to impose a standard variety which had been crystallized under the *ancien régime* as a hallmark of class distinction'. Labov (2001: 262f.) discusses the 'catastrophic view' of language change, maintaining that, whilst social catastrophes may indeed have an effect on language, it is fundamentally wrong to regard them as the only or even the most significant social factor at work.

30.3.2 Place

Diatopic variation may also have a social dimension. Séguy (1971) used data from nine linguistic atlases covering Romance varieties spoken in Spain, France, Italy, and Romania to claim that a simple logarithmic relationship obtained between geographical distance and the spread of a change from its starting-point (see also Dufrénoy 1972).[3] However, a few years later, Trudgill (1974b) put forward a 'gravity model' (also known as the 'cascade model'), demonstrating that some changes are not geographically incremental, but leap from one large population-centre to another, only spreading subsequently into the intervening territory – in other words, that the mobility of linguistic features follows much the same course as the mobility of individuals and institutions (see Labov 2003). Romance provides evidence for such a pattern; for instance, Drinka (2017: 190), discussing the geographical distribution of the perfect auxiliaries HAVE and BE according to person in central Italian varieties, points out that it is entirely in keeping with the cascade or gravity model, with larger centres tending to be more innovative and smaller communities more conservative. For a recent comparison of the 'simple distance' and 'cascade' models, see Nerbonne (2010).

---

[3] ALAn, ALC, ALF, ALG, ALLy, ALMC, ALPO, AIS, ALR.

Diatopic variation within Romance has been reduced since the Middle Ages. Local speech varieties[4] have succumbed (to a greater or lesser extent, depending on the area) to national languages, although these national languages may exhibit geographical variation as a result of the ongoing influence of local speech varieties. However, there is a striking contrast between, on the one hand, Italy, where many local varieties are still spoken and there is also substantial local variation in the national language (Cerruti 2011: 19 contends that diatopic variation is still the most significant type of variation in Italian; see also Berruto 2018), and, on the other hand, France, where local speech varieties have largely disappeared and where local and regional variation in the national language has been significantly levelled in favour of a 'supralocal, reference norm' (Boughton 2013: 132). A distinct southern French regional variety still exists; whether this, too, is yielding to the supralocal norm is a matter of debate. For further discussion and references, see Armstrong and Pooley (2010: 150–204), Jones (2011), Durand, Eychenne, and Lyche (2013), Hornsby and Jones (2013), Mooney (2016a), and Detey et al. (2016). We shall return to the question of local and regional varieties below (cf. Section 30.6).

30.3.3 Age

Variation according to age presents significant issues of interpretation. Sometimes, it can indicate a change in progress – if a form, pattern, or structure is more frequent in the speech of the middle-aged than in the speech of the elderly, and more frequent in the speech of the young than in the speech of the middle-aged, then this may be a reflexion in apparent time of a real-time change in the language (Cukor-Avila and Bailey 2013). However, this type of age-related distribution may also represent age-grading, 'a generational pattern that is cyclic or repeats as a function of cultural dictates of what is appropriate to speakers of a given age' (Sankoff and Blondeau 2007: 562), in which case change in individual speakers does not represent change in the language. Yet another possibility is 'lifespan change', in which 'individual speakers change over their lifespans in the direction of a change in progress in the rest of the community' (Sankoff 2005: 1011). The position can be summarized in Table 30.1 (adapted from Sankoff and Blondeau 2007: 563).

A good example of these complexities, involving the realization of /r/ in Montreal French, is discussed by Sankoff and Blondeau (2007).[5]

---

[4] Often misleadingly referred to as 'dialects', when in fact they might normally be considered to be separate languages – see the section on *Abstand* and *Ausbau* (Section 30.11) below.

[5] They had already emerged from Cedergren's analysis of the [tʃ] to [ʃ] change in the Spanish of Panama City (Cedergren 1973, analysed with supplementary data in Labov 1994: 94–97).

Table 30.1. *The interpretation of variation according to age*

synchronic pattern	interpretation	individual	community
flat	stability	stability	stability
regular slope with age	age-grading	change	stability
regular slope with age	lifespan change	change	change
regular slope with age	generational change	stability	change
flat	communal change	change	change

The traditional realization of this phoneme in Montreal is an apical trill. However, uvular realizations of /r/ (which are characteristic of the speech of eastern Quebec and of standard European French) have been gaining ground in Montreal. Sankoff and Blondeau demonstrate that this development involves elements of generational change, age-grading, and lifespan change.

30.3.4 Class

Social class is clearly an important factor in language variation and change, but it is protean, and, whilst attempts have been made to define it in terms of 'objective' categories, such as occupation, income, wealth, or education, these are ultimately proxies, and a large measure of self-identification is also involved. In as much as the use of different 'objective' categories may yield different results, they are sometimes treated as separate variables in sociolinguistic analyses (this is particularly true of education). Despite these difficulties, it has generally been possible to relate some linguistic variables to social class, although there is typically interaction with other social variables. For instance, Díaz-Campos, Fafulas, and Gradoville (2011) examine the intersection of age and class in three variable linguistic processes in the Spanish of Caracas: deletion of syllable-final /r/; reduction of the preposition *para* 'for' to *pa*; and deletion of intervocalic /d/. They demonstrate that, whilst lower-class speakers systematically show fewer examples of the normative variants (i.e., are more likely to make the deletion or reduction) than middle- and upper-class speakers, younger lower-class speakers are more likely to use the normative variants than older speakers of the same class. They account for this difference by showing that there is a correlation between normative usage and the amount of formal education received by a speaker. Diastratic variation can also interact with diaphasic variation. We should note that diastratic variation has been levelled in French to a greater degree than in other Romance languages (Gadet 2003: 105f.; Armstrong 2013; Coveney 2013: 80) and has to a large extent been replaced by diaphasic variation. These issues are discussed in the section on style and register below.

When discussing diastratic variation, we should distinguish between change from above and below (Labov 1994: 78). The terms 'above' and 'below' refer to the linguistic system. Change from above refers principally to the fact that the change is above the level of social awareness, although such change is usually recognised 'by the fact that it involves high-prestige features, which spread downward from the social class of highest status' (Labov 2010: 185). Normally such changes can be characterized as borrowings from other speech communities. Conversely, changes from below '[a]t the outset, and through most of their development, ... are completely below the level of social awareness. It is only when the changes are nearing completion that members of the community become aware of them' (Labov 1994: 78). In principle, change from below does not have to involve low-prestige features, but in almost all cases it appears to do so.

Going beyond traditional views of social class, Bourdieu (1982; 2001) introduces the notion of the *marché linguistique* or 'linguistic marketplace', suggesting that, just as they possess financial capital, individuals also possess cultural capital, one type of which is linguistic capital. In this sense, there is an economics of linguistic exchanges. The notion of linguistic capital corresponds to the ability to speak socially acceptable and prestigious varieties, and access to this ability is related to one's position in society.

30.3.5 Gender

The most salient aspect of gender and language has long been the so-called gender paradox, whereby '[w]omen conform more closely than men to sociolinguistic norms that are overtly prescribed, but conform less than men when they are not' (Labov 2001: 293). Although it has been demonstrated that gender differences are significant in language, Eckert and McConnell-Ginet (2003) caution against overstating these differences at the expense of other types of sociolinguistic variation, in which men and women may behave in substantially the same way. Sornicola (2009) echoes this concern with regard to Italian. Discussion of (social) gender differences in French is undertaken by the papers in Armstrong, Bauvois, and Beeching (2001). Holmquist (2008) discusses the Spanish of Castañer, in west-central Puerto Rico, noting that, although 'no single or blanket statement can be made as to the role of gender', some conclusions can be drawn: there is no significant gender correlation with stable variants, women lead in the adoption of prestige forms, and men lead in change from below. The sociolinguistic correlates of gender may be intersystemic as well as intrasystemic. Gal (1978) showed that, amongst the bilingual community of the Austrian village of Oberwart, young men were more likely than young women to use Hungarian, the language of the traditional peasant community, whilst young women were more likely than young men to use German, the more prestigious language of the newly established community of factory workers. For Romance, Maurand (1981) observes a similar situation in the village communities of Ambialet and Courris, in the Tarn, in south-west France: here, men are more likely than women to use Occitan, a language 'linked with agricultural work', whilst women are more likely than men to use French, a language 'linked with public institutions, in which its usage is dominant and exclusive'. Intersystemic correlates of gender may also exist at a micro level. Barbu, Martin, and Chevrot (2014) examine the use of a Francoprovençal relic form – the preverbal neuter clitic /i/ – by children in four villages of Haute-Savoie in the French Alps, finding that 'boys, but not girls, used the regional variant significantly more frequently with their long-term native friends than with their non-native friends', in fact using the regional variant 'twice as frequently as girls' and thus appearing as 'key actors in the maintenance and the diffusion of regional cues in local social networks'.

It should be pointed out that any analysis of gender variables in language is rendered more complex by the contemporary recognition of self-identification as an element in the definition of gender, as it is in that of class.

30.3.6 Ethnicity

Variation according to ethnicity has been particularly studied in respect of the African American and Hispanic populations of the United States (and, to a lesser extent, the native American population of the same country). Possible analogues in Romance-speaking countries are the Maghrebin and sub-Saharan African communities in France and the native populations of Latin America. Recent work showing that the speech of young urban French-speakers of immigrant descent may have significant distinguishing characteristics includes Gasquet-Cyrus (2013) for Marseille, Marchessou (2018) for Strasbourg, and Cychosz (2018) for Paris. Sometimes, the variety in question, or elements of it, may spread outside the ethnic group and be adopted by the young lower-class population as a whole. If the distinguishing features of the speech variety can be derived from a language spoken in the immigrant community, then we are essentially dealing with a contact phenomenon; but, in many cases, the 'ethnolect' is a complex mixture of elements, many of which cannot be ascribed straightforwardly to language contact.

30.3.7 Style and Register

Labov (2006: 58–86) discusses various 'contextual styles' which may be a locus of sociolinguistic variation – these are (from most casual to most formal): casual speech, interview, reading a passage, pronunciation of words in word lists, pronunciation of minimal pairs. Variation between these different styles is known as 'style-shifting'. In this connexion, we can distinguish three degrees of linguistic variable: indicators, markers, and stereotypes (Labov 1972). An indicator is a linguistic variable which is socially significant, but which does not vary in style-shifting, meaning that speakers are not generally aware of it. A marker is a linguistic variable which is socially significant, and which does vary in style-shifting (with a correlation between the distribution of the variants and the formality of the style), meaning that speakers are subconsciously aware of it. A stereotype is a linguistic variable which, like a marker, is socially significant and varies in style-shifting; but, in addition, speakers (and hearers) are highly aware of it – as a result, stereotypes are often commented on and 'corrected'. Depending on sociolinguistic circumstances, indicators may become markers, and markers may turn into stereotypes. Exemplification and discussion of these issues with regard to Romance can be found in Lefebvre's study of the French of Lille (Lefebvre 1988) and Parodi and Guerrero's discussion of Los Angeles vernacular Spanish (Parodi and Guerrero 2016). Hornsby (2009: 173) observes that, despite the levelling of regional differences in French, some 'supralocal' features may have a different status in different areas: thus, the palatalized or affricated realization of dental plosives appears to be an indicator in the Parisian *banlieue*, a marker in Grenoble, and a stereotype in Marseille.

The impact of style and register on language variation is significant in Romance generally, but especially in French. Gadet (2003: 105f.) claims that first diatopic and then diastratic distinctions have largely been levelled in French, and that diaphasic distinctions now constitute the major locus of variation in this language. Likewise, Coveney (2013: 80) claims that a large number of grammatical variables in French are 'hyperstyle variables, which – exceptionally, for sociolinguistic variables – show a greater degree of style-shift than of social stratification'. See also Armstrong (2013). Hornsby and Jones (2013: 107) attribute the major dialect levelling in France to a social structure which inhibits change from below.

Much research in the variationist paradigm has shown that there tends to be more convergence between speakers the higher the register – a logical consequence of markers being less frequent in more formal speech. However, Berruto (2012: 43) notes that, in Italy, this position is often reversed, and that there tends to be divergence between speakers in higher registers, because lower-class speakers do not have command of standard variants. This is arguably the result of a pronounced diaglossic linguistic repertoire, an issue which we discuss below (cf. Section 30.6).

For further discussion of style and register, see Chapter 27.

30.3.8 Medium

Variation according to medium generally refers to the distinction between written and spoken language, although in practice, this is often a diaphasic distinction. When, say, a formal speech is read out, we are dealing with spoken language in name only – the language is actually written. Conversely, literary works may represent, to a greater or lesser degree, the language of colloquial speech – compare Queneau's *Zazie dans le métro* ('Zazie in the Metro') of 1959, parts of which are written in what the author characterized as 'le français oral' ('oral French'). More recently, with the advent of the Internet, email, and social media, it has been argued that the 'written/spoken' dichotomy is now too simple a description of variation according to medium (see, for instance, the papers in Danet and Herring 2007, and Crystal 2006: 51, who notes that the language of the Internet 'is identical to neither speech nor writing, but selectively and adaptively displays properties of both', although 'it does things that neither of these other mediums do, and must accordingly be seen as a new species of communication'). Arguably as a result of upper character-limits for tweets and early types of text-messaging, a number of space-saving mechanisms have developed, including abbreviations for frequently used phrases (e.g., Fr. *MDR* for *mort de rire* lit. 'dead from laughing'; compare Eng. *LOL*), and the logographic use of numerals (e.g., '2' (pronounced [dø]) for Fr. *de* (pronounced [də] or [dø]); compare '4' for Eng. *for*). However, these devices are rarely used outside electronic communication. On the subject of these 'neographies' as evidence for an emerging new written register in many Romance varieties, see Kallweit (2018). There is also evidence that the rules governing social deixis (see Chapter 25, this volume) on social media are not those which apply elsewhere in either the written or the spoken language – see Williams and van Compernolle (2009) and, for a brief (journalistic) summary dealing with French, Spanish, and Italian, Lawn (2012). Jones, Parry, and Williams (2016: 618), quoting several sources, note that, in Italian, '[l]anguage use in electronic forms of communication ... shows an unexpected use of dialect by youngsters who often lack native competence, but who use dialect for expressive, non-conformist, or localizing purposes'.

Diamesic variation in Romance is discussed in more detail in Chapter 29, this volume.

30.3.9 Attitude and Lifestyle

Language variation may also correlate with social attitudes and lifestyle. For instance, Aldi (2017) finds that, in Parisian French, the distribution of some syntactic variants correlates with 'orthodox' vs 'heterodox' lifestyle. Holmquist (1985) demonstrates a correlation in the Spanish of the

Cantabrian village of Ucieda between the likelihood that a speaker will have word-final /u/ (a local variant corresponding to Castilian /o/) and the likelihood that he or she will own mountain animals, a feature of a traditional local lifestyle. The notions of social attitude and lifestyle become especially important in considering the effect of speakers' positive or negative attitudes towards their own and other communities. Labov (1963) had already demonstrated a correlation between positive attitudes to one's own community and use of local variants. These matters will be examined further in the discussion of endocentricity and exocentricity, below (cf. Section 30.9).

30.3.10 Concluding Remarks

Several times in this section we have observed that many social variables may be defined by both 'objective' quantifiable criteria and 'subjective' qualitative criteria. Although it is impossible to go into detail here, traditional variationist approaches to language have been criticized for concentrating on the quantifiable (Coupland 2007: 93f., for instance, observes that 'quantitative methods give a very indirect account of linguistic practice – an account that does not match social actors' own perceptions of meaningful speech differences') and for taking insufficient account of the fact that competing norms may exist within a single community, that identity is not monolithic, and that language may serve to create social identity as well as reflect it. For recent surveys, see Eckert (2012), Kiesler (2013), and Drummond and Schleef (2016). A survey of work on sociolinguistic variation as a creator of identity in France can be found in Jones, Parry, and Williams (2016: 615).

30.4 Transmission and Diffusion

The traditional view of language change is embodied in the metaphor of the 'family tree' (the *Stammbaumtheorie* of Schleicher 1853; 1863; 1865), which is probably still the dominant view – at least amongst non-linguists – of the historical relationships between languages (see Figure 30.1). In this model, Portuguese, Spanish, French, Italian, Romanian, and the other Romance languages are all 'related to' one another (as 'sisters' or 'cousins'), and all of them are 'descended' from Latin (note the extensions of the 'family' metaphor).

However, an arguably more accurate 'family tree' (see Figure 30.2) would represent the fact that Latin fragmented into many different dialects, essentially a continuum, and that subsequently a handful of these dialects were 'selected' to become 'standard' languages (see Section 30.10).

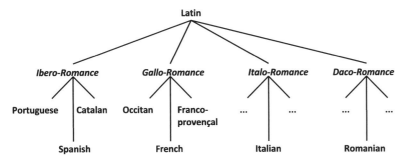

Figure 30.1 The family tree model of Romance (Version 1)

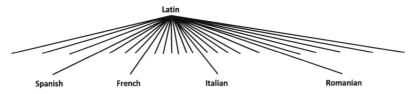

Figure 30.2 The family tree model of Romance (Version 2)

(In fact, even this representation is not strictly accurate, because the 'standard' language is often based on a dialect which has been koinéized – again, see below, Sections 30.5, 30.10.)

It is obvious that the family tree model has difficulty accounting for change due to contact. We may contrast the *Wellentheorie* ('wave theory'), put forward by Schmidt (1872) and Schuchardt (1900). In this view, changes are 'waves' or 'ripples', which propagate through a language from different points, at different rates, and to different extents, yielding a highly differentiated pattern over time.[6] By extension, a given language can be seen, at least in part, as the intersection of different influences, or successive 'waves' of contact.

Labov (2007; 2010: 305–66) seeks to reconcile these two approaches to change in an interesting way, by claiming that the 'family tree' model accounts for linguistic changes which are the result of child language acquisition, whilst the 'wave' model must be invoked to explain change resulting from imperfect learning by adults. The L1/L2 distinction turns out to be crucial. He couches the distinction in terms of 'transmission' vs 'diffusion'.

Transmission, involving first-language (L1) learners (by definition, children), is monotonic – i.e., by and large, the language continues to move in

---

[6] Bartoli (1925; 1929; 1933; 1945) suggested that, as a result of this process, 'central' areas tended to innovate more, whilst 'peripheral' areas tended to be more conservative. This is not always the case; for a rejoinder to Bartoli, see Hall (1946).

the same direction with each successive generation. The 'ratchet principle' of Lieberson (2000), regarding monotonicity in fashion, is relevant here. Through transmission, speakers acquire both structures and systems, even though there may be change from one generation to the next. That change proceeds in a particular direction is largely the result of social cohesion. Groups that are socially separated (characteristically through distance) will tend to develop differently, and their speech will grow apart – hence the splits typical of the 'family tree'. This view of the differentiation of speech varieties through the separation of communities had already been articulated by Paul (1880). It bears obvious resemblances to the arguments for speciation through separation (allopatric speciation) put forward by evolutionary biologists (see Ridley 2003). Transmission represents continuity in change.

Diffusion, involving second-language (L2) learners (who may be adults or children beyond the 'critical period' for L1 acquisition), is not necessarily monotonic. Through diffusion, speakers acquire structures, but, crucially, fail to acquire the systems which go with them and determine their distribution. The result is the piecemeal influence of one language or dialect on another – hence the rather random intersections which characterize the 'wave model'. Diffusion represents discontinuity in change. An extreme example of this discontinuity can be found in creole languages, which, in one sense, have no transmission element. Creoles, viewed as nativized pidgins, are languages which, in the words of Muysken and Smith (1995), have 'come into existence at a point in time that can be established fairly precisely'; they arise when a generation exposed to a pidgin (nobody's native language, and arguably not a language at all, but a 'minimal communication system negotiated into existence by adults who have no shared language but who need to communicate for a particular, limited purpose' – Green 1988: 420f.) acquires it as a native language, and, in so doing, vastly expands it, possibly through the 'bioprogram' (Bickerton 1981; 1984; 1988). Creoles, in this sense, are pure contact languages, representing absolute diffusion and total discontinuity. Of course, once they exist as native languages, they undergo transmission, just like all other languages.

However, creoles are an extreme example. Most examples of diffusion do not involve anything as radical as creolization. For instance, Esher (2012: 217f.; 2015) discusses the future and conditional forms of Occitan, noting that the two forms commonly share a stem and that, where they do not, the reason is usually to be found in regular sound change (although the distinction may subsequently have become morphologized). However, some varieties have adopted a new stem under the influence of French. Sometimes, this has formed the basis for a new future and a new conditional, but in the Vivaro-Alpin Occitan variety of Barcelonnette (Arnaud and Morin 1920: 312), the French stem *devr-* 'must-' has been adopted by the conditional but not by the future. This seems to be an example of diffusion – the structure has been acquired, but not the system of which it is part.

30.5 Simplification and Complexification

An abiding debate in the history of linguistics has centred round the question: Do languages grow more simple or more complex? The debate on simplification vs complexification has often been anecdotal, but it has recently been placed on a firmer footing by Trudgill (2010; 2011a; 2011b),[7] who begins by pointing out a paradox. Sociolinguists claim that language contact leads to simplification (often through the process known as koinéization or dialect levelling – see, for instance, Siegel 1985; Kerswill 2013a), whereas linguistic typologists see contact as a cause of complexification. Who is right?

Trudgill suggests that an answer to this question will vary according to sociolinguistic circumstances, and proposes the following typology:

(i) Languages exhibiting isolation (little or no contact): these languages tend to retain existing complexity and may become more complex through endogenous complexification. Icelandic is a good example, having retained its nominal case system, 'quirky' subject constructions, and various other complexities. The mainland Scandinavian languages (Danish, Norwegian, Swedish), which derive from the same ancestor, but which have had much greater contact with other languages (especially Low German during the Hanseatic period), have lost nominal case and quirky subjects; in addition, many (but not all) of their dialects have reduced the number of genders from three to two.

(ii) Languages exhibiting short-term contact involving L2 learning by adults: these languages will exhibit simplification, often drastic. Extreme examples are pidgins and creoles. Non-creole examples include mainland Scandinavian, mentioned above, and high-contact varieties of English (see especially Kortmann and Szmrecsanyi 2009).

(iii) Languages exhibiting long-term contact where territory is shared, and involving child bilingualism: these languages will exhibit complexification, mainly through additive borrowing (exogenous complexification). The extreme example is the *Sprachbund* or 'linguistic area', such as the Balkan *Sprachbund* (see Sandfeld 1930), where a variety of languages which are only very distantly related – Romanian, Greek, Albanian, Bulgarian – share a number of characteristic features which are not found in much more closely related languages (for discussion, see Joseph 2010).

---

[7] See also the papers in Sampson, Gil, and Trudgill (2009).

How does this typology fare when applied to Romance? As far as the first category (isolation leading to retention of complexity and/or endogenous complexification) is concerned, the point raised by Trudgill (2011b: 238) in his discussion of Germanic languages applies equally well:

> [a]ll the major standard language varieties in Europe today are relatively high-contact koinés and creoloids which are the result in part of simplification resulting from dialect contact. ... [C]ases of spontaneous, non-additive complexification should be looked for in relatively isolated non-standardized low-contact varieties of modern European languages in comparison with their local standards. We can also look at those languages which are spoken by small groups of speakers in tightly-knit communities and compare them to related languages.

Trudgill goes on to present instances of endogenous complexification in Germanic; the following are some plausible examples of similar phenomena in Romance:

- Cardinal numerals above 'one' (*un* (M), *une* (F)) do not vary for gender in French; exceptionally, we find separate gender forms for 'two' and 'three' (M [dø], [trwa]; F [døs], [trwas], respectively) in the Tracadie dialect of Acadian French (Cichocki 2012: 227).[8]
- In French, the second person 'plural' form of the verb exhibits a single inflexion *-ez* (/e/), regardless of whether it is functioning as a true plural or as a 'polite' singular; in central Lorraine, it has two separate inflexions, one (generally /o(w)/) indicating plurality, the other (generally /e(j)/) indicating 'politeness' (*ALLR* 1054).
- Most Romance languages have a single imperfect form of the verb. However, southern Lorraine varieties have innovated a so-called 'second' imperfect (cf. *té chantéïe* pan-Romance imperfect (< Lat. CANTABAS) vs *té chantézor* 'second' imperfect, both glossed as 'you were singing'). It has been argued that this 'second' imperfect results from the incorporation into the verb of a following adverb HORA (Latin) or *ores* (Lorrain) 'now'. Adam (1881) analyses this form as a proximate or hodiernal imperfect; Russo (2017) suggests that the contrast between the pan-Romance imperfect and this 'second' imperfect corresponds to a distinction between 'larger conceptual distance' and 'smaller conceptual distance', although this basic contrast is interpreted in a variety of ways, according to area, corresponding to more remote past vs more recent past, evidentiality vs direct perception, or irrealis/non-factive vs realis/factive.
- In the dialect of Ripatransone in the Italian Marche, most finite verbs agree with their subject in gender as well as number, though not

---

[8] It should be stressed that, although distinct gender forms for 'two' exist in some other Romance languages, such as Portuguese and Romanian, they are inherited from Latin. The Acadian forms represent a complete innovation, and cannot be traced back to Latin.

necessarily in person (see Parrino 1967; Loporcaro 2018: 309f.; and also the discussion and exemplification in Section 1.2.2.3). Loporcaro describes this agreement pattern as 'spectacular'.
- Exceptionally for Romance, the Lombard variety spoken in Monno, in the far north of the Italian province of Brescia, exhibits a type of '*do*-support', similar, but not identical, to the use of *do* as an auxiliary verb in English (cf. also discussion in Section 4.3.5). See the study by Benincà and Poletto (2004), who note (p. 56 n. 5) as a possible explanation for the existence of this phenomenon that '[u]ntil 1963 the village was reachable only by a footpath; contacts with people speaking other varieties were rare'.

As for the second category (short-term contact involving L2 learning, leading to simplification), the extreme example of creoles has already been mentioned. Other Romance examples include Angolan Vernacular Portuguese and Brazilian Vernacular Portuguese, both of which have undergone changes that 'can be characterized as structural reduction: reduced morphological marking for person or tense on verbs, for number on nouns and other elements in the NP, or for case on personal pronouns' (Holm 2009: 119). Similar developments can be found in the French spoken in many African countries (Daff 2001; Ploog 2002; 2006; Ngamountsika 2007; Loussakoumounou 2009). In koinéization (Siegel 1985; Kerswill 2013a), the contact is between varieties of the same language rather than between different languages, although the outcome is the same – simplification and/or loss of marked variants. Probably the most celebrated example from Romance comes from Spanish – Tuten (2003) points to massive simplifications of the Castilian morphological system as a result of three broad phases of dialect contact, as a result of which, for instance, its verbal morphology is considerably simpler than that of other Ibero-Romance languages. But, as pointed out by Trudgill (2011b: 238 – see above), virtually all standard languages are to some extent the result of koinéization.

Finally, there is long-term contact involving child bilingualism on shared territory, leading to complexification through additive borrowing. Romanian membership of the Balkan *Sprachbund* has already been mentioned. We should also consider the case of Istro-Romanian, spoken by a community now numbering no more than 200 on the Istrian peninsula and which has long been bilingual in Croatian. Maiden (2006), drawing on work by Kovačec (1963; 1966; 1968), notes, 'it is likely that there has been a stable coexistence of the two languages over several centuries, with Istro-Romanian limited to village and family life, and Croatian being employed in wider public spheres'. In his discussion, he focuses on

> what one might term 'structured accommodation', whereby the penetration into Istro-Romanian of a Croatian word or grammatical phenomenon is systematically attached to a particular semantic or structural context,

giving rise to distributional patterns which are native neither to Istro-Romanian nor to Croatian, but a product of the encroachment of the latter.

He gives three examples.

- For numerals between 'five' and 'eight', Istro-Romanian uses both the 'indigenous' Romance items and items borrowed from Croatian, but they are not interchangeable: the Croatian numerals appear in all and only 'lexical measure phrases' (i.e., with nouns indicating time, weight, distance, etc.); Romance numerals appear in all and only other contexts. Thus (to quote one of Maiden's examples) /ˈʃapte ˈkase/ ~ **/ˈsedəm ˈkase/ 'seven houses' vs /ˈsedəm let/ ~ **/ʃapte let/ 'seven years' (ˈʃapte < Lat. SEPTEM, ˈsedəm < Croatian *sedam*).
- Istro-Romanian has developed the systematic aspect-marking which is typical of Slavonic languages (and not usual in Romance), whereby each verb has both perfective and imperfective aspect forms. Sometimes, both forms are borrowed from Croatian; in other instances, a Romance root is common to both forms, but the perfective is formed by adding a Croatian prefix. However, in many cases, the Romance root provides the imperfective aspect form and the Croatian root the perfective: examples are 'to sleep' (imperfective /durˈmi/, perfective /zasˈpi/) and to drink (imperfective /bɛ/, perfective /poˈpi/).
- Finally, Istro-Romanian, alone amongst Daco-Romance varieties, has acquired a systematic morphological distinction between adjectives and adverbs. In both Romanian and Croatian, adverbs are normally identical to some form of the adjective (the masculine singular in Romanian, the nominative/accusative of the neuter singular in Croatian). In addition to borrowing some Croatian neuter singular adjectival forms as adverbs corresponding to etymologically Romance adjectives (e.g., /ˈteʃko/, 'heavily', alongside /ɣrev/ 'heavy'), Istro-Romanian has also taken the final -o which is characteristic of Croatian neuter singulars and added it to native Romance adjective stems to form an adverb (e.g., /plin/ 'full', /ˈplino/ 'fully').

Complex sociolinguistic circumstances may sometimes exist in which both types of contact effect seem to apply. For instance, Bolivian Spanish, almost certainly under the influence of Aymara and/or Quechua, has innovated an evidential form of the verb, which is absent from other varieties of Spanish (Laprade 1981: 222–25; Lipski 2014: 51f.). This represents complexification through additive borrowing, and tallies with the fact that there has been a long period during which substantial numbers of speakers have been bilingual in Aymara or Quechua and Spanish. However, this evidential is expressed not with a new form, but by the form which in other varieties of Spanish is the exponent of the pluperfect indicative (e.g., *habían hecho* lit. 'they had done'). In some varieties of Bolivian Spanish, this form has lost its original function and can now only convey evidentiality – there is no pluperfect indicative tense. This represents simplification, at least of the tense system, and is consistent with the fact that, in addition to bilinguals, there have long been (and still are) many Bolivians who learn Spanish as a second language. So the system of moods is complexified, whilst the system of tenses is simplified, and the overall number of forms remains the same. It appears that both types of change (additive borrowing and simplification) are at work here simultaneously, arguably because we find both types of relationship between the languages (bilingualism and adult learning of Spanish) in the speech community. It is plausible (although speculative) to suggest that these developments were in fact sequential, as follows. Spanish was originally acquired as an L2 by adult speakers of Aymara or Quechua. As there is no pluperfect in these languages, these learners simplified the Spanish tense system correspondingly. However, an awareness of the form persisted, and, when long-term bilingualism developed in at least part of the speech community, it was co-opted in a new function (which already existed in Aymara and Quechua), according to the general principles of refunctionalization discussed by Smith (2011).

30.6 Diglossia and Linguistic Repertoire

The concept of diglossia was originally introduced by Ferguson (1959), who looked at societies where two variant forms of the same language were used with different functions:[9] thus, one variety would be used for 'H' (high) functions (generally speaking, in formal contexts), whilst another would be used in 'L' (low) contexts (including colloquial speech). Diglossia is a useful notion, but Ferguson (1959: 340) himself appealed for 'further study of this phenomenon and related ones' which might 'drastically modify' his 'impressionistic remarks', and the concept has been criticized and modified in various ways (for a summary, see Kabatek 2016: 624–26), although the basic insight is largely maintained. Perhaps the most significant modification was Fishman's extension of the term 'diglossia' to situations in which the two functions were fulfilled by different languages ('exoglossic

---

[9] Some of Ferguson's examples founder on the notion of 'the same language': his four case studies involve modern standard Arabic and colloquial Arabic, the καθαρεύουσα ('katharevousa') and δημοτική ('demotic') varieties of modern Greek (the former was officially abolished in 1976), High German and Swiss German (see the section on *Ausbau* and *Abstand* below), and French and Haitian Creole (which would not normally be regarded nowadays as varieties of the same language).

diglossia'), rather than by different 'variants' of the 'same' language ('endoglossic diglossia') (Fishman 1967).

In the history of Romance, diglossia is particularly relevant to medieval western Europe, where Latin tended to fulfil 'H' functions and vernacular languages 'L' functions. However, work since Ferguson's original paper has shown that 'linguistic repertoire' is often a more complex matter than the relationship between two varieties. For instance, Pellegrini (1960) suggested that Italian-speakers in fact had access to four different linguistic codes, rather than the two codes of diglossia – moving from local to standard, these were: local dialect, regional dialectal koiné, regional Italian, and standard Italian. In similar vein, Carton (1981), discussing the Picard-speaking area of northern France, distinguished between four levels of speech: local patois, local or dialectal French, regional French, and general French (although it is doubtful whether this four-way distinction has survived into the twenty-first century – see Hornsby 2006). More recently, Hernández-Campoy and Villena-Ponsoda (2009: 192–94) have claimed that a similar situation exists in western Andalusia, involving local vernacular, Seville regional standard, common Spanish (a generalized form of Spanish which has absorbed some southern features), and standard (Castilian) Spanish. Auer (2005: 22), following Bellmann (1997), uses the term 'diaglossia' to refer to a situation in which intermediate varieties intervene between the standard language and local speech, noting that these

> intermediate forms often fulfil a sociolinguistic function by enabling their users to act out, in the appropriate contexts, an identity which could not be symbolised through the base dialects (which may have rural, backwardish or non-educated connotations) nor through the national standard (which may smack of formality and unnaturalness and/or be unable to express regional affiliation).

Historically, the development of diaglossia is characteristic of the late nineteenth or early twentieth century. Auer charts its rise and fall, from exoglossic diglossia ('Type Zero'), through a stage of endoglossic diglossia where the 'H' language is largely confined to writing ('Type A'), to spoken endoglossic diglossia ('Type B'), diaglossia ('Type C'), and post-diaglossia ('Type D'), in which there is little or no variation between local, regional, and national varieties. Post-diaglossia tends to arise through the process of unidirectional convergence, or 'advergence' ('Advergenz': see Mattheier 1996: 34) of the local and regional varieties with the national language. As noted above, it has been argued that contemporary France is a largely post-diaglossic speech community. On the other hand, diaglossia continues to be prevalent in many parts of Italy. A detailed study of diglossia and related issues with reference to Romance is Kabatek (2016).

30.7 Code-Switching and Contact Vernaculars

A phenomenon related to language contact is code-switching, in which bilingual speakers change language within and/or between sentences in the same discourse. Code-switching is a complex subject, and once again, it is not the purpose of this chapter to provide a detailed synopsis: for surveys, see Myers-Scotton (1997) and Gardner-Chloros (2009).

Myers-Scotton proposes the Matrix Language Frame model, in which one of the two languages is the 'matrix language', which sets the 'frame' (morpheme order, inflexion, and function words) and the other is the 'embedded language'. A central claim of this model 'is that although both languages are "on" during C[ode-]S[witching] production, they do not participate equally' (Myers-Scotton 1997: 221). Code-switching can have various pragmatic functions; of particular relevance to sociolinguistics is its use 'to add a dimension to the socio-pragmatic force of one's "discourse persona"' (Myers-Scotton 1997: 225). It is therefore not surprising that code-switching (and its absence) have been linked to social identity. The presence of code-switching correlates with positive attitudes to both languages; its absence to a desire to stress separateness from the 'other' community (Myers-Scotton 1997: 232f.). Jones (2005: 16) points out that, whilst code-switching is found between Jèrriais and English on the Channel Island of Jersey, speakers of Jèrriais with a positive attitude to the future of the language are less likely to code-switch away from it. Fought (2013: 393) notes that code-switching can not only serve to mark 'the complexities of minority ethnic identity' (identifying with both languages) but may also encode 'a third set of values', especially a generational difference (identifying wholly with neither language). For some relevant findings with respect to Spanish-English code-switching in southern California, see Toribio (2002).

Code-switching may become institutionalized, yielding a contact vernacular, a stable speech variety in which elements of two languages coexist in broadly equal measure (for discussion, see Matras 2000). Striking examples of contact vernaculars involving Romance are the group of Ecuadorian varieties known as Media Lengua, which derive most of their lexicon from Spanish and most of their morphology and syntax from Quechua (Muysken 1997), and Michif, spoken mainly on the Canadian prairie, where the structure of the noun phrase follows French and the structure of the verb-phrase Cree (Bakker 1997; Bakker and Papen 1997). Where contact vernaculars become of particular interest to Romance linguistics is where both languages involved are Romance. For instance, a Spanish-Portuguese contact variety known as *fronterizo* or *fronteiriço* is spoken in northern Uruguay, near the border with Brazil. Penny (2000: 164–66) notes the following characteristics of this variety: a transitional vocalic system, shading from a Spanish-like system in the south to a Portuguese-like system in the north; a transitional sibilant system, with the same characteristics; the use of Portuguese definite articles with Spanish nouns (e.g., *todo o día* 'all **the** day'; cf. Sp. *el día* 'the day'), or, occasionally the reverse; the use of *tú* as the informal second person singular pronoun (in contrast to the informal third person pronoun *você* used in most Brazilian Portuguese varieties); generalization of the third person singular inflexion of the verb to other persons; plural marking on the first element of the noun phrase only, with the other elements unmarked; mixed Spanish and Portuguese lexicon. (See also Hensey 1993.) And, in the early twentieth century, the massive migration of Italian-speakers to Buenos Aires (where in parts of the city they represented 50 per cent of the population) and Montevideo led to the emergence of a Spanish-Italian contact vernacular known as *cocoliche*. Some of the most salient characteristics of this variety, discussed by Meo Zilio (1955a; 1955b; 1955c; 1956; 1958; 1959; 1960; 1970; 1993) are: mixed Italian and Spanish phonetics and phonology; Italian noun lexemes with Spanish gender (feminine *la latte* 'the milk'; contrast masculine It. *il latte*, feminine Sp. *la leche*); Italian noun lexemes with Spanish plural in *-s*; earlier or non-standard Italian forms reintroduced under the influence of Spanish (*alcun amico* 'some friend', contrast It. *qualche amico*, Sp. *algún amigo*); simplification of the Italian system of articles; calquing of Spanish word order, Spanish use of prepositions, Spanish use of articles, Spanish use of verb forms, and Spanish derivational suffixes, using Italian forms; replacement of Italian lexemes by cognates of Spanish lexemes (*passeri* lit. 'sparrows' for 'birds', contrast It. *uccelli*, Sp. *pájaros*; *largo* lit. 'wide' for 'long'; contrast It. *lungo*, Sp. *largo*).

30.8 Language Death

'Language death' (Dorian 1981; Wolfram 2002) is the situation in which one of the languages of a bilingual community becomes so prevalent that the other language suffers from 'attrition' and then disappears. This process commonly involves simplification, often extreme – particularly the loss of morphological distinctions – as a significant proportion of the speech community become 'semi-speakers' of the language. A good example is the French variety of Old Mines, Missouri, in the United States, where we find loss of gender distinction in many adjectives, reduction of case and gender distinctions in pronouns, and loss of person and number inflection from the verb (Thogmartin 1979; Valdman 2007). However, in many 'dying' languages, complexity remains, and variation also survives, although it is no longer correlated with social categories in the normal way. King (1989: 148), in her study of language attrition in Newfoundland French, notes that 'linguistic variation in Newfoundland French, though strongly correlated with age, does not carry the weight of social meaning which variation carries in healthy speech communities', and Mougeon and Beniak (1989: 309) reach a similar conclusion in their discussion of 'language contraction' in the French of Welland, Ontario.

A noteworthy example of 'language death' in Romance is Dalmatian, which became extinct following the death of the presumed last speaker in 1898 (Maiden 2020). Maiden (2004) discusses one of the features of 'attrition' in this language – the neutralization of the distinction between the imperfect and present indicative forms of the verb. It would be possible to see this merely as a simplification; but Maiden demonstrates that it is also a morphomic change – a development which reinforces the distribution of an autonomous morphological pattern. As such, it corresponds to many developments found in other Romance languages and should be analysed as 'not abandoning complex asymmetries between form and meaning, but … making complexity itself more systematically predictable' (Maiden 2004: 107). This constitutes further demonstration that complexity can remain in a dying language – although, given that most of our information about Dalmatian derives from the last native speaker, we have no data concerning linguistic variation in this language and its social correlates (or lack of them).

30.9 Societal Typology and Language Change

It is clear that language change is not independent of the type of society in which the language is spoken.

Milroy (1987) investigated the role of social networks in language variation and change, studying a number of communities in Belfast, the capital of Northern Ireland. Speakers will characteristically be linked to (i.e., have interchanges with), for instance: (i) members of their family; (ii) their friends; (iii) their neighbours, and (iv) their workmates. Two key concepts in this regard are density and multiplexity. A network is said to be relatively dense if a large number of individuals to whom the speaker is linked are also linked to each other. A link is said to be multiplex if a speaker is linked to another individual in more than one capacity (for instance, of those listed above). The denser and more multiplex an individual's relationships, the higher their network strength score. The broad finding from Milroy's work is that the greater an individual's social network strength score, the more likely that person is to exhibit local (i.e., non-standard) variants. This has the important consequence that the role of variables such as social class, gender/sex, etc. in language variation and change may be, to an extent, epiphenomenal, or at least indirect, with any correlation mediated through network strength score. For an up-to-date discussion, see Milroy and Llamas (2013).

Following Andersen (1988: 71f.), and building on the work of Milroy and others, Røyneland (2004) and Kerswill (2018) distinguish two typological parameters of societal variation: a sociocommunicational or demographic parameter (open vs closed) and an attitudinal or ideological parameter (endocentric vs exocentric). Closed societies are essentially societies in which the majority of the population have high network strength scores (*à la* Milroy). Open societies are essentially societies in which the majority of the population have low network strength scores (*à la* Milroy). Endocentric societies set great store by solidarity within the community and are suspicious of or hostile to outside influence. Exocentric societies accept or even welcome outside influence and regard solidarity within the community as secondary. This yields a four-way typology, as follows.

Closed endocentric societies. Characteristically, these are isolated rural communities. A good example is the Protestant enclave in the *arrondissement* of Yssingeaux, in Haute-Loire (central France), studied by Nauton (1952) and Félice (1976), where the transitional Occitan–Francoprovençal speech has many aspects of phonology and morphology which distinguish it from the varieties spoken in neighbouring Catholic communities (for instance, retention of final plosives, maintenance of the diphthong /au/ in unstressed syllables; first person singular preterite inflexion in /-ɛjt/). Closedness and endocentricity here are driven by religious difference, geographical isolation, self-sufficiency, and endogamy. However, some metropolitan inner cities now exhibit the characteristics of closed endocentric societies. Inner London, where a strong sense of community holds amongst people of many different ethnic and geographical origins has led to a high degree of linguistic contact within the community and the emergence of 'new London English' or 'multicultural London English' (see Cheshire et al. 2011; Kerswill 2013b). Strikingly, it is not obvious that a similar development is taking place in Paris – Britain (2018: 294) notes: '[w]hile it is evident that at least for some linguistic features a multiethnolect has emerged in London, this is much harder to discern for Paris.' Lipski (2014: 44) implies that the increasing endocentricity of Spanish American cities (linked to an increase in population) is a factor in the emergence of distinct Latin American varieties of Spanish:

> A comparison of the time line ... of changes in Spain and Latin America with the demographic patterns of Spanish American urban zones – ports and capital cities – reveals that once cities reached a critical mass of several tens of thousands (which usually occurred during the late eighteenth or

early nineteenth century), these speech communities effectively resisted full incorporation of language changes that occurred in Spain and arrived with new settlers.

Open endocentric societies. These are typically urban centres with both a strong sense of community and strong external contacts. They tend to be sources of innovation, from which new forms diffuse outwards; they are 'optimal senders' of language change. Cities such as London and Paris have played, and to some extent continue to play, this role, which may also be played by large urban centres at a regional level, such as Seville with respect to western Andalusia (Hernández-Campoy and Villena-Ponsoda 2009: 186).

Closed exocentric societies. These are low-contact communities which none the less have a positive orientation to outside norms. Because of this orientation, they are receptive to change, but, in Kerswill's phrase (Kerswill 2018), this is essentially 'change driven by ideology, not change driven by contact'.

Open exocentric societies. These are typically very small communities, which are being subsumed into another community's identity. They are therefore likely to be transitional and unstable. These are often rural communities (compare Marshall 2004 on the village of Huntly in Aberdeenshire in Scotland), but may also be mobile suburban areas (such as outer-city Belfast). They are 'optimal receivers' of language change.

The typology sketched above is an attractive one, but we must be aware that notions such as 'open/closed' and 'exocentric/endocentric' are scalar. Societies can change from one type to another, and, of course, they do not necessarily do so abruptly. In his study of the Picard variety of Avion, a (former) mining community in the Pas-de-Calais *département* of northern France, Hornsby (2006: 128f.) notes that the mining community was characterized by high network strength scores and defines it as 'inward-looking' and having 'very narrow horizons'. For him, the closed and endocentric nature of the community explains why, exceptionally, it retained a distinctive urban dialect well into the late twentieth century – although there was in-migration, '[o]nce arrived in Avion, miners and their families formed ... communities of an exceptionally close-knit and inward-looking kind' (Hornsby 2006: 121). It is clear that Avion is now both less closed and less endocentric than it was; in particular, 'younger speakers have adopted new features by accommodating to other people who are perceived to be "modern" or socially attractive for other reasons' – these may be either outsiders or members of the speech community who have spent some time away and returned. This fact reinforces a conclusion that emerges from the recent studies cited above – namely, that endocentricity and exocentricity (i.e., attitudes) appear to be more significant determinants of language than closed vs open networks.

We noted above that Labov's work on Martha's Vineyard (Labov 1963) had already demonstrated a correlation between positive attitudes to one's own community and use of local variants. A comparable finding is made by Ferguson (2007: 299), who notes the spread of the lower-class realization of /r/ as a retroflex in Venetian at a time when Italian was making inroads into Venice, and suggests that '[i]ts salience as identity and loyalty marker in the face of outsider pressure has led to its increasing adoption by younger Venetian speakers'. Hernández-Campoy and Villena-Ponsoda (2009) paint a complex picture of language change in the Spanish city of Murcia, where many local features are yielding to more standard variants, but where two local features – the disappearance of coda /s/ and the simplification of certain consonant clusters – are not. They note (pp. 205f.) that '[t]he nonstandard realization of these features is part of the essentially southern characterization, … so deeply rooted within the Murcian speech community that they are [sic] part of the local identity there'. As was the case with at least some of the 'core' social variables discussed earlier (cf. Section 30.3), it seems once again that 'subjective' factors, such as attitude and identity, which can be difficult (although not impossible) to measure, are at least as important as 'objective' factors in sociolinguistic analysis.

30.10 Standardization

The notion of 'standard language' is an important one, at least in the history of most national languages of western Europe. A standard language can exist only in connexion with an organized speech community, and this is usually (although not inevitably) a nation-state. There were no standard languages during the Middle Ages, for instance, because nation-states did not exist. It is true that the speech of a centre of economic and political power would tend to serve as a *lingua franca* (this was already the case with Parisian French), but this is not the same as standardization. It is significant that languages which came late to nation-statehood (such as Italian and Romanian) were in general also later in establishing a commonly accepted standard.

Haugen (1966) distinguished four processes involved in standardization: selection, elaboration of function, codification, and acceptance. These are often interpreted as sequential; but, in fact, they are not (necessarily) chronological stages – they can coexist and overlap, and often do. Typologically, they can be regarded as involving form vs function on the one hand, and social vs linguistic factors on the other (although, once again, this is an idealization). Thus, selection is a social process whereby a particular form of language becomes a communicative norm, whilst acceptance is the recognition by a society that a language is appropriate for use in all or most functions. Elaboration is a process whereby a language acquires new functions, whilst codification involves fixing the form of language, essentially by choosing from amongst a pool of variants and embodying these choices in grammars and dictionaries. For Haugen (1966), a standard language involves 'maximal variation in function' and 'minimal variation in form'. It is clear that, in its purest form, such a language is an idealization.

We can link notions of elaboration and acceptance to the concept of diglossia, discussed above (cf. Section 30.6). Specifically, we might claim that elaboration was the assumption of 'H' functions by a language which had previously been restricted to the 'L' domain. Thus, in the sixteenth century, French (hitherto an 'L' language) replaced Latin (the 'H' language) as the language of the courts (by François I's *Ordonnances de Villers-Cotterêts* of 1539), and, to an extent, in other 'H' functions, too. In Spanish, this change comes later, with a *real cédula* of Carlos III in 1768. Conversely, acceptance can be seen as a process in which the 'H' language comes to encompass 'L' functions (with the caveat that this process often takes place in a society which has become diaglossic rather than diglossic – see Section 30.6 above). For instance, after the amended Tuscan literary standard had been adopted as the national language of the new Italian nation-state (established in 1861), its increasing use in a variety of everyday contexts led to the development of what Berruto (2012: 73–75) terms a 'neo-standard' language (see also Mioni 1983). Hernández-Campoy and Villena-Ponsoda (2009) make a similar, but more attenuated, point regarding the relationship between standard Spanish and what they term *español común* ('common Spanish'). Key to the acceptance of a standard language is its becoming a subject of study and medium of instruction in a mass education system, a state of affairs which only came about in the late nineteenth or early twentieth century.

Standardization is a long and complex process, but it is not unreasonable to see standard French and Spanish already starting to emerge at the end of the Middle Ages. However, the development of a standard in some other Romance languages is much less clear cut. In Italy, a literary standard (essentially, the Tuscan variety of educated Florentines) emerged at around the same time as the French and Spanish proto-standards, but was a subject of frequently heated debate (the so-called *questione della lingua* 'language question') for over three centuries, before it came to form the basis of a national language once the Italian state was created in 1861 (with the debate continuing for some time thereafter). Detailed discussion of this issue lies beyond the scope of the present chapter: for a recent survey, see Marazzini (2018). It was not until the nineteenth century that Romanian acquired a literary standard, particularly as the result of the work and writings of Ion Heliade (1802–72) (see especially Close 1974); and, as in the case of Italian, this literary standard predated the creation of the nation-state (1878). Drace-Francis (2006) examines the complex role that culture, and especially literature and literacy, played in the creation of a Romanian national consciousness, suggesting that Anderson's view of literature as 'the technical means for "re-presenting" the *kind* of imagined community that is the nation' (Anderson 2006: 25, emphasis in original) may be too simplistic.[10] What is none the less clear from the examples of Italian and Romanian is that, rather than seeing the development of a standard language as a simple consequence of nation-statehood, it is probably more accurate to see the two developments as being in a complex symbiotic relationship, in keeping with the view, already voiced above, that language does not merely reflect social identity, but may also serve to create it (see also Fishman 1972).

The standardization of languages without a nation-state may follow a comparable path. A literary standard for modern Occitan, based on Provençal, was established by Joseph Roumanille in 1853 and taken up by Frédéric Mistral, with whose name it is most associated, and the Félibrige (for a critical historical account, see Martel 2012). Since 1935, this standard has been gradually replaced by the *norma classica* of Alibèrt (1935), based on Languedocien. Regional norms exist for Gascon (Romieu and Bianchi 2005) and Auvergnat (Bonnaud 1992), with some claiming that these (especially the former) are separate languages. Despite its different circumstances (fewer speakers, greater literacy, a smaller geographical area, less geopolitical fragmentation, and, above all, the dominance of another standard language, in the form of French), the situation of Occitan is in some ways similar to that of Italian in the years before Italy became a nation-state. However, the standardization of languages where the speech community exists below the level of the nation-state may have strikingly different characteristics. Extreme examples of such standardization, which in many ways do not follow Haugen's norms, are provided by Raeto-Romance. Romansh, the first language of approximately 35,000 people in eastern Switzerland, is fragmented into five dialects with limited mutual intelligibility. Attempts have been made to standardize individual varieties (for Sutselvan, see Weinreich 2011: 271–79), but it is scarcely feasible to have multiple standards in such a small speech community. The alternative is to have an overarching standard. Bühler (1886) proposed a *romontsch fusionau*, based on Surselvan, but this did not gain traction. Latterly, *rumantsch grischun*, an interdialectal norm proposed by the Zürich academic Heinrich Schmid in 1982 (see Schmid 1986) has become widely taught in

---

[10] In fact, Anderson is talking about 'the novel and the newspaper' rather than literature in general, and is not discussing the role of literary language, but rather the role of the novel in depicting the 'simultaneity' and 'polyphony' of a community.

schools. Likewise, Dolomite Ladin, spoken as a first language by approximately 40,000 speakers in north-eastern Italy, is similarly fragmented. Here, too, an interdialectal norm has been proposed, once again by Heinrich Schmid (Schmid 1998; see also Bernardi 1999 and Valentini 2001). The explicitly planned standards of Romansch and Ladin might be likened to artificial koinés, where the admixture of elements from different dialects is determined not by spontaneous sociolinguistic processes, but by the conscious decisions of an individual or a committee. Partly for this reason, they are not universally popular in the Romansh and Ladin speech-communities (see, for instance, Posner and Rogers 1993).

Ideological aspects of standardization in general are discussed by Joseph (1987) and Milroy (2001), whilst further discussion of standardization in Romance can be found in Muljačić (1993) and Pountain (2016).

30.11 *Ausbau* Languages and *Abstand* Languages

Kloss (1967) distinguishes between *Ausbau* languages and *Abstand* languages. According to this view, there are two criteria of linguistic differentiation, which define languages known by the German labels of *Ausbausprachen* (which Kloss paraphrases as 'languages by development') and *Abstandsprachen* ('languages by distance'). *Ausbau* languages are codified, can be used for communication in all registers, and have official status (in these senses, they are standardized); they are generally distinguished from one another by the fact that they articulate different cultures. *Abstand* languages are distinguished from one another by structural difference.

It is clear that languages such as French, English, and Chinese are simultaneously *Abstand* languages and *Ausbau* languages – they are distinct from one another both structurally and culturally. On the other hand, if we take the three languages known as Serbian, Croatian, and Bosnian, we find that they are distinct at the level of *Ausbau*, but not at the level of *Abstand* – they are structurally similar (in many respects, identical) and for all intents and purposes mutually intelligible; but they are distinct in as much as they are codified separately and serve as the vehicle for different national cultures and ideologies. Meanwhile, languages such as Neapolitan, Züritüütsch (the everyday language of Zürich), and Cantonese are distinct entities at the level of *Abstand*, but not at the level of *Ausbau*: partly for cultural reasons, these varieties are generally considered (at least by outsiders) as 'dialects' of Italian, German, and Chinese, respectively, despite striking structural differences and lack of mutual intelligibility with the perceived 'roofing' language.

The *Abstand* between, say, English and Chinese is a consequence of their total unrelatedness, and is therefore unremarkable. It is more interesting to consider the *Abstand* between languages with a common ancestor, such as the Romance languages. Here, the *Abstand* is to a large extent the result of processes already discussed in this chapter. *Abstand* may in fact wax and wane with social, cultural, or political distance – for instance, Döhla (2014) demonstrates that differential object-marking in Portuguese converges with the pattern found in Spanish up to and during the period of the Iberian Union (1580–1640), when Portugal and Spain were ruled by the same king, but diverges from it once the two countries become fully separate entities again. However, speakers of languages which are *Ausbausprachen* but not *Abstandsprachen* may also attempt to create an *Abstand* more consciously, through relexification, changes to the spelling system, and even changes to the grammar. Such changes may be resisted by some members of the speech community. An interesting case involves the Romance variety known as 'Moldovan'. The idea that there might be a separate Moldovan language, as opposed to Moldovan dialects of Romanian, originates with the creation within the USSR of the Moldovan Autonomous Oblast' in 1924, which became the Moldovan Autonomous Soviet Socialist Republic later the same year, ultimately merging with Bessarabia to become the Moldovan SSR, the ancestor of the independent Republic of Moldova, formed after the break-up of the Soviet Union in 1991. 'Standard Moldovan' is largely a creation of Madan (1927), who introduced local dialect words into the language, with Slavonic calques being added subsequently, most notably by Sergievskij (1936; 1939) and his followers – the aim, at least initially, being to stress the difference between the 'socialist' USSR and 'bourgeois' Romania. With Moldovan independence, there was hesitation over what to call the national language (*limba română* 'Romanian' in the 1991 Declaration of Independence; *limba moldovenească* 'Moldovan' in the 1994 Constitution); subsequently, attempts to create an *Abstand* culminated in the publication of Stati's *Dicționar moldovenesc–român* (Stati 2003; 2011), which claims as 'Moldovan' many dialect words which are also widespread in neighbouring parts of Romania. For fuller discussion, see Deletant (1996), Dyer (1999), King (1999), Sériot (2019), and Smith (forthcoming).

Conversely, speakers of languages which are *Abstandsprachen* but not *Ausbausprachen* may seek to create an *Ausbau*, by producing works of literature and descriptive and prescriptive grammars, and by introducing the language into the school curriculum. In this sense, *Ausbau* has affinities with the processes of elaboration and codification, discussed above (cf. Section 30.10). Attempts to create an *Ausbau* for the Sutselvan variety of Raeto-Romance in the 1940s are discussed by Weinreich (2011: 279–90). A more recent and 'crowd-sourced' manifestation of *Ausbau*-related elaboration is the emergence of Wikipedias, which now exist in 31 Romance varieties. Table 30.2 lists these varieties, together with the number of articles (which provides the basis for the list order), the number of users,

Table 30.2. *Wikipedias in Romance varieties*

Language	Articles	Users	Active users
French	2,290,515	3,989,939	21,077
Italian	1,668,272	2,070,493	9,837
Spanish	1,654,540	6,092,117	15,190
Portuguese	1,053,047	2,523,183	10,648
Catalan	669,140	375,590	1,550
Romanian	415,744	542,598	998
Galician	170,504	113,199	272
Asturian	107,741	82,417	145
Occitan	86,287	43,314	93
Venetan	67,245	27,956	51
Piedmontese	65,272	22,917	36
Lombard	45,409	31,784	57
Aragonese	39,342	60,384	84
Sicilian	26,120	37,045	52
Neapolitan	14,649	24,648	25
Wallon	14,121	19,632	34
Emilian–Romagnol	12,619	20,151	30
Tarantino	9,303	9,790	10
Sardinian	6,852	18,750	31
Corsican	5,879	17,467	33
Picard	5,057	13,324	21
Norman	4,542	11,199	15
Ligurian	4,485	12,174	30
Francoprovençal	4,380	12,848	25
Mirandese	3,839	10,995	20
Romansh	3,709	16,298	25
Ladino (Judezmo)	3,569	17,692	25
Friulian	3,427	11,824	19
Extremaduran	3,248	14,487	20
(Dolomite) Ladin	1,281	765	23
Aromanian	1,245	11,891	17

and the number of 'active users' (defined as users who have edited an article within the previous 30 days.[11] (The Cyrillic Moldovan Wikipedia, which was discontinued in 2006,[12] is not included; nor are Romance-lexifier creoles.)

Sometimes attempts to create *Abstand* and *Ausbau* may go hand in hand, as currently seems to be the case with Wallon (see Francard 2009: 110–13). Finally, we should note that it is possible for 'the same' *Ausbau* language to articulate different cultures, as witness the use of Portuguese, Spanish, and French in a number of New World countries, whose cultures differ significantly from those of Portugal, Spain, and France, respectively – notions of *lusofonia*, *hispanidad*, or *francophonie* notwithstanding. Even within Europe, the use of French in Belgium and of French and Italian in Switzerland raises this sort of issue (see, for instance, Armstrong and Pooley 2010: 205–48;

---

[11] Data from https://en.wikipedia.org/wiki/List_of_Wikipedias, consulted 20 January 2021.
[12] See https://meta.wikimedia.org/wiki/Proposals_for_closing_projects/Closure_of_Moldovan_Wikipedia, consulted 20 January 2021.

Cerruti 2011: 14). In this sense, Portuguese, Spanish, and French are what Kloss (1978) labels 'plurizentrisch' ('pluricentric') languages. For detailed discussion, see Baxter (1991) for Portuguese; Thompson (1991) and the papers in Lebsanft, Mihatsch, and Polzin-Haumann (2012) for Spanish; and Lüdi (1991) and Kircher (2012) for French.

30.12 Conclusion

It will be clear at the end of this brief survey that progress is still being made on gathering and analysing Romance data and on elucidating many of the concepts and mechanisms discussed in this chapter. For instance, the methods of variationist sociolinguistics have been applied with great success to English-speaking communities, but have not been applied to anything like the same extent to most of the Romance-speaking world. As Jones and Hornsby (2013b: 2) point out, Canadian French has been extensively studied from a variationist perspective, but European French has not, and those studies that have been undertaken have been by non-French linguists, using 'analytical models [which] rest on assumptions about urban life in English-speaking societies which are largely untested in the francophone context'. 'Francophone' could be replaced by 'Romance' (with a possible proviso concerning Latin American Spanish and Portuguese). In Section 30.1 above, it was claimed that sociolinguistic variation had always been an integral part of language, and uniformitarianism was invoked to justify this view. But uniformitarianism covers the general principles at work, which are not in doubt. We must not lose sight of the fact that certain factors may be specific to certain societies – to take one example, it is not obvious that the definition of social class is identical in every Romance-speaking community, let alone in all speech-communities worldwide (Rickford 1986, although see Harrison 2013 and Lambert 2013). Even individual languages are not homogeneous and may be pluricentric: for instance, the use of pronouns of address varies substantially within Spanish, according to the society in which it is spoken (Carricaburro 1997; Uber 2011). In French, diatopic variation seems to be less significant than elsewhere in the Romance-speaking world, and style-shifting seems to be more significant than social stratification. Diaglossic repertoire – having a number of distinct but related varieties at one's disposal – appears to be a particularly significant sociolinguistic factor in Italian. It is present to a degree in many other Romance languages, but it is also found in many non-Romance languages. Standardization is to a large extent bound up with the idea of the nation-state, and its trajectory and outcome may vary according to the historical context in which the nation-state emerges and develops (or, indeed, whether a nation-state emerges and develops at all).

Above all, we have seen that language both creates and reflects social identity, and social identities – more or less by definition – are different in different societies. Much work remains to be done on all these issues, but one fact is already apparent. Whereas the Romance languages are all descendants of Latin, and from this perspective form a historically coherent group, and whilst it may even be possible to talk of a Romance 'type' of language defined in terms of, say, morphosyntax (Coșeriu 1971; 1988) or morphology (Maiden 2018), varying social history and social structures mean that the Romance languages do not form an especially coherent or exceptional group when it comes to their sociolinguistics.

Selected References

Below you can find selected references for this chapter. The full references can be found online at the following page: www.cambridge.org/Romancelinguistics

Ayres-Bennett, W. and Carruthers, J. (eds) (2018). *Manual of Romance Sociolinguistics*. Berlin: Mouton De Gruyter.
Chambers, J. K. and Schilling, N. (eds) (2013). *The Handbook of Language Variation and Change* (second ed.). Malden/Chichester: Wiley–Blackwell.
Eckert, P. (2012). 'Three waves of variation study: the emergence of meaning in the study of sociolinguistic variation', *Annual Review of Anthropology* 41: 87–100.
Ehrlich, S., Meyerhoff, M., and Holmes, J. (eds) (2021). *The Handbook of Language, Gender, and Sexuality* (second ed.). Malden/Chichester: Wiley–Blackwell.
Gardner-Chloros, P. (2009). *Code-Switching*. Cambridge: Cambridge University Press.
Hickey, R. (ed.) (2020). *The Handbook of Language Contact* (second ed.). Malden/Chichester: Wiley–Blackwell.
Jones, M. C. and Hornsby, D. (eds) (2013a). *Language and Social Structure in Urban France*. Oxford: Legenda.
Labov, W. (1994–2010). *Principles of Linguistic Change* (3 vols). Malden/Chichester: Wiley–Blackwell.
Lodge, R. A. (1993). *French: From Dialect to Standard*. London: Routledge.
Marazzini, C. (2018). *Breve storia della questione della lingua*. Rome: Carocci.
Penny, R. (2000). *Variation and Change in Spanish*. Cambridge: Cambridge University Press
Weinreich, U., Labov, W., and Herzog, M. I. (1968). 'Empirical foundations for a theory of language change'. In Lehmann, W. P. and Malkiel, Y. (eds), *Directions for Historical Linguistics: a Symposium*. Austin: University of Texas Press, 95–188.

Index

aboutness, 704, 784, 794, 797–99, 807, 809
Abstand, 925–27
acceptance, 922
Acquaviva, 422–23
Adam, 836, 912
Adamik, 106
Adams, 109–11, 552, 576, 841, 898
addition (in language contact), 848
address systems, 763–82
Adger, 655
adjective positions, 49
adstrate, 846
adverb position, 26, 51, 523, 606, 652, 660
adverbs, 414, 416, 678, 684, 837
 -*mente*, 414, 416
advergence, 916
affective suffixes, 829
affix order, 455
affrication, 55, 192, 194
age, 902–3
agentivity, 163, 499, 545, 557, 850–51
agreement, 15–16, 152, 154–55, 290, 519–42, 554, 624
 of past participle, 561–64, 627, 640–41
Aikhenvald, 690, 868
Albanian, 475–76
Alber, 316
Aldi, 907
Alexiadou, 503, 537–38
Alibèrt, 924
alignment, 544
allomorphy, 78, 88–89, 209, 256–57, 322–43, 351–52, 360, 368–69, 371, 389, 397
Almeida, 313
Alonso, 436, 445
Amiot, 430
A-movement, 624
Anagnostopoulou, 503, 537–38
analogy, 59, 67, 69–70, 72, 74, 77–78, 359, 455
analytic structures, 3–4, 377, 485, 546, 571, 582, 602, 720
anaphora, 700–5, 715
Andersen, 920

Anderson, 349, 359, 401, 418, 924
Andrade, 301, 313
animacy, 509, 619
 animacy hierarchy, 379
anticausatives, 501, 503, 549
antipassive, 506
aoristic drift, 719
apocope, 186, 191, 195, 245–46
applicative, 493, 509
Arabic, 857, 888
Aragonese, 360
Aranese, 322, 346
Aranovich, 164, 500, 579
arbitrariness, 87–88
argot, 826
argument structure, 491–93, 498, 517, 601, 648–50
Armstrong, 504
Arndt-Lappe, 316
Aromanian, 84, 264, 690
Aronoff, 89, 256, 322, 349–51, 354, 369, 371, 435, 437, 455
Arregi, 804
articles, 48
 definite, 47–48
 expletive, 53–54
 indefinite, 48
Ascoli, 140
Ashdowne, 775
Aske, 514
aspect, 388, 716–17, 720
 progressive, 592, 718
aspectual periphrases, 591–94
aspiration of /s/, 231
Asturian, 11, 102, 295–96, 307, 328, 361, 756
atlases (linguistic), 72–73, 75, 81–82, 123, 145, 901
attrition, 918
Audring, 401
Auer, 916
augment, 254, 363–64, 424–25
augmentatives, 436, 442–43, 446–48, 829
Augustine, 881
Auroux, 894
Ausbau, 818, 925–27

autosegmental representation, 280–82
Auvergnat, 924
auxiliaries, 576–82, 584–87, 589
auxiliary selection, 494, 499, 555–61, 646–52
Auxiliary Selection Hierarchy, 163, 499, 556
Avalle, 128
Ayres-Bennett, 837, 901

Babel, 866
Bach, 362
Baerman, 420
Baker, 523, 572, 606
Bakhtine, 836
Baldinger, 673
Bally, 820
Banniard, 880–81, 899
Barbosa, 536
Barbu, 905
Barra Jover, 838
Basbøll, 249
Basque, 853, 860
Bateman, 305–6
Batllori, 755
Bauche, 823
Bauer, B., 484, 588
Bauer, L., 371
Béarnais, 32, 274
Beck, 516
Becker, 337
Bédier, 132
Béjar, 564
Belletti, 20, 524–25, 606, 608, 617, 625, 789, 793
Bello, 443
Beniak, 919
Benincà, 29, 391, 657, 785
Bentley, 174, 567, 692, 811
Bermúdez-Otero, 152
Berruto, 871–72, 906, 923
Bertinetto, 719
Beyssade, 749, 759
Bianchi, 791–92, 798, 811
Biber, 147, 819–20
Bickerton, 910
bilingualism, 205, 308, 388, 848, 850–51, 853, 863, 911, 913–15, 918
binding, 538, 632–34, 700–1
bioprogram, 910
Bittner, 374
biuniqueness, 263, 270–71, 866
Blanche-Benveniste, 822
bleaching, 363, 578, 677, 680, 684
Blevins, James, 354, 366–68, 374
Blevins, Juliette, 309
Bloch, 270
Blondeau, 902
Bloomfield, 262, 367, 371, 373
Bobaljik, 438
Bocci, 791
Bonami, 338, 362
Bonet, 311
Booij, 417, 423, 455, 867
Borer–Chomsky Conjecture, 5
Börjars, 393–94
Borreguero Zuloaga, 835

borrowing, 842, 845, 850–51
 hierarchies of, 866–68
 matter borrowing, 852
 morphological, 858
 pattern borrowing, 852
 phonological, 854
 prosodic, 854–55
 syntactic, 861
Bosque, 588
Bossong, 888
Bouchard, 611
Bourdieu, 904
Boyé, 338
Brambatti Guzzo, 413
Brinton, 676, 685
Britain, D., 920
Bromberger, 277
Brown, R., 763, 776
Brugè, 620
Brugger, 620
Brunetti, 791
Brunot, 765
Buchi, 99, 101, 104
Bühler, J. A., 924
Bühler, K., 871
Burnett, 517
Burton, 107
Burzio, 70, 493–96, 565
Buthke, 855
Bybee, 367, 455

Cabranes, 329
Calabrese, A., 158, 161, 280, 282, 497
Calabrian, 287, 298, 681, 699, 713, 863
Campbell, 854, 858, 865–66
Camproux, 450
Cancila, 854
Cappellaro, 380
Cardinaletti, 572, 607, 615, 620, 635, 701, 807
Carruthers, 900
cartographic enterprise, 18
Carton, 916
case, 12, 379, 615–16, 618, 620, 625, 698
Castilian. *See* Spanish
Catalan, 11, 53, 114, 137–38, 191, 211, 302, 309, 311, 357, 405, 416, 497–98, 510, 563, 567, 585, 599, 680, 712, 715, 731, 755, 771, 797, 805
 Algherese, 210, 312
 Balearic, 49, 54, 502
 Barcelona, 642
 eastern, 212
 insular, 302
 Majorcan, 218, 220, 299, 554
 Ribagorçan, 314
 Rossellonès, 660
causatives, 111, 568, 596–600, 602, 620
 causative alternation, 501, 503, 517
Cavirani, 193
ceceo, 296
Celata, 854
Celtic, 206, 463, 481, 483
Cennamo, 548–50, 552
Centineo, 497
Cerruti, 902

Chamoreau, 858
Chevrot, 905
Chierchia, 240, 705
Chiţoran, 304–5
Chomsky, 263, 272, 276–77, 280, 282, 284, 348, 520, 522, 605, 607, 630, 664
Cicurel, 824, 827
Cinque, 26, 565, 574, 606, 611, 657, 785
Clackson, 107
Clark, 389
clash resolution, 252
class (social), 903–4
classification of Romance languages, 200, 206–7
clause types, 728–47
cleft structure, 734, 789, 792–93
Clemens, 337
clitics, 156, 615, 803
   climbing, 574–75, 591, 594, 599
   doubling, 620, 843
   expletive subject, 615
   movement, 626–30
   resumptive, 800
   subject, 154–56, 160–62, 178, 324, 536, 539, 541–42, 643, 645, 730
cocoliche, 918
coda, 194–96
code-switching, 917
codification, 135–37, 893–94, 922
Coffen, 766, 774
Colasanti, 744, 746
Coleman, 466
collectives, 472
comment, 796
common ground, 749
Company Company, 689, 837
comparative-historical perspective, 3, 5, 70, 73, 78, 80, 85, 93
comparatives, 377–78
   synthetic vs analytic, 378
complementizer, 31, 41, 43
   complementizer positions, 30–33
   dual, 31, 47
Complementizer-drop, 46
Complex Inversion, 616
complex predicates, 571–602
complexification, 911
compounds, 400, 405, 408, 410, 412, 429
conditional, 654
   synthetic, 352, 357, 362
Coniglio, 750
Conner, 686
Conrad, 819–20
contact, 80, 110–14, 205, 389–91, 474–75, 845–47, 849–50, 853, 860, 862–63, 866, 909, 911, 913, 917
conversion, 404, 426–31
Corbett, 355, 371–73, 379, 387
Cornillie, 690
corpus linguistics, 146–49
Corsican, 38, 247, 297–98
Cosentino, 20
Coseriu, 120, 871
Costa, 313
Coupland, 908
Coveney, 906

creoles, 87, 846, 910
Croatian, 388–89, 913
Crocco Galèas, 373
Crowhurst, 439–40
Cruschina, 567, 791–92, 811
Cuervo, 493, 508
Cyrillic script, 130, 136

D'Alessandro, 528, 530–31, 564, 625–26
Da Tos, 391
Daco-Romance, 81, 83, 115, 600, 760
Dadan, 36
Dalmatian, 919
   Vegliote, 61
Dardano, 842
Dardel, de, 876
Darmesteter, 430
Dasher, 690
dative shift, 9, 11
datives, 507–12, 699
De Cat, 608
De Cuyper, 504
De Mauro, 147
De Melo, 110
Déchaine, 701
Dees, 144–45
defectiveness, 388, 420
definiteness, 4, 47, 664
degemination, 222, 274, 332, 853
degrammaticalization, 684–86
deixis, 709–15
   person, 714
   spatial, 710
   temporal, 713
Delforge, 303
demonstrative systems. *See* deixis
Demonte, 609–10
dependency, 604
deponents, 112, 550–52
derivational affixes, 395
derivational morphology, 88, 348, 371, 404, 454
Désirat, 822, 825, 840
determiners, 708
detransitivization, 503
devoicing, 247, 302, 310–11, 854
Di Sciullo, 434
diaglossia, 916
dialect, 137
dialect geography, 141
dialectometry, 144–45
diamesic variation, 870–96
diaphasic variation, 841
diatopic variation, 902, 928
Díaz-Campos, 903
dictionaries, 138–39, 673, 823
Dictionnaire Étymologique Roman, 98–99
Diesing, 706
Diez, 673
differential object marking, 617, 619, 698, 926
diffusion, 910
diglossia, 126, 880, 915–16
diminutives, 436–37, 442–44, 446, 448, 829, 843
   diminutive suffixes, 441, 445, 449–54, 829

diphthongization, 85, 240, 301–4, 408
diphthongs, 190
discourse markers, 675, 685–90, 835
Discourse Representation Theory, 704
discourse tradition, 837, 892
dislocation, 795, 797, 827, 829–31
Distributed Morphology, 280, 347, 366, 402, 427, 431
distributives, 472
Dixon, 900
Dobrovie-Sorin, 566, 775
Döhla, 926
do-support, 731, 913
Drace-Francis, 924
Dressler, 371, 436, 445, 449, 454, 843
Drinka, 107, 112, 901
dual processing, 367
Dufresne, 517
Dumas, 303
Dupuis, 517

eastern vs western Romance. *See* classification of Romance languages
Eckert, 904
Eddington, 438, 440
Edmont, 141, 143
Egurtzegi, 853
elaboration of function, 922
Elcock, 97
elision, 212–16
Elordieta, 409
Embick, 493
Emilian, 301
Emonds, 523
enchaînement, 210
endocentricity, 920–21
Enger, 361
English, 508, 513, 538, 776, 827, 854, 917
Enrique-Arias, 849
epenthesis, 210–11, 302
epithesis, 191
Esher, 354, 358, 361, 364, 910
ethnicity, 905
etymology, 673
evaluative affixes, 441–48
evaluative morphology, 395, 434–36, 440–41, 454
evidentiality, 676, 690–92, 834, 915
exclamatives, 737, 739
exocentricity, 920–21
experiencer, 510
expressive morphology, 435–36, 438, 441
Extended Projection Principle, 527, 538, 807
extrametricality, 239
Eythórsson, 174

Fafulas, 903
Fagard, 678, 684
faire-infinitif construction, 598
faire-par construction, 598
Faitelson-Weiser, 451
family tree, 908–10
Fanego, 686
Fant, 276

feature theory, 276
Félibrige, 924
Ferguson, C., 915
Ferguson, R., 922
Fertig, 374
field, 820
Finco, 299
finiteness, 13–15, 31, 33, 38, 561
Finkel, 362
Fishman, 915
Fitch, 234
Fleischman, 120–21
Flobert, 551
Florentine, 81, 274, 558, 823
Flores Farfán, 865
Floricic, 338
Fløttum, 838
focus, 29–30, 35, 790, 804, 808
  focus fronting, 790
  focus types, 790
  mirative, 790–91
Folli, 505–6, 516
foot, 237, 241, 249, 258
Force, 31
Fortin, 441, 446
fortition, 194, 310
Fradin, 446
Francoprovençal, 140
Frank, 130
Frascarelli, 797–800
Frei, 895
Freitas, 313
French, 3, 22, 27, 114, 124, 139, 146, 153, 163–64, 186, 202, 204, 207, 209–11, 215–16, 223–24, 226–27, 237, 239, 242, 244–45, 248, 252–53, 259, 275, 324, 326, 338, 346, 362, 376, 397, 427, 473, 477, 479, 503, 523, 532–33, 536, 541, 562, 567, 582, 606, 616, 630, 633, 642, 678, 681, 683, 685, 704, 707, 712, 737, 771, 775, 789, 793, 809, 811, 825, 837–38, 842, 855, 887–88, 891, 901, 903, 906, 916, 923, 928
  Alsace, 860
  Belgium, 479, 481
  Canadian, 153, 294, 302–3, 556, 565, 651, 928
  Cree-French mixed language, 864
  français fondamental, 146
  français marginaux, 887
  français populaire, 823, 826, 886, 895
  Guadeloupe, 886
  Jersey, 917
  Montreal, 902
  Newfoundland, 919
  Old Mines, Missouri, 918
  Québec, 245, 248
  sign language, 485
  Switzerland, 153, 479, 481
  written vs spoken, 822, 827, 829, 907
frequency, 344, 374, 398, 582
Friedman, 690
Friulian, 250, 298–99, 315
front rounded vowels, 189, 293–94
fronterizo/fronteriço, 917
Frota, 313, 752
Fudeman, 371

functional categories, 3–54
future, 834, 885
   epistemic, 834
   evidential, 834
   synthetic, 352, 357, 362

Gadet, 906
Gal, 904
Galdi, 107
Galician, 91, 137–38, 294, 296, 307, 314, 359, 391, 756
Gallego, Á., 588
Gallo-Romance, 38, 202, 204, 206, 592
gaps, 158
García Arias, 295–96, 307
Gardani, 856–57, 867
Garrapa, 246
Garzonio, 657
Gascon, 32–33, 729, 924
Gaulish, 205–6, 483
geada, 294–95
Gehrke, 516
geminate, 853
gemination, 187–88, 195, 199, 228, 248–50, 324, 329
gender, 417, 472, 523
   ambigeneric nouns, 422
gender (in society), 904–5
Gendron, 302
generative phonology, 290
genre, 836–38
German, 392, 513, 658, 848, 860
Germanic, 112, 275, 481–82
gerund, 68, 456, 592, 600, 683
Gévaudan, dialect of, 450
Gianollo, 550
Galliéron, 123, 141–43
Giurgea, 729, 775, 792, 799–800
Giusti, 613–14, 620, 635
givenness, 784, 786, 796–97, 799
glide strengthening, 306
glottal stop, 300
Goebl, 145
Gordon, 234
Gotti, 825
Gougenheim, 146
Government and Binding, 520, 523
Government Phonology, 280–81
Gradoville, 903
grammatical relations, 614, 616
grammaticalization, 552, 576, 589, 602, 663, 675–82, 686–87, 691, 693, 715, 862
grammatization, 894
graphocentrism, 99
Greek, 111–13, 115, 117, 842, 851
   Asia Minor, 851
   Byzantine, 842
Greek-style dative, 699
Green, 832, 910
Greenberg, 434, 454, 463, 468, 480
Greene, 482
Greub, 101
Grice, 703
Griffith, 852
Guaraní, 849
Guardiano, 49

Guiraud, 824, 826
Gutiérrez-Rexach, 740

Haegeman, 761
Hajek, 307, 859
Hale, 498, 515, 564
Hall, 100, 102
Halle, 268, 276–77, 280, 282, 284, 349, 402
Halliday, 147, 820, 872
Hamp, 475–76
Han, 752
hanging topic, 800, 873
Harley, 506, 516, 645–46
Harris, A., 858, 865–66
Harris, J., 236, 286
Harris, K., 852
Hartmann, 130
Harvey, 572
Haspelmath, 178, 372, 456, 709, 851
Hasselrot, 450, 456
Haudricourt, 274–76
Haugen, 922
Haverling, 109, 113
Heliade, 923
Herman, 107, 114
Hernández-Campoy, 916, 922–23
Hernanz, 755
Hertzenberg, 708
Herzog, 899
heteroclisis, 364
hiatus, 210, 213–14, 246
Hidalgo, 831
Hill, J., 861
Hill, K., 861
Hill, V., 620, 760–61
Hinterhölzl, 797, 799
Hoffman, 852
Holmberg, 10, 639
Holmquist, 904, 907
Hopper, 676
Hordé, 822, 825, 840
Hornsby, 906, 921, 928
Horrocks, 107
Hualde, 250, 271, 412, 752
Humboldt's Universal, 389
Hummel, 682, 684
Hutter, 834
Hyman, 280
hyperbaton, 839
hyperbole, 828

Iacobini, 431, 516
ideophones, 440
Iliescu, 769
illocutionary force, 24, 31, 442, 447, 728, 747, 749–50, 752, 755, 758
imperative, 17, 394, 741–44, 752
imperfect control, 438–39
imperfectivity vs perfectivity, 550, 716–20
INDE-cliticization. *See* ne-cliticization
infinitive, 117, 428, 592, 634
   inflected, 14–15
   personal, 13
Infl, 26

inflexion
    inherent vs contextual, 867
inflexional morphology, 372, 418
inflexional vs derivational morphology, 420, 856
information structure, 784–812
interfaces, 18–21
Internet, 872, 907
interrogatives, 730, 739
intonation, 751–52, 786, 855
invariance, 263, 270–71
inverse address, 772
Iovino, 614
irrealis, 14–15, 31, 42, 45–46, 580, 663, 747
isochronism, 185–88
isogloss, 140
Istro-Romanian, 50, 52, 382, 388, 587, 913–14
Italian, 35, 54, 56, 61–62, 68, 79–82, 84–85, 114, 139, 186–87, 191, 197, 203, 227, 237–38, 240–41, 245–46, 252, 255, 336, 343, 408, 421, 423, 436, 441, 494, 499, 510, 516, 528, 532, 550, 556, 561, 565, 567–68, 585, 592, 596, 606, 642, 661, 679, 757, 770, 786, 797, 805, 823, 827, 831, 843, 853, 857, 871, 890–91, 902, 916, 918, 923, 928
    italiano dell'uso medio, 895
    italiano popolare, 824, 895
Italo-Romance, 62, 73, 81–82, 166, 361, 480, 541, 630, 699, 715, 738, 760, 853
    central, 89, 186, 227, 249, 731
    northern, 39, 151, 153, 206, 307, 542, 643, 711, 731, 733, 735
    southern, 31, 40, 42, 74, 186–87, 190, 197, 227, 249, 287, 297, 301, 584, 624, 731, 744

Jaberg, 142–43, 391
Jacobs, 800
Jaeggli, 434, 442, 537
Jakobson, 276, 864
jargons, 823–27
Jerome, 107
Jespersen's Cycle, 658, 661, 724
Jiménez, 272, 309
Jonasson, 838
Jones, Mari, 906–7, 917, 928
Jones, Michael, 265, 298
Jud, 142–43, 673
Juge, 373
Juilland, 274–76
Jurafsky, 442, 444–45

Kabatek, 837
Kager, 259
Kägi, 857
Kahane, 834
Kaiser, 619
Kamp, 704
Kato, 536
Katz, 520
Kaufman, 850–51, 860, 867
Kayne, 10, 525–28, 539, 598, 611, 615, 627, 639, 701–2
Keenan, 847
Kempchinsky, 608
Kerswill, 920–21
Keyser, 498, 515
King, 919

Kiparsky, 259, 269–70, 280
Kiss, 194
Klipple, 514
Kloss, 818, 925, 928
Koch, 130, 675, 837, 842, 872–74, 884
koinéization, 913
Koopman, 624
Kovačec, 913
Krifka, 787, 800
Kroch, 179
Kronning, 834
Kuroda, 809

L2 learning, 913
La Fauci, 553
La Spezia–Rimini Line, 206
Labov, 899, 901, 904–5, 908–9, 922
Lachmann, 132
Ladefoged, 306
Ladin, 925
Laenzlinger, 611
Lakoff, 445
Lamarche, 611
Lamiroy, 678
Landauer, 368
language death, 918
language shift, 850
Larson, 10
Latin, 3, 86, 97, 99, 110, 112–13, 117, 127, 133–34, 184–85, 188, 201, 238–39, 839, 841–42, 876–78, 880, 887, 889, 892–93, 899, 908, 916
    Christian, 107
    Medieval, 107
    submerged, 109
    vulgar, 106, 126–27, 876–79, 881, 885, 887
Lausberg, 206, 274
Lausberg Zone, 265
Lázaro Mora, 437
learnèd influence, 113, 842, 883
Ledgeway, 14, 20, 24, 33, 37, 42, 102, 392, 547, 555, 561, 618, 651, 862–63
left periphery, 20, 35, 41, 800
Lehmann, C., 677
length, 184
lengthening, 186, 188, 197, 240–41, 249
    compensatory, 250–52
lenition, 194, 200, 217, 274, 309–10
Lenz, 443
Levin, 491, 496
Levinson, 752, 763, 776
lexeme, 400
Lexical Hypothesis, 348
lexicalization patterns, 517
lexicology, 674–76, 693
liaison, 210
Liberman, 852
Lieber, 435
Lieberson, 910
Limousin, 358
Lindsey, 286
linearity, 263
Linell, 870
Lipski, 920
literacy, 882, 892, 894

Lloret, 272, 302, 309, 311
Llull, 889
Lodge, 838, 901
Lombard dialect, 731, 735
Lombardi, 20
long-distance dependencies, 624–30
Longobardi, 49, 705, 707
Longtin, 517
López, 608, 799
López Serena, 835
Loporcaro, 84–85, 100–2, 152, 161, 164–65, 172, 174, 179, 188, 204, 242, 274, 500, 559, 857, 913
Lucca, 450, 853
Lüdtke, 127, 880
Luís, 152
lunfardo, 826
Luquet, 772
Lyons, 716, 873

MacDonald, 505–6
macroparameters, 515, 638–39
Maddieson, 189, 295, 299, 306
Maiden, 62, 64, 70, 74, 78, 85, 89, 101, 242, 254–55, 322, 336, 352, 354, 356, 359, 361–64, 389, 392, 394, 425, 913, 919
Maling, 497
Malkiel, 120, 332, 673, 693
Malouf, 363
Manova, 455
Manzini, 158, 178–79, 288–89, 659, 701
Mapping Hypothesis, 706
Marandin, 749, 759
Marantz, 280, 402, 493, 516
marché linguistique, 904
Marchello-Nizia, 683
Mardale, 620, 678, 684
markedness, 8, 184, 209–10, 216, 280, 293, 309, 651
Markey, 374
Martin, 503, 905
Martín Zorraquino, 688, 692
Martinet, 274, 278
Martins, 755–56
Marx, 109, 117
Mascaró, 243
Mascioni, 270
Masini, 431, 516
mass/count distinction, 102, 447, 707
Mateu, 497–98, 515–16
Mateus, 301, 313
Matras, 850, 868
Matrix Language Frame, 917
Matthews, 373
Maxim of Quantity, 703
Mayan, 308, 477, 847
Mazzoleni, 835
McCawley, 438, 440
McConnell-Ginet, 904
McKenzie, 304
Meakins, 851
measure terms, 460–61
Media Lengua, 864, 917
medium, 907
medium transferability, 873
Megleno-Romanian, 84, 393–94, 690, 856
Meillet, 343, 677, 856, 899

Meinschaefer, 246
Meisenburg, 855
Melčuk, 371–73
Mensching, 300
Merge, 492, 666, 668
Merlini Barbaresi, 436, 445, 449, 843
Merlo, 74, 77, 321
Merovingian era, 127, 882
mesoclisis, 630
metaphony, 73, 75–76, 78, 85, 197–98, 242–43, 265, 267–71, 278–80, 284
  hypermetaphony, 74–75, 77–78
metaphor, 675, 775
metathesis, 311–12
metrical constituency, 248–53
metrical patterns, 203
metrical structure, 234, 257
Meul, 424
Meyer, 140–41
Michif, 864, 917
Michnowicz, 308
microvariation, 5, 9, 53
Migliori, 550, 552–53
Millardet, 321–22
Milroy, 919
Minimalism, 492, 520
Mioni, 871
Mirror Principle, 523–24, 606
Mistral, 924
Mithun, 455
mixed languages, 863
modality, 31, 721, 744
modals, 162, 596, 601, 690
mode, 820
Moldovan 'language', 926
Moldovan dialect, 306
Monno, 176
monoclausality, 573–74, 589, 601
mora, 237
Moravcsik, 851
Morin, 224, 250
morphological ellipsis, 413–16
Morphological Uniformity Hypothesis, 537
morphologization, 65, 71, 73, 79, 235
morphology, 70
  abstractive models, 366–67, 369
  autonomy of, 89, 256, 369–70
  Construction Morphology, 431
  constructive models, 366, 368–69
  Item-and-Arrangement, 366
  Item-and-Process, 366
  Word and Paradigm, 366, 372
morphemes, morphomic structures, 89, 92, 365–66, 919
  metamorphomes, 352, 355, 359, 368–69
  rhizomorphomes, 361–64
morphophonological alternations, 410
Mougeon, 919
Move, 492, 666, 668
movement, 26
multidimensional semantics, 446
Muñiz Cachón, 296
muta cum liquida, 193, 205
Muysken, 910
Myers-Scotton, 917

Nahuatl, 858, 861
Napoli, 435–37, 441
nasal place neutralization, 308
Natural Morphology, 371, 389
Neapolitan, 43, 392
Nebrija, 442, 893
ne-cliticization, 494, 567
negation, 715–26
negative concord, 722–23
Nencioni, 872
Nespor, 253
neuter, 101
neutralization, 269
Nevins, 92, 280, 282, 337
Newmayer, 178
Nichols, 618
Norén, 838
noun positions, 49–53
Nübling, 374
null subject, 22, 24, 37–38
Null Subject Parameter, 178
numerals, 459
   cardinal vs ordinal, 375–76
   internal word order, 468–69
   quantification, 460–61
   vigesimals, 483–84
Nurmio, 393–94

O'Neill, 348–49, 360, 369
Obenauer, 736
Ocampo, 687, 692
Occitan, 114, 137–38, 202, 222, 275, 314, 357–58, 362, 392, 450, 596, 855, 905, 910, 924
Oesterreicher, 842, 872–74, 884
Oh, 493, 516
Old Church Slavonic, 842
Oltenian dialect, 72
onomasiology, 674, 713
onset, 191–94
opacity, 270
open syllable lengthening, 187–89, 241–42, 251
optatives, 745
Optimality Theory, 256, 292, 311
orality, 843, 870–71, 875, 883, 885, 889, 895
Oresme, 888
orthography, 223, 895
Ouali, 664
out-of-the-blue announcements, 566, 809
overabundance, 390

palatal stops, 299
palatalization, 54–93, 192, 194, 196, 198–200, 275, 313, 329, 408
   of coda /s/, 313
   by yod, 55–56, 80, 192, 356
   of velars, 55–56, 58, 60–63, 65, 275, 332–33, 335, 408
   palatal~velar alternation, 65, 67–68, 70–71
Pantiscu, 161–62, 857
Paoli, 118
paragoge, 250
parameters, parametric variation, 6–12, 637–69
Parry, 907
partitive, 3, 567, 680, 707
Pasiego, 281

Passino, 300–1
passives, 831
   double passive, 588
   passive auxiliaries, 587
   periphrastic, 583, 588–89
   reflexive, 583
   SE-passives, 565–66
Paul, 910
Payne, 152
Pellegrini, 916
Penny, 917
Peperkamp, 410
periphrastic perfect, 108, 112–13
Perlmutter, 401, 493–94, 556–57, 559, 568
Pfänder, 866
Pfister, 673
phase theory, 18, 21
phi-features, 641, 643
phoneme, 261–91, 852
   inventories, 293–300
Picard, 921
pidgin, 910
Piedmontese, 307
Pike, 204
Pineda, 509
Pinkerton, 765
Pinto, 567
Pinto de Lima, 692
Placiti cassinesi, 40
Plank, 677
Platzack, 10
Plénat, 343
plurale maiestatis, 765
polarity, 755
Poletto, 29, 153, 532, 657, 661, 726, 744
politeness, 767–69, 775–76, 779
   in pronouns, 765–67
Pollock, 523, 605–6
polynormativity, 892
polysynthetic structures, 865
Pons Bordería, 837
Pons-Moll, 302
Pons-Rodríguez, 232
Popovici, 769
Pórtoles Lázaro, 688, 692
Portuguese, 91, 139, 147, 191, 244, 248, 313, 360, 363, 368, 416, 452, 520, 597, 602, 679, 726, 737, 767, 859, 926, 928
   Angolan, 913
   Azorean, 245, 294
   Brazilian, 204, 336, 419, 436, 452, 456, 535, 583, 599, 706–7, 768, 773–74, 789, 826, 913
   European, 53, 204, 550, 600, 630, 756, 768, 774
possessives, 329, 624, 836
Posta, 522
Postal, 520–23
Potts, 440, 444, 446–48, 457
Pountain, 821, 825, 842
preposition stranding, 10
prepositions, 682–84
presupposition, 697–700, 792
Prieto, 250, 439–40, 752
principle of contrast, 389
Principles and Parameters, 178, 705
printing, 135

pro-drop, 21–25, 37, 535–37, 542
progressive constructions, 679
pronouns
    clitic vs strong, 379
    personal, inflexional morphology of, 379–80
propagation, 287, 289
proper names, 53
prosodic hierarchy, 236, 316, 413
prosodic structure, 236–37, 410, 412, 751, 786
prosthesis, 191
proto-Romance, 97, 100, 104, 188
Provençal, 924
psychological reality, 92, 352, 359, 363, 365
psychological verbs, 510
Pulgram, 876
Pullum, 175, 435–36, 439–41
punctuated equilibrium, 900
Purépecha, 858–59
purism, 843, 880, 893
Pustka, 886
Puter, 306
Pylkkänen, 508

quantification, 4, 737, 794
quantity, 184, 186–88, 190, 202–3, 245
Quechua, 303, 852, 864, 914
Questione della lingua, 892–93, 923
quirky subjects, 497, 510, 911

raddoppiamento fonosintattico. See *rafforzamento fonosintattico*
Radial Category, 445
Raeto-Romance, 140
rafforzamento fonosintattico, 19, 84, 195, 211, 217, 228, 249
Raible, 887, 889
Rainer, 435
Ramchand, 516
Rao, 412
Rappaport Hovav, 491, 496
ratchet principle, 910
realis. *See* irrealis
Real-Puigdollers, 516
reanalysis, 39, 455
recomplementation, 31, 118
reconstruction, 80, 82, 98–105, 114–20
referentiality, 20
reflexives
    pleonastic, 549
refunctionalization, 363, 915
register, 126, 188, 583, 817–19, 827–29, 834–35, 842–43, 872, 895, 906
Reichenkron, 483
Reinhart, 794
relativizers, 832–33
Remacle, 891
Remberger, 300, 729, 812
Renzi, 130, 154, 646
Repetti, 249
restandardization, 881, 895
restructuring, 572, 575, 629, 634
resultative, 719
retroflex consonants, 297–98
Reyle, 704
Reynolds, 435–37, 441
Rezac, 564
rhotic, 311–12

rhyme (in syllable structure), 184, 186, 197, 202
rhythm, 204, 206, 235
rich agreement, 535
Rigau, 497–98, 515–16, 755
Ripano, Ripatransone, 15, 25, 912
Ritter, 645–46
River Plate, 144
Rizzi, 22, 28, 45, 120, 288, 537, 539, 541, 572, 607, 630, 666, 729, 750, 785, 807
Roberts, 36, 155–56, 179, 528–29, 531, 536, 539, 541–42, 564, 625–26, 639, 666
Rohlfs, 74, 143, 190, 478, 480, 483, 711, 862
Romaine, 818
Romance languages, definition of, 86
Romanian, 3, 7, 9, 11, 17–18, 31, 54, 56, 61–62, 65–67, 71, 79–82, 89, 100–1, 130, 136, 138, 163, 190, 193, 207, 238, 274, 304–5, 387, 406, 428, 449, 460, 471, 474–76, 511, 550, 565–66, 579–81, 584, 586, 592, 595, 597, 600, 602, 609, 613, 615, 617–18, 620, 627, 631–32, 648, 651, 654, 678, 683, 714–15, 736, 747, 755, 757, 760, 767–68, 772, 792–93, 799, 801, 827, 832–36, 838, 842–43, 914, 923
româna populară, 824
Romansh, 306, 359, 848, 925
roofing, 891
Rooth, 786
Roseano, 299, 315
Round, 354
Røyneland, 920
rumantsch grischun, 924
Russo, 912

Sabatini, 128, 882, 895
Sadler, 492
Sadock, 728
Safir, 537
Salentino, 310–11, 635, 665
saltatory alternations, 309
Salvi, 130
Salvioni, 168, 335
Samek-Lodovici, 805, 831
Sánchez López, 746
Sánchez-Muñoz, 818
Sanders, 271
sandhi, 19, 209–32
Sankoff, 304, 902
Sapir, 277
Sardinian, 59, 116, 120, 186, 200, 207, 227, 230, 265, 267, 272, 297–98, 316, 376, 405, 471, 520, 586, 592, 609, 642, 713, 790, 792, 812
    Campidanese, 299–300, 309–13, 342, 692
    Logudorese, 199, 265, 342
satellite, 513, 515–17
Saussure, 87, 261–62, 277, 870
Sauvageot, 146
Sauzet, 314
Savognin, 360
Savoia, 158, 178–79, 288–89, 659, 701
sayagués, 825
-sc- affix, 424–25
Scalise, 349, 434–35, 437
Scandinavian, 393, 483, 911
Schäfer, 503
Scheuermeier, 143
Schifano, 607, 654
Schleicher, 908

Schmid, 924
Schmidt, 909
Schuchardt, 120, 126, 140, 673, 876, 909
schwa, 193, 210, 239, 247, 253, 301–2, 326
Schwarzschild, 786
Schweickard, 99, 104
scripta latina rustica, 882
scriptae, 128–30, 134, 136, 148, 890–93
se as clitic, 501–7
segmentation, 866
Segre, 131
Séguy, 145, 901
Seifart, 866
selection, 922
semantic change, 674–75
semantic-pragmatic change, 690
Serrano-Dolader, 430
seseo, 297
Shlonsky, 572, 630
Sichel-Bazin, 855
Sicilian, 267, 297, 390, 483, 635, 790, 857
Siewierska-Chmaj, 775
sign languages, 846
Silverstein, 174
Silvestri, 744, 746
simplification, 911, 913, 915
Sims, 368
Skok, 63
Skutsch, 870
slangs, 826–27
Slavonic, 7, 9, 11, 63, 80–81, 130, 136, 474–76, 914
small clause, 493
Smith, J. C., 355, 363, 915
Smith, N., 910
Snyder, 516
social media, 907
social networks, 905, 919
sociolinguistic variation, 105, 873, 898–900, 904–5
sociophilology, 876–77, 879, 899
Söll, 873
sonority, 302, 306, 311
Sonority Principle, 193–94
sonority sequencing, 185, 195, 300
Sorace, 163, 499–500, 556–57, 559
Sornicola, 108, 120, 619, 904
sound change, 58, 70–71, 141, 373, 387
sources, 126–27
SOV, 860
Spanish, 11, 22, 54, 65, 147, 163, 246, 248, 257, 296, 298, 308, 346, 376, 405, 416, 427–28, 434, 436, 439, 442, 445–46, 451, 508, 550, 585, 587, 597, 602, 609, 617–18, 630, 679, 686, 709, 740, 746, 766, 770–71, 777, 779, 786, 823, 826, 830–32, 835, 858, 860, 888, 891, 904, 913, 915, 918, 923, 926, 928
  Andalusian, 231–32, 271, 296–97, 300
  Andean, 302
  Asturian, 296
  Bogotá, 777
  Bolivian, 436, 914
  Caracas, 903
  Chilean, 443, 777
  Judaeo-Spanish, 306, 712
  Latin American, 300, 443, 713
  Majorcan, 849
  Nicaraguan, 300
  Paraguayan, 849
  Puerto Rico, 904
  Seville, 916
  United States, 779
  Uruguayan, 442, 777
  Yucatán, 308
Speas, 761
spec-head agreement, 523, 525, 528, 625
speech act, 691, 729, 747–50, 759, 761
Spencer, 152, 373, 492
spirantization, 309–10
Spitzer, 448, 895
split CP, 45
split intransitivity, 545–46, 548–51, 638–39
Split Morphology Hypothesis, 401, 423, 425, 434
split *v*P hypothesis, 620
Sportiche, 624, 628
Sprachbund
  Balkan, 862, 911, 913
  Charlemagne, 112
Sprouse, 497
Squartini, 592, 691, 719
Stalnaker, 696, 749
Stammbaumtheorie, 908
standard language bias, 79
standardization, 135, 838, 842, 870, 875, 888, 890, 922–24, 928
Stark, 562
Starke, 615, 701
Stati, 926
stative, 545, 557, 649–51
Steele, 519, 534
Štekauer, 400
stem space, 352
stereotype, 906
Steriade, 304–5
Stolz, 375
stress, 184–86, 188–89, 197, 203, 206, 210, 212–14, 230, 234–59, 283, 331, 355, 396, 786
  stress timing, 204
  unstressed vowels, 190, 204, 210, 212, 214
Strong Rhyme Constraint, 186, 197
strong/weak C, 666–69
strong/weak D languages, 49
structuralism, 262–63
Stump, 354, 362, 438, 442
style, 819–20, 905
  literary, 839
style indirect libre, 840
subjectification, 690
subjunctive, 4, 14, 31, 62–63, 595, 602, 647, 654, 665, 679, 744–45, 753
substrate, substratum, 205, 274, 483, 845, 850
subtraction, 464–66
Sugisaki, 515
superlative, 377–78
superstrate, 845
supine, 428
suppletion, 82, 109, 114, 359, 371–98, 407
  caused by sound change, 387
  incursion, incursive, 373, 380, 396
  overlapping, 390, 392
  paradigmatic distribution, 397
  phonological resemblance in, 397
  strong vs weak, 373
suprasegmentals, 314–16

Surmiran, 299, 306, 392, 679
Surselvan, 679, 924
Sutselvan, 926
Svenonius, 493, 572–73, 655
Swiggers, 142
syllable
  syllable structure, 204, 210, 237, 242, 248, 270, 300–2
  timing, 204
  weight, 184, 199, 202, 237–39, 249, 257
syncope, 186–87, 191, 195, 204, 244
syncretism, 160, 358, 420, 643
synonymy, 389–90, 392–95, 397–98
synthetic structures, 3–4, 355, 357, 377, 484, 546, 571, 576, 578, 582, 602, 654, 716, 720

taboo, 827, 838, 884
tags, 759
Talmy, 512–14, 516–17
TAM, 163, 581, 653
Taraldsen, 537
Tekavčić, 274, 332
telicity, 163, 499, 502, 504–5, 514, 557, 718
Tenny, 761
tenor, 820
Terzi, 634–35
Tetun Dili, 859
thetic VS, 811
Thomason, 850–51, 860, 867
Thornton, 174
Thun, 144
tone, 314
topic, 29, 784, 793–805, 807, 809
topicality, 20
Tranel, 225
transitivity, 17, 619
Traugott, 676, 685–86, 690
Tremblay, 517
Troberg, 517
troncamento, 246
Trubetzkoy, 262, 269
Trudgill, 899, 901, 911–13
truncation, 316, 827
Turkish, 851
Tuscan, 85, 200, 391, 713
Tuten, 913
typology, 4
  typological variation, 18

unaccusativity, 163–65, 168, 170–72, 174, 493–99, 501, 517, 531, 534, 553, 556, 561, 566–67, 617, 626, 639, 651, 809
  Unaccusative Hypothesis, 493
unergativity, 163–65, 168, 171, 493–99
uniformitarianism, 928
Unitary Base Hypothesis, 435, 437
Universal Grammar, 12, 637
universals, 12–15
Ureña, 773

V2, 22, 33, 35–39, 46, 666–67, 669, 805
Väänänen, 876–78, 882, 884
van Coetsem, 850–51, 866
van der Auwera, 112
van der Hulst, 234
Vanelli, 154, 646
Varela Ortega, 341

variationist sociolinguistics, 121, 899, 906, 928
Varvaro, 60, 64, 104, 110, 121, 205
Vaugelas, 893
velar nasals, 307–8
Venetan, 587
Venetian, 307, 922
Vennemann, 389
verb positions, 25–27
Verb Second. *See* V2
verb-movement, 656
verlan, 826
Veselinova, 375
Vigara Tauste, 830
Vikings, 483
Vikner, 648
Villa-García, 118
Villena-Ponsoda, 916, 922–23
Vincent, 111, 393–94, 618, 842
Vindolanda, 877
vocative, 316, 759–60, 764, 772–73, 835, 878
Vogel, 249, 253, 410
voice (grammatical), 493, 550
voicing, 195, 210, 274, 295, 309–10, 313, 410, 412
Von Heusinger, 619
Vowel Harmony, 271
vowel length, 186–87
vowel reduction, 212, 247–48
VP-shell hypothesis, 620
Vulgate, 107

Wagner, 143, 452
Walker, 304
Wallon, 50, 52, 609, 891, 927
Waltereit, 686
Wartburg, 60, 142, 200, 206, 275, 673
Weinreich, 187, 847–48, 856, 899
Weinrich, 273
Weiss, 97, 99
Wellentheorie, 909
Wenker, 141
Werner, 374
Wheeler, 311
wh-fronting, 6
wh-in situ, 6
wh-interrogatives, 6
Wierzbicka, 445
Wikipedia, 926
Williams, E., 434, 468
Williams, W., 907
Wiltschko, 701
Winford, 851
Wolfe, 36–37
word order, 510, 531, 554, 588–89, 615, 635, 703, 754, 784, 786, 830, 860
  SVO, 27, 38, 729, 805, 860
  VSO, 617, 624, 810
Wright, 877, 899

X-bar theory, 605

Zafiu, 900
Zanuttini, 657, 726, 742, 744
Zegrean, 750
Zubizarreta, 493, 516, 786, 802, 804
Zwicky, 151, 175, 346, 435–36, 439–41, 728